PUBLIC PAPERS OF THE PRESIDENTS

OF THE UNITED STATES

Jimmy Carter

1978

(IN TWO BOOKS)

BOOK II—JUNE 30 TO DECEMBER 31, 1978

UNITED STATES GOVERNMENT PRINTING OFFICE

WASHINGTON : 1979

Published by the
Office of the Federal Register
National Archives and Records Service
General Services Administration

For sale by the Superintendent of Documents, U.S. Government Printing Office
Washington, D.C. 20402

Stock No. 022–003–01031–9

Foreword

The Presidential papers in this volume document our concerns as a nation, both the transitory and passing, and the deep and lasting questions that will occupy our attention and affect our lives for generations.

The latter part of 1978 was a time of hope and challenge for the American people, of the fruition of some important efforts and the frustration of others. Passage of the first civil service reform in nearly 100 years began the long process that will eventually make government more effective, efficient, and responsive to our needs. A major tax cut and airline deregulation helped relieve our people of excessive burdens of taxation and regulation. The time limit for ratifying the equal rights amendment was extended, giving new life to our goal of providing full equality of opportunity for more than half our people.

The final days of the 95th Congress also brought passage of the Nation's first comprehensive energy package. Although it did not include critical measures dealing with oil, passage of this legislation signaled a growing recognition in our country that the complex and difficult problems of ensuring an adequate, affordable energy supply must be faced and overcome.

The Camp David accords signed by Prime Minister Begin of Israel and President Sadat of Egypt revived the age-old dream that nations in the Middle East could transcend past enmities and learn to live in peace. Although the historic peace treaty between Egypt and Israel was not signed during the period covered by this volume, the United States was able to use its influence and good-will in a dramatic way to keep that dream alive.

It is my hope that these documents will accurately reflect the exciting moments when long efforts finally bore fruit, as well as the familiar ceremonies that define the seasons of our national life. All are part of the portrait of a people seeking to build a more prosperous nation and a more stable world where free people can fulfill their noblest and simplest aspirations, a world where justice and mercy prevail.

Jimmy Carter

Preface

This book contains the papers and speeches of the 39th President of the United States which were issued by the White House Press Office during the period June 30–December 31, 1978. The material has been compiled and published by the Office of the Federal Register, National Archives and Records Service, General Services Administration.

The material is presented in chronological order within each week, and the dates shown in the headings are the dates of the documents or events. In instances when the release date differs from the date of the document itself, that fact is shown in the textnote. Every effort has been made to ensure accuracy. Tape recordings are used to protect against errors in transcription of Presidential remarks, and signed documents are checked against the original to verify the correct printing. Textnotes, footnotes, and cross references have been provided by the editors for purposes of identification or clarity. Speeches were delivered in Washington, D.C., and other documents released there, unless indicated. All times noted are local times.

The index covers both Books I and II of the 1978 volume. In addition to the usual subject-matter entries in the index, the material has been classified in categories reflecting the type of Presidential activity or document. For example, a reader interested in the President's speeches will find them listed in the index under "Addresses and Remarks."

The Public Papers series was begun in 1957 in response to a recommendation of the National Historical Publications Commission. An extensive compilation of messages and papers of the Presidents covering the period 1789 to 1897 was assembled by James D. Richardson and published under congressional authority between 1896 and 1899. Since then, various private compilations have been issued, but there was no uniform publication comparable to the Congressional Record or the United States Supreme Court Reports. Many Presidential papers could be found only in the form of mimeographed White House releases or as reported in the press. The Commission therefore recommended the establishment of an official series in which Presidential writings, addresses, and remarks of a public nature could be made available.

The Commission's recommendation was incorporated in regulations of the Administrative Committee of the Federal Register, issued under section 6 of the Federal Register Act (44 U.S.C. 1506), which may be found in Title 1, Part 10, of the Code of Federal Regulations.

Preface

A companion publication to the Public Papers series, the Weekly Compilation of Presidential Documents, was begun in 1965 to provide a broader range of Presidential materials on a more timely basis to meet the needs of the contemporary reader. Beginning with the administration of Jimmy Carter, the Public Papers series expanded its coverage to include all material as printed in the Weekly Compilation. That coverage provides a listing of the President's daily schedule and meetings, when announced, and other items of general interest issued by the White House Press Office. Also included are lists of the President's nominations submitted to the Senate, materials released by the Press Office which are not printed full-text in the book, and acts approved by the President. This information is compiled on a weekly basis and appears at the end of each week's coverage.

Volumes covering the administrations of Presidents Hoover, Truman, Eisenhower, Kennedy, Johnson, Nixon, and the first 2 years of President Ford are also available.

This series is under the direction of Ernest J. Galdi, Acting Director, Office of the Federal Register, and is produced by the Presidential Documents Division, Robert E. Lewis, Director, and Richard L. Claypoole, Deputy Director. Editors of this book were Katherine A. Mellody, Kenneth R. Payne, Brian L. Hermes, and Rachel L. Jefferies.

White House liaison was provided by Walter W. Wurfel, Deputy Press Secretary. The frontispiece and photographs used in the portfolio were supplied by the White House Photo Office.

The typography and design of the volume were developed by the United States Government Printing Office under the direction of John J. Boyle, Public Printer.

JAMES E. O'NEILL
Acting Archivist of the United States

R. G. FREEMAN III
Administrator of General Services
August 1979

Contents

Administration of Jimmy Carter

1978

PRESIDENTIAL DOCUMENTS

Week Ending Friday, July 7, 1978

Free Enterprise Day, 1978
Proclamation 4576. June 30, 1978

By the President of the United States of America

A Proclamation

The development of the American economy has historically been the result of the interaction between the abundant natural resources of our land and the enterprising spirit of our people. Our system of economic enterprise reflects many of the same values that are embodied in our political system of democracy and civil liberty.

Excessive government regulation—regulation that does not serve the public interest—must concern us all. Unfortunately, free enterprise is sometimes easier to praise than to practice. But all who believe in free enterprise can take heart from the fact that when it is reintroduced into areas of our economy where it has long been dormant, the results can be salutary. A good example is the airline industry, where recent administrative steps toward greater competition have quickly led to both lower fares and higher profits, confirming the advisability of permanent deregulation by law.

By joint resolution (S.J. Res. 128), the Congress has authorized and requested the President to issue a proclamation designating July 1, 1978, as "Free Enterprise Day."

NOW, THEREFORE, I, JIMMY CARTER, President of the United States of America, do hereby proclaim July 1, 1978, as Free Enterprise Day. I call upon the people of the United States and interested groups and organizations to mark this observance with appropriate ceremonies and activities.

IN WITNESS WHEREOF, I have hereunto set my hand this thirtieth day of June, in the year of our Lord nineteen hundred seventy-eight, and of the Independence of the United States of America the two hundred and second.

JIMMY CARTER

[Filed with the Office of the Federal Register, 11:04 a.m. July 3, 1978]

NOTE: The text of the proclamation was released on July 1.

Interview With the President
Remarks and a Question-and-Answer Session With a Group of Editors and News Directors. June 30, 1978

THE PRESIDENT. First of all, let me say that I'm very glad to have all of you here. This is a series of meetings that we've had with leading news men and women from around the country, and it's meant a lot to us. The questions are very incisive and, I think, bring to my attention matters that sometimes are parochial in nature that I would not know about; other times, things that give me a forewarning of national issues that I wouldn't otherwise be prepared for.

ADMINISTRATION POLICIES

One of the things that I would like to emphasize today—and I've asked the staff to put these two props here—is our continuing effort to cut down on unwarranted and unnecessary Government regulation and intrusion into the private free enterprise business sector.

This pile of paper, which happens to be blank, represents the number of forms and regulations that would be required by roughly 45,000 small businesses that are now exempt from OSHA regulation. We've had very good success, particularly in the Labor Department, with OSHA and otherwise, and in HEW, in bringing about some reduction in required paperwork.

This is another example of regulations that have been required. This is the actual regulations on the purchasing of a mousetrap for the Defense Department. It used to take 500 pages to describe the regulations. Now we've cut it down to less than one page. Towels used to be 20 or 30 pages. Now it's only one paragraph.

In the Internal Revenue Service, we've simplified the tax reforms greatly so that a larger number of people could use the standard form. And because of that, the error rate this year is substantially below what the error rate has been in the past. It's a continuing effort, very difficult. I've issued a tough Executive order to all my agency leaders asking them to use their own initiative, and we've set standards for them to meet in the reduction of this regulation.

In a broader context, we've had remarkable success in airline deregulation. The Congress is still considering an airline deregulation bill, but in the actions of the Civil Aeronautics Board in international flights, and also domestic flights, we've had a dramatic reduction in the cost to passengers in acquiring the right to make these flights.

At first the airlines themselves deplored this as shaking the foundations for their profits, but now I think with the experience of a number of months they all see that this reduction of Government regulation has been greatly beneficial to them. It really has let the free enterprise system work. So, we're determined to continue this process, sometimes with disappointments and setbacks, but with a great deal of determination, not only on my part but on that of other people in this country.

We've cut out already about 85 million hours of work among American people in reducing reporting forms and requests for Government services, which is the equivalent of about 50,000 people working full time. This is what's happened in the private sector. And I would guess that many of these regulations were never adequately studied by Federal employees or leaders. The reports were never read, the forms were never examined. And I've called around this table, as a matter of fact, interested groups of Americans, you might be interested in knowing. All the State school superintendents have been here to meet with me, all the presidents of many of the major universities came here to talk to me about how they could make recommendations on legal ways to cut out forms, paperwork. And when we get their recommendations, we really try to carry them out. So, this is one item that is on my shoulders as a responsibility. We have others, of course—welfare reform, tax reform, energy policy.

The Vice President left last night for the Mideast. We're continuing our efforts there to bring about peace. He will be making a major address while he's in Israel, but will be meeting with the members of the Begin government, some of the opposition leaders as well, will be doing some symbolic things to show the Israeli people that we genuinely do care about them, that we are staunch in our commitment to their security, their freedom. He'll be making a brief visit to Egypt on the way back home.

Our SALT negotiations are continuing on a daily basis; those leading up, we hope, to a success on comprehensive test ban.

We have a kind of a long-range struggle—this is the last point I'd like to make—in the adherence to the delineation of responsibility among the different branches of Government. We've been particularly concerned in the last few weeks, months, even years, that the Congress more and more is getting into the role of administration, carrying out the provisions of law that historically have been a prerogative of the President.

Yesterday, the Congress—the House, at least—passed a very unfortunate amendment which we hope will be stopped before it becomes law, requiring every regulation issued by the Secretary of HUD to be submitted back to the Congress, and it can't go into effect for 90 days, waiting for Congress to say whether or not the regulation is advisable or not. It makes administration of Government almost impossible. And sometimes in the heat of a debate or because of an unpopular decision that's been made by myself or a Cabinet officer, you see that intrusion into the executive branch of Government by the legislative branch of Government. We hope to turn that around. I think it's unconstitutional, first of all, and it certainly is counterproductive, secondly.

Those are a few items that I thought might be interesting to you to start with. I'd like to answer your questions.

QUESTIONS

THE MIDDLE EAST

Q. Going back to the Middle East, Mr. President, for a second, I know we're most anxious not to even suggest an American solution, but what do you think the prospects are over time that those parties can somehow work out something that we can stay well clear of, except to endorse?

THE PRESIDENT. Well, let me first say that I'm convinced that Prime Minister Begin and President Sadat genuinely want peace. I don't think there's any doubt about it. Ever since Israel became a nation, it's never had 1 day free of war or the threat of war, and this is a terrible burden for a people to bear. Sadat also sees a continuing economic and political military problem for his own nation if the threat of war is there. So, that's the foundation for my belief that peace is possible.

As I said in my news conference, we've been disappointed in the last few days at the response of the Israeli Government to the questions that we asked them. And I believe that to the extent possible, it's better to let the negotiations be directly between Israel and her individual neighbors.

We have not been able so far to get Begin and Sadat to continue their discussions. There have been some periodic discussions at the Foreign Minister level and the Defense Minister level.

I believe the next step in the process, probably following the Vice President's visit, will be the promulgation, or at least the delivery to Israel of the Egyptian peace proposal. I don't know what's in it. I don't have any way to know yet. It's still in the formative stage, but I think it won't be delayed. We will receive that from Egypt, I understand, and then we will deliver it to the Israelis. Whether it's made public will be up to the Israel and Egypt Governments' desires.

My guess is that it'll be a step in the right direction but inadequate,* in which case my own inclination would be to try to bring those two nations together, at least at the Foreign Minister level, to search out the compatibility and the incompatibility of the two proposals. We may or may not participate in that conference. If called upon to do so by both governments, we would.

Following that, I think that my responsibility would be to analyze those differences and compatibilities and see if we can put forward, as we have for years, some compromise proposals which the two governments would then consider.

If all of this should ultimately fail, then, of course, the United Nations has a role to play in the Middle East and has for a long time. And as you know, the Geneva conference is the basic framework for peace as a result of the United Nations resolution, and that's always a fallback position if we fail as an intermediary or a mediator.

So, I can't give you a prediction of success, but I'm determined, as long as I'm in the White House as President, not ever to give up the hope of realizing the desire of the people involved in the Middle East.

ACCESSIBILITY TO THE PUBLIC

Q. One of your assistants said this morning, and he defended the practice, but he said this morning the constant

***

* By this term, the President wishes to make it clear that he means that the entire Egyptian proposal is unlikely to be totally acceptable to the Israeli Government. [Printed in the transcript.]

coverage by the press, as in the case of your fishing trip, where you're continuously covered, is one of the things that hinders your people-on-people contact and sort of insulates you from what the public thinks.

My question to you is, by and large, is the constant coverage just a nuisance, or how far does it go in actually hampering you doing your job?

THE PRESIDENT. I don't object to it. I was pleased yesterday when we came back in to see the literally thousands of people that stood on the jetty and were welcoming us. I would not have been quite so pleased had we not caught any fish. [*Laughter*]

But I think the sense that the American people have that the President does get tired, that I need just as much recreation now—fishing, playing tennis, walking alone in the woods, being with my family—as I did when I was a farmer, is important, and so I don't deplore that part of it. We do have adequate privacy here at the White House when we want it and at Camp David when we want it.

I don't get much privacy at home in Plains and when I go on vacations, obviously, which I haven't tried yet, but we don't get much privacy.

There's one change that has taken place that causes us some concern, but I think it's good in the long run; and that is that contrary to previous administrations, we've tried to be open. We've tried to get the American people involved in the details of a Mideast peace settlement.

In the past, as you know, most of the negotiation has been done with ultra secrecy, and only a final conclusion of an agreement was made available to the public. When SALT I was consummated with the Soviets, neither the Congress nor the American people nor the general public around the world knew what the items of dispute were and the difficult items at issue. This was the case with Vladivostok, too. An agreement was reached. It was then revealed to the public and to the Congress, and it was a matter of "take it or leave it."

Nowadays, though, because of my own inclinations and as an aftermath of Watergate and the Vietnam war and a demand to know, the specifics of negotiations are known by the public. And it makes it much more difficult to negotiate, but I think we are much less likely to make a serious mistake, as we did in Vietnam and as we may have on some of the items in negotiations on SALT.

So, I don't deplore nor regret the attention focused on me as an actual interest on the part of the American people. My private family life is completely adequate. I have privacy when I want it. And I think that it's a sound insurance policy for the American people and the Congress to be involved in the public debate on matters of great interest to our Nation, and to avoid having a tightly held, small group who in a political closet make a decision for our country and then reveal it for the first time.

This occurred during the Presidential campaign with Angola, where the public nor the Congress had ever been involved in an analysis of what occurred in Angola. After the Portuguese left, Secretary Kissinger revealed to the public that we were planning on getting involved in Angola. It was really too late; the Congress said no, and it created a very bad situation for us. So, there are two sides to it. I think it's good in the long run, and overall, I'm pleased with it.

TAX REDUCTION

Q. May I ask about the looming domestic issue starting from the other coast and trying to yell all the way to Washington, and that is Proposition 13? And I'd like to ask on the gut level how you can handle people who have risen up and taken that much into their hands to let government know that it is unresponsive.

THE PRESIDENT. I've heard about Proposition 13, even way over here in Washington. [*Laughter*]

I think there were two factors in California that may not be prevalent in all the other States that led to Proposition 13 being adopted. One was the extremely high property tax rate. California has still higher property tax rates than many other States in the Nation, even after Proposition 13 is imposed. And the other one was the accumulation of a large State surplus. These two in combination are unique, so far as I know.

Another factor was that in California, a large part of the welfare and social tax responsibility was on property. When I became Governor of Georgia, 6 months later we removed all property tax responsibility for the welfare system. It was all State. I think that's another factor that was there. This does occur, I think, in about roughly 20 States. But I think the expressions of the public that tax burdens in general are too high, that the government must economize, that taxes be reduced, is a clear message above and beyond the specific causes of the California decision.

This is something that hasn't been new. These were major issues during the campaign, even back in 1976 or 1975, and they are the kinds of things that I and Governors around the country have been pursuing as a political goal and with some degree of success.

So, I would say that the message came through clearly that the public wants lower taxes, more efficiency, less government spending, less intrusion in one's private life by government. Property taxes inherently are difficult to have uniform and fair. I think the people said we would rather have social programs financed by other means than property taxes. I think we've learned a lesson from their Proposition 13. And whether or not Proposition 13 will be repeated in other States, I think, though, would primarily relate to the three factors that I described to you earlier: State surplus, high property taxes, and the financing of social programs out of property taxes.

CAPITAL GAINS TAXATION

Q. You recently spoke out quite strongly against the Steiger amendment. Are you totally against any change in capital gains taxes? And if so, what method would you like to see implemented for better capital formation in the business community?

THE PRESIDENT. Well, around this very table, we've had meetings with the members of the Business Roundtable, others representing small business. I remember one day we had about 45 representatives of small business around this table, and their strong preference was to have tax reductions through the corporate tax rate and perhaps some accelerated depreciation and some investment tax credit, not through removing capital gains from the minimum tax.

When you analyze the beneficiaries of the Steiger amendment, as I said in my press conference, the beneficiaries are almost exclusively the very wealthy. I think 3,000 millionaires, as I said in my press conference, get an average tax reduction of $214,000, and the working families, even those with moderate incomes up to $30,000, get an average of only $1 a year tax benefit from the Steiger amendment. So, capital formation, stronger investment in new jobs and equipment, factories, is a very worthy goal.

I just think the Steiger amendment is completely the wrong approach toward

reaching that goal. There's no balance of benefits between the working American and the very wealthy.

AFFIRMATIVE ACTION PROGRAMS

Q. Mr. President, the Congressional Black Caucus has called upon you, I believe, to make a strong, perhaps, reaffirmation of affirmative action, that you do so publicly. They've also asked you to meet with them in that regard in light of the recent Supreme Court decision regarding Allan Bakke. Can we expect such a pronouncement forthcoming from you? And if so, when? And do you intend to meet with the Congressional Black Caucus?

THE PRESIDENT. Well, I meet with the Congressional Black Caucus fairly regularly and consult with them almost on a continuing basis, individual members or about individual items.

I think it's accurate to say that the Supreme Court decision on the *Bakke* case was compatible with the desires of the Black Caucus. We consulted with the Black Caucus members and others before the Attorney General presented the brief from the Justice Department. And I read the brief and approved it personally. It called for a continuation of the affirmative action option to alleviate racial discrimination, either presently extant or the apparent results of historical discrimination.

We have worked very closely through the Justice Department to reassess all the Federal programs to be sure that we not only quietly had an affirmative action program but an aggressive affirmative action program.

I mentioned procurement a while ago. We directed all the departments to purchase a certain portion of Federal supplies and equipment from black-owned and minority-owned firms. We've done the same thing with Federal deposits in banks that happen to be owned by minority Americans.

We've passed legislation this past year, which has been confirmed as legal by the Supreme Court decision in the *Bakke* case—at least indirectly—requiring, for instance, that in a public works program that a certain portion of the contracts for those public works projects had to be allotted to minority American-owned businesses.

So, we have a continuing effort to make sure that the affirmative action program goes on in the Government. And I would say that the *Bakke* decision confirms our stand and leaves adequate option in the future, not only in the university system but in all levels of American life, for affirmative action to be implemented and racial discrimination to be reduced.

NUCLEAR POWER

Q. Mr. President, I'm sure that your office was well aware of last weekend's antinuclear demonstrations across the country, particularly one in Seabrook, New Hampshire, which drew some 15,000 participants.

In August of 1976 you stated that you thought nuclear power, nuclear energy, should only be a last resort. Yet your administration continues to push for the development of nuclear energy. Do you feel that your administration is pushing more for nuclear energy than to alternate forms of energy, particularly solar and hydroelectric, which, except for the TVA project, seem to be more environmentally feasible?

THE PRESIDENT. No. We have had a dramatic change since I've been in office in, for instance, the portion of research and development funds that go to nuclear power. We've reduced that substantially. We've increased dramatically the portion

of research and development funds that go into alternate forms of energy, the various uses of coal, geothermal, solar energy, and so forth.

What we have always said is that there is a place for nuclear power. When the needs of our Nation are met to the fullest extent by conservation, by a shift from oil and gas to coal, the continued use of moderate amounts of oil and gas, enhanced use of geothermal supplies, greatly increased use of solar, then the balance should be filled in by nuclear power.

I do want to be sure that when a nuclear powerplant is proposed, that the decision be made expeditiously, that environmentalists and others have a chance to have their case considered, and that the siting of nuclear powerplants and the design of nuclear powerplants, both for compatibility with the surrounding country, recreation areas, and so forth, and also safety, is ensured.

We've never had in the past an adequate program for controlling waste disposal from nuclear powerplants. We've tried to move on this. The Congress has passed a nonproliferation act which is now in effect, which is a major step in the right direction. We have tried to expedite the licensing of nuclear powerplants. The Congress is considering this. So, I would say that we've got a very well balanced program.

I've never thought that nuclear powerplants should be abolished or prohibited. There are some States that have that desire. And when the people, through the referendum or through the legislature, decide that they do not want nuclear powerplants placed in their State, that's a prerogative that they can honor. I think we've got a well-balanced program now.

The main thing is that we still labor under confusion about the present and the future, pending the passage by the Congress of a comprehensive energy proposal. But when that is passed, I think you would see clearly that the strongest shift has been to adequate rate structure, which reduces a dependence on the scarcer forms of energy, the shift toward coal, the conservation brought about by more efficient automobiles and encouragement through tax measures of conservation matters and the shift away from oil and gas and an enhancement of the use of solar power in all its derivative forms.

HUMAN RIGHTS

Q. Mr. President, may I ask you in the Spanish language?

THE PRESIDENT. *Sí.*

Q. *Cuales son los siguientes pasos de su administracion respecto a la politica de derechos humanos en Latino America?*

THE PRESIDENT. *Bueno. El sujeto de derechos humanos es muy importante para nosotros. En el futuro será un programa de nuestro gobierno sin cesar.*

Let me speak in English. It might be easier for the others to understand and also for me, too.

The question, if I understand it right, was in the future, what will be our Government action or program for the continuation of effort on human rights. And I replied that human rights is a very important subject for us, and in the future, we will continue with the program of enhancing human rights.

In many parts of the world, this has become a burning issue, perhaps even more intense interest focused upon it than in the United States. Latin America, Caribbean, is one area. I met with the leader of the opposition parties in the Federal Republic of Germany just before lunch, and he said of all the things

that our country has done since I've been in office, the most profoundly important is our insistence upon the preservation of human rights. It permeates almost every aspect of our Government. And I think it has the strong support of the American people.

So, in all its forms, political freedom, an absence of persecution, the release of long-held prisoners, a shift toward the democratic expression of opinion by the populace, those kinds of freedoms are important to us, also the freedom from hunger and ability to have adequate health care and education. So, human rights will continue to be a cornerstone of our foreign policy and a deep personal commitment of mine.

MR. WURFEL. Thank you, sir.

THE PRESIDENT. Let me answer one more question, and then if you all don't mind, I'd like to get a personal photograph with each one of you. We won't have time for conversation, but if you'd come by we'll have——

INFLATION

Q. Mr. President, in the ongoing battle with inflation, are you discouraged about the progress that we're making against inflation, and do you think that we can in fact stop this runaway inflation and not have a recession or a depression?

THE PRESIDENT. I am discouraged about inflationary pressures. I think if you would remember back just 12 months ago or more, the overriding domestic concern by the Congress, by me, and most others, was the unemployment rate, which was very high at that time.

Since I've been in office, we've cut down the unemployment rate substantially, about 2 percent, and we've added a net increase of 5½ million jobs in our country. But lately, we've had an increase in the rate of inflation. This has been caused by several factors, the most significant of which is food costs. And I'd say the second most significant is interest charges, both of which are in the Consumer Price Index.

My guess is that food costs are leveling off, that the rate of increase will not be as great in the next 6 months as they have been in the last 6 months. Interest rates, as you know, are determined substantially by the Federal Reserve Board, which is an independent agency, and I think these interest rate increases are designed to constrain the supply of money.

There's a general attitude to be evolved in the country, and that is a genuine concern on the part of every American about inflation and a willingness to make a common sacrifice. One example of this obviously is in the passage of a budget act, an appropriations, series of appropriations bills. Every group demands that others sacrifice to control inflation. But, as I said in Texas, we've got to have someone stand up—and I'm willing to be that person—against increased demands from defense contractors, and highway contractors, local governments, veterans, educators, farmers. Each one of those groups can make an excellent case for more government spending to finance their particular interest in American life.

But I think we've got to keep a lid on spending. And I intend to use every resource at my command, including the veto, to hold down unwarranted spending on the part of Congress. I think so far Congress has been reasonable. I don't know about the final outcome of proposals.

The other thing that has to be done is in the private sector, and that's where most of the influence will come. We've had several large American corporations to agree to our deceleration formula, which means that this year the increase in prices will not be as great as the average for the preceding 2 years.

The same thing applies to wages. We've not had as much success yet with the labor unions in holding down wage demands as we have had with some of the corporations in their prices. But this is predictable.

My own sense is that the workers will have to see some willingness on the part of government and business to hold down prices before they will be willing to make a long-term sacrifice, because most of those contracts extend over a period of 3 years or so. But it's going to require a general sense that we are in it together, that we will make mutual sacrifices and some demonstration of particular elements, like the Government, that we are indeed serious. With that kind of hope being realized, then I think we can turn the tide, stop the inflation rate, and then start the inflation rate down.

I think we will have a very good demonstration on the part of the Government this year in the size of the budget, the proposal for fiscal year '80 budget, the constraints on wage rates in the Government, that will be beneficial to the private sector. And my expectation is that the private sector will respond.

So, I think we've got a good hope. It's going to be a long, tedious, slow process. We're going to have some disappointments. But the inflation rate has got to be controlled. It's my number one domestic problem, and I can only resolve it with the help of everyone.

Thank you very much. I've enjoyed it.

NOTE: The interview began at 1:03 p.m. in the Cabinet Room at the White House. Walter W. Wurfel is Deputy Press Secretary.

The transcript of the interview was released on July 1.

Federal-State Cooperative Forestry Programs

Statement on Signing H.R. 11777, H.R. 11778, and H.R. 11779 Into Law.   July 1, 1978

I have approved the enrolled bills H.R. 11777, H.R. 11778, and H.R. 11779, providing for updated and broadened programs in cooperative forestry, forestry research, and forestry extension education.

The three acts were developed through the cooperative efforts of State forestry agencies, State extension services, forest industries, conservation organizations, forestry schools, and Members of Congress working with the Department of Agriculture. The American Forestry Association through its sponsorship of an "areas of agreement" committee achieved agreement among diverse interests on key provisions. I recognize that the acts represent a consensus within the forestry community.

H.R. 11777 provides for technical assistance, cost-sharing, and resource protection programs for non-Federal forest lands, to be carried out through cooperative arrangements with State forestry agencies. It consolidates nine different programs in seven authorities into a single authority. It includes a provision allowing Federal cooperative forestry funds to be consolidated, so that each State will have more flexibility in targeting forestry programs to the specific needs and priorities of the States. I expect the Secretary of Agriculture to coordinate rural fire activities conducted under this act with the Secretary of Commerce, who has overall responsibility for general fire prevention and control activities.

H.R. 11778 modernizes and expands the 50-year-old forestry research program, providing more specific authority to meet current and future research needs. The bill provides an appropriate link to other agricultural research programs authorized by Title XIV of the Food and Agriculture Act of 1977.

H.R. 11779 expands the renewable resources extension program in cooperation with State Extension Services to provide private forest landowners with education and information about managing and using forests, rangeland, fish and wildlife, water, and other renewable resources.

These bills do contain more features which we have objected to previously—the urban forestry assistance program, the establishment of a separate rural fire emergency disaster fund, and a separate appropriation for forestry extension. While I maintain my previous position on these issues, I do not believe their presence in these otherwise worthwhile acts justifies my disapproval of the acts.

I have approved these three bills because they provide the necessary means for the Federal and State Governments and universities to cooperatively aid forest landowners and others. The bills are compatible with the policy and direction contained in my May 23, 1977, environmental message.

NOTE: As enacted, H.R. 11778 and H.R. 11779 are Public Laws 95–307 and 95–306, respectively, approved June 30, and H.R. 11777 is Public Law 95–313, approved July 1.

1978 Interim Reciprocal Fisheries Agreement With Canada

Statement on Signing H.R. 12571 Into Law. July 1, 1978

This act provides congressional authorization to bring into effect the 1978 Interim Reciprocal Fisheries Agreement with Canada. This agreement is an essential step toward allowing fishermen of each country to resume traditional fishing in the waters of the other during 1978.

Negotiations are continuing to conclude a comprehensive maritime boundary and resource agreement between Canada and the United States. Congressional approval of the agreement reflects the widespread support in the United States both for maintenance of reciprocal fishing with Canada and for the kind of comprehensive, cooperative, long-term arrangements now under negotiation.

I hope that our country and Canada can now immediately proceed to restore traditional patterns of reciprocal fishing. The interruption at the beginning of this month in these traditional reciprocal fisheries, which have continued since the 18th century, has created hardships for fishermen of both countries. Resumption of reciprocal fishing can only help the intensive efforts of both Governments to work out permanent arrangements for sharing and jointly managing our common fisheries resources, arrangements which would include mechanisms for resolving the very questions which gave rise to the present interruption.

I believe that the negotiations to conclude a comprehensive maritime agreement now being carried out by my Special Representative, Lloyd Cutler, and his Canadian counterpart offer the firm promise of a strengthened, cooperative maritime relationship which will bring benefits to the fishermen of both countries that neither country can provide on its own. Such a long-term agreement would be in the tradition of our close, cooperative relationship with Canada. In signing this act, I have asked the Secretary of State and Lloyd Cutler to make every effort with Canada to restore reciprocal fishing as soon as possible so that the important long-term maritime negotiations may proceed unimpeded.

NOTE: As enacted, H.R. 12571 is Public Law 95–314, approved July 1.

Combined Federal Campaign

Memorandum From the President.
June 30, 1978

Memorandum for the Heads of Departments and Agencies

I am pleased to tell you that Joseph A. Califano, Secretary of Health, Education, and Welfare, has agreed to serve as Chairman of the Combined Federal Campaign for the National Capital Area this fall.

This campaign, which begins in September, combines the solicitation efforts of the United Way of the National Capital Area, the National Health Agencies, and the International Service Agencies. In this single drive we will seek to do our share to meet the needs of more than 150 local, national and international health, welfare and social service agencies.

The needs of the voluntary organizations supported by the Combined Federal Campaign are great. These organizations perform essential services in helping the disadvantaged, in serving youth and the aged, in healing the sick, and in helping those in need overseas. CFC gives all of us who are Federal employees, whether civilian or military, a unique opportunity to pledge our help to people in our community, our nation, and around the world—a pledge made more convenient by the availability of voluntary payroll deductions.

I request that you serve personally as Chairman of the campaign in your organization and that you appoint one of your top assistants as your Vice Chairman. Please advise Secretary Califano of the person you designate as Vice Chairman. I am confident that Secretary Califano will have your wholehearted support in this endeavor, and I urge you to commend the campaign to everyone in your organization.

JIMMY CARTER

NOTE: The text of the memorandum was released on July 5.

Combined Federal Campaign

Memorandum From the President.
June 30, 1978

Memorandum for Federal Employees and Military Personnel

Ours is a society in which individuals traditionally share what they have with others less fortunate than themselves. The Combined Federal Campaign offers each of us the opportunity to show our individual concern for those in need of help. This one campaign combines the fundraising efforts of the local United Way, the American Red Cross, the National Health Agencies, and the International Services Agencies.

Through one gift to the Combined Federal Campaign, we can help support a wide variety of voluntary agencies. These organizations support the sick, the aged, the handicapped, the poverty-stricken and the young—those who are needy among us. Your contributions also go towards research programs and our friends in need across the seas. If you choose, your gift can be made easier through the use of payroll deductions.

While the decision to give and the amount of one's gift are, of course, personal voluntary decisions, I hope that each of you will join with me and other federal workers, civilian and military, in supporting your local Combined Federal Campaign to the fullest extent possible.

JIMMY CARTER

NOTE: The text of the memorandum was released on July 5.

Meat Imports

Proclamation 4577.   July 4, 1978

QUANTITATIVE LIMITATION ON THE
IMPORTATION OF CERTAIN MEAT

By the President of the United States of America

A Proclamation

The Act of August 22, 1964 (78 Stat. 594; 19 U.S.C. 1202 note), provides for the limitation of certain meat imports if import estimates exceed 110 percent of an adjusted base quantity for that year. The limitation applies to fresh, chilled, or frozen cattle meat and fresh, chilled, or frozen meat of goats and sheep, except lamb.

On December 30, 1977, the Secretary of Agriculture determined (43 FR 987) in accord with Section 2(b)(1) of the Act that the adjusted base quantity of meat for the calendar year 1978 is 1,183.9 million pounds. The Secretary now has estimated (in the 1978 third quarterly estimate) that the aggregate imports of meat for 1978 will be 1,492.3 million pounds. This estimate exceeds 110 percent of the previously determined adjusted base quantity for 1978.

In accord with Section 2(c) of the Act, the President must limit the import of meat to the adjusted base quantity for 1978 of 1,183.9 million pounds, unless he increases or suspends that limitation pursuant to Section 2(d) of the Act.

NOW, THEREFORE, I, JIMMY CARTER, President of the United States of America, by the authority vested in me by Section 2 of the Act, do hereby proclaim as follows:

1. The total quantity of the articles specified in item 106.10 (relating to fresh, chilled, or frozen meat) and item 106.20 (relating to fresh, chilled, or frozen meat

of goats and sheep (except lamb)) of part 2B, schedule 1 of the Tariff Schedules of the United States, which may be entered, or withdrawn from warehouse, for consumption during the calendar year 1978, is limited to 1,183.9 million pounds.

2. In accord with Section 2(d) of the Act, I determine that the supply of meat described in Paragraph 1 hereof will be inadequate to meet domestic demand at reasonable prices.

3. The limitation proclaimed in Paragraph 1 hereof is suspended during the period of calendar year 1978, which is the period that I determine to be necessary to carry out the purposes of Section 2(d) of the Act.

IN WITNESS WHEREOF, I have hereunto set my hand this fourth day of July, in the year of our Lord nineteen hundred seventy-eight, and of the Independence of the United States of America the two hundred and third.

JIMMY CARTER

[Filed with the Office of the Federal Register, 11:09 a.m., July 6, 1978]

NOTE: The text of the proclamation was released on July 5.

Small Business Energy Loan Act

Statement on Signing H.R. 11713 Into Law.
July 4, 1978

I am signing today H.R. 11713, the small business energy loan program. This act will provide Federal loans and loan guarantees to small businesses to engage in the design, manufacture, marketing, and installation of solar technologies and energy conservation practices. Senator Thomas McIntyre and Congressmen Berkley Bedell and Alvin Baldus, the sponsors of this act, have worked hard to set

up a framework for assisting small business participation in the important areas of solar energy and energy conservation.

Bringing solar and conservation technologies into wide-scale use will require a strong effort by American small businesses. I am approving this new program because I am disappointed with the past performance of the Small Business Administration in this effort. I am directing the Administrator of the SBA to marshal his authorities under this new program *and* under existing law to more actively involve small firms in solar energy and energy conservation.

Finally, I would ask the Congress to work with me in ensuring that this new program does not increase our overall budget for the Small Business Administration. I believe the SBA's resources are adequate and that this new program can be funded from within the moneys which I requested in my fiscal year 1979 budget request.

NOTE: As enacted, H.R. 11713 is Public Law 95–315, approved July 4.

The statement was released on July 5.

Highway Safety and National Traffic and Motor Vehicle Safety Acts of 1966

Message to the Congress Transmitting Two Reports. July 5, 1978

To the Congress of the United States:

The 11th annual reports on the administration of the Highway Safety and National Traffic and Motor Vehicle Safety Act of 1966 are transmitted for your consideration. The volume on motor vehicle safety contains the reporting requirements of the Motor Vehicle Information and Cost Savings Act of 1972. Also included are highlights from the second annual report to the Congress on automotive fuel economy. The highway safety document describes developments in those aspects of traffic safety in which Congress expressed special interest in the Highway Safety Acts of 1973 and 1976.

Since 1967, research has advanced the state-of-the-art of traffic safety. Safety devices have been perfected and incorporated in most automobiles on the road today. Highways have been designed and built with safety in mind, and traffic systems are better controlled. Even so, the traffic safety problem remains serious. In 1977, 46,880 of our citizens died on the nation's highways, and the number of injured ran into the millions. The direct economic cost is estimated at $43 billion annually. Had there been no traffic safety effort, and had the 1967 traffic fatality rate held constant, the 1977 toll might have been 77,000 dead and the direct economic costs would have risen to $76 billion a year.

The fact remains that the fatality rate (deaths per 100 million miles of travel) has declined steadily since 1967, as the various automotive and highway standards and programs have taken effect. The drop was especially noticeable following imposition, in January 1974, of the 55-mph national maximum speed limit, which has proven to be the single most effective safety measure instituted in this country. Cumulatively, the saving in lives since 1967 exceeds 150,000.

Despite the advances that have been made since 1967, motor vehicle accidents have remained the sixth leading cause of death in the United States. It is a national calamity that the penalties fall disproportionately on the very young and on those in their most productive years. In every age bracket from 5 to 34 years, motor vehicle accidents are either the leading or the second cause of death; among the 15 to 19-year-olds, traffic fatalities claim 38 percent of total deaths.

Persistent obstacles remain to further rapid or easy progress in reducing fatalities. Average speeds are increasing gradually. Seat belts are a simple, effective safety device, but are used by less than 20 percent of all motorists. The growing popularity of small cars, light trucks and vans increases the weight disparity within the vehicle mix and adversely affects the severity of accidents. Alcohol continues to be a contributing cause in half of all fatal accidents. Rulemaking has focused primarily on passenger cars, and many of the standards have been found to be inapplicable to light trucks and vans. Some states have repealed their motorcycle helmet laws; some have reduced or eliminated penalties for infractions of the 55-mph speed limit.

Further progress in traffic safety is feasible, but will require the dedication and cooperation of Federal, State and local governments, the automotive industry and, above all, the motoring public whose lives are at stake.

JIMMY CARTER

The White House,
    July 5, 1978.

NOTE: The reports are entitled "Highway Safety: A Report on Activities Under the Highway Safety Act of 1966 as Amended, January 1, 1977–December 31, 1977—U.S. Department of Transportation, National Highway Traffic Safety Administration, Federal Highway Administration" (Government Printing Office, 76 pages plus appendices) and "Motor Vehicle Safety 1977: A Report on Activities Under the National Traffic and Motor Vehicle Safety Act of 1966 and the Motor Vehicle Information and Cost Savings Act of 1972, January 1, 1977–December 31, 1977—U.S. Department of Transportation, National Highway Traffic Safety Administration" (Government Printing Office, 61 pages plus appendices).

Fighting in Beirut, Lebanon

Statement by the President. **July 6, 1978**

I wish today to express my deep concern at the continued bloodshed that has accompanied the fighting in Beirut over recent days. Despite appeals by Secretary General Waldheim and His Holiness the Pope—to which the United States has added its voice—and numerous efforts to achieve a cease-fire, the clashes unfortunately continue with heavy casualties among the innocent civilian population.

The fighting in Beirut is in no one's interest. It adds to the hatred and suffering accumulated over several years of tragedy in Lebanon and delays the efforts of the Lebanese Government, with the help and support of friendly governments, to rebuild national institutions and ensure security for all Lebanese.

I therefore join with those world leaders calling for an immediate end to the fighting and urge all parties with influence over the situation to spare no effort to set Lebanon once more on the road to peace and progress.

Digest of Other White House Announcements

The following listing includes the President's daily schedule and other items of general interest as announced by the White House Press Office during the period covered by this issue. Events and announcements printed elsewhere in the issue are not included.

July 4

The President returned to the White House from Camp David, Md., to meet with Vice President Walter F. Mondale, who reported on his trip to Israel and Egypt. The President and Vice President and their families then viewed the holiday fireworks display from the Residence, and then the President returned to Camp David.

July 6

The President left Camp David for visits to:

—Emmitsburg, Md., and the shrine dedicated to Saint Elizabeth Bayley Seton;

—Gettysburg, Pa., for a tour of the Gettysburg National Military Park and a visit with Mamie Eisenhower, wife of the former President;

—Mercersburg, Pa., birthplace of President James Buchanan;

—Sharpsburg, Md., for a tour of Antietam Battlefield Site;

—Harpers Ferry, W. Va.

Following the motorcade trip, the President returned to Camp David.

NOMINATIONS SUBMITTED TO THE SENATE

The following list does not include promotions of members of the Uniformed Services, nominations to the Service Academies, or nominations of Foreign Service officers.

Submitted July 6, 1978

JOSE A. GONZALEZ, JR., of Florida, to be United States District Judge for the Southern District of Florida, vice Charles B. Fulton, retired.

CHECKLIST OF WHITE HOUSE PRESS RELEASES

The following releases of the Office of the White House Press Secretary, distributed during the period covered by this issue, are not included in the issue.

Released July 6, 1978

Announcement: nomination of Jose A. Gonzalez, Jr., to be United States District Judge for the Southern District of Florida

CHECKLIST—Continued

Released July 7, 1978

News conference: on employment and producer price figures—by Charles L. Schultze, Chairman of the Council of Economic Advisers

News conference: on the adoption of an anti-inflation resolution by the National Association of Home Builders—by Ambassador Robert S. Strauss, Special Representative for Trade Negotiations, and Ernest Becker, president of the National Association of Home Builders

Announcement: adoption of an anti-inflation resolution by the National Association of Home Builders

ACTS APPROVED BY THE PRESIDENT

Approved July 1, 1978

H.R. 11777_____ Public Law 95–313
Cooperative Forestry Assistance Act of 1978.

H.R. 12571_____ Public Law 95–314
An act to amend the Fishery Conservation Zone Transition Act in order to give effect to the Reciprocal Fisheries Agreement for 1978 between the United States and Canada.

Approved July 4, 1978

H.R. 11713_____ Public Law 95–315
Small Business Energy Loan Act.

PRESIDENTIAL DOCUMENTS

Federal Law Enforcement Assistance Programs

Remarks Announcing Reorganization Legislation and a Department of Housing and Urban Development Program.
July 10, 1978

THE PRESIDENT. I think you notice from the distinguished men and women on the steps with me the importance of the subject that we will be discussing this morning. We've had a briefing for interested persons from around the Nation on this new proposal which I'm sure will be implemented without delay.

Every American is concerned about crime and every American is a potential victim of crime. But that's only part of our concern. Crime destroys the essential fabric of our society in ways that go far beyond individual suffering and loss. In that sense, we are all victims. If our communities are to be vibrant and safe, our people cannot live in fear. We cannot let criminals control our lives.

The primary responsibility for controlling crime rests with local and State officials, but the Federal Government can and does provide essential and effective support. Within the last year, we have made some progress in reducing crime. New jobs have been created. Crime rates in almost every category have gone down, but the rates are still too high and crime is still of grave concern to me and other Americans. There is clearly more that the Federal Government can and should do to solve this problem. Working in partnership with State and local governments, community organizations, and concerned citizens, we can make a safer America.

Since its creation a decade ago, the Law Enforcement Assistance Administration, LEAA, has been the Federal Government's major tool to help local communities, local officials carry out this responsibility. But it has never yet realized its full potential.

As part of our reorganization efforts, the Justice Department and the Office of Management and Budget have been working for the last 12 months, intensively reviewing LEAA. We've involved community leaders, public officials, and law enforcement specialists from throughout the Nation. We've also had valuable counsel and assistance from congressional leaders, such as Senator Kennedy and Congressman Rodino.

The proposals that I am sending to Congress today will make the Federal Government a more effective and competent partner in the fight against crime.

1241

First, we will greatly simplify the grant process, eliminating 75 percent of the paperwork. For instance, cities now requiring 40 different applications per year will in the future only have to submit one application per year.

Second, we will strengthen the partnership already enhanced by our urban policy between the Federal Government on the one hand and State and local communities on the other. For the first time hundreds of cities and counties will have the flexibility to decide how their LEAA funds can best be used to attack crime in their own communities and will receive fixed allocations of LEAA funds for that purpose. In addition, we will target resources to those areas of the country with especially severe crime problems.

Third, we will consolidate and strengthen research and statistics programs within the Department of Justice. A National Institute of Justice will be created to replace several different research units now located in the Department of Justice. It will be charged with conducting independent studies to determine how we can best solve our criminal and civil justice problems. A Bureau of Justice Statistics will be created to provide for the first time a central focus for the gathering and analysis of statistics concerning crime and concerning our justice system.

The Federal effort to help State and local governments solve their crime programs cannot be limited, however, to just improving LEAA. A sensitivity to the crime problem must be part of other Federal programs which affect the daily lives of our citizens.

Several of the Federal agencies which have been involved in our urban policy will be pooling $32 million over the next year to develop, for instance, an improved anticrime program for public housing projects. Funds will be provided by the CETA program for training and education to hire local residents for such important, preventive jobs as manning elevators and patrolling unguarded areas where the crime rate has been very high. Recreation facilities will be built by Interior Department funds for the men, women, children who reside in these projects. And LEAA funds will be provided for counseling and for other services for juveniles living in public housing projects who might be influenced or tempted to resort to a life of crime.

The programs I've announced today will have a beneficial effect on our crime problem. But if we are to be successful, we also need the support of each of the distinguished leaders who are here today from State and local governments, from community and neighborhood groups.

We have the knowledge, the ability, the determination, the commitment, and the influence, and using these more effective programs, our common effort can continue to reduce the excessive crime rate in our Nation.

I'd like now to call on the Attorney General for further remarks, and then we'll hear from distinguished Members of the Congress, and then from the Secretary of Housing and Urban Development.

ATTORNEY GENERAL BELL. Thank you, Mr. President.

This is the third ceremony we've had in the Rose Garden that bears very heavily on our effort to do something about improving our criminal justice system. The first was a meeting just like this where we joined with the Senate and House Judiciary Committees to sponsor the recodification of the criminal laws. That's now pending in the House, already passed the Senate. The second was to do something about bringing the court system into our foreign intelligence efforts—we call that the Foreign Intelligence Surveillance

Act. That has passed the Senate and is now pending in the House.

We've been somewhat delayed on revamping and revising the LEAA because it's complex. And we started out, because of some of the things they'd done in the past, with the idea that maybe it should be abolished. We finally decided the thing to do was to refurbish it in a way to take out wasted overhead on local, State, and Federal levels, and on the Federal level we reduced the payroll by 15 percent since we've been here, number one. Number two, take the fat out, not spend any more money on boondoggles, but to be sure that the money goes to the process of deterring and eliminating crime.

So, we're ending up with a three-pronged agency—research and development that will guarantee that our research is worthwhile and that it will produce something that can be developed; a Bureau of Justice Statistics, something badly needed. We oftentimes do not know what to do about the total system from police, courts, and corrections and prosecutions, without having some idea of what the statistical picture is in the country. It's been fragmented. We're bringing that together. And, of course, the grant part of the program will be a great deal better, because 70 percent of the money, as the President said, will go out almost as revenue-sharing, and the other 30 percent will be reserved for discretionary programs.

I'm quite pleased over the prospects, and I'm more pleased than that by the fact that Senator Kennedy and Chairman Rodino and some of their colleagues will be sponsoring this legislation. We hope to have it in place by October of 1979, when the present authorization for the LEAA expires. At that time, we'll be ready to move into the new system and, hopefully, both committees will agree with the President and me that we ought to go ahead

and as much as possible put the new management concept in place now, because this is a managerial problem. And when I say that, I say serious managerial problem. And we need to go ahead and move to better management.

I think that Mr. Gregg at the LEAA, who has been the Acting Administrator and is now, has done a wonderful job. Mr. President, he's one of these supergrades that goes about the Government in management capacities as he's assigned, just as you're thinking of doing in the civil service reform. And he's done a fine job. But we want to go ahead and put the new management in place as quickly as possible.

Now, it's my pleasure to present to you Senator Kennedy, who's got, I would say, as wide-ranging an interest in the administration of justice as anyone I know. It was Senator Kennedy and his staff that did a great deal of the work on the bill that's going to be introduced today. It's my pleasure to introduce Senator Kennedy.

SENATOR KENNEDY. Thank you very much, General Bell, Mr. President.

I think there are few issues which are of greater concern to the American people than their own safety and security. I think all of us are very mindful that the people who suffer the most in terms of crime are the really powerless people in our society, whether it's in the urban areas or in rural communities or in suburban areas. Usually they're the senior citizens, the poor, the disadvantaged people. I think this legislation represents the best judgment of those that have been interested in the issues of crime in the Senate. It has strong bipartisan support in the Senate. It recognizes the importance of corrections and rehabilitation.

I'm very hopeful that we'll get early consideration of the legislation and early passage of it, and it will symbolize that although law enforcement is basically a local responsibility, that there's both a symbolic and a real role for the Federal Government to work with local communities to provide for safer communities for the people that live in the cities, the suburban areas, and the rural communities of this country.

Thank you.

ATTORNEY GENERAL BELL. I'm pleased to present Chairman Rodino, a great American, one that's done as much for the administration of justice in the impeachment process and many other ways—[*laughter*]—as anyone I know. He's been a great friend and supporter of mine since I've been here.

REPRESENTATIVE RODINO. Thank you very much, Judge Bell, Mr. President, Madam Secretary, my colleagues, and friends.

Mr. President, I suppose if I don't make this short, I'm going to be charged with some kind of a crime, this tremendous heat we're under here. But I do want to tell you, Mr. President, that your administration is to be applauded for having undertaken a real review, an intense study of LEAA and the total problem of crime. I think we understand—and I know that this understanding comes as the result of many consultations on the part of the Attorney General, members of your administration, and other interested people—that we can't really successfully fight crime or really understand the causes of crime until we get the people involved. And I think that this bill, this proposal, certainly aims to do that.

First of all, it's a restructuring of LEAA. And being called the Justice Improvement Act of 1978, I think, is a hopeful sign, because I think that is what it's going to be. The innovative features of the National Institute of Justice for the purposes of doing tremendous amount of re-search—so that the States which have principal responsibility may be given the kinds of information that may set up the kinds of guidelines that will help us to understand crime, the cause of crime, and then to prevent it. And the same way with setting up the Bureau of Statistics, which I think is important.

I've been in the forefront of this battle for a long time. The bottom line seems to be that the people of America, the neighborhoods, the communities, the people, and the State governments and the Federal Government ought to recognize that this indeed won't go away as a problem until we take this kind of concerted action. And I believe that we need this kind of commitment on the part of each of us.

There was talk a long time ago in 1968 of how we were going to successfully wage this battle against crime, and we've seen that spending money wasn't the answer alone. There's got to be a total dedication, a total commitment. It won't be dollars alone. It's got to be people with understanding. And the anticrime community program, the setting up of priorities for those programs that work, removing some of the redtape, that's all going to be, I think, in the right direction.

I pledge myself to a total commitment to helping, because I think that while it may be one of those areas that seems to get a low rating when the people of America are asked what is the problem that they consider most paramount, nonetheless, I think in the hearts and minds of most of the people of America is this question: Why can't we get rid of crime? Why do we have to be afraid to walk the streets of America? Why do we have to be afraid each time to go out as free citizens?

And I think, Mr. President, that with Senator Kennedy, with myself—and I'm introducing the bill today—I think that along with Bob McClory, the ranking

Republican on our committee, I'm sure that we're going to give you the kind of support that the administration needs. And I think with your appeal to the people of America, we may be moving in the right direction.

Thank you.

THE PRESIDENT. I mentioned earlier that we have made, I think, substantial, detectable, provable progress in almost every aspect of crime statistics in the last 12 months. The Attorney General has been trying to contribute to this progress in recent days. The circuit court judge ruled that he would not have to go to jail, which does help in one category of holding down the crime statistics, and I want to express my personal congratulations to Griffin so far on his good progress. [*Laughter*]

I think that the next and the last speaker is indicative or representative of the effort that all the Cabinet members have made. Perhaps one of the prime causes for the reduction in the crime rate in the last 12 months has been the reduction in the number of people who are unemployed. We have almost 2 million fewer people unemployed now than we did when this administration took over, and we've had a net increase of 6.4 million jobs, which means that people can now earn their living rather than turn to a life of crime for the illegal acquisition of goods or money.

We have this morning a very important demonstration in Pat Harris, Secretary of the Housing and Urban Development Department, of what can be done in public housing. A very tiny portion of public housing in our country has been the focal point of excessive crime perpetrated on the residents there. And I would like to call now on Secretary Harris to explain in closing what she is doing as one of the members of the Cabinet to help in a concerted, broad-scaled

approach in our country to hold down the crime rate and to correct this defect in our democratic society.

Secretary Pat Harris.

SECRETARY HARRIS. Thank you, Mr. President, Mr. Attorney General, Members of the Senate and the House.

The program that we're announcing today is another example of the way in which the Carter administration uses existing resources in an imaginative way to achieve the goals that the President has set for his administration.

Since 1937, public housing has housed the poor of this country, and in most cases what has been provided is shelter that far surpasses in quality and in cost what could otherwise be secured by low-income families. But as the President noted, we are all aware that there are a few very large, highly visible urban projects that have not lived up to our expectations and now represent some of the worst living conditions in this country.

You know the names of these places as well as I do—Columbia Point in Boston, Stella Wright in Newark, Robert Taylor Homes in Chicago, Hunter's Point in San Francisco, Carmelitos in Los Angeles, West Dallas in Dallas. They are a very small part of the public housing program, but they account for 100 percent of the public's negative image of the program. These problem projects are often breeding grounds for crime, vandalism, delinquency, and despair. They are places that no one here would want to live in, to work in, or to raise a family in.

The Carter administration is going to do something about these projects. We realize how big this challenge is, and we do not pretend to have all the answers. What we intend to do is to make a start that can, over the next 30 months, reverse conditions in these projects and bring a better and safer living environment, employment opportunities, and hope to people living in these projects.

The way we intend to bring $209 million in assistance to local communities is completely consistent with the urban policy announced by the President on March 27 of this year. We are going to involve the local government and voluntary associations. We are going to simplify the paperwork associated with the program. We are going to coordinate the activities of other Federal agencies that can be of assistance to these projects, and we are going to make better use of already available funds. LEAA is one of the participating groups in this program.

All of us who are concerned about improving the living conditions of the disadvantaged are faced with a great challenge. Can this be done within the restrictions imposed by today's economies and the taxpayers' concern with the level of government expenditures? We believe that it can. The people of the Nation do not intend to abandon the disadvantaged. The people of this Nation instead are telling us that we must seek every possible way to make better use of the resources we have. We believe that the program announced today demonstrates that this can be done, and we will build on the results in the future.

There are many reasons to make certain that living conditions in these multiproblem projects are improved. Seventy-six percent of the households in these projects are single-parent households. Sixty-three percent of all residents are members of racial minorities, and 40 percent are elderly. But most important, 65 percent of the residents of these projects are under the age of 18.

When I think of all these young people served by public housing, I remember the young black Ph. D. in Houston who grew up in one of these projects and who today works with people of Houston to make the entire city a better place in which to live. And I think of the young white man in Newark who left a Newark public housing project to go to Harvard on a scholarship and who returned to Newark to head its housing and community development program. The protection of future leaders like the Houston Ph. D. and the Newark leader is what the HUD Public Housing Urban Initiative is all about, and I thank my fellow Cabinet members for their cooperation in getting this program under way.

Thank you, Mr. President.

ATTORNEY GENERAL BELL. Unless there's someone else that feels that they have something on their heart—[*laughter*]—we'll adjourn. Thank you.

NOTE: The President spoke at 11:30 a.m. at the ceremony in the Rose Garden at the White House.

Federal Law Enforcement Assistance Programs

Message to the Congress on Proposed Reorganization Legislation.   July 10, 1978

To the Congress of the United States:

I am today sending to Congress the "Justice System Improvement Act of 1978," which will make significant changes in programs now being administered by the Law Enforcement Assistance Administration ("LEAA") and will revitalize our efforts to help State and local governments improve their justice systems.

For the past 10 years, Federal efforts to control crime through LEAA have been uncoordinated and ineffective. In providing financial assistance to State and local governments, the LEAA program has never been as efficient or effective as originally intended. A complex bureaucratic structure has enveloped the Federal effort, involving State and local law enforcement officials in excessive regulation, complexity, and mountains of red tape—rather than providing them with needed financial and technical assistance. Compliance with procedural guidelines has often overshadowed substantive accomplishments. Further, Federal research and statistics programs have not provided the types of information needed for sound management decisions by those involved in controlling crime and improving our justice system.

With the counsel and assistance of State and local officials and of Congressional leaders, particularly Senator Kennedy and Congressman Rodino, we have devoted more than a year to an intensive, thorough review of the LEAA program. Through that review, we sought to remedy the deficiencies in the LEAA program, while at the same time building upon the program's basic strengths. The Act which I am proposing today meets that goal: it effectively addresses LEAA's weaknesses and furthers our efforts, enhanced by our urban policy, to develop an effective partnership among the Federal government, State and local governments and community organizations.

Enactment of this bill will be a major step forward in our nation's efforts to control crime and improve the administration of justice. The bill contains the following major initiatives:

—It will streamline and redirect the LEAA program
- by simplifying the grant process and eliminating unnecessary paperwork;
- by targeting funds to areas of greatest need;
- by eliminating wasteful uses of LEAA funds;
- by strengthening the role of local governments; and
- by increasing community and neighborhood participation in program decisions.

—It will also consolidate within the Department of Justice
- civil and criminal research efforts in a new National Institute of Justice; and
- civil and criminal statistical programs in a new Bureau of Justice Statistics.

LAW ENFORCEMENT ASSISTANCE ADMINISTRATION

ELIMINATING PAPERWORK

The current statute authorizing LEAA imposes 25 broad planning requirements. Implementation of these requirements has resulted in annual State plans of uncertain value and extraordinary length. Each year, State plans total about 55,000 pages often filled with needless and repetitive narrative. Over the program's history, about 500 plans filling some one-half million pages have been submitted to LEAA. Countless staff time has been devoted to plan development and review at the Federal, State and local level.

My proposal will reverse this trend. Statutorily mandated requirements regarding content of plans will be reduced from 25 to 8. Annual State plans—now averaging about 1,000 pages—will be replaced by simplified applications submitted once every three years. This change alone will decrease paperwork by as much as 75 percent.

In addition, under the Act, major local government units will be able to submit single applications for funding of all projects covering a three-year period. The impact of this change will be significant. Presently, cities like Atlanta, Denver, Detroit, Chicago, Los Angeles and Newark fill out on the average 40 project applications each year. Under the Act, they will be required to complete only one.

TARGETING FUNDS

Under the existing statute, LEAA funds are distributed to States solely on the basis of population. There is no requirement that funds be distributed according to an area's need to fight crime.

Under the Act, a priority will be placed on focusing funds to the areas with the most severe crime problems, in line with the Administration's general policy of targeting funds from government programs to areas of greatest need.

At present, 17 States have about 55 percent of the nation's serious crime and about 45 percent of the total population. Under our proposals, those 17 States would receive additional funds to distribute to their local areas with the greatest crime problems.

WASTEFUL USE OF FUNDS

The existing LEAA statute does not place any meaningful limits on how funds are to be used, or incentives for efficient use. In recent years, it has become obvious that some LEAA funds have been wasted on useless equipment, hardware, projects and programs.

To avoid future wasteful use, and to insure that LEAA funds are spent in the most productive ways, my proposal contains reasonable limits on the use of LEAA funds.

Strict limitations will be placed on the use of funds for equipment, hardware, administrative expenses, and general salary expenses. These limitations should result in additional LEAA funds for programs which will directly impact on the fight against crime and which will improve our judicial system.

LOCAL GOVERNMENTS

Under the current LEAA statute, local crime prevention and control efforts have frequently been undercut by uncertainty about funding levels, as well as by disagreements over State and local roles and responsibilities.

My proposal will eliminate the uncertainty concerning the funding level for local governments and will more clearly establish the relationship between State and local governments. Rather than having to file innumerable applications with their State governments, my proposal will enable municipalities of over 100,000 population and counties of over 250,000 population for the first time to receive a fixed allocation of LEAA funds each year.

In addition, decisions regarding funding are now made at the State level, often without adequate local consultation. Under my proposal, these cities and counties will be given greater discretion to select projects and programs particularly suited to their own crime reduction and criminal justice needs.

COMMUNITY AND NEIGHBORHOOD PARTICIPATION

All too often, a wide gulf separates law enforcement officials from the communities and people they protect. This has been particularly true of the LEAA program.

My proposal recognizes that crime prevention and justice system improvement are not solely the tasks of government or justice agencies. Private citizens and neighborhood and community organizations will have a vital role to play. The participation of neighborhood and community groups in the development and approval of State and local applications will be assured. Not only will public hearings be required before State and local LEAA funding decisions are made, but those groups will be fully represented on the State and local advisory boards that will be established to determine how LEAA funds are spent locally. These actions will reenforce the neighborhood anti-crime proposal announced recently in our urban policy.

NATIONAL INSTITUTE OF JUSTICE

Although the Federal, State and local governments spend billions of dollars each year in their effort to combat crime and improve their criminal justice systems, we do not have adequate tools to assess the impact of these dollars in reducing crime or improving our justice system.

To date, Federal leadership in developing the necessary tools has been uncoordinated, fragmented, and has generally lacked focus.

My proposal will remedy this problem by creating a National Institute of Justice within the Justice Department. The Institute will replace two existing units, the National Institute for Law Enforcement and Criminal Justice and the National Institute of Corrections, and part of a third unit, the Institute of Juvenile Development and Research. The National Institute of Justice will be authorized to undertake basic and applied research, and to conduct evaluations and sponsor demonstrations in the civil and criminal justice areas.

It will centralize the Federal effort to determine how the Federal, State and local governments can most effectively attack the crime problem and strengthen their justice system.

To ensure the independence and integrity of the Institute's efforts, its Director will have final authority for all grants and contracts made by the Institute.

An advisory board to the Institute will be composed of a broadly based group of academic experts, State and local officials, neighborhood and community leaders and citizens. The board will have authority to develop, in conjunction with the Director, policies and priorities for the National Institute of Justice.

BUREAU OF JUSTICE STATISTICS

One of the most valuable services provided by the Federal government in the criminal justice area is the compilation of statistics. However, the Federal effort here has also lacked a central focus and direction.

Under my proposal, a Bureau of Justice Statistics will be created in the Department of Justice. The Bureau will be authorized to collect, analyze and disseminate statistics on criminal and civil justice matters. As a result, the Federal government will be able to provide crime statistics which are reliable and uniform.

An advisory board to the Bureau will consist of researchers, statisticians, State and local officials and citizens. The board would have authority to recommend to the Director policies and priorities for the Bureau of Justice Statistics.

To coordinate the operation of the streamlined LEAA, the National Institute of Justice and the Bureau of Justice Statistics, the Department of Justice will establish the Office of Justice Assistance, Research and Statistics. That Office will be responsible for ensuring that each of these three organizations attacks our criminal and civil justice problems in a focused and complementary way.

The "Justice System Improvement Act of 1978" lays the foundation for an effective Federal program of financial assistance, research and statistics and is vitally important to assist States, local governments and citizens groups in combating and improving the quality of the justice programs. I urge the Congress to give this proposal prompt and favorable consideration.

JIMMY CARTER

The White House,
July 10, 1978.

Veto of the Sikes Act Amendments of 1978

Message to the House of Representatives Returning H.R. 10882 Without Approval.
July 10, 1978

To the House of Representatives:

I am returning without my approval H.R. 10882, the "Sikes Act Amendments of 1978."

The Sikes Act authorizes Federal-State cooperative programs for fish and wildlife conservation and public outdoor recreation on military reservations, National Forests, National Aeronautics and Space Administration sites, and certain Energy and Interior Department lands. It is intended to foster cooperation between the States and Federal land management agencies. H.R. 10882 would extend and increase appropriation authorizations under the Act through 1981.

I am strongly committed to the wise management and conservation of fish and wildlife on public lands; I have recommended appropriations of approximately $35 million for fish and wildlife management on public lands subject to the Sikes Act. This total includes nearly $14.4 million for Federal/State cooperative programs of the type authorized by that Act, programs I believe are valuable and important.

However, these amendments are objectionable in two respects. First, the bill would more than double the current appropriation authorizations for Sikes Act programs—from $23.5 million in 1978 to $51 million in 1979, and $61 million in 1980 and 1981. These funds would be in addition to authorizations under other, more general, land management programs which are now used for carrying out most Sikes Act activities. I insist on adequate attention to the management of fish and wildlife resources on public lands, but the appropriations for these programs must be determined in the context of an effective and efficient management program encompassing all public land resources. These amendments provide unneeded authorization levels for Sikes Act programs.

Second, and more importantly, I object to the requirement in H.R. 10882 that directs the Secretaries of the Interior, Agriculture, and Defense to report to congressional authorizing committees whenever the President's budget request for Sikes Act activities is less than the amount authorized, and requires them to state specifically why the higher amount was not requested. This requirement is designed to bring pressure on the Administration to seek separate additional funds for Sikes Act programs and invites agencies to undercut the President's annual budget he has presented to the Congress. This is an unacceptable intrusion on the President's obligations and authority as Chief Executive. This approach would limit the President's ability to make his annual budget recommendations a positive, comprehensive, and balanced statement of the Administration's policies and budget priorities.

Disapproval of H.R. 10882 will not affect planned Federal expenditures for fish and wildlife management on public lands for 1979 which may be carried out under other more general land management authorities. This Administration will continue to move vigorously ahead in cooperation with the States to implement programs for the conservation and enhancement of fish and wildlife on public lands.

JIMMY CARTER

The White House,
July 10, 1978.

NOTE: The House of Representatives reconsidered H.R. 10882 on July 11, and the bill was referred to committee.

Captive Nations Week, 1978

Proclamation 4578. July 11, 1978

By the President of the United States of America

A Proclamation

By a joint resolution approved July 17, 1959 (73 Stat. 212), the Eighty-Sixth Congress authorized and requested the President to proclaim the third week of July in each year as Captive Nations Week.

For more than two hundred years our Nation has sustained the belief that national independence, liberty and justice are the fundamental rights of all people. Today we reaffirm our commitment to these principles. In particular, we pay tribute to those individuals and groups who demonstrate their attachment to these principles in their own country and throughout the world.

Now, Therefore, I, Jimmy Carter, President of the United States of America, do hereby designate the week beginning July 16, 1978, as Captive Nations Week.

I invite the people of the United States to observe this week with appropriate ceremonies and activities and to renew their dedication to the cause of all people who seek freedom, independence, and basic human rights.

In Witness Whereof, I have hereunto set my hand this eleventh day of July, in the year of our Lord nineteen hundred seventy-eight, and of the Independence of the United States of America the two hundred and third.

Jimmy Carter

[Filed with the Office of the Federal Register, 11:07 a.m., July 12, 1978]

Federal Civil Service Reorganization

Message to the Congress Transmitting an Amendment to Reorganization Plan No. 2 of 1978. July 11, 1978

To the Congress of the United States:

I herewith transmit an amendment to Reorganization Plan No. 2 of 1978, which I transmitted to you on May 23, 1978. Except as specifically amended hereby, Reorganization Plan No. 2 remains unmodified.

Jimmy Carter

The White House,
July 11, 1978.

Amendment to Reorganization Plan No. 2 of 1978

Prepared by the President and transmitted to the Senate and the House of Representatives in Congress assembled July 11, 1978, pursuant to the provisions of Chapter 9 of Title 5 of the United States Code.

Reorganization Plan No. 2 of 1978, which was transmitted to the Senate and the House of Representatives in Congress assembled on May 23, 1978, is hereby amended by deleting the present Section 104(c) and substituting therefor a new Section 104(c) as follows:

"(c) Executing, administering and enforcing the Civil Service rules and regulations of the President and the Office and the statutes governing the same, and other activities of the Office including retirement and classification activities except to the extent such functions remain vested in the Merit Systems Protection Board pursuant to Section 202 of this Plan, or are transferred to the Special Counsel pursuant to Section 204 of this Plan. The Director shall provide the public, where appropriate, a reasonable opportunity to comment and submit written views on the implementation and interpretation of such rules and regulations;"

United States Ambassador to Syria

Nomination of Talcott W. Seelye.
July 11, 1978

The President today announced that he will nominate Talcott W. Seelye, of Bethesda, Md., as Ambassador Extraordinary and Plenipotentiary of the United States to the Syrian Arab Republic. He would replace Richard W. Murphy, who has been appointed Ambassador to the Philippines.

Seelye was born March 6, 1922, in Lebanon, of American parents. He received a B.A. (1947) and LL.D. (1974) from Amherst College. He served in the U.S. Army from 1943 to 1946.

Seelye joined the Foreign Service in 1949, and was posted in Stuttgart, Ulm, Amman, Beirut, and Kuwait. From 1960 to 1964, he was Iraq-Jordan desk officer, then officer in charge of Arabian Peninsula affairs, at the State Department.

In 1964–65 Seelye attended the National War College, and from 1965 to 1968, he was Chief of Mission in Jidda. From 1968 to 1972, he was Country Director for Lebanon, Jordan, the Syrian Arab Republic, and Iraq.

From 1972 to 1976, Seelye was Ambassador to Tunisia. He was Deputy Assistant Secretary of State for African Affairs from 1976 to 1977. In 1976 he also served as special representative to the President of Lebanon.

Interview With the President

Question-and-Answer Session With Western European and Japanese Reporters.
July 11, 1978

SOVIET DISSIDENTS

ALASTAIR BURNET [ITN, Great Britain]. Mr. President, on the eve of your going to Europe, the Russians have put on trial for his life a man who you say is innocent. Why do you think they are trying to insult you, and what can you do for Anatoly Shcharanskiy now?

THE PRESIDENT. Well, some people allege that this is an attack on the American people or our government or on me by the Soviet Union. I don't look on it in that way. I think it's an attack on every human being who lives in the world who believes in basic human freedom and who's willing to speak for these freedoms or to fight for them. The allegation that Shcharanskiy was a spy for the United States is patently false. The Soviets know it to be false. They are prosecuting Shcharanskiy because he represents an element, a small group in the Soviet Union who are fighting for the implementation of international agreements which the Soviets themselves have signed.

The Universal Declaration of Human Rights, the Final Act of the Helsinki agreements guarantee to citizens within a country the right to emigrate, to leave the country, the right to live with their own family members, the right to speak freely and even to criticize their own government. These are the things that the Soviets are attacking in the Shcharanskiy trial, the Ginzburg trial, the Orlov trial, and others. We deplore this, the actions themselves, and the violation of agreements which the Soviets themselves freely signed.

I don't believe that this trial will arouse anything throughout the world except condemnation of the Soviet Union and deploring of this unwarranted action. I don't think it will still the dissident voices. But this is not limited to a single person, nor is it a matter between the Soviet Union and the United States. It involves the whole world. And our responsibility, I think, along with that of other people who are signers, signatories, of these agreements, is to point out the violations when they occur. And we intend to continue to do so.

MR. BURNET. That is all you intend to do?

THE PRESIDENT. Well, there are other actions that are being considered, but of course, we have no mechanism by which we can interfere in the internal affairs of the Soviet Union, nor determine the outcome of the trial, nor determine the punishment, if any, which is allotted to Mr. Shcharanskiy. But we'll continue through every legitimate means to let the Soviets know of our displeasure and also to work toward the minimization of any punishment meted out to him.

INTERNATIONAL ECONOMY

JACQUES SEGUI [TV2, France]. Mr. President, let me talk about another challenge from France and Germany you have to face in Bonn at the economic summit. Does it bother you that certain European countries are actively asserting independence in economic policy?

THE PRESIDENT. Well, we have always favored in the United States, certainly in my own administration, a strong Europe, strong alliances there, politically and economically. And of course, we are participants in the military alliance to protect the freedom of Europe.

We have not studied the recent agreement that apparently is being worked upon by the European nations who have been part of the so-called Snake, now possibly to include in the future other nations involving France, Italy, and Great Britain. I noticed in the news media that Italy and Great Britain have expressed some concern about it. Until we have an analysis made of the details of this proposal, I would not want to comment about its effect on our country. I don't anticipate that there would be any obvious effort to cause a decrease in the value of the dollar nor to work an adverse trade barrier against

American goods. If these things should occur inadvertently, of course, then we would deplore it privately and maybe publicly, but I don't expect this to happen. So, the strengthening of the Economic Community in Europe is something that we do endorse.

MR. SEGUI. And political, too?

THE PRESIDENT. Obviously politically, too, yes.

U.S. ENERGY POLICY

SERGIO TELMON [RAI, Italy]. Mr. President, it is widely expected that the Europeans and the Japanese in Bonn will ask or suggest a reduction in the consumption of energy in the United States. Should the Congress fail to move on your package, what do you propose to do?

THE PRESIDENT. We discussed this subject, as you know, at the London Economic Summit, I think 14 months ago. Each one of the nations made some commitment toward goals which we would try to achieve. Our goal, as expressed, was to reduce the level of imports of oil. We've already been successful in that. The rate of importing oil in our country has dropped almost a million barrels a day. We proposed to the Congress last April a five-part energy plan. The conference committees in the Congress have now approved four of those five parts, which would encompass an additional reduction in oil imports for our country of about 2.3 million dollars (barrels a day).[1]

So, we're making every effort that we can to carry out a proposal that for the first time would give our Nation a comprehensive and understandable energy policy and reduce import levels. We're trying to increase production in our own Nation. We're trying to shift to more plentiful supplies of fuel, like coal, solar energy in some instances, nuclear power. And we're also trying to increase the price

---

[1] Printed in the transcript.

of domestic supplies of gas and oil to the prevailing world market price.

I think the Congress has made great progress already. What many people in Europe don't understand is our Nation is not only a great oil consumer, but we are a great oil-producing Nation and have habitually, historically been so. So, it's a very difficult political issue to change the structure of our laws to hold down the free import for oil and to implement strict conservation measures. But I've been pleased with what the Congress has done so far.

Through administrative action, through working closely with the Congress after this year, after they pass the first series of bills, we hope to continue this progress and, in the process, to increase production in our own country to cut down the demand for imports.

I might say that so far this year the rate of oil imports has dropped also, the first 5 months of 1978. Our increase in imports has come in manufactured goods. And one of the things that we want our trade partners to do in Europe is to increase their economic growth so that they can provide a market for our products that we want to sell. And we in the past have had a much higher rate of growth than have our trading partners who will be at the summit conference.

I think with the reduction in our own rate of growth to a more moderate level, and the increased growth in some of our trading partners' countries, that this adverse trade balance can be alleviated.

VALUE OF THE DOLLAR

HIROSHI NARITA [NHK, Japan]. Mr. President, I would like to ask a question on the dollar. In the light of the U.S. dollar's decline in these days, it is reported that at the summit meeting some other heads of government will ask the United States to stabilize and strengthen the U.S. dollars. Are you going to show them any tactical plan to protect U.S. dollars at the summit meeting?

THE PRESIDENT. The relationship between the dollar and the yen has been affected primarily by the adverse trade balance that we have with Japan. At the last summit meeting in London, for instance, we discussed the very high positive trade balance that Japan enjoyed then. The goal established by your own leaders was that this trade balance would be reduced. Instead, it's continued to go up.

I think, as the economic market leaders have recognized, the high export of Japanese goods and the relatively low imports into Japan of other goods, the yen has strengthened in comparison to other currencies, including, of course, the American dollar.

We don't anticipate intervening in the monetary markets to artifically change those basic relationships between the dollar, the yen, the deutsche mark and other currencies. But unwarranted aberrations of a transient nature we try to iron out, either by purchasing other currencies or by selling the dollar on occasion, and we cooperate with other nations as well. But the long-range trends, I think, have to be established primarily by overall market conditions, primarily trade balances. Temporary aberrations we do try to minimize.

U.S. TRADE BALANCE

MR. NARITA. Are you going to meet Prime Minister Fukuda at Bonn to reduce Japanese trade surplus?

THE PRESIDENT. Yes. One of the things that we would like to see done is for both Japan and Germany to stimulate their own economies so that the growth might be higher and so that they might be better able to buy our own goods that we would like to sell.

Another thing that we need to do is to have a successful multilateral trade negotiation. We are very eager to see tariffs and other trade obstacles removed. So far we haven't had complete success. But to the extent that these barriers to free international commerce are maintained, it makes it much more difficult for us to alleviate these basic problems that we have in trade balances.

As I said earlier, most of our trade balance now comes from the purchase of manufactured goods, not oil. Of course, the nations like Japan and Germany, who sell a lot of manufactured goods to us, like to talk about our oil imports, but they don't deplore the fact that we also buy large quantities of manufactured goods from your country and others.

But I think over a period of time, with complete understanding of one another's problems and a commitment on the part of the leaders, political and economic leaders, both within and out of government, we can bring into more near balance these very wide differences that presently exist in the trade among the developed countries of the world.

INTERNATIONAL ECONOMY

Mr. Burnet. But already, Mr. President, there are many millions of people in Europe and in America who are unemployed and are likely to stay that way. Now, if your talks fail, are we on the brink of a big recession like the 1930's?

The President. No, I don't believe so. We analyze constantly in our country— I'm sure you do in your own countries as well—the underlying economic factors. We compare them with the factors that did exist at the time of the Great Depression and the subsequent, more moderate recessions. One of the most pervasive is-

sues to be discussed at the London conference 14 month ago was the extremely high unemployment rate. This was the most severe problem that I faced as I left London and came back home.

I have only been in office 18 months, and we have had a net increase in jobs available in our own country of 6.4 million, an unprecedented growth in job opportunities. We've reduced the unemployment level by 1¾ million persons, and the unemployment rate about 2 percent, a little bit more than 2 percent.

So, we've had good success in cutting down the unemployment rate in our own country. I know that other nations have not had quite such good success yet. But our growth rate in 1977 was very high.

At the same time we were increasing employment opportunities, we also were able to buy manufactured goods from other nations. Other countries didn't grow quite so fast and couldn't buy our goods. And the present disparity in the value of the dollar and trade balances are a result of those factors.

But I don't anticipate any deterioration, further, in the economic circumstances. And if we can work in harmony with one another, try to understand both common problems and also individual, national problems, and also assess accurately how the action that we take at the summit meeting can affect other nations in the world, both those who are developed and those which are developing, I think we can act substantively to prevent a recurrence of the adverse economic circumstances, including a recession.

U.S. FOREIGN POLICY

Mr. Segui. Mr. President, Western solidarity is coming before or after U.S. interests?

The President. I find it difficult to distinguish between the two. I think that

1255

Western solidarity is a prime requirement for the realization of United States interests. We recognize this intimate tie with both Europe, Canada, and Japan—not only economically, which is what we have been discussing, but also politically and militarily. And my assessment is that these interrelationships have improved. I don't think there's any doubt that now, compared to just a few years ago, NATO is stronger. I think the European Community is stronger. I think our relationship with both Japan and Europe simultaneously is much stronger. I think that the summit conferences that have been held already—the three summit conferences—have contributed to this progress. But I never consider the interest of the United States as being separable from the common interest or well-being of the Alliance.

MR. TELMON. Mr. President, criticism is sometimes voiced on the handling of foreign policy by your administration, especially as far as the Soviet Union is concerned—up and down, human rights, up and down also in defense spending. How can you define your stand on this matter?

THE PRESIDENT. Well, I tried to express in a brief 20- or 25-minute speech at the graduation exercise in Annapolis early this year this very complicated interrelationship with the Soviet Union. We are deeply comitted to détente, both we and, I believe, the Soviet Union leaders. But we think that détente has got to be both broad-based and also reciprocal. We look upon our negotiations with the Soviet Union on the reduction of nuclear weapons as being a critical matter to ourselves and to them and to the world as far as peace is concerned.

And we have never let anything interrupt our effort, which is constant, almost daily, to bring about a successful conclusion of the SALT negotiations. These are going on at this moment between Secretary Vance and Foreign Minister Gromyko, for instance, in Geneva. We are working on the comprehensive test ban. We are trying to prevent the buildup of military forces in the Indian Ocean. We are trying to prevent the development of antisatellite capability on both sides. We are trying also to bring about a successful conclusion of the long dormant mutual and balanced force reduction talks in Vienna.

So, when matters concern mutual security plus matters of common benefit, like increased trade, we cooperate with the Soviets in an enthusiastic and determined fashion.

There are also differences between us and the Soviet Union. We have different forms of government. And I think now and definitely in the future we are going to be competitive with the Soviet Union. We believe in encouraging peace, nonintrusion in the affairs of other governments, an adherence to common agreements on the protection of basic human rights, complete freedom of determination of all nations of their own government, democratic principles. These things are opposed by the Soviet Union. They have a different philosophy of life. We have to recognize these differences.

We don't fear the competition. We are determined to meet the competition openly and appropriately, honestly and enthusiastically again. So, there's a combination there of cooperation, whenever possible, and we hope to expand the areas within which we can cooperate and to meet the competition of the Soviet Union when it's inevitable.

Overriding this is the requirement that we maintain security—of our own Nation, the security of our allies in Europe and in Japan. And we would consider any threat against Western Europe or Japan to be the same as a threat against our own territory.

So, these relationships are very complicated, and I've tried to describe them as best I can in just a few minutes.

WESTERN ROLE IN AFRICA

MR. SEGUI. Mr. President, concerning Africa, for instance, and competition, and concerning the French involvement and the role of France in Africa, do you guess now, in the future, if there is a future crisis again in Africa, then Western shall have to stay in Africa or not? I mean, Western countries, the role of Western countries is essential or not in Africa?

THE PRESIDENT. Yes, I think it's essential. As you know, some of the European nations have had a longstanding relationship in Africa, both as colonial powers and subsequent to that as very interested trade partners with large numbers of their own national citizens living within those countries—France and the Francophone countries, Germany, for instance, in Namibia, and so forth. We are working to try to resolve peacefully the threatening dispute areas.

We are cooperating with the British, for instance, in trying to solve the Rhodesian problem, to bring about majority rule in Rhodesia under a democratic form of government, to try to protect the interests of both the majority and the minority citizens, utilizing the United Nations forces to maintain peace while the electoral process can be put into effect.

We have worked very closely with the frontline nations, those nations surrounding Rhodesia. In Namibia, we are cooperating with France, with Germany, with Great Britain, with Canada, in trying to bring about a peaceful resolution of the Namibian question, withdrawal of South African forces, again establishing a democratic government there under the auspices of the United Nations.

I believe that this kind of role—peaceful, nonintrusive, not based on military action, working closely with the nationals there, the citizens of countries involved—is an appropriate role for us. I think when we have a disturbance of peace, as was the case with the violation of the Zairian border by the Katangan intruders from Angola, that we need to act in concert. My own preference, though, is to see the Organization of African Unity strengthened and any sort of peace-keeping forces be under the auspices of the African nations themselves through the Organization of African Unity.

In a special case, we do provide some military assistance or some logistical support, as we did in Zaire, to remove the nationals who were threatened there. But I think this kind of military action on our part ought to be extremely limited and done only at the request of governments involved.

U.S. RELATIONS WITH CHINA

MR. NARITA. Mr. President, regarding the East-West relations, it seems to me that the United States is willing to have normalization with Peking. When do you expect this normalization to be done, and could you tell me what the effect will be on Taiwan?

THE PRESIDENT. Well, we agree with the principles expressed in the Shanghai Communique, with the ultimate goal being normal relations between ourselves and the People's Republic of China. We don't know how rapidly this process can take place. We have deepfelt needs to protect the interest of the people on Taiwan, to see the dispute between Taiwan and the Mainland resolved by peaceful means. We intend to continue trade with Taiwan. We want to have these relationships clearly understood by the People's Republic of China.

1257

At the same time, before we can reach fully normal relations with the People's Republic, we would like to strengthen our bilateral relationships with them. We've had our Secretary of State go to visit China, as you know; my National Security Adviser has been. We've recently had a very senior scientific and technological delegation go. We'd like to increase trade with the People's Republic, as Japan has already done. But we see in the future continued trade and good relationship with both Taiwan and the Mainland.

We recognize their claim that there is only one China. We don't intend to get involved in that, but we will do what we can to maintain peace and to improve constantly our relationship with the People's Republic.

INTERNATIONAL SUMMIT CONFERENCES

MR. BURNET. A final question, Mr. President. There have been many summit conferences, and great men have got together. But do they really produce anything? Do they not just raise false hopes?

THE PRESIDENT. No, I think they produce a lot. It's impossible to compare the present world situation, following three summit conferences, with what it would have been had those summit conferences not taken place. But I know in my own case, both I, the Vice President, my whole Cabinet, all of my economic and political advisers, my military advisers prepare for months before I go to an economic summit conference. We study the particular perspective of other nations—their problems, their local political circumstances, their special needs, their plans for the future, how they interrelate with one another, how our actions might impact positively or adversely on the people in those other countries. Just the preparation for the summit conference itself is a very instructive and educational process.

And then for us to share problems with one another in a very frank and uninhibited way is also very beneficial. And I think for the world to know what we do afterwards through the communiques is constructive also. And then the last thing is that we set goals for ourselves to strive toward. It lets our own people, our own Congress, our own parliaments know what we hope to achieve. And I think the clarity of those goals, whether or not we achieve them completely, is a very constructive process.

So, I would say in summary that the summit conferences are very constructive, very beneficial to me, to the other leaders, and I think to the people we represent.

MR. BURNET. Thank you, Mr. President.

THE PRESIDENT. Thank you. I enjoyed it.

NOTE: The interview began at 3:03 p.m. in the Map Room at the White House. It was taped for later broadcast on Western European and Japanese television.

The transcript of the interview was released on July 12.

Interview With the President
Question-and-Answer Session With West German Reporters. July 11, 1978

U.S.-SOVIET RELATIONS

PETER MERSEBURGER [ARD Television]. Mr. President, in Berlin you will be facing political East-West realities. You are stressing human rights. At the same time Soviet-American relations are declining. And in Moscow Shcharanskiy is on trial. Don't you think that the two principles are contradicting each other, that human rights is undermining détente?

THE PRESIDENT. Well, we did not initiate the trial of Mr. Shcharanskiy, and we did not initiate the commitment to the preservation of human rights. As you know, the Final Act of the Helsinki agreement was signed by, I think, 35 nations, including the Soviet Union, voluntarily. They also, of course, signed the Universal Declaration of Human Rights as a member of the United Nations.

Their violation of these agreements is something that I think is earning the condemnation of the entire world, all those who believe that a person should have a right to emigrate, to live with his family, to have some possibility for free speech, to criticize one's own government. This is the principle which is on trial in the Soviet Union. We deplore this and make our criticism clear to the Soviet Union, both through diplomatic channels, through private comments, and in some cases publicly. This is not a unique American attitude. Many people throughout the world believe in these basic rights.

At the same time, we recognize that we cannot intrude into the internal affairs of the Soviet Union. We can't determine the outcome of the trial. We can't set the punishment, if any, that might be levied against Mr. Shcharanskiy, Mr. Ginzburg, Mr. Orlov, or others who have expressed themselves and who have tried to monitor the compliance with the Helsinki agreement.

We've not let this interfere in our pursuit of cooperation with the Soviet Union on crucial matters. For instance, we are negotiating, constantly, terms of a SALT agreement to limit and even to reduce the inventory of atomic weapons. We are working with the Soviet Union on a comprehensive test ban. We're trying to bring about, along with your government and others, a successful conclusion to the long stalemated mutual and balanced force reduction talks in Vienna.

So, where there are matters where we can cooperate, of mutual advantage to us,

we are proceeding enthusiastically to bring about a successful resolution of those issues. But on matters where we disagree with the Soviets, because of a difference of perspective and form of government—human rights is one example; their unwarranted intrusion into the African situation is another—we don't hesitate to let our displeasure be known.

HUMAN RIGHTS

PETER GRUBER [ZDF Television]. Mr. President, after being in office for 1½ years, if you judge your human rights policy, don't you think it's counterproductive?

THE PRESIDENT. No, I don't.

MR. GRUBER. Why?

THE PRESIDENT. I think that there is hardly a national leader in the world who doesn't now have as a constant concern or consideration the subject of basic human rights, basic human freedoms, whether or not one's own citizens condemn actions of the government or deplore actions of the government, whether or not the rest of the world looks with pleasure or displeasure on actions within a country.

In many areas of the world the recommitment to human rights initiated by us and many others, I might say, has borne rich dividends. There's been a strong shift toward democratic principles in Latin America. In Indonesia there have been tens of thousands of people liberated from prison. I think we've reexamined in our own country some possible violations of basic human rights. I think other free Western democracies have done the same. And I think the raising of this issue in a responsible, clear way has been a very constructive element throughout the world in ensuring human freedoms in which we believe so deeply.

U.S.-SOVIET RELATIONS

MR. MERSEBURGER. Mr. President, not so far ago, Soviet leader Brezhnev in Bonn agreed on the so-called indivisibility of détente. Do you think a SALT agreement, a new one with the Soviets, is only possible if the Soviets show more restraint in Africa, for instance?

THE PRESIDENT. We are deeply committed to détente. We believe that détente must be broad-ranging, and we also believe that détente must be reciprocal. We believe that world peace is a reciprocal benefit. The conclusion of a SALT agreement is a benefit to both nations and indeed to the entire world. We want to cooperate with the Soviets whenever we possibly can, and we are searching to broaden, not to narrow, the areas where we cooperate and reach agreement.

At the same time, we recognize that because of a difference of philosophy between our two governments, attitudes among our people being different, that we are going to be competitive with the Soviet Union for many years in the future, perhaps generations in the future. We are perfectly willing to be competitive. I think we can prevail, because our natural philosophy of government, based on human freedoms, is more attractive to people. We don't try to interfere with the inclination of nations to preserve their own individuality and their own freedom, contrary to the attitudes of the Soviets in some areas of the world.

We want peace. We don't want to stir up local conflagrations or conflicts. This is contrary to the attitude that the Soviets have exhibited in some areas. We have a need, I believe, over all this, to maintain our own security and the security of our allies. And we are trying to strengthen our ability to meet a possible attack, either by conventional means or by nuclear means,

which would be a holocaust for the entire world, possibly.

I think we've strengthened NATO. And we look upon these alliances, militarily and otherwise, to be an integral part of our own national policy. We, of course, feel that an attack on Western Europe would be exactly the same as an attack on the soil of the United States itself. So, these are complicated interrelationships, but I think they are fairly well defined. And we recognize that cooperation and competition is an integral part of our relationship with the Soviets now and in the future.

MR. GRUBER. There are contradictory voices coming out of Washington concerning the United States relationship to the Soviet Union. There are soft voices and there are tough voices. Which do you prefer to hear?

THE PRESIDENT. Well, the establishment of policy for our Government falls on my shoulders as President. And when we find an area of compatibility, cooperation, mutual advantage, we are very glad to discover this relationship with the Soviet Union. As I said earlier we are trying to broaden the areas in which we can cooperate.

When we disagree, of course we reserve the right as a free nation to let those disagreements be known so that they can be debated, and hopefully progress can be made even in alleviating some of those disagreements. There are some principles that must be maintained. I've mentioned a couple already—our mutual security, basic democratic principles of freedom.

We don't try to intrude into the internal affairs of other countries, but we try to demand that now and in the future international agreements are honored. And with changing circumstances in a very complicated interrelationship, there are times of expressions of cooperation and friendship; there are sometimes legitimate expressions of concern and disagreement. But this doesn't mean that we have different policies. We have one basic policy that is complicated in itself.

U.S. FOREIGN POLICY

MR. MERSEBURGER. There is some European criticism of what is called the unpredictability of the Carter administration. What is your response to that?

THE PRESIDENT. Well, I think any administration must change with changing circumstances. The world is a rapidly changing place. We have tried to have a policy that's clear. A basic principle is to strengthen the alliances that exist between ourselves and the European nations, for instance. We also try to expand the area of friendship with the newly emerging nations of the world, the ones that in the past have not been very strong or effective or active but are presently increasing their influence.

I would say that in Africa, Nigeria would be an example of that, that Indonesia would be another example, Brazil, Venezuela, India, of course. We are trying to improve our relationships with the People's Republic of China. We have a new interest in Africa, trying to preserve peace there in Namibia, Rhodesia, in the Horn of Africa.

We are trying to lower the level of conventional weapons sales, reduce the level of nuclear armaments. We have a nonproliferation policy. We're trying to understand the economic interrelationships that exist between the developed nations of the world and between us and the developing countries of the world.

So, I think that all these matters that we have addressed are individually different from one another, but collectively, they comprise the American foreign policy. It's very clear in my own mind what we hope to achieve. We spell it out for those who will listen, and with changing circumstances, of course, in the future, over a period of years, of course, our country will have to change its own policy. But we are a leading nation on Earth.

I think our policies directly affect many other people. And those many diverse peoples look upon our country with different perspectives. But there's nothing simple or easy about international economic or political or military affairs. But I think we have a very stable, very clear foreign policy that changes in an evolutionary way, not a revolutionary way.

U.S. ECONOMIC POLICIES

MR. GRUBER. You are going to Bonn to take part at the economic summit. You didn't finish your energy legislation. You couldn't reduce your trade deficit. Would you say you are going empty-handed to Bonn?

THE PRESIDENT. No. I've reexamined the commitments that we made at the last economic summit in London. We promised to reduce the level of oil imports in our country. We have done so. The first 5 months of 1978 our average imports of foreign oil were about a million barrels a day less than they had been during the year 1977. We promised to do what we could to reduce unemployment in our countries. I've only been in office 18 months, but we have had a net increase in employment in our Nation of 6.4 million jobs. We've reduced the unemployment level 1¾ million jobs. We reduced the unemployment rate by 2 percent.

We've had good progress in the Congress in implementing a national energy plan. It has five basic component parts. Already the conference committees have approved four of the five. The net result of this, when implemented, will be to reduce oil imports an additional 2.3 million barrels per day. This is a very difficult thing in our country, because, as is quite often not understood in some Europe nations, and perhaps even Japan, we are not only a very heavy consumer of oil and natural gas, but we are also one of the world's greatest producers of oil and natural gas.

And to change from a deep concern about production, which has been our Government policy in the past, to a new concern about conservation and a shift toward other more plentiful supplies of energy is not easy for a country. But we are making good progress; my prediction is that the Congress will act successfully on our energy plan before they adjourn this year.

Mr. GRUBER. So, what options will you bring to Bonn?

THE PRESIDENT. Well, that which I've just described concerning energy, to continue to reduce the level of oil imports, a presentation to the other countries of items with which they may not be familiar, that is, that our adverse trade balance has been primarily attributable this year not to oil imports, but to the importation of manufactured goods, a lot of them from Germany, a lot of them from Japan.

We have maintained and reached our goal of sustained economic growth in our country. Other nations, Japan, and Germany have not been so successful. In 1977, our economic growth rate was much higher than the average of our other trading partners who will be at the summit. We were much more able to purchase your goods than you were to purchase our goods. I think now there's a more moderate level of growth in our own Nation and perhaps an increasing rate of growth in your country and that of Japan. Perhaps in the future you'll be able to buy our goods better than you did in 1977.

The underlying economic problem is the very high adverse trade balance. We

have a negative trade balance. Germany and Japan have very high, positive trade balances. But I think that this circumstance will improve. We are all concerned about inflation. We are all concerned about unemployment. We recognize that what's good for our country almost inevitably is good for all of our trade partners. The last thing I'd want to say is we hope to bring about a successful conclusion of the multilateral trade negotiations, which have not been successful so far. We want to reduce tariffs and other impediments to free trade.

I think we are the most enthusiastic nation among those who will be at the Bonn summit in that respect. And we hope that the European nations and Japan will respond as enthusiastically as are we. We need more ability to market our own goods among our trading partners.

So, those are the three basic items: energy, trade relationships, improved inflation and unemployment circumstances.

U.S.-GERMAN RELATIONS

Mr. MERSEBURGER. There has been some confusing signals concerning German-American relations the last year— neutron bomb, disagreement on economics, nonproliferation policies. Is it perhaps, Mr. President, that the Germans expect a stronger leadership and you prefer to deal between equal partners? You expect them to be more responsible, to do more?

THE PRESIDENT. I doubt that the German Government or people look to us to dominate or to impose our will on them or anyone else. We recognize the economic and military, political strength of our country. It's not only a privilege, it's also a heavy responsibility.

We recognize clearly that what happens in our own Nation affects directly the lives of many people around the world.

This puts on my shoulders the responsibility of having very close relationships with the leaders of countries who are allies of ours. I have met personally with Chancellor Helmut Schmidt four times. Every 3 or 4 months we have been together. We have frequent exchanges of messages through diplomatic channels, and we call each other, without any crisis evolving, on the telephone fairly often just to discuss matters that are of interest to our people.

I was at Camp David this past week. Helmut called me on the phone. We had quite an extensive conversation. And I'll be spending 2 days with him before the economic summit commences. So, I think that this constant exchange of information, consultation, advice, on occasion, criticism, is healthy and constructive.

Ultimately, in a democracy we leaders are responsible to our people. And our policies can't depart too greatly from those that our people espouse. But I have no concern at all about the stability of our relationship, the commonality of our interests and purposes, and the strength of our cooperation at the government level and on a personal basis as well.

I've had the privilege not only of meeting with Chancellor Schmidt, but many of the members of his Cabinet, some of the members of the opposition parties. And I think throughout that entire gamut of responsible and distinguished leaders of the Federal Republic of Germany there's a common realization that what I've said is true, that we share so much responsibility and opportunity, that we are so closely intertwined in our destiny, the shaping of it, and that the people demand that we enhance our personal relationships. And I feel very proud of this relationship, have no concern about it at all.

MR. GRUBER. In the foreseeable future, Mr. President, can you imagine any circumstances which might allow self-determination in East Germany?

THE PRESIDENT. We would like to see a unified Germany based on self-determination. That's our ultimate goal. And we would contribute in any way we could to bring this about. That's also the goal, I believe, of all the Western allies. And we hope that some day we'll see a unified Germany.

ROLE OF CHINA IN U.S.-SOVIET RELATIONS

MR. MERSEBURGER. Mr. President, would you like to see China concerning in relation to the Soviet Union, as a lever to nudge the Soviet Union in the direction of confrontation or cooperation?

THE PRESIDENT. I think it would be a serious mistake for ourselves, for the People's Republic of China, for the Soviet Union, to try to play one against another. We develop our relationships with each country in the world on a bilateral basis, what's best for their people and ours directly. We would never use China as a lever against the Soviet Union. I think the Chinese people would resent it very deeply, and I think the Soviet Union would also.

I think it would be a counterproductive thing for us. We want to have normal relationships with China in carrying out the terms of the Shanghai Communique, and we want to increase the cooperation with the Soviet Union. But to play one against another would be a very serious mistake which we would never make.

MR. MERSEBURGER. Thank you very much, Mr. President.

THE PRESIDENT. Thank you. I've enjoyed it.

NOTE: The interview began at 3:33 p.m. in the Map Room at the White House. It was taped for later broadcast on West German television.

The transcript of the interview was released on July 12.

President's Commission on Pension Policy

Executive Order 12071. July 12, 1978

By the authority vested in me as President by the Constitution of the United States of America, and in order to create in accordance with the Federal Advisory Committee Act (5 U.S.C. App. I) an advisory commission on national policies for retirement, survivor, and disability programs, it is hereby ordered as follows:

1-1. *Establishment of Commission.*

1-101. There is established the President's Commission on Pension Policy. The Commission shall be composed of eleven members.

1-102. The members of the Commission shall be appointed by the President. The President shall designate a Chairman from among the members.

1-2. *Functions of the Commission.*

1-201. The Commission shall conduct a comprehensive review of retirement, survivor, and disability programs existing in the United States, including private, Federal, State and local programs.

1-202. The Commission shall develop national policies for retirement, survivor, and disability programs that can be used as a guide by public and private programs. Those policies must be designed to ensure that the Nation has effective and equitable retirement, survivor, and disability programs which take into account available resources and demographic changes that are expected into the middle of the next century.

1-203. The Commission shall submit to the President a series of reports. These reports shall include the Commission's findings and recommendations on short-term and long-term issues with respect to retirement, survivor, and disability programs, including, but not restricted to, the following:

(a) present overlaps and gaps among the private, State and local sectors in providing income to retired, surviving, and disabled persons;

(b) the financial ability of present private, Federal, State and local retirement, survivor, and disability systems to meet their future obligations;

(c) appropriate retirement ages, the relationship of the annuity levels to past earnings and contributions, and the role of current retirement, survivor, and disability programs in private capital formation and economic growth;

(d) the implications of the recommended national policies for the financing and benefit structures of the retirement, survivor, and disability programs in the public and private sectors; and

(e) specific reforms and organizational changes in the present systems that may be required to meet the goals of the national policies.

1-204. The Commission shall submit its final report, including its recommendations and findings, to the President prior to its termination.

1-3. *Administrative Provisions and Financial Support.*

1-301. At the request of the Chairman each Executive agency that has an interest or responsibility in the areas of the Commission's functions shall designate an individual to act as liaison with the Commission and its staff.

1-302. In performing its functions, the Commission shall seek the advice of individuals and groups interested in policies applicable to retirement, survivor, and disability programs and systems. In seeking advice from interested individuals and groups, including public and private organizations, the Commission or any committee thereof, may, among other activities, hold hearings and sit and act at such times and places as the Commission or such authorized committee may find advisable.

1–303. The Commission may request any Executive agency to furnish such information as may be helpful for the fulfillment of the Commission's functions under this Order. Each such agency is authorized, to the extent permitted by law and within the limits of available funds, to furnish such information to the Commission.

1–304. The Commission is authorized to appoint and fix the compensation of a staff, including not more than one position at the GS–18 level, as may be necessary to enable it to carry out its functions. The Commission may obtain services in accordance with the provisions of Section 3109 of Title 5 of the United States Code, to the extent funds are available therefore.

1–305. Each member of the Commission who is not otherwise employed in the Government may receive, to the extent permitted by law, compensation for each day he or she is engaged upon the work of the Commission at a rate not to exceed the maximum daily rate now or hereafter prescribed by law for GS–18 of the General Schedule, and may also receive travel expenses, including per diem in lieu of subsistence, as authorized by law (5 U.S.C. 5703) for persons in the government service employed intermittently.

1–306. The General Services Administration shall provide administrative services, facilities, and support to the Commission on a reimbursable basis.

1–307. All necessary expenses incurred in connection with the work of the Commission shall be paid from the appropriation for "Unanticipated Needs," in the Executive Office Appropriations Act, 1978, or from such other funds as may be available.

1–4. *General Provisions.*

1–401. The functions of the President under the Federal Advisory Committee Act (5 U.S.C. App. I), except that of reporting annually to the Congress, which are applicable to the Commission, shall be performed by the Administrator of General Services.

1–402. The Commission shall terminate one year after the effective date of this Order.

1–403. This Order shall be effective on the day of the first meeting of the Commission members.

JIMMY CARTER

The White House,
July 12, 1978.

[Filed with the Office of the Federal Register, 10:38 a.m., July 13, 1978]

NOTE: Additional information on the Executive order also was included in the release.

Department of Defense

Nomination of Stanley R. Resor To Be Under Secretary for Policy. July 12, 1978

The President today announced that he will nominate Stanley R. Resor, of New Canaan, Conn., to be Under Secretary of Defense for Policy.

Resor was born December 5, 1917, in New York City. He received a B.A. (1939) and LL.B. (1946) from Yale University. He served in the U.S. Army from 1942 to 1946.

Resor practiced law in New York City from 1946 to 1965 and from 1971 to 1973. He served as Under Secretary of the Army in 1965 and as Secretary of the Army from 1965 to 1971. Since 1973 he has been U.S. Representative to the negotiations on Mutual and Balanced Force Reductions being held in Vienna, Austria.

United States Ambassador to Yemen

Nomination of George M. Lane.
July 12, 1978

The President today announced that he will nominate George M. Lane, of Westminster, Mass., to be Ambassador Extraordinary and Plenipotentiary of the United States to the Yemen Arab Republic. He would replace Thomas J. Scotes, who has resigned.

Lane was born October 15, 1928, in Baltimore, Md. He received a B.A. from Cornell University in 1951 and an M.A. from Fletcher School of Law and Diplomacy in 1957. He served in the U.S. Army from 1951 to 1954.

Lane joined the Foreign Service in 1957 and served as an international relations officer at the State Department. He was posted in Beirut, Jidda, Aleppo, Rabat, and Benghazi. From 1970 to 1972, he was a personnel officer at the State Department, and from 1972 to 1973, he was an international relations officer.

From 1973 to 1974, Lane was Deputy Director, then Acting Director of the Office of North African Affairs at the State Department. From 1974 to 1976, he was Deputy Chief of Mission in Mbabane, and since 1976 he has been Deputy Chief of Mission in Beirut.

South Pacific Commission

Appointment of George Chaplin as U.S.
Alternate Representative. July 12, 1978

The President today announced the appointment of George Chaplin as United States Alternate Representative on the South Pacific Commission. He replaces D. Hebden Porteus.

Chaplin, 64, of Honolulu, has been editor of the Honolulu Advertiser since 1959. Before moving to Hawaii he was managing editor, then editor of the New Orleans Item.

Equal Rights Amendment

Letter to Members of the House Judiciary
Committee. July 12, 1978

Next week, the Judiciary Committee will be voting on H.J. Res. 638, which would extend the time for ratification of the Equal Rights Amendment. I am writing to let you, and other members of the Committee, know of my strong support for an extension of the deadline beyond March 22, 1979.

The Equal Rights Amendment is a long overdue addition to our Constitution: it will guarantee equal rights for all Americans, regardless of sex. I commend you, and the Judiciary Committee, for your efforts in 1972 proposing the Amendment and your vital support, since then, for ratification.

I am hopeful that ERA will be ratified before the present deadline expires, and I am committed to doing whatever I can to help the ratification process. But I am concerned that the current deadline may be an unnecessary barrier toward ensuring more than a hundred million Americans their constitutional rights. I do not believe that, just as we move so close to ensuring those rights, the struggle for ERA must be ended because of an original seven year deadline.

There is no constitutional requirement that ratification occur within a seven year period, nor within the period originally established for ratification. Under the Constitution, in the opinion of the Justice Department, Congress is empowered to determine the period of ratification and can change, by resolution, any previously established ratification period.

I urge the Committee to exercise its authority to extend the ratification deadline for ERA.

Sincerely,

JIMMY CARTER

NOTE: This is the text of identical letters addressed to Representative Peter W. Rodino, Jr., chairman of the House Judiciary Committee, and Representative Don Edwards, chairman of the committee's Civil and Constitutional Rights Subcommittee.

The President's Visit to the Federal Republic of Germany

Remarks on Departure From the White House. July 13, 1978

THE VICE PRESIDENT. *Mr. President, Mrs. Carter, Amy:*

Since this administration assumed office, it has established no higher foreign policy priority than the closest possible working relationship between the industrial democracies of Western Europe and Japan. The International Economic Summit Conference in Bonn is a part of that effort.

Since assuming office we have made substantial progress in assuming our share of the international economic burdens. In the past year and a half, we have added more jobs to the work force in America, 6.1 million jobs, than in any other period in the history of the United States.

In the energy field we are well along the way in establishing a basic and profound change in America's energy approach. We have established a Department of Energy. We have made substantial progress in the adoption of the most comprehensive and profound energy package ever proposed to the Congress. And this year we will use

a million barrels less of foreign oil than last year.

The President will also be visiting Berlin to renew personally on behalf of the American people our friendship and our commitment to the free people of Berlin.

Mr. President, on your mission you take with you our hopes for success and our love, and we hope a speedy return. Thank you very much.

THE PRESIDENT. We leave this morning for two trips combined into one. The first will be an official visit by me representing the United States to the people of the Federal Republic of Germany—this visit will last 2 days—to be followed by the fourth economic summit conducted by the leaders of the seven industrialized democracies.

On this journey I recognize the economic interdependence of the people of the world. And I also understand that in the free democracies, that we must demonstrate and we can demonstrate the strength, the vitality, and the cooperation that has existed among us and has been the foundation for our progress.

It's almost a cliche to say that the Federal Republic of Germany has performed an economic miracle in rising from the devastation of war to one of the leading industrial economic nations of the world. This is, of course, attributable to the tenacity and courage and the industrious nature of the German people. But it's also a tribute to the fact that they are free and that they function under the terms of a democratic society.

We demonstrated this in our own country when, because of the freedom of the human spirit, we were able to change a wilderness into a nation which is now a world leader. The Federal Republic shows that same freedom of the human spirit, a dedication to liberty, to individual human rights, and they have rebuilt their country when their industrial base and many of their cities had been thoroughly destroyed by the devastation of war.

The fact that Europe and Japan are now industrial and economic giants is, of course, a tribute to themselves, to their determination and their resourcefulness, but also a tribute to the wisdom of the United States in giving them help after the Second World War. Again, in Europe as in Japan this is a tribute to the democratic system.

In the summit conference, following my state visit to Germany, we will continue the process of cooperation, consultation, the sharing of problems and opportunities, the establishment of goals among the seven industrialized nations. We will discuss a broad range of economic issues, and I will be able to renew my own friendships with the leaders of the other countries, to explain the position, the attitude, the special problems of the United States of America, to outline our accomplishments, and to learn the same information from each of them.

We recognize that we have a responsibility to strengthen our own systems, to give a better life for our own people, to cooperate more closely. But at the same time we are not selfish in our attitudes, because history has taught us the dangers of economic chaos throughout the world and the dangers of unlimited human suffering caused by economic deprivation.

We don't expect to solve all the problems of the world, but we do expect to leave the economic summit with a more thorough understanding of the mutual nature of our responsibilities, a renewed commitment, a renewed confidence, a renewed common commitment and effort to having a better future for our people.

We'll establish goals that will be educational among ourselves, that will increase cooperation, that will let the parliaments and the congresses work in closer

harmony with the executive leaders of our countries. And I believe it will also be an educational process for the general public who observe our actions and our statements from around the world.

I leave here, finally, with a great pride in my own country, the United States of America, confidence in our system, confidence in our economic and political and military strength, recognizing the position of leadership that has been carved out by the achievements of a free society.

I will express first my friendship for the German people and then express my friendship through their leaders of those who live in Italy, France, Great Britain, Japan, Canada.

This is a sober time. It's one of reassessment, not one of discouragement; one of determination to improve the circumstances which we face. And as I leave on this trip, representing the greatest nation on Earth, I hope and I pray that I can represent the people of the United States well. Thank you very much.

NOTE: The exchange of remarks began at 8:35 a.m. on the South Lawn of the White House.

Department of Energy

Nomination of Ruth C. Clusen To Be an Assistant Secretary. *July 13, 1978*

The President today announced that he will nominate Ruth C. Clusen, of Green Bay, Wis., to be an Assistant Secretary of Energy. Her area of responsibility would be environment.

Clusen was born June 11, 1922, in Bruce, Wis. She received a B.S. from the University of Wisconsin in 1945.

Clusen was a teacher from 1947 to 1951 and in 1957–58. She has been with the League of Women Voters since 1946, and served as president from 1974 to May 1978.

Clusen has served as an environmental consultant to the Interior Department, the Conservation Foundation, the U.S. Chamber of Commerce, and the Wisconsin Department of Natural Resources. She was a member of the U.S. Delegation to the U.S.-U.S.S.R. Joint Committee on Environmental Protection in Moscow in 1974, and participated in the U.N. Conference on Human Environment in Stockholm in 1972.

Bureau of Mines

Nomination of Roger A. Markle To Be Director.   July 13, 1978

The President today announced that he will nominate Roger A. Markle, of Salt Lake City, Utah, to be Director of the Bureau of Mines at the Interior Department. He would replace Thomas V. Falkie, who has resigned.

Markle was born December 12, 1933, in Sidney, Mont. He received a B.S. in mining engineering from the University of Alaska in 1959, an M.S. in mine management from Stanford University in 1965, and an M.B.A. from the University of Chicago in 1971. He served in the U.S. Navy.

From 1958 to 1961, Markle was with Alaska Mines & Minerals, Inc., serving as mill superintendent, chief mine engineer, and then general superintendent. From 1962 to 1964, he was an instructor of adult education at the University of Alaska.

From 1965 to 1974, Markle was with Standard Oil Co. (Indiana) and its subsidiaries, in various positions related to mining and ending as manager of mine development. Since 1974 he has been president of the western division of the Valley Camp Coal Company.

Markle was appointed by the Governor to Utah's Energy Conservation and Development Council and to the Blue Ribbon Joint Legislative Committee on Energy Policy. He is chairman of the Interagency Task Force on Power Plant Siting.

United States Railway Association

Nomination of William K. Smith To Be Chairman of the Board of Directors. July 13, 1978

The President today announced that he will nominate William K. Smith, of Minnesota, to be Chairman of the Board of Directors of the United States Railway Association for a 6-year term. He would replace Arthur D. Lewis, resigned.

Smith was born April 21, 1922, in Oakland, Calif. He received a B.B.A. from the University of Minnesota in 1947. He served in the U.S. Army during World War II.

Smith joined General Mills in 1948 as a transportation clerk in San Francisco. Since that time he has been associated with the corporation's transportation department in a variety of positions and locations. In 1955 he became assistant director of transportation at the corporate headquarters in Minneapolis.

Smith has been director of transportation for General Mills since 1965 and vice president of the company since 1968.

Smith has been on the Board of Directors of the U.S. Railway Association since 1974. He has been serving as Acting Chairman of the Board since 1977.

Smith is also a board member of the Transportation Association of America and a vice president of the National Industrial Traffic League.

Civil Aeronautics Board

Nomination of Gloria Schaffer To Be a Member. July 13, 1978

The President today announced that he will nominate Gloria Schaffer, of Woodbridge, Conn., to be a member of the Civil Aeronautics Board for the remainder of the term expiring December 31, 1978, and for a new term expiring December 31, 1984.

Schaffer was born October 3, 1930, in New London, Conn. She attended Sarah Lawrence College.

Schaffer was elected to the Connecticut State Senate in 1958 and served six terms. In 1970 she was elected secretary of state of Connecticut, and she was re-elected in 1974.

Schaffer is chairwoman of the Connecticut Council on Human Services. She has served as a representative to the White House Conference on Education, and as a member of the Federal Election Commission Advisory Panel, the National Education Commission of the States, and the United States National Commission on UNESCO.

As a State senator Schaffer chaired the public welfare and humane institutions committee, the penal institutions committee, and, for three terms, the education committee.

Council on Environmental Quality

Nomination of Jane Hurt Yarn To Be a Member. July 13, 1978

The President today announced that he will nominate Jane Hurt Yarn, of Atlanta, Ga., to be a member of the Council on Environmental Quality. She would replace John A. Busterud, who has resigned.

Yarn was born October 15, 1924, in Greenville, S.C. She graduated from Saint Mary's College in Raleigh, N.C., and did postgraduate work in landscape design at the University of Georgia.

Since 1952 she has owned and managed a farm in Jackson County, Ala., where she raises cattle, row crops, and trees. She has been a member of the board of governors of the Nature Conservancy since 1969, and served as vice chairman from 1972 to 1974 and as chairman of the Georgia Coastal Islands Committee from 1969 to 1970.

Yarn was a founder of Save America's Vital Environment (SAVE) in 1970 and served as president from 1970 to 1972. Since 1977 she has been chairman of the Charles A. Lindbergh Fund, responsible for raising funds for grants in the fields of aeronautics, wildlife, exploration, natural sciences, or environment.

Federal Mine Safety and Health Review Commission

Nomination of Richard V. Backley To Be a Member. July 13, 1978

The President today announced that he will nominate Richard V. Backley, of Fairfax, Va., to be a member of the Federal Mine Safety and Health Review Commission for a 4-year term.

Backley was born July 21, 1927, in Chicago. He received an LL.B. from De Paul University in 1955.

Backley practiced law in Chicago from 1955 to 1957 and was a trial counsel for Montgomery Ward from 1957 to 1960. From 1960 to 1967, he was District Attorney for the Trust Territory of the Pacific Islands.

From 1967 to 1970, Backley was attorney adviser to the Federal Water Pollution Control Administration (now EPA) at the Interior Department. In 1970, with the enactment of the Federal Coal Mine Health and Safety Act of 1969, he became a senior trial attorney with the newly formed Division of Mine Health and Safety at Interior.

In 1974 Backley was certified as an administrative law judge. The same year he was promoted to the position of Assistant Solicitor in the Division of Mine Health and Safety, where he supervised a staff of 19 attorneys which handled all administrative proceedings involving mine safety before administrative law judges.

Since 1975 Backley has been an administrative law judge with the Civil Aeronautics Board.

Federal Coal Mine Health Activities

Message to the Congress Transmitting a Report. *July 13, 1978*

To the Congress of the United States:

I transmit herewith the 1976 Annual Report of Health Activities under the Federal Coal Mine Health and Safety Act of 1969.

I recommend that the statutory reporting requirement for this report be changed from once every year to once every three years. HEW staff resources and time could be better spent on more research rather than on the preparation of annual reports of largely repetitious material. Basic information in this field has been known for some time, and new findings develop only slowly and infrequently. All of the information contained in this report is available to Congress during annual appropriations and oversight hearings, and HEW will inform Congress immediately of any scientific breakthroughs in the field.

This report describes activities prior to the beginning of my Administration.

JIMMY CARTER

The White House,
July 13, 1978.

NOTE: The 33-page report is entitled "The Federal Coal Mine Health Program in 1976: Seventh Annual Report of Health Activities Under the Federal Coal Mine Health and Safety Act of 1969—U.S. Department of Health, Education, and Welfare, Public Health Service, Center for Disease Control, National Institute for Occupational Safety and Health."

Agreement on Namibia

White House Statement. *July 13, 1978*

The President welcomes the agreement reached yesterday in Luanda between SWAPO and the Western five contact group concerning a peaceful solution to the Namibia question. While we are awaiting a full report of the details we understand that with South African cooperation the way is now open to an early decision by the Security Council to cooperate with all the parties involved to bring Namibia to early independence.

The President appreciates the efforts of all the parties involved, including the frontline states of Africa whose cooperation has been so essential in the important progress which has been made. The United States will continue to cooperate fully in the implementation of the agreement.

Trade Negotiations in Geneva, Switzerland

White House Statement. *July 13, 1978*

The President is pleased by the announcement from trade negotiators at Geneva of progress in their presummit negotiations. He looks forward to a more detailed report from Ambassador Strauss in Bonn. Further advances will be needed to achieve a constructive outcome. The President believes the work done so far in Geneva provides a good basis for progress in this area at the Bonn summit.

Interview With the President

Question-and-Answer Session With Heinz Lohfeldt of Der Spiegel Magazine.
July 11, 1978

U.S.-GERMAN RELATIONS

MR. LOHFELDT. Mr. President, critics on both sides of the Atlantic assert that relations between the United States and its strongest ally in Europe, the Federal Republic, have reached a low point.

THE PRESIDENT. I believe that German-American relations are in fact both very good and extraordinarily close. Our two governments consult as intensely and frequently as at any other time in the history of the Western Alliance. And on our basic objectives, we agree completely. Naturally, we may sometimes differ in specific goals and approaches, but these honest differences, frankly expressed, between close friends and allies are actually a sign of the strength of our relationship.

MR. LOHFELDT. So there is no bad rapport between you and Chancellor Schmidt?

THE PRESIDENT. My personal relationship with Chancellor Schmidt is excellent. I have met with him four times since coming into office, and we consult regularly by telephone. I have the highest respect and regard for him as a wise and distinguished statesman, and as a personal friend. Our meetings have always been a source of personal pleasure and value for me, and I look forward to seeing him again in Bonn this week.

MR. LOHFELDT. Do you think that Germany should play a special role within the Western Alliance, and how would you describe this role?

THE PRESIDENT. The Federal Republic plays a vital role within the Western Alliance, in close harmony with the United States and our mutual allies. It is Western Europe's strongest economic power, it makes a large and effective contribution to NATO security, and it shares in the political leadership of the Alliance. This is not a "special" role, as you suggest, rather it reflects the deep commitment of a nation that prizes its freedom and its partnership with like-minded nations of the West.

U.S. ROLE IN EUROPE

MR. LOHFELDT. In Europe, but here in the United States as well, there is increasing talk of an American "leadership crisis." In the U.S., this crisis is reflected in the most recent, rather negative opinion polls. Within the Western Alliance, this criticism for example has been voiced by Chancellor Helmut Schmidt during his last visit to Washington. What is your response to those critics?

THE PRESIDENT. Well, I think, the stability of the Western Alliance is a proof that we don't lack leadership. There was a time, maybe a couple of years ago and before, when the commitment to NATO, for instance, was very doubtful among some of the members.

Now there is again a new spirit of commitment to a stronger NATO Alliance. Our own Congress, the people of our Nation, have a much firmer commitment to the NATO Alliance than was the case in the past. And we have a strong relationship with our allies and friends as we have ever had that I can remember in my lifetime. So, I think, there is no evidence of a lack of adequate leadership. The leadership as evidenced in this community of Western democracies is very tangible and demonstrable.

U.S.-SOVIET RELATIONS

MR. LOHFELDT. Critics charge there is no clear American foreign policy concept, and especially no clear concept for American policy towards the Soviet Union. For example, on the one hand, you and your advisers oppose the Soviet expansion in Africa, while on the other hand, your Secretary of State, Cyrus Vance, resumes the negotiations for a new SALT agreement with his Soviet counterpart, Gromyko. How do you reconcile these policies?

THE PRESIDENT. The United States seeks a détente that is both broadly defined and fully reciprocal. We recognize, however, that our relations with the Soviet Union will continue to be a mixture of cooperation and competition. For our part, we want to enlarge areas of cooperation, and my administration has engaged the Soviet Union in a broad range of efforts to limit and reduce arms. But when necessary, we will act to ensure our security and that of our allies.

If there is to be a genuine détente, the Soviet Union must recognize, as we do, the responsibility we both share to work for just and peaceful solutions to the world's problems, rather than aggravating those problems or increasing the likelihood of conflict. This is why we have expressed our concern over the actions of the Soviet Union and its ally Cuba in Africa.

MR. LOHFELDT. But you refuse to link SALT——

THE PRESIDENT. With regard to SALT, my administration has from the beginning placed the highest importance on the need to halt the upward spiral of nuclear weapons. We are prepared to conclude a SALT II agreement that truly

enhances Western security. As I said at Annapolis:

"We have no desire to link this negotiation for a SALT agreement with other competitive relationships nor to impose other special conditions on the process. In a democratic society, however, where public opinion is an integral factor in the shaping and implementation of foreign policy, we do recognize that tensions, sharp disputes, or threats to peace will complicate the quest for a successful agreement. This is not a matter of our preference but a simple recognition of facts."

MR. LOHFELDT. While you refuse to link the SALT talks to any other problem in American-Soviet relations, the Soviets are challenging the West in Africa, take American newspapermen into court, and hold trials against prominent Soviet dissidents. Don't you feel that they are exploiting the American policy of no linkage and try to test your resolve?

THE PRESIDENT. I don't believe that a trial of innocent citizens, whether they be Americans or Soviet citizens, is a test of my own resolve or an attack on the people of the United States. This problem of Shcharanskiy, Ginzburg, Orlov, and others, of American newspersons and American businessmen is really an attack on people throughout the world who believe in human freedom. And it is made in direct violation of written international agreements signed voluntarily by the Soviet Union.

The Universal Declaration of Human Rights, signed by the Soviet Union as part of the United Nations, and the Final Act of the Helsinki agreement, which was signed by the Soviet Union, along with 34 other nations in Europe and North America, calls for the preservation within each country individually of the rights of a citizen to emigrate if he chooses, or to live with one's own family, or to voice opinions even sometimes in criticism of one's own government. The Soviets have violated the various agreements which they voluntarily signed.

SOVIET DISSIDENTS

MR. LOHFELDT. The Soviets argue that the dissident trials are a purely Soviet matter and charge your administration with interference in their internal affairs.

THE PRESIDENT. When we speak out on humanitarian issues, we do so not to interfere in the internal affairs of other nations, but because of our belief in the value of the individual. Our concern for human rights is global and is not restricted to any nation or region. But my guess is that this effort in stamping out dissident voices will be unsuccessful. So, I don't look upon this action by the Soviets as an attack on me or on the American people. It doesn't damage our country. I think it arises an almost universal, justifiable condemnation of the world towards the Soviets and reveals a weakness of their own system of not being able to withstand the lonely voice of a dissident or an accurate newspaper report that is printed not in the Soviet Union, but in a foreign country.

STRATEGIC ARMS LIMITATION

MR. LOHFELDT. In view of the most recent Soviet actions, especially the trials in Moscow, the pressure of linking these actions and SALT is rapidly growing here in Washington. Senator Jackson called the resumption of the SALT talks "the wrong signal at the wrong time." What is your answer to these pressures?

THE PRESIDENT. Well, throughout history the interrelationship between the Soviet Union and the United States has demonstrated the advisability of searching out common ground on which we could cooperate to the mutual benefit of our people.

In the heat of the Vietnam war, I think in the same month that we mined the harbor of Haiphong, SALT I was signed. So, when it is obviously to the mutual benefit of our people and to the benefit of the entire world to restrict or even to reduce the level of nuclear weapon inventories, it would be a serious mistake to terminate those discussions or those conferences because of other factors which don't directly reflect on them. So, we have kept separate the negotiations with the Soviet Union on SALT.

But we reserve the right to privately and publicly criticize the Soviets when they violate the basic human rights agreements that they have signed or when through unwarranted actions they have intruded themselves or their surrogates, the Cuban troops, into the internal affairs of, for instance, African nations.

MR. LOHFELDT. Do you share Secretary Vance's optimism that a new SALT agreement will ultimately be ratified by the U.S. Senate? Right now it seems that many Senators consider the linkage a reality and would not be prepared to judge a new SALT agreement on its own merits, but rather in connection with the general Soviet behavior.

THE PRESIDENT. Yes, my belief is that the Senate will ultimately make a judgment on the merits of the agreement itself. And there is an overwhelming support for a successful and mutually beneficial SALT agreement among the American people. I think this support will be mirrored ultimately in the action of the U.S. Senate. And my experience with the Senate has been that in a showdown, when the final decision is made, they will act responsibly and in the best interest of all.

MR. LOHFELDT. Like in the debate on the Panama Canal treaties?

THE PRESIDENT. Yes. And the Mideast arms sale. They have a very difficult issue to decide now about the removal of the embargo on the sale of weapons to Turkey. But I found a majority of Senators to be very courageous and very sound in their judgment and to make the right decision.

DÉTENTE

MR. LOHFELDT. However, the escalation in the war of words between the Soviet Union and the United States has created the impression that we are witnessing the end of the era of détente and the return of the cold war. In your opinion, is the policy of détente endangered, or has it already failed?

THE PRESIDENT. Neither in the United States nor in the Soviet Union was détente ever regarded as a panacea that would end competition between two radically different systems, each with its own interests. But we value it now for the same reason we originally pursued it: as an antidote to the uncontrolled competition between the United States and the Soviet Union that might threaten us both, and the rest of the world.

Thus, the United States is fully committed to the search for relations among states that will resolve conflicts of interest peacefully. The SALT talks, for example, are a partial step toward reducing the threat of strategic nuclear weapons. While the road toward that goal is a long one, the effort is vital; and we will continue its pursuit.

I believe that the Soviet leadership shares my country's view of the importance of ensuring greater stability in our relations. We continually urge the Soviet Union to respond in kind to our efforts to reduce competition in our relations and to expand areas of cooperation.

SOVIET AND CUBAN INVOLVEMENT IN AFRICA

MR. LOHFELDT. How do you, in this context, evaluate the presence of the Soviets and the Cubans in Africa? Are they acting according to a long-term strategy, or are they just exploiting the situation of the moment?

THE PRESIDENT. In my speech at Annapolis, I spelled out the basic American approach to Africa: to work for "a continent that is free of the dominance of outside powers, free of the bitterness of racial injustice, free of conflict, and free of the burden of poverty, hunger, and disease." I believe that all people of good will can subscribe to these objectives.

In recent months, the Soviet Union and Cuba have taken a different course, which is clearly inconsistent with the independent development of free nations. Yet, whatever their motives for interfering in individual African nations, I believe the Soviet Union and Cuba will find their intrusion decisively rejected by the people of Africa. Countries that suffered through long decades of colonialism are not likely to welcome a new imperialism. And it is to help these countries maintain their rightful place in the community of nations that I and members of my administration have called attention to Soviet and Cuban actions.

SOVIET MILITARY BUILDUP

MR. LOHFELDT. You have asserted that the Soviet military buildup by far exceeds its legitimate security needs. What exactly do you mean?

THE PRESIDENT. The United States and its allies believe that the increased Soviet military buildup cannot be explained in terms of any legitimate concern with the Western defense posture. This applies in particular to the buildup of Warsaw Pact forces in Central Europe, and to the steady growth of Soviet forces for more than a decade.

MR. LOHFELDT. So what is the West supposed to do?

THE PRESIDENT. I have confidence in the strength of the West to meet this challenge—strength in military forces, in our collective will, and in our economies, political systems, and moral values. We will continue to maintain that strength. In time, we hope to convince the Soviet Union that a competition in arms adds nothing to either side's security, so that it will turn away from its overemphasis on military power and toward peaceful pursuits.

U.S.-CHINESE RELATIONS

MR. LOHFELDT. Regarding the permanent conflict between the Soviet Union and China, do you think it wise for the United States to play the "Chinese card" in order to put some pressure on the Soviet Union?

THE PRESIDENT. "Chinese card" is not a term used by my administration. The United States seeks to improve its relations with both the Soviet Union and the People's Republic of China. With regard to China, that means working within the framework of the Shanghai Communique, in the search for practical ways to normalize our relations.

MR. LOHFELDT. And you are not afraid that a closer U.S.-Chinese relationship might lead to an even more adamant Soviet attitude?

THE PRESIDENT. As the United States has made clear many times, nothing in the evolution of our policy towards China is in any way intended to affect adversely the interests of third countries, including

the Soviet Union. We believe that a productive U.S.-Chinese relationship is worth seeking on its own merits, and that a strong and secure China is in our interest.

U.S. ENERGY POLICY

MR. LOHFELDT. Mr. President, the western economy is in a severe crisis. One of the main reasons and symptoms is the weakness of the U.S. dollar, which is, first of all, caused by America's massive oil imports. What kind of a solution do you envisage to reduce these imports?

THE PRESIDENT. We have already been quite successful in carrying out the basic promises of the London Economic Summit. We agreed to attempt to cut down on the level of oil imports, and we have had good success.

MR. LOHFELDT. Really?

THE PRESIDENT. In the first 5 months of this year, without an energy law being in effect, we reduced the oil imports by almost 1 million barrels a day. And with the passage of the energy legislation, we anticipate another 2.3 million barrels a day of savings.

MR. LOHFELDT. But how are the chances for the passage of the energy legislation?

THE PRESIDENT. Agreement has been reached among the major committees of the Congress on four out of the five components of the comprehensive program we proposed to reduce consumption and increase production on energy. The fifth element of this package, the crude oil equalization tax, is still being considered by the Congress. I am working closely with the Congress to secure its passage, and I think they will decide this successfully before they adjourn for this year. I remain committed to this legislation and its objectives.

INTERNATIONAL ECONOMY

MR. LOHFELDT. In Bonn, you will, after your state visit, meet with the heads of state or government of the most important industrial countries of the West. What will you offer your partners to improve the state of the world economy?

THE PRESIDENT. The central theme of the economic summit is "concerted action," with each country sharing the responsibility of improving the world economy. Two of my highest priorities are lowering the U.S. inflation rate and reducing our oil imports.

In Bonn, I will spell out the steps we are taking to implement these policies and the reasons why I am confident we will succeed. Most of the economic problems are attributable to severe trade imbalances among us.

Last year, our Nation had a very high growth rate. We were financially able to buy goods from other countries, like Germany and Japan, for example. Our growth rate was maintained, and so we have met the goal we had established at the London Economic Summit Conference. Other nations were not quite so successful. But I hope that in Bonn other heads of government will be forthcoming in the areas of trade and growth. Progress in both areas will be important to the well-being of the world economy and, of course, to the American economy as well.

ADMINISTRATION POLICIES

MR. LOHFELDT. Mr. President, you have been in office now for some 18 months. How do you feel? Are you still optimistic about the course and the future of your administration?

THE PRESIDENT. Yes, I am. We have spelled out fairly, I think, the goals for our Nation in the time I am in the White House, and we have had some good successes.

MR. LOHFELDT. For example?

THE PRESIDENT. A year ago, my biggest problem in this country was the unemployment rate. It was almost 8 percent when I took office. I and the Congress have acted, I think, very effectively to bring this unemployment rate down. We have added a net 6.4 million jobs and cut the unemployment rate by 2 percent. We also have very good strides in reorganizing our Government. And we have tried to bring about a repairing of the spirit of our country in the aftermath of the Vietnam war and the Watergate problem. I think we have done that successfully; the attitude of our people is better.

We have still got a long way to go to solve all our problems. But we have made good progress, and I feel very optimistic about the future.

MR. LOHFELDT. Mr. President, thank you for this interview.

NOTE: The interview began at approximately 4 p.m. in the Library at the White House.

As printed above, the item follows the White House press release, which was released on July 14.

Digest of Other White House Announcements

The following listing includes the President's daily schedule and other items of general interest as announced by the White House Press Office during the period covered by this issue. Events and announcements printed elsewhere in the issue are not included.

July 8

The President has declared an emergency for the State of North Dakota because of the impact of severe storms and tornadoes which struck Grant County on July 4 and 5.

The President has declared a major disaster for the State of Wisconsin as a result of severe storms and flooding, hail, and tornadoes, beginning on or about June 25, which caused extensive public and private property damage.

The President declared a major disaster for the State of Minnesota as a result of severe storms and flooding, hail, and tornadoes, beginning on or about June 25, which caused extensive public and private property damage.

July 9

The President returned to the White House after a week's stay at Camp David, Md.

July 10

The President met at the White House with:

—Zbigniew Brzezinski, Assistant to the President for National Security Affairs;

—Frank B. Moore, Assistant to the President for Congressional Liaison;

—Senate Majority Leader Robert C. Byrd;

—the Cabinet;

—Lt. Gov. and Mrs. Richard F. Celeste of Ohio;

—Vice President Walter F. Mondale.

The President transmitted to the Congress the Special Report on Multilateral Export Controls.

The President participated in a foreign policy briefing for Members of Congress at the White House. Secretary of State Cyrus R. Vance, Secretary of Defense Harold Brown, and Dr. Brzezinski also participated in the discussions.

July 11

The President met at the White House with:

—Dr. Brzezinski;

—Mr. Moore;

—the Democratic congressional leadership;

—a group of Congressmen to discuss intelligence matters;

—Senator Dick Clark of Iowa;

—Vice President Mondale, Adm. Stansfield Turner, Director of Central Intelligence, Hamilton Jordan, Assistant to the President, and Dr. Brzezinski.

The President transmitted the following reports to the Congress:

—the 10th Annual Report of the National Advisory Council on Economic Opportunity;

—the 1977 Annual Report of the United States-Japan Cooperative Medical Science Program.

July 12

The President met at the White House with:

—Representative Morris K. Udall of Arizona;

—Dr. Brzezinski;

—Senator Quentin N. Burdick of North Dakota, Representatives Harold T. Johnson of California and Robert A. Roe of New Jersey, and administration officials to discuss urban policy;

—Senators John C. Stennis of Mississippi, Thomas J. McIntyre of New Hampshire, Henry M. Jackson of Washington, and Sam Nunn of Georgia;

—Frank Press, Director of the Office of Science and Technology Policy, who reported on his mission to the People's Republic of China.

The President attended a portion of the breakfast held for Members of Congress in the State Dining Room at the White House to discuss the situation in Turkey and Greece.

The President transmitted the following reports to the Congress:

—the annual report of the Commodity Credit Corporation for the fiscal year ended September 30, 1977;

—the annual report on the Alaska Railroad for fiscal year 1977;

—the Ninth Annual Report of the National Corporation for Housing Partnerships and the National Housing Partnership.

The White House announced that President Carter's mother, Lillian Carter, will visit the Sahel region of West Africa as an emissary of the President from July 17 to August 2. Her journey will express the President's deep interest in the problem of world hunger, the disparity between rich and poor, and the role of women in the development process. On her way to the Sahel, Mrs. Carter will stop in Paris, to meet with representatives of the Club du Sahel at the Organization for Economic Cooperation and Development, and Rome, to receive the Ceres Medal from the Director-General of the Food and Agriculture Organization of the United Nations.

July 13

The President met at the White House with:

—Dr. Brzezinski;
—Mr. Moore.

NOMINATIONS SUBMITTED TO THE SENATE

The following list does not include promotions of members of the Uniformed Services, nominations to the Service Academies, or nominations of Foreign Service officers.

NOMINATIONS—Continued

Submitted July 12, 1978

TALCOTT W. SEELYE, of Maryland, a Foreign Service officer of Class one, to be Ambassador Extraordinary and Plenipotentiary of the United States of America to the Syrian Arab Republic.

Withdrawn July 12, 1978

HOBART CALVIN JACKSON, SR., of Pennsylvania, to be a member of the Federal Council on the Aging for a term expiring June 5, 1979, vice Frell M. Owl, term expired, which was sent to the Senate on April 7, 1978.

Submitted July 13, 1978

GEORGE M. LANE, of Massachusetts, a Foreign Service officer of Class two, to be Ambassador Extraordinary and Plenipotentiary of the United States of America to the Yemen Arab Republic.

STANLEY R. RESOR, of Connecticut, to be Under Secretary of Defense for Policy (new position).

ROGER A. MARKLE, of Utah, to be Director of the Bureau of Mines, vice Thomas V. Falkie, resigned.

RUTH C. CLUSEN, of Wisconsin, to be an Assistant Secretary of Energy (Environment) (new position).

GLORIA SCHAFFER, of Connecticut, to be a member of the Civil Aeronautics Board for the remainder of the term expiring December 31, 1978, vice Lee R. West, resigned.

GLORIA SCHAFFER, of Connecticut, to be a member of the Civil Aeronautics Board for the term of 6 years expiring December 31, 1984 (reappointment).

JANE HURT YARN, of Georgia, to be a member of the Council on Environmental Quality, vice John A. Busterud, resigned.

RICHARD V. BACKLEY, of Virginia, to be a member of the Federal Mine Safety and Health Review Commission for a term of 4 years (new position).

ROY T. SESSUMS, of Louisiana, to be a member of the Mississippi River Commission for a term of 9 years (reappointment).

CHECKLIST OF WHITE HOUSE PRESS RELEASES

The following releases of the Office of the White House Press Secretary, distributed during the period covered by this issue, are not included in the issue.

CHECKLIST—Continued

Released July 10, 1978

Fact sheet: Justice System Improvement Act of 1978

Fact sheet: urban initiatives program

News conference: on Federal law enforcement assistance reorganization and a Housing and Urban Development Department urban initiatives program—by Stuart E. Eizenstat, Assistant to the President for Domestic Affairs and Policy, Deputy Attorney General Benjamin R. Civiletti, W. Harrison Wellford, Executive Associate Director for Reorganization and Management, Office of Management and Budget, Lawrence P. Simons, Assistant Secretary for Housing, Department of Housing and Urban Development, and Thomas Madden, General Counsel, Law Enforcement Assistance Administration

Released July 12, 1978

Announcement: visit of Mrs. Lillian Carter to the Sahel region of Africa

Announcement: presentation of the Ceres Medal to Mrs. Lillian Carter by the Food and Agriculture Organization of the United Nations

List: participants in the U.S. scientific and technological mission to the People's Republic of China, July 6–10

ACTS APPROVED BY THE PRESIDENT

Approved July 10, 1978

H.R. 10730_____ Public Law 95–316
An act to authorize appropriations to carry out the Marine Mammal Protection Act of 1972 during fiscal years 1979, 1980, and 1981.

H.R. 3447_____ Public Law 95–317
An act to amend chapter 83 of title 5, United States Code, to grant an annuitant the right to elect within one year after remarriage whether such annuitant's new spouse shall be entitled, if otherwise qualified, to a survivor annuity, and to eliminate the annuity reduction made by an unmarried annuitant to provide a survivor annuity to an individual having an insurable interest in cases where such individual predeceases the annuitant.

H.R. 3755_____ Public Law 95–318
An act to provide for the reinstatement of civil service retirement survivor annuities for certain widows and widowers whose remarriages occurred before July 18, 1966, and for other purposes.

Approved July 11, 1978

S. 2401_____ Public Law 95–319
Emergency Interim Consumer Product Safety Standard Act of 1978.

Editor's Note

Note Concerning the Closing Time of This Issue

The President left the White House on Thursday morning, July 13, for a state visit to the Federal Republic of Germany and meetings at the Bonn Economic Summit. Releases issued on the trip but not received in time for inclusion in this issue will be printed next week.

PRESIDENTIAL DOCUMENTS

Anatoly Shcharanskiy

Statement on the Sentence Announced at the Soviet Dissident's Trial.   July 14, 1978

I speak today with the sadness the whole world feels at the sentence given Anatoly Shcharanskiy. We are all sobered by this reminder that, so late in the 20th century, a person can be sent to jail simply for asserting his basic human rights.

It is saddest of all for the Soviet people, who in their time have known war and oppression; who yearn like all others for peace and liberty; who have seen their own Government pledge 2 years ago to respect those human rights and desires; and who now have seen that pledge broken once again.

The struggle for human liberties is long and difficult, but it will be won. There is no power on Earth that can long delay its progress.

NOTE: The statement was released at Bonn, Federal Republic of Germany.

Bonn, Federal Republic of Germany

Remarks and a Question-and-Answer Session With Reporters Following a Meeting With Chancellor Helmut Schmidt.   July 14, 1978

THE CHANCELLOR. [*in German*] Ladies and gentlemen, I would like to take this opportunity to express once again, and completely publicly, the delight not only of the Federal Republic but also of the entire German people over the visit of the American President and his Secretary of State and other advisers and people accompanying him.

We have already worked hard for 3 hours. We still have a little work ahead of us. The President will make Germans happy by taking a trip to Berlin. And then comes another bit of hard work with the so-called summit meeting on Sunday and Monday.

As far as the work so far is concerned, it will probably be best if I let the guests come forward to make a few remarks. After that there will be an opportunity for two or three questions. Then we intend to continue our work while eating.

Please, Mr. President.

THE PRESIDENT. First of all, I want to thank President Scheel and Chancellor Schmidt, the German officials for the superb welcome that they've given us, an opportunity for me to return to Bonn, to revisit Berlin and Frankfurt on this trip.

We've had an opportunity to reassess and to appreciate the firm foundation of mutual purpose and understanding and cooperation and commitment to the strong ties that bind us together politically, economically, and militarily. Under six Presidents, under five Chancellors, as Chancellor Schmidt emphasized this morning, this relationship between the

United States of America and the Federal Republic of Germany has been strong and sound. And he and I both agree that it has never been stronger nor more sound than it is today.

The bilateral discussions have been thorough. We've assessed relations between our own two countries and the cooperative attitude that we enjoy to try to preserve and to enhance peace throughout the world. We've discussed economic problems that we face together, and we have prepared ourselves very thoroughly, I believe, for a successful summit conference that will commence day after tomorrow.

These discussions are very helpful to me. I've never met any other world leader who has been of more assistance in my comprehension of economic matters than has Chancellor Schmidt.

The strength and independence of the Federal Republic of Germany is a firm foundation, as is our own, for a very frank discussion, not only of compatabilities but of differences of opinion. And these discussions are very fruitful in identifying those areas where our own national interests might be at some small variance.

The purpose of a summit conference is to resolve the differences that we can, to assess the differences that remain, to establish common goals, and to recruit the parliamentary and congressional leaders, the general public, the private sector of our free societies to join us in realizing those goals.

In every respect I feel both grateful and also confident about the relationship that exists between the people of Germany and the people of the United States.

And I look forward, Mr. Chancellor, to the continuation of our visit throughout your country and the successful conclusion of a very important summit conference with the other Western democratic leaders.

I thank you for giving me this opportunity to speak briefly to the German and American press. And as you say, we're now available for a few questions.

SOVIET DISSIDENTS

Q. Could you tell us, sir, both of you, what you think about the Ginzburg sentence and the Shcharanskiy verdict in the Soviet Union?

THE PRESIDENT. It's obvious to us that the courageous dissidents in the Soviet Union, Mr. Shcharanskiy and Ginzburg, have been accused and tried and punished, will be punished because they have supported those who sought the basic freedoms that were guaranteed in the Final Act of the Helsinki agreement, which was signed voluntarily by the Soviet Union itself, and because they supported basic commitments that are also guaranteed in the Universal Declaration of Human Rights, which the Soviet Union and other members of the United Nations have publicly and officially endorsed. We deplore this action on the part of the Soviet authorities.

Our sympathies and our support remains with Mr. Shcharanskiy, Orlov, and with Ginzburg and others. Obviously, we have no mechanism nor any desire to interfere in the internal affairs of the Soviet Union. But the arousing of public condemnation around the world for the violation of these principles of human freedom is a legitimate role for me as a leader and for the people of our country.

We seek in spite of this adverse circumstance to cooperate with the Soviet Union whenever possible. And we are continuing to make progress in some areas which are crucial to the safety of the world. Secretary Vance has just returned from a constructive meeting with the Foreign Minister of the Soviet Union on the SALT agreements. And I'll be visiting

Berlin, which is now benefiting from the Quadripartite Agreement, which is supported by the Soviet Union and the Western Allies.

So, we do condemn this action in the Soviet Union. At the same time we want to continue a peaceful relationship with all countries, and our voice will not be stilled as we consider these violations and others around the world of basic human rights.

Q. But we'll take no further action?

THE CHANCELLOR. [*in German*] I would like to add another two sentences in complete agreement with that which the President has just said. There are not only court cases in the Soviet Union. There are also cases in other countries. We Germans are particularly disturbed about the cases against Hübner and Bahro that are taking place these days in the other part of Germany. And I would like very much to make American journalists aware that there are many people in the eastern part of Europe who have to suffer under such accusations and persecutions and judgments far beyond those who at the moment are assuming such a prominent role in the public consciousness.

PRESIDENT'S VISIT TO BERLIN

Q. [*in German*] What was the reaction of President Carter to the protest of the GDR against the visit by both Chancellor Schmidt and him to Berlin?

THE PRESIDENT. The German Democratic Republic has no role to play in the assessment of compliance with the Quadripartite Agreement. This is an agreement signed by the four nations involved, and the GDR is not a part of that agreement and have no legal nor legitimate role to play as a commentator.

It is completely within the agreement for the Chancellor of Germany to visit West Berlin with me, and I think this is part of the agreement itself, that there be good relations and improved relations and strengthened relationships between the western part of Berlin and the Federal Republic of Germany. So, this is a proper action for us to take, for the Chancellor to take, and the GDR has no legitimate role to play as a commentator.

ENHANCED RADIATION WEAPONS

Q. Mr. President, can you tell us whether you and the Chancellor discussed this morning defense and NATO issues, and particularly the eventual development or deployment of the neutron weapon?

THE PRESIDENT. Yes. [*Laughter*]

Q. Have you come to any decision on either its development or deployment in Europe?

THE PRESIDENT. No, we've not reached a final decision on this, but we have a very frank and easy and free discussion about this and other matters concerning NATO. The mutual and balanced force reductions, the excessive buildup of the Soviets' very formidable middle-range missiles, such as the SS–20, these are all matters that we have discussed. But we're not prepared to reveal the substance of our discussion.

Q. Well, I wonder if Chancellor Schmidt could tell us his position as to the deployment of this weapon in Germany?

THE CHANCELLOR. I would just like to underline the very short but very precise answer of the President. Ladies and gentlemen, there will be just time for one more question.

U.S.–GERMAN RELATIONS

Q. Mr. President, can you tell us what economic differences you discussed? What are those economic differences that you have with the Federal Republic?

THE PRESIDENT. Well, there are a number of matters that we have discussed and will be on the agenda for the summit conference involving the other five' leaders. One of them, of course, is the excessive consumption of oil and other energy products in our own Nation; the adverse balance of payments that relate to the United States; the common desire for there to be vigorous growth among the Western democracies; a sharing of commitment to reduce obstacles to free trade.

I think there is no difference that I can detect in the ultimate goals that we hope to achieve. But, obviously, national interests are at variance. We are not nearly so heavily dependent, for instance, upon exports as part of maintaining employment and a vigorous economy, as are the other nations involved. Only 7 percent, roughly, of our gross national product goes to the export trade. I think maybe 25 or 35 percent of Germany's gross domestic product goes to the export of trade.

We don't have differences concerning goals. But there are normal differences of perspective because of the characteristics of our countries.

Q. Do you agree with Chancellor Schmidt that the U.S. oil imports is the greatest problem of international trade?

THE CHANCELLOR. Beg your pardon, sir, there will be another press briefing a little bit more lengthier than occasioned just now. We would like on behalf of the President as well as on my behalf to thank you all and look forward to be seeing you in some of these days. Thank you very much indeed.

NOTE: The exchange began at 1:08 p.m. in the Chancellory Lobby. The translations of Chancellor Schmidt's remarks and the German reporter's question follow the White House press release.

Following their remarks, President Carter and Chancellor Schmidt proceeded to the Chancellor's Bungalow for a working luncheon.

Earlier in the day, the President participated in the official welcoming ceremony held at Villa Hammerschmidt in Bonn. He then met with West German President Walter Scheel at the villa.

Bonn, Federal Republic of Germany

Remarks at the Bonn City Hall. *July 14, 1978*

Distinguished officials and citizens of the great city of Bonn, thank you for your welcome.

Before I came to Bonn, I was warned that three things might happen to me while I was in your city. But there has been no rain; as you can see, I'm not in the least tired; and no matter where I go, the railroad gates have always been open. Instead, I have seen a beautiful city, a green and a pleasant community with which to admire your quality of life.

Konrad Adenauer always said he chose Bonn as capital, temporary capital, of the Federal Republic, because in addition to his love for roses, he knew democracy could reach its fullest flower in this serene and gentle town along the banks of the Rhine. Despite all the changes you have undergone, you have kept that serenity and charm.

When I signed your Golden Book a few moments ago, I was surrounded by reminders of your history. And I am honored, as I stand here, to think of the history that has taken place on these very steps.

Many distinguished visitors have spoken here, among them President Charles de Gaulle and our own President John F. Kennedy. But even more important are those who spoke to you not as visitors, but as products of the soil and the soul of Germany. When Professor Gottfried Kinkel proclaimed the ideals of 1848 from these steps, one of his listeners was a young man destined to be known equally well to Americans and to Germans: Carl Schurz, the great German-American reformer.

A century later, when President Heuss spoke to you here on the night of his election in 1949, not many in his audience realized they were living in the dawn of an era when Germany and America would become the closest of partners in a global effort to secure peace, freedom, and stability for all mankind.

But that is precisely what has occurred. Today, the Federal Republic and the United States share vast responsibilities and similar interests, and Bonn has taken its place as the capital of one of our most important allies. Our security is your security, and yours is ours. That is why the United States is increasing its commitment to NATO and will help to defend your land as if it were our own.

The Federal Republic and the United States also share an attitude and a sense of duty toward Europe and to the world. Many years ago, Carl Schurz, who took so much of his guidance from this city, said something very wise to us, his adopted people. "The genuine American," he said, "must be a creative world citizen."

Today both Americans and Germans are creative world citizens, striving together to help other regions of the world achieve economic well-being and stability. And, of course, our two nations share a fundamental faith in the same values— the values of freedom, of human rights, of economic liberty, and the conviction that each person should be able to develop one's own life fully and creatively, secure from foreign oppression and secure from domestic disorder.

At a time when the enemies of democracy seem determined to test us, we are prepared to maintain our strength, because we know that democracy is the most effective means of solving problems and meeting the needs of our people. You, as citizens of the capital of one great democratic nation, and I, as a citizen of the capital of another, have this faith in common.

We understand and we share your aspirations and your commitment for peaceful reunification of all Germany.

As allies, as citizens of the world, as believers in freedom and democratic government, Germans and Americans also share an awareness of the interdependence of all people, everywhere.

As I look about this *marktplatz* today, I am conscious not only of its purely German history—this gracious rococo building behind me; this one to my right, restored from the 14th century; the great university to my left; the spires of the church above the rooftops—but I'm also conscious of its present reality: the restaurant from China, the American camera store, the shops filled with produce from France, Scandinavia, and so many other nations of Europe and the world. All of these are reminders of how closely linked have become the lives of the people of our planet.

Finally, let me say that the point is that over the past few generations, relations among us have become the province not only of governments but of our people themselves. As the world's people speak and work and live together, we all could well remember the poem of Schiller, immortally put to music by the great Beethoven, a son of Bonn, the "Ode to Joy":

"Alle Menschen werden Brüder

Wo dein sanfter Flügel weilt."
("All mankind shall be brothers where thy* gentle wings abide.")
Thank you very much, my friends.

NOTE: The President spoke at 3:20 p.m. from the balcony of the Bonn Rathaus.

Prior to his remarks, the President participated in a wreathlaying ceremony at the Memorial to the Victims of War and Tyranny.

Bonn, Federal Republic of Germany

Toast at the State Dinner.   July 14, 1978

Mr. President, Chancellor Schmidt, distinguished members of the government, economic society of the Federal Republic of Germany, ladies and gentlemen, my friends:

We who have come from Washington to visit your great country know that we are among friends. I want to express my deep appreciation for the generous reception that all of you have given to us and to offer my thanks to the citizens of the Federal Republic of Germany who have greeted us so warmly.

It's a pleasure to begin my first visit to the Federal Republic as President in the city that nurtured Beethoven—a symbol not only of German culture but also of the indomitable spirit of a free people. There are two great musicians that I have admired in Germany—Ludwig von Beethoven and President Scheel. [*Laughter*]

But Bonn is equally significant in the contemporary role as the capital of this great and vibrant nation. The political and economic development of Western Europe since World War II is one of the greatest success stories in modern history.

*"Thy" apostrophizing "Joy" or "Freedom" in this poem. [Printed in the transcript.]

Mass poverty has been replaced by mass prosperity. Century-old enemies have become political and economic allies and are together building the future of Europe.

And here in Germany you have established and maintained a strong and a stable democracy. As the capital of West Germany, Bonn symbolizes the will and the determination of free people. You are a model in a livable world—a world we can manage, a world we can afford, a world we can enjoy.

Here in this peaceful young capital in the shadow of Siebengebirge, it is possible to envision a day when all nations will have revitalized cities surrounded by rural plenty, a day when all nations will cherish freedom, will understand the function of dissent in a free society, and offer their citizens the right to share in making the decisions that affect their own lives.

As I drove through Bonn today, I saw superbly restored old buildings standing proudly beside splendid new structures. I think this growing capital city that you enjoy is as strong a testimony to the vitality of modern Germany as your remarkable deutsche mark.

The United States is very proud of its long and intimate association with West Germany. We have watched with admiration—sometimes with envy—as you became one of the outstanding economies and the outstanding trading countries of the entire world.

For the last two decades, your economy has provided a powerful stimulus for the growth in Europe. Your policies are consistently among the most constructive on the Continent, indeed, the entire world. And you play an essential role in the developing economic strength of the global economy. They are even more impressive—your policies are—in the context of your commitment to a free market system and the ideals of a free society.

That commitment is even more significant at a time when terrorist groups wrongly believe that they can force free societies to abandon our liberties. Our two nations are steadfast in our resolve to end the menace of terrorism and in our resolute conviction that democratic liberty and social justice are the best answers to terrorist threats. The application of civil protections in your exemplary basic law is ample evidence of the Federal Republic's devotion to these libertarian ideals.

The affinity between the Federal Republic and the United States goes well beyond our own bilateral interests, even well beyond those of the Atlantic community.

Our nations understand the moral force of democracy. This is the fundamental strength of the German-American partnership. Our peoples understand the meaning of fair access to opportunity and just reward. These shared convictions help us to face our problems in a spirit of cooperation. They give us the tools and the confidence to meet the challenges, difficult challenges of a modern society.

Our agenda—and the agenda for all democracies—includes a renewed commitment to global economic well-being. This, more than any other material goal, promises a future in keeping with the age-old yearnings of mankind: an end to inequities among nations, as well as among classes of citizens; a day when an interdependent world of trade and commerce can generate an adequate number of jobs, better income, and a better life in the poor two-thirds of the world; a day when the continuing transfer of capital and technology from rich to poorer countries will have spread the benefits of the industrialized nations throughout the underdeveloped world.

This transfer of funds and services is just as important to our own economic health as it is to the well-being of the less-developed countries. In 2 days, Chancellor Schmidt and I will sit down with our colleagues from the United Kingdom, France, Canada, Italy, Japan, and the European Commission to develop strategies to achieve the goals which I have just outlined. This will be the fourth economic summit conference, and I approach it with optimism.

Although we have not achieved all we had hoped in the 14 months since the last summit conference in London, I share the feelings that were expressed there in a very heartfelt way by Prime Minister Fukuda. When we met at Downing Street last year, he reminded us that the Great Depression, even the war in the Pacific, might have been prevented if world leaders had met again after the breakdown of the London Economic Conference in 1930, and suggested that while we may not achieve all we hope for, we may prevent more than we realize.

Let me say, first, that we meet acutely aware that currency fluctuations, labor migrations, crop failures, and a host of other variables respect no political or geographical boundary; that every event that once was isolated affects each aspect of today's integrated, global economy. We are mutually vulnerable to and totally and equally dependent upon each other.

Together we must seek stable, noninflationary growth and jobs for our people.

Together we must seek to expand and to liberalize international trade policies and to put an end to rising protectionist sentiment.

Together we must seek a multilateral trade agreement that enhances and not obstructs world commerce.

Together we must seek to reduce energy consumption and to encourage energy exploration and production.

Together we must seek an international monetary system strong enough and flexible enough to sustain growth and to bolster confidence.

Together we must seek to share the benefits of economic progress and expanded trade with all the developing nations and channel increased aid to the world's neediest countries.

The United States and the Federal Republic are united in our commitment to these objectives. More is at stake than our economic well-being. Economic strength gives us the means and the confidence and spirit to deter war and to ensure peace.

What we do here in Bonn this week, and at home in the weeks ahead, relates directly to our military as well as our economic security.

Our defense policy is based on a strong NATO. American security is tied as closely to the security of Western Europe today as it has been for the past three decades. We are prepared to deter war in Europe and to defend all allied territory as strongly and as deeply committed as we defend the territory of the United States itself.

Tomorrow I will visit a few of the 200,000 American NATO troops stationed in Germany and the German troops who serve with them. I will assure them of this continuing commitment of the people whom I represent.

When the NATO summit met in Washington 6 weeks ago, we agreed on a Long-Term Defense Program, 15 years, that will guarantee the men the supplies and the equipment to meet any foreseeable military threat. This was not a unilateral commitment; it was a pledge made by the Alliance itself. All the Allies agreed to increase our military budget; all of us agreed to share the responsibilities of our long-term security.

The work we do together in strengthening the global economy and providing for our mutual security gives us the confidence that we seek to reduce tension with our potential adversaries.

We realize that our relationship with the Soviet Union will continue to be competitive for a long time to come and that the Soviets will continue to pose threats and challenges to Western interests. But we also recognize the threat to peace posed by a continuation of the arms race or by our inability to move beyond confrontation.

We are prepared to broaden our areas of cooperation with the Soviet Union, to seek a genuine, broadly defined, and fully reciprocal détente. We hope the Soviets will choose to join with us in making this effort. For our part we intend to make clear that we continue to seek cooperation, but we are fully prepared to protect Western interests.

Today the United States is negotiating a SALT II agreement that will preserve and enhance our own security and that of our Allies, indeed, the entire world. Reaching that agreement is essential to meeting the broad responsibilities shared by the Soviet Union and the United States to nations and to people everywhere.

We are prepared to negotiate in other areas—to seek reductions in the level of conventional forces in Europe, to limit nuclear testing, and to put a halt to further proliferation of nuclear explosives.

But genuine détente also includes restraint in the use of military power and an end to the pursuit of unilateral advantage—as in Africa today. And détente must include the honoring of solemn international agreements concerning human rights and a mutual effort to promote a climate in which these rights can flourish.

If the Soviet Union chooses to join in developing a more broad-based and reciprocal détente, the world will reap untold benefits. But whatever the Soviets decide, the West will do whatever is necessary to preserve our security while we continue, without ceasing, the search for a lasting peace. We will maintain our own strength as a clear indication of our commitment to free, democratic institutions, and our continuing obligation to our NATO Allies.

In my very short time in the Federal Republic of Germany, I have gained a deeper sense of the fundamental strength and the mutual benefit to be derived from our partnership. I believe that we will achieve the peaceful and the prosperous world we seek together.

I hope that you will join me now in a toast to world peace and to the close and enduring German-American friendship and to the health of President Scheel. To peace, and to your health, Mr. President.

Thank you very much. Thank you, everybody.

NOTE: The President spoke at 9:25 p.m. at Schloss Augustusburg in response to a toast by President Scheel.

Wiesbaden-Erbenheim Air Base, Federal Republic of Germany

Remarks to American and German Soldiers and Their Families. July 15, 1978

THE PRESIDENT. *Chancellor Schmidt, Minister Genscher, Minister Apel, officers and men of the Armed Forces of the United States and the Federal Republic, ladies and gentlemen, friends:*

I'm very proud and happy to be with you today. To all of you, I bring greetings and the gratitude of the people of the United States of America.

I cannot think of a nobler or more important purpose than the one that you serve here. You are here in the defense of the most vital interests of all the countries of the Atlantic Alliance. Above all, Americans and Germans alike, you are here in defense of freedom.

More than economics—more even than the common threat posed by our potential adversaries—it is our commitment to freedom that unites us. We may not always live up to its concepts perfectly, but it is a concrete reality that brings meaning to our lives and which we will defend—that is, freedom—however we must. At the same time, we will continue to pursue the kind of lasting peace that all people want.

For 30 years the mission of NATO has been to prevent war by being ready to fight. That is your mission today. Hundreds of millions of people are depending upon your combat readiness, your bravery, and your capability.

Those of you who serve in Brigade '76 represent the more than 300,000 members of the United States Army, Navy, Air Force, and Marine Corps who serve in Europe in support of the NATO Alliance. As the newest contingent of American troops on this continent, you particularly symbolize your country's increased commitment to the strength of the NATO Alliance.

Those of you who serve in the Armored Brigade 14 represent the armed forces of the Federal Republic which supply more than one-half the NATO ground forces available in Central Europe.

And together your two units represent the close cooperation and the coordination that is crucial to the effectiveness of the Alliance and, therefore, to the security of our countries.

Your officers call this coordination interoperability. And after seeing a demonstration of it a few minutes ago, I call it very impressive.

You are the point of the Western sword. That sword is sharp and true, and the people and the Government of the United States are striving to keep it that way. That is why we are introducing improved equipment into the European theater—equipment like the F–15 and the F–10 (A–10) [1] aircraft and the Cobra helicopter gunship equipped with Tow antitank missiles.

That is why we have increased and repositioned our forces here. That is why, with our allies, we will meet the future needs of NATO through the 15-year, long-term defense program. And that is why we are improving our ability to provide reinforcements, should that become necessary, through such steps as increased stockpiling of weapons and equipment here in Europe.

This means that when additional troops get here in an emergency, their equipment is already stockpiled and waiting for them. This gives us more flexibility and a faster reaction time.

Military service has always involved sacrifice, even in times of peace, and especially when service is far from home. In this connection, I would like to say a few words directly to the American soldiers who are here today.

I know that many of you are experiencing tough financial hardships, especially those of you in the junior grades who have your families with you. I cannot promise you instant and complete relief. But I do want to assure you that I am acutely aware of your problem, and we are taking steps to make it easier.

These problems are closely related to the value of the dollar and the overall health of the world economy. Chancellor

---

[1] Printed in the transcript.

Schmidt and I have been discussing these issues already, and we will be discussing them in depth at the economic summit meeting tomorrow and Monday in Bonn. But we cannot rely on long-term changes in the international economy to do the job of meeting your immediate needs.

We have made some progress in the last few months, particularly the increase in allowances for junior enlisted members whose families join you here in Germany.

There have been and will be other improvements as well. In next year's budget, I have proposed to the Congress large increases in a variety of services ranging from financial counseling to dental care. And I'm asking Congress to let the Government shoulder the financial burden of travel and transportation of goods that junior members now face when your families join you here.

Problems aside, your service here brings you some rare opportunities. Germany is a beautiful and hospitable land, and this part of the Rhine Valley happens to be one of its most beautiful spots. People from all over the world come just to spend a few days here. I hope that all of you will take advantage of this chance to get to know Germany and Europe in depth.

You are here as men and women who are making an indispensable contribution to the security of life around you. I hope that you will become part of that life as much as you can. I hope that you will make German friends, both among the civilian population and among your comrades in arms.

I hope that you will begin to learn the language and something about the way of life of the German people. It will give you a new perspective on our own country and our own way of life as well.

And finally let me say, as President of the United States, as the Commander in Chief of United States military forces, I deeply appreciate the work that you are doing here. That goes for all of you—Germans as well as Americans—and certainly for your families also.

I'm glad to have this chance to visit with you, to see the wonderful demonstration of what you are doing, and I am deeply proud of your patriotism and your courage.

Thank you very much. God bless all of you.

CHANCELLOR SCHMIDT. *President Carter, soldiers, distinguished and dear American and German citizens:*

I am glad to be with you today, together with President Carter. This occasion of the being together of two heads of government with U.S. and German forces is not merely a matter of protocol. It is intended to underline the fact that the North Atlantic Alliance on either side of the Atlantic constitutes the foundation of freedom and security.

Our friend, the President of the United States, has made it clear in his remarks with great emphasis that NATO is a core of American foreign policy. This is also true to the same extent of us Germans.

Our common security is based on a threefold foundation. First, it rests on the military defense capability of NATO, that is, on our common capability of deterring a potential aggressor.

How good our common defensive capability is, the soldiers on this place gathered here know perhaps even better than we, the politicians. But let me say here that President Carter, as a former naval officer who has seen active duty, and I, as a former Minister of Defense, are not completely without some expert knowledge in this field. So, in other words, the two of us were not wholly uncritical of service when we watched your demonstrations. And I would like to say on my own judgment that I share in the pride which President Carter has expressed to you in his remarks.

Our common security, secondly, is based on the close political cooperation within our Alliance. After the NATO summit meeting which took place last May in Washington, and after my talks with President Carter yesterday and today, I may say that this field of close political cooperation is also all right, and we can also be proud of it. We take the same view of international problems and the same approach, and we are cooperating in seeking solutions to these problems.

And thirdly, our security rests on stable economic conditions, because prosperous economies and an equitable world economic order are essential elements of security.

You know, and the President has just repeated it in his remarks, that the development of the international economy causes us some concern. But I am confident that the meeting for which the heads of governments, heads of state and heads of governments, of the major Western industrialized countries will meet tomorrow in Bonn will enable us to make progress also towards ensuring higher employment figures.

I should now like to address a few remarks in particular to the soldiers of the two nations.

As members of the American and German units assigned to NATO, and on the basis and through your cooperation in your everyday life, you ensure that the Alliance lives up to its defense mission. And for this I should like, speaking on behalf of the German people, to express to you my appreciation and my thanks.

And I address these remarks in particular to the American soldiers who serve on German soil. We are aware that the presence of American soldiers in Europe will also in the future be indispensable for our security. But we are also aware that your service here, thousands of miles away from your home country, is not always easy for you. For many or even for all of you—and this goes for soldiers all over the world—personal sacrifices are involved in your service.

But I do hope that you, the American soldiers, will also feel that you are welcome to us, not only as members of the forces of an allied power, but that you are welcome to us as friends.

Let me address my final remarks to Americans and Germans alike. We are serving together the same fundamental values—freedom and dignity of man. And I thank all those who together join hands in this service.

Thank you very much.

NOTE: The President spoke at 10:12 a.m. to members of the American 4th Infantry Brigade and the German 14th Panzer Brigade following his review of a military display at the base. Chancellor Schmidt spoke in German, and his remarks were translated by an interpreter.

In his opening remarks, the President referred to Vice Chancellor Hans-Dietrich Genscher and Defense Minister Hans Apel.

Earlier in the day, President Carter and Chancellor Schmidt toured a display of NATO armaments at Rhine-Main Air Base near Frankfurt.

Frankfurt, Federal Republic of Germany

Remarks at the Frankfurt City Hall.
July 15, 1978

Chancellor Schmidt, distinguished officials of the Federal Republic of Germany and the great city of Frankfurt:

I bring you greetings and friendship from the 220 million people of the United States of America.

In a few moments I will visit the Kaisersaal and sign your Golden Book. Fifteen years ago, President John F. Kennedy signed this same historic roll, and he said, and I quote, "We are partners in peace—not in a narrow bilateral context, but in a framework of Atlantic partnership."

Today that partnership is stronger than it has ever been, and our two nations are united in an ever-broader alliance of military, economic, and political purpose.

Our military partnership is evident. I've come here from a visit to Brigade '76, where I spoke to both German and American troops and their families. At your airport, I reviewed German and American aircraft. Everywhere in Germany I see evidence of our mutual commitment, our mutual endeavor. German and American troops, working side by side, are tangible evidence of our shared responsibility and our joint commitment to the continuing freedom not only of Germany and of the Continent but of the United States and of all Allied territory.

Our economic partnership is equally visible. Tomorrow your Chancellor and I will join our colleagues from five other great nations to consider the economic problems of our regions and the world in the summit conference in Bonn.

The economic summit is one tangible sign of a continuing search for solutions to age-old problems of global inequity. The United States and the Federal Republic attend these deliberations with united purpose—to look beyond narrow self-interest to the broader interest of all nations. Our two great and free nations believe equally in our obligation to promote global—and not just national—prosperity.

Our political partnership is the bulwark of freedom for all nations. Together our people, yours and mine, demonstrate democracy in action: two free nations—one with an old culture and a new Constitution, the other with a newer culture and an older Constitution—both equally committed to the vision of a free people living at peace under governments chosen and controlled by the people.

In this vibrant city of contrast and tradition, near these buildings of such great significance to all who love liberty, it is easy to take our freedoms for granted. Here at last, the ideals of the Frankfurt Assembly are realized.

So, it is a pleasure for us to be in Frankfurt, home not only of the first German vision of democracy but of great German intellectuals and musicians, home of Goethe, of Hindemith and Humperdinck, cradle of the great house of Rothschild.

I wish I had more time to explore your ancient city and beautiful countryside. Rosalynn tells me that I will miss the best part of the trip to Germany by not joining her and Amy on her Rhine cruise from Bingen to Bonn. So, I hope to come back, my friends, to see more of the "life, bustle, and motion" that Thomas Jefferson found in Frankfurt in 1788—and that I find here today.

So, we pray for the unification of Germany as the expression of will by the people of your great nation. We pray for the continuation and even the further strengthening of cooperation and mutual commitment between the people of our two great democracies. And we pray that through political, economic, and military strength, that we might together enhance the cause of freedom and human rights around the world.

Our future in the United States is tied intimately with the future of the people of Germany. Any attack on your soil will be the same as an attack on the soil of my own country. We are bound together with unshakable bonds of friendship and mutual commitment. This gives us strength and gives us strength together.

Thank you very much, my friends.

NOTE: The President spoke at 11:40 a.m. in the Römerberg, near the Frankfurt Rathaus.

Berlin, Federal Republic of Germany

Remarks at a Wreathlaying Ceremony at the Airlift Memorial.   July 15, 1978

Chancellor Schmidt, Governing Mayor Stobbe, distinguished officials from the United States and from the Federal Republic of Germany and the great and free community of West Berlin:

I bring greetings to you from 220 million Americans and a pledge of our total commitment to you for the freedom of us all.

Thirty years ago this week, President Harry Truman was renominated by the Democratic Party, the first Marshall plan loan was made to Europe, and in this square one sound was heard above all others—the sound of Allied airplanes landing at this terminal behind us, one every 3½ minutes, carrying supplies for the free people of Berlin.

I have just met four brave men who participated in that airlift: Jack Bennett and Miller Hayes from the United States of America, Roy Jenkins and Keith Hepburn from Great Britain. And I would like for you to give them an expression of your appreciation for what they did 30 years ago.

That was the time when people everywhere began to understand that the dispute over Berlin was not a local issue, but a great defense of freedom and democracy, with permanent worldwide interest and significance.

That was the week when the people of Berlin gathered in mass rallies to cheer Ernst Reuter and other brave leaders who declared their willingness to stand fast for a better, more peaceful, more democratic world.

That was the week when the people of the Western Zones of Germany added their resources to the Allied Airlift and sent tens of thousands of gift parcels to their countrymen here in Berlin.

That was the week when German Communists visited shops in the western part of this city and warned the owners that unless they joined the party, they would lose their shops when the Western powers left Berlin. That has never happened; that will never happen.

And that was the week when the Soviet Union responded to our demand to end the blockade with the assertion, and I quote, "Berlin is in the center of the Soviet Zone and is part of that Zone." With the courage of Berliners and the determination of the people of the West, we gave the answer: *Berlin bleibt frei.* Berlin stays free.

I am sobered but proud to be with you today at this historic time, to pay my respects to the 78 Americans, Britons, and Germans who lost their lives in the Airlift and who are honored by this simple but eloquent memorial.

This effort, which it commemorates, was the beginning of the commitments, including the Atlantic Alliance, which have to this day maintained the freedom and the security of Berlin, the Federal Republic, Western Europe, and the United States.

Five American Presidents have upheld the commitments that Harry Truman made in those crucial times, and today I tell you that my Nation still upholds this commitment to freedom.

I have spent this morning visiting troops, both German and American, who are stationed in the Federal Republic as part of the NATO Alliance. The United States has 300,000 military personnel in Europe to guarantee the freedom of this Continent and our own land.

During my visit to the Federal Republic, I've seen for myself the strength of the ties that bind the Federal Republic and the United States together. And here in Berlin, the presence of our troops and the readiness of Tempelhof both bear witness to our unshakable devotion to the people of this great city.

Berlin and the Quadripartite Agreement are symbols not only of the values that can never be compromised nor negotiated but also of the practical improvements that can be achieved by those who are willing patiently to negotiate.

When the Berlin blockade was lifted in 1949, Governing Mayor Reuter declared that, ". . . much can be gained by peaceful means if one has a clear understanding of what is politically possible and . . . if one has a firm will politically."

The human benefits that have brightened the lives of Berliners, West and East, as a result of the 1971 Quadripartite Agreement are proof of what can be accomplished through détente.

Looking back over the years, we can learn from the experience here in Berlin the conditions for maintaining freedom and for reducing international tension by negotiation.

First, we must be determined to maintain our essential interests and objectives. Among these are the basic human rights to which the United States is and always will be committed.

Second, those human beings who are defended must themselves be committed to freedom, just as Berliners have so amply proven that you, being free, are committed to freedom.

Third, we must be willing to understand the perspective of others in the course of negotiating agreements which maintain our own interests.

In the 30 years that have elapsed since this Airlift began, Berliners and Americans have grown ever closer together. Every American who visits here finds not only allies in the cause of freedom but personal friends as well. We have not forgotten the aid that you sent to Americans suffering from the cold winter early last year, and we will continue to preserve, through such instruments as the Airlift Memorial Scholarships, close contact between generations that had not yet been born when our fates were first bonded together.

The Bible says a city that is set on a hill cannot be hidden. What has been true of my own land for 3½ centuries is equally true here in Berlin. As a city of human freedom, human hope, and human rights, Berlin is a light to the whole world; a city on a hill—it cannot be hidden; the eyes of all people are upon you. *Was immer sei, Berlin bleibt frei.* (No matter what happens, Berlin will stay free.)

NOTE: The President spoke at 2:23 p.m. at the memorial following his arrival at Tempelhof Field, where he reviewed American troops.

Berlin, Federal Republic of Germany

Question-and-Answer Session at a Town Meeting.   July 15, 1978

THE PRESIDENT. Governing Mayor Stobbe, this is my second visit to Berlin. Five years ago I came as Governor of the State of Georgia. And my wife and I saw the monuments by which Berlin teaches all visitors about the basic realities of our times. We saw the Wall, and we worshipped at the Memorial Church, which exists as a solid reminder of the tragedy of the past and a hopeful promise of your future. But I also experienced the warmth and the wit of your irrepressible, steadfast people. I knew when I left that someday I would want to return.

I'm pleased to enjoy the warmth and friendship of this hall, because a few minutes ago I was standing in Potsdamer Platz, looking silently at the Wall, a spectacle that so accurately reflects a wasteland of the human spirit responsible for the existence of the Wall. This demonstrates beyond the power of words the difference between those who believe in individual human rights, and those who do not.

I'm thankful that the agreements that have been reached in recent years have done so much to make life better and more humane for Berliners. And all of us in this room must certainly hope that the détente which made them possible will be permitted to continue and to progress.

Almost 30 years ago in the darkest hours of the Airlift, President Harry Truman said that the courage displayed by the people of Berlin in their beleaguered outpost is proof to the world of the strength of the democratic spirit. With the help of Lucius Clay and John J. McCloy, President Truman showed that we would stand with you when your liberty was in doubt.

And year after year, American leaders have reaffirmed their unwavering commitment to the freedom of your city. We join the British and the French in this constant pledge.

I'm honored to join the citizens of this vital and dynamic city to declare again, whatever happens, Berlin will remain free.

And now I would like for us to speak very freely with each other, as has been my own custom with meetings of this kind throughout the Nation of the United States. I will answer your questions to the best of my ability.

Thank you very much.

AMY CARTER

Q. I am a pupil, Mr. President. My question is: Does your daughter Amy learn German in school, Mr. President?

THE PRESIDENT. No, she doesn't study German yet, but on this trip she has learned a lot of German words. She's at the Berlin Zoo today, one of the greatest zoos in the whole world. And I feel sure that after she masters English and Spanish that German will be next.

FRIENDSHIP FORCE

Q. Mr. President, my name is Christel Crienitz. I am a housewife. In June I had a visitor from Minnesota within the scope of the Friendship Force organization. What do you think of this initiative, and will it be continued? And why is that trip to America still so expensive? We all want to go. [*Laughter*]

THE PRESIDENT. The Friendship Force is a project initiated by my wife when I was Governor of Georgia just between one State in our Nation and the people of northeast Brazil. When I became President, my wife, Rosalynn, desired to extend this opportunity for American people to travel to nations all over the world.

One of the best trips that we've ever had has been the exchange with your own city here and the State of Minnesota.

This Friendship Force, even at the rates charged, does not make any profit. And I think that now with the unfortunate devaluation of the dollar, you can get much more bargains in our country than you could when you were there. [*Laughter*]

I might add that we will continue the Friendship Force, because this is a project that has absolutely nothing to do with governments. It's strictly between people in one country visiting in the homes of the people in another. And I think you would testify to the fact that it has been a wonderful experience, those of you who have been to our country under this fine program.

BERLIN AND THE EUROPEAN COMMUNITIES

Q. Mr. President, my name is Bernhard Klein. I am a trade union secretary, and my question is: Does, according to your opinion, the direct election of Berlin parliamentarians into the directly elected European Parliament constitute a violation of the four-power agreement on Berlin?

THE PRESIDENT. No, it does not. I think the relationship between the elected representatives of Berlin and the Government of the Federal Republic, where you have a presence right, but not the right to vote is, one, a subject that has been resolved in the principles of the Quadripartite Agreement, and the relationship between elected Berliners and the European Community is a slightly different arrangement. Both these are within the framework of the principles and the agreement of the Quadripartite Agreement, and they are perfectly legitimate, perfectly proper.

TRANSPORTATION OF OIL

Q. Mr. President, my name is Gisela Zimmermann. I'm a secondary school teacher at the German-American John F. Kennedy School. My question is this: We witness great pollution catastrophes caused by oil tankers. You are the President of the most powerful industrial nation of the world, the country with the highest oil consumption in the world. Could you not achieve internationally binding safety codes and regulations for all oil tankers in the world that would prevent further such catastrophes and pollution in the future?

THE PRESIDENT. Last year we decided that those tankers who come into American ports, those in the United States, would have to meet much higher standards, including double bottoms and a proper care for the pumping over the side of oil wastes as the tanks are discharged. We have introduced this discussion now in international fora recently in Europe, represented by our own Department of Transportation Secretary.

As you know, many of the tankers who travel the high seas are registered in relatively small countries which have practically no control over the quality of the tankers involved. But we are trying to take a leadership role in the increasing of standards for these tankers.

I share your concern about the unnecessary waste, not only when a ship is destroyed through accident but routine pumping over the side of the ship of oil wastes. We are very eager to join with you and others in lowering this threat, and I believe that the world is becoming aroused now to join us in an effort to cut down oil spills in the waterways of the entire world.

Thank you.

QUADRIPARTITE AGREEMENT

Q. My name is Heinz Maschke. I'm a pensioner, Mr. President. My question is this, sir: Why do the three Western powers suffer all the measures of the Soviet Union for the separation of East and West? Or are there any secret arrangements between you?

THE PRESIDENT. There are no secret arrangements between our country, the British, the French on the one hand, and the Soviets on the other. So far as I know, at the time of the signing of the Quadripartite Agreement, this was a public commitment made by the American and British and French leaders. And to the best of my knowledge, there is no secret agreement now between ourselves on the Western side and the Soviets.

If there should be any proposals in the future for secret agreements, I would op-

pose them and even let the proposal be made public.

NATO

Q. Mr. President, my name is Dietmar Born. I'm a business manager. My question: On the one hand you stand up for the unlimited security of Berlin, which we gratefully acknowledge and we thank you for, Mr. President. On the other hand, however, the military odds, the military forces of the Warsaw Pact are shifting in disfavor and against Berlin all the time. Are you not afraid, Mr. President, that this will affect your credibility in the eyes of the Berliners?

THE PRESIDENT. I think it is true that in the years gone by—3, 4 years or more ago—there was some doubt on the part of the American people, including some leaders in the United States Congress, that our commitment to NATO and to its strength should be maintained at its previous level.

I've been in office now for 18 months, and there has been a renewed spirit of cooperation and total commitment to maintain and to increase our strength in the NATO area. This is exemplified by the fact that all the members of NATO now have promised to increase their actual budget commitments to NATO defense by 3 percent per year above and beyond the inflation rate.

We have also begun to allot new types of weapons with the first priority for our entire country to the Western European area: the F–15 airplane, the A–10 airplane, the most advanced types of tanks, the antitank Tow missiles, and so forth, that I reviewed this morning with Chancellor Schmidt.

So, I believe that we do have an adequate defense capability now. It is increasing, and there will never be any occasion in the future when our Nation or those others who are committed to the defense of Western Europe will lessen our alertness or lessen our commitment to make this our first priority. We consider an attack on the territory or people of Western Europe to be exactly the same as an attack would be on the territory or the people of the United States of America.

GERMAN REUNIFICATION

Q. Mr. President, my name is Petra Berndt. I'm a student here in Berlin. My question, Mr. President, is as follows: What did you mean or intend, Mr. President, when you said that the German nation had a claim and right for reunification, and how can your administration really afford to be interested in German reunification?

THE PRESIDENT. The constant commitment of the Western Allies ever since the NATO organization was formed, ever since the Second World War was over, is for the reunification of Germany, based upon the self-determination of the German people yourselves. And this is a commitment that I believe ought to be maintained and an ultimate hope that should be carefully preserved.

We are not trying to impose our will upon the German people. But when the German people approach the time of making a decision for yourselves that Germany should be reunited and Berlin again be the capital of a unified Germany, we would certainly welcome that time, and we look forward to it with our prayers and our constant hope.

EASTERN SECTOR OF BERLIN

Q. Mr. President, my name is Hans-Dieter Robel. I am a civil engineer. I would like to ask my personal question, but I would like to defer and ask a question which friends in East Berlin have asked me to put to you, Mr. President.

The U.S. carries responsibility for all of Berlin. Could you not, Mr. President, when you come back to Berlin, also visit the eastern sector?

THE PRESIDENT. Yes, I would like very much to do that. The last time I was in Berlin, I did visit both west and eastern sectors. And this is something that I would like to do in the future.

As you know, the visiting rights in both sides of Berlin are guaranteed by the original agreements and also by the Quadripartite Agreement. And when I return to Berlin, I'll try to arrange my schedule to visit the eastern sector as well.

BERLIN'S ROLE IN THE WORLD

Q. Mr. President, I'm Gudrun Hollfelder, a housewife. My question is: What do you wish the Berliners to do and what contributions can we render to realize your political ambitions, Mr. President, in the world?

THE PRESIDENT. My belief is that the citizens of Berlin, both east and west, share ultimate hopes, together with myself, with Mr. Brezhnev, Chancellor Schmidt, and other world leaders, that is, for peace, for a broadening of the cooperation that must exist between the major powers and those who live within this troubled region of the world.

In addition to that area where we agree, there are some areas of disagreement. The Western democracies believe very deeply in human freedom, the chance for each person to make one's own decision, to choose one's own government, to criticize one's own government when it betrays our trust or does not live up to our expectations.

We also believe in basic human rights, that someone should have a chance to emigrate if they choose, to rejoin one's family if one chooses, and to speak out without constraint even in the criticism of one's own government policies.

So, there are areas of agreement and areas of disagreement. And as I said a few minutes ago at the memorial to the Berlin Airlift, I would hope that those of you who profit so much by the commitment of the democratic world to basic human rights would let your own voices be expressed clearly in your own commitment to human rights, because you are a great testimony to the benefits of freedom and those rights that we all share together.

So, I think this is what you could do and what I will do to help you.

QUADRIPARTITE AGREEMENT

Q. Mr. President, my name is Klaus Teske. I'm a tool fitter, a toolmaker and a works council chairman. My question, Mr. President, is: What will the United States do so that the four-power status that was agreed for all of Berlin can also be practiced in East Berlin?

THE PRESIDENT. Well, we have no capability nor desire to intrude into the affairs of East Berlin, except to let our voices be heard and to join with other responsible authorities in carrying out the basic principles of the agreements that have been specified clearly—the original Four-Power Agreement at the conclusion of the war and the 1971 Quadripartite Agreement as well.

On occasion these rights have been challenged, the right of free visitation between the two parts of Berlin, the right of the Western Allies to show our flag on the daily trips into Eastern Berlin, and vice versa. We have every hope that when a disagreement does arise, that they might be discussed freely and clearly, that our voice might be heard without constraint by the East Berliners, the GDR [German Democratic Republic], and the Soviet Union.

As you know, the GDR has no responsibility at all for the administration of the Quadripartite Agreement nor the monitoring of compliance with it. This relates itself directly to the Soviet Union on the eastern side. But I believe that at this time, since the Quadripartite Agreement was signed 7 years ago, that there has been a great improvement. And when problems do arise, as today, for instance, when the GDR put obstructions in the free passage of people on the *autobahn,* that protests might be lodged, the public awareness of the world might be focused upon it. And I would hope that the improvements that have been made the last 7 years might continue.

I think, compared to the previous years, including the terrible occasion of the Berlin Airlift, when the blockade was established, the situation is much better than it was now (then).[1] And I believe that the reason for that is that world attention has been focused upon Berlin, its symbolism, its importance to freedom, the courage of the Berliners. And I believe that this is the best way to bring about those routine, methodical improvements that have been our experience in the past and which I hope will be our experience in the future.

We will never yield in our commitment to pointing out violations of the agreements. And I believe that world opinion and the strength of the Western Allies, the courage of the West Berliners will cause this change for the better to continue in spite of temporary aberrations or violations.

That's the best answer I can give you. It's not a very good one, but I think it's adequate.

GERMAN ANTITERRORISM LAWS

Q. Mr. President, my name is Garlinda Buchholz. I am a student. My question is, Mr. President: Repeatedly you have

---

[1] Printed in the transcript.

spoken up for human rights. What is your opinion of the antiradicals legislation in the Federal Republic of Germany?

THE PRESIDENT. I'm not familiar with the details of the legislation to which you refer. I know that all countries, including my own, has to be very careful to balance the right of dissidents to speak, but to protect the lives and the property of innocent human beings who give support and who control the government.

And my own assessment of the Federal Republic's laws is that in dealing with terrorism and other threats to peaceful human beings and to the state, that they have been very careful to preserve the basic human rights, of which I approve.

AMY CARTER

Q. Mr. President, my name is Uwe Horstmeyer. I'm 12 years old, and I'm a student. My question is: Mr. President, how much pocket money per week does your daughter Amy get? [*Laughter*]

THE PRESIDENT. Zero. [*Laughter*] The public benefits that Amy does get are limited to traveling with me and her mother—like on this trip, she came on Air Force One, which is the President's plane. And we have enjoyed staying 2 nights at the American Ambassador's home in Bonn. And as she relates to the other members of her family, particularly myself, she gets that kind of benefit. But she gets no allowance, no money, from the Federal Treasury. [*Laughter*]

That gives me a good idea. I might bring that up with the American Congress when I go back home.

BERLIN AND THE FEDERAL REPUBLIC OF GERMANY

Q. Mr. President, my name is Werner Schatt. I'm a businessman. My question is: How do you assess the allocations of the eastern side, according to

the four-power agreement? There are no ties between the western sectors of Berlin and the Federal Republic of Germany, but only communication links. Probably they refer only to the land links. What is your assessment of that allocation?

THE PRESIDENT. I think there's an equivalent assessment on the eastern side. Under the Quadripartite Agreement, the way I understand it, stronger ties of communication and relationships between West Berlin and the Federal Republic are encouraged, according to the text of the Quadripartite Agreement. It's under that kind of understanding, for instance, that Chancellor Schmidt is here with me today, and it's one of the reasons that I'm here today. I want to make sure that the strongest possible ties are encouraged between West Berlin and the Federal Republic of Germany, short of an actual political inclusion of Berlin into the rest of the balance of Germany.

So I think that as these ties of communication, transportation, trade, commerce, culture are changed, even under the Quadripartite Agreement, that change should be to strengthen them and not to weaken them.

ACCESS TO BERLIN

Q. Mr. President, my name is Heidrun Schlauss. I'm a commercial secretary, but I'm also a housewife. I would like to ask you this, Mr. President: Access traffic to Berlin was impaired by the other side since this morning. The reason given is that you are visiting Berlin and that the Federal Chancellor is with you. Will you tell the world about it, Mr. President?

THE PRESIDENT. Well, on occasion, the GDR has tried to show some ability to interfere with normal commerce and traffic. This has primarily been of a temporary or transient nature. It has no permanent damage to us, although it is in violation not only of the Quadripartite principles but also the transportation agreements between the east and the western part of Germany.

I might say that I don't believe it helps them. It focuses attention upon the GDR and their absence of free movement, their prevention of outmigration, their inability to permit their own people to speak out in dissent when they choose. And I think the focusing of the world on the differences between our free society and theirs, which is not free, is not helpful to them at all.

I visited the Wall a few minutes ago. Fifteen years ago, when President Kennedy came to visit the Wall, they covered the ugly spectacle with drapes. This morning at 2:30 a.m., the Eastern Germans came and lowered their painters on the western side of the Wall and whitewashed, trying to cover the ugly spectacle again, 15 years later. I don't think anything can hide the image of the deprivation of basic human rights exemplified by the Wall.

This is the first time in history that I've ever known when a wall was built, not to protect one's nation from foreign aggressors, but to protect one's own people from the right to escape. And so I think the interruption of traffic and the painting of the Wall are demonstrations of that.

THE BERLIN WALL

Q. Mr. President, my name is Gertrude Kempe-Rottmann. I'm a pensioner. And my question is: For how long, Mr. President, do you think we've got to live with the Wall in Berlin?

THE PRESIDENT. I don't know. [*Laughter*] I hope that it will be removed in the future, but I have no idea when it might be. I'm sorry, I can't give you a better answer, but that's the truth.

ENERGY

Q. Mr. President, my name is Gert Schulz-Lüke. I've got the foreign question for you, Mr. President, which is: What assessment or concepts do you or the U.S. have of the unhampered energy supply of Germany, based on energy that is not subject to any political influencing—and the energy supply also of Berlin?

THE PRESIDENT. I think it's obvious that almost all kinds of energy are subject to political influence and interruption. Since 1973, the world has become aware of the prospect of gross interruptions of the available energy for us all. And we've become aware of the increasing prospect of severe shortages.

My own Nation is one of the world's greatest energy producers. We're also one of the world's greatest energy users, and we waste more energy than we should. We're trying to correct this defect in our own society.

I might add that one of the best ways to preserve the flow of energy sources— oil, gas, coal, nuclear power, the use of hydroelectric power, solar power—to a people is to preserve peace on Earth.

I think the Middle East is an area which can endanger the flow of crucial energy supplies to you and also to our own country. I have probably devoted more of my own personal time trying to bring about a peaceful resolution of the differences between Israel and her Arab neighbors than any other single foreign policy since I have been in office.

And we're also trying to secure permanent peace with the Soviet Union. We deeply desire to have détente with the Soviet Union, a détente that's broad in its scope, that has reciprocal benefits for them and for us. We have, constantly, procedures intact, never interrupted, to bring about a SALT agreement, an agreement on the end of testing of nuclear explosives, the prohibition against the attack on each other's satellites, the lowering of the buildup of military forces in the Indian Ocean. These kinds of things, I think, can contribute to overall world peace.

So, I would say conservation of what we have, scientific exchange and exploration for new kinds of energy, more efficient use of energy we have, and the maintenance of world peace so that normal traffic through the oceans and through the skies will not be interrupted—those are the things that I can think of offhand that we can all do together. And I believe that we will find both new technology and new avenues to peace if we persevere together, and that's my own commitment. I'm sure it's the commitment of you and others in this area as well.

EUROCOMMUNISM

Q. Mr. President, my name is Ingeborg Skrodzki-Dorendorf. I'm a housewife. My question to you, Mr. President, is this: How do you see and assess the development of Eurocommunism and how do you assess Eurocommunism?

THE PRESIDENT. First of all, we would prefer that communism in the Western world be minimal and not increase.

Secondly, we trust the judgment of free people in free societies to make a determination that communism is not in the best interest of themselves. We have seen this occur in recent elections—in France; in Spain, which is now a democracy; also in Italy. So, the second point is that we trust free people to make their own decision, and we don't have any intention to interfere in the internal political decisionmaking process among our allies.

And the third thing I would like to say is that the best way to prevent the upsurge or strengthening of communism is to make sure that democracy works. And

this can only be possible if the people ourselves constantly assess the basic foundations or principles on which democratic systems are founded and exemplify in our own individual attitude our participation, our deep commitment to strengthen democracy and not to weaken it.

When a democratic government is corrupt, when it separates itself from its own people, when it's insensitive to the suffering of those who are not so fortunate as we, when it's resolute and is not forceful enough in defending itself against outside intrusion or threat, those things can weaken democracy.

I think the other thing that we can do to strengthen our commitment against communism is to make sure that the democracies of the world bind ourselves together in ever closer ties of friendship, cooperation, mutual defense, recognize the individuality of each of us, but pointing out those things on which we are in harmony and strengthening those ties of friendship and mutual commitment.

So, I believe that this is the best approach. I've noticed that in the last few days, particularly in France—I happened to see a television program—the foremost critics of the embarrassing trials of Shcharanskiy and Ginzburg were the Communists in France. They led the march against the Soviet Union's action in trying these innocent people and sentencing these brave people in the Soviet Union who spoke up for their own fellow citizens to have basic human rights.

So, I think that although we don't want to see communism increase, we want to do everything we can that I've outlined to prevent its growth. At the same time we have to recognize that Eurocommunism is not a monolithic structure completely dominated or encapsulated within the Soviet Union itself. And I think that gives us some additional hope that even communism itself in the Western democracies might have some beneficial aspects of democratic principles in which we believe so deeply.

Thank you.

U.S. SPACE ACTIVITIES

Q. Mr. President, my name is Gerhard Schofer. I'm a civil servant. My question is this: After the completion of the space shuttle project, do the U.S. plan further Moon missions and landings?

THE PRESIDENT. We don't have any specific plans now for additional manned missions to the Moon nor to the other planets. We have an ongoing program, however, of unmanned missiles to the outer planets as well as to the Moon.

I think these are adequate. We have proven our capability to go to the Moon. We still have that capability, of course. We now are trying to make our explorations into space, into outer space, much more efficient as far as the dollars spent compared to the results obtained. And our manned space flights will be primarily restricted to the increasing utilization of the space shuttle.

We hope to make these space flights using the shuttle a fairly routine procedure, and we hope that they might be concentrating upon those aspects of space flight that bring more direct benefits to the people here on Earth.

I think the scientific explorations, therefore, can basically be performed by instruments carried on our space vehicles, and the manned space flights will be closer in to Earth, using the space shuttle itself.

U.S. FOREIGN POLICY

Q. Mr. President, my name is Eberhard Behrend. I'm a scientist, and my question is this: Why has America, from the experiences of the Vietnam war, drawn the conclusion to withdraw the active support of freedom fighters and opposition groups in totalitarian parts of the world instead of actively supporting them and looking for a nonmilitary support of such resistance groups in the oppressed parts of the world?

THE PRESIDENT. That's a difficult question to answer. I think that I share the opinion of the American public that we should not again become involved in a military way in the internal affairs of another country unless our own security is directly threatened.

We do support the maintenance of peace. We do this through multilateral organizations like the United Nations, through multilateral teams such as we've just formed and with which we've had some success in Namibia, where we cooperated with the Federal Republic of Germany, with France, Great Britain, and with Canada. And on some occasions we work just with one other nation primarily, as is presently the case in Rhodesia, where we and the British are trying to use our good offices to bring about a peaceful resolution there.

But I don't contemplate, short of a direct threat to the security of my own Nation, the sending of troops to another country to solve an internal conflict as we did in Vietnam in the recent past.

This is not an abandonment of the principles on which our Nation was founded and which we believe. We have stood staunch in the support for basic human rights, and I think the recent world attention focused upon these violations in different countries has been a testimony to the fact that the Western democratic system and our belief in freedom is letting its voice be heard and its influence be felt. But just because we don't send troops as we did in Vietnam does not mean that we've abandoned freedom or that we will sit back and let local conflicts bring suffering upon those in whom we are deeply interested and about whom we are concerned.

GERMAN DEMOCRATIC REPUBLIC

Q. Mr. President, my name is Hertha Winkler. I'm a pensioner in the GDR in Bautzen. And I would like to direct this question to you, Mr. President: When do you come and visit us in the German Democratic Republic? Many of my friends would welcome you heartily there.

THE PRESIDENT. Let me first extend my friendship to those in the GDR, express my hope that we can find peace and a resolution of differences that stand between us still. And I want to tell you, as I said earlier, not only that the next time I come to Berlin that I would like to visit the eastern portion but I will certainly promise to go to East Berlin on my next visit.

To visit the GDR is another matter. We now have had diplomatic relations with the GDR for, I believe, about 4 years. And we're still exploring means by which we can lessen the differences between that country and our own. We have some problems with the consulate agreement. But when that basic question is resolved, then I think we could expand our relationships there.

I have visited other Eastern European nations. I was in Poland recently, and we have had visits from leaders of other Eastern European countries.

I have no objection to going there, and perhaps the next time I come to this part of Europe, we'll have an easy relationship with the GDR, which might make it possible for me to visit. But at this time, I think I'll restrict my very limited visiting time to the Federal Republic of Germany and to West Berlin.

NIKO HÜBNER

Q. Mr. President, my name is Wolfgang Netschkowski. Many Berliner citizens have asked you to do something for Niko Hübner. What can the U.S.A. do for Niko Hübner, more than just verbally protest to get Niko Hübner out of GDR prison?

THE PRESIDENT. The verbal protest is made because of the agreement on the part of the Soviets that East Berlin would be a demilitarized area. The original charge against Mr. Hübner, I understand, was because he refused to be drafted into the military forces. We did express our displeasure about this very strongly, as did the other allies involved, and made this clear to the Soviet Union and to the GDR.

As a result of this and other expressions of displeasure and the realization of the Soviets and the Eastern Germans that they did violate the agreement, they changed the charges against him from avoiding military service to a trumped-up substitute charge.

I really don't know what other action we can take, except to insist upon the honoring of the agreement that has been signed between ourselves and the Soviet Union, along with, of course, the British and French.

But we have no authority to go into the GDR and to remove someone from prison. But we have to make sure that when they do falsely charge someone against the principles expressed in the Quadripartite Agreement that our voice is heard clearly.

I think in this case it has had some success only to the extent that they changed the charge against him. But the punishment was unwarranted. It's obvious that he's an innocent person, and as you know, he's not the only one who's suffering at this time. And we hope that this can be a matter that's brought more to the focus of the world. I think the recent Shcharanskiy trial has been a matter of concern and interest to everyone, almost, on Earth, in the civilized nations.

And we hope that the problem with Herr Hübner can be now better understood by the rest of the world, and perhaps world opinion can cause his early release. But there is no specific action that I can promise you that would guarantee this early release against the desires of the Soviets or the East Germans.

BERLIN AND THE ALLIES

Q. Mr. President, my name is Irmgard Hiege. I'm a pensioner, and I've got this question for you, Mr. President: Why don't public and official circles do more to promote the personal relationships of the Berliners with the allies present in the city of Berlin?

THE PRESIDENT. I don't know now, but within a half an hour after I leave this podium, I will talk to the commanders of all the three allied services, and I will have not only an answer for you but I'll let them know about my interest in having the relationship be freer, more frequent, and more constructive.

I think it's very healthy when the Allied Forces are incorporated within the spirit of friendship and hospitality of those among whom they serve. I spoke recently—today as a matter of fact—to our forces and the German forces at Frankfurt. And I encouraged them to learn the German language, to get to know the German culture, to make personal friends of the German poeple, to shop as much as possible in the German shops, and to become a part of the German society. I think it will help them not only to understand the very great characteristics of the German people but will also make them better Americans when they come home.

So, I'll talk this over with the commanding officers here, and I think your question has already brought very good

dividends, even though I can't answer your question any better than that. Thank you.

Perhaps we could get a reply published in one of the local newspapers, since I'll have to bring this to a close in a moment. I can only take one more question, I understand.

U.S.-GERMAN EXCHANGES

Q. Mr. President, my name is Rita Schäfer. I'm a psychologist. My question is as follows: Would you help to foster existing friendship and exchange programs between our nations and to expand them in such a way that the members of the maximum number of brackets and social groupings, not only academics and professional professions, can exchange their jobs for a limited period of time in order to get acquainted?

THE PRESIDENT. Yes. This is something that would not only benefit you and others but would also benefit our own country.

I think the student exchange is one very fine example of what can be accomplished. The Friendship Force that's already been referred to earlier is one that can be greatly expanded in the future. And I think that we have a great opportunity in that there are 300,000 Americans, for instance, who serve in the military forces in Europe. And they are, hopefully, ambassadors of good will for our country and also can derive from all of you a very clear understanding of the benefits to be brought back home. But I think your question is a very good one. And I believe in these and other ways we can expand the relationship among us.

To conclude, let me say that one of the things that can be done by a President to expand the understanding between myself and you is to have this unprecedented townhall meeting. I do this in our own country. I never know ahead of time what the questions might be. I'm not nearly so familiar with your own society and your own current problems as I would be in a city in the United States, but I've tried to answer your questions as best I could.

I've derived from my brief visit here a clearer understanding of the strength and courage required by those of you who live in Berlin to maintain not only a standard of living which is even higher than that in my own country but also a spirit of freedom and a preservation of your own superb cultural traits that I hope will be permanent. We are your partners. We are your allies. We do this not just for your own benefit, because our own Nation is protected, the freedom of my own people is protected to the extent that you and your own freedoms can be preserved by joint commitment of our two nations and those of our other allies.

So, I come here not as someone who does you a favor, but as someone who benefits greatly as a President and as an American from the strong ties of friendship, economics, politics, military alliances that preserves freedom, not just for you but for us as well.

I thank you for giving me a chance to hear of your concerns, and the hospitality that you've extended to me, to my wife, Rosalynn, and to Amy. We hope to be able to come back. We hope as many of you as possible will visit our own country. And I think you would find there is warmth, a sense of common purpose and friendship, as I have found here.

God bless every one of you. Thank you for letting me be your guest.

PETER LORENZ. Mr. President, on behalf of all those in this hall and on behalf of the city, I should like to thank you most cordially for this frank and open discussion with the Berliners of this Berlin town meeting. I think we are all agreed that this was one of the highlights of your Berlin visit.

I think, Mr. President, you will have felt how close the citizens of Berlin feel associated with you, Mr. President, and the United States of America. This is of special significance that the meeting takes place here in the Kongresshalle. It was given to our city by the Benjamin Franklin Foundation. It bears the name of that President of the United States of America who so strongly promoted freedom and dignity and rights of man in the world.

You, Mr. President, are leaving no stone unturned to realize human rights in this world. And you are assured that we in Berlin, in this divided city, a city divided by a wall, do with great engagement support your efforts, Mr. President, for human rights. We are happy. We feel honored. We are grateful for your coming to Berlin. Your presence underscores the great significance and reputation of the city and the consciousness of the people of America which you represent, Mr. President.

We are most grateful to you, for you have stated here a moment ago that you support the claim and the right of the German nation to become reunited. Thank you very much from the bottom of my heart, on behalf of all of us, Mr. President.

We are very glad that you and your family, Mr. President, will spend a few pleasant hours in Berlin. When you leave Berlin in a few hours' time, our good wishes will accompany you. And thank you, sir, and thank you, American people, for the support you have given us here in Berlin.

NOTE: The President spoke at approximately 4 p.m. at the Kongresshalle, following an introduction by Governing Mayor of Berlin Dietrich Stobbe. Peter Lorenz is president of the Berlin Senate.

The participants in the town meeting spoke in German, and their remarks were translated by an interpreter. The town meeting was broadcast live in the United States.

Bonn Economic Summit Conference

Informal Exchange With Reporters.
July 16, 1978

Q. Good evening, Mr. President.

THE PRESIDENT. Good evening, everybody.

Q. How did you feel about the first session of the conference today?

THE PRESIDENT. I was pleased with it. We've not yet concluded any specific language for the final communique; that will be done tonight and tomorrow. But there was a very frank and open discussion among the seven heads of state, the Foreign Ministers, and the Finance Ministers. And this has been the habit within these summit conferences.

One of the best things about it is that we've spent literally months with staff members, Cabinet officers, and others, preparing for the summit, trying to understand the particular problems and attitudes of the other six nations, plus the European Community, which is represented here by its head.

I think that the final result of the deliberations will be good. I believe that the world economic community, when it analyzes what we do, will be pleased. And I think the attitude of all of the heads of state has been very constructive.

Q. Mr. President, just how much pressure is the United States under because of its energy consumption?

THE PRESIDENT. The other nations are no more concerned about excessive consumption and the absence of an energy policy than I am. This is a matter on which we've been working, almost without ceasing, for the last 15 or 16 months.

My own belief and my hope is that the Congress will act without delay to implement our energy policy and that the people of the United States will recognize that excessive consumption or waste of energy is not in the best interest of our own people or the rest of the world. It obviously is of much more critical importance to a country like Japan, which has to import 98 percent of its energy, and even countries like France and Germany, which have a very low supply of their own energy.

They feel not only that we compete with them for world supplies of oil and therefore drive up the price and create the ultimate shortage but that in the process we have an attitude of wastefulness based on very low-price energy in the past that they would like to see corrected. But they share our hope and our concern about the energy supply problems and the over-consumption in our own Nation.

Q. Were you able to give your fellow heads of state anything more specific other than the promise of—a lack of congressional action or anything else on the energy question?

THE PRESIDENT. Yes, the exact language is still being drafted. But I have told them what my own attitude would be—the goals that our Nation has established for the reduction of energy consumption, the shift toward greater supply of coal, solar energy, other alternative energy sources—and have spelled this out quite clearly; also, our hope that the abnormally low prices of oil in our country, which contributes to excessive waste, might be raised to the world market price and my belief that the Congress will act on this legislation, hopefully beginning with the first package Tuesday of this week.

Q. There was talk of a quota, the possibility that you might call for an oil quota.

THE PRESIDENT. No, I think that would be inappropriate for me to put in the communique, because I've not decided myself about the advisability of this action.

Q. Are you still hoping for Congress to act to prevent you having to impose quotas?

THE PRESIDENT. Yes, I hope the Congress will act on the entire package. As you know, the conference committees have agreed on four-fifths of it, which encompass an energy saving of about 2.3 million barrels per day. The remaining portion concerning the tax on oil would result in an additional 2 or 300,000 barrels a day.

So, the major portion of it has at least been agreed to by the conference committees, and I hope that Congress will act without delay.

Q. Are you pleased?

THE PRESIDENT. Yes, I'm pleased.

REPORTER. Thank you, Mr. President.

NOTE: The President spoke at 7:06 p.m. outside the U.S. Ambassador's residence.

Earlier in the day, the President attended the first and second sessions of the summit conference at the Palais Schaumburg and a working luncheon hosted by Chancellor Schmidt for summit participants at the Chancellor's Bungalow.

Later in the evening, the President attended a dinner hosted by Chancellor Schmidt at Schloss Gymnich for the summit participants.

Bonn Economic Summit Conference

Informal Exchange With Reporters.
July 17, 1978

Q. Mr. President, are you going to be discussing Berlin this morning, with the protest?

THE PRESIDENT. Yes, we'll be discussing Berlin this morning.

Q. Do you have any ideas on what you want to do?

THE PRESIDENT. No. Every year the allied leaders who are responsible for Ber-

lin try to get together to discuss it for a while. And this is what we will be discussing at breakfast, among other things.

Q. Do you have any new problems that you have to discuss?

THE PRESIDENT. We have enough problems and opportunities; we're not looking for new ones.

Q. Do you feel good about the summit?

THE PRESIDENT. Very good, yes.

Q. Can the fellows really do anything about terrorism in what they bring forth today?

THE PRESIDENT. Yes.

REPORTERS. What? [*Laughter*]

NOTE: The President spoke at 8:15 a.m. outside the U.S. Ambassador's residence.

Following the exchange, the President attended a breakfast meeting at the Chancellor's Bungalow with President Valéry Giscard d'Estaing of France, Prime Minister James Callaghan of the United Kingdom, and Chancellor Schmidt.

Bonn Economic Summit Conference

Joint Statement on International Terrorism.
July 17, 1978

The heads of state and government, concerned about terrorism and the taking of hostages, declare that their governments will intensify their joint efforts to combat international terrorism.

To this end, in cases where a country refuses extradition or prosecution of those who have hijacked an aircraft and/or do not return such aircraft, the heads of state and government are jointly resolved that their governments should take immediate action to cease all flights to that country.

At the same time, their governments will initiate action to halt all incoming flights from that country or from any country by the airlines of the country concerned. The heads of state and government urge other governments to join them in this commitment.

NOTE: Chancellor Helmut Schmidt read the joint statement during his remarks at the Bonn Stadt Theater at the conclusion of the Bonn Economic Summit Conference.

Bonn Economic Summit Conference

Remarks at the Conclusion of the Conference.
July 17, 1978

Having been fortunate enough to make an official state visit to the Federal Republic of Germany immediately prior to the summit conference, I would like to express the thanks, on behalf of all the American delegation, to President Scheel, to Chancellor Schmidt, and to the people of the Federal Republic, for their hospitality.

I have been very pleased at the results of this summit conference. The results have exceeded the expectation of all of us. The discussions and the conclusions have been carefully prepared. Each one of us has been cautious at this summit not to promise things which we could not subsequently deliver.

The assessments have been long, sometimes tedious, but comprehensive in nature. They are substantive and specific. I think each leader has gone the limit, within the bounds of political actualities, to contribute everything possible from our own individual nations to the common well-being of the world.

Our contributions have been mutually supportive. They have been different, one from another, because our capabilities and our needs are different.

We have dealt with the very serious problem of protectionism and mutually

committed ourselves to successfully concluding the multilateral trade negotiations to permit free markets to keep our people employed at home.

The Federal Republic of Germany, the Government of Japan, have generously committed themselves to increased economic growth. Other nations have joined in this commitment. The United States, recognizing our own responsibilities, and at the request of others, have committed ourselves to a comprehensive energy policy and its implementation—to cut down the importation of oil by 2½ million barrels a day by the year 1985, to raise the price of oil, which is too cheap in our own country, to the world market level to discourage waste.

We and the Canadians have recognized our need to provide some predictability, some dependability upon a supply of nuclear fuels to other nations, commensurate with a mutual profession against proliferation of nuclear explosives and the adherence to international safeguards.

We have all been concerned about inflation and have made our plans to deal with this all-pervasive threat throughout the world.

This is a time when we also recognize our strength, our stability, the benefits of peace. And our hope is that in the analysis of transient problems, with which we are trying to deal successfully, that we need not ever lose sight of the base of common purpose that binds us together in a successful endeavor in the free and democratic nations of the world.

We will be carefully monitoring progress after this summit adjourns, to make sure that those commitments made in sincerity are not forgotten nor abandoned in the months ahead.

I would like to say, finally, that we have not forgotten the developing nations of the world. We are fortunate, we've been blessed with economic and political and military strength and with a fine, high standard of living for our own people. We recognize the need to share this with other, less developed countries. And all these cumulative commitments, I think, will be very good and constructive for the entire world economy in the months ahead.

I personally believe that the strong statement on controlling air piracy, terrorism, is in itself worth the entire preparation and conduct of the summit. We are determined that this commitment be carried out individually and collectively. And our Foreign Ministers have been instructed immediately to contact other nations around the world without delay, to encourage them to join in with us in this substantive and, I think, adequate move to prevent air hijacking in the future.

I leave this summit conference with a resolve to carry out our purposes, to continue our mutual discussions and consultations, and with a new sense of confidence.

This has been a very successful meeting among us. The preparation for it was very instructive and educational, and the superb chairmanship of Chancellor Schmidt has helped to ensure its success.

NOTE: The President spoke at 7:12 p.m. at Bonn Stadt Theater following concluding statements by Chancellor Helmut Schmidt of the Federal Republic of Germany, Prime Minister Pierre Elliott Trudeau of Canada, President Valéry Giscard d'Estaing of France, Prime Minister Giulio Andreotti of Italy, Prime Minister Takeo Fukuda of Japan, and Prime Minister James Callaghan of the United Kingdom of Great Britain and Northern Ireland.

Earlier in the day, the President attended the third and fourth sessions of the summit conference at the Palais Schaumburg and a working luncheon hosted by President Scheel for summit participants at Villa Hammerschmidt.

Bonn Economic Summit Conference

Declaration Issued at the Conclusion of the Conference. July 17, 1978

The Heads of State and Government of Canada, the Federal Republic of Germany, France, Italy, Japan, the United Kingdom of Great Britain and Northern Ireland and the United States of America met in Bonn on 16th and 17th July 1978. The European Community was represented by the President of the European Council and by the President of the European Commission for discussion of matters within the Community's competence.

1. We agreed on a comprehensive strategy covering growth, employment and inflation, international monetary policy, energy, trade and other issues of particular interest to developing countries. We must create more jobs and fight inflation, strengthen international trading, reduce payments imbalances, and achieve greater stability in exchange markets. We are dealing with long-term problems, which will only yield to sustained efforts. This strategy is a coherent whole, whose parts are interdependent. To this strategy, each of our countries can contribute; from it, each can benefit.

GROWTH, EMPLOYMENT AND INFLATION

2. We are concerned, above all, about world-wide unemployment because it has been at too high a level for many years, because it hits hardest at the most vulnerable sections of the population, because its economic cost is high and its human cost higher still. We will act, through measures to assure growth and develop needed skills, to increase employment.

In doing this, we will build on the progress that has already been made in the fight against inflation and will seek new successes in that fight. But we need an improvement in growth where that can be achieved without rekindling inflation in order to reduce extremes of balance of payments surpluses and deficits. This will reduce destabilizing exchange rate movements. Improved growth will help to reduce protectionist pressures. We need it also to encourage the flow of private investment, on which economic progress depends; we will seek to reduce impediments to private investment, both domestically and internationally. Better growth is needed to ensure that the free world is able to develop to meet the expectations of its citizens and the aspirations of the developing countries.

3. A program of different actions by countries that face different conditions is needed to assure steady non-inflationary growth. In countries whose balance of payments situation and inflation rate does not impose special restrictions, this requires a faster rise in domestic demand. In countries where rising prices and costs are creating strong pressures, this means taking new measures against inflation.

—Canada reaffirmed its intention, within the limits permitted by the need to contain and reduce inflation, to achieve higher growth of employment and an increase in output of up to 5%.

—As a contribution to avert the worldwide disturbances of economic equilibrium the German Delegation has indicated that by the end of August it will propose to the legislative bodies additional and quantitatively substantial measures up to 1 p.c. of GNP, designed to achieve a significant strengthening of demand and a higher rate of growth. The order of magnitude will take account of the absorptive capacity of the capital market and the need to avoid inflationary pressures.

—The President of the French Republic has indicated that, while pursuing its policy of reduction of the rate of infla-

tion, the French Government agrees, as a contribution to the common effort, to increase by an amount of about 0.5% of G.N.P. the deficit of the budget of the State for the year 1978.

—The Italian Prime Minister has indicated that the Government undertakes to raise the rate of economic growth in 1979 by 1.5 percentage points with respect to 1978. It plans to achieve this goal by cutting public current expenditure while stimulating investments with the aim of increasing employment in a non-inflationary context.

—The Prime Minister of Japan has referred to the fact that his Government is striving for the attainment of the real growth target for fiscal year 1978, which is about 1.5 percentage points higher than the performance of the previous year, mainly through the expansion of domestic demand. He has further expressed his determination to achieve the said target by taking appropriate measures as necessary. In August or September he will determine whether additional measures are needed.

—The United Kingdom, having achieved a major reduction in the rate of inflation and improvement in the balance of payments has recently given a fiscal stimulus equivalent to rather over 1% of G.N.P. The Government intends to continue the fight against inflation so as to improve still further the prospects for growth and employment.

—The President of the United States stated that reducing inflation is essential to maintaining a healthy U.S. economy and has therefore become the top priority of U.S. economic policy. He identified the major actions that have been taken and are being taken to counter inflation in the United States: Tax cuts originally proposed for fiscal year 1979 have now been reduced by $10 billion; government expenditure projections for 1978 and 1979 have been reduced; a very tight budget is being prepared for 1980; steps are being taken to reduce the direct contribution by government regulations or restrictions to rising costs and prices, and a voluntary programme has been undertaken to achieve deceleration of wages and prices.

—The meeting took note with satisfaction that the common approach of the European Community already agreed at Bremen would reinforce the effectiveness of this programme.

ENERGY

4. In spite of some improvement, the present energy situation remains unsatisfactory. Much more needs to be done.

5. We are committed to reduce our dependence on imported oil.

6. We note that the European Community has already agreed at Bremen the following objectives for 1985: to reduce the Community's dependence on imported energy to 50 percent, to limit net oil imports, and to reduce to 0.8 the ratio between the rate of increase in energy consumption and the rate of increase in gross domestic product.

7. Recognizing its particular responsibility in the energy field, the United States will reduce its dependence on imported oil. The U.S. will have in place by the end of the year a comprehensive policy framework within which this effort can be urgently carried forward. By year end, measures will be in effect that will result in oil import savings of approximately 2.5 million barrels per day by 1985. In order to achieve these goals, the U.S. will establish a strategic oil reserve of 1 billion barrels; it will increase coal production by two-thirds; it will maintain the ratio between growth in gross national product and growth in energy demand at or below 0.8; and its oil consumption will grow more slowly than energy consump-

tion. The volume of oil imported in 1978 and 1979 should be less than that imported in 1977. In order to discourage excessive consumption of oil and to encourage the movement toward coal, the U.S. remains determined that the prices paid for oil in the U.S. shall be raised to the world level by the end of 1980.

8. We hope that the oil exporting countries will continue to contribute to a stable world energy situation.

9. Looking to the longer term, our countries will review their national energy programs with a view to speeding them up. General energy targets can serve as useful measures of the progress achieved.

10. Private and public investment to produce energy and to use it more efficiently within the industrial world should be increased. This can contribute significantly to economic growth.

11. The further development of nuclear energy is indispensable, and the slippage in the execution of nuclear power programmes must be reversed. To promote the peaceful use of nuclear energy and reduce the risk of nuclear proliferation, the nuclear fuel cycle studies initiated at the London Summit should be pursued. The President of the United States and the Prime Minister of Canada have expressed their firm intention to continue as reliable suppliers of nuclear fuel within the framework of effective safeguards. The President intends to use the full powers of his office to prevent any interruption of enriched uranium supply and to ensure that existing agreements will be respected. The Prime Minister intends that there shall be no interruption of Canadian uranium supply on the basis of effective safeguards.

12. Coal should play an increasing important role in the long term.

13. Joint or co-ordinated energy research and development should be carried out to hasten the development of new,

including renewable, energy sources and the more efficient use of existing sources.

14. In energy development, the environment and human safety of the population must be safeguarded with greatest care.

15. To help developing countries, we will intensify our national development assistance programs in the energy field and we will develop a co-ordinated effort to bring into use renewable energy technologies and to elaborate the details within one year. We suggest that the OECD will provide the medium for co-operation with other countries.

16. We stress the need for improvement and co-ordination of assistance for developing countries in the energy field. We suggest that the World Bank explore ways in which its activities in this field can be made increasingly responsive to the needs of the developing countries, and to examine whether new approaches, particularly to financing hydrocarbon exploration, would be useful.

TRADE

17. We reaffirm our determination to expand international trade one of the driving forces for more sustained and balanced economic growth. Through our joint efforts we will maintain and strengthen the open international trading system. We appreciate and support the progress as set forth in the Framework of Understanding on the Tokyo Round of Multilateral Trade Negotiations made public in Geneva, July 13th, 1978, even though within this Framework of understanding some difficult and important issues remain unresolved.

The successful conclusion of these negotiations, the biggest yet held, would mean not just a major trade liberalisation programme extending over the 1980s but the most important progress yet made in the GATT in relation to non-tariff measures. Thus the GATT rules would be brought more closely into line with the requirements of the next decade—particularly in relation to safeguards—in ways which could avoid any weakening of the world trading system and be of benefit to all trading countries developed and developing alike. A substantially higher degree of equity and discipline in the international trading system would be achieved by the creation of new mechanisms in many fields for consultation and dispute settlement. Uniform application of the GATT rules is vital and we shall move in that direction as soon as possible.

In all areas of the negotiations the Summit countries look forward to working even more closely with the developing countries. We seek to ensure for all participants a sound and balanced result, which adequately takes into account the needs of developing countries, for example, through special and differential treatment, and which brings about their greater participation in the benefits and obligations of the world trading system.

At last year's Downing Street Summit we rejected a protectionist course for world trade. We agreed to give a new impetus to the Tokyo Round. Our negotiators have fulfilled that commitment. Today we charge them, in co-operation with the other participants, to resolve the outstanding issues and to conclude successfully the detailed negotiations by December 15, 1978.

18. We note with satisfaction the renewal of the pledge to maintain an open market oriented economic system made by the OECD Council of Ministers last month. Today's world economic problems cannot be solved by relapsing into open or concealed protectionism.

19. We welcome the statement on positive adjustment policy made by the OECD Ministers. There must be a readi-

ness over time, to accept and facilitate structural change. Measures to prevent such change perpetuate economic inefficiency, place the burden of structural change on trading partners and inhibit the integration of developing countries into the world economy. We are determined in our industrial, social, structural, and regional policy initiatives to help sectors in difficulties, without interfering with international competition and trade flows.

20. We note the need for countries with large current accounts deficits to increase exports and for countries with large current accounts surpluses to facilitate increases in imports. In this context, the United States is firmly committed to improve its export performance and is examining measures to this end. The Prime Minister of Japan has stated that he wishes to work for the increase of imports through the expansion of domestic demand and various efforts to facilitate imports. Furthermore, he has stated that in order to cope with the immediate situation of unusual surplus, the Government of Japan is taking a temporary and extraordinary step of calling for moderation in exports with the aim of keeping the total volume of Japan's exports for the fiscal year of 1978 at or below the level of fiscal year 1977.

21. We underline our willingness to increase our co-operation in the field of foreign private investment flows among industrialized countries and between them and developing countries. We will intensify work for further agreements in the OECD and elsewhere.

22. In the context of expanding world economic activity, we recognize the requirement for better access to our countries' markets for the products of the developing countries. At the same time we look to increasing readiness on the part of the more advanced developing countries to open their markets to imports.

RELATIONS WITH DEVELOPING COUNTRIES

23. Success in our efforts to strengthen our countries' economies will benefit the developing countries, and their economic progress will benefit us. This calls for joint action on the basis of shared responsibility.

24. In the years ahead the developing countries, particularly those most in need, can count on us for an increased flow of financial assistance and other resources for their development. The Prime Minister of Japan has stated that he will strive to double Japan's official development assistance in three years.

We deeply regret the failure of the COMECON countries to take their due share in the financial assistance to developing countries and invite them once more to do so.

25. The poorer developing countries require increased concessional aid. We support the soft loan funds of the World Bank and the three regional development banks. We pledge our governments to support replenishment of the International Development Association on a scale that would permit its lending to rise annually in real terms.

26. As regards the more advanced developing countries, we renew our pledge to support replenishment of the multilateral development banks' resources, on the scale needed to meet the growing needs for loans on commercial terms. We will encourage governmental and private co-financing of development projects with these banks.

The co-operation of the developing countries in creating a good investment climate and adequate protection for foreign investment is required if foreign private investment is to play its effective role in generating economic growth and in stimulating the transfer of technology.

We also refer to our efforts with respect to developing countries in the field of energy as outlined in paragraph 15 and 16.

27. We agreed to pursue actively the negotiations on a Common Fund to a successful conclusion and to continue our efforts to conclude individual commodity agreements and to complete studies of various ways of stabilizing export earnings.

INTERNATIONAL MONETARY POLICY

28. The erratic fluctuations of the exchange markets in recent months have had a damaging effect on confidence, investment and growth throughout the world. Essentially, exchange rate stability can only be achieved by attacking the fundamental problems which have contributed to the present large balance of payments deficits and surpluses. Implementation of the policies described above in the framework of a concerted program will help to bring about a better pattern of world payments balances and lead to greater stability in international exchange markets. This stability will in turn improve confidence and the environment for sustained economic growth.

29. Although exchange rates need to respond to changes in underlying economic and financial conditions among nations, our monetary authorities will continue to intervene to the extent necessary to counter disorderly conditions in the exchange markets. They will maintain extensive consultation to enhance these efforts' effectiveness. We will support surveillance by the International Monetary Fund, to promote effective functioning of the international monetary system.

30. The representatives of the European Community informed the meeting of the decision of the European Council at Bremen on 6/7 July to consider a scheme for a closer monetary co-operation. The meeting welcomed the report and noted that the Community would keep the other participants informed.

CONCLUSION

31. It has been our combined purpose to attack the fundamental economic problems that our countries confront.

The measures on which we have agreed are mutually reinforcing. Their total effect should thus be more than the sum of their parts. We will now seek parliamentary and public support for these measures.

We cannot hope to achieve our purposes alone. We shall work closely together with other countries and within the appropriate international institutions; those among us whose countries are members of the European Community intend to make their efforts within this framework.

We have instructed our representatives to convene by the end of 1978 in order to review this Declaration.

We also intend to have a similar meeting among ourselves at an appropriate time next year.

NOTE: As printed above, this item follows the text of the declaration as released by the West German Government.

The President's Trip to the Federal Republic of Germany

Remarks on Arrival at the White House. July 17, 1978

THE VICE PRESIDENT. *Mr. President, Rosalynn, and Amy:*

We're delighted to welcome you back home again from an extraordinarily successful trip. I think if you asked Americans what concerned them most, it would be inflation, economic growth, the need to deal with energy. And your success on all counts in this most effective international economic summit is something that thrills us all.

We were also very gratified by the very strong and specific steps that the Western industrial democracies will now take against air piracy and terrorism. And also, I know that all Americans stood solidly behind you when you visited Berlin and reaffirmed the longstanding and unwavering commitment of the American people to the continuing freedom of that city.

Mr. President, we're delighted to have you back from this most successful trip.

THE PRESIDENT. Thank you very much.

When I was far from home in West Germany, there were two basic issues that were constantly on my mind. One was the strength and the freedom of the Western World. I told the people in Bonn, Frankfurt, throughout West Germany, that their security was our security, because we know that the defense of the United States itself is dependent upon the strength of the NATO Alliance.

We have 300,000 members of the American Armed Forces in Europe—in the Marines, the Air Force, the Navy, and the Army. I was able to visit with some of those, to talk to them personally, to talk to their families. They serve there at great personal sacrifice, but they know their purpose in life. They recognize why they make that sacrifice. They are there not only to defend territory but to defend the spirit of freedom.

We saw a demonstration of that spirit in a very exciting visit to West Berlin, a free city that could be called an island of liberty. There was an outpouring of friendship there as I rode through the streets, a demonstration that the Ber-

liners, the Germans, the Europeans know the value of our partnership. I think the impression that went through my mind in those exciting moments was that we define ourselves by the values that we are willing to sacrifice to defend, and the values that we defend in Europe can indeed make all Americans proud.

The other basic issue was the interdependence in the economic world. I met with the leaders of six other great nations to try to ensure a better life for people of our own country, a higher standard of living, more jobs, lower costs for the goods that we consume.

I can tell you in complete candor that our allies in other nations were willing to make economic sacrifices for the good of us all, so that we might sell our own products more successfully, that we might have in that way more jobs for the people of this country.

We made promises also that I intend to keep: to hold down inflation and to meet the greatest single concern of others, and that is the excessive waste of energy in this country and the excessive imports of foreign oil.

We recognize the strength of the free world. We have some problems that we've addressed very thoroughly. But overall our feeling was one of confidence, of mutual purpose, of the willingness to address the difficult issues without timidity and without fear.

So, to summarize, we realize that freedom is priceless. We realize that our own well-being at home is dependent upon the partnership that we enjoy with wonderful allies around the world. It was a good trip for us. I was proud to represent the greatest nation on Earth. And we are very glad to be home. Thank you very much.

NOTE: The exchange began at 11:30 p.m. on the South Lawn of the White House.

Citizenship Day and Constitution Week, 1978

Proclamation 4579.   July 19, 1978

By the President of the United States of America

A Proclamation

September 17, 1978, will mark the 191st anniversary of the signing, in Independence Hall, Philadelphia, of the Constitution of the United States. That great document has endured, with but few changes, as the finest foundation of government in the history of mankind.

By a joint resolution of February 29, 1952, (36 U.S.C. 153), Congress designated September 17 as Citizenship Day, in commemoration of the signing of the Constitution and in recognition of all who, by coming of age or by naturalization, have attained the status of citizenship; Congress also authorized the President to issue annually a proclamation calling upon officials of the Government to display the flag on all Government buildings on that day. By a joint resolution of August 2, 1956, (36 U.S.C. 159), Congress authorized the President to designate the period beginning September 17 and ending September 23 of each year as Constitution Week and to issue a proclamation calling for the observance of that week.

Now, THEREFORE, I, JIMMY CARTER, President of the United States of America, call upon appropriate government officials to display the flag of the United States on all government buildings on Citizenship Day, September 17, 1978, the 191st anniversary of the signing of the Constitution. I urge Federal, State and local officials, as well as leaders of civic, educational and religious organizations, to conduct suitable ceremonies and programs on that day.

I also designate as Constitution Week the period beginning September 17 and ending September 23, 1978, and urge all Americans to observe that week with ceremonies and activities in their schools, churches and in other suitable places in order to foster a better understanding of the Constitution and of the rights and duties of United States citizens.

IN WITNESS WHEREOF, I have hereunto set my hand this nineteenth day of July in the year of our Lord nineteen hundred seventy-eight, and of the Independence of the United States the two hundred and third.

JIMMY CARTER

[Filed with the Office of the Federal Register, 12:07 p.m., July 19, 1978]

Federal Civil Service Reorganization

Statement on the House Government Operations Committee's Action on Reorganization Plan No. 2 of 1978. July 19, 1978

I wish to express my appreciation for the House Government Operations Committee's vote today on the civil service reorganization plan. I especially want to thank Committee Chairman Jack Brooks for his leadership. The 31–0 committee vote count reflects the strong bipartisan support for my civil service reforms.

I look forward to the reorganization plan's becoming effective, and to the passage by Congress of the companion civil service legislation.

Federal Civil Service Reform

Statement on the House Post Office and Civil Service Committee's Action on Legislation.
July 19, 1978

I am extremely pleased that the House Post Office and Civil Service Committee has today voted to report the civil service reform act. Despite forecasts by some that this action would not come for some time, the committee has acted quickly and expeditiously. I feel that is a major accomplishment.

I congratulate Chairman Robert Nix, Vice Chairman Morris Udall, and the ranking minority member, Edward Derwinski, for their leadership in guiding the civil service reforms through the committee. I want to thank all members, both Democrats and Republicans, for the diligence and thoroughness with which they have worked.

The bill reported from committee carries forward the major thrust of my civil service reform proposal, though there were some amendments added by the committee that I opposed. I look forward to speedy House floor action on this legislation, which is so important to making our Government better serve the American people.

Federal Government Spending

Memorandum From the President.
July 19, 1978

Memorandum for the Heads of Executive Departments and Agencies

As I did at the end of last fiscal year, I again ask you to help me make sure we continue to use funds wisely. Prevention of unneeded or unwise Federal Government spending is more important than ever in this time of high inflation. Please, therefore, tell your staff not to spend or obligate funds for the sole or even primary purpose of keeping them from lapsing.

Nor should they speed up spending to avoid a shortfall that would occur solely, or even primarily, because earlier outlay estimates were too optimistic. Funds should be used only for clear and desirable program purposes.

Please issue instructions assuring that:

—obligations for the fourth quarter of the fiscal year are no higher than for the third quarter, except where seasonal requirements, essential program objectives, or procurement lead-times justify a higher level, or where more money is needed to restore program slippages to approved levels;

—orders for supplies, materials, and equipment are no more than needed to meet approved program needs;

—purchases are managed so that inventories do not exceed optimal levels;

—contracts for goods or services (for delivery extending into the next fiscal year) are let only when doing so will result in lower cost to the Government; and

—no purchases are made to compensate for what otherwise would be an outlay shortfall. Resist the temptation to buy and pay for lower priority items to make up for over-optimistic outlay estimates.

I count on your full cooperation and personal attention to save the taxpayers as much money as possible.

JIMMY CARTER

NOTE: The text of the memorandum was released on July 20.

Future Farmers of America

Remarks to the Organization's State Presidents. July 20, 1978

I was trying to remember how long I've been a member of FFA. [*Laughter*] I became a member in 1936, and as a freshman in high school, I was very small for my age, very timid, and I would say that my career that led up to the Presidency of our great country began in the Plains FFA chapter.

I learned how to cut a rafter and how to repair a tractor, how to plant an acre of peanuts. [*Laughter*] I learned how to judge a good hog or dairy cow. I learned how to be a leader in a small group which was highly competitive. I learned how to make a speech. And I learned how to broaden my area of personal interest beyond the confines of my own family and my own farm and my own community.

The Future Farmers have meant a lot to me. I went off to the Navy, and when I came home, my small business, that didn't make much money, sponsored every year a trip to Kansas City for the outstanding FFA member of the Plains chapter. We've done it ever since.

And as I prepared for this meeting with you, I thought about how closely interrelated my present duties are with responsibilities that you share with me. You've already proven your leadership capabilities. Your personal characteristics and attitudes have been assessed by other members of FFA. They've shown that they have confidence in you to lead them as I lead this country and to represent in your own life their own aspirations and the values that they hold dear.

I just came back from a trip to Europe. I rode through the beautiful fields of West Germany and saw their grain crop; barley is being harvested now. They have an excellent wheat, oat crop; sugar beets are grown in that area. And I discussed with the other leaders of the major democratic industrialized countries common problems. Every one is a responsibility of your own. One of the major considerations is employment, the control of inflation, an end to the waste of energy, more efficient operations, the removal of ob-

stacles to trade. And the most difficult single negotiating point in the multilateral trade negotiations is agricultural products.

We have an advantage over every other country on Earth—many, of course, but one that comes to mind, the one that is uniformly and universally recognized is in the production of agricultural products.

We love our land, and part even of our religious conviction is that we should be good stewards of it. We are proud of what we've accomplished, and although we do have some close interrelationships between government and the agricultural community, farmers and those associated with agriculture have always prided ourselves our own independence, our duty, and our eagerness to stand on our own feet, to make our own decisions, to be individuals, to cooperate with our neighbors, and because of the vicissitudes and uncertainties of the weather, to have confidence in the future. And when we are discouraged with drought or poor harvest or low prices, we always look to the next year, and we're not afraid. We believe in our country, and this is a characteristic that binds me closely with you.

I might add one other point. I've been in office now for 18 months, almost exactly 18 months. There's been a tremendous resurgence in the viability of American agriculture, the prosperity of farmers. Prices are up, family income is up to an extraordinary degree. Prosperity exists in our agricultural regions now. This is a good year, apparently.

Last year we set an alltime record on agricultural exports. This year we will far exceed that historic record. The rest of the world is eager for what we grow, and we meet the needs of American people as well. So, we have a lot to be thankful for.

1319

But along with our blessings derived from God and our citizenship in the greatest nation on Earth, we have a responsibility. And my responsibility is no more intent than yours. You are young, still in your formative years, still trying to expand your minds and your hearts to learn more things and to encompass more friends, to let your influence be broadened and benevolent, to understand the attitudes of other people who depend upon us for leadership and for service.

So, for all these reasons, I'm deeply grateful for your visit to me. My successes you can blame on FFA; my failures you can blame on the fact that I left farming and went into the Navy for a while. [*Laughter*] But there's no doubt that the attitudes that I learned as a member of yours and my organization have permeated my whole life, and, I think, for the better.

I'm grateful for what you mean to me and to our country. I'm even more grateful for what you will mean in the future.

Thank you very much.

NOTE: The President spoke at 10:02 a.m. in the Rose Garden at the White House.

Affirmative Action Programs

Memorandum From the President.
July 20, 1978

Memorandum for the Heads of Executive Departments and Agencies

Since my Administration began, I have been strongly committed to a policy of affirmative action. It is through such programs that we can expect to remove the effects of discrimination and ensure equal opportunities for all Americans.

With your help, this Administration has been able to develop and implement meaningful affirmative action programs

throughout the Federal government, and as a result minority employment has increased to its highest level in history.

The recent decision by the Supreme Court in *Bakke* enables us to continue those efforts without interruption. That historic decision indicates that properly tailored affirmative action plans, which provide minorities with increased access to federal programs and jobs and which are fair to all Americans, are consistent with the Civil Rights Act of 1964 and with the Constitution.

I want to make certain that, in the aftermath of *Bakke,* you continue to develop, implement and enforce vigorously affirmative action programs. I also want to make certain that the Administration's strong commitment to equal opportunity and affirmative action is recognized and understood by all Americans.

JIMMY CARTER

United States Ambassador to Malawi

Nomination of Harold E. Horan.
July 20, 1978

The President today announced that he will nominate Harold E. Horan, of Bellaire, Tex., to be Ambassador Extraordinary and Plenipotentiary of the United States to the Republic of Malawi. He would replace Robert A. Stevenson, who has resigned.

Horan was born June 16, 1927, in Houston, Tex. He received a B.B.A. (1950) and an LL.D. (1953) from the University of Houston. He served in the U.S. Army Air Force from 1945 to 1946.

Horan joined the Foreign Service in 1957 and served in Tehran, Florence, Bamako, and at the State Department. From 1969 to 1972, he was an international relations officer at the State Department, and in 1972–73 he attended the National War College.

From 1973 to 1976, Horan was detailed to the National Security Council. Since 1976 he has been Deputy Chief of Mission in Monrovia.

Budget Rescission

Message to the Congress.   July 20, 1978

To the Congress of the United States:

In accordance with the Impoundment Control Act of 1974, I herewith propose rescission of $500 million in unneeded budget authority that was made available to the Department of Labor for advances to the unemployment trust fund and other funds.

The details of the proposed rescission are contained in the attached report.

JIMMY CARTER

The White House,
July 20, 1978.

NOTE: The attachment detailing the rescission is printed in the FEDERAL REGISTER of July 25, 1978.

Privacy Act of 1974

Letter to the Speaker of the House and the President of the Senate Transmitting a Report. July 20, 1978

Dear Mr. Speaker: (*Dear Mr. President:*)

This letter forwards the Third Annual Report of executive branch activities to comply with the Privacy Act of 1974.

The report includes a summary description and assessment of agency activities during calendar year 1977, and a list of agency personal data systems subject to the Act.

The protection of personal privacy is an important priority of the Administration. Accordingly, I am sending copies of this report to the heads of each executive department and agency with instructions that they continue to review and improve the management of personal data within their agency.

Sincerely,

JIMMY CARTER

NOTE: This is the text of identical letters addressed to Thomas P. O'Neill, Jr., Speaker of the House of Representatives, and Walter F. Mondale, President of the Senate.

The report is entitled "Federal Personal Data Systems Subject to the Privacy Act of 1974—Third Annual Report of the President, Calendar Year 1977" (39 pages plus appendices).

Performing Arts Company of the People's Republic of China

Remarks on Greeting Members of the Theatrical Troupe.   July 20, 1978

It's a great pleasure for me as President of our country to welcome to the United States such distinguished artists and performers from the People's Republic of China.

You represent a great nation. I know you've already been to New York and, now, Washington. You'll be going to Minneapolis and to Los Angeles and to San Francisco, and we are glad that you have an opportunity to see our great Nation.

We have an opportunity to observe your beautiful music, performances, the dances, not only the thousands of people who see your performances themselves, but through television, millions of Americans will have an opportunity to have their lives blessed by the observance of your artistry.

I know the performances are frequent and your work is difficult, but I hope that you enjoy your visit to our Nation. You've had other cultural missions here, and our Philadelphia Philharmonic Orchestra has been to the People's Republic, but this is the most ambitious cultural exchange that we've ever had with your country.

This is a good opportunity for us to learn more about you and about your people and to contribute to the friendship that is building between our two nations.

We admire your great performances, and we believe that this will be one further step toward full normalization of relationships between the People's Republic of China and the United States of America.

And now, I would like to speak personally to a few of you very famous people.

Thank you very much.

NOTE: The President spoke at 1:35 p.m. in the Rose Garden at the White House.

Ninth Anniversary of the First Moon Landing

Statement by the President. July 20, 1978

Nine years ago today, the world paused to watch two brave men tread the surface of the Moon. It was a moment without precedent in human experience, a moment when terrestrial life reached out to touch another world. It is a source of pride for us that those men were Americans. Today, the lunar surface is crisscrossed in a half dozen places with the footprints of American astronauts and implanted with a variety of American scientific instruments.

The space shuttle, our next major manned space project, will begin regular, routine, economical operation in the early 1980's. Through it, we will use the vantage point of space to learn more

about the Earth's surface features and processes and to improve our ability to manage our resources and cope with natural phenomena. We will continue to develop technology to realize the full potential of space communications and other practical applications of space technology.

In the deeper reaches of space, we will continue to seek to expand our knowledge of the solar system and the universe of which we are a part.

As time and technology take us ever more deeply into the space age, it will continue to be our policy to conduct operations in space as required for our national well-being and to support the right of all nations to do likewise. In so doing, we remain committed to the underlying principle of the exploration and use of space for peaceful purposes and for the benefit of all mankind.

THE PRESIDENT'S NEWS CONFERENCE OF JULY 20, 1978

DR. PETER BOURNE

THE PRESIDENT. Good evening, everybody. Before I answer questions, I'd like to make one brief comment. Dr. Peter Bourne, out of consideration for my administration, has submitted his resignation this afternoon, which I have accepted with regret.

Dr. Bourne is a close friend of mine and my family. He's an able and dedicated public servant. Because of this unfortunate occurrence, he has left the Government.[1]

[1] Dr. Bourne, the Special Assistant to the President for Health Issues, resigned following the disclosure that he had issued a drug prescription for an assistant without using her real name.

There are some allegations which will be the subject of investigation, and because I would not want my comments inadvertently to affect or to influence those investigations, I will have no further comment on this subject this evening and will not answer questions on this subject.

I'll be glad to answer questions on other items.

QUESTIONS

U.S.-SOVIET RELATIONS

Q. Mr. President, you seem to be embarked on an eye-for-an-eye diplomacy with the Soviets, and they're accusing you of blackmail in terms of human rights.

My question is how far in the direction of reprisals do you plan to go, and what do you intend to accomplish?

THE PRESIDENT. We have a deep commitment in our Nation to the enhancement of human rights, not only here but around the world. The Soviets, when they signed the Final Act of the Helsinki agreement voluntarily, along with 35 or so other nations, committed themselves to certain principles to be honored among their own citizens—the right of citizens to emigrate from the Soviet Union, the right of families to be united, and the right of the government in a legitimate way, even, to be criticized by their citizens.

The recent trials in the Soviet Union have been aimed against Soviet citizens who were monitoring compliance with the Helsinki act, which the Soviets themselves signed. And we, along with voices throughout the world, have expressed our displeasure at these actions.

I have not embarked on a vendetta against the Soviet Union. I know that we cannot interfere in the internal affairs of the Soviet Union. I would like to have better relationships with the Soviets. We have continued our discussions with the Soviet Union on SALT and other matters. We would like to even enhance trade with the Soviet Union. But we have to let our own foreign policy be carried out.

I might add that in addition to those highly publicized dissidents that have been tried recently, Mr. Shcharanskiy, Orlov, and others, that there is a Lithuanian named Petkus, who has also been tried and sentenced, and when I was in East Germany recently—West Berlin— there have been two men tried in East Germany, a Mr. Hübner and also a Mr. Bahro.

I met with the six leaders of other Western democracies. All of us are concerned about this move in the Soviet Union to punish dissidents for monitoring compliance with the Helsinki agreement. But I would like to have better relationships with the Soviet Union. We have expressed our displeasure, I think, in a very moderate way.

CAPITAL GAINS TAX

Q. Mr. President, the House Ways and Means Committee seems intent on improving one of the capital gains tax cut proposals that you said here on June 26 that you saw no possibility you could accept. Would you veto the Jones or Steiger amendments, or would you accept some sort of compromise such as cutting the capital gains tax only on the sale of homes?

THE PRESIDENT. We put forward to the Congress a tax reduction and tax reform proposal that I think is adequate and necessary. First of all, it would reduce the tax burden on the American people substantially. It would permit an efficient formation of increased capital to invest back in plant and equipment and to provide better jobs for the American people. It would protect the average homeowner, the average working family against shifting the tax burden on their shoulders and away from the shoulders of the very rich, the very powerful, and the very influential. And it would also result in a simplification of the tax system.

These are principles that I feel very deeply about. In my opinion, as I expressed at the last press conference, I believe, the Jones and Steiger amendment would violate some of those principles. I will have to wait until the final tax package is placed on my desk, after it's been considered and complete action from both Houses of the Congress is concluded. At that time, I will decide whether or not that tax bill is in the best interests of our country. If it is not, I will veto it.

FEDERAL CIVIL SERVICE REFORM

Q. What are you going to do, Mr. President, to save your civil service reform? Or is it snagged now hopelessly in Congress?

THE PRESIDENT. The reorganization plans in the House and Senate that relate to civil service has been approved overwhelmingly. The House recently took action, I think 36 to nothing, to approve it. This is a key element. The Senate passed the reorganization proposal relating to civil service very strongly in the committee. The only thing they changed was one element concerning veterans preference.

The House Post Office and Civil Service Committee has passed a bill last night after long debate and some delay with some very adverse attachments to the bill, which we hope to get removed either in the Rules Committee or on the House floor or in conference.

This is a crucial element of my attempt to control the bureaucracy in the Federal Government, and it's such a burning issue in the minds of the American people, to

finally do something about waste and control of the Federal bureaucracy, that I really am convinced that the House Members and Senate Members of the Congress will not go home to face election not having acted upon it.

So, because of that, I believe that the unsatisfactory amendments will be removed, and I predict that the civil service reform bill will be passed because it's so badly needed and because the American people and I demand that something be done.

OIL PRICES

Q. You told the economic summit conference in Germany that the price of domestic oil in the United States is too low and the heart of your energy program is to raise it. But how would conservation justify the hardship that would have on American consumers and its own inflationary effect as well?

THE PRESIDENT. The long-run impact of excessive oil consumption and waste is one of the major contributing factors to the underlying inflation rate that we have now. We simply use too much oil, we waste too much oil, we import too much oil. One of the reasons is that the price is extraordinarily low. And I'm committed to a comprehensive energy package that I put to the Congress 15 months ago in April of 1977.

The Congress has still not acted finally on any one of the five crucial elements. Conference committees have completed work now on four of the five, almost completed. And the Senate has acted on one of those elements. The one that the conference committees have not yet considered is the crude oil equalization tax.

There are four basic ways, if I can remember them all, where we can increase the price of oil just to the world level price to discourage waste. One is to let the oil companies decide how much they should raise the price of oil, which I think would be very bad for the American consumer. Two other ways are for me to impose quotas or oil import fees which would result in administrative difficulties but which is presently permitted under the law.

The fourth way is much preferable, to impose a crude oil equalization tax to raise the price of oil and, within that act of the Congress, to restore that money collected immediately back to the consumers of this country. There would be no net shift away from the consumers of money. But the price of oil would be raised to encourage conservation.

That's my preference, and I still hope and believe that the Congress will take action accordingly.

Mr. Bradley [Ed Bradley, CBS News].

AMBASSADOR ANDREW YOUNG

Q. Mr. President, what effect has the statement made by Ambassador Andrew Young had on your human rights campaign, and do you agree with him that there are political prisoners in the United States?

THE PRESIDENT. The statement by Andy Young was unfortunate, and I do not agree with it. I don't think there are thousands of political prisoners in this country. He went on to explain what he meant, that 10, 15 years ago during the civil rights demonstrations and debates, that he and others were imprisoned because of their belief that the laws of the United States should be changed. They were changed. We made great progress, which Andy Young pointed out.

This is a subject that I've discussed with Andy Young. He knows that I disapprove of his statement. I do not agree. We have, I think, persisted in our human rights commitments in spite of that statement, and I've discussed this with Andy

Young. And I don't believe that he will make a similar statement again.

The fact of the matter is that Andy Young has been and is very valuable to our country. He's opened up new areas of communications and mutual trust and cooperation, among the nations of Africa in particular. At almost the same time when Andy made that unfortunate statement, he had been remarkably successful in bringing about a conclusion of the Namibian question, which could have exploded into a very unsatisfactory conflict in southern Africa.

So, I know that Andy regrets having made that statement which was embarrassing to me. I don't believe he will do it again.

NATIONAL HEALTH CARE

Q. Mr. President, you have been promising for the last 6 months to provide the American people with some sort of national health insurance. Are you going to provide that to the people this summer? Are you going to propose something and send it up to the Hill this summer?

THE PRESIDENT. By the end of this month, I will have a directive to the Secretary of HEW to consult with Governors, with mayors, with Members of the Congress, with those who provide health care in our country. And expressed in that direction to him will be the principles on which a comprehensive health care system will be established in our country.

The Congress obviously will not have time to take action on this comprehensive proposal this year, but I want the American people and the Members of Congress to know the principles under which it will be formed.

One of the very discouraging aspects of our present health care system is the enormous increase in costs that have burdened down the American people. The average increase in cost of health care per year has been more than twice as much as the overall inflation rate. I can't think of anything the Congress could do that would benefit consumers more than to pass the hospital cost containment bill that we proposed and which the Commerce Committee in the House voted down or gutted with an unsatisfactory amendment this week.

This will cost the American consumers over the next 5 years $56 billion in unnecessary health care costs and will cost the American taxpayer, through Federal expenditures, $19 billion. This is an extraordinary and unnecessary burden on the American people, but the Commerce Committee was not able to deal with it.

So, we've got to control costs even under the present system, and this year the American people will know the principles and the framework for a comprehensive health care system that cannot be acted upon this year but, I believe, the Congress will consider next year.

DR. BOURNE

Q. Mr. President, I hope that this doesn't fall within the area of legal issues that you prefer not to discuss tonight, but the health of the President himself has always been a matter of great concern to the country.

Can you say whether any of the prescriptions that were signed by Dr. Bourne were substances that went either to you or members of your family?

THE PRESIDENT. Dr. Bourne has never given me any treatment of any kind.

Q. None of those substances went to you?

THE PRESIDENT. No, sir.

PUBLIC EMPLOYEE STRIKES

Q. Mr. President, the city of Washington is vexed right now by a subway strike. We're facing a possible mail strike. Philadelphia has had a sanitation strike, Louisville, a police strike. There have been fires accompanying a firemen's strike in Memphis. How long do you think the people are going to stand for this, and what are your thoughts about strikes by public employees?

THE PRESIDENT. Well, I deplore the circumstances that finally result in a strike. We obviously prefer that through regular legal bargaining procedures that disputes can be settled without disruptive strikes. This evening, for instance, we are waiting with great interest the outcome of the postal workers' negotiations, and we hope that they will be resolved successfully before midnight, which is the deadline. If they are not, then legal procedures provide a mechanism by which some extension can be granted.

But I deplore strikes, but recognize the right of workers to conduct labor negotiations; if they aren't successful, sometimes strikes are advisable. But I prefer, of course, to see the disputes settled without strikes.

ARMS EMBARGO AGAINST TURKEY

Q. Mr. President, during your summit in Bonn, did the Western leaders bring up the subject of the Turkish embargo? And if so, what was your reaction? Could you tell us, please?

THE PRESIDENT. Yes. Every member of NATO, including five of the members who were there with me—the only exception is Japan, who's not a member of NATO—are deeply interested in removing the embargo against Turkey. This embargo was imposed, I think properly, 3 years ago. The results that were expected have not been realized. It has not resulted in any progress being made in resolving the Cyprus dispute of restoring the human rights of the Greek Cypriots, who have indeed suffered and who suffer today. It's driven a wedge between Turkey and the rest of the NATO countries, between Greece and NATO, between Turkey and Greece, between us and Turkey. And I hope that the Congress will act expeditiously to remove the Turkey arms embargo.

And there is a unanimous belief that this is the proper action within NATO, with the exception of Greece. And I believe that this action will in the long run benefit Greece as well. It's a very important subject, the most important foreign affairs subject that the Congress will consider the rest of this session.

ANTI-INFLATION POLICY

Q. Mr. President, Barry Bosworth, your Council on Wage and Price Stability head, says that there will be a restructuring of the anti-inflation program in the administration. The feeling is that the present program isn't doing the job. Is that at your instigation, and are you happy with the anti-inflation program?

THE PRESIDENT. No, it's not at my instigation. We are doing what we can from the President's office, trying to control inflation. We are cutting down the Federal budget deficit. In 1976, the budget deficit was in the 60 billions of dollars. In 1978, it was in the fifties of billions of dollars; in 1979, in the forties of billions of dollars. I hope that in the next time we can bring that down at least to the 30 billions of dollars.

We are being very constrained on the Congress in not having excessive expenditures. We also have announced that the wages of Federal employees, blue-collar and white-collar employees, will be limited to about 5½ percent. I've put a complete freeze, from my own sense of

responsibility, on executive salaries. There will be no increase this year.

We have tried to induce business and labor to have less of a price or wage increase this year and the next year than they did in the 2 preceding years. So, we're trying to do everything without mandatory controls to limit inflation.

One of the most serious needs to control inflation is to cut down on the waste of energy. This puts an enormous burden on the American people. And I hope that the Congress will act here. As I said earlier, Congress has not acted yet on the civil service reform legislation or on hospital cost containment. Airline deregulation is another bill that's being considered by Congress that will control inflation.

So, we have a comprehensive program that we put forward. In some cases, the Congress has acted, in other cases they have not. But I think the more the American people's interest is built up and the more political influence they use themselves as individuals on Congress to act against inflation, the better chance we'll have to succeed.

I think some business leaders have complied with our request; some labor leaders have acquired to our request, some have not. But we are building momentum, and I believe that we can at least let inflation top off this year. Someone's got to control it. It's got to be a partnership between the American people, the Congress, and myself. I'm doing all I can.

U.S. PARTICIPATION IN 1980 OLYMPICS

Q. Mr. President, do you agree or disagree with those who urge that American athletes boycott the 1980 Olympic games in Moscow as a protest against Soviet treatment of dissidents?

THE PRESIDENT. This is a decision that will be made by the United States Olympic Committee. My own hope is that the

American athletes will participate in the 1980 Olympics.

RODRIGUEZ CASE IN DALLAS

Q. Mr. President, Ben Reyes, a Mexican American in the Texas Legislature, said today that you called him to express your embarrassment about Attorney General Griffin Bell's decision not to initiate Federal prosecution of the Dallas policeman who shot a 12-year-old Mexican American boy while handcuffed in the rear seat of a patrol car.

Are you embarrassed by this politically sensitive decision, and did you either ask the Justice Department to prosecute the case or express your disapproval when Mr. Bell declined prosecution?

THE PRESIDENT. When I was in Texas a few weeks ago, I studied the details of this case. It's one of about 150 cases that the Justice Department has been reexamining to make sure that there was no deprivation of the political rights or criminal justice rights or civil rights of people because—who are minorities or who speak Spanish.

I think the Justice Department has done a good job. This was a particularly disturbing case, because the person killed was only 12 years old. He was handcuffed, in the custody of police officers. At that time, I called Griffin Bell, the Attorney General, and told him I was deeply concerned about it and asked him to look into the case personally. He promised me that he would, and he did.

I did not ask Griffin Bell nor his subordinates to either prosecute or not prosecute. This is a legal decision over which the President has no control. It's one made by the Justice Department officials themselves. They have decided not to prosecute this case further.

It's a very complicated legal issue. The primary reason that they quoted was that there was an enthusiastic prosecution of this case by the State officials. The relatively low sentence, I think a 5-year imprisonment for this death, was granted by the jury, and because of that, the Justice Department decided not to prosecute under the present provisions of the law. But I have no authority nor inclination to direct the Justice Department to reverse their decision.

SOVIET DISSIDENTS

Q. Mr. President, are you aware of any negotiations under way for the release of Anatoly Shcharanskiy or Alexander Ginzburg?

THE PRESIDENT. No, not specifically. I think it would be inappropriate for me to talk about the negotiations that go on between ourselves and other governments about release of prisoners in general or specifically.

Q. In principle, is the United States willing to negotiate the release of these men?

THE PRESIDENT. We would like to see the prisoners released, but I can't go into that now.

POLITICAL PRISONERS

Q. Mr. President, there's been a lot of talk about this term "political prisoner." I'd like to follow up Ed's question. What is your definition of a political prisoner? Do you believe that Ben Chavis of the Wilmington 10 is a political prisoner or not?

THE PRESIDENT. Well, it's hard for me to define in a brief period of time what is a political prisoner. I think that if there is a commission of crime involving violence, damage to another person's property or health or life, and if they are prosecuted for that under the rules of our

Government, that would certainly not come under the categorization of a political prisoner. What we deplore in the Soviet Union is the prosecution of persons who speak out, even in accordance with international agreements that have been signed by the country involved.

I might add very quickly that the Soviet Union is not the only country guilty of that.

DR. BOURNE

Q. I, too, have a question about the Bourne case, which does not touch on the allegations against him. And it is simply this: whether you agree with Dr. Bourne, as he stated in his letter of resignation, that the attacks on him were really designed to harm you through him.

THE PRESIDENT. I would prefer not to answer that question.

THE PRESIDENT'S FINANCES

Q. There have been some published analyses that you've lost somewhere in the neighborhood of $300,000 in your interest in your warehouse firms. If those allegations or analyses are true, are you considering replacing your friend, Mr. Kirbo, as trustee? [*Laughter*]

THE PRESIDENT. I would rather have made a profit on the warehouse last year. When I was sworn in as President, I agreed with the public and Mr. Kirbo and others that I would not become even knowledgeable about the details of the operation of my former businesses. And I don't know what caused the loss. I am authorized to sign the tax return, which showed the loss, but I'm not contemplating changing the trustee.

MARIJUANA

Q. Dr. Bourne, about 6 months ago, helped initiate a report of the National Institute on Drug Abuse that said paraquat, one of at least 13 herbicides being used on marijuana in Mexico, caused lung fibrosis when smoked by marijuana consumers here in the United States. The report went on to say that maybe we should halt this spraying program.

Right now in the Congress, Senator Percy has a bill which would outlaw the future expenditures of money, men, or DEA material to Mexico to spray marijuana which is later harvested, brought to the United States, and smoked. My question, sir: Are you willing to support Senator Percy in stopping the spraying of paraquat and other herbicides on marijuana in Mexico?

THE PRESIDENT. I'm not familiar with the bill. My understanding is that American money is not used to purchase the paraquat. I think Mexico buys this material from other countries, and they use their own personnel to spray it with. My preference is that marijuana not be grown nor smoked. It's an illegal—

Q. What about the $13 million a year that's being channeled into Mexico now that's being used with the helicopters to go out and spray the fields, or DEA, Drug Enforcement Administration intelligence that goes out to help eradicate these fields?

THE PRESIDENT. I favor this relationship with Mexico. When I came into office, about 75 percent, for instance, of all the heroin used in our country was coming from Mexico. Because of the work of Dr. Bourne and the officials at the DEA, the drug enforcement agency, we and the new President and officials of Mexico, President López Portillo, we've mounted a very successful campaign, and now we've almost stopped the flow of heroin, for instance, from Mexico into our country.

Marijuana happens to be an illicit drug that's included under the overall drug control program, and I favor this program very strongly.

PRESIDENT PARK OF THE REPUBLIC OF
KOREA

Q. Thank you, Mr. President. There is the press speculation in Japan and South Korea that you would invite General Park Chung Hee of South Korea to Washington in next January for talks. Could you comment on this?

THE PRESIDENT. I don't know of any invitation that is planned for President Park. I would certainly have no objection to meeting him, but we have not extended an invitation to him so far as I know.

U.S. SALES TO THE SOVIET UNION

Q. Mr. President, could you tell us how you're leaning on the sale of the Dresser equipment to the Soviet Union, and what are some of the factors involved in the decision?

THE PRESIDENT. We have taken all the action that I intend to take for the time being. We terminated the sale of a very advanced computer to the Soviet Union— roughly a $6 to $7 million sale—which would have provided a quantum jump in computer capability, multiplying the speed of the computer, I think, 20-fold. And this was supposed to have been bought by TASS, one of the Soviet news agencies, to, I think, handle the requirements for the 1980 Olympics. This was far in excess of what they needed for that purpose.

And I've put under the control agreement in our country, where different Government agencies assess the need for sales equipment that would result in increased oil production in the Soviet Union. On the particular case to which you refer, I have not cancelled that.

This sale of technology—the Germans will install it—was approved, I think, the last day of May, before we reassessed this proposal. There is still pending one element of this sale, some kind of arc welding, that I have not yet approved. I've not decided what to do about it.

AMBASSADOR YOUNG

Q. Mr. President, News Secretary Powell has indicated that in the future when U.N. Ambassador Young speaks out on issues such as human rights, that perhaps this will be a subject for discussion at the White House beforehand, perhaps indicating that he might require your prior approval on a number of topics. Will this be the case?

THE PRESIDENT. No, I don't think so. I trust Andy to realize that he will be more careful in the future. It would be almost a full-time job for me if I tried to assess— [*laughter*]—if I tried to assess every statement that Andy Young and other Ambassadors make, or other officials who have the same opportunity to consult directly with the press.

And I don't intend to get into the censoring business. I have to trust the sound judgment of those—I've made mistakes myself, and I've tried to correct them in the future. I think in this particular case Andy made a mistake. And I think he'll try to correct it on his own initiative.

THE WILMINGTON 10

Q. Mr. President, members of your administration, including yourself, have often cited the findings of Amnesty International with regard to political prisoners in other countries. Why is it, then, that you do not accept the group's finding with respect to Reverend Chavis and the Wilmington 10? And also, sir, are you not aware or concerned that what is called by some black leaders a dichotomy in your human rights policy with respect to foreign dissidents and with respect to human rights in this country is threatening your black constituency?

THE PRESIDENT. I have been concerned about human rights violations in our own country as well as others. The Justice Department reassessed the case of the Wilmington 10 after the Governor decided the action to be taken this past year. Now, so far as I know, there is no legal basis for further action on the case by the Justice Department.* The attorneys for the Wilmington 10 have the right to appeal to the Federal courts on their own initiative, and I presume that they can, under a habeas corpus request or some other. But so far as I have been able to determine from the position of the Presidency itself, having no direct responsibility for it, the case is still being considered, appeals are still permissible under certain Federal codes, and I believe that the justice system in our country has worked well.

BROOKS JACKSON [Associated Press]. Thank you, Mr. President.

NOTE: President Carter's thirty-fifth news conference began at 8 p.m. in Room 450 of the Old Executive Office Building. It was broadcast live on radio and television.

The Situation in Cyprus

White House Statement.   July 21, 1978

The Turkish Cypriots have made an important new offer regarding the presently deserted city of Varosha on Cyprus. In a message to the Greek Cypriot community, they have agreed in effect to the creation of a U.N.-supervised interim administration for Varosha as soon as intercommunal negotiations are resumed, and they have expressed a readiness to enter into discussions immediately concerning

―――――――――

*In fact, the Justice Department is analyzing the situation to determine whether it should enter the case. [Printed in the transcript.]

plans for the interim administration. This is intended to facilitate the early return of 35,000 Greek Cypriot refugees to their homes and businesses in Varosha.

The President commends this new proposal as a positive and forthcoming step on the part of the Turkish Cypriots. He especially welcomes the important new element in this proposal which will permit the United Nations to supervise the administration of Varosha. The President believes it is particularly important that no time be lost and no effort be spared in facilitating the return of thousands of refugees to their homes and in resuming meaningful negotiations under the United Nations to achieve a Cyprus settlement.

Public Lands Grazing Fee Moratorium

Statement on Signing H.R. 9757 Into Law.
July 21, 1978

Today I am signing into law H.R. 9757, the grazing fee moratorium of 1978. This legislation places a 1-year moratorium on increases in grazing fees on public lands in order to allow Congress more time to study recommendations by the Secretaries of the Interior and Agriculture.

For many years, fees charged for the privilege of grazing livestock on the Nation's public lands have been below those charged for the use of comparable private lands. However, in section 102(a)(9) of the Federal Land Policy and Management Act of 1976, the Congress clearly stated its intention that "the United States receive fair market value for the use of the public lands and their resources."

The act directed the Secretaries of the Interior and Agriculture to submit to the

Congress their recommendations for establishing grazing fees on public lands in 11 western States. Those recommendations, based on a year-long study involving extensive public participation, called for fees to be set at fair market value as determined by current land rental rates for comparable private lands. Present rates would be increased at a maximum rate of 25 percent annually to reach fair market value. Thereafter, annual adjustments would be limited to 12 percent. Under these proposals, individual operators will pay an additional $60 per year or less on average.

I strongly believe that the administration recommendations will result in a fee structure that is fair to both livestock operators and the United States. However, I am also aware of the importance of the fee structure to our livestock industry.

I am aware that the Congress is now seriously considering two bills, H.R. 10587 and S. 2475, which, among other things, would mandate a new grazing fee formula based in part on the price of beef and its cost of production. The Departments of the Interior and Agriculture have strongly opposed any formula which is not based on fees charged on comparable private lands. While I am signing H.R. 9757 to allow the Congress more time to review the administration's grazing fee recommendations, I expect that Congress and its committees will honor the principle of a fair return from the use of natural resources by commercial interests. I remain opposed to legislation which does not provide a fair return to the United States for the use of public resources. I believe it is unfair to provide a special subsidy at the public's expense to those 5 percent of all livestock operators who use public lands, while the vast

majority of operators use private lands at much greater expense.

I urge the Congress to approve the administration's grazing fee recommendations and support their implementation for the 1979 grazing year.

NOTE: As enacted, H.R. 9757 is Public Law 95–321, approved July 21.

Digest of Other White House Announcements

The following listing includes the President's daily schedule and other items of general interest as announced by the White House Press Office during the period covered by this issue. Events and announcements printed elsewhere in the issue are not included.

July 13

The President arrived in the Federal Republic of Germany at the Bonn-Cologne Airport and proceeded with Chancellor Helmut Schmidt to the U.S. Ambassador's residence in Bonn, where he stayed during his visit.

July 18

The President met at the White House with Vice President Walter F. Mondale.

July 19

The President met at the White House with:

—Frank B. Moore, Assistant to the President for Congressional Liaison;

—Zbigniew Brzezinski, Assistant to the President for National Security Affairs;

—Members of Congress to discuss the Bonn Economic Summit Conference;

—Vice President Mondale, Adm. Stansfield Turner, Director of Central Intelligence, Hamilton Jordan, Assistant to the President, and Dr. Brzezinski.

The President attended a portion of the breakfast held for Members of the Senate in the State Dining Room at the White House to discuss the situation in Turkey and Greece.

The President transmitted to the Congress the 1977 annual report of the Saint Lawrence Seaway Development Corporation.

July 20

The President met at the White House with:

—Dr. Brzezinski;

—Mr. Moore;

—Secretary of Labor Ray Marshall;

—Mayor Thomas Bradley of Los Angeles, Calif.;

—Gov. Juan F. Luis and a delegation from the Virgin Islands.

July 21

The President met at the White House with:

—Vice President Mondale, Secretary of State Cyrus R. Vance, Secretary of Defense Harold Brown, Dr. Brzezinski, and Mr. Jordan;

—Dr. Brzezinski;

—Mr. Moore;

—Carrie Lynn Christensen, Ms. United Teenager, and Senator Sam Nunn of Georgia;

—Charles L. Schultze, Chairman of the Council of Economic Advisers;

—Senator Alan Cranston of California;

—Rev. Jesse Jackson and the board of directors of Operation PUSH (People United to Save Humanity).

The President left the White House for a weekend stay at Camp David, Md.

NOMINATIONS SUBMITTED TO THE SENATE

The following list does not include promotions of members of the Uniformed Services, nominations to the Service Academies, or nominations of Foreign Service officers.

Submitted July 20, 1978

HAROLD E. HORAN, of Texas, a Foreign Service officer of Class one, to be Ambassador Extraordinary and Plenipotentiary of the United States of America to the Republic of Malawi.

JAMES DICKSON PHILLIPS, JR., of North Carolina, to be United States Circuit Judge for the Fourth Circuit, vice James Braxton Craven, Jr., deceased.

EDWARD R. KORMAN, of New York, to be United States Attorney for the Eastern District of New York for a term of 4 years, vice David G. Trager, term expired.

Submitted July 21, 1978

W. K. SMITH, of Minnesota, to be Chairman of the Board of Directors of the' United States Railway Association for a term of 6 years, vice Arthur D. Lewis, resigned.

CHECKLIST OF WHITE HOUSE PRESS RELEASES

The following releases of the Office of the White House Press Secretary, distributed during the period covered by this issue, are not included in the issue.

Released July 14, 1978

Advance text: remarks at Bonn City Hall

News conference: on the President's meetings with President Scheel and Chancellor Schmidt of the Federal Republic of Germany, Secretary of State Vance's meeting with West German Foreign Minister Genscher, and the multilateral trade negotiations in Geneva, Switzerland—by Zbigniew Brzezinski, Assistant to the President for National Security Affairs, and Ambassador Robert S. Strauss, Special Representative for Trade Negotiations

Advance text: toast at the state dinner at Schloss Augustusburg, Bonn

Released July 15, 1978

Advance text: remarks at Wiesbaden-Erbenheim Air Base, Federal Republic of Germany

CHECKLIST—Continued

Released July 15—Continued

Advance text: remarks at Frankfurt City Hall

Advance text: remarks at the Airlift Memorial, Berlin

Released July 16, 1978

News conference: on the first and second sessions of the Bonn Economic Summit Conference—by Secretary of the Treasury W. Michael Blumenthal

Released July 17, 1978

Transcript: concluding statements of Chancellor Schmidt of the Federal Republic of Germany, Prime Minister Trudeau of Canada, President Giscard d'Estaing of France, Prime Minister Andreotti of Italy, Prime Minister Fukuda of Japan, and Prime Minister Callaghan of the United Kingdom, following the final session of the Bonn Economc Summit Conference

Released July 20, 1978

Announcement: nomination of James D. Phillips, Jr., to be United States Circuit Judge for the Fourth Circuit

CHECKLIST—Continued

Released July 20—Continued

Announcement: nomination of Edward R. Korman to be United States Attorney for the Eastern District of New York

Statement: resignation of Dr. Peter Bourne as Special Assistant to the President for Health Issues and Director of the Office of Drug Abuse Policy—by Jody Powell, Press Secretary to the President

---

ACTS APPROVED BY THE PRESIDENT

Approved July 21, 1978

H.R. 2176_____ Public Law 95–320
Federal Banking Agency Audit Act.

H.R. 9757_____ Public Law 95–321
An act to impose a moratorium on any increase in the public lands grazing fee for the 1978 grazing year, and for other purposes.

H.R. 11232_____ Public Law 95–322
An act to authorize appropriations to carry out the Standard Reference Data Act, and to authorize appropriations for the National Bureau of Standards.

Equality for Women

Memorandum From the President.
July 20, 1978

Memorandum for the Heads of Departments and Agencies

Women represent more than half of the population of this country, but still do not enjoy the specific protection of the United States Constitution. They continue to face discrimination and unequal treatment in many spheres of human activity.

I have made clear before that ratification of the Equal Rights Amendment is and will remain a priority with this Administration. In addition, I am determined that every resource of the Federal government be applied to eliminating discrimination and inequality based on sex.

This Administration has made important gains, particularly in increasing the participation of women in Federal government. However, I am convinced of the need to increase our effort to achieve equal treatment for women throughout the Nation.

In response to this need, I have asked my Assistant, Midge Costanza, to focus her efforts on women's issues with particular emphasis on the Equal Rights Amendment and implementation of the International Women's Year Plan of Action. As my Assistant she will be expected to:

—participate in the development of all domestic policy decisions of this Administration which affect women;

—assure that I am fully advised of the impact on women of policy decisions, legislation and Federal programs;

—coordinate the Interdepartmental Task Force on women, established by Section 6 of Executive Order 12050;

—provide liaison and support for the National Advisory Committee for Women established by Executive Order 12050;

—monitor and provide frequent and regular reports to me on our progress in eliminating unequal treatment of women.

I am further directing that the head of each department and agency take the following actions:

—make the most of public appearance opportunities to demonstrate the Administration's commitment to the Equal Rights Amendment;

—include in public speeches, where appropriate, language emphasizing the importance of the Equal Rights Amendment and assure that similar language is included in the speeches made by officials of their agency or department;

—review the Federal women's program in their agency or department to determine how it can be strengthened and provide suggestions to Ms. Costanza for my consideration;

—designate a policy level representative from their agency or department who will serve on the Interdepartmental Task Force;

—provide professional and clerical staff support for the agency or department's representative on the Interdepartmental Task Force.

Ms. Costanza will meet regularly with department and agency heads, their staffs, and representatives of women's interests to assure full and immediate implementation of this directive.

JIMMY CARTER

NOTE: The text of the memorandum was released on July 25.

26th Anniversary of the Commonwealth of Puerto Rico

Statement by the President.   *July 25, 1978*

To the People of Puerto Rico:

Today marks Puerto Rico's 80th year under the American flag, and the 26th anniversary of the founding of the Commonwealth of Puerto Rico, a form of government freely and democratically adopted by the people of Puerto Rico. Since 1898 and as American citizens since 1917, you have made a rich contribution to the life of the United States while preserving your own unique culture and traditions within the broader community.

As you commemorate this anniversary, I would like to emphasize that the United States remains fully committed to the principle of self-determination for the people of Puerto Rico. President Eisenhower made that commitment in 1953, and this has been the position of all U.S. administrations since that time. We continue to regard it as the fundamental principle in deciding Puerto Rico's future.

My administration will respect the wishes of the people of Puerto Rico and your right to self-determination. Whatever decision the people of Puerto Rico may wish to take—statehood, independence, Commonwealth status, or mutually agreed modifications in that status—it will be yours, reached in accordance with your own traditions, democratically and peacefully.

Governor Romero Barcelo has called for a referendum after the 1980 elections in Puerto Rico to decide Puerto Rico's future status. Should the government of Puerto Rico decide to hold a referendum, I will support, and urge the Congress to support, whatever decision the people of Puerto Rico reach.

The people of the United States are proud of our cultural and political associations with Puerto Rico over the last 80 years. We know that we can best honor our friendship, and our own democratic principles, by respecting your free choice about your own future.

Indian Education Programs

Statement by the President.   *July 25, 1978*

Under my proposal for a Cabinet department of education, the Indian education programs now located in the Bureau of Indian Affairs (BIA) would be moved to the new department. I have recommended this transfer because I believe it will make Federal school-based programs more effective.

This transfer will not change the special relationships between the Government and Indian tribes and Indian people in any way. These relationships include Federal trust responsibilities, Indian self-determination, and Indian preference in hiring. My goal is to improve the delivery of education services to Indians while maintaining these special relationships.

It is especially important that we maintain educational services to Indians without interruption, protect their civil rights, preserve the integrity of the education programs, and strengthen participation of parents, tribes, and Indian people in the education of their youth. A clear recognition of the importance of these issues will help us achieve an orderly, phased transfer of the BIA programs to the new department, while protecting the interests of Indian people. I expect and hope that Indian tribes and Indian people will work with my Reorganization Project staff to assure that these objectives are met.

Throughout the Nation, our educational systems are facing important challenges. For the first time, the new department will permit a coordinated and high-level response to these challenges. I ask Indian tribes and Indian people to join with us in shaping a new department of education that is responsive to their concerns and worthy of their support.

Arms Embargo Against Turkey

Statement by the White House Press Secretary Following Senate Action.   July 25, 1978

The President is gratified at the strong bipartisan support in the Senate of the administration's request for lifting the Turkish arms embargo. This is a constructive and statesmanlike action that will strengthen the security of the United States and the solidarity of the NATO Alliance. It is an action that we believe is in the best interest of the people of Greece, of Turkey, and of Cyprus. We value both allies and respect the contribution they make to the strength of the West. We wish to do everything possible to help them maintain strong democratic societies, strong economies, and their ability to make a significant contribution to the defense of a very important segment of the NATO area.

We look forward to accelerated progress toward settlement of problems that have persisted in the Eastern Mediterranean for far too long. We desire to see all peoples of the region work in harmony to settle issues that have drawn them apart.

The size of this vote indicates the growing realization that the embargo has outlived its usefulness. The Senate action today can only encourage and enhance the positive developments of the past few days. The President hopes that the House next week will act to further encourage this progress.

NOTE: Press Secretary Jody Powell read the statement at 5:35 p.m. to reporters assembled in the Briefing Room at the White House. As printed above, this item follows the text of the White House press release.

General Services Administration

Memorandum From the President. July 24, 1978

Memorandum for Jay Solomon, Administrator of General Services

Subject: Allegations Regarding Operations of the General Services Administration

Corruption in government is intolerable. For that reason I am deeply disturbed by the allegations of wrongdoing within the General Services Administration that have recently come to my attention.

These allegations describe a pattern of misconduct extending over many years and ranging from abuse of Federal authority to criminal practices such as fraud. If these charges are true, an extremely serious breach of the public trust has occurred.

I support and commend the steps you have taken so far to bring this matter to light and to bring those responsible to justice. I will back you fully in whatever procedural, personnel, organizational, and other actions are needed.

To these ends, by copy of this memorandum, I am asking the Attorney General to provide you with whatever assistance you and others in GSA who are responsible for conducting these investigations may require, both to complete your investigations and to take appropriate and rapid remedial measures.

JIMMY CARTER

NOTE: The text of the memorandum was released on July 26.

Presidential Medal of Freedom

Remarks on Presenting the Award to Arthur J. Goldberg. July 26, 1978

THE PRESIDENT. This is a good day for me and is a memorable day in the history of our Nation.

The Presidential Medal of Freedom is an award issued very rarely. I've only given two of them before, one to Dr. Jonas Salk, who was instrumental in eliminating polio as a plague for the entire world, and the other one for Dr. Martin Luther King, Jr. This third award is one that's equally well deserved.

There are many people in our Nation who have had notable achievements, quite often in a narrowly defined field of interest. But Arthur Goldberg is a man who has devoted his life to humanitarian pursuits in the widest possible range of both interest and notable accomplishment.

As an attorney, he became an expert in labor relations, learning how to understand people, to mediate, to negotiate, quite often under the most strenuous and potentially divisive circumstances. The ability to understand conflicting ideas and to find common ground between them has been used later on in public service to the best interest of our country.

He became Secretary of Labor and performed so superbly there that his interests were retained in that field and also expanded into others. He has served as a member of the United States Supreme Court, a Justice there, and participated in notable decisions that helped to shape the attitude of our Nation toward basic civil rights, basic human rights. No one has ever doubted his purpose nor his credentials. And as our Representative to the United Nations, he brought a standard of performance there that was an inspiration to others.

Perhaps one of the most difficult international disputes ever witnessed, certainly in modern history, has been in the Middle East. And when the time came to hammer out a set of principles in writing which would be the basis for temporary periods of peace already and, perhaps, permanent peace in the future, Arthur Goldberg was the one who was able to accomplish this great achievement.

"United Nations Resolution 242" is now a standard phrase, a pat series of letters and numbers that people speak about as an unshakable basis for ultimate agreement in the Middle East. Those of us assembled here this morning who have tried to carve out mutual principles for agreement, even in the most general language, know the difficulty of it. And his language, which was adopted by the United Nations, by all the disputing parties, is still our guide in how to make progress in the future.

At Helsinki, an agreement was signed by, I believe, 34 nations, spelling out how we might have more cooperation, more exchange among nations who were potential adversaries, and the first international commitment with specific bounds for the honoring of the right of human beings to emigrate from a country, to be part of the united family, to have at least a modicum of free speech. And the signatories of that agreement at Helsinki were expected to have their activities monitored.

At Belgrade this past year, there was an international assembly to provide the first assessment of compliance with the Helsinki agreement, and Secretary Vance and I were determined to have the best possible leader there to represent our country. He was a foremost spokesman and established the principle, permanently, I hope, that there is indeed an international accountability for compliance with human rights commitments that were made at Helsinki.

There is no way nor need to outline the numbers of special ad hoc commissions and committees on which Arthur Goldberg has served our country, other Presidents. But I look upon him as a man who still has a long career ahead of him, but already has exemplified in his personal and public life principles committed to basic human rights, to legal, diplomatic, and political justice, sensitivity about the needs of those who have been deprived of the blessings of a modern society that most of us enjoy, and a man whose own personal principles have never deviated from the highest possible standard, and who has let those principles affect the at-

titude and the reputation of an entire Nation, the Nation that we love so much.

I would like now to read the citation for the Presidential Medal of Freedom.

[*At this point, the President read the citation, the text of which follows:*]

THE PRESIDENT OF THE UNITED STATES OF AMERICA AWARDS THIS PRESIDENTIAL MEDAL OF FREEDOM TO ARTHUR J. GOLDBERG

Arthur J. Goldberg, Secretary of Labor, Associate Justice of the Supreme Court of the United States, United States Representative to the United Nations, Ambassador at Large and soldier in World War II. During an eminent career of almost fifty years, Arthur Goldberg has shown his deep commitment to individual human dignity, to peace and to the cause of human rights. As a practicing attorney and counsel for the labor movement, a legal scholar, educator and a public servant, he has displayed an extraordinary capacity to bring people together, mediate differences, and to help solve the pressing problems of our age. By combining idealism and vision with wisdom and common sense, Arthur Goldberg has served his country well.

Signed, Jimmy Carter, The White House, Washington, D.C., July 26, 1978.

Arthur, congratulations. I'm very proud of you.

MR. GOLDBERG. *Mr. President, Secretary Vance, Under Secretary Christopher, Counselor Nimetz, Mr. Hansell, Mr. Chairman—my chairman—and Co-chairman, Dante Fascell and Senator Pell; this eminent member of the National Security Council, Bob Hunter; the Assistant Secretary of State, George Vest; the Deputy Assistant for Management, Ben Read; and many others—I should like to single out three, if you don't mind, of my colleagues, Mrs. Guilbert, Mrs. Passemante, Miss West, and the one who was on my tail all the time at Belgrade, Bob Oliver, the Director of the Commission; ladies and gentlemen:*

Mr. President, my wife, my children— two of whom are stranded in Alaska with three grandchildren who are very put out, so you're going to have to see them—and I wish to thank you, Mr. President, for the highest of Presidential awards. You have honored our family, and for this we are profoundly grateful. To serve our beloved country is its own reward. But to receive acknowledgement of this service by this award, particularly at your hands, Mr. President, is, I fear, more than I merit.

Mr. President, you have put respect for human rights and fundamental freedoms high on the international agenda. This respect will not be achieved overnight, as you well knew, but it cannot be denied, for it represents ultimate truth.

The poet John Milton said, "Give me the liberty to know, to utter, and to argue freely according to the conscience, above all liberties. Though all the winds of doctrine were let loose to play upon the earth, so truth be in the field. We do injuriously, by prohibiting to misdoubt her strength. Let her and falsehood grapple; whoever knew truth to be put to the worse, in a free and open encounter?"

That's the essence, I think, of human rights.

Again, Mr. President, I want to thank you for your support in my tenure as Ambassador at Large and Chairman of our Delegation in Belgrade, and also express my affectionate regards and appreciation to the members of the CSC Commission, its Director, to my friends of long standing in the State Department—Secretary Vance, Under Secretary Christopher, and their colleagues at the State Department—Dr. Brzezinski and the staff of the National Security Council, and others at the White House for their support of my tenure as Ambassador at Large and my mission to Belgrade.

I thank you very much, Mr. President, for this highest of honors.

THE PRESIDENT. Thank you very much.

Arthur's son and grandchildren couldn't get here because they were bumped off a plane in Alaska. So he and I are going to go inside and talk to them by telephone now. But I'm very proud of what this means to our country, and I appreciate very much your coming to pay your respects to a truly great American.

Thank you very much.

NOTE: The President spoke at 9:33 a.m. at the ceremony in the Rose Garden at the White House.

In his opening remarks, Ambassador Goldberg referred to Warren M. Christopher, Deputy Secretary, Matthew Nimetz, Counselor, and Herbert J. Hansell, Legal Adviser, Department of State; and Representative Dante B. Fascell, Chairman, Senator Claiborne Pell, Cochairman, and R. Spencer Oliver, Director, Commission on Security and Cooperation in Europe.

United Service Organizations, Inc.

Appointment of Two Members of the Board of Governors and Four Members of the Corporation.   July 26, 1978

The President today announced the appointment of two persons as members of the Board of Governors of the United Service Organizations, Inc. (USO), and four persons as members of the Corporation of the United Service Organizations, Inc. They are:

Members of the Board of Governors of USO:

ROBERT K. CORN, of Papillion, Nebr., a real estate developer and former postmaster of Papillion;

MRS. AL ULLMAN, vice chair of the Multiple Sclerosis Society and treasurer of the Women's Democratic Forum;

Members of the Corporation of USO:

ROBERT C. ANDREWS, of Nashville, Tenn., an Atlanta accountant;

DOROTHY C. STEPHENS, of St. Louis, Mo., director of government relations and international operations for an architectural/engineering firm;

MIKKI A. EHRENFELD, of Lincoln, Mass., director of Ehrenfeld Productions, an independent film production and free-lance photography company;

AL G. LOEHR, mayor of St. Cloud, Minn.

President's Council on Physical Fitness and Sports

Appointment of Governor Jerry Apodaca as Chairman. July 26, 1978

The President today announced that he will appoint Jerry Apodaca, Governor of New Mexico, as Chairman of the President's Council on Physical Fitness and Sports.

Apodaca, 43, has been Governor since 1974 and served in the New Mexico Senate from 1967 to 1974. He is a former high school teacher and coach and an active sports enthusiast.

Seminar on Employment

Remarks at a Reception for Participants in the Seminar. July 27, 1978

If I could have your attention, we'll wind up the work part, which is listening to my speech, and we'll start on the fun part.

Today I think most of you observed at first hand how much work my wife can get out of someone in just 1 day. [*Laughter*] And I want you to remember that she does me that way every day. [*Laughter*]

It's really been an exciting thing for me to see Rosalynn work on this program and the enormous support, advice, counsel, help, sometimes constructive criticisms, that she received from people who are interested in the same thing that she and I want to see happen in this country.

There were delegates here, or representatives here from all 50 States and a very large group from the District of Columbia, including some of the top leaders in all walks of life who can help to cement the ties between the Federal Government and those who need the services of it.

One of the constructive things that came out today was the recognition of local successes. Our country did not become as great as it is today because of what goes on in Washington, even when we have had the greatest of Presidents and the most constructive action by Congress. The strength of our Nation is derived from people like you, who in a quiet, effective way—knowing your own neighbors, your own family, your own communities' needs—in an unselfish and sometimes inspired way, you and your fellow workers evolve programs, sometimes quite unstructured, to help those that have been deprived in our society become part of the wonderful life that we enjoy in America.

This kind of success is often unrecognized, even in the local press or even in a women's organization or the Jaycees or the NAACP or the Lions Club or church. There are a lot of unheralded heroes in the United States, and you really, in a way, today represent them.

We've embarked on some ambitious programs. I've only been in office about 18 months. When I came into office, we had a very high unemployment rate, and the Congress, the private business sector, labor unions, my own administration, many of you began to decide shortly after the election in November of 1976 what could be done about it. We had 8 million people out of work. And this time last year, even, whenever I had a meeting with any group, the number one problem that I had to face as President was finding jobs for American people.

We now have the lowest unemployment rate since Lyndon Johnson lived in this house. And in the last year, we have added more jobs to the American society than ever before in history, 6½ million jobs, and we brought the unemployment rate down to a much more acceptable figure.

We've got a long way to go. Some of this improvement has been derived from government programs, comprehensive education and training programs, local public works, and so forth. And at the beginning, because all kinds of Americans were unemployed, it had to be focused upon a broad range of people. But now that we've brought down the unemployment rate very low among heads of families who are male, either black or white, we've made good progress in improving the employment rate among adult women, both black and white. But we still have some very severe pockets of unemployment.

Our young people, in particular, who belong to minority groups, still suffer severely. And that concerns me more than any other group, because I know that in the formative stages of life, it's crucial that one realize, "I am a human being, blessed by God with life, having a certain level of intelligence and competence and potential, and I want to use my one life to my own advantage and to the advantage of those around me."

But when a young person tries to become employed and to use one's talents and is rebuffed, it creates a discouraged attitude in that person that sometimes can be almost permanent. And it not only makes one feel worthless, in a self-assessment, but it alienates that person from society, and there's a reaction against one's family, against the school system, against law enforcement officials, against local, State, Federal Government, against

employers, even against the benevolent groups that work so hard to provide employment.

This is what you've come today to try to address. There is no way that any combination of Federal programs can let our people know what a wonderful opportunity exists in this country and to let them know that their lives are significant and that employment and constructive employment is possible for them.

And I hope that every one of you, certainly every group that's here, whether you come from Hawaii or Utah or Texas—I don't care which State—I hope that you will go home and try to evolve a similar meeting, maybe even larger than this one, maybe somewhat smaller, based on what you've derived here today, and let the spirit of voluntary, effective leadership be utilized to correct the deficiencies that do still exist in our country.

We've put forward an urban policy. It's been almost unanimously acclaimed by mayors and county officials and State officials. And the essence of it is a new partnership, a partnership between private citizens and government—sometimes a difficult bridge to cross—a partnership between local, State, and Federal Government, a partnership between labor and management, a partnership between people who are hungry and those who are rich, between people that don't have families and those that have a stable family life.

And I think the spirit of partnership is what you represent here today. I'd like to thank you for being willing to come and for learning at first hand from one another what a great nation we already have and with your help and dedication, how much greater it can be.

Thank you very much.

NOTE: The President spoke at 5:35 p.m. in the Grand Hall at the White House.

Advisory Council on Historic Preservation

Appointment of Joseph B. Mahan, Jr. as a Member. July 28, 1978

The President today announced the appointment of Joseph B. Mahan, Jr., of Columbus, Ga., as a member of the Advisory Council on Historic Preservation.

Mahan, 57, was an instructor and assistant professor at the University of Georgia Continuing Education Division from 1952 to 1959. He was curator of the Columbus Museum of Arts and Crafts from 1959 to 1965, and served as a consultant in sociology and anthropology to the Georgia State Office of Economic Opportunity from 1965 to 1966.

Mahan was director of education and research for the Columbus Museum of Arts and Crafts from 1966 to 1972. Since 1972 he has been executive director of Westville Village Museum in Lumpkin, Ga.

Federal Mine Safety and Health Review Commission

Nomination of Jerome R. Waldie To Be a Member. July 28, 1978

The President today announced that he will nominate Jerome R. Waldie, of Bethesda, Md., to be a member of the Federal Mine Safety and Health Review Commission.

Waldie was born February 15, 1925, in Antioch, Calif. He received a B.A. (1952) and LL.B. (1953) from the University of California.

Waldie practiced law from 1954 to 1958. From 1958 to 1966, he was a member of the California State Assembly, and from 1962 to 1966, he served as Assembly majority leader.

From 1966 to 1974, Waldie was a Member of the U.S. Congress. Since 1975 he has been an attorney in Washington.

Agency for International Development

Nomination of Calvin H. Raullerson To Be an Assistant Administrator. July 28, 1978

The President today announced that he will nominate Calvin H. Raullerson, of Lubbock, Tex., to be an Assistant Administrator of the Agency for International Development.

Raullerson was born December 18, 1920, in Utica, N.Y. He received an A.B. from Lincoln University in Pennsylvania in 1943 and an M.P.A. from New York University in 1949.

From 1950 to 1952, Raullerson was associate editor and director of research for Christian E. Burckel and Associates in Yonkers and at the United Nations. From 1952 to 1957, he was assistant to the executive director and director of educational services for the United Negro College Fund.

From 1961 to 1966, he was with the American Society of African Culture, serving as associate director in New York and in Lagos, Nigeria. From 1966 to 1973, he was with the Peace Corps, serving as Chief for East and Southern Africa, Country Director for Kenya, and Regional Director for Africa.

Since 1973 Raullerson has been at Texas Tech University. He is currently executive director of the International Center for Arid and Semi-Arid Land Studies and has also served as special assistant to the president for international programs and assistant professor of health organization management.

Raullerson has participated in a number of international conferences on African affairs.

National Health Plan

Statement by Secretary of Health, Education, and Welfare Joseph A. Califano, Jr.
July 28, 1978

I just have a brief statement which I will read, and then we will deal with the general subject tomorrow at HEW, as you know.

This administration is deeply committed to the goal of decent health care for every American, as our legislative proposals to date have demonstrated. This will be further evident tomorrow when we announce the principles on which the administration's national health plan will be based.

We are also deeply concerned that our national health plan be prudently designed, be phased in in a reasonable and cautious manner, reflect economic and budgetary realities, and avoid the imposition of excessive costs on the average American taxpayer.

Above all, we are committed to proceeding in a prudent manner which does not fuel inflationary pressures.

The President of the United States has broad responsibilities. In devising any program, however basic or important, the President must always bear in mind the impact of that program on other elements of national life and policy, especially on the economy, in inflationary times such as these.

NOTE: Secretary Califano read the statement at 5:23 p.m. to reporters assembled in the Briefing Room at the White House. As printed above, this item follows the text of the White House press release.

Digest of Other White House Announcements

The following listing includes the President's daily schedule and other items of general interest as announced by the White House Press Office during the period covered by this issue. Events and announcements printed elsewhere in the issue are not included.

July 23

The President returned to the White House after a weekend stay at Camp David, Md.

July 24

The President met at the White House with:
—David Aaron, Deputy Assistant for National Security Affairs;
—Frank B. Moore, Assistant to the President for Congressional Liaison;
—the Cabinet;
—Vice President Walter F. Mondale;
—George Meany, president of the AFL–CIO, and Secretary of Labor Ray Marshall.

The President greeted a group of Chippewa Indians from Minnesota on the South Lawn of the White House.

July 25

The President met at the White House with:
—Mr. Aaron;
—Mr. Moore;
—the Democratic congressional leadership;
—Vice President Mondale, Adm. Stansfield Turner, Director of Central Intelligence, Hamilton Jordan, Assistant to the President, and Mr. Aaron;
—Mrs. Carter, for lunch;

—James T. McIntyre, Jr., Director of the Office of Management and Budget;

—representatives of the cattle industry.

July 26

The President met at the White House with:

—Mr. Aaron;

—Mr. Moore;

—officials of the American Medical Association to discuss health issues and the national health plan;

—Representative Richard Bolling of Missouri;

—Gov. Jerry Apodaca of New Mexico to discuss his appointment as Chairman of the President's Council on Physical Fitness and Sports.

July 27

The President met at the White House with:

—Mr. Aaron;

—Democratic Members of the 94th Caucus of the Congress;

—Mr. Moore;

—John C. White, chairman of the Democratic National Committee;

—Senator Ted Stevens of Alaska and Secretary of the Interior Cecil D. Andrus.

The President transmitted to the Congress the 10th annual report of the Department of Transportation.

July 28

The President met at the White House with:

—Mr. Aaron;

—Thomas P. O'Neill, Jr., Speaker of the House of Representatives;

—Senator Edward M. Kennedy of Massachusetts to discuss the national health plan;

—Mr. Moore;

—Vice President Mondale, Robert T. Griffin, Deputy Administrator of the General Services Administration, Mr. Moore, and Mr. Jordan;

—Charles L. Schultze, Chairman of the Council of Economic Advisers;

—members of the executive committee of the National Grange;

—a group of editors and news directors (transcript will be printed next week).

The President transmitted to the Congress the 1977 annual reports on Military Awards Programs of the Department of Defense and the Department of Transportation, and the 1977 annual report of ACTION.

The President transmitted the third semiannual, fourth semiannual, and first annual reports on the National Petroleum Reserve in Alaska, to the Senate Committee on Energy and Natural Resources and the House Committee on Interior and Insular Affairs.

The President left the White House for a weekend stay at Camp David, Md.

NOMINATIONS SUBMITTED TO THE SENATE

The following list does not include promotions of members of the Uniformed Services, nominations to the Service Academies, or nominations of Foreign Service officers.

Submitted July 25, 1978

PATRICIA J. E. BOYLE, of Michigan, to be United States District Judge for the Eastern District of Michigan, vice Damon J. Keith, elevated.

JULIAN A. COOK, JR., of Michigan, to be United States District Judge for the Eastern District of Michigan, vice Lawrence Gubow, deceased.

NOMINATIONS—Continued

Submitted July 25—Continued

HARRY E. CLAIBORNE, of Nevada, to be United States District Judge for the District of Nevada, vice Bruce R. Thompson, retiring.

Submitted July 28, 1978

ANDREW L. METCALF, JR., of Michigan, to be United States Marshal for the Western District of Michigan for the term of 4 years, vice Marvin G. Washington, term expired.

JEROME R. WALDIE, of Maryland, to be a member of the Federal Mine Safety and Health Review Commission for the term of 2 years (new position).

CALVIN H. RAULLERSON, of Texas, to be an Assistant Administrator of the Agency for International Development, vice Fred O. Pinkham.

CHECKLIST OF WHITE HOUSE PRESS RELEASES

The following releases of the Office of the White House Press Secretary, distributed during the period covered by this issue, are not included in the issue.

Released July 25, 1978

Announcement: nomination of Patricia J. E. Boyle to be United States District Judge for the Eastern District of Michigan, Harry E. Claiborne to be United States District Judge for the District of Nevada, and Julian A. Cook, Jr., to be United States District Judge for the Eastern District of Michigan

Released July 28, 1978

Fact sheet: upcoming congressional floor action on Federal civil service reform and reorganization

Announcement: nomination of Andrew L. Metcalf, Jr., to be United States Marshal for the Western District of Michigan

ACTS APPROVED BY THE PRESIDENT

Approved July 28, 1978

H.R. 3489_____ Public Law 95–323
An act to amend section 216(b) of the Merchant Marine Act, 1936, to entitle the Delegates in Congress from the District of Columbia, Guam, and the Virgin Islands to make nominations for appointments to the Merchant Marine Academy, and for other purposes.

H.R. 4270_____ Public Law 95–324
An act to designate the Federal building and United States courthouse in Hato Rey, Puerto Rico, the "Federico Degetau Federal Building".

H.J. Res. 613_____ Public Law 95–325
A joint resolution to authorize and request the President to issue a proclamation designating the first Sunday of September after Labor Day in 1978 as "National Grandparents Day".

H.R. 12637_____ Public Law 95–326
An act to amend the North Pacific Fisheries Act of 1954.

S. 1291_____ Public Law 95–327
An act to declare that certain lands of the United States situated in the State of Oklahoma are held by the United States in trust for the Cheyenne-Arapaho Tribes of Oklahoma, and to authorize the Secretary of the Interior to accept conveyance from the Cheyenne-Arapaho Tribes of Oklahoma of certain other lands in Oklahoma to be held in trust by the United States for such tribes.

S. 1582_____ Public Law 95–328
An act relating to the settlement between the United States and the Ak-Chin Indian community of certain water right claims of such community against the United States.

S. 947_____ Public Law 95–329
An act to declare certain federally owned land known as the Yardeka School land to be held in trust for the Creek Nation of Oklahoma.

PRESIDENTIAL DOCUMENTS

Week Ending Friday, August 4, 1978

Interview With the President

Remarks and a Question-and-Answer Session With a Group of Editors and News Directors. July 28, 1978

THE PRESIDENT. Hi, everybody. Thank you very much. It's a pleasure to be with you and to have you come to the White House.

I'd like to take 3 or 4 minutes to outline some of the problems that I face now, some of the decisions I am making, and then spend the rest of the time answering your questions that you bring here from your own communities.

ADMINISTRATION POLICIES

When I came into office about 18 months ago, my biggest problems that I faced domestically were employment—the unemployment rate was about 8 percent—inflation, which was entirely too high, and the horrible mess in the Federal bureaucracy.

Now, 18 months later, we've done remarkably well on employment. We've added a net of 6½ million jobs, never before achieved, and we have the lowest unemployment rate that we've had since Lyndon Johnson was here as President.

Now my biggest problems are inflation and dealing with the horrible Federal bu-

reaucracy. And the one that's been the most frustrating, I think, is the bureaucracy itself. I am a manager and a businessman and an engineer by background. And to bring some order out of chaos within the Federal establishment itself has been a very difficult and trying job.

When I meet around this table every week or 2 weeks with my Cabinet, that is the most pervasive problem that they bring to me—"We cannot manage the people who work under us."

The vast majority of American Government workers are superior people. They are competent and they are dedicated. And when the civil service system was established almost a hundred years ago, the idea was to reward excellence, to encourage a person to do one's best, and to remove those who are incompetent or lack motivation and, of course, to protect the rights of workers and let managers manage.

Most of those standards of management capability brought to the Government a hundred years or so ago by the civil service system have not remained. We now find an almost lock-step promotion among employees, no matter how competent they are or incompetent, no matter how dedicated they are or how much they loaf on the job.

There's no way to distinguish adequately between those who do a good job and those who don't. And with two people sitting side by side at an office, one working hard, doing his job and his neighbor's job, the other one loafing, both being rewarded the same, really discourages those who do want to spend their one life offered in public service to constructive work.

We've put forward so far, with the greatest political difficulty, the civil service reform legislation. And I know many of you are executives—I looked down the list before I came in here—and it would be inconceivable to you to spend an average of 19 months trying to remove from employment an employee who didn't care about the success of your business and didn't care about pleasing you with a genuine display of interest and proper performance. That's what it takes.

I had them put this chart up which shows in visual terms how we have to go through this extremely complicated process to discharge one employee.

The civil service reform legislation would give us a chance to protect employees' rights much more effectively, to protect the whistleblower, the employee who points out a defect in government and who doesn't want to be punished. It would give managers a chance to manage. It would reward those who do superior work, either at the management level or the average employee level, and punish or remove those who don't perform.

Now we can't remove an employee, for all practical purposes. The only thing we can do is to transfer that employee. And, of course, where they are transferred, that just spreads the problem around; it doesn't resolve anything.

I consider this to be the centerpiece of our entire effort, to reorganize the Government and to manage as President. We want the employees to do an effective job. We want them to be responsive to the American people. That is the thing that preys on my mind today, that we are approaching a crisis stage in the Congress. We've made good progress so far, and I believe that the Congress will respond if we can maintain a public interest in this issue.

In addition to what I've just described to you, which is my primary concern, I would like to briefly outline a few other points just to precipitate your questions.

Cy Vance has had a very good report to me from the United Nations. One of the most explosive issues in Africa has been Namibia. It's been a very difficult effort that we undertook, to bring together ourselves, the French, the British, the Canadians, and the West Germans to work together with South Africa and with the so-called SWAPO organization, the South West Africa People's Organization, and we've had to work with all the black frontline presidents who are in that area.

I think that we've now reached the brink of success. A new nation will be established, formerly South West Africa, now Namibia. And if things go according to our present prospects, we will have a much greater opportunity or prospect of resolving the more difficult Rhodesian question. I have to say that all the parties involved have acted well, particularly recently, and we are very pleased with this progress.

SALT talks are continuing. The comprehensive test ban talks are continuing. We've had some setbacks recently in the Mideast, but we are determined to proceed there to success. My firm belief, knowing both men very well, is that Begin and Sadat genuinely want to bring peace to the area. Their nations would benefit enormously, economically and otherwise, with peace there. If war should erupt because of a deterioration in their interrelationship, it would be a severe blow to them, to that region, and indeed to the entire world.

I think we have a good prospect this year to have a successful conclusion of the energy effort. I'm not predicting success yet. But we have four of the five elements that would result in about 2.3 million barrels-a-day saving, already approved by the conference committees, as you know. And now these five major energy packages will go to the House and Senate for a vote.

One's already been voted on by the Senate. The most difficult of those will be natural gas deregulation and pricing. And that would still leave the mechanism by which domestic oil prices could be raised to the world market price without hurting consumers, and our proposal is the crude oil equalization tax. That one is still in doubt.

I had supper with Senator Long this week, and we discussed this at length. He feels that once the natural gas bill is out of the way, that it will take just a few days of concentrated work by the conference committee there to come to a conclusion on the crude oil equalization tax. Nobody knows what it would be, and I'm not predicting that we'll have complete success.

But those are some of the things just today that have been problems of mine, and I would be glad now to answer any questions that you might have.

QUESTIONS

COAL PRODUCTION

Q. Mr. President, there's been little evidence in the past 2 years that there's any movement toward your goal of mining a billion tons a year of coal in this country by 1985. Coal production is now what it was when you came into office, and yet, obviously, we need more coal.

Now we are receiving reports in the coal fields that the Coal Commission that you created 4 months ago is floundering, still not completed staff, still the Commission is incomplete. What is the status of the Commission and of your efforts in the coal industry?

THE PRESIDENT. I think we will reach the goal that we established. As you know, we've had a severe setback with the extended coal strike and the disputes within the industry. I don't believe there's been an adequate analysis in the news media, or among the American people, which have to derive their opinion from you all, of what the agreement achieved. My guess is that the constant disruptions, the unauthorized wildcat strikes, the dropping productivity, will be substantially enhanced* by the agreement that was reached.

You are right; only yesterday I approved the last two members of the Commission. And I think now the matter will be expedited substantially, and we will have at the conclusion of their deliberations under Jay Rockefeller, the Governor of West Virginia, as Chairman, a report back to me in a limited period of time. But it's been a very difficult matter in the aftermath of that strike, with hard feelings on both sides and some distrust on both sides, to bring together management and the coal miners and their representatives, to agree on a commission that they would mutually trust.

But I think now we have a good Commission put together, and my prediction is that we will reach that goal. Prior to the time of the strike, even with the constant disruption on a local basis of coal production, there was a substantial in-

---

*The President meant to say "reduced." [Printed in the transcript.]

crease in the production rate of coal. And I think, and Jim Schlesinger believes, that we'll reach our goal.

FEDERAL GRANTS

Q. Mr. President, relating to your dealings with the bureaucracy, is there some way that the bureaucracy can help out the smaller communities in this country who are seeking Federal grants for local projects; communities, for instance, which can't afford the expensive professional grantsmanship and planning talent? Is there any way that grants can be made more available to them or can be easier for those small communities to gain that grant money?

THE PRESIDENT. Yes, I think so. Just coincidentally, my first entree into public service was through the organization of a seven-county commission in southwest Georgia that comprised 30 towns or cities, the largest one of which was about 15,000 population. And also, coincidentally, Frank Moore, who's now my legislative assistant, was the executive director of that planning commission. He and I have known and trusted each other for a long time.

What we've done so far is to try to evolve more simplified grant procedures, cutting down paperwork, eliminating the number of forms, the frequency of forms required for application and for certification of proper spending of Federal moneys. And we've made good progress on that. We also have brought together for the first time in Washington an interagency task force to make sure that the lack of communication that previously existed is reduced.

As a Governor with a regional headquarters in Atlanta, I never could find any compatibility between HUD and HEW and Labor and EDA, which is under Commerce, and so forth, when it came to the kind of grant that you described.

And the reason for it obviously was that there was very little compatibility in Washington. You can't expect a regional office to correct a defect that exists at the heart of our Government.

Under Jack Watson, we now have an interagency task force that meets regularly, with a small staff, and I think if you would check with any regional office or those who deal with the regional offices, say, over the last number of years, you would find a substantial improvement.

So, the simplification of grant requests, the minimizing of unnecessary reports that have to be made about how grants are expended, and the coordination among the different Federal agencies are three of the things that I could mention offhand.

The last time I was out in Oregon, I had a meeting with about 35 mayors—I think 3 of the 35 were Governors—and they were highly complimentary about how housing grants and local public works grants were expedited.

And we are well ahead of our schedule, both in establishing a local public works—our new jobs programs—and also the housing program. And this is proven not because I say it, but because of the high rate of housing starts and the unanticipated rapid reduction in the unemployment rate, the creation of new jobs. And this could not have happened had we not been delivering these services more effectively.

We've still got a long way to go. I've got sense enough to know and realize that. But we are making some progress. That's a few of the things we are doing.

CIVIL SERVICE REFORM

Q. Mr. President, back to civil service reform just a minute. You said we were approaching a crisis stage in this area, and this morning Mr. Campbell told us that he's not sure that the civil service reform act will pass. If it doesn't, when will a crisis hit?

THE PRESIDENT. Well, the crisis to which I referred is in the legislative process. I think if we fail, after all the work we've done and the concentrated effort we've put on this subject to get legislation this year, it would be almost impossible to resuscitate it, to start all over again with a new Congress and proceed as far as we have now.

It was one of the most difficult political jobs I've ever had, at least in the House, just to get that bill through the Post Office and Civil Service Committee. And now, of course, it's in the Rules Committee, and now it's got to go to the floor.

The Senate has done a good job on civil service reform legislation. They did eliminate, I think ill-advisedly, the veterans preference proposal that we made. We've been very eager to see the veterans preference retained for those who genuinely deserve and need it—disabled veterans for a lifetime, and those who have been discharged in the last 10, now 15 years. But to have a veterans preference retained, say, for a naval officer who served 20 years, who has a good pension, and who comes here and bumps, because of a veterans preference, literally hundreds of other people who might do better than he does in a competitive examination, I think is ill-advised.

And when the veterans preference was originally introduced into Government employment and promotion and retention, it was designed to help a veteran in those transition years when he had been in the military service, offering his life for our country, and changed into civilian service, to let him have an advantage in getting a job. But it's been expanded from year to year into such a state that it discriminates against both other veterans, like the Vietnam veterans and disabled veterans on the one hand, and women,

blacks, and others who have to be competitive.

So, the crisis that I referred to is in the legislative process, and I think the next 2 or 3 weeks will prove whether or not we will have this crucial legislation, not just this year but perhaps for a long time in the future.

INFLATION

Q. Mr. President, we've heard this morning discussion on numerous significant issues, such as civil service, the Bonn summit.

THE PRESIDENT. That was Richard Cooper. Did Cooper talk to you all about Bonn?

Q. Yes. Could you just update us in terms of the priorities of these issues as you see it today, and also perhaps just comment briefly on what I think is terribly significant, inflation, and just how you see that one?

THE PRESIDENT. I think the American people place inflation at the top of the list of things about which they are concerned. And I would say that I spend more time dealing with inflation and all of its ramifications than any other single subject. I just finished a meeting just before lunch with Charlie Schultze to not only consider immediate inflationary indications and actions that we might take but also the long-range inflationary pressures, the underlying inflation rate tied into such things as productivity per person-hour and how that productivity has decreased in our country from 3 percent annual growth in productivity to 2 percent in the last few years. This year, the indications are that productivity rate is down to 1-percent increase per year. And this has a very severe adverse effect on our country as we compete with other nations whose productivity increase is at least 3 or 4 percent, some of them even higher.

Part of that, of course, is attributable to a shift from more mechanical production jobs to more service jobs, and that's inevitable in a highly advanced society like ours. Some of it is attributable to the fact that much of the investment capital that is available has to go into repairing the lack of investment in the past in air pollution, water pollution, better health, better safety for workers.

This is something that should have been done for the last 35 or 40 years. And since it wasn't done, now to catch up and to protect us from environmental problems and for health and safety threats, you have to put that capital investment there. This means that when you do invest $10,000 in capital, you don't necessarily get that much more increase in productivity per worker.

But I think the inflation is, overall, my most severe domestic problem. It's one over which we have a limited control or influence.

I'm trying to bring down the budget deficit as rapidly as possible. In fiscal year 1976, the budget deficit was in the 60 billions of dollars. In 1978, we had brought it down in the 50 billions of dollars. This year, we'll bring it down in the 40 billions of dollars. And when I put forward my fiscal year '80 budget, on which I'm working now, it will be in the 30 billions of dollars. We're making steady progress in spite of increasing demands on the Federal Government for services. That's one thing we can do; controlling the bureaucracy that I mentioned already, of course, is another.

Inducing business and labor to exercise voluntary constraints with a deceleration formula that's very simple and understandable—that is, that when wage negotiations are concluded, when prices are established, that those wages and prices increase this year or next year less than they did the 2 preceding years—and if this can be accomplished, we can help to overcome the adverse effects of low productivity.

When I meet with the foreign leaders in Bonn, I would say the number one concern would be employment, and particularly in, say, Italy and Great Britain, even Germany. But we recognize that the two, inflation and employment, are interrelated, and we've not ignored inflation in the last 18 months in trying to bring the unemployment rate down. I don't think any economist would claim that a 5.7-percent unemployment rate would contribute to inflation. And we've tried to be very careful in the action that we've taken not to interrelate the two adversely.

The level of Government spending, waste elimination, the encouragement of more capital accumulation are all related to the things that we've proposed, including the income tax measures that we hope the Congress will accommodate. And as we increase capital available for reinvestment among the private individual citizens and corporate structures, we want to do it fairly and equitably, hopefully in a progressive way, and not reward just those who are very rich and very powerful and very influential. But I think the attitude we've taken is good.

So, in almost every area—foreign affairs, civil service reform, employment, housing, productivity, tax reform—inflation is an overriding consideration.

Q. Mr. President, just following on the issue of inflation, what could you say to the American people and through us in answer to their question: "When is my dollar going to at least stabilize? When will the costs be at least standing still, not continue to go up? Is there a time, or what can I expect in the near future?"

THE PRESIDENT. Well, I think it would be a mistake for me to mislead anyone or to put forward a projection that I don't think is going to be realized. We've got an underlying inflation rate of 6.5 to 7 percent, something like that. And it's exacerbated by aberrations which ordinarily are on the bad side.

The two most important factors so far this year that's given us such a high rate of inflation, measured on an annual basis, is, first of all, interest rates. That's the most dominant factor of all, because the interest rates on short-term loans are a part of the Consumer Price Index, and, as you know, that's self-perpetuating. When interest rates are high, the Consumer Price Index goes up. Many wage settlements and agreements are predicated upon what the CPI is. Retirement benefits, even Government wages are in part tied to that. That's one factor.

Another one is the very rapid increase in farm prices. One reason for that is that the farm prices were extremely low last year. September farm prices kind of bottomed out. The 1977 farm act, which went into effect the first of October, gives a substantial stimulation to the income level of farmers. I would say that farm income will go up this year 25 percent, probably $5½ to $6 billion. Part of that is absorbed by increased exports, but part of it, of course, shows up in an increased price.

I think that if we can level off or top out the inflation rate the latter part of this year, that we will have accomplished a great deal. And then the reduction of the inflation rate will be a very slow, very tedious, very doubtful process.

WAGE AND PRICE CONTROLS

Q. Mr. President, you've mentioned this many times, but would you comment again on under what conditions, short of war, if any, would wage and price controls be imposed? And if so, what would be the probabilities of that?

THE PRESIDENT. I don't have any expectation of imposing mandatory wage and price controls. I said this during the campaign often; I said it after I was elected; I've said it several times since. Only if I thought the security of our Nation was endangered would I impose wage and price controls. And I have been through that process in the past, as have all of you. And my judgment is that even under the most severe national circumstances, that wage and price controls didn't work.

There was a time, for instance, during the Second World War, when our Nation was straining to have maximum productivity, say, in the manufacture of tanks and trucks and airplanes and so forth, and there was a severe shortage of civilian goods made by the same type of worker and using the same type of equipment and manufacturing capability. And if we had not had price controls on those competitive goods then, the prices would have skyrocketed. But even then there were some restraints on it. We didn't have wage controls. I think there was a pretty good patriotic attitude toward most workers, at least until toward the end of the war when we did have a series of strikes break out.

But I can't imagine any necessity for wage and price controls, unless the security of our country was actually in danger, and that would be a judgment that I'd have to make.

TAX REDUCTION

Q. Mr. President, do you see any way of harnessing Proposition 13 sentiment to the point where it helps your voluntary guidelines in restraining wage increases?

THE PRESIDENT. I can't see the direct relationship there. I do believe that Proposition 13 is an accurate expression of, first of all, the distrust of government. I'd like to restore that trust.

Secondly, I think that the people believe that government intrudes in their own lives too much. And I'd like to go along in correcting that as well.

I think people feel that government is excessively irresponsible with the taxpayers' money. And I agree with that. And we've proposed, as you know, a substantial tax reduction.

One of the facets, though, of Proposition 13 is that the emphasis there was on reducing property tax rates and with at least the visceral understanding that this would have to be made up either by Federal Government taxes or State government taxes.

California had a unique circumstance in that they had accumulated a large surplus of State taxes—I think $5.5 billion or so—and are likely to have $3 or $4 billion in surplus funds collected this year. And also, there was an extraordinarily high property tax rate in California. Even after the Proposition 13 goes into effect completely, the property tax rates in California are higher than most other States. I'm certain they are higher than any other State in the Southeast, with which I'm familiar.

So, I think there are lessons to be learned from Proposition 13, but it was a unique circumstance that would be emulated in few other States.

Another factor that I haven't mentioned is that you don't have the referendum system in many States. But I think the passage of Proposition 13 has sent a shock wave through the consciousness of every public servant—Presidents, Governors, mayors, State legislators, Members of Congress. And we've stopped and thought, what can we do to accommodate the desires expressed by the American people for modification in government and financing and taxation, as demonstrated by Proposition 13? But the exact parallel is hard to draw.

Q. Mr. President, can you tell us what you might accept in the way of a tax bill to avoid a tax increase in January?

THE PRESIDENT. Well, we've spelled out our position fairly clearly. I'm not opposed to capital gains reductions as such. I am opposed to the Steiger-Jones approach, where you eliminate the application of the minimum tax to people that, through tax shelters and other means, wouldn't pay any taxes at all. I think that is an unfair approach and it's unacceptable to me.

Other modifications in capital gains rates would be acceptable to us. One example, of course, is in the case of a homeowner who sells one's home and then who doesn't want to rebuy another home but, because of age or other considerations, wants to move into a rental apartment and so forth. That part suits me fine.

We were in favor of the accumulation of capital in an efficient way, and we worked out with the business community, the Business Roundtable and other groups that sat around this table, their preference on this approach.

A modest modification in investment tax credit, making a 10-percent investment tax credit permanent and predictable and reducing the corporate tax rates—this is what the business community preferred.

We even had a poll run among 3 or 400 business leaders of all sizes to make sure we did that. We tried to make the tax reform proposal progressive in nature so that those who earn the most taxes would pay the higher rate and to benefit the average working family members in this country, not the very high income groups of $50,000 and above, necessarily. We wanted to close some loopholes, and we also wanted to have an overall tax reduction.

In November, when we were putting this package to bed, which you have to do to present it to Congress with a budget, we thought that $20 billion would be a good figure—or 25. We found since then that because of inflation and the very rapid and unanticipated reduction in the unemployment rate, that a lower figure would be appropriate, in the neighborhood of $15 billion net.

And the last thing that we'd like to have is simplification.

So, I would say that reduction of taxes, equity improvement, progressivity, simplification are the elements of a tax proposal that we would find acceptable. I'm flexible enough. But outside of those guidelines, I would be fairly flexible.

Mr. Wurfel. Thank you, sir.

The President. One more question, and then I'll——

VIEWS ON THE PRESIDENCY

Q. Mr. President, in the early days of the campaign, you made a prayer breakfast speech in Miami on the theme of God and country—very effective. And I think the promise that you gave the electorate about spiritual leadership was helpful in your winning the election. Do you feel that since you've held office that you've fulfilled your goals in this respect?

The President. [*Laughing*] No. And I don't know whether to answer that as a politician or a Christian. As a Christian, you know, I recognize that I am sinful, that I fall short of the expectations of God and my fellow human beings. And as a politician, I know that there are many times when either I or my associates have disappointed the American people, no matter how hard we try.

I think that there has been a restoration in some areas of government of the American people's trust which have been beneficial. I tried in my acceptance speech at the convention and in my inaugural speech, which was a very brief speech, to emphasize the subject of human rights, for instance.

I felt then, during the campaign, and I feel now that the American consciousness was dealt a very severe blow by the Vietnam war and by the Watergate revelations and by the violations of law that were proven against the CIA.

I felt as an individual and as a potential President that the people were embarrassed about their own Government and felt that the Nation and its image was not as high as it had been in the past, as it was originally conceived or as the American people expected it to be. And we have tried to improve that image not by misleading anybody, but by trying to stand for things that we felt were important.

Human rights in its broadest definition is one of the notable elements in that effort. We've had a concerted commitment to bring peace to some of the troubled areas of the world, and we've tried genuinely to understand the special attitudes of billions of people, literally, who in the past had condemned the United States and what we stood for.

I think we are competing adequately with the Communist nations for the hearts and souls and trust and friendship and, to be more practical, the trade and political alignments with nations that in the past were either noncommitted at best, or oriented toward totalitarian, atheistic philosophies at worst. I think we made some progress there.

But I can't say we've done an adequate job. There's a lot of inertia, and we make a lot of mistakes. But we are trying hard, and I think we are making some progress.

Thank you very much.

NOTE: The interview began at 1 p.m. in the Cabinet Room at the White House. Walter W. Wurfel is Deputy Press Secretary.

The transcript of the interview was released on July 29.

Tchaikovsky Competition in Moscow

Remarks at a Reception Honoring Gold Medal Winners Elmar Oliveira and Nathaniel Rosen. July 31, 1978

This is a good year for our Nation, and this is a wonderful day for me.

I spend a large part of my life listening to beautiful music in the Oval Office and am an admirer for many years of those who have superlative talent and who share it with their fellow human beings.

It's been 12 years since the United States had a gold medal brought back to us from the Tchaikovsky Competition in Moscow. I believe it was 20 years ago that Van Cliburn brought back a gold medal and a first-place award in that top competition among the world's greatest musicians.

This year we have two gold medals, and I'm glad it happened while I was President. [*Laughter*]

Nathaniel Rosen, Nick Rosen, is a cellist who, through a major portion of his life, has had a superb talent. He was in a final competition in Moscow in 1966. He didn't win then, but he came back to Pittsburgh and has been admired by his fellow townsmen, by those who perform with him, and by literally tens of thousands of people in audiences who have recognized what he has to offer all of us in the enjoyment of beautiful music.

He went back this year and competed and, as you know, he won.

His wife, Jenny, has two great characteristics: One is that she's a cellist, and the other one is that she's from Macon, Georgia. [*Laughter*]

His father, David, is a violinist and, as you know, the whole family has had a mutual contribution toward competition and toward the achievement of recognized excellence.

Elmar Oliveira also brought back a gold medal to us from the Tchaikovsky Competition in Moscow this year—a superb violinist from Binghamton, New York, a man who's benefited from the musical commitment of his own family. His father, I understand, made his first violin—is that correct? And he's had a notable achievement of his own, even at an early age.

When he was 16 years old, he was one of the soloists with the New York Philharmonic Symphony Orchestra. So, today I'm pleased to recognize this great achievement for themselves, personally, for our Nation, and, indeed, for the entire world.

During the Tchaikovsky Competition this year, there were 280 competitors from 37 different nations and, as you know, they have to be great musicians before they are permitted even to compete.

This afternoon, we would also like to recognize the Board of Directors of a new Federal organization, the Institute of Museum Services. And it's a good juxtaposition, because we want American people to be able to enjoy art, music, the sciences, history, in all its forms. We are blessed not only by great performers, great composers, great artists, but also by great museums, which are not dead exhibitions of past, gone glory, but live openings for Americans' hearts and minds to understand what our Nation is, what it has been, and in addition, what it can be.

It's a continuing, learning process, a stretching of one's heart and one's mind, to understand the greatness of the world that is ours in a free and democratic society.

And this afternoon, I would like to congratulate those who are forming the new Institute of Museum Services and to congratulate and to thank these two wonderful American musicians who have honored themselves, their families, their fellow musicians, their home communities, our Nation, and the entire world with their superb talent and their superb commitment to demonstrate this talent for the blessings of us all.

Nick, congratulations. Elmar, congratulations.

We would like to meet each one of you individually, so Rosalynn and I will go and form a two-person receiving line. Two or four? Would you like to meet Nick and Elmar? And we have Joan Mondale here, too, who's the nationally famous art— Joan, come on up. I understand. Come on up.

As is so often the case in Washington, our two-person receiving line has now been expanded to five persons, and before it gets any greater, I'm going to declare this meeting adjourned and we'll meet you right over here. And I would like for the families of the two musicians to come through the line first so that we might get an individual photograph with all of you.

Thank you very much.

NOTE: The President spoke at 2:50 p.m. in the Grand Hall at the White House.

Federal Highway Administration

Nomination of Karl Bowers To Be Administrator. August 1, 1978

The President today announced that he will nominate Karl Bowers, of Estill, S.C., to be Administrator of the Federal Highway Administration. He would replace William Cox, who has resigned.

Bowers was born October 13, 1941, in Estill, S.C. He received an A.S. in business management from Virginia Southern College in 1964. He serves in the Air National Guard.

Bowers was an insurance and real estate broker from 1965 to 1974. From 1974 to 1977, he was a South Carolina State highway commissioner, serving as chairman of the State Highway and Public Transportation Commission in 1976–77. Since 1977 Bowers has been Deputy Administrator of the Federal Highway Administration.

Arms Embargo Against Turkey

Statement on House of Representatives Action To End the Embargo. August 1, 1978

I welcome today's vote in the House of Representatives which clears the way for a speedy end to the arms embargo on Turkey.

Together with last week's vote in the Senate, the House action reflects a bipartisan, statesmanlike recognition that the time has come to turn a new page in our relations with the countries of the Eastern Mediterranean.

In recent weeks, there have been signs of improvement in the web of problems affecting relations among Greece, Turkey, and Cyprus. These developments helped produce the congressional actions which will now enable us to put the embargo era behind us.

Both Greece and Turkey are valued and respected allies of the United States. We are eager to help them strengthen their economies, their democratic institutions, and their contribution to the defense of the West.

My administration will continue to press for a just and lasting solution in Cyprus. We continue to believe that the disputes in the area must be settled through peaceful procedures. Any effort to impose a military solution would be actively and unequivocally opposed by the United States.

Today's decision by the House is a crucial step toward strengthening the vital southern flank of NATO. It will soon make possible the reopening of our military installations in Turkey. And it brings all the parties concerned closer to the goals of peace and security in the Eastern Mediterranean.

National Science Board

Message to the Congress Transmitting a Report. August 2, 1978

To the Congress of the United States:

I am pleased to submit to the Congress the Tenth Annual Report of the National Science Board, entitled *Basic Research in the Mission Agencies: Agency Perspectives on the Conduct and Support of Basic Research*. This report is part of a continuing series in the Board's examination of key aspects of the status of American science.

It is now generally accepted that science and technology contribute in significant ways to our international trade balance, to productivity and economic growth, and to the solution of many of our social challenges. Perhaps less widely perceived is the fact that basic research is the foundation upon which many of our Nation's technological achievements have been built.

This report provides detailed evidence that basic research supported by Federal agencies not only contributes to America's scientific and technological advances, but also plays an active role in helping the Government meet our Nation's needs. Since taking office, I have encouraged the agencies to identify current or potential problems facing the Federal Government, in which basic or long-term research could help these agencies meet their responsibilities or provide a better basis for decision-making. As a result of this review process, my fiscal year 1979 budget proposed increased levels of funding for basic research—support that I believe is essential for the discoveries and technological innovations fundamental to both our economic well-being and our national security. The National Science Board's report illustrates well the relationship between basic and applied research, and I believe that the report will be useful to the Congress in completing its work on the R&D proposals before it.

In addition to addressing these fundamental issues the report should be helpful to the Congress and others concerned with setting priorities for future federally supported research and development, and in making our spending in this area more effective.

JIMMY CARTER

The White House,
August 2, 1978.

NOTE: The report is entitled "Basic Research in the Mission Agencies: Agency Perspectives on the Conduct and Support of Basic Research—National Science Board 1978" (Government Printing Office, 405 pages).

Assistant to the President for Public Liaison

Exchange of Letters on the Resignation of Margaret Costanza. August 2, 1978

To Midge Costanza

It is with regret that I accept your resignation as my Assistant, effective September 1, 1978.

Your work in my Administration has been invaluable, and your achievements have benefitted me as President and the people of our Nation. I am grateful for your efforts and for your friendship.

Sincerely,

JIMMY CARTER

July 31, 1978

Dear Mr. President:

This is the most difficult letter that I have ever written.

For 20 months, I have worked hard to serve you and your administration to help you keep your commitment to a partnership with the people.

My job was to keep you from being isolated—to bring you the message of what people were thinking and feeling and needing, and there were times that required my speaking out.

I listened in the White House, and I listened as I travelled throughout the country to ethnic groups, women, minorities, youth, senior citizens, and others who wished to participate.

I care about the issues of the young and the old, of minorities and women—and most especially the ratification of the Equal Rights Amendment—and I know you do too.

Although we share these common goals and concerns, it has become clear that our approaches to fulfilling them are different. I have thought about how in every government, including this one, the complexities of the problems place enormous pressures on the people whose job it is to carry out those responsibilities. Within this administration, we are people of varied backgrounds, styles and experiences, and the manner in which we carry out your charge reflects our training and orientation.

My own approach has been largely one of advocacy. I have sought to advise you on the concerns assigned to me and to present those interests and needs to you.

There are those who suggest that I should have simply carried out your policies and not voiced my own opinions and ideas openly. But that was not my style, my experience, or my interpretation of how I could best serve you and your constituents.

In recent months, I have had to deal increasingly with the subject of approach rather than that of substance, spending valuable time and energy discussing whether I have spoken out too much, what my relations are to your other senior staff, or where my office is located. The task of government is too enormous and the needs of the people are too urgent to absorb our differences in approach or to allow the time to create the atmosphere necessary to deal effectively with our goals, while sorting out the variety of our approaches.

If we could declare a recess and stop the wheels of government so that we could reconcile our diverse methods, we could perhaps come out ahead and serve the people at the same time. Since that is not possible, I have decided that at this time it is best for me to continue to search for solutions to the issues that originally brought us together, in another capacity outside the White House.

Participation in your administration may well be the most valuable experience of my life. I am mindful of that as I take my leave.

I leave with the realization that this experience will assist me as I continue to pursue my commitment to addressing the needs of the people in a different form.

I leave with the knowledge that you care about the vital issues that I have worked on, and trust that my efforts will have established a sound beginning for whomever you appoint as my successor and that the crucially important work on women's issues and domestic human rights can proceed without interruption.

I leave with the desire to cooperate in every way possible with you and your administration in the pursuit of these goals in the future.

Sincerely yours,

MARGARET MIDGE COSTANZA

Assistant to the President

[The President, The White House, Washington, D.C. 20500]

United States Railway Association

Nomination of Four Members of the Board of Directors.   August 3, 1978

The President today announced four persons whom he will nominate to be members of the Board of Directors of the United States Railway Association. They are:

JAMES E. BURKE, 58, of Freehold, N.J., vice president of the Brotherhood of Railroad Trainmen;

ROBERT G. FLANNERY, 53, of San Francisco, president and chief executive officer of the Western Pacific Railroad Co.;

STANTON P. SENDER, 45, of Washington, D.C., transportation counsel of Sears, Roebuck and Co.;

NATHANIEL WELCH, 58, of Atlanta, executive vice president of the Georgia Freight Bureau.

Bonn Economic Summit Conference

White House Statement on the West German Government's Commitment.   August 3, 1978

The President has been advised by Chancellor Schmidt of the measures that the German cabinet will propose to the legislature for 1979 tax cuts and added expenditures totaling 12.2 billion deutsche marks, in order to fulfill the German summit commitment "to propose to the legislative bodies additional and quantitatively substantial measures up to 1 p.c. of GNP, designed to achieve a significant strengthening of demand and higher rate of growth." The President was pleased to learn of these German decisions. They should provide a substantial and welcome impetus to demand and growth.

Building a healthy world economy will be a long process involving many coun-

tries; these decisions point us in the right direction. The President believes that the test of the summit is effective followup on its decisions. The German proposals indicate that good progress is being made to this end.

National Grandparents Day, 1978

Proclamation 4580.   August 3, 1978

By the President of the United States of America

A Proclamation

Our nation was shaped by the wisdom and courage of our founding fathers, and by the steadfastness of succeeding generations who have sustained their vision through two turbulent centuries of challenge and growth.

Each American family is similarly shaped and guided by its forbears. Just as a nation learns and is strengthened by its history, so a family learns and is strengthened by its understanding of preceding generations. As Americans live longer, more and more families are enriched by their shared experiences with grandparents and great-grandparents.

The elders of each family have the responsibility for setting the moral tone for the family and for passing on the traditional values of our Nation to their children and grandchildren. They bore the hardships and made the sacrifices that produced much of the progress and comfort we enjoy today. It is appropriate, therefore, that as individuals and as a nation, that we salute our grandparents for their contribution to our lives.

NOW, THEREFORE, I, JIMMY CARTER, President of the United States of America, do hereby designate Sunday, September 10, 1978, as "National Grandparents

Day." I urge officials of Government at the national, state, and local levels, and of voluntary organizations to plan appropriate activities so that the contributions that our grandparents have made may be appropriately recognized.

I urge each citizen to pause and to reflect on the influence his grandparents have had in shaping his own destiny, and on the legacy bestowed upon our contemporary society by his grandparents' generation.

IN WITNESS WHEREOF, I have hereunto set my hand this third day of August, in the year of our Lord nineteen hundred seventy-eight, and of the Independence of the United States of America the two hundred and third.

JIMMY CARTER

[Filed with the Office of the Federal Register, 10:38 a.m., August 4, 1978]

Federal Civil Service Reform and Reorganization

Remarks and a Question-and-Answer Session at a Roundtable Discussion. August 3, 1978

THE PRESIDENT. First of all, let me say how delighted I am to have this opportunity to meet with a group of highly interested citizens of our country, in the presence of distinguished public servants, and with a superb panel, whom I just met a few moments ago, with whom I'll have a discussion about one of the most important subjects that faces our Nation and the Congress this year.

I believe that the taxpayers of the United States have a right to expect a good return from their investment in the United States Government. I spent 2 years campaigning for the office that I hold, and one of the most intense desires of the American people is to have a government,

a bureaucracy, that's effective and efficient, and which serves them well.

The only group I know of who has a more intense desire to see this than the average citizen is those who give their lives in public service as career employees of the United States Government.

We began 15 months ago to assess how we could evolve amendments to the civil service laws, which have now been in effect for about 92 years, that would incorporate necessary improvements, that would let managers manage, let the superb capability of executive officers be realized for the benefit of us all; to reward dedication and excellence, and to single out those who are incompetent or lazy or not dedicated, and discipline them or inspire them or fire them.

The essence of what we proposed also includes the protection of the rights of those who are part of the civil service system, and we are also very interested in seeing the so-called whistleblowers, those who see defects in our Government, violations of the law, gross waste, protected when they point out these deficiencies, leading to correction of errors in our Government.

I'm deeply concerned about the Vietnam veterans and veterans who are permanently disabled, and I was concerned to discover that over 50 percent of all the veterans hired were either discharged before the Vietnam war or have been discharged from the service with full retirement benefits. We need to concentrate the veterans preference on those who have been discharged recently—and we define that by the last 15 years—and those who are permanently disabled.

We don't have an adequate opportunity to hire minority citizens and women, and overall, we need fairness, an incentive for better work, a clear assignment of responsibility. And in the process we have proposed embedding in the law the labor relations aspects of Government employment, which have in the past only been instituted by Executive order of the President and which could be eliminated in a time of labor dispute or crisis, simply by the stroke of a pen.

There is no way that this legislation which has been proposed and which the Congress is considering can possibly hurt any competent and dedicated public servant.

All these things are encompassed in a very far-reaching piece of legislation. Congressman Joe Fisher, who is here tonight with us, and other Members of Congress in the audience, Scotty Campbell, a professional, this panel, and I will now discuss the details of the legislation which affects many people in this area and all over the country, as a matter of fact. And following this discussion around the table, we'll have questions from the audience.

Again, let me thank you for a chance to come and, through your own presence and the television broadcast in this area, to let the people of our Government consider how we can make it even better in the greatest nation on Earth.

Thank you very much.

PANEL DISCUSSION

PERFORMANCE INCENTIVES

DWIGHT F. RETTIE. Mr. President, thank you for meeting with us. I'm a career professional, now proud to be serving with the National Park Service. I have a career that spans some 22 years of public service that has touched on four departments in our Government. I'm very pleased to tell you that I warmly welcome and grandly support much of your efforts to modernize the civil service, but I'm deeply troubled by what seems to me to be a very fundamental change represented by some of those proposals in the basic rationale and reasoning for public service.

Unlike much of private industry, the work of government can only rarely be evaluated on profit-and-loss statements or in the products of an assembly line. Most of the career people, including myself, whom I've been associated with draw their principal rewards from highly intangible, albeit deeply felt satisfactions of helping to try to make a difference in the quality of national life.

Adequate pay, of course, is important. And legislation for comparability of pay was intended to resolve that issue. But now it's suggested that the best way to recruit and motivate and retain people for quality public service is with the chance for cash bonuses and incentive pay and membership in an elite managerial corps.

Mr. President, how will it be possible to borrow from private industry a rewards-and-bonus system that seems so basically at odds with the concept of public service?

THE PRESIDENT. I've chosen a career of public service myself. Recognizing that the profit from someone who serves, as you and I and these others do, is in the better delivery of services to our fellow citizens through government, the Senior Executive Service concept is designed to let those who are competent, who are highly motivated, and who are successful in their efforts be rewarded not just with increased monetary gain, income, but also with increased responsibility, a chance to serve better, to let their own influence, their own talents be used to a much greater and fuller extent.

I think it's accurate to say that the organizations which represent the executive-level public servant is overwhelmingly in favor of this legislation. So, it's not just a matter of increased financial reward; it's also a matter of letting those who are competent and dedicated be rewarded by a chance to serve better and in a more responsible position.

CIVIL SERVICE REORGANIZATION

PAUL H. GILBERT. Mr. President, I'm Paul Gilbert, out of the Department of the Navy. I'm a civilian personnel management specialist, and I've been involved with the reorganization that we're planning to effect in the near future.

The civil service reform is designed to bring about greater efficiency and better management in the Federal sector. The proposed legislation is designed to disestablish the Civil Service Commission and set up three new organizations. I feel that the charter for these organizations will in many cases provide conflicting missions and functions. I'm concerned that we're moving toward fractionalization versus consolidation.

How do you foresee the proposed reorganization improving the efficiency of the Federal sector in such adversarial conditions?

THE PRESIDENT. Well, in one instance, the national labor relations organization, this is just a transfer of responsibility, and the major benefit there is that in the future those bargaining rights and other labor relations elements in our Government structure which have, as I've said in the past, just been a matter of a Presidential Executive order, will be incorporated in the structure of the law so that employees will have their bargaining rights protected on a permanent basis.

There is one additional agency formed, however. We will now have instead of the Civil Service Commission, which is responsible for personnel management on the one hand, and the same people responsible for the protection of the employees, we'll have two separate entities.

The Office of Personnel Management will be responsible for assuring that the civil service system works, that proper hiring techniques are prescribed, examinations, competitive relationships, to make sure that our Government is more effective.

Separated from that and removing the inherent conflict that did exist in the past will be a Merit System Protection Board, which will have as its unique responsibility the protection of the rights of those who serve in government. And a new office completely independent from the President, serving, I believe, for 7 years, removable only for cause, will be a new special counsel, completely separated from the management of the civil service system, but dedicated completely to ensuring that the rights of employees are not violated.

So, I believe that the division of those two responsibilities—personnel management on one hand, and the protection of employees on the other—is a logical division and one which was needed in the past when the civil service system has on occasion been abused.

SENIOR EXECUTIVE SERVICE

RUTH G. VAN CLEVE. Mr. President, may I ask you to comment on the Senior Executive Service? You called your reform proposal a centerpiece. I think the Senior Executive Service is the centerpiece of the centerpiece. I am a Federal employee of many, many years' standing. I hope the Senior Executive Service comes into being. I look forward to being a part of it, and look forward to that with enthusiasm.

At the same time, perhaps I should digress to point out that I have not said that, I think, before to anyone, and I believe my views and, indeed, so far as I know, the views of all of the members of this panel were not known before this enterprise was established tonight. We have all expressed within our own group great pleasure at the fact that this is as open as it is. We have not been quizzed with respect to our position.

However fortuitously, I am in favor of the Senior Executive Service, but I am concerned with the fact that many of my colleagues in the executive branch view it with grave apprehension, because they see it as introducing politics into agencies and into jobs where politics have not before been present, and where politics, in my view, and I think in the view of most of us, have no place. This is a danger which would give any of us pause, and I'd like you to comment on that danger and to tell us, if you will, how you would seek to avoid it or overcome it.

THE PRESIDENT. Let me give a brief response, and then ask Scotty Campbell to add his voice to what I say.

As you know, participation in the Senior Executive Service is voluntary. And if someone moves into that category of increased opportunity for service, also increased pay, they can at any time move back to their previous position at a GS–15 level and have their rights carefully preserved. It's an opportunity for increased service, increased responsibility, increased influence, and increased reward.

We are very concerned about some of the abuses that have taken place in the past with the unwarranted addition of political appointees that sometimes moved career public servants to the rear or out of their jobs which were desirable.

There is no limit now, under the law, as to how many noncareer appointees can be put in their jobs by the President. We have advocated and I think the Congress will go along with a limit of 10 percent, which is a very stringent limit, only half of what was proposed earlier under President Nixon, when he advocated an executive service.

In addition to that, this new, separate adjudicatory body, the Merit System Protection Board, has the responsibility, along with the special counsel, to comply with the laws, which will be very stringent, even requiring heavy penalty, to ensure that there can be no political abuse.

The law specifically spells out the definition of what is political abuse. And I believe that these four things, a 10-percent limit, the new protection board, the special counsel, and the laws prescribing prohibition against politics, will give much greater protection against politics than presently exists.

Perhaps Scotty Campbell could add an additional comment to what I've said or correct if I've made an error.

ALAN K. CAMPBELL. Just a word, Mr. President, and you indeed made no errors and pointed out the fundamental characteristics of the Senior Executive Service, which clearly is a more protected system in terms of political intrusion than is the current system; not only because of the 10-percent limitation, which the President mentioned, but in addition to that, selection to the Senior Executive Service will be made by boards that have a majority of career people on them, awards for bonuses will be recommended by boards which have a majority of career people on them.

It will also open up for career people movement to jobs as high as executive level IV's without giving up any loss of rights to the system. Therefore, we'll not have this problem of career people who have served so well being selected for Assistant Secretary positions, for example, on a political basis, and then not being able to return back to the career service.

So, what we have done here is provided a kind of high-level executive corps which will be the top managers of the Federal

Government. And may I just say that the idea has been around a long time. It was first suggested in the second Hoover Commission Report, and when former President Hoover presented that report to President Eisenhower, he said the single most important recommendation in these many, many volumes is the Senior Executive Service.

And we obviously are pleased that organizations like the National Academy of Public Administration, the National Civil Service League, people like Elmer Staats, the Comptroller General of the United States, are all very strong supporters of this. And for this intelligent audience about these kinds of organizations they know full well that these kinds of groups would not endorse a kind of service which itself could be politicized.

THE PRESIDENT. Congressman Joe Fisher would like to comment.

REPRESENTATIVE JOSEPH L. FISHER. Yes. I have thought that a Senior Executive Service, properly handled and with adequate protections, could enliven the Federal service a great deal. But one of the apprehensions that has been expressed to me many times in the last few weeks is that people will come up out of the higher grades in the civil service into this special elite corps and somehow will be found wanting, perhaps because they don't toe the line politically, and will go back, drop back to their GS–15, until, ultimately, people will be brought up into the Senior Executive Service who somehow conform or follow the right politics. And this is the apprehension I've heard and would be—I know many people here would be pleased to have a comment on this.

THE PRESIDENT. I think there are two elements that might alleviate some concern. In the first place, it's human nature for anybody to be concerned about change, and that's an understandable

attitude, particularly among those who don't have complete control over their own careers—and that is the case.

But to repeat what's already been said, in the first place, entry into the Senior Executive Service is completely voluntary. If someone does occupy a GS–15 or GS–16 level position and they don't want to go into the more advanced Senior Executive Service and perhaps be as high as an Assistant Secretary, they don't have to be. If they should get to that point of deciding, "Let me expand my life, expand my responsibilities, expand my contribution," and they don't work out, perhaps they are not compatible with the Cabinet officer, then they can always go back to their previous position without loss of pay and with their full previous rights preserved.

So, I think the insurance built in and the exciting opportunities for that executive service make a very good combination to protect the rights of employees.

Thank you very much, Mrs. Van Cleve.

MERIT PAY SYSTEM

JAMES P. SCHLICHT. Mr. President, I'm a budget specialist with the Office of Management and Budget. And I too feel that the Senior Executive Service and Merit Pay System for mid-managers are sound proposals in attaining high managerial qualities in the Federal Government. However, to have even more efficiency and productivity in the Federal work force, why doesn't this Merit Pay System extend to all professionals and totally eliminate automatic longevity step increases?

THE PRESIDENT. That was one of the things that we considered, to apply the incentive rewards all the way down at least to GS–9. We talked to many of the senior private personnel managers throughout the country in the formative stages of the legislation. They advised us not to take that big a step at once.

So, there is a mid-level, GS–13 to GS–15, where there are incentive rewards planned. This will not be the same as the Senior Executive Service, but it will reward superior managerial experience and obviously will open up to superiors a chance to observe that good work, later leading in one's career development to the Senior Executive Service.

I believe I've got the GS levels correct, but, Scotty, you might correct me.

MR. CAMPBELL. You do have them correct, and your point is exactly right. When we were deciding at what levels the incentive pay system should apply and consulted with top compensation people from the private sector, they urged us to adopt an incentive pay system, but take a small step first as we learned how to use it, and then perhaps could expand it later as we became more competent in its use. And it was for that reason that we have 13 to 15 instead of the 9 to 15, which is what I originally favored.

THE PRESIDENT. My guess is that in a year or two after this system goes into effect that there will be a persistent demand from the GS–9, 10, 11, and 12 grades that they be included in the mid-level incentive opportunity bracket. And the Congress can always amend the law to move down to lower levels, which would let these fine managerial personnel be rewarded and be given extra responsibility and opportunities.

FEDERAL EMPLOYEES' RIGHTS

WAYNE F. BUCKLE. Mr. President, I come from the American Federation of Government Employees, and we're concerned about some of the handling of employees who are given a lot of publicity in this procedure, namely, the question of getting rid of people.

One of the things that's given me a lot of concern in publicity that's happened has been making it easier to fire people. And I'm a little concerned that there can get to be too much emphasis on this question of how you get rid of people, versus the due process that ought to be given consideration in our society.

Our president, Ken Blaylock, has worked with your administration and the Congress in trying to resolve some of these problems. And I think we've come up in the bill that the House committee has reported to deal with this a little more effectively than we started out with, namely, that people who are accused of wrongdoing or who are believed incompetent can be given the right of a hearing and that the management must show a preponderance of evidence that they either have been guilty of misconduct or incompetent.

Now, I believe that this is more in line with our concepts of justice in dealing with people who will have problems. And I wonder if you are prepared to back the House legislation as it comes from the committee along those lines?

THE PRESIDENT. There are some amendments that the House committee put on with which I don't agree. I'm not qualified to understand all the technical changes that were made. But let me say that I'm convinced that under this legislation as it was proposed by us to the Congress—and it's been modified, I think, according to your desires even since then—that the rights of Federal employees will be much better protected than under the present system.

There will be a special counsel, a highly qualified attorney, completely independent of me or anyone else, responsible only to the employees themselves to guard against abuse, to investigate, to present evidence to the Merit System Protection Board, which, as you know, is a three-person, bipartisan board that serves for 7 years, isolated from politics, with a unique responsibility to preserve rights. So, I think that in the routine case, the employees' rights will be much better protected than they are now.

Let me give you a notable example from past history, perhaps the most famous person who has suffered. And that's Ernest Fitzgerald, who, through his own insistence, pointed out an example of great waste in the Federal Government. Under the present merit system, he has, through his own analysis, been punished because of that whistleblowing experience. That would not be possible under the proposed legislation. He would be protected and could not be punished, could not be silenced, in fact, may very well have been rewarded.

So, I think that the average employee will be protected even better than now, and the past abuses of whistleblowers, so-called, will be prevented in the future.

Now, I'm convinced that that's true, and I believe that your organization and Ken Blaylock, who's been superb in helping us protect employees' rights, would agree with what I've said.

MR. BUCKLE. We applaud your separation of the Civil Service Commission into the Personnel Management Office and the Merit System Protection Board.

THE PRESIDENT. Thank you, Mr. Buckle.

CEOLA B. NAYLOR. Mr. President, I'm Ceola Naylor. I'm a secretary with the Department of Housing and Urban Development. I would like to know what will be the effects of the reorganization on nonmanagerial employees such as secretaries and clericals.

THE PRESIDENT. I think part of my answer to Mr. Buckle's question would apply as well, that your basic rights would be protected. There will be a more effec-

tive analysis of competence and dedication and, I think, quicker reward.

For those who are seeking jobs, the hiring delays will be minimized. If an employee is recommended for discharge, the hearing of the case protecting the worker's rights even better would be abbreviated, so there wouldn't be these long, dragged out procedures. And I think it's good to remember that here in the presence of people who are obviously competent and dedicated, that it's an abuse for a good employee to protect one who's no good. That's an extreme minority, I know. But if you have a person sitting next to you who is a laggard or lazy or incompetent, supposedly sharing the workload, in effect you have to do that person's work, or part of it, in addition to your own.

So, I think there will be a much better recognition of achievement at all levels of employment and a much quicker correction if someone is assigned to a job and doesn't perform it.

Perhaps again I could call on Scotty Campbell to add some remarks.

MR. CAMPBELL. Just a quick comment, Mr. President. As I've traveled around the country talking to Federal employees, and as we heard from the agencies in Washington when hearings were held there, a major criticism in the Federal Government, as you are undoubtedly aware, is of the managers and the supervisors not doing an adequate job in terms of rank-and-file employees, that I have often been accused of pointing my finger at the wrong people because we have not emphasized sufficiently the problems on the managerial side. And I think that's a fair comment.

And I would guess that one of the best things that will come out of these changes is a fantastic improvement in the quality of supervision and management in the Federal Government, which will be produced by the incentive pay, the Senior Executive Service. And I think that will have an effect on the character and environment of the workplace, which will make it a much more exciting, a much more interesting place to work than it has traditionally been, and add that to the kinds of protections which will now exist in the system, which can be done speedily, which will recognize the fact that an employee doesn't have 3 years in which to fight a case, and that you will find it just a much better place to work for all employees—managers and others as well.

THE PRESIDENT. Thank you, Ceola, very much.

COLLECTIVE BARGAINING

LARRY T. SUITERS. Mr. President?

THE PRESIDENT. Yes, Larry.

MR. SUITERS. I'm a life-long resident of this area who is self-employed and who has never been a member of the Federal civil service. You have stated your opposition to expanding collective bargaining for Federal employee unions beyond Federal Executive Order 11491. Recent action by the House committee has significantly expanded collective-bargaining rights beyond those set forth in the Executive order. It has also been reported that you have indicated to Federal employee union officials that you favor a system of labor relations which approximates that which exists in private industry.

To those of us in the private sector, collective bargaining is a very broad term which includes many elements, the most significant and controversial of which are, one, the right of unions to negotiate wages and benefits, and, two, the issue of open or closed agency shops.

Would you please state the essential elements which you include in your definition of collective bargaining and indicate specifically whether or not you would accept or reject legislation which grants Federal employee unions the right as a part of the collective-bargaining process to negotiate the wages in open or closed agency shops?

THE PRESIDENT. My preference is to limit the collective-bargaining process in this legislation to what is included in the Executive order today.

There have been a few technical amendments worked out with Ken Blaylock and the union before the legislation was introduced that would expand that in some ways that I don't quite understand. But I personally don't favor some of the additions that were made by the Post Office and Civil Service Committee. I would again like to turn to the professional on my left, Scotty Campbell, to explain the small additional technical amendments that we did approve, and then perhaps Congressman Fisher would like to comment as well.

MR. CAMPBELL. Yes. First, neither the administration nor the House committee bill nor the Senate committee bill contain bargaining for wages and benefits, nor do they contain agency shop. And there is no intention on the part of either Congress or the administration to move in that direction as far as collective bargaining is concerned.

The one area of expansion in collective bargaining which the administration supports is to allow the negotiation of an agreement whereby an employee who is disciplined, discharged, suspended, may use arbitration as a means of challenging that, rather than using the statutory appeals system. We believe this serves the interest of both labor and management, because it speeds the process, does provide the employee an alternative for arbitration against the statutory appeals which, even in our new system, will not be as rapid as arbitration.

There are some other rather technical amendments that have been added in the House committee, some of them mentioned already by Mr. Buckle, with which we still disagree and hope to get them amended on the House floor or in conference.

REPRESENTATIVE FISHER. I have thought that labor relations, if you want to call them that, in the Government service are different in significant ways from labor relations in the private sector. And basically, this goes back to Mr. Rettie's opening comments having to do with, well, philosophical differences between public service and private employment.

It does seem to me in the present context that there should not be collective bargaining on pay and benefits and that the agency shop arrangement should not be in the picture. And I would agree with you, Mr. President, and the House committee and others on that.

The disputes, I think, come as to whether, within the reach of collective bargaining, should be such things as layoffs, promotions, setting job classifications, job assignments, and things like that. I haven't really thought my way through it. The House has added these things and one or two others. And I think we ought to have just a very thorough airing of this to see how far we want to go.

THE PRESIDENT. Which will probably take place in the House debate.

REPRESENTATIVE FISHER. Yes, I'm sure it will, and in the Senate.

THE PRESIDENT. Yes, I know. Mary Anne?

AMENDMENTS TO CIVIL SERVICE REFORM

MARY ANNE LECOS. Mr. President, as a long-time member of a local school board which bargained collectively with some success for many years, I approve the codification of the Executive order under which Federal employees can organize and bargain, but I am disturbed by the House committee actions which extend those rights to what I consider management responsibilities in such areas as job classification, defining layoffs and promotion standards, determining the number and types of employees assigned to jobs. I think this is totally inconsistent with your goal of achieving more efficiency and more effective management in government.

I'd like to know, Mr. President, how you feel about other committee action which has had the effect of turning the centerpiece of your legislative program into a sort of Christmas tree with the addition of such controversial and unrelated subjects as the Hatch Act revision and the reduction in the firefighters' work week.

THE PRESIDENT. I'm opposed to those very strongly as parts of the civil service reform. I don't think they are germane at all.

As you know, the Hatch Act legislation is legislation that I did support and do support. It was passed by the House and is now in the Senate. But the Hatch Act applies to a completely new category of workers not covered by civil service, the Post Office workers, tens of thousands of them.

And the abbreviation of the firefighters' week I oppose on several grounds, the most important of which I'll mention tonight is a tremendous increase in the wages paid them for a given number of hours of work. During regular working hours, the wage increase would amount to 30 percent, and in overtime, another extra 15 percent.

We just can't afford that. Just take one department, for instance, the Department of Defense. In order to provide the same level of firefighting service, they would have to employ 4,600 employees additional at the cost of tens of millions of additional dollars. And this is money that we cannot afford to spend or, I think, to waste.

I believe that some modification is needed for firefighters, but I personally believe that this legislation was too inflationary. I vetoed the legislation after it had been passed by the Congress once this year, and I don't believe it's germane to the legislation that we are trying to consider.

Civil service reform is so crucial to the better management of government and the provision of better services to the Nation and the protection of employees' rights and adequate management and promotion and reward for those who do a good job, I hate to see it delayed by the kind of amendments to which you did refer.

It still faces formidable opposition, and I think the only way that this legislation could be defeated this year, having the overwhelming support of the Congress, the overwhelming support of the American people, is for deliberate delay to be pursued. This is something that we need to guard against. And I would hope that all those who watch this program or who are here tonight will add your voices to my own and others to encourage a rapid conclusion of this very important legislation. The people are ready for it throughout the country, and the group in our Nation who would benefit most are those who have given their entire careers to public service.

HATCH ACT REFORM

MR. BUCKLE. Mr. President, in connection with this issue on the Hatch Act reform that's incorporated in the bill, as you indicated, you've given your support to Hatch Act reform in the past. As you'll recall, this went through both Houses of the Congress during President Ford's administration, and he vetoed it. It's now passed the House and is waiting in the Senate. How do you feel about helping the Senate to get it on the floor and at least let it be debated on the floor without having to be filibustered?

THE PRESIDENT. I would like to see the Hatch Act legislation come to the Senate floor and be passed, and I would be glad to sign it.

MR. CAMPBELL. Could I just add, Mr. President, to that, that we've made every effort to get the bill to the floor. We have sought a floor leader for it. The problem is that there is a threatened filibuster, and it is not clear that there are the votes necessary to overcome that filibuster in case the bill was taken up.

THE PRESIDENT. The crux of the matter though, just to repeat an important point, is that with the Hatch Act tied to the civil service reform legislation, my guess is that neither one would pass, which would be a very bad thing to have happen.

Perhaps now we might in the time remaining go to the audience. Yes?

QUESTIONS

PUBLIC PERCEPTION OF CIVIL SERVICE

Q. Good evening. Hello. My name's Eleanor Fischer, and I've been a Federal employee for 9 years. And one of the things that I've experienced as a Federal employee is a fair amount of criticism—comes from my brothers and sisters and friends and neighbors—that being a Federal employee is not in their perception a very good thing for me to do. As a matter of fact, I noticed about a week ago that I was feeling ashamed of being a Federal employee. And one of the things that I wanted to mention was that my reading about this new bill is that it is announced to be a tool that will facilitate the firing of Federal employees, which infers that there are a lot of us deserving firing.

In my experience—I train your managers, and in my experience that's really not true. So, what I would like for you to comment on is in two ways: First of all, how do you think this bill will enhance the image of the public employee in the eyes of the American people; and secondly, since you're my boss, how do you intend to use the bill as a tool to motivate people like me to feel like we make a difference, we make a contribution?

THE PRESIDENT. Thank you very much.

As President, I have some of the same feelings that you do. [*Laughter*] Some of my old classmates and friends think that I've disgraced my class by becoming a full-time Government employee. [*Laughter*] But I think that it's unfortunate that the firing aspect, which is important, but a very small increment of the total legislation, is emphasized by some people.

I think that the delineation or the distinction between a competent and dedicated Federal employee on one hand, who will be rewarded under this entire system much more quickly and much more effectively and much more assuredly than under the present civil service laws, compared to the employee who does not do a good job, but now almost moves in lockstep — you have an excellent employee and a very poor employee who come into public service at the same time. They both move together now, almost inexorably at the same rate of promotion and reward.

And I believe that many employees who don't do a good job now—knowing that they will be protected no matter how poorly they perform—will, under this new legislation, be inspired to do a much better job. I think we'll make better employees out of bad ones and superb employees out of good ones, and we'll reward those whose performance deserves reward.

The other thing that's very important is to let the public who are not involved in full-time government service know the superb contribution that is made. Nobody can deny that the Federal Government now delivers a much broader range of services than it did 10 years ago. The number of civilian employees in the Federal Government is almost exactly the same as it was 10 years ago. There's a greater responsibility on those who serve full-time, and one of the things that I believe this legislation and this debate can bring out is a recognition of the great contribution, sometimes the sacrificial contribution of the dedicated and competent public employee who gives their life to serve others.

MONITORING OF FEDERAL AGENCIES

Q. Mr. President, my name is Evangeline Jackson, and I'm president of Local 2211 with AFGE. My question tonight is similar to the first young lady's. It's obvious that the public feels that government workers receive fat checks for no work and are ensured comfortable positions, in many cases receive no reprisal for misconduct. But I have learned from my own experience that in many cases monitoring systems outside of the individual agencies are not as effective as we would hope they would be.

In many cases, quite a few agencies need to have a monitoring system set up where outside agencies, such as the Civil Service Commission, the Merit System Protection Board, the national labor relations organization that you're speaking of, could come in and monitor the functions of these agencies from time to time to see how they are handling the rights of their employees.

I would like to know if you see in the near future any chance with this reform bill of a monitoring system for individual agencies that are repeatedly accused of abusing their employees' rights?

Mr. Campbell. May I comment on that?

I think the new system, by separating what are now the conflicting roles of the Civil Service Commission, where it is, on the one hand, supposed to represent the management side of the Federal Government, carry out strong managerial policies while simultaneously protecting employee rights, has resulted in an inability of it to do its job. And, therefore, I don't think that this audience would disagree the Civil Service Commission has lost substantial credibility.

The change, in my judgment, will end that, and, indeed, the Merit Systems Protection Board, with the special counsel, will provide a monitoring system and an investigative system which will be far superior to that which we now have, because that will be its sole function, while simultaneously, the Office of Personnel Management will be able to go into agencies and in a consultive service capacity be able to help them improve their management, improve productivity, improve the quality of Federal service.

And may I say that I am sympathetic with the concern expressed here about public attitudes toward public employees, not only Federal but State and local as well, as represented by Proposition 13, that it doesn't do us any good to just deplore that; we must respond to that by improving how well we do our jobs, by improving the quality of service. And I believe when we do that, the public will then come to recognize the kind of quality which in fact, as the President has described, does exist in the Federal service.

The President. That's an excellent question. Thank you very much, Evangeline.

EMPLOYMENT OF MINORITIES

Q. Mr. President, my name is Gilbert Sandate. I represent IMAGE, a national Hispanic organization concerned with government employment opportunities for Hispanic Americans and with adequate delivery of services to our Hispanic communities across the country by our public institutions. I'd just like to make one brief observation before my question. It is disappointing to us to note that out of the 200,000 Hispanic American citizens that reside in this metropolitan area, that not one was seen fit to represent us on this select panel.

My question: Hispanic Americans are currently under-represented by 100,000 jobs in the Federal sector, if we are to reach parity with our numbers in the population. Inadequate delivery of services has cost Hispanic communities millions of dollars annually. The civil service system throughout its history has virtually excluded Hispanic Americans from full participation. The Senior Executive Service, the Incentive Pay System, and all the other facets of your package that you have presented are very fine, but if we're not represented in the senior levels—which we are not—if we're not represented in the mid-level management, or the higher level managers—which we are not—the package is virtually meaningless to the Hispanic American constituents.

What, in your opinion, does the civil service reform package do or have to offer to try to offset some of these concerns?

The President. There's no doubt in my mind that with the change in the hiring practices involved, the change in the veterans preference, that we can have a much more equitable opportunity for Americans. One of the things that we are changing is quite controversial, that is opposed, for instance, by the American Legion, of which I'm a member and of which my father was a member, is to eliminate the veterans preference, for instance, for a Navy commander who has completed his full service in the Navy, has full retirement benefits, a pension, and still can come in and seek a Federal job and get it with absolute lifetime veterans preference.

This means that many who deserve jobs, including Vietnam veterans who are recently discharged, can't compete and can't get that same job.

We also recognize that those of us who can make the political appointments, the 10 percent at the executive level that is permitted under the proposed law, have a responsibility to recognize Spanish-speaking Americans. At the executive level now, there are 109 Latin American citizens who have been selected by me to serve—I think four or five times more than ever have been before—and some of them head up major agencies in government, the community services agency and the Immigration and Naturalization Service, for instance.

So, we are trying to make progress in this correction of discrimination that's built into the civil service law now. It's not deliberate at this point, but you have to discriminate to protect those that don't need protection. And I think that if we do protect the rights of veterans who have been discharged in the last 15 years and protect the rights of preference for those who are disabled for a lifetime, that that is an adequate rewarding of veterans, and that would in effect help to solve the problem that you've described.

Perhaps Congressman Fisher or Scotty Campbell want to add a comment.

MR. CAMPBELL. Just a brief comment, Mr. President. Unfortunately, one of the provisions in the original proposal which you made to Congress, which would have broadened the hiring authority beyond the current system of restricting the selection to just a very small number, has been taken out by both the House committee and the Senate committee. And it is our hope that on the floor of one or the other of the two Houses, we will be able to get that restored, and if so, that will help us much in recruiting for minorities and women and others who have suffered discrimination.

Your point about the lack of Hispanics and other minorities and women at the executive levels is exactly right, and if you look at the levels just below them, Grades 13, 14, and 15, the percentage is just as low. That means that you aren't going to solve the problem completely by promotion policies.

There's going to have to be some reaching outside the service to find qualified people in order to do that, and I can assure you the current leadership of the Civil Service Commission is committed to doing that.

THE PRESIDENT. I might just give you two points: In the GS–16, 17, and 18 levels, 65 percent of those people are veterans. Only 3 percent——

MR. CAMPBELL. White male veterans.

THE PRESIDENT. White male veterans, excuse me. Only 3 percent of those people are women. So we recognize not only the problems with Spanish-speaking Americans, but also with women, who happen to make up a majority.

Now there is a requirement that the selection be made from the top three people on the list. And we asked to have a rule of seven so that you could select for a given opening one of the top seven. This would at least give us a broader range of selection.

We have an instance now in the Washington area where there's a vacancy, and one of the women applicants scored 100, perfect score, and she's 47th on the list. There's no possibility that she would be selected because of abuse of the veterans preference. But I want to make clear that we are trying to keep the veterans preference for those recently discharged and for those who are disabled, but remove the abuse that exsists.

REPRESENTATIVE FISHER. I might add that IMAGE the organization this young man represents, is really a wonderful organization. I've come to know it. I'd add only this: that I think there ought to be up and down and cross-wise in the agencies a much more determined effort to hire Hispanic Americans and other minority groups. It's just got to seep all through the system.

THE PRESIDENT. I might say that the panel didn't leave a vacancy, because you filled it very well.

Thank you very much, Mr. Sandate.

PROSPECTS FOR EMPLOYMENT

Q. Mr. President, my name is John Worley. I'm presently working on a business degree now and with hopes of working for the Federal Government, 1981. [*Laughter*] What I would like to know, if this act is passed, what will the job market be like for me and others my age?

THE PRESIDENT. Overall, the job market is much better now than it was 18 months ago. The unemployment rate has dropped greatly, and we have added a net of about 6½ million jobs in the entire Nation. Some of those are government jobs created specifically for groups that need special help through the local public works and CETA programs and other jobs that were designed to be filled specifically by congressional legislation.

I would say that if you are competent when you finish your college education that you would have a much better chance to get a job on your own merits, absent politics, in a free, competitive environment than you would otherwise.

My belief is that the total employment in the Federal Government is not likely to increase, but that means that each employee in the Federal Government is going to have to do a better and better job.

Productivity in the general economic sector of our Nation is not increasing very rapidly. It's increasing very, very slowly. But productivity—that is, the work done per employee—is holding its own in the Federal Government and increasing very well.

But I wish you well. We need top business graduates in the Federal Government, and I think that it's a credit to you that you want to serve with us.

Let me say in closing that we don't have time for another question. I'm very grateful to—maybe for the question, but not the answer. But go ahead. [*Laughter*] I didn't know you were already standing there.

INDEPENDENT AGENCIES

Q. Yes, sir. I'm a Government employee for the Federal Reserve System, an independent agency within the Government.

I wonder if you could state briefly what the effect of the legislation would be on those of us who are not covered by civil service.

MR. CAMPBELL. Just very briefly, there are some of the agencies excepted, such as the intelligence agencies, some of the other independent agencies, but as far as the Senior Executive Service is concerned, it is possible for independent agencies to be covered. And we hope that organizations like the Federal Reserve Board will want to be a part of that so that we can have fresh blood flowing between agencies in the Federal Government from organizations like yours as well as the regular departments.

THE PRESIDENT. Again, it would be voluntary on your part. You wouldn't have to participate if you didn't want to.

Let me say in closing that this has been a very interesting session for me and, I know, for Congressman Fisher and for Scotty Campbell and the superb panel that we've had.

I've learned a lot tonight from your questions and from listening to the answers of others. We are all partners in the same enterprise, that is, to have a great government, with dedicated public servants, trying to give better services to the people who trust us. And there's a general appreciation throughout the country of not only our country and our Government but individual employees as well. And I think we can make it even better if this exciting and sometimes confusing, sometimes dreaded legislation becomes law.

The only dread comes in because people are afraid to make a change. But I can assure you—and as you know, Scotty Campbell is the Chairman of the Civil Service Commission, and he will join me assuring you—that every aspect of this legislation as it is changing the present laws will be for the advantage of the competent and dedicated public servants who make our Government as great as it is.

Thank you very much.

NOTE: The discussion began at 8 p.m. in the Fairfax High School cafeteria in Fairfax City, Va. It was broadcast live on radio and television.

Agricultural Credit Act of 1978

Remarks at the Bill Signing Ceremony.
August 4, 1978

THE PRESIDENT. During the last 18 months, the Democratic Congress and this administration has recognized the profound need of American farmers to have a chance to meet two basic requirements. As a farmer myself for most of my life, and recognizing the attitude of American agricultural leaders and family farmers, I know that farmers don't want a handout. What they want is two basic things: first of all, to have fair prices and predictable market opportunities—and the agricultural act, the farm bill of 1977, gave them an unprecedented opportunity to have that need met.

We've seen a dramatic improvement in the economic well-being of farm families since the 1977 act went into effect last October. This year farm income will increase 25 percent, net farm income, about $5½ or $6 billion.

Last year we set a record on total farm exports in spite of very low prices for products. This year we hope to exceed even that record level of farm exports. So, we've taken care, I believe, in the best possible way, with good bipartisan cooperation between the Congress and the administration, of that one need of farmers.

The other need that farmers have is to be provided with the resources to keep their operations going, to expand them if necessary, to change the circumstances under which they operate with rapidly changing conditions in American and worldwide agricultural community. This bill, the Agricultural Credit Assistance Act of 1978, meets that other need.

In 40 years this is the most far-reaching and effective farm and rural credit legislation that the Congress has passed. After very careful analysis by us in the administration and the Congress, basic decisions were made, both to save the American taxpayers money and also to meet the needs of farmers who have requirements that have not previously been met.

There is in H.R. 11504, this legislation, an opportunity for new emergency loan programs. We are updating the level of loans that can be granted to farmers who have, in large farm operations and higher credit costs, and who have suffered from inflation and not had their suffering alleviated.

Higher loan levels are permitted for those families that are just getting started in agriculture, and for those that have very low income levels, we provide special loans at reduced interest rates.

For those that are able, established, strong economically, but still need loans, this legislation permits the interest rates to increase so there will be minimal subsidization of interest rates and that we might lend the money to farmers under existing programs more nearly at a level of the cost of money to the Government itself.

There's an expanded program for water and waste disposal which will permit better attention by farm families to the problem of environmental quality.

This is very good legislation. It's fiscally responsible. It meets the other basic need of farmers and, in partnership with the 1977 farm legislation, is a major step additionally to stability and prosperity among those who produce food and fiber and the consumers who have to pay for it.

I believe predictability and stability in farm pricing and farm production is crucial to the consumers of this Nation. And this legislation will help both the farmers and those who consume their products. I want to congratulate the House and Senate leadership for their far-reaching statesmanship in passing this legislation, their responsibility to the taxpayers, and I want to also congratulate Bob Bergland and others who made it possible for this cooperative effort to pay such rich dividends for our country.

[*At this point, the President signed the bill.*]

Thank you very much.

REPRESENTATIVE THOMAS S. FOLEY. *Mr. President, Mr. Vice President, ladies and gentlemen:*

As you've said very well, farmers are principally in need of strong income that comes from fair prices and expanding markets. But the credit availability and opportunity that this bill will provide under your leadership, leadership of your administration, is one that will offer many, many farmers, young farmers as well as established farmers, a chance to continue to seek those fair prices and expanded markets.

I want to say a word, with your permission, Mr. President, for the work that was done by the Subcommittee on Conservation and Credit in the House under the leadership of Congressman Ed Jones, who did an outstanding job, and the cooperation of the Department of Agriculture and the Secretary and all your administration, and our colleagues in the Senate, that made this legislation possible.

Thank you, sir.

THE PRESIDENT. Thank you very much, everybody. I'm very proud of this legislation.

NOTE: The President spoke at 9:51 a.m. in the Rose Garden at the White House.

As enacted, H.R. 11504 is Public Law 95–334, approved August 4.

Agricultural Credit Act of 1978

Statement on Signing H.R. 11504 Into Law. August 4, 1978

The Agricultural Credit Act of 1978, which I am signing today, gives our Nation a second important tool to improve the incomes of farmers and rural Americans. This act supplements and complements the authorities contained in the Food and Agricultural Act of 1977. That act, signed last fall, has already led to a significant improvement in the farm economy. The prices of most farm commodities have risen appreciably from their earlier depressed levels. Farm exports are higher than ever before. Farm income is expected to rise by at least $5 billion, or 25 percent, this year.

The act I am signing today will give many farmers an opportunity to refinance the debts they incurred during the past period of low prices; for some this will mean the difference between staying in farming and being driven out.

The Agricultural Credit Act of 1978 represents the most comprehensive and far-reaching farm and rural credit bill since the enactment of the Bankhead-Jones Act some 40 years ago. The revolutionary changes that have transformed agriculture during those four decades demand a new credit structure for farmers and rural people. Today's farmer must make large investments in land and machinery and operating credit. In addition, farming is a high-risk operation—a constant gamble against weather and natural disaster.

This act fulfills the modern farmer's need.

The Agricultural Credit Act of 1978 will:

—bring major credit programs of the Farmers Home Administration—farm ownership, farm operating and emergency loans—into line with the basic credit needs of modern agriculture. It does this by raising the total availability of needed credit; by increasing the loan ceilings; and by setting interest rates that reflect the cost of money;

—provide $4 billion in economic emergency loan authority to assist 60,000 or more farmers hard-pressed today because of past low prices and overburdening debt accumulated during recent periods of rising production costs. Recognizing that credit is no substitute for income, the new act

does allow eligible farmers to consolidate and refinance their debts while provisions of the 1977 farm act continue to help raise prices and incomes;

—create a special low-interest FmHA farm mortgage loan program for beginning and low-income farm families;

—extend a special cattle industry credit program for 1 year through September 30, 1979;

—authorize additional expenditures for small communities for water and sewer development;

—provide, for the first time, an effective, guaranteed farm lending program which will rely on private sector financing;

—recognize that family farm corporations, farm cooperatives, and limited family partnerships are essential to the farm economy and makes them eligible for FmHA credit programs for the first time.

I am particularly proud of the spirit of cooperation between the Congress and the administration in the evolution of this bill, which made a major contribution to the success of this legislation.

I hope that this momentum can be continued and that the Congress will soon act on three other important agricultural proposals:

—ratification of the International Sugar Agreement;

—the International Emergency Wheat Reserve; and

—reform of the crop insurance/disaster payments program.

With enactment of these measures, we will have completed work on the most comprehensive, most forward-looking set of farm programs since the New Deal. We are very close to the realization of this goal. For its part, the administration will redouble its efforts to reach accord on these unresolved issues. I call on Members of the Congress to join in this effort.

NOTE: As enacted, H.R. 11504 is Public Law 95–334, approved August 4.

National Science Foundation

Message to the Congress Transmitting a Report. August 4, 1978

To the Congress of the United States:

I am pleased to submit to the Congress the 27th Annual Report of the National Science Foundation, covering Fiscal Year 1977.

This is an important document. Many of the issues facing our Nation today, in areas such as energy, the economy, and the environment, require special knowledge and detailed information. Advances in the sciences, many of which are discussed in this report, enhance our understanding of ourselves and the world about us, and thus assist us in seeking wise and intelligent solutions to these complex problems.

Federally supported scientific progress has flourished now for several decades. This pursuit of scientific knowledge—at colleges and universities, national research centers, and other research organizations—depends heavily on judiciously allotted Federal funds, as does the education of many talented young students who might not otherwise attain the careers in science for which they are qualified.

This report describes in brief many of the National Science Foundation's activities in the past year, in support of basic and applied research, as well as education and training in science and engineering. There is a significant emphasis upon basic research, the principle mission of the NSF. In recent years, the American people have

learned that even with the help of the most advanced technology, some of our most pressing national problems can be tackled only by diligent, long-term attention. The needed basic research supported by the National Science Foundation continually enlarges our capacity to deal with many of these major national and international issues.

I believe the activities of the National Science Foundation reviewed in this Annual Report represent funds well spent in the public interest. I, therefore, commend this report to your close attention, confident that many of you will share my interest in the extraordinary range of scientific pursuits that it describes.

JIMMY CARTER

The White House,
    August 4, 1978.

NOTE: The report is entitled "National Science Foundation: Twenty-seventh Annual Report for Fiscal Year 1977" (Government Printing Office, 145 pages).

Association of South-East Asian Nations

White House Statement Issued Following a Meeting With Ministers From the Association. August 4, 1978

President Carter met today with Ministers from the Association of South-East Asian Nations (ASEAN), who are holding their first U.S.–ASEAN Ministerial Meeting in Washington from August 2–4. The President said that the United States fully supports ASEAN efforts to encourage economic, social, and cultural cooperation among its members and to promote peace and stability in Southeast Asia. He expressed admiration for ASEAN economic progress. The President told the ASEAN Ministers that the United States was prepared to embark on a long-term process of cooperation with ASEAN. The United States will respond to ASEAN's own regional priorities and programs and has agreed to set up consultative arrangements in key economic areas such as aid, energy, science and technology, food, business affairs, and trade.

Philippine Foreign Minister General Carlos P. Romulo, the spokesman for ASEAN, noted that this first joint ministerial meeting represented the culmination of intensive preparations and consultations between ASEAN and the United States. The meeting, he added, was an open dialog on the range of international issues and afforded an excellent opportunity to improve understanding and set up long-term consultative arrangements. General Romulo said the meeting reinforces the partnership and friendly relations that exist between the United States and ASEAN.

Besides General Romulo, ASEAN was represented by Ministers Widjojo and Radius, and Ambassador Ashari of Indonesia; Minister Rithauddeen and Ambassador Zain of Malaysia; Ministers Marcos, Virata, Sicat, and Peterno, and Ambassador Romualdez of the Philippines; Ministers Rajaratnam and Goh, and Ambassador Coomaraswaney of Singapore; and Ministers Pachariyangkun, Amarand, and Sribhibhadh, and Ambassador Visessurakarn of Thailand; ASEAN Secretary-General Abdullah; and Ambassador Manalo, ASEAN–U.S. Coordinator of the Philippines.

On the U.S. side, besides President Carter, Secretary Blumenthal of Treasury; Deputy Secretary Christopher of State; Dr. Zbigniew Brzezinski, Assistant to the President for National Security Affairs; Ambassador Henry Owen and Nicholas Platt of the National Security Council; Under Secretary Richard Cooper and Assistant Secretary Richard Holbrooke of State; and Anthony Gerber, State Department ASEAN–U.S. Coordinator attended.

Digest of Other White House Announcements

The following listing includes the President's daily schedule and other items of general interest as announced by the White House Press Office during the period covered by this issue. Events and announcements printed elsewhere in the issue are not included.

July 31

The President met at Camp David, Md., with:
—Vice President Walter F. Mondale, Secretary of State Cyrus R. Vance, Secretary of Defense Harold Brown, Zbigniew Brzezinski, Assistant to the President for National Security Affairs, and Hamilton Jordan, Assistant to the President;
—Vice President Mondale.

The President returned to the White House from Camp David.

The President met with leaders of religious organizations in the Cabinet Room at the White House to discuss foreign assistance programs.

August 1

The President met at the White House with:
—Dr. Brzezinski;
—Secretary Brown and Representatives George H. Mahon of Texas and Jack Edwards of Alabama;
—members of the Vietnam Veterans in Congress;

—Vice President Mondale, Adm. Stansfield Turner, Director of Central Intelligence, Dr. Brzezinski, and Mr. Jordan;

—Senator Thomas F. Eagleton of Missouri;

—James T. McIntyre, Jr., Director of the Office of Management and Budget.

The President attended a portion of the White House reception for Asian Americans held on the State Floor.

The President announced the persons who will represent the United States at the inauguration ceremonies for Julio Cesar Turbay Ayala as President of Colombia, held August 6–9. Secretary of the Treasury W. Michael Blumenthal will head the delegation, attending as Personal Representative of the President and with the rank of Special Ambassador. The members of the delegation, also with the rank of Special Ambassador, will be:

DIEGO C. ASENCIO, U.S. Ambassador to Colombia;

VIRON P. VAKY, Assistant Secretary of State for Inter-American Affairs;

JOHN V. BEHEN, president, Advisory Realty Corp., and president, Behen Storage and Warehouse Corp., Everett, Mass.;

ALBERT BILDNER, president, Business Marketing Corp. for New York City, N.Y.;

OSCAR GARCIA-RIVERA, member, U.S. National Commission for UNESCO, Washington, D.C.;

PHYLLIS LANDRIEU, vice president, Louisiana State Health Coordinating Council, New Orleans;

LUIS J. LAUREDO, director of international commerce, State of Florida, Miami;

WILLIAM B. SCHWARTZ III, First National Bank of Atlanta, Ga.;

JOAN F. TOBIN, president, Tobin Enterprises, Washington, D.C.

August 2

The President met at the White House with:

—Dr. Brzezinski;

—Frank B. Moore, Assistant to the President for Congressional Liaison;

—Members of the House of Representatives to discuss civil service reform;

—Assistant Secretary of Energy Omi G. Walden;

—Mrs. Carter, for lunch.

In a ceremony in the Oval Office, the President received diplomatic credentials from Ambasadors U Hla Shwe of the Socialist Republic of Burma, Noor Ahmad Noor of the Democratic Republic of Afghanistan, Klos Visessurakarn of the Kingdom of Thailand, Mohamed Morlai Turay of the Republic of Sierra Leone, and José Llado y Fernandez-Urrutia of Spain.

The President attended a portion of the briefing on civil service reform given by administration officials for business leaders in the State Dining Room at the White House.

August 3

The President met at the White House with:

—Dr. Brzezinski;

—Mr. Moore;

—Representatives Thomas J. Downey of New York and Bob Carr of Michigan.

The President attended a portion of the briefing on administration policies given by administration officials for civic leaders from the New Jersey area in Room 450 of the Old Executive Office Building.

August 4

The President met at the White House with:

—Dr. Brzezinski;

—Vice President Mondale, Secretary Vance, Secretary Brown, Dr. Brzezinski, and Mr. Jordan;

—Secretary of Energy James R. Schlesinger;

—Charles L. Schultze, Chairman of the Council of Economic Advisers;

—Robert J. McCloskey, U.S. Ambassador to Greece.

The President has declared a major disaster for the State of Texas as a result of severe storms and flooding, beginning about August 1, which caused extensive public and private property damage.

The White House announced that applications are now available for the White House Fellowship program for 1979–80. The program is open to all U.S. citizens, except those in civilian Federal positions. Each fellow works for a Cabinet officer or senior member of the White House staff, and participates in a program including seminars with top Government officials, leading scholars, and journalists who deal with the National Government. Application forms and additional information can be obtained by sending a postcard to the President's Commission on White House Fellowships, Washington, D.C. 20415.

NOMINATIONS SUBMITTED TO THE SENATE

The following list does not include promotions of members of the Uniformed Services, nominations to the Service Academies, or nominations of Foreign Service officers.

Submitted August 1, 1978

KARL SMITH BOWERS, of South Carolina, to be Administrator of the Federal Highway Administration, vice William Meredith Cox, resigned.

THOMAS A. WISEMAN, JR., of Tennessee, to be United States District Judge for the Middle District of Tennessee, vice Frank Gray, Jr., retired.

NORMA LEVY SHAPIRO, of Pennsylvania, to be United States District Judge for the Eastern District of Pennsylvania, vice James H. Gorbey, deceased.

NOMINATIONS—Continued

Submitted August 3, 1978

THEODORE MCMILLIAN, of Missouri, to be United States Circuit Judge for the Eighth Circuit, vice William H. Webster, resigned.

The following-named persons to be members of the Board of Directors of the United States Railway Association for the terms indicated:

STANTON P. SENDER, of the District of Columbia, for the remainder of the term expiring July 8, 1980, vice W. K. Smith, elevated.

NATHANIEL WELCH, of Georgia, for the term expiring January 10, 1983, vice Charles B. Shuman, term expired.

For terms expiring July 8, 1984

JAMES E. BURKE, of New Jersey (reappointment).

ROBERT G. FLANNERY, of California, vice Gale B. Aydelott, term expired.

CHECKLIST OF WHITE HOUSE PRESS RELEASES

The following releases of the Office of the White House Press Secretary, distributed during the period covered by this issue, are not included in the issue.

Released August 1, 1978

Announcement: nomination of Norma L. Shapiro to be United States District Judge for the Eastern District of Pennsylvania, and Thomas A. Wiseman, Jr., to be United States District Judge for the Middle District of Tennessee

Released August 2, 1978

Announcement: commitments of support by business organizations for the administration's anti-inflation policy, and anti-inflation action by the Office of Federal Procurement Policy

Released August 3, 1978

Announcement: nomination of Theodore McMillian to be United States Circuit Judge for the Eighth Circuit

ACTS APPROVED BY THE PRESIDENT

Approved July 31, 1978

H.J. Res. 1024_____ Public Law 95–330
A joint resolution making urgent supplemental appropriations for the Department of Agriculture, Agricultural Stabilization and Conservation Service, and for other purposes for the fiscal year ending September 30, 1978.

Approved August 2, 1978

H.R. 11877_____ Public Law 95–331
Peace Corps Act Amendments of 1978.

H.J. Res. 945_____ Public Law 95–332
A joint resolution making an urgent appropriation for the black lung program of the Department of Labor, and for other purposes, for the fiscal year ending September 30, 1978.

Approved August 3, 1978

H.R. 13385_____ Public Law 95–333
An act to provide for a temporary increase in the public debt limit.

H.R. 1751_____ Private Law 95–42
An act for the relief of Lucy Davao Jara Graham.

H.R. 2555_____ Private Law 95–43
An act for the relief of Michelle Lagrosa Sese.

ACTS APPROVED—Continued

Approved August 3—Continued

H.R. 2945_____ Private Law 95–44
An act for the relief of Mrs. Amelia Doria Nicholson.

H.R. 3995_____ Private Law 95–45
An act for the relief of Habib Haddad.

H.R. 4607_____ Private Law 95–46
An act for the relief of William Mok.

H.R. 5928_____ Private Law 95–47
An act for the relief of Miss Coralia Raposo.

Approved August 4, 1978

H.R. 11504_____ Public Law 95–334
Agricultural Credit Act of 1978.

H.R. 12933_____ Public Law 95–335
Department of Transportation and Related Agencies Appropriation Act, 1979.

H.R. 10569_____ Public Law 95–336
Alcohol and Drug Abuse Education Amendments of 1978.

S. 785_____ Public Law 95–337
An act to declare that all right, title, and interest of the United States in two thousand seven hundred acres, more or less, are hereby held in trust for the Paiute and Shoshone Tribes of the Fallon Indian Reservation and Colony, Fallon, Nevada, to promote the economic self-sufficiency of the Paiute and Shoshone Tribes, and for other purposes.

H.R. 1420_____ Private Law 95–48
An act for the relief of Umberto Ruffolo.

PRESIDENTIAL DOCUMENTS

Norfolk, Virginia

Remarks at the Commissioning Ceremony for the U.S.S. Mississippi. **August 5, 1978**

Senator Eastland, Senator Stennis, Governor Finch, Secretary of Defense Harold Brown, Secretary of the Navy Claytor, Admiral Kidd, Admiral Rickover, Captain Hekman, distinguished officers and men of the U.S.S. Mississippi, patriotic Americans who have listened, I am sure, with great attention to the fine address that we have just had, reminding us of the basic principles which have made our country so great:

It's good to be back here in Norfolk, on the Norfolk Navy Base, after so many years. This is where I started my naval career. It's where I started my married life. It's where my oldest son was born. And as has already been mentioned, my last tour of duty here in Norfolk was as a young officer, a lieutenant junior grade, serving on the U.S.S. *Mississippi.*

I was electronics officer, gunnery officer, doing experimental work. The U.S.S. *Mississippi* was converted into an experimental gunnery and radar ship on which we tried out new naval techniques. You just saw the finest missile-launching system on Earth, and just aft of those missiles is a 5-inch 54 gun. The first 5-inch 54 gun was fired on a ship under my supervision as electronics officer, on the U.S.S. *Mississippi.* Those were not as exciting, perhaps, as some of the new developments in a modern navy, but after World War II, they started us on the road to innovation and flexibility that has kept our Nation strong.

It's a pleasure for me as President to share this occasion with representatives of the people of Mississippi. I am very glad to see here Mississippi's Governor Cliff Finch and his daughter, Janet, who is the U.S.S. *Mississippi*'s sponsor.

I'm also glad that Marine Corps Commandant General Lou Wilson, another son of Mississippi, who has devoted his life to our Nation's service, could be with us on this ceremony.

And most of all, I'm honored to share this dais with Senator James Eastland and Senator John Stennis. Senator Eastland, as President pro tempore of the Senate, is a senior Member of that body. He's the chairman of the Judiciary Committee and has served our Nation with integrity, with distinction, and with courage for many years, and of that, Senator Eastland, I and the people of our country are very proud. Thank you very much.

Senator John Stennis has worked long and hard as chairman of the Senate

1383

Armed Services Committee to promote our national security. It's very fitting that this new guided missile cruiser be named for the home State of a man who has done so much to keep our Nation safe and strong.

In this ceremony today, we are commemorating the sources of our Nation's strength, honoring the men and women who defend it, and rededicating ourselves to the principle that our national defense is the surest protector of our liberty.

Exactly 200 years ago, early in our War for Independence, that principle led us to complete our first international alliance—with the Government of France. Fifteen hundred miles from where we are today, in the town of Pascagoula, Mississippi, the Ambassador of France is today commissioning a new American destroyer, the *Comte de Grasse*. These twin ceremonies underscore our unity with the great democracies of the world in defending freedom everywhere.

The vessel we are commissioning, on which I stand, embodies the tradition of strength. This is the fourth U.S.S. *Mississippi,* the fourth to advance our Nation's interests in peace and to maintain our security in time of war. Her predecessors served our Nation during some of the most crucial times in its history.

The first *Mississippi* was Commodore Perry's flagship on his historic voyage to Japan. The second *Mississippi* sailed with President Theodore Roosevelt's Great White Fleet, serving notice of America's emergence as a naval power early in this century. And the battleship *Mississippi,* on which I later served, earned eight battle stars in World War II, participating in some of that war's most important Pacific engagements. I'm equally proud to be here today as this new U.S.S. *Mississippi* assumes this great heritage and these great responsibilities.

This nuclear cruiser will be devoted to many varied duties, not the least of which is the assignment to protect in time of war, and to escort in war and peace, such great naval ships as the U.S.S. *Nimitz,* the nuclear aircraft carrier just behind the audience.

It's interesting to note, as Admiral Rickover pointed out to me a few minutes ago, that 58 percent of the crew of this modern warship, in fighting trim today, well-trained, have never been to sea before on another ship. This is a credit to the Navy. It shows the youth, the vigor, the competence of men who man our ships, and it shows the high technical skill needed to man a nuclear-powered warship in today's modern world.

In recent years, as Senator Stennis pointed out, we saw confidence in our Government and in our Nation falter, and belief in our national strength and character has been called into question. But our country always responded to challenge, and we have and will maintain this strength that is so crucial. We have not and we will not ever become a second-rate power in any respect, and you can depend on that.

No matter what is said, often by well-meaning people, we now maintain, the United States of America now maintains the greatest military arsenal on Earth, to protect and to preserve our freedom and liberty but, most important of all—and I speak for all men and women in uniform, or who have ever served in uniform—to preserve peace. No group of people wants peace more than those who are ready to give their lives in time of war. We possess the finest service men and women in the world—people of dedication, of conviction, and of courage.

We've put our national reputation forward, and we are known once again as the defender of basic and inalienable human rights across the globe, which we cherish and maintain here in our great country. And we've restored throughout our country the confidence that the United States stands strongest among nations and also stands strongest for what is right and decent and honorable and moral. That is the strength of our country.

We are respected by our foes, our potential adversaries, because of our strength of arms. And we are respected by our friends and our allies for the strength of our convictions. We are meeting the challenge of this great age, and we will continue to meet the challenges of this and future eras.

I have pledged as President—as a navy man—that the United States will maintain military and naval forces which can never be challenged successfully by any other power on Earth.

We will continue the development and the modernization of the submarine-launched ballistic missile component of our strategic nuclear triad to ensure that no potential adversary would dare to threaten our security.

We will enhance and support our strategic capabilities with conventional weapons such as this new cruiser. Ships like the *Mississippi* also play a vital role in our air defenses and in upgrading our anti-air warfare capabilities.

We will continue to dispatch our naval forces to patrol the waters of the world and to keep them safe for ourselves and for our allies. Our Navy, with such ships as the *Mississippi,* will always remain a strong reminder to our foes and a source of reassurance to our friends.

This great new fighting ship underscores our commitment to the security of our own people and those of our allies, our dedication to devising and deploying the finest forces on Earth, and our spirit of faith in our Nation to the causes which have made it great.

This spirit of faith and devotion is evidenced nowhere better than in you, the men and women of our Armed Forces. I know that all Americans share with me a deep appreciation for your efforts, your courage, and your dedication. You are the most important element of our Nation's defense, and I am determined that all our service persons receive the recognition which you deserve.

On this occasion, as we reaffirm our dedication to keeping those defenses strong, we must proceed, in the words of the ship's motto and the State motto of Mississippi: *Virtute et Armis.* With virtue and with arms, our strength will not falter, nor will our dedication to the ideals which have guided our Nation since its inception. We will maintain the virtue of our country through our own actions, our deeds, our public statements, and our deep commitments, and with arms we will maintain as best we can peace throughout the world and, in all cases, the security of our country.

We will remain a nation founded in freedom. We will maintain our freedom grounded in strength.

Thank you very much.

NOTE: The President spoke at 11:40 a.m. at Pier 12, Norfolk Naval Base.

Prior to his remarks, the President toured the base and then boarded the U.S.S. *Mississippi.* Escorted by Adm. Hyman G. Rickover, Deputy Commander for Nuclear Propulsion, Naval Sea Systems Command, Department of the Navy, Adm. I. C. Kidd, Commander in Chief, U.S. Atlantic Fleet, and Capt. Peter Hekman, prospective Commanding Officer, U.S.S. *Mississippi,* the President toured the ship and viewed a demonstration at the missile launcher site.

Following the ceremony, the President went to the Norfolk Naval Air Station, where he attended a reception for Virginia community and business leaders.

Wilson, North Carolina

Remarks at a Democratic Party Rally for John Ingram. August 5, 1978

Senator Bob Morgan, Senator [Governor] Jim Hunt, one of the finest products that Wilson, North Carolina, has ever produced, future Senator John Ingram, my good friend, distinguished members of the State government, and Members of Congress whom I'll mention a little later:

Let me say that I'm very proud to be the first President of the United States to come to Wilson, North Carolina. If they had known what I've seen today in the form of a welcome, all of them would have been here, just like I've come today.

It's good to come to wide-awake Wilson. [*Laughter*] And I hope that after you've lost your rooster that used to wake people up, that you'll still be able to keep the image that you have now.

I had planned today to bring Joe Califano with me. He decided not to come. He discovered that not only is North Carolina the number one tobacco-producing State, but that you produce more bricks than anyone in the Nation as well. [*Laughter*]

He did encourage me to come, though. He said it was time for the White House staff to start smoking something regular. [*Laughter*] I would like to say a word in his defense, because as I am a farmer, as I am deeply interested in the small farmers of this Nation, as I am deeply committed, and permanently, to a fine tobacco loan program, obviously I'm also interested in the health of America.

I would say that the tobacco industry, the tobacco farmers, the Federal Government, all citizens want to have an accurate and an enlightened education program and research program to make the smoking of tobacco even more safe than it is today. And we'll continue these joint programs within which I don't see any incompatibility.

I've seen great strides made in our country in recent years in the proper understanding of the farm community. My own people, the Carter family, moved to Georgia from North Carolina. They were farmers. They produced the two greatest crops in my life—peanuts and tobacco.

And as I drove in from the airport, I felt at home, because I saw the tobacco fields and the cotton fields, the sweet potato fields, the soybean fields that have made this not only a great producing area but a great marketing area. And I know that in the marketing of flue-cured tobacco, Wilson, North Carolina, has the greatest market in the entire world.

My sister moved back to North Carolina and lives not far from here in Fayetteville, North Carolina. And I think you all know, as has already been mentioned before, that I feel an additional kinship for you, because in 1976, when I, as a lonely candidate, came into North Carolina to face formidable opposition, you gave me your hand, you gave me your hearts, you gave me your votes, and you helped put me in the White House. And I won't ever forget it.

I'm particularly glad to be in North Carolina because of some of the men on the platform here today, particularly your great Democratic Senator, Bob Morgan. He's a man of courage. He's a man of great intelligence. He's a man whose roots have given him a proper perspective. And although he represents, of course, in his decisions in the Senate, the entire Nation, his heart and his soul and his great allegiance is to the people of this great State.

I served as Governor before I became President, and I've seen at first hand the superb, young leadership exemplified by Jim Hunt. He still works closely with me.

And as we have recently decided to try to make more effective the joint effort of local officials, State officials, and Federal officials in controlling crime, Jim Hunt has been in the leadership among the 50 Governors who helped to make these programs control crime better.

I'm very proud to feel, also, a certain kinship with John Ingram. If there ever was a man who was an underdog and has shown in every statewide race an ability to come from behind and win, he's it, and he's going to do the same thing in 1978.

He's a man who's not afraid to fight against political odds. And he's a man who's not afraid to fight against other odds, when he's trying to bring a correction to a system that doesn't treat American citizens fairly. He was the man who rooted out discrimination against women in insurance rates, and he's the man who rooted out discrimination against fine young men in insurance rates. And he's the one, also, who fought against the indiscriminate overcharging of tobacco farmers for insurance. And he's the man who will take the same kind of fight to Washington, to join with me and Bob Morgan to give you an even better life than you have already.

I agree with him. I think North Carolina needs a United States Senator who doesn't think that veterans benefits and tobacco loans are the same as welfare.

I would like to say a few words to you today about some of the problems that I faced when I became your President. It's not an easy job. It's a very complicated responsibility. It requires good support and understanding among the American people, and it requires a certain human sensitivity to people's needs.

I felt when I became President that the farmers of our Nation were approaching a time of repetition of the devastating years of the Hoover Depression. Prices were going down; uncertainty prevailed in farm markets. We needed a new agricultural bill to give farmers some security, some sureness about the future, some stability in their lives, and a right to produce food and fiber and other products that help the American consumer to have low prices and high quality.

The agriculture bill of 1977, passed by the Democratic Congress, has brought that improvement already to farmers' lives. It didn't go into effect until last October 1. Nineteen hundred and seventy-seven, in spite of the very lowest prices we've had in a long time, saw a world's record in the export of farmers' products overseas—$24 billion in exports in foreign markets.

Your number one export product is tobacco. Georgia's number one export product is tobacco. But we also combine that with the export of wheat, soybeans, cotton, and other basic crops, to give the rest of the world good, stable prices and high-quality products and to put our farmers back on the road to prosperity. That was a record year. But I predict today, and I believe my prediction will come true, that we'll see a new record set in 1978 in the export of American farm products overseas.

I was concerned, also, about the low family incomes of farmers. And under the new legislation passed last year, implemented for the first time this year, we will see net farm income, income after expenses, increase 25 percent—no less than $5½ billion more in the farmers' pockets, that will go to make everybody have a better life.

I would say that one of the most important problems that I have at this time is inflation. This is the kind of secret robbery that hurts every American citizen, every American family.

I'm determined to do what I can to control inflation. We have been bringing down the budget deficit. I know how North Carolina people feel. You'd rather have services met that the American people require, but you would like to have a balanced budget as well. And that's my goal along with yours.

Let me give you some quick statistics. In 1976, when I campaigned in your State for President, the Federal budget deficit was in the sixties of billions of dollars, 1976 fiscal year. In 1978, we cut it down in the fifties of billions of dollars; 1979, in the forties of billions of dollars; 1980, I promise you today that it will be down in the thirties of billions of dollars, and we're headed down to a balanced budget as fast as we can.

We're also trying to get control of the Federal bureaucracy. When I ran for President, one of the most frequent requests that I had from the American people was, "Give us a government in Washington of which we can be proud, a government that's efficient and effective." And I believe along with you that American taxpayers deserve a good return on the investment that you put in the Government in Washington, and that's what I'm going to give you.

I want to get the Federal Government out of the affairs of private citizens as much as possible. I'm a small businessman myself. I own a cotton gin, a peanut sheller. I sold fertilizing seed to farmers. I know what it means to have unnecessary reports and regulations and redtape. So, we've got some good people in office now, in Washington, who are trying to turn this trend around. It's not easy.

Last year, OSHA eliminated 1,100 regulations in 1 day, and I can tell you that this year we're going to eliminate another 1,000 regulations in OSHA. And we're trying to make the Government regulations so they're written in plain English. We're even requiring that the people who

write them sign them. And I believe that you will see this good impact in all our communities in the years to come.

Let me make one comment to you about the biggest problem that I faced and you faced when I came in office. It's already been mentioned. When I became President, we had just had a report from the Labor Department that 8 percent of all American citizens were out of work. We've changed that. In the last 18 months, we've had a net increase of 6½ million jobs for Americans. We've cut the unemployment rate almost 2 percent. And with the good leadership of Jim Hunt in North Carolina, you've cut the unemployment rate in the last year and a half by 50 percent, better than almost any State I know. So, we believe in putting people in this country back to work.

Let me say one additional word—about defense. Our country is now at peace. We haven't had an American soldier fire a gun in combat or anger in the last 18 months. And my prayer is that when I go out of office, we'll still have a nation at peace. That peace can only be ensured with a strong defense.

This morning I went to Norfolk— where I first served in the Navy on the old U.S.S. *Mississippi*—to commission a new United States Ship *Mississippi*. It's a nuclear carrier. It's designed to exemplify the high commitment that all of us have to giving our Nation a good, strong defense. We have that commitment. And we'll never see our Nation second to any in our ability to fight, if it were necessary, and to prevent fighting by our adherence to peace and a strong military establishment that will always be there, with your support.

I would like to say one other thing in closing. There is a time in our country to recognize basic human rights. One of those rights is the ability to speak, even to shout when other people are trying to speak.[1] [*Applause*] Let me say to you that that's one basic right that I would never want to see eliminated in our country. Our Nation was founded on the principle of people's liberty, people's freedom, people's individuality, a right to express ourselves, to stand on our own feet, to make our voices heard, to stand for decency and honesty and morality—a nation, through strength, to lead the rest of the world to peace.

We've never betrayed those principles. And one of the things that I wanted to do when I came into the President's office, after Vietnam, after Watergate, after the CIA revelations, was to have some standard that I could raise to make Americans once again part of their country. And as long as I'm in the White House, I not only will do everything I can in this country but I'll do everything I can throughout the world to make human rights be two words that the world will never forget. And we'll be the ones to stand more strongly for those rights.

America is a religious nation. North Carolina is a State whose families, whose communities are centered around the church. No matter what your own beliefs might be, we know that God teaches us to care for others, to preserve principles in spite of hardship, to exhibit courage when our Nation or our families or our own selves are being tested through difficult times.

We are not afraid of the future. We know that our Nation has an inherent strength derived, to a major degree, from belief in God. One of the things that I did when I was campaigning through North Carolina was to say quite openly that I was a believer in God, that I was not ashamed of it, that I was not afraid to say so publicly. As a Baptist, I also believe in

the separation of church and state. But those guidelines that often control our lives, which always should control our lives, should also control our Nation.

We've a strong nation. But we don't have to be a bully to show it. We want to be the kind of nation that arouses the understanding and the admiration and the friendship of smaller countries, those that are poor, those that are uncertain, those that are new, those whose citizens might be black or brown or yellow. We're trying to extend the influence of our Nation and its principles throughout the world in a good, decent way, to make Americans proud.

We have a good agenda for the Democratic Party. But there's no way that I can be successful as your President in putting forward those proposals unless I have a team effort.

The most important element of that team is obviously the American citizens, yourselves, who share the same principles and hopes that I do. But I also need a good team in the Democratic Party, a party which has always mirrored accurately what North Carolinians want and in which you believe.

Bob Morgan, Jim Hunt, in the future, as you know, the fine Senator John Ingram for next year, Congressman Jones, Richardson Pryor, others, your own Congressman Fountain—we have a need to have a strong team. And I hope that this year you remember all the Democratic delegation, measure them with the strictest standards. You will find them not wanting. They need your help.

If there's one characteristic of our party which has always been crucial to us, it's closeness to the people. We'll never betray your trust. We recognize that you are the ones who put us in office. We recognize that we have to please you to stay there. And we can only please you if we understand what you want our Nation to be.

---

[1] The President was referring to a group of people demonstrating near the audience.

I have great confidence in the economic strength, the political strength, the military strength of our Nation. It's not getting weaker. Don't believe anyone when they say that our Army or Navy or Air Force or Marines can't handle any challenge that comes to us from any possible adversarial foe. We are the strongest now. We'll always be the strongest militarily. And with your help, with your cooperation, with your support of good candidates, we'll keep a team, a Democratic team that will make our Nation in the future even greater than it has been in the past.

We have now and we will always have the greatest nation on Earth: the United States of America. I'm proud to be your President.

Thank you very much.

NOTE: The President spoke at 2:06 p.m. at the Wilson County Public Library. Following the rally, the President went to the Heart of Wilson Hotel, where he had a luncheon meeting with Democratic Party leaders.

Wilson, North Carolina

Remarks at Growers Cooperative Warehouse, Inc. August 5, 1978

Jim, thank you very much. I've been to a lot of tobacco auction barns in Georgia; it's the first time I've ever seen a sale on Saturday. [*Laughter*] And I especially appreciate both the buyers and the auctioneer and all of you for coming here to let me see at first hand the beautiful quality of your tobacco in North Carolina this year and to take at least part credit for the wonderful price that you are receiving for this high-quality tobacco.

As I told a large crowd earlier this day, my ancestors came from North Carolina. And they were tobacco farmers, and all of my ancestors have been farmers. Nei-

ther my father nor any of his ancestors have ever finished high school before. We grew up working people and with the realization that hard work and honest work is the foundation of agriculture all over the world.

Many kinds of crops have been almost totally mechanized. But tobacco, as you know, is one kind of production that still requires a large investment in cash money, that has a doubtful prospect each year for a successful crop and a successful market, and where hard, back-breaking labor is still a prerequisite to a profitable season.

In North Carolina, a third of the families who live on the farm make their income on 10 acres of productive land or less.

There is a lot of talk about maintaining the loan support price for tobacco on the one hand, and having a good health program on the other hand. I think anyone knows that there is no incompatibility between these two commitments. We must have stable agricultural programs, a stable price, an orderly marketing system. And because of the high quality of your crop, there's very little, if any, cost to the Government for this stable production schedule.

There are 2 million families in our country that depend for their livelihood on tobacco farmers; a fourth of them are in North Carolina. It's your number one agricultural export crop. In Georgia, tobacco is the number one agricultural export crop. And I think a good, sound education program for American citizens and a good research program for the benefit of American citizens can let us maintain good health in America and also a stable agriculture environment and industry, including, of course, the production of tobacco.

As long as I'm in the White House and have people like Bob Morgan, Congressman Fountain, and others to help me, we'll have a good loan program for tobacco in the Federal Government. You can depend on that.

Let me just add one other point. I've come here as President of our great country to learn from you, to share with you a responsibility for government. I have a lot of responsibilities on my shoulder, like you do in your own family or community circles—a responsibility to hold down inflation, a responsibility to prevent excessive Government spending, a responsibility to cut down unnecessary Government involvement in the lives of the people who comprise our private enterprise system, a responsibility to maintain the military strength of the United States, to make sure that when other nations look at us, people from all over the world say, "What is the United States of America?", that we can be proud of what they see.

Our Nation is one of great strength. God has blessed us in many ways—with a form of government now more than 200 years old, when individual human beings, no matter how different they might be from one another, could stand and speak as they choose, develop those qualities of individuality and difference that, put together, give us a strong America. He's given us good land over which we exercise stewardship, passing it down to our sons and daughters and their families to keep in a productive state. And when I assess what is the very important differences, or difference, between our country and others that's most valuable, where we have the clearest advantage over all other nations on Earth, it is in the productivity of our land and the productivity of the American farmer.

That's something that's not warlike in nature. It doesn't hurt other people. It keeps our Nation strong and influential in a good way, and it helps other people throughout the world have a better life.

I was concerned when I became President, as a farmer, about farmers. We've got a good sound administration. Bob Bergland, Secretary of Agriculture—he's not a college professor or economist exercising his theories in the Agriculture Department in Washington; he's a dirt farmer. When he came back from the war, he couldn't make a living at home. He had to go down to Florida as an itinerant farmworker. He went back up to northern Minnesota and borrowed money and rented some land and, eventually, built up a farm in his own family of about 600 acres.

He understands farmers. The Vice President does, too. And we've tried to set into progress a program, with the help of the Members of Congress and the Senate, that would turn the tide, because I could see very clearly that unless something was done, we were faced in this country with another Hoover Depression for farmers. Prices were going down; nobody knew what was going to happen next. Under the last administration, exports were turned on and turned off so many times that our foreign buyers didn't have any confidence in American markets.

On the spur of the moment, 32 oil seeds were cut off from being sold to Japan, including soybeans, including peanuts. And we saw the interruption of corn and wheat sales to other countries stopped and started so many times that they not only began to buy those products in other countries but other countries began to produce them. And it took us a long time to turn that around.

But last year, in 1977, with Bob Bergland's leadership, we had the highest level of farm exports in the history of our country—$24 billion. And as you know, farm prices were cheap. That was a lot of tons. This year, we're going to break that record again. And I can predict to you, as I did earlier today, that the net farm income in this country this year will go up 25 percent, with a net additional amount of money going into the farmers' pockets, after expenses, of $5½ or $6 billion.

Now, I know farmers, because they're in my family and they're my neighbors at home. Farmers don't want a handout. Farmers want a chance to take a chance in farming. But they want stable prices. They don't want government to disrupt their lives. They want to have an ability to get a loan with good collateral and face the future, based on their own commitment and their own hard work.

I think we've got a good partnership now between government and agriculture. And I don't think it's any accident that this year the tobacco harvest will be the best and the most profitable, perhaps, in the history of North Carolina. Opening prices for tobacco were 35 or 40 cents higher than they were last year, maybe the highest in the history of our country. A lot of it is, because of you, good quality production. Many of you signed up for the four-leaf program. Many of you didn't sign up and left those bottom four leaves voluntarily. We're getting the reputation of being producers of tobacco who are interested in quality, and that will pay rich dividends for you in the future.

Well, I'm proud of you and I'm proud of the partnership that we've formed. You've got a great commissioner of agriculture, as you well know. I was bragging about him at lunch. I'll let him tell you what I said. But anyone who can bray like a donkey and be as good a commissioner as he is, provides a fine, clear voice when he speaks of North Carolina in Washington. He's the only commissioner of agriculture I know that can let his voice be heard in Washington without using a telephone. [*Laughter*]

One more word. So, let me say once again that I'm thankful for what you've done. And I hope that you'll let me hear from you about how our Government, your Government in Washington, can be even more helpful to you as we make agriculture in our Nation continue to be the most important strategic asset of the greatest nation on Earth.

Thank you very much.

NOTE: The President spoke at 4:13 p.m. after touring the warehouse and observing a tobacco auction. He was introduced by Jim Graham, North Carolina commissioner of agriculture.

Death of Pope Paul VI

Statement by the President.   August 6, 1978

I was deeply saddened to learn of the death of Pope Paul VI, a man whose life and works have served me personally as a source of great moral inspiration. As a man of peace and profound spirituality, he will be greatly missed not only by all Roman Catholics but by all people, whatever their religious convictions.

Of Pope Paul's many contributions, two stand out for me at this sad moment: first, his untiring efforts in the ecumenical movement. Not only was he inspired in the cause of humanity to pursue greater unity of purpose within the Catholic Church, but also among all other faiths. Second, Pope Paul's world travels, at no small expense to his own physical well-being, exemplified his role of pilgrim, carrying the message of peace and love to the far corners of the world, including an inspiring visit to the United States.

During his 15 years as Pontiff, the voice of Paul VI served as a clear, moral beacon to a troubled world. With his passing, we have all been deprived of a strong voice for reason, for moderation, and for peace.

NOTE: The following announcement was released by the White House Press Office on August 10:

Mrs. Rosalynn Carter will head the U.S. delegation of five dignitaries who will attend the funeral of Pope Paul VI in Rome on Saturday.

In addition to Mrs. Carter, the delegates will be Senator Edward M. Kennedy (D–Mass.), Gov. Hugh L. Carey (D–N.Y.), Representative Robert N. Giaimo (D–Conn.), David Walters, Personal Representative of the President to the Vatican, and Leonel J. Castillo, Commissioner of Immigration and Naturalization.

On Saturday, August 12, at 6 p.m. (Rome time), the representatives will attend the state funeral for His Holiness Paul VI at St. Peter's Square. On Sunday there will be a reception for the Sacred College of Cardinals in the Consistorial Hall of the Papal Palace, Vatican City, in order to receive condolences from foreign delegations. The American delegation will attend the reception.

With the exception of Senator Kennedy, the delegation will leave by military jet from Andrews Air Force Base at 9 p.m. tonight, and arrive in Rome at approximately 1:30 p.m. (Rome time) Friday. Senator Kennedy will remain in Washington for legislative work Friday, then fly to Rome in time for the funeral.

The entire group will return to Washington Sunday evening, August 13.

Camp David Meeting on the Middle East

Statement by the White House Press Secretary. August 8, 1978

The President is pleased to announce that President Sadat and Prime Minister Begin have accepted an invitation to come to Camp David on September 5 for a meeting with the President to seek a framework for peace in the Middle East.

All three leaders agree that there is no task more important than this search for peace. Secretary Vance has informed the President that both Prime Minister Begin and President Sadat have welcomed this

meeting, and the President is gratified by their response.

Each of the three leaders will be accompanied by a small number of their principal advisers, and no specific time has been set for the duration of the meeting.

NOTE: Press Secretary Jody Powell read the statement at 11:33 a.m. to reporters assembled in the Briefing Room at the White House. As printed above, this item follows the text of the White House press release.

Fire Prevention Week, 1978

Proclamation 4581.   August 8, 1978

By the President of the United States of America

A Proclamation

Fire causes more loss of life and property in the United States than all other natural disasters combined. In the home, fire is the second most frequent cause of accidental death. Volunteer and professional firefighters bear a disproportionate burden of the human costs of fire; firefighting is still America's most hazardous profession.

Every year in this decade 7,500 U.S. citizens have died, 310,000 have been injured and more than $4 billion worth of personal property has been destroyed. America's fire incidents, casualties, and dollar loss per capita are among the very highest in the industrialized world.

As evidence of my strong personal concern about our fire problem, I have proposed a reorganization plan that would put the federal government's principal fire programs in a new Federal Emergency Management Agency. This agency would coordinate America's disaster preparedness, mitigation and response efforts. But the federal government cannot reduce America's fire losses by itself. The public and private sector—all individuals, organizations and governmental entities—must help. Together we can eliminate this unnecessary life-threatening destruction.

Now, THEREFORE, I, JIMMY CARTER, President of the United States of America, do hereby designate October 8–14, 1978, as Fire Prevention Week.

Because fire deaths most often occur in homes, I call upon American families and other property owners to install smoke detectors, to practice exit drills, and to be especially vigilant in guarding against fires caused by cooking and fires caused by smoking materials, which cause the greatest number of fires and greatest proportion of losses in homes.

I support and encourage the cooperative efforts of private enterprise and government in developing low cost residential sprinkler systems and I urge commercial and government property owners to install sprinklers in both new and older buildings, especially those buildings in which large numbers of people gather.

I urge all agencies of Federal, state and local government involved in the planning and implementation of programs directed to finding solutions to such national concerns as energy conservation, environmental protection, and economic well-being to fully consider the effects of their programs on the fire safety of the environment in which Americans live and work.

I encourage the fire service, police, prosecutors, the insurance industry, and government to work together to remove incentives for arson, and to improve arson detection and prosecution so that we can begin to eliminate this costly, often life-threatening crime.

I urge officials in private industry and in government who are responsible for using or regulating hazardous materials to seek and implement measures to significantly reduce the possibility of life loss in the event of manufacturing, transportation, or storage accidents and to assist the fire services in preparing for such disasters should they occur.

Finally, I call upon the members of the Joint Council of National Fire Service Organizations, the National Fire Protection Association, all other organizations concerned with fire safety, and the National Fire Prevention and Control Administration to provide the leadership, planning, and innovation necessary for an effective national fire prevention and control effort.

IN WITNESS WHEREOF, I have hereunto set my hand this eighth day of August, in the year of our Lord nineteen hundred seventy-eight, and of the Independence of the United States of America the two hundred and third.

JIMMY CARTER

[Filed with the Office of the Federal Register, 10:52 a.m., August 9, 1978]

General Pulaski's Memorial Day, 1978

Proclamation 4582.   August 8, 1978

By the President of the United States of America

A Proclamation

One hundred and ninety-nine years ago, the Polish patriot Casimir Pulaski gave his life fighting for freedom in the American Revolution.

General Pulaski, an exile from his native Poland, arrived in 1777 to join the Revolutionary Army. He fought courageously at Brandywine and in other battles, and he formed and commanded the famous cavalry unit, the Pulaski Legion, which fought nobly in the cause of American independence.

General Pulaski died on October 11, 1779 of wounds received in the Battle of Savannah two days earlier. Nearly two hundred years later we continue to pay tribute to him and to the millions of Americans of Polish descent who have played such an important part in founding our country, making it grow, and preserving its ideals.

Now, THEREFORE, I, JIMMY CARTER, President of the United States of America, do hereby designate Wednesday, October 11, 1978, as General Pulaski's Memorial Day and I direct the appropriate Government officials to display the flag of the United States on all Government buildings on that day.

I also invite the people of the United States to honor the memory of General Pulaski by holding appropriate exercises and ceremonies in suitable places throughout our Nation.

IN WITNESS WHEREOF, I have hereunto set my hand this eighth day of August, in the year of our Lord nineteen hundred seventy-eight, and of the Independence of the United States of America the two hundred and third.

JIMMY CARTER

[Filed with the Office of the Federal Register, 10:53 a.m., August 9, 1978]

White Cane Safety Day, 1978

Proclamation 4583. August 8, 1978

By the President of the United States of America

A Proclamation

For the more than six million Americans who suffer severe visual impairment, merely crossing the street may be a harrowing experience. This is especially true for the one-half million of our citizens who are legally blind and whose skill and resolve are tested daily in the traffic of our busy cities.

For such people, the white cane is an invaluable tool with which they can move about confidently and, most important, independently. Because the white cane is deceptively simple, many of us do not realize that special training and skill are required to use it effectively and safely. The cane is not a crutch but serves much as an extension of its user, providing assurance that the path ahead is clear and safe.

For the sighted, the white cane should serve as a reminder of the special needs of the visually handicapped person and of the importance of exercising simple courtesies which may otherwise be overlooked in haste. Observing the pedestrian's right-of-way in a crosswalk is a basic rule of traffic safety which has extra importance to the visually handicapped person who cannot see a vehicle's approach. For the sighted pedestrian, even a gesture as simple as offering to accompany a visually handicapped person across a busy intersection can make the difference between a safe crossing and a hazardous one.

To heighten public awareness of the importance of the white cane to the independence and safety of thousands of blind and visually handicapped Americans, the Congress, by a joint resolution approved October 6, 1964 (78 Stat. 1003; 36 U.S.C. 169d), has authorized the President to proclaim October 15 of each year as White Cane Safety Day.

Now, THEREFORE, I, JIMMY CARTER, President of the United States of America, do hereby proclaim October 15, 1978, as White Cane Safety Day.

On this occasion, let us all recognize the achievements of those who have overcome visual disability and blindness to lead independent, productive, and fulfilling lives. At the same time, let us all resolve to increase our awareness of the needs of visually handicapped people and observe those courtesies which enable them to move about safely and without needless constraint.

IN WITNESS WHEREOF, I have hereunto set my hand this eighth day of August, in the year of our Lord nineteen hundred seventy-eight, and of the Independence of the United States of America, the two hundred and third.

JIMMY CARTER

[Filed with the Office of the Federal Register, 10:54 a.m., August 9, 1978]

National Aviation Year and Wright Brothers Day, 1978

Proclamation 4584.   August 8, 1978

By the President of the United States of America

A Proclamation

This year, 1978, is the diamond jubilee anniversary of aviation. Seventy-five years ago on December 17, at Kitty Hawk, North Carolina, the Wright Brothers launched man into the age of powered flight. The magnitude of the heritage of Orville and Wilbur Wright is heroic. The significance of their achievement to men and women everywhere is profound.

At 10:30 in the morning on that cold and windy day Orville, aboard his fragile "Wright Flyer," was driven aloft by a four cylinder 12 horsepower engine also ingeniously fashioned by the two brothers. This first successful flight in a heavier-than-air powered aircraft lasted but 12 seconds and covered a distance of only 120 feet.

In the seventy-five years since that historic flight, the science of aeronautics and the prowess of American industry have combined to make aviation a giant among the Nation's transportation and communications systems. Air transportation has become the prime public carrier between American cities and to international points. And the movement of cargo, especially perishable goods, life saving pharmaceuticals and other high-priority items important to the public welfare and commerce, has become largely dependent upon the speed, efficiency and safety of air transport.

Aviation today is one of America's greatest enterprises and among its largest employers; a major contributor in the social and cultural enhancement of the American public and, in the international arena, an instrument of signal importance in the deterrence of aggression and as a mighty defender of peace.

THEREFORE, in this 75th anniversary year of powered flight, I, JIMMY CARTER, President of the United States of America, do hereby designate the year 1978, diamond jubilee anniversary of powered flight, as National Aviation Year. And further,

To commemorate the historic achievements of the Wright Brothers, the Congress, by joint resolution of December 17, 1963 (77 Stat. 402, 36 U.S.C. 169), designated the seventeenth day of December of each year as Wright Brothers Day and requested the President to issue annually a proclamation inviting the people of the United States to observe that day with appropriate ceremonies and activities.

Now, THEREFORE, I, JIMMY CARTER, President of the United States of America, do hereby call upon the people of this Nation, and their local and national government officials, to observe Wright Brothers Day, December 17, 1978, with appropriate ceremonies and activities, both to recall the accomplishments of the Wright Brothers and to provide a stimulus to aviation in this country and throughout the world.

IN WITNESS WHEREOF, I have hereunto set my hand this eighth day of August, in the year of our Lord nineteen hundred seventy-eight, and of the Independence of the United States of America the two hundred and third.

JIMMY CARTER

[Filed with the Office of the Federal Register, 10:55 a.m., August 9, 1978]

United States Ambassador to Jordan

Nomination of Nicholas A. Veliotes.
August 8, 1978

The President announced today his intention to nominate Nicholas A. Veliotes, of California, as Ambassador to the Hashemite Kingdom of Jordan. He would succeed Thomas R. Pickering, who is being appointed to another position.

Mr. Veliotes was born October 28, 1928, in Oakland, Calif. He served in the United States Army from 1946 to 1948. He received his B.A. (1952) and M.A. (1954) from the University of California at Berkeley, where he was a teaching assistant from 1952 to 1954.

In 1955 Mr. Veliotes entered the Foreign Service as consular and administrative officer in Naples. From 1957 to 1960, he was economic officer in Rome, and from 1960 to 1964, he was foreign affairs officer at the State Department. From 1964 to 1966, he was political officer in New Delhi and Chief of the Political Section in Vientiane from 1966 to 1969. He served as Woodrow Wilson Fellow at Princeton University from 1969 to 1970. From 1970 to 1973, he worked in the Department of State, serving as international relations officer, Special Assistant to Un-

der Secretary of State and Special Assistant to Deputy Secretary of State. From 1973 to 1975, he was Deputy Chief of Mission in Tel Aviv. He was Director of Employee-Management Relations Staff of the State Department's Bureau of Personnel from 1975 to 1976, and from 1976 to 1977, he was Deputy Director of Policy Planning Staff. Since 1977 he has been Deputy Assistant Secretary of the Bureau of Near East and South Asian Affairs.

New York City, New York

Remarks at a Bill Signing Ceremony for
H.R. 12426.   August 8, 1978

Senator Javits, Senator Moynihan, Governor Carey, Mayor Koch, distinguished Members of the Congress, the New York City and New York State officials, friends of this wonderful center of our Nation:

I'm glad to be back. The last time I was here and landed at the Wall Street Heliport, I received an even better welcome, because Ed Koch came forward and pressed an envelope in my hand. And I missed that today. [*Laughter*]

[*At this point, Mayor Koch gave the President a note.*]

This one I can read. [*Laughter*] "August 8, 1978. Mr. President, New York loves you. Sincerely, Ed Koch."

Thank you, Ed. [*Laughter*]

This is a good day for New York City. This is a good day for the United States of America.

In a few minutes, I'm going to walk over to that table, that desk owned and used by the first President of our country, George Washington, and sign a very important piece of legislation—the New York City Loan Guarantee Act of 1978.

This bill represents a crucial step in New York's long and difficult climb back towards solvency and independence, but its importance goes far beyond the limits of the five boroughs here. And I would like to talk for a few minutes about why I think this important moment is not only for New York City but for our entire country.

As President, I am proud of this greatest of cities. New York has been the Big Apple for more than two centuries. Back in 1790, when New York was already the Nation's largest city, Washington was just a swamp. New York is still the Nation's largest city, and Washington—politically, Washington is emerging from this swamp. It's a beautiful city, a little bit younger.

No longer, of course, the center of our Nation's Government, as it was in 1790, New York is still a cultural and artistic and financial and diplomatic capital—not just for the Nation but for the entire world. For artists and for business executives, for actresses and for lawyers, for editors and for scholars, and for just plain American tourists, New York is a magnet. In many aspects of life, New York is indeed the big leagues.

But there's another side of this city and to the people who live here. New York is not just a focus for ambition or financial achievement; it has long been a center of compassion as well. New Yorkers have traditionally reached out for those who needed help, not only just here but throughout the Nation and the world. New York has offered welcome and sustenance to generation after generation of newcomers who are looking for opportunity and for a better life—immigrants from abroad and people from the rural areas of our country.

When people in my part of the United States needed support for programs like rural electrification and economic development, New Yorkers gave us that support. That statue in the harbor which we flew over a few minutes ago holds up her lamp not for New Yorkers alone but for all of us.

People in other parts of the country have sometimes been jealous of the achievements of New York, and there were a few around our Nation who were willing to see the big city taken down a peg or two. I know how New Yorkers feel about that. One thing that Southerners and New Yorkers have in common is that at times we've both had to deal with regional prejudice.

But in the final analysis, this country of ours stands together. Those who thought that the United States was going to stand by while its greatest city went under were wrong.

The bill that I will sign today represents a mutual concern and a spirit of cooperation, the same spirit that our Nation must bring to bear as we seek to control other problems—problems such as inflation and energy and inefficiency in government.

Let there be no mistake about what this bill does. It is not a handout—New York has asked for no handouts and has received none—nor is it a Band-Aid or a temporary approach that simply postpones an inevitable problem. Instead, through long-term loan guarantees, the bill opens up enough breathing space for New Yorkers to complete the difficult task of restoring yourselves to financial and economic self-sufficiency.

This bill is in the national interest. It's designed to put behind us a danger that would create problems for all our cities and for the financial markets of the Nation and the world.

If New York keeps its commitments— and I'm sure it will—then this bill will not cost the American taxpayers 1 cent. It will give this great city the security and the time it needs to bring its budget into balance permanently. And under the leadership of Hugh Carey and Ed Koch, I have no doubt that that goal will be met.

One of the first actions that I took after I was elected President, before I was inaugurated, was to meet in Georgia with Mayor Beame and with Governor Carey and with other officials to commit my administration, then just being formed, to a long-term, serious, responsible, adequate, and cooperative effort to help New York help itself out of its chronic fiscal problems. This bill is the fruit of that commitment.

When we proposed this legislation 5 months ago, most people did not think it had much of a chance. That was before Secretary Blumenthal and I and many of you here convinced other Members of Congress how hard New York has worked in the past 3 years to solve your own problems—problems that were decades in the making and that were really partly the consequences of circumstances far beyond the city's control.

New York has reduced its work force by 60,000 and its real budget deficit by more than a billion dollars. Under the Federal Seasonal Loan program, New York has paid back every penny either on time or ahead of schedule, and as you well know, with interest. The people in Washington, D.C., the people in Georgia, thank you for that.

The credit for these achievements belongs to many different groups of individuals. New Yorkers have rallied to your city's colors. Groups that are usually thought of as natural enemies or competitors have worked together constructively toward a common goal. Labor and business, bankers and bureaucrats, Democrats and Republicans, politicians and ordinary citizens—all have joined together to take care of long-neglected problems. All have shown determination and courage in making the sacrifices that have been necessary

and that will continue to be necessary. And this is a message that was heard by the Congress of the United States. The successful lobbying was done by your actions, not by anybody's words.

Throughout the process, New York's leadership team has been exemplary. The State of New York has had many great Governors over the last number of years, but I don't know of anyone who has ever done more for New York City than Hugh Carey.

In 1975, New York City faced a financial emergency that was unprecedented in its magnitude and complexity. In that dark hour, Hugh Carey's personal leadership was magnificent. Without his unflinching courage, New York might not have come through this crisis at all. He is what we Southern Baptists from Georgia call a real *mensch.* [*Laughter*]

And Ed Koch is a strong mayor. He's refused to sugar-coat the difficult truths about your fiscal problems. He's never tried to mislead anyone, and New Yorkers have responded to his frankness, his honesty, and his candor.

As mayor, he's led New York in imposing tough discipline on itself. He's made the commitment to get New York's budget into true balance in 4 years' time, so that New York can once again regain its fiscal independence.

I know that Ed Koch likes to go up to people on the street and ask, "How'm I doing?" Well, if you ask me, Ed, you're doing great.

Both Hugh Carey and Ed Koch are former Members of Congress, as you know, and they have earned the trust of their colleagues on Capitol Hill. Both have been effective spokesmen for New York City at the national level.

The New York congressional delegation, every one of them in the House and Senate, have been superb, and they are owed a debt of gratitude which I'm sure you'll repay.

Obviously, a broad range of other groups have been involved in bringing this effort to a successful conclusion. The State legislature, the municipal unions, and the financial institutions have all made significant contributions, as have those leaders in the private sector who served the city through the Municipal Assistance Corporation and the Control Board.

Those who work for the city of New York have rededicated themselves to its service. Their commitment is exemplified by the six brave firefighters who gave their lives last week in the line of duty.

The New York City Loan Guarantee Act of 1978 is a step forward toward the fulfillment of America's national urban policy. It's part of a much larger effort to strengthen the fiscal and the economic base of our communities. Here in New York, in less than 2 years, we've already increased Federal aid by more than 30 percent, and we've proposed major urban legislation which will bring even more significant benefits to this city.

When I announced the national urban policy back in March, I called for a New Partnership involving the private sector of our economy, labor, citizens groups, and all levels of government—local, State, and Federal. Here in New York that New Partnership is indeed a demonstrated reality. New York is proving that with determination and commitment, our people can take control of even the most difficult and serious of problems.

We can take control of our energy problems, and we will. We can take control of our inflation problems, and we will. We can take control of the problem of inefficiency and fat and waste and poor management in government, as New York has already begun to do, and I believe that our Nation as a whole can do it as well.

The road ahead will not be easy for any of us. There's still a long way to go. Like the Nation as a whole, New York faces tough decisions and more sacrifices down the road.

In conclusion, let me say that working together we can ensure that once again, in the words of E. B. White, "New York is to the nation what the church spire is to the small village—a visible symbol of aspiration and hope and faith."

What we do here today is not an end but a beginning—a beginning of a new life, a better life for us all.

Thank you very much.

NOTE: The President spoke at 4:19 p.m. outside City Hall. Following the ceremony, the President attended a reception in the Governor's Room at City Hall, and then went to Gracie Mansion, where he and Mrs. Carter met with Terence Cardinal Cooke of New York.

The President and Mrs. Carter spent the night at Gracie Mansion and returned to the White House the following morning.

As enacted, H.R. 12426 is Public Law 95–339, approved August 8.

International Communication Agency

Nomination of James D. Isbister and Harold F. Schneidman To Be Associate Directors.   August 8, 1978

The President today announced that he will nominate James D. Isbister, of Maryland, and Harold F. Schneidman, of Pennsylvania, to be Associate Directors of the International Communication Agency.

Mr. Isbister is currently vice president of the Orkand Corp. of Silver Spring, Md., a position he has held since 1977. From 1974 to 1977, he was Administrator of the Alcohol, Drug Abuse and Mental Health Administration. He was a visiting faculty member at the London School of

Economics and Political Science in 1973 and 1974. From 1967 to 1973, he worked at the National Institute of Mental Health, serving first as executive officer and then as Deputy Director. Prior to 1967 he held positions at the National Library of Medicine, the Department of Health, Education, and Welfare, and the National Institutes of Health. He was born in Mt. Clemens, Mich., and is 41 years old.

Mr. Schneidman is currently Deputy Director for Policy and Plans of the International Communication Agency. He has been with ICA since 1957, serving as information officer in the Philippines, cultural affairs officer in Indonesia, and information officer in Italy. He was named Deputy Assistant Director for East Asia and the Pacific in 1970, and Assistant Director (Information Centers Service) in 1971. He was named to his current position in June of 1977. Born in Hazelton, Pa., Mr. Schneidman is 56 years old.

Employee Retirement Income Security Act Transfers

Message to the Congress Transmitting Reorganization Plan No. 4 of 1978. August 10, 1978

To the Congress of the United States:

Today I am submitting to the Congress my fourth Reorganization Plan for 1978. This proposal is designed to simplify and improve the unnecessarily complex administrative requirements of the Employee Retirement Income Security Act of 1974 (ERISA). The new plan will eliminate overlap and duplication in the administration of ERISA and help us achieve our goal of well regulated private pension plans.

ERISA was an essential step in the protection of worker pension rights. Its administrative provisions, however, have resulted in bureaucratic confusion and have been justifiably criticized by employers and unions alike. The biggest problem has been overlapping jurisdictional authority. Under current ERISA provisions, the Departments of Treasury and Labor both have authority to issue regulations and decisions.

This dual jurisdiction has delayed a good many important rulings and, more importantly, produced bureaucratic runarounds and burdensome reporting requirements.

The new plan will significantly reduce these problems. In addition, both Departments are trying to cut red tape and paperwork, to eliminate unnecessary reporting requirements, and to streamline forms wherever possible.

Both Departments have already made considerable progress, and both will continue the effort to simplify their rules and their forms.

The Reorganization Plan is the most significant result of their joint effort to modify and simplify ERISA. It will eliminate most of the jurisdictional overlap between Treasury and Labor by making the following changes:

1) Treasury will have statutory authority for minimum standards. The new plan puts all responsibility for funding, participation, and vesting of benefit rights in the Department of Treasury. These standards are necessary to ensure that employee benefit plans are adequately funded and that all beneficiary rights are protected. Treasury is the most appropriate Department to administer these provisions; however, Labor will continue to have veto power over Treasury decisions that significantly affect collectively bargained plans.

2) Labor will have statutory authority for fiduciary obligations. ERISA prohibits transactions in which self-interest

or conflict of interest could occur, but allows certain exemptions from these prohibitions. Labor will be responsible for overseeing fiduciary conduct under these provisions.

3) Both Departments will retain enforcement powers. The Reorganization Plan will continue Treasury's authority to audit plans and levy tax penalties for any deviation from standards. The plan will also continue Labor's authority to bring civil action against plans and fiduciaries. These provisions are retained in order to keep the special expertise of each Department available. New coordination between the Departments will eliminate duplicative investigations of alleged violations.

This reorganization will make an immediate improvement in ERISA's administration. It will eliminate almost all of the dual and overlapping authority in the two departments and dramatically cut the time required to process applications for exemptions from prohibited transactions.

This plan is an interim arrangement. After the Departments have had a chance to administer ERISA under this new plan, the Office of Management and Budget and the Departments will jointly evaluate that experience. Based on that evaluation, early in 1980, the Administration will make appropriate legislative proposals to establish a long-term administrative structure for ERISA.

Each provision in this reorganization will accomplish one or more of the purposes in Title 5 of U.S.C. 901(a). There will be no change in expenditure or personnel levels, although a small number of people will be transferred from the Department of Treasury to the Department of Labor.

We all recognize that the administration of ERISA has been unduly burdensome. I am confident that this reorgani-

tion will significantly relieve much of that burden.

This plan is the culmination of our effort to streamline ERISA. It provides an administrative arrangement that will work.

ERISA has been a symbol of unnecessarily complex government regulation. I hope this new step will become equally symbolic of my Administration's commitment to making government more effective and less intrusive in the lives of our people.

Jimmy Carter

The White House,
    August 10, 1978.

REORGANIZATION PLAN NO. 4 OF 1978

Prepared by the President and transmitted to the Senate and the House of Representatives in Congress assembled, August 10, 1978, pursuant to the provisions of Chapter 9 of Title 5 of the United States Code.

EMPLOYEE RETIREMENT INCOME SECURITY
ACT TRANSFERS

SECTION 101. *Transfer to the Secretary of the Treasury.* Except as otherwise provided in Sections 104 and 106 of this Plan, all authority of the Secretary of Labor to issue the following described documents pursuant to the statutes hereinafter specified is hereby transferred to the Secretary of the Treasury:

(a) regulations, rulings, opinions, variances and waivers under Parts 2 and 3 of Subtitle B of Title I and subsection 1012(c) of Title II of the Employee Retirement Income Security Act of 1974 (29 U.S.C. 1001 note) (hereinafter referred to as "ERISA"),

EXCEPT for sections and subsections 201, 203(a)(3)(B), 209, and 301(a) of ERISA;

(b) such regulations, rulings, and opinions which are granted to the Secretary of Labor under Sections 404, 410, 411,

412, and 413 of the Internal Revenue Code of 1954, as amended, (hereinafter referred to as the "Code"),

EXCEPT for subsection 411(a)(3)(B) of the Code and the definitions of "collectively bargained plan" and "collective bargaining agreement" contained in subsections 404 (a)(1)(B) and (a)(1)(C), 410 (b)(2)(A) and (b)(2)(B), and 413(a)(1) of the Code; and

(c) regulations, rulings, and opinions under subsections 3(19), 3(22), 3(23), 3(24), 3(25), 3(27), 3(28), 3(29), 3(30), and 3(31) of Subtitle A of Title I of ERISA.

SECTION 102. *Transfers to the Secretary of Labor.* Except as otherwise provided in Section 105 of this Plan, all authority of the Secretary of the Treasury to issue the following described documents pursuant to the statutes hereinafter specified is hereby transferred to the Secretary of Labor:

(a) regulations, rulings, opinions, and exemptions under section 4975 of the Code,

EXCEPT for (i) subsections 4975 (a), (b), (c)(3), (d)(3), (e)(1), and (e)(7) of the Code; (ii) to the extent necessary for the continued enforcement of subsections 4975 (a) and (b) by the Secretary of the Treasury, subsections 4975 (f)(1), (f)(2), (f)(4) (f)(5) and (f)(6) of the Code; and (iii) exemptions with respect to transactions that are exempted by subsection 404 (c) of ERISA from the provisions of Part 4 of Subtitle B of Title I of ERISA; and

(b) regulations, rulings, and opinions under subsection 2003(c) of ERISA,

EXCEPT for subsection 2003(c)(1)(B).

SECTION 103. *Coordination Concerning Certain Fiduciary Actions.* In the case of fiduciary actions which are subject to Part 4 of Subtitle B of Title I of ERISA,

the Secretary of the Treasury shall notify the Secretary of Labor prior to the time of commencing any proceeding to determine whether the action violates the exclusive benefit rule of subsection 401(a) of the Code, but not later than prior to issuing a preliminary notice of intent to disqualify under that rule, and the Secretary of the Treasury shall not issue a determination that a plan or trust does not satisfy the requirements of subsection 401 (a) by reason of the exclusive benefit rule of subsection 401(a), unless within 90 days after the date on which the Secretary of the Treasury notifies the Secretary of Labor of pending action, the Secretary of Labor certifies that he has no objection to the disqualification or the Secretary of Labor fails to respond to the Secretary of the Treasury. The requirements of this paragraph do not apply in the case of any termination or jeopardy assessment under sections 6851 or 6861 of the Code that has been approved in advance by the Commissioner of Internal Revenue, or as delegated, the Assistant Commissioner for Employee Plans and Exempt Organizations.

SECTION 104. *Enforcement by the Secretary of Labor.* The transfers provided for in Section 101 of this Plan shall not affect the ability of the Secretary of Labor, subject to the provisions of Title III of ERISA relating to jurisdiction, administration, and enforcement, to engage in enforcement under Section 502 of ERISA or to exercise the authority set forth under Title III of ERISA, including the ability to make interpretations necessary to engage in such enforcement or to exercise such authority. However, in bringing such actions and in exercising such authority with respect to Parts 2 and 3 of Subtitle B of Title I of ERISA and any definitions for which the authority of the Secretary of Labor is transferred to the Secretary of the Treasury as provided in Section 101 of this Plan, the Secretary of Labor shall be bound by the regulations, rulings, opinions, variances, and waivers issued by the Secretary of the Treasury.

SECTION 105. *Enforcement by the Secretary of the Treasury*. The transfers provided for in Section 102 of this Plan shall not affect the ability of the Secretary of the Treasury, subject to the provisions of Title III of ERISA relating to jurisdiction, administration, and enforcement, (a) to audit plans and employers and to enforce the excise tax provisions of subsections 4975(a) and 4975(b) of the Code, to exercise the authority set forth in subsections 502(b)(1) and 502(h) of ERISA, or to exercise the authority set forth in Title III of ERISA, including the ability to make interpretations necessary to audit, to enforce such taxes, and to exercise such authority; and (b) consistent with the coordination requirements under Section 103 of this Plan, to disqualify, under section 401 of the Code, a plan subject to Part 4 of Subtitle B of Title I of ERISA, including the ability to make the interpretations necessary to make such disqualification. However, in enforcing such excise taxes and, to the extent applicable, in disqualifying such plans the Secretary of the Treasury shall be bound by the regulations, rulings, opinions, and exemptions issued by the Secretary of Labor pursuant to the authority transferred to the Secretary of Labor as provided in Section 102 of this Plan.

SECTION 106. *Coordination for Section 101 Transfers*.

(a) The Secretary of the Treasury shall not exercise the functions transferred pursuant to Section 101 of this Plan to issue in proposed or final form any of the documents described in subsection (b) of this Section in any case in which such documents would significantly impact on or substantially affect collectively bargained plans unless, within 100 calendar days after the Secretary of the Treasury notifies the Secretary of Labor of such proposed action, the Secretary of Labor certifies that he has no objection or he fails to respond to the Secretary of the Treasury. The fact of such a notification, except for such notification for documents described in subsection (b)(iv) of this Section, from the Secretary of the Treasury to the Secretary of Labor shall be announced by the Secretary of Labor to the public within ten days following the date of receipt of the notification by the Secretary of Labor.

(b) The documents to which this Section applies are:

(i) amendments to regulations issued pursuant to subsections 202(a)(3), 203 (b)(2) and (3)(A), 204(b)(3)(A), (C), and (E), and 210(a)(2) of ERISA, and subsections 410(a)(3) and 411(a) (5), (6)(A), and (b)(3)(A), (C), and (E), 413(b)(4) and (c)(3) and 414(f) of the Code;

(ii) regulations issued pursuant to subsections 204(b)(3)(D), 302(c)(8), and 304(a) and (b)(2)(A) of ERISA, and subsections 411(b)(3)(D), 412(c)(8), (e), and (f)(2)(A) of the Code; and

(iii) revenue rulings (within the meaning of 26 CFR Section 601.201(a)(6)), revenue procedures, and similar publications, if the rulings, procedures and publications are issued under one of the statutory provisions listed in (i) and (ii) of this subsection; and

(iv) rulings (within the meaning of 26 CFR Section 601.201(a)(2)) issued prior to the issuance of a published regulation under one of the statutory provisions listed in (i) and (ii) of this subsection and not issued under a published Revenue Ruling.

(c) For those documents described in subsections (b)(i), (b)(ii) and (b)(iii) of this Section, the Secretary of Labor may request the Secretary of the Treasury to initiate the actions described in this Section 106 of this Plan.

SECTION 107. *Evaluation.* On or before April 30, 1980, the President will submit to both Houses of the Congress an evaluation of the extent to which this Reorganization Plan has alleviated the problems associated with the present administrative structure under ERISA, accompanied by specific legislative recommendations for a long-term administrative structure under ERISA.

SECTION 108. *Incidental Transfers.* So much of the personnel, property, records and unexpended balances of appropriations, allocations and other funds employed, used, held, available, or to be made available in connection with the functions transferred under this Plan, as the Director of the Office of Management and Budget shall determine, shall be transferred to the appropriate agency, or component at such time or times as the Director of the Office of Management and Budget shall provide, except that no such unexpended balances transferred shall be used for purposes other than those for which the appropriation was originally made. The Director of the Office of Management and Budget shall provide for terminating the affairs of any agencies abolished herein and for such further measures and dispositions as such Director deems necessary to effectuate the purposes of this Reorganization Plan.

SECTION 109. *Effective Date.* The provisions of this Reorganization Plan shall become effective at such time or times, on or before April 30, 1979, as the President shall specify, but not sooner than the earliest time allowable under Section 906 of Title 5, United States Code.

Digest of Other White House Announcements

The following listing includes the President's daily schedule and other items of general interest as announced by the White House Press Office during the period covered by this issue. Events and announcements printed elsewhere in the issue are not included.

August 5

The President met at the White House with Zbigniew Brzezinski, Assistant to the President for National Security Affairs, before leaving on his trip to Norfolk, Va., and Wilson, N.C.

August 7

The President met at the White House with:

—Dr. Brzezinski;
—Senator Kaneaster Hodges, Jr., of Arkansas;
—the Cabinet;
—senior White House staff members;
—James T. McIntyre, Jr., Director of the Office of Management and Budget.

August 8

The President met at the White House with:

—Dr. Brzezinski;
—Frank B. Moore, Assistant to the President for Congressional Liaison;
—the Democratic congressional leadership.

The President has declared an emergency for the State of New York because of the adverse impact of chemical wastes lying exposed on the surface and associated chemical vapors emanating from the Love Canal chemical waste landfill in the city of Niagara Falls.

August 9

The President met at the White House with:

—a group of mayors to discuss supplemental fiscal assistance;

—Mrs. Carter, for lunch.

August 10

The President met at the White House with:

—Dr. Brzezinski;

—Mr. Moore;

—Secretary of State Cyrus R. Vance, who reported to the President on his visits with President Anwar al-Sadat of Egypt and Prime Minister Menahem Begin of Israel during his recent trip;

—a group of civic leaders from Pennsylvania;

—the Cabinet, to discuss upcoming congressional floor action on civil service reform proposals.

The White House released manifests listing passengers who have flown on White House authorized military aircraft from January 7 through June 30, 1978. The lists were sent to Representative Jack Brooks, chairman of the House Committee on Government Operations, and were also made available for inspection by the press.

The President today announced the persons who will represent the United States at the inauguration ceremonies for Silvestre Antonio Guzman Fernandez as President of the Dominican Republic, held August 15–17. Secretary of State Cyrus R. Vance and Ambassador Andrew Young will head the delegation, attending as Personal Representatives of the President and with the rank of Special Ambassador. The members of the delegation, also with the rank of Special Ambassador, will be:

ROBERT L. YOST, U.S. Ambassador to the Dominican Republic;

GUS YATRON, U.S. Representative from the State of Pennsylvania;

VIRON P. VAKY, Assistant Secretary of State for Inter-American Affairs;

ROBERT A. PASTOR, staff member, National Security Council;

ABELARDO LOPEZ VALDEZ, Assistant Administrator for AID;

DENNIS P. McAULIFFE, Lieutenant General, U.S. Army, Commander of the U.S. Southern Command, Panama;

NED R. McWHERTER, speaker of the House of Representatives, Nashville, Tenn.;

DON L. TUCKER, speaker of the House of Representatives, Tallahassee, Fla.;

CLARENCE AVANT, president, Tabu Productions, Los Angeles, Calif.;

HENRY (HANK) AARON from Atlanta, Ga.;

ABRAHM F. LOWENTHAL from West Yarmouth, Mass.;

HOWARD J. SWIBEL of Chicago, Ill., attorney, law firm of Kirkland & Ellis.

The President announced today that Robert E. White, U.S. Ambassador to Paraguay, will be his Personal Representative, with the rank of Special Ambassador, to head the United States Delegation to the inauguration of His Excellency General of the Army Alfredo Stroessner as President of the Republic of Paraguay. The ceremonies are scheduled to be held August 14–16. The following people from the Embassy at Asunción have also been designated to attend the ceremonies as members of the delegation:

JERROLD MARK DION, Counselor of the Embassy;

COL. CHARLES R. WALLIS, military attaché.

August 11

The President met at the White House with:

—Secretary of Defense Harold Brown, Secretary Vance, Hamilton Jordan, Assistant to the President, and Dr. Brzezinski;

—a group of Congressmen and administration officials to discuss the equal rights amendment;

—Representative Harold T. Johnson of California;

—members of the American Society of Magazine Editors (transcript will be printed next week).

The President attended a pontifical requiem mass for Pope Paul VI at St. Matthew's Cathedral in Washington, D.C.

The White House announced that the President is naming Louis Emanuel Martin as Special Assistant to the President. His responsibilities will focus on programs and policies concerning black Americans.

NOMINATIONS SUBMITTED TO THE SENATE

The following list does not include promotions of members of the Uniformed Services, nominations to the Service Academies, or nominations of Foreign Service officers.

Submitted August 8, 1978

MARIANA R. PFAELZER, of California, to be United States District Judge for the Central District of California, vice Francis C. Whelan, retired.

TYREE A. RICHBURG, of Alabama, to be United States Marshal for the Southern District of Alabama for the term of 4 years, vice Harold S. Fountain, resigned.

Submitted August 9, 1978

NICHOLAS A. VELIOTES, of California, a Foreign Service officer of Class one, to be Ambassador Extraordinary and Plenipotentiary of the United States of America to the Hashemite Kingdom of Jordan.

HAROLD A. BAKER, of Illinois, to be United States District Judge for the Eastern District of Illinois, vice Henry S. Wise, retired.

JAMES DAVID ISBISTER, of Maryland, to be an Associate Director of the International Communication Agency (new position).

HAROLD F. SCHNEIDMAN, of Pennsylvania, to be an Associate Director of the International Communication Agency (new position).

Submitted August 10, 1978

WILLIAM E. PITT, of Utah, to be United States Marshal for the District of Utah for the term of 4 years, vice Royal K. Buttars, term expired.

CHECKLIST OF WHITE HOUSE PRESS RELEASES

The following releases of the Office of the White House Press Secretary, distributed during the period covered by this issue, are not included in the issue.

Released August 5, 1978

Advance text: remarks at the commissioning ceremony for the U.S.S. *Mississippi* in Norfolk, Va.

Released August 8, 1978

Announcement: nomination of Mariana R. Pfaelzer to be United States District Judge for the Central District of California

Announcement: nomination of Tyree A. Richburg to be United States Marshal for the Southern District of Alabama

Advance text: remarks on signing the New York City Loan Guarantee Act of 1978 in New York City, N.Y.

Released August 9, 1978

Announcement: nomination of Harold A. Baker to be United States District Judge for the Eastern District of Illinois

News conference: on the House of Representatives action on civil service reform and reorganization—by Alan K. Campbell, Chairman of the Civil Service Commission

Fact sheet: Camp David, Md.

Released August 10, 1978

Announcement: nomination of William E. Pitt to be United States Marshal for the District of Utah

News conference: on Reorganization Plan No. 4 of 1978 (Employee Retirement Income Security Act Transfers)—by James T. McIntyre, Jr., Director of the Office of Management and Budget, Secretary of Labor Ray Marshall, and Bette B. Anderson, Under Secretary of the Treasury

Fact sheet: Employee Retirement Income Security Act transfers reorganization plan (No. 4 of 1978)

Released August 11, 1978

Announcement: appointment of Vice Adm. Harry D. Train II, United States Navy, as Supreme Allied Commander, Atlantic, by the Defense Planning Committee of the North Atlantic Council

News conference: on the House of Representatives action on tax reform legislation—by Secretary of the Treasury W. Michael Blumenthal

ACTS APPROVED BY THE PRESIDENT

Approved August 8, 1978

H.R. 11832_____ Public Law 95–338
An act to authorize appropriations under the Arms Control and Disarmament Act for the fiscal year 1979, and for other purposes.

H.R. 12426_____ Public Law 95–339
New York City Loan Guarantee Act of 1978.

Approved August 11, 1978

H.R. 12138_____ Public Law 95–340
An act to name a certain Federal building in Laguna Niguel, California, the "Chet Holifield Building".

ACTS APPROVED—Continued

Approved August 11—Continued

S.J. Res. 102_____ Public Law 95–341
American Indian Religious Freedom.

S. 920_____ Public Law 95–342
An act relating to the disposition of certain recreational demonstration project lands by the State of Oklahoma.

S. 2463_____ Public Law 95–343
An act to amend the Surface Mining Control and Reclamation Act of 1977 (Public Law 95–87) to raise certain authorized funding levels contained therein, and for other purposes.

Interview With the President

Remarks and a Question-and-Answer Session With Members of the American Society of Magazine Editors. August 11, 1978

THE PRESIDENT. Hi, everybody. I apologize for interrupting Jody—*[laughter]*—and your session.

Let me say, first of all, that it's a great pleasure and an honor for me to have you here at the White House. Since I've been in office this is the 30th session we've had with special groups who represent the major news media in our country. I know that you collectively have subscriptions of, I understand, over 100 million people. And for us to be able to let you know what we are trying to do is very important to us, as well as to our country.

ADMINISTRATION POLICIES

Domestically, the main challenge that I have on a constant, day-by-day basis is to try to get control of the Federal bureaucracy so that it can be managed in an effective and efficient way to deliver services to our people. This afternoon's vote—or perhaps it might be delayed—on civil service reform is the most important single example of that.

Another one is to control budget spending, to cut down the deficit. And we've had very good success in cutting the deficit down. In 1976, when I ran for President, the deficit was in the sixties of billions of dollars. In fiscal year '78, really the first one I prepared, it was in the fifties of billions; fiscal year '79, which will start in October, in the forties of billions. And I hope that we'll cut it down another $10 billion by the fiscal 1980 year budget. So, to control the budget is very important.

The Congress has been helpful to some degree, but there is still some old, ancient, porkbarrel-type legislation that really costs a lot of money and wastes a lot of money. One is the public works bill that is being considered by the Congress next week, which adds back the unnecessary water projects that were put out last year by Congress, doubles the number of new water projects, adds literally thousands of unnecessary Federal employees. And I think that this slow process of change from wastefulness to tight management is very important.

Energy is another area over which we are trying to get control, working very closely with the private sector of our economy. We now import nine times more dollars' worth of oil than we did 6 years ago, which is an extraordinary drag on our Nation's economy—it costs us jobs, it creates inflation—and a very difficult issue with which to deal.

And of course, inflation itself, I think, is the most important single issue that concerns me, my whole administration, the people of this country and, I know, the Congress as well.

These kinds of issues have been postponed too long. We've had inflation with us for about 13 years, at roughly a 6 percent average level. And it's crept up this first half year because of high interest rates and also high food prices. We hope that the last half, it'll come down. But we still have an underlying inflation rate that's very tenacious, very difficult to reduce.

Our adverse trade balance is caused by several factors, the most important of which is the unnecessary waste of oil and other energy in our country and the excessive imports of oil. We hope that the Congress will act on this legislation which, as you know, has been before them since April of 1977. And I think that we have made good progress. But I primarily would like to point out to you not things we've already achieved, but things we are working on now.

In foreign affairs, of course, there are a series of serious responsibilities that I have as President; others before me have had the same sorts of challenges. One of the most tenacious is the Mideast. We hope to make some progress there, but we recognize the great difficulty involved. We are going ahead with SALT negotiations on an uninterrupted basis.

We've made good progress, I think, so far in reasserting, or asserting really for the first time, American influence in Africa, particularly southern Africa. We have a tenuous agreement involving Namibia. United Nations representatives have arrived there now. We have hopes that this nation—formerly South West Africa under German control many years

ago, now under South African control—will be a new, independent democracy.

We still have a serious problem with Rhodesia, trying to get the leaders of the Patriotic Front and the Salisbury Group together. We are adding our good offices under trying circumstances, working closely with the British there. In every instance, though, we are working through the United Nations with other nations, not trying to impose our will unilaterally on people, but letting majority rule prevail and letting democracy, as best we can forge it with our limited influence in some instances, be realized.

I think in the general sense—and the last thing I would like to comment—we've tried to restore the image of our country to one worthy of admiration.

I know that all of you remember just 2 years ago or 3 years ago or 5 years ago, every time the United Nations General Assembly met in New York, we were the butt of all the attacks, the butt of all the jokes, target of the vituperative speeches made by the less developed countries— small countries, black countries, new countries, weak countries. That's changed. I think they have a new understanding of our interest in them. And I think with our human rights stance, there's been a resurgence of admiration for our country, comprehension of the principles on which our Nation was founded and on which it exists.

Andy Young has done a superb job in letting those people who have formerly been excluded from consideration in many decisions made in our country—we've let them know that we care about them.

And I believe in many ways we've had some success. At home a year ago, 15, 18 months ago, the overriding concern was unemployment. The Congress did a superb job last year in laying the basis for economic stimulation and a reduction in the unemployment rate. We've had a net increase of over 6½ million jobs, never before this many added so rapidly, and the unemployment rate has dropped almost a full 2 percentage points—still pockets of very serious unemployment. And we are trying to address the inflation problem and unemployment, adverse trade balances, management of the Government—all these things as one comprehensive package.

I'll be glad to answer any questions from you now, and we'll try to break this up 2 or 3 minutes early so that I might get an individual photograph with you, all of you, if you have no objection.

QUESTIONS

ENERGY

Q. Mr. President, our magazine is releasing a survey this weekend on energy, a survey of U.S. and foreign editors, and it shows the foreigners are more concerned than Americans about energy, not only about when the oil will run out but about the devastating effects on the dollar. And my question is why you haven't tied the dollar sickness more to the energy imports we have and, also, whether you have any plans to step up your efforts to get your energy program adopted, perhaps through town meetings or those phone-a-thons that you did so well early in your administration.

THE PRESIDENT. I don't believe I've ever had a town meeting that we haven't made this basic thrust in my carefully prepared agenda for the meeting ahead of time. I answer questions, but I generally have an opening comment. I've had three fireside chats since I've been in office; two of them have been exclusively on energy. I've had one address to the Congress, other than my State of the Union message. That only address to the Congress has been on energy.

And every time I go overseas, it's obvious to me that the foreign leaders share my concern about energy. Unfortunately, we've not been able to sustain the concern among the American public about how serious overuse of energy is and oversupplies of energy from foreign sources are to the integrity of our own economic system. I think a lot of foreign leaders and people throughout the world see this as a sign of weakness on the part of our country, a lack of will to address a very difficult and challenging problem.

We have worked without ceasing, really for 20 months, even more. We began before I was inaugurated to bring to the Congress and to the people, for the first time, an energy policy. The shortage has been evident since, I'd say, no later than 1973. And the Congress is addressing it. But I think the American people, since they don't have demonstrable shortages, they don't have lines at the service station, they don't have interruptions of electricity to their homes, their houses don't get cold in the winter, in most instances they have not yet realized how serious it is.

But the deterioration of the dollar overseas is directly attributable to this factor; there are obviously some other factors. And the weakening of economic esteem for our country is directly attributable to this factor, and the high inflation rate that we experience is attributable to the same factor—overimport, overwaste of energy.

Obviously, in every case there are other factors as well. But we are trying to dramatize it. And this is one thing you can certainly do. I think your article—although I don't have any idea what it will be—will help to do this. But there's been an escalation and a waning of interest in the energy problem.

Hamilton Jordan, who is one of my chief aides, did an analysis, I think, about

April or May this year. He analyzed the number of minutes on the evening network news devoted to different issues that we considered to be crucial. And with the exception of those peaks of interest when I made those major speeches, the evening news media have practically no interest in the energy problem. CBS did have one 3-hour program, and the viewership was quite low, particularly the last 2 hours and a half. [*Laughter*]

But I think you all have not only a legitimate interest, but also you share a responsibility with me to do what you can to keep the energy problem before the American people. I would like to see it resolved by the Congress, which will be a major step forward, before it becomes a crisis for the American people.

EMPLOYMENT OF WOMEN

Q. In either May or June, depending on which statistics you read, Women's Bureau or Department of Labor statistics, the working woman became the new majority of American women; 50.4 percent, I think, was the June figure. I wonder what your administration is planning to do to support women as they undergo this extraordinary piece of social history, must learn to live with it and take part in it?

THE PRESIDENT. Let me just give you two quick statements, then perhaps you would want to ask a followup.

This morning I had a meeting around this table with a group of activists—women and men, Members of the Congress, and others—who are trying to pursue the passage of the equal rights amendment, the extension of time for its ratification, and the prohibition against the rescission of ratification already taken by some States. Not only I myself, as President, but my whole family has

worked and is working on the ERA. That would be one major step forward.

Another example that I mentioned earlier is the civil service reform legislation. At this time, women are practically excluded from the senior positions in the civil service itself. Among the executive level, I think, GS–17 and 18, 65 percent of those executives are white male veterans; only 3 percent are women. And at the present time, the civil service laws and regulations still provide a major obstacle for job opportunities for women.

There are cases where women score 100, a perfect score, on a very tough, competitive civil service examination, and they still would rank, in an order of priority for that job, higher than a hundred—they have more than a hundred people ahead of them. And we are limited at the present time by civil service regulations that only let us consider the top three. So, we are trying to make some changes in that respect.

We've consolidated, with one of our successful reorganization plans, the equal employment opportunity groups in the Government. We had seven when I became President, and now we've narrowed it down so that Eleanor Holmes Norton has, in effect, the dominant role to play there. We have, as you know, through the EEOC and also through the Justice Department, initiated several suits that are test cases that might set a standard for the resolution of the large backlog of cases where women had filed legitimate complaints about being excluded, not only from Government employment but private employment. Those are some of the things that we are doing already.

ROSALYNN CARTER

Q. A personal question, if I may. How much influence would you say Mrs. Carter has on you? Do you talk things over profoundly?

THE PRESIDENT. I would hate to admit how much. [*Laughter*]

Q. And do you fight?

THE PRESIDENT. Oh, no, we don't. We get along well. Sometimes we have arguments about things that at the time seem important, but later on, we realize are not important. But this would involve things like how late Amy can stay up at night and whether she can see a PG-rated movie or not, those kinds of things. But that's the limit.

Rosalynn is an extremely knowledgeable and sensitive person, is very strongwilled. I think she understands the consciousness of the American people and their attitudes, perhaps better than do I. She's a full partner with me in every sense of the word. And with the exception of top-secret material, where security restrains me, I share almost everything with her.

I seek her advice on matters. She is even involved in foreign affairs, and needs to be. She accompanies me on my trips. She's made several overseas trips independently of me. And I think that when a foreign leader has, in effect, underestimated her before she arrived, after they leave and they see how well she understands our Nation and how close she is to me, they are very gratified that she has come. This is particularly applicable in Latin America. She happens to speak Spanish.

She's now representing me this morning in Rome at the funeral of the Pope. I just attended a mass for the Pope at St. Matthew's Cathedral, and when I arrived there, they were very complimentary about the arrival statement that Rosalynn had made.

So, in all those ways and many others, she's a full partner with me and is an extension of myself.

When I can't go to visit a certain country for the inauguration of a President or for a substantive discussion about issues with which she is familiar, she goes and represents me. So, I'd say in many ways she's a full partner with me.

SENATOR EDWARD KENNEDY

Q. If I could ask a political question, Mr. President?

THE PRESIDENT. Of course.

Q. It seems to me, reading the publications we're representing, well, that there's a resurgence of interest in the Kennedy family. Many of us have published stories involving members of that family, to the point where it seems possible that Senator Kennedy is being groomed for a challenge to you in 1980. My question is, are you——

THE PRESIDENT. You mean, by the news media? [*Laughter*]

Q. My question is, are you prepared for a challenge by Senator Kennedy or some other Democrat in 1980?

THE PRESIDENT. Well, I take Ted Kennedy at his word. He has said he's not going to run in 1980. He said, if I run, he will support me, and I have no reason to doubt him. He's said this many times in the past. Sometimes his word has been doubted. He's always done what he said he would.

I might say that I don't fear any competition that I might get in 1980. And when I began my plans to run for President fairly early in 1972—April, as a matter of fact, of '72—I thought that my two opponents would be Senator Kennedy and Governor George Wallace. And I was perfectly willing, even eager, to meet both of them, even when I was an absolutely unknown candidate with practically little money and no nationwide organization.

So, he's a great person and a good, close friend of mine. I say that with a little bit of caution, because I don't want to exaggerate the number of close friends I have. He's one of them. I had lunch with him yesterday. I think that if you would analyze the Members of the Senate and who supported us on controversial issues when my administration had a clear preference, that he would be at the top. I don't know of another Senator among the hundred who has a higher record of support for my programs. And I appreciate this very much.

There are some times when we differ, but it's a difference with a mutual degree of respect. So, if he should decide to run, I would certainly not let that influence my decision as to whether or not I would run. But my belief is that he will not.

ENERGY AND THE ENVIRONMENT

Q. The Energy Department and EPA appear to be at rather sharp odds on protecting air and water quality, while increasing coal production. How much environmental quality is the administration willing to sacrifice to meet your stated energy goals?

THE PRESIDENT. Very little. We assessed very carefully the degree of air pollution and water pollution that would result from our energy package in its totality. And we're very cautious not to expect any sort of coal used to cause a deterioration in the quality of our environment.

We are insistent that coal, when burned, be burned as cleanly as possible. There's a specific legal limit on how much air pollution can be accommodated in industrial centers, and until a point source of pollution is retired, a new one cannot be instituted.

I think the coal industry is very eager to see this done, as well. The techniques

are being improved as time goes on. And I don't think there's any difference in opinion between the Department of Energy and the EPA. Obviously, there are some times when they disagree, but I, if necessary, resolve those differences.

We have a need to shift strongly toward increased use of coal. One of the results of the recent coal workers contract that has not been adequately assessed is the stability that it is bringing to the coal industry, that the number of wildcat strikes are going down. I think people who would be inclined to use coal now see much more clearly that their supply in the future would be more assured than was the case before the contract was negotiated.

So, I think with a complete commitment on the part of this administration and the Congress to maintain the quality of our environment, with technology being exerted to a maximum degree to make coal burning even more efficient and cleaner, and with more assured supplies of regular deliveries of coal because of better contracts and, obviously, better engineering techniques, I believe all these factors will increase the use of coal in the future. We hope to have a billion tons a year used, I think, by 1985, which is about a 40- or 50-percent increase.

RELATIONS WITH THE CONGRESS

Q. Mr. President, do you feel that under our system it's almost inevitable, or perhaps even mandatory, that an effective President have strong clashes with Congress and its dominant personalities?

THE PRESIDENT. Well, I would think so. There is an historical delineation of responsibility and perspective. The average Member of Congress has a very narrowly focused, parochial interest—not just geographical; certainly each one is interested in his or her own district—but Congress leaders tend to specialize after a period of years. They become a member of a committee or two. They then become chairman of a subcommittee. They then become, perhaps, chairman of a committee if they are quite senior. And their concentrated knowledge about a subject is highly valuable to our country, to the Congress, and certainly to me, as President.

But that means that on occasion there will be differences of opinion. I wouldn't criticize, for instance, any Member of Congress who was instrumental in passing the public works bill, which has excessive spending, excessive numbers of Federal employees required, and which authorizes projects that I think are unnecessary. These Members of Congress have been working with those projects for years. And I just think that it's time for us to save money and to have a more efficient government and to spend our money where it's needed, not wasted. So, I think the answer is that it is inevitable.

We've had good success, though, with the Democratic Congress. The news media and the people themselves have an exaggerated interest in the combat, the debate, the differences, the disputes, even the adverse votes in Congress. The positive reaction of Congress to many of my proposals, the achievements when Congress approves the proposals and even the positive votes after a subcommittee votes no—in the morning paper this will be on the headline. If the full committee the next day votes yes, this will not be on the front page in the headlines. I don't say that to criticize the news media, but to emphasize that the general public's interest is in the negative votes and the disputes.

So, even though we do have differences, we achieve an adequate degree of harmony. I'm very jealous of the prerogatives of the President; the congressional leaders are jealous of the legislative prerogatives. And when we have a serious difference,

of course, the courts make a decision or the laws are changed. But this is part of our system of government. I think it's a good system.

VIEWS ON THE PRESIDENCY

Q. If tapes had been running all during the 2 years of your administration, which 18 minutes would you choose to erase? [*Laughter*]

THE PRESIDENT. Well, let me say first of all that no tapes have been running—[*laughter*]—except when the microphone is obvious, and the tapes will be made public. We don't have tapes. I would rather not answer that question on the grounds that it might tend to incriminate me. [*Laughter*] But it's a good question.

U.S. PRODUCTIVITY RATES

Q. Mr. President, on the topic of productivity, what principal actions might the U.S. take to stimulate innovation and productivity?

THE PRESIDENT. Well, the productivity rate is still going up, quite slowly, unfortunately, 1 percent or less, whereas 7 or 8 years ago it was 3 percent per year.

Our country is going through an inevitable historical period when the productivity rate of increase is low. One reason is that we have begun to correct a longstanding defect in air and water pollution, where now, available supplies of financial investment funds are being spent not to increase production, but to improve the quality of air and water and to lessen the pollution effects. Once this is caught up, then that same amount of money can be used to increase productivity. Other countries will have to do this later on if they haven't already come to that awareness.

Another factor is the health and safety of our workers. In the past, I think we've seen evolving a much deeper concern for the health and safety of our workers, and the strength of the organizations of workers, the labor unions have let their voices be heard. That's another factor that causes us to have low productivity rate increase compared to other countries.

Another one is that our Nation has been prosperous for a long time. And we've tended to shift to a style of life that not only has a shorter work week than many nations, but which also has more of an investment or interest in service—one human being working in a career to make the life of another human being more pleasant or more healthy, and so forth. And this doesn't show up in productivity. If someone takes, say, a million dollars and builds a recreation center or a Broadway theater or a motion picture theater or produces phonograph records or has a national symphony organized, that doesn't show up in the productivity of our Nation, but it gives our people a better life.

My understanding of the statistics is that even when you have a drycleaning establishment, that that doesn't show up in productivity, although it lets us have a better life and more freedom.

So, those are some factors that can't very well be changed. I would say that labor-management harmony, longstanding contracts, a creation of more financial capital through tax measures, and so forth, so that it's very efficient, would increase investment; it would provide more jobs and more capital investment per worker. One, for instance, would be the comparison between, say, accelerated depreciation rates, which would encourage immediate investments, compared to a ridiculous capital proposal like the Steiger amendment, which only lets very rich people avoid paying their share of taxes.

So, I would say in all those factors, we will have an opportunity to improve production rates.

One other difference between our country and others—I don't want to give you too long an answer—is that we don't depend nearly so much on international trade, exports, as do other nations. I think that the percentage of our GNP devoted to exports is maybe 6 or 7 percent. Germany would be 30 percent, for instance. And it's life or death for their business community, in its totality, to be highly competitive in production so they can compete on the international market. Obviously, we have some firms in the United States who do the same thing and do it very well. But we don't have that driving force behind our whole consciousness of business and professional leaders in this country—exports, exports, exports; whereas in Germany and Japan, that is the battle cry.

And the last factor that I'll say is that in many ways, our heaviest industry is not so modern as is the case in, say, Japan and Germany, where their industrial fabric was destroyed in the Second World War and has recently been built back. This would apply, for instance, to steel production.

So, those are some of the factors that have to be improved to increase productivity.

MR. WURFEL. Thank you, sir.

THE PRESIDENT. I didn't mean to give you a dissertation.

I will answer one more question.

Q. Do you think that we are investing enough in basic research to ensure our future in this area of productivity?

THE PRESIDENT. No. That's another factor that I should have mentioned. In the last 10 years, in particular—I'd say 15 years, in particular—the percentage of GNP or business income spent on basic research and development has dropped substantially; the same with government.

One of the substantial changes that I have made in preparing the Federal budget has been to increase the portion of each major agency's budget that goes into basic research and development. This is carried out not only within government in laboratories and so forth but with direct grants to colleges and universities, in addition to that, in some appropriate ways, to encourage business through government sharing of costs to improve research and development.

I would say that the countries that have maintained a high commitment to research and development have a tendency to have much higher productivity. I think we might be suffering in 1978 because 15 years ago, there was a lessening in research and development commitment among business.

One reason, of course, is the extreme incentive that permeated the American scientific and technological industries with the space program, when during the sixties, we had a major thrust there. And this permeated the whole structure of our economy, not only in electronics, computers, but also in health care and other factors.

So, I'd say research and development is a very fruitful investment. And we're trying to turn that trend around.

We have an opportunity in some areas to do this again. I don't mean to put another man on Mars instead of the Moon, but in the energy field, for instance. And we are exploring now how we can have a composite, focused R. & D. program to alleviate our energy shortage and to make us more self-sufficient. But that, in itself, would stimulate our whole economy, would give a spirit of adventure and entrepreneurship to leaders in business and the professions and, I think, would pay rich dividends in the future in the rate of increase of our own productivity.

We've got a stable country. We've got a very strong country. And although we sometimes tend to emphasize, through the news media and through the statements of farmers like myself, through statements that come out of Wall Street or major corporations, the temporary aberrations or the temporary disappointments or the temporary statistics that show a negative factor, in general, ours is still the strongest nation on Earth, the best nation on Earth.

We're blessed with natural resources that many others don't have. And our system of government, I think, is obviously the best in the world. So, we've got a lot to be thankful for, even though we do suffer on occasion from temporary setbacks that are transient in nature.

Thank you very much.

NOTE: The interview began at 1:30 p.m. in the Cabinet Room at the White House. Walter W. Wurfel is Deputy Press Secretary.

The transcript of the interview was released on August 12.

American Indian Religious Freedom

Statement on Signing S.J. Res. 102 Into Law. August 12, 1978

I have signed into law S.J. Res. 102, the American Indian Religious Freedom Act of 1978. This legislation sets forth the policy of the United States to protect and preserve the inherent right of American Indian, Eskimo, Aleut, and Native Hawaiian people to believe, express, and exercise their traditional religions. In addition, it calls for a year's evaluation of the Federal agencies' policies and procedures as they affect the religious rights and cultural integrity of Native Americans.

It is a fundamental right of every American, as guaranteed by the first amendment of the Constitution, to worship as he or she pleases. This act is in no way intended to alter that guarantee or override existing laws, but is designed to prevent Government actions that would violate these constitutional protections. In the past, Government agencies and departments have on occasion denied Native Americans access to particular sites and interfered with religious practices and customs where such use conflicted with Federal regulations. In many instances, the Federal officials responsible for the enforcement of these regulations were unaware of the nature of traditional native religious practices and, consequently, of the degree to which their agencies interfered with such practices.

This legislation seeks to remedy this situation.

I am hereby directing that the Secretary of the Interior establish a Task Force comprised of representatives of the appropriate Federal agencies. They will prepare the report to the Congress required by this resolution, in consultation with native leaders. Several agencies, including the Departments of Treasury and Interior, have already taken commendable steps to implement the intent of this resolution.

I welcome enactment of this resolution as an important action to assure religious freedom for all Americans.

NOTE: As enacted, S.J. Res. 102 is Public Law 95–341, approved August 11.

Federal Election Commission

Withdrawal of Nomination of Samuel D. Zagoria To Be a Member. August 12, 1978

President Carter today received with regret Samuel D. Zagoria's request that his nomination to the Federal Election Commission be withdrawn from the United States Senate.

The President also announced his intention to nominate Mr. Zagoria to an appropriate high-level Government position in the near future. The President said, "Mr. Zagoria is a talented and experienced individual who can ably serve this Government in a number of important ways. I am pleased that he is still willing to serve and that he is willing to explore with us several specific possibilities."

Office of Consumer Affairs

Appointment of Esther Peterson as Director. August 12, 1978

The President today announced that he has named Esther Peterson Director of the Office of Consumer Affairs. She will assume that responsibility in addition to her present position of Special Assistant to the President for Consumer Affairs.

The Office of Consumer Affairs was created in 1971. Its responsibilities, which are detailed in Executive Order No. 11583, February 24, 1971, include assisting in the development of consumer programs in Federal agencies and assuring that the interests of consumers are presented and considered in a timely matter by those agencies. The Office is housed in the Department of Health, Education, and Welfare.

National Advisory Council on Indian Education

Appointment of Four Members. August 14, 1978

The President today announced that he will appoint four persons to be members of the National Advisory Council on Indian Education for the terms expiring September 29, 1980.

Lionel R. Bordeaux, of Rosebud, S.D., was born February 9, 1940. He received a B.A. from Black Hills State College in 1964 and an M.A. from the University of South Dakota in 1971. From 1964 to 1972, Bordeaux held a variety of positions with the Bureau of Indian Affairs. Since 1973 he has been president of Sinte Gleska College.

Frederick S. Bigjim, of Bethel, Alaska, was born July 7, 1941. He received a B.A. from the University of Alaska in 1972 and an M. Ed. from Harvard University in 1973. From 1973 to 1974, Bigjim was director and administrator of intercultural studies at Alaska Methodist University. Since November of 1976 Bigjim has been administrator/instructor of Kuskokwim Community College.

Maxine R. Edmo, of Fort Hall, Idaho, was born May 4, 1929. Edmo attended the University of Idaho. From 1969 to 1974, she was a chairperson with the Shoshone-Bannock Tribal Education Committee. Since 1975 she has been a chairperson with the Shoshone-Bannock Tribal Health, Education, and Welfare Committee.

Viola G. Peterson, of Flint, Mich., was born January 1, 1918. Peterson received an A.A. from Mott Community College. Since 1974 she has been Title IV, Part A program director for the Carman-Ainsworth Community Schools in Flint, Mich.

Columbia, Missouri

Remarks to Members of the Midcontinent Farmers Association. August 14, 1978

Senator Talmadge, chairman of the Agriculture Committee and a true friend of American farmers everywhere, and of consumers as well; Senator Eagleton, who has a very strategic position as chairman of the Appropriations Subcommittee and who watches over farmers throughout the country as if they were his own children, who does such a superb job; Senator Danforth, a very courageous man who represents this State as well; Congressman Ichord, who has welcomed me to his own district; Congressman Burlison, who in the Appropriations Committee in the House also keeps a watchful and a constructive eye on the lives and well-being of American farmers; Congressman Skelton, who serves on the House Agriculture Committee; Congressman Gephardt; Congressman Coleman; Congressman Taylor; and I want to say just a word of condolences and regrets from my wife and me to Congressman Dick Bolling, with whom I talked yesterday morning, who had a tragedy in his family when his fine wife, Jim, passed away; my good friend, Governor Teasdale, and President Fred Hinkle, who represents you well and who's been a very fine counselor, for me and for previous Presidents, who share the responsibility that I have; and to the delegates of the Midcontinent Farmers Association assembled here in such great numbers to represent yourselves and your neighbors so well:

I'm grateful that you extended me this invitation. And I'm glad to come and to talk to you about two basic subjects. One is agriculture, and we've made good progress in this respect in the last year and a half since I've been in office. The other one is also of equal importance to farmers, and that is inflation.

Sometimes it takes a great problem to arouse someone to take strong action, that's slow in coming. I tried to think of a story to illustrate this point. The Sunday before last my Sunday school teacher told about a young man who went to work for an insurance company, and his boss called him in the first week and said, "It's important that you get out and work hard and really sell these policies, because they're good for the customer, they're good for our company, they're good for you." He said, "If I feel like it, I will." At the end of the week, he hadn't sold any policies. So, his boss said, "We don't have any place for you around here."

For about 3 or 4 weeks he wandered around looking for a job, and he couldn't find one. And finally, he found a buddy in a bar, and he said, "Why don't we go and rob the local bank?" And so, they made up very careful plans to violate the law and to give them some spending money at the same time. And his buddy said, "Look, when we come out of the front door of that bank, you've got to run like mad, and don't slow down." And the young fellow said, "Well, if I feel like it, I will." [*Laughter*]

Well, he came out of that bank with a sackful of money, he ran about a block, kind of lackadaisical. And a policeman caught him by his collar, and he was tried and put in a penitentiary. The next morning the warden called him down there and said, "Well, you're a new prisoner here, and here's a cotton sack. We all work around this prison." He said, "I want you to go out in that field, and when you come in tonight, I want you to have 150 pounds of cotton in that sack." The fellow looked at the warden and said, "Well, if I feel like it, I will."

So, he came in that night; he had 25 pounds of cotton in his sack. And the warden called his biggest, strongest guard over and said, "Take this fellow in the back room and work him over." The next morning the new prisoner kind of hobbled up in front of the warden—two black eyes, knots on his head, couldn't see very well—and the warden said, "Well, here's your cotton sack. I want you to go out in that field; when you come in tonight, I want you to have 150 pounds of cotton." The

fellow said, "Boss, if it's in the field, I'll get it." [*Laughter*]

This is the kind of determination that we all need to address important issues. But sometimes it takes a little persuasion, a little crisis to bring to us the importance of our future actions.

I feel at home with you today. Both your State and mine have produced Presidents who were raised on the farm. We Presidents, from Missouri and Georgia, have another similarity, too. We both have kept the same sign in the Oval Office, the famous sign that reads, "The buck stops here." It's a constant reminder of the great opportunities and the difficult responsibilities of the President of the United States.

Although President Truman followed a career that took him away from farming, his attachment remained strong to the land and to the people who work it. And so has mine.

When I took office a little more than a year and a half ago, the farm economy was in bad shape and apparently was headed for a serious depression. It was one of the greatest problems that we had to face. The American farmer has a right to expect two things that you were not getting then: a stable and secure income and access to adequate credit at reasonable interest rates. And all Americans, on and off the farm, have a right to expect one big thing that nobody is getting today: a dollar that will still be worth as much tomorrow as it is now.

Not long ago, some of your neighbors, maybe even some of you here today, came to visit us in Washington, on tractors and with goats. Some of you may even have visited Bob Bergland's office, although I understand he was out at the time. The rumor is that he went out through the window. [*Laughter*] But we could understand clearly the message that was brought and the message that was on the hearts and minds of the farmers who stayed at home.

Things have changed for the better since then. The new programs passed by Congress have now begun to take effect. Net farm income in 1978, this year, will be up about 25 percent over last year— that's income above costs, an increase of more than $5 billion. Beef prices should be strong and relatively stable for the last half of this year, and Glenn Grimes of the University of Missouri has said that the general price of cattle will be very strong for the next 3 or 4 years. If demand stays high, which we expect it to do, stable prices, sustained, even increasing herd sizes, and adequate domestic meat production is important for farmers and also for consumers.

Our decisions have been sound, careful, and well considered. I will not permit any more expansion in beef imports this year. I will not permit unrestricted beef imports next year. And I am strongly and permanently opposed to any price controls on meat or other farm products.

Last year, in spite of low unit costs, which you well remember, we set a record for American farm exports—$24 billion— and American farmers will export even more this year than ever before in our history. We are now opening new trade offices in key foreign trade centers to promote farm exports. The time for uncertainty and for unpredictable, government-imposed embargoes on farm exports is over.

When those embargoes were imposed in the past, without notice to American farmers and without notice to our customers, it hurt us in two severe ways. One was that American farmers lost income. And secondly, those customers began to turn to other nations where the supply of vital farm products was more certain.

We know, also, that a successful multilateral trade negotiation agreement must include improved access in foreign markets for American agricultural products. We are doing everything we can—in trade negotiations, extending credit; trade promotion, to strengthen agricultural exports even more.

America's agricultural productivity and the family farm structure are among the greatest accomplishments of Western civilization. But our agriculture will remain the wonder of the world only so long as we remember a basic fact: The person most competent to make a farmer's decisions is not a bureaucrat in Washington or anywhere else; it's the man or woman on the farm. That's why I will always protect the Capper-Volstead Act of 1922, the basis for this organization.

I want to go as far as I possibly can to get the Government out of the farm business of America. That's why the first few months after I took office, I spent more hours working on the 1977 food and agricultural act, I believe, than on any other single piece of legislation.

The effects of that bill, carefully considered and passed by a wise Congress interested in you, are now being felt in record net farm income all across the country. This bill will mean fair return for farmers, reasonable prices for consumers, and a stable farm economy throughout the next 4 years.

The farmer-owned grain reserve gives you farmers a chance for better profits through a strong voice in agricultural markets. You, and not the grain dealers, can now decide the best time to sell your products, to bring profits to you and not to them. We've already helped farmers to build seven times more farm storage than American farmers did in 1976. In Missouri, you built 10 times more farm storage in 12 months than you did in 1976.

We are still working on legislation that will give farmers the financial resources to produce efficiently and to get the fair and stable income that you deserve.

Secretary Bergland and I are working with congressional leaders, including those on this stage, to consolidate the several farm disaster protection programs into one effective and efficient program.

Just last week, I signed the Agricultural Credit Assistance Act of 1978, the most substantial reform of our farm credit program in more than 40 years. You will see the beneficial effects the next time you need a loan. And the American taxpayer is protected by eliminating unnecessary Government interest subsidies. These are good ideas, and they are already starting to do the job that they were supposed to do for you.

I was able to see at first hand how Congress was capable of putting national interest above the special interests in finding solutions to long-neglected agricultural problems. But another long-neglected problem is proving much more difficult to solve. It's equally important to you. Inflation is the biggest threat we face, and we must all work together to control it.

Inflation robs all Americans of the dollars that you work so hard to earn and to save. I want to give you some straight talk—as Harry Truman would have given—about why we have inflation, and what the American people, my administration, and most of all, the U.S. Congress must do to fight it.

As long as most Americans expect inflation to continue, it will. That kind of thinking will never end unless labor, management, and government join together to act responsibly and with restraint.

I will continue to make the Federal Government do its part. For one thing, we are rooting out waste in Government, and I pledge that we will continue to do so. We are getting control over Government programs that have mushroomed out of

control for the last 40 years. No one before has ever really tried to figure out which one of these programs works and which one doesn't.

Now every one of my Cabinet members and agency leaders has begun to use zero-based budgeting, a system in which no program is taken for granted, no matter how long it's been in existence. Each program must prove its worth from the ground up every year. The benefits of this new system are beginning now to be felt.

I've also ordered them to cut paperwork and redtape, burdens that weigh on all Americans. As a result, last year we cut Government-imposed paperwork by more than 10 percent. And we're going to match that figure again this year.

One good example that you and I know very well, and which I used to dread seeing come in the mail, is the 22-page booklet which we've had to complete every few years for the agricultural census. We've now chopped it to 4 pages. And it will still give the Commerce Department every bit of census data that they need. I know how confusing that census questionnaire was. I heard about one farmer who was asked in one of the questions how his family was broken down by sex. He thought quite a while and said, well, it hadn't happened yet, but he had an uncle who had a drinking problem. [*Laughter*]

One of the most difficult jobs I have is to cut down paperwork, to cut down on forms, application blanks, reports that come in to the Federal Government.

I've now required that regulation writers go to school, that the regulations be issued in simple English language, and that the people who write the regulations sign them. This is making an impact.

I've also ordered every Cabinet Secretary to discard regulations that are no longer necessary; and if one's been required every week, to change it to 3 months; if one's been required every 3 months, to change it to annually. One result is that the Occupational Safety and Health Administration, OSHA, has now proposed eliminating more than 1,000 burdensome and unneeded regulations.

The most important contribution, however, that the Congress can make to streamline the bureaucracy is to pass my civil service reform program. We need a civil service system that rewards the competent and the dedicated employee, that disciplines those who will not work, and which lets managers manage the Federal bureaucracy. My civil service reforms will do exactly this, while protecting even better than now the legitimate rights of Government workers.

These are the tools that I need to manage the bureaucracy and to make Government work. I hope that you will urge your representatives in Congress to pass the civil service reform. The Congress hears from the special interest lobbies. They need to hear from you.

Another major goal: We must cut the Federal budget deficit, and that is exactly what we are doing. In fiscal year 1976, when I ran for President, the Federal deficit was $66.4 billion. In fiscal year 1978, the first budget that I prepared, we had cut it down to $51 billion. Next year, fiscal year 1979, the Federal deficit will be down into the forties of billions of dollars. And my goal for the next year, fiscal year 1980, is to bring the deficit down to the thirties of billions of dollars. We are making progress. I need your help. We are determined to succeed.

We are cutting unnecessary spending. We are being more careful in the preparation of the budget. And I will achieve part of this goal by limiting the pay increase of Federal workers to 5½ percent and by freezing executive salaries at zero percent increase this coming year. But they should not be required to have to

sacrifice all alone. Labor and industry must cooperate in a strong and effective effort to slow the spiral of inflation. You, the farmers of our country, must help.

I've asked industry and labor to hold down wage and price increases below the average increase of the last 2 years. Congress must help to control inflation with every vote and with every decision. Unnecessary spending must be stopped. Public works legislation now being considered would spend hundreds of millions of dollars more than it should on expensive porkbarrel projects that we do not need and will give us thousands of extra Federal bureaucrats.

The fight against inflation becomes nearly impossible when the pressures of special economic interest lobbies are successful. These lobbies care absolutely nothing about the national interest—as long as they get theirs. We will never win the fight against inflation unless we help the Congress to resist these pressures.

The hospital cost containment bill is a perfect example. Intense lobbying by the medical and hospital industry defeated the hospital cost containment legislation in the House Commerce Committee, although the vast majority of Americans and the vast majority of Members of Congress are appalled at the astronomical rise of hospital costs in recent years, costs which have been rising and are still rising at more than twice the national inflation rate. This bill would save the Federal Treasury $19 billion over the next 5 years and will save the American people $56 billion in 5 years. How does that affect you on hospital cost for your family? That's about $800 for every family in this country—$800 that your family will have to spend because the special interests so far have won the fight.

The United States Senate will soon be taking up this cost containment legislation. If Congress really wants to demonstrate its concern about inflation, it will pass hospital cost containment legislation this year. And if you really care, you will let Congress know what to do.

Another good example of important anti-inflation legislation is airline deregulation. One price that has gone down in the last year is the price of an airline ticket on overseas flights. That price has gone down because of policies set by my appointees to the Civil Aeronautics Board. We need to let those policies be embedded in the law so that domestic airline fares can also be reduced by competition under the American free enterprise system. The airline deregulation bill is an important way to get prices under control.

All of these issues are important. But in closing, I want to point to one issue more important than all, by which, no matter what else it does, the 1978 Congress will be measured, and that is its action on the most important and crucial problem, that of energy.

There is a huge and unchecked hemorrhage of American dollars flowing overseas, caused by our oil imports. More than half of American oil now comes from foreign countries. Imports are up more than 800 percent in the last 6 years, from $4.7 billion in 1972, to an incredible $42 billion today.

Oil imports in dollars are almost twice as great as all agricultural exports. This hurts our dollars. It costs Americans jobs. It robs us with unnecessary inflation and leaves our economy and even our national security at the mercy of a foreign cartel.

After more than 15 months of discussion, debate, and delay, it is time for Congress to pass a national energy plan. It's time for the American farmer to be assured of a reliable supply of oil products and natural gas. And time is running out.

Our Nation will be seriously damaged if Congress does not act this year to give us a national energy policy. I have great confidence in the United States Congress, and we all realize that a good partnership between the President and the Congress is necessary if the needs of our country are to be met.

When the Congress cooperated with me, with Secretary Bergland, with you and others, in passing the 1977 farm legislation, we proved that we could work together to find good solutions to tough problems. And now that farm bill, as you can see on your own farm and in your own family, is beginning to do the job it was supposed to do.

We must do the same thing with energy, with civil service reform, with hospital costs, with airline deregulation, and with trimming Government spending and controlling the Government bureaucracy.

We must put public interest above special interest. Only then can we beat inflation.

I, as President, need your help as American citizens. I need the help of your elected representatives. And I need it now.

This is the challenge we face together. We cannot fail our great Nation.

Thank you very much.

NOTE: The President spoke at 11:03 a.m. in the Hearnes Multi-purpose Building at the University of Missouri.

Following his remarks, the President attended a reception for Missouri State and Mid-continent Farmers Association officials in the Hearnes Multi-purpose Building.

Federal Recreation and Historic Sites in Georgia and Kansas

Remarks on Signing H.R. 8336 Into Law.
August 15, 1978

THE PRESIDENT. The President of the United States has many pleasant duties to perform. But I don't know of any legislation that I have signed since I've been in the White House, nor will sign while I'm here, that brings me more personal pleasure than does this.

Several years of my life have been spent, even before I became Governor of Georgia, developing an acute interest in, and a love for, the Chattahoochee River. It's one of the most beautiful places in our country, extremely valuable to all those who know it, who live near it, and who appreciate the quiet and seclusion and the beauty and the value of this river to our people. It's a rare occasion when within the city limits of one of our major cities, one can find pure water and trout and free canoeing and rapids and the seclusion of the Earth the way God made it. But the Chattahoochee River is this kind of place.

Standing around me are people who care as much for the river as do I, who have been down the river many times, in great crowds and also in seclusion. And I'm particularly grateful that Senator Sam Nunn and Senator Herman Talmadge are here, who worked so long and hard on this bill; Congressman Wyche Fowler and Congressman Elliott Levitas, in whose district most of this preservation will be done and encouragement for use of the river will be accomplished.

I particularly want to thank Senator Abourezk and Senator Pete Williams; and especially Phil Burton, who has husbanded this legislation through the Congress in a very effective fashion.

This legislation will provide authorization—not the appropriation of money yet—for the acquisition of property over a 48-mile stretch, from Buford Dam down to Peachtree Creek, which is in the city limits of Atlanta, Georgia, varying in width of sometimes up to 4,000 feet wide.

It will not permit Federal money to be used to acquire land that's owned by any other government entity. That land must be deeded free of charge to this national recreation area.

If I've ever seen a project that was initiated from the local level in a very unselfish way, it's this one. We came a long way in Georgia in preserving this valuable national asset on our own. And many landowners donated property, private organizations contributed money, and the intense interest of our people for many, many years has resulted in this legislation.

There's a practical benefit, also, in preserving the beauty and the quality of this area and the purity of the water. From this river, the Chattahoochee, comes water for 25 percent of the total population of Georgia, almost a million-and-a-half people.

This is a great step forward and is indicative of the need for well-preserved recreation areas to be in the immediate vicinity of major urban centers.

I want to say, also, that this legislation has broader interest than just to Georgia. There is an authorization for the preservation of the Fort Scott National Historical landmark in Kansas, and this is a very beneficial type of action by the Congress that shows a good coordination between private citizens, local, State, and Federal Government.

So, it is with a great deal of pleasure that I sign into law this legislation, House bill 8336, that will authorize the national recreation area encompassing the Chattahoochee River and the Fort Scott National Historical landmark in Kansas.

Thank you all for making this happy day possible for me and for those who love the Earth the way God made it. Thank you.

[At this point, the President signed the bill.]

REPRESENTATIVE LEVITAS. Mr. President, thank you for this opportunity that you have provided, not only to the people of Georgia but to all Americans. If there's ever been a project that started with an idea and involved citizens who wanted to see that idea fulfilled, it's been this Chattahoochee River. Citizens who cared and were concerned and were willing to sacrifice all over the State of Georgia made this possible. And I'm glad to see so many young children here today, because what has been done, the bill that you've signed, will make it possible for them and their children and their children's children to enjoy the same beauty and wonders of nature on the Chattahoochee that we have.

And I want to give you my personal thanks for your leadership as Governor and as President, not only in this but what it symbolizes for other things and for the future. Thank you, Mr. President.

THE PRESIDENT. Thank you all very much. This is a very good day for all of us.

NOTE: The President spoke at 9:32 a.m. at the signing ceremony in the Rose Garden at the White House.

As enacted, H.R. 8336 is Public Law 95–344, approved August 15.

Corporation for Public Broadcasting

Nomination of Three Members of the Board of Directors. August 15, 1978

The President today announced that he will nominate three persons to be members of the Board of Directors of the Corporation for Public Broadcasting. They are:

GEOFFREY COWAN, of Los Angeles, who would replace Joseph Hughes, whose term expired. Cowan, 36, is a lecturer in the Communications Studies Department at UCLA, and an attorney at the Center for Law in the Public Interest. From 1972 to 1974, he was director of the Communications Law Program at UCLA.

PAUL S. FRIEDLANDER, of Seattle, who would replace Gloria Anderson, term expired. Friedlander, 66, is an attorney and president of Friedlander and Sons, Inc. He is on the board of KCTS–TV and is active in civic organizations.

KATHLEEN NOLAN, of Los Angeles, who would replace Amos Hostetter, term expired. Nolan, 44, is president of the Screen Actors Guild. She is an actress in television, theater, and films. She has been a lecturer at the UCLA extension program on "Women in Media" and is on the Los Angeles Board of Human Relations.

International Atomic Energy Agency

Nomination of U.S. Representative and Alternate Representatives to the 22d Session of the General Conference. August 15, 1978

The President today announced the persons whom he will nominate as Representative and Alternate Representatives of the United States to the 22d session of the General Conference of the International Atomic Energy Agency (IAEA), which is scheduled to be held in Vienna, Austria, from September 18 to 22, 1978. They are:

DALE D. MYERS, Under Secretary of Energy, to be the U.S. Representative;

GERARD C. SMITH, Ambassador at Large and United States Special Representative for Non-Proliferation Matters, to be an Alternate Representative; and

ROGER KIRK, Deputy Representative of the United States to IAEA, to be an Alternate Representative.

Foreign Exchange Markets

White House Statement. August 16, 1978

The President has been meeting with Secretary of the Treasury Blumenthal, Chairman of the Federal Reserve Board Miller, and others in the light of his deep concern over developments in foreign exchange markets in recent days. The sharp decline in the dollar and disorderly market conditions, at a time when the U.S. trade position is showing signs of real improvement, could threaten progress toward dealing with our inflation and achieving orderly growth at home and abroad. In the light of these circumstances, the President requested the Secretary and the Chairman to consider what actions might be appropriate on their part and to recommend any future actions on his part to deal with the situation.

National Urban Policy

Remarks on Signing Four Executive Orders Implementing Urban Programs.
August 16, 1978

THE PRESIDENT. First of all, I want to thank all of you for coming here to join us again in evolving one of the most important programs that we have to face as leaders in our Nation and the private sector of our economy and the local, State, and Federal governments, the different agencies that are now being bound more closely together.

Three-fourths of the people in this country live in urban areas. And I think it's accurate to say, without casting blame on anyone, that in the past, before last year, the problems of the downtown central city and other urban areas were becoming much more crucial and critical, and people were disturbed and were losing confidence in the future.

Last week I went to New York City— and I spent a lot of time in New York during the campaign years—and there's a new attitude, a new spirit of confidence and cooperation, friendship there that's really inspirational. This is not different

from the circumstance in many of our metropolitan areas.

Some of you were with us last March when we announced a comprehensive urban policy for our Nation. This was the policy evolved after months, thousands of hours of work, because we recognize that budget limitations don't let us pump 40 or 50 billions of dollars into massive new programs in urban areas. So, we tried to evolve a proposal that would create a new partnership where people, working together, could make the existing programs more effective and where a limited amount of additional funding in new programs would pay greatly magnified dividends to our country.

We've tried to cut tape and paperwork and root out waste that has in the past existed. We now have a carefully targeted, well-coordinated, and constantly more effective set of Federal programs.

Since last March, we have submitted to the Congress all fourteen legislative proposals that were encompassed in our recommendation. Most of them have made very good progress. Some of them are now on the verge of being passed in final form. Others are being hotly debated, and I think the public and the Congress are becoming better acquainted with the reasons for their passage. But I know and I'm sure you realize that a lot can be done without legislative action.

We've already initiated almost a hundred administrative decisions that are being put into effect now to change the programs to a closer focus on actual need, to consolidate divided programs, to simplify procedures, and in general, to improve the administration altogether.

Today I'm signing four Executive orders of major importance. The first one will help to put Federal buildings in urban areas, a simple thing, but symbolically and tangibly it will have a great beneficial impact. It will tend to move jobs and people and opportunities and growth down to the formerly abandoned central city areas or those that were being abandoned in a slow and inexorable way.

I hope that this Government action and I expect this Government action will take root in the private sector and that that might be an additional commitment on the part of business and industry, professional leaders, to take the same kind of action to strengthen the backbone of our major cities and to build up jobs and further investments there.

The second Executive order will direct all Federal agencies to buy more goods and services from areas of our country that have a high unemployment rate. This, of course, will, without costing the Government any more money, help to correct a very serious deficiency. In many instances, as you well know, the highest unemployment rate exists in our neglected or deteriorating urban centers—not always, but in general. And I've asked the Federal agencies to report to me every 6 months on the progress they have made in carrying out this order to purchase goods where the unemployment rate is high.

The third Executive order will help us to assess the impact of legislative proposals, not creating massive paperwork analyses, but just to make sure that when action is taken by the Congress, sometimes in haste, sometimes in committees that are not directly responsible for urban problems, that the inadvertent damage to downtown city areas can be avoided, quite often with a substantial saving in actual tax expenditures and an increase in efficiency at the same time.

And the fourth and final Executive order will create officially an Interagency Coordinating Council, not with a new bureaucracy, but a mechanism by which for the first time, really, we can continue close consultation among the major agencies in Government responsible for the solution of urban problems.

Jack Watson on my staff is already working with key leaders in Housing and Urban Development, in Labor, Commerce, HEW, Interior, and other major Federal agencies responsible for programs that in the past have not been adequately coordinated.

As Governor, I was sometimes blessed, always aware of the presence of the Federal Regional Office in Atlanta, just a few blocks from the State Capitol. But quite often those individual Federal agency representatives would not or could not work together. I now see in retrospect that they could not work together, because you can't expect a regional office to coordinate their efforts if there's an absence of coordination in Washington.

They cannot correct defects or mistakes made in Washington. And we are being sure that from now on, as a city has a serious problem, that here in the environment around the White House, led by Jack Watson, those different agencies that in the past in good conscience have gone in different directions because they have different responsibilities, now coordinate their work to make sure that their own efforts are magnified, not duplicated, because we do have limited facilities and limited money to expend.

Well, these Executive orders will bring us closer to a coherent, coordinated, more effective urban policy.

This is not the end of our efforts, but I think we've already had tangible demonstrations of the benefits of what we've undertaken so far. And a lot of the credit goes to you from Federal agencies and from communities all over our Nation who have confidence in American people, who recognize that our lifestyles, our life patterns, are not going to be dramatically changed, that we'll live lifetimes and even our children and grandchildren will live lifetimes in major urban centers. And it's our responsibility to assure that their quality of life is not worse in the future, but is greatly enhanced.

I believe that with this new partnership which we are going to sustain, that we'll be successful in all these efforts.

Again, let me thank you for being here, and now I'd like to sign the four Executive orders.

[At this point, the President signed Executive Order 12072.]

This is involving Federal space management directing that Federal buildings be located in urban areas.

This is Federal procurement in labor surplus areas where the unemployment rate is high.

[The President signed Executive Order 12073.]

This one is the analysis of urban and community impact for actions taken by Federal agencies, and also decisions made by the Congress.

[The President signed Executive Order 12074.]

And the last one, of course, is the creation of the Interagency Coordinating Council, under the leadership of Jack Watson, and with your participation.

[The President signed Executive Order 12075.]

CLARENCE M. MITCHELL, JR. Mr. President, I'd like to exercise a little seniority and say that after 30 years or more around Washington, this is one of the most magnificent things that I've seen done here. As a resident who commutes to the city, commutes to Washington and has been doing it for a long time, I have seen the devastating effect in our great cities where Federal agencies spend millions of dollars building outside of the city limits into virgin territory, and it causes tremendous unemployment and dislocation, everything else. Also, we have seen some

awful things through the years—people being displaced for highways, dams, and things of that sort—just because there wasn't the kind of coordination that you envision here.

I must say, Mr. President, I don't think you get credit lots of times for many of the things that you do. That's why I'm exercising my seniority here.

THE PRESIDENT. I might interrupt to say I never have seen a more appropriate exhibition of the use of seniority. *[Laughter]*

MR. MITCHELL. I think you're great anyway, and I think today is another of a series of climaxes in your career as President. I think the people ought to let you know when they think you're doing a good job.

THE PRESIDENT. Thank you.

Let me just close by saying, before Pat Harris takes over and explains some further details, I really appreciate what Clarence Mitchell has said. Quite often not only myself but the members of the Cabinet, the Congress, the Federal Government, even State and local governments don't get an adequate recognition when they do make progress. My wife is going to be working for the next couple of years in trying to stimulate additional private input, aside from government, in making our urban centers more attractive.

I believe that if there's one characteristic that can describe what we have done and the characteristic of it, it would be to utilize common sense. We've not had pipe dreams, we've not put together hastily constructed, very expensive, doubtful programs to give the image of progress when the results might be counterproductive. We have made sure that they are practical and effective by letting the proposals evolve, beginning with those who are supposed to receive services and those who actually experience problems and want to correct their problems, right on up to Washington.

It hasn't been a program that was evolved in Washington and handed down to the local communities that need help. And I think if we can retain that degree of common sense, we can make sure that every time we spend the taxpayer's dollar that it's greatly magnified in its beneficial effect. That's what I want to do, and that's what your participation has helped to make progress.

Pat Harris is kind of the linchpin of making this thing work, and now I'd like to turn the program over to her, if you'll excuse me.

NOTE: The President spoke at 1:35 p.m. in Room 450 of the Old Executive Office Building. Clarence M. Mitchell, Jr., is director of the Washington bureau of the National Association for the Advancement of Colored People.

Following the President's remarks, Secretary of Housing and Urban Development Patricia Roberts Harris and other administration officials conducted a briefing on the national urban policy for Federal, State, and local officials.

On the same day, the President transmitted to the Congress a report entitled "The President's 1978 National Urban Policy Report: A Biennial Report to the Congress Submitted Pursuant to Sections 702 and 703(a), National Urban Policy and New Communities Development Act, as Amended in 1977—Prepared by the U.S. Department of Housing and Urban Development, August 1978" (Government Printing Office, 147 pages).

Federal Space Management

Executive Order 12072.   August 16, 1978

By the authority vested in me as President of the United States of America by Section 205(a) of the Federal Property and Administrative Services Act of 1949, as amended (40 U.S.C. 486(a)), and in order to prescribe appropriate policies and directives, not inconsistent with that Act and other applicable provisions of law, for the planning, acquisition, utilization, and management of Federal space facilities, it is hereby ordered as follows:

1-1. *Space Acquisition.*

1-101. Federal facilities and Federal use of space in urban areas shall serve to strengthen the Nation's cities and to make them attractive places to live and work. Such Federal space shall conserve existing urban resources and encourage the development and redevelopment of cities.

1-102. Procedures for meeting space needs in urban areas shall give serious consideration to the impact a site selection will have on improving the social, economic, environmental, and cultural conditions of the communities in the urban area.

1-103. Except where such selection is otherwise prohibited, the process for meeting Federal space needs in urban areas shall give first consideration to a centralized community business area and adjacent areas of similar character, including other specific areas which may be recommended by local officials.

1-104. The process of meeting Federal space needs in urban areas shall be consistent with the policies of this Order and shall include consideration of the following criteria:

(a) Compatibility of the site with State, regional, or local development, redevelopment, or conservation objectives.

(b) Conformity with the activities and programs of other Federal agencies.

(c) Impact on economic development and employment opportunities in the urban area, including the utilization of human, natural, cultural, and community resources.

(d) Availability of adequate low and moderate income housing for Federal employees and their families on a nondiscriminatory basis.

(e) Availability of adequate public transportation and parking and accessibility to the public.

1–105. Procedures for meeting space needs in urban areas shall be consistent with the policies of this Order and shall include consideration of the following alternatives:

(a) Availability of existing federally controlled facilities.

(b) Utilization of buildings of historic, architectural, or cultural significance within the meaning of section 105 of the Public Buildings Cooperative Use Act of 1976 (90 Stat. 2507, 40 U.S.C. 612a).

(c) Acquisition or utilization of existing privately owned facilities.

(d) Construction of new facilities.

(e) Opportunities for locating cultural, educational, recreational, or commercial activities within the proposed facility.

1–106. Site selection and space assignments shall take into account the management needs for consolidation of agencies or activities in common or adjacent space in order to improve administration and management and effect economies.

1–2. *Administrator of General Services.*

1–201. The Administrator of General Services shall develop programs to implement the policies of this Order through the efficient acquisition and utilization of Federally owned and leased space. In particular, the Administrator shall:

(a) Select, acquire, and manage Federal space in a manner which will foster the policies and programs of the Federal government and improve the management and administration of government activities.

(b) Issue regulations, standards, and criteria for the selection, acquisition, and management of Federally owned and leased space.

(c) Periodically undertake surveys of space requirements and space utilization in the executive agencies.

(d) Ensure, in cooperation with the heads of Executive agencies, that their essential space requirements are met in a manner that is economically feasible and prudent.

(e) Make maximum use of existing Federally controlled facilities which, in his judgment, are adequate or economically adaptable to meeting the space needs of executive agencies.

(f) Annually submit long-range plans and programs for the acquisition, modernization, and use of space for approval by the President.

1–202. The Administrator is authorized to request from any Executive agency such information and assistance deemed necessary to carry out his functions under this Order. Each agency shall, to the extent not prohibited by law, furnish such information and assistance to the Administrator.

1–203. In the process of meeting Federal space needs in urban areas and implementing the policies of this Order, the Administrator shall:

(a) Consider the efficient performance of the missions and programs of the agencies, the nature and function of the facilities involved, the convenience of the public served, and the maintenance and improvement of safe and healthful working conditions for employees.

(b) Coordinate proposed programs and plans for facilities and space with the Director of the Office of Management and Budget.

(c) Consult with appropriate Federal, State, regional, and local government officials and consider their recommendations for and objections to a proposed selection site or space acquisition.

(d) Coordinate proposed programs and plans for facilities and space in a manner designed to implement the purposes of this Order.

(e) Prior to making a final determination concerning the location of Federal facilities, notify the concerned Executive agency of an intended course of action and take into account any additional information provided.

1–204. In ascertaining the social, economic, environmental and other impacts which site selection would have on a community, the Administrator shall, when appropriate, obtain the advice of interested agencies.

1–3. *General Provisions.*

1–301. The heads of Executive agencies shall cooperate with the Administrator in implementing the policies of this Order and shall economize on their use of space. They shall ensure that the Administrator is given early notice of new or changing missions or organizational realignments which affect space requirements.

1–302. Executive agencies which acquire or utilize Federally owned or leased space under authority other than the Federal Property and Administrative Services Act of 1949, as amended, shall conform to the provisions of this Order to the extent they have the authority to do so.

1–303. Executive Order No. 11512 of February 27, 1970, is revoked.

JIMMY CARTER

The White House,
    August 16, 1978.

[Filed with the Office of the Federal Register, 11:38 a.m., August 17, 1978]

Federal Procurement in Labor Surplus Areas

Executive Order 12073.   August 16, 1978

By the authority vested in me as President by the Constitution of the United States of America, and in order to strengthen the economic base of our Nation, it is hereby ordered as follows:

1–1. *Procurements in Labor Surplus Areas.*

1–101. Executive agencies shall emphasize procurement set-asides in labor surplus areas in order to strengthen our Nation's economy.

1–102. Labor surplus area procurements shall be consistent with this Order and, to the extent funds are available, the priorities of Section 15 of the Small Business Act, as amended by Public Law 95–89 (15 U.S.C. 644).

1–2. *Administrator of General Services.*

1–201. The Administrator shall coordinate with and advise State and local officials with regard to Federal efforts to encourage procurements in labor surplus areas with the aim of fostering economic development in labor surplus areas.

1–202. The Administrator shall establish specific labor surplus area procurement targets for Executive agencies in consultation with the heads of those agencies.

1–203. In cooperation with the heads of Executive agencies, the Administrator shall encourage the use of set-asides or other appropriate methods for meeting procurement targets in labor surplus areas.

1–204. The Administrator shall report every six months to the President on the progress of the agencies in achieving the procurement targets.

1–3. *Agency Responsibilities.*

1–301. The Secretary of Labor shall classify and designate labor markets which are labor surplus areas. The Secretary shall provide labor market data to the heads of agencies and State and local officials in order to promote the development of business opportunities in labor surplus areas.

1-302. The heads of Executive agencies shall cooperate with the Administrator in carrying out his responsibilities for labor surplus area programs and shall provide the information necessary for setting procurement targets and recording achievement. They shall keep the Administrator informed of plans and programs which affect labor surplus procurements, with particular attention to opportunities for minority firms.

1-303. In accord with Section 6 of the Office of Federal Procurement Policy Act (41 U.S.C. 405), the Administrator for Federal Procurement Policy shall be responsible for the overall direction and oversight of the policies affecting procurement programs for labor surplus areas.

JIMMY CARTER

The White House,
August 16, 1978.

[Filed with the Office of the Federal Register, 11:39 a.m., August 17, 1978]

Urban and Community Impact Analyses

Executive Order 12074.   August 16, 1978

By the authority vested in me as President by the Constitution of the United States of America, and in order to establish an internal management procedure for identifying aspects of proposed Federal policies that may adversely impact cities, counties, and other communities, it is hereby ordered as follows:

1-1. *Urban and Community Impact Analyses.*

1-101. The Director of the Office of Management and Budget shall: (a) develop criteria for identifying major policy proposals to be analyzed; (b) formulate standards regarding the content and format of impact analyses; and (c) establish procedures for the submission and review of such analyses.

1-102. The Director of the Office of Management and Budget and the Assistant to the President for Domestic Affairs and Policy shall review the analyses.

1-2. *Agency Responsibilities.*

1-201. Executive agencies shall prepare urban and community impact analyses for major policy initiatives identified by the Office of Management and Budget, the Assistant to the President for Domestic Affairs and Policy, or the agencies themselves.

1-202. Each Executive agency shall, to the extent permitted by law, cooperate with the Director of the Office of Management and Budget and the Assistant to the President for Domestic Affairs and Policy in the performance of their functions under this Order, furnish them with the information they request, and comply with the procedures prescribed pursuant to this Order.

JIMMY CARTER

The White House,
August 16, 1978.

[Filed with the Office of the Federal Register, 11:51 a.m., August 17, 1978]

Interagency Coordinating Council

Executive Order 12075.   August 16, 1978

By the authority vested in me as President by the Constitution of the United States of America, and in order to provide for interagency coordination of the implementation of Federal urban and regional policy, it is hereby ordered as follows:

1–1. *Establishment of the Council.*

1–101. There is established the Interagency Coordinating Council.

1–102. The Council shall be composed of the heads of the following agencies, or a designated representative, and such others as the President may designate:

  (a) Department of the Treasury
  (b) Department of Justice
  (c) Department of the Interior
  (d) Department of Agriculture
  (e) Department of Commerce
  (f) Department of Labor
  (g) Department of Health, Education, and Welfare
  (h) Department of Housing and Urban Development
  (i) Department of Transportation
  (j) Department of Energy
  (k) Environmental Protection Agency
  (l) Community Services Administration
  (m) General Services Administration
  (n) Small Business Administration
  (o) ACTION

1–103. The President shall designate the Chairperson of the Council.

1–2. *Functions of the Council.*

1–201. The Council shall work with Executive agencies to involve all sectors of the Nation, including State, county and local governments, regional bodies, the private sector, neighborhood groups, and volunteer and civic associations, in a partnership to conserve and strengthen America's communities.

1–202. The Council shall facilitate cooperation and coordination of urban and regional policy implementation among and between Executive agencies.

1–203. The Council shall assist Executive agencies in coordinating timely responses to State, county and local government and community development strategies.

1–204. The Council shall identify and seek to solve interagency and intergovernmental problems which impede the effective functioning of the Federal system.

1–205. The functions of the Council shall neither substitute for nor replace Executive Office of the President clearance, review and decisionmaking procedures.

1–3. *Administrative Provisions.*

1–301. Executive agencies shall cooperate with and assist the Council in performing its functions.

1–302. The Chairperson shall be responsible for providing the Council with such administrative services or support as may be necessary or appropriate.

1–303. The Chairperson may establish working groups or subcommittees of the Council. The Chairman may invite representatives of nonmember agencies to participate from time to time in the functions of the Council.

1–304. The Chairperson shall report to the President on the performance of the Council's functions.

JIMMY CARTER

The White House,
  August 16, 1978.

[Filed with the Office of the Federal Register, 11:52 a.m., August 17, 1978]

Central Intelligence Agency

Remarks to Agency Employees.
August 16, 1978

Admiral Turner and distinguished leaders, members of the Central Intelligence Agency:

It is a pleasure for me to be back out here to meet with you and to express again my feelings about our Nation and about what you do to protect it and to make it even greater than it already is. A year and a half I was here for my first visit, the time of the swearing-in ceremony of the Director, Admiral Stan Turner.

I've told many groups that one of the most pleasant surprises that I have had as President of our country has been the quality of work done by the Central Intelligence Agency, and I want to thank you for that. You've made my job easier. The decisions that I must make on a daily basis require objective and accurate, unbiased analyses of very complicated issues. It's difficult for someone in my position to distinguish between the appearance of things and the actual facts, the reality of them. And you do a superb job in trying to bring to me and others who make opinions and then make decisions about what our Nation should do in the pursuit of our own goals and purposes, in the enhancement of our own ideals and principles.

In the last number of years, the purpose of the CIA has been changing. Your assignment is different now from what it was. There was a time not too long ago when your almost unique responsibility was to assess the activities and the potential activities of the Soviet Union. That, obviously, is still one of the important assignments that you have. But now your duties extend to the analysis of almost every region of the world, almost every country on Earth, our close allies and friends. We need to understand their special problems, their special opportunities, how we can work better with them, the attitude of their people; to study food production, agriculture, forestry, economics, mining, labor, a very, very complicated, very diverse analysis problem for you all.

I know the heroism demonstrated by many of you. Nathan Hale, who is recognized here and who died, I believe, 202 years ago, said, "My only regret is that I have only one life to give for my country." Behind me in this auditorium are commemorated 35 agents of the CIA who have given their lives for the service of our country, not adequately recognized for heroism, some not even recognized by name, 17 of them. Their names are not even known or revealed, because they lost their lives for our country in clandestine operations. But all of you represent the attitude and the commitment, the willingness to sacrifice, the patriotism of those who gave the supreme sacrifice.

I think the relations between the CIA and the American public have been substantially improved in recent months. The relationship between the CIA and the Congress has been substantially improved in recent months. Some who have been here for many, many years have had an inclination to be concerned about the increased openness, the willingness of Stan Turner and myself to let the American people know who you are, what you do, some aspects of your work which don't violate security of our country, and there's a growing appreciation for what this agency does, what you individually do for our Nation.

But there is a conflict with which you need to help me, and that is the balancing between legitimate openness which enhances your work and protects the interest of our country on one hand, and the careful preservation of security, the non-revelation of secrets which you hold which can be very damaging to our Nation if revealed. It takes intelligence, it takes sound judgment, it takes common sense to draw that distinction. But those are characteristics which you exhibit very well every day.

I'd like to say in closing that I appreciate what you are, what you do, the high professionalism, training, education, experience that you bring to your job and which you demonstrate every day with your good work, the honesty and integrity that you present to me and to your other superiors, to the Congress, to the public for critical examination.

You almost are in the position of being like Caesar's wife; you have to be even more pure and more clean and more decent and more honest than almost any persons who serve in government, because the slightest mistake on your part is highly publicized and greatly magnified, whereas your great achievements and successes quite often are not publicized and are not recognized, and they certainly are never exaggerated.

I'm glad that we have this partnership. There is now a stability in the CIA which has been brought by Admiral Turner and joined by Frank Carlucci [1] that I hope will permeate your lives for many months, many years to come.

There have been too many shocks, too many rapid changes in the past, but the policies that have now been established by Executive order, by sound decisions, by cooperation, and in the future by law, will give you a much surer sense of what the future will bring, will liberate you individually, in effect, to make your own beneficial impact in our country be even greater. I know how serious uncertainty is in a person's life.

We've assigned to the CIA, because we trust you, additional responsibilities for tasking the entire intelligence network, for preparing the budget under close supervision, for better coordination among the different agencies that have a contribution to make to security. And I am very pleased and very confident that this new assignment of authority and responsibility will be borne by you equally as well as you have demonstrated your ability to carry out functions of supreme importance to our country in the past.

---

[1] Deputy Director, Central Intelligence Agency.

So, as President of our Nation, as a partner with you in creating a better nation in the future, I express my thanks to you for a superb job and my confidence that you and I, Director Turner, and others can do even better in the future.

Thank you very much.

NOTE: The President spoke at 2:08 p.m. outside the main entrance of the Headquarters Building in Langley, Va. Following his remarks, he attended two briefings given by CIA personnel.

National Hispanic Heritage Week, 1978

Proclamation 4585.   *August 17, 1978*

By the President of the United States of America

A Proclamation

The Hispanic heritage of 16 million Americans is an essential part of our identity as a nation, and of our role as a leader among nations. As we reflect upon the countless historical, cultural, and scientific contributions that Hispanics have made to the development of our country, I want to reaffirm my commitment to ensuring the full participation of our Hispanic citizens in all levels of our society and government.

Americans have had a unique opportunity to appreciate the values of a broad diversity of cultures and the contribution each makes to our democratic and pluralistic society.

As we reach beyond our national borders to advocate the cause of human rights, we must increasingly look to our own Hispanic community as one of our primary sources of advice and counsel, particularly in the development of our relations with other nations of the western hemisphere.

Our Hispanic community is an integral element in the domestic life of our own nation, as well as in our continuing international effort to build understanding, mutual respect, and common purpose with all Hispanic nations.

In recognition of our Hispanic heritage, the Congress, by joint resolution approved September 17, 1968 (36 U.S.C. 169f), has requested the President to issue annually a proclamation designating the week including September 15 and 16 as National Hispanic Heritage Week.

Now, THEREFORE, I, JIMMY CARTER, President of the United States of America, do hereby proclaim the week beginning September 10, 1978, as National Hispanic Heritage Week. I call upon all Americans to take this occasion to reflect on the influence of Hispanic culture in our land, and to consider how each of us can be more responsive to the concerns of Hispanics.

As we observe National Hispanic Heritage Week with appropriate ceremonies and activities, I call upon all Federal, State and community agencies, all business and professional leaders, educators, the clergy, and the communications media to join with me in launching new Hispanic initiatives that will assure the full participation of Hispanic Americans in every sector of American life, at every level of leadership, and guarantee that the human and civil rights of Hispanics, other minorities and, indeed, all citizens of our country are fully protected under the law.

As part of this week's activities I have asked many of my Hispanic appointees to hold town meetings in areas of concentrated Hispanic population. These meetings will help define the problems and concerns shared by Hispanics across our nation.

The role of Hispanics is ever increasing and offers our Hispanic citizens—the fourth largest Spanish-speaking population in the world—an increasingly active and visible leadership.

IN WITNESS WHEREOF, I have hereunto set my hand this seventeenth day of August, in the year of our Lord nineteen hundred seventy-eight, and of the Independence of the United States of America the two hundred and third.

JIMMY CARTER

[Filed with the Office of the Federal Register, 11:53 a.m., August 17, 1978]

Columbus Day, 1978

Proclamation 4586. August 17, 1978

By the President of the United States of America

A Proclamation

Nearly five centuries ago an Italian navigator in the service of Spain gazed beyond the wisdom of his time and sailed west to rap at the portals of the New World. Yearly, in gratitude, we celebrate this incomparable achievement of Christopher Columbus. We honor too the courage, self-sacrifice, and perseverance that propelled him on that voyage.

These qualities can fairly be held as a standard for the people of the United States of America. When they have been foremost in our spirit, they have produced the finest moments in the history of our Republic. Let us continue to hold them fast so that we may always be open to new wisdom, but courageous and persevering in defense of the ideas we hold dear.

On October 9 we again honor the memory of Christopher Columbus and the ever-young promise of the New World.

In tribute to his achievement, the Congress of the United States, by joint resolution approved April 30, 1934 (48 Stat. 657), as modified by the Act of June 28, 1968 (82 Stat. 250), asked the President to proclaim the second Monday in October of each year as Columbus Day.

Now, THEREFORE, I, JIMMY CARTER, President of the United States of America, do hereby designate Monday, October 9, 1978, as Columbus Day. I invite the people of this Nation to observe that day in their schools, churches, and other suitable places with appropriate ceremonies to commemorate his great adventure.

I also direct that the flag of the United States be displayed on all public buildings on the appointed day in memory of Christopher Columbus.

IN WITNESS WHEREOF, I have hereunto set my hand this seventeenth day of August, in the year of our Lord nineteen hundred seventy-eight, and of the Independence of the United States of America the two hundred and third.

JIMMY CARTER

[Filed with the Office of the Federal Register, 11:54 a.m., August 17, 1978]

During the past year, I appointed a new Chairman and two Board members. To represent the public interest and advise the Congress of the Administration's position, I appointed as Chairman, William P. Adams, former Transportation Counsel for the House Committee on Interstate and Foreign Commerce. I appointed one Board member who was nominated by railroad management—Earl Oliver, a former official of the Illinois Central Gulf Railroad and the National Railway Labor Conference—and another Board member who was nominated by railroad labor—Charles J. Chamberlain, former President of the Brotherhood of Railroad Signalmen and Chairman of the Railway Labor Executives' Association. Each of these appointees is extremely well qualified and can be expected to set a high level of public service.

JIMMY CARTER

The White House,
    August 17, 1978.

NOTE: The report is entitled "Railroad Retirement Board—1977 Annual Report for Fiscal Year Ending September 30" (Government Printing Office, 88 pages).

Railroad Retirement Board

Message to the Congress Transmitting a Report. August 17, 1978

To the Congress of the United States:

I hereby transmit the annual report of the Railroad Retirement Board which summarizes its fiscal year 1977 operations under both the Railroad Retirement and Railroad Unemployment Insurance Acts.

Benefit payments under these Acts totaled almost $4 billion. Of this amount, $3.8 billion went to 1,100,000 retirement and survivor annuitants and $180 million was paid to 160,000 unemployment and sickness beneficiaries.

THE PRESIDENT'S NEWS CONFERENCE OF AUGUST 17, 1978

VETO OF THE DEFENSE DEPARTMENT AUTHORIZATION BILL

THE PRESIDENT. I have one statement, and then I'd like to answer your questions.

As President of the United States, my ultimate responsibility is to the protection of our Nation's security, and as Commander in Chief of our Armed Forces, it's my obligation to see that those forces are operationally ready, fully equipped, and prepared for any contingency. Because I take these responsibilities seriously, I submitted this spring a defense budget designed to improve our military preparedness and calling for increased spending in real terms, above and beyond the cost of inflation, especially for enhanced readiness and for the urgent requirement of strengthening our NATO forces.

Because of these same obligations, and with the concurrence of the Secretary of Defense, I have decided to veto the defense authorization bill which the Congress passed last week.

This is not a question of money. The Congress has reduced only slightly the amount of money that I recommended for our Nation's defense. It's a question of how that money is going to be spent, whether it will be concentrated in the most vital areas of need, or diverted to less crucial projects.

We must have the strongest possible defense within the budget limits set by Congress. We cannot afford to waste our national defense dollars. We need better maintenance and logistical support, more research and development, a more flexible Navy. And we need these improvements now, not 8 or 10 years in the future. The defense authorization bill does not meet any of these requirements.

There are four particularly disturbing areas in which this bill, by cutting into the muscle of our military request, could weaken our defenses and erode our contributions to NATO.

This bill, for instance, cuts $800 million for weapons and equipment for our Army forces, undermining our commitment to NATO at the very time when our allies recognize the urgent need to improve the power and the readiness of our forces in Europe.

This bill would also cut $200 million for Air Force weapons and equipment which would add flexibility and strength to our military forces, not only in NATO and this country but throughout the world.

This bill would also cause a cut of half a billion dollars, $500 million, from readiness funds. This is an unglamorous part, but it's necessary for expenditures for ship overhauls, weapon repairs, spare parts, personnel training, and the logistical support which guarantees that we can move our forces and have them act immediately when they're needed.

And this bill also cuts very heavily from military research and development funds. I had requested a substantial increase in these funds to sustain our position of technical excellence in a world where circumstances change rapidly and where weapons are increasingly dependent on advanced technology. The bill that has passed the Congress could lead to an actual decrease in these funds for next year.

The ultimate effect of this bill would also weaken our Navy by aggravating the dangerous trend away from a larger number of different kinds of ships which can maintain our military presence on the high seas, and toward a disturbingly small number of ships which are increasingly costly.

What the Congress has done with the money being cut from these vital areas is to authorize a fifth nuclear-powered aircraft carrier, which we do not need. This would be the most expensive ship ever built. Its purchase price, even estimated now, would be at least $2 billion, and the aircraft it would carry and the extra ships required to escort and defend it would cost billions more in years to come.

In order to use our dollars for their maximum effect, we must choose the armor, artillery, aircraft, and support that will immediately bolster our strength, especially in NATO. By diverting funds away from more important defense needs in order to build a very expensive nuclear aircraft carrier, this bill would reduce our commitment to NATO, waste the resources available for defense, and weaken our Nation's military capabilities in the future.

I will be glad to cooperate with Congress in passing a more responsible bill, and I urge the Members of Congress to face that duty as soon as they return from their recess. The Nation's interest and my oath of office require me to veto this bill and to seek a stronger defense for our country.

Mr. Gerstenzang [James Gerstenzang, Associated Press].

QUESTIONS

CAMP DAVID MEETING ON THE MIDDLE EAST

Q. Mr. President, your direct involvement in the Middle East summit conference next month is seeming to be a high-risk gamble. Could you say what led you to take this step and what are the risks? What happens if this effort fails?

THE PRESIDENT. Let me say, first of all, that we don't act just as a noninterested mediator or message carrier in the Mideast negotiations. Our own national security is vitally involved, not only in maintaining peace around the world but especially in the Middle East, and we have devoted our utmost effort to bringing about a peaceful resolution of the long-standing Middle Eastern disputes.

I have met in small groups and privately with Prime Minister Begin and with President Sadat on many occasions. I think I know them both quite well, and I am absolutely convinced that both men want peace and the people in both nations genuinely want peace.

All of us were pleased last November when the exchange of visits took place, Sadat going to Jerusalem, Begin going to Ismailia. It was one of the happiest few weeks of my career as President not to be involved in those negotiations and to see

them face to face, trying to work out the differences between them.

Since then, the interrelationships which brought us such high hopes last winter have deteriorated rapidly. In spite of our best efforts, recently, those peace talks broke down completely, not only at the high level of the Prime Minister and President but even at a lower level involving cabinet officers themselves. Even when Secretary Vance had scheduled a trip to the Mideast, we could not get the leaders to agree to meet.

It is a very high risk thing for me politically, because now I think if we are unsuccessful at Camp David, I will certainly have to share part of the blame for that failure. But I don't see that I could do anything differently, because I'm afraid that if the leaders do not meet and do not permit their subordinates to meet in a continuing series of tough negotiations that the situation in the Middle East might be much more serious in the future even than it is now.

So, I decided on my own, and later got the concurrence of my top advisers, including Secretary of State Vance and the Vice President and others, to invite both those men to meet with me at Camp David. We do not have any assurance of success. I do not anticipate being completely successful there and having a peace treaty signed in that brief period of time. But if we can get them to sit down and discuss honestly and sincerely their desires for peace, to explore the compatibilities among them, to identify very clearly the differences, try to resolve those differences, then I think we can set a framework for peace in the future.

It may result only in a redetermination or recommitment to continue subsequent negotiations. We might make more progress than that. But we will go there as a full partner in the discussions, depending primarily, however, on the two national leaders themselves to work out the differences between them.

I pray and I hope the whole Nation, the whole world will pray that we do not fail, because failure could result in a new conflict in the Middle East which could severely damage the security of our own country.

VALUE OF THE DOLLAR

Q. Mr. President, you're said to be very deeply concerned about the dollar. Is there a dollar crisis? What are you going to do about it? And why haven't you done something yet? And I have a followup. [*Laughter*]

THE PRESIDENT. I am deeply concerned about the dollar. And I have asked Secretary of Treasury Mike Blumenthal and the Chairman of the Federal Reserve, Bill Miller, and others to consult with one another and to give me advice on steps that can be taken by them and by me.

There are some factors that are encouraging in the long run. Recent monthly data have shown that our balance-of-trade deficit is going down. I believe that we've made good progress in seeing an increase in the economic growth of other nations overseas so that they are better able now and in the future to buy our goods than they have been in the past, when we were growing fast and we could afford to buy their goods.

The Congress can contribute. The single most important thing that Congress can do to control inflation and also to ease the pressures on the dollar and to reduce our severe adverse trade balance is to pass an energy bill. I've done everything in the world that I could do and so have my Cabinet members and all my staff members and many hundreds of people around the country to induce Congress to go ahead and act on a comprehensive energy bill. They have not yet

done so. They've been working on it since April of 1977. We still have hopes that the Congress will act successfully.

Another underlying problem, of course, is inflation, and we are dealing with that on many levels. One, of course, is to hold down the size of the Federal deficit. We've made good progress there. I know that when I ran for President in 1976, the Federal deficit was in the sixties of billions of dollars. By 1978, it was down to the fifties of billions of dollars; '79, the forties of billions of dollars, low forties; and by the 1980 fiscal year, I am determined to have it down in the thirties of billions of dollars.

We are eliminating excessive spending and demonstrating to our country and the rest of the world that we are determined to hold down inflation. But it's a tenacious thing. It would be erroneous for me to insinuate to the American people that it's easy and that we're going to solve it overnight. Everybody has got to help. But if we can top it out, the inflationary curve, this year, I think that will send a good signal to the world monetary markets.

So, we have a combination of problems, some of which we are addressing successfully, some of which are very difficult, but we are all working in concert. And I believe that the underlying economic strength of our Nation will prevent a further deterioration in the status of our Nation and a further deterioration in the dollar, particularly if the Congress will act and if we can act in this administration to address those questions that I've just described.

CAMP DAVID MEETING

Q. Mr. President, back to the summit and whatever preparations may have been made. I want to push one step further, if I may. Is there an agreement or an arrangement or even a slight arrangement already in place before you go into this big meeting?

THE PRESIDENT. Well, in my letter to both Prime Minister Begin and Sadat, I outlined some of the principles on which we should meet—not negotiating principles, but the need, for instance, to lessen the vituperation that had been sweeping back and forth between government leaders, to express in a positive fashion their determination to come to Camp David with flexibility and with an ability on the part of those government leaders to act.

The immediacy of their response—they did not delay at all, when they read my letter, to say "I will come to Camp David"—is indicative of good faith on their part. But I do not have any commitment from them to change their previously expressed positions as a prerequisite or prelude to coming to Camp David.

RELATIONS WITH THE CONGRESS

Q. Mr. President, your Agriculture Secretary was quoted as saying earlier this week that you intended to retaliate against the cheapshot artists in Congress who oppose some of your programs. What is your attitude toward Congress as you come up to the Labor Day recess?

THE PRESIDENT. I would say that in general, the Congress has been very cooperative and very constructive. I think any analysis of the accomplishments of Congress last year in the domestic field would be favorable. We addressed the most difficult questions of all successfully. The energy question was put off until this year and still has not yet been addressed.

In foreign affairs this year, I think the Congress has acted with great judgment and also with great courage to deal with some longstanding questions involving sales of weapons to the moderate Arab nations, approval of the Panama Canal treaties, removal of the embargo against Turkey, and so forth.

I have never discussed this subject with the Secretary of Agriculture, and he's never discussed it with me. But I certainly don't have any animosity against any Member of Congress. I do not have a list of Congress Members who are worthy of punishment. I have no inclination to do that; it's not part of my nature. And I think it would be counterproductive if I attempted it.

OIL IMPORTS

Q. Mr. President, earlier this year, you suggested that the time might come when you would have to move administratively to impose import fees or quotas on foreign oil. My question is, are we near that time, and if Congress should adjourn this year without passing what you consider to be a substantial energy bill, will you do it?

THE PRESIDENT. That's an option that I will maintain open for myself. Obviously there are several options that can be exercised, the most advantageous of which to consumers, to oil producers, to our own country, and, I think, to the rest of the world, is to pass the energy proposal as I presented it to the Congress— to impose a tax on oil, to reduce its waste, and to encourage more use of American oil in the first place, and to distribute the revenues from that tax back immediately to the American people. This would be a very constructive attitude.

The second one would be in the absence of congressional action, for me to impose, through Executive order under the present law, either import quotas, limiting the amount of oil that could come in, or import fees, which would charge extra for oil coming into the Nation. And, of course, the other option, which is one that I think would be at the bottom of the list, would be to permit the oil companies to unilaterally increase the price of their oil very high and to let the consumers pay for it to the enrichment of the oil companies themselves.

So, that's a list of the options that I can think of at this moment that exist for me. And my preference, of course, is for the Congress to act. But I cannot foreclose the option that I have to act unilaterally through Executive order if the Congress does not act.

MARGARET COSTANZA

Q. Why do you think Midge Costanza felt obliged to resign, and do you have a new appointee to take her place?

THE PRESIDENT. Midge resigned without any encouragement from me, and, matter of fact, I asked Midge to stay on. She left in very good spirits. She has announced to the press and has told me privately that she has several very good offers to utilize her superb services. And she's worked very closely with us, no later than yesterday, as a matter of fact, in the White House West Wing to help us choose a successor to take her place. So, I think that describes the situation quite accurately.

Q. Do you have a nominee for her replacement?

THE PRESIDENT. We have several ones whom we are considering. We have not yet made a choice.

U.S. TRADE WITH THE SOVIET UNION

Q. Do you plan to continue selective trade sanctions against the Soviet Union, since some allied nations, such as France, are unwilling to cooperate in technological boycotts?

THE PRESIDENT. We obviously don't have any inclination to declare a trade embargo against the Soviet Union to stop all trade. It's to the advantage of our country to have trade with the Soviet Union. I think embargoes that have been imposed in the past by previous administrations, for instance, an unannounced and unilateral stopping of shipments of feed grains and food grains and soybeans overseas, has been very detrimental to our country. I do not intend to do that. But we'll assess each individual sale on the basis of several criteria, one of the most important ones of which is, does this sale contribute to an enhancement of the Soviets' military capability and is this country the only reasonable source of a supply for that particular item? And we have a very well established procedure in the Government for carrying out that analysis. And I believe that my own cancellation of the sale of a very large computer a month or so ago was well-advised, but we'll have to consider each one of those additional items as they are proposed on its own merits.

It takes a long time for a decision like that to get to my desk. Most of them are simply canceled before they ever arrive— even come in to my attention. The Commerce Department and others assess it; the State Department has to approve it before it comes to me. But we'll have to assess them on an individual basis.

DEFENSE AUTHORIZATION VETO

Q. Mr. President, getting back to energy and the veto today, Senator Jackson was suggesting today, that this is going to be a big problem for the energy bill, now that you've vetoed the defense bill, because he says the aircraft carrier was kind of the glue that held that thing together, and it took them 6 months to get the bill. And he says now it's going to be a problem, and he says we've got so many headaches and this is another one. It seems rather significant to me, in that he's the man that is carrying that energy bill for you.

THE PRESIDENT. I met this morning with Senator Jackson and others to go over the reasons for my veto. He did not disagree with the reasons that I expressed. I have not had a single adviser who told me that we ought to go ahead with the nuclear aircraft carrier. The only concerns that anyone has expressed to me is that it might create additional work for Congress in correcting an error that I think they made, or that it might cause me political problems in having vetoed a bill and had a confrontation with Congress.

I don't desire to do anything with Congress but to cooperate with them. We are working now in the House, which will first take up the veto, since the bill originated in the House, to make sure that we can sustain my veto on the basis of its own merits. I don't see any reason to link the building of a nuclear aircraft carrier, which will be completed maybe in 1987, with the approval of a conference committee report on natural gas that's been negotiated now for almost 16 months.

Q. Yes, sir, but are you confident someone up there might not see it?

THE PRESIDENT. I cannot guarantee that nobody considers it, but I can tell you this: It won't be the first problem we've had with the natural gas bill. [*Laughter*]

TUITION TAX CREDITS

Q. Mr. President, the Congress appears bent on passing some sort of tuition tax relief this year. I'd like to know what your current position is now as regards to Congress passing tuition tax relief for parents with children in universities and your position on parents with children in parochial schools. Is it your intention to veto any tuition tax relief that comes down?

THE PRESIDENT. I do not favor the tuition tax credit approach to college students, and I even more strongly oppose on constitutional grounds Government financing of the elementary and secondary schools which are privately operated.

On the tax bill, I am not satisfied with the bill that the House has passed. It does not meet the basic criteria that I set for fairness, for equity, for simplicity, for progressivity and the efficient enhancement of capital investment funds.

A veto is a prerogative that a President is given under the Constitution. It's not an abnormal authority. It's one that should be a routine part of the interrelationship between the White House and Capitol Hill. And it's not only a pleasure to have that authority to make my own leverage more effective but it's a duty that falls on me. And I want to keep that option open. And I reserve the right after a bill gets on my desk to either veto it or sign it. I have no reticence about vetoing a bill that I think is contrary to the best interests of our country. My hope is that Congress would pass a bill after close consultation with us that would be acceptable.

My position on the tax credits is clear. I have not changed my position at all. I don't think anybody's position on the tax bill, the tax reduction bill, is clear. It is very, very confused, and my hope is that the Senate will correct some of the basic errors that the House made; if not, that in the conference committee the bill can be made acceptable to me. If it's not acceptable to me, I will have no hesitancy about vetoing it.

PEOPLE'S REPUBLIC OF CHINA

Q. Mr. President, during a recent interview you made the point that both we and the Chinese are patient on the subject of establishing full diplomatic relations. My question concerns the extent of that patience on your part, whether now it might be something indefinitely on the back burner or something you would like to see accomplished between now and, let's say, the end of 1980?

THE PRESIDENT. The normalization of relations with the People's Republic of China has always been a goal of my administration. It was a goal of my predecessors under the general provisions of the Shanghai Communique, that was signed by President Nixon on his historic visit to China.

The pace of negotiations must be one that's mutually set. We have a very good representative in China, Leonard Woodcock. They have a very fine representative here, a new representative not known as an ambassador, in Washington whom I've not yet met.

But we are constantly exploring ways to have better relationships with China. First of all, no matter what our relationship is with them on a bilateral basis, we want China to be a peaceful nation, to be secure, and to have their beneficial effects felt around the world. Secondly, we want our bilateral relationships with them to be better, to enhance trade, communications, student exchange, and so forth, whether or not we have diplomatic relations as such. And then, of course, the final thing is to hope for diplomatic relations when we're both willing to proceed expeditiously and when we're both willing to accommodate one another's wishes.

I can't tell you what the pace of that might be. It's not something that I could unilaterally impose upon them, and I have to judge by what their response might be.

I think there's a new impression—certainly that I have of the leadership in China—that they are more outreaching now, they're more outgoing.

The present visit of Chairman Hua, for instance, to Romania, is a good indication and an almost unprecedented thing for them to go out into the Eastern European world, and perhaps even other countries as well later on, to make visits.

So, I think that they are reaching out in a spirit of friendship. If they do, I will respond in good faith. I just cannot give you a time schedule.

RELATIONS WITH THE CONGRESS

Q. Mr. President, aside from the merits of the defense bill, which you've covered, some of your advisers are saying that part of your reason for vetoing it is a desire to undo the impression that you're a pushover, so to speak, when it comes to dealing with Congress. Do you think that you have been too willing in the past to go along with what the Members of Congress wanted, and how much does this veto have to do with an effort to make you appear tougher?

THE PRESIDENT. That really is not a factor involved in it. There have been times in the past when I've had a major difference with Congress—at least with a number of Congress Members—and have ultimately prevailed. Some of the foreign affairs debates which I just described a few minutes ago are examples of this. Early in the session last year, there was a great opposition in Congress, particularly the Democratic leadership, against reestablishing a reorganization authority for me. And they did it reluctantly, but now it's assumed to be a routine thing.

There have been cases when I have erred on the side of not vetoing a bill. I think that last year I should have vetoed the appropriation bill that authorized unnecessary water projects. If I had it to do over again, I would have vetoed it. But that's one of the rare occasions when I think I have been too lenient in accommodating the desires of Congress. But the Congress is now trying to reimpose those water projects on me as President and even additional ones that are worse.

So, I think that I've had a fairly well-balanced approach to Congress. We have close consultations with Congress on a continuing basis. I don't have any fear of the Congress. I'm sure they don't have any fear of me.

ADM. HYMAN G. RICKOVER

Q. Mr. President, in your book, "Why Not the Best?", you described Admiral Rickover as having had a great influence on your life. I wonder if in light of the veto, Mr. President, that you did discuss your decision against a new nuclear carrier of the *Nimitz* class with Admiral Rickover, and what that conversation consisted of?

THE PRESIDENT. No, I did not discuss it with him. When I had my first visit with Admiral Rickover after becoming President, it was obvious to me then and now that he's a very outspoken person. He presents his case to the Congress in an effective way, and he has a great influence on them and on me.

He pointed out then that his inclination was not to try to influence my decision on individual items in the defense budget, that he knew I had special problems as President and a special perspective that he could not have himself. And because of our close relationship in the past— which still exists, by the way—he was going to refrain from that particular aspect of my responsibilities.

He does meet with me quite frequently, and we have very frank discussions, but, I think, more in general terms. And he's not had any inclination to try to influence me on this particular matter.

Sarah [Sarah McClendon, McClendon News Service].

ROBERT T. GRIFFIN AND GEN. SAMUEL S. WALKER

Q. Sir, I want to point out to you to see if you think this is not an injustice. Robert Griffin of General Services Admin-

istration, the number two man, was fired because of his conduct there. And then a job was created for him by you, giving him $50,000 a year. Then we have a four-star general out in the Pentagon, Walton Walker, with an exemplary record, and he's having to get out of service and take retirement, which will cost the taxpayers a lot of money, simply because his position at NATO was abolished. They gave it to a Turkish general to ease the tension over the arms embargo, and there's no other four-star slot for Walton Walker, so a good man has to get out of the service. Don't you think that's an injustice?

THE PRESIDENT. I'll try to respond as best I can. [*Laughter*] In the first place, I don't know of any item that's been reported by the press in a more distorted way than the one relating to Robert Griffin. Griffin was not fired because he's incompetent. He was not fired because there was any allegation about his honesty or integrity. He was moved from the General Services Administration because he was incompatible with the director of the General Services Administration, Mr. Solomon. He was not promoted. He was transferred to another position with the same salary exactly and the same pay grade exactly. He is not a member of the White House staff. He works for the Special Trade Representative, which is not in the White House at all.

There's been a general distortion of what happened in that respect. I have no apology to make for having moved him out of GSA. I have no apology to make for having put a good man with great integrity and great knowledge in a productive job.

The general to whom you refer was recently promoted to four-star status. He was assigned to Turkey to fill a position. NATO leaders, not completely controlled by us, decided that that position would be filled by a non-American. It was no reflection on General Walker at all. There is no other four-star position in the entire Armed Forces, and he was offered a three-star position. He decided that in place of going back to a three-star position, which he had just recently occupied, that he would prefer to resign. And he is a good man also. There's no reflection on him; there's never been any reflection on him.

I've looked into both these cases myself. I'm familiar with both of them, and I can tell you that there's no reflection on either man. And they were given jobs, offered jobs compatible with their rank. General Walker performed superbly in Turkey, and I regret that he did not stay in the Army as a four-star general.

MR. GERSTENZANG. Thank you, Mr. President.

NOTE: President Carter's thirty-sixth news conference began at 4 p.m. in Room 450 of the Old Executive Office Building. It was broadcast live on television and radio.

Veto of the Department of Defense Appropriation Authorization Bill

Message to the House of Representatives Returning H.R. 10929 Without Approval. August 17, 1978

To the House of Representatives:

I am returning without my approval H.R. 10929, the "Department of Defense Appropriation Authorization Act, 1979." I am doing so because I cannot, consistently with my constitutional responsibilities, sign into law a bill that in my view would weaken our national security in certain critical areas and wastes scarce defense dollars. The Congress' inclusion in this bill of a number of lower priority programs would force out of our defense budget certain central elements of our

program, items needed now to modernize and bolster our military forces.

I believe that the defense of the United States needs to be strengthened. An adequate defense is the single most important concern I have as President. Accordingly, I submitted to the Congress in January of this year a budget request for the Department of Defense which would if enacted provide the defense we need. It requested $126.0 billion for the Department of Defense for Fiscal Year 1979. That amount was judged by me and by the Secretary of Defense to be adequate to provide for the military security of this country in Fiscal Year 1979, provided it was wisely spent.

The bill I am returning does not spend wisely. Instead, it actually would lead to less defense capability than I have requested. It does this by eliminating funds for high priority defense requirements and adding funds for purposes which do not meet our defense needs. Most notably, it would take nearly $2 billion from the total and set it aside for purchase of a nuclear-powered aircraft carrier—a ship which in the end would cost at least $2.4 billion, plus additional billions for its aircraft and the additional ships needed to defend and escort it.

We need more immediate improvements in our defense forces. A new nuclear-powered aircraft carrier would not be commissioned until 1987.

To spend $2 billion in defense dollars in that way would ignore much more serious and immediate defense needs. Other programs have been cut, during the appropriation process as well, to stay within Congressional budget limits. The effect would thus be to take away funds urgently needed by the Army, Navy, Air Force and Marine Corps for high priority programs—and to use those funds to build the most expensive ship in history.

The result would be to weaken our military security in several critical areas, particularly during the next two years, at a time when we should be strengthening it. Within the $126.0 billion allocated for defense, we cannot have both an adequately balanced defense program and the luxury of an unneeded nuclear-powered aircraft carrier.

In pushing a nuclear-powered aircraft carrier into a $126.0 billion defense budget, H.R. 10929 would result in reduction or elimination of these essential programs, and a consequent weakening of our defense posture:

—*Weapons and equipment for the Army.* I requested a $1 billion increase to strengthen our ground forces, particularly our NATO-oriented forces, by providing more helicopters, combat vehicles and ammunition for our front-line forces. Adding the nuclear-powered aircraft carrier means eliminating $800 million of that increase.

—*Weapons and equipment for the Air Force.* I requested more funds for airlift, electronic warfare equipment and electronically guided ordnance. Adding the nuclear-powered aircraft carrier means eliminating $200 million of this increase.

—*Readiness funds.* It makes no sense to have military forces if their equipment is not in condition to fight. I requested an increase of $1 billion for items which are not glamorous, but which provide the immediate fighting capability of our forces—funds (requiring appropriation but not prior authorization) for repairs of weapons, spare parts for vehicles and aircraft, ship overhauls, training of personnel, communications, and logistical support to move equipment to where it is needed. Adding the nuclear-powered aircraft carrier means eliminating half of that increase in fighting capability—some $500 million.

—*Research and development.* To sustain our position of excellence in a world of weapons increasingly dependent on technology, I requested a 3% real growth in defense research and development. Adding the nuclear-powered aircraft carrier leads to an actual reduction in research and development. The bill also shifts some R&D funds from high priority programs to less important ones.

Our Navy has for a decade been moving in the direction of larger and larger, more-and-more-costly ships, and fewer of them. As a consequence our fleet today is smaller than at any time since 1940. We need a fleet that includes more vessels that can perform our Navy's mission but that are not, as this one would be, so designed as to be prohibitively expensive to build. The Navy does not need a fifth nuclear-powered aircraft carrier. It can maintain a twelve-carrier fleet and maintain the fighting capability it needs from a conventionally powered carrier, which I shall request in my budget for next year, at a saving of $1 billion for that single ship. Without this kind of discipline and control of the cost of ships, our Navy will not long be able to carry out its missions.

For these reasons, I must withhold my approval from H.R. 10929. I adhere firmly to my request that the Congress provide $126.0 billion for defense in Fiscal Year 1979. But I ask that the Congress delete the authorization for the nuclear-powered aircraft carrier, and use that essential $2 billion of that $126.0 billion instead for as many of our programs as possible from the following critical areas:

$1 billion for Army and Air Force equipment—For helicopters, transport aircraft, combat vehicles, electronic equipment, ammunition and ordnance and other weapons and equipment.

$500 million for improving readiness in all the armed services—For a wide variety of items, ranging from repair of weapons to spare parts stockage to improved training and logistical support.

Up to $500 million for research and development—For programs proposed in my FY 79 budget but deleted by one or another Congressional action.

Naval Ships—It is crucial to maintain an appropriate overall annual level of ship construction. The Congress should return all of the general purpose ships requested in our budget.

These are the ways in which our defense dollars need to be spent. These are the ways in which they will add to our military security, by obtaining the greatest military capability for each dollar and by focusing the effort where more effort is needed.

In light of the continuing Soviet buildup, we must not reduce our own real defense capability, either by cutting the budget amount I have requested, or by substituting for high priority defense requirements programs which are less urgent or less effective.

If we do not spend our defense dollars wisely, we do not provide adequately for the security of our country. I know that the Congress and I share common goals. I ask the Congress to cooperate with me to help our armed forces use their funds in ways which produce the greatest fighting power, and to provide the men and women of our armed forces with the kinds of weapons, equipment and other items of support which they need to do their jobs.

JIMMY CARTER

The White House,
    August 17, 1978.

NOTE: The House of Representatives reconsidered H.R. 10929 on September 7, and the bill was referred to committee. For the President's statement on the House action, see page 1501 of this volume.

First Transatlantic Balloon Crossing

Telegram to the Three Balloonists on Their Successful Crossing. August 17, 1978

On behalf of all the American people, I salute your triumphant adventure. Your daring voyage through the silent sky is a welcome reminder that individual acts of bravery and skill still capture our collective imagination.

I wish to invite you to visit with me in the White House once you've returned to this country.

We all celebrate your magnificent achievement and welcome you warmly back to the earth.

JIMMY CARTER

NOTE: The telegram was addressed to Ben Abruzzo, Max Anderson, and Larry Newman, and was delivered to them after they landed their hot-air balloon, *Double Eagle II,* near Miserey, France.

Tennessee Valley Authority

Nomination of Richard M. Freeman To Be a Member of the Board of Directors. August 17, 1978

The President today announced that he will nominate Richard M. Freeman, of Glencoe, Ill., to be a member of the Board of Directors of the Tennessee Valley Authority for a 9-year term. He would replace Aubrey Wagner, whose term has expired.

Freeman was born July 2, 1921, in Crawfordsville, Ind. He received an A.B. from Wabash College in 1943 and an LL.B. from Columbia University Law School in 1948.

From 1948 to 1957, Freeman was an attorney in the law department of the Tennessee Valley Authority, counseling the resource development program and handling administrative and court litigation. From 1957 to 1967, he was a partner in the law firm of Belnap, Spencer, Hardy & Freeman, which represented industries, railroads, barge lines, and motor carriers before the Interstate Commerce Commission.

Since 1967 Freeman has been with the Chicago and North Western Transportation Co. (formerly the Chicago and North Western Railway Co.), serving as vice president—law; as one of three trustees, voting the Class A common stock, most of which is owned by employees of the company; and one of three members of the executive committee of the board. Freeman was one of two persons who worked out the formation of the Chicago and North Western Transportation Co. and the employee purchase of the Chicago and North Western Railway Co. in 1972.

Child Health Day, 1978

Proclamation 4587.   August 17, 1978

By the President of the United States of America

A Proclamation

On this, the 50th anniversary of the first Child Health Day, it is appropriate to reaffirm our strong commitment to the health and well-being of our Nation's children. Our children are our future. We all bear responsibility for assuring that they are as healthy as the healing arts permit.

After 50 years, barriers to child health care persist. The problems are now more social than technological: unequal distribution of medical personnel, inadequate access to medical services, and continuing diet problems still plague our poorer families. Despite a dramatic reduction in our

infant mortality rate in recent decades, children in some parts of the country still suffer far more than children elsewhere. This geographic inequity persists to adulthood and these same areas generally have a higher percentage of handicapped individuals as well as higher infant and child mortality rates.

We need to nurture all our children. Until mothers and children throughout the nation have equal access to comprehensive health care we can't claim to have met our responsibilities.

This is particularly important for youngsters who suffer physical, emotional or developmental handicaps. Adequate research and rehabilitative programs are essential for these children but all children need our vigilant concern. Ultimately, our goal is a nation of vibrantly healthy youngsters, psychologically and physically fit to meet any future demand.

In 1979 the United States will join other nations in observing the United Nations International Year of the Child. This will provide a chance to focus world attention on the special needs of children. Let us make this a significant year of progress in our own Nation so that we set an example for all others.

Now, THEREFORE, I, JIMMY CARTER, President of the United States of America, do hereby proclaim Monday, October 2, 1978, as Child Health Day. I am asking all the citizens of this Nation at home and abroad to unite with me in pledging our support of activities which provide for every child the promotion of health, accessible comprehensive health care services, physical and mental recreation, and the extension of cultural traditions.

IN WITNESS WHEREOF, I have hereunto set my hand this seventeenth day of August, in the year of our Lord nineteen hundred seventy-eight, and of the

Independence of the United States of America the two hundred and third.

JIMMY CARTER

[Filed with the Office of the Federal Register, 10:16 a.m., August 18, 1978]

NOTE: The text of the proclamation was released on August 18.

National Hispanic Heritage Week, 1978

Memorandum From the President.
August 17, 1978

Memorandum for the Heads of Executive Departments and Agencies

Subject: National Hispanic Heritage Week

September 10 through 16 has been designated National Hispanic Heritage Week. A series of town meetings will be held during this week in selected cities throughout the country where there are significant Hispanic population concentrations. The purpose of these meetings will be to listen to the views of the Hispanic community on current economic and social issues, particularly education, jobs, housing, health and criminal justice.

Top level Hispanic appointees in each of your agencies have been asked to participate in these town meetings. I have asked that they report to me on the views expressed at the meetings and what kind of action needs to be taken by the Departments and Agencies to deal with the problems identified. I hope you will cooperate in this effort by making available to us the Hispanic appointees who have been asked to participate in the week's activities.

The importance of National Hispanic Heritage Week should not be underesti-

mated. It is a special opportunity to reaffirm this Administration's commitment to ensuring the full participation of our Hispanic citizens in all levels of our society and government.

JIMMY CARTER

NOTE: The text of the memorandum was released on August 18.

United States Ambassador to Togo

Nomination of Marilyn P. Johnson.
August 18, 1978

The President today announced that he will nominate Marilyn P. Johnson, of Bethlehem, N.H., to be Ambassador Extraordinary and Plenipotentiary of the United States to the Republic of Togo. She would replace Ronald D. Palmer, resigned.

Johnson was born June 19, 1922, in Boston, Mass. She received a B.A. from Radcliffe College in 1944 and an M.A. from Middlebury College in 1952. She served in the U.S. Navy from 1944 to 1946.

Between 1952 and 1959, Johnson taught high school French. From 1962 to 1964, she taught English as a foreign language in Cameroon and Mali. She joined the Foreign Service in 1964, and served as cultural affairs officer in Bamako and Tunis, and public affairs officer in Niamey.

From 1971 to 1974, Johnson was Deputy Assistant Director of the Information Centers Program. She attended the Senior Seminar in Foreign Policy in 1974–75. In 1975–76 she took Russian language training. Since 1976 she has been cultural affairs officer in Moscow.

Natural Gas Legislation

*Remarks on the Congressional Conference
Committee Report on the Legislation.
August 18, 1978*

THE PRESIDENT. Good morning, everybody.

Last night the House and Senate conferees on the energy legislation reached agreement on one of the most difficult aspects of the entire energy package, and that is natural gas, ending a 30-year debate on this question. Now the conference reports will go to the House and Senate for further action.

This is a major step forward under the most difficult of circumstances, and I and everyone in our country owe the House and Senate conferees a debt of gratitude for their assistance and tenacity and their willingness to accommodate their own deeply felt personal and sectional interests in the best interests of our country.

This legislation, when passed, will give us a new national market, making available new supplies of natural gas which will be at a lower price than competitive foreign oil. The bill is specially designed to protect homeowners and small business leaders, small businesses.

It's also designed to give industry adequate supplies of natural gas at a good and competitive price. The bill encourages additional American production of natural gas, gives better prices in the future, and more sure prices in the future for those producers, at the same time protecting the interests of consumers.

We have been especially careful in natural gas legislation and the other elements of the overall energy package to protect the interests of the poor, the underprivileged, and those who don't have the flexible capability to accommodate changing prices.

The next step will be for the Senate to make a decision about the conference committee report. My hope and expectation is that the individual Members of the Senate will show the same deep interest, a willingness to be flexible, a willingness to accommodate the needs of our Nation, as have the conferees themselves.

There is no doubt that this legislation, when passed, will protect the security interests of our country. It will protect the energy interests of our country. It will help us to assure continued prosperity and jobs for the American people. It will help us to control inflation; it will also help us to have a more stable economy and to protect the integrity of the dollar overseas.

All these benefits that will come from this legislation when and if it is passed, I'm sure, will be an inspiration to the Members of the House and Senate to act expeditiously and positively on this very difficult and challenging but very important legislation.

Jim, are you prepared to answer questions?

SECRETARY SCHLESINGER. Yes, sir.

THE PRESIDENT. Secretary Schlesinger, who's done a superb job in bringing together disparate opinions and working very continuously with legislation perhaps as complex as any that's ever faced the Congress, will now answer questions that you might have.

REPORTER. Did you have to make any promises to Rangel and Corman that we should know about to get them to sign?

THE PRESIDENT. That you need to know about?

Q. That we should know about. [*Laughter*] Did you have to promise them something?

THE PRESIDENT. No. The only thing they were interested in was that I would repeat for the Congress and for the American public my interests along with theirs to protect the interests of the poor and the underprivileged, not only in this particular legislation but in other aspects.

Q. But no deals?

THE PRESIDENT. No.

NOTE: The President spoke at 11:35 a.m. to reporters assembled in the Briefing Room at the White House. Following his remarks, Secretary of Energy James R. Schlesinger held a news conference on the natural gas legislation.

Discount Rate Increase

White House Statement on the Federal Reserve Board Action.   August 18, 1978

The administration fully understands the reasons for this action. It is essential that we control inflation if we are to have a strong dollar and sustainable economic growth. As we have said, there will be a series of continuing actions over the next several weeks to deal with these problems.

NOTE: Earlier in the day, the Board of Directors of the Federal Reserve System had raised the discount rate from 7¼ percent to 7¾ percent.

National P.O.W.–M.I.A. Recognition Day

Statement on Signing H.J. Res. 963 Into Law.   August 18, 1978

American soldiers have been captured or have become missing in action during each of our country's wars.

The agony of their families has been incalculable. The prisoners themselves have suffered deprivation, starvation, abuse, torture, and sometimes death at the hands of their captors.

Their heroism in the face of these afflictions has often been greater than the heroism of men in battle; the prisoner's battle to preserve life, dignity, and honor

can go on day after painful day, sometimes for years.

And the anguish suffered by the families of Americans missing in action is prolonged by lack of certainty over the fate of a husband or son or grandson or brother.

I am proud to sign a bill honoring these Americans who have given so much and endured so much. Many of them have won through to become some of America's finest citizens—like the former prisoner of war who is one of the sponsors of this bill, Senator Hathaway. I join all Americans in gratefully recognizing their sacrifices.

NOTE: As enacted, H.J. Res. 963 is Public Law 95–349, approved August 18. The resolution requests the President to issue a proclamation designating July 18, 1979, as "National P.O.W.–M.I.A. Recognition Day."

United States International Trade Commission

Nomination of Paula Stern To Be a Member.   August 18, 1978

The President today announced that he will nominate Paula Stern, of Washington, D.C., to be a member of the United States International Trade Commission. She would replace Daniel Minchew, whose term has expired.

Stern was born March 31, 1945, in Chicago. She received a B.A. from Goucher College in 1967, an M.A. in regional studies from Harvard University in 1969, and an M.A. in international affairs (1970), an M.A.L.D. (1974), and a Ph. D. (1976) from the Fletcher School of Law and Diplomacy.

From 1972 to 1974, Stern was legislative assistant to Senator Gaylord Nelson. From 1975 to 1976, she was a guest scholar at the Brookings Institution, working on a manuscript on domestic politics and foreign policy. In 1976 she was senior legislative assistant to Senator Nelson, and also served as a policy analyst on matters related to the State Department for the Carter-Mondale Transition Team. She is now with the Carnegie Endowment for International Peace.

National Commission on Libraries and Information Science

Nomination of Charles W. Benton To Be a Member. August 18, 1978

The President today announced that he will nominate Charles W. Benton, of Evanston, Ill., to be a member of the National Commission on Libraries and Information Science.

Benton, 47, has been with Encyclopædia Britannica Films since 1953. He is presently chairman and chief executive officer of Films Inc., a subsidiary of Encyclopædia Britannica Films.

Executive Schedule

Executive Order 12076. August 18, 1978

LEVELS IV AND V OF THE EXECUTIVE SCHEDULE

By the authority vested in me as President by Section 5317 of Title 5 of the United States Code, in order to place in level IV of the Executive Schedule the positions of Senior Adviser to the Secretary of State and Special Assistant to the Special Representative for Trade Negotiations, and in order to codify other positions presently placed in levels IV and V of the Executive Schedule, it is hereby ordered as follows:

1–1. *Executive Schedule Positions.*

1–101. The following positions are placed in level IV of the Executive Schedule:

(a) Senior Adviser to the Secretary, Department of State.

(b) Director, United States Secret Service, Department of the Treasury.

(c) Assistant Secretary (Enforcement and Operations), Department of the Treasury.

(d) Adviser to the Secretary and Deputy Secretary of Defense for NATO Affairs, Department of Defense.

(e) Assistant to the Secretary for Legislative Affairs, Department of Defense.

(f) Assistant Attorney General, United States Attorneys and Trial Advocacy, Department of Justice.

(g) Director of Agricultural Economics, Department of Agriculture.

(h) Director, Office of Congressional and Public Affairs, Department of Agriculture.

(i) Chief Economist, Department of Commerce.

(j) Deputy Under Secretary for Regional Affairs, Department of Commerce.

(k) Deputy Under Secretary for International Labor Affairs, Department of Labor.

(l) Administrator, Health Care Financing Administration, Department of Health, Education, and Welfare.

(m) Administrator, Alcohol, Drug Abuse and Mental Health Administration, Department of Health, Education, and Welfare.

(n) Administrator, Health Services Administration, Department of Health, Education, and Welfare.

(o) Administrator, Research and Special Programs Administration, Department of Transportation.

(p) Associate Directors (4), Office of Management and Budget, Executive Office of the President.

(q) Special Assistant to the Special Representative for Trade Negotiations, Office of the Special Representative for Trade Negotiations.

1–102. The following positions are placed in level V of the Executive Schedule:

(a) Deputy Director, United States Secret Service, Department of the Treasury.

(b) Director, Office of Revenue Sharing, Department of the Treasury.

(c) Principal Deputy Assistant Secretary for Communications, Command, Control and Intelligence, Department of Defense.

(d) Deputy Assistant Secretary of Defense for Reserve Affairs, Department of Defense.

(e) Director of Policy Review, Department of Defense.

(f) Principal Deputy Assistant Secretary (International Security Affairs), Department of Defense.

(g) Assistant to the Secretary and Land Utilization Adviser, Department of the Interior.

(h) Executive Director, Pension Benefit Guaranty Corporation, Department of Labor.

(i) Administrator for Pension and Welfare Benefits, Department of Labor.

(j) Executive Assistant and Counselor to the Secretary, Department of Labor.

(k) Assistant Secretary, Comptroller, Department of Health, Education, and Welfare.

(l) Deputy Commissioner of Social Security, Department of Health, Education, and Welfare.

(m) Commissioner on Aging, Department of Health, Education, and Welfare.

(n) Commissioner, Automated Data and Telecommunications Service, General Services Administration.

1–2. *General Provisions.*

1–201. Nothing in this Order shall be deemed to terminate or otherwise affect the appointment, or to require the reappointment, of any occupant of any position listed in Section 1–1 of this Order who was the occupant of that position immediately prior to the issuance of this Order.

1–202. Executive Order No. 11861, as amended, is hereby revoked.

JIMMY CARTER

The White House,
August 18, 1978.

[Filed with the Office of the Federal Register, 10:59 a.m., August 21, 1978]

Mississippi River Commission
Executive Order 12077.   August 18, 1978

EXEMPTION OF ROY T. SESSUMS FROM MANDATORY RETIREMENT

Roy T. Sessums, Member, Mississippi River Commission, will become subject to mandatory retirement for age on August 31, 1978, under the provisions of Section 8335 of Title 5 of the United States Code unless exempted by Executive order.

In my judgment, the public interest requires that Roy T. Sessums be exempted from such mandatory retirement.

Now, THEREFORE, by the authority vested in me by subsection (c) of Section 8335 of Title 5 of the United States Code, I hereby exempt Roy T. Sessums from mandatory retirement until October 1, 1978.

JIMMY CARTER

The White House,
August 18, 1978.

[Filed with the Office of the Federal Register, 11 a.m., August 21, 1978]

National Lupus Week, 1978

Proclamation 4588.   August 18, 1978

By the President of the United States of America

A Proclamation

Five hundred thousand Americans suffer from Lupus erythematosus, an increasingly prevalent disease of the connective tissue. There are an estimated 50,000 new victims each year, mostly young women.

In the systemic form, lupus can affect almost any part of the body and create abnormalities in the skin, joints, kidney, heart, or other internal organs. Lupus is often fatal but even if not, its victims still endure pain and anguish.

We have made progress in understanding lupus in the last few years. Thousands of sufferers can look forward to improved treatment and the opportunity to live more productive and happier lives. Today's outlook is far from bleak, but we still need new research and alternative approaches to treatment and diagnosis if we are to eliminate lupus as a cause of human suffering and to improve life for its victims.

Now, THEREFORE, I, JIMMY CARTER, President of the United States of America, do hereby proclaim the week of September 17 through September 23, 1978 as National Lupus Week. I invite the Governors of the States, the Commonwealth of Puerto Rico, and officials of other areas subject to the jurisdiction of the United States to issue similar proclamations.

I urge the people of the United States and educational, philanthropic, scientific, medical, and health care organizations and professionals to provide the necessary assistance and resources to discover the cause and cure of lupus erythematosus and the other rheumatic diseases and to

alleviate the suffering of all persons struck by these disorders.

IN WITNESS WHEREOF, I have hereunto set my hand this eighteenth day of August, in the year of our Lord nineteen hundred seventy-eight, and of the Independence of the United States of America the two hundred and third.

JIMMY CARTER

[Filed with the Office of the Federal Register, 10:54 a.m., August 21, 1978]

World Conference To Combat Racism and Racial Discrimination

White House Statement.   August 18, 1978

This week representatives of many nations are meeting in Geneva in a World Conference to Combat Racism and Racial Discrimination.

The Conference marks the midpoint of the U.N. Decade for Action to Combat Racism and Racial Discrimination, a Decade whose initiation the United States strongly supported. But the United States is unable to participate in this potentially important Conference, although we will monitor the proceedings, because the definition of "racism" has been perverted for political ends by including Zionism as one of its forms. The United States cannot associate itself with the Decade so long as it endorses the patently false definition of Zionism as a form of racism.

Instead we hope that this Conference will return to the original purpose of the Decade, so that we might rejoin this international effort to eliminate racism throughout the world. We will work towards this end because we know the challenge that racism poses, and for more than a century we have struggled to heal its scars. We know our goals have not been fully accomplished, yet we are encouraged and deeply committed to them. Domestically and internationally, we will continue to pursue this great common purpose in the context of other uncompromised efforts.

We call on all nations to respect the original objectives of the United Nations Decade Against Racism and to resist efforts that distort its purpose and erode its moral force.

Digest of Other White House Announcements

The following listing includes the President's daily schedule and other items of general interest as announced by the White House Press Office during the period covered by this issue. Events and announcements printed elsewhere in the issue are not included.

August 12

The President met at the White House with Zbigniew Brzezinski, Assistant to the President for National Security Affairs.

August 13

The President went to Andrews A.F.B., Md., to meet Mrs. Carter and other members of the U.S. Delegation who were returning from the funeral of Pope Paul VI in Rome.

August 14

The President met at the White House with Dr. Brzezinski.

August 15

The President met at the White House with:
—Dr. Brzezinski;
—Frank B. Moore, Assistant to the President for Congressional Liaison;
—Vice President Walter F. Mondale;
—former baseball player Henry Aaron.

August 16

The President met at the White House with:
—Dr. Brzezinski;
—Mr. Moore;
—the Advisory Committee on Federal Pay.

The President received the first annual report on energy management in the Federal Government, prepared by the Department of Energy.

The President transmitted to the Congress the 1976 and 1977 annual reports of the Nuclear Regulatory Commission.

August 17

The President met at the White House with:
—Dr. Brzezinski;
—Mr. Moore;
—Louisiana civic leaders;
—Mrs. Carter, for lunch;
—Vice President Mondale, Adm. Stansfield Turner, Director of Central Intelligence, and Dr. Brzezinski.

August 18

The President met at the White House with:
—Vice President Mondale, Secretary of State Cyrus R. Vance, Secretary of Defense Harold Brown, Hamilton Jordan, Assistant to the President, and Dr. Brzezinski;
—Dr. Brzezinski;
—Mr. Moore;
—Charles L. Schultze, Chairman of the Council of Economic Advisers;
—labor and civil rights leaders to discuss the Humphrey-Hawkins full employment legislation;
—members of the International Labor Press Association (transcript begins on page 1490 of this volume);
—representatives of the United Negro College Fund.

The President has designated Edward Sanders as a Senior Adviser to the White

House and the Department of State for foreign policy, with special responsibility for Middle East affairs.

The President declared a major disaster for the Commonwealth of the Northern Mariana Islands as a result of Tropical Storm Carmen, beginning about August 9, which caused extensive public and private property damage.

The President departed the White House for a visit to Plains, Ga., the first stop in a 2-week vacation trip which will include visits to Boise, Idaho, and Jackson Hole, Wyo.

NOMINATIONS SUBMITTED TO THE SENATE

The following list does not include promotions of members of the Uniformed Services, nominations to the Service Academies, or nominations of Foreign Service officers.

Submitted August 14, 1978

RICHARD S. ARNOLD, of Arkansas, to be United States District Judge for the Eastern and Western Districts of Arkansas, vice Terry L. Shell, deceased.

Submitted August 15, 1978

The following-named persons to be members of the Board of Directors of the Corporation for Public Broadcasting for terms expiring March 26, 1984:

GEOFFREY COWAN, of California, vice Joseph D. Hughes, term expired.

PAUL S. FRIEDLANDER, of Washington, vice Gloria L. Anderson, term expired.

KATHLEEN NOLAN, of California, vice Amos B. Hostetter, Jr., term expired.

Withdrawn August 15, 1978

SAMUEL D. ZAGORIA, of Maryland, to be a member of the Federal Election Commission for a term expiring April 30, 1983, vice William L. Springer, term expired, which was sent to the Senate on April 10, 1978.

Submitted August 16, 1978

The following-named persons to be the Representative and Alternate Representatives of

NOMINATIONS—Continued

Submitted August 16—Continued

the United States of America to the Twenty-second Session of the General Conference of the International Atomic Energy Agency.

Representative:

DALE D. MYERS, of Virginia

Alternate Representatives:

GERARD C. SMITH, of the District of Columbia

ROGER KIRK, of the District of Columbia

Submitted August 18, 1978

MARILYN PRISCILLA JOHNSON, of New Hampshire, a Foreign Service information officer of Class two, to be Ambassador Extraordinary and Plenipotentiary of the United States of America to the Republic of Togo.

EDITH HUNTINGTON JONES DOBELLE, of Massachusetts, for the rank of Ambassador during her tenure of service as Chief of Protocol for the White House.

RICHARD MERRELL FREEMAN, of Illinois, to be a member of the Board of Directors of the Tennessee Valley Authority for the term expiring May 18, 1987, vice Aubrey J. Wagner, term expired.

PAULA STERN, of the District of Columbia, to be a member of the United States International Trade Commission for the term expiring June 16, 1987, vice Daniel Minchew, term expired.

CHARLES WILLIAM BENTON, of Illinois, to be a member of the National Commission on Libraries and Information Science for the remainder of the term expiring July 19, 1980, vice Frederick H. Burkhardt, resigned.

CHECKLIST OF WHITE HOUSE PRESS RELEASES

The following releases of the Office of the White House Press Secretary, distributed during the period covered by this issue, are not included in the issue.

CHECKLIST—Continued

Released August 12, 1978

Statement: withdrawal of nomination of Samuel D. Zagoria to be a member of the Federal Election Commission—by Senate Minority Leader Howard H. Baker, Jr.

Released August 14, 1978

Announcement: nomination of Richard S. Arnold to be United States District Judge for the Eastern and Western Districts of Arkansas

Released August 15, 1978

Advance text: remarks on signing H.R. 8336, a bill concerning Federal recreation and historic sites in Georgia and Kansas

Released August 16, 1978

Fact sheet: Interagency Coordinating Council

Report: on the status of the national urban policy as of mid-June

Released August 18, 1978

Biographical data: Edward Sanders, Senior Adviser to the White House and the Department of State on foreign policy

News conference: on natural gas legislation—by Secretary of Energy James R. Schlesinger

Announcement: visit of Zbigniew Brzezinski, Assistant to the President for National Security Affairs, to several Air Force command centers in the United States

ACTS APPROVED BY THE PRESIDENT

Approved August 15, 1978

H.R. 8336 _____ Public Law 95–344
An act to authorize the establishment of the Chattahoochee River National Recreation Area in the State of Georgia, and for other purposes.

H.R. 7581 _____ Public Law 95–345
An act to amend the Internal Revenue Code of 1954 with respect to the treatment of mutual or cooperative telephone company income from nonmember telephone companies, and for other purposes.

Approved August 17, 1978

S. 2424 _____ Public Law 95–346
An act to amend the Act incorporating the American Legion so as to redefine eligibility for membership therein.

Approved August 18, 1978

H.J. Res. 946 _____ Public Law 95–347
A joint resolution to designate October 7, 1978, as "National Guard Day".

S. 2821 _____ Public Law 95–348
An act to authorize appropriations for certain insular areas of the United States, and for other purposes.

H.J. Res. 963 _____ Public Law 95–349
A joint resolution designating July 18, 1979, as "National P.O.W.–M.I.A. Recognition Day".

H.J. Res. 682 _____ Public Law 95–350
A joint resolution to provide for the designation of a week as "National Lupus Week".

International Literacy Day, 1978

Proclamation 4589.   August 21, 1978

By the President of the United States of America

A Proclamation

Throughout our history, the United States has stood for the protection and promotion of human rights for all peoples. Central to these concerns are the political, social, and economic rights of all human beings. Our dedication to these rights stems from the belief that all people should be allowed to live their lives to the fullest of their capabilities, that the talent and character given each person by God should not be wasted.

Education is one of the most important gifts our society can give to its people in helping them fulfill their human potential. Especially in our modern world, adequate communication skills are essential. Education and training to promote literacy are central to our efforts to improve the lives of all people, and guarantee their basic human rights. Every illiterate adult is an indictment of us all.

In our own nation, and in nations across the world, significant efforts have been made to advance literacy, and bring its benefits to every man and woman. Our concern and dedication to this cause have brought results, but there still remains great progress to be made. Around the world, eight hundred million people lack effective reading or writing skills.

For the past 12 years, the United Nations Educational, Scientific, and Cultural Organization has set aside September 8 as Literacy Day. The United States has always joined with other nations in recognizing the need to advance literacy among people everywhere, to promote our cherished human rights.

Now, THEREFORE, I, JIMMY CARTER, President of the United States of America, do hereby proclaim September 8, 1978, as International Literacy Day, and I call upon the people of the United States to assess and strengthen our commitment to eliminating illiteracy both at home and abroad, recognizing that in so doing we are helping people everywhere open a gateway to many other human rights as well.

IN WITNESS WHEREOF, I have hereunto set my hand this twenty-first day of August, in the year of our Lord nineteen hundred seventy-eight, and of the Independence of the United States of America the two hundred and third.

JIMMY CARTER

[Filed with the Office of the Federal Register, 2:51 p.m., August 21, 1978]

International Air Transportation Negotiations

Statement by the President.
August 21, 1978

Ever since I became President, I have been seeking to introduce the airline industry to the benefits of competition both at home and abroad.

Two events highlight that effort. I am today releasing a formal statement of international aviation policy for the United States. Recently, representatives of the United States and Israel signed a new air service agreement which reflects the spirit of that policy.

Our policy seeks to encourage vigorous competition, with the goals of permitting lower fares, better service to more cities, and fewer Government restrictions on charter travel. Travelers of many countries have already benefited from recent agreements which reflect our competitive policy. I hope that our formal statement, by making our position clear, will ease the difficult process of negotiating additional air agreements with other countries.

The U.S.-Israeli agreement signed recently achieves these goals of reducing Government restrictions. It will permit healthy competition among our airlines, and, by giving Israel authority to serve four additional US. cities, it will greatly expand Israel's opportunity to provide air service between our countries.

International Air Transportation Negotiations

Statement of U.S. Policy for the Conduct of the Negotiations.   August 21, 1978

INTRODUCTION

United States international air transportation policy is designed to provide the greatest possible benefit to travelers and shippers. Our primary aim is furthering the maintenance and continued development of affordable, safe, convenient, efficient, and environmentally acceptable air services. Our policy for negotiating civil air transport agreements reflects our national goals in international air transportation. This policy provides a set of general objectives, designed particularly for major international air markets, on the basis of which United States negotiators can develop specific negotiating strategies.

Maximum consumer benefits can be best achieved through the preservation and extension of competition between airlines in a fair marketplace. Reliance on competitive market forces to the greatest extent possible in our international air transportation agreements will allow the public to receive improved service at low costs that reflect economically efficient operations. Competition and low prices are also fully compatible with a prosperous U.S. air transport industry and our national defense, foreign policy, international commerce, and energy efficiency objectives.

Bilateral aviation agreements, like other international agreements, should serve the interests of both parties. Other countries have an interest in the economic prosperity of their airline industries, as we do in the prosperity of ours. The United States believes this interest is best served by a policy of expansion of competitive opportunity rather than restriction. By offering more services to the public, in a healthy and fair competitive environment, the international air transport industry can stimulate the growth in traffic which contributes both to profitable industry operations and to maximum public benefits.

GOALS OF U.S. INTERNATIONAL AIR
TRANSPORTATION POLICY

The United States will work to achieve a system of international air transportation that places its principal reliance on actual and potential competition to determine the variety, quality, and price of air service. An essential means for carrying out our international air transportation policy will be to allow greater competitive opportunities for U.S. and foreign airlines and to promote new low-cost transportation options for travelers and shippers. Especially in major international air transport markets, there can be substantial benefits for travelers, shippers, airlines, and labor from increasing competitive opportunities and reducing protectionist restrictions. Increasing opportunities for U.S. flag transportation to and from the United States will contribute to the development of our foreign commerce, assure that more airlift resources are available for our defense needs, and promote and expand productivity and job opportunities in our international air transport industry.

TRANSLATING GOALS INTO NEGOTIATING
OBJECTIVES

United States international air transportation policy cannot be implemented unilaterally. Our objectives have to be achieved in the system of international agreements that form the basic framework for the international air transportation system.

Routes, prices, capacity, scheduled and charter rules, and competition in the marketplace are interrelated, not isolated problems to be resolved independently. Thus, the following objectives will be presented in negotiations as an integrated U.S. position:

1. creation of new and greater opportunities for innovative and competitive pricing that will encourage and permit the use of new price and service options to meet the needs of different travelers and shippers,

2. liberalization of charter rules and elimination of restrictions on charter operations,

3. expansion of scheduled service through elimination of restrictions on capacity, frequency, and route and operating rights,

4. elimination of discrimination and unfair competitive practices faced by U.S. airlines in international transportation,

5. flexibility to designate multiple U.S. airlines in international air markets,

6. encouragement of maximum traveler and shipper access to international markets by authorizing more cities for nonstop or direct service, and by improving the integration of domestic and international airline services, and

7. flexibility to permit the development and facilitation of competitive air cargo services.

EXPLANATION OF OBJECTIVES

1. *Pricing.* The United States will develop new bilateral procedures to encourage a more competitive system for establishing scheduled air fares and rates. Charter pricing must continue to be competitive. Fares, rates, and prices should be determined by individual airlines based primarily on competitive considerations in the marketplace. Governmental regulation should not be more than the minimum necessary to prevent predatory or discriminatory practices, to protect consumers from the abuse of monopoly position, or to protect competitors from prices that are artificially low because of direct or indirect governmental subsidy or support. Reliance on competition and encouragement of pricing based on commer-

cial considerations in the marketplace provides the best means of assuring that the needs of consumers will be met and that prices will be as low as possible, given the costs of providing efficient air service.

2. *Charters.* The introduction of charters acted as a major catalyst to the expansion of international air transportation in the 1960's. Charters are a competitive spur and exert downward pressure on the pricing of scheduled services. Charters generate new traffic and help stimulate expansion in all sectors of the industry. Restrictions which have been imposed on the volume, frequency, and regularity of charter services as well as requirements for approval of individual charter flights have restrained the growth of traffic and tourism and do not serve the interests of either party to an aviation agreement. Strong efforts will be made to obtain liberal charter provisions in bilateral agreements.

3. *Scheduled Services.* We will seek to increase the freedom of airlines from capacity and frequency restrictions. We will also work to maintain or increase the route and operating rights of our airlines where such actions improve international route systems and offer the consumer more convenient and efficient air transportation.

4. *Discrimination and Unfair Competitive Practices.* U.S. airlines must have the flexibility to conduct operations and market their services in a manner consistent with a fair and equal opportunity to compete with the airlines of other nations. We will insist that U.S. airlines have the business, commercial, and operational opportunities to compete fairly. The United States will seek to eliminate unfair or destructive competitive practices that prevent U.S. airlines from competing on an equal basis with the airlines of other na-

tions. Charges for providing airway and airport properties and facilities should be related to the costs due to airline operations and should not discriminate against U.S. airlines. These objectives were recognized by the Congress in legislation enacted in 1975, and their attainment is required if consumers, airlines, and employees are to obtain the benefits of an otherwise competitive international aviation system.

5. *Multiple Airline Designations.* The designation of new U.S. airlines in international markets that will support additional service is a way to create a more competitive environment and thus encourage improved service and competition pricing. Privately owned airlines have traditionally been the source of innovation and competition in international aviation, and it is therefore particularly important to preserve for the United States the right of multiple designation.

6. *Maximum Access to International Markets.* Increasing the number of gateway cities for nonstop or direct air service offers the potential for increasing the convenience of air transportation for passengers and shippers and improving routing and market opportunities for international airlines. In addition, enhancing the integration of U.S. airline domestic and international air services benefits both consumers and airlines.

7. *Cargo Services.* We will seek the opportunity for the full development of cargo services. Frequent demand for such services requires special equipment and routes. Cargo services should be permitted to develop freely as trade expands. Also important in the development of cargo services are improved facilitation, including customs clearance, integration of surface and air movements, and flexibility in ground support services.

NEGOTIATING PRINCIPLES

The guiding principle of U.S. aviation negotiating policy will be to trade competitive opportunities, rather than restrictions, with our negotiating partners. We will aggressively pursue our interests in expanded air transportation and reduced prices rather than accept the self-defeating accommodation of protectionism. Our concessions in negotiations will be given in return for progress toward competitive objectives, and these concessions themselves will be of a liberalizing character.

Proposed bilateral agreements which do not meet our minimum competitive objectives will not be signed without prior Presidential approval.

Congressional Representation for the District of Columbia

Statement on the Proposed Constitutional Amendment. August 21, 1978

The Senate will vote tomorrow on a resolution for a constitutional amendment to give District of Columbia citizens full voting representation in the Congress. I strongly urge the Senate to pass the resolution.

There should be no doubt that District citizens deserve full voting representation in Congress. First, residents of the District paid over $1 billion in Federal taxes last year, and the per capita tax payment is well above the national average. Second, District residents have fought and died in every war since the War for Independence. During the Vietnam conflict, only three States suffered greater casualties than the District. Third, virtually every other country in the free world already provides full voting representation to the citizens of its capital city.

Full voting representation for the District has strong bipartisan support. The bipartisan Task Force on the District of Columbia, chaired by Vice President Mondale, strongly recommended adoption of full voting representation. The Democratic and Republican Parties included support for the measure in their 1976 platforms.

Adoption of the resolution is a major human rights priority for my administration, and I hope the Senate will vote favorably tomorrow.

United States Ambassador to Venezuela

Nomination of William H. Luers. August 21, 1978

The President today announced that he will nominate William H. Luers of Illinois as Ambassador to Venezuela. He would succeed Viron P. Vaky, who has been appointed Assistant Secretary of State for Inter-American Affairs.

Mr. Luers was born May 15, 1929, in Springfield, Ill. He received a B.A. in 1951 from Hamilton College and an M.A. in 1957 from Columbia University. He served in the United States Navy as a lieutenant from 1952 to 1956.

He entered the Foreign Service in 1957 as consular officer in Naples. He was international relations officer in the State Department from 1960 to 1962. In 1962 and 1963, he attended Russian language and area studies at the Foreign Service Institute at Oberammergau, and from 1963 to 1965, he was political officer in Moscow. He returned to the State Department from 1965 to 1969, serving first as intelligence research specialist and then as international relations officer. From 1969 to

1973, he was political officer and then counselor for political affairs in Caracas. In 1973 he served as Deputy Director of the Office of Soviet Union Affairs at the State Department, and from 1973 to 1975, he was Deputy Executive Secretary of the Executive Secretariat. From 1975 to 1977, he served as Deputy Assistant Secretary for Inter-American Affairs.

Since 1977 he has been Deputy Assistant Secretary for European Affairs.

President's Commission on Personnel Interchange

Appointment of Lee Cassidy as Executive Director.   August 21, 1978

The President announced today he will appoint Lee Cassidy, of Wilmington, Del., as Executive Director of the President's Commission on Personnel Interchange, effective October 1, 1978.

Cassidy was born February 16, 1933, in New York, N.Y. He received a B.A. in retail business management from Adelphi University in 1955.

He is currently advertising supervisor for the plastic films division of Du Pont Company of Wilmington. He has worked for Du Pont since 1966 in a variety of advertising positions. From 1955 to 1956, he worked with Allied Stores Corp. in New York City.

Cassidy has been active in Democratic politics in Delaware, working in a number of campaigns there, serving as a member of the State platform committee in 1970, 1972, and 1974, and as a delegate to the Democratic National Convention in 1974.

From 1972 to 1974, he was a member of the Licenses and Inspections Review Board of Wilmington. Since 1975 he has been chairman of the State Public Service Commission.

Sabine River Compact Administration

Appointment of Lamar E. Carroon as Federal Representative.   August 21, 1978

The President today announced the appointment of Lamar E. Carroon, of Jackson, Miss., as Federal Representative to the Sabine River Compact Administration.

Carroon, 55, has been with the U.S. Geological Survey since 1950 and has served in a number of assignments in different areas of the country. Since 1968 he has been chief of the Mississippi District of the Water Resources Division of USGS.

Truckee, Carson and Walker Rivers and Lake Tahoe Compact

Appointment of John Russell Little, Jr., as U.S. Federal Representative.   August 21, 1978

The President announced today he will appoint John Russell Little, Jr., of Boulder, Colo., to be the Federal Representative of the United States to the Truckee, Carson and Walker Rivers and Lake Tahoe Compact. He would replace R. H. Smith, who has resigned.

Currently, Mr. Little is a regional solicitor in Denver for the Department of the Interior, a position he has held since 1974. He has the responsibility of supervising the work of 22 attorneys covering nine States and the activities of 20 major field installations of the Department of the Interior.

Mr. Little received a B.A. degree in political science from the University of Colorado in 1955 and received an LL.B. from the University of Colorado School of Law in 1956.

He served as an attorney-adviser (1956–69) and as assistant regional solicitor (1969–74) in the Denver office of the Department of the Interior before assuming his present position.

Jomo Kenyatta

White House Statement on the Death of the President of Kenya. August 22, 1978

The death of Jomo Kenyatta, the first President of the Republic of Kenya, is a very sad occasion for the people of Kenya and for their friends around the world. Jomo Kenyatta was a giant of the African independence struggle, and he was a revered leader of his country. Under his guidance, Kenya's internal development was steady and orderly; its conduct in international affairs showed a mature responsibility. President Kenyatta was dedicated to the principles of independence, majority rule, and peace and equality among nations. His voice will be missed in the councils of Africa and the world.

The United States joins with the Government and people of Kenya in mourning the loss of this great man. The close relationship between Kenya and the United States is part of his legacy to both countries.

Congressional Representation for the District of Columbia

Statement Following Senate Passage of the Proposed Constitutional Amendment. August 22, 1978

I congratulate the Senate on its historic vote this evening. I particularly want to commend Senators Byrd and Kennedy, as well as Delegate Fauntroy, for their tireless efforts to pass the proposed constitutional amendment giving District of Columbia citizens full voting representation in Congress.

Because of today's vote, and the House's favorable vote earlier this year, we are at long last on the verge of giving District citizens the representation that they deserve and that simple justice demands.

The ratification process for every constitutional amendment is naturally difficult and time-consuming. But we cannot let this opportunity to ensure human rights at home slip away. I therefore urge the States to ratify this proposed amendment as promptly as possible.

NOTE: Earlier, the Senate had passed H.J. Res. 554 by a vote of 67 to 32.

National Highway Safety Advisory Committee

Appointment of 12 Members. August 23, 1978

The President today announced 12 persons whom he will appoint as members of the National Highway Safety Advisory Committee. They are:

THOMAS J. CORCORAN, JR., general manager of Lewis Toyota Co., Topeka, Kans.;

R. ADAMS COWLEY, M.D., director of the Maryland Institute for Emergency Medical Services in Baltimore and professor of thoracic and cardiovascular surgery at the University of Maryland School of Medicine;

W. BOONE DARDEN, chief of police of Riviera Beach, Fla., and a police officer since 1948;

HOWARD G. GIBSON, a judge of the Roseville (Calif.) judicial district;

DANIEL P. KAVANAUGH, of Metropolitan Enterprises, an Oklahoma City highway construction business;

WILLIAM D. KEITH, of Carroll, Iowa, chairman of the Western Association of Railroad Passengers, a citizens group seeking increased railroad routes;

ARCHIE G. RICHARDSON, JR., of Silver Spring, Md., president and founder of the Automobile Owners Action Council, a nonprofit organization which investigates auto-related consumer complaints and conducts research;

JAMES C. SCHULTZ, of Dallas, Tex., senior vice president and general counsel of Trailways, Inc., and former chief counsel of the National Highway Traffic Safety Association;

SHEILA D. SIDLES, of Centerville, Iowa, executive secretary and a founding member of the Iowa Consumers League;

JOHN S. TREES, of Lake Bluff, Ill., vice president of Allstate Insurance Co.;

RALPH VANNATTA, commissioner of the Indiana bureau of motor vehicles;

HOWARD J. WIGDER, president of Todd Chevrolet, Inc., in Perth Amboy, N.J., and former president of the New Jersey Automobile Dealers Association.

National Labor Relations Board
Nomination of Howard Jenkins, Jr., To Be a Member. August 23, 1978

The President today announced he will nominate Howard Jenkins, Jr., of Kensington, Md., for reappointment as a member of the National Labor Relations Board for a term expiring August 27, 1983.

Mr. Jenkins has been a member of the NLRB since 1963. Prior to joining the Board, he served in several positions in the Department of Labor between 1956 and 1963. From 1946 to 1956, he was professor of law at Howard University.

Mr. Jenkins was born June 16, 1915, in Denver, Colo. He received an A.B. degree from the University of Denver in 1936 and an LL.B degree from the University of Denver in 1941.

Commissioner of Social Security
Nomination of Stanford G. Ross. August 24, 1978

The President announced today that he will nominate Stanford G. Ross, of Washington, D.C., to be Commissioner of Social Security of the Department of Health, Education, and Welfare. He will replace Mr. James Caldwell, who has retired.

Mr. Ross has been a partner in the law firm of Caplin and Drysdale since 1969. From 1968 to 1969, he served as General Counsel of the U.S. Department of Transportation. In 1967 and 1968, he was a staff assistant at the White House. He was a professor in the New York University School of Law from 1963 to 1967, and for the 2 years prior to that he was an assistant counsel of the Treasury Department in Washington.

Mr. Ross was born October 9, 1931, in St. Louis, Mo. He received a B.A. degree from Washington University in St. Louis in 1953 and a J.D. degree from Harvard University in 1956.

Federal Civil Service Reform
Statement on Senate Passage of the Legislation. August 24, 1978

The Senate's overwhelming vote this evening in favor of civil service reform is a crucial victory in the battle to cut waste and make Government more efficient.

The Senators who supported my civil service reform proposal deserve the gratitude of every taxpayer in the United States. I particularly want to thank Senators Byrd, Ribicoff, and Percy. Their dedicated work was indispensable to passing a sound civil service reform bill.

Civil service reform is the centerpiece of my efforts to meet the clear demand of the American people for a responsive and streamlined Government. Because of the Senate's action tonight, we are one step closer to a Government that offers its own employees real incentives to do a good job while fully protecting their rights.

The next step is up to the House of Representatives, which will consider the legislation when it returns from Labor Day recess. I hope the House will act promptly, so that all of us can begin to realize the benefits of a well-managed Government.

Death of the Reverend Glendon McCulloch

Statement by the President.   August 25, 1978

Rosalynn and I were deeply saddened to learn of the untimely death of our good friend, the Reverend Glendon McCulloch. He was a wise and charitable man whose life and career exemplified the finest qualities of a man of God.

For all of us whose lives he touched, Glendon McCulloch cannot be replaced. We extend our deepest sympathy to Marjorie and the other members of his family.

NOTE: Reverend McCulloch was executive director of the Southern Baptist Brotherhood Commission.

Natural Gas Legislation

White House Statement.   August 25, 1978

After nearly 2 years of effort, a Senate-House conference committee reached a natural gas compromise just last week. It does not give anyone everything they demanded—but it is *fair, balanced,* and *workable.*

The compromise will not provide massive profits for producers that overnight decontrol would allow nor does it provide unrealistically low gas prices. But what it does do is:

—Makes fresh new supplies of natural gas available for homes and industry in every region of the country at prices below alternate fuels these supplies will replace and ensures adequate supplies in every consuming State;

—Provides stability and increased markets and incentives to producers;

—Costs consumers overall no more than under existing law;

—Substantially reduces oil imports that depress our dollar.

The President cannot afford the luxury of exclusive devotion to any single regional or economic interest. Enactment of this compromise is essential to protect the stability of our strong and vital economy, and to protect our dollar and position of economic leadership in the world. The President is convinced that the U.S. Senate and House of Representatives will rise to their responsibilities as the conference committee has already done. The President expects that this matter of critical national importance will not be obscured by other issues. Now is the time for statesmanship and concern for the general welfare, not for endless contention over narrow issues.

NOTE: The statement was read on behalf of the President by Stuart E. Eizenstat, Assistant to the President for Domestic Affairs and Policy, at 2:55 p.m. to reporters assembled in the Briefing Room at the White House. Following his remarks, Secretary of Energy James R. Schlesinger and he held a news conference on the natural gas legislation and the administration's breeder reactor program.

Women's Equality Day, 1978

Proclamation 4590. August 25, 1978

*By the President of the United States
of America*

A Proclamation

August 26, 1978, is the 58th anniversary of the adoption of the 19th Amendment to the Constitution guaranteeing that the right of United States citizens to vote shall not be denied or abridged by the Federal government or any state on account of sex.

This was the successful culmination of the struggle of the American Women's Suffrage movement. The right to vote, to participate in the process of framing the laws under which we all live, is fundamental. But it was only the first step in achieving full equality for women. The late Dr. Alice Paul realized this, drafted the Equal Rights Amendment in 1923 and had it introduced in Congress over a period of 49 years, until it passed on March 22, 1972.

Women have made substantial progress toward full equality in recent years, partly as a result of the national debate on the Equal Rights Amendment, which has made many people aware of existing injustices. Despite this progress, strong action is still needed to guarantee women full equality of opportunity.

I personally believe that ratification of the Equal Rights Amendment can be the single most important step in guaranteeing all Americans—both women and men—their rights under the United States Constitution. This major step toward full equality for women has already been taken by 35 states, representing seventy-two percent of the population of this Nation. Only three more states must ratify the Equal Rights Amendment before it becomes a part of the Constitution. I believe this is too important and far-reaching an issue for arbitrary time barriers to limit full debate and an ultimate decision that truly reflects the will of the American people. In a society that is free, democratic and humane, there can be no time limit on equality.

Now, THEREFORE, I, JIMMY CARTER, President of the United States of America, do hereby proclaim August 26, 1978, as Women's Equality Day and do hereby call upon the people of the United States to observe this day with appropriate ceremonies and activities. I further urge all our people to dedicate themselves anew to the goal of achieving equal rights for women under the law.

IN WITNESS WHEREOF, I have hereunto set my hand this 25th day of August, in the year of our Lord nineteen hundred seventy-eight, and of the Independence of the United States of America the two hundred and third.

JIMMY CARTER

[Filed with the Office of the Federal Register, 4:05 p.m., August 25, 1978]

Digest of Other White House Announcements

The following listing includes the President's daily schedule and other items of general interest as announced by the White House Press Office during the period covered by this issue. Events and announcements printed elsewhere in the issue are not included.

August 21

The President has declared a major disaster for Baldwin County, Ala., as a result of severe storms and flooding, beginning about July 25, which caused extensive public and private property damage.

The President transmitted to the Congress the report on international transfers of technology required by section 24(c) of Public Law 95–92, the International Security Assistance Act of 1977.

The President departed Plains, Ga., and traveled to Boise, Idaho, where he stayed overnight.

August 22

The President began a 3-day raft trip down the Middle Fork of the Salmon River in Idaho.

August 24

The President departed Idaho and traveled to the Grand Teton National Park in Wyoming for a week's stay.

NOMINATIONS SUBMITTED TO THE SENATE

The following list does not include promotions of members of the Uniformed Services, nominations to the Service Academies, or nominations of Foreign Service officers.

Submitted August 22, 1978

WILLIAM H. LUERS, of Illinois, a Foreign Service officer of Class one, to be Ambassador Extraordinary and Plenipotentiary of the United States of America to Venezuela.

Submitted August 23, 1978

HOWARD JENKINS, JR., of Maryland, to be a member of the National Labor Relations Board for the term expiring August 27, 1983 (reappointment).

Submitted August 24, 1978

STANFORD G. ROSS, of the District of Columbia, to be Commissioner of Social Security of the Department of Health, Education, and Welfare, vice James B. Cardwell.

CHECKLIST OF WHITE HOUSE PRESS RELEASES

The following releases of the Office of the White House Press Secretary, distributed during the period covered by this issue, are not included in the issue.

Released August 21, 1978

Fact sheet: U.S. policy for international air transportation negotiations

News conference: on U.S. policy for international air transportation negotiations—by Secretary of Transportation Brock Adams

Released August 22, 1978

News conference: on the Middle Fork of the Salmon River in Idaho, site of the President's raft trip—by Wallace T. Shiverdecker, zone information officer, U.S. Forest Service

Released August 23, 1978

Transcript: informal question-and-answer session with reporters on the President's raft trip—by Press Secretary Jody Powell

Released August 24, 1978

White House statement: meeting of Zbigniew Brzezinski, Assistant to the President for National Security Affairs, with Rafael M. Nze Abuy, Roman Catholic Bishop of Equatorial Guinea

Released August 25, 1978

Fact sheet: administration's breeder reactor program

News conference: on natural gas legislation and the administration's breeder reactor program—by Stuart E. Eizenstat, Assistant to the President for Domestic Affairs and Policy, and Secretary of Energy James R. Schlesinger

---

ACTS APPROVED BY THE PRESIDENT

Approved August 20, 1978

H.R. 2777_____ Public Law 95–351
National Consumer Cooperative Bank Act.

H.R. 10787_____ Public Law 95–352
An act to authorize appropriations for activities and programs carried out by the Secretary of the Interior through the Bureau of Land Management.

Editor's Note

The President's Trip to Idaho and Wyoming

The President was in Wyoming at the closing time of this issue. Releases issued on the trip, but not received by the Office of the Federal Register in time for inclusion in this issue, will be printed next week.

PRESIDENTIAL DOCUMENTS

Week Ending Friday, September 1, 1978

Boise, Idaho

Informal Exchange With Reporters on Arrival at Boise Airport.   August 21, 1978

THE PRESIDENT. Hi, everybody. Good to see you.

Q. We're told you're not going to say anything real heavy for us, but you might say a little something.

THE PRESIDENT. Well, I'll say the most important thing. I'm glad to be in Idaho. We've been looking forward to it. I used to come out here back in the early fifties when I was working under Admiral Rickover, came into Pocatello and Arco. And I came out here when Cecil Andrus was Governor—we're very close friends—and we're really looking forward to going down the Middle Fork. I'm an old canoeist and kayaker.

Q. You're going to try that?

THE PRESIDENT. No, I think we will probably stick with the raft. But if they give me a chance, I might try the canoe at least.

Q. You better watch out for him. He's a fly-fishing enthusiast. Is there a challenge to do any particular contest as to how many and how big you're going to catch on the——

THE PRESIDENT. He brought his own fly-casting outfit. I've got mine back in

Georgia. But I'm going to have to borrow one. So, if he does win and catch the biggest fish, it's because he's fishing with his own tackle. [*Laughter*]

Q. Can we ask you one thing of small substance?

THE PRESIDENT. Of course.

Q. Apparently you met with Senator McClure last Thursday——

THE PRESIDENT. Yes.

Q. —— concerning the continuation of the atomic breeder reactor program. Have you changed your position on that?

THE PRESIDENT. No, not at all. We are strongly in favor of an adequate, very strong research and development program in the breeder field. My own background is in nuclear physics, and I'm familiar with the need for it. What I don't want to do is to firm up a specific design plan and start building the Clinch River breeder reactor, which, by the time it's finished, will be outdated and which will sap away the research and development funds that I think can be used much better to our advantage the way we have it planned.

But I think that Senator McClure agrees with this approach. His only concern, since I hadn't talked to him about it, was to be sure that our country is going to have a strong, viable, aggressive, con-

1473

tinuous research and development program in breeder reactor technology.

Q. The man right behind you here, Governor Evans, has been trying to meet with you. Apparently he will meet with you. I assume that you're going to endorse his candidacy. You want to do anything physical for us here?

THE PRESIDENT. Well, I'm not sure that he needs it. But the closer I can get to him politically, the more it helps me, he's such a good and popular Governor.

We have, I think, an excellent prospect here in Idaho and throughout the country this year to have success. And Governor Evans, as you know, is a very fine successor to Cecil Andrus. They see things the same way, and I think they are both equally popular in Idaho.

Q. Do you have any plans to sort of pontificate as you float down the Salmon River and figure out ways to increase your popularity in the polls?

THE PRESIDENT. Well, I think we're doing okay in the polls. We have addressed some very difficult subjects, and one of the polls that we will be observing very carefully is the ability of Democratic Members of Congress to be reelected in November. I think this will be a good way to assess the attitude of the American people toward me and toward the Congress.

Ordinarily, in the past, even with Presidents who have been very high in the polls, they've lost 35 or 40 members of the incumbent President's party in the House of Representatives. We hope to do better than that in November. And, of course, we've been very successful, I think, with Congress in getting people back to work. We've had good success in foreign affairs, in trying to deal with the very difficult questions of inflation. But I can't run the White House and make my decisions as President based on what's more popular. I have to make decisions sometimes when

I know that either way that I go will be unpopular.

But I think in the long run that's the kind of President the American people want.

Q. Mr. President, thank you very much.

THE PRESIDENT. It's been a pleasure.

Q. Do you see this as an unusual vacation for a President?

THE PRESIDENT. Well, I understand it's an unprecedented vacation, but I've been looking forward to this for a long time. Cecil Andrus and I have been close friends since we were first elected Governor, and he's never lost an opportunity to tell me about the beauties of Idaho. And my own background in whitewater canoeing and kayaking has prepared me to want to come out here and see the Salmon River. So, we are looking forward to it. And even if it is unusual, I think I benefit from the fact that I've decided to do it.

Q. What about the youngest member of the family staying back?

THE PRESIDENT. Who, Amy? Amy's here with us.

Q. No, the other closest member of the family, the other young man.

THE PRESIDENT. The other son?

Q. Yes.

THE PRESIDENT. Well, he had some other duties to perform. He's just finished college this year in geography, and he's a computer programer and a mapper. And he's got work already cut out for himself and couldn't get off.

My oldest son, Jack, has spent a lot of time on the whitewater canoeing trips, and he's with us, and also my middle son, Chip, and Amy, of course, who's an outstanding swimmer. We're all looking forward to it. It's really nice to be back out in Idaho.

Q. How long has it been since you spent a night in a sleeping bag? [*Laughter*]

THE PRESIDENT. Well, I'll say Amy's spent probably 10 nights in a sleeping bag, since I've been President. It's probably been 3 years since I've been in a sleeping bag.

Q. Since a scoutmaster?

THE PRESIDENT. Oh, even since then. When I was Governor, we went out every now and then.

Q. Can you swim?

THE PRESIDENT. Oh, yes, very well. [*Laughter*]

Thank you. Good to see you all; really proud to be here.

NOTE: The exchange began at 6:05 p.m.

Salmon River in Idaho

Informal Exchange With Reporters at the Conclusion of the President's Raft Trip. August 24, 1978

THE PRESIDENT. The best 3 days I have ever had. It really was great.

Q. What were the high points, Mr. President?

THE PRESIDENT. We saw mountain sheep a part of the time. We saw a golden eagle, saw a lot of—[*inaudible*]—and caught a lot of fish. We had a contest today. And I got 59 trout. We came in a little ahead of the others. The scenery was just——

Q. Did you get hung up on any rapids at all during the 2 days?

THE PRESIDENT. No. We had a little trouble on one waterfall.

Q. That was Tappen Falls. We were there.

THE PRESIDENT. I thought maybe they changed the name by now. [*Laughter*]

Q. Did you go in the water at all?

THE PRESIDENT. I went swimming.

Q. Didn't you?

THE PRESIDENT. I thought everybody did. We went swimming last night.

Q. But you didn't——

THE PRESIDENT. By accident, no.

Q. You didn't stay in long, did you?

THE PRESIDENT. I stayed in a good while.

Q. Bradley stayed in 17 seconds. [*Laughter*]

Q. Have you missed what has been going on in the world?

THE PRESIDENT. I talked to the Vice President on the phone this afternoon, got a report on several things. [*Inaudible*] I have gotten a Presidential briefing every morning at 7 o'clock from the State Department and also from the CIA. So, we had good radio communications from the outside world. Everything seems to be quiet.

Q. Did the Interior Secretary lobby you at all on the wilderness issue up the river?

THE PRESIDENT. Well, he gave me a lot of information about it. But we will have to discuss it very carefully. I think one of the best things about this region is that right through the part we went, it ought to be preserved and not destroyed. But back off from the river, where we saw flying in from the plane, were very good productive timber regions where we ought to harvest timber and let the country benefit from it. So, I like a good balance between preserving the natural beauty, unchanged, on the one hand, and harvesting growing timber in appropriate areas, which is what he is working on, and I agree with him.

Q. Are you satisfied, Mr. President, that your self-proclaimed moratorium on world crises held up?

THE PRESIDENT. So far, it has.

Q. Is it calmer now in Nicaragua? What do you hear?

THE PRESIDENT. I have gotten reports from several countries around the world. I won't go into that now.

Q. Are you going to come back and visit us again?

THE PRESIDENT. I would like to.

Q. Are you going to try the river up the other direction, now that you came down the easy way?

THE PRESIDENT. I would like to do that. I don't know if that was the easy way or not, but that was good. We have got rivers this wild in Georgia, but not as large and wild. Of course, the scenery is just—*[inaudible]*—which is really something.

Q. What do you plan to do in Grand Teton?

THE PRESIDENT. Just going to take it easy for a while.

Q. You better watch out, there are some grizzly bears over there.

THE PRESIDENT. Is that right? I am looking forward to seeing some of them.

Q. Thank you.

THE PRESIDENT. We caught three dolly vardens, which you can keep, but the rest of them, we aren't going to keep.

Q. Jody caught some.

THE PRESIDENT. Yes, our two boats today caught 111.

Q. One hundred eleven?

THE PRESIDENT. Yes.

Q. How many did you catch?

THE PRESIDENT. I don't know. Our boat caught 59. That was I and Chip and Amy and Rosalynn.

Q. I think your wife caught more than you——

THE PRESIDENT. She always does.

Q. She was fishing that time when you were overseeing the repair of the sweep.

THE PRESIDENT. Good luck to you all. We will see you later.

REPORTER. Thanks for the trip. I have enjoyed it.

NOTE: The exchange began at approximately 1:30 p.m. at the departure site on the river's middle fork.

As printed above, the item follows the White House press release.

Grand Teton National Park, Wyoming

Informal Exchange With Reporters on Arrival at Jackson Lake. August 24, 1978

THE PRESIDENT. Oh, hello, Helen [Helen Thomas, United Press International]. Did you make it?

Q. No, I didn't. But, listen, do you know your natural gas compromise is falling apart?

THE PRESIDENT. Well, I talked to the Vice President about that today. We'll do a little work on it, maybe tonight.

Q. Do you think you still can pull it off?

THE PRESIDENT. I don't know.

Q. What will you be doing here by way of activities?

THE PRESIDENT. I don't know yet.

NOTE: The exchange began at 6:10 p.m. near Brinkerhoff Lodge, where the President stayed during his visit to Wyoming.

Grand Teton National Park, Wyoming

Informal Exchange With Reporters Following a Boating Trip on Jackson Lake. August 25, 1978

THE PRESIDENT. Hello, Jody. I'm glad I didn't ram the boat into the dock.

Q. Is that the first time you've sailed in a long time?

THE PRESIDENT. A long time.

PRESS SECRETARY POWELL. I thought that looked pretty good.

THE PRESIDENT. I used to sail a lot at the Naval Academy. I went sailing one time at Sea Island at the Governors' Conference. Remember that?

MR. POWELL. It wasn't Sea Island, it was Hilton Head.

THE PRESIDENT. Hilton Head, that's right.

MR. POWELL. There was a doctor—whatever his name is—from Savannah that was Hamilton's friend. That was a beautiful boat.

THE PRESIDENT. It had a yawl.

MR. POWELL. I don't know the technical——

THE PRESIDENT. No, it was a ketch.

MR. POWELL. It was all wood and brass.

Q. Do you like the Grand Tetons?

THE PRESIDENT. Gee, that's something else, really beautiful. We went all around the island. We had a brisk wind when we went out, but there was just almost no wind coming in. It was nice.

Q. Have you been doing any work today, as well as having a little fun?

THE PRESIDENT. Well, I had a whole stack of paperwork this morning, made a few telephone calls.

Q. How does it look on the natural gas bill? Do you think you're in trouble there?

THE PRESIDENT. I made several calls last night and this morning about that.

Q. Have you talked again to the Vice President?

THE PRESIDENT. I talked to him this morning and last night. He's on the way to Texas.

Q. This coalition was unexpected, wasn't it?

THE PRESIDENT. It's the same coalition that's been evident among the conferees. You've got half on one side and half on the other that don't want a natural gas bill, and you've got the gas-producing States that want more money out of it, and you've got others that don't want any deregulation of natural gas ever. And that's why it's been so finely balanced.

As you know, we almost didn't get one vote in the House and almost didn't get one vote in the Senate to give us a majority in the conference. The same basic problem.

Q. Do you think you can put your compromise together again?

THE PRESIDENT. I don't know. Of course, what they'll vote on now is the conference committee report. It's not a matter of redrafting. But it's going to be after the 11th.

Q. Were you surprised by Senator Baker's statement the other day that he would not support cloture?

THE PRESIDENT. I talked to Senator Baker last night. He's got an open mind about it.

THE PRESIDENT. He's backing off that hard statement that he took?

THE PRESIDENT. I'm not trying to speak for him. But he said he wanted to look it over carefully and see what the entire energy package looked like. Obviously, the whole energy picture is involved, including nuclear power and gas, oil, coal, solar. It's extremely complicated, just one of those difficult things to put together.

Q. Senator McClure is indicating at this point that there was some sort of a trade-off for his vote on the possibility of putting the nuclear reactor, the breeder reactor over in Idaho?

THE PRESIDENT. No. Dr. Schlesinger and Stu Eizenstat had a press conference today and explained what happened about that. We did not change our position. I am not in favor of the Clinch River Breeder Reactor. We have always been in favor of a research and development program on breeder technology to investigate safety features, design features.

We offered a compromise in the House that was narrowly rejected. We maintain our position. We are in favor of a 3-year program on basic design work, no commitment to build. This is the agreement we worked out with McClure. The only— just to explain my position, we want to be sure that we weren't terminating the breeder program altogether. The amount of money involved, the way I understand the figures, is less than the amount the House already approved and less than the amount that the Energy Committee in the Senate had approved. But I think that Senator McClure was trying to make it look as though he had won a great victory and changed our position, possibly for his home State influence.

But we've explained that, I think, today, the ones that worked out the agreement with him. The Vice President and Stu Eizenstat and Jim Schlesinger were the ones that talked to Senator McClure about what our position was. And I think it was a very brief discussion.

Q. What Senators have you spoken to?

THE PRESIDENT. Well, I'd rather not give you a list of names—but enough, I hope.

MR. POWELL. That's enough. You won't get all——

Q. They ask if you were enjoying your vacation?

THE PRESIDENT. That's a silly question. [*Laughter*] This is so beautiful.

Q. What else do you plan on doing while you're here, Mr. President?

THE PRESIDENT. We'll go fishing two or three times. I think we'll probably go to——

Q. Can you fish right here? Or will you go away from here to fish?

THE PRESIDENT. On this lake—we had a briefing from one of the fishermen here—this lake is 400 feet deep, over 400 feet, and you fish deep for large lake trout. And we'll do some of that. We'll probably go up in the upper lake, Yellowstone, and fish a while, and maybe go to one of the streams and wade some and do some fly-fishing.

Q. I meant, did they ask you whether you were enjoying your vacation. The Senators.

THE PRESIDENT. Oh, you mean the folks back in Washington. Yes, they all envy us. I think I've got enough folks lined up in the Senate that want to go down the Middle Fork of the Salmon to keep them busy for a while. [*Laughter*] It's good to see you all.

REPORTER. Thank you.

NOTE: The exchange began at 5:10 p.m. at the dock near Brinkerhoff Lodge.

Pope John Paul I
Message to His Holiness on His Election.
August 26, 1978

Your Holiness:

On behalf of the American people, I join people the world over in welcoming your election as Pontiff of the Roman Catholic Church. We rejoice in the renewal of leadership for your Church.

In a world of rapid change, the basic needs of humanity remain the same: peace, justice, equity and the opportunity for life with dignity. These are still the supreme challenges that face us. Your voice and your efforts, in the tradition of your predecessors, can be an inspiration and a hope for all those who struggle to meet those challenges. I pray it will be heard and echoed by people of good will throughout the world.

On this happy occasion, I extend to Your Holiness my deep respect and sincere good wishes for your Papacy.

Sincerely,

JIMMY CARTER

NOTE: The following announcement was released by the White House Press Office on August 29:

President Carter today announced that he has asked Vice President Walter F. Mondale to serve as his personal representative at the September 3–4 Papal Inaugural ceremonies for His Holiness Pope John Paul I at the Vatican.

The Vice President will be accompanied by Mrs. Joan Adams Mondale, their son William, and a delegation of distinguished Americans.

Federal Reserve System
Nomination of Nancy Hays Teeters To Be a Member of the Board of Directors.
August 28, 1978

The President announced today he will nominate Nancy Hays Teeters, of Indiana, to be a member of the Board of Governors of the Federal Reserve System for the remainder of the term expiring January 31, 1984. She will replace Arthur Burns, who has resigned.

Ms. Teeters is currently chief economist of the House Budget Committee, a position she has held since 1975. From 1973 to 1975, she was a senior specialist of the Congressional Research Service, Library of Congress. From 1970 to 1973, she was a senior fellow at the Brookings Institution.

She served as a fiscal economist in the Office of Management and Budget from 1966 to 1970, and from 1957 to 1966, she was an economist for the Federal Reserve Board. She also served, in 1962 and 1963, as an economist for the Council of Economic Advisers.

Ms. Teeters was a teaching fellow at the University of Michigan from 1956 to 1957, and from 1954 to 1955. From 1955 to 1956, she was an instructor at the University of Maryland overseas division, in Stuttgart, West Germany.

She was born July 29, 1930, and received an A.B. from Oberlin College in 1952. She received an M.A. from the University of Michigan in 1957. She is a member of the American Economic Association and is a director of the American Finance Association. She is director of the National Economist Club and a member of the Cleveland Park Club.

Fishery Conservation and Management Bill

Statement on Signing H.R. 10732 Into Law. August 29, 1978

Yesterday I signed H.R. 10732, which amends the Fishery Conservation and Management Act of 1976. This bill authorizes fiscal year 1979 appropriations to implement the act, which first established the 200-mile Fishery Conservation Zone off the coast of the United States.

This bill also establishes a permit system for foreign fish processing vessels within the 200-mile limit. Under this system, Government permits would be granted to foreign fish processors to purchase fish caught by U.S. fishermen within the 200-mile zone only if domestic processors do not have the capacity or intent to process these fish. To date, domestic processors have not purchased such fish as hake and pollack, which have no domestic market. Foreign processors, however, have become interested in these fish because of clear foreign demand.

My administration is strongly committed to reducing barriers to international trade. While I am concerned that the establishment of this permit system may be viewed by some foreign nations as an interference with international commerce, the most egregious provisions have been removed at our request. Thus, during the legislative process, the administration made clear our objections to a provision which would have denied permits to processors from countries with import barriers to U.S. fish and fish products. That provision would have conflicted directly with our trade policies. I am pleased that this provision was deleted by Congress.

When Congress was considering this bill, we made clear our preference for a permit system lasting only for 2 years, rather than permanently. However, I believe that this bill will in practice cause little if any adverse impact on foreign fish processors, since most of the interest by foreign processors relates to fish species not currently consumed in the United States products.

At the same time, this bill will provide domestic processors with increased certainty about fish supplies, which will in turn provide an incentive for investments in increased capacity. It also will provide American fish processors with comparable treatment given to our fishing industry within our fishery zone. In signing this bill into law, I do not intend to set a precedent for other United States products.

NOTE: As enacted, H.R. 10732 is Public Law 95–354, approved August 28.

Meeting With State Governors

White House Statement.   August 29, 1978

President Carter announced today that he will meet Thursday at the White House with a group of Governors, headed by Gov. Julian M. Carroll of Kentucky, the new chairman of the National Governors' Association.

The meeting was arranged in order for the President to discuss with the group the energy legislation currently before the Congress and receive a report on the National Governors' Conference in Boston.

The meeting will be held at the White House at 10:30 a.m., Thursday.

The President expressed his appreciation to the Governors for the meeting, and said, "The enactment of a national energy plan is critical to every State, and I look forward to this opportunity to discuss the pending energy legislation with some of the Nation's Governors."

Federal Civilian and Military Pay

Message to the Congress Transmitting the Federal Pay Comparability Alternative Plan. August 31, 1978

To the Congress of the United States:

Under the Pay Comparability Act of 1970, an adjustment in Federal white collar pay will be required on October 1.

I have reviewed the report of my Pay Agent and the recommendations of the Advisory Committee on Federal Pay relative to pay adjustment. Their findings indicate that an average 8.4 percent increase, at a cost of $4.5 billion, will be required to achieve comparability with the private sector.

I support comparability in pay between the Federal Government and the private sector. It is essential to ensure that the Federal Government continues to attract and retain qualified and dedicated employees. The Federal Government's civilian and military personnel have given the country loyal and competent service, and I would normally have no hesitancy in ordering a pay raise achieving comparability. However, pay comparability must be viewed in the light of the overall economic situation now facing our country. For that reason, my decision about pay comparability this year is especially difficult.

Today the greatest single threat to our national economic growth and the jobs and prosperity of our people is inflation. It persists because all of us—business and labor, farmers and consumers—are caught on a treadmill that none of us can stop alone. Each group desires to raise its income to meet rising costs; eventually we all lose the inflation battle together.

To curb the wage and price spiral, I proposed last spring that in each industry and sector of the economy, wage increases this year be held significantly below the average increases for the two preceding years. The Federal Government should set an example in this effort. A Federal white collar civilian and military increase of 5.5 percent would be consistent with this guideline.

The pay act gives me the authority to propose an alternative pay adjustment which I consider appropriate in the light of, "economic conditions affecting the general welfare." Therefore I am submitting to the Congress an alternative plan for a 5.5 percent pay increase. This will allow the Federal Government to set an example for labor and industry and lead the fight against inflation by example, and not just words alone.

Accordingly, I strongly urge the Congress to support the alternative recommendation which is attached.

JIMMY CARTER

The White House,
    August 31, 1978.

FEDERAL PAY COMPARABILITY ALTERNATIVE PLAN

In consideration of economic conditions affecting the general welfare, I hereby transmit to the Congress the following alternative plan, as authorized and required by Section 5305(c)(1) of Title 5, United States Code:

The adjustment in the rates of pay of each Federal statutory pay system to become effective on the first day of the first applicable pay period that begins on or after October 1, 1978, shall be limited to a 5.5 percent increase for any position at any grade in lieu of the adjustments as determined under the comparability procedure set forth in Section 3(a) of the Federal Pay Comparability Act of 1970 (5 U.S.C. 5305).

Executive Branch Administration of the Privacy Act of 1974

Memorandum From the President. August 31, 1978

Memorandum for the Heads of Executive Departments and Agencies

Enclosed for your information is a copy of the Third Annual Report on executive branch administration of the Privacy Act of 1974, which I recently transmitted to the Congress.

The protection of personal privacy is of great concern to the American people, and an important priority of my Administration. I urge you to personally review this report and take steps to further improve your agency's administration of the Privacy Act.

The report indicates that many agencies have made substantial improvements in their implementation of the Act. I urge each of you, however, to initiate additional efforts during the coming year to reduce the amount of personal information collected and maintained by the Federal government, to avoid unwarranted disclosure of this information, and to improve the internal management of personal data systems.

I have asked the Director of the Office of Management and Budget to monitor these efforts and to keep me informed of your progress.

JIMMY CARTER

NOTE: The text of the memorandum was released on September 1.

The Cyprus Conflict

Message to the Congress Reporting on Progress Toward a Negotiated Settlement. September 1, 1978

To the Congress of the United States:

As required by Public Law 94–104, this report describes the progress that has been made towards a negotiated settlement on Cyprus in the past sixty days.

The last report described proposals submitted by the Turkish Cypriots on April 13, and noted several expressions of flexibility subsequently made by the Turkish side. In July there were further encouraging signs. Both the Government of Cyprus and the Turkish Cypriot leadership put forward fresh and promising proposals for the resettlement of the important commercial and resort city of Varosha (New Famagusta). Varosha has been deserted and under Turkish control since the 1974 fighting. Significantly, both sides foresee that progress on this issue will lead to a resumption of the intercommunal negotiations.

We have urged the two Cypriot parties to give these proposals careful consideration, and plan to continue to encourage a satisfactory compromise on Varosha, one we hope will lead them to reconvene the intercommunal negotiations under the aegis of the Secretary General of the United Nations.

Both the Congress and the Administration feel that the United States 1) should continue to play an active role in seeking a just and lasting Cyprus settlement, and 2) should continue to support the efforts of Secretary General Waldheim. On August 14, the conference committee on the Security Assistance Bill approved the language to end the Turkish Arms Embargo. I consider this action appropriate and necessary to our continuing impartial and constructive role.

JIMMY CARTER

The White House,
  September 1, 1978.

National Day of Prayer, 1978
Proclamation 4591. September 1, 1978

By the President of the United States of America

A Proclamation

Our Nation, perhaps more than any other, has always held a special cognizance of the gifts of the Creator. We were founded upon a belief in, and reverence for, the liberty of the human spirit under God and the equality of all people before the Almighty. Regardless of our individual conceptions of the Divine, Americans have always sought from Providence the help and guidance necessary to live justly and to build a better world for all who share this planet.

Today we face challenges equal to any in our history. Few generations have been given such opportunities for good or ill on Earth. We approach our responsibility confidently, but with sobering awareness that God's sea is very great, and our ship, infinitely small.

From time to time we should turn to the Almighty for help and guidance, as we have done throughout our Nation's two hundred and three years. In humility and reverence, we should pause from our daily activities to thank our Creator for the bountiful goodness that imbues our lives, and to ask for His blessing in the days ahead.

Recognizing this, the Congress by joint resolution approved April 17, 1952 (36 U.S.C. 185; 66 Stat. 64) has called upon the President to set aside a suitable day each year as a National Day of Prayer.

Now, THEREFORE, I, JIMMY CARTER, President of the United States of America, do hereby proclaim Saturday, October 7, 1978, as National Day of Prayer. I ask all Americans to join with me on that day in asking God's help that we may see and understand our responsibilities and discharge them with wisdom, strength, and patience.

IN WITNESS WHEREOF, I have hereunto set my hand this first day of September, in the year of our Lord nineteen hundred seventy-eight, and of the Independence of the United States of America the two hundred and third.

JIMMY CARTER

[Filed with the Office of the Federal Register,
  10:27 a.m., September 5, 1978]

Federal Government Travel Costs

Memorandum From the President.
September 1, 1978

Memorandum for the Heads of Executive Departments and Agencies

Subject: Reduction in 1979 Administrative Travel Costs

It is extremely important at this time, when we are trying to hold down inflation, that every effort be made to reduce Government travel costs. All travel must be limited to the absolute minimum necessary to carry out your programs.

Specifically, I ask that you reduce fiscal year 1979 administrative travel costs by 20% below the amount estimated in the 1979 budget transmitted to the Congress. Administrative travel is defined to include all travel that is not directly related and essential to the performance of a Federal program.

While I am not directing that travel for program purposes be reduced by a specific amount, I do ask that you limit all travel to purposes that are clearly necessary and cannot be accomplished effectively in any other way. The proper management of travel should permit reduction in travel budgets for program as well as for administrative purposes.

I am asking the Director of the Office of Management and Budget to provide Government-wide instructions to achieve this reduction.

I count on your full cooperation in directing your agency to help reduce the amounts spent for Government's travel.

JIMMY CARTER

Securities Investor Protection Corporation

Nomination of Adolph P. Schuman To Be a Director. September 1, 1978

The President today announced that he will nominate Adolph P. Schuman, of San Francisco, Calif., to be a Director of the Securities Investor Protection Corporation. Schuman will be nominated for the term expiring December 31, 1978, and for reappointment for a term expiring December 31, 1981. He will be designated Vice Chairman of the Corporation.

Schuman was born November 22, 1911, in San Francisco. He studied business administration and economics. He served in the U.S. Coast Guard Reserve from 1940 to 1944.

Schuman is president of Lilli Ann Corp., a women's apparel firm. He is chairman of the California World Trade Authorities Coordinating Council, a director of the Commission for National Trade Policy, and a member of the national and California regional Export Expansion Councils of the Commerce Department.

Labor Day, 1978

Message of the President. September 1, 1978

On this, the second Labor Day of my Administration, more Americans hold jobs than at any time in our Nation's history. Unemployment has been dramatically slashed. Our workers are earning more and producing more than ever before—last month, the Gross National Product passed the milestone two trillion dollar mark. Though inflation is a major concern, we are working hard to combat it and, overall, the economic picture bodes well for American citizens.

Our free market system continues to provide broad social and economic protections while maintaining respect for individual dignity and freedom of choice in the work place, as well as in the market place. Our Nation offers a working environment in which we can take pride, and the opportunity for skilled craftsmen to take pleasure in their continuing achievements.

Working Americans have good cause to celebrate this Labor Day. In the last 12 months, more jobs have been added to the economy than in any year in history. Almost a quarter of those who were unemployed when I took office are productively employed today. We have worked hard on this problem and the results are gratifying: we have brought unemployment down to the lowest level in three years, and we have done it in a peaceful, growing economy, without war or recession.

Working Americans can also take pride in the continuing effectiveness of our strong, free labor organizations. We have a vocal, articulate work force in this Nation, and an ever-better standard of living for an ever-rising percentage of our people.

We still have problems; we still have much to do. But it is good to pause and count our blessings too. We have a great deal to be thankful for on this Labor Day.

JIMMY CARTER

Digest of Other White House Announcements

The following listing includes the President's daily schedule and other items of general interest as announced by the White House Press Office during the period covered by this issue. Events and announcements printed elsewhere in the issue are not included.

August 30

The President returned to the White House following his vacation in Georgia, Idaho, and Wyoming.

August 31

The President met at the White House with Zbigniew Brzezinski, Assistant to the President for National Security Affairs.

The President attended a portion of the briefing on natural gas legislation given by administration officials for representatives of natural gas consuming businesses and industries in the State Dining Room.

The White House announced that Sarah C. Weddington will join the White House staff as Special Assistant to the President. She will serve as a senior adviser to the President and will have the lead responsibility among his advisers for women's affairs and issues.

September 1

The President met at the White House with:

—Vice President Walter F. Mondale, Secretary of State Cyrus R. Vance, Secretary of Defense Harold Brown, Hamilton Jordan, Assistant to the President, and Dr. Brzezinski;

—Frank B. Moore, Assistant to the President for Congressional Liaison;

—representatives of farm organizations to discuss the natural gas legislation;

—Secretary of Transportation Brock Adams.

During the day, the President met with various foreign policy advisers to prepare for the Camp David meeting on the Middle East, to begin September 5.

NOMINATIONS SUBMITTED TO THE SENATE

The following list does not include promotions of members of the Uniformed Services, nominations to the Service Academies, or nominations of Foreign Service officers.

Submitted August 28, 1978

NANCY HAYS TEETERS, of Indiana, to be a member of the Board of Governors of the Federal Reserve System for the unexpired term of 14 years from February 1, 1970, vice Arthur F. Burns, resigned.

BRUCE S. JENKINS, of Utah, to be United States District Judge for the District of Utah, vice Willis W. Ritter, deceased.

Submitted September 1, 1978

ADOLPH PHILIP SCHUMAN, of California, to be Director of the Securities Investor Protection Corporation for term expiring December 31, 1978, vice Jerome W. Van Gorkom, term expired.

ADOLPH PHILIP SCHUMAN, of California, to be a Director of the Securities Investor Protection Corporation for a term expiring December 31, 1981 (reappointment).

CHECKLIST OF WHITE HOUSE PRESS RELEASES

The following releases of the Office of the White House Press Secretary, distributed during the period covered by this issue, are not included in the issue.

Released August 28, 1978

Announcement: nomination of Bruce S. Jenkins to be United States District Judge for the District of Utah

Announcement: commitments by American corporations to support the administration's anti-inflation policy

CHECKLIST—Continued

Released August 28—Continued

White House statement: meeting of Zbigniew Brzezinski, Assistant to the President for National Security Affairs, with Prime Minister 'Abd al-'Aziz 'Abd al-Ghani of the Yemen Arab Republic

Released August 31, 1978

Biographical data: Sarah C. Weddington, General Counsel of the Department of Agriculture, who will be joining the White House staff as Special Assistant to the President

Fact sheet: Federal civilian and military pay adjustment

News conference: on the President's meeting with State Governors to discuss natural gas legislation—by Governors Julian Carroll of Kentucky, chairman, and William G. Milliken of Michigan, former chairman, National Governors' Conference

ACTS APPROVED BY THE PRESIDENT

Approved August 28, 1978

H.R. 11579_____ Public Law 95–353
An act to designate the Veterans' Administration center located at 1901 South First Street, Temple, Texas, as the "Olin E. Teague Veterans' Center"; and for other purposes.

H.R. 10732_____ Public Law 95–354
An act to authorize appropriations to carry out the Fishery Conservation and Management Act of 1976 during fiscal year 1979, to provide for the regulation of foreign fish processing vessels in the fishery conservation zone, and for other purposes.

S. 405_____ Private Law 95–49
An act for the relief of Chong Cha Williams.

S. 1335_____ Private Law 95–50
An act for the relief of Shin Myong Yo Purdom, also known as Myong Yo Sin.

Natural Gas Legislation

Letters to the Members of the Senate on the Conference Committee Report.
August 31, 1978

Your vote on the natural gas conference report may be the most important decision you will make during the 95th Congress. The enclosed letter describes some of the specific effects of the natural gas bill, but I want to emphasize some overall national considerations.

I personally believe that both energy producers and natural gas consumers will be benefitted by this legislation, but far more is involved than just a carefully balanced compromise between the interests of producers and consumers. Our Nation's international reputation and economic well-being are at stake.

The ability of Congress to enact into law a national energy policy has become, in the eyes of many, a test of our nation's will.

There is no doubt that action on the natural gas bill will have a direct impact on our trade deficit, on the value of the dollar, and on the rate of inflation. The reduction of more than one million barrels per day in imported oil which will result from this bill nearly equals the saving from all the other energy legislation combined. These considerations are crucial.

I realize that this may be a difficult decision for you. The personal opinions and voting history of almost everyone have had to be changed. I know that this has been true of myself and all the members of the Senate and House Conference Committees during the past 16 months.

The compromise proposal is not perfect, but it is the carefully crafted product of a sustained and sincere effort. It is highly unlikely that any new or replacement legislation can or will be evolved next year or in the near future if the Congress should reject this bill.

Our national interests are at stake. I urge you most sincerely to vote for the natural gas conference report.

Sincerely,

JIMMY CARTER

The natural gas conference report is of overriding national importance.

The problems caused by the current administrative system are substantial: supplies are inadequate in many parts of the country; the pricing structure is uncertain; and incentives necessary for increased production are clearly lacking. These problems are well recognized, but for nearly 30 years solutions have proven to be beyond our reach.

The natural gas compromise presents a rare opportunity for us to replace the existing system with an approach which is fair, balanced and workable.

Several Senate opponents argue that producers are not given enough incentives, while others maintain that the legislation excessively benefits producers to the detriment of consumers. However, opponents of the bill cannot agree on an alternative which would improve the existing system. They are united only in their opposition.

I firmly believe that the compromise does not hold special advantages for any group. The beneficiaries of this legislation will be the American people; the interest served will be the national interest.

As a compromise, the conference report does not include everything that I proposed nor does it include everything that you have supported. The report does, however, substantially increase supplies by creating a national gas market and establishing new and certain incentives for gas producers, and it provides reasonable prices for industrial and residential consumers. It strikes a fair balance between producer interests and consumer concerns, between the over-regulation of the past and the economic hardship of immediate deregulation, and between the bills passed by the Senate and House. The compromise is workable and is far superior to the status quo.

Passage of this bill is essential for several reasons.

The bill abolishes the outmoded dual market system and creates a single national gas market. Substantial additional quantities of natural gas will flow into the interstate market—where it is sorely needed—at prices below that of alternate fuels such as foreign oil, LNG, and SNG. Together with the construction of the Alaska gas pipeline, which will be greatly facilitated by this bill, these increased supplies could mean a 30 percent increase in interstate gas by 1985, a saving of approximately 1.4 million barrels per day of imported oil by 1985, and a $6 to $8 billion-a-year reduction in our trade deficit if OPEC prices rise at about the inflation rate.

With the interstate gas market opened for the first time to intrastate supplies, certain regions of the country will no longer have to suffer through gas-short winters while other regions have more than they need.

There will also be enough gas to resume home hook-ups throughout the country. And industrial users, who have had difficulty relying on gas, would be able to depend on this fuel without fear of abrupt supply cut-offs.

Under the bill's incremental pricing provisions, the industrial gas price in 1985, in almost every region of the country, will still be well below the price of fuel oil—even assuming world oil prices stay constant. Significantly, under the incremental pricing provision, the price of natural gas to industrial users will be lower than the price would have been under the Senate-passed deregulation bill.

New and easily determined production incentives will be mandated under the compromise. Prices will be set legislatively at a level that will encourage increased production. The bill abandons the vague regulatory standards of the past, and spells out in very specific fashion the prices that producers can expect. Consequently, while the compromise appears detailed, the various price determinations that must be made are relatively simple. In addition, the bill resolves the uncertainties associated with recent Supreme Court decisions and simplifies federal regulation.

As you know, the effects of enacting this compromise go well beyond the natural gas industry. During the last several months, it has become increasingly evident that Congressional action on natural gas will have a direct impact on our Nation's economic well-being.

This year our trade deficit may be the highest in the Nation's history. One of the largest contributors to that deficit is imported oil, which is now running at an annual rate of $42 billion. The approximately 1.4 million barrels per day savings resulting from the natural gas bill equals the savings of all the other energy conference reports *combined*. Because the existing gas surplus in producing states could now be used in interstate markets, the natural gas bill also provides the most immediate and direct oil import savings in the four energy conference reports.

One of the other obvious effects of not having a national energy policy has been the dollar's erosion against other currencies. Since April of last year, the dollar's value has declined 16 percent against the German mark, 34 percent against the Swiss franc, and 31 percent against the Japanese yen. Unless Congress acts soon on a natural gas bill, the world will remain convinced of our unwillingness to face the energy problem, with continuing uncertainties and pressures on the dollar in foreign exchange markets. Over the past year, leaders of the world's major economic countries have attributed a substantial part of the decline of the dollar directly to our failure to adopt a national energy plan. The Chairman of the Federal Reserve System has informed me that he shares this view.

Both the substantial trade deficit and the slide in the value of the dollar adversely affect the inflation rate. For the first six months of this year, the consumer price index rose by 10.4 percent. By stemming the decline of the dollar's value, the gas bill will help eliminate this source of inflation. At present, every 1 percent decline in the dollar's value against the currencies of the countries from whom we import adds 0.1 percent to the consumer price index.

We cannot afford to allow another Congressional Session to end without a natural gas bill and a national energy policy. If we fail to act, the consequences are clear and unfortunate—gas supplies will remain in the producing states while oil imports continue to increase; the Nation will still lack a national energy policy; the trade deficit will remain unacceptably large; we will lose an important source of strength for the dollar.

Clearly, as national leaders we must rise above competing interests, narrow regional concerns, and short-term political considerations. We must act in the domestic and international interests of our country above all else. With the eyes of the world upon us, we cannot afford to fail this test of our national will.

Sincerely,

JIMMY CARTER

NOTE: The texts of the letters were released on September 2.

Id al-Fitr

Statement by the President.
September 3, 1978

Rosalynn and I are pleased to extend warmest good wishes to our fellow citizens of the Muslim faith who will be celebrating Id al-Fitr. May this joyous occasion bring each of you the fullest measure of happiness and satisfaction.

You can take great pride in the constructive influence you have on American life by your devotion to the moral and spiritual values of your faith.

My family joins in your prayer that we will see continued progress toward the goal of peace and a greater realization of your very deep belief in the dignity and worth of every individual.

Interview With the President

Remarks and a Question-and-Answer Session With Members of the International Labor Press Association. August 18, 1978

THE PRESIDENT. Good afternoon everybody. How are you doing? I hope I'm not interrupting your meeting. [*Laughter*] Have you had a nice day so far?

I'd like to outline very briefly some of the things that have been accomplished and some of the problems that we still face, and then spend what time we have available answering your questions.

ADMINISTRATION POLICIES

As you well know, when I was inaugurated President a year and a half ago the prime concern of our Nation was unemployment. The Congress cooperated well, and with your help we were able to put into effect an economic stimulus package that's been very productive in providing jobs. We now have about 95 million Americans on the job, the highest it's ever been. We've had a net increase of 6½ million jobs just in the last year and a half. We've had about 5 million people added to the work force. As they became sure they could get a job, more have applied for jobs, and we've had a net reduction in those who are unemployed of 1.5 million.

This has been a very gratifying experience. Some key types of workers have had notable reductions. Among blue-collar workers the unemployment rate is down

30 percent. Among Vietnam veterans the unemployment rate is down 40 [33] percent. And among construction workers the unemployment rate is down 40 percent.

We have, at the same time, a continual problem with inflation that's been pressing upon us now for about 10 years, an underlying inflation rate of around 6½ percent. The only way I know to deal with this is by very tough management of the Government. Someone's got to get control of the bureaucracy, control of the energy problem, control of the economy. And there needs to be an inspiration so that all of us work together—in the private sector, labor and business, individual citizens; local, State, and Federal Government leaders, certainly myself as President, and the Congress. There is an awareness, I think, that the bureaucracy itself needs to be more effective, and we have tried to deal with some of the more controversial issues that affect us all.

Energy is now the most important as a single issue. Last night there was signed, as you know, finally, a conference report between the House and the Senate on the natural gas issue. We still have a very tough battle on our hands to get this legislation approved by the House and Senate and implemented into law.

This would leave us with one remaining item, and that's the crude oil equalization tax. It's imperative that we raise the price of crude oil up to the world market price, to stabilize markets and also to reduce the waste brought about by excessive use. And what we want to do is to impose the tax, but return the tax collected directly to consumers, so that we won't have inflation and we won't have any reduction in overall stimulus to the economy and the buying power of the American people.

The alternatives to that are not good at all. By a very thin hair, I and my predecessors, all the way back to Harry Truman, have been faced with the prospect of complete deregulation of oil and/or gas. I think Harry Truman vetoed back as far as 1950 a bill that was passed by the Congress deregulating natural gas. We've tried to make sure that the consumers are protected in this respect.

I believe that we have also a very good chance to pass the civil service reform legislation. I know this is of concern to some of you.

We would like to change into law the Executive order under which Federal employees now carry out their legitimate bargaining rights. As you know, as long as it's only an Executive order, in case of an emergency or if we had a President in office who was not friendly with labor, just by the stroke of a pen the order could be renounced and terminated. And we are trying to put this into law. There are some who are opposing the civil service reform and they might prevent this happening at all.

I think rather than my outlining to you the problems that we have and the opportunities we have with defense and foreign affairs, it might be better for me to spend the rest of the time answering your questions.

I'd be glad to answer any questions that I can, and then following that, if you don't mind, for about 3 minutes or so I would like to ask my staff to call time so that you can come by, and it might give me a chance to have an individual photograph made with you.

Yes?

QUESTIONS

OCCUPATIONAL SAFETY AND HEALTH REGULATIONS

Q. Mr. President, I am Jerry Archuleta, editor of the Oil, Chemical and Atomic Workers newspaper, from Denver, Colorado.

As far as my union is concerned, one of the greatest achievements of your administration is the change you have made in the Labor Department, and particularly in the direction that OSHA is taking.

Your appointment of Ray Marshall and Dr. Bingham have been nothing but beneficial as far as working people of this country are concerned. And thousands of lives have been saved, and many more thousands of lives have been lengthened and prolonged as a result of the changes that have taken place.

My question is: Do you think the economic impact on companies such as the textile industry or the inflationary impact on the U.S. economy should serve as constraints on your administration when it comes to protecting the well-being and the health and safety of American workers?

THE PRESIDENT. Belatedly in our country we have had an aroused citizenry influence government at all levels to give us protection that we formerly have not had—the general public in air pollution, water pollution, for instance, and the workers themselves in health and safety.

The corrective action that has been implemented has been long overdue, and we still are feeling our way along about how this can be made more effective. One thing we did, for instance, with miners, was to put the administration of the health and safety regulations under the Department of Labor itself. I think it'll be more attuned to the specific needs of workers.

We've tried to do this in such a way that it could get the approval of employers and the general public. I think for a long time, because of an inadequate commitment to what OSHA stands for, the previous administration got bogged down in sometimes frivolous and ridiculous writing of rules and regulations that not only did not protect the workers adequately but turned the general public and the employer against the program itself.

Dr. Bingham and Ray Marshall have tried to bring some order out of that chaos.

They spent too much time trying to write specific descriptions of what a safe chair might be or what a safe ladder might be or a safe handrail. And if you took this whole group and spent a week, you couldn't write all the characteristics of what is a safe ladder or chair.

Instead, we need to have strict standards enforced about the kinds of health threats that are not easily detectable by an employee or even a trained scientist—chemicals and other health threats. I think in the distinction between health on the one hand and safety on the other, we've made a great step forward.

There's a much more general acceptance now of what OSHA is trying to do. I don't think that we should ever endanger the lives of American workers, but I believe it is very healthy that Dr. Bingham, Ray Marshall, myself, all of us, as we impose improved regulations, for instance, in the cotton dust standards, that we do it in the most efficient way and the least disruptive way.

We have not backed off at all on the quality of protection of the workers' health in breathing air with cotton dust in it. At the same time, we've cut down tremendously on the potential cost of these regulations. The workers are pleased, the Department itself is pleased, and the employers are able, I think, now to make the corrective action without having to close down plants that may have been closed if the burden on them financially was just more than they could bear.

So, to summarize, we need not ever to reduce the high standards that are being set for air pollution, water pollution, safety and health of workers. At the same time, we need to have a cost-effective program and one where the regulations are practical and make common sense. This is better for the workers; it's better for the employers; it's better for our overall economy. I think it arouses support from the American public.

NATIONAL HEALTH INSURANCE

Q. Mr. President, I'm Don Stillman from the United Auto Workers magazine, Solidarity. We've seen the hospital/doctor/insurance company lobby fight vigorously against your cost containment proposals in the health care area. We are very much in favor of a national health insurance proposal, as you are. Yet, while we're in favor of phasing, we have questions about whether or not it's a practical matter to break national health insurance proposals into a number of components, one not going into effect or not going to the Congress unless the health care industry has an inflation rate that's limited in some manner.

Why do you think that breaking up of national health into a number of components would have success in the Congress?

THE PRESIDENT. Well, we've had some success already in imposing, through the Congress, improved legislation on our Nation. At the same time, I've learned about the high fragmentation of legislative responsibility within the House and Senate and the difficulty of getting comprehensive bills passed.

We would never have gotten the energy bill passed through Congress had not the Speaker of the House set up an ad hoc committee that brought together all the various committees that were responsible for energy. A typical example is the one you mentioned that creates a problem. Hospital cost containment is a relatively simple concept, certainly much simpler than energy, welfare reform, tax reform, or national health insurance in its totality.

But even that legislation—which I don't think was adequately supported, by the way, from labor—has not been passed because of the gamut it has to run. It's got to go through the Health subcommittee and committee, the Commerce subcommittee and committee, the Ways and Means subcommittee and committee, the Rules committee, then to the House floor, and then to be voted on.

And the special interest groups, the medical profession and the hospital associations, are so intense and effective in their lobbying effort to protect their enormous and unwarranted profits that they prevail in the absence of a common American interest.

I am strongly in favor, as you know, of a comprehensive and universal health insurance program for our country. My belief is that it can only be passed if the Congress and the American public are convinced that it will work, that it can be administered, that it will have a net saving for a given level of health care, compared to what we presently have, and that overall costs can be controlled.

I would hope that as the proposals are made for prevention of disease, for more universal coverage of those who are ill and need medical care, for further use of paramedical personnel rather than just medical doctors themselves, for hospital cost containment, that I would have the full support of Members of the Senate like Senators Nelson and Kennedy, for instance, who would prefer one bill implemented at one time in its totality without the involvement of the private insurers and with a pricetag that would seem to be very high, although the net cost above and beyond what we are going to spend might be still to be determined and be in doubt.

I think my approach is a better one, and on most of the elements of our proposal, Senator Kennedy and, I think, UAW were both in agreement. But it's just a matter of political judgment. I doubt that you could find any appreciable portion of the Members of the House or Senate who would favor a single proposal, implemental all at once, with a substantial pricetag on it.

You can find pretty broad support, which is increasing, I think, for the type of complete concept, but sequential implementation program that we propose.

UNEMPLOYMENT

Q. Mr. President, your administration has made substantial progress in reducing unemployment. In the past few months the rate seems to have stagnated a little bit. Are you afraid that the tight money, high interest rate policies of the Federal Reserve might lead to a further increase in the unemployment rate in the near future?

THE PRESIDENT. That's always a possibility. So far, we don't have any evidence of that. For instance, just to give you one example, housing construction is quite often the first industry to be affected adversely by higher interest rates. We've been able to sustain housing construction throughout the last 12 months or more at an annual rate of production of more than 2 million units per year.

The reduction in unemployment rate among construction workers—which I've already mentioned—is another direct indication of this sustained growth and high demand for housing. I would prefer lower interest rates, but obviously you have to have an honoring of the independence of the Federal Reserve. That's built into law, and it can't be breached.

I don't believe that the present Chairman of the Federal Reserve has any substantial difference in philosophy than my own about the proper balancing of inflation control and keeping full employment in our country.

I meet with him frequently. He and I both preserve our individuality and our mutual independence, and I think we have a very good attitude of mutual support.

We have to be careful. I think one thing that might be pointed out is that our unemployment rate now, which is hovering very close to the 6-percent level, is about as low as we anticipated would be the case at the end of 1979. What we need to guard against now is that as we reduce inflation below what it is, that we don't see a trend upward in the unemployment rate, but a continuing, at least some trend downward.

So, I think that judging by our past experience in the last 12 months or less that we've not seen any indication that the higher interest rates charged are heading us toward a recession and high unemployment.

FOOD PRICES

Q. Mr. President, Mel Stack, Retail Clerks Union. As you know, our union has taken a positive stance on the question of inflation.

THE PRESIDENT. And I thank you for it.

Q. Well, we strongly feel that wages are not at the root of the rising costs, and especially of rising food costs.

THE PRESIDENT. Yes, that's true.

Q. I must say that we were very disturbed that Barry Bosworth singled out our industry and told the Food Market Institute that he would monitor our negotiations closely. Naturally we were happy last week to hear that Mr. Bosworth was not speaking for the administration and that pronouncements about collective bargaining would henceforth be coordinated by a top-level committee.

Mr. President, would you care at this time to comment about the inflationary factors that have an impact on food prices, especially such ones as imports, grain and cattle supplies, and energy?

THE PRESIDENT. The most serious, long-range threat to our economy is the rapidly increasing import of energy. In the last 6 years our energy imports have increased more than 800 percent, an almost unbelievable amount. In 1972 oil imports were $4.7 billion; this past 12 months, they've been $42 billion—likely to be even more in the future. That has very serious results in unemployment in our country and also a higher rate of inflation.

We have experienced last winter and last year a very unusual season, and the beef industry and other agricultural production was severely hurt—beef over a long period of time, other production of food, particularly vegetables and short-life growing crops, very adversely. So, the first 6 months of this year food prices went up 18½ percent. My guess is, my prediction is, based on the economic advisers' analyses, is that the last half of this year food prices will rise much more slowly.

There's going to be a shortage of beef for the next 3 or 4 years, possibly on a worldwide basis, because it takes so long to build up a beef herd. You have to save a heifer that would have been slaughtered, let that heifer reach maturity, have the heifer bred. The heifer ultimately has a calf—the gestation period is about 9 months—and then the calf has to grow up large enough to be slaughtered, which is 30 months, at least, in that interval.

We're trying now to encourage beef producers to build up the size of their herds and to let them know that there will be some stability in market prices. I would guess the rest of this year beef prices would hover in the neighborhood from $50 to $60 a hundredweight.

I did increase the import level of beef products, and I don't have any apology to make for it. I think it was the right decision, although many beef producers thought it was a very bad decision for me to make. I feel a responsibility, though, not to try to look at each individual decision on the basis of just whether it's politically popular or not. There's got to be a common approach to inflation, how to deal with it, and sometimes even my closest friends, sometimes among labor, sometimes among farmers—and I'm a farmer—will not like exactly what I do.

But I think that we can sustain food prices at a much lower rate of inflation the balance of this year. And the longer we have experience in this administration, the better off we are.

I might add one other thing. We've tried to get the Government out of the farm business and to let there be more stability in marketing. We have world record levels of agricultural export. We set a record last year, even with very low prices per unit. We'll break that record this year. And instead of having the surplus supplies of, say, food grains, wheat, for instance, in the hands of elevator operators and grain speculators, we've increased the farm storage capacity substantially so that farmers themselves who are keeping their own grain off the market, so that they can sell it at an orderly fashion, get the profits themselves and not have the wild fluctuations in the market caused by speculation.

I think whenever food prices go up and down wildly, other prices as well, food especially, the farmers don't benefit, because the prices generally go up because other people are holding farm products off the market deliberately or because the farmers have had a very low yield. And when prices go up, the consumers pay more. When the prices come down, consumer prices come down very, very slowly.

I think all these things that I've described to you would prevent a continua-

tion of the high increases in food prices, and I believe that the action that I've taken to level off those prices in beef is typical of the proper attention we are giving to this question.

Ms. Bario. Thank you, sir.

The President. Maybe one more.

WAGE AND PRICE CONTROLS

Q. Mr. President, my name is Diane Curry, Railway and Airline Clerks Union. Administration officials have indicated that consideration is being given to some sort of incomes policy, whether guidelines, controls, or selective measures in highly unionized industries.

Would you comment on what form that policy might take?

The President. Any policy we work out concerning inflation questions or employment questions would be done very carefully and with close consultation of a wide range of people. This would apply to prices as well.

I would guess that a majority of the American people would prefer to have mandatory wage and price controls. I'm philosophically opposed to it and will not impose such controls unless our Nation faces a very serious emergency or crisis. There are no plans for any such measures as you've described.

Barry Bosworth was mentioned earlier. We do think it's better to have better consultation among my top economic advisers, including Barry Bosworth, who has a unique responsibility to hold down inflation, Charlie Schultze, who's my closest economic adviser. I have economists, as you know, who are head of the Commerce Department and the Labor Department, and of course, Mike Blumenthal, as Secretary of Treasury, is another one who's very important in shaping my own policies. The Vice President has served on both the Budget Committee and the Finance Committee in the Senate. He's familiar with the congressional aspect of that question.

But whatever we might do in the future, it would be short of any mandatory wage or price controls, and it would be carefully worked out if things should get worse on inflation so that the interests of working people and consumers would be protected. I don't have anything to predict for you, because we don't have any plans along those lines.

Let me say this in closing: I'm very grateful that you would come here to talk to me and from your questions let me learn what matters are of interest to you.

So far as I know, in almost every instance the proposals that we have made to the Congress have been compatible with the desires of your organizations whom you represent. We've worked in close harmony, and we've not always been successful, as you know.

I was quite disappointed that the labor reform bill did not pass. That was the one bill since I've been in office that I sat down and, in effect, wrote, with the help of my advisers, myself, every paragraph of it. I think it was a very moderate bill which would have brought benefits not only to working people of the country but also to employers. There was an unwarranted outpouring of distortion and political pressure from some business organizations and some rightwing organizations, highly effective, that caused the defeat of that good legislation. But we've lost some battles of that kind.

But in general, almost without exception, we have worked in harmony. And I'm grateful for that support that you've given me, and I'm grateful for the chance that we've had to support programs that you yourselves have initiated.

Our country is basically very strong and very sound economically; obviously it is, politically and militarily. And I hope that

in the future that you all will stay close to the White House staff, to Jody Powell and others that you will meet today, and if you have a specific question that comes up that you won't hesitate to call and ask.

This is a rare occasion when I have a chance to sit down with a group because of the pressures on me of time, but your opinions are very valuable to me. And I would hope that in the future, not only your questions and inquiries but also your advice and counsel and even your tough criticisms will be made available to me so that we can work in better harmony for the people that we represent. Your readers are my constituents, and I want to serve them well. And I think you can help me do it.

I thank you for coming and let me meet with you.

NOTE: The interview began at 1:30 p.m. in the Cabinet Room at the White House. Patricia Y. Bario is Associate Press Secretary.

The transcript of the interview was released on September 4.

Camp David Meeting on the Middle East

Remarks on Departure From the White House. September 4, 1978

I'm leaving now for Camp David to prepare for a very important meeting between myself, President Sadat of Egypt, and Prime Minister Begin of Israel. During the next few days, very important decisions will be made by us, working with our advisers representing three great nations, searching for peace in the Middle East which can help greatly to ensure peace in the future throughout the world; by the Congress while I'm gone, in dealing with many very important issues, including the evolution of an energy policy for our Nation.

As we meet at Camp David, no one can ensure the degree of success which we might enjoy. The issues are very complicated. The disagreements are deep. Four wars have not led to peace in that troubled region of the world. There is no cause for excessive optimism, but there is also no cause for despair.

The greatest single factor which causes me to be encouraged is my sure knowledge that Prime Minister Begin and President Sadat genuinely want peace. They are determined to make progress, and so am I.

We will need the encouragement and the prayers of everyone in our Nation, in all three nations, throughout the world, who want success to come from our deliberations. Compromises will be mandatory. Without them, no progress can be expected. Flexibility will be the essence of our hopes. And my own role will be that of a full partner, not trying to impose the will of the United States on others, but searching for common ground on which agreements can be reached and searching for exchanges of compromise that are mutually advantageous to all nations involved.

I know the seriousness with which President Sadat and Prime Minister Begin come to our country, and I have tried to prepare myself as well as I possibly could to bring success to these efforts.

It will have to be a mutual thing, and all of us will enter these discussions without prejudice toward one another, with a spirit of good will and with the realization of the sober responsibilities that fall on us.

Lastly, I would say that we will be almost uniquely isolated from the press and from the outside world. My hope is that this degree of personal interchange, without the necessity for political posturing or defense of a transient stand or belief, will be constructive.

There will be a great deal of effort made to ensure and enhance mutual trust in one another and to recognize accurately that we all want the same ultimate goal. There is no doubt in my mind about this.

I want to express, in closing, my thanks to these two great leaders for their willingness to come when the political consequences of failure might be very severe and when the prospects of complete success are very remote. We'll do the best we can, and I fervently ask the support and prayers of all those who share with us a hope that we might bring a new prospect for peace to the Middle East.

Thank you very much.

NOTE: The President spoke at 12:05 p.m. to reporters assembled on the South Lawn of the White House.

Leif Erikson Day, 1978
Proclamation 4592.   September 5, 1978

By the President of the United States of America

A Proclamation

Stories of brave men battling fearful odds fire our imaginations. We honor such men long after the memories of their adventures have been dimmed by time.

So it is with Leif Erikson. His original discovery and exploration of North America was the supreme achievement of a race of men who truly were the masters of the sea. His voyage enlarged mankind's horizons and pointed the way West for the others who were to follow.

Today we honor Leif Erikson, and in honoring him we also honor the human qualities of imagination, courage, and perseverance which characterize both his men of old and Americans of Scandinavian descent today.

As a mark of respect for the achievements of Leif Erikson and his followers, the Congress of the United States, by joint resolution approved September 2, 1964 (78 Stat. 849, 36 U.S.C. 169c), authorized the President to proclaim October 9 in each year as Leif Erikson Day.

Now, THEREFORE, I, JIMMY CARTER, President of the United States of America, do hereby designate Monday, October 9, 1978, as Leif Erikson Day and I direct the appropriate government officials to display the flag of the United States on all government buildings that day.

I also invite the people of the United States to honor the memory of Leif Erikson on that day by holding appropriate exercises and ceremonies in suitable places throughout our land.

IN WITNESS WHEREOF, I have hereunto set my hand this fifth day of September, in the year of our Lord nineteen hundred seventy-eight, and of the Independence of the United States of America the two hundred and third.

JIMMY CARTER

[Filed with the Office of the Federal Register, 1:44 p.m., September 5, 1978]

Presidential Commission on World Hunger

Executive Order 12078. September 5, 1978

By the authority vested in me as President by the Constitution of the United States of America, and in order to create in accordance with the Federal Advisory Committee Act (5 U.S.C. App. I) an advisory commission on the problems of hunger and malnutrition, it is hereby ordered as follows:

1–1. *Establishment of Commission.*

1–101. There is established the Presidential Commission on World Hunger.

1–102. The membership of the Commission shall be composed of not more than 20 persons from among citizens in public and private life as follows:

(a) Sixteen members shall be appointed by the President, who shall designate a Chairman and two Vice Chairmen.

(b) The President of the Senate and the Speaker of the House of Representatives are each invited to designate two Members of their respective Houses to serve on the Commission.

1–2. *Functions of the Commission.*

1–201. The Commission shall develop factual data as to the causes of world hunger and malnutrition. It shall review existing authorities and programs, public and private, national and international, which seek to address the problems of hunger and malnutrition; and, shall assess the extent to which those programs are meeting their objectives, and why.

1–202. In developing its data and assessing existing programs, the Commission shall review existing studies on world hunger and malnutrition, conduct additional studies where necessary, and hold such hearings or inquiries as may be helpful.

1–203. The Commission shall develop recommendations designed to significantly reduce world hunger and malnutrition; and, shall develop various options for harnessing available resources to carry out those recommendations, including policy options for improving the capacity of the United States to reduce the problems of world hunger and malnutrition.

1–204. In developing its recommendations, the Commission shall encourage public participation by holding hearings, issuing reports, and coordinating, sponsoring, or overseeing projects, studies, and other activities related to the understanding of the problems of world hunger and malnutrition. The maximum use shall be made of past and ongoing related government efforts of that nature.

1–205. The Commission shall coordinate its functions with local, state, national, and international agencies and organizations where appropriate.

1–206. An interim report on the status of its work and on its tentative recommendations shall be submitted to the President no later than July 31, 1979.

1–3. *Administrative Provisions.*

1–301. The Commission may establish subcommittees. Private citizens who are not members of the Commission may be included as members of subcommittees.

1–302. The Commission may request any Executive agency to furnish such information, advice, and services as may be useful for the fulfillment of the Commission's functions under this Order. Each agency shall designate an agency liaison with the Commission and shall, to the extent permitted by law and overriding priorities, and within the limits of available funds and personnel resources, furnish such information, advice, and services to the Commission upon the written request of the Chairman of the Commission.

1–303. The Commission is authorized to appoint and fix the compensation of a staff and such other persons as may be necessary to enable it to carry out its functions. The Commission may obtain services in accordance with the provisions of Section 3109 of Title 5 of the United States Code, to the extent funds are available therefor.

1–304. Each member of the Commission and its subcommittees may receive, to the extent permitted by law, compensation for each day he or she is engaged in meetings of the Commission or its subcommittees at a rate not to exceed the daily rate now or hereafter prescribed by law for GS–15 of the General Schedule, and may also receive travel expenses, including per diem in lieu of subsistence, as authorized by law (5 U.S.C. 5702 and 5703) for persons employed intermittently in the government service.

1–305. The General Services Administration shall provide administrative services, facilities, and support to the Commission on a reimbursable basis.

1–306. All necessary expenses incurred in connection with the work of the Commission shall be paid from the appropriation for "Unanticipated Needs" in the Executive Office Appropriations Act, 1978, or from such other funds as may be available.

1–307. The functions of the President under the Federal Advisory Committee Act (5 U.S.C. App. I), which are applicable to the Commission, except that of reporting annually to the Congress, shall be performed by the Administrator of General Services as provided by Executive Order No. 12024 of December 1, 1977.

1–4. *General Provisions.*

1–401. The Commission shall conclude its work and submit a final report to the President at least 30 days prior to its termination, including its recommendations for improving the United States' capacity to reduce the problems of hunger and malnutrition.

1–402. The Commission shall terminate on June 30, 1980 or earlier as directed by the President.

JIMMY CARTER

The White House,
  September 5, 1978.

[Filed with the Office of the Federal Register,
  1:45 p.m., September 5, 1978]

Committee for the Preservation of the White House

Appointment of Richard A. Manoogian as a Member.   September 5, 1978

The President today announced the appointment of Richard A. Manoogian, of Grosse Pointe Farms, Mich., as a member of the Committee for the Preservation of the White House.

Manoogian, 42, is president and director of Masco Corp., a diversified manufacturing firm. He is a trustee of the Archives of American Art, the Center for Creative Studies in Detroit, and the Detroit Institute of Arts.

tor of the Commission, and that William P. Hobgood will serve as Coordinator of Labor Relations Programs for the Commission.

Koleda, 36, was Director of the White House Conference on Balanced Growth, which presented its report to the President in July 1978. He is a former vice president of the National Planning Association and director of its domestic division. He has also been a Brookings Institution economic policy fellow.

Hobgood, 39, is Director of Mediation Services for the Federal Mediation and Conciliation Service. He has been active in labor relations since 1965 and has served as a mediator in several cities.

President's Commission on the Coal Industry

Appointment of Two Members, Staff Director, and Coordinator of Labor Relations Programs.   September 5, 1978

The President today announced two members of the President's Commission on the Coal Industry. They are:

JESSE CORE, 65, of State College, Pa. Core is adjunct professor of mining engineering at the Pennsylvania State University. Core retired from U.S. Steel Corp. in 1977 after a 26-year career, including 18 years as vice president. Before joining U.S. Steel Core worked as a mining engineer for several coal companies, and as a coal miner.

MARVIN FRIEDMAN, 55, vice president of Ruttenberg, Friedman, Kilgallon, Gutchess & Associates, Inc., a Washington firm of economists and manpower specialists. Friedman was previously a staff economist and assistant director of research for the AFL–CIO.

The President also announced that Michael S. Koleda will serve as Staff Direc-

National Corporation for Housing Partnerships

Nomination of Three Members of the Board of Directors.   September 6, 1978

The President today announced three persons whom he will nominate to be members of the Board of Directors of the National Corporation for Housing Partnerships. They are:

PATRICIA K. RITTER, of Hartford, Conn., chairman of the board of the Mutual Real Estate Investment Trust in New York City and director, cofounder, and former president of the Connecticut Housing Investment Fund in Hartford;

HERMAN J. RUSSELL, of Atlanta, Ga., chairman of the board of the Citizens Trust Company Bank and president and chairman of the board of Georgia-Southeastern Land Co.;

KENNON V. ROTHCHILD, of Mahtomedi, Minn., chairman of the board of directors and chief executive officer of H. & Val J. Rothchild, Inc., a mortgage banking firm, and of Rothchild Financial Corp. in St. Paul, Minn.

Camp David Meeting on the Middle East

Joint Statement Issued by President Carter, President Anwar al-Sadat of Egypt, and Prime Minister Menahem Begin of Israel. September 6, 1978

After four wars, despite vast human efforts, the Holy Land does not yet enjoy the blessings of peace.

Conscious of the grave issues which face us, we place our trust in the God of our fathers, from whom we seek wisdom and guidance.

As we meet here at Camp David we ask people of all faiths to pray with us that peace and justice may result from these deliberations.

Foreign Intelligence Surveillance Legislation

Statement Urging Passage of the Legislation by the House of Representatives. September 6, 1978

The House of Representatives is scheduled to vote this week on the foreign intelligence surveillance act, one of the most significant legislative initiatives involving our intelligence agencies in the last three decades.

This act will establish the Nation's first legislative controls over foreign intelligence surveillance conducted by the United States Government. Most importantly, those controls will be established so as to protect both the strength of our Nation's intelligence agencies and the privacy rights of our citizens.

American citizens will be assured that the intelligence agencies so vital to protecting our security will be able to perform their tasks fully and effectively. The bill also assures intelligence officers who serve our country that their proper activities in this field will be authorized by statute.

By providing clear statutory standards, this legislation will help strengthen the ability of our intelligence agencies to deal with foreign espionage and international terrorism. The strong support of this legislation by every intelligence agency clearly reflects this fact.

The passage of this legislation is also a major step toward eliminating the potential for abuse of electronic surveillance by the Federal Government. Americans will now be afforded the safeguards of a judicial warrant procedure for any electronic surveillance which might affect their rights.

This legislation has been carefully developed over several years, by executive and congressional leaders of both parties. The kind of bipartisan cooperation needed to develop legislation in the intelligence area, which is so important to the defense of our Nation, was demonstrated earlier this year by the overwhelming Senate vote, 95–1, passing the bill.

I urge the Members of the House to vote for passage of this legislation, so that we can promptly begin to implement this well-balanced, long-overdue initiative.

Department of Defense Appropriation Authorization Bill

Statement on the House of Representatives Action To Sustain the President's Veto of H.R. 10929. September 7, 1978

I am very pleased by the decision of the House to sustain my veto of the defense authorization bill. I now look forward to working closely and cooperatively with the appropriate committees of the House and Senate in enacting a new bill which will provide the strongest possible national defense, a goal which I know we all share.

1501

President's Commission on Pension Policy

Appointment of C. Peter McColough as a Member and Chairman. September 7, 1978

The President today announced the appointment of C. Peter McColough, chairman and chief executive of Xerox Corp., as a member and Chairman of the President's Commission on Pension Policy.

McColough was born August 1, 1922, in Halifax, Nova Scotia, Canada. He received an LL.B. from Dalhousie University in Halifax in 1947, and an M.B.A. from Harvard Graduate School of Business Administration in 1949. He served as an airman in England with the Royal Navy during World War II.

McColough joined Xerox (then the Haloid Co.) in 1954 as general manager of the firm's first reproduction service center in Chicago. He became president of the company in 1966.

McColough is chairman of the executive committee of the International Executive Service Corps and serves on the board of directors of the New York Stock Exchange. He is a member of the Business Council, the Business Roundtable, the Council on Foreign Relations, and the steering committee of the National Committee for Full Employment.

National Employ the Handicapped Week, 1978

Proclamation 4593. September 7, 1978

By the President of the United States of America

A Proclamation

Our country's greatest resource is its people—including those with physical and mental disabilities.

But handicapped individuals too often have had to exist on the sidelines of life because of poor education, improper vocational preparation, unavailable transportation, inaccessible buildings and other difficulties.

Now, however, local, state and Federal laws and regulations are beginning to ensure equal rights to the disabled, so that they will no longer be second-class citizens. All offices of the Federal government have been directed to improve hiring and promotion practices as they relate to handicapped individuals. The private sector, too, is being made more aware of its duties and responsibilities.

To affirm our commitment to handicapped individuals, the Congress, by joint resolution of August 11, 1945, as amended (36 U.S.C. 155) has called for the designation of the first week in October of each year as National Employ the Handicapped Week.

Now, THEREFORE, I, JIMMY CARTER, President of the United States of America, do hereby designate the week beginning October 1, 1978, as National Employ the Handicapped Week. I urge all Governors, Mayors, other public officials, leaders in business and labor, and private citizens at all levels of responsibility to help secure full employment rights for handicapped individuals and to remove all barriers that prevent their full participation in every aspect of our national life.

IN WITNESS WHEREOF, I have hereunto set my hand this seventh day of September, in the year of our Lord nineteen hundred seventy-eight, and of the Independence of the United States of America the two hundred and third.

JIMMY CARTER

[Filed with the Office of the Federal Register, 11:12 a.m., September 8, 1978]

National School Lunch Week, 1978

Proclamation 4594. September 8, 1978

By the President of the United States of America

A Proclamation

Every child needs wholesome food. The National School Lunch Program was created in 1946 to help our nation achieve that goal. It now provides nutritious lunches to 26 million children every school day.

I am proud of the success of the National School Lunch Program and of the two other nutrition-related school activities that complement its success.

One is the School Breakfast Program that now serves 2.8 million children daily. It gives all children, not just the needy, the chance to eat breakfast at school if they cannot eat at home.

The other is the Nutrition Education and Training Program that will instruct children, teachers, and school food service workers on the relationship between food, nutrition, and health.

In recognition of the National School Lunch Program's contribution to America's youth, the Congress, by a joint resolution of October 9, 1962 (76 Stat. 779; 36 U.S.C. 168), has designated the week beginning the second Sunday of October of each year as National School Lunch Week, and has requested the President to issue annually a proclamation calling for its appropriate observance.

Now, THEREFORE, I, JIMMY CARTER, President of the United States of America, do hereby urge the people of the United States to observe the week of October 8, 1978, as National School Lunch Week and to give special recognition to the role of good nutrition in building a stronger America through its youth.

IN WITNESS WHEREOF, I have hereunto set my hand this eighth day of September, in the year of our Lord nineteen hundred and seventy-eight, and of the Independence of the United States of America the two hundred and third.

JIMMY CARTER

[Filed with the Office of the Federal Register, 10:49 a.m., September 11, 1978]

United States Parole Commission

Nomination of Richard T. Mulcrone To Be a Commissioner. September 8, 1978

The President today announced that he will nominate Richard T. Mulcrone, of Shakopee, Minn., to be a Commissioner of the United States Parole Commission for a 6-year term.

Mulcrone was born May 23, 1934, in St. Paul, Minn. He attended St. Thomas College and the University of Minnesota. He served in the U.S. Army in 1954 and 1955.

In 1953 and 1954, Mulcrone was a police patrolman for St. Paul. In 1956 he was a roving gang worker, and from 1957 to 1959, he was a probation officer for Scott County, Minn. Mulcrone was with the counties of Carver and Scott, Minn., from 1959 to 1972, serving as a probation officer, director of court services, and family court referee. In 1973 he was court administrator for Scott County.

Since 1973 Mulcrone has been chairman of the Minnesota Corrections Board, which is Minnesota's first fulltime paroling authority. He has been a member of the Governor's Commission on Law Enforcement, Courts, and Corrections and the Administration of Criminal Justice, and a commissioner on the Governor's

Commission on Crime Control and Prevention. He has written several articles and a manual on juvenile delinquency, and has lectured at police training schools and universities.

Embargo Regulations Under the Trading With the Enemy Act

Memorandum From the President.
September 8, 1978

Memorandum for the Secretary of State, the Secretary of the Treasury

Subject: Determination Extending the Exercise of Certain Authorities Under the Trading With the Enemy Act

Under Section 101(b) of Public Law 95–223 (91 Stat. 1625; 50 U.S.C. App. 5 note), the exercise of certain authorities under the Trading With the Enemy Act is scheduled to terminate on September 14, 1978.

I hereby determine that the extension for one year of the exercise of those authorities with respect to the applicable countries is in the national interest of the United States.

Therefore, pursuant to the authority vested in me by Section 101(b) of Public Law 95–223, I extend for one year, until September 14, 1979, the exercise of those authorities with respect to those countries presently affected by: (1) the Foreign Assets Control Regulations, 31 CFR Part 500, (2) the Transaction Control Regulations, 31 CFR Part 505, (3) the Cuban Assets Control Regulations, 31 CFR Part 515, and (4) the Foreign Funds Control Regulations, 31 CFR Part 520.

This determination shall be published in the FEDERAL REGISTER.

JIMMY CARTER

[Filed with the Office of the Federal Register, 4:55 p.m., September 8, 1978]

Embargo Regulations Under the Trading With the Enemy Act

Letter to the Speaker of the House and the President of the Senate. September 8, 1978

Dear Mr. Speaker: (Dear Mr. President:)

Today I issued a determination that the extension for one year of the authorities currently exercised under Section 5(b) of the Trading with the Enemy Act, 50 U.S.C. App. 5(b), with respect to the countries indicated below, is in the national interest. This determination was issued pursuant to Section 101(b) of Public Law 95–223, December 28, 1977, 91 Stat. 1625.

The Foreign Assets Control Regulations, 31 CFR Part 500, prohibit persons subject to the jurisdiction of the United States from engaging in unlicensed commercial or financial transactions with North Korea, Vietnam, Cambodia or nationals of these countries. The Regulations prohibit importation or dealing in merchandise of these countries or transactions in blocked assets of these countries or their nationals absent a license from the Office of Foreign Assets Control, Department of the Treasury. Current commercial or financial transactions with the People's Republic of China are authorized as long as strategic goods are not involved. However, Chinese assets remain subject to the statute and the Regulations.

The Transaction Control Regulations, 31 CFR Part 505, are Treasury regulations which prohibit U.S. persons from engaging in unlicensed sales of strategic goods located abroad to almost all Communist countries.

The Cuban Assets Control Regulations, 31 CFR Part 515, are parallel to the Foreign Assets Control Regulations in content. However, foreign subsidiaries of

U.S. firms may engage in certain non-strategic types of trade with Cuba under Treasury license.

The Foreign Funds Control Regulations, 31 CFR Part 520, continue to block the property of Czechoslovakia and the German Democratic Republic pending a claims settlement program with those countries for the illegal expropriation of private American property following World War II. The Regulations also continue to block such assets of Estonia, Latvia, and Lithuania as a reflection of the U.S. policy of nonrecognition of the forcible incorporation of those countries into the U.S.S.R.

I have determined that these four regulatory programs should be extended because the results attendant upon the lapse of these authorities would be unacceptable in light of present U.S. foreign policy objectives. Their extension would be in the national interest of the United States for the following reasons:

(1) Current trade and financial embargoes against Cuba, North Korea, Vietnam, and Cambodia should be continued until appropriate political changes occur with respect to our relations with those countries.

(2) The Transaction Control Regulations are needed to support controls to which we have agreed with our allies with respect to the export of strategic goods to Communist countries.

(3) Freezing of Chinese, Vietnamese, and Cuban assets and controls over the remaining World War II assets of the German Democratic Republic and Czechoslovakia should continue until American claims against these countries are settled. Controls over the remaining World War II assets of the Baltic States should continue as a reflection of the U.S. policy of nonrecognition of the forcible incorporation of these countries into the U.S.S.R.

In light of these considerations, pursuant to Public Law 95–223, I have extended the exercise of these authorities for another year, until September 14, 1979.

Sincerely,

Jimmy Carter

NOTE: This is the text of identical letters addressed to Thomas P. O'Neill, Jr., Speaker of the House of Representatives, and Walter F. Mondale, President of the Senate.

Digest of Other White House Announcements

The following listing includes the President's daily schedule and other items of general interest as announced by the White House Press Office during the period covered by this issue. Events and announcements printed elsewhere in the issue are not included.

September 4

The President met at the White House with:

—Zbigniew Brzezinski, Assistant to the President for National Security Affairs;

—Frank B. Moore, Assistant to the President for Congressional Liaison;

—General Services Administrator Joel W. Solomon and Deputy Attorney General Benjamin R. Civiletti.

September 5 [1]

The President greeted President Anwar al-Sadat of Egypt and Prime Minister Menahem Begin of Israel on their separate arrivals at Camp David, Md.

---

[1] EDITOR'S NOTE: The informal nature of the meetings at Camp David precluded the announcement of daily Presidential schedules by the White House Press Office. Only those meetings and their participants which were announced have been included.

The President met in the evening with Prime Minister Begin. He then met with his foreign policy advisers.

September 6

The President met in the morning with President Sadat.

The President met with Vice President Walter F. Mondale, Secretary of State Cyrus R. Vance, and Dr. Brzezinski.

The President met in the afternoon with President Sadat and Prime Minister Begin. Following their meeting, the President met with Secretary Vance and Dr. Brzezinski.

The President met in the evening with members of the U.S. delegation.

September 7

The President met in the morning with Prime Minister Begin. Also attending the meeting were Secretary Vance, Dr. Brzezinski, Israeli Foreign Minister Moshe Dayan, and Israeli Defense Minister Ezer Weizman.

The President held morning and afternoon meetings with President Sadat and Prime Minister Begin.

The President met in the evening with President Sadat. Also attending the meeting were Vice President Mondale, Secretary Vance, Secretary of Defense Harold Brown, Dr. Brzezinski, Egyptian Deputy Prime Minister Mohamed 'Abd al-Ghani al-Jamasi, and Egyptian Foreign Minister Mohamed Ibrahim Kamel.

September 8

The President met with Vice President Mondale, Secretaries Vance and Brown, Hamilton Jordan, Assistant to the President, and Dr. Brzezinski.

The President met in the afternoon with Prime Minister Begin. Also attending the meeting were Secretary Vance, Foreign Minister Dayan, and Defense Minister Weizman.

The President met with President Sadat.

Prime Minister and Mrs. Begin hosted a dinner for the President and Mrs. Carter in the evening.

NOMINATIONS SUBMITTED TO THE SENATE

The following list does not include promotions of members of the Uniformed Services, nominations to the Service Academies, or nominations of Foreign Service officers.

Submitted September 6, 1978

The following-named persons to be members of the Board of Directors of the National Corporation for Housing Partnerships for the terms indicated:

PATRICIA K. RITTER, of Connecticut, for the term expiring October 27, 1980, vice Henry F. Trione, term expired.

KENNON V. ROTHCHILD, of Minnesota, for the term expiring October 27, 1979, vice Raymond Alexander Harris, term expired.

HERMAN J. RUSSELL, of Georgia, for the remainder of the term expiring October 27, 1978, vice Charles J. Urstadt, resigned.

HERMAN J. RUSSELL, of Georgia, for the term expiring October 27, 1981 (reappointment).

Submitted September 8, 1978

RICHARD T. MULCRONE, of Minnesota, to be a Commissioner of the United States Parole Commission for a term of 6 years, vice James R. Cooper, term expiring.

CHECKLIST OF WHITE HOUSE PRESS RELEASES

The following releases of the Office of the White House Press Secretary, distributed during the period covered by this issue, are not included in the issue.

Released September 3, 1978

Statements: support for the administration's position on the energy issue—by Governors Ella T. Grasso of Connecticut, Reubin Askew of Florida, James B. Longley of Maine, Joseph P. Teasdale of Missouri, Thomas L. Judge of Montana, Jerry Apodaca of New Mexico, Milton J. Shapp of Pennsylvania, Richard A. Snelling of Vermont, and Ed Herschler of Wyoming

CHECKLIST—Continued

Released September 5, 1978

Transcript: exchange of remarks by Vice President Walter F. Mondale and President Anwar al-Sadat of Egypt on President Sadat's arrival at Andrews Air Force Base, Md.

Transcript: exchange of remarks by Vice President Mondale and Prime Minister Menahem Begin of Israel on the Prime Minister's arrival at Andrews Air Force Base, Md.

Released September 6, 1978

Fact sheet: Marine evening dress parade ceremony (as performed at Camp David, Md., on September 7)

Released September 7, 1978

Fact sheet: President's Commission on Pension Policy

ACTS APPROVED BY
THE PRESIDENT

Approved September 8, 1978

H.R. 13467_____ Public Law 95–355
Second Supplemental Appropriations Act, 1978.

ACTS APPROVED—Continued

Approved September 8—Continued

H.R. 12602_____ Public Law 95–356
Military Construction Authorization Act, 1979.

H.R. 3532_____ Public Law 95–357
An act to amend chapter 639 of title 10, United States Code, to enable the Secretary of the Navy to change the name of a publication of the Naval Observatory providing data for navigators and astronomers.

H.R. 7161_____ Public Law 95–358
An act to amend title 10, United States Code, to allow nationals, as well as citizens, of the United States to participate in the Junior Reserve Officers' Training Corps program.

H.R. 8471_____ Public Law 95–359
An act to authorize the Governor of the State of Wyoming to exhibit the nameplate, ship's bell, and silver service of the United States Ship Wyoming without restriction as to the place of such exhibition.

H.R. 7162_____ Private Law 95–51
An act for the relief of Stephanie Johnson.

H.R. 13235_____ Private Law 95–52
An act for the relief of James Thomas Lantz, Junior, David D. Bulkley, and Arthur J. Abshire.

PRESIDENTIAL DOCUMENTS

Department of State

Nomination of Thomas R. Pickering To Be Assistant Secretary for Oceans and International Environmental and Scientific Affairs. September 11, 1978

The President today announced that he will nominate Thomas R. Pickering, of Rutherford, N.J., to be Assistant Secretary of State for Oceans and International Environmental and Scientific Affairs. He would replace Patsy Mink, who has resigned.

Pickering was born November 5, 1931, in New Jersey. He received an A.B. from Bowdoin College in 1953 and M.A. degrees from Fletcher School of Law and Diplomacy in 1954 and the University of Melbourne, Australia, in 1956. He served in the U.S. Navy from 1956 to 1959.

Pickering joined the Foreign Service in 1959 and served as an intelligence research specialist and as a political officer in Geneva. In 1964–65 he took Swahili language training, and from 1965 to 1967, he was principal officer in Zanzibar.

Pickering was deputy chief of mission in Dar es Salaam from 1967 to 1969. From 1969 to 1973, he was Deputy Director of the Bureau of Politico-Military Affairs, and from 1973 to 1974, he was Special Assistant to the Secretary of State and Executive Secretary of the Department. Since 1974 he has been Ambassador to the Hashemite Kingdom of Jordan.

United Nations

Nomination of U.S. Representatives and Alternate Representatives to the 33d Session of the General Assembly. September 11, 1978

The President today announced the persons he will nominate as Representatives and Alternate Representatives to the 33d Session of the General Assembly of the United Nations. They are:

Representatives

ANDREW YOUNG, U.S. Ambassador to the United Nations

JAMES F. LEONARD, JR., Deputy U.S. Ambassador to the United Nations

ABRAHAM A. RIBICOFF, U.S. Senator from Connecticut

JAMES B. PEARSON, U.S. Senator from Kansas

SET CHARLES MOMJIAN, a marketing executive with the Ford Motor Co. in Willow Grove, Pa.

Alternate Representatives

DONALD F. McHENRY, Deputy Representative of the United States in the Security Council of the U.N.

MELISSA F. WELLS, U.S. Representative on the Economic and Social Council of the U.N.

ANGELIQUE O. STAHL, chairman of the board of Broward Federal Savings and Loan Association in Fort Lauderdale, Fla.

JOHN W. HECHINGER, president of the Hechinger Co. in Landover, Md.

RICHARD W. PETREE, minister-counselor for political and security affairs at the U.S. Mission to the U.N.

Veterans Day, 1978

Proclamation 4595. September 11, 1978

By the President of the United States of America

A Proclamation

Among the great days of national remembrance, none is more deeply moving to Americans than Veterans Day. On this occasion, our nation traditionally joins together to salute those valiant individuals who have served in the Armed Forces.

This is a very special day. It symbolizes the debt of gratitude we owe our veterans. It reminds us that the freedom we enjoy has endured intact because millions of patriotic men and women answered their country's call to service and sacrifice.

Our veterans have not sought glory for themselves, but peace and freedom for us all. They represent the spirit that has preserved us as a great nation. They deserve our recognition for all they have done.

Now, THEREFORE, I, JIMMY CARTER, President of the United States of America, invite all Americans to observe Saturday, November 11, 1978, as Veterans Day and on this historic occasion, let us resolve anew to keep faith with those whose love of country has set them in an imperishable roll of honor.

I urge all the families and friends of our sick and disabled veterans to visit them and extend to them a grateful nation's promise that they will not be forgotten.

I call upon Federal, State, and local Government officials to mark Veterans Day by displaying the flag of the United States, and by encouraging and supporting public involvement in appropriate ceremonies throughout the country.

IN WITNESS WHEREOF, I have hereunto set my hand this eleventh day of September, in the year of our Lord, nineteen hundred and seventy-eight, and of the Independence of the United States of America, the two hundred and third.

JIMMY CARTER

[Filed with the Office of the Federal Register, 2:36 p.m., September 12, 1978]

Equal Employment Opportunity Commission

Nomination of Armando M. Rodriguez To Be a Member. September 11, 1978

The President today announced that he will nominate Armando M. Rodriguez, of Whittier, Calif., to be a member of the Equal Employment Opportunity Commission for a term expiring July 1, 1983.

Rodriguez was born September 30, 1921, in Mexico, and grew up in San Diego, Calif. He received a B.A. (1949) and M.A. (1951) from San Diego State College. He served in the U.S. Army from 1942 to 1946.

Rodriguez began his career as a teacher in the San Diego city schools in 1949. He also served as a vice principal and principal. In 1965 and 1966, he was a consultant to the California State Department of Education, and in 1966 and 1967, he was chief of the bureau of intergroup relations of that department.

From 1967 to 1970, Rodriguez was Director of the Office for Spanish Speaking American Affairs at the U.S. Office of Education. In 1969 he also served on the HEW Secretary's Committee on Easing Tensions.

From 1971 to 1973, Rodriguez was Assistant Commissioner for Regional Office Coordination at the U.S. Office of Education. Since 1973 he has been president of East Los Angeles College.

Rodriguez is a member of the National Commission on the Future of State Colleges and Universities, the National Education Task Force of La Raza, and the California School Finance Reform Commission. He is the author of numerous articles, particularly on bilingual education.

Civil Aeronautics Board

Nomination of Marvin S. Cohen To Be a Member. September 11, 1978

The President today announced that he will nominate Marvin S. Cohen, of Tucson, Ariz., to be a member of the Civil Aeronautics Board for the remainder of the term expiring December 31, 1979.

Cohen was born October 16, 1931, in Akron, Ohio. He received a B.A. (1953) and LL.B. (1957) from the University of Arizona.

Cohen was an associate with a Tucson law firm in 1957 and deputy Pima County attorney in 1958. In 1959 and 1960, he was chief civil deputy Pima County attorney. In 1961 he was first assistant city attorney for the city of Tucson.

From 1961 to 1963, Cohen was special assistant to the Solicitor of the Department of the Interior in Washington. Since 1963 he has been associated with the Tucson law firm of Bilby, Shoenhair, Warnock & Dolph.

Cohen has served as chairman of the Arizona State Bar's Group and Prepaid Legal Committee, and as secretary of Arizona Legal Services. He is a board member of the Tucson Regional Plan, and chairman of the rate structure subcommittee of the citizens advisory committee to the Arizona Corporation Commission. He has served on the Tucson Water Advisory Committee.

Presidential Commission on World Hunger

Appointment of 14 Members. September 12, 1978

The President today announced the appointment of 14 persons as members of the Presidential Commission on World Hunger. They are:

NORMAN E. BORLAUG, of Minnesota, director of the Wheat, Barley and Triticale Research and Production Programs at the International Center for Maize and Wheat Improvement in Mexico;

DAVID W. BROOKS, of Atlanta, chairman of the policy committee of Gold Kist, Inc.;

HARRY CHAPIN, the recording artist, who is the founder of World Hunger Year, a non-profit private group;

JOHN DENVER, the recording artist, who has also produced a film, "I Want to Live," directed toward the problem of world hunger;

WALTER P. FALCON, director of the Food Research Institute and professor of economics at Stanford University;

SOL LINOWITZ, Washington attorney and co-negotiator of the Panama Canal treaties (also designated Chair of the Commission);

JEAN MAYER, president of Tufts University and an expert on nutrition (Vice Chair);

BESS MYERSON, newspaper columnist and former commissioner of consumer affairs for New York City;

STEVEN MULLER, president of Johns Hopkins University and Johns Hopkins Hospital (Vice Chair);

HOWARD A. SCHNEIDER, director of the Institute of Nutrition and professor of biochemistry and nutrition at the University of North Carolina;

ADELE SMITH SIMMONS, president of Hampshire College in Amherst, Mass.;

RAYMOND C. SINGLETARY, JR., of Blakely, Ga., president of the Blakely Peanut Co. and past president of the Georgia Association of Soil Conservation Districts and the Southeastern Peanut Association;

EUGENE L. STOCKWELL, of Ridgewood, N.J., associate general secretary for overseas ministries of the National Council of the Churches of Christ in the U.S.A.;

CLIFTON R. WHARTON, JR., chancellor of the State University of New York and a specialist in economic development.

United States Ambassador to Panama

Nomination of Ambler H. Moss, Jr. September 12, 1978

The President today announced that he will nominate Ambler H. Moss, Jr., of Alexandria, Va., to be Ambassador Extraordinary and Plenipotentiary of the United States to Panama. He would replace William J. Jorden, who has resigned.

Moss was born September 1, 1937, in Baltimore, Md. He received a B.A. from Yale University in 1960 and a J.D. from George Washington University in 1970. He served in the U.S. Navy from 1960 to 1964.

Moss was vice consul in Barcelona from 1964 to 1966. From 1966 to 1969, he was special assistant to the U.S. Ambassador to the Organization of American States. From 1969 to 1970, he was Spanish desk officer at the State Department.

From 1971 to 1976, Moss was an attorney with Coudert Brothers, in Washington and then in Brussels. In 1977 he was a member of the Panama Canal Treaty negotiating team and special assistant to the conegotiator. In 1977 and 1978, he was Deputy Assistant Secretary of State for Congressional Relations. Since earlier this year, he has been an attorney with Coudert Brothers.

National Railroad Passenger Corporation

Nomination of M. Athalie Range To Be a Member of the Board of Directors. September 13, 1978

The President today announced that he will nominate M. Athalie Range, of Miami, Fla., to be a member of the Board of Directors of the National Railroad Passenger Corporation for a term expiring July 18, 1981. She would replace Mary Head, whose term has expired, and would be one of the consumer representatives on the Board.

Range was born November 7, 1918, in Key West, Fla. She attended Booker T. Washington High School in Miami.

Range became involved in public service as president of the Liberty City PTA, where she led a building drive for schools in black areas. She served as a local and county PTA president for 16 years.

In 1965 Range was elected to the Miami City Commission. She was the first black and the second woman elected to that commission. She introduced ordinances including more stringent handgun controls and updating housing and fire codes.

In 1971 Range was appointed secretary of the Florida Department of Community Affairs. She resigned in 1973 to return to private business as owner and funeral director of the Range Funeral Home in Miami.

Range is a member of the board of directors of the Florida Legal Aid Commission, and a member of the Southern Growth Conference Committee Policy Board. She is president of the Martin Luther King Boulevard Development Corp. and the Sixty-second Street Development Corp.

Civil Service Reform

Statement on the House of Representatives Action Endorsing the Proposal. September 13, 1978

The overwhelming endorsement in the House of Representatives today of my civil service reform proposal is a victory for every citizen concerned about government waste and inefficiency. The House's action, together with the Senate's favorable vote last month, demonstrates clearly that the administration and Congress together can take the tough steps needed to make the Federal Government effective and competent.

The House's commitment to civil service reform deserves the appreciation of every American. I want to commend Speaker O'Neill, Chairman Nix, and Congressman Derwinski for their dedicated efforts, and to especially thank Congressman Udall for his invaluable help on this measure.

I urge the Senate-House Conference Committee on the civil service bill to act promptly, so that we can begin to implement these reforms as soon as possible.

National Port Week, 1978

Proclamation 4596.   September 15, 1978

By the President of the United States of America

A Proclamation

Since the days of its early settlement, the United States has been dependent on water transportation for its trade. Populations tended to locate around harbors, which rapidly became the economic centers of the New World. Now there are some 170 commercial seaports in this country, as well as numerous inland ports on our navigable inland waterways. The result has been the creation of a network of ocean and inland ports that includes many of the country's most important centers of industry, distribution, finance, and education.

Ports provide the vital link between land and water carriers. The port indus-try contributes enormously to the Nation's economy. It facilitates international trade, employs significant numbers of people, provides substantial personal and business incomes, and generates revenues for State and local governments.

Now, THEREFORE, I, JIMMY CARTER, President of the United States of America, in order to remind Americans of the importance of the port industry of the United States to our national life, do hereby designate the seven calendar days beginning September 17, 1978, as "National Port Week." I invite the Governors of the several States, the chief officials of local governments, and the people of the United States to observe such week with appropriate ceremonies and activities.

IN WITNESS WHEREOF, I have hereunto set my hand this fifteenth day of September, 1978, in the year of our Lord nineteen hundred seventy-eight, and of the Independence of the United States the two hundred and third.

JIMMY CARTER

[Filed with the Office of the Federal Register, 3:25 p.m., September 15, 1978]

United States Ambassador to Lebanon

Nomination of John Gunther Dean.
September 15, 1978

The President today announced that he will nominate John Gunther Dean, of New York, to be Ambassador Extraordinary and Plenipotentiary of the United States to Lebanon. He would replace Richard B. Parker, who is being transferred.

Dean was born February 26, 1926, and became a naturalized American citizen in 1944. He received a B.S. (1949) and M.A. (1950) from Harvard University, and a Ph. D. from the Institut Hautes

Etudes in Paris in 1949. He served in the U.S. Army from 1944 to 1946.

Dean was an economic analyst for the Economic Cooperation Administration in Paris in 1950, and an industrial analyst in Belgium from 1951 to 1953. In 1953 he was assistant economic commissioner in Saigon, Phnom Penh, and Vientiane. In 1953 and 1954, he was with the Foreign Operations Administration in Saigon.

In 1955 Dean was with the International Cooperation Administration, and from 1956 to 1959, he was political officer in Vientiane. He was consular officer in Lomé from 1959 to 1960, and chargé d'affaires in Bamako from 1960 to 1961. From 1961 to 1964, he was officer in charge of Mali-Togo affairs.

In 1964 and 1965, Dean was an international relations officer at the State Department. From 1965 to 1969, he was political officer in Paris. In 1969–70 he was a fellow at the Harvard Center for International Affairs.

From 1970 to 1972, Dean was detailed to AID as Deputy Regional Director in Saigon. From 1972 to 1974, he was Deputy Chief of Mission in Vientiane. From 1974 to 1975, Dean was Ambassador to the Khmer Republic. Since 1975 he has been Ambassador to Denmark.

Dean is married to the former Martine Duphenieux.

President's Commission on Foreign Language and International Studies

Appointment of 21 Members.
September 15, 1978

The President today announced 21 persons whom he will appoint as members of the President's Commission on Foreign Language and International Studies. They are:

CAROL E. BAUMANN, director of the Institute of World Affairs at the University of Wisconsin;

ERNEST L. BOYER, Commissioner of Education at the Department of Health, Education, and Welfare;

BETTY M. BULLARD, education director for the Asia Society in New York;

PRISCILLA CHING-CHUNG, a visiting scholar in the history department at the University of Hawaii;

WAYNE FREDERICKS, executive director of international governmental affairs for the Ford Motor Co. and a former Deputy Assistant Secretary of State for African Affairs;

EDMUND J. GLEAZER, JR., president of the American Association of Community and Junior Colleges in Washington;

TIMOTHY S. HEALY, S.J., president of Georgetown University in Washington;

FRED M. HECHINGER, president of the New York Times Company Foundation and a former education columnist and editor;

VIVIAN M. HORNER, vice president for education and children's programing of Warner Cable Corp., in New York;

ALLEN H. KASSOF, executive director of the international research and exchange program of the American Council of Learned Societies and the Social Science Research Council, and a lecturer at Princeton University;

SAMUEL L. MYERS, executive director of the National Association for Equal Opportunity in Higher Education in Washington;

CONSUELO NIETO, assistant professor of education at California State University at Long Beach;

JOAQUIN F. OTERO, international vice president of the Brotherhood of Railway and Airline Clerks in Washington;

JAMES A. PERKINS, chairman and chief executive officer of the International Council for Educational Development in New York City (to be designated Chairman of the Commission);

JOHN A. RASSIAS, professor of romance languages and literature at Dartmouth College;

JOHN E. REINHARDT, Director of the International Communication Agency;

EDWIN O. REISCHAUER, chairman of the board of trustees of the Harvard-Yenching Institute and professor of Japanese history and politics at Harvard University;

SARAH I. SANTAMARIA, international business development representative for the State of Florida Department of Commerce;

COL. SAMUEL L. STAPLETON, Commandant of the Foreign Language Institute at the Defense Department;

ELONA MARIJOSIUS VAISNYS, of Mount Carmel, Conn., a free-lance writer active in the Lithuanian-American Community, Inc., and former communications specialist at Yale University;

ROBERT E. WARD, director of the Center for Research in International Studies at Stanford University.

The President also announced four Members of Congress who will serve on the Commission. They are:

SENATOR MARK HATFIELD of Oregon;

REPRESENTATIVE MILLICENT FENWICK of New Jersey;

REPRESENTATIVE LEON PANETTA of California;

REPRESENTATIVE PAUL SIMON of Illinois.

Digest of Other White House Announcements

The following listing includes the President's daily schedule and other items of general interest as announced by the White House Press Office during the period covered by this issue. Events and announcements printed elsewhere in the issue are not included.

September 9[1]

The President met in the morning at Camp David with Secretary of State Cyrus

---

[1] EDITOR'S NOTE: The informal nature of the meetings at Camp David precluded the announcement of daily Presidential schedules by the White House Press Office. Only those meetings and their participants which were announced have been included.

R. Vance, Zbigniew Brzezinski, Assistant to the President for National Security Affairs, and Hamilton Jordan, Assistant to the President.

September 10

The President telephoned the Shah of Iran in the morning and discussed the present situation in Iran. The President reaffirmed the close and friendly relationship between Iran and the United States and the importance of Iran's continued alliance with the West. The President expressed his deep regret over the loss of life and his hope that the violence would soon be ended. He further expressed the hope that the movement toward political liberalization would continue.

President Carter, President Anwar al-Sadat of Egypt, and Prime Minister Menahem Begin of Israel went to Gettysburg, Pa., for a tour of the Gettysburg National Military Park.

The President met with Prime Minister Begin. Also attending the meeting were Vice President Walter F. Mondale, Secretary Vance, Dr. Brzezinski, Israeli Foreign Minister Moshe Dayan, and Israeli Defense Minister Ezer Weizman.

September 11

The President met in the morning with President Sadat. Throughout the day, he also met with members of the U.S. delegation.

The President announced that he will nominate G. William Miller, Chairman of the Board of Governors of the Federal Reserve System, to be U.S. Alternate Governor of the International Monetary Fund.

September 12

The President met in the morning with President Sadat. Throughout the day, he also met with members of the U.S. delegation.

The President met in the evening with Prime Minister Begin.

September 13

During the day, the President met with members of the U.S., Egyptian, and Israeli delegations.

The President met in the evening with Prime Minister Begin.

The President announced that he has accorded the personal rank of Ambassador to Irving G. Tragen while he serves as Head of the U.S. Delegation to the meetings of the Inter-American Council on Education, Science and Culture, and the Inter-American Economic and Social Council. Mr. Tragen is Deputy Permanent Representative to the Organization of American States, and will head the delegations to these meetings because the Permanent Representative, Ambassador Gale W. McGee, will be unable to attend.

The President announced that he has accorded the personal rank of Minister to Jonathan Dean while he is serving as Acting U.S. Representative for Mutual and Balanced Force Reductions negotiations. Mr. Dean is serving as Acting Representative to MBFR pending the appointment of a successor to Stanley R. Resor, who was recently appointed Under Secretary of Defense for Policy. Mr. Dean was previously Deputy U.S. Representative to MBFR.

September 14

The President met in the morning with President Sadat. He then held separate meetings with, first, Secretary Vance, Dr. Brzezinski, and Mr. Jordan, and then Foreign Minister Dayan and Defense Minister Weizman.

The President held separate meetings with President Sadat and members of the Egyptian delegation.

The President transmitted to the Congress the 1977 Aeronautics and Space Report of the President.

September 15

The President met in the morning with Vice President Mondale, Secretary of Defense Harold Brown, Secretary Vance, Dr. Brzezinski, and Mr. Jordan.

Later in the morning, the President met with Secretary Vance and Foreign Minister Dayan.

The President met with Secretaries Vance and Brown, and Dr. Brzezinski. The President then had a separate meeting with Secretaries Vance and Brown to discuss defense matters.

The President met in the afternoon with President Sadat.

NOMINATIONS SUBMITTED TO THE SENATE

The following list does not include promotions of members of the Uniformed Services, nominations to the Service Academies, or nominations of Foreign Service officers.

Submitted September 11, 1978

The following-named persons to be Representatives of the United States of America to the Thirty-third Session of the General Assembly of the United Nations:

ANDREW J. YOUNG, of Georgia

JAMES F. LEONARD, JR., of New York

ABRAHAM A. RIBICOFF, United States Senator from the State of Connecticut

JAMES B. PEARSON, United States Senator from the State of Kansas

SET CHARLES MOMJIAN, of Pennsylvania

The following-named persons to be Alternative Representatives of the United States of America to the Thirty-third Session of the General Assembly of the United Nations:

DONALD F. McHENRY, of Illinois

MELISSA F. WELLS, of New York

ANGELIQUE O. STAHL, of Florida

JOHN W. HECHINGER, of the District of Columbia

RICHARD W. PETREE, of Virginia

THOMAS R. PICKERING, of New Jersey, a Foreign Service officer of the Class of Career Minister, to be an Assistant Secretary of State for Oceans and International Environmental and Scientific Affairs.

NOMINATIONS—Continued

Submitted September 12, 1978

G. WILLIAM MILLER, of California, to be United States Alternate Governor of the International Monetary Fund for a term of 5 years, vice Arthur F. Burns.

MARVIN S. COHEN, of Arizona, to be a member of the Civil Aeronautics Board for the remainder of the term expiring December 31, 1979, vice G. Joseph Minetti.

ARMANDO M. RODRIGUEZ, of California, to be a member of the Equal Employment Opportunity Commission for the term expiring July 1, 1983, vice Lowell W. Perry.

AMBLER HOLMES MOSS, JR., of Virginia, to be Ambassador Extraordinary and Plenipotentiary of the United States of America to Panama.

Submitted September 14, 1978

M. ATHALIE RANGE, of Florida, to be a member of the Board of Directors of the National Railroad Passenger Corporation for a term expiring July 18, 1981, vice Mary J. Head, term expired.

CHECKLIST OF WHITE HOUSE PRESS RELEASES

NOTE: All releases of the Office of the White House Press Secretary, distributed during the period covered by this issue, have been included in the issue.

ACTS APPROVED BY THE PRESIDENT

Approved September 9, 1978

S. 2543_____ Public Law 95–360
An act to amend title 39 of the United States Code to provide better enforcement procedures for preventing fraudulent solicitations through the mails.

ACTS APPROVED—Continued

Approved September 10, 1978

H.R. 8397_____ Public Law 95–361
An act to provide that a certain tract of land in Pinal County, Arizona, held in trust by the United States for the Papago Indian Tribe, be declared a part of the Papago Indian Reservation.

Approved September 11, 1978

H.R. 185_____ Public Law 95–362
An act to amend section 2632 of title 10, United States Code, to provide the Secretary of the department in which the Coast Guard is operating with the authority to transport Coast Guard employees to and from certain places of employment.

H.R. 12106_____ Public Law 95–363
Independent Safety Board Act Amendment of 1978.

Approved September 15, 1978

H.J. Res. 773_____ Public Law 95–364
A joint resolution authorizing and requesting the President of the United States to issue a proclamation designating the seven calendar days beginning September 17, 1978, as "National Port Week".

H.R. 8342_____ Public Law 95–365
An act to amend title 5, United States Code, to provide for the application of local withholding taxes to Federal employees who are residents of such locality.

H.R. 8771_____ Public Law 95–366
An act to amend title 5, United States Code, to authorize the Civil Service Commission to comply with the terms of a court decree, order, or property settlement in connection with the divorce, annulment, or legal separation of a Federal employee who is under the civil service retirement system, and for other purposes.

Camp David Meeting on the Middle East

Remarks of the President, President Anwar al-Sadat of Egypt, and Prime Minister Menahem Begin of Israel at the Conclusion of the Meeting. September 17, 1978

PRESIDENT CARTER. When we first arrived at Camp David, the first thing upon which we agreed was to ask the people of the world to pray that our negotiations would be successful. Those prayers have been answered far beyond any expectations. We are privileged to witness tonight a significant achievement in the cause of peace, an achievement none thought possible a year ago, or even a month ago, an achievement that reflects the courage and wisdom of these two leaders.

Through 13 long days at Camp David, we have seen them display determination and vision and flexibility which was needed to make this agreement come to pass. All of us owe them our gratitude and respect. They know that they will always have my personal admiration.

There are still great difficulties that remain and many hard issues to be settled. The questions that have brought warfare and bitterness to the Middle East for the last 30 years will not be settled overnight. But we should all recognize the substantial achievements that have been made.

One of the agreements that President Sadat and Prime Minister Begin are signing tonight is entitled, "A Framework for Peace in the Middle East."

This framework concerns the principles and some specifics, in the most substantive way, which will govern a comprehensive peace settlement. It deals specifically with the future of the West Bank and Gaza and the need to resolve the Palestinian problem in all its aspects. The framework document proposes a 5-year transitional period in the West Bank and Gaza during which the Israeli military government will be withdrawn and a self-governing authority will be elected with full autonomy. It also provides for Israeli forces to remain in specified locations during this period to protect Israel's security.

The Palestinians will have the right to participate in the determination of their own future, in negotiations which will resolve the final status of the West Bank and Gaza, and then to produce an Israeli-Jordanian peace treaty.

These negotiations will be based on all the provisions and all the principles of United Nations Security Council Resolution 242. And it provides that Israel may live in peace, within secure and recognized borders. And this great aspiration of Israel has been certified without constraint, with the greatest degree of enthusiasm, by President Sadat, the leader of one of the greatest nations on Earth.

The other document is entitled, "Framework for the Conclusion of a Peace Treaty Between Egypt and Israel."

It provides for the full exercise of Egyptian sovereignty over the Sinai. It calls for the full withdrawal of Israeli forces from the Sinai and, after an interim withdrawal which will be accomplished very quickly, the establishment of normal, peaceful relations between the two countries, including diplomatic relations.

Together with accompanying letters, which we will make public tomorrow, these two Camp David agreements provide the basis for progress and peace throughout the Middle East.

There is one issue on which agreement has not been reached. Egypt states that the agreement to remove Israeli settlements from Egyptian territory is a prerequisite to a peace treaty. Israel states that the issue of the Israeli settlements should be resolved during the peace negotiations. That's a substantial difference. Within the next 2 weeks, the Knesset will decide on the issue of these settlements.

Tomorrow night, I will go before the Congress to explain these agreements more fully and to talk about their implications for the United States and for the world. For the moment, and in closing, I want to speak more personally about my admiration for all of those who have taken part in this process and my hope that the promise of this moment will be fulfilled.

During the last 2 weeks, the members of all three delegations have spent endless hours, day and night, talking, negotiating, grappling with problems that have divided their people for 30 years. Whenever there was a danger that human energy would fail, or patience would be exhausted or good will would run out—and there were many such moments—these two leaders and the able advisers in all delegations found the resources within them to keep the chances for peace alive.

Well, the long days at Camp David are over. But many months of difficult negotiations still lie ahead. I hope that the foresight and the wisdom that have made this session a success will guide these leaders and the leaders of all nations as they continue the progress toward peace.

Thank you very much.

PRESIDENT SADAT. Dear President Carter, in this historic moment, I would like to express to you my heartfelt congratulations and appreciation. For long days and nights, you devoted your time and energy to the pursuit of peace. You have been most courageous when you took the gigantic step of convening this meeting. The challenge was great and the risks were high, but so was your determination. You made a commitment to be a full partner in the peace process. I'm happy to say that you have honored your commitment.

The signing of the framework for the comprehensive peace settlement has a significance far beyond the event. It signals the emergence of a new peace initiative, with the American nation in the heart of the entire process.

In the weeks ahead, important decisions have to be made if we are to proceed on the road to peace. We have to reaffirm the faith of the Palestinian people in the ideal of peace.

The continuation of your active role is indispensable. We need your help and the support of the American people. Let me seize this opportunity to thank each and every American for his genuine interest in the cause of people in the Middle East.

Dear friend, we came to Camp David with all the good will and faith we possessed, and we left Camp David a few minutes ago with a renewed sense of hope and inspiration. We are looking forward to the days ahead with an added determination to pursue the noble goal of peace.

Your able assistants spared no effort to bring out this happy conclusion. We appreciate their spirit and dedication. Our hosts at Camp David and the State of Maryland were most generous and hospitable. To each one of them and to all those who are watching this great event, I say thank you.

Let us join in a prayer to God Almighty to guide our path. Let us pledge to make the spirit of Camp David a new chapter in the history of our nations.

Thank you, Mr. President.

PRIME MINISTER BEGIN. *Mr. President of the United States, Mr. President of the Arab Republic of Egypt, ladies and gentlemen:*

The Camp David conference should be renamed. It was the Jimmy Carter conference. [*Laughter*]

The President undertook an initiative most imaginative in our time and brought President Sadat and myself and our colleagues and friends and advisers together under one roof. In itself, it was a great achievement. But the President took a great risk for himself and did it with great civil courage. And it was a famous French field commander who said that it is much more difficult to show civil courage than military courage.

And the President worked. As far as my historic experience is concerned, I think that he worked harder than our forefathers did in Egypt building the pyramids. [*Laughter*]

Yes, indeed, he worked day and night, and so did we—[*laughter*]——

PRESIDENT CARTER. Amen.

PRIME MINISTER BEGIN. Day and night. We used to go to bed at Camp David between 3 and 4 o'clock in the morning, arise, as we are used to since our boyhood,

between 5 and 6, and continue working.

The President showed interest in every section, every paragraph, every sentence, every word, every letter—[*laughter*]—of the framework agreements.

We had some difficult moments—as usually there are some crises in negotiations, as usually somebody gives a hint that perhaps he would like to pick up and go home. [*Laughter*] It's all usual. But ultimately, ladies and gentlemen, the President of the United States won the day. And peace now celebrates a great victory for the nations of Egypt and Israel and for all mankind.

Mr. President, we, the Israelis, thank you from the bottom of our hearts for all you have done for the sake of peace, for which we prayed and yearned more than 30 years. The Jewish people suffered much, too much. And, therefore, peace to us is a striving, coming innermost from our heart and soul.

Now, when I came here to the Camp David conference, I said, perhaps as a result of our work, one day people will, in every corner of the world, be able to say, *Habemus pacem,* in the spirit of these days. Can we say so tonight? Not yet. We still have to go a road until my friend President Sadat and I sign the peace treaties.

We promised each other that we shall do so within 3 months. Mr. President [*referring to President Sadat*], tonight, at this celebration of the great historic event, let us promise each other that we shall do it earlier than within 3 months.

Mr. President, you inscribed your name forever in the history of two ancient civilized peoples, the people of Egypt and the people of Israel. Thank you, Mr. President.

PRESIDENT CARTER. Thank you very much.

PRIME MINISTER BEGIN. Oh, no, no, no. I would like to say a few words about my friend, President Sadat. We met for the first time in our lives last November in Jerusalem. He came to us as a guest, a former enemy, and during our first meeting we became friends.

In the Jewish teachings, there is a tradition that the greatest achievement of a human being is to turn his enemy into a friend, and this we do in reciprocity. Since then, we had some difficult days. [*Laughter*] I'm not going now to tell you the saga of those days. Everything belongs to the past. Today, I visited President Sadat in his cabin, because in Camp David you don't have houses, you only have cabins. [*Laughter*] And he then came to visit me. We shook hands. And, thank God, we again could have said to each other, "You are my friend."

And, indeed, we shall go on working in understanding, and in friendship, and with good will. We will still have problems to solve. Camp David proved that any problem can be solved if there is good will and understanding and some, *some* wisdom.

May I thank my own colleagues and friends, the Foreign Minister, the Defense Minister, Professor Barak, who was the Attorney General—and now he is going to be His Honor, the Justice of the Supreme Court, the Israeli Brandeis—and Dr. Rosenne, and our wonderful Ambassador to the United States, Mr. Simcha Dinitz, and all our friends, because without them that achievement wouldn't have been possible.

I express my thanks to all the members of the American delegation, headed by the Secretary of State, a man whom we love and respect. And so, I express my thanks to all the members of the Egyptian delegation who worked so hard together with us, headed by Deputy Prime Minister, Mr. Touhamy, for all they have done to achieve this moment. It is a great moment in the history of our nations and, indeed, of mankind.

I looked for a precedent; I didn't find it. It was a unique conference, perhaps one of the most important since the Vienna Conference in the 19th century, perhaps.

And now, ladies and gentlemen, allow me to turn to my own people from the White House in my own native tongue.

[*At this point, the Prime Minister spoke briefly in Hebrew.*]

Thank you, ladies and gentlemen.

PRESIDENT CARTER. The first document that we will sign is entitled, "A Framework for Peace in the Middle East Agreed at Camp David," and the texts of these two documents will be released tomorrow. The documents will be signed by President Sadat and Prime Minister Begin, and it will be witnessed by me. We have to exchange three documents, so we'll all sign three times for this one.

[*At this point, President Sadat, Prime Minister Begin, and President Carter signed the first document.*]

I might say that the first document is quite comprehensive in nature, encompassing a framework by which Israel can later negotiate peace treaties between herself and Lebanon, Syria, Jordan, as well as the outline of this document that we will now sign.

And as you will later see, in studying the documents, it also provides for the realization of the hopes and dreams of the people who live in the West Bank and Gaza Strip and will assure Israel peace in the generations ahead.

This second document is the one relating to a framework for a peace treaty between Egypt and Israel. This is the document that calls for the completion of the peace treaty negotiations within 3 months. And I have noticed the challenge extended by these two gentlemen to each other. They will complete within 3 months—I might say that this document encompasses almost all of the issues between the two countries and resolves those issues. A few lines remain to be drawn on maps, and the question of the settlements is to be resolved. Other than that, most of the major issues are resolved already in this document.

We will now sign this document as well.

[*At this point, President Sadat, Prime Minister Begin, and President Carter signed the second document.*]

PRESIDENT CARTER. Thank you very much.

NOTE: The President spoke at 10:30 p.m. in the East Room at the White House.

Members of the U.S., Egyptian, and Israeli delegations to the summit meeting and Members of the Congress, the Cabinet, and White House staff attended the document signing ceremony, which was broadcast live on radio and television.

Camp David Meeting on the Middle East

Documents Agreed to at Camp David. September 17, 1978

A FRAMEWORK FOR PEACE IN THE MIDDLE EAST AGREED AT CAMP DAVID

Muhammad Anwar al-Sadat, President of the Arab Republic of Egypt, and Menachem Begin, Prime Minister of Israel, met with Jimmy Carter, President of the United States of America, at Camp David from September 5 to September 17, 1978, and have agreed on the following framework for peace in the Middle East. They invite other parties to the Arab-Israeli conflict to adhere to it.

PREAMBLE

The search for peace in the Middle East must be guided by the following:

—The agreed basis for a peaceful settlement of the conflict between Israel and its neighbors is United Nations Security Council Resolution 242, in all its parts.*

—After four wars during thirty years, despite intensive human efforts, the Middle East, which is the cradle of civilization and the birthplace of three great religions, does not yet enjoy the blessings of peace. The people of the Middle East yearn for peace so that the vast human and natural resources of the region can be turned to the pursuits of peace and so that this area can become a model for coexistence and cooperation among nations.

—The historic initiative of President Sadat in visiting Jerusalem and the reception accorded to him by the Parliament, government and people of Israel, and the reciprocal visit of Prime Minister Begin to Ismailia, the peace proposals made by both leaders, as well as the warm reception of these missions by the peoples of both countries, have created an unprecedented opportunity for peace which must not be lost if this generation and future generations are to be spared the tragedies of war.

—The provisions of the Charter of the United Nations and the other accepted norms of international law and legitimacy now provide accepted standards for the conduct of relations among all states.

—To achieve a relationship of peace, in the spirit of Article 2 of the United Nations Charter, future negotiations between Israel and any neighbor prepared to negotiate peace and security with it, are necessary for the purpose of carrying out all the

---

*The texts of Resolutions 242 and 338 are annexed to this document.

provisions and principles of Resolutions 242 and 338.

—Peace requires respect for the sovereignty, territorial integrity and political independence of every state in the area and their right to live in peace within secure and recognized boundaries free from threats or acts of force. Progress toward that goal can accelerate movement toward a new era of reconciliation in the Middle East marked by cooperation in promoting economic development, in maintaining stability, and in assuring security.

—Security is enhanced by a relationship of peace and by cooperation between nations which enjoy normal relations. In addition, under the terms of peace treaties, the parties can, on the basis of reciprocity, agree to special security arrangements such as demilitarized zones, limited armaments areas, early warning stations, the presence of international forces, liaison, agreed measures for monitoring, and other arrangements that they agree are useful.

FRAMEWORK

Taking these factors into account, the parties are determined to reach a just, comprehensive, and durable settlement of the Middle East conflict through the conclusion of peace treaties based on Security Council Resolutions 242 and 338 in all their parts. Their purpose is to achieve peace and good neighborly relations. They recognize that, for peace to endure, it must involve all those who have been most deeply affected by the conflict. They therefore agree that this framework as appropriate is intended by them to constitute a basis for peace not only between Egypt and Israel, but also between Israel and each of its other neighbors which is prepared to negotiate peace with Israel on this basis. With that objective in mind, they have agreed to proceed as follows:

A. *West Bank and Gaza*

1. Egypt, Israel, Jordan and the representatives of the Palestinian people should participate in negotiations on the resolution of the Palestinian problem in all its aspects. To achieve that objective, negotiations relating to the West Bank and Gaza should proceed in three stages:

(a) Egypt and Israel agree that, in order to ensure a peaceful and orderly transfer of authority, and taking into account the security concerns of all the parties, there should be transitional arrangements for the West Bank and Gaza for a period not exceeding five years. In order to provide full autonomy to the inhabitants, under these arrangements the Israeli military government and its civilian administration will be withdrawn as soon as a self-governing authority has been freely elected by the inhabitants of these areas to replace the existing military government. To negotiate the details of a transitional arrangement, the Government of Jordan will be invited to join the negotiations on the basis of this framework. These new arrangements should give due consideration both to the principle of self-government by the inhabitants of these territories and to the legitimate security concerns of the parties involved.

(b) Egypt, Israel, and Jordan will agree on the modalities for establishing the elected self-governing authority in the West Bank and Gaza. The delegations of Egypt and Jordan may include Palestinians from the West Bank and Gaza or other Palestinians as mutually agreed. The parties will negotiate an agreement which will define the powers and responsibilities of the self-governing authority to be exercised in the West Bank and Gaza. A withdrawal of Israeli armed forces will take place and there will be a redeployment of the remaining Israeli forces into specified security locations. The agreement will also include arrangements for assuring internal and external security and public order. A strong local police force will be established, which may include Jordanian citizens. In addition, Israeli and Jordanian forces will participate in joint patrols and in the manning of control posts to assure the security of the borders.

(c) When the self-governing authority (administrative council) in the West Bank and Gaza is established and inaugurated, the transitional period of five years will begin. As soon as possible, but not later than the third year after the beginning of the transitional period, negotiations will take place to determine the final status of the West Bank and Gaza and its relationship with its neighbors, and to conclude a peace treaty between Israel and Jordan by the end of the transitional period. These negotiations will be conducted among Egypt, Israel, Jordan, and the elected representatives of the inhabitants of the West Bank and Gaza. Two separate but related committees will be convened, one committee, consisting of representatives of the four parties which will negotiate and agree on the final status of the West Bank and Gaza, and its relationship with its neighbors, and the second committee, consisting of representatives of Israel and representatives of Jordan to be joined by the elected representatives of the inhabitants of the West Bank and Gaza, to negotiate the peace treaty between Israel and Jordan, taking into account the agreement reached on the final status of the West Bank and Gaza. The negotiations shall be based on all the provisions and principles of UN Security Council Resolution 242. The negotiations will resolve, among other matters, the location of the boundaries and the nature of the security arrangements. The solution from the negotiations must also recognize the legitimate rights of the Palestinian people and their just require-

ments. In this way, the Palestinians will participate in the determination of their own future through:

1) The negotiations among Egypt, Israel, Jordan and the representatives of the inhabitants of the West Bank and Gaza to agree on the final status of the West Bank and Gaza and other outstanding issues by the end of the transitional period.

2) Submitting their agreement to a vote by the elected representatives of the inhabitants of the West Bank and Gaza.

3) Providing for the elected representatives of the inhabitants of the West Bank and Gaza to decide how they shall govern themselves consistent with the provisions of their agreement.

4) Participating as stated above in the work of the committee negotiating the peace treaty between Israel and Jordan.

2. All necessary measures will be taken and provisions made to assure the security of Israel and its neighbors during the transitional period and beyond. To assist in providing such security, a strong local police force will be constituted by the self-governing authority. It will be composed of inhabitants of the West Bank and Gaza. The police will maintain continuing liaison on internal security matters with the designated Israeli, Jordanian, and Egyptian officers.

3. During the transitional period, representatives of Egypt, Israel, Jordan, and the self-governing authority will constitute a continuing committee to decide by agreement on the modalities of admission of persons displaced from the West Bank and Gaza in 1967, together with necessary measures to prevent disruption and disorder. Other matters of common concern may also be dealt with by this committee.

4. Egypt and Israel will work with each other and with other interested parties to establish agreed procedures for a prompt, just and permanent implementation of the resolution of the refugee problem.

B. Egypt-Israel

1. Egypt and Israel undertake not to resort to the threat or the use of force to settle disputes. Any disputes shall be settled by peaceful means in accordance with the provisions of Article 33 of the Charter of the United Nations.

2. In order to achieve peace between them, the parties agree to negotiate in good faith with a goal of concluding within three months from the signing of this Framework a peace treaty between them, while inviting the other parties to the conflict to proceed simultaneously to negotiate and conclude similar peace treaties with a view to achieving a comprehensive peace in the area. The Framework for the Conclusion of a Peace Treaty between Egypt and Israel will govern the peace negotiations between them. The parties will agree on the modalities and the timetable for the implementation of their obligations under the treaty.

C. Associated Principles

1. Egypt and Israel state that the principles and provisions described below should apply to peace treaties between Israel and each of its neighbors—Egypt, Jordan, Syria and Lebanon.

2. Signatories shall establish among themselves relationships normal to states at peace with one another. To this end, they should undertake to abide by all the provisions of the Charter of the United Nations. Steps to be taken in this respect include:

(a) full recognition;

(b) abolishing economic boycotts;

(c) guaranteeing that under their jurisdiction the citizens of the other parties shall enjoy the protection of the due process of law.

3. Signatories should explore possibilities for economic development in the context of final peace treaties, with the objective of contributing to the atmosphere of peace, cooperation and friendship which is their common goal.

4. Claims Commissions may be established for the mutual settlement of all financial claims.

5. The United States shall be invited to participate in the talks on matters related to the modalities of the implementation of the agreements and working out the timetable for the carrying out of the obligations of the parties.

6. The United Nations Security Council shall be requested to endorse the peace treaties and ensure that their provisions shall not be violated. The permanent members of the Security Council shall be requested to underwrite the peace treaties and ensure respect for their provisions. They shall also be requested to conform their policies and actions with the undertakings contained in this Framework.

For the Government of the Arab Republic of Egypt:

A. SADAT

For the Government of Israel:

M. BEGIN

Witnessed by:

JIMMY CARTER
Jimmy Carter, President of the United States of America

ANNEX

TEXT OF UNITED NATIONS SECURITY COUNCIL RESOLUTION 242 OF NOVEMBER 22, 1967

Adopted unanimously at the 1382nd meeting

The Security Council,

Expressing its continuing concern with the grave situation in the Middle East,

Emphasizing the inadmissibility of the acquisition of territory by war and the need to work for a just and lasting peace in which every State in the area can live in security,

Emphasizing further that all Member States in their acceptance of the Charter of the

United Nations have undertaken a commitment to act in accordance with Article 2 of the Charter,

1. *Affirms* that the fulfillment of Charter principles requires the establishment of a just and lasting peace in the Middle East which should include the application of both the following principles:

(i) Withdrawal of Israeli armed forces from territories occupied in the recent conflict;

(ii) Termination of all claims or states of belligerency and respect for and acknowledgement of the sovereignty, territorial integrity and political independence of every State in the area and their right to live in peace within secure and recognized boundaries free from threats or acts of force;

2. *Affirms further* the necessity

(a) For guaranteeing freedom of navigation through international waterways in the area;

(b) For achieving a just settlement of the refugee problem;

(c) For guaranteeing the territorial inviolability and political independence of every State in the area, through measures including the establishment of demilitarized zones;

3. *Requests* the Secretary-General to designate a Special Representative to proceed to the Middle East to establish and maintain contacts with the States concerned in order to promote agreement and assist efforts to achieve a peaceful and accepted settlement in accordance with the provisions and principles of this resolution.

4. *Requests* the Secretary-General to report to the Security Council on the progress of the efforts of the Special Representative as soon as possible.

TEXT OF UNITED NATIONS SECURITY COUNCIL RESOLUTION 338

Adopted by the Security Council at its 1747th meeting, on 21/22 October 1973

The Security Council

1. *Calls upon* all parties to the present fighting to cease all firing and terminate all military activity immediately, no later than 12 hours after the moment of the adoption of this decision, in the positions they now occupy;

2. *Calls upon* the parties concerned to start immediately after the cease-fire the implementation of Security Council Resolution 242 (1967) in all of its parts;

3. *Decides* that, immediately and concurrently with the cease-fire, negotiations start between the parties concerned under appropri-

ate auspices aimed at establishing a just and durable peace in the Middle East.

FRAMEWORK FOR THE CONCLUSION OF A PEACE TREATY BETWEEN EGYPT AND ISRAEL

In order to achieve peace between them, Israel and Egypt agree to negotiate in good faith with a goal of concluding within three months of the signing of this framework a peace treaty between them.

It is agreed that:

The site of the negotiations will be under a United Nations flag at a location or locations to be mutually agreed.

All of the principles of U.N. Resolution 242 will apply in this resolution of the dispute between Israel and Egypt.

Unless otherwise mutually agreed, terms of the peace treaty will be implemented between two and three years after the peace treaty is signed.

The following matters are agreed between the parties:

(a) the full exercise of Egyptian sovereignty up to the internationally recognized border between Egypt and mandated Palestine;

(b) the withdrawal of Israeli armed forces from the Sinai;

(c) the use of airfields left by the Israelis near El Arish, Rafah, Ras en Naqb, and Sharm el Sheikh for civilian purposes only, including possible commercial use by all nations;

(d) the right of free passage by ships of Israel through the Gulf of Suez and the Suez Canal on the basis of the Constantinople Convention of 1888 applying to all nations; the Strait of Tiran and the Gulf of Aqaba are international waterways to be open to all nations for unimpeded and nonsuspendable freedom of navigation and overflight;

(e) the construction of a highway between the Sinai and Jordan near Elat with guaranteed free and peaceful passage by Egypt and Jordan; and

(f) the stationing of military forces listed below.

STATIONING OF FORCES

A. No more than one division (mechanized or infantry) of Egyptian armed forces will be stationed within an area lying approximately 50 kilometers (km) east of the Gulf of Suez and the Suez Canal.

B. Only United Nations forces and civil police equipped with light weapons to perform normal police functions will be stationed within an area lying west of the international border and the Gulf of Aqaba, varying in width from 20 km to 40 km.

C. In the area within 3 km east of the international border there will be Israeli limited military forces not to exceed four infantry battalions and United Nations observers.

D. Border patrol units, not to exceed three battalions, will supplement the civil police in maintaining order in the area not included above.

The exact demarcation of the above areas will be as decided during the peace negotiations.

Early warning stations may exist to insure compliance with the terms of the agreement.

United Nations forces will be stationed: (a) in part of the area in the Sinai lying within about 20 km of the Mediterranean Sea and adjacent to the international border, and (b) in the Sharm el Sheikh area to ensure freedom of passage through the Strait of Tiran; and these forces will not be removed unless such removal is approved by the Security Council of the United Nations with a unanimous vote of the five permanent members.

After a peace treaty is signed, and after the interim withdrawal is complete, normal relations will be established between Egypt and Israel, including: full recognition, including diplomatic, economic and cultural relations; termination of economic boycotts and barriers to the free movement of goods and people; and mutual protection of citizens by the due process of law.

INTERIM WITHDRAWAL

Between three months and nine months after the signing of the peace treaty, all Israeli forces will withdraw east of a line extending from a point east of El Arish to Ras Muhammad, the exact location of this line to be determined by mutual agreement.

For the Government of the Arab Republic of Egypt:

A. SADAT

For the Government of Israel:

M. BEGIN

Witnessed by:

JIMMY CARTER

Jimmy Carter, President of the United States of America

NOTE: The texts of the documents were released on September 18.

United Nations

Nomination of Richard W. Petree To Be Alternate U.S. Representative for Special Political Affairs. September 18, 1978

The President today announced that he will nominate Richard W. Petree, of Falls Church, Va., to be the Alternate U.S. Representative for Special Political Affairs in the United Nations. He would replace Allard K. Lowenstein, who has resigned.

Petree was born June 4, 1924, in Jamestown, N.Y. He received an A.B. from the University of Colorado in 1948 and an M.A. from Harvard University in 1950. He served in the U.S. Navy from 1943 to 1946.

Petree was an intelligence research analyst at the State Department from 1950 to 1957, and served with the Foreign Service in Tokyo, Fukuoka, and Addis Ababa, and at the State Department. In 1972 and 1973, he was Consul General in Naha, and from 1973 to 1976, he was counselor for political affairs in Tokyo. Since 1976 Petree has been Minister-Counselor for Political and Security Affairs at the U.S. Mission to the United Nations.

minimizing the risks of disclosure of national intelligence information.

The classified annex provides helpful guidance. It differs, however, in some important respects from the views of the Executive, and in light of some recent developments of mutual concern, I feel compelled to seek some modifications in the appropriations process. In any event, I pledge that the executive agencies will continue their cooperation with the intelligence oversight committees of Congress, and I congratulate the House and Senate for supporting these committees in this difficult task.

NOTE: As enacted, H.R. 12240 is Public Law 95–370, approved September 17.

Intelligence and Intelligence-Related Activities Authorization Act for Fiscal Year 1979

Statement on Signing H.R. 12240 Into Law.   September 18, 1978

I am pleased to sign into law H.R. 12240, the Intelligence and Intelligence-Related Activities Authorization Act for Fiscal Year 1979. This is the first specific annual authorization for appropriations for intelligence functions of the Federal Government.

This act symbolizes the recent achievements of the Congress that broaden and intensify oversight of intelligence activities through a cooperative effort with the executive agencies. I would like to express particular commendation to the Permanent Select Committee on Intelligence of the House, the Select Committee on Intelligence of the Senate, and the House and Senate Armed Services Committees. The process has, I believe, enhanced congressional participation in oversight while

Days of Remembrance of Victims of the Holocaust

Statement on Signing H.J. Res. 1014 Into Law.   September 18, 1978

I have today signed House Joint Resolution 1014, designating April 28 and 29, 1979, as "Days of Remembrance of Victims of the Holocaust."

The systematic extermination of millions of human beings by the Nazis during World War II was the most terrible crime in all recorded history. In the words of the resolution, the Holocaust remains "not only a shocking symbol of Nazi brutality and destruction, but also a symbol of the danger inherent in tyranny, the pernicious quality of bigotry, and the human capacity to be cruel."

The resolution was passed unanimously by both Houses of Congress. This reflects our Nation's wholehearted conviction that the lessons of the Holocaust must never be forgotten.

Senator John Danforth of Missouri, whom I commend for having originated the resolution, chose April 28 and 29, because it was on these dates, in 1945, that American troops liberated the Dachau concentration camp. The dates chosen by Senator Danforth and embodied in this resolution thus aptly symbolize both the horror of genocide and the imperative to fight against it.

During the next few months, the President's Commission on the Holocaust will study ways in which this commemoration can best be observed, and I will issue an appropriate proclamation next spring. In the meanwhile, I wish to commend Senator Danforth, Representatives Wright, Rosenthal, Rhodes, and Vander Jagt and their colleagues, who joined in securing passage of H.J. Res. 1014.

NOTE: As enacted, H.J. Res. 1014 is Public Law 95–371, approved September 18.

Outer Continental Shelf Lands Act Amendments of 1978

Statement on Signing S. 9 Into Law.
September 18, 1978

I am signing into law today S. 9, the Outer Continental Shelf Lands Act Amendments of 1978.

Since its enactment in 1953, the Outer Continental Shelf Lands Act has provided basic authority for Federal management and development of the resources of the Outer Continental Shelf (OCS). During that time, over 16 million acres have been leased for oil and gas exploration and development. Oil and gas production from the OCS accounted for approximately 10.2 and 18.7 percent, respectively, of total domestic production of these vital resources in 1977. As part of this Nation's long-term energy program, significant additional areas are on the planning schedule for possible leasing over the next several years.

As the pace of OCS exploration and development activity has accelerated in recent years, growing concern has been expressed over its effects on coastal areas as well as the degree of competition for OCS leases within the energy industry. There has been uncertainty and controversy over the rate and location of OCS leasing and development, and States and localities have sought a greater voice in Federal OCS management. As the result of several years of hard work by the Congress, the States, the administration, industry and labor, and various concerned citizens groups, S. 9 is designed to provide a new and more effective balance between these concerns and the Nation's need for timely energy development. I am very pleased to sign these much-needed amendments into law.

The bill mandates significant changes in existing law to improve environmental safeguards, to promote greater cooperation between the Federal Government and States and localities, to reduce barriers to OCS activity on the part of small- and medium-sized energy firms, and to ensure safe working conditions for those employed on the OCS. I am convinced that by reducing the great uncertainty associated with many aspects of the OCS program in recent years and by placing a proper emphasis on environmental protection and other important objectives, this legislation will provide the needed framework for moving forward once again with a balanced and well-coordinated leasing program to assure that OCS energy resources contribute even more to our Nation's domestic energy supplies.

I am also pleased that the Congress has adopted a liability and compensation system for cleanup costs and damages caused by OCS oil spills which is generally in line with the more comprehensive legislation previously proposed by my administration. However, I continue to urge expeditious congressional action on more comprehensive legislation (H.R. 6803) which would appropriately extend coverage to virtually all oil pollution in our coastal and internal waters.

Among the many provisions I fully support there are a few about which I am concerned. First, there is a substantial increase in the annual appropriation authorization for coastal energy impact formula grants to States affected by OCS activities. While this is an essential program and I support it, in the annual appropriation process I will have to carefully weigh budget limitations and the very real needs which do exist in coastal areas affected by OCS development. Second, as outlined in my special message to Congress of June 21, 1978, I have strong constitutional and policy objections to the reservation of authority by the Congress to veto certain executive branch actions— in this case, decisions to permit the export of OCS oil and gas and to utilize lease bidding systems other than those specifically described in S. 9. I intend to treat both of these provisions as "report and wait" requirements.

Aside from these concerns, however, I applaud the passage of S. 9, which is an important part of our energy program. I congratulate all those who contributed to the passage of this important legislation, particularly Chairmen Jackson and Murphy and the other members of the Senate and House committees who helped fashion this bill. Work began long before I came

into office, but I am proud to participate in bringing this important effort to a conclusion.

NOTE: As enacted, S. 9 is Public Law 95–372, approved September 18.

District of Columbia Appropriation Act, 1979

Statement on Signing H.R. 13468 Into Law. September 18, 1978

Today I have signed H.R. 13468, which makes appropriations for the government of the District of Columbia. This bill appropriates both funds generated locally by the District and Federal funds for loans and direct payments to the District.

Congress recently took a historic step toward granting the citizens of the District equal standing with other American citizens by approving a proposed constitutional amendment to grant the District full voting representation in the Congress. If we are to make equal rights and home rule a reality for the District, we must also bring stability and predictability to the Federal payment process.

The Federal payment is intended to offset the effects of the Federal presence on the District's revenues. As such, it should be determined on a fair, objective basis and not arbitrarily changed from year to year. I favor the establishment of a formula which would consider the various factors involved in the Federal presence to determine the appropriate amount of the payment each year. My administration is working with the Congress and the District government to develop such a formula.

In signing this appropriations bill, I wish to reaffirm my commitment to the basic principles of fairness and self-determination, which must be the cornerstone of Federal-District relations. While not forgetting the close connections between the Federal Government and the District of Columbia, we must continue to move toward a greater role for the District in determining its own governmental actions.

NOTE: As enacted, H.R. 13468 is Public Law 95–373, approved September 18.

Airport and Airway Development Act Functions

Executive Order 12079.   September 18, 1978

AUTHORIZING CERTAIN FUNCTIONS OF HEADS OF DEPARTMENTS AND AGENCIES UNDER THE AIRPORT AND AIRWAY DEVELOPMENT ACT OF 1970 TO BE PERFORMED WITHOUT THE APPROVAL OF THE PRESIDENT

By authority vested in me by section 301 of Title 3 of the United States Code, it is hereby ordered as follows:

SECTION 1. The authority vested in the heads of departments and agencies by Section 23(b) of the Airport and Airway Development Act of 1970 (84 Stat. 232; 49 U.S.C. 1723(b)), with the approval of the President and the Attorney General of the United States, to perform any acts and to execute any instruments necessary to make any conveyance requested by the Secretary of Transportation under Section 23(a) of that Act may be exercised by such heads of departments and agencies without the approval of the President.

SEC. 2. Executive Order No. 10536 of June 9, 1954, as amended, is revoked.

JIMMY CARTER

The White House,
September 18, 1978.

[Filed with the Office of the Federal Register, 11:11 a.m., September 19, 1978]

Commemorative Presidential Proclamations

Executive Order 12080.   September 18, 1978

By the authority vested in me as President by the Constitution of the United States of America, and in order to simplify the procedures for the processing of approved commemorative proclamations, Section 4 of Executive Order No. 11030, as amended, is further amended by adding thereto the following new sentence:

"Notwithstanding the provisions of Section 2, the Director shall transmit any approved commemorative proclamations to the President.".

JIMMY CARTER

The White House,
September 18, 1978.

[Filed with the Office of the Federal Register, 11:12 a.m., September 19, 1978]

Naturalization Based on Military Service

Executive Order 12081.   September 18, 1978

TERMINATION OF EXPEDITIOUS NATURALIZATION BASED ON MILITARY SERVICE

By the authority vested in me as President of the United States of America by Section 329 of the Immigration and Nationality Act, as amended by Sections 1 and 2 of the Act of October 24, 1968 (82 Stat. 1343; 8 U.S.C. 1440), and by the authority of Section 3 of that Act of October 24, 1968 (82 Stat. 1344; 8 U.S.C. 1440e), it is hereby ordered that the statutory period of Vietnam hostilities which began on February 28, 1961, shall be deemed to have terminated on October 15, 1978, for the purpose of ending the period in which active-duty service in the Armed Forces qualifies for certain exemptions from the usual requirements for naturalization, including length of residence and fees.

JIMMY CARTER

The White House,
    September 18, 1978.

[Filed with the Office of the Federal Register, 11:13 a.m., September 19, 1978]

Superior Court of the District of Columbia

Nomination of Peter Wolf To Be An Associate Judge. September 18, 1978

The President today announced that he will nominate Peter Wolf to the District of Columbia Superior Court. Wolf will fill the seat vacated by former Chief Judge Harold Greene, who left the Superior Court when the President appointed him to the United States District Court for the District of Columbia.

Wolf, 43, received Bachelor's and Master's Degrees in engineering from Cornell University and attended law school at Harvard. He has engaged in civil and criminal practice since being admitted to the bar in the District of Columbia in 1962 and is now partner in the law firm of Wolf and Kovner.

Camp David Meeting on the Middle East

Address Before a Joint Session of the Congress. September 18, 1978

Vice President Mondale, Speaker O'Neill, distinguished Members of the United States Congress, Justices of the Supreme Court, other leaders of our great Nation, ladies and gentlemen:

It's been more than 2,000 years since there was peace between Egypt and a free Jewish nation. If our present expectations are realized, this year we shall see such peace again.

The first thing I would like to do is to give tribute to the two men who made this impossible dream now become a real possibility, the two great leaders with whom I have met for the last 2 weeks at Camp David: first, President Anwar Sadat of Egypt, and the other, of course, is Prime Minister Menahem Begin of the nation of Israel.

I know that all of you would agree that these are two men of great personal courage, representing nations of peoples who are deeply grateful to them for the achievement which they have realized. And I am personally grateful to them for what they have done.

At Camp David, we sought a peace that is not only of vital importance to their own two nations but to all the people of the Middle East, to all the people of the United States, and, indeed, to all the world as well.

The world prayed for the success of our efforts, and I am glad to announce to you that these prayers have been answered.

I've come to discuss with you tonight what these two leaders have accomplished and what this means to all of us.

The United States has had no choice but to be deeply concerned about the Middle East and to try to use our influence and our efforts to advance the cause of peace. For the last 30 years, through four wars, the people of this troubled region have paid a terrible price in suffering and division and hatred and bloodshed. No two nations have suffered more than Egypt and Israel. But the dangers and the costs of conflicts in this region for our own Nation have been great as well. We have longstanding friendships among the nations there and the peoples

1533

of the region, and we have profound moral commitments which are deeply rooted in our values as a people.

The strategic location of these countries and the resources that they possess mean that events in the Middle East directly affect people everywhere. We and our friends could not be indifferent if a hostile power were to establish domination there. In few areas of the world is there a greater risk that a local conflict could spread among other nations adjacent to them and then, perhaps, erupt into a tragic confrontation between us super powers ourselves.

Our people have come to understand that unfamiliar names like Sinai, Aqaba, Sharm el Sheikh, Ras en Naqb, Gaza, the West Bank of Jordan, can have a direct and immediate bearing on our own well-being as a nation and our hope for a peaceful world. That is why we in the United States cannot afford to be idle bystanders and why we have been full partners in the search for peace and why it is so vital to our Nation that these meetings at Camp David have been a success.

Through the long years of conflict, four main issues have divided the parties involved. One is the nature of peace— whether peace will simply mean that the guns are silenced, that the bombs no longer fall, that the tanks cease to roll, or whether it will mean that the nations of the Middle East can deal with each other as neighbors and as equals and as friends, with a full range of diplomatic and cultural and economic and human relations between them. That's been the basic question. The Camp David agreement has defined such relationships, I'm glad to announce to you, between Israel and Egypt.

The second main issue is providing for the security of all parties involved, including, of course, our friends, the Israelis, so that none of them need fear attack or military threats from one another. When implemented, the Camp David agreement, I'm glad to announce to you, will provide for such mutual security.

Third is the question of agreement on secure and recognized boundaries, the end of military occupation, and the granting of self-government or else the return to other nations of territories which have been occupied by Israel since the 1967 conflict. The Camp David agreement, I'm glad to announce to you, provides for the realization of all these goals.

And finally, there is the painful human question of the fate of the Palestinians who live or who have lived in these disputed regions. The Camp David agreement guarantees that the Palestinian people may participate in the resolution of the Palestinian problem in all its aspects, a commitment that Israel has made in writing and which is supported and appreciated, I'm sure, by all the world.

Over the last 18 months, there has been, of course, some progress on these issues. Egypt and Israel came close to agreeing about the first issue, the nature of peace. They then saw that the second and third issues, that is, withdrawal and security, were intimately connected, closely entwined. But fundamental divisions still remained in other areas—about the fate of the Palestinians, the future of the West Bank and Gaza, and the future of Israeli settlements in occupied Arab territories.

We all remember the hopes for peace that were inspired by President Sadat's initiative, that great and historic visit to Jerusalem last November that thrilled the world, and by the warm and genuine personal response of Prime Minister Begin and the Israeli people, and by the mutual promise between them, publicly made, that there would be no more war. These hopes were sustained when Prime Minister Begin reciprocated by visiting Ismailia on Christmas Day. That progress continued, but at a slower and slower pace through the early part of the year. And by early summer, the negotiations had come to a standstill once again.

It was this stalemate and the prospect for an even worse future that prompted me to invite both President Sadat and Prime Minister Begin to join me at Camp David. They accepted, as you know, instantly, without delay, without preconditions, without consultation even between them.

It's impossible to overstate the courage of these two men or the foresight they have shown. Only through high ideals, through compromises of words and not principle, and through a willingness to look deep into the human heart and to understand the problems and hopes and dreams of one another can progress in a difficult situation like this ever be made. That's what these men and their wise and diligent advisers who are here with us tonight have done during the last 13 days.

When this conference began, I said that the prospects for success were remote. Enormous barriers of ancient history and nationalism and suspicion would have to be overcome if we were to meet our objectives. But President Sadat and Prime Minister Begin have overcome these barriers, exceeded our fondest expectations, and have signed two agreements that hold out the possibility of resolving issues that history had taught us could not be resolved.

The first of these documents is entitled, "A Framework for Peace in the Middle East Agreed at Camp David." It deals with a comprehensive settlement, comprehensive agreement, between Israel and all her neighbors, as well as the difficult question of the Palestinian people and the future of the West Bank and the Gaza area.

The agreement provides a basis for the resolution of issues involving the West Bank and Gaza during the next 5 years. It outlines a process of change which is in keeping with Arab hopes, while also carefully respecting Israel's vital security.

The Israeli military government over these areas will be withdrawn and will be replaced with a self-government of the Palestinians who live there. And Israel has committed that this government will have full autonomy. Prime Minister Begin said to me several times, not partial autonomy, but full autonomy.

Israeli forces will be withdrawn and redeployed into specified locations to protect Israel's security. The Palestinians will further participate in determining their own future through talks in which their own elected representatives, the inhabitants of the West Bank and Gaza, will negotiate with Egypt and Israel and Jordan to determine the final status of the West Bank and Gaza.

Israel has agreed, has committed themselves, that the legitimate rights of the Palestinian people will be recognized. After the signing of this framework last night, and during the negotiations concerning the establishment of the Palestinian self-government, no new Israeli settlements will be established in this area. The future settlements issue will be decided among the negotiating parties.

The final status of the West Bank and Gaza will be decided before the end of the 5-year transitional period during which the Palestinian Arabs will have their own government, as part of a negotiation which will produce a peace treaty between Israel and Jordan specifying borders, withdrawal, all those very crucial issues.

These negotiations will be based on all the provisions and the principles of Security Council Resolution 242, with which you all are so familiar. The agreement on

1535

the final status of these areas will then be submitted to a vote by the representatives of the inhabitants of the West Bank and Gaza, and they will have the right for the first time in their history, the Palestinian people, to decide how they will govern themselves permanently.

We also believe, of course, all of us, that there should be a just settlement of the problems of displaced persons and refugees, which takes into account appropriate United Nations resolutions.

Finally, this document also outlines a variety of security arrangements to reinforce peace between Israel and her neighbors. This is, indeed, a comprehensive and fair framework for peace in the Middle East, and I'm glad to report this to you.

The second agreement is entitled, "A Framework for the Conclusion of a Peace Treaty Between Egypt and Israel." It returns to Egypt its full exercise of sovereignty over the Sinai Peninsula and establishes several security zones, recognizing carefully that sovereignty right for the protection of all parties. It also provides that Egypt will extend full diplomatic recognition to Israel at the time the Israelis complete an interim withdrawal from most of the Sinai, which will take place between 3 months and 9 months after the conclusion of the peace treaty. And the peace treaty is to be fully negotiated and signed no later than 3 months from last night.

I think I should also report that Prime Minister Begin and President Sadat have already challenged each other to conclude the treaty even earlier. And I hope they——[*applause*]. This final conclusion of a peace treaty will be completed late in December, and it would be a wonderful Christmas present for the world.

Final and complete withdrawal of all Israeli forces will take place between 2 and 3 years following the conclusion of the peace treaty.

While both parties are in total agreement on all the goals that I have just described to you, there is one issue on which agreement has not yet been reached. Egypt states that agreement to remove the Israeli settlements from Egyptian territory is a prerequisite to a peace treaty. Israel says that the issue of the Israeli settlements should be resolved during the peace negotiations themselves.

Now, within 2 weeks, with each member of the Knesset or the Israeli Parliament acting as individuals, not constrained by party loyalty, the Knesset will decide on the issue of the settlements. Our own Government's position, my own personal position is well known on this issue and has been consistent. It is my strong hope, my prayer, that the question of Israeli settlements on Egyptian territory will not be the final obstacle to peace.

None of us should underestimate the historic importance of what has already been done. This is the first time that an Arab and an Israeli leader have signed a comprehensive framework for peace. It contains the seeds of a time when the Middle East, with all its vast potential, may be a land of human richness and fulfillment, rather than a land of bitterness and continued conflict. No region in the world has greater natural and human resources than this one, and nowhere have they been more heavily weighed down by intense hatred and frequent war. These agreements hold out the real possibility that this burden might finally be lifted.

But we must also not forget the magnitude of the obstacles that still remain. The summit exceeded our highest expectations, but we know that it left many difficult issues which are still to be resolved. These issues will require careful negotiation in the months to come. The Egyptian and Israeli people must recognize the tangible benefits that peace will bring and support the decisions their leaders have made, so that a secure and a peaceful future can be achieved for them. The American public, you and I, must also offer our full support to those who have made decisions that are difficult and those who have very difficult decisions still to make.

What lies ahead for all of us is to recognize the statesmanship that President Sadat and Prime Minister Begin have shown and to invite others in that region to follow their example. I have already, last night, invited the other leaders of the Arab world to help sustain progress toward a comprehensive peace.

We must also join in an effort to bring an end to the conflict and the terrible suffering in Lebanon. This is a subject that President Sadat discussed with me many times while I was in Camp David with him. And the first time that the three of us met together, this was a subject of heated discussion. On the way to Washington last night in the helicopter, we mutually committed ourselves to join with other nations, with the Lebanese people themselves, all factions, with President Sarkis, with Syria and Saudi Arabia, perhaps the European countries like France, to try to move toward a solution of the problem in Lebanon, which is so vital to us and to the poor people in Lebanon, who have suffered so much.

We will want to consult on this matter and on these documents and their meaning with all of the leaders, particularly the Arab leaders. And I'm pleased to say to you tonight that just a few minutes ago, King Hussein of Jordan and King Khalid of Saudi Arabia, perhaps other leaders later, but these two have already agreed to receive Secretary Vance, who will be leaving tomorrow to explain to them the terms of the Camp David agreement. And we hope to secure their support for the realization of the new hopes and dreams of the people of the Middle East.

This is an important mission, and this responsibility, I can tell you, based on my last 2 weeks with him, could not possibly rest on the shoulders of a more able and dedicated and competent man than Secretary Cyrus Vance.

Finally, let me say that for many years the Middle East has been a textbook for pessimism, a demonstration that diplomatic ingenuity was no match for intractable human conflicts. Today we are privileged to see the chance for one of the sometimes rare, bright moments in human history—a chance that may offer the way to peace. We have a chance for peace, because these two brave leaders found within themselves the willingness to work together to seek these lasting prospects for peace, which we all want so badly. And for that, I hope that you will share my prayer of thanks and my hope that the promise of this moment shall be fully realized.

The prayers at Camp David were the same as those of the shepherd King David, who prayed in the 85th Psalm, "Wilt thou not revive us again: that thy people may rejoice in thee? . . . I will hear what God the Lord will speak: for he will speak peace unto his people, and unto his saints: but let them not return again unto folly."

And I would like to say, as a Christian, to these two friends of mine, the words of Jesus, "Blessed are the peacemakers, for they shall be the children of God."

NOTE: The President spoke at 8:06 p.m. in the House Chamber at the Capitol. President Sadat and Prime Minister Begin were present for the address, which was broadcast live on radio and television.

Law Enforcement Assistance Administration

Nomination of the Administrator and Two Deputy Administrators.　September 19, 1978

The President today announced three persons whom he will nominate for positions at the Law Enforcement Assistance Administration (LEAA). They are:

Norval Morris, of Chicago, to be Administrator of LEAA. Morris, 54, is dean of the University of Chicago Law School. He was director of the Center for Studies in Criminal Justice at the University of Chicago for 10 years. He has also served as director of the United Nations Institute for the Prevention of Crime and Treatment of Offenders. He has been a visiting professor or has served on the faculty of several universities in this country, England, and Australia.

Homer F. Broome, Jr., of Los Angeles, to be Deputy Administrator of LEAA for Administration. Broome, 47, is commanding officer of the commission service group for the Los Angeles Board of Police Commissioners. Broome has been with the Los Angeles Police Department since 1961, beginning as officer in charge of special operations for the community problems unit, juvenile division. He has held positions at the commander-of-police level since 1975.

Henry S. Dogin, of Armonk, N.Y., to be Deputy Administrator for Policy Development. Dogin, 43, is first deputy commissioner of the New York State Division of Criminal Justice Services. Dogin was Deputy Regional Administrator of the New York Regional Office of LEAA from 1971 to 1973, and Deputy Assistant U.S. Attorney General for the Criminal Divi-

sion from 1973 to 1975. In 1975 and 1976, he was Acting Administrator of the Drug Enforcement Administration.

Meeting With the Chief of the Liaison Office of the People's Republic of China

White House Statement.　September 19, 1978

The President received the new Chief of the Liaison Office of the People's Republic of China to Washington, Ambassador Ch'ai Tse-min, for a courtesy call this morning at 11:30. Ambassador Ch'ai arrived in Washington on August 8.

The President welcomed Ambassador Ch'ai, and they had a friendly conversation. The Ambassador conveyed regards from Chinese Premier Hua Kuo-feng, the Chairman of the Standing Committee of the National People's Congress, Yeh Chien-ying, and Vice Premier Teng Hsiao-p'ing.

The President welcomed the recent expansion in our commercial, cultural, and scientific exchanges. He asked Secretary Vance and Dr. Brzezinski to maintain close contact with Ambassador Ch'ai on international issues of mutual interest. President Carter asked Ambassador Ch'ai to convey his best wishes to Premier Hua Kuo-feng, the Chairman of the Standing Committee of the National People's Congress Yeh Chien-ying, and Vice Premier Teng Hsiao-p'ing.

Present at the meeting were Ambassador Han Hsu, Deputy Chief of the Liaison Office; Third Secretary Hsu Shangwei; Secretary of State Cyrus Vance; Dr. Zbigniew Brzezinski, Assistant to the President for National Security Affairs; Richard Holbrooke, Assistant Secretary of

State for East Asian Affairs; and Michel Oksenberg, NSC staff member.

"Criminal Defense Techniques," and author of numerous articles and a series of children's books on the law.

Equal Employment Opportunity Commission

Nomination of J. Clay Smith, Jr., To Be a Member.   September 19, 1978

The President today anounced that he will nominate J. Clay Smith, Jr., of Washington, D.C., to be a member of the Equal Employment Opportunity Commission for a term expiring July 1, 1982.

Smith was born April 15, 1942, in Omaha, Nebr. He received a B.A. from Creighton University in 1964, a J.D. from Howard University School of Law in 1967, and an LL.M. (1970) and S.J.D. (1977) from George Washington University School of Law. He served in the U.S. Army from 1967 to 1971, serving as a captain and, for a year, as a military judge in the Judge Advocate General's Corps.

From 1971 to 1974, Smith was associated with the Washington law firm of Arent, Fox, Kintner, Plotkin & Kahn, where he was primarily engaged in antitrust and trade regulation matters. From 1974 to 1976, he was Deputy Chief of the Cable Television Bureau of the Federal Communications Commission. Since 1976 he has been Associate General Counsel of the Federal Communications Commission.

Smith has served as an adjunct professor of law at Howard University Law School. He is a member of the Lawyers Committee for Civil Rights Under Law, and has served on the boards of directors of the National Conference of Black Lawyers and the Neighborhood Legal Service Program. He is coauthor of the book

United Nations Day, 1978

Proclamation 4597.   September 19, 1978

By the President of the United States of America

A Proclamation

The founding of the United Nations, on October 24, 1945, was an historic attempt to establish a framework for international cooperation.

The nations of the world now face such tasks as maintaining international peace and security; promoting basic human rights; building a better international economic order; and allocating fairly the globe's natural resources. The United Nations and its affiliated agencies bring together representatives of all nations to work together toward these goals. It holds out the vision of a truly cooperative world—a world at peace.

As one of its founding members, as its leading contributor, and as its host country, the United States feels a special pride in the Organization's accomplishments.

Now, THEREFORE, I, JIMMY CARTER, President of the United States of America, do hereby designate Tuesday, October 24, 1978, as United Nations Day.

I have appointed Clifton C. Garvin, Jr., to be United States National Chairman for United Nations Day.

I urge Americans to become better acquainted with the institutions that make up the United Nations, to consider its role in addressing the problems of global interdependence, and to help it resolve the array of critical international issues that face us in these times.

IN WITNESS WHEREOF, I have hereunto set my hand this nineteenth day of September, in the year of our Lord nineteen hundred seventy-eight, and of the Independence of the United States of America the two hundred and third.

JIMMY CARTER

[Filed with the Office of the Federal Register, 2:04 p.m., September 19, 1978]

United Nations Day, 1978

Statement by the President.
September 19, 1978

On this day marking the opening of the 33d United Nations General Assembly, I have signed this proclamation designating October 24 as United Nations Day, 1978. The proclamation is a call for increased attention and support by the American people for the U.N. and its affiliated agencies.

The U.N. is now more involved than ever before with many of the central issues of our time, and we cannot fully advance our national interests or help build a more peaceful world if we ignore the potential of the U.N.

As a peacekeeper, the U.N. at this moment has four major operations in the Middle East and in Cyprus. In addition, the Security Council is expected to adopt soon a mandate for a U.N. civilian and military presence which will implement the agreed settlement in Namibia. And the British-American proposal for settlement of the Rhodesian crisis also includes a U.N. peacekeeping role.

In the vital field of development, the U.N. system has become the world's largest purveyor of technical assistance, helping to press development programs in various fields, to uncover mineral deposits,

and to identify investment opportunities. Few U.N. activities are more critical to the United States than promotion of the rapid and orderly development of the poorer nations of the world—countries which already constitute our fastest growing export market and the source of many of our mineral requirements. And conduct of the critical North-South economic dialog is occurring largely under the auspices of the U.N.

In the promotion of human rights, which has been one of the major concerns of my administration, we have been heartened by recent advances within the U.N. system, even as we recognize that much more progress needs to be made. International organizations can play an especially vital role in this field. This December we will mark the 30th anniversary of the Universal Declaration of Human Rights, a product of the United Nations, which provides a special reason to hope and work for greater progress in human rights around the world.

Nor should the more direct benefits of our participation in the U.N. be overlooked. Americans are more protected from health hazards, air accidents, sea catastrophes, and environmental dangers than ever before because of U.N. activities. U.N. programs like the World Health Organization's smallpox eradication campaign, or the World Meteorological Organization's World Weather Watch cost relatively little, yet they save the American people several hundred million dollars every year—year after year. We could not possibly carry out these programs by ourselves except at enormous cost. It is appropriate that we acknowledge once a year the unusual contributions to our health and welfare that are provided by these critical programs.

For all of these reasons, the United Nations is of clear and growing value to the United States, and the proclamation issued today is a reflection of that concern.

In March of this year, I submitted to the Congress a special report on my views for possible reforms of the United Nations system. Among the things that I would like to see are

—more effective procedures for the settlement of disputes between nations—before they erupt into bloodshed;

—increased preparedness for dispatch of U.N. troops in peacekeeping efforts whenever and wherever needed;

—quicker and more effective reactions to reported human rights abuses;

—a study of ways we might develop autonomous sources of revenue for the international community;

—increased accountability for the expenditure of the funds contributed by 149 nations; and

—greater operational efficiency.

It is clearly in the American interest to ensure that the United Nations operates as effectively as it can, and we are now working with other U.N. members and with Secretary General Waldheim to bring this about.

As we undertake this important effort, I believe that Americans everywhere need to reflect more fully on the important contributions of the United Nations—the opportunities it provides and the direct benefits it brings. With this in mind, I ask the Congress to continue to provide the U.N. with the moral backing and financial support that have permitted the United States to play the significant role in the organization that we have since it was created.

The proclamation issued today will provide an appropriate reference point for increased attention to the United Nations and its affiliated agencies. I ask all Americans to join me in reinforcing our support for this vital institution.

Armed Forces Promotion and Disability Separation Limitations

Executive Order 12082.   September 19, 1978

SUSPENSION OF CERTAIN ARMED FORCES PROMOTION AND DISABILITY SEPARATION LIMITATIONS

By the authority vested in me as President of the United States of America by Sections 2 and 3 of an Act approved by me today (bill S. 3454 enacted by the Senate and the House of Representatives on September 7 and 12, 1978), and having determined that certain promotion limitations applicable to the Navy and Marine Corps should continue to be suspended, and having determined that the new statutory conditions authorizing a continuation of certain existing disability separation practices in the Armed Forces should be effective, it is hereby ordered as follows:

1–101. For the period beginning on September 15, 1978 and ending on September 30, 1979, the application of the following provisions of Title 10 of the United States Code is suspended:

(a) Section 5707(c), restricting the number of Navy and Marine Corps officers who may be recommended for promotion from below the appropriate promotion zone.

(b) Section 5751(a), requiring Marine Corps officers serving in the grade of brigadier general to have completed three years' service in grade to be eligible for consideration for promotion to major general.

(c) Section 5751(b), requiring certain officers to have completed specific years of service in grade before being eligible for consideration for promotion to the next higher grade.

(d) Section 5751(e), precluding officers designated for limited duty who are below the appropriate promotion zone from being considered for promotion.

(e) Section 5770, requiring certain officers to have had at least two years' sea or foreign service in grade before they may be promoted.

1–102. For the period beginning on September 15, 1978 and ending on September 30, 1979, the conditions provided for by the following provisions of Title 10 of the United States Code are effective:

(a) Section 1201(3)(B)(iv), authorizing the retirement for certain disabilities of at least 30 percent which were incurred in line of duty.

(b) Section 1203(4)(A)(iii), authorizing separation for certain disabilities of less than 30 percent which were incurred in line of duty.

(c) Section 1203(4)(C)(iii), authorizing separation for certain disabilities of at least 30 percent which were not incurred in line of duty.

1–103. Executive Order Nos. 10616, 11151, 11437, and 11554, as amended, are hereby revoked.

JIMMY CARTER

The White House,
  September 19, 1978.

[Filed with the Office of the Federal Register, 10:47 a.m., September 20, 1978]

Natural Gas Legislation

*Statement on Senate Action on the
Conference Committee Report.
September 19, 1978*

The Senate's vote today on the natural gas compromise is an important step toward putting in place a comprehensive national energy policy. The compromise is a good bill for the Nation, and it is vitally important that the Congress adopt it. I am confident the courage and determination shown by the Senate today will prevail in the week ahead, and I urge all the bill's supporters who made this vote possible today to redouble their efforts in both the Senate and the House so that enactment of the national energy act will not be delayed any further.

NOTE: Earlier the Senate had voted not to recommit the report to the conference committee with instructions for certain changes in the legislation.

Atlantic City, New Jersey

*Remarks at Groundbreaking Ceremonies at
the National Aviation Facilities Experimental
Center.   September 20, 1978*

Senator Case, Senator Williams, Governor Brendan Byrne, Congressman Hughes, Director Bob Faith, Chairman Al Marks, all the members of the New Jersey congressional delegation who are assembled here this morning, wonderful workers at the National Aviation Facilities Experimental Center, NAFEC:

I want to say how glad I am to be with you on this momentous occasion.

When I ran for President 2 years ago, I didn't carry all the districts in New Jersey, but I carried this one by a very strong majority. When I left the White House earlier this morning, my wife reminded me that the reason was that I did not come to the Second District during the campaign, she came here. [*Laughter*] And I thank you for that expression of confidence in my wife.

It is a good day for the world. It's a good day for our Nation. It's a good day for New Jersey. It's a good day for this community. I'm delighted to be here to participate in breaking ground for NAFEC's new building program.

Four years ago, I was the national chairman for the Democratic Party's election campaign. And when Bill Hughes first ran for Congress, many people said that if this young man is elected to the Congress, we will never have a chance to have NAFEC stay here where it is. Well, I think because you elected him to the Congress, NAFEC is not only here but it's being greatly expanded for the benefit of you and for our country as well. And I want to express my special thanks to him.

He has worked long, hard, difficult, grueling hours with administration officials and the FAA, other Members of Congress, to recruit support for this effort. The entire New Jersey delegation helped him strongly in the House of Representatives. And as you well know, Senators Williams and Case were responsible for getting the project approved on the Senate side.

Thanks should also go to others who have already been mentioned—Bob Faith was helpful, of course, as was the Save NAFEC Committee, Mayor Lazarow, Al Marks, Robert Gasko, Chuck Worthington, Louis Dalberth, State Senator Perskie,[1] all of Atlantic County joined in with you in helping to achieve this great victory which was fought under the most difficult circumstances. It shows that a team effort pays off.

All of you can be very proud of your role in keeping NAFEC in this State. And I think more importantly for me than the location of it is the tremendous approval

---

[1] Robert Faith, director, National Aviation Facilities Experimental Center, Joseph Lazarow, mayor of Atlantic City, Al Marks, chairman of the Atlantic County Improvement Authority, Robert Gasko, Atlantic County Freeholder, Charles Worthington, Atlantic County Executive, Louis Dalberth, director, Southern New Jersey Development Council, and Stephen Perskie, New Jersey State senator.

for expansion of this much-needed facility. The struggle was tough, the frustrations were many, but in the end the efforts of you and your representatives triumphed. And I'm glad to join with you this morning in saying that you will not be wearing Oklahoma cowboy hats after all. [*Laughter*]

Today, we in the United States are reaffirming our commitment to safe and efficient civilian aviation. And we are showing our faith also in New Jersey's ability to carry out this very difficult assignment. We are laying the cornerstone for a permanent, expanded presence of NAFEC here in New Jersey.

In the short run, this construction project will mean 1,800 to 2,000 jobs right here on the site. In addition, at least that many more will be engendered around this community for supportive construction projects. The direct investment here will be $50 million, which will mean at least $200 million in benefits, direct or indirect, to this community.

More importantly, though, in the long run, a permanent, more modern experimental center for ensuring aviation safety will mean the economic stability of this area and a better life for all the people of our country. By providing better services for testing, for research and development in areas like air traffic control, communications, navigation, airports, aircraft, we are making sure that the science of aviation keeps pace with a society whose people more and more turn to air travel to meet the needs of their lives.

Throughout its 20 years of existence and service, this facility has led the way in developing new technologies for civilian enterprise, which has given our Nation the safest possible record in the air of all modes of transportation. Its experiments here have made possible innovations in such areas as crash techniques, rescue techniques, fire safety, airway—runway designs, lighting systems, structural stress; also weight turbulence, radar, and many others of a similar benefit to American people. These innovations for which the Nation thanks you must continue.

The financing of this Phase II of NAFEC's expansion has been extremely innovative, and, of course, it's complicated. But I think we all realize now the value of this lease-back arrangement. Because of it, we are saving the taxpayers $7½ million.

This is a good day today, but 21 months from now, when the new technical and administrative complex is completed, all of you will more fully realize just exactly what your great efforts have yielded, both for this area and also for our country.

But even today it's clear that when committed and dedicated and competent people work together on a good project, when they refuse to give up hope even under the most difficult and discouraging circumstances, when they keep pushing forward for what they know is right, they cannot lose. This groundbreaking is living proof that what I've just said is true.

I thank you very much for what you've done for yourselves, your neighbors, your State, and your country.

Thank you.

NOTE: The President spoke at 10:16 a.m.

Atlantic City, New Jersey

Remarks at the United Steelworkers of America Convention. September 20, 1978

President McBride, Senator Williams, Senator Case, Governor Byrne, delegates of the United Steelworkers of America, and my other friends:

It's an honor to be introduced by one of the most outstanding leaders in America today, your president, Lloyd McBride. And it's also a pleasure to meet with and to talk to one of the finest groups of working men and women that I know, the United Steelworkers of America.

You may not know it, but you had a great deal to do with the success of the Camp David meeting. Knowing that I had to be here with you to speak today, I was able to bring to a conclusion those difficult negotiations. Late Saturday night, Prime Minister Begin finally came to me, and he said, "Mr. President, I agree to get out of the Sinai if you'll let me out of Camp David." [*Laughter*]

So, I'm here to point out to you that we are partners, we are brothers and sisters in a great effort to make our country and the world better.

And I'm also here to reaffirm my solidarity with the working people of our Nation in pursuing the goals that we share. There is no clearer expression of my commitment to this solidarity with working people than my appointment of Ray Marshall as Secretary of Labor. He's my friend and he's yours.

You who have gathered here in convention represent one of America's greatest national assets. I'm not talking about the size of your great organization alone, nor even about the enormous gains that steelworkers have realized from this union in the last 42 years. I'm talking about the broader, social vision of this international union and of the American labor movement.

You have been part of the conscience of America. Conscience is what motivated Phil Murray to organize this union in the beginning. Conscience is what motivated one of the most decent and honorable men ever to serve as a union president, my friend, I. W. Abel. And as you well know, President Abel's successor on my right here is poured out of the same crucible. These men exemplify your fight for decency and for social justice and for human rights—not just for your own members but also for millions of others who never carried a union card.

You've fought for the right of young people to have a decent education—your own children and the children of others. And we are working together this year to achieve an unprecedented increase in Federal aid to education.

You've fought for the right of older people to enjoy security and to escape the burden of doubt and fear. When I assumed office less than 2 years ago, our Nation's social security system was on the verge of financial collapse. Everywhere I went during the campaign, the elder citizens of our country would stand up and say, "What are we going to do in the future, because we are about to lose our sense of purpose and our sense of security."

You can be proud that the steelworkers union, under very difficult political circumstances, joined with my administration and the leaders of Congress to restore the integrity of the social security system. As long as I'm in the White House, as long as the steelworkers continue your momentous influence in our country, the social security system will continue to be sound. And you can depend on it.

On issue after issue, right down the line, the labor movement and my own administration have stood together. And we can be proud of what we've accomplished together.

We stood together to give 4 million Americans a chance to earn a life, a living of dignity and decency under revised and improved Federal minimum wage. We've stood together to pass the new mine safety and health legislation which Lloyd McBride and all of you have been fighting to pass for many years. That legislation greatly strengthens the thousands of miners in your union and puts the responsibility for enforcement for the first time where it belongs—in the Department of Labor under Secretary Ray Marshall.

We've stood together on occupational safety and health. Your union helped to lead the fight to pass a strong occupational safety and health bill years ago. But for 6 years, that legislation was systematically undermined by a hostile administration.

We've turned away from the nitpicking that was designed to discredit the OSHA program. Today, we are inspecting the most dangerous job sites. Today, we are attacking the most serious threats to health. The value of a human life cannot be measured on a balance sheet. And as long as I'm President and have your support, the health and safety of American workers on the job will be protected. And you can depend on that.

In the last 2 years, we have stood together to safeguard American jobs threatened by unfair foreign trade. The skills and the experience of America's steelworkers cannot be matched anywhere in the world. But the rules of international trade must be fair to America's workers. America's workers, and especially America's steelworkers, should not be forced to compete against foreign exporters who do not sell their products at a fair price. I will not permit our workers to suffer from unfair trading practices; dumping must stop.

The steps that we've taken to help steelworkers and the steel industry are already beginning to be felt. Employment in steel has increased, just this year, 24,000 jobs. Plant utilization was only 76 percent when

I became President; now the utilization of plant capacity in our country in the steel industry has risen to 90 percent. Shipments of steel throughout the world, as you well know, have dropped off at an alarming rate in the last 2 years, but shipments of domestic steel this year are already up 5 percent over last year. Industry revenues, which are needed to modernize the plants and equipment to keep you in jobs in the future, have risen substantially.

We will continue to work toward an international steel agreement with our major trading partners to deal with the problems of a depressed world steel market. I pledge to you that we will sign no agreement that is not fair to American steelworkers and to the people of the United States.

Closely related to our trade problems is the challenge of the energy crisis. Last year, foreign oil cost us in American dollars $45 billion. This is an increase of 800 percent in the last 6 years. This means that this massive export of American dollars is not only eroding the value of American dollars overseas, it's helped to build the inflation that we face at home.

It's weakened confidence in our Government, both here and throughout the world. It's cost America many jobs and will cost many more in the future. It's left our Nation far too dependent on uncertain foreign oil supplies for the energy that we must have to run our steel mills, to heat our homes and our schools, and to fuel our transportation system.

The Senate began voting yesterday on one of the most crucial parts of my national energy plan, the natural gas conference report. This legislation, when passed, will save our country, in oil imports, 2 million barrels per day by 1985, keeping jobs here at home, making us independent, letting us have a sound, sure supply of natural gas in States where it's not produced, with carefully prescribed prices, predictable prices.

As you well know, industry is now tending to move to States that produce natural gas from States that are not major natural gas producers. This legislation will let those opportunities for jobs prevail throughout our country and, at the same time, will not damage the economic strength or prosperity of the natural gas and oil-producing States, either.

We must pass this legislation to ensure that industries and communities which depend on natural gas will be assured of continued supplies. This is especially true, as you well know, in the steel industry.

I'm sure that you all remember the crisis that this Nation faced during the natural gas shortage in the winter of 1977, just after I became President.

Nationwide, more than a million Americans were laid off because American gas industry could not obtain, could not supply enough, and the rest of industry in our country could not obtain the gas it needed. Between fifty and a hundred thousand steelworkers were left unemployed. Our Nation and your own members, other working people in our country, cannot afford that kind of loss in the future.

Passage of this legislation, along with the other less controversial energy conference reports before the Congress, will give our Nation what America so badly needs—our first national energy plan. The consequences of failure for our country are unacceptable. We have debated long enough. It's time to put the interest of our Nation and the American people first and act without further delay to have a national energy policy to benefit you and all others. I ask you this morning to help me with this crucial decision that will affect your lives.

You and I have also stood together to enhance our Nation's crucial role in world affairs.

I believe that our Nation must continue to have a strong defense. And as long as I'm in the White House and you give me your support, our defense capability will be second to none on Earth. And you can depend on that.

Our Nation must continue to lead in the most difficult and important undertaking on this planet—the search for peace. And we will do that, in the Middle East and elsewhere throughout the world.

Our Nation, as you know, was damaged by Watergate, the CIA, Vietnam, and we lost a lot in the esteem of other people around the world for us and in the esteem that American people have always had for our own Government. But our basic commitments, the beliefs and ideals on which our Nation was founded, have not changed at all.

Our Nation must continue to support human rights. And I'm proud that our country stands, not only here but everywhere, for liberty and justice. And I pledge to you that as long as I'm in the White House, America will never turn its back on the struggle for human freedom and human rights around the world. And you can depend on that.

There is something clean about America. There is something decent about America. There's something idealistic about America. There's something unselfish about America. There's something strong about America. It's what makes our people love our country. And I want to see those basic commitments restored. And in that restoration will come strength based on American people themselves, where those commitments have never changed in spite of mistakes made in the past by some of our leaders.

Worldwide human rights questions are important. And we know that our own rights, our own freedoms were won in struggle, and we know that struggle still continues. It continues for you and me in the fight to have a fair and responsible labor law reform bill. I'm disappointed that because of a massive, expensive, completely distorted propaganda effort, that the Congress has not yet passed this important legislation.

Our labor law reform bill is not a grab for power by the unions, but it's a reach for justice, justice for American working men and women which is long overdue. This is the only piece of legislation that I personally helped to draft every single paragraph. It's a reasonable and responsible piece of legislation. Its purpose is to prevent a small minority of employers from flagrantly continuing to violate the law. [*Applause*] I see very clearly how you feel about this matter. [*Laughter*]

Our goal is simply to guarantee the rights which were promised American workers 43 years ago in the National Labor Relations Act, and I am determined to reach that goal. It will be at the top of our legislative priority list for next year if we don't get it this year. And I want to be sure that we have legislation of which you and I can be proud.

You represent more than a million Americans. What's always impressed me is that you've never used your influence and power to demand a handout. What you've asked for is jobs, good jobs, sound jobs, safe jobs, healthy jobs, with reasonable pay.

Our society honors work. We believe in work. That's the great strength that we have as Americans. When I took office less than 2 years ago, there were 10 million people in this country who wanted to work but could not find full-time jobs. Unemployment had more than doubled in the preceding 8 years. The unemployment rate stood at 8 percent. I pledged to work with you to provide jobs for the American people.

Working together, we have doubled the number of public service jobs in America to 725,000. We have tripled Federal support for public works. We have cut taxes for working Americans and low-income Americans by $7 billion last year. A much larger decrease in taxes will come this year, so that American people could have the purchasing power to stimulate demand for goods, to create jobs for people who produce those goods. We doubled the size of the Job Corps. We've passed our Nation's first youth employment bill to reduce the tragic unemployment rate among our young people. And we've already begun to see the results.

We've had a net increase, a net increase of 6 million new jobs in America, never before achieved. Last month, the unemployment rate dropped below 6 percent, a reduction of 25 percent since I've been in office. In New Jersey, for instance, the unemployment rate in the last 12 months has dropped almost 3 percent. I'm proud of that record. We still have a long way to go; we have a right to be proud of the gains we've made.

But the progress that we have made and the progress that we can make are both in danger. They all face a threat of the utmost seriousness—the threat of inflation.

Inflation strikes at our faith in the future. Inflation can wipe out our savings, and it can destroy your dreams.

Inflation is hardest, though, on those who have no savings and who lack the degree of economic power and security that union membership has brought to you. Inflation cruelly gouges and cheats the old and the poor. With inflation at 7

percent, which we have seen for the last 10 years, fixed incomes are cut in half every 10 years.

When there is inflation, it's often the Government and unions that get the blame. That is obviously unfair. But you and I do share, along with others, of course, a great responsibility. We must join together to fight this enemy, inflation. We must join together to help the Congress resist the special economic interests which behave as if they care nothing for the common good.

One example is the hospital cost containment legislation that I submitted earlier this year.

A couple of weeks ago, Speaker Tip O'Neill came back to Washington from a weekend in Boston. One of his friends, a working man, brought him a copy of a hospital bill which was received by one of his constituents. The man's little son was in an accident. He had fallen and struck his mouth, and four of his front teeth were driven up into his gum. He stayed in the hospital 26 hours. His bill was $2,330.99.

As we all know, those who own and operate many of our hospitals are the very ones who decide whether a patient should be admitted or not, who decide how long they stay, who decide what treatment they shall get, who decide how much to charge for that treatment. Because of this extraordinary monopoly over a certain aspect that's crucial to every American's life, the cost of hospital care is increasing at twice the rate of inflation in our country.

Something must be done. This year, we've not been successful in getting legislation passed which would have permitted hospital costs to go up only 50 percent more than the inflation rate. But with your help next year, perhaps we can be successful in defending the basic rights of American people to good health care at a reasonable cost.

Since 1950, hospital costs have gone up more than 1,000 percent. Well, the medical lobby and the hospital industry lobby so far have been successful in blocking this legislation. There would be a saving for the American people in the next 5 years, if this legislation was passed, of $56 billion. Obviously, there's a lot at stake. And so far, the consciousness of America, including yourselves, has not yet been aroused enough to convince the Members of Congress that this needed legislation should be passed. But it's time for all of us to stand up to these special interests and to all the others that refuse to look past their own selfish concerns.

Another example of important antiinflation legislation is airline deregulation.

Many of you flew in here by commercial airline service. One price that has gone down in the last year substantially is the price of an airline ticket on domestic and overseas flights. At first, the airline industry screamed that this would be devastating to them. Many airplanes on which I flew as a candidate for President would only have 25 percent or less of the seats filled. Now, because of reduced fares, those same planes are averaging 75 percent occupancy. Travel to other countries is increasing rapidly. The average working people of our country can travel in speed and comfort. And the profits of the airline companies have gone up substantially. It's been good all around.

This has mostly been done by regulatory action, the Civil Aeronautics Board, my own decisions, particularly in overseas flight. But shortly, perhaps even today, the House will vote on an airline deregulation bill that will put these enormously improved practices into law and make them permanent. We need to let those policies be embedded in the law, so that domestic airline fares can also be reduced by competition under the American free enterprise system. Government, of course, cannot do jobs like this alone in holding down unnecessary prices.

In fiscal year 1976, I began to study how I might, as President, if elected, do something about the very large Federal budget deficits. I believe in a balanced budget. When I ran for President, the Federal deficit was in the sixties of billions of dollars, $66 billion. In fiscal year 1978, the first budget that I prepared, we had cut it down in the fifties of billions of dollars—51. Next year, fiscal year '79, the Federal deficit will be down into the forties of billions of dollars. And my goal for 1980 fiscal year, which I'm preparing now, is to bring the deficit down into the thirties of billions of dollars.

This is in spite of the fact that we are giving better services to the American people, and in spite of the fact that we will probably have a total of $25 billion or more of reduced income taxes for the American people. I'm determined to exercise discipline over the Federal budget, even if it means saying no to popular proposals on occasion if that's what it takes to fight inflation.

We can get more out of what we do spend if our Government is streamlined and responsive. I talked about Government reorganization during the campaign. But it's worse by far than I thought it would be.

That's why civil service reform is so important. We need a civil service system that makes the bureaucracy manageable and rewards good performance. The civil service reforms will do this. The House passed this bill overwhelmingly. The Senate has already passed it. And I believe that if this is accomplished, we will have a better Government while fully protecting the rights of Government workers.

In waging this war on inflation, I reject the policies of the past. I will not fight inflation by throwing millions of Americans out of work. And you can depend on that. You know that such a policy was followed in the past, but it's morally wrong.

We've suffered from severe inflation for the last 10 years. Our current inflation is certainly not due to excessive wage increases or responsible Government programs. It will do no good to search for villains, whether in Government, business, or labor. But business and labor, like government, are critical to stopping inflation. As both business and labor try to catch up with past inflation and protect themselves against future inflation, prices and wages keep mounting, just to protect oneself. And in the end, no one wins.

To bring inflation under control, we must have cooperation among business, labor, government, the general public of our country. This is indisputable.

In the near future, I will announce a strengthening of our limited arsenal of weapons against inflation. I can tell you today that what we will do will be fair. It will not penalize labor or any other group in our society. At the same time, it will be tough. I will ask for restraint and some sacrifice from all. I will ask you to consider what I will have to say with open minds and in a spirit of cooperation and patriotic concern.

The problem of inflation is enormously difficult, far more complicated, far more difficult than it was a decade or two ago. Controlling this problem is not just one option among many. It is an absolute necessity. We *must* control inflation, and, in order to do it, we must work together.

I spoke of conscience at the beginning of this talk. I have no hesitation in calling upon the conscience of the United Steelworkers of America and the American labor movement when the best interests of our country are at stake. I place my faith in the broad social concern that you have shown so often in the past. I have no doubt that you will meet the challenge that faces our country once more. Together, as partners, we can and we will continue to build for the future an even greater America.

Thank you very much.

NOTE: The President spoke at 11:03 a.m. at the Atlantic City Convention Center.

Atlantic City, New Jersey

Remarks at a Democratic Party Campaign Luncheon. September 20, 1978

One of the nice things about New Jersey is that I experienced this same kind of reception and friendship and applause even before Camp David. [*Laughter*]

When I came here during the early stages of Brendan Byrne's campaign for Governor, I was really overwhelmed with the response of the people of your State, and the very wise decision that you made is a credit to you in choosing this man who has absolute integrity to administer the affairs of your State during this exciting time for New Jersey.

I just had an interview with public television, and one of the things that I could not restrain myself from saying was that since I've been coming here—1974, '75, '76, to campaign, and now as President, '78—I've seen a tremendous upsurge in the spirit of the people of New Jersey. There's a confidence in the future, an eagerness to work together, a friendship, a kind of exemplification of the finest aspects of our country that is shown by you in New Jersey and, I think, particularly by the Democrats of New Jersey. And I'm thankful for it.

I'm glad to be in the Second District and back in Atlantic City. I didn't carry all the congressional districts in New Jersey in the general election in 1976, but I carried this one. One of the reasons was that my wife campaigned here instead of me. [*Laughter*] And it was one of the few times during the campaign when I knew where my wife was, for I saw her picture on the boardwalk in Atlantic City with an enormous peanut. And I said, "Well, at least I know where she was yesterday."

But I am glad to come here to meet with you and to talk about some important things to you, to the people of our Nation, to the Democratic Party, and, I think, to the world. I don't think I'll follow any prepared text, although I gave some thought to what I would like to say.

You've showed a sound judgment in the past in the selection of the wonderful Democratic officials that have already been introduced, the sterling group of Members of Congress that have served your State, their district, our Nation so well. And you have an opportunity this year to return them to office, to elect new Democrats where Republicans now serve in the House of Representatives, and to bring to the United States Senate one of the finest candidates we have in our whole country, Bill Bradley. If you will work, I'll work to get him elected.

I have never served nor lived in Washington before I was inaugurated President. But I think what the people of our Nation were searching for was someone who had derived experience and analysis and thoughts and ideas, ideals, commitments, hopes, dreams from direct contact with the American people over a long, tough, arduous campaign; to bring some fresh ideas and thoughts to our government—the same kind of approach that Bill Bradley will bring when he arrives in the United States Senate next January.

And I know that he and I share some common beliefs, a belief that we can protect, even enhance the principles that have made the Democratic Party great; concern about those who are quite often deprived of an opportunity in our great society, those who are poor or without influence, who are not articulate, who are not well organized, those who suffer in different ways, who have not had an adequate education, who don't have a full-time job, who don't have security, who don't have wealth, perhaps who don't have good health.

These are the kinds of people that the Democratic Party has always reached out to. And we have brought them into our own hearts and into our political organization and made staunch, self-supporting, independent, proud, American political leaders out of them. And that's the essence of what the Democratic Party has as a record for which we can all be proud.

But that's not all of it. The American people obviously want that. They don't get it from the other party. But for too long, we've suffered in the Democratic Party—particularly in my part of the country—from an erroneous reputation that we were fiscally irresponsible. This is not true. And this is an additional part of Bill Bradley's belief—and I think mine as well—that we've got to have a government organizational structure that doesn't waste our tax money, that's well organized, that delivers services efficiently, that gives dedicated public servants, civil servants a chance to serve with enthusiasm and competence.

We have had good support in the Congress for making changes like this. While I was at Camp David, the House passed, with only 10 dissenting votes, the civil service reform bill, for the first time in a hundred years substantially improving the mechanism within which dedicated civil servants work—to reward good performance, to correct bad performance, to let managers manage, to let there be a new spirit of service and pride for people who are really self-sacrificing in many ways, who have given their one life to a full career of serving others. This is what we hope to open is a new vision of what dedicated, professional, career public servants can do.

This was not an easy thing. But it shows that Democrats in the White House and in the Congress can work together to make the organizational structure of our Government more efficient, more effective.

I also share with Bill Bradley a hope that we can have better budgeting procedures. I believe in a balanced budget. And I'm working hard to correct the deficiencies that existed for so many years before I was inaugurated as President.

When I ran for President in 1976 in your State, the budget deficit was in the high sixties of billions of dollars. The first budget that I prepared, fiscal year 1978, was in the fifties of billions of dollars, low fifties—51, I think. This proposal that the Congress now considers, fiscal year 1979, will be in the low forties of billions of dollars. I'm preparing the 1980 budget now. It'll be in the thirties of billions of dollars.

These reductions in deficits are what the American people demand. At the same time, we've not cut corners on delivering services to the American people. And in addition to the tremendous reduction in deficits by the end of this year, I think the Democrats in the Congress will have delivered to the American people a reduction in income taxes of more than $25 billion. This is the kind of record that makes us all proud; it's the kind of philosophy that has bound us together with the existing Members of Congress who are Democrats; it's the kind of procedure that

I'm sure will be even enhanced when Bill Bradley joins us next January in Washington.

I guess when I was elected, the biggest problem that Americans faced was unemployment. At that time in our Nation, 10 million Americans who wanted to work and who were able to work could not find a full-time job. About 8 million Americans had no job at all. The unemployment rate was 8 percent. And I and the Democratic Congress began to work on this problem together in harmony. Since then, we've had a net increase of 6 million new jobs in our country. Never before have we seen a growth in employment approaching this magnitude. The unemployment rate has dropped 25 percent, from 8 down to 6 percent. And we've begun to focus more accurately now on those who have been the chronically unemployed—minority groups, young people, women—to bring them in this circle of Americans who can stand with pride and say, "I support myself. God gave me a certain amount of talent and ability, and now I can use it for productive purposes."

There's nothing more devastating to a young person who arrives at the age of 18 or 19, finishing high school, to know that he has enormous promise within himself or within herself and to be deprived of a right to serve usefully. After a year or two of a self-realization of shame because one's life is not productive, there's an inclination for a young person to turn against society, to lash out at the structure of our country.

And these are the things that Democrats have been trying to accomplish.

We've still got some very serious problems obviously. We haven't solved all the problems. For the last 10 years, we've had an inflation rate of about 6 or 7 percent, entirely too high. And now there comes a time when we are ready to address this effectively. We won't do it as the Republicans did by putting people out of work. We intend to approach inflation by the realization that there are some things that Congress can do, some things I can do administratively, some things that labor can do, management can do, the average citizen can do, to reduce the enormous inflation rates that rob us all.

As you know, the ones who suffer most are those who live on a fixed income, those who have very modest savings. It's not right, it's not fair. It's not compatible with the ideals and principles of our country to have people suffer who occupy that position in our society.

We are trying to do some things in the Congress. One of the most important, that I mentioned to the steelworkers a few minutes ago, is the hospital cost containment bill. I don't think we're going to be successful this year in getting it passed because of the enormous influence of the lobbyists who are protecting an unwarranted position in American society. Since 1960, hospital costs have gone up more than 1,000 percent.

Not long ago, Tip O'Neill came back from a weekend in Boston and brought me a bill, a hospital bill for one of his working constituent friends. His little son had fallen down and driven two or three, four teeth, I think, up into his upper gum. The child stayed in the hospital 26 hours. The bill was $2,330.99.

This is the kind of thing that falls on people who don't have a friend who happens to be the Speaker of the House. And I think there's a time to stir up the consciousness of American people, who know that there are some things that can be done to provide equity and fairness in our society and at the same time remove the enormous burden of inflation.

Now, what we proposed to the Congress this year, which was rejected so far, is that the rate of increase of hospital charges should be limited to only 50 percent more than the inflation rate—9 or 10 percent—after 2 years. Now the increase in hospital charges are twice the inflation rate. These are the kind of things we are trying to do.

I think we'll have a successful vote this week in the Congress on another measure that we put forward as Democrats, the airline deregulation bill. Any of you who fly in our own country or overseas know that we put forward as Democrats, the in the last 20 months in the fares that you have to pay. When I campaigned around our country for 2 years, I quite often rode on a large airplane that was only 25 percent filled, or even less. Now those same airplanes are 75 percent filled, or more. The fares are cheaper. More people are flying. The airlines are making more profit.

That's the kind of thing that the Democrats are doing to demonstrate not only our fairness but our constructive contribution to the free enterprise system in America that we love so much and which quite often in the past the Republicans have erroneously claimed was their special province. We believe in tough competition to protect consumers, yes, but to make sure that those who participate in the free enterprise system as suppliers also make a better profit.

For the first time in history, political history, polling history, last month a Gallup poll showed that twice as many people now believe that the Democrats are fiscally responsible as believed the Republicans are fiscally responsible. That's a good reputation to have, and we're going to keep it.

I've watched this campaign in New Jersey with great attention. It's always easy for someone to demagog in an election for an office as important as United States Senator. We've watched with interest the Proposition 13 vote in California. And quite often that vote has been seriously distorted in this race by the opponent of Bill Bradley. For anyone to demand, for instance, that the Federal income tax be reduced enormously, like 30 or 35 percent, means that the local taxpayers, the property taxpayers will have to have enormous increases in the burden on their shoulders.

This is a point that's often distorted. But Bill Bradley understands this. We are bringing substantial reductions in income taxes at the Federal level to all of you and the people of the United States, but we are doing it in a careful and responsible way. We do not want to see property taxes raised. We want to see property taxes reduced, as Brendan Byrne and all of you were able to do in the last few years. And we are thankful for that. Bill Bradley— [*inaudible*].

Let me just make one other point before I close. We have a great country. Sometimes that greatness has not been realized nor recognized. As you all know, Congressman Peter Rodino, in the Watergate embarrassment, brought a new breath of fresh air to Washington. It took not only great courage but sound judgment and absolute integrity to do it. But in the aftermath of Vietnam and Watergate and the CIA revelations, our Nation's reputation was soiled. Many Americans turned away from our own Government and said, "It embarrasses me." The vision, the ideal, the commitment that were there 200 years ago when our Nation was formed, have somehow been lost. One of of the great responsibilities that I share with you is to restore that vision and that degree of cleanness and decency and honesty and truth and principle to our country. It's not an easy task, because the complications of dealing with foreign nations who are sovereign, over whom we

have no control, are so difficult to analyze and to utilize to meet our goals.

This past 2 weeks, we had a great step forward at Camp David because of the courage of President Sadat and Prime Minister Begin. I talked yesterday afternoon with President Sadat just before he left. And the peace negotiations will not take place, as you know, until after the Knesset votes. But I asked him if we could start immediately to deciding on a location for the peace treaty discussions. He said yes. I said, "Can we start immediately with our own Ambassadors and with an American representative analyzing all of the talks and discussions that have already taken place between Defense Minister Weizman from Israel and Secretary of War, Minister of War Jamasi in Egypt?" He said yes. So, we'll commence this without delay.

As you know, we've now sent Secretary Vance to meet today with King Hussein of Jordan, to urge him in the strongest possible way to join in the negotiations in the future. He'll go from there to Saudi Arabia to meet with King Khalid and with Crown Prince Fahd and others. He'll go from there to meet President Asad in Jordan. (Note: The President meant to say President Asad in Syria.) [1]

I think these national leaders, whether they are particularly friends of ours or not—and most of them are—believe that they can depend upon our country, depend upon the American people, depend upon the American Government to be honest, to be fair, to keep our word, and to hold high the banner of truth and justice, of freedom, of liberty, that have made us so proud in the generations in the past.

I believe that we are making great strides in bringing peace to many areas of

---

[1] Printed in the transcript.

the world. I'm proud that since I've been in the White House, there's not been a single American soldier who has lost blood in a foreign war or combat. I would like go out of office still having maintained that record. But at the same time, we have to think about others in other nations who don't enjoy the privileges and freedoms that we do. And also as long as I'm in the White House, we will keep high the banner and keep deep the commitment, not only to preserve but to enhance human rights, not only in our own country but everywhere. And you can depend upon that.

Let me say in closing that I feel a partnership with you and a kinship with you, not only as Americans but as Democrats. But there's a practical side to politics as well. You just can't point backward at achievements, analyze the present for problems, and look to the future with dreams. Elections come around, and dedicated candidates offer themselves for service. The primary battles are very difficult. I know from experience how taxing they can be on a candidate or one's family. And the support and the actual help that a candidate gets must be broadly distributed, particularly in the Democratic Party, to be effective.

You all have helped by coming here today for this luncheon. You've contributed money to the Democratic campaign effort. But I would like to ask you to do much more than this. Don't go home from this meeting thinking that you have done enough. If you are proud of what I've described in the past, if you are committed to resolving the difficulties that we face in the future, if you want to be part of a resurgent America and a strong Democratic Party that stands for the principles that you yourself espouse, if you want to see these congressional leaders—and they are leaders in the purest sense of the word—

continue to serve you, and others join them like Bill Bradley in Washington, every one of you should continue to act not only as a supporter but as a leader, a campaign manager in your own neighborhood, in your own community, in your own county or city.

You have been blessed by the fruits of our country and our party. You have an obligation to help those who represent you and me as candidates. And I would like to ask you to dedicate yourself at this moment to doing 10 times more than you had thought you would do when you arrived—to see how many people you can contact, to arouse financial and political support for the candidates in whom you believe.

I know what can be done if one is absolutely committed to achieving a goal. And I know that every one of you are competent and capable and dedicated to help us realize these goals together.

I want to thank you for what you mean to me and to our country and what you can and will mean to these fine Members of Congress and candidates who can represent us well in the future.

As Democrats, I believe together we cannot lose. Thank you very much.

NOTE: The President spoke at 12:25 p.m. in the Granada Ballroom at the Boardwalk Regency Hotel.

Employee Retirement Income Security Act Transfers

Message to the Congress Transmitting an Amendment to Reorganization Plan No. 4 of 1978.   September 20, 1978

To the Congress of the United States:
I herewith transmit an amendment to Reorganization Plan No. 4 of 1978. Ex-

cept as specifically amended hereby, Reorganization Plan No. 4 remains unmodified.

JIMMY CARTER

The White House,
September 20, 1978.

AMENDMENT TO REORGANIZATION PLAN No. 4 OF 1978

Prepared by the President and transmitted to the Senate and the House of Representatives in Congress assembled September 20, 1978, pursuant to the provisions of Chapter 9 of Title 5 of the United States Code.

Section 107 of Reorganization Plan No. 4 of 1978, which was transmitted to the Senate and the House of Representatives in Congress assembled on August 10, 1978, is hereby amended to read:

"Section 107. *Evaluation.* On or before January 31, 1980, the President will submit to both Houses of the Congress an evaluation of the extent to which this Reorganization Plan has alleviated the problems associated with the present administrative structure under ERISA, accompanied by specific legislative recommendations for a long-term administrative structure under ERISA."

Territory of the Virgin Islands

Message to the Congress Transmitting the Territory's Proposed Constitution.
September 20, 1978

To the Congress of the United States:

I am today transmitting to the Congress the proposed constitution for local self-government for the Virgin Islands, as authorized by Public Law 94–584. Until now, an organic act of the Congress provided the basis for local government in this unincorporated territory of the United States.

A locally elected constitutional convention drafted the constitution over a period of several months and held a series of public hearings and meetings throughout the Virgin Islands. The constitutional convention approved the constitution in April 1978. On July 20, 1978, the Governor of the Virgin Islands officially presented me with the constitution.

By law, I must transmit the constitution to the Congress, along with comments, within 60 days of the document's receipt. The Congress then has 60 more days to amend, modify, or approve it. As approved or modified, the constitution will be submitted to a referendum in the Virgin Islands for acceptance or rejection.

Several Federal agencies have commented on the constitution for the Executive Branch that it meets the criteria established by Public Law 94–584: it is consistent with sovereignty of the United States, its constitution, and its laws applicable to the Virgin Islands; it provides for a republican form of government with executive, legislative, and judicial branches; it contains a bill of rights; it sets up a system of local courts; and it deals with those portions of the revised organic act related to local self-government.

However, the agencies commenting on the constitution noted several matters that the Congress may wish to alter. Those comments are attached.

I commend this accomplishment of the members of the constitutional convention and the other citizens of the Virgin Islands who helped to draft the constitution. It is a significant step toward greater local self-government. It is therefore wholly appropriate that the electorate of the Virgin Islands, and not the Federal Government, has the ultimate right to accept or reject it.

To facilitate congressional deliberations, I have asked that the Attorney General and the Secretary of the Interior offer their advice and technical assistance to the committees that review the document.

JIMMY CARTER

The White House,
    September 20, 1978.

ATTACHMENT

1. Under the constitution, the aggregate public debt limitation for the Virgin Islands Government may not exceed two and one-half times its average annual revenue for the previous three fiscal years (exclusive of Federal grants). But because the constitution does not adequately define "revenue," the exact level of the new debt limitation is unclear and could conceivably be a substantial increase over the current level, depending on which receipts from various Virgin Island governmental accounts are counted as revenue. Therefore, the definition of revenue in determining the public debt limitation under the constitution should be clarified. The present debt limitation, authorized by the organic act and subsequent legislation, is primarily based on a percentage of assessed property valuation in the Virgin Islands.

2. The constitution also creates the position of Territorial Comptroller General, who would be responsible for auditing all revenues, expenditures, and programs of the local government. The relationship of the proposed Comptroller General with the current Federal Comptroller for the Virgin Islands should be clarified. Because major Federal assistance is received by the Virgin Islands, the proposed Comptroller General should complement, but not substitute for, the Federal Comptroller.

3. Section 3 of the transitional schedule of the constitution provides that, after the effective date of the constitution, "laws, executive orders, and regulations that are inconsistent with the constitution shall be void to the extent of the inconsistency." The Department of Justice advises me that section 3 cannot apply to the sources of law based on Federal authority, such as Federal statutes, executive orders, and regulations—including executive orders and regulations issued by the territorial-appointed governors. The Department, however, recommends revising in the section to remove any uncertainty about the applicability of Federal law.

United States Ambassador to Oman

Nomination of Marshall W. Wiley.
September 20, 1978

The President today announced that he will nominate Marshall W. Wiley, of Islamorada, Fla., to be Ambassador Extraordinary and Plenipotentiary of the United States to the Sultanate of Oman. He would replace William D. Wolle, resigned.

Wiley was born April 26, 1925, in Rockford, Ill. He received a Ph. B. (1943), J.D. (1948), and M.B.A. (1949) from the University of Chicago. He served in the U.S. Navy from 1943 to 1945.

Wiley joined the Foreign Service in 1958 and was posted in Taiz, Beirut, and Amman. From 1965 to 1968, he was an international relations officer at the State Department.

From 1969 to 1973, Wiley was deputy principal officer in Cairo, and from 1973 to 1975, he was director of North African affairs at the State Department. He was principal officer in Baghdad from 1975 to 1977. Since 1977 he has been Deputy Chief of Mission in Jidda.

American Expedition in the Himalayan Mountains in Pakistan

Message to Members of the Mountain Climbing Team. September 20, 1978

The American team's ascension of K2 is an inspiration to all who seek to conquer not just the highest pinnacles, but to master all that is worthy of mastery. K2 was worthy of your efforts, and you proved worthy of the attempt. I know the people of the United States, and especially Washington and California, join me in saluting you for the skill, courage and stamina exhibited in climbing the mountain that is second in height only to Everest, and perhaps second to none in difficulty. We are especially proud of James Wickwire, Lou Reichart, John Roskelley and Rick Ridgway.

Congratulations to all 14 members of the team that made this achievement possible. We are gratified for the excellent support provided by the Pakistani members, and thankful that all returned safely from this historic climb.

JIMMY CARTER

National Guard Day, 1978

Proclamation 4598. September 20, 1978

By the President of the United States of America

A Proclamation

Three hundred and forty-two years ago, the First Militia Regiment of the Massachusetts Bay Colony was organized to enable the colonists to defend themselves and their settlement. That step toward citizen self-defense was the beginning of our National Guard, the oldest military organization in the United States.

Over those three centuries, names have changed—Militia, State Troops, State Volunteers, and, finally, the National Guard—but the spirit of the citizen-soldier has been constant. It is exemplified by those who stand prepared to leave their civilian occupations, don the uniform of their Country, and serve their States and their Nation when the need arises.

In time of war, the Guard is always ready to serve. At King's Mountain, the Meuse-Argonne, Bataan, Omaha Beach, and the Iron Triangle, during the Berlin Airlift and Vietnam, the Guard has served in every major conflict in which this country has engaged.

When disaster strikes in time of peace, the Guard is equally ready to serve—as it has, in recent years, at Johnstown, Texas City, and in the wake of Hurricane Agnes.

In recognition of the debt of gratitude owed by the people of the United States to those who serve as members of the National Guard, the Congress has authorized and requested the President to issue a proclamation designating October 7, 1978, as National Guard Day.

Now, THEREFORE, I, JIMMY CARTER, President of the United States of America, ask all Americans to celebrate Saturday, October 7, 1978, as National Guard Day and to honor the Army and Air National Guard of the United States for service to their communities, to their States and to their Nation.

IN WITNESS WHEREOF, I have hereunto set my hand this twentieth day of September, in the year of our Lord nineteen hundred seventy-eight, and of the Independence of the United States of America the two hundred and third.

JIMMY CARTER

[Filed with the Office of the Federal Register, 10:36 a.m., September 21, 1978]

United States-Federal Republic of Germany Agreements on Social Security

Message to the Congress Transmitting the Agreements. September 21, 1978

To the Congress of the United States:

Pursuant to section 233(e)(1) of the Social Security Act as amended by the Social Security Amendments of 1977 (P.L. 95–216; 42 U.S.C. 433), I am transmitting the Agreement between the United States of America and the Federal Republic of Germany (F.R.G.), signed on January 7, 1976, the Final Protocol to the 1976 Agreement, also signed on January 7, 1976, and the Administrative Agreement to implement the 1976 Agreement, signed on June 21, 1978.

These U.S.-F.R.G. Agreements are similar in objective to the U.S.-Italian social security agreements which I submitted to the Congress on February 28, 1978. Such bilateral agreements, which are generally known as totalization agreements, provide for limited coordination between the United States and foreign social security systems to overcome the problems of gaps in protection and of dual coverage and taxation. In addition to remedying these problems, the 1976 U.S.-F.R.G. Agreement and Administrative Agreement would extend under specified conditions voluntary coverage rights under the F.R.G. system to U.S. citizens who have a prior connection with the F.R.G. system or who reside in the United States and were victims of persecution.

I also transmit for the information of the Congress a comprehensive report prepared by the Department of Health, Education, and Welfare, which explains the provisions of the Agreement and provides data on the number of persons affected by the agreements and the effect on social security financing as required by the same provision of the Social Security Amendments of 1977.

The Department of State and the Department of Health, Education, and Welfare join in commending this Agreement, Protocol, and Administrative Agreement.

JIMMY CARTER

The White House,
September 21, 1978.

Council on Wage and Price Stability

Message to the Congress Transmitting a Report. September 21, 1978

To the Congress of the United States:

In accordance with Section 5 of the Council on Wage and Price Stability Act, as amended, I hereby transmit to the Congress the fourteenth quarterly report of the Council on Wage and Price Stability. This report contains a description of the Council's activities during the first quarter of 1978 in monitoring both prices and wages in the private sector and various Federal Government activities that may lead to higher costs and prices without creating commensurate benefits. It discusses Council reports, analyses, and filings before Federal regulatory agencies.

The Council on Wage and Price Stability will continue to play an important role in supplementing fiscal and monetary policies by calling public attention to wage and price developments or actions by the Government that could be of concern to American consumers.

JIMMY CARTER

The White House,
September 21, 1978.

NOTE: The report is entitled "A Quarterly Report of the Council on Wage and Price Stability: First Quarter, 1978—Executive Office of the President, Washington, D.C., No. 14" (Government Printing Office, 27 pages).

Radiation Control for Health and Safety Act of 1968

Message to the Congress Transmitting a Report.   September 21, 1978

To the Congress of the United States:

I transmit herewith the 1977 Annual Report on the Administration of the Radiation Control for Health and Safety Act (Public Law 90–602) as prepared by the Secretary of the Department of Health, Education, and Welfare.

The report recommends that those sections of subpart 3, Part F of Title III of the Public Health Service Act, 42 U.S.C. 262 et. seq. (Public Law 602), which require the compilation of this annual report be repealed. This report cost $3,780 to prepare.

All of the information found in this report is available to Congress on a more immediate basis through Congressional committee oversight and budget hearings and the FDA Annual Report. We have concluded that this annual report serves little useful purpose and diverts agency resources from more productive activities.

JIMMY CARTER

The White House,
September 21, 1978.

NOTE: The 97–page report is entitled "1977 Annual Report: Administration of the Radiation Control for Health and Safety Act of 1968, Public Law 90–602, April 1, 1978—U.S. Department of Health, Education, and Welfare."

Department of Energy

**Nomination of Thomas S. Williamson, Jr., To Be Deputy Inspector General.
September 21, 1978**

The President today announced that he will nominate Thomas S. Williamson, Jr., Washington, D.C., to be Deputy Inspec-

tor General of the Department of Energy.

Williamson was born July 14, 1946, in Plainfield, N.J. He received a B.A. from Harvard College in 1968 and graduated from the University of California Berkeley Law School in 1974.

Since 1974 Williamson has been an associate at the Washington law firm of Covington & Burling. Before entering law school he was a management consultant to the training division of Alem Public Relations Consultants in Addis Ababa, Ethiopia, where he supervised the division of the company which trained U.S. Peace Corps volunteers for service in Ethiopia. He has also served as a Crossroads Africa group leader in the Cameroon and as a consultant to the Office of Planning and Evaluation at HEW.

National Forest Products Week, 1978

Proclamation 4599.   September 21, 1978

By the President of the United States of America

A Proclamation

When we Americans stop to reflect about our wealth of natural resources and the benefits they bestow, we quickly realize the worth of our Nation's forests. One-third of our land, some 740 million acres, is forested, and we get a wide range of essential products from many of these forests. Trees become houses to shelter us, books to convey our thoughts, packaging to protect our food, energy to power our factories or heat our homes.

A forest can be many things at the same time. With sound management, we need never fear running out of trees. A forest is a renewable resource. But for all its powers of regeneration, a forest is not invulnerable. If we use it unwisely or wastefully, it can disappear. If we ignore the diverse needs of our people, the forests will cease to preserve the natural watersheds, to provide a home for wildlife or a wilderness where our people can renew their spirits. Many of the earth's problems today are the result of generations of destructive deforestation that has left lands barren and wasted. We must make sure that man's works lie gently on our land, so that we may leave for future generations a richer, more abundant, more beautiful land than we inherited.

Research is helping to show the ways to get as much usable material as possible from each harvested tree, finding better methods for protecting wood products so they last longer and developing ways to recycle used wood into new products. Our scientists are also finding ways to make trees grow faster, and to protect the forest from its natural enemies of fire, insects, and disease.

The Congress has designated the third week of October in each year as National Forest Products Week to remind us of the importance of forests in our national life.

Now, THEREFORE, I, JIMMY CARTER, President of the United States of America, do hereby proclaim the week of October 15 through 21, 1978, as National Forest Products Week and ask all Americans to reflect upon the value of our forests.

IN WITNESS WHEREOF, I have hereunto set my hand this twenty-first day of September, in the year of our Lord nineteen hundred seventy-eight, and of the Independence of the United States of America the two hundred and third.

JIMMY CARTER

[Filed with the Office of the Federal Register, 2:22 p.m., September 21, 1978]

Meeting With President Gaafar Muhammed Nimeiri of the Sudan

White House Statement. September 21, 1978

President Carter met this morning with Gaafar Muhammed Nimeiri, President of Sudan and Chairman of the Organization of African Unity. President Nimeiri is in the United States on a private visit and will address the United Nations General Assembly on September 27.

The two Presidents discussed recent developments in Middle East peace negotiations resulting from the Camp David summit and issues of mutual concern in Africa. They also discussed the role of the OAU in seeking peaceful solutions to conflicts in Africa. Both leaders expressed their satisfaction with the existing cordial bilateral relationship and the focus on economic development in Sudan.

Attending the meeting were President Carter; the Vice President; Andrew Young, U.S. Representative to the United Nations; Warren Christopher, Deputy Secretary of State; Zbigniew Brzezinski, Assistant to the President for National Security Affairs; David A. Newsom, Under Secretary of State for Political Affairs; Richard Moose, Assistant Secretary of State, Bureau of African Affairs; Harold Saunders, Assistant Secretary of State for Near Eastern and South Asian Affairs; Donald C. Bergus, U.S. Ambassador to the Sudan; and Paul B. Henze, National Security Council.

The meeting lasted from 9:30 a.m. until 10:45 a.m.

United States Ambassador to the Central African Empire

Nomination of Goodwin Cooke.
September 21, 1978

The President today announced that he will nominate Goodwin Cooke of Branford, Conn., to be Ambassador Extraordinary and Plenipotentiary of the United States to the Central African Empire. He would replace Anthony C. E. Quainton, resigned.

Cooke was born July 29, 1931, in Paris, France, of American parents. He received an A.B. from Harvard University in 1953. He served in the U.S. Marine Corps from 1953 to 1955.

Cooke joined the Foreign Service in 1956 and served in Karachi, Belgrade, Rome, Brussels, and at the State Department. In 1971 and 1972, he was detailed to the Canadian National Defence College, and from 1972 to 1975, he was political officer in Ottawa.

Since 1975 Cooke has been Deputy Chief of Mission in Abidjan, Ivory Coast.

United States Ambassador to the Somali Democratic Republic

Nomination of Donald K. Petterson.
September 21, 1978

The President today announced that he will nominate Donald K. Petterson of San Luis Obispo, Calif., to be Ambassador Extraordinary and Plenipotentiary of the United States to the Somali Democratic Republic. He would replace John L. Loughran, resigned.

Petterson was born November 17, 1930, in Huntington Park, Calif. He received a B.A. (1956) and M.A. (1960) from the University of California at Santa Barbara. He served in the U.S. Navy from 1948 to 1952.

Petterson joined the Foreign Service in 1960 and served in Mexico City, Zanzibar, and Lagos. From 1968 to 1970, he was a personnel officer at the State Department, and from 1970 to 1972, he was posted in Freetown as counselor for political and economic affairs, then Deputy Chief of Mission.

From 1972 to 1975, Petterson was counselor for political affairs in Pretoria. He was an international relations officer at the State Department from 1975 to 1977 and Director of the Office of South African Affairs in 1977 and 1978. Since 1978 he has been Deputy Assistant Secretary of State for African Affairs.

Airline Deregulation Legislation

Statement on House of Representatives Action Approving the Legislation.
September 21, 1978

This is a welcome occasion. With this legislation we achieve two critical national objectives—controlling inflation and, at the same time, cutting unnecessary bureaucratic redtape.

When I announced support for airline deregulation soon after taking office, the bill had few friends. I am happy to say that today it appears to have no enemies. Industry has already benefited from it. In the last few months, price competition among domestic carriers in anticipation of this bill has brought lower fares, more passengers, and record profits.

Consumers are for it. Governors, mayors, the National League of Cities, small towns—all support airline deregulation.

The House of Representatives deserves congratulations for passing this important legislation. I particularly want to thank Speaker O'Neill, Chairman Bizz Johnson, and Representatives Glenn Anderson and Allen Ertel for their spirited championship of this effort to reduce Government meddling in the affairs of private business.

The deregulation bill will take decision-making out of the hands of five regulators and 800 Government bureaucrats who sit here in Washington and put it back in the hands of the men and women whose job it is to run the airlines. It will cut inflation. It will let free market forces operate as they should.

The Senate has already passed the bill. I hope it goes quickly to conference and reaches my desk for signature as soon as possible.

Imports From India

Proclamation 4600.   September 21, 1978

TEMPORARY STAGED REDUCTION OF RATES OF DUTY ON CERTAIN PRODUCTS

By the President of the United States of America

A Proclamation

1. The President has determined, pursuant to section 101(a) of the Trade Act of 1974 (the Trade Act) (19 U.S.C. 2111 (a)), that certain existing duties of the United States are unduly burdening and restricting the foreign trade of the United States and that one or more of the purposes of the Trade Act would be promoted by entering into the trade agreement with India identified in the fifth recital of this proclamation.

2. Pursuant to section 131(a) of the Trade Act (19 U.S.C. 2151(a)), the President, on January 14, 1975, published and furnished the United States International Trade Commission (USITC) with lists of articles which may be considered for modifications or continuance of the existing United States duties, continuance of the United States duty-free or excise treatment, or additional duties, in the negotiation of trade agreements, including the trade agreement with India identified in the fifth recital of this proclamation. The USITC, after holding public hearings, has advised the President with respect to each such article of its judgment as to the probable economic effect of such modifications of duties on industries producing like or directly competitive articles and on consumers.

3. Pursuant to section 133 of the Trade Act (19 U.S.C. 2153) and in accordance with section 4(c) of Executive Order No. 11846 of March 27, 1975, the Special Representative for Trade Negotiations designated the Trade Policy Staff Committee to afford an opportunity, through public hearings and other means, for any interested person to present his views concerning any article on the lists identified in the second recital of this proclamation or any other matter relevant to the trade agreement negotiations, including the negotiation of the trade agreement with India identified in the fifth recital of this proclamation. The Trade Policy Staff Committee has furnished the President with a summary of its hearings.

4. Pursuant to section 132 of the Trade Act (19 U.S.C. 2152) the President has received information and advice with respect to the trade agreement with India identified in the fifth recital of this proclamation, from the Departments of Agriculture, Commerce, Defense, Interior, Labor, State and the Treasury, from the Special Representative for Trade Negotiations, and from such other sources as the President has deemed appropriate.

5. Pursuant to section 101(a) of the Trade Act (19 U.S.C. 2111(a)), the President, through his duly empowered representative, on July 26, 1978, entered into a temporary trade agreement with India pursuant to which United States rates of duty on certain products would be temporarily modified, as hereafter proclaimed and as provided for in the Annexes to this proclamation, in exchange for certain measures which will benefit United States exports to India.

6. In order to implement the trade agreement referred to in recital 5 of this proclamation it is necessary to modify the Appendix to the Tariff Schedules of the United States (TSUS) (19 U.S.C. 1202) as provided for in the Annexes to this proclamation, attached hereto and made a part hereof.

Now, THEREFORE, I, JIMMY CARTER, President of the United States of America, acting under the authority vested in me by the Constitution and the statutes, including sections 101, 109, and 604 of the Trade Act (19 U.S.C. 2111, 2119 and 2483), do proclaim that—

(1) Part 2 of the Appendix to the TSUS is modified as provided in Annexes I and II to this proclamation.

(2) Each of the temporary modifications to the Appendix of the TSUS made by this proclamation shall be effective as to articles entered, or withdrawn from warehouse, for consumption on or after October 1, 1978, and each such modification will continue in force until it is superseded by a permanent modification of the appropriate provision in schedule 1, 3, 4, or 5 of the TSUS proclaimed pursuant to multilateral negotiations under the General Agreement on Tariffs and Trade.

IN WITNESS WHEREOF, I have hereunto set my hand this twenty-first day of September, in the year of our Lord nineteen hundred seventy-eight, and of the Independence of the United States of America the two hundred and third.

JIMMY CARTER

[Filed with the Office of the Federal Register, 10:45 a.m., September 22, 1978]

NOTE: Annexes I and II are printed in the FEDERAL REGISTER of September 25, 1978.

National Highway Safety Advisory Committee

Appointment of Frances H. Goodwin as a Member. September 22, 1978

The President today announced the appointment of Frances H. Goodwin, of Dallas, Tex., as a member of the National Highway Safety Advisory Committee. She would replace George Berlinger, resigned.

Goodwin, 48, is an attorney in Dallas and an associate judge of the Dallas municipal court on a part-time basis. She served as a judge of that court on a full-time basis from 1969 until 1977.

Goodwin is an expert on alcohol abuse and alcoholism and has served as chairman of the American Judges Association Committee on Alcohol and Drug Abuse and on the board of directors of the Dallas Council on Alcoholism.

Convention on the Hostile Use of Environmental Modification Techniques

Message to the Senate Transmitting the Convention. September 22, 1978

To the Senate of the United States:

I am transmitting herewith, for the advice and consent of the Senate to ratification, the Convention on the Prohibition of Military or Any Other Hostile Use of Environmental Modification Techniques, signed at Geneva on May 18, 1977.

The Convention is the result of extensive study, debate, and negotiation at the Conference of the Committee on Disarmament at Geneva and at the United Nations. It seeks to avert the dangers resulting from the hostile use of environmental modification techniques "having widespread, long-lasting or severe effects as the means of destruction, damage or injury to any other State Party."

In 1973, growing awareness of the need for protecting our environment led to the adoption of Senate Resolution 71 which urged the Executive Branch to negotiate a treaty prohibiting environmental warfare. The United States and the Soviet Union, after three rounds of bilateral consultations, tabled identical draft texts of a multilateral convention at the Conference of the Committee on Disarmament in 1975. Negotiations on the basis of these texts resulted in the document I am transmitting to you today.

I am also sending with the Convention four Understandings relating to Articles I, II, III and VIII, respectively. These Understandings are not incorporated into the Convention. They are part of the negotiating record and were included in the report transmitted by the Conference of the Committee on Disarmament to the United Nations. The provisions of the Convention and the Understandings are described in detail in the accompanying report of the Department of State.

By prohibiting the hostile use of potentially disastrous environmental modification techniques, the Convention represents one more advance in the field of arms control to which my Administration is firmly committed. I recommend that the Senate give prompt consideration to

the Convention, and advise and consent to its ratification.

JIMMY CARTER

The White House,
    September 22, 1978.

Jewish High Holy Days

Statement by the President.
September 22, 1978

On the eve of the High Holy Days, Rosalynn and I extend our heartfelt greetings to all our fellow citizens of the Jewish faith. Rosh Hashonah and Yom Kippur are supreme moments of moral and spiritual stocktaking, both in personal and in community life.

Few utterances of the human spirit are more moving and ennobling than that found in the Jewish High Holiday prayer: "May they all (all people) form one companionship to do Thy Will with a single heart."

This message has a special urgency this year in the part of the world where the Western world's great religions, including Judaism, were born. The possibility of peace in the Middle East has seldom been greater. Whether that possibility is realized will depend on the degree to which all concerned can act, in the prayer's words, "with a single heart."

Human solidarity is based on profound respect for the right of each group to be itself and to be true to its own heritage and culture. This philosophy has been translated into reality in the religious pluralism and mutual caring which are distinctive features of American democracy.

Our 200-year-old American experience with unity in diversity may be the most important cultural and spiritual example we have to offer the world. American

Jews have greatly added to that diversity and to the strength it has brought to our national life. It is with this in mind that Rosalynn and I extend our best wishes for a satisfying, peaceful, and happy New Year.

Camp David Meeting on the Middle East

Letters Accompanying the Documents Agreed to at Camp David. September 22, 1978

(A

September 17, 1978

Dear Mr. President:

I have the honor to inform you that during two weeks after my return home I will submit a motion before Israel's Parliament (the Knesset) to decide on the following question:

If during the negotiations to conclude a peace treaty between Israel and Egypt all outstanding issues are agreed upon, "are you in favor of the removal of the Israeli settlers from the northern and southern Sinai areas or are you in favor of keeping the aforementioned settlers in those areas?"

The vote, Mr. President, on this issue will be completely free from the usual Parliamentary Party discipline to the effect that although the coalition is being now supported by 70 members out of 120, every member of the Knesset, as I believe, both on the Government and the Opposition benches will be enabled to vote in accordance with his own conscience.

Sincerely yours,

(signed)
MENACHEM BEGIN

[The President, Camp David, Thurmont, Maryland]

(B

September 22, 1978

Dear Mr. President:

I transmit herewith a copy of a letter to me from Prime Minister Begin setting forth how he proposes to present the issue of the Sinai settlements to the Knesset for the latter's decision.

In this connection, I understand from your letter that Knesset approval to withdraw all Israeli settlers from Sinai according to a timetable within the period specified for the implementation of the peace treaty is a prerequisite to any negotiations on a peace treaty between Egypt and Israel.

Sincerely,

(signed)
JIMMY CARTER

Enclosure: Letter from Prime Minister Begin (Letter at Tab A)

[His Excellency Anwar el-Sadat, President of the Arab Republic of Egypt, Cairo]

———

(C

September 17, 1978

Dear Mr. President:

In connection with the "Framework for a Settlement in Sinai" to be signed tonight, I would like to reaffirm the position of the Arab Republic of Egypt with respect to the settlements:

1. All Israeli settlers must be withdrawn from Sinai according to a timetable within the period specified for the implementation of the peace treaty.

2. Agreement by the Israeli Government and its constitutional institutions to this basic principle is therefore a prerequisite to starting peace negotiations for concluding a peace treaty.

3. If Israel fails to meet this commitment, the "Framework" shall be void and invalid.

Sincerely,

(signed)

MOHAMED ANWAR EL SADAT

[His Excellency Jimmy Carter, President of the United States]

_____

(D

September 22, 1978

Dear Mr. Prime Minister:

I have received your letter of September 17, 1978, describing how you intend to place the question of the future of Israeli settlements in Sinai before the Knesset for its decision.

Enclosed is a copy of President Sadat's letter to me on this subject.

Sincerely,

(signed)

JIMMY CARTER

Enclosure: Letter from President Sadat (Letter at Tab C)

[His Excellency Menachem Begin, Prime Minister of Israel]

_____

(E

September 17, 1978

Dear Mr. President,

I am writing you to reaffirm the position of the Arab Republic of Egypt with respect to Jerusalem:

1. Arab Jerusalem is an integral part of the West Bank. Legal and historical Arab rights in the City must be respected and restored.

2. Arab Jerusalem should be under Arab sovereignty.

3. The Palestinian inhabitants of Arab Jerusalem are entitled to exercise their legitimate national rights, being part of the Palestinian People in the West Bank.

4. Relevant Security Council Resolutions, particularly Resolutions 242 and 267, must be applied with regard to Jerusalem. All the measures taken by Israel to alter the status of the City are null and void and should be rescinded.

5. All peoples must have free access to the City and enjoy the free exercise of worship and the right to visit and transit to the holy places without distinction or discrimination.

6. The holy places of each faith may be placed under the administration and control of their representatives.

7. Essential functions in the City should be undivided and a joint municipal council composed of an equal number of Arab and Israeli members can supervise the carrying out of these functions. In this way, the City shall be undivided.

Sincerely,

(signed)

MOHAMED ANWAR EL SADAT

[His Excellency Jimmy Carter, President of the United States]

_____

(F

17 September 1978

Dear Mr. President,

I have the honor to inform you, Mr. President, that on 28 June 1967—Israel's Parliament (The Knesset) promulgated and adopted a law to the effect: "the Government is empowered by a decree to apply the law, the jurisdiction and administration of the State to any part of Eretz Israel (land of Israel—Palestine), as stated in that decree."

On the basis of this law, the Government of Israel decreed in July 1967 that Jerusalem is one city indivisible, the Capital of the State of Israel.

Sincerely,

(signed)

MENACHEM BEGIN

[The President, Camp David, Thurmont, Maryland]

_____

(G

September 22, 1978

Dear Mr. President:

I have received your letter of September 17, 1978, setting forth the Egyptian position on Jerusalem. I am transmitting a copy of that letter to Prime Minister Begin for his information.

The position of the United States on Jerusalem remains as stated by Ambassador Goldberg in the United Nations General Assembly on July 14, 1967, and subsequently by Ambassador Yost in the United Nations Security Council on July 1, 1969.

Sincerely,

(signed)

JIMMY CARTER

[His Excellency Anwar al-Sadat, President of the Arab Republic of Egypt, Cairo]

(H

September 17, 1978

Dear Mr. President:

In connection with the "Framework for Peace in the Middle East", I am writing you this letter to inform you of the position of the Arab Republic of Egypt, with respect to the implementation of the comprehensive settlement.

To ensure the implementation of the provisions related to the West Bank and Gaza and in order to safeguard the legitimate rights of the Palestinian people, Egypt will be prepared to assume the Arab role emanating from these provisions, following consultations with Jordan and the representatives of the Palestinian people.

Sincerely,

(signed)

MOHAMED ANWAR EL SADAT

[His Excellency Jimmy Carter, President of the United States, The White House, Washington, D.C.]

(I

September 22, 1978

Dear Mr. Prime Minister:

I hereby acknowledge that you have informed me as follows:

A) In each paragraph of the agreed framework document the expressions "Palestinians" or "Palestinian People" are being and will be construed and understood by you as "Palestinian Arabs."

B) In each paragraph in which the expression "West Bank" appears, it is being, and will be, understood by the Government of Israel as Judea and Samaria.

Sincerely,

(signed)

JIMMY CARTER

[His Excellency Menachem Begin, Prime Minister of Israel]

United Nations Fund for Drug Abuse Control

Statement by the President.
September 22, 1978

For over 70 years, the United States of America has supported international measures to control drug abuse. Today, it is more important than ever to continue this support.

This administration recognizes that drug problems cannot be solved unilaterally but require concerted action by the world community. Drug abuse is exacting an ever greater toll on the citizens of developed and developing countries. It affects our economies, our societies, and, most of all, our culture.

The United Nations Fund for Drug Abuse Control has played a central role in this international effort. Despite limited funds it has been remarkably effective in finding cooperative ways for nations to work together on this international problem. Today I am pleased to announce that the United States will contribute $3 million to the Fund in 1978.

With the contribution, I want to extend my best wishes to Dr. Bror Rexed, the new Executive Director of the Fund.

The United States remains deeply committed to the cause of international drug control. We will continue to support the efforts of the Fund, the United Nations, and other governments.

unto set my hand this twenty-second day of September, in the year of our Lord nineteen hundred seventy-eight, and of the Independence of the United States of America the two hundred and third.

JIMMY CARTER

[Filed with the Office of the Federal Register, 11:03 a.m., September 25, 1978]

National Good Neighbor Day, 1978

Proclamation 4601. September 22, 1978

By the President of the United States of America

A Proclamation

As our Nation struggles to build friendship among the peoples of this world, we are mindful that the noblest human concern is concern for others.

Understanding, love, and respect build cohesive families and communities. The same bonds cement our Nation, and the nations of the world.

For most of us, this sense of community is nurtured and expressed in our neighborhoods where we give each other an opportunity to share and feel part of a larger family.

In recognition of the importance of fostering compassion and respect in ourselves for our neighbors, the Congress has requested the proclamation of September 24, 1978, as National Good Neighbor Day (S.J. Res. 133).

Now, THEREFORE, I, JIMMY CARTER, President of the United States of America, do hereby proclaim Sunday, September 24, 1978, as National Good Neighbor Day.

I call upon the people of the United States and interested groups and organizations to observe such day with appropriate ceremonies and activities.

IN WITNESS WHEREOF, I have here-

Civil Service Retirement Credit for Japanese Americans Interned During World War II

Statement on Signing H.R. 9471 Into Law. September 22, 1978

I am very happy to sign H.R. 9471, a bill which represents one more Government effort to redress inequities that occurred during World War II.

Three and a half decades ago, our Government overreacted to the attack on Pearl Harbor and evacuated and interned approximately 110,000 Japanese Americans who lived in our Western States.

Even at the time this action seemed shameful and indefensible to many of us. The loyalty and devotion of our Japanese American citizens—despite this Government action—has been proven many times over. Most of the internees were American citizens, and many subsequently gave their lives in defense of this country.

While we cannot undo or erase the hardships and indignities suffered by these loyal Americans, we can, in some small measure, compensate them.

Three laws have been enacted for this purpose since the end of World War II. Public Laws 82–545 and 86–782 granted special benefits for civil service pay and retirement purposes to Japanese Americans who met certain criteria and were employed by the Federal Government on

1569

July 15, 1952. The third law, Public Law 92–603, granted social security credits for privately employed adults who were confined in World War II internment camps.

All three of these laws were designed as partial compensation to working-age Japanese American internees, but they do not help those who entered Federal service after mid-1952. These Federal employees generally do not qualify for social security benefits.

H.R. 9471 will cover that group by granting civil service retirement credit for periods of confinement after age 18 in World War II internment camps to any Japanese American who later entered Federal service.

This bill represents years of unceasing effort by many Members of Congress who wished to redress the injustices suffered by this unique group of American citizens. I am pleased to have the opportunity to share in that effort today.

NOTE: As enacted, H.R. 9471 is Public Law 95–382, approved September 22.

Reorganization of Federal Audit and Investigation Functions

Letter to Senator Robert C. Byrd Urging Action on H.R. 8588.   September 22, 1978

To Senator Byrd

I urge favorable action at the earliest possible time on H.R. 8588, a bill to reorganize and consolidate audit and investigation functions and to create offices of Inspector General in twelve major domestic departments and agencies. It is a reflection of the importance of this legislation that with this Administration's support, House approval of this bill earlier this year was nearly unanimous.

The new offices created by the bill will consolidate existing audit and investigation resources under the direction of a single, Presidentially appointed official in each agency. These offices will be charged with rooting out fraud, waste, and abuse in agency programs.

I can assure the Congress that the new framework established by the bill will be put to a good and vigorous use. I intend to nominate people of the highest integrity and ability to head these offices, and I will instruct my department and agency heads to support their efforts fully.

We are pleased to have worked with the Congress, in particular with Senators Ribicoff and Eagleton, and Representatives Brooks and Fountain, in fashioning this legislation. The reorganization of audit and investigation activities complements other initiatives the Administration has underway to fight fraud and abuse in Government, including the strong whistle-blower protection provisions in the civil service reform bill, and the aggressive investigations we have launched of alleged abuses in GSA operations and CETA jobs programs.

I commend Representatives Fountain and Brooks, and Senators Eagleton and Ribicoff for their dedicated work in the development and refinement of this bill.

Sincerely,

JIMMY CARTER

[The Honorable Robert C. Byrd, United States Senate, Washington, D.C. 20510]

Digest of Other White House Announcements

The following listing includes the President's daily schedule and other items of general interest as announced by the White House Press Office during the period covered by this issue. Events and announcements printed elsewhere in the issue are not included.

September 16 [1]

The President met at Camp David with members of the U.S. delegation.

The President met in the afternoon with President Anwar al-Sadat of Egypt.

The President met in the evening with Prime Minister Menahem Begin of Israel.

The President has declared a major disaster for the State of Arkansas as a result of severe storms and flooding, beginning about September 13, which caused extensive public and private property damage.

September 17

The President met in the morning with members of the U.S. delegation.

The President held morning and afternoon meetings with President Sadat. Also attending the afternoon meeting was Secretary of State Cyrus R. Vance.

The President met in the afternoon with Prime Minister Begin.

In the evening, the President, accompanied by President Sadat and Prime Minister Begin, returned to the White House.

September 18

The President met at the White House with Members of Congress to discuss the results of the Camp David meetings.

The President announced the appointment of Robert L. Herbst, Assistant Secretary of the Interior for Fish and Wildlife, as a Commissioner of the United States Section of the Great Lakes Fishery Commission.

September 19

The President met at the White House with:

---

[1] EDITOR'S NOTE: The informal nature of the meetings at Camp David precluded the announcement of daily Presidential schedules by the White House Press Office. Only those meetings and their participants which were announced have been included.

—Zbigniew Brzezinski, Assistant to the President for National Security Affairs;
—Frank B. Moore, Assistant to the President for Congressional Liaison;
—the Democratic congressional leadership;
—Prime Minister Begin;
—producers, members of the cast, and others associated with the television series "All in the Family;"
—President Sadat.

September 20

The President met at the White House with:

—Dr. Brzezinski;
—Mr. Moore.

The President declared a major disaster for the State of Louisiana as a result of severe storms and flooding, beginning about September 15, which caused extensive public and private property damage.

September 21

The President met at the White House with:

—Dr. Brzezinski;
—Mr. Moore;
—Representative Parren J. Mitchell of Maryland;
—a group of community and civic leaders from Oregon;
—Adm. Stansfield Turner, Director of Central Intelligence.

The President transmitted to the Congress the 1976 report on the upland cotton program.

September 22

The President met at the White House with:

—David L. Aaron, Deputy Assistant for National Security Affairs;
—Mr. Moore;
—Representatives James C. Wright, Jr., of Texas, and Tom Bevill of Alabama;

—a group of Members of Congress;

—a group of editors and news directors (transcript will be printed next week).

The President left Washington in the afternoon for a trip to North and South Carolina, and returned to the White House late in the evening. (Releases issued on the trip will be printed next week.)

NOMINATIONS SUBMITTED TO THE SENATE

The following list does not include promotions of members of the Uniformed Services, nominations to the Service Academies, or nominations of Foreign Service officers.

Submitted September 18, 1978

JOHN GUNTHER DEAN, of New York, a Foreign Service officer of Class one, to be Ambassador Extraordinary and Plenipotentiary of the United States of America to the Republic of Lebanon.

RICHARD W. PETREE, of Virginia, a Foreign Service officer of Class one, to be the Alternate Representative of the United States of America for Special Political Affairs in the United Nations, with the rank of Ambassador.

PETER HENRY WOLF, of the District of Columbia, to be an Associate Judge of the Superior Court of the District of Columbia for a term of 15 years, vice Harold H. Greene.

Submitted September 19, 1978

CARIN ANN CLAUSS, of Virginia, to be United States District Judge for the District of Columbia, vice Howard F. Corcoran, retired.

H. BROOKS PHILLIPS, of Mississippi, to be United States Marshal for the Northern District of Mississippi.

J. CLAY SMITH, JR., of the District of Columbia, to be a member of the Equal Employment Opportunity Commission for the term expiring July 1, 1982, vice Colston A. Lewis, term expired.

NORVAL MORRIS, of Illinois, to be Administrator of Law Enforcement Assistance, vice Richard W. Velde, resigned.

HOMER F. BROOME, JR., of California, to be Deputy Administrator for Administration of the Law Enforcement Assistance Administration, vice Paul K. Wormeli, resigned.

NOMINATIONS—Continued

Submitted September 19—Continued

HENRY S. DOGIN, of New York, to be Deputy Administrator for Policy Development of the Law Enforcement Assistance Administration, vice Henry F. McQuade, resigned.

Submitted September 21, 1978

MARSHALL W. WILEY, of Florida, a Foreign Service officer of Class two, to be Ambassador Extraordinary and Plenipotentiary of the United States of America to the Sultanate of Oman.

THOMAS S. WILLIAMSON, JR., of the District of Columbia, to be Deputy Inspector General of the Department of Energy (new position).

Submitted September 22, 1978

DONALD K. PETTERSON, of California, a Foreign Service officer of Class one, to be Ambassador Extraordinary and Plenipotentiary of the United States of America to the Somali Democratic Republic.

GOODWIN COOKE, of Connecticut, a Foreign Service officer of Class two, to be Ambassador Extraordinary and Plenipotentiary of the United States of America to the Central African Empire.

CHECKLIST OF WHITE HOUSE PRESS RELEASES

The following releases of the Office of the White House Press Secretary, distributed during the period covered by this issue, are not included in the issue.

Released September 16, 1978

Fact sheet: Federal Emergency Management Agency reorganization plan (No. 3 of 1978)

Released September 18, 1978

Advance text: address before a Joint Session of the Congress on the Camp David meeting on the Middle East

Released September 19, 1978

Announcement: nomination of Carin Ann Clauss to be United States District Judge for the District of Columbia

Announcement: nomination of H. Brooks Phillips for reappointment as United States Marshal for the Northern District of Mississippi

CHECKLIST—Continued

Released September 20, 1978

Advance text: remarks at the United Steelworkers of America convention in Atlantic City, N.J.

Fact sheet: surface transportation legislation pending in the Congress

News conference: on the surface transportation legislation pending in the Congress—by Secretary of Transportation Brock Adams, and James T. McIntyre, Jr., Director, and W. Bowman Cutter, Executive Associate Director for Budget, Office of Management and Budget

Released September 22, 1978

Fact sheet: Federal-State partnership in rural development to achieve balanced growth in North Carolina

---

ACTS APPROVED BY THE PRESIDENT

Approved September 17, 1978

H.R. 6669_____ Public Law 95–367
National Climate Program Act.

H.R. 2931_____ Public Law 95–368
An act to amend chapter 89 of title 5, United States Code, to establish uniformity in Federal employee health benefits and coverage by preempting certain State or local laws which are inconsistent with such contracts, and for other purposes.

H.R. 10899_____ Public Law 95–369
International Banking Act of 1978.

H.R. 12240_____ Public Law 95–370
Intelligence and Intelligence-Related Activities Authorization Act for Fiscal Year 1979.

H.R. 2952_____ Private Law 95–53
An act for the relief of Master Sergeant William E. Boone, United States Army, retired.

Approved September 18, 1978

H.J. Res. 1014_____ Public Law 95–371
A joint resolution designating April 28 and 29 of 1979 as "Days of Remembrance of Victims of the Holocaust".

S. 9_____ Public Law 95–372
Outer Continental Shelf Lands Act Amendments of 1978.

H.R. 13468_____ Public Law 95–373
District of Columbia Appropriation Act, 1979.

ACTS APPROVED—Continued

Approved September 18—Continued

H.R. 12927_____ Public Law 95–374
Military Construction Appropriation Act, 1979.

S. 1633_____ Public Law 95–375
An act to provide for the extension of certain Federal benefits, services, and assistance to the Pascua Yaqui Indians of Arizona, and for other purposes.

H.R. 10878_____ Public Law 95–376
An act to extend until October 1, 1981, the voluntary insurance program provided by section 7 of the Fishermen's Protective Act of 1967, and for other purposes.

Approved September 19, 1978

S. 3454_____ Public Law 95–377
An act to amend the Act of August 29, 1974 (88 Stat. 795; 10 U.S.C. 8202 note), relating to the authorized numbers for the grades of lieutenant colonel and colonel in the Air Force and to authorize the President to suspend certain provisions of law when he determines that the needs of the Armed Forces so require, and for other purposes.

Approved September 22, 1978

H.R. 8112_____ Public Law 95–378
An act to repeal chapter 27 of title 44, United States Code.

H.R. 12915_____ Public Law 95–379
An act to amend section 2301 of title 44, relating to the National Archives Trust Fund Board.

H.R. 13087_____ Public Law 95–380
An act to authorize the issuance of substitute Treasury checks without undertakings of indemnity, except as the Secretary of the Treasury may require.

S. 2928_____ Public Law 95–381
An act to authorize appropriations for the fiscal year 1979 under the International Investment Survey Act of 1976, and for other purposes.

H.R. 9471_____ Public Law 95–382
An act to amend title 5, United States Code, to provide that Japanese-Americans shall be allowed civil service retirement credit for time spent in World War II interment camps.

S. 3107_____ Public Law 95–383
An act to amend the Bankruptcy Act to provide for uniform supervision and control of employees of referees in bankruptcy.

Asheville, North Carolina

Remarks on Arrival at the Asheville Municipal Airport. September 22, 1978

Senator Bob Morgan, Governor Jim Hunt, former Governor Bob Scott, my good friend Congressman Lamar Gudger, Congressman Hefner, and Congressman Mann, Mayor Trantham, Mayor Todd, Chairman White, Chairman McCain, many people in the audience who are responsible for my being President, who share with me the successes and the blame:

I'm glad to be back home in North Carolina—even if I am 1 week late. [*Laughter*] It is partially your credit that we finally ended the Camp David summit with success, because I was eager to come back to North Carolina, and I wasn't the only one who was eager to leave. [*Laughter*]

The last day, when everything seemed to be going wrong, Prime Minister Begin came up to me and said, "Mr. President, I promise that Israel will get out of the Sinai, if you'll let me get out of Camp David." [*Laughter*]

It's a good time for all of us in politics and government. In a person's private life, there are times of struggle, times of disappointment, times of challenge, times of failure, times of hope and times of dreams, times of success and notable achievement, times of prayer and times of thanksgiving. And I have felt throughout the last 20 months, and particularly the last 2 or 3 weeks, that your prayers were indeed with me.

We have a great country. It's always a mistake for us to overemphasize the transient or rapidly changing problems that we face. Our country has always been willing to face great challenges and to overcome difficulties and to meet difficult challenges and to answer tough questions. We've not changed. We still have the same pioneer spirit that bound us together 200 years ago, or even earlier.

My people, the Carter family, moved from North Carolina longer than 200 years ago. And we've always had a kinship with your State and a realization that there was a role for the individual human being in a democratic, free society that could contribute, no matter whether one had a service station or a peanut farm or was occupying the White House. We are party to a team effort and a team spirit that's not going to stop, not going to pause. We're going to continue to make our Nation and to keep our Nation the greatest one on Earth. You can depend on that, if I can depend on you.

I'm particularly glad to come here with Lamar Gudger. Although he is new in Congress, he's no newer than I am in the White House—[*laughter*]—and I have felt particularly close to him. I looked at a clipping from a local newspaper not too long ago, and it said that although I had

1575

very good support from the North Carolina congressional delegation, that the best support from any Congressman in Washington from North Carolina was from your friend and my friend, Lamar Gudger. I thank him, and I thank you for sending him there. And I have to make one request of you: When November comes, I want you to send him back with the biggest margin of any Democratic candidate in the whole United States.

He has helped me on things that are important to you, along, I have to admit, with other people on this platform—Bob Scott and the other Members of Congress.

When I went into the White House, we had a very serious series of problems. As a farmer, as a warehouseman, as someone who's lived in agriculture all my life, I know how bad the farm depression was 20 months ago, 24 months ago. Those of you who are interested in agriculture, think back—prices were going down that the farmers got for our products, prices that they paid for fertilizer, seed, equipment were going up much more rapidly. Net farm income was dropping.

Last year, October 1, on my birthday, we put into effect a brand new agriculture bill. And since then, farmers' spirits, farmers' well-being have been going up. This is a great stride forward.

Another problem that I had when I became President was the high unemployment rate that Bob Morgan mentioned. When I became President, there were 10 million Americans who could not find a full-time job. More than 7 million Americans did not have a job at all. The unemployment rate had been going up steadily almost for the preceding 8 years. And the Congress and I formed a partnership to try to do something about it. Since that time, we've had a net increase of over 6 million new jobs in the United States.

The unemployment rate has dropped 2

full percentage points nationwide, and it's holding steady and progressing in the direction that you want it to move. This could not have been done without cooperation. And one of the best things about our programs that we've put forward is that we've done it not depending just on government handouts and jobs—they've been important for some special groups— but we've tried to strengthen the private enterprise system to let private jobs, permanent jobs be the root of the progress we have made. And that's what we're going to do in the future.

I've always been concerned about the Government bureaucracy. I talked about it a lot during the campaign. It's one of the reasons I was elected President. I thought it was bad, but when I got to Washington, it was a lot worse than I thought it was. And we've done something about it.

Early last year, the Congress gave me the authority to reorganize the structure of Government, and we've put forward a series of reorganization plans. There's not been a single one refused by the Congress. This is an extraordinary, unprecedented achievement.

In the past, Democratic and Republican Presidents have only been successful in having the Congress approve about one out of three of the proposals made. But it shows the harmony that does exist between a Democratic Congress and a Democratic President answering the demands of the American people.

For the first time in almost a hundred years, we now have civil service reform on the verge of being passed, thanks to many of you who've let your Members of Congress know how important it is to you.

We've got hundreds of thousands of competent, dedicated public servants who work under the civil service system. They want to do a better job. They want to see excellence and dedicated employees rewarded. They don't want to see someone sitting next to them, loafing and incompetent, promoted and paid at the same rate. So, what this new law will do is to let us reward good employees, correct the defects among those that are not very good, inspire them to work harder or fire them if they don't work, and let managers manage the Government, save you money, give you better services. Everybody wins all the way around.

I just want to mention one other thing, since I'm in North Carolina and know how you feel. My professional career, as you know, was in the Navy. I was a submarine officer, and I went to the U.S. Naval Academy. I believe in a strong defense. And as long as I and these men are serving you in Washington, we're going to have a strong defense—one so strong that no one will dare to attack us with any thought that they might be successful. You can depend on that.

But there's another element of defense, and that is strength through character. We don't need to be a bully, trying to push other people around. We don't need to be combative, with a chip on our shoulder at all times. And since I've been in the White House, we have tried to reach out to others, even some of those who have not been quite so friendly with us in the past.

We put our arms around the shoulders of our close friends, who might be living next to one another in a state of war, and we've said, "Let's talk about the problems of our people and bring peace to the world." Sometimes this has been very unpopular, even with some of you.

One of the most difficult decisions that I've ever had to make in politics was to deal with the Panamanian treaty question. Some of you didn't like what we did. I realize that. But we now have a new spirit in Latin America, a strong, friendly spirit of mutual respect—not a great nation or a big brother looking down on others, but one in which we've formed a partnership to strengthen those ties of friendship, democratic principles, preservation of human rights. And with that strength, we can keep out the spread of communism in our own hemisphere.

We tried to deal fairly with the Turks and the Greeks to bring peace to Cyprus and to restore the damage that had been done to NATO. And lately, we've reached out to our friends, the Egyptians, and our friends, the Israelis, to bring them, for the first time in 30 years, after four wars, to a state of peace and friendship with open borders and trade and an end to the terrible bloodshed that's wreaked havoc in that area.

So, there is a combination of strong, staunch military commitment on the one hand, and a nation that's clean and decent and a source of pride on the other hand, where people can respect us and where the true spirit of our country can be shown to the rest of the world. And as long as I'm in the White House, I'll continue to exemplify what you are, what our Nation has been, what our Nation has been in the long past, what our Nation is now, what it can be in the future.

I believe in the spirit of commitments that were made 200 years ago, here in your State and mine, and I believe that you want us to raise a banner high of protecting human rights around the world, as we do in our own country, and that's what we're going to have if you'll continue to be partners with us.

I don't want to look too far away from you. We've also recognized that the best government is the one closest to you. I don't believe in a big brother in Washington telling you how to run your business. We've tried to get government's nose out of people's business as best we can, but not in a combative or disputive way. We've formed a good alliance with the mayors here on the platform, with the airport manager here where we stand, with Governor Hunt, and many others. And it's very important that we continue this.

We're trying to make North Carolina a kind of rural laboratory to show that small towns and cities, like where I live, and people who live on farms have a chance for a better life.

Right here where we're standing, even though you've already got some help from the Federal Aviation Administration, I can announce today there will be $2 million more coming in here next month to add 1,500 more feet to your runway, giving you an 8,000-foot runway to connect you with the outside world.

And we've tried to do away with some crazy Federal regulations. In 1 day, earlier this year, OSHA, the Occupational Safety and Health Administration, eliminated 1,100 regulations. We're trying to do the same thing in the Farm Home Administration.

I grew up in an area where there's a lot of oak wood and hickory wood that can't be used for much else except burning. And there's been a regulation that even in a farmhouse, you couldn't have a Farm Home Administration loan to put a fireplace in the living room. But we are taking that regulation out to let folks around here that have trees keep warm in the winter and not spend a lot of money on buying fuel that's produced in Oklahoma and Texas.

We had another regulation that said when you build a house, you had to provide money for curbs and gutters. Well, where I grew up in the country, we didn't need curbs and gutters. And we are removing that regulation as well.

There's another one that says you couldn't get a Farm Home Administration loan if the grade level in the particular area was more than 15 percent. There are a lot of places around this site we're standing, Asheville, where 15-percent grade looks like flat land. [*Laughter*] So, we are making changes like this to make your life better.

I might say in closing that I need your help. We've had some successes, we've got some challenges ahead. I'm very grateful to you to come out and meet me today. I ask you to help politically as well.

I realize there are a lot of Democrats here, I realize there are a lot of Republicans, there are a lot of people who don't have any party affiliation. But I hope you'll give your careful attention to electing John Ingram to the U.S. Senate and Lamar Gudger to the Congress, to give the kind of spirit that I try to exemplify in my own political life—a deep care about people who need help most, who want to stand on their own feet, make their own decisions, arrange their own lives, be proud of their own government, work closely with the local government, respect the officials, respect one another, live in a nation that's strong and peaceful.

Those are the kind of things I want; they're the kind of things you want. Together, you and I, we can have them in our country in the future.

Thank you very much. God bless every one of you.

NOTE: The President spoke at 4:50 p.m. In his opening remarks he referred to Mayors Roy Trantham of Asheville and Frank Todd of Hendersonville, N.C., John C. White, chairman of the Democratic National Committee, and Betty McCain, chairman of the Democratic Party in North Carolina.

Asheville, North Carolina

Remarks at a Reception for John Ingram.
September 22, 1978

Senator Morgan and Governor Jim Hunt,
Congressman Lamar Gudger, Wallace
Hyde, who, along with the others, helped
make it possible for me to be elected, and
your next Senator, John Ingram:

I don't have any particular remarks prepared tonight. But as I was sitting here on the stage, some thoughts went through my mind that I think are, perhaps, similar to those that went through yours.

As I listened to John Ingram talk, he obviously is a man who is quiet and sincere. He may not be as sophisticated as some of you, and neither am I, but there's a genuineness about him that appeals to me. I believe he means what he says. And I know when I first began to run for President, not many people thought I had a chance. A few of you thought so, and you helped me. And a few months ago when John Ingram decided to run for the U.S. Senate, many of you, even the strongest, most loyal, most knowledgeable Democrats, didn't think he had a chance. And when you got ready to give a campaign contribution, the chances are that you probably gave it to another fine man, Luther Hodges, or maybe some of the other candidates, Mr. Davis, or others.

But there was something in John Ingram that the people liked and trusted. It's hard to say exactly what it is, because you can't analyze the inner character of a man. But I believe a lot of women thought back about how he treated them in establishing insurance rates.

We hear a lot about the rights of women and treating them fairly and decently and giving them a chance for a job and equal pay, taking care of widows. But not many insurance commissioners around the country have been sure that insurance rates were fair to women.

A lot of young people, young men just as good as you and I, just as good as the young ladies, have long been stigmatized and condemned and made to pay higher insurance rates because a few are careless and reckless. And it's an easy thing to overlook something like that and say, "Well, all of them are not to be trusted." But in a strange way, because I think he's close to people, John Ingram said, "Well, young people can be trusted." And the insurance rates for young men and women in North Carolina are just about the lowest in the whole country because he had confidence in them.

I noticed when he introduced his wife, he was really proud of her. And I could tell that he really meant it when he called his three daughters up here and his son, and said, "These are the people that make me strong." Some might think, well, that's kind of a corny thing to do. Well, if so, I'm corny, too, because that's the way I feel about my family.

You don't have to be a college professor, you don't have to be a distinguished lawyer, you don't have to be someone who's rich to understand what people need in Washington, in the White House or in the Congress, or in the State legislature or the Governor's mansion. What you need is someone who's close to the people and who, although he might be 40, 50, 60 years old, still understands what it means to be young and what it means to be young in spirit and the special problems of those who need help.

I'm a Democrat by inheritance and by conviction and by experience. And I see some things that are special in my own party that make me proud. I think John Ingram, Lamar Gudger, represent those kinds of things; Bob Morgan represents those kinds of things; Jim Hunt represents those kinds of things.

We've always been eager to reach a hand out to someone who was in need, not down as though we were superior to them, but reach out as a brother or a sister, and say, "You're having a tough time now, perhaps you don't have a job, perhaps you haven't had a chance to get a good education, perhaps you are a farmer with just a few acres of land and not much capital, perhaps you're a young married person, you don't yet have the finances to buy a home, perhaps your parents have never been to college or your grandparents, and you, for the first time, are trying to get a better education than they."

Well, those are the kind of people that the Democrats have always cared about; even rich Democrats are concerned about those things. And in doing that, they exemplify the finest aspects of a genuine Southern—you might say—conservatism. Because we believe that the best way to invest our money and taxpayers' money is in people, to give them a chance to take whatever talent God might have given them—sometimes not much talent—but to use it, through better education programs, housing programs, farm programs, to let people stand on their own feet, answer their own questions, make their own decisions, run their own lives and, in the process, contribute, to let the rest of us have a better life.

This is not something to be scorned or condemned, when you invest in people. And I'm proud of the Democratic Party because it's what it is. I grew up as a politician, as a very young politician—I haven't been in it long—in the South. When a lot of people said, "Well, I believe in what the Democratic Party stands for; I really appreciate what Franklin Roosevelt did to change my life in the Depression or what Harry Truman did, kind of a down-to-earth, honest, tough

fighter"—I appreciate those things— "the idealism of John Kennedy." But one thing that Democrats have always had to suffer from, particularly in the South, is that we had the reputation, which we did not deserve, of being fiscally irresponsible.

Now, that's changed. The reputation has changed. The facts are that it has never been true. But last month, the Gallup Poll for the first time showed that twice as many people in this country said that Democrats are fiscally responsible than they did Republicans.

And the reason for it is that we've been trying, since I've been in Washington and long before, Democrats have, to get control of the Government, to get control of the bureaucracy, because again, the bureaucracy really consists of good people, people like you and me, who—perhaps younger—said, "I've got one life to live, and I want to spend my life serving others." At first, service in the Federal Government was a very low-paying thing; it's getting better. But they've got one life to live; they want to invest it in America.

But the problem has been that for the last 100 years, the civil service has not been modified to let them do a better job. And I thought it was a good idea, when I was running for President, to promise that we would reform the civil service to let excellent, dedicated, competent, qualified employees be rewarded, and to let those who are not so competent or not so dedicated be inspired or urged to do better, or to be transferred or fired.

I think it helps all around, because it's not good for one person to be sitting here at a desk working hard all day, competent, and for their neighbor, who's incompetent or lazy, to get the same pay, the same promotion, the same privileges, for not doing a job that the other person then has to do for them.

So, we've come close now to completely reforming the civil service system. We can let good employees be rewarded, bad ones be better, let managers manage, get a better return on your investments in government, provide better services for our people. We win all along. And that's part of what the Democratic Party is trying to do.

I believe in balanced budgets. I don't believe in wasting money, and I believe I represent in my own beliefs what most Democrats also want to see in Washington.

When I was running for President in 1976, the Federal deficit was over $60 billion, $66 billion. And I resolved to do something about it. My first budget that I presented to the Congress was in the fifties of billions of dollars. The next budget was in the forties of billions of dollars. That's the one Congress is working on now—we might get a little under forty. In 1980, the fiscal year that I'm preparing now, it's going to be well down in the low thirties. We're bringing the budget down into balance and, at the same time, we're not cutting short on the delivery of services. We're providing the needs of America, and that's what Democrats have always stood for.

As I said this afternoon at the airport, I believe in a strong defense. I spent 11 years of my life in the Navy, at the Naval Academy, on battleships, in submarines. And I know that throughout the world, people depend on us to be strong enough militarily so that no other nation can successfully even hope to challenge the United States of America. But there's more to strength than just military weapons. We've got to keep the weapons, but strength also comes from being a clean nation, a decent nation, a truthful nation.

And I think you all remember that in the last few years, we had lost that reputation. In Vietnam, and with Watergate, and with the CIA revelations where they had violated the law, a lot of people began

to lose confidence in us, and we began to lose confidence in ourselves. But I think with the close coordination of a Democratic President and a Democratic Congress, we've begun to repair that damage. And I think it's accurate to say that all over the world now there's not a single head of a nation, whether they serve in a totalitarian society or a democratic society, that every day they don't think about basic human rights—are they treating their own people fairly? And this has been like raising a banner around which we could rally once more and of which our friends and we both could be proud.

And, of course, we believe in peace. I'm proud that in the last 20 months or so we've not had a single American soldier lose a drop of blood in a foreign war. And I hope when I go out of office, we still can say the same thing. But that's peace through strength, not weakness.

So, you can see that I'm prejudiced on behalf of the Democratic Party and what it stands for. But we've got our problems. We don't claim to know all the answers. Sometimes, even in a State like yours, the Democratic Party has not worked as a team. I've been disappointed not too many years ago to see Republicans, in effect, take over in your State. But now we've come back.

And I would like to ask you tonight, as a special request from the President of the United States and the titular head of the Democratic Party, to resolve in your own minds and hearts to try to repair that damage that has occurred in the past. You've already demonstrated by coming here tonight that you believe in the same things that I believe in. But I hope that you will leave here tonight committed to making sure that we have two Democratic Senators in Washington next January.

It's not going to be easy. I recognize that. But if every one of you would not only be satisfied with what you've done tonight with a contribution—that didn't hurt any of you—but if you would go home and start thinking about what more you can do, there's no doubt in my mind that every one of you, no matter how old or young, even very young people could raise 5 or 10 times as much as you've contributed tonight. Send it in to help the candidates here on the stage, and kind of organize yourselves as campaign managers.

You're not servants. You're not followers. You're inherent natural leaders. And I think the good thing that you can do to show your leadership capability is to invest it in something you love—your country.

So, it wouldn't hurt you to organize your block, or to organize your community, or perhaps the whole town or county, and demonstrate once again that we have a spirit in the Democratic Party that wants to repair past damages, answer difficult questions, reach deep within our hearts and restore the spirit and the idealism, the truthfulness that has long exhibited what the Democratic Party stands for and what our country is.

So, help us all. Let's elect John Ingram and Lamar Gudger, and not only that, but show the people of North Carolina and our country that we are still as great as we used to be and that we can be even greater in the future.

I'm very proud of you, and I thank you for giving me your confidence to serve as President. Government can't do everything for people, and my inspiration comes from you. But I'm glad that you and I form a partnership, a kind of a political team of which I'm proud, very proud. And I'm also proud that we have a chance to exhibit this team spirit in the greatest nation on Earth.

Thank you very much.

NOTE: The President spoke at 6:34 p.m. in the Deer Park Pavilion at the Biltmore Estate. Dr. Wallace Hyde is chairman of the Ingram for Senate Fundraiser.

Columbia, South Carolina

Remarks at a Fundraising Reception and Dinner for Charles Ravenel. September 22, 1978

I think that's one of the best introductions I ever had. [*Laughter*] And it's obvious that Pug means what he says, that he's very excited about being in the same place as the President. And I suggest that in January, you send him to Washington to be with me for a long time.

As you know, I was supposed to come last week. And I'm very interested in this race in South Carolina and seeing Pug win. I thought the best thing to do was to delay the Camp David proceedings for about a week and see if I couldn't boost my own popularity a little before I came up here. [*Laughter*] And I'm very grateful to say that because of your prayers and the support of many people and the presence of two truly great men at Camp David, Prime Minister Begin and President Sadat, that we have been successful in taking the first step of what I think is inevitably going to lead very shortly to a peace treaty between Israel and Egypt.

To me, this is indicative of a kind of new tone or interrelationship among people, perhaps throughout the whole world. Those of you here in South Carolina, those of us in Georgia, are descended from people who know what it means to go through a terrible war and to live under occupation and to struggle to restore what we've lost and then to rise to new heights of achievement and common purpose.

I think this is the sense that I get throughout our own Nation now, because we have had some very bad years, with the Vietnam war and the Watergate embarrassments, the CIA revelations of violation of U.S. laws. But I think there's a determination on the part of American people to have a nation and a government of which we can be proud once again, and also a nation of which the entire world can be proud.

There's a great determination, I think, to have peace. And the change in attitude and demeanor, the dropping of ancient, unwarranted demands, the shuffling away from longstanding hatreds, the forgetting of four wars in 30 years by the two leaders of Egypt and Israel was, I think, a part of a growing sense in the world that things can be better if people can work together for a common purpose.

I was Governor of Georgia for 4 years, and I watched the campaign of Pug Ravenel 4 years ago. It was like a breath of fresh air that swept across the South. There was a lot of inspiration in it for us. I never had met Pug Ravenel. I came to South Carolina early that year to kick off the campaign of another candidate— [*laughter*]—Congressman Dorn. And it was a bad year for the Democratic Party, because the victor in the primary, because of a legal technicality, was deprived of the right to represent the South Carolina people.

This is not typical of our party. It was an extra-party thing, legal thing. I don't have any background in law; I'm not criticizing what was decided then. But it was a loss to South Carolina. And there were a lot of bitter feelings left over from it.

The supporters of other candidates felt that the party didn't come back together quickly enough to repair the divisions that had been caused, through no one's fault. Now is a different time, and if we are not successful in November—I think we will be—but if we are not successful in November, the only reason will be that you didn't grasp this additional opportunity to have the leadership of this fine young man and to heal old wounds, as we have together healed old historical wounds in the South, and to resolve together to reach

for an element of achievement and height of accomplishment and greatness of which I believe Pug Ravenel is capable.

It's nice of you to come tonight and to make a substantial contribution, and I'm grateful for your doing it. So is Pug. But that's not enough. There is probably no one here—with maybe just a very few exceptions—who couldn't give much more, and I'm sure there's no one here who coudn't go back home and raise 10 times as much among your own neighbors and friends who trust you and who would be willing to make an investment in South Carolina's future.

I hope that you won't be satisfied with just having done this small thing to help a man who, in effect, has devoted his last 4 years paying off old debts and getting prepared to present his ideas, his hopes, and his dreams for South Carolina to the people who live in this State. You know the formidable opposition he has and the immense finances that have come in to help his opponent, not only from South Carolina but from other States.

I think the financial part is something that's particularly of interest to you, because you've been blessed by God with great financial security, most of you have, and you can, among your own friends, help him in that way. But I recognize in many of you additional elements of leadership that quite often are not adequately tapped, maybe for your own professional business, yes. But I think you can take the next week or 2 weeks, or perhaps a month or two, and make an investment of your own great talent and ability in the future of our country. Organize your own family, your own block, your own community, suburb, neighborhood, your own county, on behalf of Pug Ravenel. Join in with those who've been active for him in the past. I need him in Washington.

You've got a superb United States Senator, Fritz Hollings, there, who helps me and helps you and helps the country. He's a man of great dignity, self-assurance, competence, knowledge, experience as Governor of your State, and a man of great compassion. I first heard about him when he was concerned about hungry people, mostly blacks, mostly little children that public officials had not thought about ever before. And I observed the attention that he gave them and the book he wrote about them and learned a lot from it and from him.

We need two men of that quality to represent South Carolina. And it's really up to you. A few people like this, a relatively small group in a big State can make all the difference in the world if you really care. I care. I know Pug Ravenel cares. Fritz Hollings cares. And I want all of you to care as well.

This is a time for us to make a sacrifice. We are rising now, I think, very rapidly to reach those elements of success and the goals that we've set for ourselves. I think that you can be part of it. And I would feel better knowing that we had a solid partnership, whether you might have supported another candidate in the past or not, whether you've been a completely devoted Democrat in the past or not, whether you've ever been active in politics in the past or not.

There are no defects in this man that I can discern. I know him well, and I know you know him perhaps even better. I believe that we're ready for him, and I believe with your help, he'll be in Washington next January to help me.

I'm going to go in a few minutes over to speak to a larger group. I hope you'll join us there. I want to talk about a few issues that are important to our country.

My speech will be brief. I haven't had much rest this week. I've had to double up on my trips that I couldn't take last week and had a lot of paperwork left over because we really stayed at Camp David

longer than I thought. But there are some things I want to say to you and to them. And I just want to say let's work together to send Pug Ravenel to the Senate.

You'll be doing me, your President, South Carolina, your State, and the United States, your Nation, a great favor.

Thank you.

[The President spoke at 8:45 p.m. at the reception on the grounds of the residence of Jeff Hunt, a South Carolina businessman. Following his remarks, he went to another area on the grounds where he addressed guests at the dinner at 9:25 p.m. as follows:]

THE PRESIDENT. I think when I leave here, I'll take Pug Ravenel tomorrow to Ohio and Pennsylvania to introduce me there.

MR. RAVENEL. Mr. President, I'm never leaving this State again. *[Laughter]*

THE PRESIDENT. For the last 4 years, I've been trying to get Pug to come to Plains—*[laughter]*—and he wouldn't cross the Savannah River until after this election. But I think next January he'll be making a trip. And we'll let him come home every weekend or two to let you know what he's doing in the United States Senate, representing you.

As I listened to Pug's glowing introduction, a thought went through my mind. There is a uniqueness about the Presidency, it's a lonely job. Except for prayer, you don't have any place to turn. When things go bad, you get entirely too much blame. *[Laughter]* And I have to admit that when things go good, you get entirely too much credit. *[Laughter]*

I was able to spend the last 2 weeks with two strong and courageous men. And the decisions they made violated ancient history, generations of hatred and death. Both of them took great political chances in changing their past political commitments—you might say their campaign promises; they had to violate some of them. But they were eager to reach for peace. There was a change in the Middle East in the attitude of people, and I believe that we'll make rapid progress now in bringing a peace treaty between Israel and Egypt.

President Sadat had a heart attack not long ago; so did Prime Minister Begin. And Sadat is very careful about his health. He gets up early every morning and takes a long walk, 4 kilometers, takes an hour. He's a military man, a very brisk walk. He comes back and takes calisthenics about another half hour or so; he says acrobatics, gymnastics. And then it's about 10 o'clock in the morning before he's ready to go to work.

But on several occasions I got up early and did my homework with members of my staff, and as President Sadat passed my cabin, I went out and walked with him. He's a man of great strength. One morning he said something that I thought you might be interested in. He said, "I believe that you have a sensitivity about our problems in the Middle East because you're from the South, because the South is the only part of the United States and southerners are the only people in the United States that really know what it means to suffer the tortures of the aftermath of a war in an occupation government and deprivation for a while and a struggle for the overcoming of prejudice and hatred between one race and another."

And he said, "I believe that has given you not only a special insight but perhaps an additional commitment to bring a resolution between two people that have long hated each other."

I've come here tonight still tired, haven't had any time off yet. I had to postpone this meeting from last week till tonight. I've already been to New Jersey this week, and go to two more States tomorrow; just came from North Carolina.

But I've come here because I believe in something. I believe in what our Nation has been in the past, is becoming now, and can be in the future. I believe in the Southland. I believe in the people of South Carolina, where my grandmama came from. And I believe in the people of Georgia. And I've seen just in my own political lifetime, which has been very brief, a repairing of ancient divisions.

The last President that came from the South, I think, was in 1848—not because we weren't good people, not because we weren't competent politicians, not because we weren't natural leaders, but because there were divisions that couldn't be healed; maybe because we didn't set our sights high enough, because when one of our southerners would run for President, it would probably be on a racist ticket, running against blacks or against the poor. But we've overcome that now, and we are taking the lead in the whole Nation in binding our country back together. And the rest of the country is proud of it, too.

And we have shown the way to pull white and black people together again in a spirit of harmony and friendship and mutual trust and absolute equality. We haven't repaired all the damage yet, because there are a lot of black children, as there are a lot of white children, who are very poor, who, because their parents didn't have an adequate opportunity, don't yet have one. And I think we see that clearer perhaps than folks who live in other parts of the country.

I'm a Democrat because our party has always seen better than the other party that the best investment of our natural resources and our money was in people— to give a child of ignorant parents a chance for an education, to give a sick person a chance for good health care, to tear down barriers between people, to let young married couples have a chance to own a home, to have farmers who were destitute during the Depression years have a chance to live in dignity for a change.

The Democratic Party has always been the center of reaching out to help people, not as a gift, but to repair a damage to them and to recognize in them an innate worth that God had given them and to give every human being, no matter how poor or how deprived, no matter how tiny their talents might have been, a chance to stand on their own feet, to make their own decisions, to work productively, to be a part of society.

The Democratic Party has always had a heart. And I'm proud of that. These men and women who sit on the stage with me tonight, your senior Senator, exemplify those qualities. Your next Governor, my good friend Dick Riley, exemplifies those qualities; Jack Bass typifies those qualities; your congressional delegation on my left and right, who are there working with me, show those qualities to the Nation.

I've tried to come into the White House not as someone who knew all the answers, but as someone who brought a fresh view.

I spent 2 years campaigning around this country. As you well know, when I first started, I was a laughingstock. Nobody thought I had a chance. But I worked, and my wife worked, my family worked, many of you worked. Some of you had great confidence in me. I did enter 30 primaries—and won. I've never served in Washington before, I never lived in Washington before. But I think I have a background that qualifies me at least to know what the people hunger for.

We've made some changes for the better, with the help of these men on the stage. I think we've spelled out programs in the future that will keep us busy for the next 2 years or more. I feel that we've got a task given by you, and as I was elected with your help, I think we can succeed with your help.

I'm interested in a lot of races in this country, but there is no political campaign in the United States in which I am more deeply and personally interested than to see a victory won by Pug Ravenel in November.

If you'll excuse my saying so, I think we have a lot in common, which is a compliment to me. His family moved to South Carolina about 200 years ago; mine moved to Georgia about 200 years ago. Our families were never rich. My father was a working man; so was his. My parents were not well educated. I don't think anybody in my family before me had ever finished high school or been to college; I don't know about his. But I had the chance to go off and get a good education at the U.S. Naval Academy. And Pug had a chance to go up North and get a good education because he worked four part-time jobs, had a scholarship—was an outstanding athlete; I was not. He's brought something back to South Carolina that's precious, as did I when I went off for 11 years in the Navy.

When I became Governor of Georgia, I had made friends all over the United States who had become executives in large corporations and businesses. And when I began to recruit new industry, new jobs into Georgia, I called my friends. And they helped Georgia.

Pug Ravenel has got a much broader base of friendship in that area than I ever had. And there's no doubt in my mind that those few years he spent outside of South Carolina can pay rich dividends for you in the future, because there's an intense interest among those who know Pug best, in seeing him exert a position of leadership not only for South Carolina but for the whole country. And that experience he's had as a young man will pay off greatly for you.

He's a man who's been through a political campaign and lost. I ran for Governor in 1966 and I lost. And my loss resulted eventually in Lester Maddox being Governor of Georgia. And I felt like it was a setback for me and Georgia and the South, without any criticism of him. But I think there are some things about South Carolina that can be improved, politically speaking, not in the Democratic Party, but in this election coming up.

I think this is a time for inspiration in our country and in this particular campaign. We need to forget about some things in the past. It's time we had two United States Senators from South Carolina who vote yes for matters of importance, who are willing to invest in people, who are concerned about raising standards, not lowering standards.

Pug Ravenel is a man who believes in a strong military defense; so do I. It's my profession, the only profession I ever had, except farming. But I see very clearly, as does he, that a strong defense means more than just airplanes and tanks and atomic missiles and ships. The strength of a nation also rests in the spirit of its people, in ideals that don't change, in beliefs that are realized, in trust in government, in the search for peace, repairing damage with other nations, trusting other people, setting the standard, raising a banner of human rights. These kinds of things are what make a nation great within and also make a nation great and strong in international affairs. And we need candidates who become public officials who base their own strength, their own influence, their own decisions, their own wisdom, on the folks back home, who don't get separated from them, and who try to heal differences and not create new differences.

We've still got some problems in Washington that need solving. We're making good progress on energy, good progress on civil service, but there are still some ways in which the people of this country, including you, are getting cheated, and I don't like it. I would like to have Pug Ravenel, Jack Bass, other Congressmen, Fritz Hollings, help me with it.

I'll just give you one example, because it's coming up for a decision soon and it's a tough battle, and that is inflation. Inflation robs us all, saps away our strength, particularly those who have fixed incomes or a small savings account or who live on a welfare payment or a pension. It also hurts our Nation's reputation in the world and takes away some of that greatness and strength that I just talked about.

The Congress can do a lot of things. We're trying to get the budget balanced. I believe in it. When I was elected in '76, the deficit was in the high sixties of billions of dollars. In my first budget, I cut it down to $50 billion. This year the Congress, in '79, will turn out a budget, along with me, of about $40 billion. I hope next year to have one down in the thirties of billions of dollars. We're trying to bring it down, but still give people good services.

We are trying to make our system more competitive and do away with the deprivation of people brought about by a twisting of the free enterprise system. We are going to soon pass airline deregulation to let there be competition for a change in air travel.

One of the things that presses on me is a problem with hospital cost containment. There's not anybody here in this audience who's not directly affected by the cost of medical care. And this is one of the most serious problems there is. Now, as you know, hospitals, particularly the private hospitals, are quite often owned and managed by the same people who decide whether or not you go in the hospital, how long you stay, what treatment you get, what the charges to you are.

This is not right. Last year in South Carolina—I looked up the statistics—charges for hospital care to you went up 20 percent in 1 year. Hospital costs are doubling every 5 years. This ought to be changed.

I'm not going to belabor the point, but I want to give you one example of what I mean. I have not had much success in the House in getting hospital cost containment passed, because we had a lot of pressing items on the agenda and not enough attention was given to it. And the special interest groups were putting tremendous effort in keeping it in committee, and they succeeded in the House so far this year. I hope to get it out and get it passed, still.

But Tip O'Neill, the Speaker of the House, a decent, good man, went home for a weekend. And one of his friends, a working man, came up as he was getting on the plane to go back to Washington, with tears in his eyes. He said, "Tip, I think I'm ruined." Tip said, "What's the matter, friend?" He said, "I just got a bill from the hospital, and I can't pay it. My little boy, just a child, fell down and crunched two or three of his teeth up into his gums. It wasn't all that serious. And I took him to the hospital. He stayed in there 1 day, 26 hours to be exact, and the bill is $2,330.99."

Well, that person had his problem presented to the President of the United States, because his friend was the Speaker of the House. But there are a lot of people like you around this country that are presently being cheated and charged too much for hospital care, because we've not yet been able to break the will and the influence of the special interest groups who are fighting against you. I'm determined to change that. And there are some other things, too, that I'm not going into to-

night. But I need good help, and I would like to ask you as you leave here this evening not to overlook what you've got as a possibility for South Carolina—Pug Ravenel.

You couldn't have a better three top offices if you searched the Nation over than Dick Riley as Governor, Fritz Hollings as your senior Senator, and to replace the other Senator with Pug Ravenel.

I just want to ask you one more question: Do you think that all of us together can elect Pug Ravenel to the Senate? [*Applause*] Right on. I'll do my part if you will.

Thank you very much.

Interview With the President

Remarks and a Question-and-Answer Session With Editors and News Directors.
September 22, 1978

THE PRESIDENT. I'll insist that this is the last time I follow my wife. [*Laughter*] The competition is too great. Also, I'm afraid of the consequences if my statements conflict with hers. [*Laughter*]

I want to welcome all of you to the White House. This is one of a series of meetings that we have had with top newspaper and radio-television executives from around the country since I've been in office. It's been very helpful to me, I think to Jody Powell, and to all the members of my administration here in the West Wing of the White House. Not only have we been able to get across our positions to you privately and in some depth, but we've also had a chance to derive from your own questions a clearer sense of the attitudes and questions and concerns of the American people better than we would ordinarily from the White House news media, who do a good job in their own group, of course.

ADMINISTRATION POLICIES

I think I might take just a few minutes to outline some of my present concerns and plans, and then spend all the time available answering your individual questions. As Rosalynn may have told you, we've enjoyed this responsibility that the American people have given us. We have a good, sound, and stable family life. We have had more time together by far than when I was campaigning and certainly as much as we had while I was Governor of Georgia. We have a good partnership between her and me, and my whole family works on occasion for ceremonial affairs, including my mother and my sons as well, and their wives.

I might point out to you that we've had a wide range of challenging tasks since I have been in the White House. We've put forward some very difficult decisions for Congress to make in domestic and in foreign affairs, and I think the Congress has responded superbly.

In almost every highly controversial matter, in my opinion, the Congress has ultimately made the right decision. Some of those decisions were difficult for them because of the complexity and the disputes that arise, particularly in the field of energy legislation, for instance, on domestic affairs.

I don't think we've ever had a more complicated, far-reaching, highly debated and disputed bill in the history of the Congress than this particular package of legislation. My hope and my expectation is that next week we will have a successful vote on the natural gas bill, which is the heart of the energy package. The other three measures have already been passed relatively easily, relative to the natural gas bill, through the conference committees, and I think the Senate and the House would act on them expeditiously. We have one item concerning oil taxation that may come later or perhaps even this year.

The Congress gave me full authority to reorganize the Government under the reorganization act, and we've had unanimous acceptance by the Congress for every plan we put forward; quite a dramatic change from previous administrations, even Democratic Presidents, when about one out of three were accepted—the other two were rejected by Congress. But we learned from past mistakes that had been made. We've worked very harmoniously with the Congress, and the third reorganization plan of this year has just passed the Congress, almost unanimously, this week.

We've tried to deal effectively with some of the major problems that I inherited. I won't go into detail about them. A year ago, certainly 2 years ago, the overriding concern was about employment. We had about 10 million Americans who could not find a full-time job; between 7 and 8 million who had no jobs at all—8 percent unemployment rate, it was increasing rapidly during the last 8 years. And we've turned that corner now. We have had a net increase of 6 million jobs in the country since I've been in office. And the unemployment rate now, as you know, is slightly below 6 percent, and a very stable reduction. This has been a very good achievement.

We've inherited 10 years of inflation that's of great concern to us now. I'd say on the domestic scene, this is a matter of most concern to the American people, to the political figures in our government structure at all levels, and also to me personally as President.

We're trying to deal with this effectively. One way is to make government more efficient, to hold down budget deficits. I'm determined to work toward a balanced budget as rapidly as possible.

1589

When I ran in 1976, the budget deficit was in the high sixties of billions of dollars. My first budget preparation was for fiscal year 1978. We cut it down to the fifties of billions of dollars. This 1979 will be in the high thirties or low forties of billions of dollars, and the '80 budget will be even lower. So, we have a good, steady, downward trend, strong trend downward in the budget deficit.

Civil service reform was another task that we undertook that was predicted to be completely unsuccessful. But we mounted a massive campaign on that, and as you know, now the House and the Senate have passed the civil service reform relatively intact—first time in a hundred years, it will let American public servants, who give a career of service to other Americans, be rewarded for good service. Poor service can be corrected without unnecessary delay. Managers can manage, and I think the entire government structure will benefit. Of course, the American people will, too.

Those are a few examples on the domestic scene. One that I would like to mention as a farmer is that I think we've turned around the American farm economy. The 1977 bill, which went into effect less than a year ago, has already had very beneficial results among the farm communities and farm families of our country.

In foreign affairs, I've devoted perhaps more time of all to the Mideast. It's been the most all-encompassing problem that I've addressed. This has been a highly controversial matter, because I felt at the beginning that we ought to put the controversial issue on the table, in the public consciousness, and let an open debate take place.

As you well know, I was highly criticized by many for this. It was a political risk. But I think the fact that the American people were aware of questions like Palestinian rights, for instance, addressing the problems, the sensitive problems of the West Bank and Gaza Strip, dealing with the leaders of the Arab world, a recognition of Israel's right to exist, actual peace treaties, open borders, diplomatic relations, these are phrases and terms that had never been addressed before.

The Israeli recognition of the fact that U.N. Resolution 242 and all its parts apply to these things were highly controversial when proposed. But we've had good success on that so far, and I predict a rapid conclusion of the agreement between Egypt and Israel in the Sinai and hopefully open up possibilities for increased relationships between Israel, Jordan, the Palestinians, and their other neighbors.

The Panama Canal Treaty debate was the most bitter and unpleasant experience of my Presidency. It was the most difficult political undertaking that I have ever assumed, including my campaign for President. And the Congress, I think, the Senate made a very courageous decision about this. It opened up a new era for our relationship with the entire Latin American community, and removes the onus—which we certainly didn't deserve, but which did exist in many people's minds around the world—of the last remnants of a colonial inclination on the part of our country. It was a difficult thing to do and perhaps the most troubling vote of the Members of the Senate.

The Turkey arms embargo has now been lifted—will be shortly. We hope this will lead to a resolution of the Cyprus dispute. We've opened up an avenue of better trade relationships, better defense relationships with Egypt and Saudi Arabia with the airplane sale. I think it's leading toward Israeli peace, not against Israeli peace. We've been negotiating without ceasing with the Soviet Union on SALT and other matters.

So, I think we've had some successes along the way; still have some difficult tasks ahead of us. But I believe that in general we've had good coordination of effort in the White House and a very good cooperation with the Congress, quite often on a highly bipartisan basis, particularly in foreign and defense affairs.

I'd like to answer your questions now.

QUESTIONS

NEWSPAPERS AND THE COURTS

Q. Mr. President, I wonder if you have any thoughts that you would like to share with us on the big problems of the newspaper industry now, arising, for instance, in the New York Times Farber case or the Stanford Daily raid, you know, the search warrants instead of subpoenas—or possibly the feeling in the newspaper industry that the judiciary is becoming imperialistic in their attitude towards the press?

THE PRESIDENT. Well, I might say I don't believe the judiciary is becoming imperialistic or abusive toward the press. I think all of American society, almost without exception, including the judiciary, believe that we need to carefully preserve the right of freedom of speech and the right of the news media to report accurately the news and to protect their sources.

The Hartford [Stanford] case, I think, can be resolved either by subsequent rulings or by administrative decisions through the Attorney General—he's professed a desire to do this—or perhaps even by legislation in Congress. The Farber case is one that has confused issues in it. As you know, it will now be decided by the U.S. Supreme Court. I think the New York Times and the defendants in the criminal case are perfectly willing to submit the case to the Supreme Court of the United States for final resolution. But I really

don't feel, as President, observing these issues very carefully, having talked to the Attorney General, when appropriate, and to key congressional leaders, that there is a trend in our country away from protecting the right of freedom of speech or freedom of reporting the news.

My belief is that these particular issues may have dramatized an existing problem which can be resolved quite readily by the U.S. Supreme Court decision in the Farber case, perhaps by corrective legislation or administrative decision in the other.

INFLATION

Q. Mr. President, as you are aware from the result of the newest polls, the wonderful job you did at Camp David with Mr. Begin and President Sadat was received royally. I live in a little mountain village of 2,900 people, and not many of them know Sadat from a hole in the ground, or Begin either. They talk to me about the price of bread and inflation in general.

So, my question is, you did so well on this foreign issue, why can't you get Fitzsimmons and George Meany[1] and the president of General Motors, get them up to Camp David and knock heads together to do something about inflation? [*Laughter*]

THE PRESIDENT. That sounds like a fate worse than death—[*laughter*]—to go back to Camp David, and particularly with that particular group. [*Laughter*] I never thought in my life that I would be glad to leave Camp David and come back to Washington. [*Laughter*] I told the steelworkers the other day that one of the reasons we solved, at least to a limited degree, the Mideast problem was because Begin came to see me and said, "Mr. President,

[1] Frank E. Fitzsimmons, president, International Brotherhood of Teamsters, and George Meany, president, AFL–CIO.

I will get out of the Sinai if you'll let me get out of Camp David." And perhaps if we shut them up long enough, we might. [*Laughter*]

We are now planning another step that will be a tough, strong step in controlling inflation. That will be revealed as soon as the final decisions are made on it. That will be, I think, almost all we can do within the present statutory bounds. I'm not in favor of mandatory price and wage controls, and I don't have any intention of putting them in unless our country reaches an extreme emergency, certainly not any prospect of that at all.

I believe that the international unions will be receptive to a fair and balanced inflation control policy if they feel that others will share the burden with them. And I think it's accurate to say that this is such a wide-ranging question, with many culprits, including Presidents and Congresses, including private citizens who are just homeowners and through purchasing practices encourage inflation, including the employees and employers, those who set prices, those who determine protectionist import policies, that there has to be a general sense that in the entire package of inflation control that it's balanced, that there are no special sacrificial lambs, but that everyone is making an equal sacrifice. That's my responsibility. And I think it would be a mistake to try to blame it, for instance, on a single element in that group, like labor.

I have talked privately, and in some instances publicly, including this week, with large labor groups. And as you well know, when I speak to a convention of farmers or teachers or lawyers or steelworkers or other labor organizations, they are first and foremost Americans. They are people who have families who have to go to the store themselves, who are trying to put their kids through school or through college. They're trying to buy a house or pay

for a car. And they are intensely concerned about inflation, and I think the fact is that recent polls have shown that even among union members, they would be willing to forgo any wage increase if they felt that inflation could be controlled.

And I think the balancing of that package is a difficult thing, but my responsibility. Had it not been for my 2 weeks' vacation—[*laughter*]—I would have already issued these new points to the public. But I'll do that very quickly.

MINNESOTA DEMOCRATIC PARTY

Q. Mr. President, Congressman Fraser just lost the primary election in Minnesota, and there's a better than an even chance that the Republican will win the Senate seat in the November election. And one of the national news magazines has said that Senator Wendell Anderson will also lose that seat to a Republican. That would be quite a switch for Minnesota.

Do you see that as a trend in the future, and do you plan to campaign in Minnesota?

THE PRESIDENT. No, I don't see it as a trend in the future.

Ordinarily, when a President has served for 2 years in a term, even though his popularity in the polls might be extremely high, we've had a 30- to 40-seat loss in the House, for instance. And my guess is that the Congress and I have worked harmoniously enough and that this will be realized, as the Congress Members get down to the last few days or weeks of their campaigning, by the public, that the change will be much less than that. And I feel good about it.

I think also there has been an extraordinary circumstance in Minnesota, perhaps unprecedented, where I think every statewide office is up for election, and where the death of Senator Humphrey has created confusion. And as you know,

Mr. Short, I think, was one of Humphrey's closest friends and supporters, which clouded the issue. He is much more conservative than Don Fraser.

But I don't see any trend at all against Democrats this fall. And I think after the first week in November, you will see that my prediction is accurate.

Q. Mr. President?

THE PRESIDENT. Otis [Otis A. Brumby, Jr., Marietta (Georgia) Daily Journal]?

U.S. ARMS SALES

Q. Mr. President, you speak of imports. I'd like, if I could, to ask you a question about exports, as you know, are very important to our State. We've had stories in our papers; I've seen in other papers in the area that some of your policies, the unilateral policies involving exports, have not, perhaps, had their desired effects. And I'm thinking of the major defense contracts in my area, to transport planes overseas.

What do you say to these people who have lost their jobs, who can't be hired, but they say that several thousand jobs could be created, but they can't go sell because of the unilateral actions you have taken in this area of arms sales?

THE PRESIDENT. Well, I don't have any apology to make for constraining the sale of arms. I think the type of planes, for instance, that Lockheed makes near your home, Mr. Brumby, is one of the items that have been sold with relatively slight constraint.

The C–130 or the Hercules transport plane is one that's used both for defensive purposes, for patrolling, and also in many ways for civilian use. I know when I happened to be Governor of Georgia, I took a trip through South America and saw these same planes being used to haul construction materials into the interior of Brazil, on the Amazon River. I saw the planes being used to haul fish to the inland mountain areas of Peru and to haul breeder cattle into Colombia.

So, I think that the sale of defensive arms, as you've described, have not hurt the prospect for exports, even in this particular industry to which you refer.

I am determined, though, to hold down the overall sale of offensive weapons. We have a very strict arms sales policy not to introduce a high technology weapon in an area where it doesn't presently exist, to cut down year by year the total volume of American arms sales, where in the past this volume has been going up. And this policy is constraining some of our allies and friends so far.

We've also been negotiating, talking to our friends and allies, those like France, Belgium, Great Britain, who have the ability to produce and to sell weapons, to get them to join us in this effort. And we have had several meetings with the Soviet Union—I think three so far—to try to get them to join with us in holding down the volume of weapons sales around the world.

We obviously continue to meet the requirements in a defense way of nations with whom we have mutual defense treaties, like NATO, Japan, Australia, New Zealand, and so forth. But I don't think that this necessary constraint on the volume of arms sales is at all indicative of our policy towards greatly enhancing the export of American manufactured products.

REGULATORY REFORM

Q. Mr. President, in talking to our readers, preparing for this trip, I have heard what amounts to a cry from the small business people that they are being strangled by excessive regulations, that even an owner of a small grain elevator has people coming out from the Department of Labor, from EPA and OSHA.

And we wonder if you have further plans to cut down on the bureaucratic——

THE PRESIDENT. Yes. I'm a small businessman myself, was before I came here. My son runs a grain elevator, a small one in Calhoun, Georgia. And one of the campaign commitments that I made was to cut down on unnecessary regulations.

We've done this very well, I think. And almost any small business person would tell you that within the last 20 months, those regulations and investigations that were obviously unnecessary have been eliminated. We've got a long way to go. It's very difficult to change this process.

We've also issued a directive, which is being carried out, to cut down on the volume of paperwork. The goal that we set for ourselves was a 10-percent reduction this past year. HEW, which was the biggest violator in the past, cut theirs this past 12 months by 17 percent.

We've done this by asking college presidents, small business people and others, State school superintendents—all of whom have been in this room to meet with me—to go back to their own offices and to give me a specific list of the forms and reports they have to file with the Federal Government, to detail for me and for the Office of Management and Budget where duplications exist, where they send the same information to several Federal agencies; also when they think in their own mind that a report can be abbreviated, and when it's a weekly report or a monthly report, how it might be changed into one filed every 6 months or perhaps every year. This has paid rich dividends.

We also now are writing regulations in plain English so that they can be understood. We require the authors of the regulations now to sign them. And for about a month I required every member of my Cabinet to read all the regulations that came out of their department. [*Laughter*] Two of them said that's all they did the

whole—[*laughter*]—every weekend, all the weekends for a month. But I think they got a new appreciation of what people have had to face in the past.

In OSHA we've got a remarkable woman, Dr. Eula Bingham, who is completely dedicated to cutting down on the volume of these unnecessary regulations. She's tried to emphasize writing regulations to protect workers health, like the description of requirements to eliminate chemical substances or fumes that can't be detected by the worker. That needs to be monitored very carefully.

But on safety regulations, we've tried to get away from written directives. I would challenge any of you with your superb professional capabilities to write me a regulation on what is and is not a safe chair, for instance. [*Laughter*] And that was what OSHA was trying to do.

In 1 day this year Eula Bingham terminated the application of 1,100 OSHA regulations. And although a few of those are still on the books—she has to go through a procedure to eliminate them—they are not being enforced. And I know Billy, at his service station, says that the OSHA inspections and regulations are much less onerous than they were before. [*Laughter*]

EDUCATION

Q. This has to do with the reorganization of government and, specifically, the creation of the department of education. I've talked to several self-styled and appointed-type experts in the field of education. And to pinpoint it, they're talking about education by choice, which has several other names. I realize they have two bills pending that would assist education, both at the college level for the middle income, and both at the other intermediate school level.

The question is, it seems to me that there may be a third bill that is needed to look at the overall deterioration of education and if reorganization, if that department of education will not answer that question in several ways.

THE PRESIDENT. We've had by far the greatest increase in allocation of Federal funds for education since I've been in office, than ever before, even under the halcyon days of Lyndon Johnson, when the new elementary and secondary education acts and the higher education acts were passed. I think that was in 1965. This is an achievement in itself.

We've tried to make the administration more effective, and we've tried to constrain some of the unwarranted expenditures like the very high allocation of impact aid to very rich counties. We haven't had complete success, but we are making some progress.

I personally believe that we need a department of education and committed to this when I was campaigning for President. Some of the teachers organizations who are very highly influential, as you know, in Washington and the State legislatures are divided on this issue. The American Federation of Teachers, in general, are opposed to it; the National Education Association and their affiliates around the country are in favor of it.

The reason that I feel that we need a separate department of education, among other things, is that around this table when I meet with my Cabinet, we very seldom have a question concerning education arise.

When I was Governor, I probably spent 25 percent of my time on education. Here I don't spend 1 percent of my time on education. And then quite often when the subject does come up, it involves a controversial lawsuit about the application of Federal regulations concerning civil rights and other important issues in a college or a school, and not on how to give our children a better education, using the substantial amount of Federal funds available.

Another thing that's been highly controversial is the thrust around the country of testing achievement. One of the first things I did as Governor of Georgia, was to implement a comprehensive testing program for students at the fourth grade level, the seventh grade level, and the eleventh grade level—at the fourth grade level, basically to see if the children could read and write and were prepared to go on into the higher grades; at the seventh and eighth grade level, to give them some guidance on their high school career choices; and at the eleventh grade level to give them some guidance on what they could do after they left high school.

I notice North Carolina has just done the same thing. And I strongly believe that there ought to be a testing program available for those States that want it. I am not in favor of a mandated Federal program to be conducted nationwide.

This is a matter in which I differ with some of my own administrators in the Department of Health, Education, and Welfare. But I believe the establishment of a separate department can deal more effectively with our children's needs.

I think by any measurement, our schools are not doing a good enough job, compared to the amount of money we are putting into them. This is proven, at least to some degree, by the results of the SAT tests as children get ready to go into college and so forth. But I believe the increase in expenditure of money carefully focused on basic needs, a proper sharing of State, Federal and local and private funds for children's education, and control of the schools at the local and State level—not at the Federal level—a separate department of education; perhaps some increase in testing programs around the country to encourage better performance by students; analysis of their needs; better performance by teachers—all these things, very briefly, are what I would favor seeing done.

MICHAEL DUKAKIS

Q. Michael Dukakis, the Democratic Governor of Massachusetts, has been defeated in the recent primary. The rumor is rampant in Massachusetts that you'll appoint him to a high Federal post. Is this true?

THE PRESIDENT. I have no idea. [*Laughter*]

Mike Dukakis, in my opinion, is one of the best Governors I have ever known. He's a hard-working, brilliant young man, who perhaps was not quite sensitive enough about political issues. He says what he thinks. He tries to fight for what he believes in. He's had some very difficult challenges as Governor, bringing the budget under control and so forth.

I think he's done an outstanding job. I don't know his opponent well enough to comment on the comparison between the two; Massachusetts Democrats have chosen. But I've never discussed any sort of employment with Mike Dukakis. I don't have anything in mind at all. He would be well qualified to serve in any capacity, in my opinion.

Ms. BARIO. Thank you, Mr. President.

THE PRESIDENT. Yes, sir? One other question.

POSTAL REFORM LEGISLATION

Q. Mr. President, I'd like to know if postal reform legislation now making its way through Congress meets your administration's restrained budget philosophy as described by Mr. Cutter [2] this morning?

THE PRESIDENT. No. [*Laughter*]

Q. Why not?

THE PRESIDENT. I just said one more question. [*Laughter*]

---

[2] W. Bowman Cutter, Executive Assistant for Budget, Office of Management and Budget.

I'm really out of time. I've got another meeting with a group of editors who are here, at the Woodrow Wilson Institute, studying Latin America. And these are people who are constrained to write and to study about Latin America, but have come here for 2 days, I think, to learn more about that subject. And I have to go and meet with them.

I would like to take just a moment to ask each of you, if you have no objection, to come by and let me get a quick photograph with you, and again, to express my thanks for your willingness to come to the White House and, particularly, to learn about our Government.

We don't know all the answers. I'm sure we've made a lot of mistakes. We'll make a lot in the future. But there's a good kind of a sense, I think—at least in the White House—that we are making adequate progress, a good, cooperative attitude between Capitol Hill and the White House. And of course, the most important element is how well we understand and serve the American people represented by you.

So, again, thank you very much for letting me be with you and to have the benefit of your questions and your suggestions.

NOTE: The interview began at 1 p.m. in the Cabinet Room at the White House. Patricia Y. Bario is Associate Press Secretary.

The transcript of the interview was released on September 23.

Interview With the President

Remarks and a Question-and-Answer Session With Senior Editors on Latin American Affairs. September 22, 1978

THE PRESIDENT. Well, it puts me at quite a disadvantage to follow Dr. Brzezinski in describing what our overall policy is, or even the details of Nicaragua. I think all of you have a wonderful opportunity to learn about an exciting subject. And I'm sure that many of you bring long years of experience and study to our own relationships with Latin America and about that region in general.

ADMINISTRATION POLICIES

When I came to the White House as President, I had a longstanding interest in the nations in this hemisphere to the south. My wife and I both studied Spanish in college, and we had made some trips to seven or eight of the Latin American countries while I was Governor and before I became involved in public affairs.

We tried to learn from past mistakes to see what achievements had been realized by Presidents Roosevelt and Johnson, Kennedy and others who had been successful in improving relations with the southern part of our hemisphere during their terms of office. We instituted, after very detailed analyses, some long-range proposals that we thought were needed and also well advised. We didn't want to come out with another special slogan, because I think one of the most important elements that has been missing in the past is the realization that the Latin American countries and the Latin American people are individuals.

It would be a mistake for anyone to look upon Canadians and citizens of Mexico and citizens of the United States as being a homogeneous group. And the diversity in Latin America, the Caribbean, is just as wide. So, what we attempted to do was not only to focus our own attention on peoples and countries as individuals but actually to treat them as such in our public expressions of interest and in our detailed negotiations with them on matters of importance to them.

This was spelled out fairly clearly in some speeches that I made at the Organization of American States and in my visits to the countries involved.

We also began to study some of the problems that still remain from the past. One of the important concerns that we had was the rapid escalations in commitments for weapons in South and Central America, the Caribbean.

We have tried as best we could to put an absolute lid on proliferation of nuclear explosives in this hemisphere, other than those that we ourselves retain for the defense of the hemisphere. The Treaty of Tlatelolco is one on which we've invested a great deal of effort. And we are now approaching the point where all of the Latin American countries involved, and the European and Eastern European countries who have a direct relationship, will also have espoused this commitment not to have nuclear weapons be located within this tremendous and important region of our world. It'll be the first region if we secure the remaining endorsements of the treaty—shortly from, perhaps, Argentina.

The effort that was made at Ayacucho several years ago to restrain the purchase of conventional weapons has also been supported by us. President Pérez and I and others have talked about this at length. And I believe this is another step in the right direction.

We've tried to encourage the settlement of boundary disputes, not as an intervener or even a mediator in some respects, but we've had meetings with the leaders involved, tried to bring them together in regional groups, add the services of the OAS and the United Nations on occasion to resolve these disputes by peaceful means. And I don't know of any heated dispute at this point anywhere in our hemisphere concerning boundaries themselves, unless perhaps it's between us and Canada on the fisheries disagreement off the coast of Maine. [*Laughter*]

I have personally met with 20 heads of state in this hemisphere. And this shows the degree of my interest and the degree of time that I invest in this effort, because it's very important for me, before I meet with the chief of a nation, to know as much as I can about his people and the problems and past history and interrelationships, diplomatic exchanges that have taken place or might take place in the future. But it's been a very productive thing for me.

The biggest cancer that was growing that threatened to destroy our relationship with all the nations to the south was the Panama Canal treaties. We looked upon and look upon the building of the Panama Canal as one of the greatest engineering achievements of all times; as a very benevolent thing that we did, not only for the benefit of ourselves but for the nations in Latin America, and indeed, all the world. And that's true.

But the times have passed when a major nation like ours could, in effect, control permanently territory that divided two parts of a sovereign nation from one another. And this negotiation had been going on 14 years. Although my predecessors had better political judgment than I did and delayed it until the next one took over, but—[*laughter*]—we decided to address it.

At the time, as you may have noticed, a public opinion poll by the Foreign Affairs Institute done by Gallup showed that only 8 percent of the American people favored the consummation of the Panama Canal Treaty. It was the most difficult political undertaking of my life, including even my campaign for the Presidency itself. And to achieve a two-thirds vote in the Senate on a matter that has no positive political benefit, but a lot of very negative political repercussions in some States, was a remarkable display of courage on the part of the U.S. Senate.

We still have a way to go. All our problems have not been resolved yet, even concerning the Canal treaties. But we've laid the groundwork now for a new image of the United States among all of our Latin American friends.

The other thing I would like to mention in particular is the human rights issue. I think it would be a mistake for me or anyone else in our country to try to take credit for the changes that have been made. But I do think that we have helped to dramatize the importance of basic human rights in the dealing of all leaders, in our country and other nations of the world, particularly in Latin America, towards the constituents who have to trust them for the nations' guidance.

In the past, as you know, there have been gross violations of human rights in some of those countries, and also gross violations of human rights in our own country. We've made some progress since the early sixties and fifties in removing some of these embarrassing elements of our own societal structure. And we've been trying to promote the same sort of evolutionary improvements among our friends in Latin America, with a great deal of success.

The Convention on Human Rights of the OAS—we signed it after I became President. At that time, I think we only had two signatories. Now we have 13, enough to put it into effect. The allocation of budget funds and staff for the preservation or enhancement of human rights under the OAS has been tripled just in the last few months.

There's a strong move toward the democratization of governments in Latin America among those that are very stable, among those, as you know, that are not quite so stable.

We've tried to devote some attention to the Caribbean, almost for the first time, on a multinational basis. We formed a Caribbean group of about 30 nations, the primary thrust being to provide limited financial aid for economic development. Many of these tiny island nations are not physically capable of taking care of their own needs. And they need long-term loans, sometimes soft loans, and this is one area where we try to take the lead.

I have personally encouraged my friend Pierre Trudeau to show more interest in Latin American affairs. As you know, Canada is not part of the OAS. I wish they were. But I think Prime Minister Trudeau has demonstrated, with his active involvement in the Caribbean group and other matters, that he is indeed interested.

When we signed the Panama Canal treaties he came here. And we've had a very good, improving relationship with Canada which can be an important element in this hemisphere to benefit the programs that I've outlined to you very briefly.

Zbig, I don't know what you said about Nicaragua. It is better not to have any direct comment from me, because we are trying through peaceful means to resolve the possible suffering that might take place in the future, to put an end to the suffering that's already taken place in Nicaragua. We want a stable government there. We don't want to intervene in the affairs of a sovereign country.

We are trying to work with our friends and well-meaning neighbors of Nicaragua to perhaps mediate the disputes. And I think that this is a worthy goal. We are using, to a maximum degree, the Organization of American States as a vehicle whenever possible. We've got several delegates down there, in addition to our regular ambassadorial staff, to try to bring some resolution of this difficult question.

But those are a few comments that come to mind. There may be some things that affect you.

QUESTIONS

DRUG CONTROL

Q. Mr. President, in South Florida—since you're not going to talk very much about Nicaragua—we're concerned about the drug traffic, which we seem to be the chief landing point. We also have a feeling that the Carter administration is not taking all of the steps that should be taken to stop this flow of traffic. And my question to you, sir, is do you have any plans to try to work out some sort of agreement with the countries that are the source of some of these drugs?

THE PRESIDENT. Well, we've already done a great deal, never enough in the case of drugs. When I became President, just a short time ago—sometimes it seems like a long time ago—[*laughter*]—about 90 percent of the heroin coming into this country was obtained from Mexico. And under the extremely able administration of Dr. Peter Bourne, working with Mr. Bensinger [1] and others, we worked out an agreement with President López Portillo, the new President of Mexico, to actually eliminate the poppy fields, which were the source of heroin for our hemisphere.

That's been almost completely eliminated, the heroin sources in Mexico—with aerial photographs, infrared, that shows the location of poppy fields, with the very good cooperation for the first time, really in an all-out effort along with Mexico to destroy the poppy fields once they are found, to try to shift the small farmers in the high altitude regions above 3,000 feet elevation to alternate sources of income, away from the poppies that were

---

[1] Peter B. Bensinger, Administrator, Drug Enforcement Administration.

formerly used for heroin. This has been successful.

At the same time, we tried to restrict the shift of drug production, not just from heroin to something else but to reduce it overall. We've still got a serious problem with marijuana. I think we've intercepted—over 17,000 pounds? 1,700 to 17,000 [1,700,000],[2] I've forgotten which—I saw the figures this morning—of marijuana in the last 8 months, more than any 2-year period in history.

We do still have a problem of cocaine. As you know, the coca leaves are produced in nations to the south of Colombia. Much of it is processed in Colombia, and that's been a major avenue of drugs. But we've had good cooperation now from the Colombian Government. We are forming alliances with them, actually signing documents that share responsibility. We provide some technical assistance, some helicopter services, a free exchange of information between our authorities and theirs. We've had very good, unprecedented cooperation at the top level.

But narcotics control is a major element of our relationship with the Latin American countries. They all see it as the most threatening source of corruption and even destruction of their own governmental society. And I've had long talks with President Lopez Michelsen and others, in Colombia and Mexico and different countries about this subject.

EXCHANGE OF PRISONERS; CUBA

I might say—looking at my notes—there are a couple of things that I forgot to mention.

One is that we've tried to remove the problem of prisoner exchange. And we've already signed, I think, exemplary treaties with Mexico and Bolivia, so that if Ameri-

cans are incarcerated in their prisons or their nationals are in our prisons, we can exchange those prisoners if the prisoners have no objection. This is a pattern that I think might be very well emulated in other countries around the world. We're trying now to do the same thing in Turkey, for instance. And this is another step forward.

And the other thing is a very sensitive issue that perhaps I ought not even bring up, and that's Cuba—a very serious problem for us, our relationship with Cuba.

We have opened an interests section in Havana; they have one here—not diplomatic relations at all, but it gives us an avenue of communications. And on occasion we do have our top officials meet with Cuban officials to try to work out some humanitarian projects.

There have been several hundred Cubans who have been released now; many of them have already arrived in our country. This is being done in negotiations through the State Department, administered through the Justice Department, and these are citizens with joint nationality. And there will be a large number of Cuban prisoners released before long. And we're trying to do this as a step in the right direction.

Obviously, the Cubans' heavy military presence and unwarranted intrusion into the internal affairs of African countries has been a major obstacle to any further progress.

But that kind of rounds out the things that I wanted to discuss.

INTERNATIONAL ECONOMY

Q. Mr. President, both in the conversations with some of your junior colleagues who met with us this morning and in the broadest context Dr. Brzezinski very loosely sketched for us today, cited again as a premise for assessment this absolutely transcendent factor of the trans-

---

[2] White House correction.

mutation of the world economy. People toss around phrases like "the need to redefine comprehensive international comparative advantage"—OECD comes up with "positive adjustment measure," which means progressive transference of primacy of certain industries, LDC's and so on.

This is really a question about the domestic cognates, since domestic and international are really opposite, different ends of the same poles. Question: Are we at a point where we need a comprehensive domestic strategy and articulation of the responsibilities we must go through as our part of this transformation, rather than picking out a trade adjustment here and putting down an interest pressure there? Do we need it so that there's a context of understanding to which we can all have reference as we must address this and make adjustments in our lives as well as in particular?

THE PRESIDENT. Well, I think the answer to that question is that the developing nations of the world are much more committed to an all-encompassing, new international economic order. And the developed nations of the world are much more reticent about committing ourselves to that undefined premise that might put constraints or obligations on us that we don't presently envision.

We obviously want to increase trade with the less developed countries. We want to see them get a fair and stable price for raw materials. We want to make sure that the balance-of-trade items that concern us as a tiny part of our own economy are not devastating, because they are the major part of the smaller countries' economies. We are trying to be sure that when we make decisions on sensitive items in our own Nation, like sugar or beef or tin or copper, that these decisions don't disrupt completely the economies of countries that are heavily dependent on that item. That's what I mean by what I just described.

A common fund is a phrase that's been discussed a great deal. I think we would cautiously approach a common fund if it means the pooling of several items so that you could constrain wild fluctuations in prices and supplies. But for heavy additional allocation of money to a fund from the developed countries, it would be in effect administered by the developing nations, is something that we are reluctant to do.

We have tried, however, to increase our bilateral allocation of aid to these countries, recognizing that it's not just a handout; it's a very good investment for us in the future.

We've encouraged our own industrial leaders to explore opportunities for investment in other countries, particularly in areas where it's not highly competitive with American jobs, when the unemployment rate is high here.

We've tried to increase our allocation of funds to the World Bank, the International Monetary Fund, and have actually created the Caribbean Group, a 30-nation organization, to help with economic development.

So, I think your question is an excellent one. The answer is complicated, because we feel that it's best to address these matters on a multifaceted basis rather than just giving a general commitment to the type of aid that, I would guess, is still not clearly defined in the minds of those who demand it. We don't want to have a breach of friendship in the future, because the expectation is much higher for the future than we ever intended when we made a cautious commitment.

It's a difficult subject. It's one that we haven't adequately addressed. And there's still a diversity of opinion among the developed countries of the world.

When—to close my answer—when I was in Bonn this year, we all promised that next year's economic summit, which might possibly be in Japan, sometime in the late spring, that this would be one of the top items on our agenda. And that is a very significant thing, because as we prepare for an economic summit, we literally do months and months of staff work, Cabinet-level work, and then I, myself, do a lot of work just to understand the question.

So, I'll be thoroughly schooled in it as a student before we get there. And I think this will open an avenue whereby the seven major developed countries in the Western World can be prepared to cooperate better in the future.

Maybe one more question.

CAMP DAVID MEETING

Q. Do you have any plans to apply your Camp David techniques to the solution of some of the Caribbean and Latin problems?

THE PRESIDENT. No, I don't. I had a meeting with some other editors earlier, and they asked me if I would get George Meany and Mr. Fitzsimmons and several others and go to Camp David and spend a few weeks to resolve the inflation problem. I told them that was a fate worse than death. [*Laughter*] I never had seen a time when I wanted to leave Camp David and come back to Washington until this past Sunday. [*Laughter*]

But, no, I think that would be a very rare thing. It was an extraordinary time. I think you can see, as editors, in the aftermath of Camp David the disruption of a legitimate exploration for differences. And I don't say that in a critical fashion.

But at Camp David we tried to get people to be cooperative and not to publicize differences, but to search for a common ground on which we could build an agreement. If I or Begin or Sadat had had a press conference daily while we were at Camp David, the conference, in my opinion, wouldn't have lasted 2 days, because there had to be a removal of appealing to the public.

And as you well know, both Begin and Sadat were extremely courageous in taking stands quite different from what they had espoused in the past, some of which were highly controversial and might be disapproved by those who had trusted them with leadership.

I think they both are very good and courageous people. But the enclosed nature of the Camp David environment is one that in the future I prefer to enjoy by myself with my wife. [*Laughter*]

Thank you very much. I enjoyed it.

NOTE: The interview began at 1:45 p.m. in the Roosevelt Room at the White House. It was conducted as part of the Latin American Program for Senior Editors of the Woodrow Wilson International Center for Scholars.

The transcript of the interview was released on September 23.

Supplementary Fiscal Assistance Legislation

Statement on Senate Action on the Legislation. September 23, 1978

I am pleased that the Senate has acted favorably on the Supplementary Fiscal Assistance program. The assistance provided by this bill will help our economically troubled States and localities to maintain basic services and to hold the line on tax increases. This program is an integral component of the urban policy that I proposed earlier this year. I am hopeful that the House will act quickly on supplementary fiscal assistance legislation.

Aliquippa, Pennsylvania

Remarks and a Question-and-Answer Session at a Town Meeting.   September 23, 1978

MAYOR ROSS. Good afternoon, ladies and gentlemen. My name is John Ross, mayor of Aliquippa. On behalf of the borough of Aliquippa, I welcome all of you to the Aliquippa town meeting. And now, may I present to you the President of the United States, Jimmy Carter.

THE PRESIDENT. Mr. Mayor, thank you very much.

It's a great pleasure for me to be back in this beautiful part of Pennsylvania and one of the most beautiful parts of the United States.

My wife, Rosalynn, during the campaign, spent 5 days in Beaver Valley, and all the people who were up here campaigning on the Peanut Brigade and my family and I thought that the most delightful campaign experience of our whole 1976 effort was in Pennsylvania. And we thank you for it and also thank you for the great results that helped to put me in the White House.

My mother is a great sports fan, and anybody who cares about sports knows about Beaver County. As you know, Joe Namath was a great friend of my mother's when she was in Alabama and still is. Pete Maravich played for our team in Atlanta, great athlete who began here— Tony Dorsett, another great athlete, as you know; Doc Medich, and many others. I won't try to mention all of them that came from here. But there must be something special about the climate or the training, because you have set a standard for the rest of the country in athletics.

And that's not all. We have a great song composer from Georgia, Johnny Mercer. And one of his good friends and fellow composers was also from here, and that's Henry Mancini. He was at the White House not long ago and gave a beautiful concert. And he and Johnny Mercer wrote several songs together, including "Moon River," which is one of my favorite waltzes—Rosalynn and I like to dance to it—and "Days of Wine and Roses" and many others.

So, we have not only a lot of political interrelationships with you but athletic interrelationships, cultural interrelationships, and just personal friendships.

It's a good opportunity for me as President of our great country to come here and have a frank exchange with you. Not only are you responsible for my election, but in a very important way you are responsible for how good a job I can do representing you in the White House.

There are some things that prey heavily on my mind, many ideas, but I want to defer to you this morning on your questions. There are two, though, that I would like to mention just in passing that might stimulate some questions from you.

ADMINISTRATION POLICIES

One of the great duties of a government is to police itself, to make sure that the core of our Nation in government is clean and decent and honest and open. Our Nation suffered the last few years because that has not always been true. And when it isn't true, there's a loss of trust among people like you in the government which is yours and in the elected officials which you put in office.

The Senate has already passed a very strong ethics bill. The House this week turned away many crippling amendments. And my hope is that next week our Nation will have a new standard of performance in financing and campaign contributing procedures for the Members of the Congress. I inherited many problems. This was one of them. And the Congress has cooperated.

And the General Services Administration, one of the biggest agencies in the Federal Government, not often highly publicized—we've got some serious problems.

I appointed a new Administrator, Jay Solomon, from Chattanooga, Tennessee. And he had only been there a few weeks before he began to investigate in depth, to root out the corruption that exists. The more he looked, the more he found. And he finally appointed a special investigator, and I asked the Department of Justice to help him. And now we're making some progress.

I don't know what the results will be, about the number of indictments and so forth. But we will stop that corruption of the core of our Government. What has occurred there over the last decades has amounted to hundreds of millions of dollars stolen from you, the taxpayers of our country. We are trying to set up a mechanism to prevent this happening in other agencies.

The Congress will shortly pass a bill, which I support, setting up 12 inspectors general, independent of the agency head, independent of me, who will make sure that in all the agencies of government, the major agencies, there is no tendency toward corruption.

Our new civil service reform legislation, soon to be passed by Congress, thank goodness, will help us again to have not only better use of worthy and dedicated and honest employees, but a way to correct deficiencies. And in that we'll have a special counsel, independent, to investigate and to make sure that we don't have a further corruption of your Government.

We inherited a mess, but we're getting it under control.

The other point I would like to make, because I'm here in the heart of steel country, is that we're making progress in keeping our people at work. When I became President about 20 months ago, 10 million Americans could not find a full-time job; more than 7 million had no jobs at all. We've made good progress. And you have been one of the counties, this region, that has led that progress since I've been President. The unemployment rate now in Beaver County is down to 5.1 percent.

And we've had special success in trying to turn around the problems in the steel industry itself. Employment has risen 24,-000 since the first of this year. When I became President, the utilization rate in the steel industry plants was down to 76 percent. It's now up to 90 percent. In spite of a general slowing down in the economy, domestic shipments of steel are up 5 percent; revenues of the steel companies—the second quarter of this year compared to the second quarter of last year—up 71 percent, which means that they can reinvest in keeping the plants modern and competing with steel producers in other countries.

We've put into effect, as you know, a trigger price system to stop dumping. And as long as I'm President, we won't have any worry about that any more.

So, we are making good progress in almost every aspect of your lives, with good cooperation between the Congress and the President in trying to mirror accurately in the White House what you want done for your country.

I won't go into any other items. I could spend the whole hour doing that. But I want to spend the next 50 minutes answering any questions that you have in your mind. And now, I'd like to turn, I understand, to the first microphone over here if there is a question. And I'll try to be brief with my answers so that we can cover as many questions as possible.

QUESTIONS

COMMUNITY PROGRAMS

Q. Good afternoon, Mr. President. I am Evelyn Rosmini from Aliquippa, and

I have a question for you.

Mr. President, we have lost three old-fashioned things—respect, management, and cooperation. We no longer have small-town lifestyles. Everything is deteriorating, and the youth are going to the cities.

Do you have any community development package plans for improving small-town economics so we could keep our young people in our towns?

THE PRESIDENT. Thank you, Ms. Rosmini. I think you know you mentioned a subject that's dear to my own heart, the small towns. I come from Plains, which has a total population of less than 700, and we are trying to make sure that in the allocation of Federal funds for different projects—highways, schools, health care, beautification—these needs are met.

I think it's a very serious thing when we have a barrier built between our large metropolitan centers and the more rural areas of our country. I believe it's accurate to say that in the last year almost, we have turned the corner in providing strength in the basically agricultural regions with the new farm bill that went into effect October 1, 1977, which happens to be my birthday.

We also have tried to bring together for the first time in many years the local, State, and Federal officials who work together as a team, rather than having them separated one from another. In the White House under my top assistant, Jack Watson, we have a continuing mechanism by which any mayor or county official from the smallest towns and counties in our country can come directly to me through Jack Watson to get needs met.

In the departments, of economic development under the Commerce Secretary, Housing and Urban Development, Health, Education, and Welfare, Labor, we're trying to make sure that the programs are not designed specifically for just the large metropolitan centers. I think

it's very important for us to retain the strength of our small communities and the agricultural areas. And since this is where I came from, and you can rest assured it will never be ignored as long as I'm President.

That's a good question.

URBAN RENEWAL

Q. Good afternoon, Mr. President. My name is Mrs. Etta Colbert, and I live in Aliquippa. I also live in the Logstown district of Aliquippa.

My question is, since the Logstown district, or part of it, is being redeveloped, and homes and buildings are being torn down and others are not, I would just like to know why are some of the buildings and some of the homes being torn down and others are left to stand in a very critical, deplorable condition? And that's my question. Thank you.

THE PRESIDENT. Thank you. I wish I knew the answer about your particular community, but I don't. I think it might be good for me to have Secretary of Housing and Urban Development Department, Mrs. Pat Harris, contact you directly, if you don't mind, with a telephone call and see if she can investigate the exact problems that cause you concern.

As you know, the basic decisions on which particular homes or buildings are torn down and which ones are left standing have to be, under our own system of government, a decision made by private families and also by local government and State government officials. It's not right nor proper for the Federal Government to come in and make a decision about which houses to tear down or leave. And I think this is something that must be done by the local people themselves.

But I'll ask Pat Harris, if you don't mind, to give you a call directly so that she can have one of her people look into the question, since I'm not familiar with the exact circumstances you describe.

Is that okay?

Q. Thank you very much.

THE PRESIDENT. Thank you, Mrs. Colbert.

PRAYER IN PUBLIC SCHOOLS

Q. Good afternoon, Mr. President. My name is Attorney Melvin Clark, Jr., and I'm residing in Pittsburgh, Pennsylvania.

I first would like to commend you on your splendid efforts at Camp David. I think I can speak for the majority of Americans in saying that we are extremely proud. I would like to ask my question as a representative of the Church in the Round, Aliquippa, Pennsylvania.

That question is simply, what is your personal opinion on bringing prayer back into the public schools?

THE PRESIDENT. Thank you, Attorney Clark, for your comment and also your question.

I am not in favor of the Government requiring prayer in the schools. At the same time, I'm not in favor of the Government prohibiting or preventing prayer in the schools. My own religious beliefs, which I think are compatible with the Supreme Court decisions on this, are that the first amendment to the Constitution, separating the church and the state, must be maintained.

I believe that prayer is a private relationship or communication between a person and God, and that each person should have a right to worship as he or she chooses. So, I think that prayer ought to be permitted in the schools, but not required for a particular student.

NATIONAL HEALTH PROGRAM

Q. Good afternoon. My name is Alice Feehley. I'm from Erie, Pennsylvania. I have a question for you.

Considering your principles for the national health program, you say in it that there will be no additional Federal spending until the year 1983. I want to know if that means that——

THE PRESIDENT. No additional what, Miss Feehley?

Q. Federal spending, okay?—until 1983; also that there is no adverse impact on Government budget or the taxpayer. Does that mean what we have will stay in the budget of the Government now, or does that mean we can expect no tax increase or no new Federal programs?

THE PRESIDENT. That's an excellent question, and one of the most difficult I will get today.

Let me take just a moment to describe the problem that we have. We need to have some immediate changes made in the health delivery system in our country. We need to have an emphasis on prevention of disease, the cheapest possible way to ensure a person's health. We need to have an expansion of the kind of people who can treat illness once it occurs, under the supervision of medical doctors themselves, more use of physicians assistants, registered nurses, laboratory technicians, in some instances, special instances, and so forth.

We need to have more emphasis on outpatient treatment and not require persons who don't really need it to be admitted to the hospital at very large cost.

We need to fill in some of the gaps in our present health care coverage, because at this time, the bill for the Federal Government, including health programs, is paid by those who are able to work and pay income taxes primarily, and they are exactly the ones that receive practically no benefits from the Federal health programs.

Many people are not covered by private health insurance. The most important need we have immediately, though, is to put a lid on the cost of hospital care. We have a hospital cost containment proposal in the Congress this year. I really hope it will pass. And we are fighting hard to get it passed. I'll give you the reason for it very quickly.

More and more our private hospitals are being owned and managed by exactly the people who decide whether or not you go into the hospital in the first place— what kind of health care you get, how long you stay, and how much to charge you. It's almost a monopoly, quite often, in a community. Because of that, health care has gone up since 1960 1,000 percent.

I was in South Carolina last night. I looked up the statistics: Last year in South Carolina health care went up 20 percent. The cost of health care for a given level of treatment is doubling every 5 years. This is the kind of thing that puts a tremendous, uncontrollable burden on the American people. And the charges in hospitals is going up twice as fast as the rate of inflation, which is high enough on its own.

So, we're trying to get a hospital cost containment bill passed. As soon as we can get these things done that I've just outlined to you very briefly, we'll be ready to move on a comprehensive health care package.

Another thing that we must do is to make sure that the Federal Government agencies and State government agencies and sometimes the local and private agencies are brought together to administer what we do have now in a much more effective way.

The Congress is making good progress on this. But we cannot afford just abruptly to put into effect an entire health care program that would cost the taxpayers maybe $70 or $80 or $100 billion. We've got to go into it step by step. Once we do the things that I've just described to you, we'll have a much better health care system with no additional burden on the American family for cost, and it'll be much more comprehensive, as well. So,

that's what I think we ought to do in the initial stages.

And the final conclusion of that whole process will take a good while, I would say, at least 5 years. But we're not postponing all these actions until 1983. We hope by 1983 that everything I've described to you will have already been completed.

UNEMPLOYMENT

Q. Good afternoon, Mr. President. My name is George Henderson, Jr. I'm a resident here in Aliquippa. I would like to ask you a question dealing with our educational system.

It is one thing to have had high school dropouts to be mentioned throughout various Presidential campaigns and whatever. I would like to know, have you instituted yet into your so-called repertoire of whatever you're going to do with our country a means of contacting that young, uneducated, unemployed black youth?

THE PRESIDENT. That's one of the most serious problems with the unemployment question.

I said earlier that we've added a good bit of job opportunities to our country's society. We've a net increase, just since I've been in office, of 6 million jobs, 6 million more jobs than we lost. At the same time, we've had a substantial reduction in the unemployment rate, from about 8 percent when I took over down to already less than 6 percent. But we still have pockets of unemployment in particular communities, and we have pockets of unemployment in particular kinds of Americans.

You've put your finger on the most important and unmet need, that is, young, primarily male citizens from the minority groups, either those who can't speak English well or those who are black. We've had an addition of about 725,000 public service jobs that are designed more and more to focus on the kinds of people that you've just described, black youth in particular. And in addition to that, the basic youth programs have much more than doubled.

As the general unemployment rate in the whole country among adults, both black and white, goes down, then those remaining Federal programs, which we are keeping strong, can quit worrying about those that already have jobs and focus more and more of their attention on those that still don't have jobs. We have had a substantial reduction, by the way, in unemployment among young black citizens. But we've got a long way to go. And I believe that with the help of the private sector that we can increase this employment opportunity even more.

But we've recognized, obviously, this to be our most serious unemployment problem. It's the one that has responded less to our programs so far. But it will be the top focus of our attention in the months ahead.

Thank you, Mr. Henderson.

PRESIDENT'S 1980 CANDIDACY

Q. Welcome, Mr. President. My name is Wendy Babiak, and I live in South Heights.

My first question I would like to ask you is, do you think you'll run a second term for office? [*Laughter*] And also, I'd like to ask you, if possible, and if Rosalynn wouldn't mind, could I please give you a big hug? [*Laughter*]

THE PRESIDENT. Well, the answer to one of those questions is absolutely yes. [*Laughter*] And the answer to the other one is that I'll have to ask Rosalynn about both of them. [*Laughter*] This was not on the program. [*Laughter*]

I would like to ask all of you not to tell my wife about this until I can get home and explain it. [*Laughter*] Miss Babiak, that's the nicest question I've had so far.

BEAVER CASTLE GIRL SCOUTS

Q. Hi, Mr. President.

THE PRESIDENT. Good afternoon.

Q. Welcome to the greatest county in Pennsylvania—Beaver. I'm Eleanor Vavro from Patterson Township. Beaver Falls, Joe Namath's town. Tell Lillian.

THE PRESIDENT. I'll tell her.

Q. Mr. President, I will leave all the big questions to all the people. I know there's many, many large ones. But my question is a very simple one. I will talk about something that I know something about.

How would you like to be the first President of the United States to honor us by being a member of the Beaver Castle Girl Scouts? [*Laughter*]

THE PRESIDENT. It would be a great pleasure for me. As a former—as a former—[*laughter*]—well, I wasn't a——

Q. I'll help you out, Mr. President.

THE PRESIDENT. I wasn't a Boy Scout, because I lived too far back in the country. But I was a Boy Scout leader when I got a little bit older.

Q. Great. Great. May I present this T-shirt to Amy, please? I also have a patch from the Beaver Castle Girl Scouts for you, and I also have a pin, if you will let me invest you now.

THE PRESIDENT. That'll be fine. Why don't you stand over here, and after I get the next question, I'll take the pin. And I'll give the shirt to Amy as soon as I get home.

Q. Fair enough.

THE PRESIDENT. Thank you.

TUITION TAX CREDITS

Q. Mr. President, my name is Philip Mancini. I'm from Aliquippa and a student of Quigley High School in Baden.

I would like to ask you, why did you publicly state that you would vote against the tax tuition bill as proposed by Senator Moynihan of New York if it made it through Congress?

THE PRESIDENT. For two reasons. One is, I think that we should honor the constitutional separation of church and state. As you know, we are providing, under rulings by the Supreme Court, a considerable amount of different kinds of direct aid from the Federal Government to the private schools. I think it is best to minimize the interference of the Federal Government in the private school system throughout our country

My own belief is that it is unconstitutional for the Federal Government to support to a substantial degree the curriculum and basic costs of the private school system. In addition, we have allocated for student aid, for scholarships, for loans at the college level, a much more effective means of financing than just to provide tax credits. The tax credits themselves benefit too greatly the family which is fairly well off.

And the focus of it is on the high-income families, $30,000 or more. I think as long as we have a certain amount of either Federal tax credits or Federal taxes that are collected and spent, that the money should be channeled to help most directly those families in the middle range of income and the lower range of income, where they need it much more. So, because of this strong bias towards helping very rich families and my concern about the constitutional provisions, those are the two reasons.

Thank you, Mr. Mancini.

ISRAELI OCCUPIED TERRITORIES

Q. Good afternoon, Mr. President. My name is James Hawkins. I'm from New Sewickley Township here in Beaver County. I wish to welcome you here to western Pennsylvania.

There are approximately 100,000 orthodox Christians here in the Pittsburgh area, Mr. President. Many of us have been very concerned with the treatment which our brothers and sisters, the orthodox Christians in occupied Palestine, have received for the last 30 years at the hands of the Zionist invaders, who have stolen the land and evicted them from their homeland.

We want to know why your administration has not had the courage to stand up to Menahem Begin and to the American Jewish community by simply cutting off all foreign aid to the Israelis until they give back all territories stolen from the orthodox Christians and others in occupied Palestine?

THE PRESIDENT. I thank you for your very objective and unbiased question. And I'll try to answer it as best I can. [*Laughter*]

I don't think that in addressing this particular problem of the Palestinians, nor in addressing all the broader interests in the Mideast, that my administration or I have been timid or cowardly. We have raised, as you know, for the first time in any administration, the basic problems of the Palestinians who live in the region as you described, without regard to the religious affiliation of the people involved.

Palestinian Jews, Arabs, and Christians in my opinion should have a maximum opportunity for a change, to escape the military occupation rule and to have their own government within which they can manage their own affairs, religious affairs and affairs concerning education, police, highways, and the normal administration of their lives.

One of the remarkable results of Camp David is that everything that I have just described to you has been accomplished. And the Israelis, under their spokesman, Prime Minister Begin, have agreed to this.

As soon as the negotiations can be completed, hopefully within just 2 or 3 months, there will be a self-government set up in the Palestinian area with full autonomy. The Israeli military government will be withdrawn for the first time in many years, and the people will have a chance to administer their own affairs, including the right to worship.

I believe that you would agree that this is a major step forward, the first time it has been accomplished.

Now, of course, the fact remains that many issues still remain to be resolved. And in the absence of a willingness of the Palestinians themselves to negotiate further and in the absence of a willingness, for instance, for King Hussein to negotiate further—because some of these disputes involve Jordan; many of the inhabitants of the West Bank, for instance, are Jordanian citizens—the progress we can make will be limited.

But President Sadat has committed himself to me in writing, a letter released yesterday, that in the absence of cooperation or participation by, for instance, King Hussein, he himself will continue the negotiations, not just on the Sinai relating to Egypt-Israel but also will continue the negotiations concerning the West Bank and Gaza Strip area.

We've addressed as best we could, also, the problems of the refugees and also the displaced persons who left that area as a result of different events that have occurred in the last 30 years.

So, I believe we are making great strides toward realizing the hopes that you have just outlined, to terminate military rule and to give people a chance to worship as they please. And I'm proud to report that to you and believe that we can do even more in the future when all the negotiating parties are willing to sit down and take advantage of the wonderful door that has

now been opened because of the Camp David agreement.

ANTITRUST POLICY

Q. Good afternoon, Mr. President. My name is William R. Petrelli. I reside in Hopewell Township.

The question I want to ask you is why did Attorney General Bell go against the recommendation of the Justice Department Antitrust Division and okay the merger of LTV and Lykes Company? This will cost jobs in Aliquippa.

THE PRESIDENT. I don't know. That's a decision, as you know, that's made independently of the White House.

This was a result of a lawsuit and other matters concerning enforcement of the antitrust laws. And under our Constitution, as you well know, there's a very sharp division between the rights and responsibilities of the judiciary system, the rights and responsibilities of the executive branch of Government, and the rights and responsibilities of the legislative branches of Government.

These decisions by the Attorney General, who of course does serve on my Cabinet, can be appealed and might be resolved in the future. I don't know the details of the case, have not been involved in it myself. My own commitment, however, is, after this very controversial decision is made, to minimize the damage that might be done to any community, including your own. And I pointed out a few minutes ago in my opening statement that although there are serious problems in the steel industry, that we have made progress in rejuvenating or giving new life to the American steel industry. And I think that although there are always concerns about any unemployment, the unemployment in your area is among the lowest in the whole Nation with, I think, 5.1 percent in July of this year, which are the last statistics that I have.

So, I'm not trying to evade your question. I don't know anything else about it, and I've almost told you more than I know about it already. [*Laughter*]

Q. Thank you, Mr. President.

THE PRESIDENT. Thank you, Mr. Petrelli.

EDUCATION

Q. Good afternoon, Mr. President. My name is Mike Brown, and I reside in Monaca, Pa.

First of all, let me thank you for being the person who you are and for representing us the way you've been representing us since you took office.

Mr. President, you have been a strong advocate of the department of education. By creating a separate Cabinet office, what advantages do you feel would there be that the HEW can't already do, by creating another office?

THE PRESIDENT. I was Governor of Georgia for 4 years and, before that, was in the Georgia Legislature for two terms and was the chairman of one of the committees responsible for education. Prior to that, for 7 or 8 years, I was on the local board of education. It's been one of my primary interests.

When I campaigned around the Nation for 2 years to become President, that was one of the issues that was constantly put forward to me in meetings of this kind—at first with a much more tiny crowd than this, later growing in size.

After I became President, it was startling to me that in my regular Cabinet meetings, where all the issues that are important to our country are discussed for a couple of hours on Monday mornings, that we rarely had come to my own attention any matter concerning education. I would say less than 2 percent of my time

or 1 percent is spent on education. And when it does come up at a Cabinet meeting or directly involving myself, ordinarily it's concerning a lawsuit involving civil rights or some other aspect of controversy between the Federal Government and a State or local board.

I think that the issue of education should be much more greatly dramatized and discussed at the Federal level of government. And I think a separate department of education would let us go more deeply into the reasons why we are spending an ever-increasing amount of money for education and apparently getting less results in the actual knowledge and ability of our students when they graduate from grammar school or high school.

I don't know the reasons for it. My own approach to education is fairly old-fashioned. I think we ought to get back much more to the basics of education and make sure that when a child does leave, for instance, the third grade, that child can read and write. Many of our young people can't read and write when they finish grammar school, and some of them can't read and write well when they get a high school diploma. That ought to be changed.

Another thing that concerns me very much is that we should have a concentrated commitment that even with the new department of education, that the Federal Government never gets into the role of trying to run the local school systems. That ought to be a decision made as closely as possible to the control of the parents themselves.

The essence of it is that in Washington now, in spite of the fact that we have had, since I've been in office, the greatest increase in Federal contributions to education in history—even including those great days when Lyndon Johnson put into effect the Elementary and Secondary Education

Act of 1965 and the Higher Education Act of '65—the Congress has put more into education since I've been in office than ever before—we still don't have as much attention given to education as it ought to have.

I have a great interest in education, from all my background, more than any other single subject except, perhaps, national defense. And those are some of the reasons that I think a separate department of education ought to be a good idea in our Government. It may not pass this year; I hope it will. The Senate has already taken action; it's in the House. But if it doesn't, then I'll be pursuing it again next year—I hope this year; if not, next year.

PALESTINE LIBERATION ORGANIZATION

Q. Hello, Mr. President. My name is Dan Chamvitz, and I live in Hopewell Township.

My sister happens to live in Israel. The PLO has set off bombs within 100 yards of where she works and where she lives. So, I would like to know how the United States could let the PLO, an organization which has openly killed hundreds of people, open an office and distribute propaganda in Washington, D.C.?

THE PRESIDENT. We have in our country a constitutional right to freedom of speech, one of the deepest commitments of the American people. There are a lot of organizations in our country which are obnoxious to some of us, what they stand for, what they believe in. And it's a difficult thing for a public official not to use this kind of issue to demagog and to stamp out an unpopular group, no matter how small it might be.

There is obviously no threat to our Nation's security. There is obviously no threat to the well-being of people who live in Israel if the PLO has this small information office. My own guess is that

they will learn more about our country by being here and what we stand for than we'll learn from them.

There are many groups like this that cause us concern. The Ku Klux Klan, for instance, the Communist Party, the Nazis—you know, it would be nice for us if they would just go away. But it's part of our system of government to let them have a right to speak. And I believe that as long as the American people are educated and knowledgeable about the threat of these organizations, that that's the best way to stamp them out.

I might add one other thing: I have a commitment to the people of Israel not to negotiate with nor to have private meetings with the PLO until after that organization recognizes Israel's right to exist and espouses United Nations Resolution 242, with which I know you are thoroughly familiar. So, I think we're making good progress in the Mideast.

You need not fear the little office in Washington. I believe we can handle the PLO, not by stamping them out, but by the American people.

Thank you.

WAGE INCREASES; STEEL IMPORTS

Q. *Shalom,* Mr. President.

THE PRESIDENT. *Shalom.*

Q. I am Barbara Heyman from Conway, Pennsylvania. And I personally would like to extend a *mazel tov* to you for all your accomplishments at Camp David.

THE PRESIDENT. Thank you.

Q. You recently stated that you wanted to hold wage increases to 7 percent or less. Why do you only want to give the Federal worker 5½ percent, when in fact many unions have and will exceed the 7 percent?

What further action is the Government contemplating to protect the American steel industry against foreign imports? We understand that there are about 2 million tons a month coming in with your price trigger mechanism in effect.

THE PRESIDENT. Thank you. *Shalom* to you, also. [*Laughter*] When Prime Minister Begin left the Oval Office for the last time, I gave him a little plaque that said, "*Shalom*, y'all." [*Laughter*]

It would be a mistake for anyone to blame the inflation rate on either the Federal Government, the labor unions, the working people, or industry, or the private citizens. All of us share a responsibility for controlling inflation. It's been a constant burden for the American people and a constant threat for at least the last 10 years. As you know, at one time in 1973 or '74, it got up about 14 percent. It's still running at a prevailing rate of about 7 percent, much too high.

I'm responsible directly for the Federal Government. I can't control labor unions, I can't control private industry, I can't control private citizens' lives, nor the buying patterns of housewives or others who shop for products in our country. But within the limits of my own ability and short of mandatory price and wage controls, which I do not favor and don't have any intention to implement, I have to do the best I can.

Among the top officials in Government, including all my Cabinet, the administrators, I have put a zero increase in effect. There will be no increases at all. And they—some of them willingly, some of them unwillingly—will absorb the full increase of inflation during this 12-month period. I think that their income, which is fairly high, is enough to accommodate it.

Among other Federal employees, we tried to put into effect a salary increase level about what the prevailing rate of increase had been for the last year or two, since I've been in office—not this year, last year—about 5½ percent. I don't think that will work any extraordinary

hardship on a Federal employee. It would obviously be better for them to have a 7- or 8- or 9- or 10-percent increase. I can't deny that. They'll still get their regular merit system increases, which are not limited at all.

And I think in the future with the new civil service reform legislation that I expect to sign into law shortly, they'll have a better life for themselves.

So, I'm on pretty sound ground in recommending to the Congress—I think the Congress will honor my recommendation that 5½ percent ought to set a standard or a guide for the rest of the Nation to follow.

Let me say on the steel imports, I described earlier the benefits that have been derived already from the trigger price mechanism that we put into effect. There's been an actual reduction in Japanese exports, for instance, of steel. There's been an increase, tremendous increase, in production of steel in our own country. In the last 12 months, the production of steel in our country has gone up 10 percent. So, I think we've got a good start on controlling imports.

We put a stop now to dumping in almost every incident. We are trying to hone down or to modify our trigger price mechanism to take care of unforeseen problems. And I believe that, in general, both the labor organizations and also the steel manufacturers in our country think that it's a good program. We'll continue it in effect, improve it as we go along.

PROPERTY TAXES

Q. Welcome to Beaver County, Mr. President.

THE PRESIDENT. Thank you, ma'am.

Q. I'm Elizabeth Hensley of Harmony Township. And my question relates to senior citizens and reassessment of property. Do you feel senior citizens on fixed incomes who have lived in and paid taxes on their homes for 40 years or more should have to have their property reassessed?

THE PRESIDENT. Yes, ma'am, yes, I do. It would be much better, obviously, if no one had to have their property reassessed. There are some senior citizens who are quite wealthy. Among the wealthiest people in our country are some senior citizens, not the ones about whom you have just asked me. But I think when you start excluding certain groups of citizens completely from any increase in property taxes for a number of years, you add on to the burden of others in the society, perhaps who are just as poor and just as in need as the senior citizens themselves.

One of the things that we are trying to do, however, is to make sure that as a senior citizen depends upon, for instance, social security payments to make those tax levies to the county or city, that the social security payments go up enough to accommodate the normal inflation rate.

One of the things that I'd like to warn about is that there are some demands being made now, on a nationwide basis, by the Republican leaders for a dramatic decrease in Federal income taxes, like 35 percent or some extraordinary figure of that sort under the so-called Kemp-Roth bill.

There's a given level of service to our people that has to be maintained for national defense, for social security, for education, for streets and highways and police forces. And if you drastically reduce income taxes, the only thing that you can do is to put a very large increased tax burden on property taxes, exactly what we do not want to do.

So, I think we need to cut income taxes substantially. I hope the Democratic Congress and I can do that, maybe $20 billion this year. We had about a $7 billion decrease last year. But to cut income taxes so much that you have to pile more tax burden on property taxpayers is something

that we want to avoid. So, I think we'll do everything we can to make sure that elderly citizens are protected, particularly those with low incomes. We will not exclude the rich elderly citizens from paying their part of the taxes.

We'll try to hold down property taxes as much as possible by maintaining a reasonable level of Federal income taxes and increase the social security payments and others that go to elderly citizens to accommodate for the increases in taxes and other things brought about by the inflation rate. That's in a very brief period of time the best I can do with a very complicated subject.

I know you want to pay your share. And I want to make sure you don't pay any more than your share. Thank you.

VIEWS ON THE PRESIDENCY

Q. Good afternoon, Mr. President. My name is Ken Joyce from Ambridge, Pennsylvania. There are many good communities here in Beaver County. And the next time you get a break in your busy schedule, I'd like to invite you to one of the better ones, which is Ambridge. [*Laughter*]

THE PRESIDENT. Ambridge, by the way, is one of my wife's favorites. She was there, I think, twice during the campaign. She wants to come back.

Q. Well, she can come back, too, Mr. President.

My question for you is: As a man who has risen to prominence from relative obscurity——

THE PRESIDENT. That's putting it mildly. [*Laughter*]

Q.——what is your expectation as to how history will remember you? What is your hope, your goal as a President to be remembered by history?

THE PRESIDENT. That's a hard thing to answer. Just let me briefly say that there are two things that I would like to have remembered about me. One is that I helped to restore to our Nation and to its Government a sense of purpose, of idealism, of commitment and honesty, that deserves the trust of the people of our country.

We had lost that in my opinion, in recent years, with Vietnam and Watergate and CIA and so forth. And I would like for people, when I go out of office, to say, "I've got a clean government that's decent and honest, that I can trust." If I could accomplish that, or a major part of that, on the domestic scene, I would be very, very pleased.

On the international scene, of course, the overwhelming question is peace; not peace by military might imposed on other people, but peace based on two things. One is a strong national defense capability, depending on weapons first of all, hopefully never to be used. But the other one is strength based on what our national character is, treating other people fairly and with respect, with a total commitment to the enhancement of human rights around the world and trying to lessen the tensions that have been built up, for instance, in southern Africa, between ourselves and the Soviet Union, in the Turkey–Greece–Cyprus question, to strengthen the Eastern–Western European confrontation, in the Middle East, to restore our good, friendly relationships with countries that in the past have been our enemies. These are the kinds of things that I would like to do in the international scene.

So, I would say peace based on strength in its broadest sense, on the international scene, and a restoration of people's trust and love of our own government and country, on the domestic scene.

ETHICS IN GOVERNMENT

Q. Good afternoon, Mr. President. My name's Donald Martin from Center Township.

In light of your opening remarks about corruption in the Federal Government, you know that Pennsylvania is running first or second there. [*Laughter*] And I would like to know what you feel that the average citizen can do to help to bring corruption to light and at the same time to protect our livelihood.

THE PRESIDENT. Well, first of all, I think it's good for private citizens who work in either local industries or in the government to be constantly alert to any sort of suspicious occurrences that they observe.

Secondly, I think you could elect officials who in their own past administrations have shown that they are capable of avoiding any allegations of corruption. Pete Flaherty would be an example that comes to my mind right offhand.

Third, you could help with some very controversial things in the Congress. I ran for President under a new election law that put a limit of $1,000 on contributions that could come to me from anywhere. And every contribution had to be revealed completely to the public. It cost us an enormous amount of time and money just to account for all those contributions. We need the same thing in the Congress, because you cannot imagine the extraordinary influence of special lobbying groups on Capitol Hill.

I mentioned hospital cost containment a few minutes ago. That's one example. But I think if we can ever get to the point where a Member of Congress was elected to office without any possibility of being financially indebted to the very wealthy and very well organized lobbying groups, that would be the best single thing that we could accomplish.

There's a lot of opposition to that on Capitol Hill. But I want to get that done. There's a lot of concern about it.

I was a little bit upset the other day when Amy came home and said they'd been playing a new game at school. And I said, "What is it?" She said, "Cops and GSA." [*Laughter*] So, we are trying to make government better. You can help by doing the things I described.

NATIONAL ENERGY POLICY

Q. Good afternoon, Mr. President. My name is Eli Bucan. I'm from Hopewell, Beaver County here.

Most of the questions you seemed to have answered extremely well. So, I had one, but I think it was answered properly, So, I have other ones here like, why isn't the present government moving faster in getting a good, sound energy program in the United States, and why isn't that new fuel called gasocol, I think it's called——

THE PRESIDENT. Gasohol.

Q. ——why isn't it being pushed?

THE PRESIDENT. Gasohol. I think it will be in the future. As you know we've gone for several generations in our great country without any sort of a national energy policy that people could understand that would make production in our country be equal to our needs and to cut down on the enormous drain in buying overseas oil.

In the last 6 years we've had an 800-percent increase in oil imports, from about $4.7 billion, this year $45 billion. And many people don't even know that in 1978, of all the oil we use in our country, about half of it we have to buy overseas.

My guess is that before this Congress adjourns in October that we will have a major step taken by the Congress toward a comprehensive energy bill. I believe that we've got pretty good support in Pennsylvania, at least in the Congressmen among those who are Democrats. I think you could help me by inducing both your U.S. Senators to support in the Senate next Tuesday the passage of a natural gas bill, which is a key to the rest of the energy package this year.

So, I think that after this year we'll have the major portion of a new energy policy that'll help a great deal. We've got some serious problems ahead of us if we don't.

The value of the dollar is going down, inflation rates caused to go up by excessive imports that cost Americans jobs. We are dependent on foreign supplies when we ought to be able to produce our own energy sources and so forth.

On gasohol, this is a kind of new research and development effort that I think will pay good dividends. In some countries, like Brazil, who don't have any appreciable fuel of their own, about 10 percent of their gasoline now comes from growing plants, either corn or some tuberous plants; well, you have a tuber growing underneath the ground, like a potato. And I think in the future we'll see a substantial increase in gasohol in our own country. Right now it's a little too expensive. It can't compete with other forms of gasoline. But I think you'll see that grow in the future.

And we want to shift very heavily toward other sources, too. Coal is not being adequately utilized. Solar energy would be another one.

So, with a strong research and development program, a passage this year of a natural gas bill and other bills, we'll have a major step toward recognizing and resolving the question that you've described.

Thank you very much.

I'm sorry, I don't have time for another question. We've been here now for 59 minutes, and I've only got 1 minute to close.

Let me say that I've been really impressed with the quality of your questions. Some of them have been very difficult for me to answer. And I don't claim to know all the answers. I think the best thing that I can do when I have a difficult question to address is to turn to you for help, not only in learning in a session like this but in your help in helping to pass legislation in the Congress.

Let me say this as a reminder to you. We ordinarily are concerned about and we study and we read about in the newspapers and we watch on television debates about some issues that seem to be very important at the time. But I'd like to remind you that those issues come and go; they are transient; and they don't indicate clearly in our minds the basic strength and the greatness of our country.

Sure, we've got some problems. America has always had problems; our ancestors had problems much more serious than the ones we have now. But God's blessed us in this Nation with tremendous natural resources. We are blessed by our forefathers with the kind of government structure that lets us work together as a team. And we also have individual rights, freedoms to stand on our own feet, to make our own decisions, to answer our own questions, to resolve our own differences, and to reach for greatness in the future.

So, I'd like to ask you every now and then when you're complaining about a particular thing like inflation or perhaps unemployment or perhaps steel imports or perhaps a bad education system or the wrong houses getting torn down, to remember in your conversation that we still have the best and the greatest nation on Earth. And together we'll make it even greater.

Thank you very much.

NOTE: The town meeting began at 2:30 p.m. in the Aliquippa High School auditorium. It was broadcast live on radio and television.

Aliquippa, Pennsylvania

*Remarks at a Reception for Gene Atkinson.
September 23, 1978*

THE PRESIDENT. Thank you very much. Now let me say a few words. Thank you so much. It's really tremendous for me to be among friends, between two friends who were there when I needed them, and who have formed an allegiance with me and my family that is absolutely unshakable, and that there is no way that I as President could have a closer relationship with you and the rest of my own administration than to have Pete Flaherty in the statehouse running your own affairs in Pennsylvania, and Gene Atkinson there to represent your district.

As you know, we were not very well financed in 1976. [*Laughter*] So, when we came into Beaver Valley to campaign, we didn't have any campaign headquarters and couldn't afford one. But there was one certain man who cared enough about me and who cared enough about my wife, who was in here campaigning for 5 full days, to say, "I've got a campaign headquarters and telephones. Why don't we share it?" And you know who that person was, it was your next Congressman, Gene Atkinson.

There are some things——

MEMBER OF THE AUDIENCE. Thank you, Gene Atkinson. [*Laughter*]

THE PRESIDENT. Right. Thank you, Congressman Atkinson.

MR. ATKINSON. You're welcome, Mr. President.

THE PRESIDENT. There are some things that we need in Washington, as you well know. I made a mistake, a slight mistake in the townhall meeting a while ago. We do have a limit on what can be contributed to Members of Congress, and they have to reveal it. What we need in a general election, though, is Federal financing of the entire election.

In the President's race, once President Ford and I were nominated, there was an amount of money allocated to our campaigns that got all contributors out of the picture completely. There was just one mass of contributors, and that's the taxpayers of the country, and the maximum contribution that you can make is $1 per year.

That's what we need for the Congress as well. And these two men standing next to me are the kind who want to see cleanness and decency and honesty and openness brought back into the Government, so that the only people we represent are you.

We need someone representing you in Congress who knows something about business and management—a small businessman, understands payrolls, understands how to make employees be prosperous and form a partnership with them, doing work in the graduate school at the University of Pittsburgh in business management, knowledgeable about local affairs, county commissioner—7 years?

MR. ATKINSON. 7 years.

THE PRESIDENT. And in 7 years—this is unbelievable for me; I want you all to check on it—he tells me that they've only had a 4 mill increase in property taxes in 7 years under his administration—unbelievable. That shows good knowledge not only of how local government can work well but also how to treat people who trust him and put him in office.

I hope that all of you who have helped today by coming here to meet with me and to meet with Gene and Pete will leave here with another additional commitment. You've not done enough. A financial contribution, that helps, but you can give, many of you, more.

And there's no one here who can't go back home and raise 10 times as much as you have contributed in coming here today. I know you've got 10 friends who are not here today who would be willing to give that much to get a good Congressman to represent you in Washington.

Also, you are Americans who believe in our country. And I think it's time for you to make an investment of time. Many of you, perhaps, already are. But there's also no one here who can't go back home and become, in effect, a campaign manager for Gene Atkinson, to ask your own family, your own block, your own neighborhood, perhaps a whole community, to organize for him.

When election day comes, you ought to have a list of several hundred people that you could call on the telephone, maybe beginning the night before, and say, "Would you go out tomorrow and vote for the next Congressman of the United States to represent us?" This is the kind of thing you can do, if you will.

The ones that can help most, of course, are maybe retired people, because the Congress takes actions almost every day that affect your lives. And many of you are not employed full-time, because you have reached the retirement age. You can make 150 telephone calls per day. I have done it, from my study in Plains, Georgia, to Iowa, before the first votes took place. I made 128 long-distance calls from Plains to get the nomination commitment in Iowa. So, there's no limit to what you can do if you're willing. And I hope you'll be willing, because it's an investment that you can make in a campaign for a man that will not only serve you well, but let me be able better, as President, to serve you well.

I need him there. He's a personal friend. I know how he feels about you. And there's no doubt that if you would elect and will join me in helping to elect

Gene Atkinson, you could not possibly have a better man in Washington.

Perhaps you have been here almost long enough. Now I want you to leave here, go home, go to work for Gene.

Thank you very much.

NOTE: The President spoke at approximately 4: 30 p.m. at Ciro's Top of the Mall Restaurant at the Beaver Valley Mall.

Columbus, Ohio

Remarks at Dedication Ceremonies for the Mount Vernon Plaza.   September 23, 1978

Senator Glenn, Senator Metzenbaum, my good friend Dick Celeste, Chairman Paul Tipps, Mayor Moody, my friend Les Brown, Jerry Hammond, Amos Lynch, Bill Potter, ladies and gentlemen, brothers and sisters:

How many of you think we have a great country? [*Applause*] How many of you think we can make it even better? [*Applause*]

I'm very proud to come here this afternoon to be with you, to talk for a few minutes about how you, yourselves, have helped to make the United States of America a better country. I spent 2 weeks at Camp David, and we made great progress forward toward world peace. But what you've done here is also a symbol of the greatness of our country.

Mount Vernon Avenue, as you know, in years gone by, has been one of the worst places with the worst reputation, perhaps, in the Columbus area. It was a place where housing was not good. It was a place where sanitation was not good. It was a place where health conditions were not good. It was a place where crime was high. And then you, the people of this area, decided to do something about it. Now you've got an area that's safe, healthy, clean, beautiful, and it's going to be even better in the future.

There are areas where the Federal Government has come in, with a few real estate people, and have got together with the promoters, put in a housing project, put in a place for older people, without consulting the local people, and it just didn't work. Near here you've got a few projects like that yourselves. Sawyer Towers, Sawyer Manor, and Trevitt Heights were originally planned to be places just as beautiful as this. But the occupancy rate is down; vandalism is high. And we've got a long way to go to make those places as beautiful as this.

Here you have made sure that the real estate promoters couldn't rip off the poor. Here you have made sure that you may work among the Federal, State, and local governments, along with private developers and yourselves.

The slums are gone. The people that used to live here still live here. The ones who ran the businesses before are still operating businesses here. I've seen slum development projects come in where 2 or 300 families used to live, level them to the ground with bulldozers, and the poor people had to live and move somewhere else, and then a few places for rich people sprang up to take their places.

But here in Mount Vernon Plaza and the area around, you've got more houses now, more places for people to live here now than you did before this great project started. This is the kind of cooperation that makes our country great.

One thing that I believe that you know is that we've got to have jobs for our people. When I came into office, we had about 10 million Americans who couldn't get a full-time job. About 7 million Americans didn't have a job at all. The unemployment rate was up at 8 percent, and the Democratic Congress, many others, and I went to work.

We've had a net increase in the last 20 months of 6 million new jobs in the United States. We're finding more new jobs every day. We're going to put the American people back to work, where you want to be.

I'm also concerned about areas like the ones I mentioned earlier, the Sawyer Towers, Sawyer Manors, Trevitt Heights. And I can tell you today that we are giving, through public housing, $4.3 million in loans, over $400,000 in grants, to make those places just as nice in the future as yours are here.

I believe our country is rich enough. I believe our people are intelligent enough. I believe we've got enough team spirit in our country to give every family a decent place to live, a good education for the children, safe streets to walk on, a beautiful place to look at and, also, jobs for our people and a better life for all. That's what I believe we can have.

But I have to admit to you that the Federal Government can't do it all. You've got to have good support at the local and State levels. And the main thing you've got to have is the people themselves who live in a community say, "We want to make our own area a better place to live." And once you have a little bit of beauty somewhere, that beauty can grow, because if one person sees a house in a block that's clean and painted, with a few flowers in the front yard or on the windowsill, then the next house to it wants to do the same thing. And folks start picking up trash on the streets, people start being proud of what they've got, and the first thing you know, everybody is living in a community that hasn't cost much, but is a much better place to live.

I want to remind you that we do have a great country. It's great because the people are great. We're a country that's strong, getting stronger. The Lord has blessed us in the United States of America, and we need to take care of the blessings that He's given us. We've got good land to grow crops to sell all over the world. We've got factories, steel, coal, things to make things out of, to sell in the rest of the world. But the main thing we've got is people who love peace, people who are strong, people who control their own government, people who are committed to freedom, people who are committed to equality, people who believe we can be better even than we are now. And with that kind of team spirit, a President of the United States, the Senators who represent you in Washington, your Congressman, your mayor, and your other officials can work together to realize those hopes and dreams that have always made our country what it is today—the greatest nation on Earth.

Thank you very much. God bless every one of you. We're in it together.

Let me have your attention for a moment. As President of the United States of America, proud of all of you, grateful for what you've done, I hereby dedicate the Mount Vernon Plaza for my credit, for your credit, and for a better life for all of you.

Thank you very much.

NOTE: The President spoke at 6:50 p.m. In his opening remarks he referred to Dick Celeste, lieutenant governor and Democratic candidate for Governor of the State of Ohio, Paul Tipps, chairman of the Democratic Party in Ohio, Tom Moody, mayor, and Jerry Hammond, city councilman of Columbus, Les Brown, Ohio State representative, Amos Lynch, editor of the Columbus Call and Post, and Bill Potter, executive director of the Neighborhood Development Corporation of Columbus.

Columbus, Ohio

Remarks at a State Democratic Party Reception. September 23, 1978

Senator Glenn, Senator Metzenbaum, Chairman Tipps, Chairman John White, Lieutenant Governor Dick Celeste, Con-

gressman Pease, Jim Bauman, Henry Eck-hard, State officials who have genuinely made not only Ohio but the entire Nation proud:

I'm grateful to be here with you. We belong to the right party. Which party has given Ohio two of the greatest Senators in Washington? The Democrats, right? [*Applause*] Which party has now a strong and growing majority in both houses of your State general assembly? [*Applause*] Democrats.

Which party now holds two-thirds of the statewide offices and is reaching successfully for 100 percent? [*Applause*] Democrats. Which party recognizes that one of the most important challenges of this year is to have a man in whom we have utmost faith, who cares about the people of your State, who will occupy the statehouse as Governor of Ohio? The Democrats, right? [*Applause*]

One thing that concerns me is which party is going to have a majority of Congressmen from Ohio for the first time in many years, maybe forever, who are Democrats. The Democratic Party, right? [*Applause*] We need to pick up the 12th District.

And also, I'd like to ask you another question. Which party has finally got itself out of debt and tonight is raising $100,000 to give to candidates to win the elections this fall? [*Applause*] The Ohio Democrats.

One of the greatest things is, which party welcomed a lonely peanut farmer, helped him get the nomination, and then 2 years ago, in November, gave our party's nominee a strong, solid majority in this State that put him over the top and let him become President of the United States? Again——[*applause*].

The Ohio Democrats have made tremendous strides in the past few years. Paul Tipps' leadership was an incremental part and an essential part of this progress. But he knows even better than I can say

that one man can't turn a State political organization around and achieve the tremendous victories that you've realized here in Ohio.

The Democratic Party has a certain quiet strength that becomes aroused on occasion when the needs are most visible and most urgent. The Democratic Party quite often is divided within itself. And almost invariably, that's the cause for losses on election day. The Democratic Party, quite often in different places in our Nation, has not always been unified in its efforts because of a divisive nature of hard-fought, personal campaigns in the primary elections.

You've now been able to overcome these handicaps of the past. But never in all the time of our party in the last 200 years, when it was in its unrecognized and even embryonic state in the early years, have we lost a vision of the basic elements of what we stand for.

The Democratic Party is not one that says no. We are a party that says yes. The Democratic Party is one that realizes it's best to put our Nation's investment in people. We're not a party that reaches down to others and considers them less worthy than we. We are a party that reach out to others and say, "Let me help you join the part of constructive society that's been such a blessing to me."

We're the party who believes that black and white people, those who speak good English, those who don't speak good English, those who live in the North and the South, those who are employed, those who are searching for jobs—all have an opportunity to work together for a better life for all.

On occasion, we've not been successful in achieving these ideals and goals. But we've never lost the vision of what ought to be.

We've seen a great change in our country in the last 20 months, where we've had an opportunity for a Democratic President in the White House, for the first time in 8 years, to be able to work in harmony with a Democratic Congress.

I campaigned for 2 years around our country, and I've never lived nor served in Washington before. But when I was finally inaugurated as President with your help, I knew, I think very clearly, what the American people wanted, what their needs were, what their frustrations were, what their doubts were, and what were their hopes and aspirations for the future.

When I became President, we had 10 million Americans who didn't have a full-time job. We had about 7 million Americans who didn't have a job at all. The unemployment rate had been rising for 8 years, and it reached the highest level in a long time, 8 percent. We began to work together with the help of many of you, not just for government programs but to revive the strength of our free enterprise system in which we believe so deeply.

We've had a net increase in the last 20 months of 6 million jobs. And now the unemployment rate is below 6 percent, holding steady, going down. Many people who had been deprived of a chance for employment all their lives now have a chance. People who had given up hope and weren't seeking jobs have now put their names on the unemployment roles, looking for a chance to live in dignity and self-respect for a change.

In Ohio in the last 20 months, your unemployment rate has gone from 7.8 percent down to 5.2 percent, a 33-percent decrease in unemployment in that short a period of time.

And I believe there's a new spirit in our country; that we have a conviction, exemplified by our party, that every American who wants to work can find work. And it's revived the hope and the aspirations and the confidence that people have in the future. Now we don't look upon unemployment as the most burning issue in our country. But 2 years ago, 12 months ago, it was.

I found throughout the country, too, a concern about our Government itself. Many people had lost confidence in the United States Government because of the deep wounds inflicted on our country by the Vietnam war, the Watergate scandals, the CIA revelations. A lot of people had said, "I don't want to have anything to do with politics. I've lost faith in the Government in Washington. The people that I send to hold public office have betrayed my trust." And there was a withdrawing from participation in shaping our future lives through our federal system of government.

We've begun to turn that around. I think you all know that the Congress has acted effectively to give me a chance to reorganize the structure of Government, to make it more effective, more efficient, more open. We've begun to root out corruption—it's been there for decades in the General Services Administration—to try to bring out among the employees who are very dedicated a commitment to improve their own lives, their own performance.

Civil service reform is going to pass very shortly to let those hundreds of thousands of people who have given their lives to public service on a professional career basis to be rewarded when they do good work, and those who don't do good work will either be fired or moved or inspired to do better.

We've got a chance now to let managers manage and to let the Government deliver better services in a more efficient way, to restore confidence there. The Congress is now on the verge of passing a comprehensive ethics bill to apply the strictest possible standards to Members of the Congress themselves to be sure there's no taint of scandal that might be aroused in the future, as there has been in the past, with extraordinary, unrevealed gifts, even from foreign governments.

This is the kind of thing that's now sweeping through our Federal Government in Washington in answer to the concerns and the hopes and expectations of people like you.

We've had a chance to build up our Nation's strength in other ways. We're the strongest nation on Earth economically; we're the strongest nation on Earth politically; we're the strongest nation on Earth militarily. But we had lost a way to benefit from that strength. We were condemned by the vast majority of other nations on Earth.

When I was Governor of Georgia, when I was a candidate for President, I used to flinch every year at this time when the United Nations General Assembly convened, because I knew that scores, more than a hundred other nations, would make us the butt of their jokes, the target of their attacks, condemning us in resolution after resolution because we ourselves, as a government, had betrayed what our Nation formerly stood for.

And now in the last 2 years, and as the General Assembly convenes next week, we've not seen a condemnation by the poor and the black and the brown and the yellow and the weak and the new nations of the world. We enjoy not only their respect, we enjoy their friendship and their support. It's a brand new change in international affairs that brings us rich dividends. It hasn't been easy to bring it about, but it's been brought about because you have confidence in us, and we try not to betray that confidence.

Some of the things we've undertaken have been very difficult. They've cost us politically. For 14 years, under four different Presidents, we had tried to hammer out a reasonable solution to the Panama Canal question. And most of my predecessors had been reluctant to bring it to a conclusion because I know that a year and a half ago, only 8 percent of the American people favored a treaty with Panama. And it was hard for us to see the condemnation that fell on our Nation, because we were still looked upon by many as a colonial power who had imposed its will on a tiny nation and who felt that after Watergate, after Vietnam, we had to keep a demonstration of our power somewhat as a bully.

But we worked out an equitable arrangement. And now we have a clean slate in Latin America, and people there are beginning to look on us not as a big brother handing out financial favors, but as a partner for the future.

And we've strengthened the principles of democracy. We've also restored enough strength within many of those weak countries where communism can't creep in and take over. And we're seeing many countries look to us now for guidance that didn't before. They're turning to us with open arms and an open heart. This is not a highly publicized evolutionary development, but it's very significant in the future of our country, because those people who live in our hemisphere are more important to us than we are to them.

And I think this is the kind of new image that our Nation has long deserved, but long lacked. We do have an investment in our own hemisphere. But there are other aspects of our lives that have changed. We are no longer the best friend of every scurrilous, totalitarian government on Earth. We're now understanding, as best we can, the motivations of people everywhere.

We have raised again, once for the people of the world to see, a banner of basic human rights. And as long as you have let me be in the White House, and as long as I stay in the White House, we will never abandon the hopes and dreams of people who want to emulate what we have in our country—basic freedoms, basic self-respect, individualism, based on the principles that have made our Nation great. We believe in human rights. We'll keep it that way.

We've begun to take some bold steps toward peace in areas where peace has been lacking for many years, decades, generations, sometimes even centuries.

We've tried to repair the relationships between ourselves and our former enemies, to ensure the safety of American people, to prevent wars that might start with two nations, spread to their neighbors, eventually to a region, and eventually cause a confrontation, a nuclear confrontation between the super powers.

We've moved toward restoring the relationship between Turkey and Greece, between those nations in NATO, to solve the problems on Cyprus, return human rights to that troubled island.

We've entered, for the first time, sometimes with great political danger, an effort to resolve the tortured problems of the continent of Africa. We've got friends there we didn't have before.

Secretary Kissinger, at the height of his popularity, was not permitted to cross the borders into Nigeria, the greatest black nation on Earth—strong militarily, strong politically, a great influence, a hundred million people. Now they are among our closest friends. They help us with major projects to try to bring peace to Africa. This is the kind of change that's beginning to take place.

We're working hard to get a SALT agreement with the Soviet Union. I hope it won't be long-coming in the future. We've strengthened NATO, repaired the damage that had been done between ourselves and Japan.

We've begun to work on the problems of the Middle East. I think the greatness of the leaders of Israel and Egypt has been exemplified in the last 2 weeks as they've taken a major step forward, and my prediction to you is that very shortly, after the Knesset votes, we will see a peace treaty between Israel and Egypt that I believe will last for generations in the future.

Some of these things are highly publicized, some are not. But when you arouse the slumbering problems that have been covered up too long, they are bound to be controversial.

I said last night in South Carolina that the Presidency is a lonely job. When things go wrong, the President gets too much blame. And when things go right, the President gets too much credit. It's really an exemplification by the person in the White House of what you demand and what you expect and what you will support.

I'm a farmer. And I observed with great concern during the campaign and shortly after I became President that we really had a 1930's-type depression sweeping across the farm communities of our country.

In 1977, October 1, we put into effect a new farm bill that the Members of Congress very wisely passed. We've seen a great restoration of the strength of farm families. Exports last year—highest on record in spite of very low unit prices—$24 billion. Exports this year will exceed that record. Net farm income this year will be the highest ever. It will be up $7 billion or more above last year. And farmers are beginning now to see that the Government is less and less involved in their own internal affairs.

On-farm storage lets farmers derive benefits when prices go up, and the manipulators on commodity exchanges and the large grain elevators will make less of that profit. Stable prices will benefit consumers. So, agriculture is helping as well.

We have, I think, accomplished a great deal. Many problems still face our country. In spite of the utmost efforts by myself and the Congress, we still don't have a comprehensive energy policy for our country. In the last 6 years, oil imports have increased 800 percent. In 1962 we imported $4.7 billion worth of oil. This year we will import $45 billion worth of oil.

Of all the oil used in our country now, about half of it is bought overseas. And when you take $45 billion of American money and send it overseas to pay for oil, you rob our country of that much to invest in new jobs. It creates inflation. It lowers the value of the dollar. It makes us unnecessarily dependent on uncertain foreign oil supplies in a time of crisis or national emergency.

We're trying to correct that defect in our governmental structure. And I hope and pray that before the Congress adjourns next month that they will have passed the major elements of a comprehensive energy policy.

This is the kind of difficult subject we've not been timid about facing. I think the Congress has met it well, and the people have supported us.

I've tried to restore also—and this is the last thing I want to mention—our basic system of federalism. Our country was formed when 13 States allotted certain powers to the Federal Government. They retained the other powers for themselves. And then States formed cities, towns, counties, townships. But the hope of our Founding Fathers was that there would be kind of an equal partnership, a common purpose, a team spirit of these different levels of government, and that the strongest governments will be the closest ones to the people, and that government would not intrude in the private affairs of individuals or our free enterprise system, unless it was necessary.

The few years before I became President, that structure had been, for all practical purposes, destroyed. We're trying to put it back together. We have some problems in doing it in just a few States. One of those States is Ohio. And it hurts you. No one could doubt the good intentions of all of us who serve you in Washington. I remember who put me in office, and so do the people I've chosen to work on my administration team.

I'm concerned, for instance, about the problems with Ohio coal. If the wrong decisions are made, it could cost you 12,000 jobs in your coal production industry. We need to have the kind of harmony and cooperation and partnership between Washington and Columbus, Ohio, that can solve this problem together. But we don't have it.

Every State is given the responsibility to develop air quality standards compatible with the Federal laws passed by Congress that bind us all. Forty-nine States have Governors and administrations that have evolved acceptable air quality standards. One State has not, the State of Ohio. And this prevents our resolution of one of the most difficult questions that face all of you in the prosperity and well-being of the people who look to you and your elected officials for leadership.

We've seen changes take place in some of our basic industries. Steel is one of them. As you well know, 2 years ago, before I became President, the steel industry was sliding backward. Production had dropped off. Plant capacity was unused. Steelworkers were out of jobs. Foreign imports were flooding into our country. Dumping occurred. We've solved that problem to a major degree. Since May, we've had a trigger price mechanism designed very carefully in harmony with the labor unions representing steelworkers and the steel executives as well.

We've seen this problem turn around. We've had a net increase of 24,000 steelworkers in the last year. Domestic distribution of American steel has increased 5 percent. Exports from Japan have actually gone down in steel. Profits have gone up enormously. The second quarter profits in the steel industry this year compared to last year are up 71 percent, which means that the industry is now strong enough to begin reinvesting those profits in modernization plans to provide jobs in the future for a basic industry that's important to us all. These are the kind of things that we are trying to do in the steel industry.

In some areas we've had special problems. One of my worst concerns is in Youngstown, Ohio, where we do have a serious problem.

I can't order the free enterprise system to accommodate change or to prevent change occurring. But we do need to have a partnership evolve between the local government, like in Youngstown, the State government in the Columbus statehouse, and Washington, to make sure that the damage done to the people who live there is minimal. We do not have that kind of cooperation with the Ohio State government. We need people there who can work in harmony with us, to make sure that we do have changes made to correct this deficiency.

The last problem I'd like to point out to you is one that perhaps is of most interest to me, except maybe the military, where I had my professional career planned.

When I first went home from the Navy, I was appointed to the Sumter County Library Board. Later, I became a member of the Sumter County Board of Education. I was dismayed at the low quality of our schools, and I ran for the Georgia Senate because of my hopes that Georgia could have a better system of education. When I got there, I had one request—that I be put on the education committee. And later, I became chairman of one of the most important committees in education.

I ran for Governor on a platform of better education for Georgia children, and I was elected. And I would say that 25 percent of my time as Governor was devoted to improving the educational system in our State.

You have a State that's blessed with great material wealth, people who believe and always have believed in a better future than the past was. But in this State there is a very embarrassing situation that doesn't occur anywhere else in our Nation, so far as I know. When children whom you love and whom I love don't have a stable, adequately financed, open school system, to me that's a devastating reflection on the leadership in your State. And I hope that you can do something about that on November 7 and elect State officials, particularly a Governor who cares about schoolchildren, as you and I care so deeply ourselves.

Well, I'm thankful that you would let me come here today and tonight and talk about a few things that are on my mind. I feel that we're part of a team. In the past, that was demonstrated to my benefit because I became President, elected to the highest office in our land. But my performance there is only as good as your support while I serve.

There's a good harmony that exists between myself and those men and women on this stage. And I believe that together we can correct the problems that we still face, answer the difficult questions, and face the future with the confidence that our Nation's strength deserves.

I'm proud to be a Democrat. I'm proud to represent a party and a country that's always maintained its ideals intact.

When I ran for President, a lot of people laughed at me. And still, jokes are made because I said that I want a government as good as our people, and a lot of people said we wouldn't have a very good government. That's not true, because among the American people there's a basic honesty, a basic decency, a basic unselfishness that's waiting to be tapped even more deeply. And I think that you and I, as Democrats, have a great deal to expect, because we'll have an even better future than we already have in the greatest nation on Earth.

Thank you very much.

NOTE: The President spoke at 8:26 p.m. at the Aladdin Shrine Temple. In his opening remarks he referred to Paul Tipps, chairman of the Democratic Party in Ohio, John C. White, chairman of the Democratic National Committee, Jim Bauman, Ohio State representative and Democratic candidate for the U.S. Congress, and Henry Eckhard, former chairman of the Public Utilities Commission in Ohio.

World Bank Group and International Monetary Fund

Remarks at the Opening Session of the Annual Meetings of the Boards of Governors. September 25, 1978

Mr. Chairman, Managing Director de-Larosiere, President McNamara, Governors of the Fund and the Bank, and distinguished visitors:

On behalf of the American people, I want to welcome you to Washington again for your 33d annual meeting.

We meet as a group, dedicated to the cause of international cooperation. In the political field, you and I share the belief that cooperation among leaders can lead to peace. We've learned that lesson once again in the last few days. And I know that you will join me in saluting the statesmanship and the courage of President

Anwar Sadat and Prime Minister Menahem Begin.

Your tremendous influence as leaders in your own nations can contribute greatly to maintaining the momentum toward peace, both in the Middle East and throughout the world. In the economic field, also, cooperation brings large benefits to the people who look to us for leadership.

Three decades of existence of the Fund and the Bank have brought progress and a better life for the people of the world. Like you, I want to build on that record to achieve still further economic cooperation, progress, and a better life. Since your meeting here last year, our countries, acting together, have made tangible progress on world economic problems.

The issues that remain, as you and I well know, are very difficult. But they, like other difficult questions, are not insoluble.

You assembled in this room are the economic leaders of the world. The task before you is to consolidate past gains and then to push ahead in ways that will foster economic growth in both developing and the industrialized nations.

Our goal is to achieve progress for all peoples, not just a few. The basic strategy has already been agreed. In Mexico City, at the IMF Interim Committee, agreement was reached on the general directions that economic policy should take.

Progress on those agreements has been made. The outlook for improvement is good. We must not falter. A contribution to this strategy is needed from every country represented here, no matter how great nor small, no matter how weak nor powerful.

In this effort, the United States has a major responsibility. Two months ago at Bonn, I made specific promises to our major trading partners about the actions that my country will take to this end. I pledged that the United States will fight inflation,

1627

will reduce oil imports, will expand exports.

Let there be no doubt in your mind about how seriously I take these pledges that have been made on my own word of honor and on behalf of the people of the United States. Taken together, they encompass the most urgent priorities of my own administration; my own reputation is at stake as a leader. And they are commitments that I am most fully determined to fulfill.

I've come here today to underline that determination and to describe the next steps that we will take.

I will soon announce the first phase of a long-term program to expand American exports. Removing disincentives to exports and encouraging exports are overriding tasks for my own administration. As you know, compared to many nations represented here, the export commitment has not been as great in our own country as it has perhaps among some of you.

I've also intensified my efforts, which were already great, to obtain legislation that will curtail United States imports of oil, imports which are entirely too high.

The United States Senate is scheduled to vote this week, day after tomorrow, on the key bill, natural gas regulation and pricing. This is one of the most complicated and difficult and challenging assignments that the United States Congress has ever faced.

This particular bill is expected to save 1.4 million barrels of imported oil per day by 1985. I am confident that the Senate and then the House of Representatives will do their duty to our Nation by approving this bill. I hope to have other bills comprising a strong package of energy legislation enacted before the Congress adjourns, probably, hopefully, less than a month from now.

This is essential, we know, to a sound American dollar. I intend very shortly to announce a further series of important and specific and tough measures to strengthen our fight against inflation.

These next steps will certainly not be the end of our effort, only the renewed beginning and commitment, part of a sustained effort to control these very serious problems for our own people in this country, and our relationship with your countries as well.

Every nation represented in this room understands how difficult this struggle against inflation is and what sustained commitment it demands. My administration will continue that struggle on a wide variety of fronts until we succeed. There will be obstacles and objections from special interest groups all along the way. But I will not shrink from the hard decisions and the persistent efforts that are needed.

I'm determined to maintain a sound dollar. This is of primary importance to us, and I know it is of great interest and importance to you as well. We recognize that our currency plays an international role, and we accept the responsibilities which this involves. Our countries are acting to meet our responsibilities to the system, consistent with the directives set at the IMF meeting in Mexico and as was pledged again by seven of us national leaders at the Bonn summit. The United States will do the same.

Through programs which I have just described, we will achieve the strong U.S. economy and noninflationary U.S. growth that must underlie a sound dollar and a stable international monetary system.

The outlook for progress is good. Some of the causes of our large trade deficit have already been removed. Others are now being removed. Our current account position should improve significantly next year. The United States will remain an open and vigorous economy, and an attractive place to invest.

Other steps are also required to achieve the economic progress that we all seek. In these steps, the IMF and the World Bank have, of course, a vital role to play. These two institutions are the core and the symbol of the international economic order that was built after World War II. They've shown a high capacity to adapt to new and rapidly changing needs. Strengthening and enlarging them, both institutions, is a prime goal of United States policy.

The United States is firmly committed to a strong International Monetary Fund, exercising effective surveillance over the system and with adequate resources to meet official financing needs. The United States has supported and will continue to support an increase in IMF quotas and a new allocation of special drawing rights.

I'm pleased that legislative consideration of U.S. participation in the supplementary financing facility is nearing completion. I expect final action to be taken shortly.

I might report to you that this year, the attitude of the United States Congress is better than it has been in my own memory toward supporting international financial institutions and toward foreign aid as well.

I trust that our European friends will fashion the proposed European monetary arrangements which were discussed, at least superficially, at Bonn in a way that will also strengthen the international monetary system and that will facilitate growth and trade and investment and also, quite importantly, the continued central role of the IMF.

Current European efforts to these ends are a logical step toward the greater European integration which the United States

has long supported. We also support proposals to enlarge the resources of the World Bank and its soft loan affiliate, the International Development Association, as we pledged at the Bonn summit.

Again, the Congress has met our expectations. Expanded help to developing countries contributes, we know, to the healthy world economy and to world peace. Last week, the United States Senate, as the House of Representatives had already done, met our Nation's obligations for both multilateral and bilateral aid beyond, I must admit, my own expectations.

I will seek next year to continue this commitment as part of a growing international effort to eliminate the worst aspects of human poverty. The United States Governor for the Fund and the Bank, Secretary of Treasury Mike Blumenthal, will outline our policies in more detail and our prospects for achievement in more detail when he addresses your session tomorrow.

You are gathered in Washington to address formidable challenges in both monetary and development fields. The future of all peoples in both developing and developed countries depends upon the outcome of your deliberations and subsequent action. I reiterate my Nation's commitment to the common effort that is required. I am confident that this joint effort will succeed.

Thank you very much.

NOTE: The President spoke at 3:25 p.m. in the Sheraton Hall at the Sheraton-Park Hotel to representatives of the International Monetary Fund, the International Bank for Reconstruction and Development (World Bank), the International Development Association, and the International Finance Corporation.

In his opening remarks, the President referred to Tengku Razaleigh Hamzah, Chairman of the Boards of Governors of the IBRD and IMF, Jacques deLarosiere, Managing Director of the IMF, and Robert S. McNamara, President of the IBRD.

United Nations Educational, Scientific, and Cultural Organization

Nomination of U. S. Representatives and Alternate Representatives to the 20th Session of the General Conference.
September 26, 1978

The President today announced the persons whom he will nominate to be Representatives and Alternate Representatives of the United States to the 20th session of the General Conference of the United Nations Educational, Scientific, and Cultural Organization (UNESCO), to be held in Paris from October 24 to November 28. They are:

Representatives

JOHN E. REINHARDT, Director of the U.S. International Communication Agency;

ESTEBAN TORRES, U.S. Permanent Representative to UNESCO;

HALE CHAMPION, Under Secretary of Health, Education, and Welfare;

SARAH G. POWER, chairwoman of the U.S. National Commission for UNESCO, and regent of the University of Michigan;

WILLIAM ATTWOOD, president and publisher of Newsday, Inc.

Alternate Representatives

MATHILDE KRIM, associate member of the Sloan-Kettering Institute for Cancer Research;

JOSEPH D. DUFFEY, Chairman of the National Endowment for the Humanities;

ARTHUR K. SOLOMON, professor of biophysics at Harvard Medical School;

LEILA FRASER, chief administrator to the mayor of Milwaukee;

MAURICE A. FERRE, mayor of Miami.

United States Export Policy

Remarks Announcing Administration Proposals.   September 26, 1978

One of the problems that our Nation has faced for several years, but with grow-ing concern recently, has been the very high negative trade balance. We have imported a great deal more than we have exported.

There are obviously several reasons for this. One is the extraordinary increase in the imports of oil which, as you know, have increased 800 percent in the last 6 years, so that we now import about half our total oil. This has created inflationary pressures. It has caused some doubt about our Nation's leadership, and we have been considering for a number of months what we might do about this problem.

I know the obvious cause for high trade imbalance is not exporting enough of the products that we ourselves can produce. Secretary Juanita Kreps, Secretary of Commerce, has been working with a task force recently in trying to resolve this particular aspect of our problem.

Obviously, exported goods create much needed jobs for Americans, and it corrects the defects that I've just described to you.

We've never been a nation that emphasized exports enough, because we've been so highly blessed with natural resources, approaching a degree almost of self-sufficiency.

We've never depended upon exports as have other nations who trade with us like Japan, Germany, and others. But there's a growing consciousness in our country now that we would like to accelerate, that export commitments should be a part of every producer in our country, both large, medium-sized, and small.

Many people don't know how to export. They don't know how to package goods for sales overseas, how to get their products to a transportation center, how to deliver and handle the paperwork, how to locate foreign buyers. These are the kinds of educational processes that we hope to explore, also.

Lately we've seen a slowing down in research and development commitment in our country as well, and we hope to expedite a recommitment to planning for the future, so that we can be technologically compatible and competitive with our foreign trading partners.

We also, of course, want to remove trade barriers that have been created by congressional action and by administrative action which prevent exports from going overseas, and we are negotiating with our foreign trade partners to eliminate trade barriers that prevent our own products from entering their countries. In doing this, we must be careful not to lower our standards for environmental quality or the safety or health of American workers, or our commitment to principles of human rights and others on which our Nation has been founded and exists.

Secretary of Commerce Juanita Kreps will now give you some specific proposals that have been evolved by her own department, by Members of Congress, by other members of the Cabinet, and by the business and labor leaders of our country.

Secretary Kreps.

NOTE: The President spoke at 2:33 p.m. to reporters assembled in the Briefing Room at the White House. Following his remarks, Secretary Kreps held a news conference on the proposals.

United States Export Policy

Statement by the President.
September 26, 1978

It is important for this Nation's economic vitality that both the private sector and the Federal Government place a higher priority on exports. I am today announcing a series of measures that evi-

dences my administration's strong commitment to do so.

The large trade deficits the United States has experienced in recent years have weakened the value of the dollar, intensified inflationary pressures in our own economy, and heightened instability in the world economy. These trade deficits have been caused by a number of factors. A major cause has been our excessive reliance on imported oil. We can reduce that reliance through the passage of sound energy legislation this year. Another factor is that the United States economy has been growing at a stronger pace in recent years than the economies of our major trading partners. That has enabled us to purchase relatively more foreign goods while our trading partners have not been able to buy as much of our exports. We will begin to correct this imbalance as our trading partners meet the commitments to economic expansion they made at the Bonn summit.

The relatively slow growth of American exports has also been an important factor in our trade deficit problem. Over the past 20 years, our exports have grown at only half the rate of other industrial nations, and the United States has been losing its share of world markets. Until now, both business and Government have accorded exports a relatively low priority. These priorities must be changed.

The measures I am announcing today consist of actions this administration has taken and will take to:
(1) provide increased direct assistance to United States exporters;
(2) reduce domestic barriers to exports; and
(3) reduce foreign barriers to our exports and secure a fairer international trading system for all exporters.

These actions are in furtherance of the commitment I made at the Bonn summit to an improved United States export performance.

DIRECT ASSISTANCE TO UNITED STATES
EXPORTERS

1. *Export-Import Bank.* I have consistently supported a more effective and aggressive Export-Import Bank. During the past 2 years, my administration has increased Eximbank's loan authorization fivefold—from $700 million in FY 1977 to $3.6 billion for FY 1979. I intend to ask Congress for an additional $500 million in FY 1980, bringing Eximbank's total loan authorization to $4.1 billion. These authorizations will provide the Bank with the funds necessary to improve its competitiveness, in a manner consistent with our international obligations, through increased flexibility in the areas of interest rates, length of loans, and the percentage of a transaction it can finance. The Bank is also moving to simplify its fee schedules and to make its programs more accessible to smaller exporters and to agricultural exporters.

2. *SBA Loans to Small Exporters.* The Small Business Administration will channel up to $100 million of its current authorization for loan guarantees to small business exporters to provide seed money for their entry into foreign markets. Small exporting firms meeting SBA's qualifications will be eligible for loan guarantees totaling up to $500,000 to meet needs for expanded production capacity and to ease cash flow problems involving overseas sales or initial marketing expenses.

3. *Export Development Programs.* I am directing the Office of Management and Budget to allocate an additional $20 million in annual resources for export development programs of the Departments of Commerce and State to assist United States firms, particularly small and medium-sized businesses, in marketing abroad through:

—a computerized information system to provide exporters with prompt access to international marketing opportunities abroad and to expose American products to foreign buyers;

—risk-sharing programs to help associations and small companies meet initial export marketing costs; and

—targeted assistance to firms and industries with high export potential and intensified short-term export campaigns in promising markets.

4. *Agricultural Exports.* Agricultural exports are a vital component of the U.S. trade balance. Over the past 10 years, the volume of U.S. farm exports has doubled and the dollar value has nearly quadrupled. Trade in agricultural products will contribute a net surplus of almost $13 billion in fiscal year 1978. This strong performance is due in part to this administration's multifaceted agricultural export policy, which will be strengthened and which includes:

—An increase of almost $1 billion (up from $750 million in FY 1977 to $1.7 billion in FY 1978) in the level of short-term export credits.

—An increase of almost 20 percent in the level of funding support for a highly successful program of cooperation with over 60 agricultural commodity associations in market development.

—Efforts in the Multilateral Trade Negotiations to link the treatment of agricultural and nonagricultural products.

—Opening trade offices in key importing nations in order to facilitate the development of these markets.

—Aggressive pursuit of an international wheat agreement to ensure our producers a fair share of the expanding world market.

—Support of legislation to provide intermediate export credit for selective agricultural exports.

5. *Tax Measures.* I am hopeful that Congress will work with the administration to promptly resolve the tax problems of Americans employed abroad, many of whom are directly involved in export efforts. Last February, I proposed tax relief for these citizens amounting to about $250 million a year. I think this proposal, which Congress has not approved, deals fairly and, during a time of great budget stringency, responsibly with this problem. I remain ready to work with the Congress to resolve this issue, but I cannot support proposals which run contrary to our strong concerns for budget prudence and tax equity.

My administration's concern for exports is matched by our obligation to ensure that government-sponsored export incentives constitute an efficient use of the taxpayers' money. The DISC tax provision simply does not meet that basic test. It is a costly (over $1 billion a year) and inefficient incentive for exports. I continue to urge Congress to phase DISC out or at least make it simpler, less costly, and more effective than it is now, and my administration stands ready to work with Congress toward that goal.

REDUCTION OF DOMESTIC BARRIERS TO EXPORTS

Direct financial and technical assistance to United States firms should encourage them to take advantage of the increasing competitiveness of our goods in international markets. Equally important will be the reduction of Government-imposed disincentives and barriers which unnecessarily inhibit our firms from selling abroad. We can and will continue to administer the laws and policies affecting the international business community firmly and fairly, but we can also discharge that responsibility with a greater sensitivity to the importance of exports than has been the case in the past.

1. *Export Consequences of Regulations.* I am directing the heads of all executive departments and agencies to take into account and weigh as a factor the possible adverse effects on our trade balance of their major administrative and regulatory actions that have significant export consequences. They will report back on their progress in identifying and reducing such negative export effects where possible, consistent with other legal and policy obligations. I will make a similar request of the independent regulatory agencies. In addition, the Council of Economic Advisers will consider export consequences as part of the administration's Regulatory Analysis Program.

There may be areas, such as the export of products which pose serious health and safety risks, where new regulations are warranted. But through the steps outlined above, I intend to inject a greater awareness throughout the Government of the effects on exports of administrative and regulatory actions.

2. *Export Controls for Foreign Policy Purposes.* I am directing the Departments of Commerce, State, Defense, and Agriculture to take export consequences fully into account when considering the use of export controls for foreign policy purposes. Weight will be given to whether the goods in question are also available from countries other than the United States.

3. *Foreign Corrupt Practices Act.* At my direction, the Justice Department will provide guidance to the business community concerning its enforcement priorities under the recently enacted foreign antibribery statute. This statute should not be viewed as an impediment to the conduct of legitimate business activities abroad. I am hopeful that American business will not forgo legitimate export opportunities because of uncertainty about the applica-

tion of this statute. The guidance provided by the Justice Department should be helpful in that regard.

4. *Antitrust Laws.* There are instances in which joint ventures and other kinds of cooperative arrangements between American firms are necessary or desirable to improve our export performance. The Justice Department has advised that most such foreign joint ventures would not violate our antitrust laws, and in many instances would actually strengthen competition. This is especially true for one-time joint ventures created to participate in a single activity, such as a large construction project. In fact, no such joint conduct has been challenged under the antitrust laws in over 20 years.

Nevertheless, many businessmen apparently are uncertain on this point, and this uncertainty can be a disincentive to exports. I have, therefore, instructed the Justice Department, in conjunction with the Commerce Department, to clarify and explain the scope of the antitrust laws in this area, with special emphasis on the kinds of joint ventures that are unlikely to raise antitrust problems.

I have also instructed the Justice Department to give expedited treatment to requests by business firms for guidance on international antitrust issues under the Department's Business Review Program. Finally, I will appoint a business advisory panel to work with the National Commission for the Review of the Antitrust Laws.

5. *Environmental Reviews.* For a number of years the export community has faced the uncertainty of whether the National Environmental Policy Act (NEPA) requires environmental impact statements for Federal export licenses, permits, and approvals.

I will shortly sign an Executive order which should assist U.S. exports by eliminating the present uncertainties concerning the type of environmental reviews that will be applicable and the Federal actions relating to exports that will be affected. The order will make the following export-related clarifications:

—Environmental impact statements will not be required for Federal export licenses, permits, approvals, and other export-related actions that have potential environmental effects in foreign countries.

—Export licenses issued by the Departments of Commerce and Treasury will be exempt from any environmental reviews required by the Executive order.

—Abbreviated environmental reviews will be required only with respect to (1) nuclear reactors, (2) financing of products and facilities whose toxic effects create serious public health risks, and (3) certain Federal actions having a significant adverse effect on the environment of nonparticipating third countries or natural resources of global importance.

Accordingly, this order will establish environmental requirements for only a minor fraction (well below 5 percent) of the dollar volume of United States exports. At the same time, it will provide procedures to define and focus on those exports which should receive special scrutiny because of their major environmental impacts abroad. This Executive order will fairly balance our concern for the environment with our interest in promoting exports.

REDUCTION IN FOREIGN TRADE BARRIERS
AND SUBSIDIES

We are also taking important international initiatives to improve U.S. export performance. Trade restrictions imposed by other countries inhibit our ability to export. Tariff and especially nontariff barriers restrict our ability to develop new foreign markets and expand existing ones. We are now working to eliminate or reduce these barriers through the Multilateral Trade Negotiations in Geneva.

United States export performance is also adversely affected by the excessive financial credits and subsidies which some of our trading partners offer to their own exporters. One of our major objectives in the MTN is to negotiate an international code restricting the use of government subsidies for exports. In addition, I am directing the Secretary of the Treasury to undertake immediate consulations with our trading partners to expand the scope and tighten the terms of the existing International Arrangement on Export Credits.

I hope that our major trading partners will see the importance of reaching more widespread agreements on the use of export finance to avoid a costly competition which is economically unsound and ultimately self-defeating for all of us. These international agreements are essential to assure that American exporters do not face unfair competition, and this administration intends to work vigorously to secure them.

CONCLUSION

While these initiatives will assist private business in increasing exports, our export problem has been building for many years, and we cannot expect dramatic improvement overnight. Increasing our exports will take time and require a sustained effort. Announcement of my administration's export policy is not the end of our task, but rather the beginning. To ensure that this issue continues to receive priority attention, I am asking Secretary Kreps, in coordination with officials from other concerned Government agencies, to direct the continuation of efforts to improve our export potential and performance.

I will shortly sign an Executive order to reconstitute a more broadly based President's Export Council to bring a continuous flow of fresh ideas into our Government policymaking process. I expect this Council to report to me annually through the Secretary of Commerce.

Increasing U.S. exports is a major challenge—for business, for labor, and for Government. Better export performance by the United States would spur growth in the economy. It would create jobs. It would strengthen the dollar and fight inflation

There are no short-term, easy solutions. But the actions I am announcing today reflect my administration's determination to give the United States trade deficit the high-level, sustained attention it deserves. They are the first step in a long-term effort to strengthen this Nation's export position in world trade.

Employment Tax Credit Legislation

Statement on Action by the Senate Finance Committee.   September 26, 1978

It is with great satisfaction that I note the approval today by the Senate Finance Committee of the administration's proposed legislation to provide substantial tax credits to employers willing to hire disadvantaged young workers, 18 to 24 years of age.

Continued, unacceptably high levels of unemployment for young and disadvantaged Americans, especially black and Hispanic young people, require vigorous national action. This tax credit, introduced as part of my urban policy legislation in March, would enlist the private business sector as an effective partner with government to help us move toward a solution of one of our most serious problems.

1635

International Security Assistance Act of 1978

Statement on Signing S. 3075 Into Law.
September 26, 1978

I am pleased to be able to take the action authorized by the International Security Assistance Act to fully terminate the force and effect of the embargo on arms transfers to Turkey.

The Nation is well served by the prudent decision of Congress which makes this action possible. With the removal of these restrictions, the United States will be better able to accomplish its goals in the vital Eastern Mediterranean region: to improve our bilateral relationships with Greece, Turkey, and Cyprus; to strengthen NATO's southern flank; and to help promote a just and lasting settlement of the Cyprus problem. In this effort to encourage the restoration of a stable and peaceful atmosphere in the Eastern Mediterranean, we will be fully guided by the principles set forth in the act.

This action will enable us to resume full military cooperation with Turkey and begin a new chapter in our relationship with Turkey. This relationship is important not only because of our mutual security concerns but also because of our shared commitment to democracy.

NOTE: As enacted, S. 3075 is Public Law 95–384, approved September 26.

United States-Turkey Military Cooperation

Memorandum From the President.
September 26, 1978

PRESIDENTIAL DETERMINATION No. 78-18

Memorandum for the Secretary of State

Subject: Determination and Certification Under the International Security Assist-

ance Act of 1978 Regarding Resumption of Full Military Cooperation With Turkey

Pursuant to the authority vested in me by Section 13(a) of the International Security Assistance Act of 1978, I hereby determine and certify:

(1) that the resumption of full military cooperation with Turkey is in the national interest of the United States and in the interest of the North Atlantic Treaty Organization; and

(2) that the Government of Turkey is acting in good faith to achieve a just and peaceful settlement of the Cyprus problem, the early peaceable return of refugees to their homes and properties, and continued removal of Turkish military troops from Cyprus in the context of a solution to the Cyprus problem, and the early serious resumption of inter-communal talks aimed at a just, negotiated settlement.

You are requested on my behalf to report this determination and certification to the Congress.

This determination and certification shall be published in the FEDERAL REGISTER.

JIMMY CARTER

[Filed with the Office of the Federal Register, 4 p.m., October 6, 1978]

National Farm-City Week, 1978

Proclamation 4602.   September 27, 1978

By the President of the United States of America

A Proclamation

The interdependence of farms and cities is one of the basic strengths of the Nation.

Farm people and city people have long been partners in economic and social progress. Their partnership in the use of land, labor and capital is essential if this country is to have a continuing and adequate supply of safe, wholesome food and an abundance of goods and services and reasonable prices.

To achieve a better mutual understanding of the interdependence that farm and city people bring to one another, and for the strength, well-being and benefit of all Americans, our Nation has traditionally set aside one week in November as Farm-City Week.

Now, THEREFORE, I, JIMMY CARTER, President of the United States of America, do hereby designate the period November 17 through November 23, 1978, as National Farm-City Week.

IN WITNESS WHEREOF, I have hereunto set my hand this twenty-seventh day of September, in the year of our Lord nineteen hundred seventy-eight, and of the Independence of the United States of America the two hundred and third.

JIMMY CARTER

[Filed with the Office of the Federal Register, 11:22 a.m., September 27, 1978]

Energy Coordinating Committee

Executive Order 12083.   September 27, 1978

By the authority vested in me as President by the Constitution of the United States of America, and in order to provide for the coordination of Federal energy policies, it is hereby ordered as follows:

1-1. *Establishment of the Committee.*

1-101. There is established an Energy Coordinating Committee, hereinafter referred to as the Committee.

1-102. The Committee shall be composed of the following, and such other members as the President may, from time to time, designate.

(a) The Secretary of Energy, who shall be the Chairman.

(b) The Secretary of State.

(c) The Secretary of the Treasury.

(d) The Secretary of Defense.

(e) The Attorney General.

(f) The Secretary of the Interior.

(g) The Secretary of Agriculture.

(h) The Secretary of Commerce.

(i) The Secretary of Labor.

(j) The Secretary of Health, Education, and Welfare.

(k) The Secretary of Housing and Urban Development.

(l) The Secretary of Transportation.

(m) The Special Representative for Trade Negotiations.

(n) The Director of the Office of Management and Budget.

(o) The Chairman of the Council of Economic Advisers.

(p) The Chairman of the Council on Environmental Quality.

(q) The Administrator of the Environmental Protection Agency.

(r) The Director of the Office of Science and Technology Policy.

(s) The Administrator of General Services.

(t) The Director of the National Science Foundation.

(u) The Assistant to the President for National Security Affairs.

(v) The Assistant to the President for Domestic Affairs and Policy.

(w) The Chairman of the Nuclear Regulatory Commission, who is invited to be a member.

1-2. *Functions of the Committee.*

1-201. The Committee shall ensure that there is communication and coordination among Executive agencies concerning energy policy and the management of energy resources.

1-202. The Committee shall, from time to time, develop and consider recommendations for improvements in the implementation of Federal energy policies or the management of energy resources that involve two or more Executive agencies.

1–203. The functions of the Committee shall neither substitute for nor replace Executive Office of the President clearance, review, and decision-making procedures. Those procedures shall also be used for submitting to the President any of the conclusions or recommendations developed through the Committee's energy coordinating functions.

1–204. The Committee shall meet at the call of the Chairman.

1–3. *Executive Council.*

1–301. During periods when the Committee is not meeting, the functions of the Committee are delegated to an Executive Council. Meetings may be called by any regular member of the Council.

1–302. The Executive Council shall be composed of the following, and such others as may be appropriate due to the specific matters to be considered.

(a) The Chairman of the Committee, who shall be Chairman of the Executive Council.

(b) The Director of the Office of Management and Budget.

(c) The Chairman of the Council of Economic Advisers.

(d) The Assistant to the President for National Security Affairs.

(e) The Assistant to the President for Domestic Affairs and Policy.

1–4. *Revocation of a Prior Order.* Executive Order No. 11814, as amended, which provided for an Energy Resources Council, is revoked.

JIMMY CARTER

The White House,
  September 27, 1978.

[Filed with the Office of the Federal Register,
  2:36 p.m., September 27, 1978]

Judicial Nominating Commission for the District of Puerto Rico

Executive Order 12084.   September 27, 1978

By the authority vested in me as President by the Constitution and statutes of the United States of America, and in order to create in accord with the Federal Advisory Committee Act (5 U.S.C. App. I) an advisory committee on judicial nominations for the District of Puerto Rico, it is hereby ordered as follows:

1–1. *Establishment of the Commission.*

1–101. There is established the Judicial Nominating Commission for the District of Puerto Rico.

1–102. The Commission shall have seven members appointed by the President. The President shall designate a Chairman from among the members.

1–2. *Functions of the Commission.*

1–201. The Commission shall begin functioning when the President or his designee notifies the Chairman that the President desires the Commission's assistance in identifying persons qualified to fill a vacancy on the United States District Court for the District of Puerto Rico.

1–202. Upon receiving such notification, the Commission shall:

(a) give public notice of the vacancy, inviting suggestions as to potential nominees;

(b) conduct inquiries to identify potential nominees;

(c) conduct inquiries to identify, among the potential nominees, persons who are well qualified to serve as a United States District Judge; and

(d) report to the President, within the time specified in the notification, the results of its activities, including a list of the persons whom the Commission considers to be best qualified to fill the vacancy.

1–203. In evaluating potential nominees, the Commission shall use standards provided by the Attorney General.

1–3. *Administrative Provisions.*

1–301. Members of the Commission shall serve without compensation. While engaged in the work of the Commission, members may receive travel expenses, including per diem in lieu of subsistence, as authorized by law (5 U.S.C. 5702 and 5703).

1–302. The Attorney General shall furnish to the Commission necessary administrative support.

1–303. All necessary expenses incurred in connection with the work of the Commission, to the extent permitted by law, shall be paid from funds available to the Attorney General.

1–4. *General Provisions.*

1–401. A person who is a member of the Commission shall not, during the period of membership and for one year after that period, be considered by the Commission as a potential nominee.

1–402. Notwithstanding the provisions of any other Executive order, the functions of the President under the Federal Advisory Committee Act (5 U.S.C. App. I), except that of reporting annually to the Congress, which are applicable to the Commission, shall be performed by the Attorney General in accordance with the guidelines and procedures established by the Administrator of General Services.

1–403. The Commission shall terminate on December 31, 1978, unless sooner extended by the President.

JIMMY CARTER

The White House,
    September 27, 1978.

[Filed with the Office of the Federal Register,
    2:37 p.m., September 27, 1978]

National Science and Technology Policy, Organization, and Priorities Act of 1976

Message to the Congress Transmitting a Report. September 27, 1978

To the Congress of the United States:

I am pleased to submit to the Congress the first annual report on science and technology as required by the National Science and Technology Policy, Organization, and Priorities Act of 1976.

Science and technology contribute in significant ways to many of our social needs—maintaining economic growth and productivity, feeding the world's people, improving our health and environment, and preserving our national security. They also reveal the basic structure of nature. Moreover, our science and technology draw the respect and admiration of nations throughout the world.

I believe this report, and its successors, can play an important role in providing a foundation for informed debate on scientific and technological issues, and thereby can help assure that our scientific and technological capabilities remain strong.

JIMMY CARTER

The White House,
    September 27, 1978.

NOTE: The 122-page report is entitled "Science and Technology: Annual Report to the Congress, August 1978—National Science Foundation."

California Debris Commission

Nomination of Col. John M. Adsit To Be a Member. September 27, 1978

The President today announced that he will nominate Col. John M. Adsit, Corps of Engineers, to be a member of the California Debris Commission.

Adsit, 45, has been in the Army since 1956. He has been district engineer for the San Francisco District, U.S. Army Corps of Engineers, since 1977.

International Women's Year, 1975

Message to the Congress Transmitting a Report.   September 27, 1978

To the Congress of the United States:

By mandating International Women's Year, Congress set in motion a series of fifty-two regional meetings that brought together women of all races, incomes, ethnic backgrounds and religious beliefs to consider the major issues confronting women. The culmination of International Women's Year was the National Women's Conference held in Houston on November, 1977. That conference was a turning point in American Women's long struggle for equality. In Houston, delegates elected at the regional meetings developed the *National Plan of Action*—a national agenda to achieve women's full rights and equality.

In response to the Plan's recommendations, the Administration has reviewed our programs designed to improve the opportunities for women. This Message summarizes the results of that review and forwards to the Congress the more detailed status report on Administration action on the IWY resolutions.

A keystone toward achieving equality for women would be the addition of the Equal Rights Amendment to the Constitution. By passing this Amendment, the Congress recognized the need to provide Constitutional guarantees against discrimination on the basis of sex. More than any

other single act, ratification of the Equal Rights Amendment will affirm the right of women to participate fully in American life. To ensure that women do not lose the opportunity to secure that precious right, the deadline for ratification should be extended.

Because I feel very strongly about women's equality, I sent a Memorandum last month to the heads of all departments and agencies. In that Memorandum, I directed the head of each department and agency (1) to emphasize the Administration's commitment to the Equal Rights Amendment; (2) to review the Federal Women's Program in their agency or department to determine how it can be strengthened; (3) to designate a policy-level representative from their agency or department to serve on the Interdepartmental Task Force on Women; and (4) to provide adequate staff for that representative.

However, we must not stop here. We must make every effort to help women assume their rightful place in every part of American life. This is in the national interest, for we cannot meet the important challenges of the coming decades without full participation of all our citizens, including women.

As President, I have acted upon my firm commitment to equity for women in my appointments, programs, and policies. I believe that the Federal government should serve as a model of nondiscrimination, and I shall continue to take steps toward that goal. In my Administration, women are serving in the Cabinet and at all levels of government. Still, much more remains to be done. That is why I have set in motion the Interdepartmental Task Force on Women, National Advisory Committee for Women, other key task forces, and departmental studies to recommend additional action.

My Administration is dedicated to eliminating discrimination against women. Among the crucial issues which demand our attention:

• Passage of the Equal Rights Amendment and the Resolution for Extending the Deadline for Ratification;

• Passage of pending legislation which improves the status of women as recommended in this report;

• Enforcement of all civil rights laws, particularly Title IX of the Education Amendments of 1972, which prohibits sex discrimination in Federally-financed education programs; and

• Development of improved statistical information to permit adequate evaluation of the impact of Federal programs and practices on women.

THE STATUS REPORT

International Women's Year helped raise the expectations and consciousness of American women, who now look to government, private industry, and the community for bold and energetic responses. In accepting the final report of the National Commission for International Women's Year, I reaffirmed my commitment to equality for women and my determination to help keep the spirit of Houston alive. At that time, I directed that a status report be prepared on the Administration's initial steps to implement the *National Plan of Action*. Today I am pleased to present that report with my recommendations to the Congress.

To assess our progress toward the goals described in the *National Plan of Action,* each department and agency was asked to report all current legislative and executive actions reflecting the aims and spirit of Houston. More than three hundred women, both from inside and outside the Federal government, and representing a wide range of interests, reviewed the agency surveys. Many of their sugges-

tions were incorporated into the final report, and I am grateful for their help.

A set of detailed recommendations for implementation of the *National Plan of Action* separate from this report was developed as part of this work. I shall transmit these recommendations to the Interdepartmental Task Force on Women and the National Advisory Committee for Women for review and advice.

Part I of the report sets forth those portions of the *Plan's* twenty-six resolutions calling for Federal action, and indicates the major Administration legislative and executive initiatives in the first eighteen months in those areas. In the months ahead we shall continue to *start* new initiatives to improve equity for women in areas included in *The Plan of Action* and beyond. Part II of the report describes other legislative measures which represent efforts to approach these issues in different ways.

REPORT HIGHLIGHTS

The report summarizes more than seventy-five important initiatives taken during the first eighteen months of this Administration to provide greater equity for women. These include new laws and programs, increased funding, and improved administration in areas addressed by the *National Plan of Action*. Let me highlight some of our major steps:

• More than 21 percent of my appointments within the White House and the executive branch have been women, an all-time high for any Administration. In response to my instructions, Cabinet members and agency heads also sought out and appointed women to important positions. We shall continue to do so.

• My Administration has acted:

(1) to improve Federal employment opportunities for women;

(2) to examine and make recommendations to address the problems women

business owners face in obtaining Federal grants and contracts;

(3) to enforce existing civil rights laws (*i.e.,* The Equal Credit Opportunity Act of 1974, the Fair Housing Act, Title IX of the Education Amendments of 1972, and The Civil Rights Act of 1964);

(4) to improve the collection and dissemination of data on the status of women; and

(5) to increase funding and visibility of programs serving women's needs.

• My Reorganization Plan # 1 of 1978, a major reorganization effort of the Administration, strengthens and consolidates within the Equal Employment Opportunity Commission Federal enforcement of laws and executive orders against job discrimination based on sex and race.

• I have signed and am fully implementing several important new laws—Protection of Children Against Sexual Exploitation Act of 1977, The Child Abuse Prevention and Treatment and Adoption Reform Act of 1978, the Social Security Amendments of 1977, and The Age Discrimination in Employment Act Amendments of 1978.

My Administration in its first eighteen months has initiated and supported legislation aimed at meeting the needs of women in many areas identified in the *National Plan of Action.* I urge Congress to act upon this legislation quickly.

Some of the resolutions in the *National Plan of Action* require structural as well as policy changes. My Administration has developed new operations to improve the Federal government's response to women's needs:

• The Interdepartmental Task Force on Women and the National Advisory Committee for Women were created by Executive Order in March, 1978, to advise me of additional action necessary to implement the *Plan of Action.*

• The Department of Justice Task Force on Sex Discrimination is working with each agency to survey and eliminate sex discrimination from programs and procedures throughout the Federal government. The Task Force will recommend needed changes in existing laws.

• The Interdepartmental Task Force on Women Business Owners, coordinated by the Department of Commerce, has identified barriers to business ownership for women and has made recommendations to remove them. On July 10, 1978, I asked my Cabinet to respond to the Task Force recommendations.

• The Department of Commerce Office of Federal Statistical Policy and Standards was established to coordinate data collection and to set guidelines and definitions for demographic variables.

During my Administration, other Federal programs designed to meet the needs of women have been expanded:

• The Women's Bureau in the Department of Labor, which focuses on the needs of women in the labor force, was upgraded, giving the Bureau Chief direct access to the Secretary of Labor. The Women's Bureau provides support for the Interdepartmental Task Force on Women and the National Advisory Committee for Women, operates significant programs designed to serve women, and publishes information on employed women.

• The Federal Women's Program which is in the Office of the Chairman of the Civil Service Commission, aids Federally-employed women. In conjunction with the Federal Women's Task Force on the U.N. Decade for Women, the Federal Women's Program is playing a more active and visible role in shaping Federal employment policy.

• The National Advisory Council on Women's Educational Programs is a Presidentially-appointed council which makes recommendations to Federal officials on equity for women and girls in education. During my Administration, the Council has been given an expanded mandate to help implement laws prohibiting sex discrimination in Federally-assisted education programs.

These are only a few high points of the report which surveys our progress over the past eighteen months. My Administration has been able to achieve this record in large part because of the unstinting efforts of the many dedicated women within the Government. For these efforts I am grateful.

RECOMMENDATIONS TO THE CONGRESS

For 131 years after the ratification of the U.S. Constitution, American women could not vote. Since women's suffrage in 1920, there has been considerable progress in legislative and executive action to provide equity for women. That progress has accelerated in my Administration. From 1923 to 1972, the Equal Rights Amendment languished in Congress. In 1972, Congress took a bold and affirmative step to guarantee equal rights for women. It only remains for three more states to join the majority of our nation in passing this historic amendment. ERA must be passed not only for ourselves, but to free our sons and daughters to participate fully in our nation's future.

Our nation benefits when women, as well as men, are freed from stereotypes and given a broader range of choices. Our nation benefits when all women may enter the mainstream of American life, and their talents and abilities are valued and rewarded. Our nation benefits when the freedom of all Americans is enhanced by greater freedom for American women. We can increase this freedom.

I ask you now to join with me in guaranteeing full equity for women in the United States, and to pass in an acceptable form without delay:

- H.J. Res. 638 and S.J. Res. 134 *Extension of the Deadline for Ratification of the Equal Rights Amendments.*
- H.R. 11086 (H.R. 12452) and S. 2570 *Comprehensive Employment and Training Act.*
- H.R. 50 and S. 50 *Full Employment and Balanced Growth Act of 1978 (Humphrey-Hawkins Bill).*
- H.R. 6075 and S. 995 *Pregnancy Disability Act.*
- H.R. 11280 and S. 2640 *Civil Service Reform Act.*
- H.R. 9030 (H.R. 19050) and S. 2084 *Better Jobs and Income Act (Welfare Reform).*

These bills, which are pending before Congress, will greatly enhance the civil rights, employment and economic opportunities of women. Extension of the Deadline for Ratification of the Equal Rights Amendment recently passed the House by an overwhelming majority. I congratulate the House and call upon the Senate to take similar action. The Equal Rights Amendment is needed as a constitutional protection against discrimination on the basis of sex. The Comprehensive Employment and Training Act (CETA) and the Better Jobs and Income Act (Welfare Reform), will, among other things, enable employment training and support services for displaced homemakers and low income women. In addition, CETA will protect against sex role stereotyping in Federal training programs and sex discrimination in placement in Federally-subsidized jobs. The Civil Service Reform Act and the Humphrey-Hawkins Bill will improve employment opportunities for the most recent entrants to the labor market—women and youth. And, the Pregnancy Disability Act, which is now in conference, will protect the health benefits of pregnant workers by making it unlawful for employers to discriminate on the basis of sex.

Through enactment of these bills in the appropriate form, we ensure continued progress toward the goal of full equality so that future generations of Americans— male and female—have choices and opportunities not fully realized today.

JIMMY CARTER

The White House,
September 27, 1978.

NOTE: The report is entitled "The First 18 Months: A Status Report of the Carter Administration Action on International Women's Year Resolutions, 1978."

Natural Gas Legislation

*Remarks on Senate Approval of the
Conference Committee Report.
September 27, 1978*

THE PRESIDENT. I just talked to Majority Leader Byrd and Senator Jackson, the Vice President, Jim Schlesinger, Frank Moore—all of them very eager to let me know that the Senate voted, I think overwhelmingly, compared to what we had expected, 57 to 42, in favor of the natural gas conference report. And Senator Byrd sent me word that they will work very rapidly on the other two measures that are now completed in the conference committee.

This is a remarkable demonstration of leadership on the part of the men that I've just named, one of the most difficult pieces of legislation that the Congress has ever faced in the history of our country. It's brought together a wide diversity of interests from around the country. I think it proves to our own Nation and to the rest of the world that we in this Government, particularly Congress, can courageously deal with an issue and one that tests our national will and our ability.

We have difficult decisions still left for the House to make. My expectation is that the House will act as it did August— was a year ago—to resolve the energy question and to give us a comprehensive and a valid energy policy.

I'm very grateful for the leadership that has been shown by these men and by the courageous action in the Senate this afternoon.

Thank you very much.

REPORTER. Sir, can you get it through the House if you veto the public works bill?

THE PRESIDENT. I believe we'll get it through the House.

NOTE: The President spoke at 1:31 p.m. to reporters assembled in the Oval Office at the White House.

Ethics in Government Legislation

*Statement on House of Representatives Action
on the Legislation. September 27, 1978*

I am very pleased to congratulate Speaker Tip O'Neill and the Members of the House of Representatives for their adoption of the Ethics in Government Act of 1978. This bill, which incorporates legislation submitted by me to the Congress in May of last year, will go far toward fulfilling our commitments to return integrity and efficiency to the conduct of government.

I wish also to thank Members George Danielson, Richardson Preyer, and Patricia Schroeder for their capable and sensitive leadership in winning approval of the bill.

Enactment of this legislation will follow through on commitments made during my campaign for the Presidency to:

—direct the spotlight of public attention on potential conflict of interest by requiring personal financial disclosure by senior-level officials in the legislative, executive, and judicial branches;

—assure effective oversight of agency ethics enforcement by establishing an Office of Ethics in the Civil Service Commission (to be transferred to the Office of Personnel Management under the civil service reform bill and reorganization plan);

—curb abuses of the revolving door between government and industry by closing loopholes in current statutory restrictions on government contacts by former senior officials, thereby preventing the misuse of personal influence acquired while in public service.

Since the Senate has already adopted similar measures in S. 555, the Public Officials Integrity Act, prospects appear bright for final enactment of these long-sought, far-reaching reforms to assure that Federal officials respect the high ethical standards which the American people expect and deserve.

NOTE: The statement was released on September 28.

Democratic National Committee

Remarks at a Fundraising Dinner.
September 27, 1978

I just heard the introduction of me by the Vice President, and of all the witty, clever, intelligent introductions I've ever heard, his is the most recent. [*Laughter*]

This is the most successful Presidential Democratic fundraiser in the history of the United States. And a great deal of credit is certainly due to our great chairman, John White, to Evan Dobelle, to all those who sold tickets, and to the famous people who are here who helped to draw a crowd.

Bob Strauss, our former chairman, is here. As you know, a lot has been written about Bob. Just this morning I was reading about him. I read that he's the best politician in the Carter administration— [*laughter*]—that he's the number one troubleshooter in the United States of America, that he's the least appreciated public official that's ever been known, that he has a personal savoir faire that inspires the American people to reach for greatness and to try to emulate him, that he's one of the best dressed men in the Nation, and a lot more, a lot more. If you'd like to read the entire memo from Bob, I'll share it with you later on in the future. [*Laughter*]

One of the other great people that always attracts a crowd was introduced a little earlier—my mother, Lillian. She always has the ability to put her finger right on the most incisive element in a certain episode, no matter how small or great. As soon as I returned from Camp David with President Sadat and Prime Minister Begin, I had a brief television program with them, went upstairs, the phone was ringing. Mother was on the phone. She was campaigning for someone in Arkansas. She very quickly asked me the most important question. She said, "Jimmy, is Anwar Sadat already married?" [*Laughter*]

She's the only one in the family that knows how to handle the press. She stays in Plains and—sometimes she stays in Plains. And not too long ago—this is a true story—she had a young woman who came to interview Mother about me from a very famous newspaper in Paris. And the young woman was cross-examining Mother—and she doesn't like women news reporters very much as it is— [*laughter*]—but the questions got more and more aggressive and abusive. And finally she said, "I understand that your son said he would never tell a lie." And Mother said, "That's right."

She said, "Is your son absolutely honest?" Mother said, "I think he's reasonably honest, yes." And she said, "He wouldn't tell any kind of lie?" Mother said, "Well, I think on occasion in his life he's told maybe a little white lie." And the woman turned on her tape recorder very quickly. She said, "What do you mean by a little white lie?" And Mother said, "Well, just a little white lie." And the woman said, "Well, define it for me, define it." And Mother said, "I don't know how to define a little white lie." The woman said, "Well, at least you could give me an example." Mother sat there for a while, and she said, "Well, I guess I could. Do you remember a few minutes ago when you came in the front door and I said that you were a very attractive young lady?" She said, "That was a little white lie." [*Laughter*]

I'm proud of our Democratic Party officials. I'm proud of Bob Strauss, the other people that serve with me. I'm proud of my family—my mother, my wife, my sons, their wives. I'm proud of the team that we have created in the last 2 years to serve our Nation.

Two years ago, I completed a long travel through this country, promising the people that we would try to create a government as compassionate and as competent as were the American people themselves. Our party has always been known as a party of compassion. But in the last 2 years, we have also proven that we have a party of competence. Along with effective new programs, we've proved that the Democratic Party is the party of fiscal responsibility.

I would like to announce to you that I've just received a news report from the wire services—AP, UPI, Reuters, Jerusalem Television, State Department, and the OPS Center—that the Knesset voted for peace, 85 [84]; against the removal of the settlements, 19. So, we've made a great step forward, and I'm very grateful for that.

That's indeed good news, and it's sure proof of the tremendous courage of Prime Minister Begin, the Israeli members of the Knesset who have now formed a possible partnership for the rest of our lives with their neighbors, the Egyptians, under the leadership of President Sadat. I'm very proud of this decision by them. We've got a great country, and we've got great friends and partners around the world.

Ours has been a party that believes in a strong United States, strong not just in military weapons—we're the strongest on the Earth in military weapons; not just the strongest economically—we're the strongest on Earth economically; not just the strongest in our political structure, our free enterprise system—we are the strongest politically and in our societal structure. But we are strongest as well in our commitment to basic principles which never change, principles that are challenged every now and then under the most difficult circumstances by war, by corruption, by embarrassment, by failure on the part of some leaders. But the American people always stand staunch and never falter in our commitment to higher ideals and a greater nation in the future.

The Democratic Party represents those commitments, those ideals in the purest sense of all. Ours is the oldest political party on Earth. It's also the youngest political party on Earth, always eager for new ideas, always eager to meet change without fear, always eager to reach a hand out to someone not quite so fortunate as we—not down with a condescending air or as though we were doing someone else not quite so good as we a favor, but a party that believes in other people and the fact that they should have a right to take whatever God-given talent they might own and use those talents to the utmost.

We've corrected some of the defects in our party. In the past, at least in the South, where I come from, we've always had the image of a party with a big heart. Our Members of Congress, even our most conservative Senators, have always voted for social security, Medicaid, Medicare, to give people a chance in life. But quite often we've had the wrong impression in the minds of the American people about our party's commitment to effective management, how to make government be efficient.

And after the last few years of embarrassment under Republican administrations, I thought it was particularly important for us in this new administration to run the Government well, to take control of it and let the people know that someone was in command. And the partnership that we have between the executive and the legislative branches of Government now are proving that we have achieved that very difficult task successfully.

Republicans talk about tax cuts. Democrats cut taxes. Republicans talk about balanced budgets, and they run up huge deficits, which we inherited. Democrats draw up responsible budgets, and we cut back Republican deficits. Any person who's lucky enough to be President and smart enough to be a Democrat—[laughter]—knows that his success, my success, is based on our long party history of great national and international purpose—the desire to keep the United States sound and strong; the desire to assure peace and liberty throughout the world; the desire to help those who are poor and weak and timid and inarticulate; the desire for vigorous and sustained and economic growth to give us confidence in the future; the desire to protect our great American natural beauty of pure air, of clean water;

the desire to keep power, political power, where it belongs, in the hands of our people, in the hands of government closest to the people, no matter whether they might be young or old, consumers or producers, wage earners, retired people, farmers, city dwellers.

We not only reach out to people but we bring them into the heart of things, into our hearts individually and personally and into the heart of our political organization to let their own lives be magnified and influenced. This is the essence of the Democratic Party, the party of Thomas Jefferson.

That's why our party produces great leaders like my colleague, Fritz Mondale, the best Vice President I guess this country has ever had. Others have had perhaps equal potential. I don't know about that. But Fritz takes on the full duties of a President on occasion. He's an equal partner with me. There's nothing that I do that he doesn't share.

Our great Speaker, Tip O'Neill, who preceded Fritz Mondale, Majority Leader Bob Byrd, who won a remarkable victory today in the Senate—and I thank him for it—Jim Wright, Alan Cranston, all of our Democratic leaders in the House and Senate, chairmen and other members who have constructed already for the 95th Congress a superb record—we have a Congress that will not be forgotten.

The people won't forget that Congress helped to shore up crucial partnerships, crucial to us with our historic allies around the world who had begun to feel neglected. They won't forget the Congress that worked with me to strengthen NATO and to strengthen our defense around the world. They won't forget the Congress which has helped to restore the moral authority of our Nation.

As I've said recently in some campaign speeches, when I was Governor of Georgia, when I was a candidate, I actually used to shrink up inside every year this time when the United Nations General Assembly convened, because I knew that my Nation, which I love, would be the butt of every joke and the target of every attack for more than two-thirds of the nations in the world. And I'm proud that in the last 2 years that has not been the case, and we've now got new friends among the poor nations, the small nations, the new nations, and the nations whose people are black and brown and yellow. We've made hundreds of new friends, and I'm proud of that.

These are some of the promises that I made to the American people during my 2 years of campaigning; they're part of our Democratic platform, as you well know.

Two years ago I promised the American people a responsible government, one that was lean and efficient and manageable. And that's what the Congress has helped me give them.

Two years ago I promised the American people that we would get control of the bureaucracy, restore incentives and the work ethic to our civil service system, let good employees be rewarded, let poor employees be inspired to do better or transferred or perhaps discharged, let managers manage, let our Government be a source of pride and not despair, admiration and not condemnation. That's what we've done.

Two years ago I told the American people that the Democrats believed that competition and market forces in a free enterprise system should determine prices, and we proved what we meant by making good progress on the airline deregulation bill, which I hope will pass, and by administrative decisions of the CAB, that's lowered fares and boosted profits of the airlines of the United States. I'm proud of that, too.

Two years ago I said that Democrats believed in a free economic system with minimum intrusion by Government in the private affairs of American citizens, and we've proved it by eliminating regulations, almost as fast as the other party used to write them, and we're beginning to rewrite the ones that are left in plain English so ordinary Americans, even Democrats—[*laughter*]—can understand them.

And 2 years ago I promised to maintain our national security and to keep our Nation strong, and we've done that. The defense establishment has never, never been so strong. But we've done more than guarantee our basic security with military strength; we've cut wasteful military expenditures.

We put in a superb new management team under Harold Brown and the new Joint Chiefs of Staff to head our military establishment. We've brought our strategic thinking into the 21st century.

We are now working on the last phases of a SALT II agreement with the Soviet Union, which I hope to consummate very soon. And we have stopped the spread of nuclear weapons and the capability to have nuclear explosions around the world. The Congress did that; I'm grateful to them.

But that's not all we've done. Two years ago I said that peace is more than just the absence of war. Peace is the unceasing effort to preserve human freedom and to preserve basic human rights. And we've made that effort. It's becoming increasingly successful. There's not a day that I have been President that we've not sought to narrow the gap between the values that we hold most dear as a people and our actions abroad in dealing with other people. Our goal is freedom and peace and justice for all. That's America's most cherished purpose, and we are strong in the pursuit of it.

I said 2 years ago that we would remove fraud, waste, and corruption from the Government, and we are doing it—not overnight; it took a long time to create the mess that we inherited, and we can't eliminate it in 1 year. But we'll get rid of it, and you can depend on that.

Two years ago I promised the American people that we would get control of our runaway energy problem. It's been the most difficult legislative task, I believe, that the Congress has ever undertaken in the history of our Nation. And at long last we are getting the tools to do this job. I was excited by the work that Scoop Jackson has done in the Senate and others who worked with him.

Two years ago I promised the American people that we would revitalize our educational system and to focus the attention of it on the poor and the deprived children who haven't had an adequate chance in life, whose parents perhaps are illiterate and haven't had the will or the motivation or the vision to inspire those little kids. Even compared to the halcyon days of Lyndon Johnson, the Congress has voted the largest increases in funds for school and education in history, and it's focused accurately on those who need it most.

Two years ago when I campaigned around this country, the common question asked me by almost every group that had elderly citizens in it is, "How are we going to deal with a bankrupt social security system?" I promised them that we would act responsibly and restore integrity to that system, and we've kept that promise. It hasn't been easy, politically speaking, but we've done it.

Two years ago I said my administration would have an urban policy for the first time to revitalize our cities, to inspire the mayors and Governors and others, private citizens, in a new partnership. And we have that policy now.

Two years ago I told the American people that we had to bring our Federal budget under control. The last full year before my election in 1976, the budget deficit was $66 billion. We cut that deficit the first year to $51 billion. We'll get it down, with the great help of the Congress, at least to $40 billion this year, maybe a little lower. And we're going to cut it significantly further next year. And we're going to keep right on cutting the budget deficit with good management and sound programs as fast as the strength of the economy permits. We've kept that promise without yielding our commitment to let Americans have a better life.

One of the biggest problems we inherited, as you well know, was 10 million American adults who could not find a full-time job, 6 or 7 million who couldn't find a job at all. In just the short period of a year and a half, we've had a net increase of about 6½ million full-time jobs in the United States. The unemployment rate has dropped 25 percent in that short time, and we're going to keep it going down.

And you ought to realize that we have cut the budget deficit, given jobs, better education, strengthened our defenses. At the same time, last year we had a multibillion dollar tax cut, and we have on schedule now another tax cut for the American people of about $20 billion. That is the kind of fiscal responsibility that American people deserve, to meet our people's needs while balancing the Nation's books.

Of course, Democrats have always believed in service, but carefully budgeted, efficiently delivered service. We can cut crime, we can build roads, we can deliver jobs, we can feed our people without huge deficits if we eliminate the waste and the bloat in government. This is responsible leadership. This is sound fiscal policy, and the American people know it.

It's not callous nor hardhearted for a government to deliver food to a hungry person without waste, with efficiency. It's not callous nor hardhearted management to give our children a better education without waste, and efficiently.

For the first time in political history, a recent Gallup Poll showed that twice as many of the American people now believe that Democrats are fiscally responsible as believe that Republicans are fiscally responsible. The Republic has finally woken up to know the truth about Democrats, compared to Republicans, and I'm thankful for that.

Well, let me say in closing that we're getting control of our energy problems. We're getting control of the bureaucracy. We're bringing new efficiency to government. We're taking control of foreign affairs. Our Nation is strong again, proud again, secure again in its place in the world. And we've made a good start on the most difficult task of all, solving our economic problems in the areas of unemployment, in budget deficits. Now it's time to put all our efforts into solving the most complicated and intractable and corrosive problem of all, and that's inflation.

Inflation hurts every one of us, not just the poor, not just the elderly. It saps away our national strength and will and confidence. Very soon I will announce a new package of anti-inflation measures. They'll be tough. They will require sacrifice from business, from labor, from government, from every family, every segment of our society. They will be tough, but they'll be fair.

I would like to caution all of you Democrats—those in my administration, those in the Congress—that we here in Washington must set an example. We cannot pass legislation that's identifiably wasteful. If we do, it will sap away the strength that we have to inspire the American people to solve this very difficult problem on their own.

The best birthday present I could get from the Congress is to pass the air deregulation bill, to pass the hospital cost containment bill, to send me appropriations bills and authorization bills that are solid and firm and cut to the bone without any waste. This is how the Congress can show its determination to join the fight against inflation.

If we fail here, it will be almost impossible to succeed elsewhere. This is the most pressing of the hundreds of large and small restraints that are necessary to win this battle. This is the future of our Democratic Party, a future in which we maintain our vision, even heighten our vision, while governing with prudence and responsibility that builds the confidence of our people in us.

I'm proud of what we've achieved in the last year and a half. I'm proud of the groundwork we've laid for future achievement. But there's more to do if the United States is to realize the full promise of our people. We must succeed in giving the women of America equal rights. And we must succeed in honoring the greatest of all Democrats, Hubert Humphrey, in meeting the yearnings of the poor people of our Nation by passing a full employment bill with his name on it, the Humphrey-Hawkins bill.

It's obvious to me, I'm sure it's obvious to you, that we cannot rest on past achievements. We cannot be complacent. We have work to do as Democrats and as Americans. Let's do this work for our country together.

Thank you very much.

NOTE: The President spoke at 9:57 p.m. in the International Ballroom at the Washington Hilton Hotel. In his remarks, he referred to John C. White, chairman, and Evan S. Dobelle, treasurer, Democratic National Committee.

Camp David Agreements on the Middle East

Letter to Prime Minister Menahem Begin of Israel on the Knesset's Vote on the Agreements.   September 27, 1978

Dear Mr. Prime Minister:

I have just learned of the Knesset's favorable vote on the Camp David agreements and I want to extend my warmest personal congratulations to you. This action by the representatives of the Israeli people takes us another step toward the goal we seek of a peaceful Middle East.

I deeply admire the courage and skill with which you presented the agreements we reached at Camp David. You know that I understand the difficult choices that face you and your colleagues if peace is to become a reality. Your firm leadership on these vital issues has provided a new and impressive demonstration of your statesmanship.

With best wishes.

Sincerely,

JIMMY CARTER

[His Excellency Menachem Begin, Prime Minister of Israel]

NOTE: The text of the letter was released on September 28.

American Education Week, 1978

Proclamation 4603.   September 28, 1978

By the President of the United States of America

A Proclamation

Our founders assumed that an educated electorate was essential to a strong, healthy democracy. Freedom of speech, thought and inquiry are part of the basic structure of our society, and we share a fundamental belief that education can provide the key to overcoming all our problems. We have come a long way toward providing access to schools for all our people, and we provide enormous resources for education. We can be proud of that progress, as we are proud of the progress of many of our students, both youngsters and adults. But we must also recognize that many young Americans still emerge from our schools inadequately prepared to take up the responsibilities of adult life. Others have not been sufficiently challenged to develop their full potential.

Teaching has never been easy, and inspiring students is more difficult still. Perhaps it is even harder today than in the past, but it is no less crucial to the well-being of our people and of our society.

The theme of this year's American Education Week, "Education Can Turn Things Around," expresses our faith in the power of education. We expect our teachers to provide the skills, knowledge and background for understanding that will allow all Americans to make the best use of their God-given abilities. If they are to succeed, we must support these goals for human achievement in all aspects of our society. We can do this by placing our priorities and our emphasis on the lasting instead of the trivial, by rewarding quality and accomplishment, by respecting true knowledge, by raising important questions and seeking honest answers, by valuing and nurturing the capabilities of every human being.

Now, THEREFORE, I, JIMMY CARTER, President of the United States of America, do hereby designate the week beginning November 12, 1978, as American Education Week.

It is appropriate that we honor what is right and good in education in America today—the dedicated, searching teachers who demand much of themselves and their students, who push beyond failure and discouragement to light the spark of understanding. It is appropriate, also, to recognize our responsibility as parents, grandparents, neighbors and citizens, to support the efforts of our schools to meet our high expectations, so that now and in generations to come our people may become a truly educated people.

IN WITNESS WHEREOF, I have hereunto set my hand this twenty-eighth day of September, in the year of our Lord nineteen hundred seventy-eight, and of the Independence of the United States of America the two hundred and third.

JIMMY CARTER

[Filed with the Office of the Federal Register, 12:12 p.m., September 28, 1978]

Budget Rescission

Message to the Congress.   September 28, 1978

To the Congress of the United States:

In accordance with the Impoundment Control Act of 1974, I herewith propose rescission of $10.8 million in employment and training funds appropriated to the Department of Labor.

The details of the proposed rescission are contained in the attached report.

JIMMY CARTER

The White House,
September 28, 1978.

NOTE: The attachment detailing the rescission is printed in the FEDERAL REGISTER of October 4, 1978.

Administrative Conference of the United States

Appointment of Seven Members of the Council.   September 28, 1978

The President today announced the appointment of seven persons as members of the Council of the Administrative Conference of the United States. They are:

Government representatives

JOAN Z. BERNSTEIN, General Counsel of the Environmental Protection Agency

MICHAEL J. EGAN, Associate Attorney General

MARGARET A. McKENNA, Deputy Counsel to the President

MICHAEL PERTSCHUK, Chairman of the Federal Trade Commission

Public representatives

WALTER GELLHORN, professor emeritus at Columbia University School of Law (reappointment)

IRA M. MILLSTEIN, a New York attorney and adjunct professor of law and trade regulation at New York University School of Law

OTIS M. SMITH, of Detroit, Mich., general counsel of General Motors and a former justice of the Michigan supreme court.

The Administrative Conference was created in 1964 to develop improvements in the legal procedures by which Federal agencies administer regulatory, benefit, and other Government programs. Its members include agency heads, other Federal officials, private lawyers, university professors, and other experts in administrative law and government.

Board for International Food and Agricultural Development

Appointment of David Garst as a Member. September 28, 1978

The President today announced the appointment of David Garst, of Coon Rapids, Iowa, as a member of the Board for International Food and Agricultural Development for a 3-year term.

Garst was born September 10, 1926, in Des Moines, Iowa. He graduated from Stanford University in 1950 with a major in economics and agricultural policy. He served in the U.S. Army.

Garst has been part owner of the Garst Co. since 1940. He is presently half owner, and the company farms 15,000 acres. It is also heavily involved in cattle breeding.

Garst is also sales manager of Garst and Thomas, a large seller of seed corn and sorghum seed. Through other companies in his community, he is involved in other aspects of the farm service industries. Garst was an adviser on agricultural policy to the Carter-Mondale campaign in 1976. He is a member of the National Agricultural Marketing Association and a director of the United States Feed Grain Council. In the 1950's, Garst traveled to Eastern Europe to demonstrate and sell farm equipment.

United Service Organizations, Inc.

Appointment of Maxine E. Flournoy and Jeff Wald as Members of the Board of Governors. September 28, 1978

The President today announced the appointment of two persons as members of the Board of Governors of the United Service Organizations, Inc. (USO). They are:

Maxine E. Flournoy, of Alice, Tex. Flournoy served in the Women's Airforce Service Pilots (WASP's) during World War II as a pilot. She has also served as a company pilot and, with her husband, operates an oil well drilling company.

Jeff Wald, of Los Angeles, president of Jeff Wald Television Productions and Wald-Nanas Associates, and a member of the board of governors of Cedars-Sinai Medical Center in Los Angeles.

Country Music Month, October 1978

Message of the President. September 28, 1978

As modern American society becomes more and more hectic and complex, there is a desire in all of us to return to the simple things in life.

This perhaps in part explains the growing popularity—even in our busiest metropolitan areas—of country music. And designated as "Country Music Month," October invites us all to return, at least vicariously, to the hills and the farms of America and to retrace the everyday emotions and experiences of country life.

Country music is part of the soul and conscience of our democracy. It unfolds the inherent goodness of our people and of our way of life. It captures our indomitable spirit and pulsates with the sorrows, joys and unfailing perseverance of ordinary men and women who sustain our national vitality and strength.

I welcome the opportunity to applaud the Country Music Association on its sponsorship of this annual observance, and I encourage more Americans to share in the enjoyment and cultural enrichment that country music can bring.

JIMMY CARTER

THE PRESIDENT'S NEWS CONFERENCE OF SEPTEMBER 28, 1978

THE PRESIDENT. I'd like to comment first on two very courageous actions that have been taken recently.

CAMP DAVID AGREEMENTS

The first is by the Israeli Knesset, their parliament, late last night, when they voted overwhelmingly by more than a 4-to-1 margin for peace in the Middle East, including the removal of the Israeli settlers from the Sinai, which is Egyptian territory.

This is a continuation of the courageous action that has already been

1653

demonstrated by Prime Minister Begin, who led the parliament debate, gave his full weight to this peace move, and by President Sadat who cooperated at Camp David in making it possible.

Since the Knesset vote, I have talked to Prime Minister Begin; also, just a few minutes ago, since lunch, to President Sadat. Both of them agree that there are no remaining obstacles to proceeding as rapidly as possible to conclude a peace treaty between Israel and Egypt.

I'm very proud of this action on their part. We will cooperate again as full partners in the negotiations to conclude the final terms of the Israeli-Egyptian peace treaty.

NATURAL GAS LEGISLATION

The other courageous vote that was taken yesterday was by the United States Senate, under the great leadership of Majority Leader Robert Byrd and committee chairman, Senator Scoop Jackson, to approve the natural gas legislation. This is a bill that will provide the centerpiece for establishing a United States energy policy. It's very good for consumers, particularly in those States that are faced with a very urgent shortage of natural gas in years to come. It's also fair to producers. I think it would make us much less dependent upon imported foreign oil.

And I congratulate the Senate on this action. Now the House must act on the same legislation. I hope that they will do so expeditiously and expect that this will be the case.

RAILWAY LABOR DISPUTE

One other report, briefly: We have not been successful, after 28 hours or more of negotiation, to reach a settlement between the striking railway workers and the rail lines. We now have almost a complete shutdown of rail service in our country. I have just recently issued an order establishing an emergency board which will take over the responsibility for negotiating a settlement between the workers and the railroads themselves.

This is necessary action. I think it's accurate to say that both sides do want a settlement. The differences between them are relatively small compared to what they were originally. This will take the railway workers back on the job. If there is any opposition to this action, then I would not hesitate to go to Federal court to enforce it. And I believe that this is the first step to getting our railway service back into operation in our country.

Mr. Pippert [Wes Pippert, United Press International].

QUESTIONS

ISRAELI SETTLEMENTS; PRESIDENTIAL TRIP TO MIDDLE EAST

Q. Mr. President, what will you do to make Prime Minister Begin comply with your understanding that Israel must eventually withdraw from the West Bank and, further, to build no settlements there during the 5 years of negotiation? And will you consider a Christmas trip to the Middle East for the signing of the peace treaty?

THE PRESIDENT. There's nothing that I can make Prime Minister Begin do. He's an independent leader of an autonomous and independent nation, and I can only use persuasion and depend upon the mutual trust that exists between me and him.

There were 20 or 30 very crucial issues that were obstacles at the beginning of the Camp David negotiations. This was one of them. And I would guess that it was after midnight Saturday, less than 24 hours after the final agreement was signed, that we reached these agreements.

There are two elements of the dispute. One is at what time will the agreement not to build any more settlements be concluded. Prime Minister Begin's interpretation is that this is to be maintained, the prohibition against new settlements, during the negotiations concerning the Sinai with Egypt. My very clear understanding is that it related to the negotiation for conclusion in the West Bank, Gaza Strip, of the establishment of a self-government.

The other question concerns whether or not Israel would initiate new settlements after this negotiating period was concluded and the self-government was established. I think the best answer to that is that this is an honest difference of opinion.

The best answer I can give is to quote from a statement by Foreign Minister Dayan, who was with us at that midnight meeting, and this is a statement he made at the Ben Gurion Airport on the 19th of September, when he arrived in Israel. "Let us not delude ourselves"— I'm quoting him—"I have no doubt that when we enter into deliberations with the other three parties concerning what is to happen in the area in the 5 years of transition"—that's the West Bank, Gaza Strip— "this question will come up and will be discussed and agreement will have to be reached on this subject."

So, the degree of participation of the residents of the West Bank has still got to be determined. But it's an honest difference of opinion. It would certainly be no obstacle to the progress towards peace.

But I can't say that we've resolved it yet. There's no personal animosity between myself and Prime Minister Begin. I certainly do not allege any improper action on his part. It's just an honest difference of opinion, which I think will be resolved.

As far as my going to the Middle East is concerned, nothing would please me more than to participate in the signing of a peace treaty at an early date. But that's still to be negotiated. The only request that President Sadat made of me in the entire Camp David proceedings was that

I come to Egypt. I promised him that I would sometime in the future.

AIRBASES IN THE NEGEV

Q. May I follow up? If Prime Minister Begin persists, would you consider cancelling the U.S. agreement to build airbases in the Negev for Israel?

THE PRESIDENT. No. The letter to Israel concerning the two airports to be put in the Negev—I have already directed that that letter be sent to Israel. It's not being sent from me to Prime Minister Begin; it's being sent from Defense Secretary Harold Brown to Defense Minister Weizman.

We have not agreed to build the airbases. We've agreed to consult with the Israelis and participate in the cost of those rebuilt airbases, to the degree that we negotiate in the future. We will certainly participate in the cost, the degree to be determined in the future.

PRESIDENT'S RATING IN THE POLLS

Q. Mr. President, I'm sure you've been enjoying your big resurgence in the polls lately, but I wonder if you're fairly confident you can keep them up there.

THE PRESIDENT. I'm not sure about that. I hope so. My interpretation is that the polls have been much more accurate the last week or two than they were before. [*Laughter*] But I'll do the best I can.

I think it's not an accurate conclusion that the culmination of our efforts on, say, natural gas, civil service reform, and other major endeavors in the Congress, is the result of the Camp David accords. Obviously my own reputation as a capable leader was enhanced by that agreement, but we've been working very long months to bring about the conclusion of some highly controversial issues. And I will continue to do the best I can, but my actions will never be predicated on what is the most popular. But I'll do what I think is best for our country, and I'll take my chances on whether the people approve or not.

CAMP DAVID MEETINGS; HUMPHREY-HAWKINS BILL

Q. Mr. President, it was recently reported that you said in a meeting with the Congressional Black Caucus that a Camp David-type meeting on the Humphrey-Hawkins full employment bill would be ill-advised——

THE PRESIDENT. Yes, that's correct.

Q. ——causing John Conyers to storm out, as everyone knows. And I was wondering, first, why would such a meeting be ill-advised, and secondly, if Camp David meetings are to be focused on international affairs, might such a meeting take place involving the principal ones in South Africa and Rhodesia, where these situations could be equally as violent and turmoil could equally exist?

THE PRESIDENT. I've been in office now for 20 months. I've faced many very difficult issues, in foreign affairs and domestic affairs. I've never called a caucus or a meeting at Camp David except once in my life. This was a unique set of circumstances where I felt that extended negotiations over several days—as you know, it turned out to be 2 weeks—in almost complete seclusion, was absolutely necessary to reach an agreement.

I would guess that this might never again occur. It may on very rare occasions. But I don't ever intend to use a Camp David meeting to settle matters that ought best to be resolved within the Congress, where they can best handle them. I will use my utmost influence to determine the outcome of those deliberations in the Congress.

As far as the Humphrey-Hawkins bill goes, I think it's very important that this bill be passed. It's a full employment commitment of our country, which I share. We have helped to get the bill passed through the House. It is now on the Senate calendar. I talked to Majority Leader Byrd since lunch about this. He's proceeding as rapidly as he can. He's trying to get a time certain, an agreement by some Republican Members of the Senate to vote on the Humphrey-Hawkins bill.

But it's just not appropriate and I think it would be ill-advised for me to take a. group of Senators or Congressmen in the last 2 weeks of the session up to Camp David to spend a week or two in seclusion. It's just impractical.

STRATEGIC ARMS LIMITATION

Q. Mr. President, we hear reports that you feel pretty good about how the SALT negotiations are coming along these days. How close are we to a SALT agreement now?

THE PRESIDENT. The issues that divide us and the Soviet Union on SALT have been constantly narrowed over the last 18 months of negotiation. Now the issues are quite few.

I also talked to Secretary Vance since lunch. He's been meeting today and yesterday with Foreign Minister Gromyko of the Soviet Union. I think that both men are negotiating aggressively and in good faith to reach a conclusion of the differences.

I don't know what the outcome will be. It takes two to reach agreement. We hope to conclude a SALT agreement this year, and I will be meeting with Foreign Minister Gromyko Saturday to capitalize upon the progress that I hope that Vance and Gromyko are making now. I don't see any insurmountable obstacles. But if the Soviets are forthcoming and cooperative and are willing to compromise some of their positions, we will have an agreement.

FRAUD BY WELFARE RECIPIENTS

Q. Mr. President, it's been reported this week that some Federal employees who are on the payroll and also drawing welfare benefits have been charged. It's also reported outside of Washington recently that the Federal Government has made what amounts to a conscious decision not to pursue fraud by individual welfare recipients and leave that instead to the local and State governments. Are you aware of this policy, and do you approve of it?

THE PRESIDENT. When I came into office, we were determined, I and my administration, I think shared by the Congress, to proceed aggressively to eliminate fraud from government. We've got a problem in GSA. We've had good success in other areas, including the rooting out of people who have tried to defraud the Government by drawing welfare payments when they were on a payroll and didn't deserve it, according to the law.

My own inclination would be to let the Justice Department decide whether or not an indictment and a prosecution should be pursued or whether a repayment of the funds with some penalty would be adequate. I'm not familiar with the individual cases. But the fact is we have initiated, for the first time, an attempt to root out these violators of the law and to make them provide some recompense to the Government that's according to what is proper and right.

I wouldn't say that every case ought to be pursued as a criminal proceeding, to put them in jail. Sometimes they might be discharged from their job, sometimes to repay the money, sometimes to pay a penalty. If it's a gross case, I would favor them going to jail.

INFLATION AND INTEREST RATES

Q. Mr. President, the Fed's discount rate is now nearly 10 percent. You're about to announce some top anti-inflation measures. How can any anti-inflation program be credible when you have interest rates this high, and do you think 10 percent interest rates is the proper way to fight inflation?

THE PRESIDENT. The discount rate is not that high, but I think it's too high and I wish it was lower.

There are three entities in the Government that have a great individual, independent impact on either controlling inflation or enhancing inflation. One is the President and my Cabinet members—in the preparation of the budget, do we advocate reducing the deficit; do we advocate spending too much.

The other one is the Congress, who makes the final determination on the budget and also prescribes, to a major degree, tax policy. The third, of course, is the independent Federal Reserve.

My own hope is that our present efforts to control inflation will be so successful that those interest rates now, as determined by the Federal Reserve, can be brought down.

When I came into office, we had a budget deficit of almost $70 billion—I think, $66 billion. By the end of this congressional session, I hope that we will almost have brought that down below $40 billion, maybe even lower. We're cutting down the Federal deficit. We have a very tight constraint on spending. This is important in controlling inflation.

I'm going to be very persistent in my own role as President in holding down unwarranted spending in individual bills that come to me from the Congress. I think the time for wasteful spending is over. And I think if we can show that we can get inflation under control through those actions by me and the Congress, that would be an inducement for the Federal Reserve to start bringing the interest rate down.

1657

But each one of those elements of our Government—Federal Reserve, Congress, President—are independent. I can't control the other two. I can set a good example; that's what I'm trying to do.

STRATEGIC ARMS LIMITATION

Q. Mr. President, going back to SALT, the military is pushing an idea of digging a lot of holes in the ground for our land-based intercontinental ballistic missiles. So, you truck them around; the Russians never know which hole the missile is in. The theory is the Russians have to hit all the holes in order to get all the missiles. Do you think that's a good idea, and how does that affect the SALT negotiations?

THE PRESIDENT. That is one among many ideas. I think over a period of time, it has become obvious that our fixed silo-type intercontinental ballistic missiles are becoming more and more vulnerable because of the accuracy of the Soviet missiles—ours are even more accurate—and the MIRVing of the Soviet missiles, where they have many warheads on each missile—which we've had for a long time.

The so-called multiple aim points, or many silos for each missile, is one idea that has been put forward. It has some very serious defects. I can only mention two at this time. One is, how do you vertify that all the holes don't have missiles in them? It's obvious that we would be keeping the agreement, and we would not violate it. We don't know that that would be the case on the other side. And I believe that we would find, as we proceed further with it, that it would not only be very difficult if the Soviets adopted this same policy, but very expensive as well.

But that is one option that we are considering. And I would guess that by the end of this year, we would have gone through all the options including that one. And at that time, certainly at the time that SALT II agreement is reached, I will explain to the American people in the most careful and complete terms what our future plans for adequate strategic strength will be, probably going for the next 5 years.

That's just one of the options now. It has some very serious defects. It's being considered.

LEBANON

Q. Mr. President, there's a report that you are working for a settlement in Lebanon and that Syria and Israel would be involved. Could you verify this, sir?

THE PRESIDENT. This is a subject that President Sadat raised with me several times at Camp David. It's one in which we've been involved, as you know, for many months.

There's a tragedy in Lebanon that the rest of the world has not adequately addressed, including ourselves. The suffering of the people of Lebanon, through no fault of their own in almost every case, has been extraordinary.

Obviously, the responsibility for resolving the Lebanon question rests primarily on the shoulders of those who live there. My commitment has been to strengthen the Sarkis government, politically, economically, and militarily. We gave them some aid so that the President of that country can control the affairs of the country itself. When we were flying back from Camp David on the helicopter, President Sadat and I were talking about this; Prime Minister Begin joined in the conversation. All three of us committed ourselves to renew our support for the Sarkis government, the Lebanese Government. So, they have the prime responsibility.

The next two nations, I would say, that are the most intimately involved are Syria, which has large forces in Lebanon—invited in by the Lebanese Government because they cannot maintain order by themselves under existing circumstances—and Israel, who obviously wants a stable government, stable people on their northern border.

Other countries more removed geographically also have an intense interest and influence in Lebanon. I would say two of them would be Saudi Arabia and Egypt.

More distantly, other countries that have a direct historical interest, like the United States and France, would be involved. All this could be done under the aegis of the United Nations.

But I think it's time for us to take joint action to call a conference of those who are involved, primarily the people who live in Lebanon, the different factions there, and try to reach some solution that may involve a new charter for Lebanon. I'm not in favor of a partitioned Lebanon. I'd like to see a unified Lebanon, at peace, with a strong enough central government to control the situation there and protect its own people.

PRESIDENTIAL VETOES AND INFLATION

Q. Mr. President, I understand that you're considering vetoing the public works/water projects bill and, in addition to that, that you're considering vetoing four other bills—tuition tax credit, surface transportation, tax cut bill, and Labor-HEW. Can you tell us, is this part of your anti-inflation program? Will you veto the bills? Or is this a President Carter who has come down from Camp David and is now trying to show that he can handle his own Congress as well as the Israelis and the Egyptians?

THE PRESIDENT. I don't want to show that I can handle the Congress. What I want to do is to work in harmony with the Congress. I think we've done that to a substantial degree, a provable degree.

The legislation to which you refer causes me deep concern, because some of it is wasteful, some of it has elements in it which I consider to be unconstitutional. And my own objection to certain features of that legislation has been well known to the Congress and also to the public.

The public works bill has now passed the conference committee, and both the House and Senate have adopted the conference report. This bill in its present form is completely unacceptable to me. And I will decide whether or not to veto it when it gets to my desk. It's up to the leaders of the Congress to decide when to submit it to me. My objection to some of its features are well known.

I think that we have got to establish a policy in Washington, the Congress and I, particularly in these crucial days when inflation is our number one concern, at least on the domestic scene, that will be an example for the rest of the Nation to follow.

If we continue the age-old policy of porkbarrel allocations in the public works bill, this is a horrible example to set for the rest of the country. It would make it very difficult for me to control inflation if the Congress and I couldn't set a good example for the rest of the Nation. So, I'm willing to meet the Congress on this issue—we have an honest difference of opinion with some of the Members of the Congress—and have it resolved in a constitutional and appropriate way.

If it involves a veto, the Congress has a right to express their displeasure by attempting to override my veto. I'm going to do the best I can, if I do veto the bill, to get enough votes to sustain my veto. There have been some allegations made that the Congress might try to connect this bill with the energy bill. I don't believe they will do that. The proper way for the Congress to express its displeasure over the veto of the public works bill is to try to override the veto. I believe the energy legislation is too important for any responsible Member of the House of Representatives to connect it with the public works bill.

Judy [Judy Woodruff, NBC News].

INFLATION AND UNEMPLOYMENT

Q. Mr. President, President Ford said this week that you made a mistake last year in concentrating on unemployment rather than inflation. Do you agree with that, first of all, and secondly, do you wish that you had moved sooner to do something about inflation?

THE PRESIDENT. No, I don't agree with that at all. When I was running for President, after I became President, I never singularly attacked the unemployment problem without also trying to deal with the inflationary problem. President Ford left me with a $66 billion deficit. We've tried to turn that around and cut down deficit spending. We've been remarkably successful.

At the same time, we have provided the American people with a much better life, better education programs, better housing programs, better transportation programs, substantial tax reductions—$6 or $7 billion last year; perhaps as much as $20 billion this year.

I believe that we have seen in 1977 a very substantial reduction in the inflation rate. The last 6 months of 1977 the inflation rate was down quite low, 4½ to 5 percent; an average for the entire year of about 6 or 6½ percent. It grew this year more than we had anticipated for several reasons, the most important of which was the high food prices that occurred the first 6 months of the year.

We have always had a very strong anti-inflation program. Since we have had very good luck so far, success in bringing down

the unemployment rate, adding 6½ million new jobs, bringing the unemployment rate down about 25 percent already, we are now able to focus our attention much more specifically on inflation.

It's much more of a threat now than it was a year ago. But I'm determined to deal with inflation as effectively as we have already proven we could deal with unemployment.

EGYPTIAN-ISRAELI PEACE NEGOTIATIONS

Q. Mr. President, you said in your opening statement that both President Sadat and Prime Minister Begin said there are no remaining obstacles to concluding the Sinai treaty. Have they set a date yet for starting these talks? And how long would you estimate that it would take to go through the formalities that still remain?

THE PRESIDENT. I would hope that we could commence the talks within 2 weeks, but no specific date has been set. Both Prime Minister Begin and President Sadat today, when I talked to them on the phone, on their own initiative said that they were expecting us to be full partners, as I was at Camp David, and they could see no obstacle to the peace talks beginning without delay.

I think it will take 2 weeks to prepare for the talks. There are some official responsibilities that President Sadat has in his own country that will take place and be concluded within 2 weeks. But that would be the approximate timeframe. I'm not trying to be presumptuous, because no date has been set.

Q. If I could follow that up, Prime Minister Begin is supposed to be sending a letter dealing with the Israeli position on the West Bank. Has that letter been received yet? And would any delay on that letter perhaps hold up these talks on the Sinai?

THE PRESIDENT. Prime Minister Begin has sent me a letter expressing his position, and I've also sent him a letter expressing my position. Now I think the next step would be for me and him, in good faith and in a friendly, cooperative attitude, to try to work out the differences between us.

Q. Will you make those letters available?

THE PRESIDENT. I'll think it over. I can't answer because I would really—it suits me okay for the letters to be made available, but I can't unilaterally release the letter that I sent to him or received from him without his approval.

My own inclination is to let all the correspondence be made public that relates to the Mideast settlements. We've done that so far, even when we had differences of opinion. But I would have to get his permission before we could release the letters.

STEEL INDUSTRY

Q. Mr. President, your trigger price program for steel has managed to reduce the foreign imports. But foreign steel still takes a large part of the U.S. market, and the floor under steel prices does drive up the inflationary forces. What modifications, if any, do you plan in your trigger price program?

THE PRESIDENT. Well, as you know, the steel trigger price program went into effect, I think, only in May. We've only had a few months of experience with it. So far, it's been very successful.

We've had a net increase this year of, I think, 24,000 jobs in the steel industry alone. And in spite of a fairly dormant construction industry we've had 5-percent increase in the shipments of domestic steel. I understand that the Japanese steel exports have actually gone down this year. The most important measure, I think, of success so far is that a year or so ago the steel industry plants were only being used at about 76-percent capacity. Now that use has increased to almost 90-percent capacity. So, we've got a very vigorous steel industry now.

I think the price of steel has been held reasonably well under control. We are obviously fine-tuning the trigger price system as we get more experience with it. There are special kinds of steel that might be involved. And we have some problems still in Europe, because the steel price, as you know, is based on Japanese cost. But I think we've stopped the unwarranted dumping of foreign steel on our American market. I think we've protected the jobs of steelworkers, and we've added a new degree of prosperity to the steel industry.

I believe that the second quarter this year, compared to the second quarter of last year, steel industry profits were up 71 percent, which means that they have a lot more to invest back into more modern plants and more jobs for better steel production in our country.

EGYPTIAN-ISRAELI PEACE NEGOTIATIONS

Q. Mr. President, can you tell us a little more, sir, about the nature of your participation in this next round of talks? You mentioned full partnership. Will you be personally involved with that, or will Secretary Vance be?

THE PRESIDENT. I would guess that I would not be personally involved, except in a case where the leaders of the other two nations were involved. If there was a dispute about a particular drawing of a line, or a phased withdrawal, or something of that kind that could not be resolved at the Foreign Minister or delegate level, then I would get involved if necessary.

I wouldn't want to see the talks break down because of any timidity on my part. I consider it to be one of the most important responsibilities that I have. I would guess, though, that the negotiations will be carried on at a fairly high level, below the President and Prime Minister level.

I understand from Prime Minister Begin that the leader of his delegation will be Foreign Minister Dayan. I don't know yet who will head the Egyptian delegation, and I've not yet decided on the American delegation leader. But it'll be at a fairly high level.

And the principles for settling the Sinai disagreements have all been resolved. Now the details, which I don't think are going to be highly controversial, are the only things remaining to be resolved. The exact decision of whether a particular road intersection or a hilltop would be at the first withdrawal line, those are the kind of things that would be settled. And I believe we have a good relationship between the two leaders that wouldn't cause a deterioration in the negotiations.

FRANK CORMIER [Associated Press]. Thank you, Mr. President.

THE PRESIDENT. Thank you very much. I enjoyed it.

NOTE: President Carter's thirty-seventh news conference began at 4 p.m. in Room 450 of the Old Executive Office Building. It was broadcast live on radio and television.

Emergency Board To Investigate a Railway Labor Dispute

Executive Order 12085.   September 28, 1978

CREATING AN EMERGENCY BOARD TO INVESTIGATE A DISPUTE BETWEEN THE NORFOLK AND WESTERN RAILWAY COMPANY AND CERTAIN OF ITS EMPLOYEES

A dispute exists between the Norfolk and Western Railway Company and certain of its employees represented by the Brotherhood of Railway, Airline and Steamship Clerks, Freight Handlers, Express and Station Employes, a labor organization;

This dispute has not heretofore been adjusted under the provisions of the Railway Labor Act, as amended; and

This dispute, in the judgment of the National Mediation Board, threatens substantially to interrupt interstate commerce to a degree such as to deprive a section of the country of essential transportation service:

Now, THEREFORE, by the authority vested in me by Section 10 of the Railway Labor Act, as amended (45 U.S.C. 160), it is hereby ordered as follows:

1-101. *Establishment of Board.* There is established a board of three members to be appointed by the President to investigate this dispute. No member of the board shall be pecuniarily or otherwise interested in any organization of railroad employees or any carrier.

1-102. *Report.* The board shall report its finding to the President with respect to the dispute within 30 days from the date of this Order.

1-103. *Maintaining Conditions.* As provided by Section 10 of the Railway Labor

Act, as amended, from this date and for 30 days after the board has made its report to the President, no change, except by agreement, shall be made by the Norfolk and Western Railway Company, or by its employees, in the conditions out of which the dispute arose.

JIMMY CARTER

The White House,
September 28, 1978.

[Filed with the Office of the Federal Register,
5 p.m., September 28, 1978]

Emergency Board To Investigate a Railway Labor Dispute

Appointment of the Membership.
September 28, 1978

The President today announced the appointment of the three members of the Emergency Board to investigate the Norfolk and Western labor dispute. They are:

Paul H. Hanlon, of Portland, Oreg., to be Chairman of the Emergency Board. Hanlon has served as Chairman of four previous Emergency Boards under the Railway Labor Act and is the impartial umpire under the Ford/United Auto Workers contract. He is a member and former officer of the National Academy of Arbitrators.

Jerre S. Williams, of Austin, Tex. Williams is a professor of law at the University of Texas. He has previously served on Emergency Boards under the Railway Labor Act. He is vice president of the National Academy of Arbitrators and an author of several books on labor law. He was the first Chairman of the Administrative Conference of the United States, serving from 1967 to 1970.

Jacob Seidenberg, of Falls Church, Va. Seidenberg is an attorney and holds a Ph. D. in economics. He is a former Chairman of the Federal Impasse Service Panel, has served previously on Emergency Boards under the Railway Labor Act, and he is a member of the National Academy of Arbitrators.

Multilateral Trade Negotiations

Message to the Congress Transmitting Proposed Legislation.   *September 28, 1978*

To the Congress of the United States:

I am today submitting to the Congress a proposal for legislation to extend for a brief period the authority of the Secretary of the Treasury under Section 303(d) of the Tariff Act of 1930 to waive the application of countervailing duties. I hope that the Congress will be able to enact the necessary legislation before adjournment *sine die.*

If not extended, the waiver authority will expire on January 2, 1979. This would seriously jeopardize satisfactory conclusion of the Multilateral Trade Negotiations (MTN) underway in Geneva. Unless the waiver authority is extended to cover the period during which the results of the MTN will be under review by the Congress, our ability to press ahead with the negotiations would be sharply limited.

As stipulated by the Congress in the Trade Act of 1974, negotiation of a satisfactory code on subsidies and countervailing duties is a primary U.S. objective in the MTN. The United States is seeking through such a code improved discipline on the use of subsidies which adversely affect trade. In our view, a satisfactory subsidy/countervailing duty code must include (1) new substantive rules on the use of internal and export subsidies which adequately protect United States agricultural and industrial trading interests insofar as they are adversely affected by such subsidies, and (2) more effective provisions on notification, consultation and dispute settlement that will provide for timely resolution of disputes involving the use of subsidies in international trade.

My Special Representative for Trade Negotiations has informed me that the prospects for reaching agreement by year end on a subsidy/countervailing duty code which meets basic U.S. objectives are good—provided that the waiver authority can be extended until such a code has been submitted to, and acted upon, by the Congress under the procedures of the Trade Act of 1974. In this connection, the legislation I am proposing would provide that the countervailing duty waiver authority will expire as scheduled on January 2, 1979, unless we are able to report to the Congress before that date that a subsidy/countervailing duty code has been negotiated among the key countries participating in the MTN and that the MTN itself has been substantially concluded.

Under the countervailing duty waiver authority, the imposition of countervailing duties may be waived in a specific case only if "adequate steps have been taken to eliminate or substantially reduce the adverse effect" of the subsidy in question. This provision and the other limitations on the use of the waiver authority which are currently in the law would continue in effect if the waiver authority is extended. Thus, U.S. producers and workers will continue to be adequately protected from the adverse effects of subsidized competition.

A successful conclusion to the MTN is essential to U.S. economic policy. If the waiver authority is not extended, such a successful conclusion will, as I have noted, be seriously jeopardized. Accordingly, I urge the Congress to act positively upon this legislative proposal as quickly as possible.

JIMMY CARTER

The White House,
September 28, 1978.

PROPOSED LEGISLATION

Section 303 of the Tariff Act of 1930 (19 U.S.C. 1303) *as amended,* is further amended by adding the following new sentence at the end of Subsection (d) (2).

"The four-year period specified in the first sentence of this paragraph shall be extended until August 1, 1979, provided that before January 3, 1979, the President informs both Houses of Congress that agreement on a code governing the use of subsidies and countervailing duties has been reached and that the Multilateral Trade Negotiations as a whole have been substantially completed and provided further that any determination by the Secretary of the Treasury made pursuant to this section and in effect on January 2, 1979, shall, notwithstanding any expiration date set forth therein, remain in effect until August 1, 1979, unless prior thereto the Secretary has reason to, and does, revoke such determination."

Department of Education Legislation

Statement on Senate Action on the Bill. September 28, 1978

I welcome the Senate's passage of the department of education bill.

Education is a key factor in the development not only of individual citizens but of the country as a whole. Yet it is often overlooked or, at best, given second-rate attention in important policy discussion. I believe that this is unacceptable in a nation where all levels of government spend ever-increasing amounts of money for education while getting less results in the actual performance of our students.

Creation of a department of education, which I set as a priority in this year's State of the Union address, is one important step we can take to improve education in America. It will bring to the Cabinet the leadership needed to direct broad attention to education matters. It will establish Cabinet-level accountability for Federal education programs, exposing them to far greater scrutiny by the President, the Congress, and the public.

Decisions on the running of local school systems need to be made at the community level, as close as possible to the control of the parents themselves. A department of education will enable the Federal Government to do a better job of helping States and local communities carry out their educational responsibilities.

I want to thank Majority Leader Byrd and Chairman Ribicoff for their leadership in gaining Senate passage of the department of education bill. I urge the House of Representatives to act promptly on this measure.

NOTE: The statement was released on September 29.

Death of Pope John Paul I

Statement by the President.
September 29, 1978

It was with deep sadness that I learned of the sudden death of Pope John Paul I. In the brief weeks of his reign, Pope John Paul captured the imagination of his Church and of the world. He held out the promise of combining his predecessors' finest qualities, reaffirming what is enduring and strong in the Catholic tradition, while expanding the frontiers of the Church to cope with the needs of the modern world. The warmth of his personality and his understanding of the lives of ordinary people were evident to all. We are all made poorer by his death.

Office of Management and Budget

Nomination of John Patrick White To Be Deputy Director. September 29, 1978

President Carter today announced that he will nominate John Patrick White to be Deputy Director of the Office of Management and Budget. White, since May 1977, has been Assistant Secretary of Defense for Manpower, Reserve Affairs and Logistics.

White was born in Syracuse, N.Y., on February 27, 1938. He received his undergraduate degree in industrial and labor relations from Cornell University in 1959, his masters degree in economics and public administration from Syracuse University in 1964, and his doctorate in economics from Syracuse in 1969.

From 1969 to 1977, White was with the the Rand Corp., Santa Monica, Calif. He was a member of Rand's board of trustees and served as senior vice president from 1975 to 1977.

From 1964 to 1968, White was on the faculty of Le Moyne College in Syracuse, N.Y. He served with the Marine Corps from 1959 to 1961.

White is married to the former Elizabeth Lucille Michaud. They live in McLean, Va., and have four children.

Department of the Interior

Nomination of Larry E. Meierotto To Be an Assistant Secretary. September 29, 1978

The President today announced that he will nominate Larry E. Meierotto, of Washington, D.C., to be an Assistant Secretary of the Interior. He would replace Ronald Coleman, resigned.

Meierotto was born October 8, 1945, in Dallas, Oreg. He received a B.A. from the University of Portland in 1967.

In 1971 Meierotto served as assistant director for administrative services for the State of Idaho, and in 1972 he was special assistant to the Governor of Idaho and special assistant to the budget director. In 1974 he was a planner with the Idaho Department of Environmental and Community Services, and later served as coordinator of then-Governor Cecil Andrus' reelection campaign.

In 1975 Meierotto was director of special projects for the Pacific Northwest Regional Commission. In 1976 he served as special assistant to then-Governor Andrus. In January 1977, he moved to Washington to serve as Special Assistant to Secretary of the Interior Andrus. Since August 1977, he has been Deputy Assistant Secretary for Policy, Budget and Administration.

Rural Electrification Administration

Nomination of Robert W. Feragen To Be Administrator. September 29, 1978

The President today announced that he will nominate Robert W. Feragen, of Reston, Va., to be Administrator of the Rural Electrification Administration for a term of 10 years. He would replace David Hamil, resigned.

Feragen was born January 28, 1925, in Minot, N. Dak. He received a B.A. (1950)

and M.F.A. (1952) from the State University of Iowa. He served in the U.S. Army from 1943 to 1946.

Between 1952 and 1961, Feragen was an assistant professor at Texas A&M College and at the State University of New York. From 1961 to 1963, he was information director for the East River Electric Power Cooperative in Madison, S. Dak., and from 1963 to 1971, he was information director for the Basin Electric Power Cooperative in Bismarck, N. Dak.

Feragen was general manager of the Northeast Public Power Association in Littleton, Mass., from 1971 to 1974, and general manager of Massachusetts Municipal Wholesale Electric Co. from 1974 to 1978. Since earlier this year he has been Deputy Administrator of the Rural Electrification Administration.

Feragen is a member of the American Public Power Association and chairman of its legislative and resolutions committee. He served on the Governor's Commission on Public Power in Massachusetts.

Consumer Product Safety Commission

Nomination of Samuel D. Zagoria To Be a Member. September 29, 1978

The President today announced that he will nominate Samuel D. Zagoria, of College Park, Md., to be a member of the Consumer Product Safety Commission. He would replace John Byington, who has resigned.

Zagoria was born April 9, 1919, in Somerville, N.J. From 1946 to 1955, he was a reporter and editor for the Washington Post. He was a Nieman Fellow at Harvard University in 1954.

From 1955 to 1965, Zagoria was administrative assistant to Senator Clifford P. Case. He was a member of the National

Labor Relations Board from 1965 to 1969. Since 1969 he has been director of the Labor-Management Relations Service, sponsored by the U.S. Conference of Mayors to provide local governments with information on municipal labor-management relations.

Zagoria is the author of numerous articles and the editor of the book "Public Workers and Public Unions."

Federal Employees Flexible and Compressed Work Schedules Act of 1978

Statement on Signing H.R. 7814 Into Law. September 29, 1978

It gives me great pleasure today to sign into law the Federal Employees Flexible and Compressed Work Schedules Act of 1978, which will permit Federal agencies to experiment with alternatives to the traditional 5-day, 40-hour week. I congratulate Representatives Patricia Schroeder, Stephen Solarz, and Gladys Spellman, and Senators Gaylord Nelson, Thomas Eagleton, and Jacob Javits, for their leadership on this bill. I add my special thanks to committee chairmen Robert Nix, Abraham Ribicoff, and Harrison Williams. I would also like to thank Herbert Harris and Joseph Fisher for their support of this bill.

During the campaign I made a promise to encourage the introduction of more flexible work alternatives to benefit, among others, persons with children, students, and the older or handicapped worker. I am pleased that the Congress also recognized the potential of flexible work arrangements and has now given me the opportunity to carry out that campaign pledge.

We hope that flexible work schedules will increase Government productivity and responsiveness to public needs and provide a new pool of talent for Government service. We expect that some Federal agencies will remain open to serve the public for a greater number of hours each day by using flexible time schedules.

We also will be studying the impact of these work schedule alternatives on the use of mass transportation facilities and energy conservation. Finally, we believe that the quality of individual, family, and working life can be improved when persons are given some voice in the selection of their work arrangements.

While the advantages appear to be substantial, these schedules have not yet been tested within the full range of environments that characterize Federal employment. Therefore, before making a decision to amend Federal laws permanently, this legislation wisely establishes an experimental period of 3 years during which we can evaluate various innovations in a large number of agencies.

This bill also contains a very important provision, introduced by Representative Solarz, which would allow a Federal employee whose personal religious beliefs may occasionally require absence from work to request overtime to make up the time lost. Such overtime work would be compensated with an equal amount of time off, in lieu of overtime pay. I am especially pleased that this provision comes in time for the High Holy Days of the Jewish faith. Congressman Solarz deserves special commendation for his sensitivity to this religious problem and for his innovative solution. The Civil Service Commission will immediately issue interim regulations implementing the compensatory time-off provisions.

NOTE: As enacted, H.R. 7814 is Public Law 95–390, approved September 29.

Digest of Other White House Announcements

The following listing includes the President's daily schedule and other items of general interest as announced by the White House Press Office during the period covered by this issue. Events and announcements printed elsewhere in the issue are not included.

September 23

The President met at the White House with Zbigniew Brzezinski, Assistant to the President for National Security Affairs.

September 25

The President met at the White House with:

—Vice President Walter F. Mondale, Secretary of State Cyrus R. Vance, Secretary of Defense Harold Brown, Hamilton Jordan, Assistant to the President, and Dr. Brzezinski;

—Dr. Brzezinski;

—the Cabinet;

—Ambassador Andrew Young, U.S. Representative to the United Nations;

—Representatives Thomas A. Luken and Willis D. Gradison of Ohio, and baseball player Pete Rose;

—Vice President Mondale;

—Senator Edward M. Kennedy of Massachusetts;

—Representative John Conyers, Jr., of Michigan.

The President announced the delegation to the ceremonies celebrating the independence, within the British Commonwealth, of the Government of Tuvalu. The ceremonies are scheduled for September 29 to October 1 in Funafuti. Tuvalu is in the South Pacific. The delegation will be:

ELIZABETH G. STEVENS, who is active in civic affairs and politics in Washington, D.C., and will head the delegation;

JOHN P. CONDON, U.S. Ambassador to the Dominion of Fiji;

LEO J. MOSER, political adviser to the Commander in Chief of the Pacific Forces in Honolulu, Hawaii.

The President attended a portion of the reception hosted by members of his family on the South Grounds of the White House for supporters of the 1976 Presidential campaign.

September 26

The President met at the White House with:

—David L. Aaron, Deputy Assistant for National Security Affairs;

—Frank B. Moore, Assistant to the President for Congressional Liaison;

—the Democratic congressional leadership;

—the Congressional Black Caucus;

—Vice President Mondale, Frank C. Carlucci, Deputy Director of Central Intelligence, Dr. Brzezinski, and Mr. Jordan;

—Mrs. Carter, and Harold Hughes, director, and Douglas E. Coe, executive director of the Fellowship Foundation;

—James T. McIntyre, Jr., Director of the Office of Management and Budget;

—Members of Congress, representatives of business and labor, and administration officials to discuss United States export policy.

The President attended a portion of the briefing on hospital cost containment legislation given by administration officials in the East Room at the White House.

September 27

The President met at the White House with:

—Dr. Brzezinski;

—Mr. Moore;

—a group of Members of Congress to discuss the public works appropriations legislation;

—Vice President Mondale and Charles L. Schultze, Chairman of the Council of Economic Advisers;

—Senator J. Bennett Johnston of Louisiana.

The President attended a portion of the reception for presidents of the U.S. Jaycees in the White House Family Theater.

September 28

The President met at the White House with:

—Dr. Brzezinski;

—Mr. Moore;

—Secretary of Transportation Brock Adams, Senator Howard W. Cannon of Nevada, and Representatives Harold T. Johnson and Glenn M. Anderson of California, to discuss issues concerning the airlines;

—Eric G. Sandstrom, commander-in-chief of the Veterans of Foreign Wars.

The President attended a portion of the reception held for United States religious leaders on the State Floor of the White House.

The President has designated Elwood T. Driver, a member of the National Transportation Safety Board, to be Vice Chairman of the Board.

September 29

The President met at the White House with:

—Dr. Brzezinski;

—Mr. Moore;

—Secretary Brown, Gen. David C. Jones, Chairman of the Joint Chiefs of Staff, and other Defense Department officials, Frank Press, Director of the Office of Science and Technology Policy, and Mr. McIntyre;

—members of the National Association of Farm Broadcasters (transcript will be printed next week);

—Vice President Mondale and the Congressional Black Caucus.

The President attended a portion of the briefing on energy given by administration officials for representatives of farm organizations in the East Room at the White House.

NOMINATIONS SUBMITTED TO THE SENATE

The following list does not include promotions of the members of the Uniformed Services, nominations to the Service Academies, or nominations of Foreign Service officers.

Submitted September 26, 1978

The following-named persons to be Representatives and Alternate Representatives of the United States of America to the Twentieth Session of the General Conference of the United Nations Educational, Scientific, and Cultural Organization:

Representatives:

JOHN E. REINHARDT, of Maryland
ESTEBAN EDWARD TORRES, of Virginia
HALE CHAMPION, of the District of Columbia
SARAH G. POWER, of Michigan
WILLIAM ATTWOOD, of Connecticut

Alternate Representatives:

MATHILDE KRIM, of New York
JOSEPH D. DUFFEY, of the District of Columbia
MAURICE A. FERRE, of Florida
ARTHUR K. SOLOMON, of Massachusetts
LEILA FRASER, of Wisconsin

Submitted September 27, 1978

B. AVANT EDENFIELD, of Georgia, to be United States District Judge for the Southern District of Georgia, vice Alexander A. Lawrence, retired.

COLONEL JOHN MILEY ADSIT, 397–28–2973, United States Army, to be a member of the California Debris Commission, under the provisions of Section 1 of the Act of Congress approved 1 March 1893 (27 Stat. 507) (33 U.S.C. 661), vice Colonel Henry Augustus Flertzheim, Jr., reassigned.

1669

NOMINATIONS—Continued

Submitted September 27—Continued

DONALD E. O'BRIEN, of Iowa, to be United States District Judge for the Northern and Southern Districts of Iowa, vice William C. Hanson, retired.

Submitted September 29, 1978

LARRY E. MEIEROTTO, of the District of Columbia, to be an Assistant Secretary of the Interior, vice Ronald G. Coleman, resigned.

ROBERT W. FERAGEN, of Virginia, to be Administrator of the Rural Electrification Administration for a term of 10 years, vice David Hamil, resigned.

SAMUEL D. ZAGORIA, of Maryland, to be a Commissioner of the Consumer Product Safety Commission for the remainder of the term expiring October 26, 1978, vice S. John Byington, resigned.

SAMUEL D. ZAGORIA, of Maryland, to be a Commissioner of the Consumer Product Safety Commission for a term of 7 years from October 27, 1978 (reappointment).

CHECKLIST OF WHITE HOUSE PRESS RELEASES

The following releases of the Office of the White House Press Secretary, distributed during the period covered by this issue, are not included in the issue.

Released September 25, 1978

News conference: on hospital cost containment legislation—by Secretary of Health, Education, and Welfare Joseph A. Califano, Jr., Ambassador Robert S. Strauss, Special Representative for Trade Negotiations, James T. McIntyre, Jr., Director of the Office of Management and Budget, and Charles L. Schultze, Chairman of the Council of Economic Advisers

News conference: on the installation of a solar energy system on the West Wing of the White House—by Omi Walden, Assistant Secretary of Energy, and Hugh A. Carter, Jr., Special Assistant to the President for Administration

CHECKLIST—Continued

Released September 26, 1978

News conference: on U.S. export policy—by Secretary of Commerce Juanita M. Kreps

Released September 27, 1978

Announcement: nomination of Donald E. O'Brien to be United States District Judge for the Northern and Southern Districts of Iowa

Announcement: nomination of B. Avant Edenfield to be United States District Judge for the Southern District of Georgia

ACTS APPROVED BY THE PRESIDENT

Approved September 26, 1978

S. 3075_____ Public Law 95–384 International Security Assistance Act of 1978.

S. 3119_____ Public Law 95–385 An act to transfer certain real property of the United States to the District of Columbia Redevelopment Land Agency.

S. 3120_____ Public Law 95–386 An act to enhance the flexibility of contractual authority of the Temporary Commission on Financial Oversight of the District of Columbia.

Approved September 27, 1978

S. 1103_____ Public Law 95–387 District of Columbia Reciprocal Tax Collection Act.

S. 2556_____ Public Law 95–388 An act to change the name of the District of Columbia Bail Agency to the District of Columbia Pretrial Services Agency.

Approved September 29, 1978

S.J. Res. 133_____ Public Law 95–389 A joint resolution to authorize and request the President to issue a proclamation designating September 24, 1978, as "National Good Neighbor Day".

H.R. 7814_____ Public Law 95–390 Federal Employees Flexible and Compressed Work Schedules Act of 1978.

PRESIDENTIAL DOCUMENTS

Interview With the President

Remarks and a Question-and-Answer Session
With Members of the National Association
of Farm Broadcasting. September 29, 1978

THE PRESIDENT. Good afternoon, everybody. Sorry to interrupt your meeting. [*Laughter*]

ADMINISTRATION POLICIES

I was just looking over yesterday's Washington Post. And my staff had counted 13 articles in one newspaper about fraud or corruption or misspent public funds. And this is one of the challenges that we've accepted since I've been President, is to try to root out this kind of legitimate concern that American people have about government.

We will have legislation very shortly establishing the firmest possible restraint on major public officials in the Congress and my administration concerning ethics. We're setting up 12 inspectors general, who will supervise independently the proper performance within the major agencies.

We've now embarked, as you know, on a very difficult task of correcting some of the deficiencies that have existed for decades, really, in the General Services Ad-

ministration. I think the civil service reform, which is likely to pass very shortly, will mean that public employees who are overwhelmingly excellent, honest, dedicated, competent, will be given a chance to be rewarded for that kind of performance. And we are encouraging the protection of the so-called whistleblowers, and in the process of civil service reform, we have a special counsel who again is independent of me or anyone else who can investigate allegations of improper performance.

This is an ongoing process. It's not an abrupt crusade. It's something we've been doing for a long time. But I hope it'll pay dividends, because every time we do have a revelation of a bad performance or improper spending of funds or even just mismanagement, certainly corruption and fraud, it creates a very bad core problem in government that we'd like to root out.

I think I might outline just in a couple of minutes a few of the things that we are working on now in the last stages of the congressional session, and just briefly cover some foreign affairs, and then let you ask me questions that are of concern to you.

I think we have now a good chance to pass the major portion of the natural gas and other energy policy bills. And we'll get four bills passed, maybe half of another bill, which would include everything except the crude oil equalization tax—that would be carried over till next year—a few other smaller items.

Civil service reform is something we've struggled with now for 20 months. The conference committee concluded its work yesterday in a spirit of harmony. I think that will be concluded now.

Airline deregulation, which has been hung up because it's tied to an airline noise bill, has now been separated. I met with the key conferees yesterday, and they are prepared to move on that.

We have many other items that are important. The full employment bill, of course, is important; the equal rights amendment extension is important to over half the American people. And we have in addition a wide range of mandatory bills, appropriations bills and authorization bills which must be presented to me in a fiscally responsible way, otherwise they'll face disapproval here in the White House.

We've now had almost exactly a year of experience with the 1977 farm act, which was perhaps the most far-reaching legislation that was passed in 1977. I think the results have been good. We are making remarkable progress in improving the net farm income. We've made good progress in increasing farm exports; last year set an all-time record in spite of very low unit prices. This year we expect to improve upon that.

We still are trying to assess any needs for change. We're going to have good crops, I think, this year in some of the basic commodity items, and the set-aside programs we're trying to orient and also to describe so that they'll be constructive. We're trying to increase the quality of our farm products, both at the shipping points and all kinds of grains. And, of course, we're trying to leave the bottom four leaves of tobacco plants—do different things that the farmers can do on their own that might cut down the volume when that volume is comprised of marginal quality of portion of shipments for sales.

In foreign affairs, we are progressing slowly, sometimes haltingly, but I think in a good spirit, with the Soviet Union in concluding a SALT agreement, hopefully this year. I'll meet tomorrow morning with Foreign Minister Gromyko, who's been meeting the last 2 days in New York with Secretary Vance on that and a comprehensive test ban.

We've had good success, as you know, well-publicized effort at Camp David in trying to make a major stride toward peace in the Middle East. Yesterday, I spoke by telephone both to President Sadat and to Prime Minister Begin. They're both pleased with the Knesset vote. And I see really no difficult problems to be resolved in concluding a peace treaty between Egypt and Israel. The only holdup in an immediate commitment to negotiations is just the technicalities of getting the delegations chosen, determining a site, and there are holy days or important national days both in Egypt and Israel which will be concluded about 2 weeks from now.

So, I don't see any problems there. I'd be surprised if some insurmountable problem did arise. I won't go into other details on foreign and domestic policy. I'd rather spend my time with you answering your questions.

QUESTIONS

BEEF IMPORTS

Q. Mr. Carter, would you sign the Bentsen bill on the countercyclical cattle imports if it got to your desk?

THE PRESIDENT. No, I wouldn't approve the Bentsen bill as it was drafted.

I've let Lloyd and others know about my own concerns on details. I think it will certainly be modified as it goes to the House, and then to the conference committee.

We now have a level of beef imports that I don't intend to increase this year. But I think I ought to have some flexibility there, because quite often there is a legitimate need for increased beef imports. The fact is, in the past this has worked fairly well.

But I studied the Bentsen bill fairly thoroughly when it was first passed through the Senate and expressed some concerns about it, through Bob Bergland, to the House and to the conferees. I don't remember the details of all the items that I didn't like. But there's a good basic philosophy behind it which has been, I think, effectively used by most Presidents. But I think that the President needs flexibility in controlling beef imports.

AGRICULTURE LEGISLATION

Q. Mr. President, Charlie Rankin from the Lower Rio Grande Valley of Texas.

We've been apprised this morning of the situation concerning your veto of water projects. Have you had a chance to look at the agricultural appropriations bill and contemplate vetoing any of the porkbarreling projects in there, trying to work out something? [*Laughter*]

THE PRESIDENT. From what I know about the agriculture bill, it's reasonably acceptable. The bill has not gotten to my desk. My staff has not thoroughly assessed it, but my first hearing about it is favorable.

AMERICAN FARMING

Q. Mr. President, I'm Jack Crowner from Kentucky. What is your opinion now of the mood of the American farmer—with a big production in the Government

program that we had for set-asides, apparently did not take too well advantage of.

THE PRESIDENT. I think that will probably be determined more accurately on November 7, when you see the results of the campaigns.

Compared to a year ago, the life of the American farm family and also, I think, the attitude of the American farm family has improved dramatically. I hear this in my own travels through the farm regions, from my own home area, which suffered badly last year. And the statistics prove that the farmers should basically be satisfied.

I think the increase—in addition to what I've already described on exports and net farm income—you have an increased right of farm families to control their own basic marketing procedures, with a dramatic growth in on-farm storage. And we are also trying to set up export offices in different key regions of the world, which will help. I think this combination will let the farmers have a much more aggressive sales policy overseas.

We are now getting some orders for grain from countries that didn't formerly trade with us. The People's Republic of China is one, and there's a large possible market there. Bob Strauss is trying to protect the American farmer, too, in his negotiations on trade agreements. I think in general the attitude is good now.

LOCK AND DAM PROJECT IN ILLINOIS

Q. Mr. President, my name is Chuck Lilligren from Minneapolis. If there were proper user fees along with it, would you approve of new construction of Lock and Dam 26 in Alton, Illinois?

THE PRESIDENT. This has been a matter of great debate. My inclination is to approve it, provided the water use fees are compatible with what guidelines I laid down for Senator Long and others in the Senate debate.

INDICTMENTS OF GSA PERSONNEL

I just got a memo here that a Federal grand jury Friday indicted 18 persons on charges stemming from the Government's investigation of the scandal at the General Services Administration. Where is that, Jody?

PRESS SECRETARY POWELL. That's in Baltimore. That's a Baltimore indictment.

THE PRESIDENT. That's the first indictment. Well, I hope we can get it straightened out.

PREDATOR CONTROL

Q. Mr. President, would you consider rescinding or at least modifying the stringency of Mr. Nixon's Presidential order that banned the use of 1080 in the control of coyotes? Sheep ranchers and goat ranchers in Texas—I'm from Texas, my name is Peeples—are suffering ruinous losses. I know of them going out of business, and it's because of an animal that is not endangered. You have it within your power with the sweep of a pen to do something about it.

THE PRESIDENT. I don't know how to answer that question. I've never discussed it with Cecil Andrus or Bob Bergland. But my present inclination would be to leave the Executive order intact. I've not made a study of it, but that's my present thought.

COTTON DUST REGULATION

Q. Mr. President, Ernie Houdashell, from Amarillo, Texas. Recently the Occupational Safety and Health Administration released the long-awaited cotton dust standards. And in doing so, they put an economic bind, a tremendous bind on some segments of the cotton industry, possibly, that's going to close down some segments of the cotton industry. Are you ever going to do anything about OSHA as far as the people, these regulations? They're running without control, so to speak, and they are endangering industries like the cotton industry. These cotton dust standards, they're not well founded according to some experts.

THE PRESIDENT. I doubt if there's any regulation that's been issued within the last 12 months that I put more time on personally than I did the standards on cotton dust. You're talking about cotton dust in textile mills, right?

Q. Right.

THE PRESIDENT. Previously, the Republican administration had advocated standards and a method for enforcing them that would have cost the industry an estimated $7 billion, if I remember correctly. I think that's an accurate figure.

After quite a deep study by my Council of Economic Advisers, also by my group that controls inflation and tries to prevent extraordinary burdens being placed on producers and then consumers, and meeting with the director of OSHA, who I consider to be one of the best administrators in the Government, and also Ray Marshall, we modified those standards considerably and cut that cost, I would say, to a fourth of what it was previously.

I think the present regulation is very reasonable, the one that we've issued now. And I'm sure that there are some who don't want to change the standards at all. But this has been a matter of concern to administrations long before I became President, and we've improved it greatly. I think the regulation we issued is——

Q. It's being challenged in the courts now by the National Cotton Council. They are——

THE PRESIDENT. I understand that, and that's their prerogative. But I think the courts, when they review it, will rule in our favor.

FARM SUPPORT FOR THE ADMINISTRATION

Q. Mark Oppold, Cedar Rapids, Iowa. We are glad to have your wife in our city today, visiting.

How concerned are you about capturing the farm vote in 1980, and what measures will the administration take to bring the vote to your side 2 years from now?

THE PRESIDENT. Well, I hope the Democratic nominee for President gets the farm vote in 1980, no matter who it might be. [*Laughter*]

I would rather my administration and the Democratic Congress be judged on its record. Farmers are responsible people. I think they make judgments by the degree of freedom they have to produce crops; the degree of control they have over their own destiny; the amount of detectable interest in their specific problems derived from an administration, including the Congress, on kind of a personal basis; the degree of increase in sale of their products, domestically and overseas; and the amount of net income that they realize, which is a bottom-line thing, after they've worked for a year on the farm.

I think on all these issues I've just described—and I could go on—our record has been good. But obviously we want to have an equally good record in the next 2 years. I'm willing to rely on the statistics and the facts and the actual achievements, not just on words or claims or goals that are set and sometimes not realized.

PEANUT LEGISLATION

Q. Mr. President, are you pleased with the way the new peanut bill is working?

THE PRESIDENT. That's one bill that I have deliberately not been involved in because of my family's deep involvement in peanuts.

When I was running for President, I promised the public that I would stay aloof from that particular legislation. And

I issued a directive to Bob Bergland, and I asked Senator Talmadge and also Tom Foley to leave me out of that particular legislation. And I think, though, that it seems to be working. I don't have placards and tractors blocking my entrance to my home when I go home to Plains. [*Laughter*] So, I presume it's working well.

The general philosophy behind it—of course, I was thoroughly familiar with it before I was elected President. I was involved as one of the leaders in the peanut industry. But I think, there again, the trend has been toward decreasing Government involvement and the tight constraint on the peanut farmers' production and an increase in sales and promotion.

I think that the approach is one that's been good.

SUGAR PRICE SUPPORTS

Q. I'm Dave Bateman, from Fargo, North Dakota. And there are two things that concern us out there—obviously, as you know, water. We think we know how you feel about Garrison Dam. What about sugar? Will we have a sugar bill? We've got the largest contiguous acreage of sugar beets in the country out there, and our farmers are rightly concerned whether we'll have a bill or not.

THE PRESIDENT. I would like to see a bill passed. There's a wide range of opinion about what the price level for sugar should be, all the way from 14 cents to 17 cents, and this involves an enormous amount of money.

I think the Ways and Means bill that came out of the House would be the maximum that I could accept on sugar prices.

Q. Is that 15 cents?

THE PRESIDENT. That's 15 cents, with no annual built-in increase.

Q. No escalator clause in there at all?

THE PRESIDENT. That's correct. That's

what the Ways and Means Committee advocated.

In the Senate, as you know, the Church-Long bill calls for 17 cents. If something like that should prevail over my objection, this would really be the only agricultural product where you set the prevailing nationwide price to accommodate the highest cost of production anywhere in the Nation. Even sugarcane producers in Hawaii, you know, would find that the 17 cents to be excessive, for instance. And of course, sugar beets, you can produce sugar for probably less than 15 cents.

I've never promised any farm group, even when I was eagerly seeking their support in the campaign, that I would guarantee them a profit. And I think that this level that I've described is adequate.

FARMER PROTESTS

Q. Mr. President, Jerry Urdahl from Wisconsin. What's your opinion of the American Agriculture Movement?

THE PRESIDENT. I think it's all right.

This is a movement that originated last year because of despair and a feeling that top Government officials and the general public did not understand the legitimate grievances and concerns—sometimes actual suffering—that existed in the farm families of our country.

Whether or not you would approve of blocking traffic with tractors—and I don't approve of that kind of law violations; that was a rare occurrence—I think the dramatization of the farmers' plight to the entire public, indeed the entire world, was a very constructive thing. It helped me to get from the Congress and helped many Congress Members to vote for an excellent 1977 farm bill. And I think it kept vividly in the minds of the American people that the farmers are a crucial element in our economic strength and need to be protected in the future.

So, whether you agree with specific occurrences that were highly publicized and exaggerated or not is beside the point. I think the American farm movement did a great service to agriculture and to the country.

TERRORISM

Q. Mr. President, getting away from agriculture, but since your meetings on world peace, there was a threat that there would be now terrorism brought to the United States. I'm Bob Miller from Ohio. In our highly populated area, there has been some concern on this. What do you visualize?

THE PRESIDENT. There's always a threat of terrorism. And I don't know yet what the Mideast peace proposal will do toward the trend.

But, in recent months, in the last 6 or 9 months—I've forgotten the exact period of time—the incidence of terrorism worldwide had dropped. And this was especially true of the incidence of terrorism against Americans and American installations throughout the world.

There are deep feelings about the Mideast, as you know, on both sides. And I've seen threats that the oil fields in Saudi Arabia would be attacked or that American installations around the world would be attacked because of the Camp David accords. We'll continue to be vigilant about it.

One of the major conclusions that was reached at Bonn at the summit conference which was not highly publicized was that the seven nations agreed for the first time that if airplanes were hijacked, for instance, that we would exert the most stringent economic sanctions, through the right to land and take off airplanes, to have air service, against any country that harbored terrorists or hijackers or who kept captured planes in their territory.

We've since contacted every nation in the world which has commercial air service—and that's almost all of them—and urged other nations to join in with us. And a substantial portion of them—I couldn't tell you the exact percentage today—have also combined with us in means by which terrorism could be constrained. I hope that downward trend, accelerated by the airline hijacking concurrence among the world's leaders, will continue. But if it should turn around, we will obviously just do the best we can to restrain it.

I think many people in the Mideast, even in other confrontation states, don't feel as deeply against the major move toward peace as some of the leaders indicate.

Most people were amazed a year ago, or less than a year ago, at the overwhelming roadside response of Israelis toward President Sadat and of the Egyptians toward the Prime Minister of Israel, Begin, and his negotiating team. They thought there would be some animosity. But there was an overwhelming sense of appreciation that "you've finally brought peace to us."

I think some of the other nations would find this to be true, when and if their leaders show the same courage that has been exhibited by Begin and Sadat. I think the people out there want peace.

So, I think the threat of terrorism is probably exaggerated. But if it should occur, attempts, I think we are prepared to meet it.

RELATIONS WITH THE FARM PRESS

Q. Mr. President, do you feel that you and your administration have been treated fairly by the farm broadcasters and telecasters and the farm press?

THE PRESIDENT. I think so; yes, sir.

In general, I think the press has been very fair to us. The only thing that has concerned me about the press has been that all the time we were trying to work on very broad-ranging problems, that we were criticized because we didn't have instant success. And a lot of people took the campaign promises that I made over a 2-year period and, at the end of my first year, said, "Carter has not kept his campaign promises, because he hasn't done all these things he promised."

This includes an energy policy. Nobody had had the temerity or foolhardiness as President before to try to bring about that accomplishment. Civil service reform in a hundred years, nobody had tackled it; government reorganization, these sorts of things. With that one exception, which is predictable and understandable, I think the press has been very fair.

And now that I have had some success—I'd say notably the Camp David meetings and, I think recently, accomplishments in the Congress—there's probably been too much credit. So, I think if you balanced it out over a 20-month period, 18-month period—[*laughter*]—the excessive criticism for a while and now the excessive credit would pretty well balance out. [*Laughter*]

FARM INCOME

Q. Larry Steckline from Kansas. The figures we get indicate quite a difference between farm and nonfarm income. Are you happy today with farm income?

THE PRESIDENT. No. I think we still see that farm income is—I started to say *the* lowest—among the lowest in the Nation per capita, and also certainly the lowest in the Nation per person, compared to the tremendous capital investment required, even in a fairly prosperous State like Wisconsin.

I remember when I was running for President and campaigned in Wisconsin, I got some figures on the dairy industry from the University of Wisconsin and others. And if I remember right, the average dairy farm at that time, which was '76, had a capital investment of $180,000. The average net income for the family was $7,000. The average size of the family was, I think, five people, which is an extremely low per capita income. And the fact was that the dairy farmer could very well have sold his farm and invested it at 5-percent interest and made $9,000 income without having to work at all.

So, I don't think the general public yet realizes how low farm income is, compared to other farm income, for laborers, and certainly they don't for a farm family that has a tremendous capital investment. There's still a wide disparity there that I hope to help close.

MR. WURFEL. Thank you, sir.

FARM PRICE CONTROLS

Q. Mr. President, Ken Root from Oklahoma City.

THE PRESIDENT. Well, I'll get this one, and then we'll——

Q. Do you have, following this question, in case farm prices started up, say, like they did in 1973, would there be any chance that you would cut it off at the other end by imposing any price controls if a situation like that reoccurred?

THE PRESIDENT. Absolutely not; I would never do that.

I need to go. I have another appointment. But if you don't object, I would like for you to come by and let me get an individual photograph with you before you leave. I don't have time for other questions as you come by, just a handshake and a photograph, and then we'll send them to you after you get home.

NOTE: The interview began at 1:18 p.m. in the Cabinet Room at the White House. Walter W. Wurfel is Deputy Press Secretary.

The transcript of the interview was released on September 30.

Fighting in Lebanon
Statement by the President.
September 30, 1978

I have just been reviewing the dangerous situation in Lebanon with Secretary of State Vance.

The fighting today was particularly destructive and it seemed to be spreading. I was therefore greatly relieved to learn that President Asad of Syria had been personally involved in bringing about a cease-fire, which is holding for now. I call urgently on all involved to negotiate a permanent end to the cycle of confrontations which has gone on far too long and at such a heavy cost in innocent lives.

I hope other friends of Lebanon will join with the United States in efforts to bring an end to the tragedy in Lebanon and to assist President Sarkis of Lebanon in all appropriate ways as he tries to restore stability and calm.

Humphrey-Hawkins Full Employment Legislation
Statement by the President.
September 30, 1978

Today marks the 8th annual dinner of the Congressional Black Caucus. From its inception, the caucus has played an instrumental role in the development and passage of legislation benefiting all Americans.

Since taking office, I have found the caucus, under the leadership of Congressman Parren Mitchell, to be an extraordinarily talented group of legislators, always having the interests of the Nation and their constitutents as a primary concern. For that reason, I have met regularly with the caucus throughout my Presidency, and I look forward to the guidance and counsel I will get from our future meetings.

A member of the caucus, Congressman Gus Hawkins, drafted, with the late Senator Hubert Humphrey, a landmark full employment bill, which I endorsed in my campaign and have strongly supported since the beginning of my administration.

Among the caucus' most outstanding achievements has been the effort to make all Americans aware of the need for a legislated commitment to a full employment policy.

Over the next 2 weeks, the debate over this legislation will intensify. Throughout that debate, we should never lose sight of the fact that the Humphrey-Hawkins bill is designed to help all Americans, not just blacks or other minorities. A full employment commitment of the Federal Government will benefit men and women of every color and economic status.

I continue to regard the passage of the Humphrey-Hawkins bill as one of the highest legislative priorities of my administration. Working with the Congressional Black Caucus and the Full Employment Council, led by Coretta Scott King, my administration has been working to ensure passage this year of this long overdue and much needed legislation.

We have been successful so far in the House of Representatives, which overwhelmingly passed the Humphrey-Hawkins bill this year. The bill is now before the Senate, and through the leadership of Senator Byrd, the bill has now been placed on the Senate calendar. We are now working with the Senate leadership to secure a time agreement on this bill so that we can be certain the 95th Congress will not adjourn without passage of the Humphrey-Hawkins bill. If the Members of the Senate allow this bill to come to a vote, I have no doubt that we will succeed.

Congressional Black Caucus

Remarks at the Caucus' Annual Dinner.
September 30, 1978

Chairman Parren Mitchell, Vice Chairperson Shirley Chisholm, members of the Black Caucus, distinguished black religious leaders from all over the Nation, ladies and gentlemen, brothers and sisters:

I think in the last 2 days, everybody knows how I stand on the Hawkins-Humphrey full employment bill. And I want to make sure that the chairman of the Black Caucus is with us. So, I brought tonight a big button that says, "Justice Through Jobs, Pass Humphrey-Hawkins, Sponsored by the National Council of Churches." I want to make sure that Parren Mitchell wears this, too.

This is a great evening—two hotels full of great Americans who believe in progress, who have proven it, sometimes at the risk of your own lives, who know the greatness of our country, believe it can be even greater. Gus Hawkins is here. He met me outside. And he's one of those who has had the sensitivity and the tenacity, the influence in the Congress to make great progress on a bill in which we are all interested.

There's another great man who worked with him who couldn't be here tonight. Of all the white men I've ever known, he was closest to the black people of our country. Of all the druggists I've ever known, he was closest to being a preacher, and that's Senator Hubert Humphrey. He was one of those, like you and like myself, who didn't believe in the trickle-down theory of government services.

There are a lot of definitions of that. I think Senator Humphrey had the best. He said the Republican theory, the trickle-down theory, was if you feed a horse enough oats, eventually the sparrows will have something to eat. [*Laughter*] But those of you who are assembled tonight in this tremendous audience, the biggest in history for a Black Caucus banquet, I and my administration are trying to put an end to the trickle-down theory.

I'm very grateful that tonight we are honoring the black churches. As all of you may know, I grew up in the South. [*Laughter*] And I've seen from my earliest days a remarkable demonstration of the interrelationship, within the black churches, of a courageous stand for spiritual progress and a courageous stand for the progress of material things—a person's body, an end to embarrassment through racism, an end to poverty, an end to hunger, an end to the war between people in a country, an end to a war between people in different countries. This is the kind of thing that has always been held high as a commitment of the great black leaders of our Nation. Martin Luther King, Jr., was the most famous, a man who inspired us all. But he was one among many during the time of his life, and he inspired many who have come along since him.

I'm not a preacher; I'm a farmer. But I thought this evening it might be good— I tried to think of a theme for my talk, which is going to be fairly brief—but I thought if you wouldn't mind, I would use a text—[*laughter*]—that would signify very clearly what I want to talk about tonight.

This comes from the 25th Chapter of Matthew, the words of Jesus talking about a king: "Then shall He say also unto them on the left hand, Depart from me, ye cursed, unto everlasting fire, prepared for the devil and his angels: For I was hungry, and ye gave me no meat; I was thirsty, and ye gave me no drink; I was a stranger, and ye took me not in; I was naked, and ye clothed me not; and in prison, and ye visited me not. Then shall they also answer him, saying, Lord, when saw we thee hungry, or athirst, or a stranger, or naked, or sick, or imprisoned, and did not minister unto thee? Then shall he answer them, saying, Verily I say unto you, inasmuch as ye did it not unto one of the least of these, ye did it not to me. And these shall go away unto everlasting punishment: but the righteous into life eternal."

The Black Caucus who serve in Congress, still in the minority, have been inspired to courageous action, unity in the face of pressure, tenacity in the face of discouragement, because they believe in these principles. And they see themselves uniquely responsible not only for all Americans but particularly for those who have been hungry and thirsty and alone and in prison and naked.

This has given them strength to carry on in the tradition of the great black leaders of this Nation who have held high a banner which has made us all sometimes ashamed and then proud of our achievements together.

The American Government is one of the greatest institutions on Earth, an institution that is lumbering on occasion, frustrating on occasion, confused on occasion. But it derives its strength and it derives its direction in a time of crisis from those who are strong willed and whose commitments never falter and whose aims are sure and whose goals are clear.

I've been in office 20 months, in the highest elected office, perhaps, in the whole world. And I have forged to my own benefit as President, to the benefit of those in the minority in this country, and to the benefit of all American people, a good alliance with the members of the Black Caucus, and I'm thankful for it.

When I took office a few months ago, our country had the highest unemployment rate since the Great Depression.

Ten million Americans could not find a full-time job; 7 million Americans couldn't find any job at all. The unemployment rate was 8 percent. And we started working together, the Congress and I and many of you who are not in government. We've added a net of 6½ million jobs; we've cut the unemployment rate 25 percent; we've allotted 6 billion new dollars for youth employment; we've tripled CETA jobs; we've doubled Job Corps jobs; we've quit making poor people pay for food stamps. We've made some progress.

We've made some progress, but we can't afford to rest on our laurels, because Gus Hawkins, Hubert Humphrey, the members of the Black Caucus knew and still know that we can never stop moving toward full employment until every man and every woman in the United States who's able and willing to have a job has a job. And I'm determined to see this bill passed this year, because I don't want to hear the unemployed child or man with a dependent family cry out this verse, "Inasmuch as ye did it not to one of the least of these, ye did it not to me."

Twenty months ago, when a Democratic administration came in after 8 years, the civil rights laws that you had struggled and suffered to have passed were being unenforced. They laid dormant. Tens of thousands of cases that had been presented to your Government had not been heard. There was no administrative thrust behind them. Government contracts—your tax money being spent for good projects—never found a black contractor to fill the need for work; bank deposits avoided the black-owned banks. Women were still deprived of a basic constitutional right for equality.

We had court cases coming along—the *Bakke* case, challenging the right to consider race in admission to colleges, with far-reaching impact that might have con-demned absolutely the affirmative action commitment of us all. And people like Drew Days and Eleanor Holmes Norton worked with many of us to bring about improvements in employment opportunities.

We still have a long way to go. And I predict to you that next week, the bill that will extend the constitutional amendment time for the equal rights amendment will pass the Senate, and we'll still have a chance in our country to give women the same basic constitutional right that the rest of us have.

Human services were neglected for 8 years. Educational funds were not focused on a poor child, a child whose parents were illiterate because they never had a chance to get an education. We know what Lyndon Johnson tried to do in 1965 with the Elementary and Secondary Acts, the Higher Education Acts. But those had not been realized in their dreams. And this year, we have increased funds allotted for educational programs focused on those who need it most, more than any time in the history of our country, including even those great days when Lyndon Johnson was President.

And Pat Harris has seen very clearly that our central cities were deteriorating. Housing was absent. And she and I and Mary Berry and the Black Caucus and many of you have worked to correct these defects in our society. We now have an urban policy that will let us have better cities where the poor people live. We're determined to carry it through. We're working together. We'll never change our commitment.

We also saw a silent robbing of those who live on fixed incomes, who have a small pension, who live on slowly changing welfare payments, who have a part-time job. We inherited a very high inflation rate. For 10 solid years, inflation has been too high. Waste in government was robbing us all. Deficit spending was caused by inefficiency.

We've tried to make the government more responsive to meet people's needs at the delivery end of the cycle, because you've never seen a hungry child fed with waste or educated with inefficiency. You've never seen a house built with a cumbersome bureaucracy, and you've never seen people's needs met with ever-increasing Federal deficits to put a burden on us all.

And Bill Beckham in the Treasury Department, Bunny Mitchell and Louis Martin in the White House, the Black Caucus, and you and I have moved to correct these deficiencies. We've got a long way to go. Inflation is still with us. But together, I believe that we can turn that corner and let people have a stable and a predictable and a sure future.

We inherited, also, the aftermath of the Vietnam war, a war that was distorted because it was waged against people far away, whose skins were yellow. Our draft laws, the policy of the Department of the Army and others, had been oriented to draft and send overseas the poor and the black who couldn't afford to send their sons to college.

Our country had a consciousness that we were not committed to the purity of peace; we were committed to the filth of war. Now we've changed that attitude. Clifford Alexander is now the great Secretary of the Army, and we are staying strong to preserve the peace. But we've also got a fine leader of the Peace Corps, Carolyn Payton. And we're trying to extend the influence of our country in a beneficent way, not a condemnatory way throughout the world.

I'd like to mention one other thing that concerns me, because this is one of the greatest defects that our country has sustained for a full 200 years, and that is a foreign policy that was misapplied. As I said to the Democratic fundraiser early this week, as a Governor of Georgia, as a candidate for President, I used to shrink up and dread the day each fall when the United Nations General Assembly began its deliberations, because I knew that my country, which I love, would be the target of every attack and the butt of every joke among two-thirds of the nations on Earth.

We were despised and condemned by the small nations, the new nations, the weak nations, the nations whose people were black or brown or yellow. We had ignored the great continent of Africa. Our Nation had espoused and supported racist regimes, dictatorships. Our own Secretary of State was not permitted to go into Nigeria 3 or 4 years ago—as you know, one of the greatest nations on Earth, with about a hundred million people and great wealth, very influential.

But now I don't dread to see the General Assembly called to order, because we've got new friends all over the world. And they've been brought to our side not by me, although my commitment is there, but by people like Terry Todman, Don McHenry, and a man who's not afraid to speak out when he sees something wrong, Andy Young.

The General Assembly is in session now, you know. Is Andy Young here tonight? He's a Black Caucus member, and he's a preacher. [*Laughter*]

Well, let me tell you this: I don't know of anyone who serves in the administration of Jimmy Carter who has done more for our country throughout the world than Andy Young. [*Applause*] And one other comment—I was going to make it even if you hadn't stood up—[*laughter*]—as long as I'm President and Andy Young is willing to stay there, he'll be the United Nations Ambassador.

There are a lot of other people I could mention. I spoke to this group last year, and there was a lonely sign down in front that said, "Thank you, Mr. President, for endorsing D.C. voting rights." But I don't believe anybody felt at that time that a year later the Congress would have passed overwhelmingly, both bodies, a constitutional amendment to give those rights.

And I'd like to recognize and thank Walter Fauntroy for his tremendous leadership, Clarence Mitchell, our 101st Senator, and three members of the Black Caucus who will, unfortunately, be retiring this year: Barbara Jordan, who electrified our country, who inspired the world with her great address at the Democratic National Convention, when I was nominated; Congressman Bob Nix, who was the leader, who's getting the civil service reform bill through the Congress this year—one of the great achievements of all times; and Yvonne Burke, who's going to be the next attorney general of California.

Well, let me close by saying that some people criticize you and me, and it's an honor when they do. [*Laughter*] Some people say we are too impatient. Do you think we're too impatient?

AUDIENCE. No.

THE PRESIDENT. Some people say we are too ambitious for those that we care about. But I don't believe we're too ambitious. Some people say—and you've heard it many times—"They are never satisfied." [*Laughter*] But can we afford to be satisfied when we've got hundreds of thousands of young black men walking the streets looking for a job?

AUDIENCE. No.

THE PRESIDENT. Can we afford to be satisfied when our cities are crumbling and particularly those areas where poor people live and are at the mercy of landlords who don't care about them, often, and who need our help?

AUDIENCE. No.

THE PRESIDENT. Right. Can we afford to be satisfied when we have literally millions of young people still struggling for an adequate education because they can't speak English well or because their parents never had a chance to learn?

AUDIENCE. No.

THE PRESIDENT. No, we can't. Can we afford to be satisfied when we're still spending more on nuclear weapons than we are on peace?

AUDIENCE. No.

THE PRESIDENT. Can we afford to be satisfied when we realize that for many people, even in our own country, equality is still just a dream?

No, we cannot afford to be satisfied.

I'm proud that you and I are able to walk together. I'm proud of the partnership that binds us, one to another. I'm proud of a recognition of unrecognized and unfulfilled dreams. I'm proud to share with you experience of the past when progress has been made. I'm proud to know people in this audience who have exhibited, even in a position of prominence, a great sensitivity and love for those who yearn for a better life.

There's a person here who helped to begin this movement, and I don't even need to call her name. She's a woman who refused to sit in the back of a bus. And her name is Rosa Parks. She's here. Where is she?

Rosa Parks, would you come up here? In the midst of that historic event that began the Montgomery bus boycott, Martin Luther King, Jr., came up to an old woman, and he was concerned about her strenuous effort to correct the deprivation of human rights. And he said, "Honey, aren't you tired and worn out?" She said, "My feet are tired, but my soul is rested."

Well, we've got a long way to walk in the future. We'll walk together. Our feet may be tired, but when we get through, our soul will be rested.

Thank you very much.

NOTE: The President spoke at 10:14 p.m. in the International Ballroom at the Washington Hilton Hotel. In his opening remarks, he referred to Representative Parren J. Mitchell of Maryland, chairman, and Representative Shirley Chisholm of New York, vice chairperson, Congressional Black Caucus.

Kennedy Space Center, Florida

Remarks at the Congressional Space Medal of Honor Awards Ceremony.   *October 1, 1978*

Governor Askew, Senator Chiles, Senator Stone, Senator Stevenson, who is the chairman of the Subcommittee on Energy and Technology, Congressman Tiger Teague—who is the retiring chairman of the Committee on Science and Technology, and who has done so much to bring our space program to our Nation and who wrote the legislation establishing the Space Medal of Honor—Congressman Fuqua, Congressman Gibbons, Congresswoman Boggs, ladies and gentlemen; many of you who have helped in past years to make the achievements commemorated this afternoon possible:

This is one of the most exciting events of my life. For a number of weeks since I planned to come here, I've been thrilled at the prospect of meeting these famous men on my right, who have done so much to inspire all those who love our country and who have confidence in the future of human beings.

A few minutes ago, we watched a simulated takeoff and flight of *Apollo XI*. And my palms are still sweating with excitement and nervousness, and I might say that I was not the only one. The astronauts' palms were sweating even more than mine. [*Laughter*]

I believe it's accurate to say that we are here today to recognize and honor six American pioneers of the farthest and highest of all frontiers, the frontier of space. We honor them for individual human qualities, dedication, skill, extraordinary courage. But we do more than that. What those men have done is the most visible part of a vast and continuing collective accomplishment of many people.

Tens of thousands of Americans, many of you, including scientists, engineers, administrators, skilled workers, others, have contributed directly to the success of the American space enterprise. They in turn have had the support of an entire nation and the good wishes of an entire planet.

The glory that belongs to the six recipients this afternoon of the Space Medal of Honor belongs equally to those who helped them, and in a real sense, to all humanity who prayed for them and who supported them. This does not diminish the glory of these American heroes. It enlarges their glory.

It's fitting that these ceremonies take place today on the twentieth anniversary of the founding of the National Aeronautics and Space Administration. And it is, of course, fitting that they take place here, where the ships that took men to the Moon were launched and where we will take our next great step into space with the first flight of the space shuttle, which I sincerely hope will be before my next birthday. I have every assurance from those involved that there will be no slippage in the present schedule as it now stands.

The age of space, as Dr. Frosch[1] said, can now be characterized as having

_____
[1] Robert A. Frosch, Administrator, National Aeronautics and Space Administration.

reached the threshold of its maturity. It began 21 years ago this week with the launching of *Sputnik I*. That remarkable achievement galvanized our own space efforts. We have met the challenge fully; indeed, we have gone far beyond that challenge. And as Americans, we are proud of these achievements and glad of the benefits that have been brought to our Nation and, indeed, to the entire world.

We speak often of progress. But there's nothing in scientific and technological experience to compare with the enormous leaps we've made in the brief span of the two decades of the space age. We have performed what any generation would have considered miracles. We've taken the stuff of fantasy and dreams, and we've turned it into accomplishment and reality.

The dreams of a few visionaries have become a part of the everyday life of hundreds of millions of people. Consider what we have done in just one quarter of a human lifetime. We've put men in orbit around the Earth and around the Moon. We've put machines in orbit around the Earth, the Moon, the Sun, and the planet Mars. We've learned to maneuver in space, to dock ships together in space, and even to walk in space. On board Skylab we've learned to live and work in a weightless environment for many weeks at a time.

We've begun the exploration of the inner planets and the outer planets. Two American *Vikings* have been sending back valuable scientific data from the surface of Mars for more than 2 years.

Pioneer X has passed Jupiter and is on its way to interstellar space. It will be the first tangible product of human hands to leave the solar system. Its flight time may turn out to be longer than the life of civilization that launched it. And of course, its destination is unknown. But

like the entire effort of space exploration, it is a striking symbol of human curiosity, human ingenuity, and the very human desire to communicate with others.

And of course, the greatest event of all: We went to the surface of the Moon, not once, but six times. And each time, the astronauts returned safely to their home planet, Earth, and to their home country, the United States of America.

In the 9 years since a man took that one small step, the giant leap it represented has almost come to be taken for granted. Yet, at the outset, many doubted it could be done at all. And many more doubted it could be done in so short a time. But it was done. And it was done magnificently. The goal was met. And this great space center is deservedly named for the man who summoned his fellow citizens to an extraordinary adventure, President John F. Kennedy.

We went to the Moon, in part, as a matter of national pride. But when we got there, we discovered something very interesting. Through the eyes and the cameras of the astronauts, we looked back at the Earth, above the strange horizon of the Moon in a pitch black sky. We saw our own world as a single delicate globe of swirling blue and white, green, brown. From the perspective of space, our planet has no national boundaries.

It's very beautiful, but it's also very fragile. And it is the special responsibility of the human race to preserve it. Of all the things we've learned from our explorations of space, none has been more important than this perception of the essential unity of our world.

I learned this morning that while I was at Camp David with President Sadat and Prime Minister Begin, that scientists at Cal Tech discovered a new miniplanet whose orbit comes between that of Earth and that of Mercury. The new miniplanet has just been named Ra Shalom—Ra being the Egyptian sun god, and as you know, *shalom* being the word for peace.

This, I think, vividly demonstrates that we on Earth have a responsibility to unify the people of the world in peace and harmony and preserve the life of those that were observed so distantly by the astronauts from the Moon.

Space has brought us a great deal of human knowledge and also a great deal of technical knowledge. It may also have brought us a measure of wisdom. Today we celebrate the accomplishments of the past in the spirit of the men we honor; we also look toward the future, a future that is as exciting as anything that has gone on before.

The first great era of the space age is over; the second is about to begin. It will come into its own with the new space shuttle, the heart of our new space transportation system, when it becomes operational. With its ability to lift a payload of up to 32 tons into orbit on mission after mission, the shuttle will give us a regular, frequent, and economical access to space. Like the sea, the land, and the air, space will become an environment in which human beings can live and work for the welfare of their own species.

Paradoxically, the most exciting thing about the space shuttle is that it will make our use of space in the future routine and perhaps not very exciting.

The first generation of space activities was driven in large part by a single, exciting transcendent goal: the quest for the Moon. In the second generation, thanks to the versatility of the shuttle, our activities in space will be enormously varied.

We've invested so far some $100 billion over the history of our American space programs. It's now time for us to capitalize on that major investment even more. We've already reaped many practical benefits from space. Over the next generation, these benefits will increase geometrically.

Communication satellites have already made global communications instantaneous, reliable, and cheap. They've brought remote areas of the Earth out of their isolation. We will continue to develop them.

Weather satellites have already saved billions of dollars, thousands of lives through early warnings of hurricanes and floods. We will continue to develop them. We've greatly strengthened our national security through defense space applications. We will continue to develop these capabilities.

Photoreconnaissance satellites have become an important stabilizing factor in world affairs in the monitoring of arms control agreements. They make an immense contribution to the security of all nations. We shall continue to develop them.

Earth resources satellites have already proved their value to many countries through remote sensing. They tell us about everything from the location of mineral and energy deposits to the condition of our crops, from the motion of icebergs to the health of the oceans. We will continue to develop and to use these satellites for the benefit of all people of the world.

Aboard the shuttle on many of its missions will be the European-built laboratory, the space lab. Scientists of many nations will use the space lab to do research in all branches of science and engineering. No one can say where this research will lead, but carefully selected experiments could yield direct benefits in the coming decades.

I'm often asked about space factories, solar power satellites, and such other large-scale engineering projects in space. In my judgment, it's too early to commit the Nation to such projects. But we will continue the evolving development of our technology, taking intermediate steps that will keep open possibilities for the future.

During the period of the *Saturn-Apollo* missions, we were pilgrims in space, ranging far from home in search of knowledge. Now we will become shepherds tending our technological flocks, but like the shepherds of old, we will keep our eyes fixed on the heavens.

We are committed to the practical use of space. But we are equally committed to the scientific exploration of the solar system and the universe.

In the 1980's, the 1990's, we will continue the direct reconnaissance of the solar system. Through the eyes of our remote cameras, we will see Mars and Venus, Jupiter and its moons, Saturn with its moons and rings, and comets and asteroids. The study of other planets, their climate, geology, geophysics, perhaps their biology, will increase our understanding of our own planet. We will seek to learn more about the Sun.

Many missions will aim at this goal in the years to come. In one of them, an instrumented probe will journey far above the plane of the solar system to look down at the never-before-seen polar regions of the Sun.

And finally, we will look out from Earth orbit to the very end of the universe, notably by means of the space telescope. In its orbit 300 miles above the Earth's surface, the space telescope will at last let us see the universe without interference from the Earth's obscuring atmosphere.

It will be the centerpiece of astronomy for the decade beginning in the mid-eighties. Its contributions may dwarf all but the most fundamental discoveries of the past, leading to a quantum growth in our understanding of the basic nature of time, matter, and energy.

In the coming generation, the scope and the range of our space activities will reflect the range of our requirements and interests as a vigorous, responsible, and free society. Those activities will be measured against all the needs of our country. We will be encouraging other countries to participate both in the work and in its benefits. But we will not give up the leadership of the United States in space.

And finally, let me say, in the last analysis the challenge of space takes us very close to the heart of things. It brings us face to face with the mysteries of creation, of matter, of energy, of life itself. The men we honor today met that challenge, and they were equal to it. Our Nation met that challenge and was equal to it. And in the final two decades of the twentieth century, America will reach out once more to the beauty and to the mystery of space, and once again America, you and I, will be equal to that great task.

Thank you very much.

NOTE: The President spoke at 4:14 p.m. at the Vehicle Assembly Building of the Shuttle Landing Facility, John F. Kennedy Space Center.

Following his remarks, the President presented the awards to Neil A. Armstrong, Col. Frank Borman (USAF, Ret.), Capt. Charles Conrad, Jr. (USN, Ret.), Senator John H. Glenn, Jr. (Col., USMC, Ret.), and Rear Adm. Alan Shepard (USN, Ret.). He also presented a posthumous award to Betty Grissom on behalf of her husband, Lt. Col. Virgil I. Grissom (USAF).

Earlier in the day, the President toured various facilities at the Center and received briefings from NASA officials.

Orlando, Florida

White House Statement on the President's Meeting With United Nations Secretary General Kurt Waldheim. October 1, 1978

President Carter and Secretary General Waldheim discussed the crisis in Lebanon, and both expressed their deep concern and sorrow at the loss of life and further destruction as a result of the latest fighting in Beirut and surrounding villages.

The President and the Secretary General urged that all involved make every effort to observe the cease-fire accepted on the 30th of September.

They urged that a framework be developed for a political solution of the crisis in Lebanon and agreed to do all they can to this end.

NOTE: The statement was released at Orlando, Fla.

Orlando, Florida

Remarks at a Reception of the International Chamber of Commerce. October 1, 1978

I think it's accurate to say that I was just introduced by one of the Nation's greatest political leaders and a man who's been an inspiration to me and, I'm sure, to all of you, and I appreciate it very much.

I was talking to Kurt Waldheim a few minutes ago, the Secretary General of the United Nations, and we only had about 10 minutes to discuss all the problems of the world. And in the midst of it, I got a happy birthday call from President Ford, which I appreciated very much. I called him on his birthdays; he called me on my birthday. We have a very good interrelationship too, because, as you know, we have a very small fraternity of Presidents and ex-Presidents. [*Laughter*] And we feel the burdens of the office very deeply. And he's been extremely helpful to me.

Earlier, when I was planning on this trip, I called Amy and said that we were going to be down here in Florida to celebrate the birthday of one of the world's greatest and most admired leaders. And

she said, "Yes, I know, Daddy." And I was swelling up with pride. She said, "This is Mickey Mouse's 50th birthday." [*Laughter*]

I had a thrilling afternoon, one of the great days of my life, and a birthday that I will never forget. We went to the space center at Cape Canaveral, Cape Kennedy, the Kennedy Space Center, and I gave medals of honor to five of our heroic astronauts and also posthumously to the widow of Virgil Grissom. And to remember what they have done for our country is one of the great events of my life. And to shake hands with Neil Armstrong and the others there was really a momentous occasion.

I think this is typical of what Florida has helped our Nation to realize. It's not really a coincidence that when great events take place in our country, that your State is often at the heart of the great accomplishment.

This is the first time in 20 years that the International Chamber of Commerce has met in our Nation. And as you know, this is the first time that this tremendous convention has appeared in any nation except in the capital city of that country. And it's because of leadership of men like Reubin Askew, with the help of men and women like you, that this has been made possible.

I'm going to speak briefly this evening to the group in convention, and the thrust of my remarks will be that business, tourism, exchange of people and products can transcend international borders even greater than governments can through political means. And I think had we had the same interrelationships back 30 or more years ago that we have now, the course of the world would have been quite different.

One of the things I'm going to say is that our two most ferocious allies, whom we hated and despised and did all we could to defeat, Japan and Germany, are now among our greatest allies and friends. They were our greatest enemies. Now they're our greatest allies. And had we had the same trade relationships and business interrelationships and cultural interrelationships among people like you who are leaders in your own right, the course of world events might very well have been quite different. But I want to express my thanks to you, as President of the United States, for your generosity and your leadership in honoring our country and your State by bringing this tremendous convention here.

It's typical of you, and I know that you are proud, as am I, that you've been able to accomplish this great feat. It'll help us in many ways, those of us who serve in government, those of you who serve in business and the professions, to have a better life for our own people and, I think, in the process have a better life for all people around the world.

Thank you very much from the bottom of my heart.

NOTE: The President spoke at 7:35 p.m. in King Stefan's Banquet Hall at Walt Disney World. He was introduced by Gov. Reubin Askew of Florida.

Orlando, Florida

Remarks at the Opening Session of the 26th World Conference of the International Chamber of Commerce. October 1, 1978

Thank you, Governor Askew, Secretary General Waldheim, President McGregor, delegates and officers of this great congress, distinguished guests:

It's indeed an honor to be here for many reasons. I'm especially grateful to be on the same program with Secretary General Kurt Waldheim, who has my deepest admiration and appreciation, who leads the United Nations with courage and sensitivity and effectiveness, and with whom I sympathize very deeply. I have 50 States to deal with; he has 150 states. And his complicated responsibilities greatly transcend my own.

I'm also glad to come to Disney World. me so graciously in his remarks. We worked very closely on many occasions, and it's a reassuring fact for myself and all other national leaders to have him in that position of responsibility.

I'm also glad to come to Disney World. I was looking forward to seeing Fantasy Land, particularly because it's the source of inspiration for my economic advisers. [*Laughter*] I think perhaps some of you can see the origin of ideas that you get from advisers as well while you're down here.

I think it's a wonderful thing that you have assembled in our country. And I'm very pleased to welcome the International Chamber of Commerce to its third conference on United States soil and proud that you've returned here, even though the interval has been 20 years. It's a tribute to Governor Reubin Askew and your other gracious hosts in Florida that now, for the first time in your history, I understand you are not meeting in the capital city of the host nation.

I come here proud, but also sobered. A few hours ago, I walked among the launching pads at Cape Kennedy and placed medals around the necks of five astronauts who had led the way to space, and in the hands of one widow, Mrs. Virgil Grissom, whose husband gave his own life after great and courageous feats. There is no prouder testimony than that center of space exploration to what mankind can accomplish, calling on our creativity, our resources, using our vast technology for exploration rather than conquest, channeling our competition internationally into peaceful means and peaceful ends. These are the accomplishments of a privileged nation, privileged in our resources, privileged in our place in the world.

It is these very privileges that sober me, for I believe that they constitute the moral obligation of our times. I want to talk tonight about the responsibilities that privilege imposes, especially on those who hold positions of leadership, as do all of you, whether in government or private corporations, or who lead our societies in other ways.

We meet at an unusual time in our world's history. It's a moment of relative calm. We are more or less free of overt, international warfare, more or less free of the severe dislocations that have disrupted our economies in the past. Yet, in this moment, we must face the deeper problems of humanity. None of us can ignore hunger, although we may never personally experience hunger. We cannot ignore the problems of overpopulation or the unequal division of the world's goods, even though we might obviously have gotten and retained more than our share.

We've all learned that in an interdependent world, we can only advance when we advance together. As human beings, our sense of mercy and justice is offended when injustice so freely reigns.

It's in this time of relative calm that we can assess our reasons, weigh our obligations, and decide how best to exert and apply our efforts to these great obligations that you and I face together as leaders.

There is one responsibility that transcends all others, and that is the cause of peace. Leaders often underestimate the wisdom of our people and how much our people desire peace.

We saw a dramatic demonstration of this recently. Almost a year ago, when two brave leaders, President Sadat and Prime Minister Begin, took the first long step toward peace, their people rejoiced on the streets. Where they expected hatred, there was obvious demonstration of friendship and even love. Where they expected displeasure or condemnation, there was overwhelming rejoicing.

My belief is that the great hunger for a peaceful world imposes on us the obligation to use the resources we control constructively, to use them to minimize frictions that can lead to war. And my belief is that the people of other neighboring countries, even in the Middle East, also equally yearn for peace, even though some leaders may not yet recognize this fact.

As the leader of my own Government, there is no responsibility that I take more seriously. It guides every decision I make about our Nation's defense forces. For I know that our unquestioned strength is the surest guarantee for liberty for ourselves and perhaps even stability and security in the world.

But I also know that the pursuit of military strength alone is not enough. We must have the confidence and the courage to pursue every avenue for peace, and to realize that this pursuit is not a sign of weakness. That is why Secretary Vance and I have just spent long hours, even yesterday, with Foreign Minister Gromyko, negotiating in earnest hope of an early agreement on a strategic arms limitation treaty between our countries.

But government does not bear the sole responsibility for peace. Throughout history, the forces that can unite us also have often driven us apart. Ideology, religion, allegiance to national soil, all have the power to bring war among peoples, or to enable them to find peace and concord.

This audience possesses another such powerful force. Within this century we've seen narrow economic interests cause the friction that led to devastating wars. But we've seen the same economic forces lift humanity above the bitterest previous divisions.

Most of us here can remember the days when the United States was engaged in total war against Germany and Japan, countries that are now our closest allies. Largely through the bonds of trade and commerce, these nations have become our partners in seeking a prosperous global future.

I've often wondered what would have happened if we had the same bonds of trade and commerce before 1939 or before 1941. That's why I'm such a staunch advocate of global commerce. That's why I'm determined to increase substantially United States trade with other nations, including the Soviet Union and the People's Republic of China.

I will not compromise, of course, our Nation's security nor that of our allies, but I believe that fruitful economic relationships can advance the security of all peoples on Earth.

Let me repeat that governments cannot achieve this goal alone. Every company, every corporation, every economic leader involved in international commerce can aggravate tensions by encouraging protectionism, by setting nation against nation and rich against poor, or it can work to overcome and to prevent these same negative forces.

That responsibility weighs heavily on all of us who are in positions of privilege. We know that if power or profit is pursued for itself, and nothing more, that we are not worthy of our gifts, but more importantly, our world will suffer. Without leaders of vision, we can never solve the problems that most sorely afflict us and those that threaten us even more in the future.

There is another responsibility that is imposed upon us, that of simple justice—justice among nations of the world, justice among the peoples within each nation.

It's not too much to believe that all people should have an equal opportunity to enjoy life's rewards, whether they were born in a poor country or a rich one, whether they were raised by poor parents or by those of wealth.

The world's governments have a responsibility to pursue social justice. In the United States we've increased our foreign aid appropriations and raised a strong voice on behalf of human rights, political rights, social rights, economic rights in our own country and throughout the world. We recognize that trade and free economies also offer a good hope of improving living standards and a better chance of protecting individual freedoms in the broadest definition of the word "freedom."

It's very important that we all work to bring all nations of the world, especially the Eastern nations, the OPEC nations, and the underdeveloped nations, more closely into the world financial and economic organizations, like the International Monetary Fund, the World Bank, regional banks, and others. To meet our own responsibilities, we're expanding our exports, sustaining our economic growth at the rate which permits us to buy from other nations, and taking tough but sensible steps to preserve the value of the dollar as a reserve currency.

These actions will help to distribute the world's wealth more equitably in the future. But I know as well that you represent multinational companies; some of you can often do more than governments to determine how fairly the world's rewards are shared.

The International Chamber deserves great credit for the contributions that you've made, for the ethical code you developed, for your work with the United Nations, and your many other progressive and admirable acts. Organizations like your own and the companies your members represent have brought the benefits of trade, technology, education, and medicine to parts of the world that had been too long without them.

But you realized as well as I how often a few corporate leaders have been known to exploit weak nations, to abuse poor and inarticulate workers, to tolerate racism, and often to overlook bribery, payoffs, and corruption by trusted employees. You know how often some have been unworthy of the great power and influence they possess. And you know as well as I that power long abused cannot be maintained. It cannot be maintained, not only because it's wrong but because it defies the historical trend of our times.

For the past few decades, nationalism was a vision which inspired and moved people around the world to create a nation that was independent, no matter how small or weak it may have been. Now that revolution, nationalism, has largely been completed. And other goals are emerging—goals of justice, equity, human rights, and freedom.

These are the wave of the present and the wave of the future. We should not fight this wave. We should ride it, be part of it, encourage it, let it nurture a better life for those who yearn and for those of us who already enjoy. If we can marshal our resources in the cause of right, if we can pursue peace and justice as energetically as we pursue power and profit, then we can achieve these goals and in the process win the fight against our other modern evils, such as international terrorism, which threaten many of us.

These are all shared responsibilities, ones you must take as seriously as I. But there are some very specific responsibilities

of the United States Government which I would like to mention briefly here this evening, because they affect everyone here and those you represent back home.

The United States has a responsibility to contribute to global economic stability and well-being. There are three important steps our Nation is taking, based on the commitments I made 2 months ago in Bonn.

The first is to reduce inflation. I will soon announce a tough new program designed to bring inflation under control. We've already acted to make sure that the Government sets an example, cutting unnecessary spending, reducing Federal pay increases, removing unnecessary regulations, cutting the Federal deficit, and letting the free market set prices wherever it can.

We've tried a quick experiment relating to the international and domestic airlines. Fares have been drastically reduced. The number of passengers has been greatly increased. The profits of the airlines have also grown. Soon I will ask for an expanded anti-inflation program with balanced and reasonable sacrifices from business, labor, and every other segment of our economy, along with government.

The second step is to reduce our dependence on foreign oil. We are on the verge of enacting a comprehensive energy program—I predict that it will be done before the Congress adjourns—which will increase our domestic production, shift to more plentiful supplies of fuel, and reduce the waste of all forms of energy in our country.

Energy is a worldwide problem, and our responsibilities extend far beyond our own borders. We will never attempt to obstruct exploration and the development of worldwide energy resources. Our great technology is available for others to use.

The third pledge we made at Bonn was to expand our export and to broaden world trade and investment, and I might add, while discouraging the excessive speculation in currencies that unsettles foreign exchange markets. We will expand our exports to get our current account deficit under control.

Recent statistics are encouraging. And factors that have already come into existence will enhance this trend in the coming months. The rate of growth of our Nation is now much more in phase with the rate of growth of our trade partners. A lower valued dollar will make our own products more attractive. And controlling inflation in our country, minimizing the imports of oil over a period of time, will help to expand our exports as contrasted with our imports.

U.S. trade relationships and export performance are not just a domestic concern. As our trade encourages peace, our export growth will spur the world economy.

U.S. food production is a great world resource, and more stable storage and supplies will increase agricultural exports at more predictable and reasonable prices to help feed the hungry people of the world. It also reduces our trade deficit, which in turn strengthens the dollar.

We accept and will honor the responsibilities that go with the dollar's role as an international reserve of currency. Our present policies are designed to fight inflation and achieve that goal, and I have no doubt that the dollar will rise in response to its fundamental value and the emerging economic trends which I have just described. Stable, noninflationary growth enables public and private institutions to meet their obligations to the poor two-thirds of the world.

We must do more to help these countries by trade, by aid, by other measures. Private enterprise has a large responsibility here. World prosperity depends at least as much on the wisdom and foresight of private business leaders as on the good sense of government.

I described the steps the U.S. Government is taking, not because they will solve all our problems—because they won't—nor because they are unusually brave ones—because they are not. I mention them as an indication of how deeply I believe my Nation has a responsibility in the world.

Each of these steps involves some sacrifice for the American public. In many cases they require deferral of goals we would prefer to pursue. But the American public is ready to meet this challenge. I have no doubt about that. I think my Nation has come to the recognition that only through vision, accommodation, and occasional sacrifice can we be worthy of our privilege, that only by fulfilling our obligations can we win many of the rewards that are truly worth possessing.

I believe, as I know you do, that the best way to achieve the world we seek is through a free political and economic system. This means a political system in which governments answer for their actions to their people. It means an economic system in which resources are allocated as much as possible by private, not government decisions.

I believe in a free market system. I prospered in it as a business man. I know it's the best route for progress for all. But here, again, it would be a mistake to blame government for protectionist decisions. Hardly a week goes by that I don't have some very conservative businessman or a group of businessmen come to me to ask for government protection of his own interests, at the same time deploring protectionism for all others.

In choosing the theme for your 26th conference, "Enterprise, Freedom, and the Future," the International Chamber has recognized the essential linkage between free people, free nations, and free enterprise. Our future course will be determined by our ability to sustain these freedoms. We must meet our responsibilities to others, to keep and enhance these freedoms which we cherish. Any abuses of our power and influence will lead to international constraints and controls and a lack of freedom.

Peace and freedom are our first priorities. So long as we have a free play of ideas and information, so long as we maintain a climate that stimulates invention, innovation, competition, our public and private institutions will have the intellectual ferment and the technological progress we need to produce social and economic progress. I know the deliberations that follow here in Florida will be stimulating and productive. And I'm sure that you will leave Disney World ready to launch a new assault on the problems that command our future attention.

I now declare the 26th Congress of the International Chamber of Commerce opened.

Thank you very much.

NOTE: The President spoke at 8:35 p.m. in front of the Magic Kingdom Castle at Walt Disney World. In his opening remarks, he referred to Ian McGregor, president of the International Chamber of Commerce.

International Mediation Group for Nicaragua

Designation of William G. Bowdler as U.S. Representative.   October 2, 1978

President Carter has named Ambassador William G. Bowdler as the United States Representative on the International Mediation Group, which will be going to Nicaragua to provide good offices in an effort to reach a peaceful settlement of the current difficulties in that country.

Ambassador Bowdler expects to meet in the next few days with the representatives of the Dominican Republic and Guatemala, the other two countries in the mediation group, and will be going to Nicaragua with them later this week to commence the mediation process.

As the Secretary General of the OAS has announced, the Government of Nicaragua as well as the broad opposition front in Nicaragua have indicated their acceptance of this conciliation effort.

Ambassador Bowdler is a career Foreign Service officer who has served as Ambassador to El Salvador, Guatemala, and South Africa. In addition, he was the senior adviser for Latin American affairs on the National Security Council staff from 1965 to 1968. During the past 5 months, he has been serving in the Department of State as Director of the Bureau of Intelligence and Research. He holds the rank of Career Minister.

In naming an experienced diplomat and negotiator as U.S. Representative, President Carter said he hoped that all sides participating in the conversations will work constructively to develop an enduring, democratic solution.

Diplomatic Relations Act

Statement on Signing H.R. 7819 Into Law. October 2, 1978

It is with pleasure and pride that I have signed into law the Diplomatic Relations Act.

I am pleased, because its enactment is a reflection of what Congress can accomplish when skillful and dedicated leaders of both Houses work closely together in a common cause, with full cooperation and participation from the executive branch—

in this instance, especially from the State and Justice Departments. I particularly want to thank Congressmen Dante Fascell and Joe Fisher and Senators Paul Sarbanes and Mac Mathias for their superb efforts on behalf of this legislation.

The pride that I feel stems from the fact that this significant step, so important in our conduct of foreign relations and to our own citizens, has been achieved under this administration after years of unsuccessful efforts.

The Diplomatic Relations Act repeals previous U.S. statutes on diplomatic immunity, which were established to fit conditions of 18th century diplomacy. Under these laws, complete immunity from local jurisdiction was extended to all members of foreign diplomatic missions—from Ambassadors to private servants, for any and all activities, official or private, while in the United States. Such broad legislative protection is outmoded in terms of current activities and goes far beyond the requirements of international law as set forth in the Vienna Convention on Diplomatic Relations of 1961, now subscribed to by 122 countries.

The act establishes the privileges and immunities provisions of the Vienna Convention as the essential United States law on the subject. It provides a workable basis for substantially reducing those occasional controversies involving diplomatic immunity which result in personal hardship to innocent victims, who otherwise would have little or no legal recourse. The reforms of the act are consistent with the original purposes of diplomatic immunity. They ensure the legitimate, unimpaired conduct of official relations between the representatives of sovereign states.

Two features of the Diplomatic Relations Act are especially noteworthy: (1) the requirement that foreign diplomats carry automobile liability insurance and

(2) the "direct action" provision, which allows an injured party to sue the insurance carrier directly in those instances where diplomatic immunity may continue to be invoked.

I congratulate the Congress on action in a long-ignored but vital area. This bill will help to usher the United States into the modern world of diplomatic law and practice.

NOTE: As enacted, H.R. 7819 is Public Law 95–393, approved September 30.

Rhode Island Indian Claims Settlement Act

Statement on Signing H.R. 12860 Into Law. October 2, 1978

I have signed into law H.R. 12860, the Rhode Island Indian Claims Settlement Act. Once implementing State legislation has been enacted, this act will settle once and for all the decades-old controversy over Indian claims in Rhode Island, particularly in the town of Charlestown. Most importantly, this law resolves those claims in the best possible way—by mutual agreement of the Indian claimants, the State, the town, the local landowners affected by the claims, and the Federal Government.

The need for a legislative settlement has been apparent since 1975, when the Narragansett Indians began pressing claims to aboriginal tribal lands in Charlestown. Their ancestors had been dispossessed of those lands during the 19th century, and they claimed that because these transactions had been consummated without congressional approval, they violated the 1790 Indian Nonintercourse Act.

I applaud the parties to the controversy, Senators Pell and Chafee, and Representatives Beard and St Germain, for their constructive approach to this most difficult problem. I am gratified to see that attempts to resolve such Indian claims can be made in an atmosphere of cooperation.

Interior Secretary Andrus and I support and encourage just and amicable settlements of legitimate claims. I hope that other Indian claims which are now the source of friction among Indian and non-Indian citizens of this country can also be settled in the way the people of Rhode Island have done—in a climate of harmony.

NOTE: As enacted, H.R. 12860 is Public Law 95–395, approved September 30.

Federal Pesticide Act of 1978

Statement on Signing S. 1678 Into Law.
October 2, 1978

I am pleased to sign into law S. 1678, amendments to the Federal Insecticide, Fungicide, and Rodenticide Act. This bill culminates 2 long years of hard work by the chairmen of the Senate and House Agriculture Committees, Senator Talmadge and Representative Foley. The bill's sponsor, Senator Leahy, Senator Lugar, and Representatives de la Garza and Fithian have pursued this effort with dedication and care.

These amendments make numerous, important revisions to the FIFRA, most of which were sought and supported by the Environmental Protection Agency on behalf of the administration. With these amendments, the important task of registering pesticides may move forward in a more streamlined and efficient manner, while providing a sound basis for protection of public health and the environment. I am also pleased that vital health

and safety information will once again be made available for public use and scrutiny.

S. 1678 is a fine example of cooperation between the Congress and the executive branch in making regulatory programs meet their underlying purposes without imposing overly bureaucratic, unduly costly, or unnecessary requirements. This act represents a step forward in the twin causes of better protection of the environment and reform of our regulatory processes.

NOTE: As enacted, S. 1678 is Public Law 95–396, approved September 30.

Futures Trading Act of 1978

Statement on Signing S. 2391 Into Law.
October 2, 1978

I have signed into law S. 2391, the Futures Trading Act of 1978. This legislation extends appropriation authority for the Commodity Exchange Act to strengthen regulation of the Nation's highly volatile futures trading industry and to improve the administration of the Commission.

The Commodity Exchange Act provides a Federal regulatory framework to ensure fair practices and honest dealing on commodity exchanges and to provide a measure of control over manipulative activity which may cause financial injury to producers and consumers. While these amendments do not reflect all of the recommendations of the administration, I believe that they provide a suitable basis for moving forward with the work of the Commission. Further, I expect that various administrative deficiencies on the part of the Commission which have come to light in recent months will be corrected.

In signing this bill, however, I must note my serious objections to a provision which requires the approval of congressional committees before a user fee system may be implemented by the Commission. This "committee approval" requirement is one of several types of legislative veto devices which I and the Attorney General view as unconstitutional, a position which I communicated to the Congress on June 21, 1978.

Accordingly, I believe that the Commission should treat this provision as a requirement that it submit the proposed fee plan to the appropriate committees, but that regulations establishing the system be promulgated as final unless the Congress, within a reasonable period of time, acts by legislation, subject to Presidential approval or disapproval, to overturn such regulations.

NOTE: As enacted, S. 2391 is Public Law 95–405, approved September 30.

10–4 Day

Statement by the President.   October 2, 1978

This year marks the 20th anniversary of Citizens Band radio. CB is now a widely used emergency communications system. It helps keep motorists safe on our Nation's highways by providing faster notification of highway accidents, increased detection of reckless driving, and more information to reduce traffic delays. The CB is also effective in emergencies unrelated to motor vehicles. By allowing for citizens' participation in public safety, we greatly enhance that safety.

The growth of CB use in recent years is extraordinary. The Federal Communications Commission has now issued nearly 14 million licenses. More than 20 million Americans have used a CB radio at one time or another.

While CB is primarily for emergency use, the nonemergency channels bring enjoyment and companionship to millions of Americans, including my own family.

In recognition of the fine service provided by Citizens Band radio, I join with CB organizations across the country in celebrating "10–4 Day," October 4, 1978.

Strategic Arms Limitation Talks

Nomination of Herbert S. Okun for the Rank of Minister While Serving as State Department Representative to the Talks. October 2, 1978

The President today announced the nomination of Herbert S. Okun, of Chevy Chase, Md., for the rank of Minister during his assignment as the State Department Representative to the Strategic Arms Limitation Talks.

Okun was born November 27, 1930, in New York City. He received an A.B. from Stanford University in 1951 and an M.P.A. from Harvard University in 1959. He served in the U.S. Army from 1952 to 1954.

Okun joined the Foreign Service in 1955, and served in Munich, Moscow, Belo Horizonte, Brasília, and at the State Department. From 1969 to 1970, he was Special Assistant to the Secretary of State, and from 1970 to 1973, he was Alternate Director of the Office of Soviet Affairs at the State Department.

In 1971 and 1972, Okun was Deputy Chairman of the U.S. Delegation to the U.S.–U.S.S.R. Talks on Prevention of Incidents at Sea. In 1973 and 1974, he was political adviser to the Commander in Chief of Allied Forces, Southern Europe. From 1975 to 1978, he was Deputy Chief of Mission in Lisbon. Since earlier this year he has been the State Department Representative to SALT.

Domestic Clothespin Industry

*Message to the Congress Transmitting a
Report.   October 2, 1978*

To the Congress of the United States:

In accordance with section 203(b)(2) of the Trade Act of 1974, enclosed is a report to the Congress setting forth my determination that import relief for the U.S. clothespin industry is not in the national economic interest, and explaining the reasons for my decision.

JIMMY CARTER

The White House,
    October 2, 1978.

IMPORT RELIEF ACTION

CLOTHESPINS FROM THE PEOPLE'S
REPUBLIC OF CHINA (PRC)

As required under sections 406(b) and 203(b)(2) of the Trade Act of 1974, I am transmitting this report to Congress setting forth the action I will take with respect to clothespins covered by the affirmative finding on August 3, 1978, of the U.S. International Trade Commission (USITC) under section 406(a)(3) of the Trade Act. As my action differs from that recommended by the USITC, I have included the reasons for my decision.

After considering all relevant aspects of the case, including those considerations set forth in section 202(c) of the Trade Act of 1974, I have determined that import relief for the domestic clothespin industry would not be in the national economic interest for the following reasons:

1. The imposition of import relief would not be an effective means to promote adjustment in the industry. While imports from the PRC have become an increasingly important component of U.S. imports, other foreign sources still accounted for seventy-three percent of all U.S. imports in 1977. Foreign sources, other than the PRC, are able to supply clothespins to the U.S. market at prices significantly below the prices charged by U.S. producers. Moreover, existing foreign capacity would not be a limitation on foreign producer ability to increase shipments to the U.S. Thus, third country suppliers would likely fill any excess U.S. demand resulting from a limitation of any kind on imports of clothespins from the PRC.

2. It should be noted that the USITC has instituted an investigation under section 201 of the Trade Act of 1974 to determine whether clothespins from all foreign suppliers are being imported into the United States in such quantities as to be a substantial cause of serious injury, or threat thereof, to the domestic industry. A determination on this case by the USITC is due by November 21, 1978. The import problems facing the domestic clothespin industry will considered further within the context of this pending escape clause case.

Domestic Clothespin Industry

*Memorandum From the President.
October 2, 1978*

Memorandum for the Special Representative for Trade Negotiations

Subject: Determination under Sections 406 and 202 of the Trade Act; Clothespins from the People's Republic of China

Pursuant to sections 406(b) and 202 of the Trade Act of 1974 (P.L. 93–618), I have determined the action I will take with respect to the report of the United States International Trade Commission (USITC), transmitted to me on August 3, 1978, concerning the results of its investigation of a petition for import relief filed by the Clothespin and Veneer Products Association on behalf of the domestic industry producing clothespins provided for in items 790.05, 790.07 and 790.08 of the Tariff Schedules of the United States.

After considering all relevant aspects of the case, including those considerations set forth in section 202(c) of the Trade Act of 1974, I have determined that provision of import relief is not in the national economic interest.

The imposition of import relief would not be an effective means to promote adjustment in the domestic industry. While imports from the PRC have become an increasingly important component of U.S. imports, other sources still accounted for seventy-three percent of U.S. imports in 1977. Foreign sources, other than the PRC, are able to supply clothespins to the U.S. market at prices significantly below the prices charged by U.S. producers. Moreover, existing foreign capacity would not be a limitation on foreign producer ability to increase shipments to the U.S. Thus, third country suppliers would likely fill any excess U.S. demand resulting from a limitation of any kind on imports of clothespins from the PRC.

In addition, it should be noted that the USITC has instituted an investigation under section 201 of the Trade Act of 1974 to determine whether clothespins from all foreign suppliers are being imported into the United States in such quantities as to be a substantial cause of serious injury, or threat thereof, to the domestic industry. A determination on this case by the USITC is due by November 21, 1978. The import problems facing the domestic clothespin industry will be considered further within the context of this pending escape clause case.

This determination is to be published in the FEDERAL REGISTER.

JIMMY CARTER

[Filed with the Office of the Federal Register, 10:57 a.m., October 2, 1978]

Budget Deferrals

Message to the Congress.   October 2, 1978

To the Congress of the United States:

In accordance with the Impoundment Control Act of 1974, I herewith report 30 deferrals of fiscal year 1979 funds totalling $1,178.2 million. The deferrals are primarily routine in nature and do not, in most cases, affect program levels.

The details of each deferral are contained in the attached reports.

JIMMY CARTER

The White House,
October 2, 1978.

NOTE: The attachments detailing the deferrals are printed in the FEDERAL REGISTER of October 4, 1978.

Ceramic Tableware Imports

Proclamation 4604.   October 2, 1978

TERMINATION OF INCREASED RATES OF DUTY ON CERTAIN CERAMIC TABLEWARE

By the President of the United States of America

A Proclamation

1. By Proclamation No. 4125 of April 22, 1972, the President proclaimed increased duties on certain types of ceramic tableware that are defined in items 923.01 through 923.15 of the Tariff Schedules of the United States (TSUS). These increased duties were to be effective from May 1, 1972, through April 30, 1976, unless modified or terminated earlier. This action was taken under the following legal provisions: section 350(a) (1)(B) of the Tariff Act of 1930, as amended (19 U.S.C. 1351(a)(1)(B)); and sections 201(a)(2), 302(a)(2) and (3), and 351(a) of the Trade Expansion

Act of 1962 (19 U.S.C. 1821(a)(2), 19 U.S.C. 1902(a) (2) and (3), and 19 U.S.C. 1981(a)).

2. By Proclamation No. 4436 of April 30, 1976, the President proclaimed the extension and modification of the increased rates of duty then in effect on imports of some of the articles of ceramic tableware provided for in items 923.01, 923.07, 923.13, and 923.15 of the TSUS. This was done under section 203(h)(3) of the Trade Act of 1974 (19 U.S.C. 2253 (h)(3)).

3. I have determined, pursuant to section 203(h)(4) of the Trade Act of 1974 (19 U.S.C. 2253(h)(4)) and section 351(c)(1)(A) of the Trade Expansion Act of 1962 (19 U.S.C. 1981(c)(1)(A)), after taking into account the advice of the U.S. International Trade Commission and after seeking the advice of the Secretaries of Commerce and Labor as required by those sections, that it is in the national interest to terminate the increased rates of duty currently in effect on imports of the articles of ceramic tableware now provided for in items 923.01, 923.07, 923.13 and 923.15 of the TSUS.

Now, THEREFORE, I, JIMMY CARTER, President of the United States of America, acting under the authority vested in me by the Constitution and the statutes, including section 203(h)(4) of the Trade Act of 1974 (19 U.S.C. 2253(h)(4)) and section 351(c)(1)(A) of the Trade Expansion Act of 1962 (19 U.S.C. 1981(c) (1)(A)), and in accordance with Article XIX of the General Agreement on Tariffs and Trade (GATT), do proclaim that—

(1) The modifications of tariff concessions on ceramic tableware provided for in items 533.28, 533.38, 533.73, and 533.75 in Part I of Schedule XX to the GATT made by Proclamations Nos. 4125 and 4436 are terminated;

(2) Subpart A, part 2 of the Appendix to the TSUS is modified by deleting items 923.01, 923.07, 923.13, and 923.15, including the superior headings thereto;

(3) The modifications of Part I of Schedule XX to the GATT and of the Appendix to the TSUS made by paragraphs (1) and (2) hereof shall be effective as to articles entered, or withdrawn from warehouse, for consumption on or after the date of publication of this Proclamation in the FEDERAL REGISTER.

IN WITNESS WHEREOF, I have hereunto set my hand this second day of October in the year of our Lord nineteen hundred seventy-eight, and of the Independence of the United States of America the two hundred and third.

JIMMY CARTER

[Filed with the Office of the Federal Register, 10:18 a.m., October 4, 1978]

NOTE: The text of the proclamation was released on October 3.

United States Ambassador to Morocco

Nomination of Richard B. Parker. October 3, 1978

The President today announced that he will nominate Richard B. Parker, of Manhattan, Kans., to be Ambassador Extraordinary and Plenipotentiary of the United States to the Kingdom of Morocco. He would replace Robert Anderson, who has resigned.

Parker was born July 3, 1923, in the Philippines, of American parents. He received a B.S. in 1947 and an M.S. in 1948 from Kansas State College. He served in the U.S. Army from 1943 to 1947.

Parker entered the Foreign Service in 1949, and was posted in Sydney, Jerusalem, Beirut, and Amman. In 1957–58 he was an international relations officer at the State Department, and from 1958 to 1961, he was Libyan desk officer.

From 1961 to 1964, Parker was political officer in Beirut, and in 1964–65, he was on detail as a Woodrow Wilson Fellow at Princeton University. From 1965 to 1967, he was counselor for political affairs in Cairo, and from 1967 to 1970, he was country director for the United Arab Republic.

From 1970 to 1974, Parker was Deputy Chief of Mission in Rabat. He was in Algiers from 1970 to 1977, as Chief of the U.S. Interests Section, chargé d'affaires ad interim, and then U.S. Ambassador. Since 1977 he has been Ambassador to Lebanon.

National Mediation Board

Nomination of George S. Ives To Be a Member. October 3, 1978

The President today announced that he will nominate George S. Ives, of Bethesda, Md., for reappointment as a member of the National Mediation Board for a term expiring July 1, 1981.

Ives was born January 10, 1922, in Brooklyn, N.Y. He received an A.B. from Dartmouth College in 1943 and an LL.B. from Cornell University Law School in 1949.

In 1949 and 1950, Ives was legal assistant to the Chairman of the National Labor Relations Board. From 1950 to 1953, he was an associate attorney with Simpson, Thatcher & Bartlett in New York, and from 1953 to 1958, he was administrative assistant to Senator Irving Ives, his father.

Ives was in private practice in law and labor arbitration from 1959 to 1969. He has been a member of the National Mediation Board since 1969.

Overseas Private Investment Corporation

Nomination of J. Bruce Llewellyn To Be President. October 3, 1978

The President today announced that he will nominate J. Bruce Llewellyn, of The Bronx, N.Y., to be President of the Overseas Private Investment Corporation. He would replace Marshall T. Mays, resigned.

Llewellyn was born July 16, 1927, in New York City. He received a B.S. from City College of New York and LL.B. and J.D. degrees from New York Law School.

Llewellyn was assistant director of housing for the New York City Housing and Redevelopment Board from 1962 to 1965. In 1965 he was executive director of the Upper Manhattan Small Business Development Corp., and from 1965 to 1966, he was Regional Director for the U.S. Small Business Administration in New York.

In 1966 and 1967, Llewellyn was executive director of the New York Small Business Development Center, and from 1967 to 1969, he was deputy commissioner of the New York Housing and Development Administration's Department of Rent and Housing Maintenance. Since 1969 he has been president of Fedco Foods Corp., a supermarket chain with 18 stores in Manhattan and The Bronx.

Llewellyn is treasurer of the South Bronx Overall Economic Development Program and a member of the board of the Freedom National Bank and the Urban National Corp. He is a past chairman of the board of Coalition Venture Capital Corp., and president of One Hundred Black Men, Inc.

Rutherford Poats, who has been serving as Acting President of OPIC, will join the National Security Council staff, where he will deal with a wide range of international economic issues, including economic relations among industrial countries and aid to developing countries.

Energy and Water Development Appropriations Bill

Remarks Announcing Intention To Veto H.R. 12928. October 3, 1978

THE PRESIDENT. There are no problems more serious in our country than inflation, the high tax burden on our people, and waste in government.

These are concerns that press very heavily on me as President. And they are concerns that have caused me to decide that later this week I will veto the public works bill recently passed by Congress.

It's important that I and the Congress set an example for the rest of the Nation in controlling inflation. And this public works bill is exactly the wrong example. It's inflationary; it's wasteful; it spends the taxpayers' money in a very inefficient and inappropriate way.

I do agree that public works projects in this country are necessary. But the bill is absolutely unacceptable.

In the first place, it mandates, it requires me to hire 2,300 new employees, which I may or may not consider necessary, at an average salary per year of about $25,000, a total cost of $57 million.

In addition, this bill restores six unnecessary water projects that were deleted by the Congress last year at a cost of about $580 million.

In addition, the Congress has added 27 new water projects above and beyond what was recommended, at a total cost of about $1.8 billion, or about three times as much as I recommended.

I, along with the people of our country, am tired of seeing the taxpayers' money wasted, and I am determined to see the fight against inflation succeed. That's why I'm going to veto this unreasonable bill later on this week.

I think that we've got to set an example for fiscal responsibility. We cannot afford to fail in our fight against inflation. And I urge the Members of the Congress to sustain my veto and to come back immediately with a reasonable bill that spends the American taxpayers' money wisely and which builds projects that will be of benefit to our country, which are sound, advisable, and needed.

Thank you very much.

REPORTER. Can you win the veto fight, sir?

THE PRESIDENT. I'm determined to win it, yes.

NOTE: The President spoke at 4:25 p.m. to reporters assembled in the Oval Office at the White House.

Martin Luther King, Jr. Center for Social Change

Remarks at a White House Reception for Friends of the Center. October 3, 1978

It's a great honor for me to welcome my good friends to the White House this evening and an honor to be joined by my special friends on this program.

The Morehouse College Choir, which you've all heard with great pleasure, is memorable in itself. Martin Luther King, Jr., sang in it. Is that right, Coretta? And Martin Luther King II is now studying at Morehouse. I happen to be a Morehouse brother myself. And the choir sang on a special day for me, the day of my Inauguration. So, I'm very deeply grateful to them and moved whenever I hear them.

I'm also proud of my friend, Daddy King. He is, I think, described pretty well—if you will forgive my saying so—as St. Paul instructed us. He has borne all things, he's believed all things, hoped all things; his love never failing, his spirit triumphant, his voice still strong in the praise of the Lord, whom he has served all his days.

I'm also grateful that Henry Ford II has come. His family's charities, often without public knowledge or recognition, have sustained many of those in this group and those who are loved by others in this group, when projects were looked on as social experiments, experiments that have changed our society. And I think that Henry Ford himself has been a great bridge between those who've been blessed with material wealth and those who have suffered from poverty and injustice. And I want to express my thanks, as President, to you and what you and your family have meant and still mean to our country.

I'm glad to see my friend Andy Young here. He was at the side of Martin Luther King, Jr., during most of his ministry. He was with him at the time of his death. As our Ambassador to the United Nations, Andy Young accurately represents the principles that were the foundation of Martin Luther King, Jr.'s life. And he has put forward our own Nation in its best posture, depending on understanding, brotherhood, love, compassion, nonviolence, in the most effective possible way.

And I would like to mention Coretta King, who out of her own personal grief was strengthened and not weakened, who assumed the position of leadership, and who is trying now to share the dreams of her husband with the rest of us and, indeed, with the whole world in creating an international center to nurture the great change which he fought for, prayed for, and died for.

We are here today to remember Martin Luther King, Jr., and what he stood for and what his accomplishments were. He brought together the conscience of white Americans and the courage of black Americans in a bond of love that broke down the barriers that had existed for centuries. He helped us to overcome our ignorance of one another and our fear of doing what many of us knew was right. In a period of great hostility and difficult social change, when many compromised too much and others compromised not enough, he walked a steady path of conviction. And our people, both black and white, sooner or later learned to follow in his footsteps.

He was not alone in calling on, working for, sacrificing for the changes that he sought, so that more than anything else his own voice and the voice of his people could be heard throughout this Nation, throughout the world, and we're all better for it.

Since the time of Christ, so far as I know, there have been two major nonviolent revolutions. The first one freed India from outside domination, when a quiet little man walked the dusty roads and preached the principle of nonviolence and human love. And the other, led by Dr. King, freed the United States, the country which we all love, from the domination of racism and prejudice.

I'm grateful that the power of these revolutions did not die with the men who led them, who gave such eloquent expression to their goals and to their methods. Unlike violent revolutions, the power of nonviolence lives on. It does not depend on the ability to accumulate weapons and arms. It does not depend on hatred to perpetuate it. It does not depend on terror or maiming or suffering or death. It's available not just to the strong and domineering and the eloquent, but it's also available to the poor and the meek and those who are often inarticulate or even ignorant. Nonviolence is effective among the young and not just the old.

I think this is why our traditional national structures have been changed for the better. And certainly in my lifetime, perhaps even in the entire history of our country, there's not been a change so profound, no one that was so greatly needed, no one that's been consummated with such uniform benefits for all—those who espoused the change originally, those who fought it bitterly until it was obvious that it was inevitable.

This kind of commitment depends on the strength of convictions. It depends on the capacity to love. It depends on an ability to accept blows and suffering and not to return them. It depends on loving through to a victory that transcends that kind of victory that can be won by force, because it involves, as Christ taught, a victory brought about by changing the hearts of people who were enemies.

It's ever more important if we are to gain full human rights around the world for us to set an example of freedom from threat and torture, of freedom from disease and hunger, of freedom of ideas for all people without requiring that people be sacrificed for the worthy causes that they espouse.

That's what makes the Martin Luther King, Jr. Center for Social Change so important. It's the primary repository for the documents and films and photographs, verbal statements of those who brought about the civil rights movement.

Quite often I have leaders come to visit me as their first stop, and their second stop is in Atlanta to think back and to pay tribute to a man who served our Nation, who served me, who served all Americans so well.

Of course, we've not overcome all the injustices and inequities that he and others set out to change and to make right. But we've passed many a milestone already along that difficult road.

I said last year, in honoring Martin Luther King, Jr., with the highest civilian honor that I, as President, can bestow, the Presidential Medal of Freedom, that he made our Nation stronger because he made us better. And tonight I'd like to add that he made our world better because he made our Nation stronger.

We are better able to stand the assaults and attacks and criticisms of those who would deny freedom and justice everywhere, maybe able to hold fast, sometimes turning the other cheek to abuse, but with our feet willing only to move forward, not backward, until at last we all overcome together.

Thank you very much.

NOTE: The President spoke at 4:44 p.m. in the East Room at the White House.

Ambassador at Large
Nomination of Henry David Owen.
October 3, 1978

The President today announced that he will nominate Henry David Owen, of Washington, D.C., to be Ambassador at Large for economic summit affairs.

As U.S. Representative to the International Summit Preparatory Group, Owen will represent the President in international preparations for economic summit meetings and in international followup on these meetings. In order to discharge these duties, Owen will coordinate U.S. Government preparation and followup on summit agenda issues for the Secretary of State and in conjunction with other departments and the National Security Council.

Owen was born August 26, 1920, in New York City. He received an A.B. from Harvard University in 1941. He served in the U.S. Navy from 1942 to 1946.

From 1946 to 1955, Owen was an economist at the State Department. In 1955 he became a member of the Policy Planning Staff at State. From 1962 to 1966, Owen served as Deputy Counselor and Vice Chairman of the Department's Policy Planning Council. From 1966 to 1969, he was Chairman of the Policy Planning Council.

From 1969 to 1978, Owen was director of foreign policy studies at the Brookings Institution. In 1976 he was appointed a part-time consultant to the U.S. Government for economic summit affairs.

Owen is the author of numerous articles and publications. He is the editor of "The Next Phase of U.S. Foreign Policy" and coeditor (with Charles Schultze) of "Setting National Priorities."

Customs Procedural Reform and Simplification Act of 1978

Statement on Signing H.R. 8149 Into Law.
October 4, 1978

I have signed H.R. 8149, the Customs Procedural Reform and Simplification Act of 1978. This is the first major legislation in more than 20 years to streamline Customs clearance of merchandise and passengers.

During those 20 years, the value of U.S. imports and duties collected has increased fivefold; the number of travelers entering the United States each year has more than doubled, from 130 million to over 270 million.

This bill responds to that growth in three major ways. First, it enables the Customs Service to improve procedures for handling the documentary and financial aspects of import transactions, while ensuring timely collection of import statistics. Second, it expedites Customs procedures for processing goods and travelers at a reduced administrative cost. Third, it ensures due process of law for persons accused of Customs violations.

Under this new law, the Customs Service can improve its automation in processing imports and reducing the number of financial transactions between importers and the Government. I am especially pleased with the increase in the personal exemption for travelers from $100 to $300 and the new 10 percent rate of duty for all tourist purchases, which, along with expedited passenger clearance, will make entering the country a quicker and more pleasant experience.

The tourist economies of the Virgin Islands, Guam, and American Samoa will also benefit from an increase of $200 to $600 in the personal exemption, 5 percent flat rate of duty for all goods purchased in those islands, and a new provision which permits the exemption and the flat rate to apply to purchases shipped home as well as those accompanying the traveler.

My administration is strongly committed to eliminating cumbersome procedures, reducing paperwork, facilitating the flow of world trade, and improving the Government's responsiveness to the needs of the traveling public. This bill addresses each of these goals. I am pleased to sign it.

NOTE: As enacted, H.R. 8149 is Public Law 95–410, approved October 3.

United States Arms Control and Disarmament Agency

Nomination of Jane Cahill Pfeiffer To Be a Member of the General Advisory Committee. October 4, 1978

The President today announced that he will nominate Jane Cahill Pfeiffer, of Greenwich, Conn., to be a member of the General Advisory Committee of the U.S. Arms Control and Disarmament Agency. She would replace Joseph Martin, Jr., who has resigned.

Pfeiffer was born September 29, 1932, in Washington, D.C. She is a graduate of the University of Maryland.

Pfeiffer was with IBM for 20 years, serving as vice president for communications and government relations from 1972 to 1976. Since 1976 she has been an independent management consultant. She has recently been named chairman of NBC.

National Council on the Humanities

Nomination of Eight Members. October 4, 1978

The President today announced eight persons whom he will nominate to be members of the National Council on the Humanities for terms expiring January 26, 1984. They are:

CHARLES V. HAMILTON, 48, the Wallace S. Sayre Professor of Government at Columbia University and author of several books and numerous articles on the black experience and politics in America;

LOUIS J. HECTOR, 62, a Miami, Fla., attorney and trustee of the University of Miami;

M. CARL HOLMAN, 59, president of the National Urban Coalition and a former Deputy Staff Director of the U.S. Commission on Civil Rights;

JACOB NEUSNER, 46, professor of religious studies and the Ungerleider Distinguished Scholar of Judaic Studies at Brown University, author of numerous scholarly and popular books on Judaism;

MARY BETH NORTON, 35, associate professor of American history at Cornell University;

SISTER JOEL READ, 52, president of Alverno College in Milwaukee and a professor of history there;

LEON STEIN, 66, editor emeritus of Justice, published by the International Ladies' Garment Workers Union, senior advisory editor at Arno Press, and editor of numerous books on the labor movement and other aspects of American history; and

HARRIET M. ZIMMERMAN, 47, a Ph. D. candidate in Old Testament studies at Harvard Graduate School and active in civic organizations such as the United Jewish Appeal and the Atlanta Jewish Welfare Federation.

Veto of Energy and Water Development Appropriations Bill

Remarks on Vetoing H.R. 12928. October 5, 1978

Good morning, everybody. Two days ago I said that my concern about inflation, my determination to reduce wasteful Government spending would compel me to veto the public works appropriations bill. In just a moment I will sign this message to the Congress and thereby veto the bill.

This has not been an easy decision for me to make. It's something I do not enjoy. But I have a deep commitment to controlling unnecessary spending and also controlling inflation. And I will continue this process, no matter how unpleasant it is, as long as the Congress sends me unacceptable legislation which is not compatible with fiscal responsibility.

As I said Tuesday, there has never been a question of the need to develop our energy and water resources. The question is one of fiscal responsibility, equity, or fairness in the allocation of scarce Government funding for worthwhile projects and restraint in overall spending.

I urge each Member of Congress to support my veto and to work with me immediately to develop a responsible bill that can be passed this year, one that would give our Nation the energy and water resources that we actually need at a cost that we can afford.

[*At this point, the President signed the veto message.*]

Thank you very much.

NOTE: The President spoke at 10:03 a.m. to reporters assembled in the Oval Office at the White House.

Veto of Energy and Water Development Appropriations Bill

Message to the House of Representatives Returning H.R. 12928 Without Approval. October 5, 1978

To the House of Representatives:

Today I am returning H.R. 12928, the Energy and Water Development Appropriations bill, to the Congress without my approval. This bill would hamper the Nation's ability to control inflation, eliminate waste and make the government more efficient.

I respect the hard work and good intentions of the Members of Congress who have prepared this legislation. I share with the Congress a commitment to a strong program of water resource development. Wise development and management of water resources are vital to American agriculture's continued prosperity,

and to community and economic development in key areas of our Nation. I have proposed $2.5 billion this year to support nearly 300 water projects—including twenty-six project starts, the first proposed by any President in four years. Much of the water development funding in this bill is sensible and necessary.

H.R. 12928 also contains energy research and development programs which are important to our Nation's energy future. These appropriations are generally in accord with national needs, and I support them.

But this bill also contains provisions for excessive, wasteful water projects and ill-advised limitations on efficient program management; these require that I disapprove H.R. 12928 in its present form.

The bill would require expenditures on water projects which have already been evaluated objectively and found to be unsound or to fall short of planning, design and environmental assessment requirement. These requirements are essential to ensure that tax dollars are well spent and that future cost over-runs and litigation are avoided. The bill attempts to mandate an unnecessary major increase in the size of the Federal bureaucracy. And it uses funding procedures which conceal from the taxpayers the true size of excessive Federal spending commitments.

In its present form, this bill appears to appropriate less than my FY 1979 Budget. In fact, however, it commits the Federal government to 27 additional new projects and reinstates six projects halted last year—three for construction and three for planning. These added water projects represent a total long-term commitment, including inflation, of $1.8 billion in excess of those I proposed. Yet only a little more than $100 million is appropriated in this bill for these projects.

ADMINISTRATION'S 1979 REQUEST FOR WATER RESOURCE PROJECTS COMPARED WITH THE
AMOUNTS CONTAINED IN H.R. 12928

($ in millions)

	President's Request	Bill	Difference
Number of projects:			
New construction starts_____	26	53	+27
Six projects halted last year*_____	—	6	+6
Total _____	26	59	+33
1979 appropriation for projects:			
New construction starts_____	640	104	−536
Six projects halted last year *_____	—	8	+8
Total _____	640	112	−528
Actual total cost of projects:			
New construction starts_____	640	1,821	+1,181
Six projects halted last year*_____	—	586	+586
Total _____	640	2,407	1,767

Purchasing water projects on the installment plan does not reduce their cost to American taxpayers. Nor does it justify funding projects which fail to meet reasonable standards. We can achieve an efficient Budget only if we are prepared to admit the true costs of the actions we take.

No challenge the Congress and the Executive Branch must face together is more painful than the exercise of budgetary discipline in each individual case. But only consistent, determined discipline will enable us to achieve our shared objectives of controlling inflation, balancing the budget and making government more efficient. The action I am taking today is part of that effort.

This appropriations bill is a true and difficult test of our resolve to discipline the Federal budget. Each bit of additional spending always looks small and unimportant against the total Federal budget. The temptation to look the other way in each case is always great. But both Congress and the Executive Branch must recognize that there is no one single dra-matic act which will control the budget. Budgetary control must be achieved by the cumulative impact of hard choices such as the one I am presenting to the Congress today.

Following are my specific objections to this bill:

—*Funding is reinstated in this bill for unsound water projects.* Six projects not funded last year by the Congress after thorough review determined them to be unwise investments would receive funding this year. The six projects would cost more than $580 million to complete. Three of these would be funded for construction and three for further study, even though no additional analysis is needed to augment the exhaustive information now available. One of the projects funded for further study would require an investment of over $1 million per farm family served. The majority of

---

*Includes three projects funded for construction (total cost: $302 million) and three projects funded for further study (total cost: $284 million).

another "study" project's water supply "benefits" are to serve one catfish farm and several "potential" catfish farms. One project funded for construction, whose major benefit category is flatwater recreation, would be the sixth Corps of Engineers reservoir in a 50-mile radius. American taxpayers simply should not be forced to fund projects which provide such questionable public benefits.

—The bill commits the Federal government to excessive new water project construction starts. I requested funds for 26 new water project construction starts costing a total of $640 million, including an allowance for inflation. This is the first time a President has recommended new starts in four years. This request was well-considered and reflects my commitment to a strong continued program of water resource development. I believe these initiatives are of high priority in meeting agricultural, flood damage reduction, economic development, environmental and other needs. However, the bill goes far beyond this large request. It includes initial funding for an additional 27 projects which, allowing for inflation would add $1.2 billion in total costs. In addition to unacceptable long-term budgetary impact, many of these projects lack required planning or engineering information, present unresolved economic or environmental problems, fail to meet legal requirements or meet low-priority needs.

There are competing uses for every Federal dollar and difficult choices must be faced. Every program in government, no matter how vital, must focus first on matters of highest priority. The President and the Congress must join in this difficult effort. Particularly with taxes and inflation a major concern of every American, I cannot support undertaking expenditures such as a $412 million project where planning is incomplete, or a $117

million project which, without adequate consideration of the concerns of local farmers or of the availability of less damaging alternatives, would take large amounts of valuable farm, pasture and forest land out of production and displace 140 people. Other projects funded in excess of my recommendations post similar serious problems.

—*I would be forced to enlarge the Federal bureaucracy substantially and unnecessarily.* This bill would mandate the hiring of more than 2,300 additional Federal employees in the Corps of Engineers and the Bureau of Reclamation—far exceeding actual need. This requirement is inconsistent with efficient program management and would cause growth in this segment of the Federal work force that would be difficult to reverse.

—*The true costs of the bill far exceed the amounts appropriated.* I believe that funds to meet the full cost of all new water projects should be appropriated when the decision to go forward is made so that the true cost to the taxpayer is known and considered. Appropriating the full amount also helps ensure that, once a project is begun, funds are available to permit speedy, efficient completion. This bill continues the practice of committing the government to major financial investments for what appears on the surface to be very small appropriations. Thus, in making a relatively small appropriation of $103.6 million for new water project construction, H.R. 12928 is actually committing the government to total expenditures of $1.8 billion. At the same time, adding new starts each year without taking their full costs into account greatly increases the risk that budget pressures in the future will cause costly delays.

—*By eliminating funding for the Water Resources Council, the bill would seriously impair efforts to better coordinate water resources programs.* The Water

Resources Council, composed of all the agencies with water programs, is our best assurance of consistent and efficient implementation of water programs throughout the government and close working relationships with other levels of government. The Administration's new water policy stresses the need for systematic management of water resource programs and for increased coordination with state and local governments, and Congress recognized the importance of these objectives and of the Water Resources Council in reauthorizing the Council and its small staff this year.

I am pleased to note that the energy research and development portions of the bill are acceptable and meet important national needs. In a constructive step, this bill provides that decisions on the Clinch River Breeder Reactor project—or possible alternatives—will be determined in the Department of Energy authorization bill, the appropriate place to resolve this issue.

Vital energy programs and sound water development investments are important and shared goals of the Congress and my Administration.

Yet the American people have the right to expect that their government will pursue these goals effectively, efficiently and with the budgetary discipline and careful planning essential to reduce inflation and continue economic growth. Citizens rightly demand sound programs to meet their needs. They rightly demand restraint and judgment in the allocation of public funds. And they expect those of us in public office to demonstrate the courage needed to face hard choices.

I call upon the Congress to join me in meeting our shared responsibility to the American people. I urge you to revise this bill expeditiously so that vital water

and energy programs can continue unhampered by waste and inefficiency.

JIMMY CARTER

The White House,
   October 5, 1978.

NOTE: The House of Representatives reconsidered H.R. 12928 on October 5, and the bill was referred to committee.

Veto of Energy and Water Development Appropriations Bill

*Letter to Members of Congress Urging Support of the Veto of H.R. 12928.
October 5, 1978*

To Members of Congress

The Producers Price Index for finished goods rose 0.9% in September (an annual rate of 11.4%).

I urge you to help me *control inflation* and to set an example of leadership for the nation by supporting my veto of the public works bill.

JIMMY CARTER

United States Ambassador to Iceland

*Nomination of Richard A. Ericson, Jr.
October 5, 1978*

The President today announced that he will nominate Richard A. Ericson, Jr., of Oakland, Calif., to be Ambassador Extraordinary and Plenipotentiary of the United States to Iceland. He would replace James J. Blake, who has resigned.

Ericson was born May 24, 1923, in Honolulu, Hawaii. He received a B.S.F.S. from Georgetown University in 1955. He served in the U.S. Army from 1943 to 1947.

Ericson joined the Foreign Service in 1947 and served as economic officer in

Tokyo. From 1958 to 1960, he was Chief of the Near East and Asia Division of the Bureau of Intelligence and Research. From 1960 to 1961, he was staff assistant in the Bureau of East Asian and Pacific Affairs. From 1961 to 1962, he was special assistant to the Deputy Under Secretary of State for Management.

In 1962 and 1963, Ericson was detailed to the National War College. From 1963 to 1965, he was political officer in London, and from 1965 to 1968, he was counselor for political affairs in Seoul. From 1968 to 1970, he was counselor for political affairs in Tokyo.

From 1970 to 1974, Ericson was Country Director for Japan, and from 1974 to 1976, he was Deputy Chief of Mission in Seoul. Since 1976 he has been Deputy Director of the Bureau of Politico-Military Affairs at the State Department.

United States Ambassador to Mauritius

Nomination of Samuel R. Gammon.
October 5, 1978

The President today announced that he will nominate Samuel R. Gammon, of Bryan, Tex., to be Ambassador Extraordinary and Plenipotentiary of the United States to Mauritius. He would replace Robert V. Keeley, resigned.

Gammon was born January 22, 1924, in Sherman, Tex. He received a B.A. from Texas A&M University in 1946 and an M.A. (1948) and Ph. D. (1953) from Princeton University. He served in the U.S. Army from 1943 to 1946 and 1950 to 1952.

Gammon joined the Foreign Service in 1954 and was posted in Palermo and Milan and at the State Department. In 1962 and 1963, he was officer in charge of Italian affairs. From 1963 to 1967, he was

principal officer, then consul general, in Asmara.

From 1967 to 1970, Gammon was counselor for political affairs in Rome. In 1970 and 1971, he was detailed to USIA as Deputy Assistant Director for Europe. From 1971 to 1973, he was executive assistant to the Deputy Under Secretary of State for Management.

From 1973 to 1975, Gammon was Deputy Executive Secretary in the Executive Secretariat at the State Department. Since 1975 he has been Deputy Chief of Mission in Paris.

United States Tax Court Nominating Commission

Appointment of the Membership.
October 5, 1978

The President today announced the appointment of the six members of the Tax Court Nominating Commission, established by Executive Order 12064 (June 5, 1978):

ROBERT MUNDHEIM, General Counsel, Department of Treasury, Chairman;

JEROME KURTZ, Director, Internal Revenue Service;

CARR FERGUSON, Assistant Attorney General, Tax Division, Department of Justice;

RUTH SCHAPIRO, partner, Proskauer, Rose, Goetz & Mendelsohn, New York City, member of the Advisory Committee of the New York Institute on Federal Taxation;

SHERWIN SIMMONS, partner, Trenam, Simmons, Kemker, Scharf, Barkin, Frye & O'Neill, Tampa, former chairman, taxation section, American Bar Association;

LAWRENCE STONE, partner, Irell and Manella, Los Angeles, former professor of law, University of California at Berkeley, and co-author of "Federal Income Estate and Gift Taxation" (1972).

The President also requested the assistance of the Commission in filling the vacancy on the Tax Court which will be created by the retirement of the Honorable Arnold Raum on October 27, 1978. He directed the Commission to make special efforts to consider well-qualified women and members of minority groups as possible nominees.

Presidential Commission on World Hunger

Statement by the President. October 5, 1978

Farmers around the globe are preparing to gather one of the largest harvests on record. Yet, despite this abundance, hundreds of millions of people will remain hungry and malnourished. Some Americans are among them. Theirs is a daily experience which saps the strength and will and prevents maximum human development. Their numbers will grow unless we find means to raise world food production and improve food distribution, reduce population growth, and help these men, women, and children raise themselves out of the poverty that lies at the root of their hunger.

The United States has a stake in helping to solve this problem, not only because of our humanitarian concerns but for other reasons as well. We cannot have a peaceful and prosperous world if a large part of the world's people are at or near the edge of hunger. So long as food shortages exist in developing countries, the possibility remains of another world food crisis like that of 1973–74. Such a crisis could trigger another ruinous cycle in food prices and thus contribute powerfully to inflation.

With the support of the American people and the Congress, this administration will intensify its efforts to meet the world hunger problem. To this end, we must look for ways to tap the talents and commitment of the American Nation in an effective international effort.

To assist in this vital effort, I have signed an Executive order creating a Presidential Commission on World Hunger. Ambassador Sol Linowitz, who will be its Chairman, has already served our country in many capacities—most recently as Ambassador to the OAS and as conegotiator in the Panama Canal treaties. None of his assignments, however, have been as important to the future hopes of mankind as the one he and his colleagues will undertake over the next 2 years—that of helping to alleviate hunger and malnutrition throughout the world.

I have asked the Commission to analyze the nature and dimensions of the problem, to assess the performance of existing programs, and to recommend actions this Nation can take to reduce world hunger and malnutrition. I have also asked the Commission to inform the American public of these recommendations and assist in their implementation. The Commission will provide me with a status report by July 31, 1979, and a final report by May 31, 1980.

I am confident that this new venture, which will entail close cooperation between the private sector and U.S. legislative and executive branches of Government, will produce a notable advance in the war on hunger.

NOTE: On October 5, the President participated in the inaugural session of the Commission in the Roosevelt Room at the White House.

Acquisition of the Museum of African Art by the Smithsonian Institution

Statement on Signing S. 2507 Into Law. October 5, 1978

I am pleased to sign into law today S. 2507, a bill which authorizes the Smithsonian Institution to assume reponsibility for Washington's Museum of African Art and furthers an important goal of this administration by providing for greater understanding between the people of the United States and the people of Africa in the years to come.

It is unfortunate that until recently the traditional art forms of the continent of Africa were regarded as having only anthropological interest. But thanks in no small part to the effective programs of the Museum of African Art, the magnificent creations of the cultures of Africa have now been recognized as forming one of the truly major art traditions of the world, one whose rediscovery in the West can be traced in the work of many of this century's greatest artists, and one which represents a substantial part of the heritage of millions of our citizens.

The Museum of African Art, through the dedicated work of its founder and director, Warren Robbins, has amassed a remarkable collection of traditional African art objects, all of which are being donated to the people of the United States. In providing for the acceptance of this gift, S. 2507 pledges the faith of the United States to the continuance of the Museum of African Art as part of our great national museum, the Smithsonian Institution, where its collections will be exhibited to the general public free of charge. For its part the Smithsonian, which already has fine collections of European art, the arts of the Americas, and of the Near and Far East, will be responsible on behalf of all of us for the preservation, care, and continued development of this superb collection of African art.

During his last months, Senator Hubert Humphrey drafted the text embodied in S. 2507, which was introduced after his untimely death by Senator Wendell An-

derson and Congresswoman Lindy Boggs. Together with them, committee chairmen Claiborne Pell and Lucien Nedzi deserve our special thanks.

As I sign this bill, I am privileged to guarantee future generations of Americans the opportunity to visit the Museum of African Art and to look at, study, and learn from its great collection.

NOTE: As enacted, S. 2507 is Public Law 95–414, approved October 5.

Veto of Energy and Water Development Appropriations Bill

Statement on Action by the House of Representatives Sustaining the Veto of H.R. 12928. October 5, 1978

This has been a tough fight. I am gratified by the result, but I can take little personal pleasure from a fight among friends, whatever the outcome.

We took a long step in the battle against inflation this afternoon. The Nation owes a debt to the Congress for its wise and responsible action.

As I said earlier this week, there has never been a question of the need to develop our energy and water resources. I will work with the Congress to develop legislation that provides the energy and water projects we need—and can afford.

The hard work and dedication that went into the original legislation will not be wasted. Working together, I hope the Congress and the administration will be able to agree on legislation that protects our citizens from the devastation of drought and floods, that channels water from resource-rich to resource-poor areas, that develops our necessary energy resources.

Equal Employment Opportunity Functions

Executive Order 12086.   October 5, 1978

CONSOLIDATION OF CONTRACT COMPLIANCE FUNCTIONS FOR EQUAL EMPLOYMENT OPPORTUNITY

By the authority vested in me as President by the Constitution and statutes of the United States of America, including Section 202 of the Budget and Accounting Procedures Act of 1950 (31 U.S.C. 581c), in order to provide for the transfer to the Department of Labor of certain contract compliance functions relating to equal employment opportunity, it is hereby ordered as follows:

1–1. *Transfer of Functions.*

1–101. The functions concerned with being primarily responsible for the enforcement of the equal employment opportunity provisions under Parts II and III of Executive Order No. 11246, as amended, are transferred or reassigned to the Secretary of Labor from the following agencies:

(a) Department of the Treasury.

(b) Department of Defense.

(c) Department of the Interior.

(d) Department of Commerce.

(e) Department of Health, Education, and Welfare.

(f) Department of Housing and Urban Development.

(g) Department of Transportation.

(h) Department of Energy.

(i) Environmental Protection Agency.

(j) General Services Administration.

(k) Small Business Administration.

1–102. The records, property, personnel and positions, and unexpended balances of appropriations or funds related to the functions transferred or reassigned by this Order, that are available and necessary to finance or discharge those functions, are transferred to the Secretary of Labor.

1–103. The Director of the Office of Management and Budget shall make such determinations, issue such orders, and take all actions necessary or appropriate to effectuate the transfers or reassignments provided by this Order, including the transfer of funds, records, property, and personnel.

1–2. *Conforming Amendments to Executive Order No. 11246.*

1–201(a). In order to reflect the transfer of enforcement responsibility to the Secretary of Labor, Section 201 of Executive Order No. 11246, as amended, is amended to read:

"Sec. 201. The Secretary of Labor shall be responsible for the administration and enforcement of Parts II and III of this Order. The Secretary shall adopt such rules and regulations and issue such orders as are deemed necessary and appropriate to achieve the purposes of Parts II and III of this Order.".

(b) Paragraph (7) of the contract clauses specified in Section 202 of Executive Order No. 11246, as amended, is amended to read:

" "(7) The contractor will include the provisions of paragraphs (1) through (7) in every subcontract or purchase order unless exempted by rules, regulations, or orders of the Secretary of Labor issued pursuant to Section 204 of Executive Order No. 11246 of September 24, 1965, so that such provisions will be binding upon each subcontractor or vendor. The contractor will take such action with respect to any subcontract or purchase order as may be directed by the Secretary of Labor as a means of enforcing such provisions including sanctions for noncompliance: *Provided, however,* that in the event the contractor becomes involved in, or is threatened with, litigation with a subcontractor or vendor as a result of such direction, the contractor may request the United States to enter into such litigation to protect the interests of the United States." ".

1–202. In subsection (c) of Section 203 of Executive Order No. 11246, as amended, delete "contracting agency" in the proviso and substitute "Secretary of Labor" therefor.

1–203. In both the beginning and end of subsection (d) of Section 203 of Executive Order No. 11246, as amended, delete "contracting agency or the" in the phrase "contracting agency or the Secretary".

1–204. Section 205 of Executive Order No. 11246, as amended, is amended by deleting the last two sentences, which dealt with agency designation of compliance officers, and revising the rest of that Section to read:

"Sec. 205. The Secretary of Labor shall be responsible for securing compliance by all government contractors and subcontractors with this Order and any implementing rules or regulations. All contracting agencies shall comply with the terms of this Order and any implementing rules, regulations, or orders of the Secretary of Labor. Contracting agencies shall cooperate with the Secretary of Labor and shall furnish such information and assistance as the Secretary may require.".

1–205. In order to delete references to the contracting agencies conducting investigations, Section 206 of Executive Order No. 11246, as amended, is amended to read:

"Sec. 206. (a) The Secretary of Labor may investigate the employment practices of any Government contractor or subcontractor to determine whether or not the contractual provisions specified in Section 202 of this Order have been violated. Such investigation shall be conducted in ac-

cordance with the procedures established by the Secretary of Labor.".

"(b) The Secretary of Labor may receive and investigate complaints by employees or prospective employees of a Government contractor or subcontractor which allege discrimination contrary to the contractual provisions specified in Section 202 of this Order.".

1–206. In Section 207 of Executive Order No. 11246, as amended, delete "contracting agencies, other" in the first sentence.

1–207. The introductory clause in Section 209(a) of Executive Order No. 11246, as amended, is amended by deleting "or the appropriate contracting agency" from "In accordance with such rules, regulations, or orders as the Secretary of Labor may issue or adopt, the Secretary or the appropriate contracting agency may:".

1–208. In paragraph (5) of Section 209(a) of Executive Order No. 11246, as amended, insert at the beginning the phrase "After consulting with the contracting agency, direct the contracting agency to", and at the end of paragraph (5) delete "contracting agency" and substitute therefor "Secretary of Labor" so that paragraph (5) is amended to read:

"(5) After consulting with the contracting agency, direct the contracting agency to cancel, terminate, suspend, or cause to be cancelled, terminated or suspended any contract, or any portion or portions thereof, for failure of the contractor or subcontractor to comply with equal employment opportunity provisions of the contract. Contracts may be cancelled, terminated, or suspended absolutely or continuance of contracts may be conditioned upon a program for future compliance approved by the Secretary of Labor.".

1–209. In order to reflect the transfer from the agencies to the Secretary of Labor of the enforcement functions, substitute "Secretary of Labor" for "each contracting agency" in Section 209(b) of Executive Order No. 11246, as amended, so that Section 209(b) is amended to read:

"(b) Pursuant to rules and regulations prescribed by the Secretary of Labor, the Secretary shall make reasonable efforts, within a reasonable time limitation, to secure compliance with the contract provisions of this Order by methods of conference, conciliation, mediation, and persuasion before proceedings shall be instituted under subsection (a)(2) of this Section, or before a contract shall be cancelled or terminated in whole or in part under subsection (a)(5) of this Section.".

1–210. In order to reflect the responsibility of the contracting agencies for prompt compliance with the directions of the Secretary of Labor, Sections 210 and 211 of Executive Order No. 11246, as amended, are amended to read:

"Sec. 210. Whenever the Secretary of Labor makes a determination under Section 209, the Secretary shall promptly notify the appropriate agency. The agency shall take the action directed by the Secretary and shall report the results of the action it has taken to the Secretary of Labor within such time as the Secretary shall specify. If the contracting agency fails to take the action directed within thirty days, the Secretary may take the action directly.".

"Sec. 211. If the Secretary of Labor shall so direct, contracting agencies shall not enter into contracts with any bidder or prospective contractor unless the bidder or prospective contractor has satisfactorily complied with the provisions of this Order or submits a program for compliance acceptable to the Secretary of Labor.".

1–211. Section 212 of Executive Order No. 11246, as amended, is amended to read:

"Sec. 212. When a contract has been cancelled or terminated under Section 209(a)(5) or a contractor has been debarred from further Government contracts under Section 209(a)(6) of this Order, because of noncompliance with the contract provisions specified in Section 202 of this Order, the Secretary of Labor shall promptly notify the Comptroller General of the United States.".

1–212. In order to reflect the transfer of enforcement responsibility to the Secretary of Labor, references to the administering department or agency are deleted in clauses (1), (2), and (3) of Section 301 of Executive Order No. 11246, as amended, and those clauses are amended to read:

"(1) to assist and cooperate actively with the Secretary of Labor in obtaining the compliance of contractors and subcontractors with those contract provisions and with the rules, regulations and relevant orders of the Secretary, (2) to obtain and to furnish to the Secretary of Labor such information as the Secretary may require for the supervision of such compliance, (3) to carry out sanctions and penalties for violation of such obligations imposed upon contractors and subcontractors by the Secretary of Labor pursuant to Part II, Subpart D, of this Order,".

1–213. In order to reflect the transfer from the agencies to the Secretary of Labor of the enforcement functions "Secretary of Labor " shall be substituted for "administering department or agency" in Section 303 of Executive Order No. 11246, as amended, and Section 303 is amended to read:

"Sec. 303. (a) The Secretary of Labor shall be responsible for obtaining the compliance of such applicants with their undertakings under this Order. Each administering department and agency is directed to cooperate with the Secretary of Labor and to furnish the Secretary such information and assistance as the Secretary may require in the performance of the Secretary's functions under this Order.".

"(b) In the event an applicant fails and refuses to comply with the applicant's undertakings pursuant to this Order, the Secretary of Labor may, after consulting with the administering department or agency, take any or all of the following actions: (1) direct any administering department or agency to cancel, terminate, or suspend in whole or in part the agreement, contract or other arrangement with such applicant with respect to which the failure or refusal occurred; (2) direct any administering department or agency to refrain from extending any further assistance to the applicant under the program with respect to which the failure or refusal occurred until satisfactory assurance of future compliance has been received by the Secretary of Labor from such applicant; and (3) refer the case to the Department of Justice or the Equal Employment Opportunity Commission for appropriate law enforcement or other proceedings.".

"(c) In no case shall action be taken with respect to an applicant pursuant to clause (1) or (2) of subsection (b) without notice and opportunity for hearing.".

1–214. Section 401 of Executive Order No. 11246, as amended, is amended to read:

"Sec. 401. The Secretary of Labor may delegate to any officer, agency, or employee in the Executive branch of the Government, any function or duty of the Secretary under Parts II and III of this Order.".

1–3. *General Provisions.*

1–301. The transfers or reassignments provided by Section 1–1 of this Order shall take effect at such time or times as the Director of the Office of Management and Budget shall determine. The Director shall ensure that all such transfers or reassignments take effect within 60 days.

1–302. The conforming amendments provided by Section 1–2 of this Order shall take effect on October 8, 1978; except that, with respect to those agencies identified in Section 1–101 of this Order, the conforming amendments shall be effective on the effective date of the transfer or reassignment of functions as specified pursuant to Section 1–301 of this Order.

JIMMY CARTER

The White House,
    October 5, 1978.

[Filed with the Office of the Federal Register, 10:26 a.m., October 6, 1978]

Sikes Act Amendments of 1978

Statement on Signing H.R. 13745 Into Law. October 5, 1978

Today I am signing into law H.R. 13745, the Sikes Act Amendments of 1978.

On July 10, 1978, I vetoed an earlier version of this legislation which would have more than doubled the 1978 authorized funding level under the act and would have required the Secretaries of the Interior, Agriculture, and Defense to explain Presidential budget requests for less than the amount authorized.

As stated at that time, I am strongly committed to the sound management and conservation of fish and wildlife on public lands. However, annual appropriations for these programs must be set in the context of an effective and efficient overall public land management program. In my view, the reporting requirement contained in

H.R. 10882 constituted an unacceptable intrusion on the authority of the President to present his budget recommendations to the Congress.

I am pleased, therefore, that the Congress has reenacted legislation extending the Sikes Act through 1981, while deleting the objectionable provisions of the earlier bill. This administration will continue its efforts, in cooperation with the States under this and other laws, to ensure the conservation and enhancement of fish and wildlife on Federal lands.

NOTE: As enacted, H.R. 13745 is Public Law 95–420, approved October 5.

The statement was released on October 6.

Amtrak Improvement Act of 1978

Statement on Signing S. 3040 Into Law. October 5, 1978

I am today signing into law S. 3040, the Amtrak Improvement Act of 1978.

This legislation authorizes the appropriation of $755 million in Federal funds in fiscal year 1979 for the National Railroad Passenger Corporation's (Amtrak) operating expenses and capital expenditures. The bill also directs the Secretary of Transportation, in conjunction with Amtrak, to conduct a study of Amtrak's basic route structure for railroad passenger service and to submit his final recommendations regarding that system to the Congress by December 31, 1978.

For several years attempts have been made to put Amtrak on a more stable financial footing and to discontinue services that have large operating losses without providing substantial public benefits. This bill provides a procedure for bringing about a quick, significant restructuring of Amtrak's route system. Without this legislation, restructuring would have to be done on a route-by-route basis, in a time consuming manner, with no assurance that the final result would coincide with national transportation needs and priorities. Under these circumstances it would be very difficult to control the future growth of Amtrak's deficit. For this reason, I am signing the bill.

However, S. 3040 also contains a provision requiring that the final recommendations of the Secretary of Transportation regarding the Amtrak route system must lay before Congress for a period of 90 calendar days, during which they may be disapproved by a simple resolution adopted by either the Senate or the House of Representatives.

In my message to the Congress of June 21, 1978, I specifically indicated that I regard such congressional control over the exercise of statutory discretion by the executive branch as unconstitutional. Accordingly, I am directing the Secretary of Transportation to treat this provision in S. 3040 as a "report and wait" provision.

I am also concerned over the "Buy American" provision in this bill. S. 3040 would require that Amtrak's purchase of goods costing over $1 million be limited to those mined, produced, or manufactured in the United States. However, there are provisions in the legislation permitting the Secretary of Transportation to waive these "Buy American" requirements under certain conditions. I expect the Secretary to exercise his discretionary waiver authority in a manner that is consistent with the public interest, including our obligations under international agreements.

NOTE: As enacted, S. 3040 is Public Law 95–421, approved October 5.

The statement was released on October 6.

Meeting With President Spyros Kyprianou of Cyprus

White House Statement.   October 6, 1978

President Carter and Cypriot President Spyros Kyprianou met this morning from 10:15 to 10:45 in the Cabinet Room for a useful and friendly exchange of views on how progress could be made towards a just and lasting solution of the Cyprus problem which would meet the needs of all the people of Cyprus and contribute to lasting peace in the Eastern Mediterranean.

President Carter expressed the desire of the United States Government to work actively for a just and lasting settlement of the Cyprus problem within the framework of the United Nations.

Attending the meeting on the American side were Deputy Secretary of State Warren Christopher; Matthew Nimetz, Counselor of the State Department; Dr. Zbigniew Brzezinski, Assistant to the President for National Security Affairs; and Paul B. Henze, NSC staff member. Accompanying President Kyprianou were Foreign Minister Nikos Rolandis; George Pelaghias, Director General of the Ministry of Foreign Affairs; and Nicos G. Dimitriou, Cypriot Ambassador to the United States.

the States to ratify the equal rights amendment to the Constitution.

Our concern for human rights must begin at home, and the rights of citizenship must be protected, regardless of sex. I believe it is past time for that protection to be written into the Constitution of the United States. That is why I have been so strongly committed to ERA, and why I urged the Senate to take the action it took today.

I want to again commend the many citizens organizations that have worked so closely with us to obtain passage of the extension and to thank Senator Birch Bayh and Majority Leader Robert Byrd for their outstanding leadership on this issue.

I hope that States which have not yet ratified the amendment will now take speedy advantage of this additional opportunity to do so.

Human rights also includes economic opportunity. With the passage of the ERA extension, we can devote full attention to passage of the Humphrey-Hawkins full employment bill before the end of this session. I have asked Louis Martin and Anne Wexler of my staff to chair a White House task force to coordinate administration activities in support of this legislation. Hamilton Jordan will meet with this task force and representatives of citizens groups supporting the legislation at noon on Monday.

Equal Rights Amendment and Humphrey-Hawkins Full Employment Legislation

Statement on Senate Action on the ERA Extension Resolution and a White House Task Force on the Employment Legislation. October 6, 1978

I am delighted by today's passage of the Senate resolution extending the time for

Federal Communications Commission

Nomination of Anne P. Jones To Be a Member.   October 6, 1978

The President today announced that he will nominate Anne P. Jones, of Arlington, Mass., to be a member of the Federal Communications Commission for a term expiring June 30, 1985. She would replace Margita White, whose term has expired.

Jones was born February 9, 1935, in Somerville, Mass. She received a B.S. in social sciences from Boston College in 1958 and an LL.B. from Boston College Law School in 1961.

From 1961 to 1968, Jones practiced law with a Boston firm. From 1968 to 1978, she was with the Securities and Exchange Commission, where she served as attorney adviser, then Special Counsel in the Division of Corporate Regulation; legal assistant to Commissioner James J. Needham; and Associate Director, then Director of the Division of Investment Management Regulation.

Since last January, Jones has been General Counsel to the Federal Home Loan Bank Board.

Railroad Retirement Board

Nomination of Earl Oliver To Be a Member. October 6, 1978

The President today announced that he will nominate Earl Oliver, of Chicago, for reappointment as a member of the Railroad Retirement Board for a term expiring August 28, 1983.

Oliver was born February 25, 1917, in Monticello, Ky. He received a B.A. from Oklahoma A&M College.

Oliver worked for the Chicago and Northwestern Railway from 1941 to 1947 as a secretary, chief clerk, safety inspector, assistant trainmaster, and trainmaster. He was with Illinois Central Gulf Railroad from 1948 to 1975, working in various labor relations positions, then as manager of personnel, director of personnel, vice president for personnel, and finally senior vice president for personnel and adminis-

tration. After his retirement in 1975, he did staff work for the National Railway Labor Conference and the Railroad Labor-Management Committee. He was appointed to the Railroad Retirement Board in 1977.

United States Advisory Commission on International Communication, Cultural and Educational Affairs

Nomination of Lewis Manilow To Be a Member.   October 6, 1978

The President today announced that he will nominate Lewis Manilow, of Chicago, Ill., to be a member of the United States Advisory Commission on International Communication, Cultural and Educational Affairs for a 3-year term.

Manilow, 50, is a Chicago attorney and president of the Museum of Contemporary Art of Chicago.

From 1969 to 1975, Manilow was chief executive officer in the development of the New Community of Park Forest South. He is chairman of the League of New Community Developers. He is also a producer of plays in Chicago and New York, a governing life member of the Art Institute of Chicago, and a founding member of Illinois Advocates for the Arts.

National Commission on Social Security

Nomination of Three Members. October 6, 1978

The President today announced three persons whom he will nominate to be members of the National Commission on Social Security for 2-year terms. They are:

JAMES J. DILLMAN, a Sheboygan, Wis., attorney, vice chairman of the Wisconsin Retirement Fund board of trustees, and a member of the Wisconsin Retirement Research Committee;

MILTON S. GWIRTZMAN, of Newton, Mass., an author on tax policy and economic policy and a practicing attorney;

DAVID H. RODGERS, of Spokane, Wash., deputy commissioner of insurance for eastern Washington, formerly manager of the employee benefits office of the Aetna Life Insurance Co.

International Development and Food Assistance Act of 1978

Statement on Signing H.R. 12222 Into Law. October 6, 1978

I am today signing into law H.R. 12222, the International Development and Food Assistance Act of 1978.

This legislation authorizes the appropriation of $1,794 million for U.S. bilateral and multilateral economic assistance for fiscal year 1979 to carry forward our programs to encourage development in the world's poor countries and to promote peace and stability abroad. The bill endorses the use of our foreign assistance resources to meet the basic human needs of poor people in developing countries through a policy of equitable growth.

These provisions bring us closer to our foreign policy goals, and I fully support them.

However, H.R. 12222 contains a constitutionally objectionable provision for a legislative veto. The bill requires the President to develop a new personnel system for the Agency for International Development, and to submit the new system to Congress for review by March 15, 1979. The objectionable provision allows either House of Congress to strike down the proposed changes by adopting a disapproving resolution up to 90 days after they are submitted.

The provision for disapproval by either House exemplifies the kind of unconstitutional device to which I strongly objected in my June 21, 1978, message on the legislative veto. As I noted in that message, ". . . the legislative veto injects the Congress into the details of administering substantive programs and laws. . . ." and it infringes ". . . on the Executive's constitutional duty to faithfully execute the laws."

I agree that the Agency's personnel management needs to be strengthened to assure the success of our development assistance programs. Accordingly, I am directing the Administrator of AID, Mr. Gilligan, to undertake an urgent study of the Agency's personnel system. The study will include appropriate recommendations for revitalizing the system to meet AID's special requirements, consistent with my program for civil service reform.

The administration will advise and consult the proper congressional committees throughout its review. New regulations will be submitted to Congress by March 15, 1979, as called for. The Administrator of AID will implement the new regulations at the end of the 90-day congressional review period unless a statute, subject to my approval under Article I, Section 7 of the Constitution, is enacted overturning them. This approach ensures respect of congressional intent in a way that is constitutionally appropriate.

NOTE: As enacted, H.R. 12222 is Public Law 95–424, approved October 6.

Digest of Other White House Announcements

The following listing includes the President's daily schedule and other items of general interest as announced by the White House Press Office during the period covered by this issue. Events and announcements printed elsewhere in the issue are not included.

September 30

The President met at the White House with:

—Zbigniew Brzezinski, Assistant to the President for National Security Affairs;

—A. A. Gromyko, Foreign Minister of the Union of Soviet Socialist Republics, and other Soviet officials, Vice President Walter F. Mondale, Secretary of State Cyrus R. Vance, Secretary of Defense Harold Brown, Ambassador Paul C. Warnke, Director of the United States Arms Control and Disarmament Agency, Malcolm Toon, U.S. Ambassador to the Soviet Union, Dr. Brzezinski, and other U.S. officials, to discuss the strategic arms limitation talks;

—Foreign Minister Gromyko and Secretary Vance.

The White House announced that Dr. Brzezinski will visit France, the Federal Republic of Germany, and the United Kingdom October 2–4 for consultations. This trip is part of continuing consultations by Dr. Brzezinski with our allies.

The President has asked Vice President Mondale to head the U.S. delegation to the funeral of Pope John Paul I in Rome.

October 1

The White House announced that Mrs. Lillian Carter will head the U.S. delegation to Rome for the funeral of Pope John Paul I. Vice President Mondale will be unable to head the delegation because of this week's legislative agenda.

October 2

The President met at the White House with:

—David L. Aaron, Deputy Assistant for National Security Affairs;

—Frank B. Moore, Assistant to the President for Congressional Liaison;

—Vice President Mondale.

In a ceremony in the Oval Office, the President received diplomatic credentials from Ambassadors George Ashley Griffith of Grenada, Horst Grunert of the German Democratic Republic, Sean Donlon of Ireland, and Tabarak Husain of the People's Republic of Bangladesh.

October 3

The President met at the White House with:

—Mr. Aaron;

—Mr. Moore;

—the Democratic congressional leadership;

—Ambassador Toon and Mr. Aaron, to discuss SALT and U.S.-Soviet relations;

—Adm. Stansfield Turner, Director of Central Intelligence, Hamilton Jordan, Assistant to the President, William J. Perry, Under Secretary of Defense for Research and Engineering, and Mr. Aaron;

—Governor Ricardo J. Bordallo of Guam;

—Mrs. Carter, for lunch;

—the Cabinet, to discuss anti-inflation strategy and various pieces of legislation.

The President today announced the members of the delegation to the funeral of Pope John Paul I. They are:

MRS. LILLIAN CARTER, Personal Representative of the President;

THOMAS F. EAGLETON, U.S. Senator from Missouri;

ELLA GRASSO, Governor of Connecticut;
MICHAEL BLOUIN, U.S. Representative from Iowa;
PETER SARROS, Acting Personal Representative of the President to the Vatican;
FRANCIS X. BELLOTTI, attorney general of Massachusetts;
EDWARD KOCH, mayor of New York;
ERNEST MORIAL, mayor of New Orleans;
WILLIAM FITZGERALD, State senator from Michigan;
MARIO OBLEDO, California secretary of health and welfare; and
GERARD DOHERTY, a Boston, Mass., attorney.

October 4

The President met at the White House with:
—Mr. Aaron;
—Mr. Moore;
—James T. McIntyre, Jr., Director of the Office of Management and Budget;
—Robert O. Anderson, chairman of Atlantic-Richfield.

The President attended a portion of a White House briefing on energy given by administration officials in the East Room for a group of business leaders.

October 5

The President met at the White House with:
—Dr. Brzezinski;
—Mr. Moore;
—a group of Republican Members of Congress to discuss natural gas, energy, and other legislation;
—Secretary of the Treasury W. Michael Blumenthal, G. William Miller, Chairman of the Board of Governors of the Federal Reserve System, Charles L. Schultze, Chairman of the Council of Economic Advisers, and Mr. McIntyre;
—Speaker of the House of Representatives Thomas P. O'Neill, Jr.

The President attended a briefing in the Old Executive Office Building given by administration officials for State and local officials, labor leaders, and other Democratic citizens from the State of Michigan.

The President has named Ambler H. Moss, Jr., U.S. Ambassador to Panama, and Lt. Gen. Dennis P. McAuliffe, Commander in Chief, U.S. Southern Command, Panama, as the U.S. delegation to the inauguration of the new President and Vice President of Panama.

October 6

The President met at the White House with:
—Vice President Mondale, Secretaries Vance and Brown, Andrew J. Young, U.S. Representative to the United Nations, Dr. Brzezinski, and Mr. Jordan, to discuss the situation in Lebanon and other foreign policy issues;
—Mr. Moore;
—Dr. Schultze;
—Representative Robert C. Krueger of Texas;
—Michael Forrestal, president, and C. William Verity, Jr., chairman, U.S.-U.S.S.R. Trade and Economic Council, to discuss the council members' recent trip to the Soviet Union.

The President transmitted to the Congress the 10th annual report on the National Housing Goal.

The President left the White House for a weekend stay at Camp David, Md.

NOMINATIONS SUBMITTED TO THE SENATE

The following list does not include promotions of members of the Uniformed Services, nominations to the Service Academies, or nominations of Foreign Service officers.

Submitted October 2, 1978

HERBERT S. OKUN, of Maryland, a Foreign Service officer of Class one, for the rank of Minister during the tenure of his assignment as the State Department SALT Representative at Geneva, Switzerland.

NOMINATIONS—Continued

Submitted October 3, 1978

HENRY DAVID OWEN, of the District of Columbia, to be Ambassador at Large.

RICHARD B. PARKER, of Kansas, a Foreign Service officer of the Class of Career Minister, to be Ambassador Extraordinary and Plenipotentiary of the United States of America to the Kingdom of Morocco.

J. BRUCE LLEWELLYN, of New York, to be President of the Overseas Private Investment Corporation, vice Marshall Trammell Mays, resigned.

GEORGE S. IVES, of Maryland, to be a member of the National Mediation Board for the term expiring July 1, 1981 (reappointment).

Submitted October 4, 1978

JANE CAHILL PFEIFFER, of Connecticut, to be a member of the General Advisory Committee of the United States Arms Control and Disarmament Agency, vice Joseph Martin, Jr., resigned.

The following-named persons to be members of the National Council on the Humanities for terms expiring January 26, 1984:

> CHARLES V. HAMILTON, of New York, vice Frank Everson Vandiver, term expired.
>
> LOUIS J. HECTOR, of Florida, vice Martin Luther Kilson, Jr., term expired.
>
> M. CARL HOLMAN, of the District of Columbia, vice Hanna Holburn Gray, term expired.
>
> JACOB NEUSNER, of Rhode Island, vice Sheldon H. Solow, term expired.
>
> SISTER JOEL READ, of Wisconsin, vice Sidney Hook, term expired.
>
> LEON STEIN, of New York, vice Irving Kristol, term expired.
>
> HARRIET MORSE ZIMMERMAN, of Georgia, vice Jeffrey Hart, term expired.
>
> MARY BETH NORTON, of New York, vice Richard R. St. Johns, term expired.

Submitted October 5, 1978

RICHARD A. ERICSON, JR., of California, a Foreign Service officer of Class one, to be Ambassador Extraordinary and Plenipotentiary of the United States of America to Iceland.

NOMINATIONS—Continued

Submitted October 5—Continued

SAMUEL RHEA GAMMON, of Texas, a Foreign Service officer of Class one, to be Ambassador Extraordinary and Plenipotentiary of the United States of America to Mauritius.

Submitted October 6, 1978

ANNE P. JONES, of Massachusetts, to be a member of the Federal Communications Commission for a term of 7 years from July 1, 1978, vice Margareta E. White, term expired.

EARL OLIVER, of Illinois, to be a member of the Railroad Retirement Board for the term of 5 years from August 29, 1978 (reappointment).

CHECKLIST OF WHITE HOUSE PRESS RELEASES

The following releases of the Office of the White House Press Secretary, distributed during the period covered by this issue, are not included in the issue.

Released September 30, 1978

News conference: on their meeting to discuss the strategic arms limitation talks—by Secretary of State Cyrus R. Vance and Foreign Minister A. A. Gromyko of the Soviet Union

News conference: following the meeting between Secretary Vance and Foreign Minister Gromyko—by Jody Powell, Press Secretary to the President

Released October 1, 1978

Advance text: remarks on presenting the Congressional Space Medal of Honor Awards at the Kennedy Space Center, Fla.

Announcement: designation of Mrs. Lillian Carter to head the U.S. delegation to Rome for the funeral of His Holiness Pope John Paul I

Released October 2, 1978

News conference: on tuition tax credit legislation—by Secretary of Health, Education, and Welfare Joseph A. Califano, Jr.

Fact sheet: administration actions to improve health services and facilities in rural areas

Released October 3, 1978

News conference: on the equal rights amendment extension legislation—by Sarah C. Weddington, Special Assistant to the President

CHECKLIST—Continued

Released October 3—Continued

Fact sheet: H.R. 12928, the energy and water development appropriations bill

Released October 4, 1978

News conference: on the energy and water development appropriations bill—by Cecil D. Andrus, Secretary of the Interior, James T. McIntyre, Jr., Director of the Office of Management and Budget, Charles L. Schultze, Chairman of the Council of Economic Advisers, and Clifford L. Alexander, Secretary of the Army

Statements: commendation of the President on his intention to veto the energy and water development appropriations bill—by Governors Robert W. Straub of Oregon, John V. Evans of Idaho, J. James Exon of Nebraska, and Michael O'Callaghan of Nevada

News conference: on the equal rights amendment extension legislation—by Ms. Weddington

Statements: commendation of the President on his intention to veto the energy and water development appropriations bill—by Governors James B. Hunt, Jr., of North Carolina and Jerry Apodaca of New Mexico

Released October 5, 1978

News conference: on the Presidential Commission on World Hunger—by Sol Linowitz, Chairman of the Commission

Released October 6, 1978

News conference: on the agreement reached between the Environmental Protection Agency and the Republic Steel Corporation concerning Republic's compliance with clean air and water standards, modernization of facilities, and continued employment of steelworkers in the Warren and Youngstown, Ohio, areas—by Jack H. Watson, Jr., Assistant to the President for Intergovernmental Affairs, Douglas M. Costle, Administrator, Environmental Protection Agency, W. J. De Lancey, president, Republic Steel Corporation, Lloyd McBride, president, United Steelworkers of America, and Senator John H. Glenn, Jr., of Ohio

News conference: on U.S. arms sales—by Jessica Tuchman Mathews, staff member, National Security Council

ACTS APPROVED BY
THE PRESIDENT

Approved September 30, 1978

H.R. 12935_____ Public Law 95–391
Legislative Branch Appropriation Act, 1979.

H.R. 12936_____ Public Law 95–392
Department of Housing and Urban Development—Independent Agencies Appropriation Act, 1979.

H.R. 7819_____ Public Law 95–393
Diplomatic Relations Act.

H.R. 12772_____ Public Law 95–394
An act to facilitate the exchange of certain lands in the State of Oregon, and for other purposes.

H.R. 12860_____Public Law 95–395
Rhode Island Indian Claims Settlement Act.

S. 1678_____ Public Law 95–396
Federal Pesticide Act of 1978.

H.R. 3702_____ Public Law 95–397
Uniformed Services Survivors' Benefits Amendments of 1978.

S. 3069_____ Public Law 95–398
An act to provide that members of the Sisseton-Wahpeton Sioux Tribe may request the Secretary of the Interior to acquire certain lands, and to provide that the tribe shall have a preference right to purchase certain lands held in trust by the United States for tribal members.

S. 3002_____ Public Law 95–399
An act to modify a portion of the south boundary of the Salt River Pima-Maricopa Indian Reservation in Arizona, and for other purposes.

S. 3271_____ Public Law 95–400
An act to amend the pilot project workfare provisions of the Food Stamp Act of 1977.

H.R. 11401_____ Public Law 95–401
National Aeronautics and Space Administration Authorization Act, 1979.

S. 3468_____ Public Law 95–402
An act to amend the Agricultural Act of 1949 to ensure that the interest rates on price support loans for upland cotton are not less favorable to producers than the interest rates for such loans on other commodities.

S. 1896_____ Public Law 95–403
An act to amend the Hazardous Materials Transportation Act to authorize appropriations for fiscal year 1979.

S. 2701_____ Public Law 95–404
An act to amend the Water Resources Planning Act (79 Stat. 244, as amended).

ACTS APPROVED—Continued

Approved September 30—Continued

S. 2391_____ Public Law 95–405
Futures Trading Act of 1978.

S. J. Res. 165_____ Public Law 95–406
A joint resolution to provide for a temporary
extension of certain Federal Housing Administration mortgage insurance and related
authorities, of the national flood insurance
program, of the crime insurance and riot re-
insurance programs, of certain rural housing
authorities, and for other purposes.

H. J. Res. 1140_____ Public Law 95–407
A joint resolution to amend section 8 of the
Export-Import Bank Act of 1945.

H.R. 1427_____ Private Law 95–54
An act for the relief of Marie Grant.

H.R. 3460_____ Private Law 95–55
An act for the relief of William J. Elder and
the estate of Stephen M. Owens, deceased.

H.R. 5097_____ Private Law 95–56
An act for the relief of Doctor Daryl C.
Johnson.

H.R. 6760_____ Private Law 95–57
An act for the relief of Charles M. Metott.

Approved October 2, 1978

S. 3375_____ Public Law 95–408
Federal District Court Organization Act of
1978.

S. 3272_____ Public Law 95–409
An act to amend the Packers and Stockyards
Act, 1921, and for other purposes.

Approved October 3, 1978

H.R. 8149_____ Public Law 95–410
Customs Procedural Reform and Simplification Act of 1978.

Approved October 5, 1978

S.J. Res. 154_____ Public Law 95–411
A joint resolution authorizing the President
to invite the States of the Union and foreign
nations to participate in the International
Petroleum Exposition to be held at Tulsa,
Oklahoma, from September 10, 1979,
through September 13, 1979.

H.R. 12443_____ Public Law 95–412
An act to amend section 201(a), 202(c)
and 203(a) of the Immigration and Nation-

ACTS APPROVED—Continued

ality Act, as amended, and to establish a
Select Commission on Immigration and Refugee Policy.

S. 3342_____ Public Law 95–413
An act to name a lake which has been completed as part of the Papillion Creek basin
project as the "Standing Bear Lake".

S. 2507_____ Public Law 95–414
An act to authorize the Smithsonian Institution to acquire the Museum of African Art,
and for other purposes.

H.J. Res. 1088_____ Public Law 95–415
A joint resolution providing financial assistance for the city of New York.

S. 1265_____ Public Law 95–416
An act to amend chapter 21 of title 44,
United States Code, to include new provi-
sions relating to the acceptance and use of
records transferred to the custody of the
Administrator of General Services.

H.R. 12508_____ Public Law 95–417
An act to amend the Immigration and Nationality Act to facilitate the admission into
the United States of more than two adopted
children and to provide for the expeditious
naturalization of adopted children.

H.R. 8812_____ Public Law 95–418
An act to name a certain Federal building in
Jonesboro, Arkansas, the "E. C. 'Took' Gath-
ings Building".

H.J. Res. 1007_____ Public Law 95–419
A joint resolution authorizing and requesting
the President to proclaim the 7-day period
beginning on May 4, 1979, as "Asian/Pacific
American Heritage Week".

H.R. 13745_____ Public Law 95–420
Sikes Act Amendments of 1978.

S. 3040_____ Public Law 95–421
Amtrak Improvement Act of 1978.

H.R. 11291_____ Public Law 95–422
An act to authorize appropriations for the
Federal Fire Prevention and Control Act of
1974, and to change the name of the National Fire Prevention and Control Administration to the United States Fire Administration.

ACTS APPROVED—Continued

Approved October 5—Continued

H.R. 8449_____ Private Law 95–58
An act for the relief of Lourdes Marie
Hudson.

Approved October 6, 1978

H.R. 1920_____ Public Law 95–423
An act to amend section 5064 of the Internal
Revenue Code of 1954 to provide for refund
of tax on distilled spirits, wines, rectified
products, and beer lost or rendered un-
marketable due to fire, flood, casualty, or
other disaster, or to breakage, destruction,
or other damage (excluding theft) resulting
from vandalism or malicious mischief while
held for sale.

ACTS APPROVED—Continued

Approved October 6—Continued

H.R. 12222_____ Public Law 95–424
International Development and Food Assistance Act of 1978.

H.R. 11567_____ Public Law 95–425
An act to amend the Securities Exchange
Act of 1934 to authorize appropriations for
the Securities and Exchange Commission for
fiscal years 1979 and 1980, and for other
purposes.

H.R. 9071_____ Private Law 95–59
An act to confer jurisdiction upon the United
States Court of Claims to hear, determine,
and render judgment upon the claim of John
T. Knight.

Elkins, West Virginia

Remarks on the Occasion of the 42d Annual Mountain State Forest Festival.
October 7, 1978

I might say first of all it is not a coincidence that five Presidents have been here to the Mountain State Forest Festival. Not only is this a great part of the Nation and a wonderful and enjoyable thing for us to do, but when Harley Staggers and Jennings Randolph *suggest* to the President—*[laughter]*—that he attend the festival in Jennings Randolph's hometown, Harley Staggers' district, it's quite an inappropriate thing to turn them down in the invitation. *[Laughter]*

I'm also thankful that one of the greatest majority leaders of all time, Bob Byrd, was willing to let me off 3 or 4 hours this afternoon to come. *[Laughter]* I doubt that he would have given me an excuse to go anywhere else in this last week of the 95th Congress.

It is great to be with my friends—with Queen Sylvia, who I hope will visit me in the Oval Office before too long; Governor Jay Rockefeller, one of the great Governors of our country, helpful to me in many important issues, particularly important to your State; Senator Randolph; Congressman Staggers; Mayor Martin; members of the victorious Elkins High Tigers. *[Applause]* I don't know what to say about the Tigers getting a louder applause than the President, but—*[laughter]*——

It's good to be with you. In spite of the light shower, this is a beautiful fall day. And I can't think of a more beautiful place in the United States to be than right here with you.

I'm especially glad to participate in the Mountain State Forest Festival and to help salute West Virginia's forest industry, your unique heritage, and your great and unexcelled future. I'm here to reaffirm that commitment to your future, to the development of the natural resources and the rich human resources of West Virginia. I want the Government that I lead to be the kind of government that will simply let the greatness of the American people be realized.

I feel at home here. I grew up near a town about one-tenth as large as Elkins and not too far from a county seat of Americus, Georgia, about exactly the same size as yours, a town where people also depended on the land for a living.

We learned how to work, and my people still work, like yours. We had a good life, and we still have a good life, like yours.

We take care of each other. We share the pleasures of a country life. We want our children to have opportunities even that we did not enjoy. And we want to be sure that future generations can see a nation that's strong and free, proud, decent, honest.

We want our young people to grow up and stay in the community and have sound reasons for doing so. We want jobs for them that are secure, exciting, fulfilling, and that use the talent that God has given each one of us.

That's why when I first came to Washington as President, about 20 months ago, I was determined that the Federal Government would take certain stances, would help rural development, help to overcome the problems that we share, and make sure that there's a full partnership between Washington and the rest of the country.

It's been a pleasure to work with these men on the stage with me, with Governor Rockefeller and with Jennings Randolph and with Harley Staggers and with Bob Byrd and with others in the West Virginia congressional delegation. We are working to make sure that West Virginia's great potential is realized.

It's been a special privilege for me to admire for many years, to know and to grow to understand and to appreciate your senior Senator, Jennings Randolph. I work with him every day. No State has a more strong, vigorous, able, experienced, dedicated spokesman for the things that make our Nation great and strong. Nearly everywhere you look in the United States—in Georgia, in Hawaii, in Alaska, California, New England, and of course, here in West Virginia, you can see something that Jennings Randolph has done for common, ordinary, average, good, working American people.

He deserves credit for some of the most far-reaching and exciting ideas that any United States Senator has ever had. More than 20 years ago, he sat down with a roadmap of the United States and drew on that map the lines that presently comprise the Interstate Highway System of our Nation. He had the dream many years before the Congress finally took action. And all of us benefit from it.

He is the prime spokesman for the programs that have made the disadvantaged, the unemployed, and the handicapped people of our country enjoy a good life. He's been a strong and stalwart leader and protector of the integrity and the reputation, the respect, and the well-being of American veterans.

Like my own mother, one of the youngest people on Earth, his youth and his vigor have been used to help those who are just getting started in life, or perhaps have tried to get started and haven't been able. It's not an accident that he was the man, long before the Congress ever took action, long before the Constitution of the United States was ever amended, that thought it was right for 18-year-old American citizens to have a vote. If they were able to fight and die, they ought to have a vote. And it was Jennings Randolph who made this possible for our whole country.

He deserves credit for preparing for changing times. He's always had a vision to look to the future, and he's also had the experience and the competence and the respect of his fellow Senators to let his dreams come true for all of us. He's helped us get through Congress steps to evolve a national energy policy, and I wish we had listened to him 20 years ago when he first began to talk of this great need.

We have a lot to be thankful for. One of those is that he is a personal, good friend. Mike Mansfield, who was the majority leader of the Senate after Lyndon Johnson, before your own Bob Byrd, said that no human being who has ever served in the Congress of the United States touched more people in a beneficial way than Jennings Randolph. And I don't believe you could pay a higher compliment to a man than that.

I'd also like to say a word, if you have no objection, about Harley Staggers. Not many districts can claim a more effective and hard-working Congressman. He's keeping our transportation system strong. And I think that many who know and depend upon a sound railroad system realize that every now and then, you hear about a Staggers amendment for transportation, a Staggers amendment for better health, a Staggers amendment for better energy programs, and he's the author of those great changes that the Congress adopts.

He's improved our railroad system more than any other person in the Congress. He's been a key man in the energy program. This year, it's no accident that when the Speaker appointed a committee to evolve our national energy policy—this was last year—that one of the chairmen there—there were three men who did the work—Harley Staggers was in the leadership role. He's made sure that we have a future for synthetic fuels, that we use coal to the best advantage, and that we locate these new and exciting plants where you all know the coal is, in West Virginia. And I think our new energy policy is going to depend on you much more than it has in the past because of him. Well, he's been a great credit to you and a great help to me.

I think you can count on me to continue to work with these men and others to see that the Federal Government serves your needs—determined by the people here, not in Washington. Too often in the past, Washington simply wrote checks for projects they decided over there in some obscure bureaucracy that people like you needed. Too often, regulations which were written in Washington prevented the American people from doing a good job and prevented government from being effective. We're trying to do something about those programs.

This past week, my White House staff met with Jay Rockefeller, local officials from around your State, to decide what Federal, State, and local people could do together for West Virginia. We let you make the decisions. They looked at dozens of programs. Most of them identified small problems that had been an obstacle—applications sit around too long, regulations are too complicated. And they evolved, before they left Charleston this week, over $200 million worth of projects for housing, economic development, more jobs. Here in your State, these meetings help you to help yourselves. The first Federal grant will be $4.7 million to the State of West Virginia, to be used as a revolving loan to help keep 20,000 threatened jobs.

The first use of this fund will be not too far from here, in Morgantown, by keeping safe 800 jobs in that city's largest factory. The second grant will be $14 million, matched by $67 million in local funds and other sources, to help build and to renovate the downtown shopping area and the civic center of Charleston. It complements and adds on to a $5 million EDA grant that I announced the last time I was in your State.

This is the kind of initiative that the Federal Government is carrying out to not only let you solve your problems, let you have a better life, but which prevents the deterioration of the downtown urban centers that quite often has been caused in the past.

Well, I won't go on and on naming things that we are trying to do, but I would like to say that we are trying to do the best we can with a partnership that's important—not just one man, not just a powerful Senator, not just an influential congressional leader, not just a President, but all of us as a team.

We got started less than 2 years ago. We faced 8-percent unemployment, much higher in some parts of your State. We faced serious inflation, which has been with us now for 10 years. We faced an energy crisis with no energy policy. We had record high Federal budget deficits, a $66 billion deficit. When I was running for President in 1976, Government spending, Government bureaucracy were out of control. The people were fed up with waste and mismanagement. But working with Senators Byrd and Randolph, Congressman Staggers, and others, we've been able to do something already about these problems.

We've cut unemployment in our whole Nation by one-fourth, down to 6 percent, with over 6½ million net new jobs. We're facing up to inflation now. We look upon it as our number one domestic problem.

We want to stop the outrageous increase in hospital costs. We're getting control of runaway government. We've reformed our civil service system. We've cut down already the Federal deficit by $28 billion, from $66 billion the first year, to this coming year, just begun, of $38 billion. It's on the way down.

We are cutting back paperwork, eliminating unnecessary regulations, stopping government interference in the private lives of American people. We've tried to keep pace with changing times by keeping our Nation strong militarily, economically, and politically.

We've strengthened our Armed Forces. We've kept our alliances with our friends intact. We've got a foreign policy based on peace and on human rights that we can be proud of. We've been working hard not only at Camp David but throughout the world to ensure that we can continue our record, because since I've been in office, thank God, not a single American soldier has shed blood in a foreign land.

And finally, let me say that we've done all this because of, not in spite of, the people of this country, by keeping open our system of government, letting you participate, letting you know what's going on.

Sometimes you see our mistakes and you see the confusion when a new idea is debated and evolved in government. But by working for a government as good as you are, as kind as you are, as competent as are the people of West Virginia, we hope to reach the heights of which we are capable.

We have still a lot to do together. We cannot rest because we've had some successes already. But we can at least be confident that we are facing the future honestly, and we are working for solutions for the good of all.

If I can tap the strength and the courage, the ability, the dedication, the patriotism of the people of West Virginia and others like you in our country, we'll have an even greater nation than we have already. And as you well know, we still live in the greatest nation on Earth.

Thank you very much.

NOTE: The President spoke at 1:43 p.m. at Elkins High School Wimers Field. Following his remarks, he rode in the festival parade and then returned to Camp David, Md.

Federal Civilian and Military Pay Increases
Executive Order 12087.   October 7, 1978

ADJUSTMENTS OF CERTAIN RATES OF PAY
AND ALLOWANCES

By the authority vested in me as President by the Constitution and the laws of the United States of America, it is hereby ordered as follows:

1–1. *Adjusted Rates of Pay and Allowances.*

1–101. *Statutory Pay Systems.* Pursuant to the provisions of subchapter I of Chapter 53 of Title 5 of the United States Code, the rates of basic pay and salaries are adjusted, as set forth at the schedules attached hereto and made a part hereof, for the following statutory pay systems:

(a) The General Schedule (5 U.S.C. 5332(a)) at Schedule 1;

(b) the schedules for the Foreign Service (22 U.S.C. 867 and 870(a)) at Schedule 2; and

(c) the schedules for the Department of Medicine and Surgery, Veterans Administration (38 U.S.C. 4107) at Schedule 3.

1–102. *Pay and Allowances for Members of the Uniformed Services.* Pursuant to the provisions of Section 1009 of Title 37 of the United States Code, the rates of monthly basic pay (37 U.S.C. 203 (a) and (c)), the rates of basic allowances for subsistence (37 U.S.C. 402), and the rates of basic allowances for quarters (37 U.S.C. 403(a)) are adjusted, as set forth at Schedule 4 attached hereto and made a part hereof, for members of the uniformed services.

1–103. *Executive Salaries.* The Executive Salary Cost of Living Adjustment Act (Public Law 94–82, 89 Stat. 419) provides for adjustments in the rates of pay and salaries as set forth at the schedules attached hereto and made a part hereof, for the following:

(a) The Vice President (3 U.S.C. 104) and the Executive Schedule (5 U.S.C. 5312–5316) at Schedule 5;

(b) Congressional Salaries (2 U.S.C. 31) at Schedule 6; and

(c) Judicial Salaries (28 U.S.C. 5, 44

(d), 135, 173, 213, 252, 792(b) and 11 U.S.C. 68(a)), at Schedule 7.

1–2. *General Provisions*

1–201. *Effective Date.* The adjustments in rates of monthly basic pay and allowances for subsistence and quarters for members of the uniformed services shall be effective on October 1, 1978. All other adjustments of salary or pay shall be effective on the first day of the first applicable pay period beginning on or after October 1, 1978.

1–202. *Superseded Orders.* Executive Order No. 12010 of September 28, 1977 is superseded.

JIMMY CARTER

The White House,
  October 7, 1978.

[Filed with the Office of the Federal Register, 10:05 a.m., October 10, 1978]

NOTE: The pay schedules attached to the Executive order are printed in the FEDERAL REGISTER of October 11, 1978.

Democratic National Committee

Remarks in Conjunction With the Committee's "Get Out the Vote" Campaign. October 10, 1978

Good morning, everybody. I've come here to join forces with Senator Wendell Ford, who's the chairman of the Senate reelection committee, with Jim Corman, who's the chairman of the same committee in the House, and with Chairman John White, who heads the Democratic National Party.

One of the most important things that we can do as Americans is to encourage people to participate in our government processes. But during the last 20 years, there's been an alarming and an unprecedented reduction in the inclination of American people to participate in their own government processes. They've stopped voting. And this is a very serious indictment of our own process of encouraging people to control their own affairs.

In 1950, two-thirds of the American people voted. In 1978, so far, two-thirds of the American people have not voted. Of all the nations on Earth who permit their citizens to vote, we are number one in nonparticipation. There is no other country that approaches the United States in citizens not participating in the choosing of their own leaders.

Our very Nation's government basis was that leaders should govern with the consent of the governed, that laws should be made by the consent of the governed. And in our country lately, the trend has been away from this commitment. There are many reasons for it. Some have been because of disillusionment evolving from the war, from Watergate. Some of the reasons have been because American citizens don't think their voice makes a difference.

My wife was in Ohio this past week, and in the last several Governors elections and in also the Presidential elections, the outcome was determined by one vote per precinct. So, every citizen's voice should and does count.

Americans realize, I believe, as a body, that the future is important. And they recognize that leaders like the President of the United States and Members of the Senate, Members of Congress, Governors, mayors, have a responsibility.

Part of my responsibility the next 4 weeks will be to encourage Americans to take part in the election process. We've organized now and will implement, beginning today, a 4 weeks' crusade among Democratic Party officials—Senator Ford, Jim Corman, John White, and others— a crusade to get people to participate.

I have asked my family members, my Cabinet members, and local and State officials throughout the country to join in this effort. During the last few days before the November vote, I'll make a personal commitment of several days to encourage people to participate in the process, as the President of our country.

We have a need to remind people, "If you don't vote, you're the loser." "If you don't vote, you are the loser"—that will be our slogan. That will be the motivation for my own effort. And I hope that we can correct one of the most serious defects in the democratic system of our Nation. I think our government will be better if our people participate in choosing our leaders and if the leaders of the government at different levels know that the people care who we are and what we do.

Our government's strength is derived directly from the people themselves, and I hope that this effort will be successful.

After I leave, Senator Ford and Congressman Corman, Chairman White will explain the details of our effort. But I would like to ask the news media, particularly, to publicize the fact that our Nation's strength does depend upon participation of people in the government process on election day and subsequent to that, and that if they don't vote, then they, the individual voters, are the losers.

Thank you very much.

NOTE: The President spoke at 9:30 a.m. at the Democratic National Committee Headquarters.

Foreign Relations Authorization Act, Fiscal Year 1979

Statement on Signing H.R. 12598 Into Law. October 10, 1978

I have signed into law H.R. 12598, the Foreign Relations Authorization Act of 1979.

H.R. 12598 authorizes fiscal year 1979 appropriations for the Department of State, the International Communication Agency (ICA), and the Board for International Broadcasting (BIB) in the aggregate amount of $1,904,992,000. In addition, the bill contains a number of provisions sought by the administration which will allow us to conduct foreign affairs better.

H.R. 12598 also permits more than 800 senior Foreign Service officers, whose pay is at $47,500, to retire voluntarily between October 1, 1978, and December 31, 1979, and compute their annuities on the basis of their highest single year's salary. This is commonly referred to as "high one" retirement authority. Currently, annuities of all civil service and other Foreign Service employees are based on the average of their highest 3 years' salaries.

This extraordinary retirement bonus—only for high-ranking Foreign Service officers paid at the statutory ceiling of $47,500—will serve as an inducement to retirement at most only 17 months earlier than they might otherwise elect under the "high three" computation formula.

I strongly oppose this provision. Enactment of a "high one" bonus for the Foreign Service introduces a new one-time retirement benefit, despite my call for a moratorium on nonessential Government retirement liberalizations. This call came during the deliberations of the new President's Commission on Pension Policy, which was established to review the Nation's retirement and disability systems, including Federal employee retirement systems.

Nevertheless, I am signing H.R. 12598 despite the "high one" retirement provision, because the bill authorizes urgently needed appropriations for State, ICA, and BIB, while also creating new tools to help these agencies carry out their foreign affairs programs. In this regard, I note that

the conference report on H.R. 12598 explains that the Senate, which did not include "high one" in its version of the bill, acceded to the House: ". . . because of the serious personnel surplus in senior Foreign Service ranks. It is not to be construed as a precedent for broadening other Government retirement inducement authorities now or in the future. Both the House International Relations Committee and the House Post Office and Civil Service Committee Chairmen have agreed that enacting this provision will not constitute a precedent for other U.S. Government personnel systems."

In approving H.R. 12598, I am taking in good faith the conferees' assurances that the bill's "high one" retirement authority will not serve as a precedent for other Government retirement programs.

NOTE: As enacted, H.R. 12598 is Public Law 95–426, approved October 7.

Departments of State, Justice, and Commerce, the Judiciary, and Related Agencies Appropriation Act, 1979

Statement on Signing H.R. 12934 Into Law. October 10, 1978

Today I have signed H.R. 12934, which makes appropriations for the Departments of State, Justice, and Commerce, the judiciary, and related agencies.

Although I have signed this appropriation bill, I strongly oppose a provision which compromises this Government's ability to fulfill its legally binding financial obligations to the United Nations and its specialized agencies. The Congress has enacted unacceptable prohibitory language in reducing the appropriation for

"Contributions to International Organizations" by declaring that no part of the appropriation "may be made available for furnishing of technical assistance by the United Nations or any of its specialized agencies." If allowed to stand, this action would cause the United States to violate its treaty obligations to support the organizations of the United Nations system. Withholding of, or assigning conditions to, U.S. contributions to assessed budgets of these organizations would make it virtually impossible for these organizations to accept such contributions, would seriously impair their financial and political viability, and is contrary to the policy of collective financial responsibility continuously advocated by this Government since establishment of the United Nations system.

This precedent would also weaken the ability of organizations of the United Nations to withstand efforts by other governments to impede their effective work. The United States has consistently opposed the Soviet Union's withholding of its assessed contributions to those programs of the United Nations which the Soviet Union has found politically unpalatable. Our efforts to stem such politicization of organizations of the United Nations would be severely weakened if the action of the Congress is allowed to stand.

Accordingly, I intend to recommend promptly to the Congress the restoration of funds for this appropriation and the elimination of the language which jeopardizes our ability to support these international organizations. It will be important that the Congress respond positively to my recommendation so this Government can meet its clear obligations under the United Nations Charter and related treaties.

NOTE: As enacted, H.R. 12934 is Public Law 95–431, approved October 10.

Federal Employees Part-Time Career Employment Act of 1978
Statement on Signing H.R. 10126 Into Law.
October 10, 1978

I have today signed the Federal Employees Part-Time Career Employment Act of 1978, an important legislative contribution to the broad effort to make the Federal Government more effective and manageable.

This act will facilitate part-time Federal employment. It will help us tap the energies and talents of people who, for various reasons, are unable to work full time—older people, the handicapped, students, women, especially those with family responsibilities, and others.

Along with the recently enacted "flexitime" bill, this legislation will provide more flexible—and more productive—working arrangements for Federal employees.

I congratulate Senators Gaylord Nelson and Thomas Eagleton and Representatives Patricia Schroeder and Yvonne B. Burke for their leadership on this bill. And I thank Chairmen Abraham Ribicoff and Robert Nix for their support.

This legislation puts the congressional stamp of approval on an effort to which my administration has been strongly committed.

Last September, I directed Federal agencies to open up opportunities for men and women seeking part-time employment. This effort, coordinated by the Civil Service Commission, has led to a shift toward part-time jobs. It has also confirmed the experience of private industry that expanded part-time employment can improve productivity and the quality of working life.

These efforts will continue under the Federal Employees Part-Time Career Employment Act of 1978.

NOTE: As enacted, H.R. 10126 is Public Law 95–437, approved October 10.

Bill Authorizing the Susan B. Anthony Dollar Coin

Statement on Signing S. 3036 Into Law. October 10, 1978

I have signed into law S. 3036, the Susan B. Anthony Dollar Coin Act of 1978. This act authorizes the Secretary of the Treasury to replace the current dollar coin with the "Anthony dollar," a smaller, more easily handled coin. I am confident this act—and the new dollar—will substantially improve our coinage system as well as cutting Government coin production costs.

I am particularly pleased that the new dollar coin will—for the first time in history—bear the image of a great American woman. The life of Susan B. Anthony exemplifies the ideals for which our country stands. The "Anthony dollar" will symbolize for all American women the achievement of their unalienable right to vote. It will be a constant reminder of the continuing struggle for the equality of all Americans.

NOTE: As enacted, S. 3036 is Public Law 95–447, approved October 10.

Vietnam Era Veterans

Message to the Congress.   October 10, 1978

To the Congress of the United States:

I am submitting this Message to report on the progress of Veterans of the Viet-

nam-era, and to describe the actions I will take to respond to the special problems a number of these Veterans still face.

Veterans of World War I, World War II and Korea have received the recognition and gratitude they deserve. They are honored and remembered as men and women who served their country. This has not always been the case for those who served during the War in Vietnam. In many ways, their service was more painful than in other eras: the selection process was often arbitrary; the war was long and brutal; the changes in warfare and innovations in medicine meant that fewer soldiers were killed than in other wars, but a far greater percentage survived with disabling injuries.

Because the war did not have the full backing of the American public, neither did those who fought in Vietnam. Many civilians came to confuse their view of the war with their view of those who were called upon to fight it. They confused the war with the warrior. Yet I know that all Americans join me in stating that the courage and patriotism of those who served in Vietnam have earned them full measure of honor and respect.

It is a tribute to the caliber of those who served that most Vietnam-era Veterans have already adjusted very successfully to civilian life. Still, in many ways, the effects of the war in Vietnam linger on. We have only begun to understand the full impact of the conflict. As part of healing its wounds, we have recognized our obligation to forget many harsh words and rash acts, and to forgive those who resisted the war. Of even greater importance is our determination to recognize those who did serve and to show our appreciation for the sacrifices they made.

I have directed the Secretary of Defense to honor the memory of all those who fought and died as well as those who are missing in action in Southeast Asia in ceremonies this fall at Arlington Cemetery.

As for those who did return, our review has found their personal and family median incomes are substantially higher than similar-aged non-Veterans, and their unemployment rates have been lowered. For the third quarter of 1978, Vietnam-era Veterans aged 20–34 had a 4.7% unemployment rate as compared to a 6.7% rate for the third quarter of 1977. Although rates vary from month to month, it is fair to say that most Vietnam-era Veterans have moved into the mainstream of economic life. Vietnam-era Veterans are making comparable or better use of their Veteran benefits than Veterans of previous wars. To date, nearly 65% have utilized their GI Bill benefits, which is far greater than under the World War II or Korean programs. We should not fail to recognize the hard work and determination that typify most Vietnam-era Veterans who have been successful in their military to civilian transition.

But for many Veterans—especially minority and disadvantaged Veterans—the transition to civilian life has led to unemployment, poverty and frustrations. The key to making our Veterans' programs successful—and efficient—is to target them carefully on those who continue to need help. By using our resources more skillfully and coordinating our efforts more closely, we can aid those ex-servicemen and women who are most in need of government assistance.

In my written State of the Union message to you last January, I indicated that my Administration would undertake a government-wide review of the status of the Vietnam-era Veteran and the programs designed to serve them. Since that time, the Veterans Administration, the Department of Labor, the Department of Defense, the Department of Justice, the Department of Health, Education, and Welfare, the Community Services Administration, the Council of Economic Advisors, the Office of Management and Budget, and the Domestic Policy Staff have reviewed the status of these ex-servicemen and women and have prepared recommendations for improved government performance. On the basis of that policy review, I have ordered improvements in four areas of Veterans affairs:

• EMPLOYMENT OPPORTUNITIES
• EDUCATIONAL OPPORTUNITIES
• OTHER VETERANS SERVICES AND BENEFITS
• MILITARY STATUS

In order to implement my decisions in these areas and improve delivery of services to veterans, I have established an interagency Veterans Federal Coordinating Committee, composed of representatives of eight agencies, operating under the direction of the Executive Office of the President.

I am also conferring upon the Veterans Administration the status of a Cabinet Agency, for the purpose of attending Cabinet meetings. The Veterans Administration is a large and important part of our government. Its presence at Cabinet meetings will be useful for other departments with overlapping responsibilities, and for the Veterans Administration itself, which will have a stronger voice.

To better understand some of the issues that will continue to confront the Vietnam-era Veteran, I am instituting a survey of public attitudes toward those Veterans. This study will help us identify the real areas of concern, as well as accurately portray the public's overall support of Veterans' benefit programs generally.

I. Employment Opportunities

Most Vietnam-era Veterans are now doing better economically than non-veterans of the same age and background. In 1977, Vietnam-era Veterans aged 20–39 had median personal incomes of $12,680 compared to $9,820 for similar-aged non-veterans. When compared by family income, the figures are $15,040 and $12,850 respectively. For Vietnam-era Veterans aged 20–34, the unemployment rate of 7.4% for September one year ago declined to 4.9% in September, 1978. As in all other sectors, unemployment rates for Veterans are substantially lower than they were when this Administration took office. We have hired nearly 98,000 Vietnam-era Veterans in public service jobs as part of the Administration's Economic Stimulus Package. Jobs and training assistance for Veterans became a top domestic priority when the Administration took office; the results are now clearly visible.

But if the overall employment picture for Vietnam-era Veterans is encouraging, the unemployment problems of minority, disabled, and disadvantaged Vietnam-era Veterans are cause for continued concern and attention. Black Vietnam-era Veterans, a significant percentage of whom saw active combat, face unemployment rates of 11.2% for the third quarter of 1978 compared to 15.9% for the third quarter of 1977. For the more seriously disabled Veterans, the unemployment rate is estimated to range as high as 50%. We have made great strides in every area of employment since the beginning of my Administration, but these jobless rates are still far too high. There is a clear need to better coordinate employment and employment assistance programs so that they are targeted on those Veterans most in need.

With that in mind, I have ordered a comprehensive review of the overall system for delivery of employment services to veterans. The review will yield further suggestions for improvement, but I have already initiated action to:

• *improve the participation of Veterans in all Comprehensive Employment and Training Act (CETA) programs.* We have designed a number of ways of making sure CETA prime sponsors take account of the special needs of Veterans. They include: inspecting grant plans and monitoring local prime sponsor systems to assure consideration of the Vietnam-era Veteran and seeking to have better Veterans representation on prime sponsor councils.

• *continue operation of a national Help Through Industry Retraining and Employment (HIRE) program at a $40 million level, and supplement it with a $90 million HIRE II program, paid for with carry-over funds from the original HIRE effort.* HIRE I is a national contract program operated through State Employment Services across the country, and through the National Alliance for Business. It hires and trains Veterans, members of Veterans' families eligible for Veterans' preference, and disadvantaged non-veteran youth for jobs in the private sector. HIRE II will decentralize sponsors to contract for and operate it in cooperation with State Employment Security agencies. HIRE II will be available exclusively for Veterans. Participants will also have access to all of the training, public employment and outreach services available through other CETA programs.

• *Secure from Congress authority to spend in Fiscal 1979 HIRE funds appropriated in 1977.* Without this extension the unobligated funds would have reverted to the Treasury.

• *continued support will be given for the special outreach programs for Veterans operated by the National Alliance for Business and selected community organizations.* One of the most important contributions government can make to Vietnam-era Veterans is to support outreach programs. They extend Veterans services to those who are unaware of the availability of assistance or intimidated by the idea of seeking it. We have extended our outreach efforts through HIRE II program and Veterans organizations. The National Alliance for Business and 13 other private programs funded by the Department of Labor must have continued backing.

• *maintain current funding levels for the Disabled Veterans Outreach Program (DVOP).* DVOP was originally funded as part of the economic stimulus package, but the program deserves to continue at its current level of $30 million. DVOP employs 2,000 disabled Veterans to help find jobs for other disabled Veterans. So far, 26,000 disabled Veterans have found work through the program and it continues to be targeted at those Veterans with the severest employment problems.

• *improve coordination between Department of Labor and Veterans Administration employment programs.* These programs will become more efficient as departmental policy links are clarified by a new high-level joint committee appointed by the Secretary of Labor and the Veterans Administrator. Money-wasting duplication of effort will be ended.

• *order all Federal agencies to make greater use of the Veterans Readjustment Appointment (VRA) authority to bring Vietnam-era Veterans, especially the disabled, into government service.* I have already submitted legislation to liberalize and extend the authority to June 30, 1980. The bill has passed both Houses of Congress and is now in conference.

II. Educational Opportunities

Vietnam-era Veterans are in the process of becoming the best educated group of Veterans in our history. Already, 65% of Vietnam-era Veterans have taken advantage of the GI Bill. That compares to a final rate of some 51% for World War II Veterans and 43% for Veterans of the Korean War. The Nation has spent nearly $25 billion on the GI Bill for Vietnam-era Veterans compared with $14 billion for those who served in World War II and $4.5 billion for Veterans of the Korean conflict.

But these readjustment assistance benefits often have not been utilized by those Vietnam-era Veterans who need them the most. Many members of minority groups and those lacking a high school diploma have not taken full advantage of the GI Bill. For them, outreach efforts must be intensified and eligibility expanded. At present, eligibility for most benefits under the GI Bill generally ends ten years after discharge. Although these provisions are more liberal than for Veterans of previous wars, we will:

—submit legislation to the Congress that would extend eligibility beyond ten years for these Veterans the Veterans Administration defines as in need or educationally disadvantaged.

—continue a VA program called "Operation Boost" designed to seek out Veterans who are unaware of the time limit that is fast approaching for many of them.

III. Other Veterans Services and Benefits

In general, Veterans benefits have been generous for Vietnam-era Veterans, but these and other benefits to which they are entitled need to be targeted better on those who really need them. Among those

benefits and services requiring improvement are ones relating to:
- Disabled Veterans
- Incarcerated Veterans
- Readjustment counselling and substance abuse treatment.

DISABLED VETERANS

Individuals with service-connected disabilities are especially in need of greater assistance from the government. That is particularly true for Vietnam-era Veterans, who suffered a 300% greater loss of lower extremities than Veterans of any other war. Altogether, 512,000 have sustained some kind of disability.

Our vocational rehabilitation programs must reflect our paramount concern for those Veterans who have service-connected disabilities. The current VA program is based on a 1943 model and requires major updating. I will submit legislation to the next Congress that will modernize and improve that program.

READJUSTMENT COUNSELING AND SUBSTANCE ABUSE TREATMENT

The frequent image of the Vietnam Veteran as unbalanced, unstable and drug-dependent is simply not borne out by available information. Most Veterans have adjusted well and the incidence of drug abuse, although greatly increased while in service, has for the most part declined to pre-Vietnam levels or lower. Nevertheless, there is evidence that suggests a significant minority of Vietnam Veterans have experienced problems of readjustment which continue even today.

Vietnam-era Veterans under age 34 have a suicide rate 23% higher than non-Veterans of the same age group. The number of hospitalized Vietnam-era Veterans identified as alcoholics or problem drinkers more than doubled from 13% in 1970 to 31% in 1977. And, although the drug abuse problem has declined, Vietnam-era Veterans account for 39% of all inpatients and 55% of all outpatients being treated by the VA for drug dependence problems.

The government is addressing these concerns, but more must be done:

—The Administration has already proposed legislation which would authorize psychological readjustment counseling to Vietnam-era Veterans and their families. The proposal is aimed at those Veterans who are not classified as mentally ill but nevertheless need some kind of counseling. I urge Congress to enact this proposal prior to adjournment.

The Administration also requested legislative authority to contract for halfway houses in the treatment of Vietnam-era Veterans with substance abuse problems. This authority, together with the activation of 20 new VA substance abuse treatment units in this coming fiscal year, should provide needed resources to treat those with continuing alcohol and drug abuse problems.

—Finally, more research needs to be done into the problems of Vietnam-era Veterans. I am directing both the Veterans Administration and the National Institute of Mental Health to initiate studies in this area. A major study contracted for by the Veterans Administration to be submitted next year should enable us to better identify the nature and extent of problems being experienced by Vietnam-era Veterans.

INCARCERATED VETERANS

Like Veterans of all wars, a certain percentage of Vietnam-era Veterans end up in prison after returning home. Available data suggest that there are about 29,000 Vietnam-era Veterans in State and Federal prisons. Many of these Veterans received discharges which entitle them to VA benefits. Unfortunately, we lack comprehensive information about imprisoned Veterans.

I have directed the Law Enforcement Assistance Administration (LEAA) to compile accurate data about incarcerated Veterans. I have also asked the LEAA and the Bureau of Prisons to develop an information dissemination program for criminal justice system officials aimed at informing Veterans of the benefits available to them.

IV. MILITARY STATUS

Ninety-seven percent of all Vietnam-era Veterans received discharges under honorable conditions after completing service. It is only fair that those few individuals with discharges under other than honorable conditions be presented with the fullest possible justification for the action taken against them. Because of the serious harm such a discharge can do to a Veteran seeking a responsible place in society, the government must assure that discharge review is readily available to insure fair and humane treatment.

In this connection the Administration will:

—grant assistance to Veterans seeking discharge review. The Department of Defense has agreed to provide indices of discharge review/correction board cases to selective regional offices of the VA.

—submit legislation to modify the provisions of PL 95–196 which automatically barred VA benefits for combat Veterans discharged because of unauthorized absences of 180 days or more.

CONCLUSION

No steps we take can undo all the damage done by the war. There is no legislation that can bring those who died back to life, nor restore arms, legs, eyes to those who lost them in service. What we can do is to acknowledge our debt to those who sacrificed so much when their country asked service of them, and to repay that debt fully, gladly, and with a deep sense of respect.

JIMMY CARTER

The White House,
    October 10, 1978.

Veterans Readjustment and Career-Conditional Appointment Program

*Memorandum From the President.
October 10, 1978*

Memorandum for the Heads of Departments and Agencies

A major goal of this Administration has been to insure that employment opportunities for Veterans are concentrated on those areas where there is the most need—Vietnam-era and disabled Veterans.

As you are aware, since 1970, Federal agencies have had the authority to appoint certain Vietnam-era Veterans—generally with less than 14 years formal education and within one year after separation from active duty—to jobs at levels up through GS–5. In turn, these appointments can be converted to career-conditional positions. Administration supported legislation now pending in House-Senate conference would further extend and liberalize this authority by allowing appointments up to GS–7 and by removing the education limitation for disabled Veterans.

In 1974, the Congress charged the Civil Service Commission with responsibility for the evaluation of this program as it is implemented by your agencies. The Commission is mandated with obtaining, on at least a semi-annual basis, reports from Federal agencies with respect to their records on these Veterans' readjustment appointments and resulting conversions to career-conditional positions.

I am concerned with the wide disparity between agencies in the utilization of Veterans readjustment and resulting career-conditional conversion appointments. While some agencies have done a commendable job others have virtually ignored the Veterans readjustment and career-conditional appointment program. Access to Federal employment can be enhanced for Vietnam-era and disabled Veterans with fuller utilization of the Veterans readjustment appointment authority outlined in 38 U.S.C. section 2014.

I have directed the Chairman of the Civil Service Commission to contact each agency with a request for a specific plan of action to include goals and timetables for the implementation of the Veterans readjustment program. I expect your full cooperation on this matter.

JIMMY CARTER

Veterans' Federal Coordinating Committee

Memorandum From the President.
October 10, 1978

Memorandum for the Secretary of Defense, the Attorney General, the Secretary of Commerce, the Secretary of Labor, the Secretary of Health, Education, and Welfare, the Administrator of Veterans Affairs, the Chairman of the Civil Service Commission, the Director of the Community Services Administration

We have recently completed an interagency policy review of Federal programs affecting Veterans of the Vietnam War era. I have sent a Message to the Congress reporting on the findings of that review as well as proposing ways the Administration can improve the delivery of services and expand available benefits where necessary, to these Veterans. While there already are generous benefits and services available for Veterans, what is required of us is better identification of the special needs of Veterans in general, and service-disabled Veterans in particular, and developing methods for improving the delivery of services to meet these needs. I have decided to establish a Veterans' Federal Coordinating Committee that will be chaired by the Assistant to the President for Domestic Affairs and Policy and the Director of the Office of Management and Budget. Specifically, the Committee is charged with:

(a) Setting appropriate goals and taking such other actions as are needed to assure the delivery of services to Veterans. It will assume the employment responsibilities previously charged to the Interagency Jobs for Veterans Advisory Committee.

(b) Fostering greater coordination and linkage of programs affecting Veterans both within the Federal Government and, where appropriate, between Federal programs and those of State and local governments.

(c) Insuring full implementation of the decisions made as part of the Policy Review Study.

I am requesting that you designate a member of your staff for the purpose of representing your department or agency on this Committee.

JIMMY CARTER

Ralph H. Metcalfe

Statement on the Death of the Representative From Illinois.   October 10, 1978

With deep regret I learned today of the death of Representative Ralph H. Metcalfe. His life was genuinely inspiring. As a famed Olympic sprinter—second only to Jesse Owens in 1936—as a strong, independent voice for the people of Chicago and most recently, as a visionary leader in the Panama Canal Treaty ratification, he was uncompromising in the pursuit of excellence.

He stood always for equity. His political energy was invested always on behalf of his constituents, and his unexpected passing deprives his community, his colleagues, and the Nation of a staunch and honest leader.

United States Arms Control and Disarmament Agency

Resignation of Paul C. Warnke as Director of the Agency and Negotiator for the Strategic Arms Limitation Talks. October 10, 1978

The President has accepted with deep regret the resignation of Paul C. Warnke as Director of the United States Arms Control and Disarmament Agency and SALT negotiator, to be effective later this month.

In accepting the resignation, the President said that Mr. Warnke's service has enhanced the security of the United States and made a lasting contribution to world peace.

His courage and competence have helped to bring the United States within sight of a new SALT agreement as well as enabling us to make solid progress in many other arms control initiatives, the President said.

Mr. Warnke's resignation, which is for personal reasons, reflects the fact that when he undertook his present assignment, he informed the President that he could remain only for a limited period of time because of personal commitments.

Mr. Warnke will accompany Secretary Vance when he goes to Moscow for SALT

talks later this month and will leave his position shortly thereafter.

Corporation for Public Broadcasting

Nomination of Howard A. White To Be a Member of the Board of Directors. October 10, 1978

The President today announced that he will nominate Howard A. White, of Brooklyn, N.Y., to be a member of the Board of Directors of the Corporation for Public Broadcasting. He would replace W. Allen Wallis, resigned.

White, 50, is senior vice president and general counsel of ITT World Communications, Inc., and executive director of its legal and regulatory administration department. He worked for the Federal Communications Commission from 1962 to 1966 as an attorney and as Assistant Chief of the Common Carrier Bureau.

Federal Election Commission

Nomination of Max L. Friedersdorf To Be a Member. October 10, 1978

The President today announced that he will nominate Max L. Friedersdorf, of Alexandria, Va., to be a member of the Federal Election Commission.

Friedersdorf was born July 7, 1929, in Grammer, Ind. He received an A.B. from Franklin College in 1952 and an M.A. from American University in 1970.

From 1952 to 1960, Friedersdorf was a reporter and editor with the Indianapolis News, Chicago Daily News, Louisville Times, and Franklin (Indiana) Evening Star. From 1961 to 1970, he was an administrative assistant and press secretary for the U.S. House of Representatives.

In 1971 Friedersdorf was Director of Congressional Relations for the Office of Economic Opportunity, and from 1971 to 1973, he served as Special Assistant to the President. He was Deputy Assistant to the President from 1973 to 1975 and Assistant to the President for Legislative Affairs from 1975 to January 1977. He is presently staff director for the United States Senate Republican Policy Committee.

THE PRESIDENT'S NEWS CONFERENCE OF OCTOBER 10, 1978

LEGISLATION IN THE 95TH CONGRESS

THE PRESIDENT. I have a brief statement to make to begin with.

As all of you know, we are approaching the end of the 95th congressional session with a great deal of work still to be done. We are searching for a fair tax bill that would be simple, equitable, progressive in nature. The Senate, after it completes its deliberations on the tax bill, will take up the full employment and balanced growth legislation, which expresses in clear legislative terms a commitment that has been longstanding in our Nation, that any American has a right to a job and this right must be balanced with stable pricing structures.

The passage of this legislation was very greatly needed, and I hope the Senate will act expeditiously on it. The House has already passed it overwhelmingly.

The most important bill left in the House is on energy. We've been working on a comprehensive energy policy for our Nation now for 18 or 20 months. The most important single element in the energy package is natural gas—a difficult, complicated, highly debated question.

In addition to that, we will have bills designed to conserve energy, to shift to coal—a more plentiful supply of energy—utility rate reform and, also, energy taxes and credits to encourage people to take actions to make their houses more efficient and their businesses more efficient and to save energy throughout the Nation.

The most important single portion of this legislation is on natural gas. Because of our excessive dependence on foreign oil, we've seen the value of the dollar decline. Large sums of American money have gone to foreign nations unnecessarily, and the excessive imports have caused at least 1 percent to be added to our inflation rate.

The vote on these bills in the House will come at the end of this week. The natural gas bill will result in a decrease by 1985 of 1.4 million barrels of imported oil per day. I believe that this vote is the most important that will be cast by the Members of the Congress during this year, and it will be a measure of the effectiveness of the Congress, of our government, and also a measure of achievement for the year. I sincerely hope that the House Members will vote affirmatively on the natural gas legislation and other packages of the energy policy for our country at the end of this week.

Mr. Cormier [Frank Cormier, Associated Press].

QUESTIONS

TAX LEGISLATION

Q. Mr. President, you mentioned taxes. Almost certainly the tax bill you get from Congress will significantly exceed your own goals. Do you think that a tax veto is inevitable?

THE PRESIDENT. Well, the goals that the tax bill will exceed—I presume you mean the amount of money that it will cost the Treasury, right?

The House bill is within the guidelines that I established for the cost to the Treasury. I think it would not be excessively inflationary. The Senate is still deliberating on the tax bill so far as I know, unless they've just recently finished it, and what they are considering would not be satisfactory in its present form. If the House and Senate conferees, the rest of this week, can get together and take the best elements of both the House bill on the one hand and the Senate bill on the other and combine them, then we can have an acceptable tax bill to present to me and which I will sign.

The bill must be simple, fair, equitable, progressive in nature, that is, putting the tax burden where people can most afford it and a substantial reduction in tax burden on our people. If it meets those requirements, then I will sign it. But at the present time, the issue is still in doubt.

Q. Would you hesitate to veto it if it doesn't meet those criteria?

THE PRESIDENT. No, I would not hesitate to veto it if it does not meet those criteria.

EGYPTIAN-ISRAELI PEACE NEGOTIATIONS; ISRAELI OCCUPIED LANDS

Q. Mr. President, are the separate peace talks that open on Thursday between Israel and Egypt linked in any way to negotiations on other Arab lands under Israeli occupation? And have you ever answered King Hussein's questions concerning the clarification on the sovereignty issues?

THE PRESIDENT. The two discussions on the Sinai, which relates to Egypt and Israel only, on the one hand, and the West Bank, Gaza Strip discussions on the other are not legally interconnected. But I think throughout the Camp David talks and in the minds of myself, Prime Minister Begin, and President Sadat, they are interrelated. We have been trying to induce the Jordanians, and to some lesser degree, so far, the Palestinians who live on the West Bank, Gaza Strip area to participate in the talks.

We hope that they will both participate, along with the Egyptians and the Israelis. There's no doubt in my mind that while the negotiating teams are in Washington, we will discuss both the Sinai questions leading to an Egyptian-Israeli peace treaty and also the questions concerning the West Bank and Gaza Strip.

I have not yet responded to the questions that King Hussein sent to me. I saw him on one of the television programs reading the questions. They're in the process of being assessed by the State Department, and I presume when they get to me——

Q. They were given to you privately, were they not?

THE PRESIDENT. No, they were not. I've not yet received them personally. But I do know basically what's in them. It's important that this be done expeditiously, and I will not delay it, but it'll be several days.

ARKADY SHEVCHENKO

Q. Mr. President, what is your view of the Shevchenko defection case, in which a high-level Russian defector had his whereabouts revealed by a paid woman companion who says that the funds for her companionship came from the CIA?

THE PRESIDENT. If the figures the woman quoted were accurate, which they aren't, it would be highly inflationary—[laughter]—contrary to my policy there.

But Mr. Shevchenko, I understand, had large sums of money paid to him by the United Nations when he terminated his service there and, I understand, had other bank accounts as well. I've also heard that he's writing a book, or more than one book, and will receive in the future substantial advanced payments for that authorship.

The payments that we have made to him, the CIA, I'm not familiar with completely—I'm sure that Admiral Turner would be glad to answer that question. But they don't equal what the woman said was paid for her services or favors.

RESIGNATION OF PAUL WARNKE; SALT NEGOTIATIONS

Q. Mr. President, does Mr. Warnke's resignation have anything to do with the idea that perhaps he's not the right man to try to sell this treaty to the Senate? And second, to the SALT treaty, can you say today that you will submit a SALT agreement to the Senate for ratification, or are you still holding out the possibility that you might just do it in an executive capacity?

THE PRESIDENT. Mr. Warnke came to help us with the SALT negotiations as Director of the ACDA organization with the understanding that he would only stay for a limited period of time.

At that time, last year, we thought that we would have a SALT agreement in 1977. Several months ago he told me that for personal reasons he would still like to step down. Quite early this past summer I induced him to stay on. He will be the head of the Arms Control and Disarmament Agency until after Secretary Vance's upcoming trip to Moscow, after which he will step down. I wish he would stay on. He's a very good man, and he will be available to testify to the Congress even after he returns to private life.

I have not yet decided how to submit the agreement or the treaty to the Congress. I think it would depend upon when it was concluded, but my preference would be to submit it as a treaty.

Q. But you don't rule out the other, sir?

THE PRESIDENT. My preference is to submit it as a treaty.

RHODESIAN SITUATION

Q. Mr. President, will you see Ian Smith now that he's in the United States? And there's a second part to that question. Are you aware of any agreement Henry Kissinger made with Smith, such that the United States would give Rhodesia full diplomatic recognition and an end to sanctions in return for a trend toward majority rule?

THE PRESIDENT. I'm not familiar with that executive agreement. I do not intend to see Mr. Smith. He's had a meeting with the Members of the Congress who invited him over and also had, I think, a 2-hour meeting with Secretary Vance. There's no reason for me to meet with him.

I think that the essence of it is, what we're trying to do is to end the bloodshed in Rhodesia. We've not caused the bloodshed. We've not caused the war. But we have put forward publicly, without any secrecy about it, along with the British, to the frontline Presidents, to the patriotic front, to the Smith regime, our proposals that there be all-parties conferences where people that are in dispute can get together and talk and try to work out a means by which free and democratic elections can be held in Rhodesia, so that anyone who is qualified can run for office and let the people of Rhodesia decide what kind of government they want.

This is a proposal that Mr. Smith and his regime have not been willing to accept. But this is what we propose. If the parties in dispute prefer a different proposal and agree upon it, we would have no objection to that.

REVELATION OF CLASSIFIED INFORMATION;
SALT NEGOTIATIONS

Q. Mr. President, we are currently prosecuting a former CIA warrant officer for allegedly selling a manual on one of our spy satellites to the Soviets. Can you tell us whether or not the Soviets having that manual has in any way compromised U.S. security, and whether or not it has affected our SALT negotiations because it might make it more difficult for us to verify their strategic weapons systems?

THE PRESIDENT. I would not want to comment on that particular case. Whenever the Soviets discover any information about our classified material, it's obviously potentially damaging to our country. It has not affected our SALT negotiations. I stated publicly, I think for the first time a President has done so, down at Cape Kennedy, Cape Canaveral, two or three Sundays ago, that we did have aerial surveillance. And I think that it's important for the American people to know that in the past and present and in the future, that our aerial surveillance capability would be adequate to affirm that the agreement on SALT, those in existence and those in the future, would be adequate.

So, the revelation of any secret information or classified information is something to be avoided. It has not affected the SALT talks. Our ability to verify compliance will be adequate in the future.

VASCHENKO FAMILY

Q. Mr. President, a family of Russian Pentecostals, the Vaschenkos, are seeking asylum and are lodged in the U.S. Embassy in Moscow. They said in letters that have been smuggled out that the embassy is bringing subtle, emotional pressure to expel them into the hands of the Russians, probably at great risk. Did you direct the embassy to seek their ouster, or are you willing to give them asylum and visas?

THE PRESIDENT. They are Russian citizens, as you know, and have been in the embassy in the Soviet Union, in Moscow, the American Embassy, for months. We have provided them a place to stay. We provided them a room to live in, even though this is not a residence with normal quarters for them. I would presume that they have no reason to smuggle out correspondence to this country since they have the embassy officials' ability to transmit messages. I have not directed the embassy to discharge them from the embassy, no.

INFLATION

Q. Mr. President, the current underlying inflation rate is between 7 and 8 percent. Under your new anti-inflation program to be revealed soon, could we expect that rate to drop very much next year?

THE PRESIDENT. Well, I would hope so. I've been working on the anti-inflation package for a number of weeks, as you know, as you may know. I think that when the Congress completes its work, then I'll be able to put the final touches on the anti-inflation program and reveal it to the public and pursue it aggressively.

My best effort at this moment in dealing with inflation is to be involved in the passage or the modification of laws during these last few days of the congressional session. And this is what I've been trying to do, sometimes with private meetings with conference committees, sometimes with individual Members of Congress, on a rare occasion with a veto of a bill that I found to be unacceptable.

But I would hope and I believe that the anti-inflation proposals that I make, along with a tight constraint on budget spending by the Congress and myself, would be adequate to bring down the inflation rate next year.

EQUAL RIGHTS AMENDMENT

Q. Mr. President, when do you think the ERA amendment will be fully ratified?

THE PRESIDENT. I don't know. We've been very pleased to have the Congress extend the time for 3 years. But that's a decision on ratification for the States to make. So far, 35 States have ratified it. Three more need to do so to make 38, or a three-fourths majority. But I'm not qualified to predict when those three States might take that action. I hope without delay.

DEPARTMENT OF EDUCATION

Q. Mr. President, how high a priority do you still set on the creation of a department of education—first, at this session of Congress and, if it doesn't happen at this session, then the next one?

THE PRESIDENT. I have advocated and have worked hard this year for the establishment of an independent department of education. I don't think that education in our country has gotten an adequate hearing in my own administration or previous ones, because it has been a part of HEW, with health and welfare the dominant portions of that Department.

I think at this point, it's unlikely that the bill will pass this year. The Senate did pass the bill. The House was not able or willing to take it up. But I still have it as an important goal of mine to establish this department.

I think it's important that a more efficient delivery of educational opportunity to children in our country be achieved. I think the primary control of the schools, obviously, ought to be at the local and State level, but I think it'll make it more effective.

Q. In that connection, does it trouble you that the Congress appears to be wanting to drop Headstart from that department?

THE PRESIDENT. I think that issue has already been resolved. We don't want to do anything to weaken Headstart, and I believe it's been a belief on the part of those who've managed Headstart in the past that it ought not to be part of the education department. And when I was a young man, just home from the Navy, I headed up the Headstart program in Georgia the first year, believe in it, and want to strengthen it, not weaken it. But I don't believe that it's likely that Headstart will be a part of the new department of education.

EGYPTIAN-ISRAELI PEACE NEGOTIATIONS

Q. Mr. President, to follow up Helen's [Helen Thomas, United Press International] opening question on the Middle East, you said there was no doubt that the subject of the West Bank would come up in the talks as well as that of Sinai. One of the Egyptian delegates has indicated that the Egyptians might be unwilling to sign a peace treaty without evidence of Israeli flexibility on the future question of settlements on the West Bank. Have the Israelis given any indication yet—for example, have they yet responded in this question of the exchange of letters and come around to the U.S. position on the future settlements in the West Bank?

THE PRESIDENT. I don't believe that your opinion accurately expresses what President Sadat has told me. I don't think he would let any single element of the West Bank, Gaza Strip settlement prevent a conclusion of a treaty between Egypt and Israel.

And I think the Israelis have been very forthcoming, in my experience with them at Camp David over long days of negotiation, concerning the West Bank and Gaza Strip. I think they're acting in good faith to set up an autonomous governing entity in the West Bank, Gaza Strip, to withdraw their military government very expeditiously. And I think the settlements issue still remains open, but it's subject to a negotiation.

And last time I had a press conference, I read the statement that Foreign Minister Dayan made in Israel—which I think is adequate—combined with a cessation of settlement activity altogether, between now and the time the self-government is set up.

The role of our Government—our position has always been that the settlements in occupied territory are illegal and are an obstacle to peace. I've not changed my opinion. But to summarize, I don't believe that this one issue, if unresolved expeditiously, would prevent the peace treaty between Israel and Egypt.

IRAN

Q. Mr. President, I'd like to ask you about Iran. How do we view the situation involving the Shah there now? Is he secure? How important is it to U.S. interests that the Shah remain in power? And what, if anything, can the United States Government do to keep him in power?

THE PRESIDENT. The strategic importance to our country, I think to the entire Western World, of a good relationship with a strong and independent Iran is crucial. We have historic friendships with Iran. I think they are a great stabilizing force in their part of the world. They are a very important trade partner. They've acted very responsibly.

My own belief is that the Shah has moved aggressively to establish democratic principles in Iran and to have a progressive attitude towards social questions, social problems. This has been the source of much of the opposition to him in Iran.

We have no inclination to try to decide the internal affairs of Iran. My own hopes have been that there could be peace there, an end to bloodshed, and an orderly transformation into more progressive social arrangements and, also, increased democratization of the government itself, which I believe the Shah also espouses. He may not be moving fast enough for some; he may be moving too fast for others. I don't want to get involved in that specifics.

PRESIDENT'S POPULARITY IN WESTERN STATES

Q. Mr. President, could I just ask you a political question? You've been making a rapid rise in the polls lately, but some Democrats out in the West don't seem to believe that. Governor Lamm said something to the effect that you're about as popular in the West as Sherman in Georgia—[*laughter*]—and he said he was not even sure you would feel welcome there, was not sure it would be of benefit to Democrats out there even if you came out to campaign for them. I was just wondering, sir, how do you think that situation has developed?

THE PRESIDENT. I don't think my popularity with Governor Lamm has fluctuated very much since I've been in office. It's always been about the same as you've just described. [*Laughter*] But I've been to Colorado to campaign in his presence and, also, for Senator Haskell and the congressional delegation, and was well received there.

I think it's accurate to say that most of the Western Governors and, I think, most of the Members of the Congress from the West have been strongly supportive of the basic positions that I've taken on issues that were highly controversial. And I feel at ease and I feel very welcomed when I go there.

Obviously, public opinion polls go up and down. They went up substantially at the end of the Camp David agreement; I think it's inevitable that they'll go down somewhat. But I can't modify my own positions on issues or my basic commitments to the American people on the basis of public opinion polls. And if I happen to be unpopular with a particular Governor or a group of people, I'll just have to accept that and do the best I can.

TAX LEGISLATION

Q. Mr. President, I know you've answered one tax question, but what do you think of the $142 billion, 5-year tax cut bill passed by the Senate? Do you think there are enough safeguards in it against inflation? And what do you think of the concept of passing annual tax cuts so far for as long as 5 years ahead?

THE PRESIDENT. I'm really not qualified to answer that question, because I've not studied the actions that the Senate has taken in the last few hours. It would be very difficult to consummate as far-reaching and as controversial and as innovative a concept as that in the last few hours of a congressional session.

This is something in which the House has not been involved, and for that to be analyzed completely as to its impact on the American taxpayers in such a short time would be very difficult.

In general, I believe that the Senate-passed bill has a much greater tax reduction than I can accept and has some features in it which I cannot accept.

My hope is, as I expressed originally, that the House and the Senate conferees, over the next 2 or 3 days, can reach an agreement, extracting the most acceptable elements from the House bill, combining them with the most acceptable elements of the Senate bill, so that I can sign the final bill as passed.

If not, then there will be no tax bill this year, because I will veto it. The only option would be for the Senate and the House to come back in a special session after the election, which I would not favor personally.

If this should occur, and I hope it won't occur—a veto—then, of course, early next year tax reduction would again be at the top of the agenda so that it could be passed as soon as possible, making some provisions of it, as appropriate, even retroactive to the first of the year.

But my hope and expectation is still that the House and Senate conferees can meet and resolve the differences between them. I will be meeting tomorrow with the chairmen of the two committees from the House and Senate, and, hopefully, the three of us can agree on an acceptable package.

RHODESIAN SITUATION

Q. Mr. President, a followup on the Rhodesia question. You indicated that if an all-parties conference would take place, this would be an advantage to possibly settling the problems in Rhodesia. Would you host such a conference in the United States?

The PRESIDENT. I have no preference about where it should be held. I think it would be better, perhaps, to hold it where the parties to the conference prefer.

Two or 3 weeks ago, I instructed Secretary Vance to propose to the frontline Presidents and others that an all-parties conference be held in New York. This was not acceptable to some of them, and the idea was not carried to completion.

But the important thing is to get the members who are in dispute, who head armed forces that are killing each other in Rhodesia, Zimbabwe, and the surrounding areas, and bring them to a table to talk about the differences and try to resolve them.

I believe that this is the best approach. And, as I say, we are not wedded to a particular plan, although I think that the Anglo-American plan, so-called, has been accepted in its basic elements by all the frontline Presidents and, on occasion, major parts of it by the Smith internal group and also the patriotic front. It's a good basis for negotiation.

So, we're doing the best we can to end the bloodshed and to bring peace without any tendency to force people to come to a certain place or to force people even to accept the elements of the settlement that we think are best.

FEDERAL BUDGET

Q. Mr. President, there was a time when you spoke of a balanced Federal budget by 1981, and now the Senate is talking of that as a factor in whether or not there would be a gigantic tax cut. If and when do you ever see a balanced Federal budget, and how important is that any more as a long-range consideration?

THE PRESIDENT. I still have a balanced budget as a goal, an important goal. You have to judge very carefully how much you can reduce taxes, which takes money away from the Federal Government that it could use to balance a budget on the one hand, and how much that tax reduction would stimulate the economy to bring in additional revenues at a lower tax rate.

I've been trying to bring the Federal deficit down. As I've said many times, when I was running for President in 1976, the deficit was $66 billion. The Congress is very likely to pass a budget this year of about $38 billion deficit. So, we've cut down the deficit $28 billion already, in just 2 years. And I would hope that this trend would continue downward. The

1980 budget deficit, I hope, would be even less—you can't predict what the economic forces will be—and then the following year, I hope to get it down further.

I would certainly like to have a balanced budget, but it depends to a great degree on the strength of the economy and what tax reductions we give. By the end of this year, if things go well on the tax bill, we will have reduced taxes on the American people $25 billion. Had we not given a tax reduction, of course that would be additional revenue to help balance the budget. So, you have to balance the budget itself on one hand, how much deficit you have, against tax reductions to the people to keep jobs available and the economy growing. That's a very difficult thing to do. We are just doing the best we can. It's unpredictable what will occur.

VALUE OF THE DOLLAR

Q. Mr. President, I'd like to ask you about the future of the dollar, sir. Do you feel that the inflationary—anti-inflationary steps that you plan to take after Congress leaves, combined with making good on the pledges at Bonn which would occur if Congress acts on your energy plan, would that in sum be sufficient to turn the dollar around, or do you feel you have to do more than that in order to stem the erosion of the value of the dollar against other currencies?

THE PRESIDENT. Well, you have to do more than any two particular items. I think the most important thing the Congress can do is to pass an energy package to give us an identifiable American energy policy. I think this would restore confidence in our Government, confidence in our people—more than anything I can think of, among foreign nations who trade with us and who trade in our currency and therefore cause it sometimes to go down in an unwarranted degree.

Obviously, controlling inflation is another very major step forward that we can take to strengthen the dollar. We have done other things as well. We're trying to increase our exports to reduce our balance of trade deficit. We have sold additional amounts of gold, which is predictable policy now, and I think this helps to strengthen the dollar.

And one of the most important things that is occurring outside of our control, but modified in a beneficial way at Bonn, was to strengthen the economies of our major trading partners, notably Japan and Germany. As their economies are stronger, they can buy goods more from other countries, including ourselves.

So, I think all these factors combined would lower our trade deficit and lead to a stronger dollar.

Mr. Cormier. Thank you, Mr. President.

The President. Thank you, Frank.

note: President Carter's thirty-eighth news conference began at 4 p.m. in Room 450 of the Old Executive Office Building. It was broadcast live on radio and television.

Legal Services Corporation

Nomination of Six Members of the Board of Directors.   October 11, 1978

The President today announced six persons whom he will nominate to be members of the Board of Directors of the Legal Services Corporation for terms expiring July 13, 1981. They are:

Michael Kantor, of Pacific Palisades, Calif., an attorney, former executive director of Action for Legal Rights, and former consultant to the National Legal Aid and Defender Association;

Robert J. Kutak, an Omaha, Nebr., attorney and currently a member of this Board;

F. William McCalpin, an attorney in St. Louis, Mo., and director and president of the Missouri Legal Aid Society;

Revius O. Ortique, Jr., a New Orleans attorney, currently a member of this Board, and a member of the executive committee of the National Legal Aid and Defender Association;

Howard R. Sacks, a professor and former dean at the University of Connecticut School of Law and executive director of the National Council of Legal Clinics;

Ramona Toledo Shump, of Topeka, Kans., an interviewer for the department of human resources, Topeka WIN program (a job placement service for Aid to Dependent Children), active in community affairs.

Department of Commerce

Exchange of Letters on the Resignation of Sidney L. Harman as Under Secretary. October 11, 1978

To Sidney Harman

I accept your resignation as Under Secretary of Commerce with genuine regret.

You have made significant contributions during the early years of the Administration, especially in the areas of Quality of Working Life and Minority Economic Development.

Your design and execution of the program to revitalize the domestic shoe industry has been a significant achievement.

I wish you the best of times in your continuing life and work.

Sincerely,

Jimmy Carter

———

Dear Mr. President:

Please accept my resignation as Under Secretary of Commerce effective December 1, 1978.

I have appreciated the opportunity to serve you and your Administration and I thank you for the confidence and responsibility you placed in me through this appointment.

I believe that the programs I initiated at your instruction are now in good order and that the time is appropriate for me to move to other activity in the private sector.

I shall, of course, be available at your call for any assignment you determine will be of service to you.

Faithfully yours,

Sidney Harman

[The President, The White House, Washington, D.C. 20500]

Department of Education

Letter to the Speaker of the House of Representatives. October 11, 1978

To Speaker Tip O'Neill

The creation of a separate Department of Education is one of my priorities for the 95th Congress.

I have followed closely the progress of H.R. 14067, the Department of Education Organization Act, through the Government Operations Committee and Rules Committee. I am grateful for your help in obtaining a rule for consideration of the bill on the House floor.

Education is an important factor not only in the development of individuals but of the country as a whole. I believe that the current organizational status of Federal education programs is unacceptable in a nation where all levels of government invest substantially in education programs while getting less results in the actual performance and job prospects of our students.

The running of local school systems is the responsibility of states and local communities. I believe that a Department of Education will enable us to do a better

job of helping states and localities carry out their responsibilities. As you know, the Senate has passed the Department of Education Organization Act by a large margin. We believe that a large majority of Members of the House support H.R. 14067. I appreciate your scheduling this bill for floor action this week. I ask that you bring up the bill on Thursday and complete action that day if at all possible.

Thank you for all of your help.

With warmest personal regards,

Sincerely,

Jimmy Carter

[The Honorable Thomas P. O'Neill, Jr., Speaker of the U.S. House of Representatives, Washington, D.C. 20515]

Inspector General Act of 1978

Remarks at the Bill Signing Ceremony. October 12, 1978

The President. I have been trying to wait until Chairman Brooks arrived, but apparently he is caught in the traffic and won't be here for a few minutes. But we'll go ahead anyhow, and I hope he will come in before long. He's been one of the originators and a strong supporter of this, along with Congressman Fountain in the House and with very strong support from Senator Ribicoff and Tom Eagleton and others in the Senate.

I think it's accurate to say that the American people are fed up with the treatment of American tax money in a way that involves fraud and mismanagement and embarrassment to the Government. I consider and these Members of the House and Senate behind me consider the tax money to be a matter of public trust. We've not yet completely succeeded in rooting out the embarrassing aspects of government management—or mismanagement. This bill will go a long way toward resolving that problem.

It establishes 12 Inspectors General who will be within the agencies involved, the 12 major agencies. They will be appointed by me. They will be confirmed by the Senate. They will come under the Hatch Act to prevent any politicization of the functions. They will make their reports to the Attorney General if law violations are involved. They'll make frequent, periodic reports to the head of the agency. They'll make reports to the Congress.

When they make a report directly to the Congress, the head of the agency cannot modify that report in any way. The head of the agency can append comments.

These Inspectors General will be responsible for auditing, and they will be responsible for investigating any allegations of fraud or mismanagement.

In addition, there is a provision in the bill that protects whistleblowers. If someone comes from within the agency, meets with the Inspector General, reports something that's a violation of the law or an example of gross mismanagement or waste, the Inspector General has the authority to protect the identity of that person, if that person so requests, to make sure that there is no punishment inflicted on that person who brings attention to the public of mismanagement or fraud.

One thing that I would like to add is that this has been a very good, cooperative effort. The agencies involved have agreed that the Inspectors General should be added to their departments. I have cooperated completely with the Members of the House and Senate, and I think the men behind me—especially, as I say, Chairman Brooks, who's been the main one to negotiate with me, L. H. Fountain, and 12 others who originated the bill— deserve an awful lot of credit.

The House and Senate have worked in cooperation, too. And I particularly want to congratulate, again, Senator Eagleton and Senator Ribicoff and others.

It's very important for us to put this bill into effect as rapidly as possible, and the responsibility of mine is to choose people for Inspectors General who will be both competent and whose integrity is unquestioned.

So, I'm very grateful that we have this chance to protect the taxpayer's dollar, to root out corruption, fraud, waste, mismanagement in the most effective and enthusiastic fashion. It's with a great deal of pleasure that I sign into law House bill 8588, to establish Inspectors General in 12 departments in Federal Government.

[At this point, the President signed the bill.]

Mr. Chairman, I'm glad you arrived. I said all the good things about you before you got here.

REPRESENTATIVE BROOKS. Well, you did a beautiful job on the legislation, really, because you followed it and knew what it was about. Thank you.

THE PRESIDENT. Well, I'm very proud. Thank you very much, Lawton.

As you all know, Lawton Chiles has been one of the guiding lights in bringing about correction of some of the abuses in the general services agency and other places where fraud has been apparent. And my intention is to add at least 100 inspectors and auditors to the general services agency next year as rapidly as possible to conclude that investigation effectively.

Thank you, Lawton, for your good work.

I might say that this has been a bipartisan effort, too. Frank Horton and others here have been very helpful. Chuck Percy, thank you very much. Joe, good luck, and thank you very much.

It has been remarkable that the members of the Cabinet have cooperated as well as they have. *[Laughter]* But I think that's a tribute to the forcefulness of the Members of the House and Senate. Thank you all very much.

Would you like to say a word? Mr. Chairman, would you like to say a word?

REPRESENTATIVE BROOKS. I want to say it's a pleasure to work with you, and I must say that your delineation of what the bill will do and can do for the Government was outstanding. And I'm glad you're not in the Congress, or you'd be running the whole thing, instead of just 99 percent of it. [*Laughter*]

REPRESENTATIVE FOUNTAIN. Mr. President, I would like to say that I think this legislation, which we've been working on idea-wise for many years—we thought the Advisory Commission on Intergovernmental Relations would do a lot of it. It's done some good, but it hasn't gone this far. But I think this will fit into your reorganization plan, and the key point that you mentioned, the fact that the Inspectors General will be appointed by you and have the power of the appointment of the President, confirmed by the Senate, and the independence that he'll have to investigate and not have to ask someone, is a significant thing about this bill.

And I think it has potential for saving and preventing the expenditure of billions of dollars so you won't have to cut out all the services you might otherwise have to cut.

THE PRESIDENT. That's a good point.

I might say that the standards for inspection and auditing will be worked out by the General Accounting Office, working closely with the Office of Management and Budget. This will be implemented under the provisions of the law and, as Tom Eagleton said during the debate, by executive direction.

So, we'll move enthusiastically. And I think the harmony and the partnership being established between the executive and legislative branch of Government to root out fraud and corruption and mismanagement is a very constructive step.

SENATOR PERCY. Mr. President, I think in the absence of Chairman Ribicoff, Senator Chiles——

SENATOR CHILES. Tom, I think, had something.

SENATOR EAGLETON. Well, I'll just be brief. I thought the ceremony was going fine till Brooks arrived. [*Laughter*] I have nothing to add.

REPRESENTATIVE BROOKS. That was correct. [*Laughter*]

THE PRESIDENT. Frank Horton would like to say a word.

REPRESENTATIVE HORTON. Well, Mr. President, I want to echo everything that's already been said and thank the administration for their support of this legislation. We already have in existence Inspector Generals in several of the departments. And it was a result of legislation that we had passed in the last Congress that set up the Inspector General in HEW.

And Tom Morris, through the work that he's been doing there—HEW has already uncovered a lot of abuse. And as a result of that, I got a letter from somebody in Texas one time which was based on a report in one of the national magazines, and they wrote and said, well, all this has been discovered, all this fraud and abuse. What has the Congress done about this? And I wrote back and said we were the ones that got the Inspector General started. So, I think we'll see a lot of excellent results.

And this is certainly one of those steps in the right direction to cut down on Government expenditures.

THE PRESIDENT. I agree. Chuck, would you like to say a word?

SENATOR PERCY. I just echo what has been said. The General and I have been talking about the Office of Public Integrity in the Justice Department. We're going to try to emphasize the importance of that in legislation we're marking up today. I think we have a tremendous responsibility in government to ensure that the standards are even higher than in private life. And for that reason, I think great emphasis is being placed by Congress and the administration on this area, and I think we're going to get to the bottom of it.

THE PRESIDENT. Thank you.

Thank you very much.

NOTE: The President spoke at 9:13 a.m. in the Cabinet Room at the White House.

As enacted, H.R. 8588 is Public Law 95–452, approved October 12.

Inspector General Act of 1978

Statement on Signing H.R. 8588 Into Law.
October 12, 1978

I am pleased to be signing H.R. 8588, a bill to reorganize and consolidate audit and investigation functions and to create offices of Inspector General in 12 major domestic departments and agencies. I think it is a reflection on the importance of this legislation that the final version of the bill was approved by unanimous votes in the Senate and House.

The new offices created by the bill will consolidate existing audit and investigation resources under the direction of a single, presidentially appointed Inspector General in each agency. By combining these resources under an Inspector General, who will be directly accountable to the agency head, the Inspectors General will be of prime importance to my administration in our continuing, concerted effort to root out fraud, abuse, and waste in agency programs. Over the long term, this legislation will be of great value to this administration's commitment to improving economy, efficiency, effectiveness, and integrity in the administration of Federal programs.

I can assure the Congress that the new framework established by the bill will be put to a good and vigorous use. I intend to nominate people of the highest integrity and ability to head these offices, and I will instruct my department and agency heads to support their efforts fully.

We are pleased to have worked with the Congress in fashioning this legislation. The reorganization of audit and investigation activities complements other initiatives the administration has under way to fight fraud and abuse in Government, including the strong whistleblower protection provisions in the civil service reform bill and the aggressive investigations we have launched of alleged abuses in GSA operations and CETA job programs.

I commend Representatives Fountain and Brooks and Senators Eagleton and Ribicoff for their dedicated work in the development and refinement of this bill.

NOTE: As enacted, H.R. 8588 is Public Law 95–452, approved October 12.

Egyptian-Israeli Peace Negotiations

Remarks of the President, the Israeli Foreign Minister, and the Egyptian Defense Minister at the Opening Ceremony. October 12, 1978

THE PRESIDENT. *Distinguished Ministers, Mr. Vice President, Mr. Secretary, friends:*

For 2,000 years in the Middle East, people have cried, "Peace, peace," when there was no peace. The burden of war has lain heavily on this troubled ground. But less than 1 month ago, President Sadat of Egypt and Prime Minister Begin of

Israel created a chance for true peace. In their negotiations at Camp David, they displayed the wisdom and the courage necessary to forge a framework for peace in the Middle East.

Everyone who shares their dream of bringing division and bitterness to an end in the Middle East will join me in welcoming their representatives to Washington as they take their next vital steps toward turning that framework into a lasting structure of peace.

No one who is aware of the history of our own generation or of this century or, indeed, of the last 20 or more centuries can overlook the historic importance of this event—the moment when Egyptians and Israelis meet to begin negotiating the terms of a treaty which will define in a practical and concrete way relations of peace between them.

Our meeting today gives us a measure of what has been accomplished and what remains to be done to make peace and dignity a reality for all the people of the Middle East. We have certainly not resolved all the issues, nor removed all the risks. We have established, however, principles and procedures for resolving the negotiations ahead.

Again, we invite Jordan, the inhabitants of the West Bank and Gaza, and others who are ready to seize this opportunity to join with us in our search for peace. The alternative is drift, stalemate, continued enmity, and perhaps even another war.

The talks that begin today deal primarily with that part of the Camp David framework related to a peace between Egypt and Israel, to establish the specific terms by which Egypt will assume its full exercise of authority and sovereignty over the Sinai, under which security will be assured to both nations, both peoples, and under which the two countries will live and work together as peaceful neighbors.

This peace between these two great nations must be the foundation and the first step toward the larger, even greater, more important result which we all seek— a comprehensive and a lasting settlement between Israel and all her neighbors. A peace treaty between Egypt and Israel should be complemented by progress toward fulfillment of the provisions of the general framework agreement which was concluded at Camp David dealing with the West Bank and Gaza and the just solution of the Palestinian question in all its aspects.

In the days since Camp David, we've seen difficult but important decisions made in both Egypt and Israel, decisions which demonstrate the firm commitment of the leaders, the government, and the peoples to this great effort, decisions which demonstrate their willingness and their ability to turn the existing commitment to peace into an early reality.

With President Sadat's striking vision of the future, he's made even more clear his nation's determination to achieve peace, not only for Egyptians but for all those involved in or affected by recent conflict, a peace that answers their yearning for an end to bloodshed, an end to destruction, and assures the legitimate rights of all who have suffered or who might suffer in the future through never-ending war.

In these recent days Prime Minister Begin has displaced once again his courage and his statesmanship, his determination in dealing with the very difficult decisions which are necessary and must be taken for peace. I appreciate how hard, how difficult it has been for him to make some of the decisions and for the members of his government to join in with him. They touch the very heart of every citizen of Israel. The Knesset's decisions confirm what we in this country have always known and believed, that Israel's greatest wish is to live at peace and in good neighborly relationships with all the countries around Israel.

The United States is committed without reservation to seeing this great process through until each party to the Arab-Israeli conflict is at peace with all the others. Our own national interests are deeply involved.

The question of peace or war in the Middle East affects the well-being of every American. But beyond this, the generations-old cycle of tragedy and suffering speaks to America's moral conscience and to our deep and lasting concern for human rights and the expansion of human potential for peoples everywhere.

We will work hand in hand with all involved parties until the job is done and peace is assured.

Minister Moshe Dayan, Minister Kamal Hassan Ali, Minister Ezer Weizman, Minister Butrus Ghali, the Egyptian, Israeli, and American peoples and people throughout the world are depending on you now. Our assistance is available.

My own personal involvement is assured to you. Our hopes are with you, and our prayers.

Thank you very much.

FOREIGN MINISTER DAYAN. *Mr. President, members of the Egyptian delegation, the Israeli delegation, distinguished guests:*

Allow me to thank on behalf of the Israeli delegation the President of the United States for his hospitality and initiative in advancing the peace process in the Middle East.

Primarily, we appreciate your role in the negotiations between the Egyptians and the Israelis. It is our hope and belief that we have reached the stage in which we can finally conclude a peace treaty.

I know that we still have to overcome many obstacles, but with you and your aides' help, Mr. President, and the constructive spirit of the parties, we can accomplish peace.

Thank you very much again, and I am happy that immediately after this distinguished ceremony here, we shall go to the Blair House to our working meeting.

Above all, this is the purpose of being here.

Thank you very much.

DEFENSE MINISTER HASSAN ALI. *Mr. President, Israeli delegation, American delegation, and guests:*

Permit me at the outset to convey to you President Sadat's warm greetings and best wishes.

We are honored to present to you greetings from 40 million Egyptians. They are grateful to you, Mr. President, and to the American people for your genuine interest in peace in the Middle East. They will always remember your great contribution in Camp David to the cause of peace.

Mr. President, we are very happy to be here to continue our endeavor for peace. We are thankful to you for inviting us to conduct the negotiation in your beautiful country. Your invitation is a symbol of the American commitment to a just and lasting peace in the Middle East. It is also another affirmation of your pledge to act as a full partner in the peace process.

We attach the greatest importance to the continuation of this partnership until a comprehensive peace is achieved in our area, a comprehensive peace which ensures the fulfillment of the legitimate rights of the Palestinian people and enables them to play a constructive role in a peaceful Middle East.

Mr. President, the peace-loving people of Egypt have welcomed the outcome of the Camp David meetings. Our people hope that the two frameworks will serve as a solid foundation for a comprehensive peace to be built in good faith by all parties.

We came here with good faith and earnest hope. We also came here determined to devote all the necessary time and energy to achieve our goals. We sincerely hope that our coming negotiations will be another success to be added to the achievement of Camp David.

We should encourage other Arab parties to join with us in this great pursuit. We also hope to continue our joint effort until peace prevails throughout the area.

My colleagues and I are looking forward to a very fruitful cooperation with our good friend, Secretary Vance, and his assistants.

Thank you, Mr. President.

NOTE: The President spoke at 11:02 a.m. in the East Room at the White House. In his opening remarks, he referred to Secretary of State Cyrus R. Vance, head of the U.S. delegation to the negotiations.

Following the ceremony, the U.S., Egyptian, and Israeli delegations proceeded to Blair House for the first working session.

National Science Board

Nomination of Seven Members.
October 12, 1978

The President today announced seven persons whom he will nominate to be members of the National Science Board for terms expiring May 10, 1984. They are:

LEWIS M. BRANSCOMB, of Armonk, N.Y., vice president and chief scientist for IBM Corp., former Director of the National Bureau of Standards, and an expert in atomic physics;

EUGENE H. COTA-ROBLES, of Santa Cruz, Calif., academic vice chancellor and professor of biology at the University of California at Santa Cruz, an expert in bacteriology and microbiology;

ERNESTINE FRIEDL, of Durham, N.C., a professor of anthropology at Duke University;

WALTER E. MASSEY, of Providence, R.I., dean of the college and professor of physics at Brown University;

DAVID V. RAGONE, of Ann Arbor, Mich., dean of the College of Engineering at the University of Michigan, an expert in metallurgical engineering;

EDWIN E. SALPETER, of Ithaca, N.Y., the James Gilbert White Professor of Physical Sciences at Cornell University, an expert in astrophysics;

CHARLES P. SLICHTER, of Champaign, Ill., professor of physics and in the Center for Advanced Study, Loomis Laboratory of Physics, at the University of Illinois.

Pension Benefit Guaranty Corporation

Appointment of Three Members of the Advisory Committee.   October 12, 1978

The President today announced the appointment of three persons as members of the Advisory Committee to the Pension Benefit Guaranty Corporation for terms expiring February 19, 1981. They are:

RICHARD H. FAY, a Washington, D.C., attorney who deals with Employee Retirement Income Security Act (ERISA) and Federal taxation problems, and a former legislative assistant to several Senators and Congressmen;

DAN M. McGILL, of Bala Cynwyd, Pa., chairman of the insurance department at the University of Pennsylvania, chairman of the Pension Research Council, and chairman of the governing board of the Leonard Davis Institute of Health Economics;

JOHN F. TOMAYKO, of Bethel Park, Pa., assistant to the president of the United Steelworkers of America, where he has worked on the negotiation and development of various pension and benefits plans.

Goodloe E. Byron

Statement on the Death of the Representative From Maryland. October 12, 1978

I am saddened by the untimely death yesterday of Representative Goodloe E. Byron.

Representative Byron was unusually close to the people of his district; he was never too busy to act as their friend and advocate in their dealings with the Federal Government.

He introduced the legislation which created the Monocacy Battlefield National Park, and he further expressed his love of the outdoors by sponsorship of the legislation I signed in March which protects and preserves for all time the Appalachian Trail.

The delight of many thousands of tourists and hikers will be his best memorial.

Mrs. Carter and I extend our deepest sympathy to Representative Byron's family.

Civil Service Reform Act of 1978

Remarks at the Bill Signing Ceremony. October 13, 1978

THE PRESIDENT. I think this is a happy day for our country, and I want, first of all, to express my deep appreciation to those who are assembled around me and to many others who serve in the Congress who have made this remarkable achievement possible.

Seven months ago, we began an effort that many people predicted would end in failure, but this ceremony commemorates the courage and the ability, the dedication of the Members of the Congress to a very noble effort.

During my campaign for President, I made reorganization of the Government a top priority, and this monumental civil service reform bill takes a long step toward meeting that commitment to the American people. It's a centerpiece of our efforts, joint efforts to bring efficiency and accountability and competence to the Federal Government that will exceed what we have known in the past.

This legislation provides a fundamental and, I think, long overdue reform of the Federal bureaucracy. Ninety-five years ago, a civil service was created to put an end to the abuses brought about by the political spoils system. Today, I'm happy to sign this bill which marks the first major change in the civil service in nearly a century.

This bill changes the rules in a constructive fashion, a carefully considered fashion. It puts incentive and reward back into the Federal system. It allows Federal employees to be encouraged, transferred, or discharged for the right reasons if they cannot or will not perform. And it prevents discouraging or punishing them for the wrong reasons, for whistleblowing or for personal whim in violation of basic employee rights. This bill will make the bureaucracy more responsible. It will build in incentives. Excellence can now be rewarded.

In being fair to Federal employees, we must also and will be fair to those who pay our salaries, the American taxpayers. Our Nation was built on a system of rewards and incentives in the private sector of our lives. "You get what you pay for" is part of the American folk wisdom. Civil service reform will help taxpayers get what they have been paying for.

Promotions will no longer be automatic. From now on, promotions and pay increases will be a sign of jobs well done in the Federal Government, just as it is in every successful American private business. Employees who use imagination, initiative, and bold vision will be able to benefit in ways that they could never do before. Those who believe in government the most and who dedicate their careers to lives of public service have the greatest stake in making it work.

It's an honor for all of us to do the people's business. It's time to match this high purpose with even higher performance by the President and by all those who work with me in our Nation's service.

This is a great piece of legislation. Now all of us—elected officials, appointed officials, tenured civil servants, newcomers to public service—have to get busy and make it work.

Again, let me thank these men and women in the Congress who have made it successful and sign this measure with a great deal of pride and gratification for their superb achievement.

Thank you very much.

[At this point, the President signed the bill.]

I would like to ask a few of the Members of Congress to comment briefly. They've been great allies and partners in this effort, which was sometimes very difficult, and I believe the sensitivities of all those who have been affected by the legislation and will be in the future have been adequately addressed.

I'd like to start by calling on Mo Udall to say just a word, if you will, Mo.

REPRESENTATIVE UDALL. Thank you. Let me take my 60 seconds to congratulate everybody, but to throw up a word of caution. Remember right after the Bay of Pigs, John Kennedy couldn't find anybody who had dreamed up this great episode. *[Laughter]* And he quoted an old adage. He said that victory has a thousand fathers, but defeat is an orphan. And there are a lot of fathers and mothers of this legislation around here who deserve a lot of credit. But I think the job now,

as the President has said, is for all of us to make it work.

I was in this room 8 years ago with another President, a great reform called postal reform—*[laughter]*—you all remember that. I was one of the fathers of it. *[Laughter]* But we learned—we were going to have efficient and inexpensive postal service. And we learned that reform has consequences that you don't like sometimes, but the best reforms aren't going to work unless people make them work.

So, it's up to all of us in the Congress to give the oversight and follow through on this thing. It's up to Scotty Campbell and the people in the executive branch and the President to help make it work. It's up to all of us.

But I think we've got a good beginning here, and I have high hopes for this great reform, Mr. President.

THE PRESIDENT. Thank you, Mo.

Chairman Robert Nix.

REPRESENTATIVE NIX. Mr. President, I would just like to thank the members of the Post Office and Civil Service Committee for their dedication in helping to achieve this great result. And I particularly want to thank Mo Udall and everyone else who has been a participant in this great effort. I'm honored and pleased, and particularly so because I go out of Congress at the end of this session.

THE PRESIDENT. Everyone would agree that it would have been impossible without bipartisan support. We could not have done it had the Republican leaders not joined in in the effort to make our Government more responsible and more effective.

I'd like to ask Ed Derwinski if he would say a word.

REPRESENTATIVE DERWINSKI. Thank you, Mr. President.

We felt that this was a bipartisan cause, and we are aware of the fact that our bipartisan effort has had proper influence in the White House in many other fields. [*Laughter*] We're glad, as Republicans, to have a role in government, as small a group as we are—[*laughter*]—and we think that this reform will do a hell of a lot better than the postal reform that Mo referred to you. You were the father of that. [*Laughter*]

This is a good bill. And, Mr. President, you should know that Scotty Campbell is one hell of a lobbyist, and you ought to turn him loose on a few other troubles that you have.

THE PRESIDENT. Senator Abraham Ribicoff.

SENATOR RIBICOFF. Mr. President, you gave the country the leadership; Congress gave you the cooperation to make this possible. I want to pay tribute to the entire membership of the Governmental Affairs Committee, and the cooperation from Senator Percy, and the staffs, majority and minority staffs of the Governmental Affairs Committee, who worked so hard and effectively.

I also want to pay tribute to Mo Udall, who headed up the House conferees. I have never worked with a group of conferees so constructively and so effectively. And the difficult parts of those bills to be reconciled were made possible through the great cooperation we had from the House conferees.

THE PRESIDENT. I might point out that an integral part of the entire reform effort was a reorganization plan that was approved, of course, by the Senate committee and also by the House committee separate from Post Office and Civil Service. And that was headed up by Chairman Jack Brooks.

Jack, thank you.

REPRESENTATIVE BROOKS. Thank you. Mr. Chairman, last night, or rather this morning, at about quarter to one, we passed your reorganization bill number 4, you'll be pleased to know.

THE PRESIDENT. Good.

REPRESENTATIVE BROOKS. I want to say that for the record I did not vote—you can look at the record—I didn't vote for that lousy post office bill. I thought it was rotten then. [*Laughter*] But this is a great program, and I think that any President, if he's going to manage the vast executive branch, has got to have a civil service, a personnel system that's responsive and effective and so you can manage it.

And I think that you proposed this and Congress supported it. I think you now have the tools to have a shot at managing this vast bureaucracy in a way that'll make it work for the people and not against them.

THE PRESIDENT. Thank you very much, Mr. Chairman.

Again, in the Senate it was a very superb demonstration of bipartisan effort. And I'd like to call on Senator Chuck Percy to make a comment, who was very helpful in every way.

SENATOR PERCY. Thank you, Mr. President.

I think we know why Camp David was a success, and we know why civil service reform is a success and why you became President. It's that determination and stick-to-itiveness and setting a goal and just never flinching from it, and we're grateful for that leadership.

I was particularly gratified to work once again with Senator Ribicoff as our chairman. I think both of us had tremendous admiration for Mo Udall, who really waltzed us through that conference in beautiful style. I've never had a better feeling as we left a conference—almost as good as when we went into it. [*Laughter*]

My colleague from Illinois, Ed Derwinski, was just a tower of strength. And

Chairman Nix, we appreciate your support.

I think that probably when you get down to a couple of words, what we're trying to do in a sense is make Federal employees proud of being a part of the Federal system. And Chairman Campbell, all through this, even when I decided to try to hold hearings in Illinois, in four cities, to have it understood by 110,000 Federal employees and by our 11 million people what we were trying to accomplish, his backing and support was just—we couldn't have done it without him.

And I think, in a sense, when we left those hearings, people did understand what we were trying to accomplish. Probably no two words in the English language have had more rhetoric about them than "substantial evidence"—that is, except the border dispute on 242. [*Laughter*] But taking an example there, we found that when we were going to merit fire as well as merit hire, substantial evidence for nonperformance is well understood in administrative law, and we think we won't have the problems we've with 242.

So then, I think that people understand this law, and it can be applied, and it's going to be a giant step forward in improving the efficiency and effectiveness of the civil service.

THE PRESIDENT. Thank you, Senator.

It would be good to point out that the original draft of the legislation and every stage of its consummation was monitored and supported to a major degree, finally, I think, overwhelmingly, by those employees who are affected most directly by the legislation itself. Employees at the top civil service ranks, those who are appointed and serve relatively temporarily, those at the bottom ranks and middle ranks helped Scotty Campbell draft the original proposals and worked with the Congress throughout.

Ken Blaylock, one of the leaders of a large group, as you know, of Federal employees, did yeoman service at great political cost to himself potentially. But I think his courage and his ability to explain in definitive and clear terms to those employees who were concerned has been instrumental in the final passage of this legislation. And I'd like to ask if Ken Blaylock will say a word.

MR. CAMPBELL. This will be his second speech, Mr. President.

MR. BLAYLOCK. Mr. President, I've already spoken to the group while we were waiting earlier, but let me say this—the real emphasis now has been said many times here—there's a lot of players, everybody's intent was the same. But now we've got to make it work, and we've just opened the door. And again, the American Federation of Government Employees and AFL–CIO, who, by the way, all of you know, lent great support to our efforts, we're just proud to have played a role in the development of this piece of legislation.

And thank you, Mr. President.

THE PRESIDENT. Thank you, Ken, very much.

I think if anybody deserves to speak twice, it would be Ken.

Scotty, you haven't said anything.

MR. CAMPBELL. We started before you, Mr. President.

THE PRESIDENT. Well, I don't want to close the ceremony without recognizing Scotty Campbell. I think in every person's remarks, certainly including my own, we know who was the guiding light for this legislation. And Scotty, because of his superb professional ability and his own integrity, his deserved trust that was built up among all people toward him, made this success possible. And I want to express my own thanks to him on behalf of the American people for his leadership now and for his leadership in the future.

I think it was an awareness that Scotty would be instrumental in implementing this legislation that made many people accept it in faith. And our confidence in you, Scotty, is complete. And I believe the confidence of all those who serve the Federal Government in you has made it possible for this success to be achieved.

I want to express again my thanks to all of you for a wonderful step forward in making our Government better for the American people.

Thank you very much.

NOTE: The President spoke at 9:30 a.m. in the State Dining Room at the White House. Kenneth Blaylock is president of the American Federation of Government Employees, and Alan K. Campbell is Chairman of the United States Civil Service Commission.

As enacted, S. 2640 is Public Law 95–454, approved October 13.

Civil Service Reform Act of 1978

Statement on Signing S. 2640 Into Law. October 13, 1978

History will regard the Civil Service Reform Act of 1978 as one of the most important laws enacted by this Congress.

Congress has done an extraordinary job in shaping this landmark legislation and enacting it in just over 7 months.

The ceremony today and the legislation it honors would not have been possible without the skilled, consistent leadership of Representative Morris Udall. I am also grateful for the bipartisan efforts of Representatives Edward Derwinski, and Chairmen Robert Nix and Jack Brooks on the House side, Chairman Abraham Ribicoff and Charles Percy on the Senate side, and the superb work done by Jim McIntyre and Scotty Campbell. We all owe a debt to these men.

In March, when I sent my proposals to Congress, I said that civil service reform and reorganization would be the centerpiece of my efforts to bring efficiency and accountability to the Federal Government. It will be the key to better performance in all Federal agencies.

In August, Congress approved Reorganization Plan No. 2 of 1978, which restructured the central institutions of Federal personnel management. This Civil Service Reform Act of 1978, which I sign today, adds the muscle to that structure.

This legislation will bring fundamental improvements to the Federal personnel system.

It puts merit principles into statute and defines prohibited personnel practices.

It establishes a Senior Executive Service and bases the pay of executives and senior managers on the quality of their performance.

It provides a more sensible method for evaluating individual performance.

It gives managers more flexibility and more authority to hire, motivate, reward, and discipline employees to ensure that the public's work gets done. At the same time, it provides better protection for employees against arbitrary actions and abuses and contains safeguards against political intrusion.

The act assures that whistleblowers will be heard, and that they will be protected from reprisal.

It moves Federal labor relations from Executive order to statute and provides a new agency, the Federal Labor Relations Authority, to monitor the system.

And it provides for systematic research and development in personnel management to encourage continuing improvements of the civil service system.

We know that legislation of this kind is possible only when highly respected men and women from outside government come forward and declare their support to Congress and the Nation. In this instance, many did so, and I am grateful for their contributions.

I would particularly like to acknowledge the efforts of Stanton Williams of PPG Industries and his colleagues of the Business Roundtable; the pivotal role of Ken Blaylock of the American Federation of Government Employees, and of Tom Donahue of the AFL-CIO; David Cohen of Common Cause; and John Gardner; the former Cabinet officers and former Civil Service Commissioners; and the organizations of State and local government officials who came forward to support the legislation; and the many, many professional and academic organizations who expressed strong support.

Now this bill is law, but this is just the start of a continuing effort to improve the Federal Government's services to the people. By itself, the law will not ensure improvement in the system. It provides the tools; the will and determination must come from those who manage the Government.

Our aim is to build a new system of excellence and accountability.

I am asking every executive, every supervisor, and every Federal employee to take part in this renewal. I am expecting all members of the Cabinet and all agency heads to give continuing personal attention to the implementation of this legislation.

The changes we expect will not happen all at once. But I pledge to you today that this administration will move to implement the civil service reforms with efficiency and dispatch.

We have already called a conference of 400 line executives and managers, together with agency personnel directors, to give concrete advice on making the act work as intended. It will be held in less than 2 weeks.

This historic bill goes to the very heart of what the American people are asking for: a government and a civil service that work. That was my campaign promise to the American people, and it gives me great personal pleasure to sign the bill that keeps that promise.

NOTE: As enacted, S. 2640 is Public Law 95-454, approved October 13.

Federal Compliance With Pollution Control Standards

Executive Order 12088.   October 13, 1978

By the authority vested in me as President by the Constitution and statutes of the United States of America, including Section 22 of the Toxic Substances Control Act (15 U.S.C. 2621), Section 313 of the Federal Water Pollution Control Act, as amended (33 U.S.C. 1323), Section 1447 of the Public Health Service Act, as amended by the Safe Drinking Water Act (42 U.S.C. 300j-6), Section 118 of the Clean Air Act, as amended (42 U.S.C. 7418(b)), Section 4 of the Noise Control Act of 1972 (42 U.S.C. 4903), Section 6001 of the Solid Waste Disposal Act, as amended (42 U.S.C. 6961), and Section 301 of Title 3 of the United States Code, and to ensure Federal compliance with applicable pollution control standards, it is hereby ordered as follows:

1-1. *Applicability of Pollution Control Standards.*

1-101. The head of each Executive agency is responsible for ensuring that all necessary actions are taken for the prevention, control, and abatement of environmental pollution with respect to Federal facilities and activities under the control of the agency.

1-102. The head of each Executive agency is responsible for compliance with applicable pollution control standards, including those established pursuant to, but not limited to, the following:

(a) Toxic Substances Control Act (15 U.S.C. 2601 *et seq.*).

(b) Federal Water Pollution Control Act, as amended (33 U.S.C. 1251 *et seq.*).

(c) Public Health Service Act, as amended by the Safe Drinking Water Act (42 U.S.C. 300f *et seq.*).

(d) Clean Air Act, as amended (42 U.S.C. 7401 *et seq.*).

(e) Noise Control Act of 1972 (42 U.S.C. 4901 *et seq.*).

(f) Solid Waste Disposal Act, as amended (42 U.S.C. 6901 *et seq.*).

(g) Radiation guidance pursuant to Section 274(h) of the Atomic Energy Act of 1954, as amended (42 U.S.C. 2021(h); see also, the Radiation Protection Guidance to Federal Agencies for Diagnostic X Rays approved by the President on January 26, 1978 and published at page 4377 of the FEDERAL REGISTER on February 1, 1978).

(h) Marine Protection, Research, and Sanctuaries Act of 1972, as amended (33 U.S.C. 1401, 1402, 1411–1421, 1441–1444 and 16 U.S.C. 1431–1434).

(i) Federal Insecticide, Fungicide, and Rodenticide Act, as amended (7 U.S.C. 136 *et seq.*).

1–103. "Applicable pollution control standards" means the same substantive, procedural, and other requirements that would apply to a private person.

1–2. *Agency Coordination.*

1–201. Each Executive agency shall cooperate with the Administrator of the Environmental Protection Agency, hereinafter referred to as the Administrator, and State, interstate, and local agencies in the prevention, control, and abatement of environmental pollution.

1–202. Each Executive agency shall consult with the Administrator and with State, interstate, and local agencies concerning the best techniques and methods available for the prevention, control, and abatement of environmental pollution.

1–3. *Technical Advice and Oversight.*

1–301. The Administrator shall provide technical advice and assistance to Executive agencies in order to ensure their cost effective and timely compliance with applicable pollution control standards.

1–302. The administrator shall conduct such reviews and inspections as may be necessary to monitor compliance with applicable pollution control standards by Federal facilities and activities.

1–4. *Pollution Control Plan.*

1–401. Each Executive agency shall submit to the Director of the Office of Management and Budget, through the Administrator, an annual plan for the control of environmental pollution. The plan shall provide for any necessary improvement in the design, construction, management, operation, and maintenance of Federal facilities and activities, and shall include annual cost estimates. The Administrator shall establish guidelines for developing such plans.

1–402. In preparing its plan, each Executive agency shall ensure that the plan provides for compliance with all applicable pollution control standards.

1–403. The plan shall be submitted in accordance with any other instructions that the Director of the Office of Management and Budget may issue.

1–5. *Funding.*

1–501. The head of each Executive agency shall ensure that sufficient funds for compliance with applicable pollution control standards are requested in the agency budget.

1–502. The head of each Executive agency shall ensure that funds appropriated and apportioned for the prevention, control and abatement of environmental pollution are not used for any other purpose unless permitted by law and specifically approved by the Office of Management and Budget.

1–6. *Compliance With Pollution Controls.*

1–601. Whenever the Administrator or the appropriate State, interstate, or local agency notifies an Executive agency that it is in violation of an applicable pollution control standard (see Section 1–102 of this Order), the Executive agency shall promptly consult with the notifying agency and provide for its approval a plan to achieve and maintain compliance with the applicable pollution control standard. This plan shall incude an implementation schedule for coming into compliance as soon as practicable.

1–602. The Administrator shall make every effort to resolve conflicts regarding such violation between Executive agencies and, on request of any party, such conflicts between an Executive agency and a State, interstate, or a local agency. If the Administrator cannot resolve a conflict, the Administrator shall request the Director of the Office of Management and Budget to resolve the conflict.

1–603. The Director of the Office of Management and Budget shall consider unresolved conflicts at the request of the Administrator. The Director shall seek the Administrator's technological judgment and determination with regard to the applicability of statutes and regulations.

1–604. These conflict resolution procedures are in addition to, not in lieu of, other procedures, including sanctions, for the enforcement of applicable pollution control standards.

1–605. Except as expressly provided by a Presidential exemption under this Order, nothing in this Order, nor any action or inaction under this Order, shall be construed to revise or modify any applicable pollution control standard.

1–7. *Limitation on Exemptions.*

1–701. Exemptions from applicable pollution control standards may only be granted under statutes cited in Section 1–102(a) through 1–102(f) if the President makes the required appropriate statutory determination: that such exemption is necessary (a) in the interest of national security, or (b) in the paramount interest of the United States.

1–702. The head of an Executive agency may, from time to time, recommend to the President through the Director of the Office of Management and Budget, that an activity or facility, or uses thereof, be exempt from an applicable pollution control standard.

1–703. The Administrator shall advise the President, through the Director of the Office of Management and Budget, whether he agrees or disagrees with a recommendation for exemption and his reasons therefor.

1–704. The Director of the Office of Management and Budget must advise the President within sixty days of receipt of the Administrator's views.

1–8. *General Provisions.*

1–801. The head of each Executive agency that is responsible for the construction or operation of Federal facilities outside the United States shall ensure that such construction or operation complies with the environmental pollution control standards of general applicability in the host country or jurisdiction.

1–802. Executive Order No. 11752 of December 17, 1973, is revoked.

JIMMY CARTER

The White House,
  October 13, 1978.

[Filed with the Office of the Federal Register,
  3:40 p.m., October 13, 1978]

Federal Compliance With Pollution Control Standards

Statement on Signing Executive Order 12088. October 13, 1978

I am pleased to sign this Executive order, which will ensure that Federal facilities and Federal activities live up to the spirit and the letter of the Nation's environmental protection laws. This administration is committed to the goals of achieving and maintaining a clean environment. The Federal Government itself should be the leader in that effort, and this order will help establish that leadership.

I am confident that the Congress will support this action. Over 100 Members of the House of Representatives have written to me expressing their concern with the Federal Government's laggard efforts in the past, and Representatives Paul Rogers and Timothy Wirth deserve particular credit for their continuing attention to this problem.

From now on, all Federal facilities must comply with the same Federal, State, and local environmental standards, procedural requirements, and schedules for cleanup that apply to individual citizens and corporations. I personally will review requests for exemptions, and I will grant them only in cases where I find that national security or the paramount interest of the Nation is at stake. I have ordered that the Administrator of the Environmental Protection Agency and the Director of the Office of Management and Budget attempt to resolve any conflicts that may arise between Federal agencies and other units of government.

For the fiscal year which is now beginning, the Federal Government will spend over $484 million to correct problems at facilities that are currently in violation of pollution laws and to prevent future violations from occurring at other facilities.

Federal Compliance With Pollution Control Standards

Memorandum From the President. October 13, 1978

Memorandum for the Heads of Executive Departments and Agencies

Today, I signed Executive Order No. 12088 which sets forth the policies which are to govern compliance with environmental standards by Federal facilities.

Federal agencies shall exercise leadership in the attainment of the Nation's environmental goals. This Executive Order makes the head of each executive agency responsible for ensuring that Federal facilities are at all times designed, constructed, operated, and maintained in compliance with all Federal, State and local environmental requirements. Consistent with existing law, there will be no exemption from these requirements except in the interests of National security or in extraordinary cases where an exemption is otherwise in the paramount interest of the United States.

The FY 1979 Budget which I submitted to the Congress provided for pollution control equipment at Federal facilities that are not in compliance with Federal environmental requirements. This policy also will govern the preparation of subsequent budgets. I have asked the Director of the Office of Management and Budget, in consultation with the Administrator of the Environmental Protection Agency, to monitor the use of funds appropriated for pollution abatement at Federal facilities so that we can be sure that Federal agencies actually comply with environmental requirements in the most direct and effective manner.

I know I can count on your cooperation in this effort.

JIMMY CARTER

Power Rates Charged by the Southwestern Power Administration

Statement on Signing S. 2249 Into Law.
October 13, 1978

I am pleased to sign today S. 2249, a bill which will prohibit discrimination based on distance from the source of power in rates charged by the Southwestern Power Administration, an agency of the Department of Energy.

The main purpose of the bill is to provide for termination of a transmission service charge levied upon Associated Electric Cooperative, Inc., of Springfield, Missouri. The bill permits the Southwestern Power Administration to renegotiate all aspects of its contract with this cooperative to more correctly reflect the value of services rendered, while continuing the current practice of charging different rates for different classes of service. The transmission charge will be terminated upon completion of the new contract. Finally, S. 2249 does not prohibit the Southwestern Power Administration from recovering the transmission service charges levied prior to the effective date of the act.

Senator Eagleton, the chief sponsor of the bill, deserves credit for his hard work in developing this legislation, which will contribute to the resolution of a long-standing dispute between a Missouri elec-

tric cooperative and the Southwestern Power Administration.

NOTE: As enacted, S. 2249 is Public Law 95–456, approved October 13.

National Jogging Day, 1978
Proclamation 4605.   October 13, 1978

By the President of the United States of America

A Proclamation

Millions of Americans have come to view jogging as an enjoyable, affordable, and effective way to keep in shape.

Most medical authorities agree with them, saying that a reasonable and regular program of jogging improves the heart, the circulatory system, and the lungs, while helping runners take off, or ward off, excess weight.

Everyone who has run knows that its most important value is in removing tension and allowing a release from whatever other cares the day may bring. It is a blessing to our Nation that so many of our people have rediscovered this simple pleasure.

By Joint Resolution (H.J. Res. 685) the Congress has designated October 14, 1978, as National Jogging Day.

Now, THEREFORE, I, JIMMY CARTER, President of the United States of America, do hereby declare October 14, 1978, as National Jogging Day.

IN WITNESS WHEREOF, I have hereunto set my hand this thirteenth day of October, in the year of our Lord nineteen hundred seventy-eight and of the Independence of the United States of America the two hundred and third.

JIMMY CARTER

[Filed with the Office of the Federal Register, 5:01 p.m., October 13, 1978]

Wild and Scenic River Designation

Letter to the Speaker of the House and the President of the Senate. October 13, 1978

Dear Mr. Speaker: (Dear Mr. President:)

In accordance with the Wild and Scenic Rivers Act, I am pleased to transmit a proposal to designate a 50.4-mile segment of the Illinois River within the Siskiyou National Forest in Oregon as an element of the National Wild and Scenic Rivers System.

This recommendation is based on a careful study by the Secretary of Agriculture and reflects the involvement of a broad spectrum of concerned government and private organizations at the national, State and local levels. Designation of this segment of the Illinois River will protect its free-flowing character and preserve its outstanding scenic and recreational values. It will also complement the adjoining Rogue Wild and Scenic River.

I, therefore, strongly concur with the Secretary's recommendation to preserve the unique and irreplaceable natural values of the Illinois River through its designation as a Wild and Scenic River, and I urge speedy Congressional approval.

Sincerely,

JIMMY CARTER

NOTE: This is the text of identical letters addressed to Thomas P. O'Neill, Jr., Speaker of the House of Representatives, and Walter F. Mondale, President of the Senate.

Digest of Other White House Announcements

The following listing includes the President's daily schedule and other items of general interest as announced by the White House Press Office during the period covered by this issue. Events and announcements printed elsewhere in the issue are not included.

October 8

The President returned to the White House from Camp David, Md., to attend a concert by Leontyne Price in the East Room. He then returned to Camp David.

October 9

While at Camp David, the President discussed energy legislation with 15 Governors in a telephone conference call.

October 10

The President met at the White House with:

—Zbigniew Brzezinski, Assistant to the President for National Security Affairs;
—Frank B. Moore, Assistant to the President for Congressional Liaison;
—Senator Muriel Humphrey of Minnesota, Representative Augustus Hawkins of California, and a group of administration officials and citizens, to discuss the Humphrey-Hawkins full employment legislation;
—Foreign Minister Moshe Dayan of Israel and members of the Israeli delegation to the peace negotiations.

The President has declared a major disaster for the State of California as a result of landslides, beginning on October 2, which caused extensive public and private property damage.

October 11

The President met at the White House with:

—Senate Minority Leader Robert C. Byrd;
—Dr. Brzezinski;
—Mr. Moore;
—representatives of the American Association of Editorial Cartoonists;
—John M. Carey, national commander of the American Legion;

—Senator Adlai E. Stevenson of Illinois;

—Acting Foreign Minister Butrus Ghali and Defense Minister Kamel Hassan Ali of Egypt.

October 12

The President met at the White House with:

—Secretary of the Treasury W. Michael Blumenthal, Senator Russell B. Long of Louisiana, and Representative Al Ullman of Oregon, to discuss tax legislation;

—Dr. Brzezinski;

—Mr. Moore;

—members of the New York congressional delegation;

—Vice President Walter F. Mondale, Adm. Stansfield Turner, Director of Central Intelligence, Hamilton Jordan, Assistant to the President, and Dr. Brzezinski;

—Mrs. Carter, for lunch;

—James T. McIntyre, Jr., Director of the Office of Management and Budget;

—a group of Congressmen to discuss energy legislation.

October 13

The President met at the White House with:

—Vice President Mondale, Secretary of State Cyrus R. Vance, Secretary of Defense Harold Brown, Dr. Brzezinski, and Mr. Jordan;

—Mr. Moore;

—Senator Daniel Patrick Moynihan of New York;

—Charles L. Schultze, Chairman of the Council of Economic Advisers;

—a group of editors and news directors (transcript will be printed next week).

The President attended a portion of the annual meeting of the National Alliance of Business, Inc., in Room 450 of the Old Executive Office Building.

The President transmitted to the Congress the 1977 annual report of the National Credit Union Administration and the 7th annual Railroad Safety Report.

NOMINATIONS SUBMITTED TO THE SENATE

The following list does not include promotions of members of the Uniformed Services, nominations to the Service Academies, or nominations of Foreign Service officers.

Submitted October 7, 1978

JOHN PATRICK WHITE, of California, to be Deputy Director of the Office of Management and Budget, vice James T. McIntyre, Jr.

Submitted October 11, 1978

LEWIS MANILOW, of Illinois, to be a member of the United States Advisory Commission on International Communication, Cultural and Educational Affairs for a term of 3 years (new position).

The following-named persons to be members of the National Commission on Social Security for terms of 2 years (new positions):

JAMES J. DILLMAN, of Wisconsin.

MILTON S. GWIRTZMAN, of Massachusetts.

DAVID H. RODGERS, of Washington.

HOWARD A. WHITE, of New York, to be a member of the Board of Directors of the Corporation for Public Broadcasting for the remainder of the term expiring March 26, 1980, vice W. Allen Wallis, resigned.

The following-named persons to be members of the Board of Directors of the Legal Services Corporation for terms expiring July 13, 1981:

F. WILLIAM McCALPIN, of Missouri, vice Roger C. Cramton, term expired.

MICHAEL KANTOR, of California, vice Glee S. Smith, Jr., term expired.

ROBERT J. KUTAK, of Nebraska (reappointment).

REVIUS O. ORTIQUE, JR., of Louisiana (reappointment).

HOWARD R. SACKS, of Connecticut, vice J. Melville Broughton, Jr., term expired.

RAMONA TOLEDO SHUMP, of Kansas, vice Glenn C. Stophel, term expired.

NOMINATIONS—Continued

Submitted October 12, 1978

MAX L. FRIEDERSDORF, of Indiana, to be a member of the Federal Election Commission for a term expiring April 30, 1983, vice William L. Springer, term expired.

The following-named persons to be members of the National Science Board, National Science Foundation, for terms expiring May 10, 1984:

LEWIS M. BRANSCOMB, of New York, vice Russell D. O'Neal, term expired.

EUGENE H. COTA-ROBLES, of California, vice William H. Meckling, term expired.

ERNESTINE FRIEDL, of North Carolina, vice Wesley G. Campbell, term expired.

WALTER EUGENE MASSEY, of Rhode Island, vice T. Marshall Hahn, Jr., term expired.

DAVID V. RAGONE, of Michigan, vice Joseph M. Reynolds, term expired.

EDWIN ERNEST SALPETER, of New York, vice William A. Nierenberg, term expired.

CHARLES PENCE SLICHTER, of Illinois (reappointment).

CHECKLIST OF WHITE HOUSE PRESS RELEASES

The following releases of the Office of the White House Press Secretary, distributed during the period covered by this issue, are not included in the issue.

Released October 10, 1978

News conference: on the results of the review of Federal policies affecting Vietnam era veterans—by Vice President Walter F. Mondale, Max Cleland, Administrator of Veterans Affairs, and Ernest G. Green, Assistant Secretary of Labor for Employment and Training

Fact sheet: Vietnam era veterans

Released October 11, 1978

Fact sheet: U.S. civil space policy

Released October 12, 1978

Fact sheet: Inspector General Act of 1978

Released October 13, 1978

Fact sheet: Civil Service Reform Act of 1978

Transcript: remarks of Alan K. Campbell, Chairman of the U.S. Civil Service Commission, and other speakers participating in the bill signing ceremony for S. 2640, the Civil Service Reform Act of 1978

ACTS APPROVED BY THE PRESIDENT

Approved October 7, 1978

H.R. 12598_____ Public Law 95-426
Foreign Relations Authorization Act, Fiscal Year 1979.

H.R. 12841_____ Public Law 95-427
An act to prohibit the issuance of regulations on the taxation of fringe benefits, and for other purposes.

H.R. 10822_____ Public Law 95-428
An act to improve the operations of the national sea grant program, to authorize appropriations to carry out such program for fiscal years 1979 and 1980, and for other purposes.

Approved October 10, 1978

H.R. 12930_____ Public Law 95-429
Treasury, Postal Service, and General Government Appropriations Act, 1979.

H.R. 11005_____ Public Law 95-430
An act to provide authorization of appropriations for the United States International Trade Commission for fiscal year 1979.

H.R. 12934_____ Public Law 95-431
Departments of State, Justice, and Commerce, the Judiciary, and Related Agencies Appropriation Act, 1979.

H.R. 13349_____ Public Law 95-432
An act to repeal certain sections of title III of the Immigration and Nationality Act, and for other purposes.

H.R. 10581_____ Public Law 95-433
An act relating to judgment funds awarded by the Indian Claims Commission to certain Indian tribes, and for other purposes.

H.R. 11400_____ Public Law 95-434
National Science Foundation Authorization Act for Fiscal Year 1979.

H.R. 9214_____ Public Law 95-435
An act to amend the Bretton Woods Agreements Act to authorize the United States to participate in the Supplementary Financing Facility of the International Monetary Fund.

S. 409_____ Public Law 95-436
An act to designate the Meat Animal Research Center located near Clay Center, Nebraska, as the "Roman L. Hruska Meat Animal Research Center".

H.R. 10126_____ Public Law 95-437
Federal Employees Part-Time Career Employment Act of 1978.

ACTS APPROVED—Continued

Approved October 10—Continued

S. 425_____ Public Law 95–438
An act to authorize the President of the
United States to present on behalf of the
Congress a specially struck gold medal to
Lieutenant General Ira C. Eaker, United
States Air Force (retired).

S. 286_____ Public Law 95–439
An act to repeal certain requirements relating to notice of animal and plant quar-
antines, and for other purposes.

S. 1267_____ Public Law 95–440
An act to amend sections 3303a and 1503 of
title 44, United States Code, to require mandatory application of the General Records
Schedules to all Federal agencies and to resolve conflicts between authorizations for disposal and to provide for the disposal of Federal Register documents.

S. 2946_____ Public Law 95–441
An act to authorize the Secretary of Agriculture to relinquish exclusive legislative
jurisdiction over lands or interests under his
control.

S. 2951_____ Public Law 95–442
An act to authorize the Secretary of Agriculture to accept and administer on behalf
of the United States gifts or devises of real
and personal property for the benefit of the
Department of Agriculture or any of its
programs.

S. 3045_____ Public Law 95–443
An act to amend the Farm Credit Act of
1971 to extend the term for production credit
association loans to producers or harvesters
of aquatic products.

S. 3067_____ Public Law 95–444
Civil Rights Commission Act of 1978.

S. 3092_____ Public Law 95–445
Humane Methods of Slaughter Act of 1978.

S. 3274_____ Public Law 95–446
An act to designate the United States Department of Agriculture's Bee Research Laboratory in Tucson, Arizona, as the "Carl
Hayden Bee Research Center".

S. 3036_____ Public Law 95–447
An act to amend the Coinage Act of 1965
to change the size, weight, and design of the
one-dollar coin, and for other purposes.

ACTS APPROVED—Continued

Approved October 10—Continued

H.R. 1445_____ Private Law 95–60
An act conferring jurisdiction upon the
United States Court of Claims to hear, determine, and render judgment upon the
claim of Commander Edward White Rawl-
ins, United States Navy (retired).

Approved October 11, 1978

H.R. 13125_____ Public Law 95–448
An act making appropriations for Agricul-
ture, Rural Development, and Related
Agencies programs for the fiscal year ending
September 30, 1979, and for other purposes.

S.J. Res. 29_____ Public Law 95–449
A joint resolution to authorize the President
to issue a proclamation designating that
week in November 1978, which includes
Thanksgiving Day as "National Family
Week".

H.R. 12026_____ Public Law 95–450
Indian Peaks Wilderness Area, the Arapaho
National Recreation Area and the Oregon
Islands Wilderness Area Act.

S. 3467_____ Public Law 95–451
An act to designate the United States Department of Agriculture's Pecan Field Station in Brownwood, Texas, as the "W. R.
'Bob' Poage Pecan Field Station".

Approved October 12, 1978

H.R. 8588_____ Public Law 95–452
Inspector General Act of 1978.

H.R. 9945_____ Public Law 95–453
An act to amend the Act creating the Indian
Claims Commission to repeal the provision
limiting the activities of Commissioners during the two years following their terms of
office.

Approved October 13, 1978

S. 2640_____ Public Law 95–454
Civil Service Reform Act of 1978.

H.R. 12603_____ Public Law 95–455
An act to amend the Great Lakes Pilotage
Act of 1960 in order to relieve the restrictive
qualification standards for United States registered pilots on the Great Lakes.

S. 2249_____ Public Law 95–456
An act to prohibit discrimination in rates
charged by the Southwestern Power Administration.

H.R. 13635_____ Public Law 95–457
Department of Defense Appropriation Act,
1979.

PRESIDENTIAL DOCUMENTS

Week Ending Friday, October 20, 1978

Interview With the President

Remarks and a Question-and-Answer Session With Editors and News Directors.
October 13, 1978

THE PRESIDENT. Well, I hate to interrupt your meeting with Jody.

95TH CONGRESS

You've come at a very interesting time—the last few days, or few hours, I hope, of the 95th Congress and when a considerable amount of domestic legislation is being decided. The rapid pace of the congressional session, according to some of the oldtimers, is unexcelled in previous years. And I think that confusion abounds on the Hill, but a lot of preparatory work has been done by the subcommittees and committees. And I think that we will have a successful session.

I signed this morning one of the most far-reaching and important pieces of legislation that has been considered since I've been in office, and that's a complete reform of the civil service system, the key to better management of the entire Government structure. And I'm very grateful for the rapid movement on this complicated legislation. It's the first time in 95 years that the civil service has been changed in any appreciable degree.

The Congress will decide on the energy legislation, possibly today. The Senate has completed most of the component parts. The House has now come out of the Rules Committee with a decision, which is compatible with what they decided early last year, that the entire package would be considered as a unit. There will be a test on calling the previous question, a test on the rule, and then a vote on the entire package, whether it should be accepted or rejected. We don't know the outcome, of course, but we're working very hard on that. And I've probably made—well, I have made dozens of calls, beginning early last week, on the energy question.

Hospital cost containment, which I consider to be the most important single controlling factor on inflation in the future, has now passed the Senate. It will be considered very quickly, within the next few minutes, as a matter of fact, by the Ways and Means Committee in the House. If it should pass there—we're working very hard to get it passed—it will go through the Rules Committee, hopefully get on the calendar in the waning days of the session.

Airline deregulation, another very important anti-inflation measure, has already been proven in practice, primarily through the international decisions that have been made by the CAB, with my own encouragement, to reduce rate costs drastically for passengers and also freight, coincidentally, and with an enormous increase in the use of airlines and a remarkable increase in profits for the airline companies themselves. We hope to establish this principle in law. The bill has passed in very fine form, even better than we originally submitted it to the House and Senate. We're now waiting for a vote.

The full employment, planned growth bill, sometimes known as the Humphrey-Hawkins bill, will be voted on in the Senate, also within the next few minutes or hours.

ADMINISTRATION POLICIES

We have a lot going on in foreign affairs right now. We had our first meeting with the Israelis and Egyptians yesterday at Blair House. I had met with the key negotiating teams earlier, both the Israelis, first, and the Egyptians. We've put forward a draft treaty. The group will be using this as a basis for their negotiations. And we have an excellent negotiating team representing our country, all of whom were involved in the Camp David discussions. And I'm available, of course, at any moment, day or night, to come in and help resolve problems or insurmountable difficulties.

In the meantime, Cy Vance will leave this evening, going to South Africa. He'll be meeting with the Foreign Minister, Botha, and the new Prime Minister, Pieter Botha, P.W. Botha, and others there. He's being joined by the Foreign Ministers of Canada, Great Britain, and Germany, and by a key official in the French Government.

We hope that we can induce the South Africans to be more forthcoming in quickly resolving the Namibian question, perhaps giving us some help on the Rhode-

sian question as well. Cy will go from there to Moscow, where we will have another discussion between him and Gromyko, possibly by the President, Brezhnev, as well, on SALT.

My primary domestic concern is still to control inflation. We've had a remarkably good congressional session, I believe, the first 2 years of my own service with the Congress, in getting the budget deficit down and implementing some very stringent attitudes in the Congress that are somewhat unprecedented.

The risky vetoing of the defense authorization bill and subsequent vetoing of the public works appropriations bill, I think, have proven that I and the Congress, working together, want to eliminate unnecessary spending and set an example for the rest of the country to emulate.

Those are just a few of the things that I thought about a minute ago that I might mention to you in opening, and now I'll spend the rest of my time answering your questions.

QUESTIONS

U.S. SPACE POLICY

Q. Mr. President, I come from Cape Canaveral, where you visited 2 weeks ago. There was a big spread in the local newspapers yesterday that you were ordering cutbacks in the space program. And there are also rumors going around the Kennedy Space Center that as soon as the shuttle becomes operational, you will order even more cutbacks in an austerity program. So, my question is this: What kind of space policy can we expect from your administration, sir?

THE PRESIDENT. I think a very aggressive space policy. Anyone who reads the documents that have been prepared very carefully, very thoroughly by the Defense Department, the CIA, NSC, all those who will use them, including Agriculture,

Commerce, and finally approved by me, would say that it's a very sound program based on scientific need and actually capitalizing now upon the great exploratory efforts that have been made in space. We look upon the space shuttle as a way to change dramatic, very costly initiatives into a sound, progressive, and innovative program to utilize the technology that we have available to us.

We'll continue interplanetary space exploration. We'll have a greatly expanded effort concerning astronomy assessments of the Earth, weather, communications. We'll expand our effort to bring into the space program now both foreign countries and also private firms in our Nation. And I think it is accurate to say that the space shuttle, which is approaching completion—we hope the first orbital flights will be less than a year from now—will open up a broad vista of new uses for our technology.

So, we're not going to minimize or decrease our commitment to space at all. I think the spectacular efforts to send men to the Moon and to make the first orbital flights, and so forth, have been just a precursor to now the more practical and consistent and effective use of our space technology.

So, it's not a matter of playing down the importance of space; it's a matter of using what we've already learned in the most effective way.

THE RHODESIAN SITUATION

Q. Mr. President, you have still refused to meet with Mr. Smith from South Africa. Recently he stated that he would be willing to sit down and talk to all the guerrillas in attempts to reach some type of peace settlement. Have you changed your mind about talking to Mr. Smith?

THE PRESIDENT. No, there's no need to meet with Mr. Smith. We don't recognize the Smith regime as being legal. In fact, only one country in the world does, and that's South Africa.

Mr. Smith and Mr. Sithole came over here on a tourist visa. They've had access to the public media in an unrestricted way. They've met with congressional committees in an unrestricted way. They've had extensive discussions with Secretary Vance, both since they've been over here and previously in Rhodesia. There's no need for me to meet with them.

I was encouraged, if it's true, that Smith is now saying he's willing to meet with all the other parties involved in the dispute for an all-parties conference.

What we want is to end the bloodshed. What we want is to have democratic elections in Rhodesia with an established constitution based on democratic principles. We want anyone who desires, to run for public office, and we want the people in Rhodesia, black and white, to be able to vote on an equal, one-person-one-vote basis, to choose their own leader. This is something that we've advocated from the very beginning, and Smith so far has refused to accept all these principles.

If he is now willing to move from his previous position and meet with the other parties in dispute, the patriotic front and others, that would suit us very well. I think it's also important that I emphasize we're not trying to force an Anglo-American solution on anyone.

If the patriotic front and the so-called internal group of Smith's regime can agree on any other alternative, we are perfectly glad to support what they propose.

I think it's true that all of the frontline Presidents, the Presidents of countries surrounding Rhodesia, have endorsed the principles of the Anglo-American plan. But we're not trying to force our will on anyone.

But the matter has been thoroughly discussed, and I don't see any reason for me to meet with Mr. Smith.

SAFETY STANDARDS FOR YOUTH CAMPS

Q. Dave Ferguson, from Connecticut. Mr. President, first of all, I'd like to just say that if you or Mrs. Carter needed a place to stay on your trips up to Connecticut next week, we'd be glad to put you up. [*Laughter*]

THE PRESIDENT. Okay.

Q. Senator Ribicoff estimates that every year 100 children are killed and 200,000 are injured while attending youth camps. Many people feel that these numbers could be reduced if Federal legislation were passed that established camp safety standards and methods of enforcing these standards, and they feel that State efforts have been inadequate.

Congressmen Sarasin and McKinney recently wrote to you asking that your administration change its position and endorse passage of such a bill. Will you support passage of such an act next session? And if not, why not?

THE PRESIDENT. I don't know. I never have had this come to my attention, except just in a very tangential way. My general philosophy concerning all of government is that the best governments to administer programs of that kind are the ones that are closest to the people.

I think local governments in a county or a township area or a State government obviously would be much better qualified to administer safety regulations and safety laws concerning boating and mountain climbing and horseback riding and so forth, than would the Federal Government.

Obviously, there could be some cooperation there when requested by the local and State authorities, because part of the money in some categories does come from Federal allocations. But my inclination would be to let local and State people handle this particular safety question and let the Federal Government respond to their requests for legitimate and proper assistance.

INFLATION

Q. Mr. President, I'm from Lebanon, New Hampshire. Earlier in the day, Mr. Eizenstat said that you would soon be announcing some tough things in the fight against inflation. Could you give us any idea what those might be?

THE PRESIDENT. No, not yet. It's very difficult for me to put my final approval on an anti-inflation package until I see what the Congress action will be during these last few hours. I have a thick document that's a culmination of literally weeks of work on my desk now, with a series of options that I have thoroughly discussed with large groups around this table and smaller groups in my office.

As soon as the Congress completes its work and goes home, it won't take me but just a short while, just a few days, to make my final judgments on all those options. But they would have to be based upon the budget levels, the action on either accepting or rejecting things like hospital cost containment, my own decision concerning a tax reduction bill.

There's no way that I can do it before I see what the Congress does in its final stages. But the work has been done, basically, with that one exception.

RELATIONS WITH THE CONGRESS

Q. Mr. President, Dave Cooper, from the Akron, Ohio, Beacon Journal. Do you see now anything changed in the institutional relationship between the Presidency and Congress in light of some of the successes of the last several weeks?

THE PRESIDENT. No, I don't really believe so. I think the first year I was in office I was maybe a little overly hesitant about using my own influence and authority. I was, and still am, heavily dependent upon the leadership in the Congress to give me advice and counsel, and I've tried to work with them in an attitude of partnership and sharing of responsibility under the aegis of constitutional provisions.

I've had good luck. I believe that any objective assessment of the accomplishments of the 95th Congress will show that they deserve a great deal of credit for courage and also for hard work. I have never seen a group work harder than they have, and I've been a Governor and I've been in the legislature myself.

I've only had, I think, six vetoes since I've been in office. I think the first 20 months of President Ford's administration—Majority Leader Byrd told me the other day—I think he had something like 46 vetoes. So, I think this is a good indication of our good relationship.

I don't hesitate, though, to use the veto when I must, even though it's politically dangerous and, certainly, when the outcome is uncertain.

What I've tried to do, though, is when we propose legislation originally, to meet with the congressional leaders involved, and then as we see trends developing in the Congress, in either House or within the committee, that I think are contrary to my policies, to invite the Members of Congress here, both Democrats and Republicans, and point out my concerns and see if we can't work out an agreement before the decision by them is made.

On the nuclear aircraft carrier and on public works, I tried as hard as I could to avoid a confrontation with Congress. But I think some Members of Congress felt—in fact, some of the Democratic leaders of Congress told me on more than one occasion—that they thought that a President has no right to assess the advisability of individual public works projects. And they feel very deeply about this, because

very rarely in the history of our country has a President exerted this influence or right.

I feel an obligation to do it. So, to summarize, I think I've got a good division of my own authority versus that of Congress. I think it's completely constitutional in nature. I think we have a good mutual respect. I think the results of the Congress will prove this.

My vetoes will be rare, but I consider a veto to be a legitimate prerogative of the President, and even a duty of a President, so that there is no domination of the White House by the Congress itself, or vice versa.

MARIJUANA

Q. Mr. President, Jim Cameron, from Boston, Massachusetts. There's a question of some concern to the millions of young persons in this Nation: What will be the fate, or any changes in your attempts at marijuana law reform since the departure from your staff of one of its greatest champions, Dr. Bourne?

THE PRESIDENT. I don't think any change in policy. Peter Bourne and I were always compatible on this matter. I had favored during the campaign the State laws calling for decriminalization, with a fairly substantial fine that might be levied for possession of small quantities and a more heavy emphasis on controlling those who distribute marijuana and the more dangerous drugs. But I don't envision any change in our policy since Dr. Bourne's departure.

ARAB RESPONSE TO CAMP DAVID AGREEMENTS

Q. I'm with the Baltimore Jewish Times, and I was wondering how you felt about Saudi Arabia's lack of cooperation in the peace talks, especially in light of the arms sales and the leverage you should have gained through them.

THE PRESIDENT. I have not been disappointed with the Saudi Arabians' response to the peace talks. We obviously would like for everyone in the world to endorse the Camp David agreements without any caveats at all. But none of the Saudi Arabian leaders, nor has King Hussein, condemned the talks or rejected them or closed the door for future support and encouragement.

There are three elements that any Arab leader cannot, in good conscience, endorse or avoid. One is the matter of sovereignty over the West Bank, Gaza Strip. And of course, when I say "Arab leaders," I'm including President Sadat. The other one is the question of eastern Jerusalem and the control of the Moslem holy places by Moslems. And the third one is the resolution of the Palestinian question.

We always use the phrase "in all its aspects." And I think that this concern by the Saudis has been expressed in very moderate terms. They have been complimentary about the progress that might evolve from the Camp David talks, and I have not detected any attitude on their part, even surreptitiously, to influence others to condemn the talks or to work against them.

I have just completed today my own response to King Hussein's questions. And after my response has gone through the State Department and NSC, just so they can see what I've decided, that response will be submitted to King Hussein. And I would guess that a copy of my answers to his questions would go to the Saudi Arabians. But we've not given up hope in getting further participation.

I might add one other thing, that is, that a conclusion of an Egyptian-Israeli peace treaty, I think, will remove a lot of the opposition to the Camp David agreements that is presently predicated on preventing such a peace treaty. I think there's a lot of posturing going on by

people who do not want to see a treaty between Israel and Egypt. Once that treaty is concluded, I hope that some of the opposition might dissipate. That's just a hope; I can't predict it yet.

CONGRESSIONAL HEARINGS ON
ASSASSINATIONS

Q. Mr. President, Bill Sumner, from the St. Paul Pioneer Press.

THE PRESIDENT. Good to see you.

Q. I don't know if this has gone past you or not, but were you able to follow any of the assassination hearings, and if you were, have you reached any sort of conclusion about them?

THE PRESIDENT. I've just followed them through the press. I've not been involved in them in any way. My own sense is that they've been thoroughly investigated, and I haven't detected in the last 3 or 4 years or more of investigations that anyone's minds have been changed. There are Americans who will always consider the assassination of President Kennedy to have been the result of an international plot of some kind, originating in the Soviet Union or in Cuba or somewhere else. And I've never seen anything that contradicted what the Warren report said in any substantive degree.

So, I think it's legitimate for the Congress to continue to investigate the Kennedy assassination. I'm not sure that anyone's mind will be changed, and no substantive, new evidence has been brought to light.

I think there were some interesting facts brought forward in the Martin Luther King, Jr., assassination. But whether there was any proof that the original conclusion that James Earl Ray was responsible for it, I haven't detected that. So, I would say that both assassinations have been thoroughly investigated. It's a legitimate function of Congress. I don't think any material change has resulted in the final conclusion at the time of the trial or the original investigation.

LEGISLATIVE PROCESS

Q. I'm Tom Leathers, from Kansas City. Congress these last few days will make all sorts of decisions on all sorts of bills in rather a hurryup fashion. Is this the best way to run the Government, do you think?

THE PRESIDENT. Well, short of a dictatorship—[*laughter*]—I believe it's the best way. And I think, obviously, our system is better than a dictatorship.

I get frustrated sometimes at the inertia of Congress at some moments and also the overly hasty action of Congress in others. But I have to say that sometimes within the White House itself, even on my own desk, there is inertia at times because of different reasons—sometimes deliberate, sometimes because of an overload of work, and sometimes, perhaps, I have to act too hastily.

It's good for the American people to remember, though, that some of the matters the Congress seems to be deciding hastily have been debated and considered over 20 months, and that the members of a subcommittee or even a large full committee quite often are highly expert in that particular question, particularly the members of their staffs. And, of course, a Congress Member who's been there 8, 10, or more years tends to focus his or her attention on specific matters or subjects that relate to their committee assignment.

So, I've been really impressed with the professionalism of Congress. And something that seems to be hasty is often that way only because the press and the American public have not been aware of the long, tedious negotiations and investigations that have gone on in prior months.

Energy, for instance, probably has been considered as thoroughly as any other sub-

ject that has ever been addressed by the Congress. The civil service reform is the same way. Even the tax bill, which I thought was handled in a very abrupt and unpredictable fashion, the ultimate conclusion will be adequate.

I'm here, having 10 days after the Congress passes a bill, with all my staff to assess what they have done. If I think a mistake has been made on the tax bill or any other major bill, then I can veto it. And the worst consequence would be that the Congress would either come back in a special session—which I hope will not be the case—or could consider a bill, a replacement bill very early the next year, maybe even with retroactive provisions in the case of taxes.

I haven't decided what to do about that particular bill. I just use it as an example of one that has been considered very precipitously. I think, though, in general, the literally hundreds of bills that Congress does consider are carefully considered.

PROGRAMS FOR THE HANDICAPPED

Q. Mr. President, Aubrey Bowie, from Greenville, South Carolina. What is the administration's position on funding for voc-rehab and other programs for the handicapped, and is it in conflict or agreement with what Congress wants to do?

THE PRESIDENT. I think we're fairly compatible with Congress on vocational rehabilitation and other matters. I believe that the total HEW budget will only be slightly above what I advocated originally. There might be some categories where they are higher, like in the National Institutes of Health. But I think in general, we've been compatible. The differences might be a matter of 3 or 4 percent, or 5 percent, just a difference of judgment.

But we've done, I think more—this Congress has, with my full support—to aid handicapped people than has ever been done before. I don't say that particularly in a bragging way, because a lot of the work is a culmination of many years of effort by the Congress and by my Republican predecessors. But I think the handicapped people in our country have benefited tremendously in the last year's action by the Congress, including both legislation, executive decisions made by me and Joe Califano, and budget allocations of funds.

Mr. WURFEL. Thank you, sir.

THE PRESIDENT. Thank you very much. I might take one other question.

NATIONAL RURAL POLICY

Q. Mr. President, I'm Joe Parker, from North Carolina. Governor Hunt has made a big thing of balanced growth in our State. As you know, we are a State of small cities. We heard Mr. Eizenstat this morning talk about urban policy. What, if anything, does the administration plan to do on framing a national rural policy, and will it be as comprehensive as the urban policy?

THE PRESIDENT. Well, of course, our urban policy was designed to incorporate smaller cities and communities, as well as the very large ones. It was specifically not designed just for the major cities. Because of Governor Hunt's interest, we are using North Carolina, in effect, as an experimental region for rural growth and improvement of community life, with special attention given by Cabinet members, with some small allocation of funds. And I believe that what is decided in North Carolina as an outcome of these experiments that have been initiated by Governor Hunt, working with me and my staff members, will be a good precursor to what we can do on a nationwide basis.

I doubt if we'll have to have as complicated and as far-reaching a nationwide effort to determine what ought to be done. We've done a lot of work on this as we concluded our urban policy, and now

we're trying to experiment and try out some of the ideas in North Carolina. North Carolina is not exclusively the place that we are attempting these things, but we have focused our attention more on North Carolina because of Governor Hunt's interest.

If you all don't mind, I'd like to close now—I've got another meeting—and take 2 or 3 minutes to get an individual photograph with you.

NOTE: The interview began at 1:15 p.m. in the Cabinet Room at the White House. Walter W. Wurfel is Deputy Press Secretary.

The transcript of the interview was released on October 14.

Employee Retirement Income Security Act Transfers

*Statement on Congressional Action on Reorganization Plan No. 4 of 1978.
October 14, 1978*

I welcome the Congress approval of the ERISA reorganization plan.

This reorganization plan, the fourth to be submitted and become effective this session, can be implemented right away and will have immediate tangible results. It will reduce jurisdictional overlap and duplication by clearly dividing responsibility for ERISA regulation between the Departments of Labor and Treasury. It will reduce substantially ERISA's administrative burden on both businesses and labor unions by reducing the time required to process applications for exemptions from prohibited transactions and accelerating the issuance of the remaining regulations. ERISA has been a symbol of unnecessarily complex governmental regulation, and this plan will simplify significantly the administration of the act.

I want to thank Chairmen Ribicoff and Brooks, Senators Javits, Bentsen, and Williams, and Congressmen Dent, Ullman, Gibbons, Pickle, Conable, and Erlenborn for their support and leadership on this plan.

Agricultural Foreign Investment Disclosure Act of 1978

Statement on Signing S. 3384 Into Law.
October 14, 1978

Today, I am signing into law S. 3384, the Agricultural Foreign Investment Disclosure Act of 1978.

This legislation establishes a nationwide system to monitor foreign purchases of U.S. farmland and directs the Secretary of Agriculture to evaluate the effects of such foreign investment on family farms and rural communities. The bill establishes a series of detailed reporting requirements that will apply to all foreign citizens who hold or acquire a significant interest in American agricultural land.

For some time, many of our Nation's farmers have expressed concerns that increased foreign investment in U.S. farm real estate has driven land prices up. There have also been fears that foreign investors may be more willing to subdivide their land or divert it to other uses. While recent surveys by the Commerce Department and the General Accounting Office suggest that foreign ownership of domestic farmland is still very low, I recognized that we need more information on farmland ownership patterns before we reach definite conclusions.

S. 3384 should help fill that information gap. Together with a study under way in the Agriculture Department to determine the best long-range approach to monitoring foreign investment in U.S. real estate, this legislation will help give

us a sound, factual basis for future policy decisions.

I must, however, caution those who expect immediate results from the studies required by S. 3384. The information obtained through the bill's reporting requirements will have to be analyzed carefully. The policy options that arise from such analysis will have to be considered in the light of overall U.S. trade policies, including our opposition to unnecessary restrictions on international investment flows. It will be particularly important to evaluate whether various economic trends, including higher real estate prices and absentee ownership of land, are actually due to foreign investment and whether they reflect other domestic social and economic factors.

At a time when government efficiency is at the front of our people's minds, I am glad that the Congress has given us an opportunity to evaluate the efficiency and effectiveness of this monitoring system by requiring a report from the Secretary of Agriculture at the end of 1 year. I hope that that evaluation, which will coincide with the completion of the study required by the International Investment Survey Act, will provide a sound basis for shaping future Federal efforts in this area.

NOTE: As enacted, S. 3384 is Public Law 95–460, approved October 14.

National Energy Legislation

Statement on Congressional Approval of the
Legislation.   October 15, 1978

Eighteen months ago, I said that our decisions about energy would test the character of our people and the ability of our Nation to face its most difficult problems. Today the Congress has proven that we can meet that test.

1783

By its vote today, the Congress has given us an energy plan that will advance our national security, ensure our freedom of action in foreign affairs, and protect our economic interests at home and abroad. We will begin down the other side of the mountain, away from the ever-mounting demand for energy and ever-shrinking supply. It sets our Nation on a course of conservation, exploration, and application of new technologies. It does so in a way that gives producers incentives that are adequate and consumers the supplies they need.

The result will not be overnight miracles. This is not the end of the road, but it is a beginning, and an important one.

We have declared to ourselves and the world our intent to control our use of energy and thereby to control our own destiny as a nation.

95th Congress

Statement by the President.   October 15, 1978

I want to congratulate the Congress on a record of accomplishment unmatched in more than a decade. The American people can be justly proud of the work this Congress has done in solving some of the Nation's most pressing problems.

When the 95th Congress assembled 21 months ago, its Members knew they had been elected to tackle the country's basic concerns. Our people wanted action to put the economy back on course, to deal with such long-neglected and critical problems as energy, to make our Government more efficient, and to equip our Nation for the challenges of a changing world.

Now that the Congress has adjourned, its Members can look back with satisfaction on the record that has been compiled.

In these 21 months, the Congress has made progress on nearly all the crucial areas of concern to our people. This progress was made possible by the sense of cooperation, harmony, and trust that developed between my administration and the Congress. The accomplishments of this Congress truly reflect a commitment to executive-legislative cooperation that has been unparalleled in recent years.

The most important achievement is the national energy act, which, along with the creation of the Department of Energy, will give our Nation the tools we need to start down the road away from excessive dependence on foreign oil. The act will protect our consumers and producers, enhance our national security, and remove one of the most pressing causes of inflation and economic instability.

The Congress acted in other ways to ensure our economic future. The economic stimulus plan enacted last year has helped us make the fastest progress against unemployment in more than 25 years, and the Humphrey-Hawkins act sets goals for future noninflationary progress in the same direction. The improvements in the CETA program, the social security system, and the food stamp program all mean that the benefits of our economic progress will be more fairly shared among all our people.

At the same time, the Congress has shown an awareness of the urgent problem of inflation, demonstrating its sense of fiscal responsibility, especially in sustaining my vetoes of the public works and defense bills.

Every sector of our economy will feel the impact of bills passed during this Congress:

—For our rural areas, the Congress enacted an historic farm bill which has already brought new prosperity to our farmlands.

—For the people of our urban areas, the Congress enacted nearly all of the elements of our urban policy and provided responsible help to our largest city with the New York City Assistance Act.

—For all of us, the Congress has made steady progress toward a healthier environment through improvements in the clean air and water pollution acts and a landmark strip mining bill. At the same time, it has removed unneeded regulation in areas, such as the airline industry, where the market can do a better job.

Because of this Congress efforts, we now have the tools we need to make Government more efficient, through six reorganization plans, new Inspectors General, and the first reform of the civil service system in nearly a century. The ethics bill will help ensure that those who hold Federal offices always deserve the public's trust.

Finally, this Congress has shown that it understands that human justice and human rights are the irresistible trend of our times. It helped extend justice at home with its approval of the ERA deadline extension and the proposed amendment to grant full voting representation to the District of Columbia. It supported human rights abroad and insisted, through the antiforeign boycott legislation and the corrupt foreign practices bill, on a decent standard of conduct for American actions overseas.

Time and again, the Congress showed that it was willing to make courageous decisions to advance our national interest. History will prove the wisdom of congressional action on the Panama Canal treaties and the Turkish arms embargo. The world has already seen the dramatic progress toward peace in the Middle East that the Middle East arms sale helped bring about.

I extend my deep appreciation and congratulations to the congressional leadership, especially Majority Leader Robert Byrd and Speaker Tip O'Neill, for their extraordinary efforts on behalf of the American people. Of all the reasons for the 95th Congress success, the most important has been their wise and dedicated leadership. I look forward to working with them again in the 96th Congress.

Pope John Paul II

Statement on the Election of the Pope.
October 16, 1978

I add my congratulations and my sense of joy to that felt around the world at the selection of Pope John Paul II.

Twice in 8 weeks, the College of Cardinals has had to choose a new leader for their Church and for the world—and twice they have given us choices which have filled the Church and the world with new hope.

Like his predecessor, Pope John Paul II has shared the experiences of working people and understands the daily victories and defeats of human life.

A theologian and a worker, he also understands, in a way few in this Nation ever can, the most extreme tests that life presents. He knows what it is to struggle for faith, for freedom, for life itself; and his insight into these modern dilemmas will enrich, and be enriched by, the enduring traditions of his own Church.

During our visit to Poland early this year, Rosalynn and I gained a sense of the spiritual resilience of the nation that has given the world this new Pope. Of all Americans who share my sense of warmth and gratitude for this new leader, Polish Americans have reason for special pride.

NOTE: An announcement of the U.S. Presidential Delegation to the Investiture of Pope John Paul II, held at the Vatican on October 22, is printed on page 1808 of this volume.

Restoration of Citizenship Rights to Jefferson F. Davis

Statement on Signing S.J. Res. 16 Into Law. October 17, 1978

In posthumously restoring the full rights of citizenship to Jefferson Davis, the Congress officially completes the long process of reconciliation that has reunited our people following the tragic conflict between the States. Earlier, he was specifically exempted from resolutions restoring the rights of other officials in the Confederacy. He had served the United States long and honorably as a soldier, Member of the U.S. House and Senate, and as Secretary of War. General Robert E. Lee's citizenship was restored in 1976. It is fitting that Jefferson Davis should no longer be singled out for punishment.

Our Nation needs to clear away the guilts and enmities and recriminations of the past, to finally set at rest the divisions that threatened to destroy our Nation and to discredit the great principles on which it was founded. Our people need to turn their attention to the important tasks that still lie before us in establishing those principles for all people.

NOTE: As enacted, S.J. Res. 16 is Public Law 95–466, approved October 17.

Water Research and Development Act of 1978

Statement on Signing S. 2704 Into Law. October 17, 1978

Today I am signing S. 2704, the Water Research and Development Act of 1978. This legislation brings together two important concerns of mine: greater support for basic research and a vigorous search for practical ways to solve the in-creasing problems of water quality and quantity in various parts of the Nation. The national water policy announced earlier this year will be strengthened by the water research program enacted by this bill, which is based on legislation I requested in 1977.

The Office of Water Research and Technology in the Department of the Interior will be the agency responsible for putting this legislation into action. It will provide for new research in saline water conversion, water re-use, water conservation, water problems of urbanizing areas, and other water-efficient technologies. It will support 54 water research institutes throughout the Nation. It will assist in the training of water scientists and engineers, the transfer of water research results to water managers at the local and State levels, and the demonstration of technology to solve critical water problems wherever they exist.

I particularly want to congratulate Congressman Lloyd Meeds and Senator Mike Gravel for the work they have done on this bill. I am pleased to sign S. 2704.

NOTE: As enacted, S. 2704 is Public Law 95–467, approved October 17.

Tribally Controlled Community College Assistance Act of 1978

Statement on Signing S. 1215 Into Law. October 17, 1978

I am pleased today to sign into law S. 1215, the Tribally Controlled Community College Assistance Act of 1978. This legislation authorizes additional Federal assistance to community colleges controlled by American Indians on their reservations.

This past summer, the "Longest Walk" brought attention to the special needs of

Indian communities and their special relationship to the Federal Government. This act provides a needed base of stable funding for postsecondary education on our Indian reservations, and provides American Indians with greater educational opportunities near their families, their tribes, and their places of employment.

I appreciate the efforts of Senator Abourezk and Representative Blouin in securing passage of this legislation, which will enable American Indian citizens to make greater contributions to their communities and to their Nation.

NOTE: As enacted, S. 1215 is Public Law 95–471, approved October 17.

Director of the Presidential Personnel Office

Appointment of Arnold J. Miller.
October 17, 1978

The President today announced the appointment of Arnold J. Miller, of Burtonsville, Md., as Director of the Presidential Personnel Office. He replaces James F. Gammill, Jr., who is going back to his studies in economics and finance.

Miller, 37, is officer-in-charge of the Washington office of Contract Research Corp., a Massachusetts-based management consulting and executive recruitment firm. He was one of the founders of the firm in 1973.

Before the founding of Contract Research Corp., Miller was manager of national projects for Abt Associates in Cambridge, Mass. He has done graduate study at Harvard's Russian Research Center, and is the author of "Manpower Programs for Offenders: A Technical Assistance Guide" and "An Operational System for the Jacksonville, Florida Concentrated Employment Program."

Special Congressional Medal Honoring Marian Anderson

Remarks at the Presentation Ceremony.
October 17, 1978

THE PRESIDENT. First of all, I'd like to ask Marian Anderson to come up with me.

On very rare occasions, there are people who appear in the world community who are an inspiration to literally millions of people because of their superb talent, because of their sensitivity to others' yearnings for status in life or opportunity or a joy of living, and who at the same time exemplify the characteristics of citizens of a nation like our own whose ideals and aspirations and standards all of us cherish. Marian Anderson is one of those rare people. Her musical talent is exceptional, unique, recognized and enjoyed by people everywhere. She's brought joy to millions of people, and she exemplifies the finest aspects of American citizenship.

She's never considered herself to be a crusader for the downtrodden or brown or yellow or black people of our planet. But she's done as much to elevate their souls, their spirit, and their status among other human beings as anyone else who's ever lived.

No one in this country could ever forget Easter Sunday in 1939, when Marian Anderson let her beautiful voice be heard in a quiet but forceful way, saying that black people have rights in this country that have not yet been recognized.

That was a long time ago. It was 15 years before the Supreme Court ruled that there should be equality of rights in our country. And she did it in such a way that tore the heart of those who were afflicted by their own conscience, but inspired those who wanted more courage to bring about a realization of what our Nation is, and wasn't at that time.

I think it's accurate to say that she is one who has enjoyed great success, and she's been eager to share that success with many others, through scholarships, through her own humanitarian efforts, and through the example of a life, she's expanded her influence in a beneficient way to encompass the lives of many others.

It's a great honor for me to deliver to her on behalf of the American people a special gold medal that was mandated to be designed and produced for her by the Congress of the United States. I've never had an experience like this before. This is indeed an honor for me. And I think the recognition of her and what her life means to our country by the Congress is indeed well deserved.

It's a great honor to me as President, on behalf of more than 200 million American citizens—indeed, not in a presumptuous way, on behalf of many hundreds of millions of people around the world—to give her this token of our esteem, our appreciation, our admiration, and our personal love.

Miss Anderson, it's a great honor for me to present this medal to you.

MISS ANDERSON. Mr. President and Mrs. Carter, I am without the proper words to express to you today the depth of my feelings. I have always loved America, and without getting on a soapbox to say so, we tried to do in our medium that which we felt was more like us to do. And we do hope in some places there was some good.

When Mrs. Carter spoke to me about the possibility of receiving the medal, and we waited for days, weeks, and months, I just wondered whether or not this was going to have to be given posthumously. [*Laughter*]

But here we all are, and this is about the happiest moment of my life. And I can't find all the words that I would like to say, but this much is true: I could not have been here at this moment on this spot without people all over the world, many of whom I did not know and never will, sending up prayers now and then, that we would be always under His protection. And I believe that we were. That President Carter and Mrs. Carter are the kind of people that they are is like a beacon in a desert. And they mean so much to so many people whom they don't know and never will know.

And I am so thrilled at this moment, that I don't know that I can get back to my seat or not. [*Laughter*] But I am eternally grateful, eternally grateful, because whatever has been done, so many people have had a part in it. And I thank the dear Lord up above for all that He has done, and I hope that He shall be with me forever, as I hope He will be with you, because without Him, we are naught.

Thank you.

THE PRESIDENT. Miss Anderson's autobiography is entitled, "Oh Lord, What a Morning," and the final words in that autobiography, I thought, were appropriate to be read after she made her response. And I'm quoting the last paragraph in her autobiography.

"There are many persons ready to do what is right because in their hearts they know it is right. But they hesitate, waiting for the other fellow to make the first move, and he in turn waits for you. The minute a person whose word means a great deal dares to take the open-hearted and courageous way, many others follow. Not everyone can be turned aside from meanness and hatred. But the great majority of Americans is heading in that direction. I have a great belief in the future of my people and my country."

PHOTOGRAPHIC PORTFOLIO

President Jimmy Carter

Overleaf: With President Anwar el-Sadat of Egypt and Prime Minister Menahem Begin of Israel at Camp David, Maryland, September 7. *Above:* Town meeting in Berlin, Federal Republic of Germany, July 15. *Left:* With Western and Japanese leaders during the Bonn Economic Summit Meeting, Federal Republic of Germany, July 17. *Right:* On the Middle Fork of the Salmon River in Idaho, August 22.

Left: Signing the Civil Service Reform Act of 1978 in the State Dining Room, October 13. ***Below:*** Addressing the Congressional Black Caucus dinner in Washington, D.C., September 30. ***Right:*** Witnessing the signing of documents agreed to at the Camp David meeting on the Middle East, in the East Room, September 17.

Above left: Breakfast with members of the White House Correspondents Association in the State Dining Room, November 16. *Below left:* Speaking at the "Get Out the Vote" rally in New York City, November 2. *Above:* Prior to an address to the Nation on the anti-inflation program, in the Oval Office, October 24. *Below:* Presenting a special congressional medal to Marian Anderson on the State Floor, October 17.

Left: Meeting with administration officials to discuss the 1980 fiscal ye[ar] budget in the Cabinet Room, December 8. *Below:* Greeting guest[s] at the 50th birthday party receptio[n] for Mickey Mouse in the East Roo[m], November 17.

We thank you for those fine words.

When the mayor of Atlanta, Maynard Jackson, was inaugurated, I was Governor. And I went to a beautiful inauguration ceremony; with two exceptions, the best one I've ever been to. [*Laughter*]

The entire group of thousands of people were thrilled by the beautiful voice of Mattiwilda Dobbs, who is an aunt of Maynard Jackson, the mayor of Atlanta, and a native of my own State. I think that those of you who have seen the back side of this medal, perhaps when it fell on the floor, can see a world being held in God's hands. And we have now, to close our ceremony, Mattiwilda Dobbs, who will sing, "He's Got the Whole World in His Hands."

NOTE: The President spoke at 3:27 p.m. in the Grand Hall at the White House.

Egyptian-Israeli Peace Negotiations

White House Statement Following Meetings With the Israeli and Egyptian Delegations. October 17, 1978

The meeting with the Israeli delegation, beginning at 2:10 p.m. in the Cabinet Room, lasted 1 hour. The President was accompanied by Vice President Mondale; Zbigniew Brzezinski, Assistant to the President for National Security Affairs; Alfred L. Atherton, Ambassador at Large; and William Quandt, National Security Council staff member. On the Israeli side were Foreign Minister Moshe Dayan; Meir Rosenne, Legal Adviser, Ministry of Foreign Affairs; Defense Minister Ezer Weizman; Ely Akim Rubenstein, Assistant Director General, Ministry of Foreign Affairs; and Simcha Dinitz, Israeli Ambassador to the United States.

The meeting with the Egyptian delegation, beginning at 4 p.m. in the Cabinet Room, lasted 1 hour. The President was accompanied by Vice President Mondale; Zbigniew Brzezinski, Assistant to the President for National Security Affairs; Alfred L. Atherton, Ambassador at Large; and William Quandt, National Security Council staff member. On the Egyptian side were Dr. Butrus Ghali, Acting Foreign Minister; Lt. Gen. Kamal Hassan Ali, Minister of Defense; Ashraf Ghorbal, Egyptian Ambassador to the United States; and Usama al-Baz, Under Secretary, Ministry of Foreign Affairs.

The President welcomed this opportunity to get a firsthand report from the heads of the Egyptian and Israeli delegations about the status of the talks in Washington. He reviewed with both delegations the progress made so far in the conference and the issues that remain to be resolved. The President and the Israeli and Egyptian delegates expressed their satisfaction with the progress so far. They reaffirmed their determination to continue that progress, so that the negotiations can be completed as soon as possible.

Veterans Disability Compensation and Survivors Benefits and Housing Benefits Bills

Remarks at the Bill Signing Ceremony. October 18, 1978

THE PRESIDENT. This morning I've come to sign two very important bills involving our veterans, those who are disabled and those who have served in Vietnam—in fact, all the Americans who have honored our country by offering their lives for liberty and freedom.

Since our Nation was first founded, Americans have felt obligated to honor those who have offered their lives in this noble purpose.

In my own State, and in the area in which Jack Brinkley and I live, for instance, the land was settled by drawings of lottery cards by those who had served in the Revolutionary War. And many of the families who moved into the western part of Georgia and other parts of our country acquired their land by having served in the war to give our own country its initial status and freedom.

These two bills this morning, House bill 11886 and House bill 12028, continue this process to honor veterans in the first place and to give them an opportunity for a reasonable competitive relationship with other citizens who may not have suffered in the war.

One thing that we need to protect all citizens against is the impact of inflation. The disabled veterans compensation has been increased in these bills by 7.3 percent, which equates to the inflation rate last year.

There has been an increase in the maximum home loans to be guaranteed, from $17,500 to $25,000, and the rights of veterans to acquire certain categories of condominiums and also mobile homes has been included.

We also have recognized the importance of improved energy conservation and special provisions have been made for homes that would include these features. In addition to that, of course, we have increased the allocation of funds for modifying homes to accommodate those veterans who are severely disabled, up to a maximum now of $30,000.

The active duty requirements for veterans to receive loan guarantees in the Vietnam war have now been equated with those requirements for veterans who have served in the Korean and the World War II.

As many of you have known, who are related directly to veterans, we've had a problem in finding cemetery space for those who have died. And these bills will provide that not only will there be a better opportunity for making available limited space in Federal cemeteries, but also a new program for enhancing services through State cemeteries for veterans will be included.

We've never had an unidentified or unknown soldier from the Vietnam war. All those who died and whose bodies were recovered have been identified. But this bill recognizes that at Arlington, where our Nation focuses its attention upon veterans, that there should be a means to honor those who died in Vietnam, and a special plaque will be installed there as a result of these two bills.

I might add my thanks to the Members of Congress who serve in this important realm of legislative responsibility—Congressman Jack Brinkley, who happens to be my own personal Congressman from the Third District, Congresswoman Margaret Heckler, who was to be here this morning, and many others.

As you know, in the Senate Alan Cranston has been one of the leaders in meeting the needs of veterans. Although it won't be signed this morning, because it has not yet arrived on my desk, I will sign the veterans pension bill of 1978 as soon as it does arrive in my office.

I want to congratulate all those who have been instrumental in improving the lot of veterans. We quite often have not recognized them adequately, particularly those who served in the Vietnam war. This is a major step in the right direction. And I'm very proud as President to sign these two bills and want to again congratulate those in the Congress who have made this step forward possible.

Congressman Brinkley and Max Cleland, all of those who worked so hard, I want to thank you for it.

Jack, you might want to say a word.

REPRESENTATIVE BRINKLEY. Thank you very much, Mr. President. It's a joy for me to be here representing the Third District of Georgia, which is the district encompassing Plains, Georgia, and to have had an active part in the role of the Veterans Committee of the House of Representatives. The housing subcommittee, on which Elizabeth Lunsford is majority counsel, deals with housing, which is important, basic, and fundamental for veterans. Our housing bill touches retirees, other veterans, and active duty military personnel. It streamlines the law and brings it up to date. It's important to the economy and to the quality of life of these men, and we're just grateful to have had a part in it.

Thank you very much, Mr. President.

THE PRESIDENT. Thank you, Jack. Max?

MR. CLELAND. It's an honor to be with you this morning, and I'm especially grateful to you for having representatives of the major veterans organizations with us today. Without their help, this legislation couldn't be possible.

Thank you, Mr. President.

THE PRESIDENT. Thank you, Max, very much.

I think the Congress has made it possible to improve greatly the attention paid to Vietnam veterans. And we've seen substantial improvement in their employment opportunities and in the services given to them.

As all of you know, in the past number of years, we have not honored Vietnam veterans from our hearts or actions as previous veterans of other wars were honored. And I'm very glad to see this defect in our societal attitudes corrected by the

Congress. I'm glad to be a part of it.

Thank you.

NOTE: The President spoke at 9:30 a.m. in the Cabinet Room at the White House. Max Cleland is Administrator of Veterans Affairs.

As enacted, H.R. 11886 is Public Law 95–479, and H.R. 12028 is Public Law 95–476, both approved October 18.

Veterans Disability Compensation and Survivors Benefits and Housing Benefits Bills

Statement on Signing H.R. 11886 and H.R. 12028 Into Law.   October 18, 1978

I am pleased to sign into law today H.R. 11886, the Veterans' Disability Compensation and Survivors' Benefits Act of 1978, and H.R. 12028, the Veterans' Housing Benefits Act of 1978.

Our Nation owes no greater responsibility or debt of gratitude than to the men and women who served their country in battle and came back with disabling injuries. Because of that debt, we have gladly provided compensation payments.

However, in the last year, inflation has reduced the value of that compensation, and, unlike social security or other programs, there is no automatic inflation adjustment. H.R. 11886 will increase these payments by 7.3 percent, so that beneficiaries do not unfairly bear the brunt of inflation.

Inflation has also driven up the cost of housing, as most of us know. H.R. 12028 will expand the opportunities for our veterans, especially the younger, Vietnam era veterans who are entering a very expensive housing market for the first time.

This bill will increase the maximum home loan guarantee to a more realistic level, expand the VA home loan program to purchasing condominiums and mobile

1791

homes, and encourage energy-saving home improvements. This bill will also increase the maximum grant for specially adapted housing for the severely disabled to $30,000.

These two bills will go far to improve and modernize veterans benefit programs that are critical to the well-being of those who have bravely served our Nation.

As I sign these two bills today, I am also looking forward to signing soon the Veterans' and Survivors' Pension Improvement Act of 1978.

NOTE: As enacted, H.R. 11886 is Public Law 95–479, and H.R. 12028 is Public Law 95–476, both approved October 18.

Comprehensive Older Americans Act Amendments of 1978

Remarks at the Bill Signing Ceremony. October 18, 1978

THE PRESIDENT. This morning it's a great pleasure for me to sign House bill 12255, which is the amendments to the Comprehensive Older Americans Act, a foundation for the security and better life of Americans who reach their retirement age.

This legislation, which is quite comprehensive in nature, will strengthen the Federal Council on Aging, on which I rely for constant advice, sometimes prodding, sometimes counsel, sometimes criticism, but which has been a very effective voice within the White House for the senior citizens of our country.

One of the things that's interesting to me and, I think, will be exciting to older Americans and those who care about them is that this bill provides for a White House Conference on the Aging in 1981. And we will—in fact, we have already begun to plan for that conference to assess where we stand in our country on meeting the needs of older Americans, and also to improve the delivery of those kinds of services and opportunities.

Another very interesting feature of this legislation is that it moves even further to terminate, or to minimize, at least, the discrimination against Americans because of their age, because of their race, or because of their ethnic background.

One of the results of a very rapid improvement in Federal programs for the aging has been confusion in administration. And this bill recognizes and corrects that defect by consolidating Titles III, V, and VII of the Older Americans Act. This would provide now for a better administration in a coordinated way of social programs, housing programs, programs to deliver food, the establishment of centers for elderly Americans.

One of the things that I hope this act will provide and ensure is a more narrow focusing of attention and services on those who have the greatest economic and social need. We want to broaden opportunities to additional older Americans, but when there is a limited supply of funds or facilities, of course, those should be given on a top-priority basis to those who have the greatest need of all.

The bill also extends for 3 years the employment opportunities for older Americans under the ACTION programs, and this, I believe, will be a reassuring note to older Americans who want to have at least partial or part-time employment in resolving some of the other problems in American society.

I particularly want to thank Senator Tom Eagleton, whose wife is here with us this morning, and also John Brademas, who's with us with his mother. And I'd like to ask Congressman John Brademas if he has a comment to make before I sign the bill.

REPRESENTATIVE BRADEMAS.   Well, you're very kind, Mr. President.

I suppose one of the reasons that I was so committed to seeing the passage of this legislation is that I have a very articulate champion of it in my own family in the person of my mother, who is a 77-year-old retired schoolteacher, who is a great supporter of Jimmy Carter and John Brademas. [*Laughter*]

THE PRESIDENT. John, I'm afflicted by the same situation in my own family. [*Laughter*] I've got a one-woman lobby in my home. [*Laughter*] That's a great opportunity for us both to have.

Rosalynn, would you like to comment?

MRS. CARTER. I'm just very pleased to be here and very pleased for Jimmy to have the opportunity to sign this bill.

THE PRESIDENT. Thank you.

MRS. CARTER. I, as you know, meet with Nelson every other week and stay in touch with what's going on in the legislature with the legislation as it goes through both Houses, and it's just a great thrill for me to be here this morning to see Jimmy sign this bill.

THE PRESIDENT. Thank you.

Nelson, would you like to make a comment?

MR. CRUIKSHANK. Well, thank you, Mr. President.

The course of this bill through the House and the Senate has been a little like the perils of Pauline at several points. But due to the efforts of John Brademas and Senator Eagleton, they steered through all the narrow passages, and it came out a good bill that's going to do a lot for the older people in this country. And it's going to make the administration of the program better and more effective. And now the task, after you sign this, Mr. President, will be for all of us to pitch in and make it work. And we'll have to work as hard as the congressional people have worked on this as we get to working on carrying out its provisions.

THE PRESIDENT. Very fine. Well, I'll sign it now so we can all go to work and implement the opportunities that Congress has given us.

Thank you very much.

NOTE: The President spoke at 10:03 a.m. in the Cabinet Room at the White House. Nelson Cruikshank is Counsellor to the President on Aging.

As enacted, H.R. 12255 is Public Law 95–478, approved October 18.

Comprehensive Older Americans Act Amendments of 1978

Statement on Signing H.R. 12255 Into Law.   October 18, 1978

With great pleasure, I am signing into law H.R. 12255, the Comprehensive Older Americans Act Amendments of 1978. These amendments to the Older Americans Act of 1965 are an important step toward more effectively meeting the special needs of our elderly citizens.

In a relatively short time, the Nation has greatly expanded programs for older Americans. We have dramatically reduced poverty among the elderly. We have established a wide array of Federal, State, local, and private services to help maintain our older citizens in their own homes, rather than institutions, and to maximize their independence and dignity. Now we are improving these services by strengthening their coordination and planning at all levels of government.

These amendments consolidate several separate, overlapping titles of the Older Americans Act into a single title covering all services. They also improve planning for these services to add efficiency at all levels of government and eliminate countless hours of paperwork and administrative burdens.

Moreover, they require better targeting of these resources on low-income and minority elderly.

The amendments continue the Older American Community Service Employment program for low-income older persons. Congress expanded eligibility under the program to individuals with somewhat higher incomes than poverty level. But I hope that the program administrators will ensure that those in greatest need can have the first opportunity to participate.

The amendments also extend for 3 years ACTION's three Older American Volunteer programs: Retired Senior Volunteers, Foster Grandparents, and Senior Companions. These programs provide volunteer opportunities for persons age 60 and over to serve meaningfully the infirm, the mentally retarded, and other individuals in their communities.

The amendments will help expand the ability of the elderly to protect their rights in two ways: by authorizing a private right of action for judicial redress of age discrimination, and by requiring the U.S. Commission on Civil Rights to study racial and ethnics discrimination in programs for the elderly.

Further, the amendments strengthen the role of the Federal Council on Aging, which I rely on for advice, and provide for a White House Conference on Aging in 1981. This Conference will provide a national forum to reassess the progress we have made and to prepare for challenges that will confront the Nation's elderly citizens over the next generation or two.

In summary, I particularly want to recognize the work of Congressman John Brademas and Senator Thomas Eagleton, who helped shape these important amendments which represent the continuation of the Nation's commitment to find effec-

tive ways to assist our older citizens. I am proud to sign them and reaffirm that commitment.

NOTE: As enacted, H.R. 12255 is Public Law 95–478, approved October 18.

Codification of the Interstate Commerce Act

Statement on Signing H.R. 10965 Into Law.   October 18, 1978

I have signed into law H.R. 10965, a bill which revises and codifies the Interstate Commerce Act and related laws as subtitle IV of title 49, United States Code, "Transportation."

The goal of this bill, to codify the Interstate Commerce Act and related statutes, is a laudable one. As its title reveals, this legislation is intended merely to restate existing law, not change it. However, section 10706 of the bill might be construed to authorize the Interstate Commerce Commission to shield from the antitrust laws intermodal rate bureaus to which rail carriers are parties. In fact, the administration believes the Commission does not possess such power, and this important issue is currently in litigation. It would, therefore, be highly inappropriate for a codification of existing law to resolve this dispute or to influence the pending litigation.

Further, the division of litigating responsibility between the Commission and the Department of Justice is not entirely free from doubt under present law.

I understand that both the bill and its legislative history state that the Congress has no intention of changing existing law or of resolving issues of ICC authority or of influencing pending litigation. With that understanding, I am approving this bill.

NOTE: As enacted, H.R. 10965 is Public Law 95–473, approved October 17.

President's Personal Representative to the Vatican

Designation of Robert F. Wagner. October 18, 1978

The President has asked Robert F. Wagner of New York to serve as his Personal Representative to the Vatican. Wagner succeeds David Walters, resigned.

In his capacity as the President's representative, Wagner will visit the Vatican from time to time to exchange views on international and humanitarian subjects of interest and concern to the Vatican and to the U.S. Government.

Wagner has been a senior partner since 1975 in the law firm of Finley, Kumble, Wagner, Heine and Underberg in New York. In 1968 and 1969, he was United States Ambassador to Spain, and from 1954 to 1965, he served as mayor of New York City. Wagner has served in the New York State Assembly and as vice chairman of the Port Authority of New York and New Jersey. He was a lieutenant colonel in the U.S. Air Force during World War II.

Baltimore, Maryland

Remarks at a Fundraising Dinner for Harry Hughes.   October 18, 1978

Senator Sarbanes; Governor Blair Lee; Mayor Schaefer; Congressman Long and Congressman Mikulski, Gladys Spellman; candidates who will in the future be Members of Congress, Joe Quinn, Sue Ward; Chairman Rosalie Abrams; Louis Goldstein; my good friend Harry Hughes; Steven Sachs; ladies and gentlemen, friends who have made one of the wisest decisions and who will make other wise decisions in November that Maryland has ever seen:

Speaking of polls, I thought until recently that the most famous one in the world was Dr. Brzezinski. But I think that—[laughter]—recently, we've had an election of a new Pope. And when I came on the stage, I remembered Congresswoman Barbara Mikulski, and then I remembered the Baltimore Sun. And I've gotten very confused about this.

I do want to say that it's good to be back in the State that offered to me and my predecessors Camp David. That was a great achievement for peace; thanks to you for making it possible. My esteem in the country has gone up substantially since then. It's very nice now that when people wave at me, they use all their fingers. [Laughter]

I believe things are getting better all over, and I think particularly in Maryland. As I sat here a few minutes ago and looked at and listened to Blair Lee, I tried to think of some descriptive words that were appropriate for him. I think statesman and a Christian gentleman fit him very well.

He's brought credit to the office that he fills, and he's acted in an exemplary way—a kind man, a gentle man, a confident man, an honest man, one who's generous, and I think, one who's been quite unselfish and dedicated. It's an honor for me to be with a man like him.

And I also believe that he has set a tone in the political structure of Maryland that will be filled and perhaps even enhanced by Harry Hughes when he becomes Governor early next year.

It's nice to have a man in the Governor's office, as Harry Hughes will be, who is fiscally knowledgeable and responsible, a man who's campaigned around this State as a relative unknown, who was not expected to win, but who didn't depend upon powerful political allies to put him in office, who cast his lot directly with the people whom he met on the street and in factory shift lines—people who have to work for a living, people who have admired the spirit and ideals of Maryland, but sometimes have been disappointed in the realization of those dreams and ideals—a man who understands what it means to have a fair and equitable distribution of State funds and, I think, above all, a man who will bring permanently throughout his terms of office as Governor a basic character, a basic integrity to the politics of Maryland, which will be an inspiration to all of us and a source of great gratitude on the part of people who will put him in office.

I'm very grateful to be on the stage with Harry Hughes, your next Governor.

I might give you a warning, however. I was really a little disappointed to see the recent poll result which showed the Democratic candidates so far in the lead.

One of my responsibilities as Governor,* as the titular head of the Democratic Party, is to work with Chairman John White and to try to monitor what goes on throughout the country in all 50 States— with 435 House of Representatives races and about 35 or 40 U.S. Senate races and about two-thirds of the Governors being elected this year. And quite often, I have seen a person with an immense, almost unshakable lead in the early polls be defeated, not because the candidates slacked off or quit working or became overconfident, but because the supporters of that

*Reference should have been "President." [Printed in the transcript.]

candidate took for granted a victory and didn't go out and work just as hard as they would if he was an underdog or fighting a very tough, close battle in the public opinion polls.

You've come here tonight to contribute financially to the election of Harry Hughes. But it would be a tragedy if all of you who are highly motivated, who believe in him, and who want better things for Maryland won't go back to your own home with your family, with your neighbors, with your block, with your community, with your city, and exert your leadership in recruiting a massive turnout on election day for him.

It's not impossible that this bright vision for Maryland, this breath of fresh air that's sweeping across Maryland might be lost unless you and Harry Hughes, his family, all of us, including myself, do our utmost to get him elected.

Do you promise that after tonight you'll work just as hard for him as you worked for anyone in the primary; do you promise to do that? [*Applause*]

If so, we'll have a great victory. And I think it's very good for a candidate to have a tremendous victory on election day, because this tells the people to rally to him, it tells the legislature to give him support, it gives him the strength politically to carry out campaign promises. It lets him epitomize the finest aspects of our political system, the finest aspects of the Democratic Party.

We've always been a party of compassion and competence, compassion *and* competence. Sometimes we haven't lived up to that reputation or that commitment. But I believe it's accurate to say that now the American people are beginning to realize that the Democratic Party can be both. No one has ever doubted that the Democrats cared about others. We are a party with the heart. We are a party who reaches out to those who are less fortunate than we. We've been extremely interested in seeing good programs implemented to let people get an education, let people have a job, to let people have a home, to see cities improved, to see highways built.

We've always had that reputation. And we're trying to carry it out, not only on the State level but also at the local and Federal level.

I was very proud the other day—having campaigned several times with Mayor Schaefer, with Bob Embry in Baltimore, having learned what a real urban renewal program ought to be—to see Baltimore recognized and your mayor receive an award in Germany for having the finest urban renewal program in the world. It's a credit to you, and it shows what a party can do.

We are forming now an urban policy on a nationwide basis patterned substantially after what has been done in Baltimore, forming a new partnership between local, State, and government officials, private individuals, just private homeowners, working people, retired people, to let our country be more clean, more decent, and have a better place to live.

The Congress last year passed a new farm bill to let our agricultural families who have been deprived in the past of an adequate level of income have a better life. And Maryland is a great agricultural State.

And the Members of your Congressional delegation who are here on the stage with me have helped to forge now, not a division between urban and rural dwellers, but kind of a new partnership there as well.

We believe in basic rights of human beings. One of those basic rights is the chance for a job. When I campaigned around the country for 2 years, the single most important issue that was brought up every time I had a political meeting was the high unemployment rate.

When I became President about 20 months ago, 10 million Americans did not have a full-time job; 7 million Americans or more didn't have any job. We had an 8 percent unemployment rate. Since then we've had an unprecedented achievement. The Congress has passed laws that have been implemented effectively. Our economy has been stimulated. And we've had a net addition to over 6 million jobs. The unemployment rate has been brought down 25 percent, a very good demonstration of what the Democratic Party stands for, to let people stand on their own two feet, resolve their own problems, support themselves, be constructive members of a societal structure.

We've tried to bring to the Federal Government a kind of breath of fresh air. The Congress has now passed very stringent ethics bills, which I will sign into law in the next few days, requiring all executive offices in the Government, all Members of Congress to account for their incomes, to make sure that any conflict is identified or preferably avoided. And the Congress has done this enthusiastically on their own, because there have been embarrassments about top public officials.

We're trying to root out fraud. As you well know, here in Baltimore, in the General Services Administration, a few bad managers are giving our Government a bad name. But we're trying to bring some resolution of this problem. And the Congress has also passed a new Inspectors General bill to establish 12 offices, independent, within the largest agencies, to root out and detect fraud and mismanagement and waste from your Government, which I head.

We're now getting ready to embark on a massive program for anti-inflation. And I've tried to bring to the Government the proper basis for management itself. When I ran for President, we had a Federal deficit of almost $70 billion, $66 billion. We've tried to cut that down, to cut the deficit down. And this year the Congress has completed appropriations bills with a deficit cut down to less than $40 billion. Next year it's going to be lower. My goal is to have a balanced budget. And if the economy permits it, I'm going to work with you to bring about a balanced budget in our country.

There's no place for waste, and at the same time we've strengthened education programs, strengthened our highway programs, strengthened our urban development programs, cut down the Federal deficit, we've also cut taxes substantially—$8 billion last year; the Congress has just passed another bill to reduce taxes 19 or more billion dollars more.

And I think the combination of those three things shows that we have a firm grip now on the fiscal management of our Government.

We're trying to eliminate unnecessary regulations—and those that are written, to write them in plain English. We're making the people that write them sign them. And we're trying to make it so people can understand them, even peanut farmers from Georgia.

We've tried to put "free" back into our free enterprise system. One of the things we've already done is to tackle the airline industry. We've lowered fares dramatically. The airlines objected strongly, and now they've increased their passenger capacity and utilization greatly. Their profits are up. Everybody is benefiting. The Congress has now passed a law to make sure that this is permanent.

We're going to move on other sections of the transportation industry in the future. We're trying to get government's nose out of the business of the people, let the free enterprise system work, make government a model for others, remove the things that are embarrassing and restore some fiscal integrity and fiscal management principles to government and give our people better services at the same time. And so far, we've done it. We're going to keep on doing it in the future.

I'd just like to mention two other things. One is that in your city, in your State, there are tens of thousands of dedicated public servants who work for the Federal Government, as do I. They have sacrificially, in many instances, dedicated their one life on Earth to a career of serving other Americans. Quite often they don't get credit for what they do. And sometimes in the past they've not been permitted to do their best.

For the first time in 95 years, I proposed to the Congress civil service reform legislation to let superb employees be recognized and to utilize their talent and ability and dedication; to inspire those who have not done too well to do better or to be transferred or discharged; to let managers manage; and to let Federal employees be proud of their own careers and let the American people be proud of them.

I'm very grateful that the Congress has now passed, in an intact form, the civil service reform legislation. This will help, again, to give better management to your Government and to mine.

We've also maintained the strength of our country in other ways, not just a strong government itself, but a strong nation, a strong defense. Although our military might is unequaled anywhere in the world—and it will be kept that way—it's not just a quantity of weapons or even the resolve of American people to defend ourselves or even the sacrificial dedication of service people that makes us strong. In the past we had been weakened because many

Americans had lost confidence in what our Government stood for: the Vietnam war, the Watergate tragedy, the CIA revelations, and other things had induced the American people to feel that our country was not clean enough, it wasn't decent enough.

We didn't raise a banner high, around which people could rally and of which people could be proud. But now I think we've committed ourselves on a worldwide basis to try to exemplify in our foreign dealings what Americans feel in our own hearts.

We're not supporting every tinhorn dictatorship around the world any more. And we have let people know that our protection, our support, our enhancement of basic human rights, in which we believe in America, is also a burning, intense, permanent belief around the world. And as long as I'm President, the United States will be identified in the minds and hearts of people everywhere as the Nation that stands irrevocably and permanently for basic human rights. It's an important thing; it'll be maintained.

And the last thing that I'd like to mention is something that we've already covered, and that is peace throughout the world. We've been fortunate in the last 2 years. Not a single American service person has shed blood in any conflict anywhere on Earth. I hope that I can go out of office at the end of my service having maintained that record.

But we're also trying to use our good offices to bring an end to bloodshed in other parts of the world: in the Middle East, with a permanent peace there for the first time in history; in Lebanon. Secretary Vance left Pretoria, South Africa, this morning, having tried to put together an end to the potential bloodshed and dispute in Namibia. We've been working on the problems in Rhodesia. He's on the way to the Soviet Union this afternoon to continue his discussions on SALT. Warren Christopher, Deputy Secretary of State, left at 3 o'clock this afternoon, going to Greece. And we hope we can finally bring some resolution of the problems between Greece and Turkey and the Cypriots who have suffered so much on Cyprus.

So, we're trying as best we can to represent what you want our Nation to be, what all of us want the Democratic Party to be; but you can help us accomplish, if you are part of it, because as I said during the campaign many times, we want a government that's as good and honest and decent and compassionate and competent as the American people.

And this is the kind of government that we're trying to achieve in Washington. It's the kind of government that I know that Harry Hughes will achieve in Annapolis for Maryland, beginning next year, with your help.

Thank you very much.

NOTE: The President spoke at 7:20 p.m. at the Baltimore Civic Center. In his opening remarks, he referred to Rosalie Abrams, chairperson of the Maryland Democratic Party, Louis Goldstein, Democratic candidate for Maryland comptroller, and Steven Sachs, Democratic candidate for Maryland attorney general.

Veto of United States Aquaculture Bill

Memorandum of Disapproval of H.R. 9370. October 18, 1978

MEMORANDUM OF DISAPPROVAL

I have withheld approval from H.R. 9370, "A bill to establish new Federal programs and assistance for the development of aquaculture in the United States."

While the underlying purpose of the bill—development of an active aquaculture industry is sound, I am concerned that the numerous broad-reaching programs established under the bill are premature. H.R. 9370 would establish a National Aquaculture Council to assess the state of aquaculture in the U.S. and to prepare a National Aquaculture Development Plan—a detailed set of Federal activities to expand the commercial potential of certain aquatic species. It would establish substantial new programs of Federal assistance to carry out the plan and undertake demonstration projects in aquaculture. The bill also would create a Federal Aquaculture Assistance Fund to provide financial assistance and support to the aquaculture industry through a new Federal loan guarantee program and a new Federal insurance program.

The Administration recognizes the importance of aquaculture, the need for effective programs to support this, and the concept of an assessment of the aquaculture industry. In fact, many of the actions that the bill would require are already underway. Federal agencies are now involved in a wide variety of aquaculture activities, and they already have the legislative authorities they need to provide research and technical and financial assistance to the aquaculture industry. For example, the Small Business Administration can assist small business concerns which are engaged in aquaculture. The Department of Commerce, through its aquaculture research activities and the Sea Grant program, is supporting marine research, development, and advisory services. The Department of the Interior spends about $15 million yearly on freshwater aquaculture at its fish hatcheries, research and development laboratories, and cooperative fishery units. The Agriculture Department provides a complete range of information and technical assistance related to aquaculture. Additionally, the Farm Credit Administration

is authorized to extend credit to harvesters of aquatic products.

We also have in place a way to coordinate the aquaculture programs of the Federal Government—namely, the Interagency Subcommittee on Aquaculture of the Federal Council on Science and Technology.

Given this array of Federal activities, I believe we should more carefully assess the need for additional programs in this area. In particular, I am concerned about offering major new government subsidies such as the loan guarantee and insurance programs unless and until a clear need for them has been established. Accordingly, I must withhold my approval of the bill.

My Administration will continue to assess the needs of aquaculture and the effectiveness and adequacy of the Federal programs in this area. We look forward to reviewing these programs next year with the sponsors of this measure in the hope we can agree on additional improvements in the government's aquaculture program.

JIMMY CARTER

The White House,
    October 18, 1978.

NOTE: The text of the memorandum of disapproval was released on October 19.

Equal Rights Amendment

Remarks on Signing H.J. Res. 638.
October 20, 1978

Lot of happy faces this morning. [*Laughter*] Much more pleasant than you looked 2 months ago.

As is well known, the Constitution does not require that the President sign a resolution concerning an amendment to the Constitution of the United States. But I particularly wanted to add my signature to those of the Speaker of the House and to the President pro tem of the Senate, to again demonstrate as strongly as I possibly can my full support for the ratification of the equal rights amendment.

We still have 15 States of the 50 who have not ratified this amendment to the Constitution, which would give a simple acknowledgement that women should have equal rights under the laws of our Nation.

This has not been an easy effort. And although it's a well-deserved recognition of the fact that equal rights have not indeed been extended to women, there's been a gross distortion of what this amendment does.

I believe that a thorough debate, an accurate analysis of what the significance of this amendment is, will lead to ratification of the constitutional amendment.

It's a very important effort. We now will have three additional years to let the public be well educated, to let the legislatures of the remaining 15 States be thoroughly acquainted with the beneficial consequences of the ratification amendment and a chance to inspire all those who believe in equal justice and basic human rights in our country to show this by their full support of the passage of this amendment.

I and all my family, my Cabinet members, the Democratic Party officials, all of us are eager to work with those who have been so courageous and persistent in pursuing this great effort.

I think it is accurate to say that a few weeks ago even, the issue was in doubt. But because of the extremely effective effort made by Birch Bayh, Don Edwards, many others, certainly including the majority leader of the Senate, the Speaker of the House, this has been made possible for us all.

And now, as President of the United States, it's a great pleasure for me to sign the law passed by Congress, the resolution extending the time of 3 years for the ratification of the equal rights amendment. And in doing so, I urge all the people of the country to join me in correcting a basic defect in the American Constitution in providing equal rights for the women of our country.

[At this point, the President signed the resolution.]

Let me say that this is enough of ceremonies, and now it's time for all of us to go to work. *[Laughter]* I hope that we can start our efforts among the people of our country very early and not wait until the final few hours of intense debate in the State legislatures before we mount an effective effort.

I think Sarah Weddington here on my staff will be a major asset, and of course, my wife, my daughter-in-law Judy, who's working almost full-time. She's going to have to take a brief respite around the first part of December to deliver my first granddaughter. *[Laughter]* But other than that, we'll be working full-time.

And I want to thank all of you who have been so notable in your efforts, sometimes under the most discouraging circumstances. But I think that the truth has prevailed in the Congress, and I'm sure it will prevail in the rest of our country in the months ahead.

Thank you again, very much.

NOTE: The President spoke at 10:08 a.m. at the ceremony in the Cabinet Room at the White House.

No Public Law number was assigned to H.J. Res. 638.

National Family Week, 1978
Proclamation 4606.   October 20, 1978

By the President of the United States of America

A Proclamation

Families differ, but the values of family life are unchanging—warmth, love, compassion, support, and understanding. Families are the building blocks of civilization. Our social and individual achievements, be they great or small, can generally be traced to early family influences. Family values are our most fundamental and lasting heritage.

Changing social patterns have threatened family stability. In today's increasingly complex world it is important to maintain the values and continuity of family life. All families are important, but the extended family, the foster family and the adoptive family play a special role by relieving the isolation of those who lack the comfort of a loving nuclear family.

Thus, National Family Week offers the opportunity to pay special tribute to those who open their homes and provide the warmth of family life to those who would otherwise be alone. We salute all families as we focus attention this week on opportunities to restore their strength and help them meet the challenges of contemporary society.

Now, THEREFORE, I, JIMMY CARTER, President of the United States of America, in accordance with a joint resolution of Congress, do hereby proclaim the week of November 19, 1978, as National Family Week and call upon the American people to observe this week with appropriate thoughts and actions in their houses and communities.

IN WITNESS WHEREOF, I have hereunto set my hand this twentieth day of October, in the year of our Lord nineteen hundred seventy-eight, and of the Independence of the United States of America the two hundred and third.

JIMMY CARTER

[Filed with the Office of the Federal Register, 10:29 a.m., October 23, 1978]

Thanksgiving Day, 1978
Proclamation 4607.   October 20, 1978

By the President of the United States of America

A Proclamation

Since 1621, the people of this country have gathered each year to celebrate with a feast their good fortune in their continuing ability to provide for families and friends.

On this Thanksgiving Day, we reaffirm our faith in our heritage of freedom, and our spirit of sharing.

In the spirit of Thanksgiving, Americans humbly recognize how fortunate we are to be strong—as individuals, and as a nation. It is that strength which allows us to display compassion for those around the world who face difficulties that our forefathers, blessed with the American land, were able to overcome.

While Providence has provided Americans with fertile land and bountiful harvests, other nations and peoples have not been so favored. Each year growing food supplies give us greater cause for giving thanks, yet one person in six worldwide still suffers from chronic hunger and malnutrition.

Two hundred years ago the Continental Congress proclaimed a day of thanks, and asked for deliverance from war. This year, let us observe Thanksgiving in the spirit of peace and sharing, by declaring it a day of Thankful Giving, a day upon which the American people share their plenty with the hungry of other lands.

Now, THEREFORE, I, JIMMY CARTER, President of the United States of America, in accordance with Section 6103 of Title 5 of the United States Code, do proclaim Thursday, the 23rd of November, 1978, as Thanksgiving Day.

I call upon the Governors, Mayors, and all other State and local officials to broaden the observance of Thanksgiving to include the practice of Thankful Giving in their celebration, inviting Americans to share with those abroad who suffer from hunger.

I call upon the American people to make personal donations to religious or secular charities to combat chronic hunger and malnutrition, and to support the concept of Thankful Giving in order that we may one day assure that no individual anywhere will suffer from hunger, and that we may move to a day of universal celebration in a more perfect community within our nation and around the world.

IN WITNESS WHEREOF, I have hereunto set my hand this twentieth day of October, in the year of our Lord nineteen hundred seventy-eight, and of the Independence of the United States of America the two hundred and third.

JIMMY CARTER

[Filed with the Office of the Federal Register, 10:30 a.m., October 23, 1978]

Appointments of Additional District and Circuit Judges

Statement on Signing H.R. 7843 Into Law. October 20, 1978

The omnibus judgeship act, which I am signing today, creates an unprecedented number of new positions in the Federal judiciary—35 new judgeships on the courts of appeals and 117 on the district courts, increasing the size of the Federal bench by over one-quarter. These new judges will help us catch up on court backlogs and provide prompt, efficient administration of justice in this country.

Judicial decisions affect every American. It is imperative to select our top legal minds for these openings. At the appellate level, the 13 panels of the Circuit Judge Nominating Commission, which I established by Executive order, will screen candidates to ensure that only the most qualified individuals are considered. Similar commissions have been established in 18 States to consider candidates for district judgeships.

I will sign another Executive order which will set standards and guidelines for the selection of district court judges.

This order will encourage the creation of nominating commissions in States where they do not now exist, and it will set minimum standards for judicial selection in all States—even those that do not yet have commissions.

This act provides a unique opportunity to begin to redress another disturbing feature of the Federal judiciary: the almost complete absence of women or members of minority groups. Of 525 active judges, only 29 are black or Hispanic, and only 9 are women—and almost half of these have been appointed during my administration.

I am committed to these appointments, and pleased that this act recognizes that we need more than token representation on the Federal bench.

Last May I signed an Executive order requiring that judicial selection commissions actively recruit qualified minority and female lawyers as circuit judge candidates. I intend to write each Chairman of each panel to remind them of this obligation.

The Senate has historically played an important role in judicial selection, particularly at the district court level, and I ask the Senators—and their commissions, where they exist—to work with me to achieve a more representative judiciary. To further this goal, I will not nominate any judges in a circuit until I have had an opportunity to review *all* candidates for that circuit. All candidates for a district court will be reviewed in the same fashion before any final decisions are made.

I am happy to sign the omnibus judgeship act today. Our Nation needs these new judges, and it is important that they be the most qualified lawyers available. In filling these judicial openings, we must bear firmly in mind the vital issues these men and women will deal with—issues that will affect our national life well into the 21st century.

NOTE: As enacted, H.R. 7843 is Public Law 95–486, approved October 20.

Domestic Copper Industry

Letter to the Speaker of the House and the President of the Senate Transmitting a Report.   October 20, 1978

To Speaker Thomas O'Neill (To Vice President Walter Mondale)

In accordance with section 203(b)(2) of the Trade Act of 1974, enclosed is a report to the Congress setting forth my decision that import relief on unwrought, unalloyed copper is not in the national economic interest, and explaining the reasons for my decision.

Sincerely,

JIMMY CARTER

IMPORT RELIEF ACTION
UNWROUGHT, UNALLOYED COPPER

As required by section 203(b)(2) of the Trade Act of 1974, I am transmitting this report to Congress setting forth the actions I will take with respect to unwrought, unalloyed copper covered by the affirmative finding, on August 23, 1978, of the U.S. International Trade Commission (USITC) under section 201(d)(1) of the Trade Act. As my decision differs from that recommended by the USITC, I have included the reasons for my decision.

After considering all relevant aspects of this case, including those considerations set forth in section 202(c) of the Trade Act of 1974, I have determined that import relief is not in the national economic interest for the following reasons:

1. Import relief would impose significant costs on U.S. consumers of unwrought, unalloyed copper (refined copper). The increases in refined copper prices resulting from provision of relief could create incentives for circumvention of relief through increased imports of other copper products such as scrap, blister, and fabricated items. This would effectively reduce the level of protection provided to the domestic copper industry. Moreover, domestic copper fabricators would be faced with higher refined copper input costs and, at the same time, possible increased import competition in fabricated products.

2. Domestic copper market conditions have improved during 1978 and there is an improving outlook over the next several years for both the U.S. and world copper markets. U.S. and world copper prices have risen during 1978 and the world inventory overhang has declined. Domestic refined copper production increased during the first part of 1978; and imports have begun to decline from the high levels prevailing during the first part of the year.

3. Provision of import relief would subject U.S. jobs in other industries to possible foreign retaliation against U.S. exports or compensation by the United States in the form of reducing import restrictions on other products.

4. Import relief would adversely affect U.S. international economic interests. It would be contrary to our efforts to reduce trade barriers in the MTN and to develop cooperative international solutions to the world copper industry's problems in

the context of discussions in the UNCTAD Integrated Program for Commodities. Import relief would also affect our bilateral relations with Canada and with LDC copper producers, such as Chile, Zambia, and Peru, who are heavily dependent on copper exports as a source of foreign exchange earnings.

5. Trade adjustment assistance benefits have been and will continue to be available to copper mine, smelter, and refinery workers.

NOTE: This is the text of identical letters addressed to Thomas P. O'Neill, Jr., Speaker of the House of Representatives, and Walter F. Mondale, President of the Senate.

Domestic Copper Industry

Memorandum From the President.
October 20, 1978

Memorandum for the Special Representative for Trade Negotiations

Subject: Determination Under Section 202(b) of the Trade Act, Unwrought Unalloyed Copper

Pursuant to section 202(b)(1) of the Trade Act of 1974 (P.L. 93–618, 88 Stat. 1978), I have determined the action I will take with respect to the report of the United States International Trade Commission (USITC), transmitted to me on August 23, 1978, concerning the results of its investigation of a petition for import relief. This petition was filed by the Anaconda Co., Asarco, Inc., Cities Service Co. (Minerals Group), Copper Range Co., Cyprus Mines Corp., Duval Corp., Hecla Mining Co., Inspiration Consolidated Copper Co., Kennecott Copper Corp., Magma Copper Co., Phelps Dodge Corp., and Ranchers Exploration and Development Corp., on behalf of the domestic industry producing unwrought, unalloyed

copper, provided for in item 612.06 of the Tariff Schedules of the United States.

After considering all relevant aspects of the case, including those considerations set forth in section 202(c) of the Trade Act of 1974, I have determined that import relief is not in the national economic interest for the following reasons:

1. Import relief would impose significant costs on U.S. consumers of unwrought, unalloyed copper (refined copper). The increases in refined copper prices resulting from provision of relief could create incentives for circumvention of relief through increased imports of other copper products such as scrap, blister, and fabricated items. This would effectively reduce the level of protection provided to the domestic copper industry. Moreover, domestic copper fabricators would be faced with higher refined copper input costs and, at the same time, possible increased import competition in fabricated products.

2. Domestic copper market conditions have improved during 1978 and there is an improving outlook over the next several years for both the U.S. and world copper markets. U.S. and world copper prices have risen markedly during 1978 and the world inventory overhang has declined. Domestic refined copper production was up slightly during the first part of 1978; and imports have begun to decline from the high levels prevailing during the first part of the year.

3. Provision of import relief would subject U.S. jobs in other industries to possible foreign retaliation against U.S. exports or compensation by the United States in the form of reducing import restrictions on other products.

4. Import relief would adversely affect U.S. international economic interests. It would be contrary to our efforts to reduce trade barriers in the MTN and to de-

velop cooperative international solutions to the world copper industry's problems in the context of discussions in the UNCTAD Integrated Program for Commodities. Import relief would also affect our bilateral relations with Canada and with LDC copper producers, such as Chile, Zambia, and Peru, who are heavily dependent on copper exports as a source of foreign exchange earnings.

5. Trade adjustment assistance benefits have been and will continue to be available to copper mine, smelter, and refinery workers.

This determination is to be published in the FEDERAL REGISTER.

JIMMY CARTER

[Filed with the Office of the Federal Register, 4:46 p.m., October 20, 1978]

Egyptian-Israeli Peace Negotiations

White House Statement Following Meetings With the Israeli and Egyptian Delegations. October 20, 1978

President Carter met this afternoon with the Israeli and Egyptian delegations to the peace talks. The President's meetings followed the presentation Thursday evening of a revised United States negotiating draft of the main articles of the peace treaty between Egypt and Israel.

During the meetings with the President, both sides reviewed the progress of the negotiations and the remaining issues to be resolved. The meetings were held prior to consultations that both delegations will conduct with their governments.

As stated earlier today, the parties will be consulting separately with their governments about the current status of the negotiations. The President's meetings this afternoon were designed to assist those consultations.

Ambassador al-Baz of the Egyptian delegation has gone to London to consult with Vice President Mubarak, who is on a tour of several European capitals. Vice President Mubarak intends to return to Cairo to give President Sadat an up-to-date report on the status of the negotiations.

Israeli Foreign Minister Dayan and Defense Minister Weizman, along with Professor Barak and Dr. Rosenne, are returning to Israel Saturday night for consultations with their government. Both the United States and Egyptian delegations were informed of this decision in advance. The ministers plan to be in Israel several days, returning to the conference about midweek next week. Working contacts between members of all three delegations here in Washington will continue during their absence.

In addition to the President, those attending the meetings on the American side were: Dr. Zbigniew Brzezinski; Ambassador Alfred Atherton; Herbert Hansell, Counsel, State Department; William Quandt, NSC staff; Hamilton Jordan, Assistant to the President.

In addition to Ministers Dayan and Weizman, members of the Israeli delegation included: Ambassador Simcha Dinitz; Ely Rubinstein, Assistant Director General, Ministry of Foreign Affairs.

In addition to Minister Hassan Ali and Minister of State Butrus Ghali, members of the Egyptian delegation included: Ambassador Ashraf Ghorbal; Ambassador Abdallah al-Erian, legal adviser.

United States Arms Control and Disarmament Agency

Nomination of George M. Seignious II To Be Director. October 20, 1978

The President today announced his intention to nominate retired Army Lieutenant General George M. Seignious II to be Director of the U.S. Arms Control and Disarmament Agency. Seignious has served as the "at large" member of the President's SALT negotiating delegation since September 1977.

General Seignious was born June 21, 1921, in Orangeburg, S.C. He graduated from The Citadel in 1942, receiving a Regular Army commission as second lieutenant of infantry. During World War II, he served in Europe with the 10th Armored Division and rose from platoon leader to assistant operations officer of the Division.

Seignious' duty assignments have included serving as military assistant and executive assistant to the Secretary of the Army; Director of the Policy Planning Staff in the Office of the Assistant Secretary of Defense (International Security Affairs); military adviser to Governor Harriman and Ambassador Vance at the Paris Peace Talks on Vietnam; Commanding General of the 3d U.S. Infantry Division; U.S. Commander in Berlin; and adviser to Ambassador Rush during the Quadripartite Negotiations in Berlin in 1971.

In 1971 and 1972, Seignious served as Deputy Assistant Secretary of Defense (Security Assistance) and director of the Defense Security Assistance Agency. From 1972 to 1974, he was Director of the Joint Staff for the Joint Chiefs of Staff. He retired from the Army in 1974, and since then has been president of The Citadel.

Digest of Other White House Announcements

The following listing includes the President's daily schedule and other items of general interest as announced by the White House Press Office during the period covered by this issue. Events and announcements printed elsewhere in the issue are not included.

October 14

The President met at the White House with Zbigniew Brzezinski, Assistant to the President for National Security Affairs.

The President transmitted to the Congress:

—the 1977 annual reports of the Great Lakes Basin Commission, the Missouri River Basin Commission, the New England River Basins Commission, the Ohio River Basin Commission, and the Upper Mississipppi River Basin Commission;

—the 13th Annual Report of the Department of Housing and Urban Development.

October 15

The President departed the White House for a stay at Camp David, Md.

October 16

The President returned to the White House from Camp David.

October 17

The President met at the White House with:

—Dr. Brzezinski;

—Adm. Stansfield Turner, Director of Central Intelligence, and Dr. Brzezinski;

—Mrs. Carter, for lunch;

—James T. McIntyre, Jr., Director of the Office of Management and Budget.

October 18

The President met at the White House with:

—Dr. Brzezinski;
—Billy O. Hightower, national commander, Disabled American Veterans;
—Secretary of Commerce Juanita M. Kreps, Ambassador Robert S. Strauss, Special Representative for Trade Negotiations, and labor and management representatives of the men's apparel industry;
—Vice President Mondale.

The President attended a White House reception for the World Congress of Postal, Telegraph and Telephone International.

His Majesty Hassan II, King of Morocco, has accepted President Carter's invitation to make a state visit to the United States in November. The King will visit Washington on November 14 and 15 for discussions with the President and other senior United States officials. Details of the visit are being discussed between the two governments.

October 19

The President met at the White House with:

—Dr. Brzezinski;
—Senator Daniel K. Inouye of Hawaii;
—Senator Ted Stevens of Alaska.

The President attended a portion of the briefing by administration officials for Ohio civic and community leaders held in Room 450 of the Old Executive Office Building.

The President went to Blair House for a working lunch with the Egyptian, Israeli, and American delegations. The White House announced that the luncheon was a continuation of the talks the President had with both the Egyptian and Israeli delegations in the White House on Tuesday. The President continued to review with the delegations the status of the talks, including the progress made and the issues remaining.

The White House announced the members of the U.S. Presidential Delegation to the Investiture of Pope John Paul II at the Vatican. They are:

THE HONORABLE THOMAS P. O'NEILL, JR., Speaker of the House of Representatives (Personal Representative of the President);
MRS. THOMAS P. O'NEILL, JR.;
THE HONORABLE ZBIGNIEW BRZEZINSKI, Assistant to the President for National Security Affairs (Personal Representative of the President);
THE HONORABLE EDMUND S. MUSKIE, United States Senator from Maine;
THE HONORABLE ROBERT F. WAGNER, Personal Representative of the President to the Vatican;
MR. PETER SARROS, Deputy Personal Representative of the President to the Vatican;
MRS. PATRICK J. NUGENT;
THE REVEREND STANLEY E. MILEWSKI, chancellor, Orchard Lake Schools, Mich.;
THE HONORABLE JOSEPH P. ADDABBO, United States Congressman from New York;
THE HONORABLE FRANK ANNUNZIO, United States Congressman from Illinois;
THE HONORABLE DEWEY F. BARTLETT, United States Senator from Oklahoma;
MR. MATHEW W. BIESZCZAT, Cook County Commissioner, Ill.;
MR. JOHN F. CONNELLY, chairman of the board, Crown Cork & Seal Co.;
THE HONORABLE JAMES J. DELANEY, United States Congressman from New York;
THE HONORABLE EDWARD J. DERWINSKI, United States Congressman from Illinois;
MR. STAN FRANCZYK, Polish American columnist;
MR. JOHN FERRARO, president of the Los Angeles City Council;
THE HONORABLE J. JOSEPH GARRAHY, Governor of Rhode Island;
THE HONORABLE MARY ANNE KRUPSAK, Lieutenant Governor, State of New York;

Dr. Eugene Kusielewicz, president, Kosciuszko Foundation;

The Honorable John J. LaFalce, United States Congressman from New York;

The Honorable Patrick J. Leahy, United States Senator from Vermont;

Mr. Raymond E. Majerus, director of Region 10, United Auto Workers;

Mr. Aloysius A. Mazewski, president, Polish-American Congress and Polish National Alliance;

The Honorable Barbara A. Mikulski, United States Congresswoman from Maryland;

The Honorable Henry J. Nowak, United States Congressman from New York;

The Honorable Azie Taylor Morton, Treasurer of the United States;

The Honorable Lucien N. Nedzi, United States Congressman from Michigan;

Mr. Francis J. O'Connor, O'Connor, Thomas, Hammer, Bertsch & Norby;

The Honorable Dan Rostenkowski, United States Congressman from Illinois;

Mr. Jack Spitzer, president, B'nai B'rith International;

The Honorable George G. Tapper, former State Senator, Florida;

Mr. John Wojtylo of Detroit, Mich., cousin of Pope John Paul II;

The Honorable Clement J. Zablocki, United States Congressman from Wisconsin;

The Honorable Leo C. Zeferetti, United States Congressman from New York.

October 20

The President met at the White House with:

—Dr. Brzezinski;

—Charles L. Schultze, Chairman of the Council of Economic Advisers.

The President has accorded the personal rank of Ambassador to Michael B. Smith in connection with his position as U.S. negotiator on textile matters. Smith, 42, is a Foreign Service officer who has been detailed to the White House since 1971.

NOMINATIONS SUBMITTED TO THE SENATE

NOTE: The Congress having adjourned *sine die* on Sunday, October 15, no nominations were submitted during the period covered by this issue. The first session of the 96th Congress will begin on Monday, January 15, 1979.

CHECKLIST OF WHITE HOUSE PRESS RELEASES

NOTE: All releases of the Office of the White House Press Secretary, distributed during the period covered by this issue, have been included in the issue.

ACTS APPROVED BY THE PRESIDENT

Approved October 14, 1978

H.R. 1337_____ Public Law 95–458
An act to amend the Internal Revenue Code of 1954 with respect to excise tax on certain trucks, buses, tractors, et cetera, home production of beer and wine, refunds of the taxes on gasoline and special fuels to aerial applicators, and partial rollovers of lump sum distributions.

H.R. 13991_____ Public Law 95–459
An act to provide for the United States to hold in trust for the Susanville Indian Rancheria of Lassen County, California, approximately one hundred and twenty acres of land.

S. 3384_____ Public Law 95–460
Agricultural Foreign Investment Disclosure Act of 1978.

S. 2916_____ Public Law 95–461
Drug Abuse Prevention and Treatment Amendments of 1978.

H.R. 13692_____ Public Law 95–462
An act granting the consent of Congress to the Historic Chattahoochee Compact between the States of Alabama and Georgia.

H.J. Res. 685_____ Public Law 95–463
A joint resolution to designate October 7, 1979, the Sunday of "Fire Prevention Week" as "Firefighters' Memorial Sunday"; to designate October 14, 1978, as "National Jogging Day"; and to designate and authorize the President to proclaim, February 11, 1979, as "National Inventors' Day".

ACTS APPROVED—Continued

Approved October 17, 1978

S. 415_____ Public Law 95–464
An act to amend the Anadromous Fish Conservation Act to include fish in Lake Cham-
plain that ascend streams to spawn.

H.R. 12932_____ Public Law 95–465
An act making appropriations for the Department of the Interior and related agencies
for the fiscal year ending September 30,
1979, and for other purposes.

S.J. Res. 16_____ Public Law 95–466
A joint resolution to restore posthumously
full rights of citizenship to Jefferson F. Davis.

S. 2704_____ Public Law 95–467
Water Research and Development Act of
1978.

S. 2801_____ Public Law 95–468
An act to designate the building known as
the Ozark National Forest Headquarters
Building in Russellville, Arkansas, as the
"Henry R. Koen Forest Service Building".

H.R. 8394_____ Public Law 95–469
An act to provide for payments to local governments based upon the acreage of the National Wildlife Refuge System which is
within their boundaries, and for other
purposes.

S. 2376_____ Public Law 95–470
An act to authorize withholding from salaries
disbursed by the Secretary of the Senate
and from certain employees under the jurisdiction of the Architect of the Capitol for
contribution to certain charitable organizations.

S. 1215_____ Public Law 95–471
Tribally Controlled Community College Assistance Act of 1978.

H.R. 8811_____ Public Law 95–472
An act to amend section 7447 of the Internal
Revenue Code of 1954 with respect to the
revocation of an election to receive retired
pay as a judge of the Tax Court.

H.R. 10965_____ Public Law 95–473
An act to revise, codify, and enact without
substantive change the Interstate Commerce
Act and related laws as subtitle IV of title
49, United States Code, "Transportation".

S. 682_____ Public Law 95–474
Port and Tanker Safety Act of 1978.

Approved October 18, 1978

H.R. 6503_____ Public Law 95–475
An act to amend the Intercoastal Shipping
Act, 1933, and for other purposes.

ACTS APPROVED—Continued

Approved October 18—Continued

H.R. 12028_____ Public Law 95–476
Veterans' Housing Benefits Act of 1978.

H.R. 11302_____ Public Law 95–477
Environmental Research, Development, and
Demonstration Authorization Act of 1979.

H.R. 12255_____ Public Law 95–478
Comprehensive Older Americans Act
Amendments of 1978.

H.R. 11886_____ Public Law 95–479
Veterans' Disability Compensation and Survivors' Benefits Act of 1978.

H.R. 12929_____ Public Law 95–480
An act making appropriations for the Departments of Labor, and Health, Education,
and Welfare, and related agencies, for the
fiscal year ending September 30, 1979, and
for other purposes.

H.R. 12931_____ Public Law 95–481
An act making appropriations for Foreign
Assistance and related programs for the fiscal
year ending September 30, 1979, and for
other purposes.

H.J. Res. 1139_____ Public Law 95–482
A joint resolution making continuing appropriations for the fiscal year 1979, and for
other purposes.

H.R. 9998_____ Public Law 95–483
Ocean Shipping Act of 1978.

H.R. 10600_____ Private Law 95–61
An act for the relief of Thomas Joseph
Hunter and Rose Hunter.

Approved October 19, 1978

H.R. 13797_____ Public Law 95–484
An act to authorize establishment of the
Fort Scott National Historic Site, Kansas,
and for other purposes.

Approved October 20, 1978

S. 3486_____ Public Law 95–485
Department of Defense Appropriation Authorization Act, 1979.

H.R. 7843_____ Public Law 95–486
An act to provide for the appointment of
additional district and circuit judges, and for
other purposes.

H.R. 14026_____ Public Law 95–487
An act to provide means for the acquisition
and retention of title to certain lands by the
village corporation organized pursuant to
the Alaska Native Claims Settlement Act for
the Natives of the Village of Kake, Alaska,
and for other purposes.

ACTS APPROVED—Continued

Approved October 20—Continued

H.R. 13167_____ Public Law 95–488
An act to amend the Internal Revenue Code of 1954 to insure that the deduction for contributions to a black lung benefit trust be allowed for any such contributions which are made for the purpose of satisfying unfunded future liability, and for other purposes.

H.R. 13803_____ Public Law 95–489
An act to terminate the authorization of the navigation project on the Columbia Slough, Oregon.

S. 1318_____ Public Law 95–490
An act to permit the State of Hawaii to use the proceeds from the sale, lease, or other

ACTS APPROVED—Continued

Approved October 20—Continued

disposition of certain real property for any public purpose.

S. 3259_____ Public Law 95–491
Federal Information Centers Act.

S. 3373_____ Public Law 95–492
An act to amend title 10, United States Code, to authorize the Secretary of Defense to provide transportation to the Girl Scouts of the United States of America in connection with International World Friendship Events or Troops on Foreign Soil meetings, and for other purposes.

H.R. 11035_____ Public Law 95–493
An act to incorporate the United States Capitol Historical Society.

Wichita, Kansas

Remarks at a Rally for Bill Roy and John Carlin. October 21, 1978

Senator Bill Roy—doesn't that sound good? Well, it sounds good for the whole country; Governor John Carlin—that also sounds great—Congressman Dan Glickman; Congresswoman Martha Keys; distinguished officials of the Democratic Party in Kansas, which is constantly growing day by day, larger and larger, stronger and stronger; my fellow Americans who realize that we have a great country and we want to see it even greater:

It's an honor for me to come back to Kansas.

When I was first elected Governor of Georgia, there was a man whom I met in just a few days after the election, a man who was an inspiration to me and to all the other Governors who served with him, who was kind of a guide for us, and who set an example of sound management and integrity, competence, and that was Bob Docking.[1] And I think it's good that Kansans remember the sound statesmanship that has been exemplified in him and

---

[1] Former Governor of Kansas.

in your congressional delegation by Democrats.

I've enjoyed replacing Republicans in the White House. [*Laughter*] We've been trying to turn the country around, trying to manage the Government better, trying to cut redtape. When I got there the Republicans were cutting redtape, but they were cutting it lengthwise. [*Laughter*]

We've had a good experience in the last 20 months. But I look forward to seeing the Congress reconvene next January with Bill Roy as the first Democratic Senator to come from Kansas in, I believe, 46 years.

As you well know, he's a man of unique character and ability and background and experience. I think out of more than 200 million Americans, there are only 350 people who have both a degree in medicine and one in law. And he's had an ability as a Member of Congress, in the House of Representatives, to assess long before some of us realized it the intense need to give better services to people, particularly in the rural and small areas, emergency medical care, and at the same time cut the cost of this kind of care that all of us need. He set up health maintenance organizations, which gave us a mechanism by which people could cooperate in preventive health care, and at the same time set up mechanisms also to spread health care in an emergency way throughout our regional areas where doctors and medical care had been scarce.

He's a man who knows how to manage money, a sound and an effective legislator, and I look forward to being with him next year. He's a man also who has Kansas blood in his veins. He's quite independent, and I don't have any doubt that when his judgment comes down to what does the President want on the one hand and what do the people of Kansas want on the other, that he's going to vote with Kansas, and I'll forgive him for that ahead of time.

And I look forward to my next trip back to Wichita, back to Kansas when you will have a Democratic Governor.

John Carlin is the kind of candidate who in a leadership position in the Democratic Party makes a Democratic President proud. He's young. He's effective. As a speaker of your house, he's shown his wide grasp of the factors that make Kansans' lives better—good fiscal management, a sound and a fair tax structure.

And one of the things I particularly like about John Carlin, as a peanut farmer, is that he's a farmer himself. [*Laughter*] I'm not saying that he and I are going to plot against the other Americans, but we want to make sure that the farm families of this country don't suffer.

I've read a great deal about John Carlin before I came to Kansas. The only criticism that I've seen mentioned in the national press, that we read in Washington, is that some people have accused him of being too fiscally responsible. [*Laughter*] And I think that's a very fine criticism to make of a man who will serve as a Governor of a State like Kansas.

I don't want to see anybody in office who wants to waste money that the taxpayers send up. I think an efficient, effec-

tive government is the best one to deliver proper services to people, particularly when the philosophy of Kansan people needs to be adequately represented in the Governor's office. And I know John Carlin will do that.

Dan Glickman is a freshman Congressman, but he acts like one who's been there 20 years. [*Laughter*] My staff analyzed his record in the 95th Congress. There were nine major amendments that the Congress passed with Dan Glickman's name on them. And that is almost unprecedented. It shows that he has an intense commitment to hard work and effective work for you in Washington. And his service on the Agriculture Committee and, as you know, on the Science and Technology Committee fits in perfectly with Kansans' lives and particularly the region around Wichita, because you have equal to all other communities in the Nation a commitment to the future, in space, aviation, technology, as well as being the foremost wheat-producing State and one of the largest and best agricultural production States in the Nation.

And Dan Glickman fits in so well in his committee assignments—I think that's what has made him so strong, because he represents what you want with such an effective voice.

And I can't pass by an opportunity, although this is not her district, to mention Martha Keys, a woman with great influence, intellect, intelligence, courage, and who, even though this is only her second term, has become a foremost leader on perhaps the most important committee in the Congress, the House Ways and Means Committee.

She's responsible for health care, welfare, taxation, energy; and the legislation that the Congress has passed this year has her mark on it. And when she puts a mark on legislation, you can rest assured that the people of Kansas come out very well with her influence. I'm very proud of her.

I'd like to mention just a few things briefly that are on my mind this morning as I talk to you as President of your country.

All of us, I believe, in this audience realize that agriculture provides the industry that's the basic strength of our Nation. In the last 21 months or so, I've had an opportunity as a new President to analyze the strategic balance that exists between our country on the one hand and the others nations of the Earth on the other.

We believe, in fact we know that we have a superior position in politics, in government, economics, military might. But there are a lot of nations who compete with us in those varying aspects of international life. The one sound, stable, unchanging advantage that we have over all others is the land that God gave us, over which we act as stewards. Our productivity in agriculture is increasingly important now. But in the future, it gives us an assurance of a good life, an assurance of a beneficial impact and influence in other nations that's one of the proudest possessions of myself as President, of other members of our government, and indeed of the Western free world.

We cannot only correct many of our economic problems with our tremendous agricultural production, but we can use this influence to benefit the lives of many others. I think all of you know that in January of 1977, when I became President, the farm families of this country were in trouble. The people in Georgia, where I live, many of the people in Kansas, as well, were discouraged.

There were some predictions that agriculture in America was facing another depression, where the low relative income of American farm families was going to be even lower. Prices had hit the bottom; exports were faltering; the Government was

becoming more deeply intrusive in the lives of farm families, in the marketing of wheat, corn, basic feed grains, sorghums. The farm families quite often sold their crops cheap that went into the massive grain elevators. Commodity prices were manipulated. Sometimes prices went up, and the beneficiaries were not the farmers, because they had lost control over the food that they had produced.

That's been changed. The new farm legislation supported by your own Members of Congress, of course, went into effect almost exactly a year ago. Farm family income has gone up in 1 year $7 billion, between 20 and 25 percent more. We've tried to get government out of the lives of farmers. We've increased farm storage tremendously to let the farmers themselves have much more control over when they market their products, so that they can get the benefits of the changes in farm prices. And at the same time, we've tried to stabilize those prices.

We see American farm production continuing to go up. This year in the United States, the average corn production per acre is 100 bushels. At the same time, we don't feel that we need to worry about this good production, because we're working as hard as possible to increase the markets for American farm products.

Last year, we set an all-time record, even in dollars, with very low prices, as you well remember. We exported $24 billion worth of farm products in 1977. In 1978 we'll beat that record. We'll go to $26.6 billion in farm exports.

In just a few minutes, not coincidentally in Wichita, I'm going to sign a new agricultural export bill that will greatly enhance American farm export levels in the years to come.

These kinds of changes that have been made in the Government help us all. They're typical of the approach to American farm life of the Democratic

Party. But this is just one example out of many that I could mention.

The Democratic Party has always been a party of two things: one, compassion. We've always been concerned about people who need help. We've never believed in handouts, but we do believe in extending a hand to help someone, to help people stand on their own feet, support themselves, make their own decisions, become an integral part of a dynamic society.

We believe in children having a good education; young couples having an opportunity to buy a home; good highways to carry our products to market, to let us visit one another.

We believe in a strong defense. We also believe that we have to let people be employed. One of the greatest hungers in the life of a person is to let that one life, given by God, be used in a beneficial way.

I can't think of anything more devastating to a young man or woman, 18, 19, 20 years old, as they approach adulthood and begin to take their place in the community, than not to have a job and day by day by day be identified in one's own mind, in one's own family, in one's own community, as a failure, a nonproductive member of a great American society.

When I became President, we had 10 million Americans who did not have a full-time job, 7 million or more who had no job and who were looking for jobs. The Democratic Congress worked well with me. And we set up programs primarily to open up job opportunities in the private sector, because five out of six of the jobs in our country don't relate to government at all.

We've cut the unemployment rate 25 percent in just a short time that we've been in office. We've had a net increase of more than 6 million jobs in our country. This is the kind of approach that I think is proper for the Democratic Party to have.

We recognized some longstanding defects. We did not have, as you may have heard, a comprehensive national energy policy. And you know I said that it was the moral equivalent of war. I was beginning to feel it was the moral equivalent of the Hundred Years War. [*Laughter*] But the Congress has now passed a good energy bill. And it'll be improved by administrative action, and it'll probably be improved in the future by changes that Congress might make.

We've got a new Department of Energy now, and I think we can guarantee to you here not only a good market for energy products produced in your State but an assured supply of reasonably priced products in the years to come. We'll start conserving more. We'll start shifting to the more plentiful supplies of energy, and we'll have a chance to cut down on the enormous imports that have bled from our Nation, about $45 billion per year. We now import about 50 percent of our total oil. We want to turn that around.

We've also tried to root out fraud, mismanagement, waste from the Government.

I was concerned when I became President, when I was running for President, about the enormous budget deficits. It rubbed me wrong, as someone who's worked all my life for my own living, to see the budget deficits in Washington continue to go up and up and up.

When I was a candidate back in 1976, the budget deficit was almost $70 billion. We have already cut that budget deficit down to just a little above $40 billion, and we're moving in the right direction. And I'll keep as one of the major goals of my own administration a balanced budget. That's what I want to see while I'm still in the White House.

I think some of the most sacrificial and dedicated workers that I know of in the country are those who work for the Government. I'm not just talking about in the White House but other places as well. They are people who have offered their whole life's career to serving others.

But we had kind of a disgrace in the civil service system. And now the Congress has reformed the civil service for the first time in 95 years, and we are letting good, dedicated, competent, hard-working employees in the future be recognized and rewarded—and those who don't work quite so hard, we're going to inspire them to do a little bit better. If they don't, they're going to be transferred. If they don't improve, they'll be discharged.

And now managers can manage. But we're trying to put into our Government itself the same sort of fiscal management that has epitomized the successful elements of a free enterprise system.

I might say in passing that we're trying to make the free enterprise system better, a little bit more free. I think if you all would think back in the last few years, any of you who have flown in a commercial airline, you know that the rates have dropped tremendously. And you know why that's happened? Because we have gotten a Government regulatory agency to let the airlines compete with each other. In other words, we have gotten Government's nose out of the people's business and the rates have gone down; those empty airplanes have started filling up. It doesn't cost as much to haul one passenger, and the airlines are making more profit. And this is a very excellent example of what we are trying to do in Washington.

Well, I could go on and on. But I do want to mention two more things before I close. One is in foreign affairs.

I think all of us realize that 2 years ago, 3 years ago, the American people were disheartened, we were embarrassed, we were alienated from our Government. Sometimes we Americans were even ashamed of our own Government. The Vietnam war, the CIA revelations, the Watergate scandals, all made us feel that our country was not quite so clean, not quite so decent, not quite so honest, not quite so open as it ought to be. But we've turned that around as best we could. No one's perfect.

We've not only tried to bring that kind of attitude to government, we've also raised high a banner for the world to see of the principles and ideals on which American life has been founded for the last 200 years. And there's not a single leader in the world among 150 nations who doesn't think every day now about basic human rights. And as long as I'm in the White House, they're going to keep on thinking about that.

And the last thing I want to mention is this: We are a strong people. We're a people who have never been afraid of a challenge. We don't like to be pushed around. We have the strongest military strength in the world. We're going to keep it that way.

But we also believe in peace. And I thank God that since I've been in the White House, we've not had a single American soldier shed blood in a foreign country. And I hope I can go out of office having maintained that record of peace built on strength, not just for ourselves, but we are trying every day, through the most intense, concerted effort, to bring peace to others around the world who have been suffering more than we have.

Cy Vance just left South Africa a few days ago, 2 days go, where he's trying to make sure that Namibia doesn't erupt into war, trying to bring peace to Rhodesia. He's negotiating today in Moscow to have concluded a good SALT agreement that'll protect us in the future.

We had good luck at Camp David in trying to bring—[*applause*]—and I think one of the reasons that we had this success so far is because of the commitment of American people to extend a hand of moderation and conciliation and help to others like President Sadat and Prime Minister Begin who genuinely want peace for their people. But that's escaped the Holy Land, as you know, for hundreds and hundreds of years. And I hope we will be successful in our negotiations.

So, I've tried to outline as briefly as I could some of the characteristics, some of the achievements, some of the remaining problems of the Democratic Party.

We don't claim that we know all the answers. But we have an innate strength as Democrats, in that we cast our lot directly with you. We derive our strength from you, our counsel and advice from you, our criticisms, in a constructive way, from you.

We try to stay close to you, because I said during the campaign many times— sometimes the press teased me about it— that I want a government in Washington as good and decent and honest and truthful and competent as the American people. That's what we want to have. And I believe that we'll have it.

One of the best ways to guarantee it is to give me in Washington, from Kansas, a good Democratic team to work with. That's important.

You've come here today to help the candidates in whom you believe, for U.S. Senate, for Governor, for Congress. And I hope every one of you will go away from this meeting, not with a sense that you've done enough by coming here, but with a determination to make your own lives a kind of a focal point for success for the candidates in whom you believe. Each one of you has the character and ability and influence to be kind of a one-person cam-

paign manager for Bill Roy, John Carlin, for your candidates for Congress.

And I want you to pledge to me as Americans that you'll not only vote but that you will work between now and November 7. And with these candidates being successful, with your help, we'll make the greatest nation on Earth even greater in years to come.

Thank you very much.

NOTE: The President spoke at 12:40 p.m. in the Exhibition Hall at the Century II Convention Center.

Wichita, Kansas

Remarks at a Bill Signing Ceremony for S. 3447.   October 21, 1978

As I said in the other room, with a peanut farmer in the White House and a dairy farmer in the statehouse, I think the Kansas farmers will at least have very strong voices in State and Federal Government.

There's no doubt that agriculture is the stable element in our Nation's economy. And quite often in the past it's not been adequately recognized.

This morning I come before you to sign a very important piece of legislation. Last October we put into effect the agricultural bill, an omnibus bill of 1977. There have been substantial improvements already in the income level of American farmers and also in the level of exports. But I have felt with increasingly bountiful harvests, which have been very obvious this year throughout the country, that even greater emphasis ought to be placed on exports.

Last year we had very low farm prices, as you know. But in spite of those very low prices per unit, we had the highest export level in the history of our country, about $24 billion. This year we've increased it even more to about $26.6 billion. But the Congress has worked very well—as you know, Dan Glickman is a member of that committee—in describing some of the problems in increasing agricultural exports in the future.

In the first place, we do not have competitive trade offices around the world to sell our agricultural products. When I was Governor of Georgia, we had—just one State—six different international trade offices located in different capitals and trade centers around the world—in Rio de Janeiro, in São Paulo in Brazil, in Bonn, Germany, in Brussels, Belgium, and Toronto, Canada, and so forth—just to sell Georgia products. And the Congress has now well recognized that we don't have that same capability of having trade offices where you have a merchant there whose sole responsibility is to sell American agricultural products. And in the future we will have this capability.

The Congress mandated between 6 and 25 trade offices to be established under the Department of Agriculture to sell American farm products in a competitive way in the future.

Another thing that we decided to do in this legislation is to give special loans, well-secured loans, from 3 years up to 10 years to establish grain reserves that might enhance the shipment of American grain overseas, to be sure that we had breeder livestock sales, to increase the export of our American beef and pork and poultry. We've not been competitive in exports of livestock in the past. Other countries have, as you well know.

And also to provide marketing facilities. There are some nations that want to buy our products. They don't have an easy or convenient way to unload wheat or corn or sorghum in their dockyards. And so, we can give short loans now for these countries, well secured, they're not giveaway programs to let them buy our agricultural products.

We are increasing the stature of the representatives of the Agriculture Department in our consulates and in our embassies around the world so that they can have a higher level of authority in pursuing their single purpose of increasing American markets overseas.

Another thing that we've tried to do is to increase the possibility of nations to buy American products.

We've changed recently the right of the Soviet Union to buy from 8 million metric tons of grain up to 15 million metric tons of grain without going through the procedure of getting approval for it. We've got the grain on hand. We want the Soviets to buy it.

And as you know, one of the things that has devastated our markets in the past have been embargoes imposed by previous administrations. As long as I'm in the White House there are not going to be any embargoes to prevent the shipment of American products overseas.

And just one other point that I believe is important. We have also authorized short-term CCC loans to the People's Republic of China to buy American wheat, sorghum, and corn. In the past we have lost this tremendous market completely. One out of four people on Earth live in the People's Republic of China. And they've been going to Canada, going to Australia, going to Argentina, going to Brazil, buying beans, corn, and wheat. They have not bought any from us in the past. In the future we hope to open that market as well.

So, what we are trying to do is to join in with you in letting the Federal Government, for a change, not be an obstacle to the sale of American farm products, but to be an avenue by which that sale might be enhanced, because we don't want a surplus to accumulate here in our country that forces the price down, and I don't want to put a constraint on American farmers about what you can produce.

I want to get the Government's nose out of the farmers' business rather than stick it deeper into the farmers' business. And I think this is a very good approach that the Congress has done.

Jim Cramer was in the White House, I think last Valentine's Day, representing the American farm movement, to add his voice to the counsel and advice, along with many others, on what we ought to do to improve American markets. This is one of the things that has resulted from his visit there. And I want to express my appreciation to him personally and to all of you who have helped me.

This is the second bill that I've ever signed outside Washington. The other one was when I went to New York to sign a bill to try to keep New York out of bankruptcy. [*Laughter*] But this is not designed to keep American farmers out of bankruptcy, because you're no longer on the verge of bankruptcy. But this is to make your lives more profitable in the future.

And it's a great pleasure for me as President of the United States to come to Wichita, Kansas, to sign into law a bill that will give us a greatly enhanced opportunity in the future to sell the superb products that you produce so well in your great State.

Thank you very much.

[*At this point, the President signed the bill.*]

Well, we've got a new law.

NOTE: The President spoke at 1:21 p.m. in Meeting Room 201 at the Century II Convention Center. Jim Cramer is the Kansas delegate to the American Agriculture Movement.

As enacted, S. 3447, the Agricultural Trade Act of 1978, is Public Law 95–501, approved October 21.

Wichita, Kansas

Remarks at a Reception for Bill Roy and John Carlin. October 21, 1978

Since I couldn't get anybody to introduce me, I decided to introduce myself. [*Laughter*] I'm Amy's father and Billy's brother—[*laughter*]—Rosalynn's husband and Lillian's son. [*Laughter*]

I'm not going to make another speech, because you've already heard me tell you what I think our party stands for and the great qualities of Bill Roy and John Carlin and your great Congressman, Dan Glickman. And I know that you agree with me.

What I would like to do is to emphasize to you the last thing I said in my talk. It is never an easy thing for a Democrat to be elected in Kansas. And I think we have a history of political elections to prove that what I've said is true. Things are looking good for the Democrats all around the country. But it's because we've been underdogs. It's because we have worked harder. It's because we've recognized that we were not and will not be as well financed, and it's because we had fervent, committed, enthusiastic, sacrificial supporters to give us political strength when we couldn't buy it.

And I know that all of you have already contributed to the campaigns of those with me on the stage. But you haven't given as much as you can, and you haven't given as much as you ought to.

There is no greater investment that you could possibly make than to have a better government—a State government and a Federal Government. And I hope that every one of you will consider how you can even sacrifice to make the political campaigns of these good men more successful.

Some of you may have already given a

thousand dollars to Bill Roy's campaign, and maybe your wife or husband has also given a thousand dollars. That's all you can give legally. And I don't want you to do anything illegally. [*Laughter*] But there's no reason that you can't contact your friends, your neighbors, other members of your family, and help them raise additional money.

The last 2 or 3 weeks of a campaign is when Republicans have been most successful in the past, when they have upset Democrats who are favored in the polls, because they can have a massive blanketing of the news media, radio, television, newspapers. And we need to protect ourselves from that. All we want is the Kansas people to know the truth. And this can be done by word of mouth.

It's extremely important that you concentrate on election day as well.

In 1960, two-thirds of the American people voted on election day. In recent elections, two-thirds of the American people did not vote on election day. And sometimes, as you know, a campaign turns on very, very few votes. In Ohio, recently, almost every major campaign has been decided on less than one vote per precinct.

And I hope that all of you will remember this and organize in your own way an effective "Get Out the Vote" campaign on election day. So, organize ahead of time additional recruits to campaign actively. Give financially as much as you can and make sure that on election day you, your family, your neighbors, your whole community is reminded that if you don't vote, you are the loser.

We're going to make an effort all over the Nation to remind people to vote, but there is absolutely no substitute for direct contact from a citizen who is known by someone who says, "I believe we ought to vote today."

Now, I know what can be done. When I was campaigning for President, my first test was in Iowa. In the entire State of Iowa, less than 30,000 people went to the Democratic caucuses to choose the delegates to the national convention. It was in January of 1975. In those last few days from my bedroom in Plains, Georgia, with the telephone, I called an average of 125 or 130 people long-distance every day to ask them to give me their support for President. And I consider those telephone calls to have been the difference, perhaps, between my having been elected President and losing.

And there's no reason that any of you, whether you've got a secretary to place the calls or whether you do it on your own, can't go down a portion of a telephone book and call those that you know and say, "Tomorrow or today is election day. Let's all go out and support John Carlin, support Bill Roy, support Dan Glickman, and have a good strong team in whom we can have confidence to lead our State and to lead our Nation." I'm very serious about this, and I want you to be serious as well.

That's my speech. I'm going to leave in a few minutes to go to Minnesota. But as I do leave, I hope that you will not take lightly what I've asked you to do. It's a tremendous investment in a better life for you and a better life for the people that you love. And I hope that you won't overlook this opportunity to make our Nation one of which you can be proud and feel that you are part of a team.

Now, if you don't mind, I'd like to take the rest of my time—I'm going to go through the crowd, and I'll have to keep moving, but I'd like to shake hands with as many people as I can reach in a few minutes.

NOTE: The President spoke at 1:43 p.m. in the Service Club Room at the Century II Convention Center.

Rochester, Minnesota

Remarks at the Rochester Municipal Airport.
October 21, 1978

Senator Anderson, Governor Perpich, Mayor Smekta, Chairman Scott, National Chairman John White, Congressman Oberstar, Congressman Nolan, next Senator Bob Short, Congressman Mike Freeman, in the future, and Gerry Sikorski:

Thank you very much for welcoming me here.

I've been wondering where Fritz Mondale was, and I should have guessed he was in Minnesota. [*Laughter*]

This is the first time that he and I have ever been together on a campaign trip since the election, and it's no accident. Not only is Minnesota his home, but we consider the elections this year in your State to be unequaled in importance in the entire Nation.

I particularly want to thank Gerry Sikorski and your fine mayor for being present to welcome us. I felt surely they'd be in Poland or either in Rome today, one or the other. [*Laughter*] But I think all of us recognize the tremendous resurgence or surgence of Poles throughout the world; that I predict that next January, when the new Congress is sworn in, that there will be a fine young Polish American Congressman from the First District of Minnesota.

I'm very grateful and somewhat sobered to come back to your State. As a Governor for 4 years who served with Wendy Anderson, as a Democrat throughout my life, as someone who has been interested in government earmarked by honesty and decency and openness and responsibility and character and truthfulness and compassion, I think I can say as a Georgian, as an American, as President, that your State and the Democrats in it have long exemplified those attributes above and beyond any other State party in our country. And I want to thank you for it.

There are a lot of reasons. One is that there's an ease with which Minnesotans can participate in government. And as I said many times during the campaign, I think government ought to be as good and honest and decent and truthful and compassionate and competent and as filled with love as the people of this country. But you have another reason, as well.

The last time I came to your State, it was not a happy occasion. I came here to pay the Nation's last tribute to a man who exemplified more than anyone I have ever known what is good about politics, about government, about public service, and about our country.

Hubert Humphrey was a man who was an inspiration to me and, I'm sure, to all of you. He was courageous, he was a fighter. He never backed down in the face of difficulty or a severe challenge or an obstacle. He never was afraid to show emotion. No one ever doubted that his heart was big, because he was genuinely concerned about a person who was black or who could not speak English well or who was poor or who was a Native American or someone who didn't have a job or didn't have a home or had a small farm deeply in debt or didn't have a friend or was struggling to get started in a profession or politics. Everybody knew that there was one man in this Nation to whom they could turn, not just for sympathy, because he was not just a sympathetic type person. But he considered that unfortunate American to be as good as he was, and he wanted to give that person a chance to prove it in a society, in a system that he cherished and loved so much.

I remember the difficult days in the South in 1964 when he was running for Vice President. Democrats were fairly scarce in Georgia. Muriel Humphrey came to Georgia to campaign with my mother, Lillian, and my wife, Rosalynn. Bob Short, who will be your next Senator, was there running the nationwide campaign for Hubert Humphrey to be Vice President—a close friend, a loyal friend who came into the South to say, "We've got a man from Minnesota in whom you can have trust."

This was a fine demonstration of leadership, and of course, our Nation's loss came when Hubert Humphrey was not elected President in 1968 because the Democratic Party was divided. And because the Democratic Party could not heal its wounds after the 1968 convention in Chicago, Hubert Humphrey was not elected President. And Richard Nixon was elected President. That should have taught Democrats a lesson.

People are different. Fritz Mondale is different from me. You've got candidates running for Congress, some from the northern part of Minnesota who might be quite conservative on some issues, some from the cities who might be identified as quite liberal. The U.S. Senate candidates are different from one another, but there's a basic underlying commitment of the Democratic Party that does not change. And as President I have stood there in the White House with Fritz Mondale many times and recognized that only because of party loyalty and a common purpose and a common commitment and common ideals and common beliefs, could we prevail. And the Democratic candidates and the Democratic Members of Congress from the South or the West or the North, in a time of trial for our country, domestic or foreign trials, have a tendency to stand together.

And I would like to urge you, if I don't do anything else while I'm here, to remember Hubert Humphrey, to remember what happened to him when our party was divided, to remember what he stood

for, to remember his friends and commit yourselves now to give the Democratic candidates a tremendous victory on November 7. That's what I want you to do. Will you do it? Will you do it? [*Applause*] Very good.

We still enjoy Hubert Humphrey's legacy. The Humphrey-Hawkins bill will give us a chance on the one side to put Americans to work. We've had remarkable success in the last 20 months. The unemployment rate in Minnesota has been cut to less than half what it was. You've got an unbelievably low unemployment rate. But the Humphrey-Hawkins bill is now ready to reach out, to give other people who are hard to employ, the last ones hired, the first ones fired, a decent chance in life. And at the same time it commits us to careful planning for the future, not just to control unemployment but to control inflation, to work together with the Congress, the President, Governors, mayors, employers, workers, farmers, to say, "What can we do to bring down both unemployment and also inflation at the same time and engender in our country a better use of the tremendous resources, human and natural resources that God gave us?"

I want particularly to mention today, Senator Wendell Anderson. He and I were elected Governor together. We served together for 4 years, a bright, young, shining star among the 50 Governors of our Nation. But it's remarkable what he has accomplished since he's been in the Senate.

The problems that I face are broad. Energy has been one of the most difficult, challenging, complicated, confusing issues we ever faced. We've never had an energy policy before. Wendy Anderson just happens to serve on the Energy and Natural Resources Committee. And he was one of those in the Senate who was able, working with Scoop Jackson and others, to

1823

come forth with a proposal that the Congress ultimately accepted.

I inherited 20 months ago a budget deficit of $66 billion. I believe Democrats ought to be fiscally responsible. I don't think we ought to waste money. I think we ought to manage the Government well. I think we ought to be efficient, because you've never educated a child, you've never fed a hungry person, you've never built a house or a road with waste and inefficiency. Wendy Anderson just happens to serve on the Senate Budget Committee, and we have already been able, in 2 years, to cut the budget deficit of the United States by more than $28 billion. And it's still on the way down, and I need Wendy Anderson to help me get it down.

I'm not going to go down a whole list of things he's done, because that would take too much time. But I would like to say this: I believe that our country has now and always must have the strongest defense capability on Earth. Wendy Anderson just happens to serve on the defense committee in the Senate, the Armed Services Committee. And he, along with me next year, is committed to bringing to our Nation a new SALT agreement hammered out with the Soviets, protecting our interests, to be another major step in eliminating the threat of nuclear war, not only for our own country and the whole world. And I need Wendy Anderson in Washington to help me get that SALT agreement ratified by the Senate.

Rudy Perpich has been a good heir to the Governorship of your great State. I think he's brought a new tone to Minnesota politics which is very valuable. He's shown already that he knows how to cut taxes. He's pledged himself to cut taxes even more in a responsible way, not in a ridiculous way.

He's a tough Iron Ranger who knows how to fight against waste. He believes in a better education for children. He wants to take care of the health of Minnesotans, not just in Rochester, which has the greatest medical center on Earth, but throughout his State as well. And he's proven that he has the ability to understand just common, ordinary, everyday, good people. He's one of us. He's one of you. And I hope you'll give him your support.

And I'd like to mention one other person before I close, who's a fine young candidate, who stayed home today from Rome to be with me. And that's Gerry Sikorski.

He was born in a rural community like I was. His family knows what it means to live under a Republican administration, because they lost their farm during the great Hoover Depression. Gerry's father worked on a railroad yard for 40 years. His family knows what it means to be poor, to struggle, to have difficulties and to overcome them.

This young man went to college because of his father's hard work. He graduated near the top of his class and, as you know, has been the attorney for a township, which gives him a good insight into the quality of life, not only in rural areas, not only in the life of a poor family, but also, he knows what makes a city great.

This district needs a Democratic Congressman. And I hope that you will help me, and I hope that you will help our Nation, and I hope that you will help yourselves by sending Gerry Sikorski to the Congress with a great victory on November 7.

I've observed Hubert Humphrey and Muriel Humphrey, Wendy Anderson, your congressional delegation. I can tell you that Minnesota does not send rubberstamps to Congress. You keep the congressional delegation toes to the fire. And whenever there's a conflict in Wendy Anderson's mind between what the President wants and what the people of Minnesota want, he listens to the voices back home. And that's the way it ought to be.

But I'm thankful that in the White House, I've got a man who's a full partner with me, who does the best he can, almost always successfully, to be sure that the President wants what the Minnesota people want—and that's Fritz Mondale.

I think I can say without anyone disputing this that there has never been in the history of the United States a closer and more valuable partnership between the President of our country and the Vice President of our country, than between Jimmy Carter and Fritz Mondale. And I'm thankful for that.

There are no decisions which I make in which he is not involved. He is my foremost adviser, my closest confidant. He's the man to whom I turn when I have a problem or have trouble or a difficulty that I can't resolve. He knows this country well. He knows the Members of Congress. His ideals, his standards, his integrity is absolutely impeccable, and you know that. But I would like to thank you for training a man and giving to me a man to serve as Vice President with the qualities that Fritz Mondale has brought to my administration. Thank you very much.

Of course he helps me in domestic affairs, presiding over the Senate. But when I got in trouble at Camp David a few weeks ago, and it became obvious to me that the situation was hopeless and that both the Egyptians and the Israelis were ready to leave and go home, I put in a call to Fritz Mondale.

I said, "Fritz, what are your plans for the day?" And he said, "I have three States to visit. My promises have already been made." And I said, "I would like for you to cancel that trip and come to Camp David," which he did. And it doubled the ability that I had to deal

effectively with Prime Minister Begin and President Sadat, because I never had any doubt that when Fritz Mondale was talking to President Sadat or to Prime Minister Begin or their delegations, that he spoke with the same authority and the same voice as though I was there myself.

But the most important thing was that there was no doubt in the minds of Sadat and Begin that when Fritz Mondale spoke, he was speaking for the President of the United States. And we are indeed fortunate in this country to have a man like him as Vice President. I sincerely hope that you will not tell him what I said about him. [*Laughter*]

Let me close by saying this: It's no accident, as I said earlier, that Fritz and I have come together here. This is the most important State in the Nation for elections this year. You've come here to see a President. You've come here because you're interested in government. But your coming here is not enough.

I would like for every one of you when you leave here to resolve in your own heart to make a contribution to your country by sending to Washington two Democratic United States Senators, eight Democratic Members of Congress, and keeping in office a fine Democratic Governor and his administration.

You believe that all of us when we get in office should do a good job. But the responsibility is also on your shoulder. And I have seen many fine candidates lose an election—that close—because their best friends, allies, neighbors, relatives, supporters took an election for granted or were not willing to invest a tiny bit of one's own character and ability and finances in a successful campaign.

There is no one here that can't go home, no matter how old or young you might be, and become a campaign manager for the candidates that you admire so much. Organize your own home, your own block, your own community, and let's make November 7 be a tremendous victory for the Democratic Party and for our Nation.

We've got the greatest nation on Earth. If you work hard enough between now and November, then in the future it can be even greater than it already is.

Thank you very much. You do your part; I'll do mine.

NOTE: The President spoke at 4:23 p.m. In his opening remarks, he referred to Ulric Scott, State Democratic-Farmer-Labor chairman, and John C. White, Democratic National Committee chairman.

Minneapolis, Minnesota

Remarks at a Bill Signing Ceremony for H.R. 8533. October 21, 1978

It's a rare thing for me to sign a major piece of legislation outside Washington. I've only done it twice. Once was when we approved the legislation which would save New York City from bankruptcy, and I decided to go to New York to do this. It was much better received up there than it was in Washington. [*Laughter*]

And the other time was earlier today in Wichita, Kansas, when I signed the Farm Trade Act of 1978, which will greatly enhance our ability to export farm products to foreign nations. This bill is far-reaching in its effect. It will authorize a further expansion of exports.

Last year, as you know, in spite of very depressed unit farm prices, we had the highest level of exports in history, $24 billion. This year, we'll hit $26.6 billion, perhaps a little more; next year, even higher figure. And I know in your own region here it's absolutely crucial that we have a continuation of sustained farm exports, particularly with the bumper crops

that we have experienced in recent months.

A third of our grain which is exported is transported down the Mississippi River—one-third. Eleven percent of our total exports go through the Mississippi River Transportation System, much higher percentage than that in bulk cargo of all kinds.

One of the serious problems in the past in increasing this rate of transport of products that are produced here in Minnesota and other parts of the Midwest has been the Locks and Dam 26 in Illinois. And for many years, there has been an attempt made to have authorization passed to improve this system. The Congress has now passed this legislation. It's not yet been signed by the President. And I wanted to come here where you are so heavily interested in this project to put my signature on the bill which will make it law.

This is an authorization bill. At the same time ever since Franklin Roosevelt was President, there has been an attempt made to let those who use our waterways contribute to the improvement and construction of projects that would enhance the use of the waterways, waterway user fees. This bill authorizes that to be done.

Beginning in 1980, 4 cents per gallon of fuel sold for use in barge transport will go into a trust fund. And that will build up by 1985 to 10 cents a gallon. By 1985 we'll have $100 million a year going into this trust fund that will then be used exclusively for the improvement of our waterway system itself. I think this is a very good step in the right direction.

Along with this the Congress has directed that an entire study be made of the concept of water user fees to be sure that they can be extended throughout the country and used in the most effective way; and also a study to be made of the Mississippi River Basin, particularly its transportation system. All of these provisions are in the bill before me now.

I would particularly like to thank the Minnesota congressional delegation. Senator Wendell Anderson serves on the Energy and National Resources Committee and also on the Budget Committee, which is very helpful in passing legislation important to your State, as you can well see. And of course, Senator Humphrey, both Hubert and his wife, Muriel, have been of great help in getting this legislation passed.

The Members of the House have done the same. I want to express my thanks to them. Also, since we are signing this bill outside Washington, I think it's good to recognize for the media itself some others who have worked very hard on this legislation: Senator Stevenson—Adlai Stevenson of Illinois; Senator Russell Long, who is chairman of the Finance Committee and very interested in the Mississippi, of course; and Senator Domenici; Senator Jennings Randolph from West Virgina, who was the founder of the Interstate Highway System and who's been a very heavy contributor throughout his own legislative career, which is distinguished— which I hope will continue for 6 more years after this year—who has been instrumental in helping me. And of course, in the House, Bizz Johnson, and the chairman of the Ways and Means Committee, Al Ullman.

But I'm very proud to recognize all those Members of the Congress, your own delegation, particularly, from Minnesota.

And now I will sign into law House bill 8533, which will authorize the future construction of Locks and Dam 26, in Alton, Illinois, and make even more effective the use of the Mississippi River for transporting your products both to other parts of our country and to overseas export.

Thank you very much.

[At this point, the President signed the bill.]

We are very honored tonight to have with us not only the Vice President, who's worked as a partner with me on this, but also Brock Adams, who's the Secretary of Transportation. And I'd like to see if Brock has a word to say.

NOTE: The President spoke at 7:15 p.m. in the Lake of the Isles Room at the Minneapolis Auditorium.

As enacted, H.R. 8533 is Public Law 95–502, approved October 21.

Inland Waterways Authorization Bill

Statement on Signing H.R. 8533 Into Law. October 21, 1978

Today I have signed into law H.R. 8533, an act that authorizes the replacement of Locks and Dam 26 at Alton, Illinois, and establishes the principle of user charges on the inland waterways.

Many people in Congress worked to make this bill possible. I want to express my particular appreciation to Senators Wendell Anderson, Adlai Stevenson, Russell Long, Pete Domenici, and Jennings Randolph, and to Chairmen Bizz Johnson, Glenn Anderson, and Al Ullman, who helped to fight for Locks and Dam 26 and for an adequate user charge.

The act I have just signed takes an historic first step by providing a fuel tax on commercial operators on the waterway system. Until now, the costs of building, maintaining, and operating the navigation facilities that waterway operators use have been borne entirely by the general taxpayers, with no contribution from users. Every administration since that of Franklin D. Roosevelt has tried to change this situation. This bill makes substantial progress toward accomplishing this long sought goal.

The bill provides for a tax that will start at 4 cents per gallon in 1980, and increase to 10 cents per gallon in 1985. The proceeds from this tax will be deposited in a trust fund for use in construction of new waterway projects. While this is less than the cost recovery I had requested, it is a major step in that direction.

The act also provides for a comprehensive study to be carried out by the Secretary of Transportation for the purpose of fully assessing the impacts and effects of various types and levels of user charges. We are looking forward to carrying out this study and making recommendations based on it to a future Congress. I intend to continue to work hard for an adequate level of cost recovery on the waterway system.

The bill is also important because it authorizes a much needed new lock and dam at Alton, Illinois. Many in the Midwest have long been concerned with the condition and capacity of Locks and Dam 26. Farmers who depend on water transportation to move their grain to market, and others who rely on our waterways for supplies of chemicals, fuels, fertilizers, and other bulk commodities, know the importance of a smoothly functioning waterway system. There is no question that significant physical deterioration has occurred in the present facility at Alton and that an increase in its capacity will be needed before long. This law meets these concerns by authorizing a new, modern facility with a single 1,200-foot lock designed to meet the needs of waterborne traffic in this area for many years to come.

The prolonged and lively debate over this authorization has raised fundamental issues of national transportation policy. My decision to support the authorization for construction of a new facility at Alton was made in the context of careful con-

sideration of all the transportation factors involved.

The careful consideration that the administration and the Congress gave to this issue illustrates the new era of budgeting restraint we are entering. In the future, we can only afford to invest in the highest priorities and the most needed projects. This applies not only for waterway and other transportation facilities but in every area of Federal spending.

The Upper Mississippi River Basin Commission is required to carry out comprehensive studies of the future transportation requirements of this region. We are very hopeful that these studies, along with the analysis of user charges, will lead to a prudent program of future waterway investment, together with a fair and just cost recovery mechanism. If we can accomplish these goals, we can continue to provide this region with the transportation system it must have.

NOTE: As enacted, H.R. 8533 is Public Law 95–502, approved October 21.

Minneapolis, Minnesota

Remarks at a Fundraising Reception for Governor Rudy Perpich.   October 21, 1978

How many of you are supporting Rudy Perpich for Governor? You supporting him? [*Laughter and applause*]

Okay. I want to ask you another question. How many of you have contributed all that you can afford—[*laughter*]—to his campaign, or the maximum amount? Well, I think it would be very nice for me if all of you would raise your hands—[*laughter*]—and be telling the truth. How many of you have called 50 people and asked them to vote for Rudy Perpich? [*Laughter*] Be truthful. Okay, I can tell you it is not any problem at all for you to call 150 people a day. If you would just give 1 day as an investment in good government in Minnesota, it would pay rich dividends. There is no reason why every one of you can't be a focal point for a campaign organization for Rudy Perpich to be reelected Governor.

He's done a good job. All of you recognize that. He's brought tough, competent, down-to-earth, kind of people-to-people government, which is a continuation of the tremendous standard that has been set in the past by Wendy Anderson, by Hubert Humphrey, by Fritz Mondale, [Lieutenant] Governor Olson, and others. And I think it's very important to you in this difficult Democratic year in Minnesota, when two U.S. Senators, the Governor, all eight Congressmen are at stake, to invest some extra time in their reelection.

And it's not enough for you to come here tonight and give a substantial or a modest contribution. I don't think there's anyone here who can't call 2 or 300 people who know you, who trust you, who would listen to your voice, and say, "Vote for Rudy Perpich on November 7."

Obviously, that includes the entire DFL slate. But I'm particularly here to encourage you to help him. It's important to me that you do this; it's important to your country. He has been successful in bringing a combination of concern and compassion and good government, reduce taxes, a realization on the part of the Minnesota people that the State government is in firm hands. And as you know, he's the kind of person that's absolutely trustworthy to represent your interests in the State.

So, I'm asking you, as President of the United States—[*laughter*]—to work for him, okay? [*Applause*] Good deal.

Let me say one other thing. I'm not going to make a speech, because I'm going to make one later on, and perhaps some of you will come in and listen to me then. But I would like to shake hands with as many of you as possible. And the only way I see to do it without causing a tremendous traffic jam is for me to start over here. And if you would kind of get along the chain, all the way back to the back door, I'll reach as far as my hand will reach.

And every time—if you're going to help Rudy Perpich, like I asked you, come shake hands with me. If you are not going to help him, I'll shake hands with you later on when you change your mind, okay? [*Laughter*]

Thank you very much.

NOTE: The President spoke at 7:25 p.m. in the Plaza Room at the Minneapolis Auditorium.

Minneapolis, Minnesota

Remarks at a Democratic-Farmer-Labor Party Victory Rally. October 21, 1978

Vice President Mondale, Senator Humphrey, Senator Anderson, Congressman Bruce Vento, Jim Oberstar, Rick Nolan, next Senator Bob Short—next Senator Bob Short—Chairman White, Chairman Scott, Mike Freeman, enthusiastic delegates of the DFL:

This has been a good week for me. In the first place, last Sunday, the Congress went home, which was a gracious blessing to the President. [*Laughter*]

I was amazed to see the stock market go down instead of up. [*Laughter*] My brother Billy has not been in the news all week. [*Laughter*] He has the only gas station listed in Fortune 500. [*Laughter*]

My daughter Amy had a birthday on the 19th, and she's gotten to be quite a young lady. She was 3 years old when I was elected Governor, and she's a very fine child. We get to see more of her now than we used to. She had John Travolta come and eat supper with us for one of her birthday presents.

She wanted to see both his movies and we wouldn't let her go because she's not old enough. Amy said, "Well, Daddy, I'd like to remind you that I'm a preteenager." And I said, "Amy, you've been a preteenager for a long time, ever since you were born." And she said, "Yes, but now I'm a double-digit preteenager." [*Laughter*] We don't let people use "double-digit" around the White House any more until we get inflation under control. That's what we're going to do next. [*Laughter*]

I've come here tonight to speak to you briefly about our country from the perspective of the President. When I think back on my own relatively brief political career, I think in a strange way my life has been centered around Minnesota.

Those of us who believe in our Nation, who believe in the highest principles of public service, who believe in politics in a decent and clean fashion, who have never been afraid to address difficult questions, look upon Minnesota as an example for the other states. And we look upon the dean, the founder of the DFL, Hubert Humphrey, as an idol throughout the country.

I've been to Minnesota twice before this since I've been President. The first time I stopped in Minneapolis and asked Senator Humphrey to ride with me on Air Force One when he returned back to Washington after a long, sustained treatment for his terminal illness.

On the way back to Washington, I asked him if he would visit Camp David with me. He said he had never been there. And so the following month, Senator Humphrey and I and his doctor spent the entire weekend alone at Camp David. I've never learned more in a briefer period of time in all my life about people, about Minnesota, about farmers, about

older citizens, about poor people, about those who are black or brown or yellow, who can't speak English well.

I've never learned more about the proper interrelationship between our own country and others. He talked to me about some of the needs of repairing damage that had been done to our country by the Vietnam war, by the CIA revelations, by Watergate; how he traveled in many nations when he was Vice President.

We discussed together the dread that he felt as a major leader, that I felt as a Governor, a candidate for President, as President, every fall when the United Nations General Assembly convened, to know that the Nation that we loved would be the butt of every joke and the target of every attack by the small and the weak and the new nations of the world; and how we needed to repair the damage that had been done to our basic government structure.

He talked to me about his love for Israel, his long relationship with those in this country who support and strengthen and sustain that fine young democracy which has been plagued by war four times in 30 years. He knew President Sadat. He knew Prime Minister Begin. He knew the other leaders of Israel. He taught me about them, and we compared notes about what we knew.

And this entire weekend served to strengthen my commitments to make our Nation's Government more nearly meet the standards that Hubert Humphrey set in his own life, that he helped to establish in the DFL in Minnesota, that he helped to bring to Washington in a clean and a pure and a decent fashion.

And our Nation's better, as you well know, because he lived and because he served you and because he served me.

I believe that a government should be competent. I think it ought to be well organized. I think the Government should put its budget together in a careful way so that the taxpayers' money should not be wasted and so that there should be the utmost service rendered to those who need it for a given level of Government expenditures.

My own background is as a working person, a farmer; my training is as an engineer and a scientist. And I've tried to bring to the Government those principles, because you can't educate a child, you can't feed a hungry person, you can't build a home with waste and mismanagement and fraud. And for too long the people in our country have had a growing doubt about the ability of government to handle its own affairs.

And I think with the help of those on the stage with me tonight, particularly Fritz Mondale, we've made progress in that respect. I won't repeat what he's already said so well. But we've done a few additional things.

One was to recognize the quality of the civil servants of our country, people who believed in government, entered it at a very low wage, knew that they had one life to live on Earth, one career to contribute. They didn't ever get any glory or fame. They didn't ever hear a crowd applaud. They quite often were not recognized for what they achieved. They were often castigated or criticized when someone else made a mistake.

And now, after 95 years, we have reformed the civil service system to reward and encourage those who are competent and who do a good job, who contribute well; to identify those who don't do so well, who are not competent, who are not well motivated, perhaps lazy, so that they can be encouraged to do better, or transferred or discharged.

And we now have a civil service coming on that will let managers manage and make us proud once again of our Govern-

ment. This is the kind of thing we've tried to bring to make government more competent.

I believe in the free enterprise system, and I particularly believe in the free, competitive part of it.

In the past, in our Government—too often in the past we've established regulatory commissions or passed laws ostensibly to protect consumers. But over a period of years of abuse and political pressure and intrigue, and intense focusing by special interest groups on those regulatory agencies, their purpose has been subverted. And instead of protecting the consumers against the regulated industry, they've turned and protected the regulated industry against consumers. We're trying to change that and I believe we can change it.

One quick example is the airline industry. We've got in the last few months a tremendous reduction in air fares. Formerly empty planes are now full. Traffic has gone up tremendously. Profits have gone up tremendously. And I'll predict that within the next few years the Civil Aeronautics Board will find that its existence is no longer needed. Consumers will benefit. Airlines will benefit. Our Nation will benefit as well.

So, competence in managing the Government is very good indeed.

Another thing that we need, of course, is a government that's compassionate, that understands the needs of others. And I think here is where Fritz Mondale has contributed to my own administration in a way that's brought credit to you and to those that I've mentioned already, particularly Senators Humphrey.

We also have a need to have a strong defense, a strong nation politically, a strong nation economically. We're not trying to use this strength to benefit ourselves at the expense of others. We are strong enough now not to have to depend on every cheap, tinhorn dictatorship in the world. We're supporting human rights. And as long as I'm in the White House, we'll continue to do so.

I don't believe there is a national leader on Earth who can now spend a full day without asking himself or herself, "How does my own administration, how does my own nation measure up in the opinion of our citizens or those around the world in protecting basic human rights?" And this applies not only in the totalitarian governments that will stay that way for many years in the future, but it applies to those countries, many, several at least in Latin America, that are now changing from a totalitarian dictatorship into a free and open democratic system.

This is a good trend. And I believe that we've now raised the banner whereby we can once again be proud that our Nation's Government stands for the same principles that the citizens have always espoused and which were the foundation for our Government and our Nation 200 years ago.

The last point I'd like to make is this: We have become, as Fritz Mondale said, a nation committed not only to peace for our own people, but a nation committed to peace for others. I thank God that since I've been President, not a single American soldier has shed blood in a foreign country. And I hope I leave office with that record.

We've become involved, at considerable political risk, in trying to negotiate peace in other parts of the world. Secretary Vance earlier this week was in South Africa, meeting there with leaders of four other Western nations—France, England, West Germany, Canada—to try to induce the South African Government to support peace, democracy, majority rule, one-person-one-vote principles in the nation of Namibia and also the nation of Rhodesia.

He left there to go to the Soviet Union, and he's now negotiating with Foreign Minister Gromyko and President Brezhnev, trying to bring back to me response to proposals that would secure an effective and adequate SALT agreement to remove the threat of nuclear weapons that endangers the lives of all those on Earth. And I need Wendy Anderson and I need the whole Democratic group to help me next year get it ratified.

Warren Christopher, the Deputy Secretary of State, is in Greece. We are trying to secure peace on the island of Cyprus and to eliminate the animosity that existed for several years between Greece and Turkey, our allies.

I've personally become involved, as you know, in trying to negotiate a peace in the Holy Land between Israel and Egypt. We had good success at Camp David. But we only formed a framework or an outline for peace. Many differences still exist.

I have found the last 2 weeks that it's much more difficult to negotiate the details of a peace treaty than it was a general outline of a peace treaty. And it's exceptionally difficult when the Prime Minister and President each are thousands of miles away, rather than just a few yards away from me and away from each other. But we are being persistent in this effort.

The Israeli delegation has now left to go back to Israel for a report to the Cabinet the first of next week, consultations with Prime Minister Begin, and to receive new instructions from their own country.

I met yesterday afternoon with Foreign Minister Dayan and Defense Minister Weizman. Last night, late, I met for 3½ hours with the Israeli delegation to try to go into details of the differences that still remain between themselves and the Egyptians. This morning at 6:45 I was meeting with the Egyptian delegation—making good progress each time we met. But the outcome is not assured, and we still need the hopes and the prayers of the people of this country to realize a final peace treaty between Egypt and Israel in the next few weeks.

And I ask you to remember that in the past, the successes that we have achieved in all these areas of a troubled world have only been possible because I don't speak with an isolated, hollow voice. We have not tried to evolve foreign policy in a secret, closed closet.

We have put forward the principles of negotiation and a frank description of the problems so that you could become involved in assessing those problems and helping me to find solutions. Sometimes this has not been a popular nor an easy process. But there is no doubt that when Fritz Mondale or I meet with a foreign leader—Begin, Sadat, or others—they know that we don't speak idly, that we speak because the Congress gives us its backing and because the people of the United States, more than 200 million of you, are involved in the process as full partners.

So, I believe that our Government now has become more competent. It has not lost its attitude of compassion and concern. And we have become the epitome for many in our search for peace through strength.

My closing message to you tonight is this: You've made a great investment in the DFL. You've made a great investment in having an exemplary State government. You've made a great investment in sending distinguished leaders to Washington. And I urge you during the next 3 weeks to commit yourselves to an extra commitment, an extra effort, even sacrificial in nature, to overcome differences among you and to have the full Democratic slate elected in November, to give me strength to make our Nation even stronger.

Thank you very much.

NOTE: The President spoke at 8:20 p.m. in the Minneapolis Auditorium Arena. In his opening remarks, he referred to John C. White, Democratic National Committee chairman, and Ulric Scott, State Democratic-Farmer-Labor chairman.

National Productivity Council
Executive Order 12089.   October 23, 1978

By the authority vested in me as President by the Constitution of the United States of America, and in order to provide for coordinated and effective Federal programs to improve productivity in the public and private sectors, it is hereby ordered as follows:

1–1. *Establishment of the Council.*

1–101. There is established the National Productivity Council.

1–102. The Council will be composed of the heads of the following agencies, or a designated representative, and such others as the President may designate:

   (a) Department of the Treasury.
   (b) Department of Commerce.
   (c) Department of Labor.
   (d) Office of the Special Representative for Trade Negotiations.
   (e) Council of Economic Advisers.
   (f) Office of Management and Budget.
   (g) Office of Science and Technology Policy.
   (h) Council on Environmental Quality.
   (i) Civil Service Commission, and
   (j) Council on Wage and Price Stability.

1–103. The Director of the Office of Management and Budget will serve as Chairman of the Council.

1–2. *Functions of the Council.*

1–201. The Council will work with Executive agencies to assure that activities designed to improve productivity in the private and public sectors are carried out in a manner that realizes maximum benefit from the resources invested. As part of this responsibility the Council will identify opportunities for cooperative or innovative projects to be undertaken by the agencies, as well as overlapping or duplicative programs which should be eliminated.

1–202. The Council will identify issues pertaining to private and public sector productivity and productivity improvement, and will make assignments to Council members or other Executive agencies for studying and resolving the issues.

1–203. The Council will identify major policy issues with productivity implications for consideration by the President, including the need for legislative initiatives.

1–204. The Council will serve as the focal point within the Executive Branch for liaison with elements of the private sector concerned with improving productivity, and will seek the advice and assistance of business, labor, and academic leaders, as well as representatives from State and local governments and others concerned with productivity.

1–205. The Council will serve as the focal point within the Executive Branch for liaison with organizations of foreign governments involved in efforts to improve productivity.

1–3. *Administrative Provisions.*

1–301. Executive agencies shall cooperate with and assist the Council in performing its functions.

1–302. The Chairman shall be responsible for providing the Council with such administrative services and support as may be necessary or appropriate.

1–303. The Chairman may establish working groups or subcommittees of the Council. The Chairman may invite representatives of nonmember agencies to participate from time to time in the functions of the Council.

1–304. The Chairman shall report to the President on the performance of the Council's functions.

JIMMY CARTER

The White House,
October 23, 1978.

[Filed with the Office of the Federal Register, 2:45 p.m., October 23, 1978]

National Productivity Council

Statement on Signing Executive Order 12089. October 23, 1978

The American people place inflation at the top of the list of things about which they are concerned. One of the major factors fueling inflation is the slowdown in productivity growth in our country. Productivity per person-hour has decreased from a 3.2 percent annual growth rate to 1.6 percent in recent years. This also has a very adverse effect as we compete with other nations whose productivity growth has been much higher.

Improvement in the growth of productivity is essential, therefore, to the social and economic welfare of the American people. This improvement can be realized if the public and private sectors work together to make the best possible use of technology, capital, and human resources. The Federal Government can make major contributions in improving the utilization of these resources.

This Executive order establishes the National Productivity Council. It will serve as the mechanism for coordinating Federal programs which support productivity improvement in public and private sectors, and for assuring that maximum benefit is realized from these programs. It will be the focal point in the executive branch for productivity efforts, superseding the National Center for Productivity and Quality of Working Life, whose authorization expired at the end of this last fiscal year.

Members of the Council will include those departments and agencies with significant responsibilities related to productivity improvement in the private and public sectors—the Departments of Commerce, Labor, and the Treasury, and the Civil Service Commission—and those agencies with a special interest in productivity improvement—the Council of Economic Advisers, Council on Environmental Quality, Council on Wage and Price Stability, Office of Management and Budget, Office of Science and Technology Policy, and Office of the Special Representative for Trade Negotiations. The Director of the Office of Management and Budget will serve as Chairman of the Council.

As its first item of business I will be asking the Council to undertake several items of study and research which will assist in setting priorities and goals for Federal productivity efforts during the next few years. One of the top priority items of study will be determining the appropriate role of the Federal Government in supporting the productivity improvement efforts of State and local governments. In all of these studies the Council will be seeking advice and assistance from business, labor, and academic leaders, as well as from representatives from State and local governments and others concerned with productivity improvement. I believe that through a cooperative effort we will be able to increase productivity growth and make a significant contribution to controlling inflation and improving the state of our economy.

National Productivity Council

Memorandum From the President.
October 23, 1978

Memorandum for the Heads of Departments and Agencies

Subject: Productivity Improvement Program

Today I have signed an Executive order establishing a National Productivity Council. I have established this Council in recognition of the vital role productivity plays in the Nation's economy by helping control inflation, making U.S. goods more competitive in world markets, and increasing the real income of the American worker.

The Council will serve as the focal point in the executive branch for efforts to improve productivity in the private and public sectors of our economy. One of its major functions will be to assure that these efforts are themselves carried out in the most productive fashion.

I would like to highlight the major responsibilities for improvement that are assigned by statute to the executive branch, and identify the departments and agencies to which I look for leadership in carrying out these responsibilities:

- Technological innovation, including improved management systems and production methods—Department of Commerce;

- Collection and dissemination of information on productivity and productivity improvement—Department of Commerce;
- Productivity growth through improved and innovative utilization of employee skills and capability—Department of Labor (in cooperation with the Department of Commerce);
- Protecting and improving the quality of working life of employees in conjunction with productivity improvement—Department of Labor (in cooperation with the Department of Commerce);
- Productivity measurement—Department of Labor;
- Labor-Management cooperation in productivity growth—Department of Labor;
- Productivity of the Federal Work Force—Civil Service Commission (in cooperation with the Office of Management and Budget); and
- Assuring that productivity concerns are taken into account in regulatory policy—Office of Management and Budget (including assuring consideration of productivity in regulatory analyses provided for in Executive Order 12044).

Improved productivity is vital to the social and economic well-being of our Nation. The Federal Government can make a major contribution to improving productivity. I expect all agencies to cooperate with and assist the Council in meeting its responsibilities so we realize maximum benefit from the Federal effort to improve productivity growth.

JIMMY CARTER

Small Business Conference Commission

*Appointment of Five Members.
October 23, 1978*

The President today announced the appointment of five persons as members of the Small Business Conference Commission. They are:

ANN M. DAVIS, of Rancho Palos Verdes, Calif., director of community relations and public affairs at KACE–FM Radio, and a member of the board of a trucking company and a beer distributorship;

MARGARET S. HANSSON, of Boulder, Colo., founder and chief executive officer of Genac, Inc., a corporation manufacturing new products for handicapped children and adults, and a consultant to various agencies working with young people starting new small businesses;

SHEPARD LEE, of Auburn, Maine, owner of several automobile and recreational vehicle dealerships there, and a former Maine State Chairman of the Small Business Administration Advisory Council;

ARTHUR LEVITT, JR., of New York City, chairman of the board of governors and chief executive officer of the American Stock Exchange (also designated Chairman of the Commission);

STEVEN E. WEINSTEIN, of Atlanta, Ga., chief executive officer of Second Realty Co. and several other real estate companies in Atlanta.

Advisory Commission on Intergovernmental Relations

Appointment of Governor Bruce Babbitt as a Member.   October 23, 1978

The President today announced the appointment of Bruce Babbitt, Governor of Arizona, as a member of the Advisory Commission on Intergovernmental Relations.

Babbitt, 40, has been Governor since 1977. He is a former attorney general of Arizona and former special assistant to the Director of VISTA.

Missouri River Basin Commission

Appointment of Millard W. Hall as Chairman.
October 24, 1978

The President today announced the appointment of Millard W. Hall, of Lincoln, Nebr., as Chairman of the Missouri River Basin Commission.

Hall, 42, is director of the Nebraska Water Resources Research Institute at the University of Nebraska. He also serves as a professor of civil engineering there. Before going to Nebraska in 1975, Hall was director of the Land and Water Resources Institute at the University of Maine.

Airline Deregulation Act of 1978

Remarks on Signing S. 2493 Into Law.
October 24, 1978

THE PRESIDENT. I think we have more people here today than we had when we tried to organize the campaign to get this legislation passed. [*Laughter*]

It is a special pleasure for me today to sign into law the Airline Deregulation Act. This legislation will permit us to achieve two critical objectives. One is to help our fight against inflation. And the other one is to ensure American citizens of an opportunity for low-priced air transportation.

It will also mean less Government interference in regulation of an increasingly prosperous airline industry. All of us here today worked long and hard for this legislation. And the product is well worth that labor.

In recent months, thanks to the actions of the Civil Aeronautics Board, under the leadership of Chairman Alfred Kahn, we've seen the beginning of real competition among domestic airlines. Competition has already helped both consumers and the industry. It has brought lower fares, more passengers, and higher profits. In the future, of course, regulation of air safety will continue, as it has in the past, under another Government agency.

With this act, airlines can reduce their fares up to 50 percent, opening up air travel to millions of Americans who would not otherwise be able to afford it.

There will also be more competition for air routes. In the past, it was almost impossible for a new carrier meeting all the safety and financial requirements to receive permission to serve the public. But under the new bill, the opportunities for entry of new airlines in this service will be greatly improved.

The bill also provides a more efficient program for guaranteeing good quality services of airlines to our smaller communities. And the bill fulfills the commitment to lift the heavy hand of Government regulation, by phasing out route approval at the end of 1981, phasing out domestic fare regulation by the end of 1983, and phasing out all activities of the Civil Aeronautics Board by 1985.

For the first time in decades, we have deregulated a major industry. When I announced my own support of airline deregulation soon after taking office, this bill had few friends. I'm happy to say that today it appears to have few enemies. Governors, mayors, consumer advocates, all supported the bill. And all will benefit from the increase in competition and the guarantees of quality services to smaller communities. Taxpayers will benefit from the orderly phasing out of the functions of the Civil Aeronautics Board and from the sound precedent this bill sets for dealing with other over-regulated industries.

This bill would not have been possible without the early leadership of Senator Ted Kennedy, who's here with us, and Senator Howard Cannon, who worked in a yeoman's way for the passage of this legislation. I want to especially thank them for first raising this issue and bringing it to public attention.

I also want to thank Chairman Bizz Johnson and Glenn Anderson—who's not here—and Allen Ertel. Glenn is back here—[*laughter*]—Bizz Johnson is not here—and Allen Ertel for the cooperation and leadership that they showed in passing this exemplary anti-inflation legislation.

Chairman Bizz Johnson couldn't come, is that correct?

Well, it's with a great pleasure that I sign now into law Senate bill 2493, to deregulate the airline industry of our country. It's a major step forward for consumers, for the airline industries as well, and especially for those who use air transportation for their purposes.

[*At this point, the President signed the bill.*]

I'd like to ask Chairman Howard Cannon if he would like to make a comment.

SENATOR CANNON. Well, thank you very much, Mr. President. I certainly agree with you that this is a great day in deregulation of the regulatory structure. I think it's extremely important to the country. I think, as you do, that it's going to be important not only to the consumers but important to the air carriers as well, though they did not believe so at the be-

ginning. And I'm delighted to see that it's finally signed into law.

THE PRESIDENT. Thank you.

Ted Kennedy?

SENATOR KENNEDY. Mr. President, I just want to join in commending you for your leadership in this important legislative achievement and also for the bipartisan support that was received. It was really a bipartisan effort.

It meets the objectives which you've established in the problems of inflation, getting the Federal Government out of an important industry. It's going to mean more jobs and better services for people. And I hope that we can do the same in other areas of economic regulation.

THE PRESIDENT. Glenn Anderson, who's very much present.

REPRESENTATIVE ANDERSON. Yes, very much present. [*Laughter*]

Well, thank you, Mr. President. I want to say that I'm very pleased with the legislation. I think that we have worked out a good bill. The committees have worked hard to iron out any differences we might have had at the start. And I think that's one of the reasons we do find there's very few opponents to the bill today.

And I would be remiss if I didn't say that the support of the administration in helping us get this bill through both Houses was very, very obvious, and we thank you very much for it.

THE PRESIDENT. I particularly want to thank two people that I mentioned briefly. One is Alfred Kahn, the Chairman of the CAB. He and his predecessor had, within the bounds of the law, put as many of these reforms into effect as was possible. And they proved, as the law was being considered, that these reforms worked. And it made it possible, I believe, to convince those who did doubt the efficacy of this bill that it was a good piece of legislation. I thank you for that.

And I especially want to thank Allen Ertel, who, in the last weeks of the legislative session, introduced an amendment on the floor of the House that removed a lot of objectionable amendments that had been imposed on the bill in committee and brought into compatibility as best as was possible the House bill and the superb Senate bill that had already been passed.

I'd like to ask the last person, Brock Adams, if he would like to make a comment. Brock is the Secretary of Transportation, and this will greatly impact on the quality of our transportation system.

SECRETARY ADAMS. Mr. President, I just am deeply pleased that this has happened. It was a promise that I made to you early on. We all knew it was going to be difficult. And I appreciate your deep support and that of all of those in the White House as well as those in the Congress for making it possible. It will make the average American family have a chance to really travel. And I'm glad it's there for you, and we're pleased.

THE PRESIDENT. Very good.

This is a great step forward in controlling inflation. Quite often we don't have a chance to do anything positive to control inflation. We can put the brakes on and not spend money. But this is a major step forward. And I hope it's a precursor to what the Congress can help me do next year to minimize regulation of other crucial industries, particularly in the transportation field.

Thank you all very much for a wonderful bill.

NOTE: The President spoke at 4:05 p.m. at the ceremony in the Cabinet Room at the White House.

As enacted, S. 2493 is Public Law 95–504, approved October 24.

Anti-Inflation Program

Address to the Nation.   October 24, 1978

Good evening.

I want to have a frank talk with you tonight about our most serious domestic problem. That problem is inflation. Inflation can threaten all the economic gains we've made, and it can stand in the way of what we want to achieve in the future.

This has been a long-time threat. For the last 10 years, the annual inflation rate in the United States has averaged 6½ percent. And during the 3 years before my Inauguration, it had increased to an average of 8 percent.

Inflation has, therefore, been a serious problem for me ever since I became President. We've tried to control it, but we have not been successful. It's time for all of us to make a greater and a more coordinated effort.

If inflation gets worse, several things will happen. Your purchasing power will continue to decline, and most of the burden will fall on those who can least afford it. Our national productivity will suffer. The value of our dollar will continue to fall in world trade.

We've made good progress in putting our people back to work over the past 21 months. We've created more than 6 million new jobs for American workers. We've reduced the unemployment rate by about 25 percent, and we will continue our efforts to reduce unemployment further, especially among our young people and minorities.

But I must tell you tonight that inflation threatens this progress. If we do not get inflation under control, we will not be able to reduce unemployment further, and we may even slide backward.

Inflation is obviously a serious problem. What is the solution?

I do not have all the answers. Nobody does. Perhaps there is no complete and adequate answer. But I want to let you know that fighting inflation will be a central preoccupation of mine during the months ahead, and I want to arouse our Nation to join me in this effort.

There are two simplistic and familiar answers which are sometimes proposed—simple, familiar, and too extreme. One of these answers is to impose a complicated scheme of Federal Government wage and price controls on our entire free economic system. The other is a deliberate recession, which would throw millions of people out of work. Both of these extreme proposals would not work, and they must be rejected.

I've spent many hours in the last few months reviewing, with my own advisers and with a number of outside experts, every proposal, every suggestion, every possibility for eliminating inflation. If there's one thing I have learned beyond any doubt, it is that there is no single solution for inflation.

What we have, instead, is a number of partial remedies. Some of them will help; others may not. But we have no choice but to use the best approaches we have and to maintain a constant search for additional steps which may be effective.

I want to discuss with you tonight some of the approaches we have been able to develop. They involve action by Government, business, labor, and every other sector of our economy. Some of these factors are under my control as President—especially Government actions—and I will insist that the Government does its part of the job.

But whether our efforts are successful will finally depend on you as much as on me. Your decisions—made every day at your service station or your grocery store, in your business, in your union meetings—will determine our Nation's answer to inflation as much as decisions made here in the White House or by the Congress on Capitol Hill.

I cannot guarantee that our joint effort will succeed. In fact, it is almost certain not to succeed if success means quick or dramatic changes. Every free government on Earth is wrestling with this problem of inflation, and every one of them knows that a long-term disease requires long-term treatment. It's up to us to make the improvements we can, even at the risk of partial failure, rather than to ensure failure by not trying at all.

I will concentrate my efforts within the Government. We know that Government is not the only cause of inflation. But it is one of the causes, and Government does set an example. Therefore, it must take the lead in fiscal restraint.

We are going to hold down Government spending, reduce the budget deficit, and eliminate Government waste.

We will slash Federal hiring and cut the Federal work force.

We will eliminate needless regulations.

We will bring more competition back to our economy.

And we will oppose any further reduction in Federal income taxes until we have convincing prospects that inflation will be controlled.

Let me explain what each one of these steps means.

The Federal deficit is too high. Our people are simply sick and tired of wasteful Federal spending and the inflation it brings with it.

We have already had some success. We've brought the deficit down by one-third since I ran for President—from more than $66 billion in fiscal year 1976 to about $40 billion in fiscal year 1979—a reduction of more than $25 billion in the Federal deficit in just 3 years.

It will keep going down. Next year, with tough restraints on Federal spending and moderate economic growth in prospect, I plan to reduce the budget deficit to less than one-half what it was when I ran for office—to $30 billion or less.

The Government has been spending too great a portion of what our Nation produces. During my campaign I promised to cut the Government's share of our total national spending from 23 percent, which it was then, to 21 percent in fiscal year 1981. We now plan to meet that goal 1 year earlier.

Reducing the deficit will require difficult and unpleasant decisions. We must face a time of national austerity. Hard choices are necessary if we want to avoid consequences that are even worse.

I intend to make those hard choices. I have already vetoed bills that would undermine our fight against inflation, and the Congress has sustained those vetoes. I know that the Congress will continue to cooperate in the effort to meet our needs in responsible, noninflationary ways.

I will use the administrative and the budgetary powers of my office, including the veto, if necessary, to keep our Nation firmly on the path of fiscal restraint.

Restraint involves tax policy as well as spending decisions. Tax reduction has never been more politically popular than it is today. But if future tax cuts are made rashly, with no eye on the budget deficits, they will hurt us all by causing more inflation.

There are tax cuts which could directly lower costs and prices and help in the fight against inflation. I may consider ways to reduce those particular taxes while still cutting the budget deficit, but until we have a convincing prospect of controlling inflation, I will oppose any further reductions in Federal income taxes.

To keep the Government to a manageable size, I'm ordering tonight a cut in Federal hiring. This order will mean a reduction of more than 20,000 in the number of permanent Federal employees already budgeted for this fiscal year and will cut the total size of the Federal work force.

I've already placed a 5½-percent cap on the pay increase for Federal employees, and Federal executive officers are receiving no pay increases at all.

It's not enough just to control Government deficits, spending, and hiring. We must also control the costs of Government regulations.

In recent years, Congress has passed a number of landmark statutes to improve social and environmental conditions. We must and we will continue progress toward protecting the health and safety of the American people. But we must also realize that everything has a price and that consumers eventually pick up the tab. Where regulations are essential, they must be efficient. Where they fight inflation, they should be encouraged. Where they are unnecessary, they should be removed.

Early this year, I directed Federal agencies to eliminate unnecessary regulations and to analyze the costs and benefits of new ones. Today, for instance, the Occupational Safety and Health Administration, sometimes called OSHA, eliminated nearly 1,000 unnecessary regulations.

Now, we can build on this progress. I've directed a council of my regulatory departments and agencies to coordinate their regulations, to prevent overlapping and duplication. Most important, the council will develop a unified calendar of planned major regulations. The calendar will give us, for the first time, a comprehensive list of regulations the Federal

Government is proposing, with their costs and objectives.

As President, I will personally use my authority to ensure that regulations are issued only when needed and that they meet their goals at the lowest possible cost.

We are also cutting away the regulatory thicket that has grown up around us and giving our competitive free enterprise system a chance to grow up in its place.

Last year we gave the airline industry a fresh shot of competition. Regulations were removed. Free market forces drove prices down, record numbers of passengers traveled, and profits went up. Our new airline deregulation bill will make these benefits permanent. For the first time in decades, we have actually deregulated a major industry.

Next year we will work with Congress to bring more competition to others, such as the railroad and trucking industries.

Of all our weapons against inflation, competition is the most powerful. Without real competition, prices and wages go up, even when demand is going down. We must therefore work to allow more competition wherever possible so that powerful groups—government, business, labor—must think twice before abusing their economic power. We will redouble our efforts to put competition back into the American free enterprise system.

Another reason for inflation is the slowdown in productivity growth. More efficient production is essential if we are to control inflation, make American goods more competitive in world markets, add new jobs, and increase the real incomes of our people.

We've made a start toward improving productivity. The tax bill just passed by the Congress includes many of the investment incentives that I recommended last January. Federal support for research and development will continue to increase, especially for basic research. We will coordinate and strengthen Federal programs that support productivity improvements throughout our economy.

Our Government efforts will attack the inflation that hurts most, inflation in the essentials—food, housing, and medical care.

We will continue to use our agricultural policies to sustain farm production, to maintain stable prices, and to keep inflation down.

Rising interest rates have always accompanied inflation. They add further to the costs of business expansion and to what consumers must pay when they buy houses and other consumer items.

The burden of controlling inflation cannot be left to monetary policy alone, which must deal with the problem through tight restrictions on money and credit that push interest rates up. I will work for a balanced, concerted, and sustained program under which tight budget restraint, private wage and price moderation, and responsible monetary policy support each other. If successful, we should expect lower inflation and lower interest rates for consumers and businesses alike.

As for medical care, where costs have gone up much faster than the general inflation rate, the most important step we can take is to pass a strong bill to control hospital costs. This year the Senate passed one. Next year I will try again, and I believe the whole Congress will act to hold down hospital costs—if your own Members of Congress hear from you.

Between now and January, when the new Congress convenes, I will be preparing a package of specific legislative proposals to help fight inflation.

The Government will do its part, but in a country like ours, Government cannot do the job alone. In the end, the success or failure of this effort will also rest on whether the private sector will accept—and act on—the voluntary wage and price standards I am announcing tonight.

These standards are fair. They are standards that everyone can follow. If we do follow them, they will slow prices down so that wages will not have to chase prices just to stay even. And they point the way toward an eventual cure for inflation, by removing the pressures that cause it in the first place.

In the last 10 years, in our attempts to protect ourselves from inflation we've developed attitudes and habits that actually keep inflation going once it has begun. Most companies raise their prices because they expect costs to rise. Unions call for large wage settlements because they expect inflation to continue. Because we expect it to happen, it does happen; and once it's started, wages and prices chase each other up and up. It's like a crowd standing at a football stadium. No one can see any better than when everyone is sitting down, but no one is willing to be the first to sit down.

Except for our lowest paid workers, I'm asking all employees in this country to limit total wage increases to a maximum of 7 percent per year. From tonight on, every contract signed and every pay raise granted should meet this standard.

My price limitation will be equally strict. Our basic target for economy-wide price increases is 5¾ percent. To reach this goal, I'm tonight setting a standard for each firm in the Nation to hold its price increases at least one-half of one percentage point below what they averaged during 1976 and 1977.

Of course, we have to take into account binding commitments already in effect, which will prevent an absolute adherence to these standards. But this price standard is much lower than this year's inflation rate, and more important, it's less than the standard for wage increases. That difference is accounted for by rising productivity, and it will allow the income of America's workers to stay ahead of inflation.

This is a standard for everyone to follow—everyone. As far as I'm concerned, every business, every union, every professional group, every individual in this country has no excuse not to adhere to these standards. If we meet these standards, the real buying power of your paycheck will rise.

The difficulty with a voluntary program is that workers fear that if they cooperate with the standards while others do not, then they will suffer if inflation continues.

To deal with this concern, I will ask the Congress next January to enact a program that workers who observe the standards would be eligible for a tax rebate if the inflation rate is more than 7 percent. In other words, they would have a real wage insurance policy against inflation which might be caused by others. This will give our workers an additional incentive to observe the program and will remove their only legitimate reason not to cooperate.

Because this is not a mandatory control plan, I cannot stop an irresponsible corporation from raising its prices or a selfish group of employees from using its power to demand excessive wages. But then if that happens, the Government will respond, using the tools of Government authority and public opinion.

Soon after they raise prices or demand pay increases that are excessive, the company or the union will feel the pressure that the public can exert, through new competition to drive prices down or removal of Government protections and privileges which they now enjoy.

We will also make better use of the $80 billion worth of purchases the Government makes from private industry each year. We must be prudent buyers. If costs rise too fast, we can delay those purchases, as your family would, or switch to another supplier. We may not buy a fleet of cars this year, for example, if cars cost too much, or we may channel our purchases to suppliers who have observed our wage and price standards rather than to buy from those who have not.

We will require firms that supply goods and services to the Government to certify their compliance with the wage and price standards. We will make every effort, within legal limits, to deny Government contracts to companies that fail to meet our wage and price standards. We will use our buying power more effectively to make price restraint and competition a reality.

The Government now extends economic privileges to many parts of the private economy—special franchises, protected wages and prices, subsidies, protection from foreign competition. If wages or prices rise too fast in some industry, we will take that as a sign that those privileges are no longer needed and that this protection should be removed. We will make sure that no part of our economy is able to use its special privilege or its concentrated power to victimize the rest of us.

This approach I've outlined will not end inflation. It simply improves our chances of making it better rather than worse. To summarize the plan I'm announcing tonight:

We will cut the budget deficit.

We will slash Federal hiring and reduce the Federal work force.

We will restrain Federal pay.

We will delay further tax cuts.

We will remove needless regulations.

We will use Federal policy to encourage more competition.

We will set specific standards for both wages and prices throughout the economy.

We will use all the powers at our disposal to make this program work.

And we will submit new anti-inflation proposals to the Congress next January, including the real wage insurance proposal I've discussed tonight.

I've said many times that these steps will be tough—and they are. But I also said they will be fair—and they are. They apply equally to all groups. They give all of us an equal chance to move ahead.

And these proposals, which give us a chance, also deserve a chance. If, tomorrow or next week or next month, you ridicule them, ignore them, pick them apart before they have a chance to work, then you will have reduced their chance of succeeding.

These steps can work, but that will take time, and you are the ones who can give them that time. If there's one thing I'm asking of every American tonight, it is to give this plan a chance to work—a chance to work for us.

You can help give it that chance by using your influence. Business and labor must know that you will not tolerate irresponsible price and wage increases. Your elected officials must know how you feel as they make difficult choices.

Too often the only voices they hear are those of special interests, supporting their own narrow cause. If you want Government officials to cut inflation, you have to make sure that they hear your voice. I have heard you with unmistakable clarity.

Nearly 40 years ago, when the world watched to see whether his nation would survive, Winston Churchill defied those who thought Britain would fall to the Nazi threat. Churchill replied by asking his countrymen, "What kind of people do they think we are?"

There are those today who say that a free economy cannot cope with inflation and that we've lost our ability to act as a nation rather than as a collection of special interests. And I reply, "What kind of people do they think we are?"

I believe that our people, our economic system, and our Government are equal to this task. I hope that you will prove me right.

Thank you, and good night.

NOTE: The President spoke at 10 p.m. from the Oval Office at the White House. His remarks were broadcast live on radio and television.

Anti-Inflation Program

White House Fact Sheet on Details of the Program.   October 24, 1978

THE PRESIDENT'S ANTI-INFLATION PROGRAM

FEDERAL GOVERNMENT ACTIONS

The Federal Government alone cannot solve the inflation problem, but it must take the lead. The administration will do everything in its power to ensure that its actions are consistent with the objectives of the anti-inflation program.

Budgetary Policy

Substantial progress has been made in reducing the rate of unemployment. But further progress in reducing unemployment will depend on our success in reducing the rate of inflation. The budget that will be submitted in January will give top priority to moderating inflation. To achieve that goal the President will:

—Put a tight rein on the growth of Federal spending. He has pledged to cut the share of Gross National Product accounted for by Federal spending from 23 percent in FY 1976 to about 21 percent in FY 1980, 1 year ahead of his previously announced schedule.

—Reduce the Federal deficit. In fiscal year 1976, the Federal deficit was $66 billion. In just 3 years, by 1979, the deficit will be cut to below $40 billion. In the 1980 budget, the deficit will be reduced still further—to less than one-half the 1976 deficit.

In order to contribute to these goals, the President has imposed severe limits on the hiring of Federal employees. Effective immediately, for an indefinite period, Federal agencies will be permitted to fill only one out of two vacancies as they occur.

Regulatory Policy

Programs to protect the environment and the health and safety of workers and consumers are vital. But the achievement of these critical objectives should not place unnecessary burdens on the economy. Regulatory agencies are now required to analyze major new regulations to identify and compare benefits and costs. In addition, the President has:

—Directed the formation of a Regulatory Council. This Council will include all regulatory departments and agencies. The Council will have the important task of coordinating duplicative and overlapping regulations, in concert with the Office of Management and Budget's efforts to enforce the regulatory-process Executive Order 12044.

—Directed the new Regulatory Council to develop a unified *calendar* of major regulations. The calendar will provide, for the first time, a comprehensive list of major regulations to be proposed by the various agencies of the Federal Government. This calendar will facilitate a comprehensive and consistent approach to the evaluation of costs and benefits of proposed regulations. The Council will help to ensure that regulatory objectives are achieved at the lowest possible cost.

—Pledged to use his authority to ensure that regulations are issued only when necessary and that they achieve their goals at the lowest possible cost.

—Directed each executive branch regulatory agency to include additional regulations that have a major economic impact in the "sunset" reviews that are required by E.O. 12044.

PRIVATE SECTOR ACTIONS

Success of this anti-inflation effort will depend upon the cooperation of the private sector. To this end, the President has set forth explicit numerical standards of behavior for pay and prices in the year ahead.

Pay Standard

Annual increases in wages and private fringe benefits should not exceed *7 percent*.

—Workers earning less than $4 per hour will be exempt as well as wage contracts already signed.

—In new collective bargaining situations, a contract in which wage and fringe benefit increases average no more than 7 percent annually over the life of the contract will be consistent with the standard. In evaluating a contract for consistency with the standard, cost-of-living clauses will be evaluated using a 6-percent-per-year rate of price inflation over the life of the contract.

—No more than an 8-percent pay increase should be included in the first year of a multiyear contract.

—Increases above the standard will be acceptable to the extent that they reflect changes in work rules and practices that show demonstrable productivity improvements.

—The standard does *not* apply to individual workers. The standard applies to *average* pay increases for *groups* of workers. Firms will be expected to divide their work force into three categories:

(a) management employees, (b) groups of employees covered by separate collectively bargained contracts, and (c) all other employees.

Price Standard

Individual firms are expected to limit their price increases over the next year to *one-half of one percentage point* below their average annual rate of price increase during 1976–77.

—If wage-rate increases for a firm decelerate by more than one-half percentage point from the 1976–77 base period, greater deceleration in prices will be required in order to ensure that savings are reflected in prices.

—The standard does not apply to specific products, but to a firm's overall average price.

—Firms unable to meet the one-half percent deceleration standard due to *unavoidable* cost increases must demonstrate, as an alternative, that their before-tax profit margins are no higher than in the best 2 of the last 3 years.

OBJECTIVES FOR THE PROGRAM

The pay and price standards have been developed to be consistent with one another.

—The deceleration standard for prices can be related to the wage standard by adding 0.5 percentage point to the 7-percent wage standard to reflect scheduled increases in legislatively mandated payroll costs and deducting 1¾ percentage points for productivity growth. The result is a 5¾-percent economy-wide rate of increase in unit labor costs. If firms reduce their average price increases by the price standard—that is, if they reduce their average price increase by one-half percentage point below the average rate of price increase in 1976–77—the result would be a 5¾-percent increase in prices of non-food commodities and services. The pay and price standards are thus consistent with one another.

—Because of the allowances necessary to deal with a complex economy—such as the treatment of wage contracts already signed and the existence of some uncontrollable cost increases—widespread observance of the standards would lead to an overall rate of inflation of 6 to 6½ percent in the year ahead, well below the rate of inflation in 1978 to date.

REAL WAGE INSURANCE

The President will recommend to the Congress a program of "real wage insurance." Under this program, workers who are members of groups that meet the pay standard would receive a tax rebate if the rate of inflation in the year ahead exceeds 7 percent. The program will be developed for submission to the Congress in January. Although final decisions remain to be made, the broad outlines of the program are as follows:

—The amount of the rebate would be equal to the difference between the actual rate of inflation and 7 percent, multiplied by an individual worker's pay, up to some reasonable limit.

—Workers who are members of groups that meet the 7-percent pay limitation would be eligible for the real wage insurance.

—The rebate would be paid *only* if the rate of inflation in the year ahead actually exceeds 7 percent.

INCENTIVES FOR COMPLIANCE

The administration will interpret wage and price increases above the standards as indications of inflationary conditions, such as shortages, excessive market power, or shelter from competition. Thus, increases in excess of the standards will trigger actions by the Government such as:

—Reexamining various restrictions on imports and, where possible and appropriate, relaxing them.

—Asking regulatory agencies to review rate levels and other rules in light of the standards for wages and prices.

—Seeking modification in those regulations that set minimum levels for prices or wages in specific situations.

GOVERNMENT PURCHASES

The Federal Government itself is a major purchaser of goods and services. By channeling its procurement to those firms whose price and wage decisions meet the standards, it can realize long-term savings in its procurement budget and simultaneously take the lead in fighting inflation.

—To the extent consistent with legal requirements and ensuring national security, the President will direct Government agencies to limit purchases to those firms observing the pay and price standards.

—After January 1, the Government will require firms awarded contracts in excess of $5 million to certify that they are observing the standards.

—This program will be administered by the Office of Federal Procurement Policy (OFPP) of the OMB.

—Specific procedures to carry out this policy will be announced soon by OFPP and by the Council on Wage and Price Stability (CWPS).

MONITORING

The Council on Wage and Price Stability will be expanded by about 100 persons to monitor the adherence to the wage and price standards by firms and employee groups.

1847

—CWPS has the authority to obtain, where necessary, required information on prices, profits, and wage rates. It will publicly identify areas of the economy and firms that are not complying with the standards.

—In addition CWPS will monitor on a regular basis wage and price developments of individual firms whose annual sales exceed $500 million. It will also monitor individually all major collective bargaining settlements.

Assistance for Minority and Disadvantaged Small Businesses

Statement on Signing H.R. 11318 Into Law. October 25, 1978

I am pleased to sign H.R. 11318, a bill which assists minority and socially and economically disadvantaged small businesses through investment, procurement, management, and technical assistance programs in the Small Business Administration (SBA). This bill also sets up ways for small businesses to participate more in Federal Government contracting.

I am aware of the past shortcomings of SBA's 8(a) Business Development program. This program is intended to channel noncompetitive procurement contracts to socially and economically disadvantaged businesses so as to build them up to the point where they can compete on their own in the Federal procurement process. H.R. 11318 provides statutory guidelines for eligibility in this program; it also provides the management and technical assistance tools needed to develop these businesses. The regulations implementing this program will be uniform and governmentwide.

H.R. 11318 will also make it less expensive for minority enterprise small business

investment companies (MESBIC's) to get capital from SBA, which will help struggling businesses to become successful enterprises.

By requiring that all Federal procuring agencies consult with SBA in establishing realistic goals for small business participation in Federal contracts, H.R. 11318 will increase the number of contracts going to all small businesses. This bill also creates Offices of Small and Disadvantaged Business Utilization in each Federal agency with procurement powers to further the cause of small business in the contracting and subcontracting process. Furthermore, the administration will take administrative steps to strengthen the subcontracting provisions of the bill even further.

This bill addresses a matter of deep concern to this administration—making minority-owned businesses into full and equal partners in the free enterprise system. As a result of racial or ethnic prejudice or social bias, too many Americans have too long been kept from realizing their full potential in the small business community. H.R. 11318 goes a long way in helping small and disadvantaged businesses grow in our economy. Special thanks are due to Congressman Joseph Addabbo, Congressman Parren Mitchell, and Senator Sam Nunn for their efforts in drafting this significant legislation.

H.R. 11318 principally benefits ethnic minorities, although others also face disadvantages in their entrepreneurial efforts. More must be done to assist women business owners into the economic mainstream. My own Interdepartmental Task Force on Women Business Owners gave me its recommendations and findings early this summer. I have since directed that a new interagency committee follow up these recommendations with the cooperation of all departments and agencies.

I shall soon announce new steps to aid women entrepreneurs and businesses owned by women.

NOTE: As enacted, H.R. 11318 is Public Law 95–507, approved October 24.

Advisor to the President on Inflation and Chairman of the Council on Wage and Price Stability

Remarks Announcing the Appointment of Alfred E. Kahn.   October 25, 1978

Last night, I outlined a government- , and in fact, nationwide program to improve our chances to control inflation. In order to help me coordinate this entire program, I have asked Alfred Kahn, who has been the Chairman of the Civil Aeronautics Board, to be Advisor to the President and Chairman of the Council on Wage and Price Stability.

Obviously this will be a very challenging and important responsibility for him. He will work directly with me, with the Secretary of Treasury, Labor, Commerce, the Special Trade Representative, the Chairman of the Council of Economic Advisers, and others, to make sure that our efforts are given the maximum chance to succeed.

Very few occurrences in the Government this last year have been of more significance to our Nation nor more gratifying to me than Chairman Kahn's proving in the CAB that we could actually have better service with lower costs, higher profits, and a chance to let our free enterprise system show its vigor and its strength and its value to our Nation. This has occurred in the deregulation of the airline industry, and Chairman Kahn has been responsible for that progress.

We will endeavor to ensure that our Nation's response to inflation is effective and is flexible and that we remove the obstacles to decreasing prices, decreasing costs, decreasing wage increases.

One thing I'd like to point out is that this will be a very good opportunity for Government and the private sector of our Nation to work in harmony. We will be making every effort to get mayors, county officials, Governors, Members of Congress, and the executive branch of our Federal Government to work with the private sector to make as much progress as possible.

I believe in our free enterprise system and believe that free competition can bring about a realization of our hopes to control inflation. I'm very proud that Alfred Kahn has agreed to come and help me in this very important position.

I would like to express my deep thanks to Robert Strauss, our Special Trade Representative, who for the last 6 months has used his tremendous enthusiasm and his influence and competence to arouse the Nation's concern about inflation and to bring about this appointment. He came to me several weeks ago, suggested that I go on television, make a major speech to the Nation about the problems of inflation, some of the opportunities for resolving those problems. And he was the first to suggest that I appoint Alfred Kahn to be my assistant, my adviser, in handling the inflationary problem. And I want to express my personal thanks to Bob Strauss, who is our Special Trade Representative, for the good work he has done.

I'd like now to introduce to you Chairman Alfred Kahn, the new Advisor to the President, my new partner in controlling inflation in our country.

NOTE: The President spoke at 1:52 p.m. to reporters assembled in the Briefing Room at the White House. Following his remarks, Mr. Kahn and Charles L. Schultze, Chairman of the Council of Economic Advisers, spoke to the reporters.

Civil Aeronautics Board

Letter on the Resignation of Alfred E. Kahn as Chairman. *October 25, 1978*

To the Members and Staff of the Civil Aeronautics Board

When I talked to Chairman Kahn about accepting the position as my counselor on inflation policy, he expressed very deep concern about what the effect of his leaving might be on the Civil Aeronautics Board. He told me that he felt a heavy responsibility for helping the Board through these very important transitional months of adjustment to the new deregulation legislation, which the Board and I have strongly supported. I offered at once to do everything I could to set his concerns at rest.

I have a particular desire to communicate directly with you in any event, because you at the Board have presented my Administration with one of its great success stories, and I wanted to express my deep appreciation to you for the work you have been doing.

I want to explain to you, also, that Chairman Kahn leaves you only with the greatest reluctance, and only because I persuaded him that I need his services worse than you do. I know that you still have very challenging tasks ahead, but your direction, I believe, is now set; and you have demonstrated to the world the benefits of restoring the air transport industry to the free enterprise system.

In order further to set your minds at rest, I am immediately naming Board Member Marvin Cohen as Chairman Kahn's successor. Chairman Cohen, I am convinced, will give the Board dynamic and dedicated leadership in the years ahead, and help you to continue your proud record of accomplishment in the public interest.

I would understand it if you felt a particular concern with this departure of your Chairman just after Congress has passed a bill that contemplates eventual abolition of the Civil Aeronautics Board. I have two observations I should like to make about that prospect. First, this will be an event of historic significance—a case of a government regulatory agency moving forthrightly to deregulate the industry it is charged with supervising, and then to terminate its existence when it has become unnecessary. It is a task worthy of your most dedicated and imaginative efforts; and one in which you may take great pride.

Second, you and I know that there will remain very important responsibilities of the Federal Government towards the air transportation industry—effectuating our recently developed liberal international aviation policy, engaging in much more thorough antitrust regulation, providing essential consumer protections, and developing and administering a new small communities service subsidy program. These are responsibilities of the government that will continue for as long into the future as any of us can see. And when I contemplate with satisfaction the elimination of the Civil Aeronautics Board, therefore, I do not at all contemplate the disappearance of your jobs: there is still and will continue to be important work to be done, and we will need you to continue to do it.

I conclude, once again, with an expression of my deep appreciation to you for your devoted, successful and historic efforts.

JIMMY CARTER

Federal Election Commission

Recess Appointment of John W. McGarry as a Member. October 25, 1978

The President today announced the appointment of John W. McGarry as a member of the Federal Election Commission.

McGarry, 56, was nominated to be a member of the FEC last April, but his nomination was not confirmed before the Senate adjourned. He was special counsel on elections to the Committee on House Administration of the U.S. House of Representatives.

McGarry was born June 11, 1922, in Boston, Mass. He served in the U.S. Navy during World War II, and after the war graduated from Holy Cross College and earned a law degree at Georgetown Law Center.

From 1959 to 1963, McGarry served as assistant attorney general of Massachusetts. He then combined private law practice with services as chief counsel for the Special Committee To Investigate Campaign Expenditures, which was created as a temporary unit every 2 years until 1972 to oversee House elections.

McGarry served as special counsel on elections to the Committee on House Administration from 1973 to 1978.

United Nations Sponsorship of Week Devoted to Disarmament

Statement by the President. October 25, 1978

October 24 marked the beginning of a week devoted to fostering the objectives of disarmament, proclaimed by the United Nations General Assembly in the Final Document of the Special Session on Disarmament last June.

The United States is committed to balanced, effective, and verifiable arms control and disarmament measures. We are currently engaged in arms control negotiations of unprecedented scope, with the goals of reducing the threat of war and maintaining our national security and that of our allies. These negotiations include the Strategic Arms Limitation Talks and talks aimed at a comprehensive ban on nuclear testing, mutual and balanced force reductions (MBFR), and a ban on chemical weapons.

With the support of many other governments of the international community, these efforts give real meaning to Disarmament Week. They are an important contribution to mankind's quest for a peaceful world.

Veto of Amendments to the Small Business Act and the Small Business Investment Act

Memorandum of Disapproval of H.R. 11445. October 25, 1978

I am withholding my approval of H.R. 11445, omnibus amendments to the Small Business Act and the Small Business Investment Act. Because I recognize very personally the needs of the small business community and the dedication of Congressman Neal Smith and Senator Gaylord Nelson, Chairmen of the respective House and Senate small business committees, in developing this legislation, it is with great regret that I must take this action.

Having spent most of my adult life as a small businessman, I share with the Congress a strong commitment to the small business people of our country and I recognize the need for greater attention to small business needs by the Federal Government. Since I took office we have reduced the burden of Federal regulations on small business, proposed significant tax reductions and increased lending under the guaranteed loan program by 40%. In May of this year I signed an Executive Order calling for a White House Conference on Small Business to be held in January, 1980. This conference will involve over 25,000 small business people throughout the country helping us to develop a small business policy for this country. I intend to work with the Congress and particularly with Chairmen Smith and Nelson to develop and implement such a policy.

This legislation does have beneficial features. However, it is precisely because of my commitment to small business and an effective Small Business Administration, that I must withhold my approval from H.R. 11445. This bill, in its present form, is not the best we can do for small business in the United States and is inconsistent with the tight budget situation we will face in the next few years. Disapproval of the bill would not interrupt any existing SBA programs since SBA programs are already authorized for fiscal year 1979, nor would it interfere with Administration plans regarding the White House Conference on Small Business, since $4,000,000 has already been appropriated for the Conference in fiscal year 1979. This Conference is an important priority of mine and of my Administration.

The bill authorizes over $2 billion in expenditures in excess of our budget projec-

tions through 1982. It continues a duplicative program of farm disaster lending by the SBA with excessively deep interest subsidies and terms which we believe to be wasteful. This has led to an unwarranted amount of farm disaster lending which should be done by the Farmers Home Administration. This Administration has proposed that farm lending be consolidated in the Department of Agriculture which has the farm credit expertise and extensive field network necessary to operate the program effectively and efficiently. The Congress has failed to act on this recommendation.

Even more important is the effect this bill would have on the operations of the Small Business Administration. The bill virtually mandates significant staff increases. It would also interfere with the ability of the Administrator of the SBA, my primary small business advisor and representative, to effectively run that agency. The legislation imposes specific titles and responsibilities upon agency officials and specifies funding and personnel levels for activities throughout SBA down to the smallest detail. These legislative strictures run counter to my efforts to better manage the Federal Government.

The bill also distorts the role of SBA's Chief Counsel for Advocacy. I supported the establishment of this office as a means to insure that the views of small business were adequately reflected in the policy-making processes of the Government. But the legislation tends to move the Chief Counsel for Advocacy into policy and administrative areas more properly those of the Administrator of the SBA. This bill also might begin to isolate the Chief Counsel for Advocacy from the executive policy-making process by calling for an annual report to Congress which could not be reviewed or coordinated with any other agency of the Executive Branch. Current statutes provide the Chief Counsel with sufficient authorities to evaluate small business issues and serve as an ombudsman to small business interests.

I am also concerned by the loan pooling provision in this bill that would authorize private dealers to issue a new class of 100 percent federally guaranteed securities which would compete directly with the Treasury and other federally-backed securities in the bond markets.

I look forward to working with the Congress and the small business community who worked on this bill to develop a program to meet the needs of small business. It is my great hope that early in the next Congress an approach will be fashioned to meet the needs of the small business community, with the full involvement of my Administration.

JIMMY CARTER

Foreign Intelligence Surveillance Act of 1978

Statement on Signing S. 1566 Into Law.
October 25, 1978

I am pleased to sign into law today the Foreign Intelligence Surveillance Act of 1978. As I said a year and a half ago at the beginning of the process that produced this bill, "one of the most difficult tasks in a free society like our own is the correlation between adequate intelligence to guarantee our Nation's security on the one hand, and the preservation of basic human rights on the other."

This is a difficult balance to strike, but the act I am signing today strikes it. It sacrifices neither our security nor our civil liberties. And it assures that those who serve this country in intelligence positions will have the affirmation of Congress that their activities are lawful.

In working on this bill, the Congress dealt skillfully with sensitive issues. The result shows our country benefits when the legislative and executive branches of Government work together toward a common goal.

The bill requires, for the first time, a prior judicial warrant for *all* electronic surveillance for foreign intelligence or counterintelligence purposes in the United States in which communications of U.S. persons might be intercepted. It clarifies the Executive's authority to gather foreign intelligence by electronic surveillance in the United States. It will remove any doubt about the legality of those surveillances which are conducted to protect our country against espionage and international terrorism. It will assure FBI field agents and others involved in intelligence collection that their acts are authorized by statute and, if a U.S. person's communications are concerned, by a court order. And it will protect the privacy of the American people.

In short, the act helps to solidify the relationship of trust between the American people and their Government. It provides a basis for the trust of the American people in the fact that the activities of their intelligence agencies are both effective and lawful. It provides enough secrecy to ensure that intelligence relating to national security can be securely acquired, while permitting review by the courts and Congress to safeguard the rights of Americans and others.

This legislation is the first long step toward the goal of establishing statutory charters for our intelligence agencies. I am committed to that goal, and my administration will work with the Congress to achieve it.

Many people played important roles in securing passage of this bill.

I am convinced that the bill would not have passed without the leadership of Attorney General Bell; the personal commitment of the Director of Central Intelligence, Admiral Turner; and the work of Admiral Inman of the National Security Agency and Directors Webster and Kelley of the FBI. I extend my personal appreciation to these men and their staffs.

My administration's bill was based on some fine work during the Ford administration under the leadership of Attorney General Levi. His contribution to this legislation was substantial, illustrating the bipartisan nature of this process.

There was strong, effective, and bipartisan leadership in the Congress as well. I particularly want to commend Senators Kennedy, Bayh, and Garn for helping to guide this bill to overwhelming approval in the Senate. Chairman Boland and Congressman Morgan Murphy of the House Intelligence Committee and Chairman Rodino and Congressman Kastenmeier of the House Judiciary Committee undertook the hard work of moving the bill through the House. And, once again, I am indebted to the efforts of Speaker O'Neill and Majority Leader Wright.

I wish as well to express my appreciation to the Vice President, who long supported this foreign intelligence reform in the Senate and who assured the wholehearted commitment of the executive branch to this important legislation.

I have said so often, one of the central goals of my administration is to restore the confidence of the American people in their governmental institutions. This act takes us one more step down that road.

NOTE: As enacted, S. 1566 is Public Law 95–511, approved October 25.

Ethics in Government Act of 1978

Remarks on Signing S. 555 Into Law. October 26, 1978

THE PRESIDENT. I'm very pleased this morning to participate in a ceremony that has great significance for our country. During my own campaign for President, I promised the American people that I would do everything in my power to guarantee integrity in the executive branch of Government, and also obviously I have been joined with great enthusiasm by the Members of Congress and members of the judiciary as well.

On May 3 of 1977, shortly after I became President, I proposed legislation to the Congress to meet these commitments. And today I'm pleased to sign into law the Ethics in Government Act of 1978, which gives us added tools to ensure that the Government is open, honest, and is free from conflicts of interest.

I am pleased that no major provision of my own original proposal has been deleted or weakened, and that the Congress, with our support, has actually extended important provisions to the legislative and judicial branches of Government. This is a good indication of cooperation in extending these ethical standards throughout the entire Government of our country.

This bill will provide for mandatory, personal financial disclosures for high officials in the executive branch of Government, for all Members of the Congress, and for all senior members of the judicial branch of Government as well.

The ultimate authority for—or responsibility for endorsing and interpreting the provisions of the act lies in the executive branch of Government. Substantially, it broadens protection against abuses caused by postemployment conflicts of interest, so that people who have been employed in the Government cannot use this employment to go and enrich themselves by going into an area of private employment which would use their influence recently derived from Government service. It closes the revolving door that has been so significantly abused in the past.

This legislation also establishes a Special Office of Government Ethics in the new Office of Personnel Management, which was brought about by a revision of the civil service system of our country.

This bill responds to problems that developed at the highest level of Government in the 1970's.

If in the future there are ever substantial allegations of criminal violations by the President or the Vice President, by Members of the Congress [Cabinet] or senior members of the President's staff, a Special Prosecutor will be appointed by a panel made up of U.S. Court of Appeals judges of the District of Columbia to prosecute or investigate and see if a prosecution is necessary. This Special Prosecutor could only be removed on the basis of extraordinary impropriety or incapacity, which gives the Special Prosecutor in the future, if needed, a great protection in carrying out his responsibilities without interference.

I'm hopeful, of course, that this authority will rarely be needed, but I believe it is necessary in response to the lessons that we have learned to the embarrassment of our country in the past.

Enactment of this legislation would not have been possible without the outstanding leadership and enthusiastic personal involvement by Speaker Tip O'Neill. And I would like to point out too that Congressman George Danielson, the floor manager of the bill in the House, and Senator Abe Ribicoff, the floor manager in the Senate, did truly outstanding jobs in their successful efforts on behalf of this legislation. Senator Percy, Senator Robert Byrd, Senator Case, and Representatives Pat Schroeder, Richardson Preyer, Samuel Stratton, James Mann, and others deserve congratulations for their excellent work on this bill.

There was a great deal of pressure from many sources to weaken the provisions of this ethics legislation. That pressure was successfully withstood by those that I've described. I'm very pleased that we've achieved this milestone in the history of safeguards against abuse of the public trust by Government officials.

I believe this act will help to restore public confidence in the integrity of our Government, and I think it might serve as a bellwether or a guide to other elements of our government at the State and local level who might wish to imitate what has been done so well by the Congress this year.

It's with a great deal of pleasure that I sign the ethics legislation, which guarantees higher standards of performance and accountability to the public in all the branches of the Federal Government.

[At this point, the President signed the bill.]

Mr. Speaker, I thank you.

SPEAKER O'NEILL. I recall the first session that we ever had, when I had been designated as Speaker of the House, with the President of the United States. It was down in Georgia, and he had four goals. One of them was an economic stabilization package. Secondly was a strong ethics package. Thirdly was reorganization, and fourth was an energy package. It took us a little while to accomplish them all, but we did do them, and I think we did them well.

And so, Mr. President, those are the four goals of the first 2 years. They were the main goals, and the ethics package, as I say, was one of them. And I'm pleased to be here in the participating of your signing this legislation.

Thank you.

THE PRESIDENT. Thank you very much.

Senator Case, would you like to make a comment?

SENATOR CASE. Mr. President, Mr. Speaker, this is a very poignant moment for me. Twenty years ago Dick Neuberger and I introduced the first disclosure bill in the Congress. And it's kind of nice to have it come to fruition before I leave. And so, I thank you for asking me here.

I thank you, Tip, for your leadership, and I'm grateful indeed for all the Members of the House and Senate who came to see the light.

Thank you.

SPEAKER O'NEILL. You've been a good man, Senator.

THE PRESIDENT. Thank you very much.

NOTE: The President spoke at 10:03 a.m. at the signing ceremony in the Cabinet Room at the White House.

As enacted, S. 555 is Public Law 95–521, approved October 26.

Anti-Inflation Program

Memorandum From the President. October 26, 1978

Memorandum for the Heads of Executive Departments and Agencies

There is no more important goal for my Administration than restraining inflation. A crucial part of this effort is managing government more efficiently. With that goal in mind, I am imposing an indefinite limitation on the hiring of Federal civilian workers, as of October 25, 1978.

I ask that you limit the number of new full-time permanent appointments in your agency to not more than 50 percent of the *new* vacancies occurring after October 25, 1978. In other words, for each two *new* vacancies, you may appoint one new permanent employee. You may not fill such vacancies as exist on October 24, 1978 except by use of the appointments permitted as a result of new vacancies.

I am instructing the Office of Management and Budget and the Civil Service Commission to issue instructions on this directive. In addition, I delegate authority to the Director of the Office of Management and Budget to grant specific exemptions in a very limited number of cases, when such exemptions are necessary to assure that essential services are provided and fundamental needs are met.

I ask that, as you carry out this directive, you do it in a way that protects the operations in your agency that directly affect the public—for example, Social Security claims processing and check issuance, and veterans' benefit payments. You should absorb as much of the impact as possible in the support and overhead operations of your agency.

It is within your power to determine whether the government succeeds in this part of the battle against inflation. I urge you to do everything possible to assign your staff where the need is greatest, so that vital and basic services may continue uninterrupted. Contracting with firms and institutions outside the government must not be used to circumvent the intent of this directive.

I urge you to give this matter your personal attention and support.

JIMMY CARTER

Strategic Arms Limitation Talks

Designation of Ambassador Ralph Earle II as Chairman of the U.S. Delegation.
October 26, 1978

The President announced today that Ambassador Ralph Earle II, who has been serving as Alternate Chairman of the U.S. Delegation to the Strategic Arms Limitation Talks (SALT), will become Chairman of the Delegation upon the resignation of Paul C. Warnke, effective October 31, 1978.

Earle was born September 26, 1928, in Bryn Mawr, Pa. He received an A.B. from Harvard College in 1950 and an LL.B. from Harvard Law School in 1955. He served in the U.S. Army from 1950 to 1952.

Earle practiced law with the firm of Morgan, Lewis and Bockius in Philadelphia from 1956 to 1968, as an associate and then a partner. In 1968 and 1969, he served as Principal Deputy Assistant Secretary of Defense and Acting Assistant Secretary of Defense for International Security Affairs.

From 1969 to 1972, Earle was Defense Advisor to the U.S. Mission to NATO. In 1972 and 1973, he was a consultant for SALT in the Office of the Secretary of Defense. He was the ACDA Representative on the U.S. Delegation to SALT from 1973 until May 11, 1977, when he became Alternate Chairman of the U.S. Delegation.

Nashville, Tennessee

Remarks at a State Democratic Party Rally.
October 26, 1978

Governor Blanton, Senator Jim Sasser, Congressman Jones, Congressman Gore, Administrator of the GSA Jay Solomon, Mayor Fulton, Speaker Ned McWherter, Lieutenant Governor Wilder—*I'd also like to recognize Mrs. Clifford Allen,*[1] *who is here; we think so much of her—members of the Tennessee supreme court, members of the State legislature, the Governor's cabinet, my friends from Tennessee:*

Thank you very much for coming.

Second only to Georgia in the primary, does anybody here know which State gave me the biggest margin of victory when I ran for President? [*Applause*] Right on. And I've come to thank you for that.

Not too long ago, the Congress and I restored full citizenship to President Jefferson Davis. And since Camp David, the Congress and the people of the country have done the same to me, and I want to thank you for that, too.

For any Democrat coming to Tennessee, and particularly coming to Nashville, is a homecoming, because Andrew Jackson, one of the greatest Presidents who ever lived, the father of our party, has made Tennessee a homecoming place for all Democrats.

He was a man of great courage. He was a man who was independent. He was a man who loved his home State. He was a man who founded the principles of our party, that said that those who hold public office have to put our faith, our confidence, our responsibility to the average, common, good American citizens who put us in office.

That was Andrew Jackson's commitment. That's the commitment of the Democratic Party today, and we're going to keep it that way.

There has been a time in the last few years when Tennessee strayed temporarily from the Democratic Party and from the

---

[1] Wife of the U.S. Representative from Tennessee who died June 19.

principles of Andrew Jackson. But that time is gone. And in the last few years, we've seen a major shift back toward Democrats by Tennessee, and that's going to keep on the next 2 weeks.

Georgia, my own State, has always been close to Tennessee. We share a lot with you. When it snows in the north Georgia mountains and the northwestern part of our State, our State legislators have to come through Tennessee to get home to Atlanta to act as legislators. We've always kept those borders open, except one time when General Sherman crossed them on the way from Tennessee through Atlanta. But with that one exception, we bind ourselves to you.

We'll keep those lines open. And I'm proud to say that as Tennesseans, I consider you my brother, and I'm glad to be here as that, too.

In addition to Andrew Jackson, Tennessee has provided some great Democratic statesmen: James K. Polk, President of the United States; Cordell Hull, one of the greatest Secretaries of State our country has ever seen; Estes Kefauver, who ought to have been President of the United States.

Kefauver was a man who went throughout the country, standing on street corners, standing in factory shift lines early in the morning, shaking hands with the American citizens and saying, "What can I do for you if I'm the nominee of the Democratic Party?"

I believe he entered 13 primaries. He won 11 of them. He wasn't elected President, but he set a standard of campaigning that I followed very closely when in 1976 I entered 30 primaries and won a fairly good number of those—[*laughter*]— which gave me an avenue to the White House.

I want to recognize, too, a great United States Senator who served at the same

time, Senator Albert Gore, who's been an inspiration to a lot of southerners.

As you well know, when the South was going through those difficult days of changing from a segregated society to one where we gave all American citizens equal rights, regardless of color, Albert Gore, Estes Kefauver set a standard for the rest of us to follow. Their courage has made the southland a better place to live for blacks and whites. And I want to thank them for what they meant to me and to my own people.

I'll always remember the Democratic convention when Frank Clement made an inspiring address, and his son, Bob,[2] has brought the same kind of approach to Democratic politics in this State. And he supported the Democratic nominees as a loyal Democrat should, in this same status with the same tradition as his father, Frank.

I can't come to Tennessee, especially Nashville, without mentioning Dick Fulton, a man who was in the Congress, who could have stayed there as long as he wanted to, who was doing a great job, but felt that he could do a better job and be closer to you if he came home as mayor of Nashville. And I hate to miss him in Washington, but I'm glad you've got him. And I'm very thankful that he's doing such a great job here as your mayor, and I want to make sure that everybody knows about that.

Some people said he came to Nashville to be closer to country music. [*Laughter*] But that's not true any more, because you can't get any closer to country music that originates in Nashville than you do in the White House when I turn my record-player on or my radio on—that's the kind of music I really love.

---

[2] Tennessee public service commissioner and candidate for Governor during the State Democratic primary.

And we've had a lot of great music performers from your city come to entertain us and many others in the White House since I've been President. The night before last, my wife and I were on the telephone talking to June Carter and also to her husband, as you know, about the unfortunate loss of Maybelle Carter. She set not only a standard in country music that's inspired Johnny Cash and many others as well as her own family, but she also set a standard of common, ordinary people who love one another, expressing their views, their hopes, their dreams, their fears to the world through music. And I want to thank you for her.

As June knows, I always claim kinship with her, particularly after I started running for office. And that family means a lot to me and to the rest of the country.

I just want to mention two other people. Al Bissell, a great mayor of Oakridge, has provided us with a standard of leadership at the municipal level, and I predict that his son, Keith, will do an equally good job as public service commissioner next year.

Jay Solomon, a Tennessean, came to Washington at my request. He didn't much want to come, but he's a great businessman from Chattanooga, and he took over as Administrator of the General Services Administration, the GSA. And he's done as much to let us know about waste and corruption in Government as anyone. He's fighting the battles for you to make the Federal Government be better, cleaner, more decent, more honest. He's the kind of fellow who issues the contracts now after he opens the bids. And I want to thank Tennessee for giving me Jay Solomon.

I've really come here today to get you to work hard for the nominees for Governor, United States Senate, State offices, and the U.S. Congress, whom you have already chosen in an open, tough, difficult, closely contested Democratic primary.

You've chosen a man to come to Washington with me 2 years ago, who's done an outstanding job already. And I want to express my deep thanks to you for sending Jim Sasser to Washington, who has already carved out for himself a position of leadership.

One of the most important responsibilities of any Senator is to pass the appropriations bills, deciding where money goes for every possible service the National Government provides. Jim Sasser just happens to be on the Appropriations Committee. Another important job, of course, is preparing the budget to cut down on deficits and to make sure the Congress toes the line when they spend your money. It just happens that Jim Sasser is on the Senate Budget Committee.

Another important job is to give government reorganization a chance to let us have a better government. We've passed now a very fine civil service reform law to put our good civil servants to work a little harder for you. It just happens that Jim Sasser is chairman of the Civil Service Reform Committee, and I want to thank Tennessee for giving me this strong ally and friend and supporter in Washington.

I've only got one complaint to make about Jim Sasser. He's a little too independent. [*Laughter*] When it comes down to deciding what I want him to do, compared to what Tennessee wants him to do, he always does what you want him to do.

Now I want to comment on one man who's had maybe a more difficult youth than I had. When I was 14 years old, because of the TVA and because of the REA, we got electricity and running water in the house I lived in. Jake Butcher didn't get it until he was 16 years old. [*Laughter*] He's a man who comes from humble beginnings. He's a man who exemplifies in my mind the true spirit of Tennessee. He's worked hard. He has cast his lot with the people of this State. He's a competent, successful businessman.

When I was Governor of Georgia, I spent about 25 percent of my time trying to bring industry into my State. I spent that time trying to revive the possibility of jobs for Georgians, to make sure we were a dynamic, growing State, to make sure the State government was run economically and efficiently as a business ought to be. And you have a true treasure coming up next year in Jake Butcher as your Governor. And I hope every one of you will help him.

I have particularly admired his positive campaign. He has not run a negative campaign. He's pointed out to you how Tennessee could be a better State with good leadership. And he has got a particularly soft spot in his heart for senior citizens. If he's elected Governor—and I'm sure he will be—he's promised all those over 65 years old that you will not have to pay sales tax on food. That shows where he stands. That shows one of the things that he will do.

And now I want to mention a woman who, next January, is going to make Jim Sasser senior Senator from Tennessee—Jane Eskind.

In the Tennessee primary—and there's no other like it in the whole United States—you had nine candidates for the Democratic nomination for U.S. Senator. Nobody thought Jane Eskind had a chance. Jane Eskind thought she had a chance. She put her political future in your hands. And she came through on top.

The reason is that she's tough, competent, she knows government. She'll come with a clear eye and a clean-sweeping broom. She's cast her lot with the little people, the common, ordinary, good working people of Tennessee. And she'll bring to Washington the true spirit of Andrew Jackson. And I hope all of you will help her when November 7 comes.

I'll have to express my thanks as a peanut farmer to Ed Jones, the dean of the Tennessee congressional delegation and one of the leading members of the Congress in passing agricultural legislation for our country.

Albert Gore, Jr., fits in well with Tennessee. He's on the committee responsible for science and technology. And Tennessee, with a dynamic economy and a clear vision of the future, is certainly benefiting from his incumbency, and I'm sure he'll go back into office.

And you've got here in Nashville a man to fill some big shoes, your next Congressman, Bill Boner. Ron Arline will be the next Congressman; Gordon Ball, Margaret Francis. We've got the most wonderful Democratic slate you've ever had, and I hope you'll help me get all of them elected in 2 weeks, November 7, Tuesday after next. Will you do that for us? [*Applause*] Very good.

Now I'd like to say just a word about our Nation. Tennessee is the Volunteer State. You got that title and that reputation because you've always been willing and eager to defend our Nation when it was in trouble. And as your Governor pointed out, since I've been in office, we've not called on a single Tennessean nor a single American to lose a life or to shed blood in conflict in another country. And I want to keep that record as long as I'm in the White House.

Our Nation has taken the leadership in trying to preserve peace for our own people, in trying to bring peace to others. We are negotiating now to conclude a SALT treaty, to make sure that we lessen the threat of nuclear weapons for people in our own country and throughout the world. We are trying to negotiate, with some success already, peace in the Middle East, between Israel and Egypt. This is a difficult undertaking, and we need your help, your prayers, and your support.

We are trying to strengthen our ties with our own allies, to let NATO be stronger. We've got a strong defense, ever improving. We're the strongest nation on Earth militarily, and as long as I'm in the White House, we're going to stay number one in defense.

Tennesseans believe in hard work. So do I. When I was elected President, we had 10 million Americans, 10 million Americans who could not get a full-time job. We had 7 million Americans or more who couldn't get a job at all. But we put America back to work. We've had, since I've been in office, an increase of 6 million net new jobs for America, and we're going to keep on giving our people a chance to work for themselves and for our country.

We are trying to provide better education, better housing, better highways, a good agricultural program. With your Congressmen's help, we passed a farm bill about a year ago that's already improved farm income 25 percent. We've got the highest level of agricultural exports in the history of our country last year. This year, it's going to be even higher; next year, higher still.

We're trying also to make sure that we have a good energy program, and for the first time in the history of our Nation, we now have a good, sound energy policy that's going to be better in the future with your help.

[The day before] [3] yesterday, I signed a bill to deregulate the airline industry.

---

[3] Printed in the transcript.

We're trying to get Government's nose out of the business of the people of this country, and we've made good progress already. We've had a decrease in airline fares, a tremendous increase in the number of people who can now afford to fly in airplanes, and the profits of the airline industry have gone up. And by 1985, we will have eliminated a major Federal regulatory agency, the CAB, the Civil Aeronautics Board, because we've proven that the American free enterprise system can work if competition is put in and the consumers are protected. That's the kind of government we're trying to give you.

The Democratic Party has always been a party with a heart. We believe in people and giving our people a better chance to live. But we're also a party that knows how to manage government. When I was running for President in 1976 and you helped me so much, we had a Federal budget deficit of $66 billion. In 1 year, we cut it down to the fifties. We've now cut it down to the forties. By the end of next year, we'll have cut it in half, and we're going to keep on working until we have a balanced budget for the Federal Government and responsible to you.

At the same time, we've cut taxes. Better services, lower taxes, lower budget deficits, better management, zero-base budgeting—these are the kind of things that we believe are important.

We're cutting out corruption. I signed an ethics bill this morning to make public officials accountable for where their income is derived and how they spend the money and whether they are honest. This will go a long step forward.

And the next big undertaking is to control inflation in our Nation. For the last 10 years, the inflation rate in our country has averaged 6½ percent. As I said the other night, the 3 years before I became President, it averaged 8 percent. And I want to ask your promise as the last thing today, will you help me with our anti-inflation program to control inflation in this country? Will you help me? [*Applause*] Right on.

Well, I want to close by saying this: You've shown your confidence in me as a Georgian, as a neighbor, as a southerner, as an American. The Presidency of the United States is not an easy job. But I feel at ease with it, in spite of the difficulties, in spite of the challenges, in spite of the promises that need to be kept, in spite of the problems that face me every day, because I cast my lot with you when I ran for President. I also stood on street corners, in factory shift lines, went through city halls and courthouses, met you on the street, shook hands, asked for your advice and your support.

That's where my strength comes from, from you. That's where the strength of Andrew Jackson came from, from you. And I hope to maintain your confidence in me and improve your confidence in the Federal Government by good management, by peace, by openness, by strength, and because you control me and your Government.

This is what the Democratic Party stands for also. And I hope on November 7 that all of you will do the best you can to elect the fine slate of Democratic officers and make the greatest nation on Earth even greater in the future.

Thank you very much.

Are we going to win in November? [*Applause*] Right on. Are you going to work and help us win? [*Applause*] Right on.

Thank you very much. I love every one of you.

NOTE: The President spoke at 12:18 p.m. at Legislative Plaza.

Nashville, Tennessee
Remarks at a State Democratic Party Fundraising Reception.   October 26, 1978

Governor Blanton and Senator Sasser, distinguished Members of the Congress from Tennessee, Speaker, and Lieutenant Governor, who have honored me by your presence, and good, solid, strong, dedicated, sacrificial, committed, determined Democrats:

It's good to be with you.

Jim Sasser said that there's so much excitement and so much enthusiasm, the Democratic candidates have such a wonderful support in Tennessee this year, he wishes that this is the year he was to run for the Senate again—[*laughter*]—almost.

I don't think you could have sent anyone to Washington who could have done a better job so quickly and earned the respect and admiration of his fellow Senators and of the President than you have with Jim Sasser, and I thank you for him.

I'm not going to make another speech to you, because you don't need it. And I've already made one speech pointing out what the Democratic Party is trying to do both here in Tennessee and throughout the country.

In 1974 I was a nationwide campaign coordinator for the Democratic Party. I read the little almanac every time I went into a State. I was going to go to Memphis to meet with Jim Sasser and some of those who are on the stage with me, to try to see what could be done to rejuvenate a dormant Democratic Party in Tennessee.

The political almanac said—and I can almost quote it—"The most Republican State in the Nation is Tennessee." You've changed that, and I'm thankful for it.

Well, we've got a long way to go. As a neighbor of yours and one who has been interested in politics for the last number of years, I've watched with a great deal of interest the almost unique primary system that you have in Tennessee, where a lot of people run and where the one who gets a plurality wins.

In Georgia, we have a runoff 2 or 3 weeks after the first primary. You don't do that in Tennessee. And quite often it creates scars, because those who are defeated—and I've been defeated—can't build up enthusiasm to support those whom the people have chosen.

I'm thankful that this year in Tennessee that's not the case. Every single candidate for the U.S. Senate and for Governor have endorsed and are working for the nominees that you've chosen. I'm glad of that.

It's been a long time though since Tennessee had a chance to choose a Democratic Governor and two Democratic United States Senators. It's going to require a lot of work. Many of you have already helped. You wouldn't be here at this particular fairly exclusive meeting had you not had a deep commitment to the Democratic Party and what it stands for and if you were not supporting the candidates who are waging such a tough battle for election.

The Republican nominees are formidable, they are well known, they are well financed. Had I let characteristics like those make much of an impression on me, I would never have entered 30 primaries, and I would never have gotten the nomination and been elected for President.

We know that in the last few days of a campaign, the candidate who can convince the people that he or she is closest · to them is dependent upon them for the election success and will serve them and rely on them after they are in office. Those are the candidates who win.

There have been an enormous number of upset victories in our Nation the last

3 or 4 years. You've seen them all over the country. And that's the reason, because people have gotten doubtful about those who are proud, those who are aloof, those who forget about a particular constituency and cast their lot on a nationwide basis; those who might forget that their unique responsibility is, first of all, to be an American, yes, but secondly, to represent Tennessee.

In the last two or three decades in the South, Democrats have been afflicted by an undeserved reputation that Republicans are more fiscally responsible, are better managers, and are more attuned to competence and efficiency. That reputation has now changed. Had it not been changing, I would never have been elected President.

But I ran my campaign talking about zero-based budgeting, cutting down the Federal deficit, cutting the size of the Federal work force; getting Government's nose out of private people's business; making sure that the free enterprise system had an opportunity to be stronger even than it already is; putting my confidence in government at the lowest possible level, closest to the people, rather than concentrating it in Washington.

Of course, I also talked about a strong defense; also talked about better lives for farmers and talked about peace. But now we've changed that earlier reputation, and I noticed with a Gallup poll this summer that by a 2-to-1 margin the people of our country now believe that the most fiscally responsible party is not the Republicans, but the Democrats.

I believe now you have an opportunity to put a man in the Governor's office who will maintain competence, efficiency, dynamism, who understands the distinction that ought to be drawn between government and the private sector; who understands the problems of working people; who's shown that the free enterprise system works in an honorable way; and who can bring to government a vision of what Tennessee can be—with new jobs, new industry, lower taxes, a better life for senior citizens, a better education system.

These are the kinds of things for which the groundwork's been laid. But Jake Butcher is the kind of person who didn't have to run for Governor. The Lord knows it's not an easy thing to run for a major political office, with one's family involved, with a deep, unshakable commitment. He and Sanya have been willing to go out, as is indicated on this poster, and put himself before you to serve Tennessee. And I hope you'll put him in the Governor's office and give me a good partner here in Tennessee with whom I can work the next 4 years.

I just want to say a word, too, about Jane Eskind, who I think has a campaign that pretty closely parallels mine in 1976. It would be good for Tennessee to have her as a U.S. Senator. She understands the intricacies of government from the point of view of one who is deeply interested. She's been a loyal public servant without holding elective office.

I'd never served in Washington myself, and I know the advantage that I had, along with Jim Sasser, of coming there, as Jay Solomon has done, with kind of a fresh point of view. But she understands the intricacies of government. And she, I remember, in 1976, led a voter registration drive in Tennessee and added 250,000 new voters to the rolls. She didn't have to do that, but she did a good job with it. And she is running a very aggressive, very competent campaign.

I want to say this in closing: It's not easy for them to run; it wasn't easy for me to run. I did it because I wanted to, and I'm enjoying being President. I never have claimed to know all the answers, but I think as long as I put my faith in you, as they will do, I can avoid some of the mistakes that have been made in the past.

You've come here maybe feeling that you've done enough. I bet everyone in this room has been blessed socially, politically, economically. We've enjoyed the fruits of a free society. Some of you may have come from humble background, maybe even from illiterate parents who had to work every day for a living. But you've done well. And I hope that you will see in the next 10 or 12 days that the most important thing that you could possibly do with your time, your influence, or your money is to help good candidates be elected on November 7.

There's no one in here who's not competent enough to be, in effect, when you go back home, a campaign manager for Jake and for Jane and for Keith and for others; to call your own friends and your own neighbors, to see your business associates or those who have confidence in you, and say, "Let's help these candidates restore to Tennessee, which has in the past been heavily oriented toward the other party, a new fresh Democratic spirit." It will really help me as a President to do a better job and help you to have a better State and a better Nation.

And I'd like to ask every one of you, if you will do that, to actually work between now and November 7 to actually raise extra money for them and use your influence in a beneficial way for Tennessee. Would you say when I ask you, "I will"? Will you do that for us? [*Applause*] Right on, thank you.

I came here to thank you and to hear you say that. Thank you very much.

NOTE: The President spoke at 1:15 p.m. in the Grand Ballroom at the Hyatt Regency Hotel.

Miami Beach, Florida

Remarks at a State Democratic Party Rally.
October 26, 1978

My good friend Bob Shevin; Florida's next Governor, Bob Graham; Congressman Claude Pepper—[applause]—go ahead and applaud; great—Congressman Bill Lehman; Congressman Dante Fascell; Mayor Haber; Chairman Duran:

Let me say that it is a great honor and pleasure for me as President of the United States to come back down to Florida, my neighboring State, first of all, to pay my thanks to you for supporting me when I ran for President, and to let you know that I'm here to support some men who can do a great job for you on November 7. Will you help them in 12 days to be elected? [*Applause*]

Florida needs a Governor who will continue the absolutely superb work of my friend, Governor Reubin Askew, one of the greatest Governors who ever served any State in this country.

Florida needs a Governor who knows what it means to work, a man who has held, during the campaign, more than a hundred jobs, spending a day alongside Floridians like you on farms, in factories, grocery stores, working in hotels, learning what it means to take care of a home, trying to see at first hand what could be done to make Florida an even greater State.

Florida needs a man who can come from a position as an underdog and be triumphant over nine other very worthy, dedicated, competent candidates who

challenged him. Florida needs a man who knows about education, who served as the chairman of the Senate Education Committee, who's worked as a teacher, who knows what it means to give our young people, indeed our old people as well, a chance to continue to stretch minds, to stretch hearts throughout their life's existence.

Florida needs a Governor who understands your basic natural resources, your basic human resources. He wants to see those resources developed in the most effective way. Florida needs a Governor who's eager to freeze property taxes. I think that's one of the best campaign promises I know of, and he's the kind of man who will keep that promise.

Florida needs a man who, as Governor, will be dedicated to law enforcement, to eliminate the threat of crime that causes concern among all those who live in this beautiful State. And Florida needs a man who can join with the Members of Congress in the great State legislature to make sure that our elderly citizens, our retired citizens still have an enjoyable, secure, and fruitful life, to let their own existence be meaningful as long as they live on this Earth. That man is Bob Graham. I hope you'll help him get elected.

I'd like to say a word about Claude Pepper. *Él es un buen hombre, un buen candidato. Es muy importante ayudarle. Es necesario tenerle en el Congreso de los Estados Unidos. Es un amigo de mí.* [He's a good man, a good candidate. It's important that you help him. It's necessary to have him in the Congress of the United States. He's a friend of mine.] And I hope that you will give him every support on November 7.

He's a man of courage. He's a man of vision. He's been an inspiration to many of us who have lived in the South in eliminating discrimination against people who were weak, poor, black, who couldn't speak English very well or who were old.

It's a great honor for me to be on the same stage as Claude Pepper. And I know you're going to give him one of the greatest margins of victory of any congressional candidate in the United States. He deserves it.

I also want to recognize Bill Lehman, who, along with Claude Pepper, is one of the greatest friends that Israel has. He serves on the Budget Committee. He helped me get civil service reform. He's a loyal, dedicated man who is so well liked that he doesn't even have any opposition on November 7. And he's going to help all the other Democratic candidates, Bill Lehman. Thank you, Bill.

There are many of you here who have a great interest in Latin America, in foreign affairs, in peace and defense. And you've got a strong supporter and a strong fighter for the things in which you believe in Dante Fascell, who's one of the great congressional leaders in international affairs and who also takes care of his own district.

Well, you can see that we have in the Democratic Party a good team. I've been President now for less than 2 years, but I believe that we've done what you want your Government to do in many aspects of life in Washington. Do you want a government of which you can be proud, that fights for human rights throughout the world? [*Applause*] That's what we've tried to bring in Washington through our Nation's foreign policy.

There have been times in the past when we could not be proud of everything our President did or everything our Nation's Government stood for. But I think it's accurate to say now that throughout the world, we have raised high a banner of which we can be proud; a nation that in its domestic affairs and foreign policy is clean and decent and represents the ideals

and commitments and principles on which our Nation was founded 200 years ago.

Do you want a government whose officials are honest and who are free of embarrassment and corruption? Do you? [*Applause*] That's what we're trying to bring to Washington.

This morning before I left the White House I signed a bill called the Ethics Bill of 1978. It requires that in the future, Presidents, Vice Presidents, Cabinet members, all top civil servants, all the Members of Congress, all the top members of the judiciary, all our judges, have to account for their net worth, their incomes, make sure that the public has available to them an assessment of whether or not that candidate or that public official is honest.

We've been fighting to get this legislation now in our country for over 20 years. It has not been possible until this morning. And from now on, your public officials will have to account to you, and it will not only make them honest, but it will keep them honest. And they'll have to prove it.

Let me ask you another question. Do you want a government that's able to put American people back to work? [*Applause*] Right on. I knew you'd say yes.

When I took over as President 21 months ago, we had 10 million Americans who could not find a full-time job. We had 7 million Americans who couldn't find a job of any kind. The unemployment rate was 8 percent. In the last 20 months, we have brought the unemployment rate down 25 percent. And we have also added, in doing so, over 6 million more jobs than we had when I was inaugurated President.

The Congress deserves a lot of credit for this, because they've emphasized not jobs in government, but jobs in the private sector, permanent jobs.

We still have a long way to go. Many of our young people, many of those who belong to minority groups still are not employed. And we want to be sure that in the months to come we give them an opportunity to expend their one life on Earth in a productive way and feel that they are part of society, doing a useful job in their life, not alienated from society because they can't get a job they want.

Let me ask you another question. Do you want a government that will get the regulatory agencies and government agencies' nose out of the private sector's business and let our free enterprise system work in the United States? [*Applause*] Well, that's the kind of government we're trying to bring you in Washington.

As I got off the plane at the airport a few minutes ago, I was met by Frank Borman, one of the great heroes of our country, one of the astronauts that went to the Moon, now president of Eastern Airlines.

When I came in as President, I promised that we were going to deregulate the airline industry, to make sure that we eliminated the artificial holding up of prices to those who wanted to fly on our commercial airlines. We have reduced those fares tremendously. The number of passengers has gone up greatly, and the profits for Eastern Airlines, Delta, Pan Am, and all the others have gone up as well.

I'm committed in the future to bringing deregulation to other industries and make sure the free enterprise system in our country has a chance to have competition, which is good for our industry and also good for consumers. That's another goal that we've set for ourselves, that if you'll help us, we're going to meet.

I've got two or three more questions to ask you.

Do you want a government that works hard to control the threat of atomic weapons, which could destroy us all? Do you? [*Applause*]

We're negotiating every day to bring about a good SALT agreement with the Soviet Union, to cut down the level of atomic weapons. And the Congress has already passed a very good nonproliferation bill which prevents countries who don't have atomic weapons from having them in the future.

Two years ago there was a general belief that the atomic genie was out of the bottle, that nobody could stop the spread of atomic weapons. But we've been successful so far. And I believe that next year we'll have a chance to approve in the Congress a SALT agreement that will give our Nation less atomic weapons but greater security in the bargain.

And I'd like to ask you another question. Do you want to make sure that the United States is always number one in military strength? [*Applause*] That's what we've got now, and that's what we're going to keep, because with strength comes the ability to use our influence in a beneficial way around the world.

Our country is now respected by others. We are no longer the butt of all the jokes. We're no longer the target of all the attacks by the small nations, the weak nations, the new nations, the nations whose people might be brown or yellow or black. We've spread our influence in a beneficial way, and we've let our potential adversaries, the Soviet Union and others, know that we're going to stay strong.

But strength is not just military might. It's also economic strength. It's also political strength, based on freedom and the right of each individual person to make one's own influence felt.

Let me ask you another question. Do you want a government that can cut down the Federal deficit? [*Applause*] I thought you'd say that, too.

When I was running for President down here in 1976, our budget deficit, Federal deficit, was $66 billion. The first year we cut it down to the fifties of billions of dollars. The Congress and I have now cut it down a little below $40 billion. And before I've been in office one more year, we're going to cut the Federal deficit down below half what it was when I came in office. And we are going to continue to work for a balanced budget for your Federal Government.

Do you want a government that cuts your income taxes? [*Applause*] Okay, okay. Last year, we cut income taxes $8 billion. This year, the Congress has already passed a bill that would cut our income taxes about $19 or $20 billion more. When I get back to Washington and get that bill, do you think I ought to sign it? [*Applause*] I'll take your advice. I've decided to sign the bill.

I'm just going to ask you three more questions. One is, do you want a government that will keep our social security system sound? [*Applause*] Well, as you well know, 2 years ago, when I came down here to campaign among you, the first question I ever got from retired people or those who were approaching retirement were, "Is the social security system going into bankruptcy?"

At that time, in 2 more years, our social security system would have been bankrupt. Now the Congress has a social security system that will be sound and secure and dependable the rest of this century. And I can predict to you that forever, as long as any of us live, we're going to have a social security system on which you can depend.

And now, the two most important things: There is a great challenge that presents itself to us that we have not yet solved. I talked about it to you 2 nights

ago; the anti-inflation program that I outlined is badly needed. It's tough. It's necessary. It's fair. With the exception of peace for our Nation and the security of our Nation, next year the most important responsibility which I will have on my shoulders is to control inflation.

There are going to be a lot of special interest groups who are selfish, who will not want to join me in controlling inflation. As you well know, the ones who suffer most are the ones who live on a fixed retirement income, who have very low-paying jobs, or who are insecure. I want to ask you to help me every way you can to join in against the inflationary threat to us, and if you will join me and help me and point out those who violate the guidelines I've set down, which are fair, then I believe we can have success.

Will you help me fight inflation this next year? [*Applause*] Good deal.

And the last question I want to ask you is this: Do you want a government that will help bring peace to the Middle East? [*Applause*] Very good.

We've made good progress, as you know. The people of Israel, the people of Egypt want peace. They have two courageous leaders, President Sadat and Prime Minister Begin. I want peace as well. And we've had an excellent relationship to date. It's not going to be easy to conclude the details of a peace treaty between Israel and Egypt. I need your help, your support, and your prayers.

I believe that we can be successful. But I think that this is one of the greatest opportunities that any President has ever faced, to bring to that troubled land in the Middle East peace, which has escaped those people for thousands of years.

We'll be negotiating, starting again tomorrow. The Israeli delegation returns to Washington this evening. Secretary Vance will be working on this almost full-time. I will help when my help is needed. And

I pray that before Christmas, I will be going to the Middle East to join in signing a peace treaty that will bring permanent, good relations between ancient enemies, Egypt and Israel.

Well, you can see that we are trying to do our best. We've had some successes, some partial success, some great challenges still ahead of us. I want to have a government that can be justifiably proud of what it is. I want to make sure that our Nation has a reputation of being clean and decent. I want our strength to depend upon the finest characteristics of the American people. I hope that you will help between now and November 7 to encourage all your friends, all your neighbors to vote.

In 1960, two-thirds of the American people went to the polls to vote. In recent elections, two-thirds of the American people did not go to the polls and vote. It's important that you do so. If you will help me to elect these fine candidates whom I've come down to Miami to help, we can make a great nation of which we are all so proud an even greater nation in the future.

Thank you very much. God bless all of you.

NOTE: The President spoke at 5:35 p.m. at the North Shore Community Center Park. In his opening remarks, he referred to Robert L. Shevin, Florida attorney general, and Alfredo Duran, State Democratic Party chairman.

Miami Beach, Florida

Remarks at a Fundraising Reception for Bob Graham. October 26, 1978

It's always exciting to me to come to Florida, but particularly when I have a chance to participate in seeing a bright,

new political star flash across the Florida heavens, and that's what's happening here. And running on the same ticket with Claude Pepper—[*laughter*]—is Bob Graham, an older, more experienced politician, but equally as exciting.

This is a happy day for me to come back down here, because you gave me so much support and help when I needed it. When I was flying in, I thought there was a day of mourning in Florida. I saw over the Eckerd Drug Stores black drapes—[*laughter*]—I didn't know what happened.[1]

But we've got in Bob Graham a young man who has proven already that he knows how to reach the consciousness of a doubtful electorate and knows how to understand at first hand the ideals and the needs and the yearnings and the fears and trepidations and the hopes of average, ordinary working people who comprise this State.

I've watched his campaign with a great deal of interest. And I've seen his former opponents, Bob Shevin and others, come forward in a very generous and courageous way, immediately after the campaigns were over, and say, "We give you our support, because we know you and we have confidence in you."

At this moment in Bob's campaign, prospects look very good. And I congratulate you and him for it. But if there's one thing I've observed in this Nation the last 3 or 4 years, it is that upsets can happen. And I thank God for it. And you know what the polls looked like just a few weeks before Bob Graham was nominated to represent the Democratic Party. It would be a serious mistake for those who

---

[1] Jack Eckerd is the Republican gubernatorial candidate.

have confidence in the Democratic nominees to take anything for granted.

You've come here with a generous heart, with a willingness to help the Democratic ticket, and particularly Bob Graham, financially. That's not enough. He's being outspent by a great and widening margin. And the impact of a highly professional television campaign and a radio campaign in the last few days can be a very dangerous development in a well-organized political effort.

He needs all the help you can give him. If you haven't given the limit, I hope you will do so. If you have and your wife or husband also have, my plea to you is to take a checklist of your friends who have confidence in you, whether they be Democrats or Republicans, call and ask them for an equally generous contribution.

If you were raising money for some other worthy cause of a benevolent nature, you would drop your own professional responsibilities and work for several days or several weeks in preparation for a highly publicized fundraising banquet at which you might possibly be the master of ceremonies or be recognized there.

Those investments pay rich dividends. But I can think of no investment that would pay any more dividends than to have a continuation of an honest and a competent gubernatorial administration in Florida. Things could turn sour in Florida with the wrong kind of leader, and your good life could change. And I would like to ask you the next few days—we only have 12 days until the campaign is over—to invest several of those days in being a campaign manager for Bob Graham.

Call your friends and neighbors, those who have confidence in you, and ask them to go and vote and to contribute their time and finances as well. That's not too much to ask to make an investment in the future of your State and your Nation.

I'll do the best I can as President to represent you well. I have great responsibilities on my shoulders, as you well know. And one of the greatest sustaining factors that can encourage a President in times of potential discouragement or potential failure is to have a strong Governor on whom a President can depend.

So, if you believe in the things that I'm working to achieve, if you're grateful for the good life that you have here in Florida now, and you're willing to make an investment in the future, I hope you'll make that sacrificial effort the next few days.

The Democratic Party has always been one of compassion. We've reached our hands and hearts out to those who were less fortunate than we. We've stood for the elimination of racial discrimination, sex discrimination. We've tried to give people better jobs, better homes, better education, better transportation, a brighter future, a strong Nation militarily. We've stood for peace around the world.

Our motives are above suspicion. We are a compassionate, concerned party. But we are also a competent party. You can't educate a child nor feed a hungry person nor defend a nation or its principles with waste, corruption, or inefficiency.

And you again have a man here who's proven in his own life that he is honest and he is competent. When you have a combination of compassion on the one hand and competence on the other, that's a combination that's hard to beat.

Nobody can beat Bob Graham November 7 if you help him. Will you help him? [*Applause*] If you'll help him, I will, too.

Thank you.

NOTE: The President spoke at 6:20 p.m. in the Jade Promenade Room at the Fontainebleau Hotel.

Full Employment and Comprehensive Employment and Training Act Bills

Remarks on Signing H.R. 50 and S. 2570 Into Law.   October 27, 1978

THE PRESIDENT. I see a lot of smiling faces. [*Laughter*]

With the signing of this Full Employment and Balanced Growth Act of 1978, this Nation is putting its long-term economic goal of full employment with stable prices into law. This act requires that the Congress and the President and the Federal Reserve Board cooperate in probably an unprecedented way in indicating each year the policies that will be followed to achieve these goals.

This was the last major piece of legislation among many important acts that bore the name of a great and compassionate American, Hubert Humphrey.

I think everyone agrees that he's with us in spirit. He knew how destructive unemployment was to our Nation and to individual American citizens who could not find a way to utilize the talent that God had given them. He knew how important it was to the social and economic fabric of our Nation to have people employed. He dreamed of the day when everyone who wanted a job could find a job.

Congressman Gus Hawkins, who coauthored this legislation, from its very inception continued in an effective and a yeoman's way to guide the leadership in the House to pass this legislation. And then, of course, he was joined with a very effective ally in the Senate, Muriel Humphrey. And we derived success because of their great work.

I want to express my thanks to the Full Employment Action Council, which was ably chaired by Coretta King, and also to the Congressional Black Caucus, under the leadership of Parren Mitchell, to House Speaker Tip O'Neill, and to Senate Majority Leader Bob Byrd, whose unflagging support and hard work in the final few hours of the legislative session translated these two legislative proposals into the bills which I am about to sign. And I would also like to thank Leon Keyserling, whose work in drafting this legislation and his persistence in seeing it through to a successful conclusion helped to make this fine day possible—[*applause*]—go ahead and applaud for them all.

The unemployment rate in our country was 8 percent on Election Day in 1976. And one of my first actions as President, working with Senator Humphrey and others, was to propose legislation to put Americans back to work.

A part of that legislation created the largest public service jobs program and the largest training program, combined, in the history of our country since the New Deal days of the Great Depression. The results have been dramatic. Unemployment has been reduced 25 percent, more than 6½ million new jobs have been created, a record not matched in so short a period of time in the 200-year history of our country, even during wartime. Over 1½ million Americans have been taken off the unemployment rolls.

I'm also signing today the Comprehensive Employment and Training Act Amendments of 1978, because the programs in it provide major tools in our effort to reach the unemployment goals of the Humphrey-Hawkins bill by 1983.

I'm pleased that the Congress has passed our recommendations to extend CETA and more sharply to target its programs to those who are most in need of help.

The Congress also gave the Secretary of Labor, Ray Marshall, the authority that we requested to investigate and to deal effectively with some examples of fraud and abuse which have in the past occurred in the public jobs programs. These few unscrupulous people who would use these programs as political plums or for personal gain deserve condemnation and punishment. They are a threat to the opportunities of people who have been unable fully to participate in our economy. We intend to see that such abuses are ended.

My administration is committed to attacking the specter of youth unemployment, which threatens to sap the will and waste the potential of a sizable portion of an entire generation of Americans. Extending the youth employment and demonstration projects act is critical to the success of this effort.

Our targeted tax credit proposal, approved as part of the tax bill, would also help millions of young people find employment in the private sector of our economy. I'm particularly proud that Congress approved this and the Private Sector Initiative program. We will establish now private industry councils throughout our Nation, letting labor, business, community leaders, government leaders at all levels form a full partnership to make our CETA program more effective even than it has been in the past.

Hubert Humphrey said, and I'd like to quote him, "A Humphrey-Hawkins bill is a first step, but an indispensable one, toward an era of full employment, steady economic growth, and reasonable price stability. It is no panacea. It is no miracle cure, but with it, national economic policy will be required to be directed toward achieving specific, measurable economic goals."

Although attaining the unemployment and the inflation goals of this bill will be very difficult, we will do our best to reach them. The CETA legislation, with its attack on structural unemployment, is a key to that effort. But I must warn you that our fight against inflation must succeed if we are to maintain the steady economic growth necessary to avoid an increase in unemployment and to achieve the goals in the Humphrey-Hawkins bill.

Success in fighting inflation is critical to success in fighting unemployment. In the future, we can see from this bill that all Americans, not any particular kind of American, will be benefited. There will be required 2-year programs and 5-year programs expressing from the point of view of myself, my entire administration, the Congress, the Federal Reserve, and the private sector, specific goals to achieve in employment, inflation, unemployment, production, real income of Americans, productivity, how much each American worker can produce, price levels, balanced growth, a downward trend in the Federal share of the GNP spent, improving our trade balance, and working toward a balanced budget.

Those are the requirements in this bill, the elements that any President would want to assess and in which a President and the Congress needs the utmost cooperation from every other element of American society.

The Federal Reserve Board will have to make now semiannual written reports to the Congress specifying its own contribution—for controlling inflation, yes, but to meeting the other goals as well.

I'm very grateful that those assembled behind me on this stage and in front of me in this audience have been so successful in bringing to a conclusion this long struggle to provide for our Nation an inspiration, a motivation, and a mechanism by which we can have in the future both full employment and balanced growth for our great country.

It's with a great pleasure now that I sign both these bills into law, and then I would like to call on a few carefully selected people to make brief remarks. [*Laughter*]

[*At this point, the President signed the bills.*]

I would like to ask Muriel Humphrey to say a word, if she would.

SENATOR HUMPHREY. Well, I have a very full heart today, and it's a lot of emotion for me—a little difficult for me to speak. I see many friends, wonderful people in the audience here, on stage as well as in the audience, who have given hours, years of work towards attaining this bill. I'm very, very proud to have been a part of the success that we have obtained for this bill.

Hubert, I think, over the years, felt it was a very, very great way, it was an ideal and a goal that he hoped could be accomplished. And I think now we're seeing the result of it. Hubert Humphrey had a good many times been involved in different bills that we know about—the equal rights bills and some very important ones—but most of the time, he gave over the honor to someone else to have his name on those bills. I think that the Humphrey-Hawkins bill is the only bill that has the distinction of having his name, and I must say I thank everyone. I see so many different ones that I want to say thank you to, I don't dare to mention the names— [*laughter*]—especially the President.

THE PRESIDENT. Thank you very much.

Now I'd like to call on Gus Hawkins.

REPRESENTATIVE HAWKINS. Mr. President, and friends—[*applause*]—the same to you, thanks.

I'm sure that Hubert Humphrey would have enjoyed the exuberance of this occasion, would have had a very wonderful speech to say. It's been such a long struggle that some of us have given out, I think, in talking. [*Laughter*]

THE PRESIDENT. He would not have been one of those. [*Laughter*]

REPRESENTATIVE HAWKINS. I'm quite sure that as I supported your energy program and also looked at the economies in the White House, I was a little afraid today that you had extended this economy to these pens. I'm very pleased to know that you have not done that. [*Laughter*]

I'm quite sure that when time is settled and individuals have had an opportunity to read the Full Employment and Balanced Growth Act, even our critics, they will begin to agree with some of us that it really is a modern-day Magna Carta of economic rights, not between the people and an unwise ruler, but a contract between the people and a magnificent President who gave us the assistance needed to get the bill through.

And I'm quite sure that none of us is so naive as to believe that this is the end. It is only a beginning. The bill must be implemented. It is significant today, Mr. President, that you're signing also the CETA bill, which begins the implementation of the full employment act. Those who have said that the full employment bill is only a symbol, that it has no program, no money, or practically nothing else in it, I think will be delighted to know, if not excited, that at least in the beginning of the implementation of the full employment act, this, the first bill— the first step, as Hubert Humphrey would have said—has certainly a program. It provides, directly, jobs, more than 600,000 directly, and that it has more than $11 billion in it. Now, if that isn't money, then I'm quite sure it may disturb even you and your economy program, Mr. President.

So, I think we're on the way. Those that also would say we are raising the expectation of people, well, I can only say that I hope that we are. I hope that we are keeping alive the hopes of millions of Americans who believe that in a meaningful job at decent wages, that that is something which America can afford to give to them. And I hope that we forever keep that hope alive, that expectation. To me, that is not asking for too much.

THE PRESIDENT. Congressman Hawkins just told me that he and Senator Humphrey began work on this bill in 1971. And it's been a long and difficult struggle, and the bill is filled with great and important substance. If it wasn't, the struggle would not have been so great, and so many people would not have been sweating, now that they've read what's in the bill. [*Laughter*]

It's going to put a great responsibility on me as President, on every member of my Cabinet, on the Federal Reserve Board, on every Member of the Congress, on labor, business, to carry out the mandates of this legislation.

It is very important and, I think, will transform not only the employment opportunities and growth but the basic planning mechanism by which the economic future of our Nation can be assessed, goals can be set, and mechanisms to reach those goals can be made possible.

It's very important legislation, and I thank Gus Hawkins and Senator Humphrey, both Senators Humphrey, for this work.

I'd like to call now on Coretta King, who was the first one to talk to me about this legislation when I was still Governor of Georgia. [*Laughter*]

MRS. KING. This is indeed a great historical occasion, perhaps as significant as the signing of the Civil Rights Act of 1964

and the Voting Rights Act of 1965. Perhaps in the future, history will record that it may be even more significant, Mr. President, because I think it deals with an issue on a basic human right that's the most basic of all human rights, the right to a job. And that is a central priority now of our economic policy with the signing of this act into law today.

I want to express my appreciation to all of those persons in the Full Employment Action Council, Full Employment Committee, the National Committee for Full Employment, as started 4 years ago in a coalition effort working for a full-employment economy. Gus Hawkins was there that day, Leon Keyserling was there that day, and a number of other people who are in this audience.

I am representing my cochairperson, Murray Finley of Amalgamated Clothing and Textile Workers, who could not be here. And with me, Irving Bluestone of the United Auto Workers and Jay Clayman of IDUD. In the audience are other members of our coalition representing the Urban League, the NAACP—Mr. Hooks was supposed to have been up on the platform, I believe—who are all members of the 84 organizations in the coalition, including Dr. Howard Spragg of the National Council of Churches.

As President Carter said in 1974, I called him and he was still Governor, and asked him if he would join our committee. And he asked if I would send the material, and later on, he signed his card as a member of the National Committee for Full Employment. Now, we'd selected only one Governor, and we very carefully selected him. [*Laughter*] I don't know; maybe we were prophetic, because here he is today as the President who signs this legislation and makes it a law.

I want to express my appreciation on behalf of the coalition to both authors of the bill. I think of Senator Muriel along with Senator Hubert Humphrey—who could not be here today, but is with us in spirit—and Muriel has worked untiringly. And Gus Hawkins, who has worked very closely with us, the Congressional Black Caucus, and the majority leader in the Senate and in the House, and all of the persons who have worked untiringly— this is a unique coalition, and, Mr. President, we are going to stay in business to help with the implementation of this thing.

And also, I would like to say that this bill is a tribute, or this law now, this act, is a tribute to the dedication of Senator Humphrey and Gus Hawkins and both Senators, but it's also a tribute to Martin Luther King, Jr., because in 1968, he started a crusade calling for a job and income for all people who needed a job. He did not live to carry out that campaign, and so in 1974, we felt that we had an obligation, a mandate, to pick it up and to carry it forward. And now today, I am sure Martin Luther King, Jr., is with us in spirit, because his concern was that all people in our society would be able to share equally in the fruits of this great Nation.

Thank you.

THE PRESIDENT. All the members of my Cabinet, of course, will join in the carrying out of the mandates of this bill, but I'd like to call on Ray Marshall, Secretary of Labor, to represent the Cabinet and to say just a closing word.

SECRETARY MARSHALL. Mr. President, this act represents a real victory, I think, for the American people. It would be very difficult to think of a problem that this country has that would not be materially improved by full employment. And I think that either in material terms, in terms of the lost output that the country suffers as a result of unemployment, or in terms of the human suffering that goes with unemployment, no other problem

could parallel it. We've done a lot of talking about full employment for the last 30 years, and now we have committed ourselves to achieving it.

So, I think it's a great day. I think that—I heard that this was the largest signing of any bill that we had had in the White House, and I think that indicates the feeling that people have. But it also indicates the number of people who were involved in making this program successful. I'm proud to have had a part in it and to be Secretary of Labor at the time that it gets signed.

Thank you.

THE PRESIDENT. Thank all of you.

NOTE: The President spoke at 2:03 p.m. at the ceremony in the East Room at the White House.

As enacted, H.R. 50, the Full Employment and Balanced Growth Act of 1978, is Public Law 95–523, and S. 2570, the Comprehensive Employment and Training Act Amendments of 1978, is Public Law 95–524, both approved October 27.

Public Rangelands Improvement Act of 1978

Statement on Signing H.R. 10587 Into Law. October 27, 1978

I have signed into law H.R. 10587, the Public Rangelands Improvement Act of 1978.

This act builds on previous legislation, most recently the comprehensive Federal Land Policy and Management Act of 1976, to improve the management of the public rangelands. It clarifies several legal authorities, thereby helping resolve some of the conflicting demands that have hampered effective management of these lands. It should also increase cooperation between the Federal Government and those who use the public rangelands.

H.R. 10587 will further the national policy of a sound and balanced approach to the Federal management of the public lands. Those lands are increasingly important because of their energy, agricultural, environmental, and recreational resources. After generations of disagreement, all those interested in the public lands are beginning to find better ways of balancing the wide range of demands that press on these vital resources.

In particular, the bill recognizes the historical importance of the public rangelands to the western livestock grazing industry and provides a basis for an improved grazing program in the future.

While I had hoped that the Congress would adopt the recommendations of the Secretaries of the Interior and Agriculture to require Federal grazing fees to be set at fair market value, the fee provisions in H.R. 10587 will bring fees more into line with rates charged on comparable private grazing lands.

I have approved the Public Rangelands Improvement Act because I believe it will lead to improved Federal management of our Nation's public land resources.

NOTE: As enacted, H.R. 10587 is Public Law 95–514, approved October 25.

Meeting With King Khalid of Saudi Arabia

White House Statement. October 27, 1978

The President is delighted that King Khalid of Saudi Arabia was able to accept his invitation for lunch today. He is very thankful for his Majesty's rapid recovery, and we are honored that His Majesty chose to visit the United States for medical treatment at the Cleveland Clinic.

During the luncheon, the President and His Majesty discussed a number of important issues of mutual interest, including their joint commitment to peace and security in the Middle East. The President took the opportunity to explain personally to His Majesty the efforts made to that end in the Camp David accords, and discussed with His Majesty the current status of the negotiations foreseen in those accords. His Majesty assured the President that Saudi Arabia appreciates greatly the efforts which the President is making to help bring lasting peace to the area and desires to remain in close contact with the United States about them.

As is characteristic of our exchanges with the Saudi leadership, these discussions were carried out in an atmosphere of longstanding friendship, deep mutuality of interest, and well-tested spirit of cooperation.

The luncheon lasted approximately 90 minutes. The participants were as follows:

Saudi Arabian Side

His Majesty Khalid bin Abd al-Aziz al-Sa'ud, King of Saudi Arabia;

His Royal Highness Prince Sultan bin Abd al-Aziz al-Sa'ud, Minister of Defense and Aviation;

Dr. Rashad Pharaon, Presidential Advisor;

His Excellency Ali Abdallah Alireza, Ambassador of Saudi Arabia to the United States;

His Excellency Mohammed al-Nowaizer, Minister for Royal Diwan;

His Excellency Ahmed Abd al-Wahab, Chief of Royal Protocol;

Dr. Fadl al-Rahman, King Khalid's personal physician.

U.S. Side

The President;

Secretary of State Cyrus Vance;

Secretary of the Treasury W. Michael Blumenthal;

Secretary of Defense Harold Brown;

Dr. Zbigniew Brzezinski, Assistant to the President for National Security Affairs;

Hamilton Jordan, Assistant to the President;

Alfred L. Atherton, Jr., Ambassador at Large;

John C. West, United States Ambassador to Saudi Arabia;

Harold H. Saunders, Assistant Secretary of State for Near Eastern and South Asian Affairs;

William B. Quandt, National Security Council staff member;

Isa Sabbagh, interpreter;

Dr. Rezavai, heart specialist, Cleveland Clinic.

1978 Nobel Peace Prize

Message of Congratulations to Recipients President Anwar al-Sadat of Egypt and Prime Minister Menahem Begin of Israel. October 27, 1978

Today the world is sending you its congratulations. In honoring you with its Peace Prize, the Nobel Committee has ratified a decision already made by millions around the world.

I add my own congratulations, for this honor you so fully deserve.

Through all the generations of leaders in your region of the world, none have wanted peace more than the two of you—and none have taken the risks, or displayed the courage, that you have in this quest. I know that the Middle East would not be so near to peace today were it not for your determined efforts, and I know that the same qualities that have earned you this award will guide your nations toward the lasting peace that all peoples of your region desire.

Time and again in the last year, you have overcome the obstacles that stood in your way, for you understood the importance of your goal. I know that this award will be an occasion for you and for all of us to rededicate our efforts, for it makes clear how much the people of the world value your search.

The work you have done so far must not be left uncompleted. Everything I have learned about your character, your commitments, and your courage gives me confidence that the promise of this moment will be fulfilled.

JIMMY CARTER

Bill To Rename a Federal Building for Justice William O. Douglas

Statement on Signing S. 3540 Into Law. October 27, 1978

I am pleased and honored to sign S. 3540, a bill to rename the Federal building in Yakima, Washington, for one of the town's and the Nation's most respected and beloved citizens—Justice William O. Douglas.

Justice Douglas' distinguished career on the United States Supreme Court spanned 36 years, the longest service on the Court in history. This remarkable man is respected around the world for the leadership and compassion he has shown as a fierce protector of individual rights, an advocate of the defenseless against oppression, and an activist on behalf of environmental preservation.

Justice Douglas richly deserves the recognition Congress has provided him by passing this bill.

NOTE: As enacted, S. 3540 is Public Law 95–538, approved October 27.

National Commission for the Review of Antitrust Laws and Procedures

Appointment of the Membership of a Business Advisory Panel on Antitrust Export Issues. October 27, 1978

In his September 26, 1978, announcement on export policy, the President announced that he would appoint a business advisory panel to work with the National Commission for the Review of Antitrust Laws and Procedures on antitrust export issues.

Today he announced the membership of that panel. The eight members are:

Rufus Phillips, president of Airways Engineering Corp. in Washington, a firm which exports construction engineering technology and has designed airports and ports in over 30 countries. Phillips will serve as Chairman of the panel.

Robert P. Beshar, director of National Semiconductor, a firm with over $1 billion annual sales, with extensive export and foreign production involvement. Beshar is a former Deputy Assistant Secretary of Commerce, director of the Bureau of International Commerce, and National Export Expansion Coordinator.

Seth M. Dabney, general counsel and secretary of Caterpillar Tractor Co. in Peoria, Ill. Caterpillar is one of the largest exporters from the United States, with about one third of its $6 billion annual sales due to exports of heavy equipment and diesel engines.

Barry Hawk, a professor at Fordham Law School in New York City and author of numerous articles on international antitrust.

Mary Gardiner Jones, vice president of Western Union and a former Commissioner of the Federal Trade Commission.

William Kennedy, a New York attorney, former international counsel and now counsel to General Electric Corp. Kennedy was actively involved in the preparation of the "Antitrust Guide for International Operations" released by the Justice Department in 1977.

Otis Smith, vice president and general counsel of General Motors Corp.

Jack Valenti, president of the Motion Pictures Association of America and the Motion Picture Export Association of America.

Digest of Other White House Announcements

The following listing includes the President's daily schedule and other items of general interest as announced by the White House Press Office during the period covered by this issue. Events and announcements printed elsewhere in the issue are not included.

October 21

The President met at the White House with David L. Aaron, Deputy Assistant for National Security Affairs.

Following his trip to Kansas and Minnesota, the President went to Camp David, Md.

October 24

The President returned to the White House from Camp David.

The President met at the White House with:

—the Cabinet;

—Mike Rossman, world light heavyweight boxing champion;

—James T. McIntyre, Director of the Office of Management and Budget, Charles L. Schultze, Chairman of the Council of Economic Advisers, Ambassador Robert S. Strauss, Special Representative for Trade Negotiations, Frank B. Moore, Assistant to the President for Congressional Liaison, and Members of Congress, to discuss the anti-inflation program;

—Secretary of State Cyrus R. Vance, Secretary of Defense Harold Brown, Paul C. Warnke, Director of the U.S. Arms Control and Disarmament Agency, Zbigniew Brzezinski, Assistant to the President for National Security Affairs, and Hamilton Jordan, Assistant to the President.

October 25

The President met at the White House with:

—Dr. Brzezinski;

—Senator Ernest F. Hollings of South Carolina;

—Robert R. Bowie, Deputy Director, National Intelligence, Central Intelligence Agency, Dr. Brzezinski, and Mr. Jordan;

—Ted Leszkiewicz, national commander of the American Veterans of World War II, Korea and Viet Nam.

The President greeted participants at the briefing held by administration officials for southern black leaders in the State Dining Room at the White House.

The President went on an inspection tour of Camp Hoover, Va.

October 26

The President met at the White House with Dr. Brzezinski.

The President announced the United States Delegation to the independence celebrations of Dominica on November 3. Frank V. Ortiz, Jr., American Ambassador to Barbados, will head the delegation, attending as Personal Representative of the President with the rank of Special Ambassador. Mrs. Ortiz will ac-

company the Ambassador. The members of the delegation, also with the rank of Special Ambassador, will be:

JOHN D. ARCHBOLD of Upperville, Va.;
MICHAEL L. MADUFF of Chicago, Ill.;
GABRIELLE K. McDONALD of Houston, Tex.;
HAROLD E. ROGERS, JR., of San Francisco, Calif.;
HENRY L. STRAUSS of Denver, Colo.

October 27

The President met at the White House with:

—Secretaries Vance and Brown, Dr. Brzezinski, and Mr. Jordan;

—Dr. Brzezinski;

—Mike Mansfield, U.S. Ambassador to Japan;

—Alfred E. Kahn, Advisor to the President on Inflation and Chairman of the Council on Wage and Price Stability, and Barry P. Bosworth, Director, Council on Wage and Price Stability, and Dr. Schultze;

—Administration officials to discuss the fiscal year 1980 budget.

NOMINATIONS SUBMITTED TO THE SENATE

NOTE: The Congress having adjourned *sine die* on Sunday, October 15, no nominations were submitted during the period covered by this issue. The first session of the 96th Congress will begin on Monday, January 15, 1979.

CHECKLIST OF WHITE HOUSE PRESS RELEASES

The following releases of the Office of the White House Press Secretary, distributed during the period covered by this issue, are not included in the issue.

Released October 24, 1978

Advance text: remarks on signing S. 2493, the Airline Deregulation Act of 1978
Advance text: address to the Nation on the anti-inflation program

CHECKLIST—Continued

Released October 25, 1978

Transcript: remarks on his appointment as Advisor to the President on Inflation and Chairman of the Council on Wage and Price Stability—by Alfred E. Kahn, and Charles L. Schultze, Chairman of the Council of Economic Advisers

Statements: support for the anti-inflation program by government officials, leaders of business and labor organizations, and civic groups

Released October 26, 1978

Advance text: remarks on signing S. 555, the Ethics in Government Act of 1978

Released October 27, 1978

Statements: support for the anti-inflation program by leaders of business and labor organizations and civic groups

Advance text: remarks on signing H.R. 50, the Full Employment and Balanced Growth Act of 1978, and S. 2570, the Comprehensive Employment and Training Act Amendments of 1978

ACTS APPROVED BY THE PRESIDENT

Approved October 21, 1978

H.R. 12264_____ Public Law 95–494
An act to designate certain lands in the State of Wisconsin as wilderness.

H.R. 12250_____ Public Law 95–495
An act to designate the Boundary Waters Canoe Area Wilderness, to establish the Boundary Waters Canoe Area Mining Protection Area, and for other purposes.

S. 1081_____ Public Law 95–496
An act to amend certain laws relating to the Osage Tribe of Oklahoma, and for other purposes.

H.R. 12051_____ Public Law 95–497
An act relating to the application of certain provisions of the Internal Revenue Code of 1954 to specified transactions by certain public employee retirement systems created by the State of New York or any of its political subdivisions.

S. 2588_____ Public Law 95–498
An act to declare that the United States holds in trust for the Pueblo of Santa Ana certain public domain lands.

ACTS APPROVED—Continued

Approved October 21—Continued

S. 2358_____ Public Law 95–499
An act to declare that the United States holds in trust for the Pueblo of Zia certain public domain lands.

H.R. 8755_____ Public Law 95–500
An act to make specific provisions for ball or roller bearing pillow block, flange, take-up, cartridge, and hanger units in the Tariff Schedules of the United States, and for other purposes.

S. 3447_____ Public Law 95–501
Agricultural Trade Act of 1978.

H.R. 8533_____ Public Law 95–502
An act to amend the Internal Revenue Code of 1954 to provide that income from the conducting of certain bingo games by certain tax exempt organizations will not be subject to tax.

H.R. 12556_____ Private Law 95–62
An act for relief of Batavia Turf Farms, Incorporated.

Approved October 24, 1978

S. 2411_____ Public Law 95–503
An act to amend chapter 315 of title 18, United States Code, to authorize payment of transportation expenses for persons released from custody pending their appearance to face criminal charges before that court, any division of that court, or any court of the United States in another Federal judicial district.

S. 2493_____ Public Law 95–504
Airline Deregulation Act of 1978.

H.R. 11658_____ Public Law 95–505
An act to amend title XI of the Merchant Marine Act, 1936, to permit the guarantee of obligations for financing Great Lakes vessels in an amount not exceeding 87½ per centum of the actual or depreciated actual cost of each vessel.

H.R. 13767_____ Public Law 95–506
An act to amend the Federal Property and Administrative Services Act of 1949 to permit the recovery of replacement cost of motor vehicles and other related equipment and supplies.

H.R. 11318_____ Public Law 95–507
An act to amend the Small Business Act and the Small Business Investment Act of 1958.

H.R. 12165_____ Public Law 95–508
An act to extend until the close of June 30, 1981, the existing suspension of duties on certain metal waste and scrap, unwrought metal, and other articles of metal, and for other purposes.

ACTS APPROVED—Continued

Approved October 24—Continued

H.R. 11686_____ Public Law 95–509
Department of Energy National Security and
Military Applications of Nuclear Energy Authorization Act of 1979.

H.R. 13418_____ Public Law 95–510
An act to amend the Small Business Act by
transferring thereto those provisions of the
Domestic Volunteer Service Act of 1973 affecting the operation of volunteer programs
to assist small business, to increase the maximum allowable compensation and travel expenses for experts and consultants, and for
other purposes.

Approved October 25, 1978

S. 1566_____ Public Law 95–511
Foreign Intelligence Surveillance Act of
1978.

S. 3412_____ Public Law 95–512
Comptroller General Annuity Adjustment
Act of 1978.

H.J. Res. 1147_____ Public Law 95–513
A joint resolution authorizing and requesting
the President to designate the seven-day period beginning on May 28, 1979, as "Vietnam Veterans Week".

H.R. 10587_____ Public Law 95–514
Public Rangelands Improvement Act of
1978.

S. 1185_____ Public Law 95–515
Interstate Horseracing Act of 1978.

H.R. 10161_____ Public Law 95–516
An act for the relief of Eastern Telephone
Supply and Manufacturing, Incorporated,
and other matters.

H.R. 11945_____ Public Law 95–517
An act to authorize the Secretary of the
Army to return to the Federal Republic of
Germany ten paintings of the German Navy
seized by the United States Army at the end
of World War II.

H.R. 12112_____ Public Law 95–518
An act designating Gathright Lake on the
Jackson River, Virginia, as Gathright Dam
and Lake Moomaw.

S. 1626_____ Public Law 95–519
An act to clarify the status of certain legislative and judicial officers under the provisions of title 5, United States Code, relating
to annual and sick leave, and for other purposes.

ACTS APPROVED—Continued

Approved October 26, 1978

H.R. 5029_____ Public Law 95–520
Veterans' Administration Programs Extension Act of 1978.

S. 555_____ Public Law 95–521
Ethics in Government Act of 1978.

Approved October 27, 1978

H.R. 13481_____ Public Law 95–522
An act to name the post office and Federal
building in Portland, Maine, the "Frederick
G. Payne Building".

H.R. 50_____ Public Law 95–523
Full Employment and Balanced Growth Act
of 1978.

S. 2570_____ Public Law 95–524
Comprehensive Employment and Training
Act Amendments of 1978.

H.R. 7296_____ Public Law 95–525
An act to designate the new Terminal Radar
Approach Control Federal Building in
Hempstead, Long Island, New York, as the
"Charles A. Lindbergh Federal Building".

H.R. 12116_____ Public Law 95–526
An act to amend the District of Columbia
Self-Government and Governmental Reorganization Act to repeal the authority of
the President to sustain vetoes by the Mayor
of the District of Columbia of acts passed by
the Council of the District of Columbia and
repassed by two-thirds of the Council, to
change the period during which acts of the
Council of the District of Columbia are subject to congressional review, and for other
purposes.

H.R. 7305_____ Public Law 95–527
An act to designate a certain Federal building in Champaign, Illinois, the "William L.
Springer Building".

H.R. 13808_____ Public Law 95–528
An act to designate the "Omar Burleson
Federal Building".

H.R. 13809_____ Public Law 95–529
An act to designate the "George Mahon
Federal Building".

H.R. 13892_____ Public Law 95–530
An act to amend title 28 of the United
States Code to provide that the requirement
that each United States attorney and United
States marshal reside in the district for which
he is appointed shall not apply to an individual appointed to such a position for the
Northern Mariana Islands if such individual
is at the same time serving in the same capacity in another district.

ACTS APPROVED—Continued

Approved October 27—Continued

H.R. 14223_____ Public Law 95–531
An act to designate a certain Federal building in Bloomington, Illinois, the "Leslie C. Arends Building".

H.R. 14295_____ Public Law 95–532
An act to designate the "Paul G. Rogers Federal Building".

H.J. Res. 747_____ Public Law 95–533
A joint resolution to consent to an amendment of the constitution of the State of New Mexico to provide a method for executing leases and other contracts for the development and operation of geothermal steam and waters on lands granted or confirmed to such State.

H.J. Res. 816_____ Public Law 95–534
A joint resolution to extend the authority of the Federal Reserve banks to buy and sell certain obligations.

S. 2049_____ Public Law 95–535
An act to establish fees and allow per diem and mileage expenses for witnesses before United States Courts.

S. 2403_____ Public Law 95–536
An act to consent to certain amendments to the New Hampshire-Vermont Interstate School Compact, approved by Public Law 91–21.

S. 3336_____ Public Law 95–537
Contract Services for Drug Dependent Federal Offenders Act of 1978.

S. 3540_____ Public Law 95–538
An act to rename the United States Federal building in Yakima, Washington, the "Justice William O. Douglas Federal Building".

H.R. 1396_____ Private Law 95–63
An act for the relief of Mrs. Sun Pok Winer.

H.R. 1446_____ Private Law 95–64
An act for the relief of Lester Bruce Priday.

H.R. 1449_____ Private Law 95–65
An act for the relief of Geoffrey Parnham.

ACTS APPROVED—Continued

Approved October 27—Continued

H.R. 2662_____ Private Law 95–66
An act for the relief of Christopher Robert West.

H.R. 2940_____ Private Law 95–67
An act for the relief of Daniel Crowley.

H.R. 4535_____ Private Law 95–68
An act for the relief of Kazuko Nishioka Dowd.

H.R. 5230_____ Private Law 95–69
An act for the relief of Jung In Bang.

H.R. 5933_____ Private Law 95–70
An act for the relief of Jonathan Winston Max.

H.R. 6801_____ Private Law 95–71
An act for the relief of Hye Jin Wilder.

H.R. 7604_____ Private Law 95–72
An act for the relief of Margaret Somerville Jefferis.

H.R. 8810_____ Private Law 95–73
An act for the relief of Kim In Hyung.

H.R. 8927_____ Private Law 95–74
An act for the relief of Monika Grantz.

H.R. 9352_____ Private Law 95–75
An act for the relief of James William Dibben.

H.R. 9568_____ Private Law 95–76
An act for the relief of Renate Irene McCord.

H.R. 9610_____ Private Law 95–77
An act for the relief of Raymond Vishnu Clemons.

H.R. 9611_____ Private Law 95–78
An act for the relief of Craig Day.

H.R. 9613_____ Private Law 95–79
An act for the relief of Eustace John D'Souza.

H.J. Res. 489_____ Private Law 95–80
A joint resolution granting the status of permanent residence to certain aliens.

S. 1484_____ Private Law 95–81
An act for the relief of Michael Bruce Holland.

Buffalo, New York

Remarks at the Greater Buffalo International Airport.   October 28, 1978

Governor Carey, Senator Moynihan, Congressman LaFalce, Congressman Nowak, National Democratic Chairman John White, Chairman of Erie County, Joe Crangle, Mayor Griffin, and my good friends who gave me a strong support when I was running for President and have given me a warm welcome this morning in spite of the cold weather:

I'm glad to be back with you. Thank you very much.

I know how difficult it can be to be an incumbent President or Governor in these days. I'm sure New Yorkers will know what I mean when I told the political Democratic rally in Maryland not long ago that just since Camp David, Americans have been waving at me with all five fingers. [*Laughter*]

And I think it's the same way with Hugh Carey, who came into office facing tremendous problems for New York State. You needed a man with courage, who was not afraid to tell the truth, even though sometimes it was not politically popular. You needed a man who was honest even when it hurt. You needed a man who thought taxes were too high. And for the first time in many, many years since I can remember, in New York State taxes are on the way down. Hugh Carey has reduced income taxes $1.3 billion.

I think the most serious problem that I saw in New York State when I campaigned here in 1975, 1976, was the economy, jobs. Everywhere I went, people would tell me, "My father—my uncle— my son—my wife—cannot get a job." Since Hugh Carey has been your Governor, the unemployment rate in New York State and here in Erie County, as well, has dropped 35 percent. It's still on the way down, thanks to this man.

When I was Governor of Georgia, 25 percent of my time was spent with economic development, bringing in new industry, new jobs, strengthening those that were there. Hugh Carey has been very successful in doing this. And the thing I like about his administration is that he's had a well-balanced emphasis between New York City, which was in desperate trouble—and he's gotten it out of trouble—and upstate New York.

The community development program that used to provide Buffalo, for instance, with $8 million, will now provide you $24 million. Hugh Carey knows the Congress.

He can work with Hank and John and Pat to make sure that your voice is heard clearly and strongly in Washington.

One of the things that had been dragging out for years and years was social security claims. And since Hugh Carey has been Governor, New York has now been awarded from the Federal Government in back claims $214 million. That's money that was going to come out of your pockets; now it's paid back to you because you deserve it.

Hugh's very generous, too. One of the things that causes him political problems is he's not the kind of politician who runs forward and says, "I did this; I did that; I claim credit for the good works that you have seen." He was very generous in giving me and Midge Costanza and my son Chip credit for moving rapidly to deal with the serious problem of the blizzard in Buffalo. But Hugh Carey was a man who called me on the phone immediately and said, "Mr. President, we need some help." And because I knew him and trusted him, and I knew his good relationship with your congressional delegation, with your mayor, your Erie County chairman, I was sure that he spoke for the people. And so I sent Chip up here, and we dealt with the blizzard problem.

Love Canal was a problem I didn't understand. I was not here living with the contamination problem. But Hugh Carey, with his sensitivity, jumped on it right away. And I have to tell you that he's done a lot more at the State level than I and my people have done at the Federal level. And I want to express my thanks to him for dealing with your problem.

If you can get wet, so can I.[1] *[Laughter]*

I just want to mention a couple of other things, because I want to be brief. I don't

---

[1] It had begun to rain, and the President declined the use of an umbrella.

want you to get wet any more than you have to.

We are now trying to deal with inflation. It's my biggest single domestic problem. One of the things that I want to be sure the Congress does next year is to pass a hospital cost containment bill, because hospital costs have been going up in this country. Hospital costs have been going up twice as fast as the inflation rate. But Hugh Carey, with his dynamic leadership, has passed the best hospital cost containment bill in the Nation, and I hope to get just half as good a bill through the Congress next year as Hugh Carey has already gotten for you here in New York State.

The taxpayers of New York State are enjoying the lowest Medicaid cost of all 50 States—the lowest of all 50 States. That's quite an achievement. Hugh, I have admiration and thanks for what you've achieved.

Let me say that he needs your help. He's got a tough, hard race, as was the case with myself when I started running for President. He started out as an underdog, because he was dealing with thankless problems. And as I said before, he's the kind of person—you noticed in his introduction to me, did not claim credit for anything. But he's got a tough race on his hands. And I hope you'll recognize that he's a sound leader knowing local, State, and Federal Government; that can work with Hank, that can work with John, that can work with Pat, that can work with me, and give you a better life in a great State in the years ahead. Help him on November 7. He and I together will help you the next few years. I won't say how many. *[Laughter]*

Recently, the world was thrilled by the selection of a great new Polish Pope. Maybe you heard about it here in Buffalo. *[Laughter]* I had very limited authority to appoint a delegation to go to Rome. You can imagine how many thousands of people wanted to go, and there could only be a tiny group. But I looked around the leadership of Congress to try to pick people that I thought were representative of the great Italian Americans and the great Polish Americans of our country. And it didn't take me long to decide that John LaFalce and Henry Nowak ought to be the ones to represent me.

As you know, in the selection of a Pope, when a Pole won, you couldn't also have an Italian at the same time. But you are lucky here in the Niagara frontier to have a good Pole and a good Italian American to serve you in Congress. That makes a great combination that can't be beat. And I might say with Pat and Hugh, you've also got some winning Irishmen to make out a ticket very well. [*Laughter*]

I don't believe that any new Senator has ever arrived in Washington and made a greater, more beneficial impact for his people back home than Pat Moynihan has done. As you know, he is eloquent. He is courageous. He is dynamic. And when he speaks, people listen. He has analyzed, in the most definitive way, how Federal laws ought to be changed to make the allocation of your tax money back to you more fair. He's been to see me many times about this. And when he speaks, the southern Members of Congress, those from the Sun Belt, say, "Well, I think it's fair to give more public works money, more transportation money, more welfare money, more education money, more highway money to those areas like Buffalo, like New York, which have in the past been deprived."

I have a great admiration for Pat Moynihan. He's a sound man, a good man, an inspirational man. And not only is he superb in domestic affairs, but he has that rare combination of being very knowledgeable in international affairs as well. And I hope you'll keep him in the Senate

as long as he wants to stay, because he makes a good partner for us to serve you better.

Pat, I want to express my thanks to you.

Just a word about my own administration. And I can be much briefer about this. [*Laughter*]

When I came into the White House about 21 months ago, we had 10 million Americans who couldn't find a full-time job. Seven million had no jobs at all. We've cut the unemployment rate already 25 percent. We've added 6½ million net new jobs. We've cut the unemployment rate, the unemployment numbers, 1½ million.

We've given better services to our people, stronger defense, better highways, better education. We've tried to give what people need, because I spent 2 years learning what our Nation hungered for. At the same time, we've cut taxes. Last year we cut your income taxes $8 billion. And with Pat's help this year, we've evolved a tax bill that will cut your income taxes about $20 billion more.

It's not been easy. It's not been easy to give better services, a stronger defense, revise our programs to benefit you and cut taxes at the same time.

There's one other thing that bothers me, though, and that's the Federal deficit. When I was running for President in 1976, the Federal Government deficit was more than $66 billion. We've already cut it down over $25 billion. And by the end of next year, we will have cut the Federal budget deficit more than half.

We are working on it some more. And my goal is still to balance the Federal budget. If you'll help me, I believe we'll be able to do it.

We've reorganized the Government. This week I signed an ethics bill, passed by the Congress, that requires all major public officials—Presidents, Vice Presidents, Cabinet members, all the Members of Congress, the Federal judges—to reveal to you every year what their net worth is, what their income is, where it comes from, just to make sure we remove all temptation for Federal Government officials to perform illegally or to betray your trust in them.

We have reorganized the Federal Government. We've tried to bring some order into the civil service system. In over 95 years, nobody had tackled the civil service system. We've got fine, decent, even self-sacrificial public servants. They want to do a good job. But they couldn't do it, because the bureaucracy had them constrained. You'd have two people sitting side by side at adjacent desks, one of them competent, eager, hard-working, conscientious; the other one either incompetent or lazy. They got the same recognition, the same salary, the same promotions. And you could imagine how this affects civil servants.

So, we passed a reform bill, first time, as I said, in 95 years. Now that good employee will be rewarded, and the other employee will either be inspired to do better or be transferred or fired. And we also are going to make managers manage.

The most serious problem that I have other than the security of our Nation is inflation. I'm determined to keep Federal spending down. I'm determined to keep the bureaucracy efficient. I'm determined to encourage State and local governments to join in with me to get the Congress to pass legislation like the hospital cost containment bill that didn't pass this year.

I'm determined to inspire employers to hold their prices down and workers, knowing that prices are going to be held down, to restrain their wage demands. I need your help in doing this. It's not going to be easy. It's not going to be quick. But it's vitally important that we succeed.

One thing we are trying to do is to get the Government's nose out of the people's business. I believe in the free enterprise system. I believe in the free enterprise system, but too long, the regulatory agencies, that were designed originally to protect consumers, have been cheating consumers and protecting the very corporations that are so powerful that they were supposed to regulate.

We've tried a good experiment this year. With the Congress help, we've worked on the airline industry. We have deregulated the airline industry. Rates went down. Passengers and goods hauled went way up. Profits went up as well. And that's just the kind of thing we're going to do in the future to other industries.

So, if you will help me, we'll control inflation together, and that'll solve the last major domestic issue we have. It'll also provide more jobs in the process. Will you help me with that? [*Applause*] Right on. I thank you.

And now I'd like to close by saying this: On international affairs, of course, this is a unique responsibility of a President, to keep our Nation strong. Militarily, we're the strongest nation on Earth. We're going to stay there. We are going to stay there, because, through strength, we can use our influence, which is tremendous, around the world, not only to keep peace for our own people but to give peace to others.

We're negotiating now a SALT agreement with the Soviet Union to cut down the threat of nuclear weapons destroying us all. The Congress passed a very good bill this year, nonproliferation, it's called, to prevent nations that don't have atomic explosives from ever having them.

We're working in Africa to try to bring peace there instead of bloodshed. And I'm very thankful that since I've been President, not a single American has shed blood in any foreign conflict, and I hope to keep that record until I go out of office.

We have become the champions of human rights. We are not scorned and despised as we formerly were. The United States has become an object of admiration. And we had some success, as you know, at Camp David recently.

We are moving toward peace in the Middle East. It's slow, it's tedious, it's not sure. We still need your encouragement. We still need your prayers.

We've had trouble in recent hours with the Israeli settlements issue on the West Bank. The Egyptians had decided to withdraw their negotiators. I contacted President Sadat last night and said, "Leave your negotiators in Washington." He sent me word this morning, "I'll do what my friend Jimmy Carter asked me." They're going to stay there and negotiate.

But we've still got a lot of problems in our country. But I'd like to ask you, in closing, not to forget about the strength of our country. Every day there are some things about which you can complain, a little aberration in the normal progress of our great Nation. But God's really blessed us. He's given us the strongest nation on Earth, the most freedom that anybody can have, a chance to use our talents as we see fit, economic blessings of all kinds, rich land, and great influence around the world.

And if you will help me and keep a Democratic team together that's strong and forceful, depending on you for our authority and our incumbency, we'll make the greatest nation on Earth in the future even greater.

Thank you very much.

NOTE: The President spoke at 10:45 a.m.

Hartford, Connecticut

Remarks at a Fundraising Reception for Governor Ella Grasso.   October 28, 1978

My good friend, Governor Ella Grasso; Lieutenant Governor Killian; Senator Abe Ribicoff, about whom I'd like to speak in a few minutes; Congressmen Cotter, Moffett, Dodd, and Giaimo—one of the greatest and strongest congressional State Democratic coalitions that I have ever known, wonderful men—Bill Ratchford, who will join them in January in the Congress; former Governor John Dempsey; Chairman John Dempsey, Jr.; Bill O'Neill, who's the next Lieutenant Governor; Hank Parker, State treasurer; Ed Caldwell, State comptroller; Carl Ajello, attorney general; and Barbara Kennelly, the next secretary of state:

As you know, Barbara Kennelly comes from a great Democratic family. I believe if there's one thing that epitomizes Connecticut politics, it is that the Democrats comprise a family. I noticed when Ella Grasso introduced me, she first mentioned my favorite joke writer, my mother—[*laughter*]—who thinks that Ella Grasso is absolutely beautiful. And then she mentioned my wife, Rosalynn, and then she mentioned my son Chip, who hasn't even come yet, and and last she mentioned me, the President of the United States. [*Laughter*]

But when you start talking about the Baileys—and I'm very grateful that Mrs. John Bailey [1] is here as an honored guest—the Dodds, the Dempseys, you can see that what the Democratic candidates in Connecticut represent is kind of a solid family structure. It provides cohesion and strength. It provides a mechanism by

---

[1] Wife of the former State and National Democratic chairman.

which standards and ideals can be maintained and passed on from one election to another, continuity in principle, dedication, consistency in purpose, a closeness to one another.

That's why I think that I'm lucky to be in Connecticut. That's why I think that you're lucky to have Ella Grasso as your present and future Governor.

The first time I met Ella, I don't think she believed that I was going to be President, although I told her so. [*Laughter*] She wanted to talk to me about my term as Governor, because I had been successful in reorganizing the structure of State government. And she has taken 200 fragmented State agencies, and now she's bringing them down to 22 major State organizations which can do a better job for you and save money.

I've seen her also inherit a $71 million deficit, and she's changed that, over a 3-year period, to a $200 million surplus that she's using to keep local property taxes down. And I think this is the kind of administration that I admire, that you appreciate, and that you want to have continued.

She's a person who cares deeply about people. She's worried about your government, its structure, deficits, tax cuts. But I think that when I came through Connecticut campaigning for 2 years, '75 and '76, the overwhelming concern that I felt in your State was about the strength of our economy, the high and growing unemployment rate.

When I became President, we had 10 million people in our country who were looking for a full-time job and could not find one. Over 7 million people could not find a job at all, and I, the Congress, the Governors, others began to work on this serious problem.

We've had remarkable success. We've added a net of 6½ million new jobs in our country, never before achieved, even in time of war. And we've cut the unemployment rate by 25 percent nationwide. But in Connecticut, under Ella Grasso's leadership, the unemployment rate has been cut 50 percent. And the good thing is that she's done it not by creating jobs that are paid for by taxpayers, but by creating new taxpayers, providing jobs in the private industry sector.

She's brought in 260 new plants, factories, and employers just since she's been in office. And this has been done with a great care to invest favorably in the future. She's been very careful not to cause a deterioration in the quality of life for those who live here. She hasn't lowered standards or given special tax breaks to bigshots in order to get jobs coming into Connecticut.

She's not turned her back on the Connecticut people. She's given you and those you care for a new chance in life, and she's set kind of a standard for us to emulate in Washington.

One of the things that I struggled for most eagerly but unsuccessfully was a good hospital cost containment bill. Ella Grasso was able to get one in Connecticut, and she's cut hospital costs 30 percent already.

Well, I've just about decided to ask her to quit Connecticut and come to Washington to help me. But to show you how much I think of Connecticut, I'm going to sacrifice my own future administration and let you keep her for 4 more years, perhaps.

I'd like to mention not in passing but in a very important way your own congressional delegation. I think if there's one person who has helped me more than any other to control inflation in the House by being a sound and mature statesman in managing the fiscal affairs of Congress, it's been Bob Giaimo.

As you know, he's on the Appropriations Committee permanently, and he has been the chairman of the House Budget Committee. There's not a more responsible, difficult job that could have been awarded him by the other Members of Congress, and he's done a superb job in this. I'm very grateful to you for letting me have him in Washington.

Toby Moffett serves on the Government Operations Committee, responsible for Government reorganization, and Toby has the reputation of being one of those Members of Congress who really keeps his foot, one in Washington, one in his own district, takes care of his own constituents, and helps Presidents and the rest of the Nation as well.

Bill Cotter—in the South, people would think he's my brother, but, you see, he's not. [*Laughter*] He serves on the very powerful Ways and Means Committee. And because of his superb ability and his growing seniority, he's in a position to help you and me in the future. Health, welfare, taxation, energy, many other crucial subjects come before the Ways and Means Committee, and this is a very great credit to him and to you.

I'd also like to mention Chris Dodd. Perhaps above all other committees, the one that decides which legislation is seriously considered by the 435 Members of the House, which legislation is called up first, which legislation can be amended, the extent of the amendments, it's the Rules Committee. And service on the Rules Committee is a great honor for a Member of the House of Representatives and a great credit for the State which sent him to Congress. And I want to congratulate Chris Dodd on doing such a fine job in this important position.

Bill Ratchford, scheduled to go to Congress next January, has already proven in Connecticut that he's an expert on the problems of our senior citizens. But that's not all. He rode on the airplane here with me, and I asked him, "What is the most important issue that you would like me to mention?" And he said, "I would like to be known as the man who, when I come to Washington next year, is going to help you, Mr. President, to control inflation in our country." You couldn't have a better platform than that.

It almost becomes a personal thing for me when I mention the next person that I'd like to talk about. If there is one man who, ever since I have known him, exemplifies in the finest way the rare word "statesman," it's your Senator, Abraham Ribicoff.

He's a man of great courage, and there may have been times, even since I've been in the White House, when he has cast a vote that was not popular among many people in Connecticut. But as time has gone by, his sound judgment and his knowledge of domestic and foreign affairs has proven him to be right. He runs the committee responsible for all Government reorganization. And I would say that above all other Members of the Senate, he has helped me most in my dealing with the Middle East crisis. And I could not have been successful in Camp David had it not been for the leadership and the courage and the knowledge of Abraham Ribicoff, and I want to thank him again.

Now I want to say a word about my own administration. [*Laughter*]

Part of a family life is teamwork. I've not been President very long; as you know, I haven't been in politics very long. But I've tried to bring to the White House the kind of attitude that would make you proud of our Government once again.

There was a time, 2, 3, 4 years ago, when the people of our Nation lost confidence in our Government because of the war in Vietnam, because of Watergate, because of the CIA revelations. But we've tried to tackle those serious problems in an open and effective way, depending on you, the people of our country, to give us guidance.

We've accomplished a great deal already in putting our people back to work. We provided better services in strengthening our cities, education, highways, a stronger defense. At the same time, we've been able to cut taxes—last year, $8 billion, this year, $19 billion more.

I have also been concerned about the budget deficits. When I ran for President in 1976, the budget deficit for the Federal Government was over $66 billion. Now, to give better services, to cut taxes, and also to reduce the deficit is not an easy combination to achieve. But we've already cut the Federal budget deficit more than $25 billion. By the next budget, which I'm now working on, we will have cut the budget deficit for the Federal Government more than half.

And this congressional delegation that you're sending to Washington and I pledge ourselves to continue our efforts, with a strong economy, to get the Federal Government budget balanced in the years ahead.

With Abe Ribicoff's leadership, the Congress passed and I signed this week a new ethics bill. The vast majority of top Government officials are honest, decent, sensitive, wanting to be accountable to you. But I pledged in the campaign that we would let it be more open. So, I signed a bill this week that requires all the Members of Congress, the President, the Vice President, the Cabinet members, every person who has any kind of top leadership role in the executive branch of Government, all the Federal judges, to reveal their net worth and to reveal their source of income to the people of our country, not only to prove they're honest but to remove temptations which sometimes afflict those in positions of power.

This is a good step forward, and I hope that in this respect and also by proceeding on our platform goals, that confidence in our Government will be restored.

We have the strongest military force on Earth, and we're going to keep it that way. I lived and worked as a young officer in Connecticut, in New London, when I was in submarines on two different occasions, and I know how much your own State has contributed to a strong national defense. With that strength can come steps toward peace. We're negotiating a new SALT agreement with the Soviet Union. We're working on it every day.

Very early next month Abe Ribicoff will take 10 other Members of the Senate to the Soviet Union to explore new ways whereby we might guarantee peace with them and a growing sense of friendship.

Peace is important to us, and I'm very proud of the fact that so far since I've been in the White House, not a single American person, no soldier, sailor, marine has shed blood in any conflict overseas. And I hope that I go out of office with that same record.

We've tried to maintain a strong moral leadership. I want our Nation's Government to have the reputation all over the Earth of being clean and decent. We're struggling with difficult issues in South Africa, in Cyprus, strengthening NATO, exploring ways for new peace and recognition between ourselves and our former adversaries in Asia.

And as you know, we've been lucky so far, after Camp David, in trying to bring peace to the Mideast. This is not an easy thing to do. There are ancient, historical enmities, distrust, hatred, repeated wars. The negotiating effort is not yet over. We need your support and we need your prayers.

In recent days we've had a problem, as you know, with the Israeli settlement announcement. President Sadat had sent word to his delegation to come back to

Egypt. But I got in touch with President Sadat, and he informed me this morning that as long as I wanted the Egyptian negotiators here, that he would leave them in Washington to negotiate a peace treaty. And I'm thankful for that.

Both sides want peace, and I think as long as our Nation is strong, as long as foreign leaders know that I don't speak with a hollow voice, that when I speak, the Congress knows what we are trying to accomplish, the congressional leaders like those on the stage here with me, Governors and citizens like you understand and support me, it gives my voice great authority and great influence which it would not have otherwise.

And I have tried to raise again the banner of principle—the principles on which our Nation were originally founded. And as long as I'm in the White House, we will have the reputation of being the nation, the strong nation that will always insist upon an enhancement of basic human rights around the world.

So, to close, let me say this: We've got a good Democratic team. I feel very proud to be the leader of the Democratic Party, to see the cohesion that we enjoy giving strength to our country. I have no fear of difficult challenges. There are no easy answers to problems that have afflicted our Nation for a long time. But with a strong congressional delegation, a strong Governor and State administrators, State legislature to work with me, there is no doubt that if we can earn your confidence—and we're determined to do so—and keep that confidence and support, that we will make the greatest nation on Earth even greater in the future.

Thank you very much.

NOTE: The President spoke at 1:20 p.m. in the Capitol Ballroom at the Hartford Hilton Hotel. In his opening remarks, he referred to John Dempsey, Jr., State Democratic Party chairman.

Hartford, Connecticut

Remarks at a State Democratic Party Fundraising Reception. October 28, 1978

I've come to Connecticut for two basic reasons. One is to thank you for your great support of me and my programs, and the wonderful congressional delegation that you've sent to Washington, particularly Abe Ribicoff, who's here with me this morning, and to let you know how deeply I need for you to support strongly our Democratic nominees, and particularly your wonderful Governor, Ella Grasso.

I have only got a few minutes. I would like to take a chance to shake hands with you rather than making a speech. But there are two things I want to say. First of all, your coming here today is very helpful financially to Governor Grasso. But it's not enough, because all of you are able to help her even more financially among your friends and neighbors and relatives, and I hope you will do so. You could not possibly make a better investment in the future of Connecticut and the future of our country.

And each one of you can become a campaign manager for her, because you have the influence, the prestige, and the ability to do so. And I hope that you will in this last 9 or 10 days of this election year.

The other thing I'd like to comment on to you, at the request of Senator Abe Ribicoff, is about the Middle East. We've had some luck, as you know, at Camp David, and we intend to continue our efforts until we have peace in the Mideast.

We have two great leaders there who were honored yesterday with the highest peace award in the world: President Sadat and Prime Minister Begin. The people of Israel, the people of Egypt want peace, and so do the people who live in the West Bank, Gaza Strip, Jordan, Syria, and, of course, Lebanon. It is a slow, uncertain, tedious process. It's not enjoyable to get involved in the negotiation of every single word, every phrase, every punctuation mark, every paragraph, to overcome years, generations, even centuries of hatred and animosity and bloodshed and distrust. But the spirit is there, and the desire is there. We need your help, and we need your support.

I told a group a few minutes ago that because of the problems with the Middle East settlements and the furor that it aroused in Egypt, that President Sadat had told his delegation to come home. But I contacted him last night, asked him to rely on us to bring about a peaceful resolution. And this morning, he informed me that his delegation will stay in Washington as long as it's necessary to have a peace treaty.

The last thing I want to say is to ask you to be patient with me and Abe Ribicoff and others. There are times when I have made statements or taken action during the last 12 months—and Senator Ribicoff has done the same—when, for a few days or maybe even weeks, it seemed that we had made a serious mistake.

Our commitment to Israel, our allegiance to Israel, is unshakable. And sometimes there are nuances or complications or facts that can't be revealed at the time. But over a period of weeks, I think you've always seen that when Abe Ribicoff votes in the Congress for a controversial issue, like, for instance, the sale of F–5's to Egypt, it seems to some that he may have made a mistake or that I may have made a mistake in advocating it. But we would never have induced President Sadat to come to Camp David had it not been for that vote.

And so, I hope that you will be patient with us and give us your moral support and your active support as we struggle with this very difficult question.

I want to see peace throughout the world. But with the exception of our own Nation itself, I can't think of any issue that's more sensitive nor more important than to bring peace, permanent peace, and a recognition of Israel by her neighbors. If you'll help me, I'll help you and we'll bring that about.

Thank you very much. I love you all.

NOTE: The President spoke at 1:53 p.m. in the Plaza Room at the Hotel Sonesta.

Lynn, Massachusetts

Remarks at a State Democratic Party Rally. October 28, 1978

Speaker O'Neill; Speaker Tom McGee; Senator Ted Kennedy; Paul Tsongas, next Senator from Massachusetts; Ed King, next Governor of Massachusetts; his running mate, Tommy O'Neill, next Lieutenant Governor; my good working companions in Washington, Congressman Harrington, Congressman Markey; Mayor Marino, who has welcomed me so well to Lynn; Mike Connolly, the next secretary of state; Bob Crane, the next treasurer; Francis Bellotti, next attorney general; Thad Buczko, State auditor; and John Marino, who will be the next Congressman from the 10th District:

I also want to say that you've already welcomed two great, young newcomers—Jim Shannon, the Fifth Congressional seat candidate, and of course we know Nick Mavroules is a great friend of all of ours, and I welcome you all.

It is an honor for me to come back to Massachusetts. You treated me well in 1976, not only by giving me your votes for President but also by ensuring that I had as the leader of the House of Representatives perhaps the greatest Speaker of all time—I believe the greatest Speaker of all time—Tip O'Neill.

He's been a brother, a father, an adviser, a friend, a counselor, a critic, an adviser. He's a man who believes in his country. He says next year we have four priorities, in increasing order of importance: first, to get hospital cost containment passed; second, to have a SALT agreement ratified; third, to get inflation under control; fourth, to see the Red Sox win the National [American] League pennant, and then go on to win the World Series, right, Tip?

The day after we had a new Polish Pope elected, Tip O'Neill called me up and said, "I've got a good recommendation for the next Secretary of State." I knew before he told me that he was talking about Carl Yastrzemski, and Tip wanted to take him over to the investiture of the new Pope. But when Cy Vance steps down, I'll call on Carl to help me as Secretary of State.

Let me say this in recognition of Ted Kennedy: Of all the hundred Members of the Senate who have given me good support this year, the Senator who has been my most consistent supporter in domestic and foreign affairs has been your great Senator, Ted Kennedy, and I want to thank him in front of all of you.

It's very important that we have representing Massachusetts next year a fine, new Democratic Senator, Paul Tsongas. He represents what the Democratic Party is, a man who believes in meeting basic human needs, a man who's honest, practical, competent, and close to you. He's a man who believes in the economic development of Massachusetts, who wants to put our people back to work. He serves on the Banking Committee. He's responsible for urban affairs. He's responsible as well for defense. He's a very strong supporter of having our Nation have a strong defense capability.

We are now the strongest nation on Earth. And with the help of people like Paul Tsongas, we're going to stay that way, and you can depend on it.

He's one of the leaders in developing for our country a new energy policy. Because of his ability and his knowledge of New England, particularly Massachusetts, he was chosen to serve on the ad hoc committee to develop a new energy bill. And you couldn't go wrong and you won't go wrong Tuesday after next when you elect Paul Tsongas to be the next Senator from your great State.

You've got a good Democratic team in Ed King and Tommy O'Neill. They believe in holding down property taxes. They're tough enough to deliver on promises. They believe in making the city stronger, and they are for the working people. And I hope you'll give them your strong support.

I think you know it's a balanced ticket, and the Democratic Party is certainly broad enough to encompass those who might disagree on some issues. But they believe that their strength, politically, their counsel, when they're in office, will come to you, and I hope you'll give them your strong support.

I'd like to talk just a few minutes about my own administration and the importance of a Democratic team. When I went in office 21 months ago, we had 10 million people in this country who could not find a full-time job. We had 7 million people who could find no jobs at all. When I campaigned through your State in '75 and '76, through Connecticut, Vermont, New Hampshire, Maine, the most important single question asked me was, "Can we put our people back to work?" The Congress and I have worked hard at this with the help of great Governors like your own Mike Dukakis, with Governors around the country.

We've cut the unemployment rate already by 25 percent. We've added a net increase of 6½ million jobs. The unemployment rate has dropped 1½ million, and we're going to keep on until every person in this country who wants a job can find a job. That's our great task, a very important one.

In Lynn, your employment has gone up twice as fast even as the national average that I've just described to you.

We've lowered taxes. Last year we lowered your income taxes $8 billion, this year almost $20 billion more. We've added good services—for you, the highest increase in allocation of money for education in the history of our Nation. We've also had good programs, as you know, for highways. We've strengthened our country's defense. We're improving the allocation of funds to areas like your own, where the need is greatest. We're rebuilding our cities. We formed a good partnership between local, State, and Federal officials. At the same time, we've seen a need to make our Government more efficient, more effective.

One of the big problems that we had was with our civil service. It was formed 95 years ago. It had never been changed nor improved. Quite often we would have two Federal workers sitting side by side. One would be competent, dedicated, hard-working. The one sitting next to him or her would be incompetent or lazy. With the new civil service reform, we're going to recognize the hard, dedicated worker, and the ones who haven't been working well are going to be reinspired, transferred, or fired. And we're going to let managers manage, and in the future you can depend on your Government being more effective and more efficient.

I think all of you remember just 2 or 3 years ago there was a great dissatisfaction, even distrust of our Federal Government by the people of this country. After the war in Vietnam, after the Watergate scandals, after the embarrassments of the CIA, there was a great feeling that public offi-cials could not be trusted. I advocated that we require a change in accountability of public officials to you, the people of this country.

Under the great leadership of Tip O'Neill, the Congress passed and I signed just this week a new ethics bill. It requires the President, the Vice President, the members of the Cabinet, all top employees in the executive branch of Government, every Member of Congress, all Federal judges, to reveal their net worth, to let you the people know how much income they have and where that income comes from. So, from now on, there will be much less temptation to violate the laws or to do something embarrassing or unethical, and that's a great step forward, thanks to your Speaker and my Speaker, Tip O'Neill.

In addition to better services and lower taxes, I was very concerned in 1976 about the high Federal Government deficit. When I ran for President, the Federal deficit was over $66 billion. I've not been in office yet 2 years, but the Congress and I together have already reduced the deficit by $25 billion. I'm now preparing the 1980 fiscal year budget. I'm going to cut the Federal deficit to less than half what it was when I was elected.

And with the help of the Members of Congress, we've dedicated ourselves, with a strong economy, to having a balanced budget for the Federal Government of the United States in the future.

The biggest problem that I have and that you have still on our shoulders is to control inflation. It robs those who are least able to afford it. The other night I spoke to the Nation on television to outline what I would do as President, what business leaders and employers would do to hold down prices below 6 percent increase per year.

I asked the working people of this country that if we are able to control government waste and spending and hold down prices, to also hold down their wage demands. It is going to be a very difficult undertaking. I need your support, and I hope the people of this country will rally to me to control this blight on our economy, give us a stronger nation that can keep jobs coming to us by holding down inflation.

I would like to say one other thing in closing about international affairs. It's very important for our country's military capability to be strong, because with strength comes confidence and influence in the rest of the world. We've tried to provide leadership that in the past was missing. We've not felt a necessity to endorse and support every tinhorn dictatorship around the country [world] [1] that violated human rights. We've tried to raise a banner for our country to follow of common decency, honesty, and self-respect.

I think we've been successful to a great degree. As you well know, in times gone by, every time the United Nations met in the fall of the year in New York, our country was embarrassed by being the target of every attack, the butt of every joke. This is no longer the case. And I believe that the nations of Asia, Europe, Africa now see us as a nation that can be trusted, a nation that's strong, a nation that's going to stay strong.

We're negotiating every day with the Soviet Union to bring about a SALT agreement to reduce the threat of atomic weapons that hang over our heads, those of the Soviet Union and indeed the entire world. The Congress has already passed a bill that was called the nonproliferation bill to keep nations who don't presently have atomic weapons from getting them.

The Republican Senator from this State has said that he wants us to put a moratorium on negotiating with the Soviets to limit nuclear weapons. This would be a serious mistake, to stop trying for world peace, to stop trying for nuclear weapons. And as long as I'm in the White House, we'll continue to negotiate to keep our Nation's strength, to cut down on nuclear weapons, and eliminate this great threat from the entire world.

I'm grateful that since I've been in office, not a single American member of our Armed Forces has shed blood in a foreign country. And I hope I can go out of office at the end of my term with that record still intact.

But we're not trying to bring peace just to our own country. We're trying to bring peace in other troubled areas of the world. In Southern Africa, in Namibia, in Rhodesia, in Cyprus, wherever there's a threat of bloodshed that might spread to other countries and eventually to us, we are working day and night to try to alleviate tensions, to eliminate hatred, and to build up friendships.

One of the most complicated and longstanding disputes in the entire world, as you know, is in the Middle East. There's no doubt in my mind that the people of Israel want peace. There's no doubt that the people of Egypt want peace. This also applies to those who live on the West Bank, in Jordan, in Syria, in Lebanon.

We've already made some progress. President Sadat, Prime Minister Begin have been very determined and very courageous in seeking common ground on which they could build an agreement. Lately, we have had some problems with the settlement issue on the West Bank. There was a chance yesterday that the Egyptian delegation might withdraw. They had orders to do so. But I contacted President Sadat. This morning, he sent me word that his delegation would stay here and continue to negotiate until there's a peace treaty between Israel and

---

[1] Printed in the transcript.

Egypt. And I hope before this year is over, I can go over and sign a peace treaty with those two, bring peace to that troubled region.

I'd like to emphasize that the Presidency is sometimes a lonely job. And it's only with a team effort that I can be successful, that the Congress can be successful, that gubernatorial and local officials can be successful in meeting your needs in an effective way.

We have been making progress in lower taxes, better services, a more open government, more effective delivery of the things that you need in your own lives. We've built up our Nation's defense. We've increased the influence and the esteem of our own Nation around the world. We've protected human rights, and we're working hard toward peace. We've put our people back to work, and we are trying to control inflation.

Every one of these issues, many others like them, are very difficult. It requires the support of you and people like you around the country. I can be much more effective in domestic and foreign issues if when I speak, foreign leaders and others know that I don't speak with a hollow voice, that the Congress gives me its backing and that you support me in my efforts to lead this Nation. I hope you'll support the entire Democratic ticket in Massachusetts.

The next 9 or 10 days will be very important to you. I hope that you'll make a small investment of time, money, and your influence to shape the kind of government you will have in the future and elect these fine candidates who have already been chosen in an open, free, democratic primary.

Please do this, because I want to see the Democratic team stay together which has served you so well in Massachusetts. We've got the greatest nation on Earth. If you'll help me and the others on the stage with me in the future, we'll have an even greater nation, the United States of America.

Thank you very much, everybody.

NOTE: The President spoke at 4:37 p.m. at the Lynn City Hall. In his opening remarks, he referred to Thomas W. McGee, speaker of the house of the Massachusetts General Court.

Lynn, Massachusetts

Remarks at a Reception for Paul Tsongas and Edward King. October 28, 1978

Well, it's a great pleasure for me to come back to Massachusetts. I would like to say just a few words. I don't have much time to spend with you, and I particularly would like to meet every one of you individually, if you have no objection.

I just had a tremendous welcome and an unbelievable crowd in Lynn to meet me and Paul Tsongas and Ed King. And this is a ticket in Massachusetts that will do an outstanding job for you. I talked to them about better services to the American people, higher standards of ethics and morality, decency, honesty, openness, reduced taxes, better management of government, more efficiency, cutting the budget deficit, stronger defense, and a search for peace in the Mideast and around the world.

This is a very important agenda, very difficult to achieve. And it takes a strong team to do it. Part of that team, of course, is comprised of elected officials. But the most important part of it are Americans like you who have been blessed by God with great material wealth, influence, social status, and ability to influence others as well.

We've only got 9 or 10 days left in this election. It's going to be close. It would be a serious mistake for us to take anything for granted. You've helped by making a substantial financial contribution, which

I'm sure did not hurt any of you. [*Laughter*] I hope that you will not consider this to be your complete fulfillment of an obligation for a better State and a better Nation.

If you haven't given the limit, I hope you will. Get your husbands or wives to do the same and contact your own friends and neighbors, those who have confidence in you, to contribute as well. Democrats and Republicans can help. And I think it's very important that each one of you kind of anoint yourself this next week and a half to be a campaign manager for the Democratic candidates in whom you have confidence. You couldn't possibly make a better investment in your own State and Nation, your own future, and a future for people who care for you and about whom you are deeply concerned.

I need for you to join our Democratic team and to be part of it. And you can do this by helping me elect these fine men to the offices they seek. They've been nominated in an open, free, democratic primary. No one would doubt that at all. And I hope that you would now give them your full support. They particularly need your support after they are in office, and so do I. I need them; they need you; I need you.

Thank you very much for letting me come.

NOTE: The President spoke at 5:27 p.m. in the Olde Storeroom at the Colonial Hilton Inn.

Portland, Maine

Remarks at the Annual Jefferson-Jackson Day Dinner.   October 28, 1978

Senator Hathaway, Senator Ed Muskie, Chairman Hal Pachios, Joe Brennan, John Quinn, Mark Gartley, Chairman John White, fellow Democrats:

I feel at home in Maine.

I'm your President, and I have the deepest feelings about those who serve with me in positions of major importance, positions of public trust. I remember history as well. Hal Pachios said that he wasn't sure whether or not I was familiar with nature food. I grew up on a farm during the Hoover Depression. [*Laughter*] I'm quite familiar with hickory nuts, persimmons, and boiled rabbit. And later, when the Democrats came in, I graduated to buttermilk, Maine potatoes, and peanuts.

I don't have much time with you. I wanted to talk soberly and frankly tonight. I don't care whether you applaud or not.

I didn't come up here to waste my time. I've had a long week. The duties of my office are sometimes burdensome, sometimes create loneliness, always serious. My decisions affect the future of our Nation, in fact, many other nations around the Earth. This could have been my 1 day off this week, but I wanted to come here, because I, as the President of our country and as the leader of the Democratic Party, am very interested in what happens in Maine 10 days from now on November 7.

I can't carry an election for you. I can't stay here and hold your hand to make sure that Bill Hathaway is the next Senator from Maine or that Joe Brennan is the next Governor, Mark Gartley and John Quinn your next Members of Congress. I can't do that.

I thought a lot about Maine. My son's been up here to campaign for these candidates. He didn't have to. The Vice President's been up here to campaign. He didn't have to. My wife has been up here to campaign with Bill Hathaway and with the other candidates. She didn't have to. We believe in them.

I have a great admiration for the character and the spirit of the people of

Maine. I believe that Ed Muskie and these candidates on my right exemplify that historical attitude and spirit of the people of your State.

Bill Hathaway is perhaps not a very good politician. He doesn't brag on himself. He's not a flashy person. He doesn't dwell on press statements. He doesn't attack a serious problem in a superficial way. When there's a serious matter that affects Maine, like the Indian claims question in which I have been deeply involved since the first week I was in the White House, I've never observed nor ever expected Bill Hathaway to demagog that issue or to try to get a single vote out of it.

He's worked quietly behind the scenes, effectively. He has known the attitude of Maine people. He's known the attitude of Maine public officials. He's recognized that there is a sharp difference of opinion, even between him and some of the other Democratic candidates. Sometimes I did not agree with Bill Hathaway's approach to this question. But he didn't particularly care, because he was searching for a permanent solution that would be good for the people whom he loves. And I think he deliberately was willing to sacrifice perhaps some of his own political benefit in order to serve you well.

I don't quite know what you call that. I don't call it being naive, because he knew what he was doing. I don't think he was trying to be a martyr, because obviously he did not want to sacrifice himself. I call it integrity and courage.

My own opinion, as one who's visited here, I think, five times, is that that is what Maine is, what your original pioneers were, what you believe in, how you feel—whether you're a Democrat or Republican, that doesn't matter. There's a certain staunchness and courage and quietness about a resident of Maine. At least that's my opinion as someone from

Georgia observing what you are. I believe I'm right.

His fellow Senators, in 6 short years, have recognized what Bill Hathaway is. He serves on the Finance Committee, and everyone who serves on that committee or the Budget Committee, like Ed Muskie or others, know that there is one man who cannot be swayed by a powerful chairman, who cannot be swayed by sometimes a demagogic majority to violate in writing the tax laws in this country what's best for the average working family of our Nation. And that's Bill Hathaway. He has never changed. He believes in tax reform, whether it wins him a vote or not.

And I'll bet you that you will not see a single powerful, selfish lobby making a major campaign contribution to Bill Hathaway. And there's a good reason, because he's protecting your interests and not the special interests.

He has a couple of special subcommittees where he devotes the focal point of his time. One concerns employment, and the other one concerns small business. It would not have been possible for us to bring down the unemployment rate 25 percent in just 21 months, never before achieved in this country, had it not been for people like him. And he hasn't been one who wanted to create an enormous number of Government jobs, to take your tax money and pay someone else to work for the Government.

He believes in the free enterprise system of this country in its finest and most decent and most open and most competitive form, creating jobs that are permanent, because there's nothing more debilitating to a young person or an old person than to know you've got one life to live on this Earth and to see your God-given talents being wasted because you can't produce something and earn a living for you or your family. And the small business people of this country—I was one of them—very seldom have a true champion. We've had one in Bill Hathaway, not because he seeks votes, because he never publicizes what he does. But whenever I have a difficult issue that addresses itself to these two particular problems, I don't have to worry about the motivations or the final vote of Bill Hathaway.

He's a man with a heart. He exemplifies one characteristic of the Democratic Party, and that's compassion. We've never been one to turn our backs on those that are poor, unemployed, illiterate, without influence, black, or perhaps not able to speak English well. We don't consider ourselves reaching down to somebody to give them a chance. We reach out to them and say, "Join us in a society and use your own talent and ability, stand on your own feet, meet your own needs, contribute to a greater nation." That is the attitude that Bill Hathaway exemplifies in his service.

He's an expert on the problems of the elderly. There are some who work on the same committee that constantly publicize to the organized groups representing the elderly in this country how much they do. As I said before, Bill Hathaway is not a good enough politician to make it a major commitment to publicize his own achievements. He's a man who understands that we've got to have a strong nation, a strong defense. And if there ever has been one effective protector of the defense contribution of Maine to the rest of the Nation, in all forms, it's been Bill Hathaway.

He's never tried to violate what was best for our country to put Maine before other nations, to make us waste money, but he has been there in a careful, persistent way, saying, "This is what I think, it's best to make our Nation strong."

Sometimes the polls have not looked good for him or for some of the other candidates on the stage with me. If I had been worrying about polls, I'd still be growing peanuts. Two weeks after I announced my candidacy for President, Gallup ran a public opinion poll on the next President. There were 38 names on the list. Mine wasn't even on the list. [*Laughter*]

And I might say in closing about Bill Hathaway specifically that he's a gentleman. When I rode back from the 1974 Maine Democratic convention with him, and he said, "What are you going to do after you quit being Governor," I said, "I'm going to run for President." He never said a word. He looked up at the ceiling, shook his head a little bit, but he never embarrassed me by saying a word, and I appreciate that. [*Laughter*]

But I remember when Bill Hathaway ran for the Senate. The seat was held by a Republican. I don't believe that there had ever been an elected Democratic Senator to hold that seat. I doubt if 5 percent of you thought he had a chance when he began to run. But he brought that seat to the Democratic Party, and he has used it well for you and for the rest of the country.

There is a difference between the two parties. I inherited the White House after a long campaign about 21 months ago. Ten million Americans didn't have a full-time job. The budget deficit was $66.6 billion. The average American was embarrassed about our own Government. Every time the United Nations convened in the fall, I, as a Governor and a candidate for President, shrank inside, because I knew that my country, which I love, was going to be the butt of every joke, the target of every attack by two-thirds of the nations in the entire world.

It was an embarrassing thing. We were looked on as warmongers. Our Government put its arms around every tinhorn dictatorship in the world, to the embarrassment of our friends and allies and the American people as well.

Our farmers were facing a new depression. Their income was going down; prices were below the cost of production. There was a problem with exports. The Government had its nose too deeply into the affairs of the farm families. The wild fluctuations in prices were exacerbated by embargoes against the sale of American farm products to foreign countries, not just the Soviet Union but countries like Japan. The farmers didn't know where to turn.

Human rights was a phrase that could not have been used without laughter by some of the high officials in our own Federal Government. There was waste, corruption, a steady stream of top Republican officials going to jail. Civil servants who give their whole careers to serving others were not able to do a good job for us because of a bureaucracy that was strangling them.

The Congress had passed laws concerning education, housing, highways, and the Republican administration would subvert the will of Congress, impound money required to be spent for the benefit of us all by law.

The so-called free enterprise system was increasingly deprived of a key element, and that was competition. That is what the Republican Party meant to our country. No person can change it. I don't claim to have changed all that, but I do tell you that a Democratic team—the President, Vice President, Cabinet members, reinspired civil servants, Members of Congress, Governors, mayors, county officials, and average American citizens—have begun to change some of those aspects or characteristics of our Government.

I believe it's now attaining a reputation of a government that's clean and decent and honest, and that accurately represents the principles and the ideals on which our Nation was originally founded. We've got a long way to go. We are the strongest nation on Earth militarily. We're going to stay that way. But we're trying to use our strength not to push other nations around.

We could have made a great deal out of punishing the people of Panama. I could have got a lot of votes by doing that. We could have been a bully and gotten away with it, and a lot of folks would have said, "We've a great President now, because we've shown those Panamanians that we are indeed a powerful nation." But we have not used our power in an abusive way. We have used our power, our influence, our strength to enhance peace.

I thank God that since I've been in office, not a single American soldier has lost his life or shed blood fighting in a foreign country. I hope I can go out of office saying the same thing.

But we've not only tried to provide peace for ourselves; we've tried to use our good influence along with our allies and friends, not by ourselves—we've worked with Great Britain to try to bring peace and democratic government, one person-one vote, majority rule to Rhodesia. We're trying to do the same thing in Namibia.

We've lessened the tensions, strengthened NATO, removed disharmonies, and taken a step toward peace with Turkey, Greece, Cyprus. We're trying to restore normal relations with some of our former adversaries associated with the Vietnamese war.

We are negotiating every day to bring a new SALT agreement between ourselves and the Soviet Union to lessen the fear of world destruction with nuclear weapons. The Congress passed a new law, nonproliferation bill, that prevents nations that don't have atomic explosives from ever having them. It has not been an easy thing.

I called Sadat and Begin to Camp David to try to induce them to utilize their great courage and vision, representing their own people's hunger for peace, to come closer together. We've made some progress. We've got a long way to go. But the point is that we've turned our Nation around now, and we have goals of which we can be proud.

I need help in the Congress, Democratic help. There are 435 Members in the House. Do you know how many votes we get on an average bill of the kind I've just been talking about from the Republican side? Sometimes as many as 3, sometimes as many as 12. There's a great difference between the Democratic Party and the Republican Party. If there wasn't, I would not be here tonight.

We've got 10 days to go before the election. It's going to be a tough campaign. Our candidates don't have enough money. You've paid only $15 to come here tonight, I see—most inexpensive Jackson-Jefferson Day banquet I've ever come to. All of you can afford more. There's not a single person in this room that couldn't contribute a hundred to a thousand dollars to the candidates on this stage on my right.

You could not possibly make a better investment in the future of your family, your State, or your country. There's no one here who couldn't expend, in the next 10 days, 40 hours to help the candidates that you have come here professing to support.

I don't doubt your seriousness or your dedication, nor your loyalty. I don't believe you would lie to a President, and I would like to ask every one in this room—think about it a few minutes—who will work on the telephone or handing out pamphlets or in the headquarters or among your neighbors and family and friends, all of you who will devote 40 hours between now and election day to help the Democratic candidates win, would you please rise? [*Applause*] That makes my trip to Maine worthwhile. And I thank you for it.

Let me close by saying this: We are partners. We are partners. In the past, our Nation has sometimes been divided on issues. At one time, it was divided by war. Your ancestors in Maine were on one side, my ancestors in Georgia were on the other. But our Nation was united, and we need to make sure that it stays united and also strong, that it represents what we are.

When Sadat and Begin were at Camp David the last 10 days, they never saw each other except for a visit to Gettysburg. And we agreed before we left that we would not talk about the Middle East, because they were in such disharmony that I thought it would exacerbate and be an obstacle to a peaceful agreement. But we went to Gettysburg, and while there, we read about a man from Maine. His name was Joshua Chamberlain. He fought in the war, and later he served as Governor of your State.

More than a hundred years ago he wrote, "A government has something more to do than to govern and to levy taxes. It is something more than a police to arrest evil and to punish wrong. A government must also encourage good, point out improvements, open roads of prosperity and infuse life into all right enterprises. It should combine the insight and the foresight of the best minds of the State, for all the high ends for which society is established and to which man aspires. That gives us much to do."

Those words mean a lot to me as a Georgian. Those words mean a lot to me as President. We live in the greatest nation on Earth, economically, militarily, politically, socially, I hope morally. With your help, as teammates of mine, along with Bill Hathaway and the other Democratic candidates, we can make our great

Nation even greater in the future. That's my prayer.

Thank you very much.

NOTE: The President spoke at 7:43 p.m. at the Stevens Avenue Armory. In his opening remarks, he referred to Harold Pachios, State Democratic Party chairman, and John C. White, Democratic National Committee chairman.

Protection for the Privacy of Rape Victims

Statement on Signing H.R. 4727 Into Law. October 30, 1978

I am pleased to sign H.R. 4727, an important change in the rules of evidence to protect the rights of victims of rape.

This bill provides a model for State and local revision of criminal and case law. It is designed to end the public degradation of rape victims and, by protecting victims from humiliation, to encourage the reporting of rape.

There is no question that victims of rape and other sex crimes, predominately women, are reluctant to report these crimes. Too often rape trials have been as humiliating as the sexual assault itself. By restricting testimony on the victim's prior sexual behavior to that genuinely relevant to the defense, the rape victims act will prevent a defendant from making the victim's private life the issue in the trial.

The thousands of women who met last year in Houston for International Women's Year urged Federal, State, and local governments to provide this basic protection for rape victims. I am pleased that the Federal Government is serving as a model in this regard, and I urge all criminal jurisdictions to follow the Federal example in providing this essential pro-

tection for women. I congratulate Congresswoman Elizabeth Holtzman for her sponsorship of this legislation and her leadership in this area.

NOTE: As enacted, H.R. 4727 is Public Law 95–540, approved October 28.

Great Bear and Bob Marshall Wildernesses in Montana

Statement on Signing H.R. 13972 Into Law. October 30, 1978

I am very pleased to sign H.R. 13972, which designates the Great Bear Wilderness and enlarges the Bob Marshall Wilderness in the State of Montana.

This act adds 345,771 acres of some of Montana's most rugged and beautiful backcountry to the National Wilderness Preservation System. The area is comprised of mountainous terrain with outstanding scenic, watershed, wildlife, and primitive recreation values. It forms a critical ecological link between Glacier National Park and the Bob Marshall Wilderness and protects a large segment of the Flathead River.

Establishment of the Great Bear Wilderness is the product of years of work by a tireless and dedicated conservationist, the late Senator Lee Metcalf of Montana. He introduced the legislation leading to the wilderness study of the area. And now, thanks to the effort of his wife, Donna Metcalf, and his colleagues in the Senate and House of Representatives, another of the Nation's most beautiful pristine areas will receive appropriate protection and recognition as part of the National Wilderness Preservation System.

I am proud to honor Senator Metcalf's memory in signing this important bill.

NOTE: As enacted, H.R. 13972 is Public Law 95–546, approved October 28.

Domestic Bicycle Tire and Tube Industry

Letter to the Speaker of the House and the President of the Senate Transmitting a Report.   October 30, 1978

Dear Mr. Speaker: (Dear Mr. President:)

In accordance with section 203(b)(2) of the Trade Act of 1974, enclosed is a report to the Congress setting forth my decision that import relief for the domestic bicycle tire and tube industry is not in the national economic interest, and explaining the reasons for my decision.

Sincerely,

JIMMY CARTER

IMPORT RELIEF ACTION
BICYCLE TIRES AND TUBES

As required under section 203(b)(2) of the Trade Act of 1974, I am transmitting this report to Congress setting forth the action I will take with respect to bicycle tires and tubes covered by the affirmative finding on September 1, 1978 of the U.S. International Trade Commission (USITC) under section 201(d)(1) of the Trade Act. As my action differs from that recommended by the USITC, I have included the reasons for my decision.

After considering all relevant aspects of the case, including those considerations set forth in section 202(c) of the Trade Act of 1974, I have determined that import relief for the domestic bicycle tire and tube industry would not be in the national economic interest for the following reasons:

(1) The imposition of import relief in the form of a tariff increase would not be an effective means to promote the permanent adjustment in the domestic industry. The sole remaining domestic producer has the most modern plant available, and very little can be done to improve current operating efficiency. In addition, corporate profits are high, and the profit margin on bicycle tires and tubes remains respectable in spite of low capacity utilization levels.

(2) At current profit levels, it is unlikely that the remaining domestic manufacturer will cease producing bicycle tires and tubes. Should the corporation eventually decide to terminate production, much of the plant's equipment could be modified to produce other kinds of recreational tires made by the company.

(3) The relative stability in the domestic producer's market share indicates that domestic demand is less price sensitive than is import demand. Consequently, its market for domestically-produced tires and tubes is expected to remain intact.

(4) It is estimated that any loss in employment resulting from a denial of import relief would be small, and that those separated would be eligible for adjustment assistance. The Department of Labor estimates that the reemployment prospects are probably fair for potentially separated workers.

(5) Import relief would be inflationary. It is estimated that the consumer cost of the relief recommendation made by the USITC would be between $4.4 and $7.5 million for the first full year of relief.

(6) The foreign policy consequences of granting relief measures are adverse. The world trading community would view this as a sign of growing protectionist sentiment. Moreover, because other petitions of the industry are now being investigated under the antidumping and countervailing duty statutes, it would also be seen as an attempt to harass foreign exporters through duplication of remedies.

(7) A duty increase such as recommended by the USITC will not place

effective restraints on import competition but may merely accelerate the movement of production facilities out of Korea and Taiwan and into such countries as India, Indonesia, and Thailand.

(8) Provision of import relief would subject U.S. jobs in other industries to possible foreign retaliation against U.S. exports or compensation by the United States in the form of reduced import restrictions on other products.

NOTE: This is the text of identical letters addressed to Thomas P. O'Neill, Jr., Speaker of the House of Representatives, and Walter F. Mondale, President of the Senate.

The text of the letters was released on October 31.

Domestic Bicycle Tire and Tube Industry

Memorandum From the President.
October 30, 1978

Memorandum for the Special Representative for Trade Negotiations

Subject: Determination Under Section 202(b) of the Trade Act; Bicycle Tires and Tubes

Pursuant to section 202(b)(1) of the Trade Act of 1974 (P.L. 93–618, 88 Stat. 1978), I have determined the action I will take with respect to the report of the United States International Trade Commission (USITC), transmitted to me on September 1, 1978, concerning the results of its investigation of a petition for import relief. This petition was filed by the Carlisle Tire and Rubber Company, the sole domestic producer of pneumatic bicycle tires provided for in item 772.48 of the Tariff Schedules of the United States (TSUS), and tubes for bicycle tires, provided for in TSUS item 772.57.

After considering all relevant aspects of the case, including those considerations set forth in section 202(c) of the Trade Act of 1974, I have determined that import relief is not in the national economic interest for the following reasons:

(1) The imposition of import relief in the form of a tariff increase would not be an effective means to promote the permanent adjustment in the domestic industry. The sole remaining domestic producer has the most modern plant available, and very little can be done to improve current operating efficiency. In addition, corporate profits are high, and the profit margin on bicycle tires and tubes remains respectable in spite of low capacity utilization levels.

(2) At current profit levels, it is unlikely that the remaining domestic manufacturer will cease producing bicycle tires and tubes. Should the corporation eventually decide to terminate production, much of the plant's equipment could be modified to produce other kinds of recreational tires made by the company.

(3) The relative stability in the domestic producer's market share indicates that domestic demand is less price sensitive than is import demand. Consequently, its market for domestically-produced tires and tubes is expected to remain intact.

(4) It is estimated that any loss in employment resulting from a denial of import relief would be small, and that those separated would be eligible for adjustment assistance. The Department of Labor estimates that the reemployment prospects are probably fair for potentially separated workers.

(5) Import relief would be inflationary. It is estimated that the consumer cost of the relief recommendation made by the USITC would be between $4.4 and $7.5 million for the first full year of relief.

(6) The foreign policy consequences of granting relief measures are adverse. The world trading community would view

this as a sign of growing protectionist sentiment. Moreover, because other petitions of the industry are now being investigated under the antidumping and countervailing duty statutes, it would also be seen as an attempt to harass foreign exporters through duplication of remedies.

(7) A duty increase such as recommended by the USITC will not place effective restraints on import competition but may merely accelerate the movement of production facilities out of Korea and Taiwan and into such countries as India, Indonesia, and Thailand.

(8) Provision of import relief would subject U.S. jobs in other industries to possible foreign retaliation against U.S. exports or compensation by the United States in the form of reduced import restrictions on other products.

This determination is to be published in the FEDERAL REGISTER.

JIMMY CARTER

[Filed with the Office of the Federal Register, 4:11 p.m., October 31, 1978]

NOTE: The text of the memorandum was released on October 31.

Federal Regulatory Management

Memorandum From the President.
October 31, 1978

Memorandum for the Heads of Executive Departments and Agencies

Subject: Strengthening Regulatory Management

I am deeply committed to seeing that the regulatory agencies perform their important missions without imposing unnecessary costs. Last March I issued Executive Order 12044 as a first step toward ensuring that regulations achieve their statutory goals in the most effective and balanced way. To reinforce this effort,

I am establishing a Regulatory Council, to include all Executive Departments and Agencies with major regulatory responsibilities. The independent regulatory commissions will be invited to join. I am also extending the Regulatory Analysis Review program and accelerating the "sunset" process under Executive Order 12044.

The Regulatory Council will help inform me, the public, and the Congress about the cumulative impact of regulation on the economy. It will publish, at least every six months, a unified calendar of major regulations, using the criteria defined in the Executive Order. This calendar will state the goals and benefits, legal requirements, and expected timetables of the regulations, along with available estimates of economic impacts. The first calendar will be published no later than February 1, 1979.

My Executive Office agencies and I will work with the Council and the calendar. The Council will help ensure that regulations are well coordinated, do not conflict, and do not impose excess burdens on particular sectors of the economy. OMB will use the calendar in its key role of overseeing agency compliance with the Executive Order.

The Council will consult with the Congress and the public as it proceeds. In the next few weeks, I will meet with the Council to discuss the development of the calendar, identify cross-cutting issues, and emphasize the need to regulate in the least costly, most effective manner. The Council will be chaired by a member for a one year term. The first chairman, serving through January 1, 1980, will be Douglas Costle. The departments should participate in their capacities as regulators.

The regulatory calendar will be used by the Regulatory Analysis Review Group that I established on an interim basis early this year. This group assists agencies in analyzing the economic consequences of proposed major rules and in exploring alternative approaches. The group discusses and submits formal comments on 10 to 20 of the most important regulations proposed each year. Today, I am extending this program through June 30, 1980.

The above steps will further improve the process of issuing new regulations. The Executive Order also requires agencies to prepare lists of existing regulations for "sunset" review. As part of my effort to eliminate unnecessarily inflationary regulations, I am asking you to review these lists and identify additional major regulations which can be modified or eliminated to reduce costs. Candidates for such reviews should be submitted to OMB by December 1, 1978.

These steps will accelerate our progress toward a regulatory system that meets the needs of the public at the least cost. Your personal attention to this effort is essential to its success.

JIMMY CARTER

APPENDIX

Regulatory Council

Department of Treasury
Department of Justice
Department of Agriculture
Department of Commerce
Department of the Interior
Department of Labor
Department of Health, Education, and Welfare
Department of Housing and Urban Development
Department of Transportation
Department of Energy
General Services Administration
Environmental Protection Agency
Veterans Administration
Administrative Conference of the United States

The independent regulatory commissions will be invited to join the Council. Agencies in the Executive Office of the President will participate with it.

Occupational Discrimination Based on Pregnancy

Statement on Signing S. 995 Into Law. October 31, 1978

I am pleased to sign into law today legislation that protects American women from occupational discrimination on the basis of pregnancy.

I am convinced that discrimination based on pregnancy, childbirth, and related medical conditions constitutes discrimination based on sex. As its passage of this bill shows, the Congress shares that conviction—and shares as well my unalterable opposition to such discrimination.

This bill, an amendment to title VII of the historic Civil Rights Act of 1964, stands for the principle of equal justice under law. It does not bestow favored treatment on America's 42 million working women. Nor does it diminish in any way the rights and benefits of their male coworkers. It simply requires employers who have medical disability plans to provide for disability due to pregnancy and related conditions on an equal basis with other medical conditions.

This legislation does not introduce any novel employment practices. Some States already prohibit sex discrimination based on pregnancy. Under this new law, this kind of protection now applies to all workers throughout the country covered by title VII.

NOTE: As enacted, S. 995 is Public Law 95–555, approved October 31.

Congressional Delegate for the Territory of American Samoa

Statement on Signing H.R. 13702 Into Law. October 31, 1978

Today I am signing into law H.R. 13702, which provides the territory of American Samoa with a nonvoting Delegate to the United States House of Representatives. American Samoa became a member of the American political family through a voluntary act of cession by the chiefs of Tutuila and Manua at the turn of the century. Since that time, the people of American Samoa have demonstrated their attachment to this Nation by their patriotic service in the Armed Forces and have contributed greatly to our sports and cultural life.

American Samoa has made significant strides toward self-government in union with the United States. In 1960 American Samoans adopted their own locally drafted constitution, which was approved by the Secretary of the Interior. In 1969 American Samoan leaders began to take an active part in the territory's budgetary process. In 1970 the people of American Samoa elected a delegate at large to represent them in Washington, and in 1977 they elected their own Governor.

The United States should recognize, in view of this history, that American Samoa is a permanent part of American political life, deserving of representation in the United States Congress. The American Samoa Delegate legislation provides that recognition.

By signing this bill, I am signaling to the world that the United States remains committed to the well-being of American Samoa, to the development of democratic representation, and to our close brotherhood with the people of American Samoa.

NOTE: As enacted, H.R. 13702 is Public Law 95–556, approved October 31.

President's Commission on Foreign Language and International Studies

Executive Order 12090. October 31, 1978

By the authority vested in me as President by the Constitution and statutes of the United States of America, in order to extend for five months the life of the President's Commission on Foreign Language and International Studies, Section 4 of Executive Order No. 12054 of April 21, 1978, is amended to read as follows:

"Sec. 4. *Termination and Final Report.* The Commission shall submit its final report to the President not later than eleven months after its first meeting and shall terminate thirty days thereafter.".

JIMMY CARTER

The White House,
  October 31, 1978.

[Filed with the Office of the Federal Register, 4:12 p.m., October 31, 1978]

National Climate Program

Memorandum From the President. October 31, 1978

Memorandum for the Heads of Departments and Agencies

I have just signed into law the National Climate Program Act (P.L. 95–367). I am pleased to commit the Nation to this Program of improving our understanding of climatic changes, both natural and man-induced.

Much of the responsibility for implementing this Act falls on the Secretary of Commerce. In addition to those responsibilities specifically assigned to the Secretary of Commerce in the Act, I shall also expect the Department of Commerce to prepare the preliminary and final 5-year plans and the biennial revisions identified in Sec. 5(d)(9). Working closely with all other involved agencies, including but not limited to those identified in Sec. 5(b)(2), the Secretary of Commerce will define, as an integral part of the plans, the role of each agency in carrying out the Program. The plans shall reflect the Administration's ongoing and proposed climate program efforts and will be promulgated by me after appropriate review in the Executive Office of the President.

Each involved Department and Agency will assign a policy officer to work with the Secretary of Commerce or her designee to assure that the goals, objectives, assignments of responsibilities, and allocations of resources, detailed in the plans, are consistent with the mission responsibilities of each Department and Agency. If any issue arises where a consensus of views cannot be reached among these officers, the matter shall be brought to the attention of the Director, Office of Management and Budget, and the Director, Office of Science and Technology Policy, for resolution.

The Director of the Office of Science and Technology Policy will maintain cognizance, for me, of the status of Program coordination and recommend from time to time any program and procedural changes deemed necessary.

JIMMY CARTER

Value of the Dollar in Domestic and International Markets

Remarks Announcing Measures To Strengthen the Dollar. November 1, 1978

THE PRESIDENT. Last week, I pledged my administration to a balanced, concerted, and sustained program to fight inflation. That program requires effective policies to assure a strong dollar.

The basic factors that affect the strength of the dollar are heading in the right direction. We now have an energy program passed by Congress; our trade deficit is declining; and last week, I put in place a strong anti-inflation program.

The continuing decline in the exchange value of the dollar is clearly not warranted by the fundamental economic situation. That decline threatens economic progress at home and abroad and the success of our anti-inflation program.

As a major step in the anti-inflation program, it is now necessary to act to correct the excessive decline in the dollar which has recently occurred. Therefore, pursuant to my request that strong action be taken, the Department of the Treasury and the Federal Reserve Board are today initiating measures in both domestic and international monetary fields to assure the strength of the dollar.

The international components of this program have been developed with other major governments and with central banks. They intend to cooperate fully with the United States in attaining our mutual objectives.

Secretary Blumenthal and Chairman Miller are announcing detailed measures immediately.

Thank you very much.

SECRETARY BLUMENTHAL. In the past few months the United States has taken action to correct the imbalances that have characterized our economy. We have passed an energy bill which will lead to a reduction of our dependence on imported oil. We have implemented a program to enhance exports as a national priority. We have launched a tough and determined anti-inflation campaign. We have taken steps to reduce the Government's preemption of the Nation's financial resources by cutting dramatically our budget deficit. We have also moved decisively toward undoing the overregulation of our great economy. We have enacted a tax bill which will enhance capital formation and improve productivity. More must and will be done, but the prerequisites for improved economic performance are in place.

Recent moves in the dollar exchange rates have not only exceeded any decline related to the fundamental factors but plainly are hampering progress toward the price stability, balance-of-payments improvement, and enhanced climate for investment and growth which these measures are designed to bring about.

The time has, therefore, come to call a halt to these developments. At the President's direction, Chairman Miller and I are today announcing comprehensive corrective actions.

Effective immediately, the Federal Reserve is raising the discount rate from 8½ to 9½ percent, and is imposing a supplementary reserve requirement equal to 2 percentage points of time deposits of $100,000 or more.

In addition to domestic measures being taken by the Federal Reserve, the United States will, in cooperation with the Governments and central banks of Germany and Japan, and the Swiss National Bank, intervene in a forceful and coordinated manner in the amounts required to correct the situation. The United States has arranged facilities totaling $30 billion in the currencies of these three countries, which will finance the U.S. contribution to the coordinated market intervention activities of the four participating countries.

That $30 billion in the currencies of these three countries are being raised through a drawing of the U.S. reserve tranche of the International Monetary Fund; through the sale of SDR's to Germany, Japan, and Switzerland; through a substantial increase in the Federal Reserve swap lines with the Bundesbank, the Bank of Japan, and the Swiss National Bank; and through our intention to issue foreign currency denominated securities. Together, this will make up the $30 billion package.

In addition, the Treasury will increase its gold sales to at least 1½ million ounces monthly, beginning in December.

The currency mobilization measures will be described in more detail, and Under Secretary Solomon is here to answer any questions. We'll have a brief break so that you can digest this and give you a few minutes, and then we'll go into the details of it.

The fact is that the foreign exchange situation that this program is designed to correct has gotten out of hand. It must end, and it will end. The dollar's deterioration has already led to a rise in import competitive prices, which further fuels inflation and perpetuates a vicious cycle. And the image of the American economy and its leadership is adversely affected by this.

We feel that failure to act now would be injurious to the American and to the world economy. Our economy is strong. Steps have been taken to strengthen it further, and the fundamental economic conditions and growth trends in the four nations that are a party to this agreement are moving toward a better international balance.

Assisted by the actions we have now announced, this will provide an improved framework for a restoration of more stable exchange markets and the correction of the recent excessive exchange rate movements.

Thank you very much.

NOTE: The President spoke at 9 a.m. to reporters assembled in the Briefing Room at the White House.

Following Secretary Blumenthal's remarks, Anthony M. Solomon, Under Secretary of the Treasury for Monetary Affairs, and he held a news conference on the Treasury Department and Federal Reserve System measures.

White House Forum on Inflation

Remarks and a Question-and-Answer Session by Telephone With Participants in the Forum in St. Louis, Missouri. November 1, 1978

AMBASSADOR STRAUSS. Charlie, may I interrupt you now and ask if you would take your seat. President Carter is coming to the phone now and is just on the phone. Good morning, Mr. President.

THE PRESIDENT. Good morning, Bob. How's the meeting going so far?

AMBASSADOR STRAUSS. Well, Mr. President, I'm joined here by Charlie Schultze and Ray Marshall and Fred Kahn and Lee Kling, Esther Peterson, and probably a thousand people here under the sponsorship of the Regional Commerce and Growth Association in St. Louis. And we're going to have a good day, Mr. President. Everyone here is optimistic and everyone is—well, they've got the kind of looks on their face you'd like to see. [*Laughter*]

THE PRESIDENT. Bob, that's good to hear.

I think everyone knows that we've had excellent response so far from our anti-inflation effort, following up a very successful first 20 months in getting the unemployment rate down. I noticed that in St. Louis, for instance, the unemployment rate has gone down at least 25 percent. And we look on that great city as a model for good labor-management relations and a strong center for business locations that affect not only our country but the entire world.

But we've had inflation preying upon our American economy now for 10 years with an average inflation rate of 6½ percent, and of course, it's gotten worse in recent years. And I finally decided that we needed to move in a bold and aggressive way throughout this country to recruit volunteers to help me fight inflation.

The Congress has done a good job. We've been able to cut the unemployment rate on the one hand, but also we've cut taxes drastically, $28 billion, and also cut the deficit down by $25 billion in the brief period of time I've been in office.

We had two basic decisions that we could have made. One was to impose Federal mandatory wage and price controls throughout the free enterprise system, which I think would be a very bad thing to do and which I do not intend to do; and secondly, to deliberately create a recession, which would throw millions of people out of work. This is what did occur shortly before I became President. But as I announced the other night, we chose instead to invoke a series of voluntary actions by both business and labor, hoping to recruit as many Americans as possible to join in a crusade.

I'm determined, Bob, and everybody there, to make this program work. It will be my top responsibility on domestic affairs in the months ahead. I do not intend to see it fail. We have an excellent team committed to make it work, not only in our own administration but throughout the Congress and the Government, and we've had good response from responsible labor leaders and also from the rank and file of workers throughout our country as well as the business community.

I might say that I'll do my share or more. I've pledged to cut the Federal deficit further, which we will do. I've pledged to freeze Federal employment, only filling one out of two vacancies that occur. We will have lower Federal employment in the future. I've pledged to cut down substantially the percent of the gross national product of our Nation that the Federal Government spends and to cut down unnecessary regulations and the cost of regulation itself without causing a deterioration in the quality of our own lives.

I think the only chance this program has to work is for it to be an extended, deep, permanent commitment by a wide range of groups. It has to be a nationwide, team effort. We're not going to have immediate success. Trends are in the right direction, however.

I think we have taken bold action this morning to sustain the value of the dollar in international markets, and I believe that this will have a beneficial effect in controlling inflation. It was a difficult decision for me to make, but I have no doubt that it was the right decision to make. And it's typical of the kind of action that is going to be taken regardless of political consequences to control inflation in our country.

I would like to add once more, before I take questions, Bob, that I need from everyone assembled in St. Louis and, in fact, throughout the country, not just a nodding of one's head and saying, "This is a good program; we hope it works," but I need active support. I need positive support. And I need well-publicized support from all the leaders that are assembled there together with you.

And I hope that this first meeting of its kind in St. Louis will act as a pattern for us to copy throughout the country and as a massive demonstration of American support for a much needed and effective program to control inflation in our Nation.

Now, Bob, I'd like to take questions that anyone there might have.

AMBASSADOR STRAUSS. Mr. President, thank you very much.

To be certain that we secured representative questions, Mr. President, we have asked three people to participate in this part of it. The first gentleman from whom you will hear is Mr. Robert Kelly, who's president of the St. Louis Labor Council, AFL–CIO. Mr. Kelly not only has a question, Mr. President, but Mr. Kelly this morning advised Lee Kling and me that he also had a statement that he wished to make. And I now will ask Mr. Kelly to proceed. Bob Kelly.

MR. KELLY. Mr. President, first let me thank you for trying to tackle this very huge problem.

Yesterday the executive council of the AFL–CIO expressed a number of concerns with your proposed plan to halt inflation. The officers of the St. Louis Labor Council, along with you and the executive council, do agree that inflation is our number one enemy. We in St. Louis also share many of the same concerns voiced by the executive council in Washington. Yet the executive council does not determine the collective bargaining goals of the affiliated unions in Missouri. In the final analysis, the members of our public and private sector unions who will negotiate contracts over the next year must determine for themselves what they need to provide food, housing, energy, medical care for their members and families.

In St. Louis we've already proven that we can work in harmony with industry to the mutual benefit of the community. As a result of this reasonableness shown on both sides of the bargaining table, you will find that our recent contract settlements here have on an average already come well within your suggested wage guidelines.

If industry will do its share to hold down the prices at or below the guidelines in levels in the future, we in the area labor movement have already demonstrated that we will hold up our end of the bargaining on the wage side.

Now, my question is twofold: Your program calls for all Americans to make a sacrifice, and particularly on workers to bite the bullet on their wage requests and businessmen to limit their price hikes. What most workers would like to know, however, is what assurance you have that prices and that the other factors that cause inflation can be controlled. And second, judging from the press reports of Congressmen's negative reaction to your safety-valve tax credit program, what are the realistic chances of congressional approval of that plan?

THE PRESIDENT. Mr. Kelly, that's a very fine statement, and I appreciate what you had to say.

We got about as much support for our program from Mr. Meany as we had anticipated. We knew that he preferred mandatory wage and price controls, which I do not intend to implement. But he also said that he was willing to cooperate and, of course, was not demanding that the international unions refuse to cooperate with our voluntary program. And I believe that there will be a growing cooperation, not only as you've already demonstrated in Missouri but throughout the country, from the working people of our Nation and also, of course, the organized labor movement itself.

It's my responsibility to carry out my part of the bargain, Mr. Kelly, and this is in answer to your question. I don't intend

to violate any of the commitments that I made in my speech last week. We will cut down the Federal deficit. We will maintain a commitment to good programs for the American people. We will protect the interests of the average consumer and the average working person in our Nation. We will eliminate waste. We will make sure we have adequate regulation, but without unnecessary burdens that would cause jobs to leave our country and without causing the price of American products to go up.

The first proof of acceptance, of course, will come from the business community. We are in the process now of contacting the 500 largest employers in our Nation to get them to agree to comply with the standards that we've prescribed, which is roughly 5¾-percent increase on an average in prices, but one-half percentage point below the average increase in price for the last 2 years. And I think that as we go along, as contracts are negotiated by labor, you will be able to see the degree of compliance by the business community itself.

I'm very determined that the Congress will pass the real wage insurance program that I advocated. My own assessment of the telephone calls that we've made to key Congress Members has been very positive. This will be a top priority of ours, and I believe the Congress will realize that one of the bases on which we can have success in controlling inflation is to give workers a guarantee that they will not lose if they comply with the 7-percent guideline standard. And I don't believe Congress will fail, because there's a general, broad support in our country for controlling inflation.

This will be a very simple request to the Congress. We will have the legislation drafted before the Congress goes into session in January. It will be thoroughly discussed with the key Members of Congress and individual Members before the Congress convenes, and I think I can assure you that we will be successful in getting this legislation passed to be an insurance program for real wages for American workers who comply with our standards.

Mr. KELLY. Thank you, Mr. President.

AMBASSADOR STRAUSS. Thank you, Mr. Kelly.

And now, Mr. President, the next gentleman from whom we will hear is one of America's most distinguished business leaders, a man you know, Hal Dean, chairman of the board of Ralston-Purina, and who's president of the City Progress Association of Missouri. Hal, would you stand up when you ask your question, please?

Mr. DEAN. Good morning, Mr. President.

THE PRESIDENT. Good morning, Mr. Dean. It's good to hear from you.

Mr. DEAN. Thank you very much. I know you've had a busy morning. We would like to say thank you for choosing St. Louis yourself, and your administration coming out here and saying hello to us.

I certainly applaud Bob Kelly's remarks. I cannot speak for all of the business leaders of either St. Louis or the country, but I can assure you that I know the character of the business leaders of St. Louis, and we are going to cooperate with you on your program. And I can say for my own company that you will receive complete cooperation.

You have consistently said that our problems of inflation did not have single nor short-term solutions. Mr. Bill Miller, head of the Federal Reserve System, has also advocated the necessity of the longer range approach. He has outlined a specific 8-point program dealing with what I feel are basic and fundamental issues. He addresses fiscal and monetary restraints, including the ultimate balancing of the Federal budget, regaining productivity by encouraging capital formation, reducing the role of government in our economy, restricting present burgeoning regulatory issues, and becoming less dependent on foreign energy.

My question: Do you agree that these corrective actions, approached forcefully and consistently, will be successful in bringing inflation under control, and can you politically stand behind such a program?

THE PRESIDENT. The answer to both your questions is yes. I'd like to go down and explain very briefly each one of those items I jotted down hastily as you asked your question.

Fiscal and monetary responsibility is very important to me. I believe the action that we've taken this morning to sustain the value of the dollar will be well received in international markets and also in domestic markets as well. We have a need to keep the dollar strong. We're not going to try to fix an exchange rate and hold to it, but we want to eliminate aberrations in the international markets. My own belief is that the dollar is now undervalued. We have not yet benefited in our foreign exchange adequately from a lower priced dollar, but this will come along.

Fiscal responsibility in budgeting is something that I've espoused over and over, and I think we've already proven it by lowering the Federal deficit by the end of the budget I'm preparing now, more than 50 percent below what it was when I was running for President.

Secondly, I want to reduce the percentage of the gross national product spent by the Federal Government. This answers two parts of Bill Miller's standards. One is that we have fiscal responsibility. The other one is that we keep Government's nose out of the affairs of the free enterprise system and individual persons' decisions as much as possible.

On deregulation, I think that Alfred Kahn, who's with you this morning, has shown vividly that to utilize the free enterprise system in a highly competitive way, as it's designed to be and as it ought to be, is a very beneficial thing, not only for the consumers of our Nation but also to control inflation in general and also to provide higher profits for well-managed and competitive industries.

The budget that I'm preparing for 1980 will be a tight one. It will be adequate. I think part of it, as I've described publicly in my directives to all agencies, is that we need to increase productivity. One means for that, as you well know, being the head of a major corporation that's used this effectively, is in research and development. And I have directed in the preparation of the 1980 fiscal year budget that basic research and in research and development in general should not be reduced as a percentage of the total Federal budget.

Regulation, unnecessarily, is a very great and costly burden on American business, on our economic society. We've now got a council of regulators. I appointed a Chairman yesterday, Doug Costle, and they will make sure that regulations are actually needed, that unnecessary ones are eliminated, that they be simple, nonintrusive, and that whenever one is issued to protect the quality of Americans' lives, which is very important, that we have a very careful assessment of the economic cost.

On energy, the Congress has finally passed, after an excessive delay, the basic elements of our energy plan. We will continue to improve upon it as time goes on, and I think you will see in the coming weeks that our administrative actions based on the law that now gives us this authority will be very forceful in cutting down the imports of oil.

I might point out that the tardiness of the Congress action may result in high import levels of oil in this particular quarter, but this is an action on the part of our importers that can be corrected and will be corrected in the future.

So, Bill Miller's basic thrust in fiscal responsibility in all its elements are feasible. They are the kind of commitments that I have undertaken. I think the Congress itself, Democrats and Republicans, liberals and conservatives, agree that we've got to comply with these basic premises in order to control inflation, to keep our economy growing, to keep people's jobs intact, and to give us a vigorous influence around the world as the great strength of our country warrants.

Mr. Dean, I want to thank you again for your question and a chance to answer those specific elements of it.

MR. DEAN. Thank you, Mr. President.

AMBASSADOR STRAUSS. Mr. President, the final question will come from Mr. William E. Douthit, who is president of the Urban League of St. Louis. Mr. Douthit, will you please ask your question?

MR. DOUTHIT. Mr. President, as we all know, inflation hurts the poor and the unemployed more than anyone. And your program calling for wage and price restraints confronts, in my opinion, the excess money side of the inflation equation. On the other side we need to increase production and put more people to work. Under your program, what incentives does business have to do this?

THE PRESIDENT. Well, I think for business, Mr. Douthit, to have an assurance of stability in the future, the value of the dollar, sustained economic growth, responsible government actions, increased opportunity for exports, these kinds of assurances to business are the best guarantees that we will have investments in new equipment, new factories, new jobs, and higher productivity that would ensure success for all our efforts.

In the past, I think there's been too much doubt in the business community about the attitude of government, about the sustained growth, about research and development, about export opportunities, about excessive imports of fuel, about stable prices of fuel, higher productivity in our country of fuel—these kinds of questions are the ones that we've tried to address already since I've been in office with the full cooperation of the Congress.

The sustaining of the value of the dollar is also a very important element, because as you know, when the dollar decreases in value overseas, the indirect but very predictable consequence of this is a higher inflation rate here at home. And this is a combination that's very complicated. Although the Federal Reserve is an absolutely independent agency, I can tell you that there's a very close coordination between the Congress leaders in tax policy, between the executive branch of Government, represented primarily by the President, and by Bill Miller, who's the Chairman of the Federal Reserve. And we have a commitment to keep these three branches of Government independent, but we do coordinate our efforts and we share responsibilities and we share problems.

So, I think that it's important that we have this sustained, constant, long-range commitment with a maximum degree of harmony within the government itself. I'm sure of that.

What we need now is a public profession of support from the hundreds of business and labor leaders throughout the country that can either make or break this program. I'm determined as President to make it successful, to make it succeed. Our country needs it. The American people support it.

And it was no accident that we chose St.

Louis as the place for this first conference on inflation, because you are the center for nationwide distribution systems, you're the headquarters for some of our most important corporations. And I think the relationship there between labor and management has been very good in the past, setting example for the rest of the country.

The question that you asked is a good one, and I think that the answer is that we can succeed in controlling inflation if we all cooperate. I'm determined as President to provide that leadership. I have no doubt that the Congress, labor, business, and the American public will support it.

I want to again express my thanks to Bob Strauss, for the members of my own team who are there with the St. Louis leaders, and hope that this example, having been set in St. Louis, will be followed throughout the country.

I believe we've got an opportunity now to capitalize on the tremendous economic strength of our country to solve this serious but, I believe, transient problem of inflation if we all work together. And I have no doubt that we will work together in the true spirit of Americans who are willing to sacrifice special advantage for the benefit of our country.

Thank you very much, Bob, and everybody who's assembled there.

AMBASSADOR STRAUSS. Thank you, Mr. President. Thank you.

NOTE: The President spoke at 10:30 a.m. from the Oval Office at the White House to the forum being held at the Alfonso J. Cervantes Convention Center.

Also participating in the forum were Ambassador Robert S. Strauss, Special Representative for Trade Negotiations, Charles L. Schultze, Chairman of the Council of Economic Advisers, Secretary of Labor Ray Marshall, Alfred E. Kahn, Advisor to the President on Inflation, S. Lee Kling, Assistant Special Counselor on Inflation, and Esther Peterson, Special Assistant to the President for Consumer Affairs.

Education Amendments of 1978 and the Middle Income Student Assistance Act

Remarks at the Bill Signing Ceremony.
November 1, 1978

THE PRESIDENT. It took me all morning to read this bill. [*Laughter*]

It's a great pleasure for me to take part in this ceremony of recognizing a historic achievement on the part of the Congress.

In 1965 I was a State senator in Georgia, very interested in education, and I was invited to meet with the Secretary of HEW in the final preparation of the 1965 Elementary and Secondary Education Act and the Higher Education Act.

I think more than any other Congress in history, perhaps even including those who served in 1965, this Congress has been the most education minded and has done the most in dollar terms for education in our country. The totality of what has been accomplished in these two bills is very difficult to assess, certainly in a brief period of time.

It opens up aid to the most disadvantaged children, more than 2 million additional children who live in very poor neighborhoods or whose families suffer from poverty or deprivation will be aided by this legislation. The legislation also emphasizes additional progress in the basic skills, the ability to read, to write, and to perform mathematical problems.

I think this opens up a way also to enhance the already improving interrelationship between the Federal, State, and local governments in the administration and the support, financially, of the American education system. There is no encroachment in these bills by the Federal Government into the administration or decisionmaking process of the local school system. We've been careful about that.

There's an increased ability in budget-ing to remove the abuses in the so-called Impact Aid legislation that has been on the books for too long and which heavily favors some undeserving communities at the expense of others.

There's a substantial reduction available now to reduce paperwork by simplification of administration of grant programs and by reducing the reporting required and still leaving accountability intact.

We have made major steps forward in bilingual education, long overdue progress, and improving the educational opportunities of Native Americans, American Indians, and providing additional assistance in guaranteeing the educational rights of women.

Again, within the bounds of other laws and constitutional provisions, this legislation will provide an additional emphasis and impetus to the desegregation of our schools to remove deprivation of human rights, of basic civil rights. And there's additional aid available in this legislation also for students who attend private schools.

I would like to point out that in the legislation concerning middle-income student assistance relating to the colleges, this legislation is completely compatible with the recommendations made by me to the Congress earlier this year. I'm very grateful that it has materialized in this fine fashion. It provides substantially increased student aid for students from low- and middle-income families, increases the income level of families that are eligible for loans, provides additional guarantees of interest to be paid by the Federal Government for students who are still in college, and expands the college students who are covered by a net increase of 2 million.

I'm particularly grateful to the Members of Congress who played the leadership role in this major effort. I won't try to mention them all, but I would like to mention especially Senator Williams, Senator Pell, who's here, Congressman Carl Perkins, Congressman Ford, and others who have worked in a yeoman fashion to make this success possible.

I'd also like to thank Joe Califano and Mary Berry and Commissioner Boyer [1] for the good work they did on behalf of my own administration.

The students of America, of all ages, can benefit greatly from this new legislation. It encompasses a total of about $12 billion in additional aid focused particularly among those who need it most, from the pre-elementary grades, all the way up through college. And I want to express on behalf of the American people my thanks to all who have been responsible for making this success possible.

Thank you very much, everyone.

[*At this point, the President signed the bills.*]

I'd like to ask Claiborne Pell if he has a comment to make. Do you favor the legislation? [*Laughter*]

SENATOR PELL. I think it will do exactly what you say and will mean there's no reason why any American youngster feels that he cannot achieve higher education because of financial reasons, providing he can cut the mustard and is willing to extend himself.

Thank you.

THE PRESIDENT. Joe, would you like to comment?

SECRETARY CALIFANO. Mr. President, I think it makes you a great education President. This is the largest increase in the history of elementary and secondary education aid since the program began, and for the first time in the history of this

country, every single student who can get into college is eligible for a loan to help him or her get through college. And I think that just puts your brand on education the way it is in your bones. So, I think it's great.

THE PRESIDENT. Thank you. Does anyone else have a comment? Bill?

REPRESENTATIVE FORD. Thank you, Mr. President. I recall when you announced the initiative on the higher education legislation here at the White House. There were many people across the country who said that it was much too ambitious, that it couldn't be done, that the Congress would not respond well. I think it speaks very well of your leadership and the way in which you were able to convince the Congress that the time had come to make this bold step, that this legislation you now sign is the largest single infusion of higher education money for middle-income and working-class families since the G.I. bill at the end of World War II.

And I agree with Joe Califano. I was here in 1965, as he was. We thought that we would never again see a Congress like that. This Congress in response to your leadership will go down among other things as a great education Congress, and your name in the books for all of history in education is certainly assured.

THE PRESIDENT. Thank you for those comments.

I might say in closing that there's been a great deal of publicity given to the lack of passage, absence of passage of the tuition tax credits. This was a proposal that I personally did not favor. I think the Congress acted wisely in this respect. This provides a much greater benefit to college students who need it most. It's a carefully balanced program, and I think the benefits to be derived, compared to the dollars spent from the Federal Treasury, are greatly an improvement over what was proposed as an alternative.

[1] Mary F. Berry, Assistant Secretary for Education, and Ernest L. Boyer, Commissioner of Education, Department of Health, Education, and Welfare.

But the sum total of this largest appropriation since the program began for elementary and secondary education, and the greatest improvement in history for college student loans and grants, is a notable step, and again, let me thank all of you for making this possible. I'm very proud to be part of it.

Thank you very much.

NOTE: The President spoke at 2:05 p.m. in the State Dining Room at the White House.

As enacted, H.R. 15, the Education Amendments of 1978, is Public Law 95–561, and S. 2539, the Middle Income Student Assistance Act, is Public Law 95–566, both approved November 1.

Education Amendments of 1978 and the Middle Income Student Assistance Act

Statement on Signing H.R. 15 and S. 2539 Into Law. November 1, 1978

In early 1978 I proposed several major initiatives for education: a record $12.4 billion budget request for the Office of Education programs—a 17-percent increase over the previous year—including an additional $1.4 billion in our college student aid programs; and major legislative proposals.

Today I am pleased and proud to be able to join with my colleagues from the Congress and friends from the education community and sign into law the Education Amendments of 1978 and the Middle Income Student Assistance Act. Combined with the appropriations bill for fiscal 1979 I signed earlier this month, these bills represent an historic expansion of Federal assistance to education.

The administration's proposals for the reauthorization of the Elementary and Secondary Education Act of 1965 were intended to reaffirm and strengthen our commitment to equal educational opportunity for disadvantaged children; to ensure mastering the basic skills of reading, writing, and mathematics; to forge a new Federal, State, and local partnership; to achieve increased budget control over Impact Aid; to reduce excessive paperwork; and to address the unique educational needs of bilingual, American Indian, and female students; to aid desegregation of school systems; and to increase aid to private school children, especially through Federal programs for instructional materials, compensatory and bilingual education.

To my great pleasure, the amendments include the major proposals which we made to Congress last February, in particular, the new Title I provisions for supplemental funds to school districts with large numbers or proportions of children from poor families, and matching grants to stimulate States to establish compensatory education programs. As a result, more than 7 million disadvantaged children—almost 2 million more than last year—will be served.

The Middle Income Student Assistance Act, which I am also signing today, is similar to the G.I. bill as a landmark in the Federal commitment to aid families with college students. Responding to my original proposals to the Congress, this bill provides more generous Basic Educational Opportunity Grant—Pell grants—to low-income students, and makes eligible students from families with income up to about $25,000. An additional 1.5 million students from middle-income families will be eligible for the Basic Grants program.

The bill also expands the Guaranteed Student Loan program so that the Government will pay interest for *any* student eligible for a federally guaranteed loan of up to $2,500 per year while the student is still in college.

The expanded commitments to education represented by these two bills fully support the assertion that this has been the most education-minded Congress since the midsixties. This year with the help of education and parent associations, we have together taken an historic step in the evolution of the Federal role in education.

The Nation is deeply indebted to the work of the members of the Senate Human Resources Committee-Education Subcommittee and the House Education and Labor Committee-Education subcommittees. In particular, I wish to extend my personal thank you to Senators Williams and Pell, Congressmen Perkins and Ford, and to Secretary Califano, Assistant Secretary Mary Berry, and Commissioner of Education Ernest Boyer for the bills I am signing today.

NOTE: As enacted, H.R. 15, the Education Amendments of 1978, is Public Law 95–561, and S. 2539, the Middle Income Student Assistance Act, is Public Law 95–566, both approved November 1.

Small Business Conference Commission

Executive Order 12091. November 1, 1978

By the authority vested in me as President by the Constitution of the United States of America, and in order to increase the membership and alter the functions of the Small Business Conference Commission, it is hereby ordered that Sections 1–101, 1–201, 1–204 and 1–402 of Executive Order No. 12061 of May 18, 1978, are amended to read as follows:

"1–101. There is established a Small Business Conference Commission. The Commission shall be composed of eleven members.",

"1–201. The Commission shall provide advice with respect to the holding of a White House Conference on Small Business to be held in early 1980.",

"1–204. Prior to the White House Conference on Small Business, the Administrator of the Small Business Administration shall hold open regional and local meetings or conferences. These open meetings shall seek to identify the specific issues which should be addressed at the Conference and shall solicit candidates for Conference delegates. The Commission shall review the issues addressed at these regional and local meetings.", and

"1–402. The Commission shall terminate on April 30, 1980, or 60 days after the conclusion of the White House Conference on Small Business, whichever is sooner.".

JIMMY CARTER

The White House,
　　November 1, 1978.

[Filed with the Office of the Federal Register,
　　4:43 p.m., November 1, 1978]

Federal Anti-Inflationary Procurement Practices

Executive Order 12092. November 1, 1978

PROHIBITION AGAINST INFLATIONARY
PROCUREMENT PRACTICES

By the authority vested in me as President and as Commander in Chief of the Armed Forces by the Constitution and statutes of the United States of America, including Sections 2(c) and 3(a) of the Council on Wage and Price Stability Act, as amended (12 U.S.C. 1904 note) and Section 205(a) of the Federal Property and Administrative Services Act of 1949, as amended (40 U.S.C. 486(a)), and in order to encourage noninflationary pay and price behavior by private industry and labor, and to provide for the procurement by Executive agencies and Military Departments of personal property and services at prices and wage rates which are noninflationary, it is hereby ordered as follows:

1–101. The Chairman of the Council on Wage and Price Stability shall:

(a) Monitor company pay and price practices in order to determine compliance with the standards set forth in Section 1–102 of this Order;

(b) Promulgate regulations and guidance to further define these standards, and provide for appropriate exemptions and exceptions;

(c) Publish, or cause to be published, in accordance with procedures designed to ensure fairness and due process, the names of individuals or companies which are not in compliance with the standards;

(d) Promulgate procedures to be used in proceedings before the Council on matters pertaining to the standards, and take such other action as may be necessary and consistent with the purposes of this Section.

1–102. Noninflationary wage and price behavior shall be measured by the following standards:

(a) For prices, noninflationary price behavior is the deceleration by companies of their current rate of average price increase by at least 0.5 percentage points from their historical rate of annual price increase during 1976–1977 except where profits have not increased.

(b) For pay, noninflationary pay behavior is the holding of pay increases to not more than 7 percent annually above their recent historical levels.

(c) These standards, which shall be further defined by the Chairman of the Council on Wage and Price Stability, shall be subject to certain limitations and exemptions as determined by the Chairman.

1–103. In order to ensure economy and efficiency in government procurement, the head of each Executive agency and Military Department shall ensure that their contracts incorporate, on and after January 1, 1979, a clause which requires compliance by the contractor, and by his subcontractors and suppliers, with the standards set forth in Section 1–102 of this Order.

1–104. Each Executive agency and each Military Department shall comply with the directions of the Administrator for Federal Procurement Policy, who, in accord with Section 6 of the Office of Federal Procurement Policy Act (41 U.S.C. 405), shall be responsible for the overall direction of the implementation of Section 1–103 including the issuance of regulations and procedures for determining exceptions and granting exemptions.

JIMMY CARTER

The White House,
    November 1, 1978.

[Filed with the Office of the Federal Register, 4:49 p.m., November 1, 1978]

President's Commission on the Holocaust

Executive Order 12093.   November 1, 1978

By virtue of the authority vested in me as President by the Constitution of the United States of America, and in order to create, in accordance with the provisions of the Federal Advisory Committee Act (5 U.S.C. App. I), an advisory committee on the establishment of a memorial to the victims of the Holocaust, it is hereby ordered as follows:

1–1. *Establishment and Membership.*

1–101. There is established the President's Commission on the Holocaust.

1–102. The Commission shall consist of not more than thirty-four members as follows:

(a) The President shall appoint twenty-four members of the Commission and shall designate one of these members to chair the Commission.

(b) The Speaker of the House of Representatives and the President of the Senate are each invited to designate five members of their respective Houses to serve as members of the Commission.

1–2. *Functions of the Commission.*

1–201. The Commission shall submit a report to the President and the Secretary of the Interior containing its recommendations with respect to the establishment and maintenance of an appropriate memorial to those who perished in the Holocaust.

1–202. The Commission's report shall examine the feasibility of obtaining funds for creation and maintenance of the Memorial through contributions by the American people.

1–203. The Commission shall recommend appropriate ways for the nation to commemorate April 28 and 29, 1979, which the Congress has resolved shall be "Days of Remembrance of Victims of the Holocaust."

1–3. *Administrative Provisions.*

1–301. To the extent permitted by law, the Secretary of the Interior shall provide all necessary administrative services, facilities, support, and funds necessary for the performance of the Commission's functions.

1–302. Each member of the Commission who is not otherwise employed in the Government may receive compensation for each day such member is engaged in the work of the Commission at a daily rate to be determined by the Secretary of

the Interior. Such rate shall not exceed that payable pursuant to the Federal Advisory Committee Act.

1–303. Members of the Commission shall be entitled to travel expenses, including per diem in lieu of subsistence, as authorized by law (5 U.S.C. 5702 and 5703) for persons in the Government service employed intermittently.

1–304. The functions of the President under the Federal Advisory Committee Act which are applicable to the Commission, except that of reporting to the Congress, shall be performed by the Secretary of the Interior in accordance with guidelines and procedures prescribed by the Administrator of General Services.

1–4. *Final Report and Termination*

1–401. The Commission shall submit its final report to the President and the Secretary of the Interior not later than six months from the date of its first meeting.

1–402. The Commission shall terminate not later than thirty days after submitting its final report.

Jimmy Carter

The White House,
   November 1, 1978.

[Filed with the Office of the Federal Register,
   4:50 p.m., November 1, 1978]

Office of Management and Budget

Recess Appointment of John P. White as Deputy Director. November 1, 1978

The President today announced the recess appointment of John P. White as Deputy Director of the Office of Management and Budget. White was nominated October 7, 1978, but was not confirmed by the Senate before they adjourned.

White, 40, had been Assistant Secretary of Defense for Manpower, Reserve Affairs and Logistics. Prior to joining the Defense Department in 1977, he was with the Rand Corporation.

Contract Disputes Act of 1978

Statement on Signing H.R. 11002 Into Law. November 1, 1978

I am pleased today to sign H.R. 11002, the Contract Disputes Act of 1978. This is landmark legislation in at least two respects.

First, it provides for the first time a uniform statutory base for the resolution of claims and disputes arising in connection with Federal contracts. The previous process was a mass of confusing and sometimes conflicting agency regulations, judicial decisions, decisions of agency boards of contract appeals, and statutes. This act will provide a much more logical and flexible means of resolving contract disputes. It should lead to savings for Federal agencies and their contractors.

Second, apart from the creation of the Office of Federal Procurement Policy in 1974, it represents the first enactment into law of major recommendations of the Commission on Government Procurement.

I particularly would like to recognize the hard and effective work of Senator Lawton Chiles and Congressman Herb Harris in getting this legislation enacted. Senator Chiles was also a member of the Commission on Government Procurement and was, therefore, instrumental in the creation of the system reflected in this act.

NOTE: As enacted, H.R. 11002 is Public Law 95–563, approved November 1.

Special Pay for Sea Duty

Executive Order 12094. November 1, 1978

By the authority vested in me as President and as Commander in Chief of the Armed Forces of the United States of America by sections 305, 305a and 403 of title 37 of the United States Code and in order to implement increased rates of special pay for enlisted personnel serving on sea duty, it is hereby ordered as follows:

1–101. Executive Order No. 11157, as amended, is further amended by revising Part II thereof to read as follows:

"PART II—SPECIAL PAY FOR SEA DUTY AND DUTY AT CERTAIN PLACES

"Sec. 201. Provided they have over three cumulative years of sea duty, enlisted members of a uniformed service who are in pay grade E–4 or above and who are entitled to receive basic pay shall be entitled to receive, additionally, career sea pay while on sea duty. The period of sea duty shall include the date of reporting and the date of detachment as stated in orders. Career sea pay shall be at the rates prescribed in section 305a of title 37, United States Code.

"Sec. 202. (a) For the purpose of entitlement to career sea pay, the term "sea duty" shall mean duty performed by enlisted members:

"(1) while permanently assigned for duty to a vessel, ship-based staff, or ship-based aviation unit pursuant to orders issued by competent authority and serving in a ship whose primary mission is accomplished underway, including—

"i. periods not to exceed the first 30 consecutive days of temporary additional duty ashore; and

"ii. periods not to exceed the first 90 days during which messing or berthing facilities, or both, are temporarily out of service in order to permit alterations or repairs.

"(2) while temporarily assigned for duty to a vessel, ship-based staff, or ship-based aviation unit pursuant to orders issued by competent authority and serving in a ship whose primary mission is accomplished underway. The period of service shall include periods not to exceed the first 30 consecutive days of further temporary additional duty ashore from the ship.

"(3) while permanently or temporarily assigned for duty to a vessel or ship-based staff pursuant to orders issued by a competent authority and serving in a ship whose primary mission is accomplished in port, but only during periods while the ship is away from its home port for at least 30 consecutive days.

"(b) For the purpose of this section, the word "vessel" or "ship" shall mean a self-propelled vessel that is in an active status, in commission or in service and is equipped with berthing and messing facilities.

"Sec. 203. The Secretaries concerned (within the meaning of section 101(5) of title 37, United States Code) with respect to personnel of the uniformed service within their respective departments, are hereby authorized to prescribe such supplementary regulations, not inconsistent herewith, as they may deem necessary or desirable for carrying out the provisions of sections 305 and 305a of title 37 and this Executive Order. Such regulations shall be uniform for all the services to the fullest extent possible.

"Sec. 204. Enlisted members entitled to receive basic pay shall be entitled to receive, additionally, pay at the rates prescribed by section 305(a) of title 37 of the United States Code while on duty at places that are outside the 48 contiguous States and the District of Columbia and that are designated for this purpose by the Secretary of Defense or, in the case of

enlisted members of the Coast Guard when it is not operating as a service in the Navy, by the Secretary of Transportation. Subject to provisions of section 305 of title 37 of the United States Code, an enlisted member who is permanently assigned to duty at a place so designated is entitled to receive that pay during a period of authorized leave, temporary additional duty, temporary duty, or hospitalization or while on an operational aircraft flight, but not more than 30 days while he is away from that place. Enlisted members shall be entitled to special pay under this section when attached to ships undergoing repair and overhaul in designated foreign-duty areas for extended periods when entitlement to special pay for sea duty has been terminated. Such enlisted members shall be entitled to special pay for sea duty under the same conditions as an enlisted member on temporary additional duty or temporary duty in that designated foreign-duty area.

"Sec. 205. Unless otherwise entitled to special pay in accord with the second sentence of section 204 hereof, during periods spent on temporary additional duty or temporary duty or on operational aircraft flights, pay in accord with section 204 shall accrue to enlisted members only for periods of eight continuous days or more in duration at one or more places designated, including the dates of arrival at and the dates of departure from those places.

"Sec. 206. (a) No enlisted member shall be entitled under this order to receive both career sea pay and pay for duty prescribed in sections 204 and 205 hereof for the same period of time.

"(b) No enlisted member shall be entitled to receive career sea pay while in receipt of monetary allowance in lieu of rations, except during a period when messing facilities are temporarily out of operation to permit alterations or repairs not to exceed 90 days, provided such member is not authorized leave during such period."

1–102. Executive Order No. 11157, as amended, is further amended by revising section 401(c) thereof to read as follows:

"(c) The term "sea duty" shall mean service performed by either an officer or enlisted member in a self-propelled vessel that is in an active status, in commission or in service and is equipped with berthing and messing facilities."

JIMMY CARTER

The White House,
November 1, 1978

[Filed with the Office of the Federal Register, 10:21 a.m., November 2, 1978]

Emergency Board To Investigate an Airline Labor Dispute

Executive Order 12095.   November 2, 1978

CREATING AN EMERGENCY BOARD TO INVESTIGATE A DISPUTE BETWEEN WIEN AIR ALASKA, INC. AND CERTAIN INDIVIDUALS

A dispute exists between Wien Air Alaska, Inc., and certain individuals represented by the Air Line Pilots Association, a labor organization.

Section 44 of the Airline Deregulation Act of 1978 (Public Law 95–504) directed that the provisions of Section 10 of the Railway Labor Act, as amended, be invoked despite the fact that the National Mediation Board has failed to find that the dispute in its judgment substantially threatens to interrupt interstate commerce to a degree such as to deprive a section of the country of essential transportation service.

Now, THEREFORE, by the authority vested in me by Section 44 of the Airline

Deregulation Act of 1978 (Public Law 95–504) it is hereby ordered as follows:

1–101. *Establishment of Board.* There is established a board of three members to be appointed by the President to investigate this dispute. No member of the board shall be pecuniarily or otherwise interested in any organization of airline employees or any carrier.

1–102. *Report.* The board shall report its findings to the President with respect to the dispute within 30 days from the date of this Order.

JIMMY CARTER

The White House,
November 2, 1978.

[Filed with the Office of the Federal Register, 10:28 a.m., November 2, 1978]

Industry and Trade Administration

Executive Order 12096.   November 2, 1978

COMPENSATION OF CERTAIN OFFICIALS IN THE INDUSTRY AND TRADE ADMINISTRATION, DEPARTMENT OF COMMERCE

By the authority vested in me as President of the United States of America by Section 703(a) of the Defense Production Act of 1950, as amended (50 U.S.C. App. 2153(a)), it is hereby ordered as follows:

1–101. The compensation for the position of Senior Deputy Assistant Secretary for Industry and Trade, Industry and Trade Administration, Department of Commerce, is fixed at the rate now or hereafter prescribed by law for level V of the Executive Schedule (5 U.S.C. 5316).

1–102. The compensation for the position of Deputy Assistant Secretary for Trade Regulation, Bureau of Trade Regulation, Industry and Trade Administration, Department of Commerce, is fixed at the highest rate now or hereafter prescribed by law for grade 18 of the General Schedule (5 U.S.C. 5332).

1–103. The compensation for the positions of Deputy Director, Bureau of Trade Regulation, and Director, Office of Industrial Mobilization, Bureau of Trade Regulation, Industry and Trade Administration, Department of Commerce, are fixed at the highest rate now or hereafter prescribed by law for grade 17 of the General Schedule (5 U.S.C. 5332).

1–104. This order supersedes Executive Order No. 11759 of January 15, 1974.

JIMMY CARTER

The White House,
November 2, 1978.

[Filed with the Office of the Federal Register,
10:29 a.m., November 2, 1978]

Veto of the Navajo and Hopi Relocation Bill

Memorandum of Disapproval of H.R. 11092.
November 2, 1978

MEMORANDUM OF DISAPPROVAL

I am withholding my approval of H.R. 11092, the "Navajo and Hopi Relocation Amendments of 1978." I have no objection to the authorization in this bill to fund the important and difficult work being performed by the Relocation Commission to administer the partitioning of land which has been jointly used by the Navajo and Hopi Tribes. My failure to approve this bill will not affect the ability of the Commission to continue its work, because appropriations for this fiscal year have already been approved.

My objections to the bill center on section 4, which would provide for a one-house veto of the relocation plan which is finally adopted by the Relocation Com-

mission. I have previously informed the Congress of my view that such legislative veto devices are unconstitutional intrusions into the day-to-day administration of the law by the Executive Branch, including independent agencies such as the Relocation Commission. Congress is constitutionally empowered to overrule agency decisions executing the law only by enacting legislation subject to the veto power of the President under Article I, section 7 of the Constitution.

Where either Congress or the President is dissatisfied with the execution of the law by an independent agency or commission, legislation agreeable to both or enacted over the President's veto is an appropriate and constitutional means for overturning the result reached by that independent agency. If the Constitution required less, there would in fact be no true independence for agencies such as the Relocation Commission. This principle was adhered to by the Ninety-third Congress when it enacted the Navajo and Hopi Indian Relocation Commission Act in 1974 and is one from which we should not depart.

The bill also contains a provision which would oust incumbent members of the Navajo and Hopi Indian Relocation Commission if they happened to be Federal, State or local elected officials. This provision in section 2 has constitutional implications since it would allow for Congressional removal of officers in the Executive Branch. Further, as a matter of fairness and equity, interruption of the tenure of appointed officials by the imposition of new "qualifications" should not be lightly undertaken. Accordingly, I would suggest that the Ninety-sixth Congress, in any consideration of a similar bill, give due consideration to these problems.

The Administration will work with the Congress next year to develop any needed legislation to improve the operations of the Relocation Commission. The Commission needs to operate more effectively and I look forward to working with Congressional leaders such as Senator DeConcini and Congressman Udall toward this end.

JIMMY CARTER

The White House,
    November 2, 1978.

Veto of Bill Providing for Maritime Industry Relations With Federal Officials

Memorandum of Disapproval of H.R. 11861. November 2, 1978

MEMORANDUM OF DISAPPROVAL

I am withholding my signature from H.R. 11861, which would require the Secretaries of Commerce and the Navy to meet at least four times a year with representatives of the maritime industry and to submit an annual report to the President and Congress on their activities and recommendations.

Both the Maritime Administration of the Commerce Department (MARAD) and the Navy already have numerous contacts with the maritime industry and with each other to study, develop, and implement the goals of the Merchant Marine Act. Navy and MARAD are currently working to improve their cooperation in this area by adding the Secretaries of Commerce and Navy to an existing interagency advisory board on maritime matters. They are also arranging to have the board meet at least four times a year, and at least one of these meetings will be open to maritime industry representatives.

In addition, in order to assure that the concerns that generated this bill are fully addressed, I am directing both Secretaries

to consult regularly with maritime industry officials to discuss issues of mutual concern.

In light of these actions, I see no reason for this legislation. It is not necessary to achieve our goal of an adequate merchant marine. It would mandate a change in administrative functions which are currently satisfactory. It is an undue legislative intrusion into administrative activities which are the appropriate responsibility of the Executive Branch, and the required report would be an additional and unnecessary government expense. For these reasons, I am disapproving this bill.

JIMMY CARTER

The White House,
    November 2, 1978.

Veto of Bill To Establish the Legionville National Historic Site in Pennsylvania

Memorandum of Disapproval of S. 1104. November 2, 1978

MEMORANDUM OF DISAPPROVAL

I am withholding my approval from S. 1104, a bill that would authorize the establishment of the Legionville National Historic Site in the State of Pennsylvania. I am withholding my signature because I do not believe the Legionville site is of sufficient national significance to merit the cost of establishing and maintaining it as a national historic site.

The site does not meet the national significance criteria for historical areas established by the Department of the Interior. The Pennsylvania State Historic Preservation Office judged the site of only local significance. A National Park Service report made in June 1977 agreed. Further, the site has been altered by such modern intrusions as a railroad and an interstate highway.

The career of General "Mad" Anthony Wayne has been amply commemorated at other designated sites and I do not believe the added expense of acquiring and developing this site is a worthwhile expenditure of Federal funds.

JIMMY CARTER

The White House,
    November 2, 1978.

Public Telecommunications Financing Act of 1978

Statement on Signing H.R. 12605 Into Law.
November 2, 1978

I am pleased to sign the Public Telecommunications Financing Act of 1978. This bill carries out my commitment to a strong, secure public broadcasting system.

Public broadcasting has made great strides since President Johnson signed the Public Broadcasting Act of 1967, setting the framework for today's public system. The television system has grown from 124 local stations to 282 and the radio system from 93 to 215. Public television and radio have set new standards in children's programs, drama, music, science, and history. Documentaries, news analyses, and live coverage of speeches and hearings have brought government closer to the American people.

Public broadcasting has also proved itself a valuable teaching tool for both in-school and adult instruction. It has pioneered such innovations as captioning for the deaf, subchannel reading services for the visually impaired, and signal transmission by satellite.

The bill I am signing will enable public broadcasting to continue this impressive record of development and service. It accomplishes almost all the objectives I set out in my message to Congress on public broadcasting a year ago. Senators Howard Cannon and Ernest Hollings and Representatives Harley Staggers and Lionel Van Deerlin were the leaders on this bill, and I congratulate them for their hard and effective work.

In addition to extending Federal support at increasing levels through 1983, the bill makes important changes to the system:

—It revamps the facilities grant program, with the goal of extending the reach of public radio and television signals to the tens of millions of Americans who cannot receive them. The program is also opened to allow use of the most efficient technologies, including cable TV and lower power broadcast stations.

—It will increase participation of minorities and women in public broadcasting and ensure full enforcement of the laws against discrimination.

—It strengthens fiscal accountability and limits administrative overhead.

—It minimizes the involvement of the Board and staff of the Corporation for Public Broadcasting (CPB) in program selection, thereby strengthening the system's insulation from political control.

—It requires public broadcasters to operate in the sunshine, with meetings and records open to the public.

—It will increase participation by independent producers and will help them by having CPB act as a clearinghouse for information about funding sources.

—It requires CPB to initiate long-term planning for the system.

Under this bill, public broadcasting will be able to step up production of first-rate radio and television programs here in the United States. CPB has already moved to increase the proportion of funds going to this purpose toward the levels suggested in my message. Now that the bill has passed, CPB and the stations can go to work creating the institutions that will assure a constant flow of excellent, innovative programs. CPB can use multiyear grants to build up production centers to focus on such areas as news coverage, programs aimed at women and minorities, and children's programing. Such centers, along with vigorous local programing, can help continue public broadcasting's progress toward a central role in our Nation's communications system.

I do have one reservation about this bill. I regret it retains the provision forbidding public stations to editorialize. I recommended deleting that clause, because public broadcasters should have the same first amendment rights as other broadcasters.

In addition to signing the bill, I am issuing guidelines on direct grants by Federal agencies. This bill does not cover those grants, but they provide a substantial proportion of the funds available for innovative programing. The guidelines will improve coordination of these grants, help inform producers and public broadcasters about their availability, and help ensure that these funds are never used for improper political control of program content.

The public broadcasting system is constantly evolving in response to the public's needs and to the opportunities presented by new telecommunications technologies. This bill is a step in that process. The House Communications Subcommittee is already considering future steps as part of its comprehensive effort to modernize the Communications Act. I look forward to the report of the Carnegie Commission on the Future of Public Broadcasting, due this winter, to help chart public broadcasting's course for the 1980's.

NOTE: As enacted, H.R. 12605 is Public Law 95–567, approved November 2.

Reclamation Safety of Dams Act of 1978

Statement on Signing S. 2820 Into Law. November 2, 1978

I am signing today S. 2820, the Reclamation Safety of Dams Act of 1978, a bill that provides much-needed aid to preserve the structural safety of dams under the stewardship of the Bureau of Reclamation.

The act provides that the costs of construction and maintenance needed as a result of simple aging and normal deterioration will continue to be shared with beneficiaries under terms of current contracts and agreements.

I do note, however, that the bill exempts from normal cost-sharing requirements any upgrading undertaken as a result of new hydrologic or seismic data or due to changes in state-of-the-art criteria. This could apply even when a project may have vendible outputs and the beneficiaries are normally required and able to share the capital costs. I am concerned that in these cases, the Federal taxpayer is assuming a cost which is generally a normal expense for project beneficiaries.

However, dam safety is a very important matter that needs attention now. Therefore, I am signing this act.

I also believe the public interest demands that we reform cost-sharing policies for future projects. We need a more uniform and equitable balance between the Federal Government and the projects' direct beneficiaries. I announced such an initiative in my water policy message last spring, and I plan to propose to the next session of Congress a more coherent and fair policy. That proposal would ensure that the public's safety is protected, that the Federal taxpayer does not pay the entire cost of safety repairs, and that project beneficiaries pay their fair share of the costs.

NOTE: As enacted, S. 2820 is Public Law 95–578, approved November 2.

Retirement Pay for Marine Corps Sergeants Major

Statement on Signing H.R. 10343 Into Law. November 2, 1978

H.R. 10343 authorizes a change in the calculation of retirement pay for two retired Marine Corps Sergeants Major, so that they will be treated in the same manner as all other retired senior enlisted advisers of the military services. I view the bill as exceptional private relief legislation meant to remedy an anomaly in existing law and as having no precedential value. On that basis I have decided to approve the bill.

NOTE: As enacted, H.R. 10343 is Public Law 95–581, approved November 2.

New York City, New York

Remarks at a "Get Out the Vote" Rally. November 2, 1978

Governor Carey, Senator Moynihan, Mayor Koch, Lieutenant Governor Krupsak, Mario Cuomo, Members of Congress:

Thank you very much, everyone, for coming out today for a tremendous rally that is going to prove to the people of the world that the people of New York care about your own city, care about your own State, and care about this Nation by voting on November 7. Will you do that? [*Applause*] Thank you very much.

Last week I made a speech about inflation. And the next day I told Mike Blumenthal that I was coming to Wall Street for a rally, and Mike Blumenthal said, "If there's one thing that Wall Street needs, it's a rally." This is a tremendous one for people; it's a tremendous demonstration of your interest in your own government.

One thing that I'd like to say today is this: I come here as your President, as President of all the people of our country, Democrats and Republicans. One thing that has been of great concern to me in the past is the tremendous decrease in the number of people who care enough about our Nation to vote on election day. In 1960 two-thirds of the people of our country voted. Recent elections have shown that two-thirds of the people of our Nation do not vote. We live in trying times, times when public servants who are elected by you need to know that you care about our country.

I'd like for you to think back, just for a few minutes, 2 or 3 years ago when I first came to New York State, to New York City, to campaign for President. Your city was in a state of crisis. Bankruptcy was the immedate prospect for you all. When I walked the streets of your city, there was an attitude of despair; the spirit of New York was lost.

But things have changed under the dynamic leadership of a courageous man— Governor Hugh Carey. He's a man who knows how to form and to use a team based on the principles of American democracy. Working with Pat Moynihan and the congressional delegation from New York, working with Mayor Beame and now Ed Koch, Hugh Carey has let me know, as President, what I could do to help your city and to help your State.

Shortly after the election in 1976, even before I was inaugurated, Hugh Carey and your mayor came down to Georgia to talk to me and to outline in specific terms what the Congress and the President could do, if we cared, to resolve New York City's financial crisis and to put this State back on the road to prosperity.

Hugh Carey inherited a State deficit of a billion dollars. You now enjoy a State surplus of $600 million. Hugh Carey saw that taxes on your shoulders were too great. He has reduced State taxes $1.3 billion.

Hugh Carey cares about people, people of all kinds, and he's provided services to you, a strong anticrime program to make your streets and your homes safer.

Hugh Carey was concerned about the unemployment rate in this State, and the unemployment rate in the last 21 months has dropped in New York State 35 percent.

He's a Governor who believes in economic development of all kinds, all over New York, and he's a man who believes in tough, competent fiscal management. Hugh Carey is one of my staunchest allies in trying to fight against inflation.

We tried unsuccessfully this year to get a hospital cost containment bill through the Congress, because costs of hospital care have gone up twice as fast as the very high inflation rate in our Nation. I was not successful. I'm going to continue to fight next year. And a beautiful pattern for us to use in Congress is what Hugh Carey has already done in New York State.

There was 1 State among all 50 last year where the costs of hospital care went down. Do you know what State that was? New York—the only one. The next best State in holding down hospital costs had an increase of 9 percent. You, now, in your State have the lowest Medicaid cost of any State in our entire Nation.

These are the kinds of things that quite often have not been emphasized enough by Hugh Carey, who's a modest man. But we require a Democratic team, and we re-

quire the ability to work together, and particularly we need to have your trust, your confidence, and your support.

This is a very close election in prospect for you in November. Hugh Carey was in Congress 14 years. The people there trust him; they trust Ed Koch. And they know that those two men who serve you are thoroughly aware of the congressional procedures and also thoroughly aware of the needs of New York City and New York State.

I'd like to point out one other thing: We have a great population in New York of leaders from almost every nation on Earth. This is a living demonstration, in your great community of millions of people, of how basic human rights can be achieved here through good services, jobs, lower taxes, safer streets, equal opportunity, which can be used as a pattern for other nations around the world.

When I have a problem in dealing with international affairs—bringing human rights to Northern Ireland, bringing human rights and peace to the Mideast—I know that I can refer to and depend upon the advice and the counsel and support of your great Democratic Party leadership here—Hugh Carey, Ed Koch, Pat Moynihan, and others.

It's a very great influence that you enjoy in helping to guide me in making decisions that affect your own ancestors, your own relatives, in troubled areas of the world.

November 7 is a time for you to take a few minutes and to express your views of support for good leaders, particularly Hugh Carey and his good team, and also to show this country and the rest of the world that you have confidence in the future of our Nation and that you are willing to invest a small portion of your time and effort to let your voice be heard. It strengthens me in dealing with your problems to know that you care enough to vote.

I believe the best way to make sure that we have equitable and fair treatment in our country for average citizens is to make sure that on election day your voices are the ones to be heard. The voice and influence of powerful, selfish special interest groups are always heard through high-priced lawyers and very effective lobbyists.

The time for the average citizen to let your voice be heard is on election day. And I hope there will be a demonstration next Tuesday that you really care.

When I was elected President, we had 10 million Americans who were looking for a full-time job and could not find one. The unemployment rate was 8 percent. In the last 21 months we have added a net increase of 6½ million jobs and cut the unemployment rate 25 percent. If you care about this kind of progress in the future, then you yourself will vote on November 7.

I've embarked, as you know, on a tough, sometimes unpopular program to control inflation in our Nation, to stabilize the value of the dollar, to have integrity and purpose and responsible monetary policy for our country. If you care about the maintenance of this effort and the success of it, then on November 7, next Tuesday, you will vote.

We have strengthened our democratic influence around the world by bringing our allies to our side in military matters, in political matters, and—in a vivid demonstration of cooperation yesterday—in stabilizing the dollar, controlling inflation, and having a strong, growing economy in our country. If you care about our Nation having a good relationship with our allies, in meeting our own needs and their needs around the world, then on November 7, next Tuesday, you will vote.

We've got a good path laid out for ourselves. The Congress in the last few days has finally passed, for the first time, a national energy policy. Our deficits have been drastically reduced. We've got a good, sound anti-inflation program announced and making good progress.

Our trade deficits are going down. Our exports are going up. The prospect for the future looks good. If you care about this kind of progress economically, that affects every family in America, then next Tuesday, you will vote.

On economic matters—controlling inflation, having a responsible monetary policy—I mean business. I do not intend to fail, and I will not fail if you'll help me. And you can help by voting next Tuesday. Will you do that for me? [*Applause*] Thank you.

It's going to take a while. There are no easy answers. We've had too high inflation for the last 10 years. We're going to have some more high inflation before we turn the corner and get it under control. Do not be discouraged. Stick with me, stick with my program, and we will be successful.

The last thing I want to mention is this: Our country is strong. It's strong militarily, the strongest on Earth. It's going to stay that way. Our country is strong economically, the strongest on Earth. It's going to stay that way. Our country is the strongest politically in the whole Earth. It's going to stay that way. We've raised the banner of principle, of honesty, of decency, of protection for human rights. We're going to maintain that banner high. It's going to stay that way.

But the only way we can keep this strength and to make sure that we let our Nation, which is already the greatest on Earth, be even greater in the future is for you to keep a Democratic team in office and let your support be felt by voting next Tuesday. If you do, we'll be successful in carrying out our programs; you'll have a better life; our Nation will be even greater than it is today.

Thank you very much. Help us all the way I've said.

Thank you.

NOTE: The President spoke at 12:35 p.m. from the steps of the Federal Hall National Memorial. In his opening remarks, he referred to New York Secretary of State Mario M. Cuomo, Democratic candidate for Lieutenant Governor.

Following his remarks, the President attended a fundraising luncheon for Governor Carey at the Arthur Krim residence.

While at the Krim residence, the President also met with Prime Minister Menahem Begin of Israel and Secretary of State Cyrus R. Vance. Prime Minister Begin was in New York City to receive an award from the New York Council of Churches.

Flint, Michigan

Remarks at a "Get Out the Vote" Rally. November 2, 1978

Senator Don Riegle; Congressman Dale Kildee; Speaker Bobby Crim; Mayor Rutherford; your next United States Senator, Carl Levin; your next Governor, Bill Fitzgerald; and my good friends from Flint, Michigan:

It is true that almost exactly 2 years ago, at the end of a long 2-year campaign in all 50 States, Vice President Mondale and I chose this auditorium to close our campaign effort. We came here for sound reasons. Flint is a famous community, the birthplace of one of our greatest corporations—the greatest on Earth, perhaps—the epitome of what it means to be an honest, decent, hard-working American, the birthplace of enlightened labor leadership, and a place which epitomizes in the finest way what our Nation is, what our Nation has been, what our Nation can be in the future.

It was mentioned that 1960 was the year when John Kennedy was elected President and was the last year that Michigan chose a Democrat to be Governor.

In 1960 two-thirds of the American people went to the polls the first week in November to vote. The projections are that next week, two-thirds of the American people will not vote. This rally today is an opportunity for me as President of all the people of our country, Democrats and Republicans, to remind you of the great responsibility that we as Americans have to demonstrate that we are able to manage our own affairs, to run our own government, to set our own standards, to form a team, and to make a great nation even greater in the future.

Will you help me next week by electing this Democratic ticket and going out to vote? [*Applause*]

I am going to breathe a sigh of relief when Carl Levin comes to Washington as your new United States Senator.

There are many problems which I have as President of our great country. One is to fight inflation, which has been hanging over our head and putting a burden on the working people of this country for the last 10 years. This is not an easy assignment. It requires cooperation from labor, from business, from agriculture, from the private homeowner. It also requires the most intense cooperation from your own elected leadership.

Carl Levin's opponent has already discounted the effort to fight inflation. I believe that you want a United States Senator that will help me help you control inflation. Is that right? [*Applause*] Very good.

I worked hard for 2 years to be elected to this office I hold, because I wanted to be President of the United States. I cast my lot, when not 1 percent of the American people had ever heard my name, with workers in factory shift lines, with people on street corners, with elderly, retired citizens, with young students, with those who believe that our Nation could be better, could be more honest, could be more decent, could be more filled with justifiable pride than was the case 2 or 3 years ago, when our Nation had been embarrassed with the failures of a Republican administration, when our farmers were facing another recession, or even depression. Prices were down. Every month or two the Republican administration would declare an embargo against the sale of American grain products overseas. And I pledged in my campaign and never, as long as I was President, would we ever embargo the sale of American farm products to foreign markets, and we'll never do it. And we are now setting records every year in the export of farm products overseas.

We also had a problem with unemployment. When I was elected President, we had 10 million Americans who were looking for a full-time job and could not find it. Seven million Americans could not find a job at all. Congress helped me, and we set a goal for ourselves to add new jobs to the American societal structure.

Since then we have had a net increase of 6½ million new jobs. The unemployment rate is down 25 percent; in Michigan, 35 percent. It needs to come down further, and I need a United States Senator there to represent Michigan, along with Don Riegle, who wants to be Senator, who will work at it, who will help me get the inflation rate down, help me get better life for farmers and put our people back to work.

Carl Levin will not be my man. He has proven that he's a man who is not afraid to fight powerful political figures, and Carl Levin is not afraid to fight the bureaucracy. He has proven this in his own community, and he will prove it, when he gets to the Senate, for the entire State of Michigan and also for the country that we both love. It's very important to control the bureaucracy, to cut down waste, to initiate ethics, and to make sure that our public officials are honest. Carl Levin is a man who's not afraid to tackle the bureaucracy, and I need somebody that will come there and work full-time with me to bring some order out of government.

I'd like to remind you of this: Now the polls show a slight advantage for the Democratic candidate for Senate. But the last few days can make a difference. I've seen it happen over and over and over the last 2 or 3 years, when people got complacent, took a victory for granted, and the Democrats got out-spent on television, radio, billboards, telephone calls, newspapers, the last few days.

Carl Levin's opponent will spend over $2 million on his campaign for reelection. Carl Levin, as is typical with Democrats, will spend about one-third that amount.

What can make the difference? Being a better candidate? Yes. We have that advantage. But what Carl Levin needs is friends, supporters, neighbors, those who believe in a greater Michigan, who will get out and work these last 4 days in a sacrificial way and be, in effect, every one of you, a campaign manager for the Democratic ticket. If so, we'll go over the top next Tuesday night.

I'd like to tell you about two things that happened to me in the last few weeks. One was last week. I was in the State of Connecticut. When I campaigned there 2 or 3 years ago, that State was quite discouraged. Industry was moving out every week. The unemployment rate was extremely high. Connecticut has a dynamic Governor, Governor Ella Grasso. She believes that the Governorship ought to be a place for dynamism, aggression, and a hard fight day by day to make her State better. She has brought in the last year 260 new industries and cut the unemployment rate in half.

I believe Michigan is ready for that kind of dynamic and aggressive fighter as a Governor, and we have that opportunity in Bill Fitzgerald. Will you help put him in office? [*Applause*]

He's raised legitimate issues. He's interested in a highly publicized health problem. He's taken the position that's responsible and courageous. He is a man who believes that the Governor's office ought to be a place for action. He's also a man of great respect in this entire country.

Recently, I had to send a small delegation to Rome to represent me as the President and our country as a nation at the funeral of the Pope, and I chose Bill Fitzgerald to go along with my mother and just a few others to represent our Nation. This is the kind of leadership we need. This is the kind of leadership we will have next year with Bill Fitzgerald.

He told me he only made one mistake on that trip, to play poker with my mother. He should not have done it. [*Laughter*] And because his personal finances and his campaign treasury were reduced by my own mother, I hope you'll help him even more this next 4 days to win his election.

Let me close by saying that we need in Washington a strong team. We need, as we relate to you, a strong relationship between your State administration and the Democratic team in Washington. We've worked hard to bring down unemployment in our country. We've got a long way to go. We are working hard to bring down inflation, which has been with us more than 10 years. We've got a long way to go.

Yesterday, I signed two bills that give the greatest Federal aid to education in the history of our country from preschool years, elementary, secondary, and aid to college students of all ages and of all incomes. We've also sustained a rate of growth of housing construction in our country, over 2 million per year. We've been sensitive in meeting the legitimate needs of our country, but we've also brought a new concept to Washington.

The Democratic Party has always been a party of compassion, a party that recognized that we needed to extend a hand to those who are less fortunate in our society, to let them be able to stand on their own feet, to make their own decisions, to support themselves, to play a role in government, to be respected members of a community. We still have that unique characteristic which has given the Democratic Party the support for generations of the working people of this country. But we've also realized that you cannot educate a child, you cannot feed a hungry person, you cannot build a home or repair highways with waste, corruption or inefficiency.

I believe in tough management. When I was running for President, we had a Federal deficit of more than $66 billion. In giving better services to our people, we have been able to cut the deficit down already by more than $25 billion. In the budget I'm working on now, we'll cut the Federal deficit more than half, and with the help of people like Don Riegle, Carl Levin, Congressman Kildee, we are working forward in the future to having a balanced budget for the Government of the United States of America.

How can you give better services, balance the budget without raising taxes? We've been able to do it. Last year, aided by the Democratic Congress, we cut taxes by $8 billion. This next week, as soon as I get the final bill from the Congress, I will sign it to reduce income taxes another $20 billion.

So, we've been able to give better services, cut the deficit and cut taxes, a pretty good achievement if I do say so myself.

We're trying to stabilize the value of the dollar. We had great luck yesterday by taking bold action to make sure that America is economically strong, that we are not afraid to make difficult decisions, and the rest of the world cooperated with us.

We've proved in the process that our allies and our friends will sustain the United States in a common effort to balance the world economic system and give us a more stable future. The Congress has now passed for the first time in our history a national energy plan to give us adequate supplies of energy at reasonable and predictable prices, to cut down our imports of foreign fuel, let our Nation be self-sufficient, to shift us toward more plentiful supplies of fuel like coal, solar energy, to preserve the precious fuel oil, gasoline for use in mobile equipment, as is constructed in your own State, and to give homes a chance to have an adequate supply of natural gas in the future. This is a great step forward, and we will continue to make our Nation strong in itself.

I believe that we can have a government that's efficient as well. For 95 years we've had a civil service system that steadily grew more and more bureaucratic in nature and which prevented good, qualified, dedicated, hard-working civil servants from being adequately rewarded. You would have two workers sitting side by side at adjacent desks, one, as I've just described, working hard, trying to do a good job, dedicated, efficient; another one unqualified, lazy, without motivation. They both got paid exactly the same amount, exactly the same pay increases, exactly the same promotion. There was no motivation for better performance, managers could not manage.

Now we've got a new civil service reform bill. We can reward the dedicated and competent employee in the Federal Government. The other one who's not been working well, we can inspire them to do better, transfer them to a more fitting job, or discharge them if they don't work. This is what I believe is best for our

country. It's what we're going to continue to do.

I agree with the people of Michigan that we need a strong nation, not just politically, not just economically, but militarily as well. We have the strongest military defense capability on Earth. And as long as I'm in the White House, we're going to keep it that way—number one. It's going to stay that way.

We need to be strong so that we can maintain peace. This is important for our own country, yes. I'm very proud of the fact—and I hope I can go out of office still saying the same thing—that since I've been President, we've not had a single American in uniform shed blood in a foreign country. This is a notable achievement.

And it's true because we are strong, but it's also true because we are now repairing the damage that was done to our country, through the Vietnam war years, the Watergate scandals, and the revelations about the CIA. There's a new spirit in our Nation, but there's also a new respect for our Nation among the other countries of the world. We want to preserve peace for ourselves, yes, but we also believe that as long as we have a country that has a reputation for honesty, openness, decency, with a spirit and the ideals and the commitments on which our Nation was founded, that our influence can be beneficial and helpful in the other trouble spots of the world.

This is important to us. It's important to others. One of the great things that we have been able to do is to raise high the banner of human rights, and our country is now looked upon as the nation that stands foremost in the protection of basic human rights. And we'll have that reputation again as long as I'm in the White House.

Let me say that we've also tried, with some success, so far, to bring peace in southern Africa, to bring peace to Cyprus, to bring peace in the Middle East. A few hours ago in New York I was with Prime Minister Begin. Cy Vance, the Secretary of State, is meeting with him there all day today. We had some success, some good luck at Camp David because of the tremendous courage of President Sadat, Prime Minister Begin, who represent the hunger in their people's hearts for peace.

I believe that if we keep on working together and if I, when I speak, my voice is recognized as representing what you want, with decisions made openly, after public debate, with the knowledge of the Congress, that my voice will not be hollow and not be discounted by other leaders. And I believe that through strength, through a common commitment of the American people to restore the greatness of our Nation, we can be successful in the Middle East and live in a world at peace.

Tuesday, 4 days from now, will be a time for you to make a decision. Do you want to continue an increase in jobs in our country, to control inflation, to deal with the bureaucracy, to have a better life for farmers, to cut down the Federal deficit, improve education, housing, highways, strong defense, human rights, peace? If so, don't leave those responsibilities to me or to those who seek public office. Share those responsibilities with us. There is no reason why every one of you in the next 4 days cannot become in effect, as I said, a campaign manager for candidates in whom you have confidence.

Coming to this rally this afternoon is appreciated. It shows your interest in the future of Michigan, in the future of our country. But if you don't vote Tuesday and if you don't encourage your relatives, your neighbors, and those who will listen to your voice to vote, then by default you have let your Nation down.

We've got the greatest country on Earth. With your help, between now and next Tuesday, we will elect this fine Democratic slate, and in the future, because of you, we'll have an even greater nation than it is today.

Thank you very much, partners. We'll work together for the next 4 days.

NOTE: The President spoke at 5:08 p.m. at the Industrial Mutual Association Hall. In his opening remarks, he referred to Bobby D. Crim, speaker of the Michigan House of Representatives.

Skokie, Illinois

Remarks at a "Get Out the Vote" Rally. November 2, 1978

Senator Stevenson, Congressman Mikva, Alex Seith, Mike Bakalis, distinguished Democrats who will be elected Tuesday if you will help them, supporters of one of the finest Congressmen I have ever known:

I'm glad to be back in the 10th District.

I might say that every aspect of a President's life is not pleasant. It's not easy. Sometimes decisions have to be approached with a great deal of trepidation and caution. Sometimes there are discouragements. Since the Camp David negotiations began, I've not taken any time off. I've been working on the weekends and also during the week.

One good thing about a President is that I can set priorities for myself. I can do what I think is the most important thing for the Nation that I love. And the most important thing to me at this moment is to see Abner Mikva return to Congress next year.

It's not an accident that many knowledgeable and distinguished Democrats come into this district to add their voice of support for Congressman Mikva. We all want to have a better nation. We all want to meet our responsibilities of public office.

It's an exciting thing to come tonight to see democracy in action, to see dedicated Americans who are willing to fight to have a nation that's even greater than it is. And it's an inspiration to me as President to be in a rally with this degree of enthusiasm and fervor and commitment and support and success that's going to be demonstrated next Tuesday night.

We've got a candidate for the United State Senate here, whom I've known for several years. When the Democratic Party has met in its annual conventions or its midterm conventions, we have chosen a man from Illinois, who was not well known even in his own State, to come and give us advice and counsel in shaping the policies and the goals and ambitions of our party in foreign affairs. And I'm very grateful to have a man here with me tonight who intends not only to continue using his great knowledge and ability and influence to have a better success in dealing with other countries but who has pledged himself to cut the deficit every year, to cut taxes—and he will—to have fiscal responsibility in his administration as U.S. Senator, and who's casting his own future on a door-to-door campaign for the Senate, and one whom my mother, Lillian, loves—Alex Seith.

My mother has been into Illinois twice to campaign with Alex. The first time she pronounced his name wrong. [*Laughter*] And she couldn't remember how to say it, and she finally remembered that Seith reminded her of Jimmy's teeth, and she got it right from then on. [*Laughter*]

From that point on, his fortune has turned. And he has surprised and startled the political world throughout our country by the success of his campaign, because

he's been sound, firm, strong, consistent and because he's cast his lot, not with powerful political figures, but with people on street corners and in their homes, when he's gone door to door to let you know what a United States Senator can be who cares about you and who will be a very fine partner for Adlai Stevenson.

There's also a young man that I've learned to respect, admire, and even love, a young man who comes from a family of immigrants, Greek immigrants, who came here believing in the future of our Nation, who knows what it means to work hard for a chance in life, who, through superb dedication, confidence, and ability and, above all, an understanding and a compassion for the average people of Illinois in particular, has come from nowhere in politics, who has never been ahead in any poll conducted before election night, who has never lost an election, and who will win next Tuesday night for Governor— Mike Bakalis.

I'd like to talk to you very quietly for a few minutes about some thoughts that are on my mind.

Four days before the election in 1960, the people of the Nation went to the polls to vote, and the outcome of that election hung on the results in Illinois. It was very close. John Kennedy was elected President of our country. In that election two-thirds of the American people went to the polls to vote. In recent elections and the predictions for next Tuesday night, two-thirds of the American people will not vote.

We've seen poll results—I have, as President, the last few days—that show that the Democrats on a nationwide basis have a substantial advantage over Republican candidates, on an average. That's all voters. But among those who are likely to go to the polls and vote, the Democratic advantage is slashed in half.

There have been a lot of upsets in elections in our country, particularly the last 3 or 4 years. Issues are difficult, complicated. Public opinion is volatile. People have a distrust of candidates. They think they promise too much or won't do a good job when they're in office or might lose touch with voters.

The outcome of the election next Tuesday night will depend upon how many supporters go to the polls and vote. This is the first time that Abner Mikva has ever been ahead in the polls, and, as you know, he has won by the narrowest margin time after time.

I came this afternoon from Flint, Michigan. Two years ago, the night before the election, I met Fritz Mondale—we had been campaigning independently, but we met together in Flint, Michigan, late at night, both tired, to try to convince the Michigan people to vote for us. And I recall then that in the primary in Michigan, where 50 delegates' votes hung in the balance, I carried that State by less than 2,000 votes, not even 1 vote per precinct.

Last election, 2 years ago, Abner Mikva was elected to the Congress by 201 votes, much less than 1 vote per precinct. It is important that those who have confidence in him care enough about our Nation to invest your own time and energy and effort in determining the outcome of the election.

It would be a devastating blow and a tragedy for the 10th District of Michigan—of Illinois—[*laughter*]—for the State of Illinois, and for the United States if Abner Mikva is defeated. Will you work hard with all your effort the next 4 days to get other people to vote, to vote yourself, to have elected the finest Congressman that we could possibly return to Washington—Abner Mikva? Will you do that? [*Applause*] Good deal.

I want to ask you a couple more questions. Take your coats off and roll up your sleeves. Let's get to work. I want to ask you a few questions. I want to ask you a few questions, and I'll be very brief.

When I was elected President, there were 10 million people in this country who were looking for jobs, who couldn't find a full-time job. Since then, with Democratic leadership depending on you for your support and advice and counsel and criticism, we have had a net increase of 6½ million jobs in this country. We've already cut the unemployment rate 25 percent. We've got a long way to go. Do you care enough about your Nation to work hard between now and November 7 to elect Congressman Mikva, so that he can help me put America back to work? [*Applause*] Good deal.

Jobs are important, but we also have very serious problems that we have not yet solved with inflation. I have spelled out to the Congress, to the American people, indeed, to the world, a commitment on my part to make sure that we get inflation under control.

I inherited a Federal deficit of over $66 billion. I'm now preparing next year's budget, and I will have cut the deficit more than 50 percent in 2 years.

We're trying to eliminate waste, corruption in government. We're trying to add service and dedication and hard work to the civil service system. We're trying to open government so you'll know what is going on.

The Congress has passed an excellent ethics bill that will require everyone who holds a high position in the executive branch of Government, every Member of Congress, every Federal judge to reveal net worth, the source of income, so that it will remove all temptation to violate the confidence that you place in them.

We're trying to make our government efficient and effective. You can't educate a child with waste and inefficiency. You can't feed a hungry person with waste and inefficiency. These are the kinds of things that we're trying to do to get compassion, on the one hand, and competence, on the other, blended in together.

I need all the help I can get. Do you care enough about your country between now and next Tuesday to work hard to elect Abner Mikva to help me get inflation under control? [*Applause*] Good deal.

Ever since I've been in office, we've been building housing units at the rate of over 2 million per year, a very fine achievement. In addition to that, yesterday I signed into law the finest pair of education bills that have ever been passed in our country, to help from kindergarten, elementary, secondary schools, college— over $12 billion to give young people a better education in our Nation. We are not cutting back on good services for the American people.

So, we're cutting the deficit; we're giving better services; we're also cutting taxes. Last year we cut income taxes $8 billion. This year we're cutting taxes $20 billion more. That's a good combination—lower deficits, better services, lower taxes. I need your help to keep Abner Mikva in Congress. Will you work between now and next Tuesday to keep him there to help me carry on this program economically? [*Applause*]

I just want to ask you one more question. Alex Seith, Mike Bakalis, Abner Mikva, as well as your incumbent Senator, Adlai Stevenson, would help me to form and to keep an outstanding Democratic team, a team of elected officials, responsible to you, to make our Nation as great as possible.

We now have the strongest nation on Earth—militarily, economically, politically.

Our political system has been damaged in the last few years. Think back 3 years ago. There was a great alienation of American people from government. We had been embarrassed by a war in Vietnam. We had been embarrassed by the revelations of Watergate. We had been embarassed by knowledge that our own CIA had violated the law.

There was a general distrust of the American Government. Every fall, I dreaded to see the United Nations General Assembly meet, because I knew that the United States, the country that I loved, would be the butt of every joke, the target of every attack by two-thirds of the nations on Earth.

Farmers were facing another depression. Workers were discouraged.

These kinds of things had created in our own Nation's image a reasonable doubt among people of our country. We were attaching ourselves to every totalitarian government and tinhorn dictatorship possible, with almost no attention to the preservation and enhancement of basic human rights.

We now have the strongest military defense capability on Earth. We're going to stay number one. But we use it not to abuse other people, not to be a bully; we use this strength, combined with our economic strength and combined with our political and moral and ethical strength, to show the rest of the world that our Nation is honest, our Nation is competent, our Nation is decent.

And we have reraised the banner of human rights. And as long as I'm President, our country will be in the forefront and will be known by every nation on Earth as a people who stand and will protect and will enhance basic human rights everywhere on Earth. And you can depend on that.

For about 2,500 years the Middle East has been torn by distrust, by hatred, and by war. Finally, about a year ago, there was a move made by President Anwar Sadat to bring peace between Israel and Egypt. A very courageous Prime Minister

Begin welcomed him there and exchanged visits.

But as you know, the peace talks broke down, and I invited both men to come to Camp David. They came, not because of me, not because of my influence with them, not because of my personal characteristics, not even because I was President of the United States, but they came because they realized that when I spoke to them either publicly or in private, that I did not speak with a hollow voice, that the Mideast issues for the first time had been openly debated. The American people had been involved in the debate. The Congress was part of a democratic team committed to peace in the Middle East. And they came trusting our Nation. We had good luck at Camp David as a first major step.

This morning I met with Prime Minister Begin. Cy Vance, Secretary of State, spent all day with him. Yesterday he was with the Egyptians and the Israelis. And I believe that our Nation's influence now, our integrity, and our influence is strong and sound and dependable enough so that working with them—courageous leaders—with your backing and involvement, we can finally bring peace to the Mideast. It's what I want.

And I want to ask you this question in closing: Do you care enough about world peace to invest part of your life—at least 4 days of your life—in electing candidates that you know will help and strengthen me as I try to represent you well in international affairs, to keep our Nation strong, firm, dynamic, trusted, and a major element for peace? Will you do that for me? [*Applause*] Very good.

It's good of you to come. It's good of you to applaud.

I would like to ask you to do something specific that's very easy. I would like for you to promise me that between now

and Tuesday, that each one of you will contact at least 50 other people and get a promise from them that they will go to the polls Tuesday and vote—preferably for the Democratic ticket, but at least vote. Every one that will—think about it awhile; don't lie to your own President. [*Laughter*] But if you will promise to get 50 people to vote between now and Tuesday, would you please stand? [*Applause*] Thank you very much. You have made my trip worthwhile.

Good luck. Thank you very much.

NOTE: The President spoke at 7:43 p.m. in the Niles East High School gymnasium.

Earlier in the evening, the President attended a fundraising reception for Representative Mikva at the Newton Minow residence.

Following his remarks at the rally, the President proceeded to the home of Mayor Michael A. Bilandic of Chicago, where he spent the night.

Domestic High Carbon Ferrochromium Industry

Letter to the Speaker of the House and the President of the Senate Transmitting a Report. November 2, 1978

Dear Mr. Speaker: (Dear Mr. President:)

In accordance with Section 203(b)(1) of the Trade Act of 1974, enclosed is a report to the Congress setting forth my determination to provide import relief for the U.S. High Carbon Ferrochromium Industry and explaining the reasons for my decision.

Sincerely,

JIMMY CARTER

IMPORT RELIEF—HIGH-CARBON FERROCHROME

As required under Section 203(b)(1) of the Trade Act of 1974, I am transmitting this report to Congress setting forth my decision with respect to high carbon ferrochromium covered by the affirmative finding on September 6, 1978, of the U.S. International Trade Commission (USITC) under Section 201(d)(1) of the Trade Act. As my action differs from that recommended by the USITC, I have included the reasons for my decisions.

After considering all relevant aspects of the case, including those set forth in Section 202(c) of the Trade Act of 1974, I have determined that import relief in the form of an increased tariff of 4¢ on any high carbon ferrochromium (HCF) entering the United States at less than a value of 38¢ per pound would be appropriate because:

(1) The additional duty on HCF would provide the domestic industry with the opportunity to operate at a reasonable rate of return.

(2) The additional duty on HCF would raise the U.S. import price to a level sufficient to minimize the likelihood that the EC minimum import price and Japan's duty paid import price would divert HCF exports to the U.S.

(3) The additional duty would protect the most competitive U.S. producers from bearing the burden of the current world oversupply situation while less efficient EC and Japanese producers are being protected.

(4) Since the volume of business involved is small, and prices substantially depressed, the inflationary impact would be minimized.

(5) The proposed remedy should minimize any adverse effect on foreign suppliers in that shipments of high carbon ferrochromium entering the United States at not less than 40¢ per pound would not bear any additional duty.

NOTE: This is the text of identical letters addressed to Thomas P. O'Neill, Jr., Speaker of the House of Representatives, and Walter F. Mondale, President of the Senate.

Domestic High Carbon Ferrochromium Industry

***Memorandum From the President.
November 2, 1978***

Memorandum for the Special Representative for Trade Negotiations

Subject: Determination Under Section 202(a) of the Trade Act; High Carbon Ferrochromium

Pursuant to Section 202(b)(1) of the Trade Act of 1974 (P.L. 93–618, 88 Stat. 1978), I have determined the action I will take with respect to the report of the United States International Trade Commission (USITC) dated September 6, 1978, concerning the results of its investigation, as requested by the House Ways and Means Committee, of the domestic industry producing ferrochromium, containing over 3% by weight of carbon, provided for in Item 607.31 of the Tariff Schedules of the United States.

After considering all relevant aspects of the case, including those set forth in Section 202(c) of the Trade Act of 1974, I have determined to provide import relief for the domestic industry. Relief should be granted in the form of an increased tariff of 4¢ on any high carbon ferrochromium entering the United States at less than a value of 38¢ per pound for the following reasons:

1. The domestic industry is currently operating at unprofitable levels. Even the most competitive domestic firm (which supplies over half of all domestic production) is operating with substantial losses

due to the price and volume of import competition this year.

2. Other importing countries have protected their producers. The European Community has established minimum prices for high carbon ferrochromium imports. The Japanese market does not appear to be fully open. The U.S. industry thus bears virtually all of the burden of adjustment during the current period of world overcapacity (the U.S., Japan, and EC constitute 90 percent of the free world high carbon ferrochrome market.

3. The additional duty on HCF would raise sufficiently the U.S. import price, minimizing the likelihood that the EC minimum import price and Japan's duty paid import price would divert HCF exports to the United States. This would provide the principal domestic producer with the opportunity to operate at a reasonable rate of return.

4. The recommended relief would not be inflationary. Market prices would be restored to levels assuring a fair return after imports have unduly depressed prices.

This determination is to be published in the FEDERAL REGISTER.

JIMMY CARTER

[Filed with the Office of the Federal Register, 11:51 a.m., November 3, 1978]

Gresham, Oregon

**Remarks at a "Get Out the Vote" Rally.
November 3, 1978**

Governor Bob Straub, Congressman Bob Duncan, Congressman Les AuCoin, Senator Cook, Chairman Klonoski, Chairman of the Democratic National Committee John White, and my friends:

How many of you are going to vote next Tuesday? [*Applause*]

In 1960, when John Kennedy was elected President of our country, two-thirds of the American people went to the polls to vote. In recent elections and the projections for next Tuesday, two-thirds of the American people will not vote.

It's very important for all Americans to know that the government is yours, that candidates who know you will vote will be much more cautious about following your mandates and desires. And also you have a responsibility and an opportunity in a free and democratic nation to exercise your will at the ballot box.

Yesterday, I was in Flint, Michigan, the last place I stopped before the great election 2 years ago, when I was chosen to be your President. In the primary in Michigan, out of more than a million votes, I won by less than 2,000, which meant that less than one person per precinct decided who won that State. Last night, I was campaigning for Congressman Abner Mikva in the 10th District of Illinois. He won 2 years ago with 201 votes, less than one-half vote per precinct.

It's extremely important that if you care about your Nation that you work hard enough to get other people to vote and also vote yourself.

I'm very glad to come to beautiful Oregon. When Fritz Mondale, the Vice President, was here a few days ago, there were heavy rains. Today, when the President comes, there is no rain. You can see how much it pays off to have a President.

I would like to emphasize again the importance of your participation in the democratic processes.

It's not easy holding public office these days. I guess one of the most difficult jobs in the world is to be President of the United States. It's also one of the best jobs of all, because I represent the greatest nation on Earth.

It's getting better every day, with your help. We have a young, vigorous, dynamic, confident, competent administration. Our Nation is the strongest on Earth. It's the strongest militarily, and it's going to stay that way. It's the strongest politically, because we believe in the dignity of every human being, the right of people to stand on their own feet, to make their own decisions, to control their own government, to let their own individuality be expressed. And we're trying to spread this philosophy, this commitment, these ideals around the world.

We now have a country where people can trust the Government once again. I remember just 3 or 4 years ago when many Americans were ashamed of our own Government. The Vietnam war was one that turned many people against our own country; the revelations in Watergate, where many of the top officials, as you know, in our Government went to jail. The CIA was violating the laws of our Nation. Corruption, scandal pervaded our Government. We've changed all of that. We're trying to bring a government of honesty, openness, and decency, of which not only we can be proud, but which will earn the respect of the rest of the world.

It's only through strength of character, it's only through strength economically that my own influence can be used, as your President, to bring peace, not only to our own people but to other trouble spots of the world as well. I hope that I can go out of office at the end of my term by saying what I can say today, that not a single American in uniform has shed blood in a foreign country since I've been President. We're going to try to keep that peace.

We've also raised high the banner of human rights, and as long as I'm in the White House, we will protect basic human rights, not only in our own country but in every country on Earth, and you can depend on that as well.

I want to tell you why I came to Oregon at this particular time. I want to let you know the importance of government, the importance of your participation, and also to get out as many people as possible to vote next Tuesday and to ask you to vote for a superb Democratic ticket, headed in Oregon by my good friend and a great Governor, Bob Straub. I want you to help him.

Some people say that Governor Straub is not a good politician because he takes difficult stands on controversial issues. And I think that's true.

Oregon is the birthplace of the referendum, where people can put on the ballot issues that you consider to be important to yourselves. He analyzes those issues. He doesn't try to guess what's the most popular thing to do. He's not wishy-washy in his own decisions. He lets the people know where he stands. He's a strong and courageous leader, and he's helped Oregon tremendously since he's been in office.

If he has one fault, it's that he's overly modest. When he came into office, Oregon had the fourth highest unemployment rate in the United States, 12 percent unemployment. Bob Straub has brought that unemployment down to 5 percent. He's cut it more than in half, and now Oregon is at the top in employment, not unemployment.

He's tried to protect the environment in Oregon at the same time—at the same time—he has helped to improve business and jobs. Seventy-two new businesses have been brought into Oregon to provide jobs for you and those you care about; 175 existing Oregon businesses have expanded. But at the same time Bob Straub believes that the good quality of life that is enjoyed in your State—and there is no better quality of life anywhere on Earth—

ought to be preserved. And you need a Governor that'll keep your environment clean and make sure that the land is used well and the forest industry is protected, the forest harvests are expanded, that more trees are planted. And I hear this from Bob Straub every time I talk to him. And you need to keep him in office to protect you and the quality of your life in the future.

What kind of industry do you want in Oregon? Clean industry, right. That's the kind I want throughout the country, and Bob Straub is setting an example for other States to follow. I might point out that Bob Straub also believes in lower taxes, at the same time opening government so you can understand it better and participate in it, but giving better services to the people as well.

Many of you are still students, and Oregon now has the highest State support for education in over 30 years, which is a very good commitment and a better life for you and those you care about.

He's fighting for lower utility rates, lower rent for elderly people, and also fighting to give lower costs for dental care for elderly people. He believes, as I do, that we can tackle tough problems and be successful.

As you well know, Congressman Bob Duncan, Congressman Les AuCoin are very strong supporters of what I'm trying to do in Washington. I inherited, when I went into office, a very serious series of problems. We had over 10 million people in our country who could not find a full-time job. Since then, we've had a net increase of 6½ million new jobs. On the way here from Illinois this morning on Air Force One, I got a report that last month we added 642,000 jobs in our country, and we cut down the unemployment rate another two-tenths of 1 percent. It's now 5.8 percent, the best it's been in many, many years.

I've been concerned, as have you, about the stability of our own economy. I want to say just a word about the prospect for a recession next year.

In the last 2 weeks many economists, advisers of mine, have been predicting that if the American dollar was not stabilized on foreign markets, that inflation rates would go up much higher next year than this year and that we would face an almost sure recession.

Last Saturday night I met with my top economic advisers to consider what to do. And we made a decision that we believed then and believe even more strongly now would not only stabilize and strengthen the dollar overseas; it'll expand American export, create more jobs for American citizens, and make sure that we do not have a recession in 1979. This is what we believe we can accomplish. If you will help us with our anti-inflation program, we'll be successful. Will you help me with that by using all of your influence in the future? [*Applause*]

This is a program that requires cooperation and teamwork from Democrats and Republicans alike, from employers and employees alike, from those who live in cities, those who live on the farms, because all of us have to make equal sacrifices to control rampant inflation.

We've had a very high inflation rate now for 10 years. The 3 years before I became President, we had an average inflation rate of 8 percent. It's not quite that high now, and we want to hold it down.

In the last 2 days, the value of the dollar has gone up against the deutsche mark, for instance, in Germany 8 percent. As you know, day before yesterday, the stock market went up more than it ever had in history, over 35 points. That's an indication of confidence in our Government.

When I began running for President, nobody thought I had a chance, but I stuck to it and won. When I made my anti-inflation speech—[*applause*]—with your help. When I made my anti-inflation speech, a lot of people said we don't have a chance to win. But I don't intend to lose, and we're going to fight inflation until we whip it. We're going to keep Americans employed. We're going to keep a strong dollar. We're going to keep jobs going, and our Nation is going to stand as a bulwark against depression throughout the world.

It takes a good team effort, a good Democratic team effort, and I want to ask all of you to think back—sometimes in a very brief life, since a lot of you are quite young—how things were 2, 3 years ago, before Bob Straub was your Governor and before we had a Democratic administration in Washington. We've still a long way to go. We haven't solved all our problems. We don't claim to have done that. But we are trying to recognize for a change that our Nation is one of which we can be justifiably proud.

Our military and economic and political strength is not being used to abuse other people. We no longer have any need to espouse every totalitarian regime in the world to make us look good. We've been willing to treat the Panamanians fairly. We've injected our beneficial impact into South Africa to bring peace, an end to apartheid, majority rule, one person-one vote in that troubled continent.

We're working to bring peace to Cyprus. We're trying to have a SALT agreement negotiated with the Soviet Union, to remove once and for all the threat of nuclear destruction from the entire world. And I intend to succeed in having a good SALT agreement in the next few weeks.

The Congress has passed a nonproliferation bill, the first time we've ever had one which will prevent nations that don't presently have nuclear explosives from ever having them. We're making progress toward peace, and, as you know, not too long ago, I invited President Sadat of Egypt and Prime Minister Begin to Camp David, and we had some good luck there. We're going to keep working until we have peace in the Middle East, and you can depend on that.

So, what is it fair to say that we want in an American Government, in the government of Oregon? What do we want our Nation to be? We want it to be strong, and we'll keep it that way. We want it to be peaceful in its attitude, and we're going to keep it that way. We want our influence to be felt in a beneficial way around the world, and we'll keep it that way. We want us to help bring peace to areas which are troubled. We want to keep our young people from having to give their lives in war.

We want to remove the threat of nuclear destruction. We want our people to have jobs. We want to control inflation. We want the American economy to be strong. We want farmers to be prosperous. We want young people to get a good education. We want homes to be built, a good highway system to be maintained.

These are the kinds of things we are working to achieve in this administration, and we also at the same time want to have a competent, tough, and efficient government. We don't waste money any more.

When I was running for President, we had a Federal deficit of over $66 billion. I've not been in office very long yet, but in the preparation of the next budget, on which I'm working now every week, we will have cut the Federal deficit more than half in two. And we're going to continue to work until we have a balanced budget for the Government of the United States.

Well, I want to come to a close in my own speech, to ask you first of all to participate by voting and encouraging other people to vote next Tuesday. Secondly, I'd like to ask you to vote for the Democratic candidates, and particularly those who are running a tough race against very high financial odds.

There's no doubt in my mind that Bob Straub's opponent will have two and a half times as many dollars to spend on his campaign as does your Governor. I want you particularly to help him to be elected, because Bob Straub is a man who deserves support, particularly from young people, who believe in the idealism of American life and the strength of our country and a good quality of existence, with good jobs, growing industry in the future in Oregon. That's very important. But most of all, I want you to make sure that you feel that you're a part of the American political existence. When you vote, your influence is felt. And I want to make sure that young people like yourselves, who are idealistic, who are not afraid of change, who believe in openness of government, who believe in principles that haven't changed for the last 200 years, who believe in courage in the face of difficulty, who don't believe problems are too great to overcome, who don't believe the questions are too difficult to answer—you are the ones on whom the future of the United States depends.

We have got the greatest nation on Earth now. With your help and your participation, your support and your confidence, we're going to have an even greater nation in the years ahead, when you're the leaders of our country.

Thank you very much.

NOTE: The President spoke at 10:15 a.m. in the Amphitheater at Mt. Hood Community College. In his opening remarks, he referred to Democratic Senatorial candidate Vern Cook and Jim Klonoski, State Democratic Party chairman.

Sacramento, California
Remarks at a "Get Out the Vote" Rally. November 3, 1978

Are the Democrats going to win next Tuesday? [*Applause*] Are you going to help? [*Applause*] Right on.

Senator Cranston, Governor Jerry Brown, Lieutenant Governor Merv Dymally, the great congressional delegation, Speaker Leo McCarthy, my friends in Sacramento, California, and all those who observe this tremendous demonstration of what it means to have a democratic society where each human being—their influence, their voice, their vote—can make a difference in the future of our Nation:

I would like to say first of all how proud I am to be in Sacramento, where for 26 years you have been blessed with one of the greatest Members of Congress who ever served—my friend, John Moss. It's a sad day for us to see him step down.

Also, I hate very much to surrender to Sacramento one of the greatest Congresswomen I've ever known, a strong, dynamic, forceful person, who will be your next attorney general—Yvonne Burke.

California needs an attorney general who's tough, competent, concerned about crime control, who will work with the United States Attorney General to control crime in your State. It'll be a great pleasure to have her as a partner with us, controlling crime and protecting the lives of people here.

I want to say, too, that I come here to add my own voice of admiration and support and confidence in one of our Nation's greatest Governors; one who's brought a breath of fresh air to the political scene of the United States; a man who's been able, through his leadership, to reinspire California; who inherited some difficult problems, but who's worked to solve them, and who'll be solving those problems in California for the next 4 years—my friend and your Governor, Jerry Brown, who will win a tremendous victory next Tuesday.

More than any other political figure I know, Jerry Brown is sensitive to the will of the people of his State. He recognized the mandate given to him last June, and he's followed that mandate, not only with enthusiasm and commitment but with effectiveness. He's been able to cut State spending $3 billion. He's been able to cut State taxes $1 billion. He's been able to return to local government, to hold down property taxes $4 billion. This is just a start. He's the kind of man that can lead you to even greater life in a greater State in the future, and I'm very proud to be here on his behalf.

We have a good partnership between the Federal and the State Governments. And also there's a great partnership that exists in the Jerry Brown-Merv Dymally team. He inherited a tremendous unemployment rate in California when he became Governor. But with Merv Dymally's help, there's been a great emphasis on restoring the economic soundness of the life of California.

There have been 1 million new jobs available for Californians with the Brown-Dymally team. Corporate profits are at an all-time high. Personal income is at an all-time high. New industries are moving in California as they've never done before. You've got more foreign investments here than any State in the entire Nation.

And we need to keep this team intact for a better economic life, brighter prospects, jobs, lower taxes, lower property taxes, more savings, tougher State government. So, I hope you'll support with all your enthusiasm—you, your friends, your relatives, anyone you can influence, by helping to vote—a great victory for Jerry

Brown, Merv Dymally next Tuesday.

We're also trying to do a good job in Washington. You've got a great leader, who's recognized by his own peers in the United States Senate as the Democratic whip, working with Bob Byrd. Your great Alan Cranston is a man on whom I depend to help me both with domestic affairs and also foreign affairs.

You have a great congressional team: Phil Burton, who's a tough in-fighter, who believes in saving money, who has great influence with his fellow Members of Congress; Norman Mineta, an expert on urban affairs; Bizz Johnson, who is responsible for assuring that the airline industry will be deregulated—lower fares, more passengers, higher profits in the future; Jim Corman, who's heading up the entire Democratic effort throughout the country this year to elect Congress Members for the next session; John Burton; Pete Stark; Ed Roybal, who's trying to emphasize a much greater influence, through votes, by Spanish-speaking Americans all over our Nation. We are rapidly growing, very important constituency in our country. So far, the voter turnout among Americans who speak Spanish has not been high enough. It's a great hope of the future. And I want to encourage an increased participation in politics, particularly Democratic politics, by those whose ancestors were from Latin America, who speak Spanish, and who are enlightened, strong, representing the principles and ideals of a Democratic Party. Jerry Patterson—and I particularly want you to help Dennis Kazarian, Norma Bork, and in this area, I'm especially pleased to be here on behalf of Vic Fazio and Bob Matsui, who I'm sure you are going to send to the Congress in January.

Now I want to say a word about myself. I've come here as President of our entire country, Democrats and Republicans. In 1960 in the United States, two-thirds of the American people went to the polls to elect John Kennedy President and to vote for the Democratic ticket. Two-thirds voted. The projections for Monday, unless people are inspired to run their own affairs, are that two-thirds of the American people will not vote.

It's very important that you go to the polls and cast your ballot. It's not enough to come to a rally or even to work for a candidate during a long, tedious, trying, difficult campaign. Every time we have three people who do not vote, two of them ordinarily are Democrats. And when you have polled the opinion of all voters and then poll the ones who are most likely to vote, the Democratic lead in almost every election is cut in half.

It's important for us to project our own voice, our own influence, to assess our Nation's needs, and to help resolve difficult problems.

It's not easy being an incumbent in these days. But I think we've brought a new light, not only to California, under Jerry Brown's leadership, but to our Nation as well.

I'd like for you to think back just 2 or 3 years, at the situation as it was before we had a Democratic administration in Washington. Our Nation was discouraged. People had lost confidence in our Government. We were involved in a war in Vietnam. We had the Watergate scandals, when top people in our Government were being sent to prison. The CIA revelations showed that important elements of the American Government were violating the law and getting away with it.

When I became President, 10 million Americans could not find a full-time job. The unemployment rate was 8 percent.

Every time the United Nations General Assembly met in New York in the fall, we were all embarrassed, because our great Nation, which we love, became the butt of every joke and the target of every attack by two-thirds of the nations on Earth.

We had lost our spirit. We were not identified as one that was trying to search for peace throughout the world. We were attaching ourselves to disreputable administrations in other countries in order to pursue doubtful political goals. We had lost touch with the idealism that made our Nation great.

We've tried to turn that around. We've cut the unemployment rate by 25 percent. We've added 6½ million net jobs. We're trying to get inflation under the control. If you'll help me, we'll succeed.

We've now gotten the dollar back into a strong position. We've raised the banner of human rights. We've made sure that we're meeting the services of our people. We've cut taxes $28 billion. We're trying to bring some order out of chaos in the civil service system. We're letting the people who do a good job be rewarded, letting managers manage. We've cut the deficit almost 50 percent already. So, these kind of things on the domestic scene are the results of a good Democratic team.

I'd like to mention, as well, that we have the strongest nation on Earth. We're the strongest politically; we're the strongest economically; we're the strongest militarily.

We do have the strongest defense, and we're going to stay that way. But we use our defense strength not to abuse others, not to impose our will on smaller nations, but to work for peace—peace for ourselves and peace for others. Since I've been in the White House—and I hope as long as I'm there—there has never been an American in uniform who shed blood in a foreign country in conflict. And if you'll help me, we'll maintain that peaceful record.

We've raised the banner of human rights. And as long as I'm in the White House, our Nation will always be identified as the Nation that will insist and fight for basic human rights, not only in our own country but throughout the world.

We're searching for peace, as well, to remove the threat of atomic destruction. We're negotiating every day with the Soviet Union to have a SALT agreement, and I hope before too many weeks goes by, we will be successful. The Congress has passed a nonproliferation bill that prevents nations who don't have atomic explosives from ever having them in the future.

We are also searching for peace in southern Africa, to have majority rule, one person-one vote, an end to apartheid.

In Cyprus we're trying to bring the Greek- and the Turk-Cypriots into understanding, to bring peace to that troubled region.

And in the Mideast, I've been negotiating, as you know, with President Sadat, Prime Minister Begin. And if you'll stick with me and give me your voice, we'll bring peace to the Mideast in the next few weeks.

Let me summarize what I want to say in just a few words. First of all, this is your country, ours or your governments at the Federal, State, and local level. Your voice cannot be heard unless you're willing to vote and to get other people to participate in the democratic processes.

It's always a mistake to take for granted a political victory. Some of the Democratic candidates are far ahead in the public opinion polls. I've seen, in the last few days of a campaign, those apparent victories turn into disappointment and defeat. Other Democratic candidates have very close races, because their opponents can outspend them with an almost unlimited political campaign chest.

We are trying, as a Democratic team, to meet the needs of our people, to strengthen the income of American farm families—which has increased already 25 percent—to increase farm exports, to have predictable government policies. We're trying to bring peace to ourselves and to the world, maintain a strong defense, put our people back to work, cut down inflation, stabilize the dollar, have a strong economy. These are the kind of things that benefit all those who live in this Nation. And above all, we're trying to have a government that's honest, decent, trustworthy, admired by other people in the world, known as one that protects human rights and protects peace, of which the American people can be truly proud.

It's important that you keep this Democratic team together. It's important that you participate Tuesday by giving us your vote and your support. And I ask you to do so, to make the greatest nation on Earth even greater in the future with a strong Democratic team and you being part of it.

Thank you very much, everybody. God bless you all.

I also want to ask everybody to vote against Proposition 6.

NOTE: The President spoke at 1:20 p.m. at the K Street Mall. In his opening remarks, he referred to Leo T. McCarthy, speaker of the California State Assembly.

Proposition 6 is an initiative statute on the California ballot which would prohibit the employment of homosexuals in the State school system.

Duluth, Minnesota

Remarks at a "Get Out the Vote" Rally. November 3, 1978

Vice President Mondale, Senator Humphrey, Senator Anderson, Governor Perpich, Congressman Oberstar, Governor Schreiber, Chairman John White, Bob Short, my friends who are going to have a great Democratic victory November 7, next Tuesday, if you work, and I hope you will work:

Mayor Beaudin met me at the airport, and as we drove in, he talked about the changes that have taken place in northeast Minnesota in the last 3 years. One of the best things that happened to me was shortly after the Ohio, California primaries, a young man, compared to me, came down to Plains and said, "I've just finished reading your book, Jimmy, called, 'Why Not the Best?', and I've offered to volunteer my services to be your Vice President." [*Laughter*]

That's not exactly the way it happened, but I wanted to come back to Minnesota and thank you for Fritz Mondale, the greatest Vice President I know.

Elections are exciting; elections are precarious, unpredictable; elections are times when the people of the country which we all love have an opportunity to be part of government, to stand on our own feet, to make our own decisions, to show what democracy means, to show what freedom means, what individuality means.

In 1960, our country went to the polls, and we elected John Kennedy as President. Two-thirds of the American people voted. The projections are that Tuesday, this year, two-thirds of the American people will not vote.

Tonight, I'm going to discuss some of the reasons for that, but I would like to point out to you that when three people don't vote on election day, ordinarily, two of them are Democrats, because Democrats quite often are those who have newly arrived on the scene of full citizenship. They are people who quite often have come up out of poverty, who might be black, who might not speak English very well, whose parents have only been here a short time, who have recently got a job or recently finished an education, who have recently become interested in politics and government. So, a strong vote on election day almost always ensures that people like DFL candidates, Democrats throughout the country will be elected.

There's a real reason for the fall-off in voter participation, and I'd like to ask you to think back 3 or 4 years about what our country was. There was a great alienation, distrust, withdrawal by the people of our country from their Government.

We had been embroiled for many years in the Vietnam war; 50,000 young Americans had died. Watergate, an unprecedented scandal in our Nation, resulted in revelations day by day which were an embarrassment to us all. Top officials in the heart of our Government—in the White House, the Attorney General, and others—not only were embarrassed but were guilty of crimes. Many of them went to prison. Our CIA was accused, with some basis, of plotting murder and violating the law.

Our farmers were facing another Hoover Depression; income was down. When we had a slight surplus in feed grains, food grains, in a completely unpredictable way, the leaders of our Government would declare an embargo and would not let us ship our goods overseas to world markets.

When I became President, 10 million American adults could not find a full-time job. Seven million Americans couldn't find a job at all. In your region of Minnesota, the unemployment rate was 9 percent throughout the Iron Range, Northview, and here in Duluth, the unemployment rate was 9 percent.

Mayor Beaudin told me tonight the unemployment rate here is less than 4 percent; the same throughout the northeast.

We saw in times gone by a time when the elderly people were beginning to worry about their own future. Social security, which had begun under a Democratic President many years ago, was facing immediate bankruptcy.

These kinds of things had torn at the very fabric of our country. And I, as a Governor and a candidate for President, shrank up inside every autumn when the United Nations General Assembly began its deliberations in New York, because I knew that the country that I loved was likely to be the target of every attack, the butt of every joke by two-thirds of the nations on Earth. We were not beloved, we were not even respected by every nation that was small or new or weak, or whose people were brown or black or yellow.

Our country had lost its spirit. But there was a hunger within us and a strength within us that was indomitable, and we began the long journey back. It was not an accident. It's not been easy. We have not yet won all the battles. We've not answered all the questions. We've not solved all the problems.

But the progress that we have made has been because of a strong team spirit, a spirit that epitomizes what Hubert Humphrey's life meant, what he stood for, a concern about common, ordinary working people who don't want a selfish benefit from government, but just want a chance in life to be an individual, to take whatever talent God might have given us and use that talent to the utmost, to be free and proud, proud of ourselves, proud of our family, proud of our country. That's not asking too much. And that's what we've tried to bring back.

Your State is known throughout the Nation as setting an example for the rest of us in honesty, in decency, and concern about one another, voter participation. This is what we need to have Tuesday. But we can't take anything for granted. I doubt if any time in recent years has there been a threat that the Governor's office,

both Senate offices might go to the Republican Party, responsible for that kind of America that I've described in a very few words.

Miners now have a good life. The social security system is sound. In the last 21 months we've added 6½ million net new jobs in our country. We've cut the unemployment rate down by 25 percent. Day before yesterday, I signed two bills, the most progressive and far-reaching help for education in the history of our country—over $12 billion that will now go from the Federal Government into better elementary and secondary education, better aid for students who want to get a college education and who couldn't otherwise afford it.

At the same time, we've not been wasteful. The Democratic Party has always been a party with a heart, we've always been compassionate. But we've also built very laboriously, recently, a reputation for competence, for efficiency, because you can't educate a child, you can't feed a hungry person, you can't build a house, you can't have a good school system with waste and inefficiency.

I was concerned, as a responsible fiscal person, because when I ran for President, we had a deficit of over $66 billion. We've already cut that deficit over $25 billion. And the budget I'm preparing now for submission next year to Congress will more than cut that deficit in half. And we're trying to work for a balanced budget.

At the same time we've been careful about your own pocketbook, not just concerned about deficits and better services, but we've cut taxes $8 billion last year in income tax cuts, another $20 billion this year.

We've tried to bring to you the elements of life that Americans have a right to demand and which epitomize what you've had here in Minnesota with an enlightened and a progressive government.

I wouldn't say that I'm tired, but I haven't had much rest since we began the summit talks at Camp David. And I didn't have to come here tonight, because I'd like to be going back to Washington to be with my family for a change. But I've come here, and so has the Vice President, because I care about what happens in Minnesota Tuesday night when the election returns come in. It's important to the country. And it's a completely legitimate thing for a President to care who the Governor of a State is and who the Members of the Senate are.

We didn't get where we are by giving up. And in the last few weeks I've heard some of the most important and prominent and even loyal Democrats from Minnesota saying, "I'm afraid we've lost one of our Senate seats. I'm afraid we have an insurmountable obstacle to overcome." That's not the spirit of America. That's not the spirit of the DFL. It's not the spirit which I try to epitomize as President.

Many of you come here tonight because you are loyal, and I appreciate your being here. And perhaps you've worked hard in the past elections to have DFL nominees elected. You've proven that with the superb public servants that you've elected to represent your State here and also in Washington.

But it's not a time to give up. We've 3 more days, and there's no reason why everyone here tonight shouldn't put in 30 hours on the telephone, walking the streets, asking your family, your neighbors, your community to support the candidates Tuesday night and win a victory for Minnesota and for our country.

We are not a nation that's ever surprised when we win a victory, because there's a spirit within our country that far surpasses in most cases what govern-

ment is. But I'm afraid that in your State this year, because of divisions within your party, that your public officials might be better than the people themselves. And I've come to ask you not to let them down. They are great nominees. They're different from one another. Fritz Mondale and I are different from one another. He has constituencies that I'm not very familiar with, and so do I have people who know me better than they know him. But we work as a team with our differences intact, and out of that comes strength.

I spent last night with a Croatian family in Chicago, Mayor Michael Bilandic. His parents haven't been here long. I met his mother. She doesn't speak English very well; I could hardly hear what she said. But she said every night she kneels down beside the bed, and she prays for me as President. And she prays that our country will be even greater.

Marty Schreiber comes from next door in Wisconsin. He's running against a cute Republican candidate who said the other day that elderly people are millstones around the neck of young Americans. That's the kind of philosophy that represents the Republican Party. It's the kind of philosophy that's brought me here to you tonight. I don't consider my mother to be a millstone around my neck. And I don't believe you consider your parents to be that either.

I've got great burdens on my shoulders. I asked for them, and I enjoy my job. But I need help in Washington and also in the State offices of this country from people who share a common philosophy with me. We intend to continue to put Americans back to work, to add jobs, to give people the basic right to support themselves, to take whatever talent or ability God might have given them and use it in a useful way.

We're trying to control inflation. When I became President, we had an average inflation rate for the preceding 3 years of 8 percent. It's a very intractable problem. It's not easily solved, but I announced last week a strong anti-inflation program, and as I had a philosophy during the campaign, I did not intend to lose, I don't intend to lose in the fight against inflation if you'll help me, and I hope you will.

I'm a farmer. I come from a working family. My family happens to have been in this country 100 years before it was a nation. We've lived in Georgia for more than 200 years. No one in my family before me ever finished high school. I know what it means to work for a living. I know what it means to have a better chance in life, and I want to be sure that the Government continues to give good services to our people. But I deeply believe that the best government is the one closest to the people.

I think there are roles to play for the Federal Government that can be enhanced, for we need a Federal Government that the bureaucracy is a source of pride and trust. When we inherited this job, the civil service was 95 years old and had not been reformed. It had deteriorated in quality. You'd have two people sitting side by side, one dedicated and competent, hard-working; another right next door at the adjacent desk, incompetent, lazy, in the wrong job.

The Congress has now changed that. We've got civil service reformed. Now we can reward that good employee. We can inspire the other one or maybe transfer the other one or maybe discharge the other one. We can let managers manage. We'll have a better Government for you. The budget is coming under control. These signs of progress mean that we have a competent government that's still compassionate.

Wendy Anderson, for instance, serves on the Budget Committee. He's a junior Senator, as you know, but he is so respected by his peer group that he's been given assignments commensurate with his background, his experience here as Governor and his own competence as a man.

I'm deeply dedicated to a strong defense. Our Nation is the strongest nation on Earth militarily. And as long as I'm President, our Nation will always be number one in military strength, and you can depend upon that.

It just happens that Wendy Anderson is on the Armed Services Committee, and he realizes that we don't just need a strong defense for the safety of America. We certainly don't want a strong military to impose our will on others. We want a strong defense because we love peace. There has not been a single American who has shed blood in combat since I've been President, and I hope I can complete my term as your President with that record still intact.

We are working every day with the Soviet Union to have a good SALT agreement, to remove the threat of nuclear weapons from their destructive power over the entire Earth. The Congress has passed a nonproliferation bill that prevents nations who don't have atomic explosives from ever having them in the future.

And we've tried to set an example for others. We've raised high a banner that represents the spirit and the commitment and the ideals of America, a banner that says, "Human Rights." And as long as I'm President and I have a strong Democratic team to support me, we will be the nation known throughout the world as the people who believe in basic human rights here and in other nations as well. And you can depend upon that as well.

Let me close by saying this: You have the right and, I hope, the duty to make a very important decision for you and your future on Tuesday night. Hubert Humphrey, Muriel Humphrey have been inspirations to all of us. Wendy Anderson, Bob Short will make a great team in Washington to help me. Rudy Perpich, here, Marty Schreiber, great Governors, epitomizing what we know is best for our country.

If you want jobs, if you want inflation controlled, if you want to cut the Federal deficit, make government more responsive to you, give our farmers and city dwellers a better life, our children a better education, a government of which we can be proud, a statesman-like attitude toward foreign affairs, military strength designed to bring world peace to us and others throughout the world, then work hard the next 3 days, vote Tuesday, send a strong Democratic team to victory. And I will be deeply appreciative as President of the United States.

Thank you very much.

NOTE: The President spoke at 8:35 p.m. at the Duluth Arena Auditorium. In his opening remarks, he referred to John C. White, Democratic National Committee chairman.

Following the rally, the President returned to Andrews Air Force Base, Md.

Digest of Other White House Announcements

The following listing includes the President's daily schedule and other items of general interest as announced by the White House Press Office during the period covered by this issue. Events and announcements printed elsewhere in the issue are not included.

October 28

The President met at the White House with Zbigniew Brzezinski, Assistant to the President for National Security Affairs.

Following his return to the White House from the trip to New York, Connecticut, Massachusetts, and Maine, the President met with W. Michael Blumenthal, Secretary, and Anthony M. Solomon, Under Secretary for Monetary Affairs, Department of the Treasury, Federal Reserve Board Chairman G. William Miller, Charles L. Schultze, Chairman of the Council of Economic Advisers, and Alfred E. Kahn, Advisor to the President on Inflation, to discuss the forthcoming Treasury Department and Federal Reserve measures to strengthen the dollar in domestic and international markets.

The President left the White House for a stay at Camp David, Md.

October 30

The President returned to the White House from Camp David.

The President has declared an emergency for the State of California because of the impact of brushfires which occurred in the County of Los Angeles between October 23–25.

The President and Mrs. Carter hosted a Halloween party at the White House for members of the White House staff and their guests.

October 31

The President met at the White House with:

—Dr. Brzezinski;

—James T. McIntyre, Jr., Director of the Office of Management and Budget, Stuart E. Eizenstat, Assistant to the President for Domestic Affairs and Policy, and Mr. Schultze, to review the fiscal year 1980 Federal budget;

—Vice President Walter F. Mondale, Adm. Stansfield Turner, Director of Central Intelligence, Hamilton Jordan, Assistant to the President, and Dr. Brzezinski;

—His Imperial Highness Crown Prince Reza of Iran;

—Douglas M. Costle, Administrator of the Environmental Protection Agency and Chairman of the Regulatory Council;

—Vice President Mondale, Under Secretary Solomon, Mr. Miller, Mr. Schultze, and Mr. Eizenstat, to discuss the measures to strengthen the dollar in domestic and international markets.

In a ceremony in the Oval Office at the White House, the President received the first books of the "Public Papers of the Presidents, Jimmy Carter, 1977" from Joel W. Solomon, Administrator of General Services, James B. Rhoads, Archivist of the United States, John J. Boyle, Public Printer, Fred J. Emery, Director, and Ernest J. Galdi, Deputy Director, Office of the Federal Register. Also participating in the ceremony were the following Federal Register staff members: Martha B. Girard, Robert E. Lewis, Richard L. Claypoole, Margaret M. Donohoe, Katherine A. Mellody, and Kenneth R. Payne.

November 1

The President met at the White House with:

—Vice President Mondale, Secretary of State Cyrus R. Vance, Dr. Brzezinski, and Mr. Jordan;

—Mrs. Carter, for lunch.

November 2

The President met at the White House with Dr. Brzezinski.

The President left the White House for a 2-day trip to New York, Michigan, Illinois, Oregon, California, and Minnesota.

NOMINATIONS SUBMITTED TO THE SENATE

NOTE: The Congress having adjourned *sine die* on Sunday, October 15, no nominations were submitted during the period covered by this issue. The first session of the 96th Congress will begin on Monday, January 15, 1979.

CHECKLIST OF WHITE HOUSE PRESS RELEASES

The following releases of the Office of the White House Press Secretary, distributed during the period covered by this issue, are not included in the issue.

Released November 1, 1978

Advance text: remarks announcing measures to strengthen the value of the dollar in domestic and international markets

News conference: on the Treasury Department and Federal Reserve Board measures to strengthen the dollar—by W. Michael Blumenthal, Secretary, and Anthony M. Solomon, Under Secretary for Monetary Affairs, Department of the Treasury

ACTS APPROVED BY THE PRESIDENT

Approved October 28, 1978

S. 1315_____ Public Law 95–539
Court Interpreters Act.

H.R. 4727_____ Public Law 95–540
An act to amend the Federal Rules of Evidence to provide for the protection of the privacy of rape victims.

H.R. 7749_____ Public Law 95–541
Antarctic Conservation Act of 1978.

H.R. 11671_____ Public Law 95–542
An act to designate a certain Federal building in Big Stone Gap, Virginia, the "C. Bascom Slemp Building".

H.R. 12634_____ Public Law 95–543
An act to designate a building in Pittsburg, Kansas, as the "Joe Skubitz Social Security Administration Center".

H.R. 13187_____ Public Law 95–544
An act to designate the United States Post Office and Federal Building in Griffin, Georgia, the "John J. Flynt, Jr. Federal Building".

H.R. 13514_____ Public Law 95–545
An act to name a certain Federal building in Shreveport, Louisiana, the "Joe Waggonner Federal Building".

H.R. 13972_____ Public Law 95–546
An act to designate the Great Bear Wilderness, Flathead National Forest, and enlarge the Bob Marshall Wilderness, Flathead and Lewis and Clark National Forests, State of Montana.

ACTS APPROVED—Continued

Approved October 28—Continued

H.R. 13989_____ Public Law 95–547
An act to amend section 1445(b) of the Food and Agriculture Act of 1977 to modify the formula for distribution of funds authorized thereunder for agricultural research.

H.R. 1392_____ Private Law 95–82
An act for the relief of Maria Miraflor Carabbacan.

H.R. 1400_____ Private Law 95–83
An act for the relief of Stefan Kowalik.

H.R. 1402_____ Private Law 95–84
An act for the relief of Rosario A. Calvin.

H.R. 1406_____ Private Law 95–85
An act for the relief of Lilia Araujo.

H.R. 1750_____ Private Law 95–86
An act for the relief of Anthony Rogers.

H.R. 1779_____ Private Law 95–87
An act for the relief of Gilberto Taneo Gilberstadt.

H.R. 1931_____ Private Law 95–88
An act for the relief of Juana Todd Atherley.

H.R. 1936_____ Private Law 95–89
An act for the relief of Lee So Ryung.

H.R. 1938_____ Private Law 95–90
An act for the relief of Santos Marquez Arellano.

H.R. 2253_____ Private Law 95–91
An act for the relief of Ruben P. Din.

H.R. 2369_____ Private Law 95–92
An act for the relief of Natividad Casing and Myrna Casing.

H.R. 2553_____ Private Law 95–93
An act for the relief of Young Gun Kim.

H.R. 2758_____ Private Law 95–95
An act for the relief of Carmen Prudence Hernandez.

H.R. 2759_____ Private Law 95–96
An act for the relief of Sealie Von Kleist Hernandez.

H.R. 2939_____ Private Law 95–97
An act for the relief of Derrick Mariano Tan.

H.R. 2944_____ Private Law 95–98
An act for the relief of Ricky Lee Trautvetter.

H.R. 3217_____ Private Law 95–99
An act for the relief of Meeja Sa Foster.

H.R. 3618_____ Private Law 95–100
An act for the relief of Martha Castro Fitz Maurice.

H.R. 3625_____ Private Law 95–101
An act for the relief of Peter Neal Smith.

H.R. 3835_____ Private Law 95–102
An act for the relief of Pece D. Van Arsdol.

ACTS APPROVED—Continued

Approved October 28—Continued

H.R. 4875_____ Private Law 95–103
An act for the relief of Elizabeth D. Yee Kraus.

H.R. 5163_____ Private Law 95–104
An act for the relief of Marinelle Khristy Cruz.

H.R. 6934_____ Private Law 95–105
An act for the relief of Donna Marainne Benney.

H.R. 7387_____ Private Law 95–106
An act for the relief of Noel Abueg Emde.

H.R. 7419_____ Private Law 95–107
An act for the relief of Vasilios Georgios Valcanos.

H.R. 8308_____ Private Law 95–108
An act for the relief of Jae Keun Christianson.

H.R. 10407_____ Private Law 95–109
An act for the relief of Ling-Yung Kung.

S. 337_____ Private Law 95–110
An act for the relief of Miriama Jones.

S. 579_____ Private Law 95–111
An act for the relief of Imelda C. Jayag Potter.

S. 612_____ Private Law 95–112
An act for the relief of Timmy Lao Olavere.

S. 973_____ Private Law 95–113
An act for the relief of Young-Shik Kim.

S. 1110_____ Private Law 95–114
An act for the relief of Juanita Binabise.

S. 1154_____ Private Law 95–115
An act for the relief of Jin Syen Suh.

S. 1165_____ Private Law 95–116
An act for the relief of Chester Chun Ket Young (also known as Chun-Kit Yeung).

S. 1166_____ Private Law 95–117
An act for the relief of Maria Elena Jumalon.

S. 1563_____ Private Law 95–118
An act for the relief of Do Sook Park.

S. 1618_____ Private Law 95–119
An act for the relief of Sang Yun Yoon.

S. 2248_____ Private Law 95–120
An act for the relief of Susanna Shu-hui Jean.

S. 2294_____ Private Law 95–121
An act for the relief of Joselyn Buccat Lalley and Jodelyn Buccat Lalley.

S. 2446_____ Private Law 95–122
An act for the relief of Caroline Valdez Sulfelix.

S. 3042_____ Private Law 95–123
An act for the relief of Mary Jo Natividad and Regina Natividad.

ACTS APPROVED—Continued
Approved October 28—Continued

S. 3051_____ Private Law 95–124
An act for the relief of Tsutomu Tanaka.

S. 3109_____ Private Law 95–125
An act for the relief of Ricardo Rosas Salazar.

Approved October 30, 1978

S. 3112_____ Public Law 95–548
An act to amend the Act of October 19, 1965, to provide additional authorization for the Library of Congress James Madison Memorial Building.

H.R. 12509_____ Public Law 95–549
An act to amend the Immigration and Nationality Act to exclude from admission into, and to deport from, the United States all aliens who persecuted any person on the basis of race, religion, national origin, or political opinion, under the direction of the Nazi government of Germany, and for other purposes.

S. 1403_____ Public Law 95–550
An act to provide for conveyance of certain lands near Dixon, New Mexico, to the University of New Mexico.

H.R. 13416_____ Public Law 95–551
An act to amend title 10, United States Code, to modernize the permanent faculty structure at the United States Military Academy, and for other purposes.

H.R. 13372_____ Public Law 95–552
An act to increase the price of migratory-bird hunting and conservation stamps and to provide for consultation by the Secretary of the Interior with State and local authorities before migratory bird areas are recommended for purchase or rental, and for other purposes.

S. 3551_____ Public Law 95–553
An act to make technical corrections in the North Pacific Fisheries Act of 1954.

S. 3189_____ Public Law 95–554
An act to further amend the Mineral Leasing Act of 1920 (30 U.S.C. 201(a)), to authorize the Secretary of the Interior to exchange Federal coal leases and to encourage recovery of certain coal deposits, and for other purposes.

H.R. 1405_____ Private Law 95–126
An act for the relief of Jennet Juanita Miller also known as Jennet Juanita Flowers.

H.R. 1428_____ Private Law 95–127
An act for the relief of Mrs. Angelita Short.

ACTS APPROVED—Continued
Approved October 30—Continued

H.R. 1450_____ Private Law 95–128
An act for the relief of Hildegard G. Blakeley.

H.R. 1777_____ Private Law 95–129
An act for the relief of Cathy Gee Yuen.

H.R. 1798_____ Private Law 95–130
An act for the relief of Kwong Lam Yuen.

H.R. 2256_____ Private Law 95–131
An act for the relief of Edmundo Alfredo Oreiro Espinueva.

H.R. 2292_____ Private Law 95–132
An act for the relief of Boulos Stephan.

H.R. 2558_____ Private Law 95–133
An act for the relief of Doctor John Alexis L. S. Tam and Yeut Shum Tam.

H.R. 2658_____ Private Law 95–134
An act for the relief of Nora L. Kennedy.

H.R. 3090_____ Private Law 95–135
An act for the relief of Fidel Grosso-Padilla.

H.R. 4404_____ Private Law 95–136
An act for the relief of Susan Spurrier.

H.R. 4530_____ Private Law 95–137
An act for the relief of Elisabetta Basso Gallizio.

H.R. 6664_____ Private Law 95–138
An act for the relief of Lily Lirio Galindo.

H.R. 7550_____ Private Law 95–139
An act for the relief of Johanne Lapointe.

S. 142_____ Private Law 95–140
An act for the relief of Gaspar Louis Sayoc.

S. 1006_____ Private Law 95–141
An act for the relief of Concrete Industries (Monier), Limited.

S. 2379_____ Private Law 95–142
An act for the relief of Jesusa Navarro Romero and Antonio Angeles Romero.

S. 2509_____ Private Law 95–143
An act for the relief of Rodolfo N. Arriola.

S. 2671_____ Private Law 95–144
An act for the relief of Masami Yamada.

S. 2687_____Private Law 95–145
An act for the relief of Doctor Allan Joseph Cawley.

Approved October 31, 1978

S. 995_____ Public Law 95–555
An act to amend title VII of the Civil Rights Act of 1964 to prohibit sex discrimination on the basis of pregnancy.

H.R. 13702_____ Public Law 95–556
An act to provide that the Territory of American Samoa be represented by a non-voting Delegate to the United States House of Representatives, and for other purposes.

ACTS APPROVED—Continued

Approved October 31—Continued

S. 3084_____ Public Law 95–557
Housing and Community Development
Amendments of 1978.

H.R. 1753_____ Private Law 95–146
An act for the relief of Marina Houghton.

H.R. 2259_____ Private Law 95–147
An act for the relief of Rogelio M. Encomienda.

H.R. 3613_____ Private Law 95–148
An act for the relief of Irma Victoria Bolarte Alvarado.

H.R. 7653_____ Private Law 95–149
An act for the relief of Jackson Ormiston Edwards Cuffy and Merle Cleopatra Edwards Cuffy.

H.R. 9075_____ Private Law 95–150
An act for the relief of John F. Johnson.

S. 1401_____ Private Law 95–151
An act for the relief of Elvi Engelsmann Jensen.

S. 3066_____ Private Law 95–152
An act for the relief of Yom Chong Ok.

S. 3106_____ Private Law 95–153
An act for the relief of Debbie Agatta Hepburn.

S. 391_____ Private Law 95–154
An act for the relief of Brigitte Marie Harwood.

S. 1826_____ Private Law 95–155
An act for the relief of Kainoosh-Fard Bullock and her son, Kami Bullock.

H.R. 1940_____ Private Law 95–156
An act for the relief of Dimitrios Panoutsopoulos, Angeliki Panoutsopoulos, and Georgios Panoutsopoulos.

Approved November 1, 1978

S. 3595_____ Public Law 95–558
An act to amend section 202(d) of the Magnuson-Moss Warranty Federal Trade Commission Improvement Act to extend the deadline for filing a report of rulemaking procedures.

S. 2534_____ Public Law 95–559
Health Maintenance Organization Amendments of 1978.

H.R. 8389_____ Public Law 95–560
An act authorizing the President of the United States to present a gold medal to the widow of Robert F. Kennedy.

H.R. 15_____ Public Law 95–561
Education Amendments of 1978.

ACTS APPROVED—Continued

Approved November 1—Continued

S. 976_____ Public Law 95–562
An act to amend the Perishable Agricultural Commodities Act.

H.R. 11002_____ Public Law 95–563
Contract Disputes Act of 1978.

H.R. 11209_____ Public Law 95–564
An act to provide for the establishment, ownership, operation, and governmental oversight and regulation of international maritime satellite telecommunications services.

S. 2788_____ Public Law 95–565
United States Railway Association Amendments Act of 1978.

S. 2539_____ Public Law 95–566
Middle Income Student Assistance Act.

S. 1562_____ Private Law 95–157
An act for the relief of Datronics Engineers, Incorporated.

Approved November 2, 1978

H.R. 12605_____ Public Law 95–567
Public Telecommunications Financing Act of 1978.

H.R. 7577_____ Public Law 95–568
Economic Opportunity Amendments of 1978.

S. 1029_____ Public Law 95–569
An act to authorize the Smithsonian Institution to construct support museum facilities.

H.R. 11003_____ Public Law 95–570
An act to clarify the authority for employment of personnel in the White House Office and the Executive Residence at the White House, to clarify the authority for employment of personnel by the President to meet unanticipated needs, and for other purposes.

H.R. 14224_____ Public Law 95–571
An act to authorize and direct the Secretary of the Interior to acquire certain lands for the benefit of the Mille Lacs Band of the Minnesota Chippewa Indians.

S. 2075_____ Public Law 95–572
Jury System Improvements Act of 1978.

H.R. 14145_____ Public Law 95–573
An act to amend title 28 of the United States Code to make certain changes in the divisions within judicial districts and in the places of holding court, and to require the Director of the Administrative Office of the United States Courts to conduct a study of the judicial business of the Central District of California and the Eastern District of New York.

S. 3081_____ Public Law 95–574
Federal Railroad Safety Authorization Act of 1978.

ACTS APPROVED—Continued

Approved November 2—Continued

S. 1487_____ Public Law 95–575
An act to amend title 18 of the United
States Code to eliminate racketeering in the
sale and distribution of cigarettes, and for
other purposes.

H.R. 12140_____ Public Law 95–576
An act to amend the Federal Water Pollution Control Act to provide additional authorizations for certain operating programs
under the Act.

H.R. 13597_____ Public Law 95–577
An act to authorize the Architect of the
Capitol to install solar collectors for fur-
nishing a portion of the energy needs of the
Rayburn House Office Building and House
Office Building Annex Numbered 2, and for
other purposes.

S. 2820_____ Public Law 95–578
Reclamation Safety of Dams Act of 1978.

S. 2247_____ Public Law 95–579
An act amending section 312 of the Immigration and Nationality Act.

S. 1835_____ Public Law 95–580
An act to establish a Rural Transportation
Advisory Task Force, and for other purposes.

H.R. 10343_____ Public Law 95–581
An act to provide for recalculation of the
retired pay of individuals who served as
sergeant major of the Marine Corps before
December 16, 1967.

H.R. 12393_____ Public Law 95–582
An act to provide for nationwide service of
subpoenas in all suits involving the False
Claims Act, and for other purposes.

H.R. 4319_____ Public Law 95–583
An act to amend subchapter III of chapter
83 of title 5, United States Code, to provide that employees who retire after 5 years
of service, in certain instances may be eligible to retain their life and health insurance
benefits, and for other purposes.

S. 3371_____ Public Law 95–584
An act to repeal certain provisions of law
establishing limits on the amount of land
certain religious corporations may hold in
any Territory of the United States.

ACTS APPROVED—Continued

Approved November 2—Continued

H.R. 3185_____ Public Law 95–585
An act to amend the Act commonly known
as the Miller Act to raise the dollar amount
of contracts to which such Act applies from
$2,000 to $25,000.

H.R. 1422_____Private Law 95–158
An act for the relief of Julio Ortiz-Medina.

H.R. 1748_____ Private Law 95–159
An act for the relief of Carmela Scudieri.

H.R. 1775_____ Private Law 95–160
An act for the relief of Karin Ehard.

H.R. 1787_____ Private Law 95–161
An act for the relief of Paz A. Norona.

H.R. 2291_____ Private Law 95–162
An act for the relief of Carmen Cecilia Blan-
quicett.

H.R. 3307_____ Private Law 95–163
An act for the relief of Anthony Casamento.

H.R. 7795_____ Private Law 95–164
An act for the relief of Veronica Judith
Hudson.

H.R. 8192_____ Private Law 95–165
An act for the relief of Andrée Marie
Helene McGiffin.

H.R. 8751_____ Private Law 95–166
An act for the relief of Francesco Giuttari.

S. 464_____ Private Law 95–167
An act for the relief of Sameek Keshary
Ray.

S. 2079_____ Private Law 95–168
An act for the relief of Lawrence Youngman.

S. 2349_____ Private Law 95–169
An act for the relief of Margaret Perry.

Approved November 3, 1978

H.R. 7971_____ Public Law 95–586
An act to validate certain land conveyances,
and for other purposes.

H.R. 7101_____ Public Law 95–587
An act to amend certain provisions of law
relating to land claims by the United States
in Riverside County, California, based upon
the accretion or avulsion, and for other purposes.

H.R. 4533_____ Private Law 95–170
An act for the relief of Gary Daves and Marc
Cayer.

PRESIDENTIAL DOCUMENTS

Veto of Bill To Change District of Columbia Retirement Program

Memorandum of Disapproval of H.R. 6536. November 4, 1978

MEMORANDUM OF DISAPPROVAL

I am withholding my approval from H.R. 6536 which would make certain changes in the retirement program for police, firefighters, teachers and judges of the District of Columbia.

This action today in no way alters my commitment to the basic principles of fairness and self-determination which must be the cornerstone of Federal-District relations. Included among our actions to fulfill this commitment have been (1) support of full voting representation, (2) support for expansion of "Home Rule" for the District and (3) support of efforts to provide greater equity and predictability to the financial relationship between the Federal government and the District.

I have also proposed removal of the Federal government from the District's Budgetary process by 1982, as well as the development of an equitable Federal payment process on the District's revenues. This process must rest on an objective, equitable basis and not be used as a device to balance the District's budget. To achieve movement toward that goal, I recommended a Federal payment for Fiscal Year 1979 totaling $317 million—the highest total ever recommended by a President.

It is against that background that my Administration last year expressed its willingness to work with the Congress and the District to develop a sound, reasonable solution to the District's current financial difficulties with its pension program for police, firemen, teachers and judges. Previous Administrations have declined to acknowledge any Federal responsibility for the District's current pension funding problems. In the bill that passed the House of Representatives, my Administration announced its willingness to assume sixty percent of the cost of making a transition to an actuarially sound system. This would have obligated the Federal Government to make payments of $462 million over 25 years. Instead, the Congress ultimately adopted a different method of funding which identified the Federal responsibility as that portion of the unfunded liability attributable to employees who retired prior to Home Rule. This would require the Federal government to pay more than $1.6 billion over that same period.

This proposal fails to recognize that a large part of that liability derives from abuses of the disability retirement statutes which were permitted to flourish by those responsible for their effective administration. It undervalues or ignores the significance of Federal assistance through the Federal funding of benefits for thousands of District employees who participate in the Federal Civil Service Retirement System. I am therefore of the view that the enrolled bill overstates the degree of Federal responsibility.

Although the bill's benefit and disability retirement reforms are desirable, its failure to apply these reforms to current employees constitutes a serious and costly deficiency. While the bill contains a penalty clause, the purpose of which is to reduce the Federal payment if abuse persists, the application of basic statutory reforms to all employees would be a far more effective and efficient means of preventing a recurrence of the abuses which have prevailed in recent years.

Accordingly, I am compelled to withhold my approval from this bill.

I realize that many members of Congress have worked long and hard with the Administration on this question. I agree with them that there is indeed a Federal responsibility to see that this program is converted to one which is actuarially sound and which minimizes opportunity for abuse.

I look forward to working with the Congress and the elected representatives of the District of Columbia early in the next session to develop acceptable retirement funding and reform legislation. We are prepared to consider a reasonable Federal financial contribution, providing that provisions are included that fully remedy the problem of retirement abuses. Work-

ing together, I am sure we can place the District retirement programs on a sound basis in a manner which both limits the extent of Federal financial responsibility, while also recognizing the Federal responsibility in this area.

JIMMY CARTER

The White House,
   November 4, 1978.

NOTE: The text of the memorandum of disapproval was released on November 5.

Veto of Bill Concerning Shipping Rebating Laws

Memorandum of Disapproval of H.R. 9518. November 4, 1978

MEMORANDUM OF DISAPPROVAL

I have decided not to sign into law H.R. 9518. This legislation, which would impose severe enforcement measures in the area of ocean shipping rebating, reflects concern with the possible disparity in enforcement of our anti-rebating laws against US-flag carriers but not against foreign flag operators. I share that concern, and any disparity that exists must be eliminated.

The United States is currently engaged in important discussions with several European countries and Japan in an attempt to reach cooperative agreements involving a number of shipping problems, including rebating. Rather than taking immediate unilateral action undermining these efforts, I have directed the Secretary of State, in cooperation with the Federal Maritime Commission and other agencies to pursue these talks vigorously and to report to me on their progress. I am also directing the Administration's Maritime Policy Task Force to provide, by an early date, a set of recommendations that will address both the substance of our rebating laws as well as procedures for enforcement, taking into account the inherently international character of ocean shipping.

In the interim, I am asking the Federal Maritime Commission to step up its enforcement efforts against illegal rebating under the authority now provided in the Shipping Act of 1916. The Administration is committed to assist the FMC in these efforts, and I urge the FMC to seek the assistance of the Department of State in obtaining any necessary cooperation from foreign governments.

Although I am withholding my signature on H.R. 9518 I believe the bill represents an important signal to foreign countries that we must work together to secure a cooperative shipping regime. I commit my Administration to work with the next Congress to develop a comprehensive maritime policy for the United States, in which the concerns reflected by this bill as well as broader policy issues can be fully addressed.

JIMMY CARTER

The White House,
    November 4, 1978.

NOTE: The text of the memorandum of disapproval was released on November 5.

"Get Out the Vote" Rally in Jackson, Mississippi

Remarks by Telephone to Participants in the Rally. November 5, 1978

Good afternoon. This is Jimmy Carter—at Camp David, as a matter of fact.

I've been out campaigning in the last number of weeks in 31 different States, recognizing how important it is to Democratic candidates to have a large vote. Since most of the Democratic voters are working people, quite often we are not inclined to vote as strongly and as eagerly as are the Republicans, because the special interest groups that really want something for themselves out of government are always the ones that are most eager to go and vote.

You've got a wonderful candidate, Maurice Dantin, and I really need him to be in the Senate to represent, first of all, the United States; secondly, Mississippi; and then third, of course, to help me on key issues as they come up in the Senate.

I was in Flint, Michigan, the other night, and I recall that I won the Michigan primary and got about 50-something delegates by less than one vote per precinct. And I went directly from there to the 10th District of Illinois, where the incumbent Congressman won by only 201 votes out of about 200,000 votes cast.

We've seen a very close race in Mississippi evolve, and I know that every vote will count. So, as President, I want to encourage all of you to do as southerners have always done, and that is to show that you run your own government and that your strong expression of opinion and will on election day is the guide for not only your future Senator, Maurice Dantin, but also a guide to me as President.

We only have a few hours left, the rest of the day and all day Monday, and then, of course, you can work on Tuesday as well. But there's no reason why everyone at this rally, 600 or 700 people, can't put in 15 or 20 hours of solid work between now and the close of election day Tuesday for Maurice Dantin and the entire Democratic ticket there in your State.

It's not enough just to come to a rally on Sunday afternoon and express your opinion that Maurice should be the next

Senator. You know how close the race might be. And I hope that everyone there will promise this afternoon before you leave to put in 15 hours of solid work on the telephone, with your neighbors, in your community, at campaign headquarters, to get people to go and vote, and vote for Maurice Dantin. He'll be a great United States Senator. I'll certainly be proud to have him in Washington next January. And as President, I'm counting on you to express in a democratic way your right to control your own government.

So, thank you very much for letting me be part of this wonderful Sunday afternoon rally for a very fine candidate. Now our confidence has to be in you. I know you won't let me down. I know you won't let your party down. I know you won't let your country down. I know you won't let Maurice Dantin down.

Good luck. As soon as you adjourn, go to work.

NOTE: The President spoke at 4:15 p.m. from the tennis courts at Camp David, Md., to the rally being held in the Main Ballroom at the Holiday Inn—Medical Center.

Uniformed Services University of the Health Sciences

Statement on Signing H.R. 13903 Into Law. November 4, 1978

I am today signing into law H.R. 13903, because congressional intent is clear that this bill does not affect my authority to make recess appointments to the Board of Regents of the Uniformed Services University of the Health Sciences.

NOTE: As enacted, H.R. 13903 is Public Law 95–589, approved November 4.

The statement was released on November 6.

Solar Photovoltaic Energy Research, Development, and Demonstration Act of 1978

Statement on Signing H.R. 12874 Into Law. November 4, 1978

I am signing today H.R. 12874, the Solar Photovoltaic Energy Research, Development, and Demonstration Act of 1978, a bill that authorizes an aggressive program of research, development, and demonstration of solar photovoltaic energy technologies.

The bill's long-term goal is to make electricity from photovoltaic systems economically competitive with electricity from conventional sources. I share that goal, and in my amended budget for fiscal year 1979 I asked the Congress for $105 million for photovoltaics research.

However, this bill also establishes specific numerical objectives for the Solar Photovoltaic Research, Development, and Demonstration program. These specific objectives are very optimistic. Technical and economic obstacles could make it difficult to meet these goals without massive Federal investments, or even with such investment. The Congress recognized that these objectives may be unrealistic and specifically provided that the Secretary should request changes in the goals if obstacles arise. Congress also recognized the risks involved in premature commercialization of solar photovoltaic technologies. It is still too early to concentrate on commercialization of photovoltaics. Photovoltaic systems hold great promise, but in the short run we must emphasize research and development, including fundamental work on the physical properties of these systems, so that this promise can be realized.

Therefore, I will not propose to the Congress that a broad Federal solar photovoltaic purchase program tied to the specific goals of this act be undertaken soon. Rather, consistent with congressional intent, we will focus on research and development that will accelerate cost reductions. We will also continue, where appropriate, small, carefully targeted photovoltaic purchases to meet technical objectives. This approach should lay a firm foundation for the advancement of solar power from photovoltaics in the future.

NOTE: As enacted, H.R. 12874 is Public Law 95–590, approved November 4.

The statement was released on November 6.

Veterans' and Survivors' Pension Improvement Act of 1978

Statement on Signing H.R. 10173 Into Law. November 6, 1978

I am pleased to sign H.R. 10173, the Veterans' and Survivors' Pension Improvement Act of 1978. This bill creates a new pension program for needy disabled veterans and their survivors. It removes the most glaring inequities of the old program and directs pension payments to those veterans and their survivors most in need. It will assure higher income standards for the neediest eligible veterans and their survivors and indexes these income standards to changes in the cost of living, as is now done with social security benefits.

This bill substantially carries out the recommendations for reform of the pension program submitted by the Veterans Administration earlier this year. It should save the taxpayers money in the years ahead, because it redirects available resources to those veterans and survivors most in need.

I congratulate the Congress, particularly Chairmen Alan Cranston, Ray Roberts, Herman Talmadge, and Sonny Montgomery, in passing this measure which generally meets the administration's reform objectives and confines the cost to reasonable levels.

NOTE: As enacted, H.R. 10173 is Public Law 95–588, approved November 4.

Presidential Records Act of 1978

Statement on Signing H.R. 13500 Into Law. November 6, 1978

During my campaign, I promised to work to make the Presidency a more open institution. So, I am especially pleased to sign the Presidential Records Act of 1978, which will ensure that Presidential papers remain public property after the expiration of a President's term.

In the past there were no statutory restrictions on the disposition of Presidential papers. Retiring Presidents, Vice Presidents, and their staffs could take their papers with them as their own private property. Under the new law, all but the most personal of these papers will remain in the hands of the Federal Government after an administration leaves office.

Once the documents are processed, they will be available to the public under the Freedom of Information Act. The exceptions provided for in the new law are sharply limited and carefully drawn. An outgoing President can restrict access for a period of up to 12 years to especially sensitive materials, such as those relating to a Presidential appointment or those which would constitute an unwarranted invasion of the privacy of a citizen. As a safeguard, the legislation also provides for the resolution of constitutional questions raised by disputes over the release of Presidential records. Of course, classified foreign relations and national security information will continue to be protected after the 12-year period under Executive order and the relevant Freedom of Information Act exemptions.

Even though the bill does not take effect until January 1981, I will ensure that the Presidential papers created during my current term will be preserved and made available as part of the rich historical record for future generations of scholars.

I wish to commend Congressmen John Brademas, Jack Brooks, Richardson Preyer, and Frank Thompson, and Senators Abraham Ribicoff, Gaylord Nelson, and Charles Percy for their leadership on behalf of this legislation.

Last week, I signed into law the Ethics in Government Act, which will require financial disclosure on the part of high-level Government officials and will subject the President and Vice President and others to the scrutiny of a Special Prosecutor if substantial allegations of criminal misconduct are ever made. The Presidential Records Act of 1978 carries forward my commitment to making sure that our Government is not above the law, and merits the trust of the people from whom a President and his Government derive their power.

NOTE: A enacted, H.R. 13500 is Public Law 95–591, approved November 4.

Friendship Force From Berlin, Federal Republic of Germany

Remarks on Greeting the Berlin Citizens on Their Arrival in the United States. November 7, 1978

THE PRESIDENT. *Ambassador von Staden, Chairman Max Schmeling—* where's——

ALFRED INGENWERTH. [*Referring to Mr. Schmeling*] He is not on board.

THE PRESIDENT. He's not on board.

MR. INGENWERTH. I am the flight director—[*inaudible*].

THE PRESIDENT. Okay. Well, we heard that he's done a great job in arranging this flight. We're very proud that you could come.

My wife and I have had a chance to visit West Berlin twice. Both times we were received with open arms, friendship, hospitality, and warmth. And we are very grateful that you have come to our country to learn about us and to see if we could respond with an equal amount of hospitality and friendship to you.

This is a very fine opportunity for the great people of West Germany and the great people of the United States to know one another better. We are very grateful also that the Friendship Force idea, which is my wife, Rosalynn's, idea, has been carried out so successfully during the last 16 months.

We've now had 18 exchanges between our country and foreign nations, involving more than 20,000 people, and your support of this program has been a very good demonstration of how valuable it is.

When I was in Berlin for the town meeting, many of the people in the audience had been to our country in the former Friendship Force flight. And their enthusiasm for the exchange was very inspirational to us.

I hope that while you are here, not only would you receive the welcome of myself as President, my wife, Rosalynn, and our family, but also your host families, whom I'm sure you will grow to know and to love, and also the people of the United States.

This is an important night to us. It's our election night. We're choosing about 35 Senators and 435 Members of our House of Representatives, I think 36 Governors, and many members of our State Legislatures. So, perhaps when you get to your host family, you will see how the election results will come in through the television broadcasts.

I will go from here to the White House, and I will be on the telephone a large part of the night calling and congratulating the winners and calling and consoling the losers. I hope we won't have any Democrats who are losers.

I might say this in closing: You are fortunate in many ways in coming to this area immediately adjacent to Washington, D.C., our National Capital. I hope that while you are here you will enjoy yourselves, because Americans like to enjoy themselves as well.

There are many exciting places for you to visit, and of course, you can learn about the history of our Nation, of which we are, of course, very proud. But I think the most important thing which you will learn is how the family with whom you stay lives, what they believe, what they are, what their interrelationships are with their neighbors, and how grateful they are to make new neighbors now across the ocean, those of you who have come here from Germany.

We are very, very grateful to have you. We've exchanged visits, as you know, with your Chancellor, Helmut Schmidt, and his wife. They're very good friends of my wife, Rosalynn. And this additional exchange will be the cement that ties your great democracy even closer with our own.

Thank you very much for coming. Welcome. And now I would like to walk down the aisle and shake hands with each of you.

NOTE: The President spoke at approximately 7 p.m. on board the airplane which had brought the Friendship Force members to Dulles International Airport, Va. In his opening remarks, he referred to German Ambassador to the United States Berndt von Staden and Max Schmeling, former heavyweight boxing champion and chairman of the German committee of the Friendship Force.

White House Forum on Inflation

Question-and-Answer Session by Telephone With Participants in the Forum in Hartford, Connecticut.   November 8, 1978

AMBASSADOR STRAUSS. Mr. President?

THE PRESIDENT. Yes, Bob.

AMBASSADOR STRAUSS. Can you hear us all right?

THE PRESIDENT. I hear you fine, yes.

AMBASSADOR STRAUSS. Mr. President, we're in, as you know, in Hartford, Connecticut, and Charlie Schultze, Fred Kahn, Ray Marshall, Esther Peterson, Lee Kling, and myself are here for our second inflation forum, much the same format we had in St. Louis.

Before we begin, Mr. President, I want to tell you that I was very brief when I opened this meeting, and I asked everyone to be exceedingly brief. And Schultze told this crowd that I didn't have the nerve to say that to you. Now, Mr. President, I do want to say to you that we were all a little lengthy in St. Louis, even including our Washington call. [*Laughter*] So, now I've shown this crowd I'm not afraid to say that to you, Mr. President.

I'll begin with the first question. The first question will be asked of you, Mr. President by Johnny Driscoll, whom you know, who's president of the Connecticut State Labor Council, AFL–CIO.

Mr. President, before he takes his question to you, would you make such statement as you would care to make?

THE PRESIDENT. Bob, you've taken up so much time telling me to be brief, I think I'll go just right directly to the question. [*Laughter*]

John Driscoll, go ahead.

MR. DRISCOLL. Mr. President, we sympathize with you in the tremendous problem that you're trying to deal with in the matter of inflation. And I'm very pleased that you have decided to take your case to the country in this way, to ask how people feel about it.

When you were sailing out of New London with the Navy, I don't know whether you had much of a chance to find out how Connecticut people act, but I hope you did find out then, or since then, that we do like to have questions answered. And I'd like to pose one to you which occurred to me after I read your proposals on this matter; and that is, in connection with wages and prices, you've proposed a pretty self-monitoring plan with regard to wages.

Every employer will be making sure that wages are held down to that 7 percent, compensation of all kinds held down to that 7 percent. But there isn't that much of an incentive or that much of a monitoring process, as I can see it, for prices.

The question is, why did you not use the same kind of built-in control by using the Federal income tax to either give an incentive to management to hold prices down, or to in effect "disreward" them, if I can use that term, if they fail to hold the line.

THE PRESIDENT. John, I think it's obvious that the people of Connecticut have spoken very clearly about tough government budgeting and management, with the results of the election yesterday.

Also, I think it's good to point out that in the last 21, 22 months since I've been in office, the people of your area have benefited substantially because of our economic policies. I think in January of '77, when I became President, you had about an 11-percent unemployment rate in the city of Hartford, and that's been cut almost exactly in half, down to 5.6 percent. In fact, in Greater Hartford, the unemployment rate is less than 4½ percent. But inflation for the last 10 years has been holding at about 6½ percent average. The

3 years before I became President, as you know, it averaged about 8 percent.

We tried to provide a very balanced program and believe we succeeded. The labor wage standard increase would be 7 percent, which is some reduction over previous years' experience, and, of course, we've asked business throughout the Nation, employers who set prices, to hold their own price increases ½ percent below the average increase for the last 2 years, which works out, if everyone could comply, to about a 5¾-percent increase.

So, the standards on prices are a little bit more stringent than labor; I think well balanced. We will be monitoring constantly about 4 or 500 of the top businesses in the country to make sure that they do comply. We will use every legal means at our command to induce them to comply— the arousal of public interest, the awarding of contracts on Government purchases, which consist, as you know, of enormous billions of dollars each year, about $85 billion a year.

And of course, the income tax incentive was designed to help labor by assuring any employee group that if they do comply with the 7-percent wage increase standard, that they will be guaranteed that their real wages will not fall. If the inflation rate goes above 7 percent, of course, there will be an income tax reduction credit for them.

So, I believe that in general it's a very well-balanced program. I'm going to do my share by holding down the budget, by holding down the Federal work force, by holding down Federal pay, by reducing the deficit down to less than half what it was when I ran for President, by reducing unnecessary Federal regulations, and I intend to be tough and persistent. And if I can get the help from labor and business, I can succeed as the leader of our country.

So, it's a well-balanced program—tight constraints on business and labor, voluntarily imposed, some tough Government actions that can be taken against business on prices. But in general, John, if you all will help me, I think we'll be successful.

AMBASSADOR STRAUSS. Thank you, Mr. President.

Mr. President, the next question will come from Mr. Edward Bates, who is chairman of the Connecticut Mutual Life Insurance Company of Hartford.

Mr. Bates.

MR. BATES. Mr. President, certainly for our company there is a very strong commitment to your voluntary program. And I believe a similar commitment prevails among our business community generally here in the Hartford area.

I have an equally strong belief that the success of the program will depend on what government does in its own area. You've made reference to areas that may require additional legislation. Could you share with us those areas that might be under consideration, either legislation to control inflationary Government spending or to alleviate the inflationary cost of legislatively mandated regulation?

THE PRESIDENT. Mr. Bates, I appreciate your promise to help us with this program. And I think you accurately represent the attitude of most business leaders in our Nation as well.

It's too early for me to outline in any specific terms what the legislative proposals will be. Both through regulation, administrative decision, and legislation, however, we will do everything we can to carry out the purposes that I've described. To reduce budget expenditures is one thing that's directly under my control, and the 1980 fiscal year budget will be very tight, very tough, very closely patterned to meet the needs of our people without inflationary pressures.

One very important success that we had in the Congress this past year—and we intend to build on it—is the deregulation of major industries, the insertion of higher degrees of competition into our free enterprise system. I think we've had proven success in the airline area. The ICC is moving on its own initiative to deregulate other aspects of transportation, and we'll persist in this same effort through legislation there.

On taxes, I outlined in my anti-inflation speech the fact that we would not approve reductions in general income taxes in the future until inflation is under control. I think that Charlie Schultze, or others there with you, Alfred Kahn, can better outline details of what we might do. But I can tell you ahead of time, before they even talk, that this package is still in a formative stage. But we'll try to put it together in an anti-inflation effort.

Some of the efforts will be repetitions of what we attempted unsuccessfully to get in 1978. A notable example is in hospital cost containment, which I'm sure would be very favorably supported by the insurance industry, and also by all those who need medical care.

AMBASSADOR STRAUSS. Thank you, Mr. President.

Mr. President, the third and final question will come from Mary Heslin, who's commissioner of the department of consumer protection, State of Connecticut.

MS. HESLIN. Good morning, Mr. President. I appreciate this opportunity to speak to you. I feel that the thousands of Connecticut consumers that voice their concern to us here have now the opportunity, I think, in turn to be voiced nationally.

We hear repeatedly at the various consumer forums that we have provided throughout the year two major consumer concerns, one being that of the increased food prices and the second one being that of health care costs. In these two areas, people are most vulnerable; consumers feel most frightened and most frustrated.

And I should like to ask at this time what government actions are planned to assist the consumer in restoring some of that confidence.

THE PRESIDENT. Miss Heslin, I know you've done a great job in Connecticut in protecting consumer interests, and I'll try to do the same thing from the White House on a nationwide basis.

One of our top priority legislative efforts in 1979 will be to pass hospital cost containment legislation. As you know, it was approved by the Senate. It was blocked by the special interest groups in the House, in committees. And I think an arousal of public interest in this legislation will prove that it is needed and will make our efforts successful.

In some major States, I'd say notably New York State, also Connecticut, of course, we have had good, proven results there when State legislation on hospital cost containment has been implemented. The hospitals' medical-care providers have not been suffering, and consumers have benefited greatly. In New York State, as a matter of fact, last year hospital costs actually went down 6 percent. And this is a very fine achievement and, of course, Connecticut had very good success as well.

In food prices, of course, this is something that's very difficult to regulate. And I don't have any intention of imposing price standards on food. This would be a very serious mistake, in my opinion. The market forces, however, on the worldwide basis, will determine food costs in our country.

I think it is accurate to say that in some of the major areas of the world, recent estimates show that there will be bumper crops this year. Our own Nation has had the best corn crop in history. Stocks of food in storage are fairly high. They are primarily under the control of farmers.

I think food prices will be much more stable than they were in the past. We will monitor very closely any sort of international decisions to make sure that inflation is not pressed upon us too highly. My own guess is compatible with most economists', and that is that food prices will not increase in 1979 nearly so much as they did in 1978.

So, in my decisions as President, I'll try to do the best I can to moderate food price increases, to stabilize price levels, and on hospital cost containment, go all out, with your help, to pass beneficial legislation.

AMBASSADOR STRAUSS. Thank you, Mr. President.

Mr. President, do you have a concluding statement that you would care to make?

THE PRESIDENT. Yes, Bob, I do, very briefly. This is an effort that has not been successful in spite of many attempts in the past to control inflation in our country. I am determined, as I said earlier, to be persistent and tough in my own leadership role in controlling inflation from the responsibilities that I have as President of our country.

I need to have voluntary aid and support in many hundreds of decisions made by private citizens in our country, leaders in labor, leaders in business. We are asking mayors, county officials, Governors, and others to support our program. And I believe that if we can arouse the interest of Americans, which already exists, accentuate this interest, let them know that the fight is not hopeless, that we can succeed.

This is a major battle, and as Alfred Kahn has said and you have said, many others have said, it's a battle that we cannot afford to lose. And I do not intend to lose this battle against inflation in our country. And I need all the help I can get, and I'm sure, with your help, we will succeed.

AMBASSADOR STRAUSS. Thank you, Mr. President.

NOTE: The President spoke at 9:30 a.m. from the Oval Office at the White House to the forum being held in the Lincoln Theater at the University of Hartford.

Also participating in the forum were Ambassador Robert S. Strauss, Special Representative for Trade Negotiations, Charles L. Schultze, Chairman of the Council of Economic Advisers, Alfred E. Kahn, Advisor to the President on Inflation, Secretary of Labor Ray Marshall, Esther Peterson, Special Assistant to the President for Consumer Affairs, and S. Lee Kling, Assistant Special Counselor on Inflation.

Appropriations Bill for the Nuclear Regulatory Commission

Statement on Signing S. 2584 Into Law. November 8, 1978

I have signed S. 2584, which authorizes the Nuclear Regulatory Commission's fiscal 1979 appropriation, and contains provisions relating to the national effort to develop a nuclear waste management policy and program.

On March 13, 1978, I established an Interagency Review Group (IRG) chaired by the Secretary of Energy and charged with developing a national strategy for dealing with the long-term management of nuclear waste. The IRG mandate recognizes the fact that numerous Federal agencies, as well as State and local interests, must be involved in the formulation of such a national policy, and in its implementation. The Nuclear Regulatory Commission has been encouraged to participate in the work of the IRG to the extent it deemed appropriate, in light of its position as an independent regulatory agency.

This bill directs the Commission, in cooperation with the Department of Energy, to study possible extension of the Commission's licensing authority over Federal radioactive waste storage and disposal activities not presently licensed. It also requires the Commission to report on means by which States might participate more fully in the process of site selection, licensing, and developing radioactive waste storage and disposal facilities. These studies, which are to be completed by March 1 of next year, will give the Commission an additional opportunity to contribute to the important work of the IRG. I expect the Commission to take the IRG's work on these subjects into full account and to closely coordinate its activities with the Department of Energy on these matters. I expect that the Commission's studies will serve as a useful supplement to the IRG's fundamental role in developing administration policy regarding nuclear waste management.

The policy being developed by the IRG is of paramount importance to me and to the Nation in reaching a viable resolution of nuclear waste problems. I look forward to receiving the IRG report in the near future, confident that the studies to be done by the Nuclear Regulatory Commission under this bill will contribute to those solutions.

NOTE: As enacted, S. 2584 is Public Law 95–601, approved November 6.

Veto of Bill Concerning Tax Structure in United States Territories

Memorandum of Disapproval of H.R. 13719. November 8, 1978

I have withheld my approval of H.R. 13719, which would have authorized special Federal payments to Guam and the

Virgin Islands to offset the local revenue losses during calendar years 1978 through 1982 caused by the Revenue Act of 1978.

Because income taxes paid by territorial residents to the governments of Guam and the Virgin Islands are based on the U.S. Internal Revenue Code, tax changes intended to reduce Federal income tax liabilities in the United States have a corresponding effect in reducing territorial tax liabilities. H.R. 13719 would have authorized direct grants to the territories to offset revenue losses associated with the 1978 tax Act.

While recognizing the defects in the current territorial tax structures which H.R. 13719 was designed to alleviate, particularly the effects of periodic Federal tax reductions on local revenues, I do not believe the bill provides an acceptable long-range solution. By replacing reasonable local tax efforts with direct Federal payments, the bill is simply another attempt to manage territorial deficits without addressing the underlying economic and financial problems which have led to those deficits. We can no longer afford a piecemeal approach to the growing revenue problems of the territories.

Accordingly, although I am disapproving H.R. 13719, I am directing the Secretaries of the Interior and the Treasury to study the financial situation of both the Virgin Islands and Guam and to recommend a plan designed to help those governments achieve a higher degree of financial stability without perpetuating a piecemeal system which is costly to the Federal government and which does not sufficiently encourage responsible financial management in these territories.

JIMMY CARTER

Civil Service Reform Act of 1978
Memorandum From the President.
November 8, 1978

Memorandum for the Heads of Departments and Agencies

On October 13, I signed the Civil Service Reform Act of 1978. The Reform Act provides us with the tools to make major changes in the management of our government. However, the Act will not cause those changes to occur automatically. In very large part, our success will depend on your efforts to implement the Act's purposes vigorously and effectively.

As you know, I gave a great deal of personal attention to developing the reform legislation and supporting it in Congress. When I signed the bill at the White House, I publicly pledged "to implement the civil service reforms with efficiency and dispatch." I intend to give the same close personal attention to implementing the Reform Act as I did to its development and passage. To assist me, I am asking Scotty Campbell, Chairman of the Civil Service Commission, to meet with each of you as soon as possible to review implementation objectives and needs. We must start immediately in translating the statutory mandate into reality.

Let me call your attention to some of the major features of the Reform Act that I believe offer significant prospects for improving the way we carry out the responsibilities with which we are charged. The Act:

—Creates a Senior Executive Service as a government-wide corps of more than 8,000 top executives to manage Federal programs of all types.

—Bases the compensation of Senior Executives and GS13–15 managers on individual and organizational performance.

—Provides the statutory framework for new systems of performance appraisal within the agencies as a basis for advancement and retention of employees.

—Gives managers throughout government more flexibility and authority in all phases of personnel management so they can hire, motivate, reward, and discipline employees as necessary to carry out their programs.

—Provides employees with fairer protection of their legitimate rights, including protection against political abuse.

Implementation of these and other features of the Reform Act call for your personal leadership and commitment. I know that I can count on you in this important effort and that you will give Scotty Campbell your full cooperation and support.

JIMMY CARTER

President's Commission on the Holocaust

Appointment of the Membership and Advisers to the Commission. November 8, 1978

The President today announced the 24 persons he will appoint as members of the President's Commission on the Holocaust. The Commission was announced by the President on May 1 at the White House reception in honor of Israel's 30th anniversary, and was formally established by Executive order on November 1. The purpose of the Commission is to make recommendations on establishing and funding an appropriate memorial to victims of the Holocaust, and to recommend ways for the Nation to commemorate April 28 and 29, 1979, the "Days of Remembrance of Victims of the Holocaust."

The 24 members of the Commission announced today are:

ELIE WIESEL, the Andrew Mellon Professor of Humanities at Boston University, a recognized authority on the Holocaust and survivor of Nazi concentration camps. He will serve as Chairman of the Commission.

HYMAN BOOKBINDER, Washington representative for the American Jewish Committee;

ROBERT MCAFEE BROWN, professor of ecumenics and world Christianity at Union Theological Seminary in New York City;

RABBI GERSON COHEN, chancellor and Jacob H. Schiff professor of history at the Jewish Theological Seminary of America in New York City;

LUCY S. DAWIDOWICZ, an author and historian whose books include the award-winning "The War Against the Jews 1933–1945";

KITTY DUKAKIS, of Brookline, Mass., who is active in cultural exchange and scholarship programs between the United States and Israel;

BENJAMIN EPSTEIN, national director of the Anti-Defamation League of B'nai B'rith;

RABBI JUDA GLASNER, of Los Angeles, an author and civic leader, retired as rabbi of several congregations in California;

ARTHUR J. GOLDBERG, U.S. Representative to the Conference on Security and Cooperation in Europe, and former Supreme Court Justice;

RABBI ALFRED GOTTSCHALK, president of the Hebrew Union College-Jewish Institute of Religion in Cincinnati;

FATHER THEODORE HESBURGH, president of Notre Dame University;

RAUL HILBERG, professor of political science at the University of Vermont and an historian of the Holocaust;

RABBI NORMAN LAMM, president of Yeshiva University in New York;

FRANK LAUTENBERG, national president of the United Jewish Appeal;

ARNOLD PICKER, of Golden Beach, Fla., a retired attorney, now active in civic and philanthropic affairs;

RABBI BERNARD RASKAS, of the Temple of Aaron Congregation in St. Paul, Minn., who is active in national rabbinical organizations;

HADASSAH ROSENSAFT, a lecturer and author on the Holocaust, and a survivor of Bergen-Belsen, who remained in the camp over 5 years following liberation and supervised the resettlement of the survivors;

BAYARD RUSTIN, president of the A. Philip Randolph Institute, former assistant to Dr. Martin Luther King, Jr.;

MARILYN SHUBIN, campaign director of the Atlanta Jewish Federation and national vice president of the National Council of Jewish Women;

ISAAC BASHEVIS SINGER, the award-winning Yiddish writer;

SIGMUND STROCHLITZ, a New London, Conn., automobile dealer, vice president of the American Friends of Haifa University, active in community affairs, and a survivor of concentration camps;

MARK TALISMAN, director of the Council of Jewish Federations and Welfare Funds;

TELFORD TAYLOR, professor emeritus of law at Columbia Law School, who served as chief counsel for the U.S. War Crimes Office at Nuremberg, Germany, from 1946 to 1949;

GLENN WATTS, president of the Communications Workers of America.

The Commission will also include 10 Members of Congress, 5 from each House, to be appointed by the President of the Senate and the Speaker of the House of Representatives.

The President also announced 27 persons whom he will ask to contribute their advice to the Commission because of their scholarly expertise and community service. They are:

SYLVIA BECKER, of Atlanta, Ga., vice chairman of the Zachor Holocaust Research Center;

MICHAEL BERENBAUM, professor of history at Zachor Institute for the Holocaust, Wesleyan University, Middletown, Conn.;

IRVING BERNSTEIN, executive vice chairman of the United Jewish Appeal;

THOMAS BUERGENTHAL, a Fulbright and Jaworski professor of international law at the University of Texas, and chairman of the Human Rights Committee of UNESCO;

YAFFA ELIACH, professor of history at Brooklyn College and director of the Center for Holocaust Studies;

MICHAEL GETTINGER, former executive director of the Atlanta Jewish Welfare Federation;

HELEN GINSBERG, of Denver, president of the Babi Yar Park Foundation, a Holocaust memorial park;

AARON GOLDMAN, president of Macke Corporation and active in civic affairs;

ISAAC GOODFRIEND, cantor of Ahavath Achim Synagogue in Atlanta;

GRACE COHEN GROSSMAN, curator of the Spertus Museum in Chicago, a Holocaust memorial and documentation center;

RABBI MARVIN HEIR, dean of Yeshiva University of Los Angeles and director of the Simon Wiesenthal Center on the Holocaust there;

RICHARD KRIEGER, executive director of the Jewish Federation of North Jersey and a consultant to Israel's Holocaust memorial, Vad Yeshem;

MILES LERMAN, of Vineland, N.J., vice chairman of the Zachor Holocaust Research Center;

PAUL LEWIS, of Dallas, Tex., a builder who has donated his time and money to building Holocaust memorials in 10 cities across the United States;

FRANKLIN LITTELL, chairman of the board of the National Institute on the Holocaust and chairman of Temple University's Department of Religion;

FRANK LOGUE, mayor of New Haven, Conn., who personally directed creation of that city's Holocaust memorial;

STEPHEN LUDSIN, president and founder of the Remembrance of the Holocaust Foundation;

BENJAMIN MEED, founder and president of the Warsaw Fighters and Ghetto Resisters Organization;

WILTON S. SAUG, a Cleveland attorney and president of the board of the Cleveland Jewish News;

JAY SCHECTOR, developer of the Holocaust studies curriculum for the New York City school system;

RICHARD SCHIFTER, a Bethesda, Md., attorney;

NATHAN SHAPELL, a Los Angeles builder, author, and philanthropist, and a Nazi camp survivor;

ABRAHAM SPIEGEL, a Beverly Hills businessman and philanthropist, and survivor of a Nazi camp;

RABBI MARC TANNENBAUM, an American Jewish Committee official and expert on the Holocaust;

SIGGI WILZIG, a Clifton, N.J., bank president and philanthropist, and survivor of a Nazi camp;

IRVIN ZIFF, national executive director of Jewish War Veterans;

SOLOMON ZYNSTEIN, founder and president of the American Federation of Jewish Fighters, Camp Inmates, and Nazi Victims.

Merit Selection of United States District Judges

Executive Order 12097.   November 8, 1978

STANDARDS AND GUIDELINES FOR THE MERIT SELECTION OF UNITED STATES DISTRICT JUDGES

By virtue of the authority vested in me as President by the Constitution and the statutes of the United States of America, including Section 7(a) of the Omnibus Judgeship Act of 1978, providing that the President shall promulgate and publish standards and guidelines for the selection of nominees for United States district court judgeships, it is hereby ordered as follows:

1–1. *Nomination of District Judges.*

1–101. Whenever a vacancy occurs in a district court of the United States, the President shall nominate as district judge to fill that vacancy a person whose character, experience, ability, and commitment to equal justice under law qualifies that person to serve in the federal judiciary.

1–102. The Attorney General shall assist the President by recommending to the President persons to be considered for appointment who are qualified to be district judges and by evaluating potential nominees. The Attorney General shall receive recommendations of such persons from any person, commission or organization.

1–103. The use of commissions to notify the public of vacancies and to make recommendations for district judge is encouraged. The Attorney General shall make public the suggested guidelines for such commissions.

1–104. Before making recommendations, the Attorney General shall consider whether:

(a) Public notice of the vacancy has been given and an affirmative effort has been made, in the case of each vacancy, to identify qualified candidates, including women and members of minority groups;

(b) The selection process was fair and reasonable;

(c) The person or persons recommended meet the standards for evaluation set forth in Section 1–2 of this Order.

1–105. In evaluating proposed nominees, consideration will be given to reports of Department of Justice investigations and all other relevant information concerning potential nominees and their qualifications.

1–2. *Standards for Evaluating Proposed Nominees.*

1–201. The standards to be used in determining whether a person is qualified to serve as a district judge are whether that person:

(a) Is a citizen of the United States, is a member of a bar of a state, territory, possession or the District of Columbia, and is in good standing in every bar in which that person is a member;

(b) Possesses, and has a reputation for, integrity, good character, and common sense;

(c) Is, and has a reputation for being, fair, experienced, even-tempered and free of biases against any class of citizens or any religious or racial group;

(d) Is of sound physical and mental health;

(e) Possesses and has demonstrated commitment to equal justice under law;

(f) Possesses and has demonstrated outstanding legal ability and competence, as evidenced by substantial legal experience, ability to deal with complex legal problems, aptitude for legal scholarship and writing, and familiarity with courts and their processes;

(g) Has the ability and the willingness to manage complicated pretrial and trial proceedings, including the ability to weigh conflicting testimony and make factual determinations, and to communicate skillfully with jurors and witnesses.

1–3. *Amendments of Existing Orders.*

1–301. Section 3(b) of Executive Order 12059 of May 11, 1978 is amended to read as follows:

"(b) The Panel for the District of Columbia Circuit shall have the additional function of recommending nominees for the United States District Court for the District of Columbia. In exercising this function, the panel shall use the standards set forth in Executive Order 12097 and shall forward its recommendations to the Attorney General.".

1–302. Executive Order 12084, of September 27, 1978 is amended in the following respects:

(1) Section 1–202(d) is amended to read as follows:

"(d) report to the Attorney General, within the time specified in the notification, the results of its activities, including a list of persons whom the Commission considers to be best qualified to fill the vacancy.".

(2) Section 1–203 is amended to read as follows:

"1–203. In evaluating potential nominees, the Commission shall use the standards prescribed in Executive Order 12097.".

JIMMY CARTER

The White House,
November 8, 1978.

[Filed with the Office of the Federal Register,
2:50 p.m., November 8, 1978]

Amateur Sports Act of 1978
Statement on Signing S. 2727 Into Law.
November 8, 1978

I have today signed S. 2727, the Amateur Sports Act of 1978.

The President's Commission on Olympic Sports reported that the frequent disputes between some of our amateur sports organizations have hindered the grassroots development of amateur sports as well as the performance of United States athletes in international and Olympic competition. This legislation, based on the recommendations of the President's Commission on Olympic Sports, establishes procedures and guidelines to resolve disputes without placing the Federal Government in control of amateur sports. The act designates the United States Olympic Committee as the coordinating body for amateur sports, restructures the Olympic Committee and many of its constituent organizations, and gives the Olympic Committee a mandate to resolve disputes through arbitration.

I hope that this legislation will strengthen United States participation in international amateur sports competition and broaden opportunities for all Americans to enjoy amateur sports.

NOTE: As enacted, S. 2727 is Public Law 95–606, approved November 8.

Veto of Bill Concerning Government Ban of Tris in Sleepwear

Memorandum of Disapproval of S. 1503. November 8, 1978

MEMORANDUM OF DISAPPROVAL

I am withholding my approval of S. 1503, a bill which would authorize Government indemnification, upon a judgment by the U.S. Court of Claims, of businesses which sustained losses as a result of the ban on the use of the chemical Tris in children's sleepwear.

In 1971 and 1974 the Government established strict fabric flammability standards on children's sleepwear to protect children against burns. To meet these flammability standards, the clothing industry treated fabric by using substantial quantities of the flame-retardent chemical Tris. In 1975, information became available that Tris was a carcinogenic risk to humans. Some firms stopped using Tris after this test information became available, but other firms did not.

On April 8, 1977, the Consumer Product Safety Commission ruled that children's sleepwear containing Tris was banned as a "hazardous substance" under the Federal Hazardous Substances Act. This led to the removal of Tris-treated children's sleepwear from the marketplace. Both the imposition of flammability standards and the subsequent ban on Tris-treated fabrics have caused expenditures and losses by industry.

The imposition of strict flammability standards to protect the Nation's children was fully justified. After it was discovered that Tris was hazardous to health, the removal of Tris-treated sleepwear from the marketplace, again to protect the Nation's children, was also fully justified.

S. 1503 would establish an unprecedented and unwise use of taxpayer's funds to indemnify private companies for losses incurred as a result of compliance with a federal standard. The Government could be placed in the position in the future of having to pay industry each time new information arises which shows that a product used to meet regulatory standards is hazardous. This would be wrong. Producers and retailers have a basic responsibility for insuring the safety of the consumer goods they market.

If this bill became law the potential would exist for compensation of firms who marketed Tris-treated material after they knew, or should have known, that such products constituted a hazard to the health of children. Extensive, costly, and time-consuming litigation would be required to determine, in each instance, the liability involved and the loss attributable to the ban action in April 1977, without regard to profits the claimants may have earned on Tris-treated garments in earlier years.

While it is most regrettable that losses have resulted from the regulatory actions taken to protect the safety and health of the Nation's children, no basis exists to require a potential Federal expenditure of millions of dollars when the actions of the Government were fully justified. Accordingly, I am compelled to withhold my approval from this bill.

JIMMY CARTER

Veto of Bill Concerning Government Ban of Tris in Sleepwear

Letter to the Administrator of the Small Business Administration. November 8, 1978

To Administrator Vernon Weaver

Today, I withheld my approval from S. 1503, the TRIS Indemnification Bill, because it would:

—establish an unwise precedent for paying industry for losses which occur when a product is used to meet a regulatory standard and the product is later found to be hazardous and eliminated from the marketplace;

—open the door for compensation of businesses which marketed TRIS-treated products after it was known, or should have been known, that TRIS was proving to be hazardous;

—result in complex, expensive and time-consuming litigation, particularly by large retailers who have substantial sums at stake and can finance such litigation.

I understand that some small cutting and sewing firms involved have received loans from the Small Business Administration, specifically under the 15 USC 636 (b), to help them continue in business and to preserve the livelihoods of their employees. I ask that SBA continue this work but, in addition, assist other eligible firms to the fullest extent possible under existing loan programs. This would allow affected firms which are facing financial difficulties time to recover and, where appropriate, to seek redress through the judicial systems for any losses they may have incurred.

JIMMY CARTER

[The Honorable A. Vernon Weaver, Administrator, Small Business Administration, 1441 C Street, N.W., Washington, D.C. 20416]

National Energy Bills

Remarks on Signing H.R. 4018, H.R. 5263, H.R. 5037, H.R. 5146, and H.R. 5289 Into Law. November 9, 1978

THE PRESIDENT. This is a day of great progress for our Nation and of great personal satisfaction to me as President. And I think it's a vindication of our system of democratic government.

Today I'm very proud to sign into law the five essential elements of our national energy program. Today we can rightfully claim that we have a conscious national policy for dealing with the energy problems of the present and also to help us deal with them in the future.

Enacting these five bills, as everyone here knows, has been a difficult and sometimes a painful political process. It's required confidence, dedication, vision, and hard work. But I know of no task which we faced at the outset of my own administration which was more important to the economic health and well-being and, indeed, even the national security of our country.

Events of the past 18 months have underscored the importance of this legislation. A severe natural gas shortage during one of our more severe winters, a crippling and unpredictable coal strike, the severe imbalance of payments in our Nation's trade, a deterioration in the value of the American dollar, and more recently in Iran a threat to a major source of world supplies—each of these problems has either aggravated or portends the aggravation of our domestic inflationary pressures. And each of them has been made worse or would be making them worse in the future without this legislation on the desk before me.

The energy bills that I am about to sign encompass the three major principles that I outlined to the public and to the Congress in April of 1977: first of all, that we must learn to use energy efficiently. We can no longer afford to run our factories, our schools, our homes, our public buildings as though energy were cheap enough and plentiful enough to waste. That's the first principle.

Second, that we must provide adequate incentives and predictability in the Federal Government, its laws and regulations, to encourage additional production of available expendable energy supplies in our own country.

And, third, that we must shift toward more abundant supplies of energy than those that we are presently using at such a great rate, to coal, with which our Nation is blessed, and also, of course, with the renewable supplies of energy, particularly of solar energy itself.

The conservation incentives that are embedded in this legislation are considerable and they are very substantial. They constitute a major step toward a conservation ethic in our country.

I believe that we all know that conservation is the easiest and the cheapest way to either create or to save an additional barrel of oil or a thousand cubic feet of gas or a Btu of energy. Mostly these incentives, as encompassed by the wisdom of the Congress, rely on natural market forces of a free enterprise system to accomplish the purpose. The government regulatory intrusion is minimized, and I hope and believe that with additional experience in the administration of these laws, this trend can be accentuated and made more rapid itself.

The Natural Gas Pricing Act of 1978, one of the bills that I am signing today, will end 30 years of debate over how natural gas should be regulated, how it should be priced. One of the major altercations of President Harry Truman with the Congress was his veto of a bill relating to this same subject. This act will for the first time provide a uniform national market for natural gas, with adequate incentives for producers to increase their production in a sustained and dependable and efficient way, and also to guarantee consumers increased long-range supplies of this valuable source of energy and also with predictable and moderate price increases.

The coal conversion and the energy tax legislation will shift our consumption away from the scarce resources toward those that are more abundant through tax incentives and tax penalties, yes, but also with tax credits for solar and other renewable energy. And they will move us toward a time when our society is no longer so heavily dependent upon finite and rapidly depleting sources of energy.

The promise of solar energy, use of biomass and others has been too long neglected as a major source of supply. And we are cooperating, not only within our own country but with our foreign friends, in the evolution of more efficient ways to use these inexhaustible supplies of energy.

The utility rate reform bill will encourage State regulatory agencies to prescribe electric rates so that there will be a more readily available supply of adequate electrical energy, that rate structures will be oriented toward conservation. And this gives the Department of Energy and interested citizens standing and the ability to intervene in protecting themselves and protecting the Nation's resources.

I would like to say also that overall, these bills, the utility rate reform, energy taxes, energy conservation, coal conversion, natural gas bills which I am signing, will enable us to save by 1985 about 2½ million barrels of oil per day. This is not as great as the original goal in the proposals that we made to Congress, but it's a substantial basis on which we can predicate future achievements in additional conservation of energy.

All of you here today in the audience and standing behind me have earned my deepest respect for your hard work on this bill. I would particularly like to congratulate the leaders of Congress. Tip O'Neill in the House, Bob Byrd in the Senate provided superb leadership when the prospects for success in this effort were very doubtful, when many people gave up hope that our Congress was able to deal with so sensitive, complicated, challenging, and, I would say, politically sacrificial an issue. There are no political benefits to be derived in solving the hundreds of disputes which have now been resolved, but I think a grateful nation will recognize in historical terms the great achievement of these leaders.

The key chairmen of the committees, Harley Staggers, Al Ullman, Lud Ashley, John Dingell in the House, Scoop Jackson, Russell Long in the Senate, have made this success finally possible. And I particularly want to thank the members of the Cabinet, but especially Jim Schlesinger and his fine group, who worked so laboriously and with such tenacity and with such confidence in the face of discouragement to make this success possible.

There are many others outside the Federal Government, some assembled here today. The Governors, the mayors, county officials, business leaders, labor leaders, private citizens, consumer groups, farmers, all rallied here, sometimes in this room, to meet with me personally, to meet at breakfasts and luncheons and suppers and banquets, to look at slide presentations, to listen to the arguments, and then to use their influence in hammering out the details of this legislation.

We also benefited greatly from the direct and indirect aid given to us by our foreign friends, and I would particularly like to recognize the presence here today of representatives of the Federal Republic of Germany, of Great Britain, Italy, of France, of the European Community, Mexico, Canada, all of whom have come today to recognize this achievement.

In closing, let me say that we've acquitted ourselves well as a nation. While the world watched, our people have shown the will and the courage to face this complex problem in a nation which was politically divided because we are one of the

world's greatest consumers of energy. We are also one of the world's greatest producers of all kinds of energy. We've been a leader in technological development. We've got long-range habits evolved that are difficult to change. And we've been so greatly blessed by God with apparently unlimited energy sources that we've not ever acquired the realization until recently that conservation must be an important part of our future lives.

And now with this legislation, we face the continuing challenge of the future with new tools and also with a new resolve. The greatness of our Nation has been proven, and the future greatness of our Nation is more assured than before this legislation was passed.

I would like to thank all of you as I sign the legislation now.

This one that I've just signed is the public utility regulatory policies act; this legislation is the Energy Tax Act of 1978. The next is the National Energy Conservation Policy Act—the men and women around me know how much blood, sweat, and tears went into every one of these. [*Laughter*] This is the Powerplant and Industrial Fuel Use Act of 1978.

Dr. Schlesinger has just returned from a visit to the People's Republic of China, to Japan, and he is determined, as am I, to administer this legislation well and, through our administration, to prove the wisdom of the Congress. And of course, as problems evolve or as regulation becomes unnecessary, we will ask the Congress in a sequential and predictable and evolutionary way to modify the bills as required.

This last one is the Natural Gas Policy Act of 1978.

I would like to ask Tip O'Neill to say a word.

SPEAKER O'NEILL. Mr. President, this has to be the biggest crowd that I've ever seen in the swearing in of a bill. [*Laughter*]

And this crowd truly means that this is one of the most important pieces of legislation to have passed the Congress of the United States, I would say, in a century. Because of the diversity of ideas and because of the parochialness of the problem of energy, we did have a struggle. But with your great leadership, Mr. President, the Congress of the United States enacted this bill. And I think it augurs well for the country, for the democracy for which we stand for, the Congress, and the world itself. So, I congratulate you, Mr. President, on your leadership.

THE PRESIDENT. Congressman Harley Staggers, the chairman.

REPRESENTATIVE STAGGERS. Mr. President, I want to congratulate you and commend you for your leadership. Without your leadership this bill would never have been enacted—I can tell you that—without your persistence and perseverance. So, the country owes a lot to you. I can say that. It's not a perfect bill. I didn't agree with all of it by a long way, but I worked for it, because you said and most of them said it would be good for America. And I think it's the best thing we could get. So, it showed it on our side that it's the best bill that we could possibly get out.

There are so many that need to be commended that I'm just not going to try to do that, but John Dingell did such a great job on our side, and I know that Tip O'Neill was always on top of it on our side; Lud Ashley, completely, all the time, and, of course, the Senators. There were so many of those that were in the conference that were really working hard to get it done. We just hope and pray that it'll be good for America and that we will have synthetic fuels in place to take the place of all other fuels by the time we deregulate gas. [*Laughter*]

Thank you very much.

THE PRESIDENT. Thank you very much.

Someday someone could write a book about the passage of this legislation. One of the most remarkable achievements was the formation of an ad hoc committee in the House by the Speaker and led by Lud Ashley, working very closely with the others assembled around him. And this made it possible to expedite in the House the passage of legislation which might have been blocked even permanently by the diversity of committees that are responsible for the passage of the legislation. This is not because of any defect in the House, but because of the extreme complexity of the legislation: Almost every committee in the House could have had some jurisdiction over this legislation. And I'm very grateful to Tip for his great leadership and for Harley Staggers, who's already spoken. And I'd like to ask Lud Ashley, the leader of the ad hoc committee, to make a comment.

REPRESENTATIVE ASHLEY. Well, thank you, Mr. President. I've got to be very candid with you. I hope you never send us a legislative package like the number you did on us last April. [*Laughter*]

THE PRESIDENT. You've got my promise. [*Laughter*]

REPRESENTATIVE ASHLEY. But if you find it necessary, Mr. President, I hope that I'll be able to play a part in the efforts as I have this time.

You're quite right that whenever you have a bill over which has been said the last rites as many times as this one, so many close votes, why, there are a number of people, most of whom are in this room, who claim credit—for example, the 207-to-206 vote. [*Laughter*] And since most of them are in the room, I'd like to say thanks to whoever it was. [*Laughter*]

THE PRESIDENT. We had a lot of people saying last rites, but nobody ever gave the benediction. [*Laughter*]

John Dingell is one who held the negotiations together on many of those occasions when Lud Ashley pointed out that the benediction was about to be said. And he's been a stalwart leader, one involved in this fight for many years. And I think that John, along with myself and everyone here, has learned a great deal in the process, has had to modify previous positions taken, but has believed in the future of our country adequately enough to retain the true measure of leadership. And I'd like to ask John Dingell if he would say a word.

REPRESENTATIVE DINGELL. Thank you, Mr. President. I feel about this about like I do about the elections—I'm glad they're over. [*Laughter*]

Mr. President, you've given great leadership, and we're proud of it. I don't think anything here can be said without mention of what Tip O'Neill and Harley Staggers and Lud Ashley and my friends and colleagues in the Senate and Jim Schlesinger did. It was an enormously difficult undertaking. I don't believe we've ever seen a larger pile of legislation signed at one time, embodying one piece of legislation. The complexity, the difficulty, and the bitterness and trouble that surrounded this legislation exceeds anything I've ever seen. But it has been accomplished. It is a good piece of legislation. And it is going to start moving the country forward.

Mr. President, I should advise that we look forward to working with you next year, and I should advise that the staff is at this moment looking into the successor of this legislation—hopefully in single pieces. [*Laughter*]

Thank you.

THE PRESIDENT. I came back from my western trip, and there was an almost unanimous belief in the Congress and among the news media that the natural gas legislation was dead. And it was the superb leadership of Bob Byrd, who, in effect, resurrected this legislation and led it

in the Senate to be passed. With his usual modesty he's asked that I not call on him for a statement, but I'd like to make the statement for him. And I'd like for us now to recognize the great leadership that he showed in this.

Another man who played a great leadership role in the Senate, not quite so reticent about making a statement—[*laughter*]—is my good friend, Wendell Ford. And I'd like for him to speak for the Members of the Senate who worked so strongly and so effectively on this important legislation.

Wendell?

SENATOR FORD. I thank you, Mr. President. Being reticent is not true. Bob Byrd said, "You will speak." [*Laughter*] And I have recognized leadership the last 4 years I've been in the Senate. Bob Byrd has given me the leadership I think I needed whenever I needed it. I think everyone in this room understands that. [*Laughter*]

Mr. President, I too, along with the others, wish to compliment you for the character that you displayed when you said to the Congress and to this country that we need energy legislation, no longer could we solve our energy problems with wishful thinking.

And I want to say that at no time was I disappointed with the effort and the work that was done by the administration. I think a group of men that only a few have been recognized, but I'd like to recognize them as a total, the conference committee. You know, you have to work with people to really understand their true character. And I was impressed with the desire, uppermost in the minds and hearts of every member of that conference committee, that this country would be strong through this energy bill. And so, I compliment them, Mr. President. I think you would, too, on the basis that this country comes first, regardless of their personal feelings.

And so, as we look to a new Congress, the ability to work together, find the rough edges in what we've done to polish this piece of legislation, I believe this country will recognize even though they call it a stack here—I love it a little more than that, because I do have some blood in it—but I do believe that this will be a singular moment in the history of this country. As we say to the rest of the world, the free market system will work, and we're going to get to it.

I thank you for the opportunity to be here today.

THE PRESIDENT. Thank you.

Bob Byrd has finally agreed to say a word. Thank you. [*Laughter*]

SENATOR BYRD. Mr. President, someone has said "Be bold and mighty forces will come to your aid." You're the first President who has sent to the Congress a comprehensive national energy policy proposal. It is a subject that has been around a long time. It is one of the most divisive, controversial, emotional, longstanding issues that we have had to confront the Congress in many years.

As you pointed out, Mr. Truman vetoed a bill, and so did Mr. Eisenhower, that dealt with natural gas pricing or deregulation in one form or another. So, this has been the toughest of all the issues as far as I am concerned that I have ever seen come before the Senate. And I want to congratulate you as President of the United States for having the courage and the vision and the stick-to-it-iveness to propose and to see this legislation through to its fruition.

I also want to congratulate Speaker O'Neill and the Members of the House who worked so effectively and diligently to make this day possible.

When I was in Europe in July at your request, the foremost questions on the minds of Mr. Callaghan, the Prime Minister of England, Chancellor Schmidt of Germany, and the leaders of Belgium, dealt with energy. And they wanted to know when the United States was going to do something about its energy problem and whether or not it had the discipline, the self-discipline and the willpower to do that. And I assured those leaders that the Congress, much to their surprise, had not buried the legislation, was going to enact the legislation, and was going to put the package on your desk before we adjourned. They had heard quite to the contrary.

And I think that that assurance helped in the forthcoming Bonn Summit, which you attended, because they saw from the congressional perspective that the legislation was not dead—and of course, repeatedly the tombstones had been erected over this legislation. Never was I once in doubt. And I assured those leaders we were going to do it. We did it, and so, today it's with particular gratification to my heart that that word has been kept.

Now finally, I want to say that the men on my side of the aisle—Henry Jackson, Russell Long, Wendell Ford, all of the other Senators who participated in committee, in the floor debate, and in conference—did a magnificent job, and I personally am in their debt, as I feel that the Senate is and as I feel that the country is.

Dr. Schlesinger, Frank Moore, Dan Tate, Bob Thompson, the other people on your staff worked very closely with the leadership in both Houses, and I think that to all of them and to you great credit is due. And finally, to our Nation I think this is a great day.

There's a statue in Atlanta, Georgia, on which there is the inscription, as you should know. It's erected to the memory of Benjamin Hill, and that inscription is as follows:

"Who saves his country saves all things, saves himself, and who lets his country die lets all things die, dies himself ignobly, and all things dying curse him."

The Congress of the United States, working with the President, has not let the country die, but has worked to save our country.

THE PRESIDENT. Just one more brief comment. There have been comments made about courage and vision. There was also a good bit of ignorance involved. And this spring and summer I began to see very clearly why my predecessors had never proposed to the Congress a comprehensive energy bill. [*Laughter*] And everyone deserves a lot of credit. But I would like to ask to make the closing comment Jim Schlesinger, who was the guiding light in the evolution of the original proposal, who was involved in every discussion in the Congress, who was involved in the hammering out of compromises, and of course on whose shoulders will now fall the responsibility of implementing the legislation and also administering the Department of Energy and perhaps in the future proposing the modifications to the legislation as we achieve progress in our country in the future.

I'd like to recognize and to thank, I'm sure on behalf of everyone here, Jim Schlesinger and ask him to make a closing comment.

SECRETARY SCHLESINGER. Thank you, Mr. President.

It is now 18 months or more since you signed the letter of transmittal in the Rose Garden. Those of us who have worked on the national energy act thought for a while that we were taking on a lifetime calling—[*laughter*]—that like the Council of Trent, the natural gas conference might go on forever. [*Laughter*]

We have come, as we sinologists say, to the end of a long march. And we have come to the end of that march because

of the leaders assembled here and to Senator Jackson, Senator Long, Chairman Ullman, others who could not be here. We are grateful to all of them, Mr. President; to you in particular for your tenacity in staying with this legislation.

Two points, Mr. President: First, it is the most massive legislative package ever to come out of the Congress. It is a good beginning, as you indicated, but we have received here about 60 to 65 percent of the savings in oil in 1985 that you originally suggested. And we will have to do better. There may be additional legislation for John Dingell and others to think about.

At a time where a single country in the Middle East in turmoil can cause difficulties for the entire industrial world, potential trouble, we shall have to do better.

Secondly, Mr. President, we have the problem of implementation. The FERC [Federal Energy Regulatory Commission], under Charlie Curtis, is working diligently with industry, with outside groups to see to it that the natural gas legislation acquired in pain will work.

Mr. President, next week we will publish our coal regulations. There are many who have said that the coal conversion bill has been emasculated. They will be proved wrong, Mr. President. [*Laughter*] Within a few weeks the very commentators who suggest that will be talking about the excessive authority that has been given to the Federal Government— [*laughter*]—in that coal conversion legislation.

Once again, Mr. President, thank you for staying with this legislation.

THE PRESIDENT. Thank you, Jim.

I might point out that none of these men who worked so hard on the legislation was defeated Tuesday, which is a good sign for the future.

And I would like to emphasize that this was a bipartisan effort. There was a very strong nonpartisan or bipartisan commitment to passing this legislation. I want to express on behalf of the entire Nation my thanks, not only to the Democratic leaders but also to the Republican leaders of the Congress who made this possible.

NOTE: The President spoke at 9:07 a.m. at the ceremony in the East Room at the White House.

As enacted, the bills, approved November 9, are as follows:

H.R. 4018, Public Utility Regulatory Policies Act of 1978—Public Law 95–617;

H.R. 5263, Energy Tax Act of 1978—Public Law 95–618;

H.R. 5037, National Energy Conservation Policy Act—Public Law 95–619;

H.R. 5146, Powerplant and Industrial Fuel Use Act of 1978—Public Law 95–620;

H.R. 5289, Natural Gas Policy Act of 1978—Public Law 95–621.

Jean Monnet

Letter to Mr. Monnet on His 90th Birthday. October 25, 1978

To Jean Monnet

I salute you on your 90th birthday—an occasion for celebration on both sides of the Atlantic. For many decades you have been one of the world's foremost leaders in helping to create the foundation of a united Europe. Your goals have always been world peace, equality among peoples, economic prosperity and, most important, uniting individuals on the basis of common interests and mutual respect.

Much of your dream has already come true: The European Coal and Steel Community, Euratom, and the European Economic Community have brought nations and peoples of Western Europe closer together than ever before in cooperative effort. I am proud that the United States has consistently supported these moves toward European unity. Your hope that the United Kingdom would join the European Community has come to pass, and we now hope that direct elections to the European Parliament will involve Western European peoples ever more directly in the Community's development.

I wish to express my deep admiration for your unique and vital contribution in creating this increasingly united Europe. And I want to underscore your special achievement in fostering the enduring relationship between the United States and Western Europe.

As Europe moves toward new forms of unity, you can count on the United States to maintain and strengthen that relationship. The stronger and more united Western Europe becomes, the more opportunities for effective partnership open up between all the main industrial regions. The Summit meetings in which Europe, Japan, and North America come together to concert their economic policies are, in a very real sense, a tribute to you. I hope that we will now be as ingenious in finding new ways to improve this intercontinental cooperation as you were in promoting unity in Europe.

Few men have left such a profound impact on their time. Few have been so innovative in creating institutions which strengthen peace and prosperity.

Your profound knowledge of the United States, combined with your energy, vision, and deep commitments, make you a true Atlantic, as well as European, statesman. On behalf of the American people and government, I salute you.

JIMMY CARTER

[Mr. Jean Monnet, Houjarray, par Monfort l'Amaury, Seine]

NOTE: The text of the letter was released on November 9.

1985

Great Lakes Fishery Commission

Appointment of Frank R. Lockard as a Comissioner of the U.S. Section. November 9, 1978

The President today appointed Frank R. Lockard, 39, of Waverly, Ind., as a Commissioner of the United States Section of the Great Lakes Fishery Commission, to succeed Lester P. Voigt, resigned.

Lockard has been the director of the division of fish and wildlife, Indiana Department of Conservation, since 1973.

Lockard was born in St. Francis, Kans., and graduated from Colorado State University with a B.S. degree in 1961.

He served in the U.S. Army from 1961 to 1963 and in the Army Reserve from 1963 to 1967. He was previously the chief of fisheries and a fish management supervisor in Indiana before becoming the director of the division of fish and wildlife. He has been a member of several wildlife societies and is presently the president of the Midwestern Association of Fish and Wildlife Commissioners.

THE PRESIDENT'S NEWS CONFERENCE OF NOVEMBER 9, 1978

Held in Kansas City, Missouri

THE PRESIDENT. I'm glad to be in Kansas City, and I would like to call on Mr. Scott Feldman [KNBC–TV, Kansas City] for the first question.

FARM SET-ASIDE PROGRAMS

Q. Thank you, Mr. President. It's been suggested that American farmers would be immensely helped if the Government were to drop its set-aside programs and urge farmers to produce simply everything they could, while at the same time the Government would push agricultural exports even harder.

My question to you, sir, is would you consider dropping the farm set-aside program, and how far will your administration go in demanding in world trade talks that the United States not open its market any wider to foreign goods unless those countries let in more American farm goods?

THE PRESIDENT. Thank you, Mr. Feldman.

I think it's highly likely that we will have set-asides. On a nationwide basis, we have had very good crop in corn, this year in particular, averaging for the first time over 100 bushels per acre.

The policy of our own Government, my administration, has been to try to increase farm income, and we've increased farm income about 25 percent.

We've also, every year, set records on farm exports. We have gotten recent information that the worldwide feed grain stocks are fairly high, but we anticipate very large exports of farm products this coming year.

I would say a moderate set-aside program, continued storage of farm products under the farmer's control, not so that the middle grain dealers can make the extraordinary profits as they have in the past, no embargoes on the shipment of farm products in the future, as they have been under previous administrations— this combination, I think, is the best to pursue.

I don't believe that the erection of tariffs or trade barriers would help us at all in the agricultural economy, because we export so many more agricultural products that we import. But we have recently signed a bill—as a matter of fact, in Kansas—passed by the Congress, that would improve greatly our opportunity to export farm products in the future with additional loans for those that might purchase our farm products, with additional opening of farm export offices to represent our farmers in foreign countries where markets are possible.

Mr. Pippert [Wes Pippert, United Press International].

RESULTS OF THE ELECTION

Q. Mr. President, I'm very interested in your assessment of the election, and a couple of specific questions: Why did Democrats do so poorly in this region of the Middle West; and secondly, with regard to Congress, how much does the more conservative nature of the Senate jeopardize approval of a SALT agreement, either as a treaty or as an executive agreement? And will the new makeup of the Senate make you hesitate to introduce such legislation as urban aid and welfare reform?

THE PRESIDENT. I hope I can remember those four questions. Well, in the first place, I think the Democrats did fairly well on a nationwide basis. We lost some very key races, some of them in the Midwest. I'd say one of the most serious was the loss of the Senate seat, Dick Clark in Iowa. But I just rode in from the airport with the new Governor-elect of Kansas, who happens to be a Democrat.

I think there was a general expression around the country of approval for the Democratic Party and its policies. I don't look on it as a referendum of whether I've done a good job or not. We retained well over 60 percent of the Members of the House of Representatives, Congress, about 60 percent in the Senate, and about 60 percent in the Governorships.

The election of Republican Senators and their effect on the SALT ratification—I think both liberals and conservatives, Democrats and Republicans favor

an agreement with the Soviet Union which would limit the threat of nuclear arms in the future. We have been negotiating the SALT II agreement now for almost 2 years, even longer, including the time my own predecessors spent on this effort. And I believe that if the SALT treaty is well balanced—and it certainly will be—it will be infinitely superior to no treaty at all and much better than the SALT I agreement under which we presently live.

So, I believe that we will have a tough fight in the Senate, as we've always anticipated, but I don't anticipate that partisanship will play a role in the passage or ratification of the SALT agreement.

I would never be hesitant about presenting any sort of controversial legislation to Congress because I feared failure. If I had had this inclination toward fear, I would not have been able to sign an energy bill this morning; we would not have had the Panama treaties ratified; we would not have had many achievements that we've already realized.

So, I wouldn't let the makeup of the Congress, which is still heavily Democratic by the way, prevent my introducing bills that I thought were good for the country.

Mr. Brooks Jackson [Associated Press].

DEFENSE SPENDING

Q. Mr. President, as you draw up the budget for next year, which you will be doing the next few weeks, you're facing the choice between, to some extent, guns and butter. We've committed to our NATO Allies to let the military budget grow. At the same time, you want to hold down, decrease the Federal deficit to $30 billion or below.

Is it true, as reported, that you've decided to let the whole military budget grow by about 3 percent faster than the rate of inflation while ordering a $4 billion, $5 billion cut of the projected gross of social programs? And if so, where are those cuts going to come from—Amtrak subsidies or Federal pensions or farm programs or where?

THE PRESIDENT. Well, I've been working on the 1980 fiscal year budget for months. I had my first hearings, preliminary hearings with the agency heads last April or May, and now almost daily, I meet with the Office of Management and Budget on future decisions to be made in the budget itself. I won't make final decisions on the fiscal year '80 budget until sometime next month, after meeting with the heads of the different agencies and departments of the Federal Government to let them appeal, in effect, decisions that the OMB, Office of Management and Budget, and I have made together.

There's no way that I can cut down the ability of our Nation to defend itself. Our security obviously comes first. And we have encouraged our NATO Allies in particular to increase their expenditures for a joint defense of Europe, and therefore us, by 3 percent a year above the inflation rate. I intend to honor that commitment. The final figures, though, on individual departments, and clearly the Defense Department, have not yet been decided.

I might point out I will meet my goal, which I announced in the anti-inflation speech a couple of weeks ago, of having a budget deficit less than half what it was when I was running for President. The budget deficit will be below $30 billion. It's going to be a very tight, very stringent, very difficult budget to achieve, but I will achieve it. And I'm sure Congress will back me in this effort. I'm also continuing a freeze on hiring of Federal employees. I have limited this year, with the Congress approval, the pay increases for Federal employees—there is no increase

at all for executives in the Federal Government. And I'll do other things as well to control inflation.

I consider it to be my top domestic commitment, and I don't intend to fail.

MEAT IMPORTS

Q. Mr. President, Jim Fitzpatrick, Kansas City Times.

Do you intend to sign the meat import bill, and if not, why not?

THE PRESIDENT. The bill has not gotten to my desk yet. And I expect to receive it tomorrow or Saturday. I'll make a decision then.

I might point out that I'm strongly in favor of the countercyclical approach to beef imports, where on a predictable basis, when the supply of beef in this country is high, that imports would be lower, and vice versa.

There are some factors that concern me about the beef import bill. One is the—I understand to be a severe limitation on the President's right to make decisions in case of emergency. But I'll have to assess the bill in its entirety. If I should make a decision against the legislation, however, because of the feature that I just described to you, then I would work with the Congress to include early next year a countercyclical approach. I think it's a very good approach. And I'll just have to make a decision before the end of this week.

Judy [Judy Woodruff, NBC News].

REVENUE ACT OF 1978

Q. Mr. President, the tax bill that you have signed contains cuts in capital gains taxes, which is the opposite of what you would have liked. It also contains cuts for people in the middle-income level, who are making between $10,000 to $15,000 a year. That is not going to be enough to offset the increases in social security taxes.

Why did you sign the bill?

THE PRESIDENT. Well, there were many features about the tax bill which were not my original preference. The reforms included in the bill—and they're substantial—did not measure up to what I asked the Congress to do. The final reduction in capital gains taxes was substantially below that approved by either the House or Senate. It was as low as the conference committee could go.

I think that we do need tax reduction, and the bill involves about $21 billion in tax reductions—and a part of it, by the way, is the continuation of the present tax reductions, which would have increased $13 billion, roughly, had I not signed the bill at all.

We did the best we could in the last few days—as a matter of fact, the last few hours—of the congressional session to make the bill more acceptable to me. In balance, it was acceptable. It was necessary. And I think that we do benefit greatly from the fact that the people of our country will not be saddled with $20 to $30 billion in increased taxes at the first of next year, had I not signed the bill.

I've not given up on my hope that we can have additional reforms in the future. And I think the capital gains reductions were reasonable, compared to what the House and Senate had both considered.

SOCIAL SECURITY PAYMENTS

Q. In line with that, Mr. President, last week in Kansas City, Senator Eagleton expressed concern over the social security tax increase, the bill that was passed. He termed it as a bad bill and one that needed to be reviewed. Do you agree with the review and possibly a reduction in the social security tax increase?

THE PRESIDENT. The original proposal that I made to the Congress last year, in 1977, was that the social security be handled slightly different from the way it was and that we have a reduction, as you know, in social security payments. The Congress—and I approved, finally—decided that the social security system was in such imminent danger of bankruptcy that it had to be saved; and it was saved by increase in rates.

I have no present plans to advocate a substantial change in the present legislation. If so, if I did have a reduction in social security payments, that reduction would have to be made up by allocations of funds from the general Treasury. I know for a fact that Senator Long, head of the Finance Committee in the Senate, is strongly opposed to this procedure. And I think even if I desired it, it would be highly unlikely that we could achieve it. It's one of the options that we will consider, but I certainly have no present plans to do so.

ANTI-INFLATION PROGRAM

Q. Mr. President, considering George Meany's reaction to your anti-inflation proposals, and in view of the fact that negotiations are coming up in a number of industries, major industries, during the next few months, what do you intend to do to keep the unions involved to adhere to your 7-percent wage cap?

THE PRESIDENT. Well, Mr. Meany did not reject the voluntary wage and price standards that I proposed. He expressed a preference that the Congress be called back into session to impose an extensive, mandatory Government wage and price standard throughout the entire free enterprise system of our country. I do not have any intention of doing this. And if I attempted it, I have no feeling at all that the Congress would approve.

In the absence of that, Mr. Meany, I think, made clear in one of the Sunday afternoon talk shows that he did encourage individual labor unions to cooperate, within the bounds of their desires and what's best for their own members. So, I've got, I'd say, a minimal, at least, degree of support from the AFL–CIO president. Of course, he recognized, as do I, that we have international presidents, themselves, to make decisions. There are several thousand bargaining units in the country. We've gotten fairly substantial encouragement from the UAW, one of the major labor unions, and also from the Teamsters, who will be negotiating a contract next year.

I'm determined, as is Alfred Kahn and other members of my administration, to make the anti-inflation package work. I don't intend to back down. I'll do everything I can that's legal within the bounds of my own authority and my influence with Congress to assure that the anti-inflation package is successful. And I think that most labor members, in organized unions or otherwise, feel that it's much better for them to control inflation than it is to let it run rampant, even if they were to get some small increases in—temporary increases in wages that are then overcome by increased inflation.

Everybody wants inflation to be controlled, including the members of labor unions.

Q. Mr. President, Stan Karmack, KCMO, Kansas City. We have confirmed with the Hershey Corporation this morning that the price of a Hershey bar is going up 9.3 percent. Since that is above your wage and price guidelines, will you try to put the bite on the Hershey bar? [*Laughter*]

THE PRESIDENT. If the report is true, then I would disapprove it strongly. We do have some persuasion that we can exercise. I would hope that the Hershey Company and all other companies would comply with our policy proposed, that any increase that they implement would be at least one-half percent below the average of their increase for 1976 and 1977. I'm not adequately familiar with the Hershey prices in the past to see if this is in compliance with it.

But through purchasing policies of the Federal Government, through competition, through the disapproval expressed by myself, other leaders of our Nation, and individual consumers, I would hope that any deviation from our policies could be controlled.

THE MIDDLE EAST

Q. Mr. President, question on the Middle East. Do you agree with President Sadat's view that the two agreements, the one on the West Bank and the agreement now being negotiated for peace between Israel and Egypt, have to be linked in some way?

THE PRESIDENT. Well, there's never been any doubt in my mind, nor President Sadat's, nor Prime Minister Begin's, that one of the premises for the Camp David negotiations was a comprehensive peace settlement that includes not just an isolated peace treaty between Israel and Egypt but includes a continuation of a solution for the West Bank, Gaza Strip, and ultimately for the Golan Heights as well. There is some difference of opinion between the two leaders about how specifically it should be expressed in the Sinai treaty.

I personally favor the presently negotiated language, which in the preamble does say that both nations commit themselves to carry out the comprehensive peace agreement as was agreed at Camp David. This is a matter for negotiation between the two leaders.

I have heard President (Prime Minister) [1] Begin say in my presence that he did not desire a separate peace treaty with Egypt. And, of course, this is also the opinion and strongly felt view of President Sadat.

We've been negotiating on the Mideast peace agreement for months. I have personally put hundreds of hours into it. We have reached, on more than one occasion so far, agreement on the text between the negotiators themselves. When they refer the text back to the leaders at home in Egypt and Israel, sometimes the work that has been done is partially undone. But I think that the present language as approved by the negotiators is adequate, and our presumption is to adhere to that language as our preference. But I would like to point out that we are not trying to impose our will on the leaders themselves or on those nations, and we hope that they will rapidly reach a conclusion.

There's no doubt in my mind that this kind of difference in language and how a linkage is actually expressed is a matter for negotiation. It does not violate the commitments made at Camp David, no matter what the decision might be as reached jointly by Egypt and Israel.

FARM SET-ASIDE PROGRAMS

Q. Mr. President, may I retrack to the '79—Sam Nelson, Commodity News Service—may I retrack to the '79 feed grain set-aside program?

THE PRESIDENT. Yes.

Q. You said you plan on a moderate program. Is a 20-percent acreage set-aside considered by you moderate, and do you plan to wait until the November 15 deadline to make your announcement?

THE PRESIDENT. I did not plan to wait until the November 15 deadline. I intend to move on it as quickly as I can. We did

_____
[1] Printed in the transcript.

want to wait until after today, because as you know, this is the date on which we get November crop estimates. And we wanted to have that information available before we put the final touches on the decision.

I would not want to give you any figure yet, because I haven't decided. But I will try to decide that either this week or very early next week. I don't intend to wait until the 15th.

RESULTS OF THE ELECTION

Q. Mr. President, looking at the won-and-lost column of the Democratic candidates for whom you campaigned in this election, how would you assess your impact in these races?

THE PRESIDENT. I would say when they lost, I had a substantial impact. When they won, they did it on their own merit. [*Laughter*]

Q. Mr. President, may I follow up? Seriously, do you believe that in modern times that a President coming into a city to campaign for a candidate really does sway the voter one way or the other?

THE PRESIDENT. It's hard to say. My time to campaign around the country is very limited. There are hundreds and hundreds of candidates, as you know. I think I tried to help roughly 50 candidates for the Congress, in the Senate and House, including Governors, I believe. And a few more than half those won. But I couldn't say that my presence either caused a victory or a defeat.

We did choose for my own presence those elections in almost every instance where there were marginal prospects for victory. When you go into a State, for instance, like California, it's obvious that Governor Brown was a heavy favorite. There were other Democrats running for the Congress, for instance, in the Sacramento area, whose elections were quite doubtful, and the same thing applied all over the country.

So, I don't think the President has too much of an impact on an individual race. The major purpose of my last swing was to encourage American people to get out to vote. The vote turnout was higher than we anticipated. It was not nearly high enough. I think three voters out of eight went to the polls. Five voters out of eight did not. But that was the primary purpose of my last swing, to help Democrats, yes, but to get out a large vote. I doubt that my presence had much of an impact on the outcome of those who won.

AGRICULTURAL ECONOMY

Q. Mr. President, Steve Saunders from KBCM Radio. You've already mentioned the countercyclical measure and the set-aside program. But aren't you playing with the profits of agriculture, maybe one of the only facets of our economy by itself that can help with the inflation problem, the devaluation of the dollar problem, and the balance-of-trade deficit, all in one, by not signing the countercyclical bill, by waiting until this late for that set-aside program, when most farmers wanted it earlier, and by allowing about 50 percent of the world's reserves of grain stocks to build up in this country?

THE PRESIDENT. No. [*Laughter*] We inherited a situation in the agricultural communities that was very depressing and of great concern to me. The farmers were actually faced with another depression. The Congress passed, with bipartisan support last year, a comprehensive agriculture bill. It went into effect the first day of October 1977. Since then, farm income has increased $7 billion this year compared to last year, a 25-percent increase in farm income.

In spite of very depressed prices in 1977, the exports hit an alltime record. This year, we expect to export over $27 billion, which is substantially above the alltime record set last year. We'll continue this balanced approach.

The farmers will have to do some sacrificing along with all other Americans. We can't concentrate all of our government's effort and ignore inflationary pressures, erect trade barriers just to protect farmers. I'm a farmer myself, and I never have met a farmer who, in a showdown, wanted to do something deleterious or harmful to his own country just for selfish advantage.

I think we've been very fair with farmers; I continue to be fair with the farmers; and of course my own stand is corroborated by the action taken by the Congress. And my decisions will be made very shortly, before the statutory limit, after the information on production that was received today, with which I'm not yet familiar. And I'm not waiting until the last minute.

The reporter with the large diamond ring on her finger.[2] [*Laughter*]

NATIONAL ENERGY BILLS

Q. Mr. President, you said when the energy bill finally passed that you were not pleased with all aspects of it and that you would work year after year to try to improve it. What specifically will you propose in January to change the energy bill that you signed today?

THE PRESIDENT. I don't know yet. As was pointed out this morning in the signing ceremony, this is one of the most difficult legislative tasks that the Congress has ever undertaken, possibly, in the history of our country. It's complicated; it's contentious; it's very difficult to understand. It has international implications, and politically I don't think anyone could win from it. It was not something that's politically attractive.

---

[2] Ann Compton of ABC News had recently announced her engagement to be married.

The proposal that I made originally with substantial taxes imposed on oil, the taxes to be refunded to the American people immediately, would have saved additional oil consumption. The bills that I signed this morning will result in savings of about 2½ million barrels of oil per day by 1985. The original proposals would have saved an estimated 4½ million barrels per day. So, we've got about 60 or 65 percent of what we asked for. But we do now have a comprehensive energy policy for the first time.

As we go into the implementation of this legislation, we'll obviously have some accomplishments, which means that regulation can be reduced. We'll obviously find some defects, I'm sure, in this complicated legislation, that I'll try to correct. But I've not given up on my original proposal that there should be a constraint on the excessive consumption of oil and therefore the excessive importation of oil. How we'll go about it, I don't yet know.

THE PRESIDENT'S RELIGION

Q. Mr. President, you're in the Bible Belt of the United States. And I was wondering if it's made a difference to you that you're a born-again Christian, in the last 2 years in office?

THE PRESIDENT. I think my religious beliefs are well known. And in my own opinion, a deep religious faith is a very sound basis on which to make difficult decisions and to have some assurance that you are doing the proper things. But I've been very careful not to interrelate my Christian beliefs with my responsibilities as President. But it is a great personal gratification for me to have that religious faith.

NICARAGUA

Q. Mr. President, you're being confronted with a growing number of pleas to help bring about a mediated peace in the Latin American country of Nicaragua. Is the U.S. going to act to prevent further bloodshed and repression, or do you feel that your hands are tied because you don't want to interfere in the internal affairs of another country? What can you do?

THE PRESIDENT. We are participating actively and daily in the negotiations to bring about a settlement in Nicaragua. I get daily reports from Mr. Bowdler. He was one of the three major negotiators there. We're working in harmony with two other Latin American countries in this effort.

We are trying to bring about a resolution of the Nicaraguan question. And I think you know in the last few weeks since these negotiations began, the bloodshed has certainly been drastically reduced. It's one of the most difficult tasks that we've undertaken.

And we proposed others to be the negotiators at first. We were unable to find an acceptable group. With our absence, both sides—I guess all sides, there are many more than two—wanted the United States to be negotiators. So, we are negotiating actively now to reach an agreement in Nicaragua to control bloodshed, to minimize disputes, and to set up a government there that will have the full support of the Nicaraguan people.

RIGHT-TO-WORK LAWS

Q. Mr. President, Bill Stilley of Raytown and William Jewell College Radio Station, KWPB. Missouri voters defeated the right-to-work amendment Tuesday. And I was wanting to know what effect do you see will this have on the right-to-work movement in efforts to repeal section 14(b) of Taft-Hartley?

THE PRESIDENT. I think obviously the outcome of the vote in Missouri will have a great effect on attempts that might have been made in other States to repeal right-to-work or to establish right-to-work laws.

This is a matter that I doubt the Congress will address in any concerted fashion during the coming year. So, I don't think that the Missouri decision will have a great effect on the National Government. It's a very highly controversial issue. The Missouri people spoke, I think, clearly, by a 3-to-2 margin. And I think this would be certainly a discouragement for an attempt in other States to impose right-to-work.

MR. JACKSON. Thank you, Mr. President.

THE PRESIDENT. Thank you very much. I've enjoyed being here. And I'm going now to speak to the 50th anniversary of the FFA organization of our country, of which I was a member early in my life.

NOTE: President Carter's thirty-ninth news conference began at 12 p.m. in the Grand Ballroom at the Muehlebach Hotel. It was broadcast live on radio and television.

Kansas City, Missouri

Remarks at the National Convention of the Future Farmers of America.
November 9, 1978

President Ken Johnson, former FFA adviser of Plains High School, L. K. Moss, fellow members of the FFA:

I'm proud to be with you today as a man who comes on behalf of 220 million Americans to say congratulations on your 50th anniversary.

I'm not here as a senior statesman of the FFA, to give you advice and counsel on how to run your lives. When I was in my final stages of campaigning for Governor, I went to Macon, Georgia, to attend the Governor's Honors Program, a group of the 400 brightest students in Georgia who were honored each summer with an 8-week training course. And they have a special day called Careers Day, and I was invited to be the main speaker.

I was very proud of myself. And when I was introduced by the host, a young man from south Georgia, he said, "We are very glad to have with us"—at that time—"State Senator Jimmy Carter. He's from Plains, Georgia. He went to Georgia Southwestern College, where he studied chemistry. He went to Georgia Tech, where he studied engineering. He graduated from the U.S. Naval Academy, where he studied naval science. He did graduate work in nuclear physics at Union College in Schenectady, New York. Now he's growing peanuts." [*Laughter*] "And he's here to tell us how to plan our life's career."

Well, my speech was over before I got the audience back. So, I'm not here to give you advice on how to plan your life's career.

The first thing I joined in my life was the Baptist Church. The second thing I joined in my life was the FFA. Our great organization was then only 9 years old. And as I began to prepare this talk—I don't have any text at all—I thought I would give you some observations from the point of view of the President of the United States and from the point of view of the secretary of the FFA Chapter in Plains, about the changes that have taken place in those years since I became a member of this great organization and began to learn about myself, my community, my Nation, my responsibilities.

In 1937, when I joined the FFA, farm life was much more similar to farm life in the time of Christ or the time of the pharaohs thousands of years ago than it was similar to farming today. We had no tractors on our farm. We had no hybrid seed to plant. Fertilizers were very limited. Excessive cultivation robbed our crops of their basic strength. The only pesticide we had was arsenic, applied by hand. We had no indoor plumbing. We had no running water. We didn't have electricity until I was 14 years old. Our life was confined to a tiny community. And the center of my own existence was my family; close-knit, mutually dependent on one another. Americans were not mobile then. It was a very rare occasion for a family to move. How different it is today.

We still have the greatest agricultural economy on Earth to provide food, fiber for other people not so fortunate as we. Our productivity has increased enormously. Farm population has gone down. Mechanisms, chemicals, advanced pesticides of all kinds have become an integral part of life. Family structures are not nearly so sound nor stable. With the advent of television and extensive news media coverage available to us, the horizon of our knowledge and our community within which we exist has increased tremendously.

Change has taken place so rapidly that many of us are concerned about it; it causes us trouble and doubts about the future, uncertainty. Americans are mobile. A dwelling place is a transient thing. But some things in the life of Americans—you as young men, I, when I was 13, 14 years old—don't change. The needs of a human being or a nation, the basic needs, have not changed. The basic values on which we predicate our lives as individuals and as a nation haven't changed. The aspirations of free people for the future have not changed.

It's not even necessary for me to say that you as leaders now will shape our own great Nation's future. Many people have said this to you in your own local chapters, even in your own homes. But one point I want to make to you is that you need not wait until the future, until you have finished college or have established a family or have a sound, dependable income, to begin to shape the future of the United States of America. Tap now and invest in your own community—no matter how broad it might be, even to the limits of the shores of our country—the advantages and characteristics of youth. Idealism, hope, innovation, and ability and eagerness to change things that you do not like; tough criticism of the status quo without fear of punishment or being fired from a job or disruption of a family; the exemplification of courage in making difficult decisions, taking unpopular stands—these are things that sometimes are almost unique with young people of your age.

I know all of you, because you are leaders in FFA, have a commitment in your personal lives to stretch your mind; to learn more about God's world, the technicalities of it, the history of it, the future of it, the expanding universe, the microscopic, even atomic, details that escaped knowledge just a few generations ago; and also to stretch your hearts to encompass more friends, to know more people, to love others, to know about them, to search for truth. I think it's accurate to say that the excitement of one's life depends on how deeply you become involved as a person in knowing and helping to shape the community within which you live, no matter how small or how large that community might be.

Leadership has characteristics that have challenged men and women for centuries. As a young man, and as President, I've learned some things about leadership. One is that the fear of failure is one of the greatest obstacles to progress. How timid we are when we challenge some obstacle or engage in some contest or set a high goal for ourselves. How timid we are that we might fail in the effort and perhaps be the subject of ridicule or criticism or scorn. And so we are tempted to sit quietly and not do anything and let the world pass us by. Or perhaps we become so obsessed with our own personal problems or transient problems that are temporary in nature that we have no driving inclination for personal and superb achievement commensurate with our own native ability and potential.

I acknowledge as a politician that attacking problems can sometimes be dangerous. This morning I signed a comprehensive energy bill, five major pieces of legislation, perhaps the most difficult, complicated, far-reaching that the Congress has considered in its long existence. There was no political benefit to be derived, because it's highly contentious, separates from one another producers from consumers.

The Panama Canal treaties, finally approved by the Senate, were difficult for the Members of the Senate to address. There was no political gain to be derived from taking a courageous stand to treat this small country with deference, as a powerful nation should.

The Mideast questions are some that we might very well avoid, because any failure there now or in the future could redound to the discredit of the leaders who tried to bring peace.

Inflation, my biggest domestic challenge of the present and the future months—there is no way to win, because when you try to control inflation, control spending, it's inevitable that you aggravate very fine special interest groups, perhaps students, perhaps farmers, perhaps the aged, perhaps some who are unemployed, because there has to be a limit to Federal spending or a reduction of deficits and a much sounder management of Government money than has been the case in the past.

Even when you are successful partially—in cutting the unemployment rate 25 percent, adding 6½ million new jobs, increasing farm income 25 percent in the last year, trying to impose economic justice on our Nation—you still become identified with not necessarily the solution, but you've become identified with the remaining portion of the problem.

It's always a mistake to try for universal approbation, universal approval, because if you fear making anyone mad, then you ultimately probe for the lowest common denominator of human achievement.

I have found it much more difficult to be a leader in a time of calm than in a time of crisis. Leaders are very popular in a time of crisis, because it's easy to arouse support for the interests of those who are concerned with the crisis itself. But to take action to prevent a future crisis that can't be easily detected nor proven is a very difficult task indeed.

Leaders in FFA at the national, State, or local level, Governors, Presidents, have a lot of advisers, very valuable. But the most difficult decisions of all, the toughest decisions almost invariably, I have found, must be made alone.

I've also found that the less you know about a subject, the easier it is to make a decision about it. When you know the complexities of a question and have to balance one set of arguments against another, learn the details of a complicated issue, it's much more difficult to make a decision. But if you take a simplistic approach, only look at the surface of a question, one side of an argument, it's indeed quite easy to make a decision.

I agree with President Harry Truman, who said he wished he had economic advisers with only one hand, because they always say, "On one hand this, and on the other hand this. Now, Mr. President, you make the decision."

As a candidate, as a young leader, and now as President, I've also found that there is absolutely no substitute for detailed knowledge nor for hard work. I planned my Presidential campaign for 2 years before I made my plans public, and I campaigned, I and my family and many helpers, for 2 more years.

In the energy bill passed this morning, there were literally tens of thousands of hours of work put in by me, my assistants in the executive branch of Government, the Members of the Congress, their staff members and advisers.

When I prepared to go to Camp David to meet with President Sadat and Prime Minister Begin, I put in hundreds of hours studying the history of the Middle East, the character of the two leaders, the attitudes of the people involved, the issues involved, the disputes, the future.

Only with tenacity and knowledge and hard work can any achievement be reached. I've never seen an exception to this, at least in my own life.

Everyone has limits on authority or influence. You do, and so do I. The Constitution of the United States puts very severe limits on a President. This is often seen in a President's struggle to deal with the problems of the day.

Franklin Delano Roosevelt was well known as one of the most powerful and influential Presidents of history. But in the last 7 years of his administration, ever since 1938, until he died in 1945, he was never able to get a single important piece of legislation through the Congress.

Woodrow Wilson, a great and inspiring leader, was not able to implement through the Senate of the United States the ratification of the League of Nations, which might very well have prevented World War II.

John Fitzgerald Kennedy, an inspirational leader, admired by the world, had a very ineffective dealing with the Congress on major legislation like civil rights and others.

Lyndon Baines Johnson, who was very effective in dealing with the Congress, was never able to extricate our country from a bitter and divisive war in Vietnam.

Teddy Roosevelt said that the White House was a bully pulpit. Franklin Delano Roosevelt said that the primary purpose of a President was to be a moral leader. And it's aways a danger for those in positions of leadership to moralize or to preach to others or to ascribe superior characteristics to oneself or to those one leads. And it's very difficult for Americans to realize that we are not superior to other people.

We need to have increased trust in our Nation, the recognition of its innate strength, trust in its elected officials, the overwhelming majority of whom are honest and sincere and dedicated and only wanting to do one thing, and that's a good job, if for no other reason just to be elected. But I believe they're all dedicated in trying to have a better country through a better government.

In the past we have seen trust in government lost, and the only way I know to restore trust in government is for the government to be trustworthy, to be be open and honest, ethical, committed to peace, epitomizing the ideals and aspirations on which our country was originally founded.

Well, for you and for me, present, potential, and future leaders, we face possibly an escalating or growing prospect for change and for conflict within our country's people.

Ours is a nation of diversity. We've now got about 150 other nations on Earth. Social, economic, military, political interrelationships change very rapidly, and the conflicts are inevitable. But we have a great responsibility as a leading nation and as leaders within our Nation to orient this change and this conflict in a constructive way toward better security for all, obviously for our own country: strength, not based just on military might but on the strength of convictions, on the strength of the quality of our government—solving an age-old problem about which I spoke often to young people during the campaign: Liberty—on the one hand, to do what you choose, to be an individual, to stand on your own feet, to make your own decisions, to shape your own life; and on the other, equality of opportunity sometimes in conflict one with another, because we might say if we are superior and have a superior position in life, why should not we enjoy the benefits of it? Why should we grant equality to someone not so competent, not so rich, not so powerful, not so influential as we? But our Nation's moved a long way since 200 years ago, when it was founded on freedom and equality, to correlate the innate conflict between these two ideals.

And ours ought to be a nation, and you ought to have a life, dedicated to peace. Diversity can be shaped into a common purpose. But we have to understand the ideas involved in the historic life of our Nation. We have to express clearly the underlying ideas in the historic life of our Nation. And then we have to implement progress based on the innate ideas in the historic life of our Nation.

Your leadership, my leadership as President even, must be shared. In Government, I have to share responsibility with the Congress, with the courts, State and local officials. And so do you. But the fount of power in our country rests in an informed public—an informed public— a public that's aware of the alternatives that we have available to us, to explore those alternatives through open debate, through democratic processes, through freedom of speech, and then shape common goals that are worthy of a great nation like our own.

All of you are leaders; young people are potential leaders, but leaders toward what? Toward hatred? Toward division? Toward prejudice? Toward a defiance of the law? Toward a tearing of the fabric of the society that sustains us? Toward the destruction of one's body with drugs, alcohol? Obviously, for you, no, because this is completely contrary to what the FFA stands for. But knowing this and being blessed with your present leadership capability, where others look to you with that blue jacket on and say, "There is a member of the Future Farmers of America, what is she or he like?"

There's a great opportunity for you to repair the damage that has been done through inadvertence or laziness or withdrawal from among your own circle of friends, to raise high the banner of idealism and commitment and truth and honesty and compassion and love and competence, human rights that epitomizes our Nation.

Those are the things that you can do. So, whether one is the secretary of a local FFA Chapter, which I was, or the President of the greatest nation on Earth, it's our responsibility together as partners, as common leaders, to bring out the best in the people who observe us and to make even greater the greatest nation on Earth.

Thank you very much.

NOTE: The President spoke at 2 p.m. in the Municipal Auditorium Arena. In his opening remarks, he referred to J. Ken Johnson, national president of the Future Farmers of America.

Inspector General Act of 1978

Memorandum From the President. November 8, 1978

Memorandum for the Secretary of Agriculture, the Secretary of Commerce, the Secretary of Housing and Urban Devel-

opment, the Secretary of Interior, the Secretary of Labor, the Secretary of Transportation, the Director, Community Services Administration, the Administrator, Environmental Protection Agency, the Administrator of General Services, the Administrator, National Aeronautics and Space Administration, the Administrator, Small Business Administration, the Administrator of Veterans Affairs

Subject: Implementation of the Inspector General Act

One of the highest priorities of my Administration is the detection and prevention of fraud, waste, and inefficiency in the operation of Federal programs. As you know, I take very seriously our obligation to conduct the public's business with the utmost integrity.

On October 12 I signed a bill establishing Offices of Inspectors General in each of your departments and agencies. It places under these officials virtually all of your audit and investigative resources. I would like to select these Inspectors General personally and send their names to the Senate for confirmation as soon as possible. Therefore, please suggest at least three candidates of exceptional integrity and ability to me without delay. I will also seek the names of potential appointees from other sources.

I also want to ensure an early, well-coordinated effort to establish the new offices. I am therefore asking Jim McIntyre to see which present resources and functions should be assigned to the new offices and to set the process up quickly and efficiently.

JIMMY CARTER

NOTE: The text of the memorandum was released on November 10.

National Parks and Recreation Act of 1978

**Statement on Signing S. 791 Into Law.
November 10, 1978**

It is with great pleasure that I sign the National Parks and Recreation Act of 1978. This bill is the most significant conservation legislation to pass the 95th Congress. This new law reaffirms our Nation's commitment to the preservation of our heritage, a commitment which strives to improve the quality of the present by our dedication to preserving the past and conserving our historical and natural resources for our children and grandchildren. It honors those who helped to shape and develop this Nation; it acknowledges our need to receive strength and sustenance from natural beauty; and it addresses the pressing need to improve recreational opportunities in our urban areas.

Specifically, this bill:
—Establishes 15 new units in the National Park System and authorizes increased land acquisition and other improvements in numerous existing units;
—Designates 1,974,005 acres in 8 National Parks as wilderness;
—Authorizes $725 million over the next 5 years to renovate recreation facilities in urban areas;
—Establishes 8 new rivers as components of the Wild and Scenic Rivers System; and
—Designates 17 new rivers to be studied for addition to the Wild and Scenic Rivers System.

Many of the specific items in this act were included in my 1977 environmental message to the Congress, and I want to thank the Congress for moving forward with these administration proposals. This bill also includes the administration's

Urban Park and Recreation Recovery program, which will provide $725 million of assistance to urban areas for use in augmenting their urban recreation programs. The passage of this legislation is a great achievement.

However, I must note my reservations regarding the constitutionality of one of the bill's provisions, Sec. 1301, which would require the Secretary of Agriculture to seek the permission of Congress to exercise his existing power to exchange certain Federal lands in the State of Montana for certain private lands in that State where an exchange involves more than 6,400 acres. It is my view, and that of the Department of Justice, that the execution of laws such as those empowering the Secretary of Agriculture to exchange Federal land for non-Federal land may not be invalidated or otherwise controlled by Congress except by legislation subject to the President's veto power under Art. I, Sec. 7 of the Constitution. For this reason, I have directed the Secretary of Agriculture to report to the Congress, pursuant to the reporting requirement of Sec. 1301, the details of land-for-land exchanges covered by Sec. 1301 and to listen to any concerns which may be expressed by the specified congressional committees. At the same time, I have instructed the Secretary that he may consummate any land-for-land exchanges covered by Sec. 1301 which are, in his opinion, otherwise authorized by statute, irrespective of the acreage involved.

A great number of people contributed to the passage of this legislation. I would like to give special recognition to the efforts of Representative Phil Burton and Senator James Abourezk. Without their exceptional leadership this legislation would not be before me today. I am proud that this administration has taken an active part in the passage of this legislation.

I look forward to working with the Congress to assure its swift implementation.

NOTE: As enacted, S. 791 is Public Law 95–625, approved November 10.

Child Nutrition Amendments of 1978

Statement on Signing S. 3085 Into Law. November 10, 1978

I am signing into law S. 3085, the Child Nutrition Amendments of 1978. This legislation funds school food programs, the child care food program, and substantially expands the Special Supplemental Food Program for Women, Infants, and Children (WIC).

The amendments contain administration proposals to increase management efficiency and to establish national income standards to assure that only those persons in need receive program benefits. Other administration proposals in the amendments will reduce our expenditures for school feeding programs, simplify recordkeeping for the school breakfast program, and extend the child care food program, which provides nutritious meals to children in day care centers.

There are significant problems with this legislation which can be corrected by the next Congress. The spending levels for fiscal year 1980 and thereafter are higher than the substantial WIC increases that I recommended to the Congress. These increases and the failure of Congress to adopt administration proposals to achieve savings by more carefully targeting benefits to those most in need make it more difficult to reduce the budget deficit and cut spending. Furthermore, an entitlement feature for WIC in fiscal 1980 limits my ability, and that of Congress, to control costs through annual appropriations.

I am signing this act, however, because of the strengthening of these other child nutrition programs and because of WIC's success in improving the health of low-income pregnant and nursing women and young children. It has reduced anemia and the number of underweight infants at birth, and has dramatically reduced infant mortality rates. The WIC program is fully consistent with my commitment to preventive health measures and may actually reduce hospital expenditures and Medicaid costs.

I am nevertheless signing the bill because key members of the House and Senate committees have assured me that they will promptly enact a reduction of at least $50 million in the 1980 entitlement and will actively explore other cost-saving reforms. The Secretary of Agriculture is already preparing several of these reforms which I will submit in my budget and legislative program to the next Congress.

NOTE: As enacted, S. 3085 is Public Law 95–627, approved November 10.

Appropriations Bill for the Pennsylvania Avenue Development Corporation

Statement on Signing S. 1829 Into Law.
November 10, 1978

I am signing today S. 1829, a bill which authorizes appropriations for the Pennsylvania Avenue Development Corporation (PADC) for fiscal years 1979 through 1983. The bill also provides PADC with other authorities that will facilitate carrying out the Pennsylvania Avenue development plan.

This action underscores my commitment to the preservation and enhancement of one of our Nation's most historic streets. I am confident that the co-operative efforts of the Pennsylvania Avenue Development Corporation, the Congress, the government and people of the District of Columbia, and the American business community will result in the revitalization of this area and will demonstrate what can be achieved when the public and private sectors unite for a common purpose.

I am however concerned because the provisions of this bill establishing the San Antonio Missions National Historical Park would lead to unacceptable entanglements of the Federal Government in the operations of active churches. I have therefore directed Secretary Andrus to consider implementation of the portions of the bill relating to restoration and maintenance of the Missions only if they pass into secular ownership and use.

NOTE: As enacted, S. 1829 is Public Law 95–629, approved November 10.

Consumer Product Safety Commission

Statement on Signing S. 2796 Into Law.
November 10, 1978

Today I am signing S. 2796, a bill which provides continuing authorization for the Consumer Product Safety Commission and makes certain amendments in that Agency's authority.

The Consumer Product Safety Commission has had a troubled 5-year history, but it has a crucial mission: to protect Americans' health and safety. In considering this legislation, the administration and Congress reviewed the problems faced by this Agency and decided to extend its life for 3 additional years. At the end of that period, there will be a "sunset" review. The CPSC has new, vigorous leadership, and this bill gives it more flexible procedures. It now has the opportunity to do an effective, responsible job.

This bill also requires the Commission to review all of its regulations within the next 18 months. This provision is an important contribution to our effort to update outmoded regulations throughout the Government and eliminate unnecessary ones.

This bill also addresses the difficult problem of exports of products which do not comply with U.S. safety standards. While the work that Congress has done in this area has been generally constructive, I am concerned that the shipment-by-shipment notification required by this bill will impose unnecessary burdens on American exporters, and my administration will work with Congress to attempt to reduce these burdens. United States policy governing the export of hazardous products has been proliferating on a piecemeal basis. A number of statutes applicable to differing types of products address the export issue in different ways. An interagency task force, chaired by Esther Peterson, my Special Assistant for Consumer Affairs, has been evaluating the laws in this area with the goal of developing a more uniform policy. We expect to announce recommendations in this area by the end of the year.

NOTE: As enacted, S. 2796 is Public Law 95–631, approved November 10.

Endangered Species Act Amendments of 1978

Statement on Signing S. 2899 Into Law.
November 10, 1978

I am signing into law today S. 2899, the Endangered Species Act Amendments of 1978.

In addition to providing needed authorization for the endangered species program, the bill establishes a special seven-member Cabinet-level committee. The Committee will be authorized to exempt programs and activities of Federal agencies from the requirement not to jeopardize the continued existence of endangered or threatened species. While I believe that this new exemption process is not necessary, I hope that as the Committee carries out its responsibilities, it will make the utmost efforts to protect the existence of the species inhabiting this planet. In the past, the act has worked well without this exemption process, because all agencies have made efforts to resolve conflicts and, where necessary, to pursue alternate courses of action. This consultation and cooperation should continue under these new amendments, minimizing the number of requests for exemptions. Destruction of the life of an endangered or threatened species should never be undertaken lightly, no matter how insignificant the species may appear today.

I am asking that the Committee members be exceedingly cautious in considering exemptions, and that the exercise of possible national security exemptions by the Secretary of Defense be undertaken only in grave circumstances posing a clear and immediate threat to national security.

In some ways these amendments improve the Endangered Species Act. The consultation process will be strengthened; funds are authorized from the Land and Water Conservation Fund to purchase endangered plant habitat; and provisions for enforcement against commercial violators of the act are improved. Of course, the most welcome provision is the reauthorization of appropriations for the act, which expired on September 30, 1978.

I recognize that this has been a difficult issue. Many Members of Congress have worked very hard to preserve the essence of the Endangered Species Act while allowing flexibility which many perceived to be necessary. I congratulate Senators John Culver, Jennings Randolph, Howard Baker, and Malcolm Wallop and Congressmen John Murphy, Robert Leggett, John Dingell, David Bowen, and Ed Forsythe for their hard work, especially in the hurried last hours of the 95th Congress.

My administration will make every effort to implement these amendments properly and to work with the Congress to secure continued authorization for the Endangered Species Act in the future.

NOTE: As enacted, S. 2899 is Public Law 95–632, approved November 10.

Psychotropic Substances Act of 1978

Statement on Signing S. 2399 Into Law. November 10, 1978

Today I am pleased to sign S. 2399, which enables the United States Government to meet the obligations contained in the Convention on Psychotropic Substances.

The United States played a key role in the drafting of the convention in 1971. The treaty sets up a system for controlling drugs such as amphetamines and barbiturates similar to the existing system for narcotics. The passage of S. 2399 ensures that we will be able to fulfill all our obligations under the convention and work more effectively with other governments to curb the illegal trafficking of these drugs.

The treaty must now be ratified, and I look forward to working with the Senate to see that this is done early in the 96th Congress.

NOTE: As enacted, S. 2399 is Public Law 95–633, approved November 10.

Congressional Visit to the People's Republic of China

Announcement of the Visit by a Bipartisan Congressional Delegation. November 10, 1978

The Chinese People's Institute of Foreign Affairs of the People's Republic of China has invited a bipartisan congressional delegation to visit China during November.

The delegation will depart November 10 and return November 27. The group will be led by Senator Edmund S. Muskie, Democrat of Maine, who will be accompanied by his wife.

Other members of the group include Senators Bob Packwood (R-Oreg.), Patrick Leahy (D-Vt.), Dick Stone (D-Fla.), Representative Butler Derrick (D-S.C.), Tom Bevill (D-Ala.), Tim Lee Carter (R-Ky.), and James Scheuer (D-N.Y.), who will be accompanied by their wives, and Representative Wyche Fowler (D-Ga.), who is single and will be joined by his father.

The Congressmen will be accompanied by Frank Moore, Assistant to the President for Congressional Liaison, and his wife; David Dean, Department of State, former Deputy Chief of Mission, Peking; Madeleine Albright, National Security Council; and Richard Faulk, Department of State.

Since the first congressional delegation went to the People's Republic of China in 1972, more than 100 Members of Congress have visited China.

The exchange relationship fulfills that part of the Shanghai Communique in which both sides pledged to foster broader understanding and engage in cultural and scientific exchanges.

This will be the third congressional delegation to visit China in 1978.

Digest of Other White House Announcements

The following listing includes the President's daily schedule and other items of general interest as announced by the White House Press Office during the period covered by this issue. Events and announcements printed elsewhere in the issue are not included.

November 5

The President went to Camp David, Md., for a weekend stay following his return to Andrews Air Force Base, Md., from the 2-day trip to 6 States to attend "Get Out the Vote" rallies.

The White House announced that the President has withheld his approval from H.R. 11580.

November 7

The President returned to the White House from Camp David.

The President has amended his October 29 declaration of an emergency for the State of California. The original declaration was because of damage due to the impact of brushfires occurring on October 23–25 in the County of Los Angeles.

November 8

The President met at the White House with:

—Zbigniew Brzezinski, Assistant to the President for National Security Affairs;

—Vice President Walter F. Mondale, Adm. Stansfield Turner, Director of Central Intelligence, Hamilton Jordan, Assistant to the President, and Dr. Brzezinski;

—Vice President Mondale;

—Gov. Michael S. Dukakis of Massachusetts;

—James T. McIntyre, Jr., Director of the Office of Management and Budget.

November 9

The President met at the White House with Dr. Brzezinski.

November 10

The President met at the White House with:

—Secretary of State Cyrus R. Vance, Dr. Brzezinski, and Mr. Jordan;

—Dr. Brzezinski.

NOMINATIONS SUBMITTED TO THE SENATE

NOTE: The Congress having adjourned *sine die* on Sunday, October 15, no nominations were submitted during the period covered by this issue. The first session of the 96th Congress will begin on Monday, January 15, 1979.

CHECKLIST OF WHITE HOUSE PRESS RELEASES

NOTE: All releases of the Office of the White House Press Secretary, distributed during the period covered by this issue, have been included in the issue.

ACTS APPROVED BY THE PRESIDENT

Approved November 4, 1978

H.R. 10173_____ Public Law 95–588 Veterans' and Survivors' Pension Improvement Act of 1978.

H.R. 13903_____ Public Law 95–589 An act to amend title 10, United States Code, to provide that a member of the Board of Regents of the Uniformed Services University of the Health Sciences whose term of office has expired shall continue to serve until a successor is appointed.

H.R. 12874_____ Public Law 95–590 Solar Photovoltaic Energy Research, Development, and Demonstration Act of 1978.

H.R. 13500_____ Public Law 95–591 Presidential Records Act of 1978.

S. 1816_____ Public Law 95–592
Native Latex Commercialization and Economic Development Act of 1978.

S. 703_____ Public Law 95–593
An act to improve the administration and operation of the Overseas Citizen Voting Rights Act of 1975, and for other purposes.

H.J. Res. 1173_____ Public Law 95–594
A joint resolution relative to the convening of the first session of the Ninety-sixth Congress, and for other purposes.

H.R. 9701_____ Public Law 95–595
An act to amend the Budget and Accounting Procedures Act of 1950 to require that the Comptroller General provide for a financial audit with respect to pension plans for officers and employees of the Federal Government and its agencies and instrumentalities, to require that an annual report, including a financial statement and an actuarial statement, be furnished to the Congress and the Comptroller General with respect to such plans, and for other purposes.

S.J. Res. 160_____ Public Law 95–596
A joint resolution to initiate preliminary studies for the restoration and renovation of the Pension Building in Washington, District of Columbia, to house a Museum of the Building Arts, and for other purposes.

H.R. 5646_____ Public Law 95–597
An act to amend the Regional Rail Reorganization Act of 1973 to require ConRail to make premium payments under certain medical and life insurance policies, to provide that ConRail shall be entitled to a loan under section 211(h) of such Act in an amount required for such premium payments, and to provide that such premium payments shall be deemed to be expenses of administration of the respective railroads in reorganization.

Approved November 6, 1978

H.R. 8200_____ Public Law 95–598
An act to establish a uniform Law on the Subject of Bankruptcies.

H.R. 11733_____ Public Law 95–599
Surface Transportation Assistance Act of 1978.

H.R. 13511_____ Public Law 95–600
Revenue Act of 1978.

S. 2584_____ Public Law 95–601
An act to authorize appropriations to the Nuclear Regulatory Commission for fiscal year 1979, and for other purposes.

H.R. 12467_____ Public Law 95–602
Rehabilitation, Comprehensive Services, and Developmental Disabilities Amendments of 1978.

S. 990_____ Public Law 95–603
Federal Physicians Comparability Allowance Act of 1978.

Approved November 8, 1978

H.R. 13650_____ Public Law 95–604
Uranium Mill Tailings Radiation Control Act of 1978.

S. 2774_____ Public Law 95–605
An act to extend the boundaries of the Toiyabe National Forest in Nevada, and for other purposes.

S. 2727_____ Public Law 95–606
Amateur Sports Act of 1978.

S. 2981_____ Public Law 95–607
An act to amend section 5 of the Department of Transportation Act, relating to rail service assistance, and for other purposes.

S. 1214_____ Public Law 95–608
Indian Child Welfare Act of 1978.

S. 3083_____ Public Law 95–609
Quiet Communities Act of 1978.

S. 274_____ Public Law 95–610
An act to amend title 10, United States Code, to prohibit union organization of the armed forces, membership in military labor organizations by members of the armed forces, and recognition of military labor organization by the Government, and for other purposes.

H.R. 10898_____ Public Law 95–611
An act to amend the Regional Rail Reorganization Act of 1973 to authorize appropriations for the United States Railway Association for fiscal year 1979.

S. 2093_____ Public Law 95–612
An act to provide that the Exchange Stabilization Fund shall not be available for payment of administrative expenses; and for other purposes.

S. 2522_____ Public Law 95–613
An act to extend the programs of assistance under title X and part B of title XI of the Public Health Service Act.

S. 553_____ Public Law 95–614
An act to amend the boundary of the Cibola National Forest, designate an intended wilderness area, and for other purposes.

ACTS APPROVED—Continued

Approved November 8—Continued

H.R. 9251_____ Public Law 95–615
Tax Treatment Extension Act of 1977.

H.R. 2329_____ Public Law 95–616
Fish and Wildlife Improvement Act of 1978.

Approved November 9, 1978

H.R. 4018_____ Public Law 95–617
Public Utility Regulatory Policies Act of
1978.

H.R. 5263_____ Public Law 95–618
Energy Tax Act of 1978.

H.R. 5037_____ Public Law 95–619
National Energy Conservation Policy Act.

H.R. 5146_____ Public Law 95–620
Powerplant and Industrial Fuel Use Act of
1978.

H.R. 5289_____ Public Law 95–621
Natural Gas Policy Act of 1978.

S. 2450_____ Public Law 95–622
An act to amend the Community Mental
Health Centers Act to revise and extend the
programs under that Act, to amend the Public Health Service Act to revise and extend
the programs of assistance for libraries of
medicine, the programs of the National
Heart, Lung, and Blood Institute, and of the
National Cancer Institute, and the program
for National Research Service Awards, to establish the President's Commission for the
Study of Ethical Problems in Medicine and
Biomedical and Behavioral Research, and
for other purposes.

S. 2466_____ Public Law 95–623
Health Services Research, Health Statistics,
and Health Care Technology Act of 1978.

ACTS APPROVED—Continued

Approved November 9—Continued

S. 3151_____ Public Law 95–624
Department of Justice Appropriation Authorization Act, Fiscal Year 1979.

Approved November 10, 1978

S. 791_____ Public Law 95–625
National Parks and Recreation Act of 1978.

S. 2474_____ Public Law 95–626
Health Services and Centers Amendments of
1978.

S. 3085_____ Public Law 95–627
Child Nutrition Amendments of 1978.

H.R. 7320_____ Public Law 95–628
An act to revise miscellaneous timing requirements of the revenue laws, and for
other purposes.

S. 1829_____ Public Law 95–629
An act to amend the Pennsylvania Avenue
Development Corporation Act of 1972; to
provide for the establishment of the San
Antonio Missions National Historical Park;
and for other purposes.

H.R. 14279_____ Public Law 95–630
Financial Institutions Regulatory and Interest Rate Control Act of 1978.

S. 2796_____ Public Law 95–631
An act to amend the Consumer Product
Safety Act to extend the authorization of
appropriations, and for other purposes.

S. 2899_____ Public Law 95–632
Endangered Species Act Amendments of
1978.

S. 2399_____ Public Law 95–633
Psychotropic Substances Act of 1978.

Veto of Bill To Extend Certain Nurse Training Programs

Memorandum of Disapproval of S. 2416.
November 10, 1978

MEMORANDUM OF DISAPPROVAL

I am withholding my approval from S. 2416, a bill that would extend a series of programs authorizing special Federal support for the training of nurses.

Although I support a number of its provisions, this bill would continue several Federal nurse training programs whose objectives have been accomplished and for which there is no longer a need. Moreover, the funding authorizations are excessive and unacceptable if we are to reduce the budget deficit to help fight inflation.

For the past 22 years, the Federal government has provided substantial financial support for nursing education. From 1956 through 1977, almost $1.4 billion was awarded for student traineeships, loans, and scholarships; for construction and basic support for nursing education programs; and for projects to improve nursing education and recruitment.

With the help of this support, the number of active nurses has more than doubled since 1957 to over 1,000,000 in 1978.

Ten years ago, in 1968, there were 300 active nurses per 100,000 population in the United States. By the beginning of 1977, this ratio had risen to 395 per 100,000 population.

The outlook is also good for adequate, sustained growth in the supply of nurses. There is, therefore, no reason for the government to provide special support to increase the total supply of professional nurses.

This year the Administration proposed to extend only the authorities for special projects in nursing education and for nurse practitioner training programs, in order to focus Federal nurse training support on areas of greatest national need. This proposal was based on the concept that future Federal assistance should be limited to geographic and specialty areas that need nurses most.

S. 2416 would authorize more than $400 million for fiscal years 1979 and 1980, mostly for continued Federal funding of a number of unnecessary special nurse training programs, at a potential cost to the taxpayer far above my budget. At a time of urgent need for budget restraint, we cannot tolerate spending for any but truly essential purposes.

I must point out that nursing training is primarily undergraduate education, and nursing students are eligible for the assistance made available by the government to all students, based on need. I recently signed into law the Middle Income Student Assistance Act, which will significantly expand our basic grant and student loan guarantee programs. Nursing students are also eligible for National Health Service Corps scholarships.

Disapproval of this bill will not cause an abrupt termination of funding of the nurse training programs, since funds are available for fiscal year 1979 under the continuing resolution.

If the Nation is to meet its health care needs at reasonable cost, Federal nursing and other health professions programs must make the greatest contribution to adequate health care at the most reasonable cost. This bill does not meet that test.

The Administration is now conducting a major review of its support for all health professions training, including nursing. Legislative proposals in this area will be made to the 96th Congress. These proposals will recognize the key role of nurses in our society and the need for nurses to play an even greater role in the efficient delivery of health care services.

JIMMY CARTER

The White House,
    November 10, 1978.

NOTE: The text of the memorandum of disapproval was released on November 11.

Veto of Bill To Exempt Apparel Items From Tariff Reductions

*Memorandum of Disapproval of H.R. 9937.
November 10, 1978*

MEMORANDUM OF DISAPPROVAL

I have decided not to sign into law H.R. 9937. This bill is an amendment to the Bank Holding Company Act which would authorize the General Services Ad-

ministration to sell certain silver dollar coins at negotiated prices. I have determined that this legislation would not be in the national interest because of an unrelated amendment which exempts all textile and apparel items from any tariff reductions in the Multilateral Trade Negotiations (MTN) now underway in Geneva.

I am determined to assist the beleaguered textile industry. We are committed to a healthy and growing textile and apparel industry. This legislation would not advance that cause, and could even harm the entire U.S. economy.

This bill would not address the real causes of the industry's difficulties. In return for any transient benefits, the bill would prompt our trading partners to retaliate by withdrawing offers in areas where our need for export markets is the greatest—products such as tobacco, grains, citrus, raw cotton, paper, machinery, poultry, and textile-related areas such as mill products and fashion clothing. The loss of these export areas is too high a price for our Nation to pay.

The cost of this bill might be even higher; at best, it would cost us many opportunities for export; at worst, it could cause the collapse of the trade talks and further restrict the growth of the world economy. If the two and a quarter million workers in the textile and apparel industry are to survive in their jobs, we must work to keep the world economy strong and international trade free.

Just within the last year we have taken a number of steps to improve the condition of the U.S. textile and apparel industry:

—We negotiated a renewal of the International Multifiber Arrangement through 1981, providing more responsive controls over disruptive imports.

—We have negotiated 15 new bilateral export restraint agreements which are firmer and fairer than earlier versions, covering 80 percent of all imports from low-cost suppliers. And we are negotiating more.

—We have improved our monitoring of imports and implementation of restraints, through steps such as the new legislative initiatives I have approved.

—We have, despite the proposed small reduction in tariffs, the highest textile and apparel tariffs in the developed world.

—We have begun discussions with exporting countries not now under restraint to seek appropriate levels for their shipments.

—We have established a pilot program to improve productivity in the men's tailored clothing industry, and we have begun an export promotion program for the entire textile and apparel complex.

—And we have begun a review of existing and proposed Federal regulations affecting this industry to assess their impact.

This, however, is not enough. I pledge that we will do more:

—We will intensify our review of existing bilateral restraint agreements to be sure they really work, and if there are harmful surges we will work promptly to remedy them.

—We will not allow the effectiveness of our restraint agreements to be undermined by significant increases in shipments from uncontrolled suppliers, and we will maintain a world-wide evaluation of the imports of textile and apparel into the U.S. and seek appropriate action, country-by-country, where warranted.

—We will be prepared to expand the pilot project underway in the men's tailored clothing industry so that other sectors may benefit from that experience, and we will speed proposals for a similar program in the ladies apparel industry.

—We will negotiate strenuously for removal of non-tariff barriers to U.S. textile and apparel exports, including restrictive "rules of origin."

—The Office of the Special Representative for Trade Negotiations will begin a new policy review and report to me quarterly on developments in the domestic textile and apparel industry, with special emphasis on imports and exports, so that appropriate actions can be taken more promptly.

These steps, like those of the past year, will not be the limit of our assistance to this vital industry. But each step that we take must be directed toward the long-term health of this industry and the United States economy as a whole—unlike H.R. 9937 which on balance is detrimental to the textile industry, to its two million workers, and to the Nation as a whole.

JIMMY CARTER

The White House,
November 10, 1978.

NOTE: The text of the memorandum of disapproval was released on November 11.

Veto of Meat Import Bill

Memorandum of Disapproval of H.R. 11545. November 10, 1978

MEMORANDUM OF DISAPPROVAL

I have withheld my approval of H.R. 11545, the Meat Import Act of 1978.

I do so because the bill would severely restrict Presidential authority to increase meat imports and would place a floor or minimum access level for meat imports that I believe is too low. It deprives a President of the only anti-inflationary tool available in this area.

Current law allows the President substantial flexibility to increase meat imports when, in his judgment, domestic supplies are inadequate to meet demand at reasonable prices. I am convinced that this flexibility must be preserved as a weapon against inflation.

Under this bill, however, authority to increase meat imports would be tied to declaration of a national emergency or natural disaster, or to a restrictive price formula. Under this formula, the farm price of cattle would have to increase faster than the retail meat price by more than ten percent during the first two calendar quarters of a year. Under this formula, quotas could have been relaxed only once in the last ten years.

I also believe that the United States must avoid imposing excessive restrictions on our trading partners who supply us with meat. H.R. 11545 would impose those restrictions by stipulating a minimum access level for meat imports of 1.2 billion pounds, instead of the 1.3 billion my Administration recommended. I am concerned that the bill's lower level could harm our trade relations with the meat exporting countries and thus impair their long-term reliability as sources of additional meat supplies when our own production is low, particularly at a time when we are negotiating for greater access to foreign markets for both our industrial and agricultural products.

If the Congress had enacted H.R. 11545 without these objectionable provisions, I would have been pleased to sign it, as my advisers make clear repeatedly. The bill would have amended the Meat Import Act of 1964 to provide a new formula for determining meat import quotas. The new formula would have adjusted meat import quotas up when domestic production of meats subject to the quota went down. Under the 1964 meat import law, quotas are adjusted in the opposite way, so that as domestic production declines, the limits on meat imports are tightened, at exactly the wrong time. This defect has often compelled Presidents to increase or suspend the meat import quota, in order to ensure supplies of meat

at reasonable prices. The new counter-cyclical formula would, in most years, automatically make the necessary adjustment in the meat import quotas, without involving the President in the normal operation of the meat trade.

This Administration supports such counter-cyclical management of meat imports; in fact, the Department of Agriculture was instrumental in developing the formula which the Congress approved. But for all the advantages of the new formula, it is still an untested mechanical formula which may not respond ideally to all future situations. This is why I find the restrictions on the President's discretion to increase meat imports so objectionable and why my Administration's support for H.R. 11545 was so clearly conditioned upon removal of those restrictions and on increasing the minimum access level for meat imports to 1.3 billion pounds annually.

I am prepared to work with the Congress next year to pass a counter-cyclical meat import bill which will provide the stability and certainty the cattle industry requires, while preserving the President's existing discretionary authority and setting an acceptable minimum access level for imports.

JIMMY CARTER

The White House,
November 10, 1978.

NOTE: The text of the memorandum of disapproval was released on November 11.

Anti-Inflation Program

Statement on Administration Measures To Implement the Program. November 11, 1978

I have taken four actions which underscore my commitment to restraining inflation and to implementing an anti-inflation program which is fair but tough.

These actions are a clear indication that the Federal Government is prepared to do its part to reduce inflation. These actions also call upon important sectors of our economy to participate in the fight against inflation. If we are to succeed in that fight, no sector of our economy can be exempt.

First, I have vetoed S. 2416, the Nurse Training Amendments of 1978. These amendments would authorize expenditures far in excess of our budget request and the needs of our nurse training programs. In addition, the amendments would continue certain financial assistance programs for undergraduate nurses which are no longer necessary, in light of the number of nurses in our country and the expansion of educational assistance programs for all undergraduates.

Second, I have vetoed H.R. 9937, which would have terminated my authority to negotiate reductions in United States tariffs on textiles and textile products in the Multilateral Trade Negotiations. Acceptance of an exemption for the textile industry would inevitably have led to a request for similar treatment for other industries. In order both to increase our exports and reduce inflationary pressures, we are attempting to negotiate mutual reductions of tariffs and nontariff barriers to trade around the world. By completely exempting an entire industry from these negotiations, we risk a series of retaliatory actions by our trading partners on those agricultural and industrial products which have the greatest potential for increased U.S. exports. In addition, we would seriously threaten the successful conclusion of the Multilateral Trade Negotiations, which is vital to relieving inflation pressures here and abroad.

Third, I have vetoed H.R. 11545, the Meat Import Act of 1978, which would have deprived me and future Presidents of a major anti-inflation tool. While I favored the act's countercyclical formula for determining the level of meat imports, we clearly stated during congressional deliberations that I could not accept a bill which limits my existing discretionary authority to expand meat imports or which limits meat imports to less than 1.3 billion pounds a year. This bill does not meet either of those requirements: It severely restricts a President's authority to expand meat imports and permits only 1.2 billion pounds of meat to be imported a year.

Fourth, the Department of Agriculture, with my approval, will today announce a 1979 feed grain program that is essentially the same as the one for this year. The most recent crop reports show that our country, as well as the rest of the world, will have the greatest levels of feed grain production and the largest total supply in history. As a result, over the next 12 months, the average price of feed grain will be virtually the same as during the past year. The balance of supply and demand together with the program I have approved will likely result in feed grain prices late in 1979, and through most of 1980, that are well within the targets of the anti-inflation program I recently announced.

Under the 1979 program, producers who participate will be offered a target price of $2.20/bushel (up 10¢ from 1978) if they set aside 10 percent of their land. In addition these farmers will be eligible for a diversion payment of 10¢/bushel (down 10¢ from 1978) in return for diverting an additional 10 percent of their acreage. Without any set-aside program in 1979 these farmers would face a disastrous reduction in their income. This set-aside program is a carefully balanced one, which is fair to producers, to consumers, and to taxpayers.

2011

Veterans Day

Remarks at Ceremonies at Arlington National Cemetery. November 11, 1978

My good friend and fellow veteran, Max Cleland, distinguished officials of the Government of the United States, representatives of patriotic organizations, particularly those who are dedicated to the memory of men and women who have offered their lives for the freedoms which we all cherish:

I'm very grateful to be here today as President to honor all those who have served our Nation in war.

It is appropriate that on this 60th anniversary of the armistice that ended World War I, the Congress has restored Veterans Day to November 11. I might add that as Governor of Georgia, helped and abetted and encouraged and advised by Max Cleland, who was a Georgia State Senator, our State never changed. We always recognized November 11, and we never changed the date at all.

I'm also proud that the veterans of World War I are sponsoring this observance. My father was a veteran of World War I. He was a first lieutenant in the Army. And that particular war has played a special place in my life, because, as a young man, I saw the devastating after-effects of that war—injuries lingering on, delayed death because of gas and other poisons. I wished that World War I might truly have been the war than ended all wars, that November 11, 1918, could have remained Armistice Day for all times, and that no more Americans, no more people anywhere on Earth might ever again have been called upon to offer their lives in combat.

Those who then proclaimed the great goal of a permanently peaceful world were later dismissed as foolish dreamers because their dream did not come true. Today we know that peace is more than an impractical ideal promoted only by dreamers. It is a practical and an urgent necessity in a world grown too small and too vulnerable to contain the hatred and destruction that war can unleash. It was a good dream in 1918, even if it did not come true, and it is important that we study the reasons those noble efforts failed and were followed by conflicts even more terrible than World War I.

We must never forget the consequences of failure to create a world in which peace can become a personal and permanent blessing for all mankind.

Historian Bruce Catton, who wrote about the War Between the States, said of the cost of war, of the death of young soldiers in cold tents and steaming swamps, of the grief of "a woman on a farm in Indiana or Mississippi, learning that the child who had run barefooted across the meadows in spring, has now gone under the turf in some place whose name she had never heard before."

When we come to honor those who died, we must remember, too, those who were bereaved by the loss of those we knew and loved.

On this day, we also thank those who returned with the memory of war's desolation, some with physical pain which they will always bear. They, perhaps more than others, are determined to build a wiser world.

It's fitting that we praise especially here today no famous men. We come instead to honor those who fought and died without recognition, their names and deeds known only to those who were their fallen comrades, and of course, known to God. So much that is good in this Nation depends on the unknown actions of humble men and women who understand the importance of duty, done without public recognition or the blare of trumpets. The strength of our Nation lies in our willingness to do what we must, each of us each day, wherever may lie our particular duty.

These unknown soldiers best symbolize such acts of quiet courage by ordinary people whose reward is that their Nation and their freedoms remain secure for future generations. They may not have succeeded in achieving the permanent peace they sought. But that does not make their contribution less valuable. They each preserve the dream so that another generation could try again and for our own generation to have a time of respite from war in which to seek a peace that might at last endure.

As President, I try to remember the lessons of history. Our first President knew the terrible responsibility of leading a ragged army of civilians, or enduring the hardships of battle and of nature and of helplessly watching his own men die of wounds and exposure in order to create our free Nation. He warned us bluntly—and I quote George Washington—"To be prepared for war is one of the most effectual means of preserving peace."

I will, as President, make our own preparations so thoroughly that no enemy will ever wish or dare to test us.

I seek to do everything in my power to make peace for ourselves and to help other nations make peace. We Americans cannot hope to have the assurance of permanent peace even when wars are distant from us. In a world where missiles can circle the Earth in a matter of a few minutes, time and space no longer protect us. We must be ever vigilant and ever prepared. But our only true hope for survival and for the survival of liberty and human opportunity is to create a world in which no person or no nation need be so desperate as to risk the devastation and destruction of war.

We are fortunate that no Americans are dying in battle anywhere in the world today. But if we forget why those who are buried here died, then will their sacrifice have lost its meaning. Then, if we forget, they will have paid too high a price.

If we are to honor our dead, whether from World War I, World War II, Korea, Vietnam, or the earlier wars that established our freedom and independence as a nation, we must honor their dream of a world where men and nations live in freedom and settle their inevitable differences peaceably, justly, and without resorting to violence or force.

I pray each day that we can at last secure the dream for which so many Americans have died, that no more of our children or grandchildren need ever lie here beside these unknown soldiers in nameless graves because we could not hold onto the blessings they gave us and realize the dreams they died to leave us.

[*At this point, a plaque honoring Vietnam era veterans was unveiled.*]

I'd like to say in closing that there is no unknown soldier from the war in Vietnam who is to be buried at Arlington. But in a sense, all who served in Vietnam were unknown soldiers, because their service to our country has not been adequately realized. They were no less brave because our Nation was divided about that war. They were not welcomed back as other heroes have been, but often ignored as though their presence among us was an awkward reminder of the anguish that accompanied that war at home.

Vietnam veterans knew the same pain when a bullet struck its mark, the same loss when they returned home without a leg or an arm or were unable to see the land or the familiar faces they had known. They were no different from veterans of other wars, except that more of them did not understand why they suffered and more of them were further wounded by the attitude of those who stayed behind. Too often, instead of appreciation and support, they have been criticized and rebuffed because they answered the call of duty. Often our Nation's response to their heroism hurt more than their wounds.

So, it is fitting for all those who served in Vietnam be especially honored here at the Tomb of the Unknown Soldiers, because we can never fully realize what it has cost them to answer their Nation's call. We have paid a bitter price not asked of the veterans of any other war in history, and we owe them a special debt.

We have sought to remedy this in the last 2 years. This plaque is not the final tribute our Nation will pay to those who served in Vietnam, but the Congress and I and Max Cleland and others were determined that this plaque be placed here today as an important symbolic act of appreciation to them. The four figures on the plaque represent the men and women in all five services—Army, Navy, Marines, Air Force, and Coast Guard—who participated in the war on land, sea, and air. The plaque states, and I quote:

"The people of the United States [of America] pay tribute to those members of its Armed Services [Forces] who served honorably in Southeast Asia during the Vietnam conflict."

I think it has been especially fitting for Max Cleland, the Administrator of the Veterans Administration, to join me in unveiling this plaque. He personifies the dedication and sacrifice of those who served in Vietnam, and their determination to rebuild their own lives and to build a world in which such sacrifices will never be demanded again.

NOTE: The President spoke at 11:51 a.m. at the Amphitheater after laying a wreath at the Tomb of the Unknowns.

Interview With the President

Question-and-Answer Session With Bill Moyers of the Public Broadcasting Service. November 13, 1978

VIEWS ON THE PRESIDENCY

MR. MOYERS. Mr. President, a philosopher you have read and quoted, Søren Kierkegaard, once wrote an essay called "For Self-Examination." Confession and examination have a long history in your church, although not usually on television. With your permission, I'd like to ask a few questions for self-examination.

If there is a single dominant criticism by your supporters of the Carter administration, it is that for the first 18 months there was no single theme, no vision of what it is you want to do. Are you going to try to, in the next 2 years, mold a Carter vision of the country?

THE PRESIDENT. Well, I think it was also Kierkegaard who said that every man is an exception. And the multiplicity of responsibilities that a President has, the same issues that our Nation has to face, I think, causes some lack of a central focus quite often.

We're dealing with the question of a strong national defense, some concern about the good intentions of potential adversaries like the Soviet Union on the one hand. At the same time we are struggling valiantly to find common ground on which we can assure peace between us and better friendship and a minimization of the distrust.

We, at the same time—we're dealing with SALT, are trying to bring peace to the Mideast, to Cyprus, to Namibia, to Rhodesia, to Nicaragua, exerting a leadership role in our country that the rest of the world sometimes expects. And then, of course, on domestic issues, they are so broad—trying to have a strong farm economy, increase exports, stabilize prices with an anti-inflation program, meet the necessary demands of many interest groups in our Nation who are quite benevolent. So, to bring some tightly drawn, simplistic cohesion into this broadly diverse responsibility is almost impossible.

I think in some cases previous Presidents have had their thrust identified with a simple slogan only in retrospect. I know that Roosevelt's New Deal was identified well into his term, and when he used the expression in a speech, he had no idea that it would categorize what he'd brought to the country. So, I think that only when an administration is looked at in maybe at least a recently historical perspective can you get a central theme.

We are trying to restore trust in government. We're trying to have enhancement of world peace, focusing on human rights, and at the same time exemplify what I tried to express in the campaign, and since I've been in office, as well, that my party and what I stand for is a proper blending of both compassion and competence.

In the past we've not been able to bridge that gap adequately. I think we've made a step in the right direction, but how to bring one or two phrases or a slick, little slogan to identify an administration in its formative stage or even in its productive stage is almost impossible.

MR. MOYERS. If I could put it another way, T. S. Eliot once said that every large, new figure in literature changes our perception of literature. I think the same is probably true of the Presidency. It represents something of what the country is all about. You're the most recent representative of that tradition, and I'm wondering if, 2 years into your administration, you know what it is you'd like to leave.

THE PRESIDENT. I don't think my goals have changed much since I began thinking about running for President, even 4 years before I was elected, and in the last 2 years.

There's no doubt that our Nation had been damaged very severely by the Vietnam war and by the Watergate scandals and by the CIA revelations. And I think our people were also beginning to suspect that many key public officials were dishonest, not exactly forthcoming in telling the truth, and that there was no respect for our own country among the vast majority of nations in the rest of the world. There was some doubt about our own allies and friends that we espoused who were personifications of human rights violations.

And I think in all those respects—how people look upon our government, either from the point of view of an American citizen and also foreign leaders and citizens—that we've made good progress toward reaching the goal of restoring that accurate image of a good nation with integrity and purpose, openness, and also with a President who speaks accurately for the people themselves.

One problem has been that in the openness that I've tried to create, there comes with debate on complicated issues an absence of clarity. The simplest decisions that I have to make, as I told the FFA convention in Kansas City last week, are the ones about which I know least, that the more you know about the subject, all the complexities on both sides, the detailed, intricate arguments, the more difficult it is to make a decision. If you don't know much about a subject, you can make a very quick and easy decision.

But I think that we have made good progress in correcting some of the defects that existed in our Government, and I feel that history will look with favor now.

MR. MOYERS. As you talk, it occurs to me that not since 1960 has a President finished two terms in the White House.

Kennedy was elected and assassinated, Johnson was elected and discredited, Nixon was elected and disgraced, Ford was appointed and defeated. Would you like to be the first President to finish two terms since 1960?

THE PRESIDENT. Well, I haven't decided that yet. I would like to be worthy of that honor, and if I decided to run for reelection in 1980, I intend to win. But I can see why it's difficult for a President to serve two terms. You are the personification of problems, and when you address a problem, even successfully, you become identified with it. And that's what the responsibility of the Presidency is.

MR. MOYERS. Is that why, Mr. President, this disorder has been growing around the Presidency? For almost 15 years now, there is a sense of almost as if the American people or a substantial representative of the American people have silently withdrawn their support from the Presidency, no longer look to it as the symbol of the Nation as a whole.

THE PRESIDENT. I think that's true. But there were some special circumstances that relate to those Presidents you mentioned. Kennedy was assassinated. I don't think that was any reflection on the Presidency itself. It was just a tragic occurrence that I hope will never be repeated.

Johnson was, I think, looked upon by the country as primarily the one responsible for the continuation of the Vietnam war, and the war was around his neck like an anvil, pulling him down. I think he did the best he could to terminate the war, and I know he suffered personally because of the loss of American lives in Vietnam.

Nixon, of course, his successor, had the special problem with Watergate, and Ford was identified with the pardon of Nixon and didn't have long enough to get himself established, I think, to stay in office.

So, there have been special circumstances, but I don't believe that it is inherent in the office that you would be forced out of office because of some adverse occurrence.

MR. MOYERS. You don't agree with one of your predecessors that it's a splendid misery?

THE PRESIDENT. No. I think that was President Nixon who said it was a splendid misery.

MR. MOYERS. Quoting before him some earlier—it was Adams, I think——

THE PRESIDENT. Before Watergate, yes.

No, I've not been miserable in the job. I might point out that it's voluntary. Nobody in my memory has been forced to serve as President. And as a matter of fact, in spite of the challenges and problems and, sometimes, disappointments and criticisms, I really enjoy it.

MR. MOYERS. What's the hardest part?

THE PRESIDENT. I think the hardest part is the attempt to correlate sharply conflicting ideas from worthy people. The easy problems don't arrive on this desk. You know, the easy problems are solved in the life of an individual person or within a family or perhaps in a city hall or a county courthouse or, at the worst, in a State capitol. The ones that can't be solved after all those intense efforts arrive here in the White House to be solved, and they're quite difficult ones. And I think the attempt to correlate those conflicting ideas probably bring about the most serious challenge to a President.

MR. MOYERS. You said not long ago, "I feel like my life now is one massive multiple-choice examination, where things are put in front of me and I have to make the difficult choice." Can you give me an example of that?

THE PRESIDENT. Yes. I haven't found anything easy about this job. But I didn't expect it to be easy when I came here. Well, I mentioned one earlier, the fact that we have to be very protective of our Nation's security and cover every eventuality if we don't make progress toward peace with the Soviet Union.

At the same time, we have to explore every possibility to have a peaceful relationship with the Soviet Union, to alleviate tensions and to find common grounds on which we can actually build friendships in the future. And these two are not only extremely complicated, each side of that possibility, but apparently are in conflict.

U.S.-SOVIET RELATIONS

MR. MOYERS. What do you think the Soviets are up to, Mr. President? I mean, do you see them as primarily a defensive power, seeking to solidify their own position in the world, or do you see them as an aggressive power, seeking to enlarge their position in the world?

THE PRESIDENT. Well, to be perhaps excessively generous, but not too far off the mark, I think, first of all, they want peace and security for their own people, and they undoubtedly exaggerate any apparent threat to themselves and have to, to be sure that they are able to protect themselves. At the same time, as is the case with us, they would like to expand their influence among other people in the world, believing that their system of government, their philosophy is the best. This means that we have to plan in the future, in the presence of peace between us, to be competitive with them and able to compete both aggressively and successfully.

But I would say that those are their two basic motives, as is the case with us—security for themselves and to have their own influence felt in the rest of the world as much as possible.

MR. MOYERS. There is a school of thought which says that their aim is to achieve superiority over us in both conventional and strategic weapons and that we must therefore not settle to be equal with them, but to have superiority over them. These are the hard choices you're talking about. Where do you come out in that debate?

THE PRESIDENT. They will never be superior to us in national strength nor overall military strength. We are by far the stronger nation economically. Our productivity capacity is superior, and I think always will be.

We've got a vibrant, dynamic social and political system based on freedom, individuality, and a common purpose that's engendered from the desire of our own people, not imposed from above by an autocratic government. I think our absence of desire to control other people around the world gives us a competitive advantage once a new government is established or as they search about for friends. We are better trusted than the Soviet Union. They spend more than twice as much of their gross national product on military matters, but we are still much stronger, and we will always be stronger than they are, at least in our lifetimes.

We are surrounded by friends and allies—Canada in the north, Mexico in the south—two open and accessible oceans on the east and west. The Soviets, when looked at from the perspective of the Kremlin, are faced with almost a billion Chinese, who have a strong animosity and distrust toward the Soviets. Toward the west, in Eastern Europe, their allies and friends can't be depended on nearly so strongly as our own. They have a difficult chance to have access to the oceans in an unrestricted fashion; their climate is not as good as ours; their lands are not as productive.

And so, I think that in any sort of present or future challenge from the Soviet Union, our Nation stacks up very well, and I thank God for it.

MR. MOYERS. But do you think the number one mentality which you hear many people espouse is a healthy mentality? Is the whole question of being number one one that can ever result in anything but an increasing escalation of tensions and increasing arms expenditures?

THE PRESIDENT. In nuclear weapons, which is, you know, where our competition with the Soviets is most direct, we've both accepted the concept of rough equivalency; that is, we are just about equal. They have heavier warheads; we have more of them. We have three different systems for delivery of warheads—if we ever need to, and I don't think we ever will have to—that are mutually supportive. We have a much higher developed electronics technology; our surveillance systems are probably as good or better than theirs. Our submarines are quieter than theirs.

We've got an advantage in having a tremendous reservoir of a free enterprise business system that can be innovative and aggressive. We have a much closer correlation between the production of civilian or peaceful goods on the one hand and military on the other.

So, I think that in the case of nuclear weapons, we have an equivalency with them, and they recognize it, and vice versa. Both of us realize that no one can attack the other with impunity. We can absorb, even if we had to, an attack by the Soviets and still destroy their country, and they know it, and vice versa.

So, I think that the horrible threat of surety of mutual destruction will prevent an attack being launched. We don't intend to evolve and neither do the Soviets intend to evolve a capability to destroy the other nation without ourselves being destroyed by nuclear forces.

In the case of land weapons, as I said before, the Soviets have vulnerable borders. They have neighbors whom they can't trust as well as we. And they face even in the nuclear field three other nuclear powers who are potential adversaries in case of a crisis—the Chinese, the British, and the French—in addition to ourselves. We don't have any of those as potential adversaries for us.

But I think for any nation to have a macho attitude, that we're going to be so powerful that we can dominate or destroy the other nation, would be counterproductive. And I don't think that even if we wanted to do that, either we or the Soviets could have that capability.

IRAN

MR. MOYERS. Let me apply the multiple-choice, difficult options equation to a couple of other contemporary and very live issues. One is Iran. What are the options facing you there?

THE PRESIDENT. Well, we look on the Shah, as you know, as a friend, a loyal ally, and the good relationship that Iran has had and has now with ourselves and with the other democracies in the world, the Western powers as being very constructive and valuable. Also, having a strong and independent Iran in that area is a very stabilizing factor, and we would hate to see it disrupted by violence and the government fall with an unpredictable result.

The Shah has been primarily criticized within Iran because he has tried to democratize the country and because he's instituted social reforms in a very rapid fashion. Some of his domestic adversaries either disagree with the way he's done it, or thinks he hasn't moved fast enough or too fast, and deplore his breaking of ancient religious and social customs as Iran has become modern.

MR. MOYERS. But he was also criticized, Mr. President, for running a police state—political prisoners——

THE PRESIDENT. That's exactly right. I think the Shah has had that criticism, sometimes perhaps justified—I don't know the details of it. But I think there's no doubt that Iran has made great social progress and has moved toward a freer expression of people. Even in recent months, for instance, the Shah has authorized or directed, I guess, the parliament to have all of its deliberations open and televised, something that we don't even do in our country here.

MR. MOYERS. You think this is all too late?

THE PRESIDENT. Well, I hope not. I don't know what will come eventually. I would hope that a coalition government could be formed rapidly. At the present time there's a quasi-military government. The Shah has reconfirmed his commitment to have open and democratic elections, maybe within 6 months or 8 months. I hope that would be possible.

Our inclination is for the Iranian people to have a clear expression of their own views and to have a government intact in Iran that accurately expresses a majority view in Iran.

MR. MOYERS. But can we do anything to encourage that, or are our hands tied?

THE PRESIDENT. No, we don't try to interfere in the internal affairs of Iran.

MR. MOYERS. We did put the Shah in, but you're saying we can't keep him in.

THE PRESIDENT. I think that's a decision to be made by the people of that country.

MR. MOYERS. Does it hurt you sometimes to have to sit back and do nothing when you know there are large stakes in a part of the world beyond your influence?

THE PRESIDENT. Well, we don't have any inclination to be involved in the internal affairs of another country unless our own security should be directly threatened. And that's a philosophy that I have espoused ever since I've been in the national political realm.

I just think we've learned our lessons the hard way, in Vietnam and in other instances, and we've tried to be loyal to our allies and loyal to our friends, to encourage one person-one vote, majority rule, the democratic processes, the protection of human rights. Obviously, we have not always succeeded in encouraging other people to measure up to our own standards, but I think we've been consistent in our effort.

MR. MOYERS. But this is again where some criticism arises in some circles in this country, who say the Soviets have a stake in what happens in Iran and they are free to move clandestinely or any other way that they wish. But if we take the position that you're espousing, we'll sit back and do nothing when we should be in there covertly or clandestinely or overtly, taking a tough stand, saying that we may not like the Shah but we need him in power. You're saying that day is over, that we cannot do that.

THE PRESIDENT. No, we have made it clear through my own public statements and those of Secretary Vance that we support the Shah and support the present government, recognizing that we don't have any control over the decisions ultimately made by the Iranian people and the stability of that region. The absence of the success of terrorism, of violence, the anarchy that might come with the complete disruption of their government is a threat to peace.

We don't have any evidence that the Soviets, for instance, are trying to disrupt the existing government structure in Iran nor that they are a source of violence in Iran. I think they recognize—they have a very long mutual border with Iran, and a stable government there, no matter who its leaders might be, is valuable to them.

This might change. If it becomes obvious that the Shah is very vulnerable and that other forces might come into power, the Soviets might change their obvious posture. But that's the observation that we have now.

EGYPTIAN-ISRAELI NEGOTIATIONS

MR. MOYERS. What about the Middle East, Mr. President?

THE PRESIDENT. I have put hundreds of hours in both preparation and direct negotiation with the leaders in the Middle East, particularly Egypt and Israel. And Secretary Vance, even to the extent of abandoning some of his other responsibilities in foreign affairs, has tried to bring about a successful conclusion of the peace treaty negotiations. There, again, we don't have any authority over anyone else. We can't use pressure to make the Israelis and Egyptians come to a peaceful settlement of the disputes that have divided them.

The Camp David framework, which was almost miraculous in its conclusion— it seems more miraculous in retrospect than it did at the time—is a sound basis for peace between Egypt and Israel. There's no doubt that both nations would be highly benefited by peace.

MR. MOYERS. But yet the talks seem to be at an impasse as of tonight.

THE PRESIDENT. The present disagreements, compared to the benefits to be derived, are relatively insignificant. The benefits are so overwhelming, in comparison with the differences, that I hope that the Egyptians and Israelis will move toward peace.

MR. MOYERS. What's holding it up tonight?

THE PRESIDENT. At Camp David it was a framework, it was an outline that had a lot of substance to it, but it required negotiation of details and specifics. And there is no way that you could have a peace treaty with all of the ends tied down and all of the detailed agreements reached, the maps drawn, the lines delineated, time schedules agreed, without going far beyond what the Camp David outline required.

And so, both sides have demanded from the others additional assurances far above and beyond what Camp David said specifically. This is inherent in the process. And I think in some cases, in many cases, the two governments have reached agreement fairly well.

Now I don't know what's going to happen. We hope that they will continue to work in reaching agreement, to understand one another, to balance the consequences of failure against the benefits to be derived from the success, and be flexible on both sides.

These are ancient arguments, historical distrust not easy to overcome. And the frustrating part about it is that we are involved in the negotiations, but we can't make Israel accept the Egyptians' demands, nor vice versa. We have to try to tone down those demands and use our influence. I don't know what will happen about it. We just pray that agreements will be reached.

MR. MOYERS. Are you asking both sides to make further concessions?

THE PRESIDENT. Oh, yes—every day and night. We ask both sides to please be constructive, to please not freeze your position, to please to continue to negotiate, to please yield on this proposal, to adopt this compromise. These have been and are our efforts on a constant basis.

It would be horrible, I think, if we failed to reach a peaceful agreement between Israel and Egypt——

MR. MOYERS. What would happen?

THE PRESIDENT. ——and then see our children, our grandchildren, future generations look back and say these little tiny technicalities, phrases, phrasing of ideas, legalisms, which at that time seemed to be paramount in the eyes of the Egyptian and the Israeli agreements, have absolutely no historical significance. And that's basically what the problems are.

MR. MOYERS. Are you saying that the impasse as of today is because of technicalities and not major principles?

THE PRESIDENT. Yes, compared to the principles that have already been resolved and the overall scope of things, the disagreements now, relatively, are insignificant.

MR. MOYERS. Egypt wants to tie the present negotiations, I understand, to some future resolution of the Gaza Strip and the West Bank. Israel is resisting that. Who's being more stubborn?

THE PRESIDENT. Well, I wouldn't want to start saying who's being more stubborn. I think there's adequate stubbornness to be allotted to both sides.

MR. MOYERS. You mentioned grandchildren, and I heard you say after Camp David that at one critical moment that was resolved because of somebody thinking about grandchildren. Would you tell me about that?

THE PRESIDENT. It might be a mistake to attach too much importance to it, but during the last few hours of negotiations at Camp David, when it looked like everything was going to break down then, Prime Minister Begin sent me over some photographs of me and him and President Sadat and wanted me to autograph them. And the issue at that time was Jerusalem, which was an almost insurmountable obstacle that we later resolved by not including it at all in the framework. And instead of just putting my signature on it, which President Sadat had done, I sent my secretary, Susan Clough, over and got

the names from one of his aides of all his grandchildren.

So, I personally autographed it to his granddaughters and grandsons and signed my name, and I carried it over to him in one of the most tense moments and I handed it to him. And he started to talk to me about the breakdown of the negotiations and he looked down and saw that I had written all of his grandchildren's names on the individual pictures and signed them, and he started telling me about his favorite grandchild and the characteristics of different ones. And he and I had quite an emotional discussion about the benefits to my two grandchildren and to his if we could reach peace. And I think it broke the tension that existed there, that could have been an obstacle to any sort of resolution at that time.

MR. MOYERS. What does that say to you about the nature of these problems and their resolution?

THE PRESIDENT. Well, you know, when you put the problems in the focus of how they affect people, little children, families, the loss of life, the agreements and the need for agreement becomes paramount. When you put the focus in the hands of international lawyers and get it down to technicalities—is a certain event going to take place in 9 months or 8½ months or 10 months; is this going to happen before that; is this demarcation line going to go around this hill or through the hill, on the other side of the hill; can the observation towers be 150 feet high, 200 feet high, 125 feet high—the human dimension of it becomes obviously paramount. But when the negotiators sit around a table and start talking, the human dimension tends to fade away, and you get bogged down in the legalisms and the language and the exact time schedule, when from a historic perspective they have no significance.

Another problem has been—and this has been one of the most serious problems—at Camp David we didn't have daily press briefings, and this was the agreement when we started here in Washington, that neither side would make a direct statement to the press. As you know, this has not been honored at all, and it's created enormous additional and unnecessary problems for us.

MR. MOYERS. You mean leaks from both governments are——

THE PRESIDENT. Not just leaks. I mean, almost every day I see interviews in the national television of at least one of the sides in the dispute.

And also at Camp David I was working directly with the heads of state. Here we work with the negotiators, and the negotiators then refer their decision back to the head of state or the cabinet. The cabinet reverses themselves, reverses the negotiators on a language change or one word, and in effect you get the most radical members of the governments who have a major input into the negotiating process, rather than having the heads of state there 100 yards away so that they can resolve those issues once and for all.

So, I think the followup to Camp David has been much more time-consuming and much more frustrating than it was when the three of us were primarily leading the discussions.

VIEWS ON THE PRESIDENCY

MR. MOYERS. I read that the Camp David log showed that you spent 27½ hours with Sadat and 29 hours with Begin, and 9 hours alone with Sadat and 6 hours alone with Begin, with no one else in the room, the way FDR used to do with Churchill.

Do you think that you could resolve most of these large issues we face if you could just get people in a room like this and talk to them? It used to be said

Lyndon Johnson could have done much better had he been able to persuade people one on one instead of having to use television and public speeches. Do you think that other problems you face could be resolved if you could meet nose to nose, in a sense, with the adversaries?

THE PRESIDENT. I couldn't guarantee success, but I think, obviously, the likelihood of success would be better.

MR. MOYERS. This goes back to something you said earlier, too, where what you try to do is never seen in the singular way in which you're trying to do it, that you become many things to many people. How do you resolve those contradictions?

THE PRESIDENT. Well, that's inevitable. The most pressing problem on my hands, on my shoulders, is not to present to the people of the world a simplistic and simple character as a President or as a person.

The agenda for an average day for me is incredibly complex, you know, and I shift from one subject to another—from domestic affairs to foreign affairs, from one country to another, from one issue to another. And there's no way for me to say what I did in this one single day in a few words, so that the complexities are inevitable. The only thing I know to do about it is to try to address each item on its own merits and make a decision that I think at that time is the best for my country and my people.

The advantage of having good advisers is very great, and I do have good advisers. I've been criticized because I studied details of issues too much, but that's my nature. And I think on occasion it pays rich dividends, in that I am able to understand the complexities of an issue when a final decision has to be made and not depend entirely on advisers who don't have the knowledge that I, as President, can have uniquely.

But this is a fond hope, I guess, of every politician, to be universally admired, to have all of your themes clearly defined, to have everything packaged beautifully so it can be examined from all sides without doubt, to have one's character be recognized clearly, and to have universal approbation of the people that you try to represent. All those things are hopeless dreams.

Mr. Moyers. Pat Caddell made a speech recently in which he said—Pat Caddell is one of your associates—in which he said that a President can succeed by doing poorly because the people out there don't think he can do well. Do you think that's true?

The President. [*Laughing*] I hope I don't have to prove that.

Mr. Moyers. You were criticized, I know, talking about details, for keeping the log yourself of who could use the White House tennis courts. Are you still doing that?

The President. No—and never have, by the way.

Mr. Moyers. Was that a false report?

The President. Yes, it was.

Mr. Moyers. But seriously, is the job too big? Is the United States Government, which is a $500 billion enterprise, now too big to be managed by a single chief executive?

The President. No. I wouldn't want to—I say that, recognizing that no one person can do it all. But the structure of the American Government is still the best that I can imagine. There's a tremendous sharing of responsibility between the different branches of the Federal Government, an adequate sharing of responsibility between myself and Governors of States and mayors and county officials at the local level of government, between government and private citizens. These balances have been evolved historically, and I think they've grown to their present

state because in each instance when a change occurred, tests were made and the best arrangement triumphed.

But it would be a serious mistake to try to run a government like this with, say, a committee. And I'm thankful that my Cabinet can be either hired or fired by me. I consult with my Cabinet or listen to them, but I make a decision. I don't have to have a vote and go by the majority vote in my own Cabinet. And if you had, say, a three-person President, one perhaps involved with foreign affairs, one with domestic affairs, one managing the bureaucracy itself, I think it would be much worse than what we have now.

I like the constitutional arrangement, where you have an executive with constitutionally limited powers and a voice with which to express the aspirations and hopes of our country accurately, I hope, to the people.

Mr. Moyers. Was Camp David the high of your administration so far?

The President. Well, I'd say the first 12½ days were probably the lower of my administration; the last half day at Camp David was one of the highest. It's hard to say.

Mr. Moyers. What's been the lowest moment for you? Were you aware, for example, this summer of the growing doubts about your competency to be President?

The President. Well, there was a rash of news reports, cover stories in the weekly magazines, and editorial comments around the Nation expressing concerns about my ability to run the Government.

I'm not sure they were any more condemnatory nor critical than they were about previous Presidents, all the way back to Abraham Lincoln; even before. Each President has been criticized and castigated as incompetent and dastardly, even.

MR. MOYERS. Your polls had fallen very sharply this summer as well.

THE PRESIDENT. Well, they had—not as low as the polls fell for, say, Harry Truman during his own administration, but lower than I liked. But I never had any particular concern about that, because I could see in the evolutionary stage, for instance, in my dealings with Congress, progress being made toward eventual decisions by Congress that showed that the 95th Congress had a very good record of achievement. And I think in the confrontations I had with the Congress, when we disagreed on two or three items, I prevailed because I think I was right and established principles that will be good for the future.

But I've never had any doubt about my own resolution. I recognize my own limitations and faults. I'm not omniscient. I'm certainly not omnipotent. I have limited powers, limited authority, and I try to overcome those inherent defects in the office itself as best I can.

ADMINISTRATION PROGRAMS

MR. MOYERS. What people were saying in circles where I was listening was that Jimmy Carter accepted an energy bill that was not what he wanted; Jimmy Carter settled for a tax bill that was at odds with his conviction; Jimmy Carter had set aside an aggressive fight for welfare reform; he lost his hospital containment costs; he didn't push on education. In a sense, people were saying that Jimmy Carter, who said he was going to bring competency and efficiency to government, was being routed on every front and settling, compromising for what he had said before he didn't want. And from that came a perception, I think, of a weak President, of a President who is being defeated in one front after another.

THE PRESIDENT. The final legislative agenda as it was passed, I think, is a great credit to the Congress and shows a good compatibility between them and me and has been a matter of pride for all of us.

The fact that we had very few Members of the Congress defeated in the last election, compared to previous off-year elections, is good. We still have more than 60 percent Democrats in the House, about 60 percent in the Senate, I think about 60 percent in the Governorships, is an endorsement of what the Democratic Party has done.

But I think I need to be fair in saying that there have been times when I've had to compromise, below what I had asked the Congress to do or had demanded of the Congress. We got about 65 percent of the energy bill that we originally proposed to Congress in ultimate savings in imported oil, about 2.5 million barrels a day savings compared to 4.5, for instance.

I would like to have gotten the entire thing. I'm not out of office yet and will come back to try to get some more in the future.

MR. MOYERS. But take the tax bill, Mr. President. During the campaign, you said repeatedly our tax system is a disgrace to the human race. The tax bill you signed was a bill that gave the biggest breaks to the wealthiest taxpayers and the smallest breaks to the smaller taxpayers. Did you sign that bill in conscience?

THE PRESIDENT. That's not exactly fair, because although the bill fell far short of the reforms that I advocated, the bill does bring substantial tax reductions to all taxpayers. And it's a fairly balanced bill, as far as that goes.

It was necessary that a bill be passed, and compared to the version that the House passed or compared to the version that the Senate passed, the compromise that was brought about was superior to either one of those.

Had I vetoed that bill after the Congress sent it to me, we would have had an enormous increase in taxes on the American people as of the first of the year; not only the loss of roughly $20 billion in tax reductions that we've added, but also we would have lost, say, roughly $13 billion in tax reductions that had been passed the previous year.

So, there was a case that was a difficult decision to make. When I met a few days before the Congress adjourned with the leaders of the House and Senate—Al Ullman in the House, Russell Long in the Senate—and said, "This is what I will and will not accept," they complied with my request substantially. And although it was short of what I would have preferred, my vetoing of that bill would have been a very serious mistake.

MR. MOYERS. This explanation, this rationalization, which is necessary in this town on a lot of compromises, raises the question about where you think the Democratic Party is going. As you know, Democrats have a tradition of using the Government's powers to correct the imbalances and the injustices of the capitalist economy, to innovate, to equalize, to take risks. Republicans are elected generally to manage, to stabilize, to pull in the horns a little bit.

Howard Baker is going around town saying—the minority leader of the Senate—saying that "The Democrats are singing our song, and it's a Republican song." And what a lot of people are saying has been reborn in Washington is a conservative administration with a Democratic President with Republican intuitions. Do you think that's fair? Isn't the Democratic Party coopting the Republican philosophy?

THE PRESIDENT. No, I don't think so. The Democrats have always been a party of compassion and concern about the people of our country. We've always been eager to extend a helping hand to somebody who hasn't had an adequate chance in life to stand on one's own feet, to make one's own decisions, to control one's own destiny, to have an education if they didn't have one, to have a house to live in, to have better health care, better food, security in one's old age, better highway systems. These are the kinds of things that the Democratic Party has always espoused and has always pursued.

I saw quite early in my administration as Governor of Georgia that we had an undeserved reputation as Democrats of not being fiscally responsible and not being competent in management. One of the major thrusts of my own Governorship was to reorganize the government, to get control of the bureaucracy, to cut taxes, to budget carefully, and I ran my campaign for President on that platform. And we've had remarkable success since I've been here.

We will have cut the budget deficit more than half compared to what the Republican administration had when they went out of office.

We will have passed civil service reform to get the bureaucracy under control, for a change. We've had $28 to $30 billion in tax reductions. At the same time we've had the largest allocation of increased funds for better education the country's ever seen. We've had help to cities and other local governments that's almost unprecedented. We've sustained a home building rate of over 2 million a year.

So, we've been able to combine, through tough, competent fiscal management, both the delivery of good services to our people and also tight budgeting, cutting down deficits, cutting taxes. And the combination of those two, in my opinion, is not incompatible. You can't educate a child with inefficiency and waste and corruption. You can't feed a hungry person with inefficiency or waste or corruption. And I think that this is a reputation that the Democrats have now assumed, legitimately so, of competent management, that we did not enjoy in the past.

And I can understand why the Republicans are complaining, because they can no longer allege successfully that the Democrats can't be both compassionate, concerned, and competent.

Mr. MOYERS. If you were a teenage black youth in the ghetto, if you were one of those millions of people who are surplus in our economy, who have no positive role in our economy or our society, would you have taken much encouragement from the results last week of that election?

THE PRESIDENT. Well, that's hard to say, when you analyze the results. The Republicans picked up a few extra seats in the House—I think about a dozen—and a few extra seats in the Senate. That obviously should not bring encouragement to anyone that the Republicans have more seats.

Mr. MOYERS. I mean the rhetoric that many Democrats use, the rhetoric almost everyone used, in talking about cutting back, retrenching, cutting taxes, all of which would add up to a different kind of approach to government than the traditional Democratic posture.

THE PRESIDENT. I see what you mean. That's hard to say, because for a single person who's out of a job, the most important thing is to get a job. In the last 20 months or so, we've added almost 7 million net new jobs to the American economy. We've cut the unemployment rate about 25 percent.

In the case of agriculture, we've increased farm income, net farm income about 25 percent, and as I say, sustained additional commitments to better education, better housing, and so forth.

Now, however, there's a general feeling among those who are in the very low levels of income and those retired people who have a fixed income, that the most serious threat to our Nation is inflation. And I think the Congress candidates and those running for Governor as well recognize that controlling inflation had to be given a very high priority.

With that comes a need to have tight budgeting decisions made, a reduction in deficits, and a demonstration to the Government and also to the private parts of our economy that we are going to be fiscally responsible.

I think in the long run the alleviation of inflation in a person's life is almost as important as an increase in wages or an increase in prices that one can get for products sold.

So, there is a new emphasis, I think, on the control of inflation, but it doesn't mean that we've abandoned searching for new jobs, nor the better life for the people who live in our country.

Mr. MOYERS. But it is likely, isn't it, that if you succeed in your inflation fight, some people will be put out of work?

THE PRESIDENT. I don't believe that's the case. We don't project that to happen. I think there will be an increase in the number of jobs available every year that I'm in office. The rate of increase might slack off and level off some, but I don't think there will be a net loss in the number of jobs in our country.

Mr. MOYERS. A lot of private economists are forecasting a turndown by 1980. How can you avoid that if you really keep the pressure on interest rates and housing construction and the pressures to stop the growth of inflation? Do you have some new trick in the hat?

THE PRESIDENT. No. There is no trick, and there again it's a difficult decision that you just have to balance. But whether we can continue to build up enormous deficits by spending money we don't have, and benefit the American people, is a serious question. I don't think we can.

I think we've got to have careful budgeting, a more accurate focusing of Government services to meet the needs of those who need it most; combined with a restoration of confidence in our Government's ability to handle both fiscal, monetary, and administrative affairs. And there are times when those are in conflict. But we now have 10 years of inflation that's averaged about 6½ percent, and I think that almost every economist, even those who think we might have a recession next year, agrees that we have got to cut down on the inflation rate.

VIEWS ON THE PRESIDENCY

MR. MOYERS. Some of your people this morning were telling me that they sense a new attitude on your part, a new spirit of confidence. And they attribute it to the fact that in your mind you've made some very tough decisions on the inflation front and are going to stick with them. Is that true? Are their perceptions accurate?

THE PRESIDENT. I don't feel that I'm more confident or more aggressive or more sure of myself than I was before. We've made some difficult decisions ever since I've been in office. It seems to me, almost daily, difficult decisions have had to be made. But, obviously, the longer I'm in office, the more I'm aware of the needs. I understand the Government structure better. I know more of the leaders both within Washington and outside Washington who help to shape our Nation's policies and shape its future.

We've now finished the 95th Congress work. I think they passed about 6 or 700 bills which help to clarify my own programs. We're trying to take advantage of what the Congress has decided, and I think I'm certainly more aware of and

more sure of the opportunities and limitations of the Presidency itself.

MR. MOYERS. What have you learned about this town?

THE PRESIDENT. I like Washington very much. We came here as newcomers.

MR. MOYERS. To say the least.

THE PRESIDENT. To say the least. I didn't know the congressional leaders. I didn't know the news media representatives, except those who followed me in the campaign. Neither did they know me. I had a lot to learn about the bureaucratic structure of the Government. I was not privy of course to secrets involving national defense or international relations, and I really spent 18 months or so not only as a President but also as a student trying to learn what I didn't know before.

There have been no serious disappointments on my part. I told some news people the other night at a supper at the Mansion that there were two things that had been unpleasant surprises. One was the inertia of Congress, the length of time it takes to get a complicated piece of legislation through the Congress, and the other was the irresponsibility of the press.

MR. MOYERS. Irresponsibility of the press?

THE PRESIDENT. Yes.

MR. MOYERS. What do you mean?

THE PRESIDENT. Well, quite often news reports have been inaccurate when I think a simple checking of the facts with a telephone call or a personal inquiry could have prevented a serious distortion of the news. And also there's a sense of doubt or even cynicism about the Government and about programs or proposals, brought about I'm sure by the Vietnam experience, of the fact that the public was misled during Watergate and perhaps even the CIA, as I mentioned earlier.

But I think that a lot of that was caused by my relative inaccessibility and by the lack of knowledge on my part of the press and vice versa. And in the last few months we've taken steps to make sure that we understand each other better, so that I have an ability and my Cabinet Members have an ability to present the facts clearer to the American people through the press, and vice versa.

MR. MOYERS. Is this the work of your media czar, Mr. Rafshoon? What did he tell you about how to get the message out?

THE PRESIDENT. Well, it was a common belief that all of us had that we needed to have a clearer access to the public through the press in an undistorted way, a truthful way, not to try to cover up any mistakes we made, and also to have it understood among those who report the news that they can have access to me or to Jody Powell or to Hamilton Jordan or members of the Cabinet or others if there is a question that arises approaching a deadline, that they can make a telephone call and say, "Is this or is this not accurate?"

We all recognize the devastating consequences of ever making a misleading statement or telling a falsehood, because our credibility would be damaged. And we've bent over backwards (not)[1] to do that. But I think that we've made some progress in this respect.

And I understand the Congress a lot better now. I know the speed with which legislation can be expected to move through the Congress. I understand the complexities of the committee system, the interrelationships between the House and the Senate.

And also I think we're doing a much better job in letting the press have access to the facts.

MR. MOYERS. The hour is past. Should we stop?

---

[1] Printed in the transcript.

THE PRESIDENT. I think perhaps we'd better, if the hour's over.

MR. MOYERS. Well, on behalf of Public Broadcasting, I thank you for your time.

THE PRESIDENT. Thank you, Bill.

NOTE: The interview began at 1:30 p.m. in the Oval Office at the White House. It was taped for later broadcast on the Public Broadcasting Service.

Anti-Inflation Program
Remarks at a Briefing for Federal Sub-Cabinet Officials. November 13, 1978

This is my first chance to meet with you as a group. But I have had a chance to get to know many of you since I've been President. And I'm very grateful to be here with you this afternoon to discuss an important subject.

I'd like to ask, first of all, how many of you are willing to join in with me and Alfred Kahn, Charlie Schultze, the Cabinet, and others in helping to control inflation during this next year and in the months after—would you just raise your hand so I know where I stand? [*Laughter*] Any who did not raise their hand are excused. [*Laughter*]

Last year I spoke at Notre Dame at the graduation exercise, and I told them about a man who was arrested for being drunk and for setting a bed on fire. And when he got up in front of the judge he said, "I plead guilty to being drunk, but the bed was on fire when I got in it." [*Laughter*] And I want to make clear at the beginning that I don't assume responsibility for all the inflationary problems that have piled up on my shoulders in recent months. [*Laughter*]

As I said in my anti-inflation talk a couple of weeks ago, this has been a chronic problem for our Nation the last 10 years, averaging about 6½ percent, as you well know. But you and I together have before us a very difficult, tedious, thankless battle to combat inflation. You are the leaders of our Government, enjoying positions of great responsibility, quite often not recognized for what you contribute. But still, if we fail, the responsibility will be yours as well as it is mine.

I think it's important on us to assess very carefully the inventory that we have with which to work, what Federal resources, what decisionmaking authority and power do we have to combat inflation; to set an example for others who work with us and for others around our Nation who observe us very closely.

We have already committed ourselves to a very tight budgeting procedure. The fiscal year 1980 budget will be stripped of every degree of waste and inefficiency possible to detect. We've already had success, as you know, in cutting down the level of the Federal budget deficit. This has been observed and in some cases appreciated. But I'm not here this afternoon to brag on ourselves. I'm here as President, as a partner of yours to ask for your help.

Many of you have insights and abilities and experience which I don't have. And I hope that you will leave this meeting this afternoon with an awareness of our goals, with a clearer knowledge personally of those with whom you will be working; but above all, with a commitment on your own initiative, without further request or encouragement or inspiration from any of us on the stage, to do what you can within the sphere of your own influence to be effective in controlling inflation.

As you well know, inflation hurts everyone in our country, particularly those who are least able to make their own decisions because of limited income, limited influence, limited awareness, limited flexibility. Those who are most defenseless are the ones who need defense most from us.

Also, I think it's accurate to say that in order to control inflation that sacrifice is going to be demanded from everyone. Very beneficial, very influential, very eloquent interest groups will make their voices heard in a competitive way. And because you are much closer to the delivery end of government services, those pressures on you will perhaps be even greater than they are on me or on members of the Cabinet or on the White House staff members.

And I know as well, you in some ways are part of the interest groups themselves. Because of the relatively narrow focusing of your own responsibility, you will be tempted to be a spokesman for those that you serve and say, "Above all other interests in government, I demand or I request or I will use my own influence with the Congress or with the budgeting authorities to serve those who look to me for their needs to be met."

I'd like to ask you to avoid that as much as possible and to put yourself in my position, looking at the Government as an entity and recognizing that the interest groups, however deserving, must be considered in the overall framework of how well they will be served if inflation is controlled.

I can't see any political benefit to be derived from the efforts that are required of us. There won't be enormous sums of money to hand out. And we will have to be as pure as Caesar's wife in making sure that the decisions we do make that require sacrifice, through the most intense observation and analysis, are obviously fair and just.

As you deal with contractors and grantees, suppliers of goods and services to the Government, I hope that you will demand of them and inspire in them a cooperative attitude with us. The influence that you can exert personally can spread like waves on a pond to include others and to get them brought up into a realization of the tremendous benefits to be derived for our country with an objective and enlightened control and reduction of inflationary pressures.

I think it's obvious that there is no need for us to reduce the quality of services. This is not an incompatibility with what I've just described. We've been successful in the last 2 years in having the needs of our people met and, at the same time, having substantially reduced waste, promoted efficiency, cut the deficits all at the same time. We've provided for our country's defense as never before in history.

And I think we've had a sustained level of the production of housing units for our people, increased allocation of funds for public recreation areas, education, health, social benefits that have brought credit to our administration. And that can obviously continue in the future as it has in the past. But the delivery of services must be more efficient and the assessment through zero-base budgeting techniques and through your own analyses of the priority allocation of limited Federal funds must be more intensely focused.

We've got a good opportunity through our reorganization efforts, which have been approved by the Congress, through the new civil service reform legislation, which gives us an additional opportunity for professional public servants to expend their efforts and energies more effectively, to make sure that we can deliver services even better than we have in the past.

I'd like to touch on another very sensitive subject, and that is fraud and corruption. In the last number of years, certainly not just since we've been in office, there have been embarrassing revelations of violation of regulation, violations of

ethics, even violations of the law. Several people have been indicted within the last few months. Other investigations on a preliminary basis have already revealed practices that bring shame to our Government. I recognize as accurately as you that this is a very tiny minority in the Government, perhaps even a lower portion than would be the case in an average nongovernmental organization.

But we have an additional responsibility to root these kinds of practices out on our own initiative. It's not enough for the Administrator of the General Services Administration, working with the Attorney General, to try to reveal and correct and, secondarily, to punish those who are culpable.

But the devastating impact of this kind of revelation on the honest and sincere, dedicated, competent public employee is the most serious consequence of fraudulent practices. All of you remember clearly and vividly—in fact, the entire world remembers the reflection that was brought on the White House itself by the Watergate revelations and how the CIA is just struggling to overcome the adverse publicity brought to it by revelations of illegal practices.

But obviously, the White House, the Cabinet is an entity that deserves to be respected and honored and the CIA has the same character of professionalism and competence and dedication and patriotism that deserves recognition and honor.

The General Services Administration is the same way. It deserves to be recognized and honored for its good performance. The Small Business Administration is now becoming scrutinized much more closely. As you know, recently, legislation was passed for the establishment of 12 Inspectors General offices, and at the same time, the GAO has reported that $4.3 billion in unresolved audit findings hang over the Federal Government.

The point I want to make to you is that in our eagerness to set a good example to inspire the Nation to help us to control inflation in all its multitudinous and deleterious aspects, that the rooting out of improper practices is the responsibility not just of the President or Cabinet Members or the Attorney General. It's the responsibility of you and all those who work with you and under you.

And I would hope that you would not wait until a highly publicized revelation of improper practices becomes obvious before you take the initiative on your own to reexamine even accepted practices that might not be completely appropriate and to be sure that any standing practices that might have been condoned are reexamined for absolute propriety.

We have a team effort in order to make our Government more effective and respected, and I know that you will join in with me in making this possible. Charlie Schultze has spoken to you. Alfred Kahn has spoken to you. The Cabinet members are on the stage behind me. The White House staff and others are eager to cooperate.

The recent elections, I think, have given a clear message to the Congress, to Governors, to county and city officials, that this must be a joint effort to realize the two principles on which my own party's success has been predicated; a compassion and understanding for those who need assistance and services on the one hand, and competence on the other.

We have to get maximum benefit from every dollar spent, every person employed, every decision made. Unwarranted Government regulation must be minimized. The competitive nature of the free enterprise system must be enhanced. And I know that I can count on you to join in with this effort with other leaders of our Government to be successful.

I do not intend to fail as President in

making sure that the Government is efficient, competent, and honest. And I would like to be sure that a close observation of how we perform can be a real inspiration to our Nation. With you as partners, a member of the same team, I have no doubt that we will be successful.

Thank you very much.

NOTE: The President spoke at 3:15 p.m. in the Interdepartmental Auditorium at the Department of Commerce. Charles L. Schultze, Chairman of the Council of Economic Advisers, and Alfred E. Kahn, Advisor to the President on Inflation, also participated in the briefing.

Visit of King Hassan II of Morocco

Remarks at the Welcoming Ceremony. November 14, 1978

THE PRESIDENT. It is indeed a great honor for me as President of our country and for the people of the United States to welcome His Majesty, King Hassan II of Morocco.

Your Majesty, we are grateful that you have come to pay us a visit, along with Crown Prince Sidi Mohammed. This reminds us with a great deal of pleasure of the visit 11 or 12 years ago (21 years),[1] when you came as Crown Prince with your own father, the revered King Mohammed V.

It's impossible for the people of the United States of America to forget the early days of our own Nation's existence. Our Declaration of Independence was in 1776. And 1 year later, in 1777, Morocco recognized our people, our new Government as a nation. Your country, Your Majesty, was the first nation on Earth to ever give us this diplomatic relation and

---

[1] Printed in the transcript.

recognition. And we will ever be grateful to you for having confidence in us and in the spirit of freedom and independence which our struggling forefathers had espoused to the world.

Only 10 years later, in 1787, there was signed a treaty of friendship and commerce between the United States of America and the nation, the people of Morocco.

These relationships have bound us together in common purpose, mutual understanding, and friendship for centuries. But we still recognize your leadership and your great nation not only as our nearest neighbor in Africa, but we recognize your country as indeed the crossroads of north and south, east and west, because of the ancient history of your people, the ancient and benevolent nature of the reign of your family and the pride with which you espouse ideals and commitments that are so precious to the people of my country.

Ever since World War II, we have enjoyed the closest possible political and military alliance with your nation. Our sailors, our airmen, our diplomats, our business leaders, our scholars, our students have been welcomed in your country. And we deeply appreciate this ancient and also this modern special privilege of being the friends of the people of Morocco.

You have shown great courage in trying to retain the cohesion of the Arab world and, at the same time, being forceful in your expression of support for the peace initiative taken by President Sadat a little more than a year ago when he went to Jerusalem. He was criticized by many, but he was praised and supported by you. And I know that your beneficent influence in the future will help our Nation, and those others who are struggling for peace, ultimately achieve success.

Your Majesty, as a statesman, admired and respected throughout the world, as a representative of a great people, as a scholar and a leader throughout the continent of Africa, and indeed, your entire region of our planet, we are grateful for our relationship with you and for your kind visit to our country.

There is no doubt in my mind that our own discussions with our advisers and other leaders and the private discussions that I intend to have with you will be very constructive both for the people of your country and my own and also for the enhancement of peace in your troubled region and indeed throughout the world.

Thank you, Your Majesty, for being here with your fine family, and I want again to express our welcome to you on this wonderful day in the history of my own country.

Thank you and welcome.

KING HASSAN. Mr. President, I have come to visit you with consideration, friendship, as much as faults in English. [*Laughter*] But I shall try to translate or to write the feelings of my people and my own feelings for yourself and your country.

You have built all your election, Mr. President, on rights of men, in the time where you are the first nation in the world. For us, the small peoples, this philosophy and this policy is very important, and it is a big encouragement, because we have no weapons, we have not your army; we have only our faith and our rights. But I think that faith and rights are the best weapons to live or to die.

Mr. President, you told us in few words, but in full words, the history between the United States and the Kingdom of Morocco. My hope and my wish is to build with you our modern history on the same level as our old history.

I have the mission to bring on my shoulders and to convey in my heart the friendship of my people to the American people. I pray God to help me to be a good servant for my people and for the friendship between the United States and Morocco. And I pray God, I pray God to help you in your work, Mr. President, and to preserve the United States of America.

THE PRESIDENT. Thank you very much.

NOTE: The President spoke at 10:45 a.m. on the South Lawn of the White House.

Emergency Board To Investigate an Airline Labor Dispute

Appointment of the Membership.
November 14, 1978

The President today announced the members of the Emergency Board to investigate the dispute between Wien Air Alaska and the Air Line Pilots Association. This Board was created by Executive order on November 2, 1978. The members are:

John N. Gentry, of Reston, Va., a lawyer and labor relations specialist. Gentry is a member of Wirtz and Gentry, a labor and public interest consulting firm. His professional activities relate to manpower, education, labor relations, and dispute resolution. He is president of the National Manpower Institute and is a former Deputy Assistant Secretary of Labor for Labor-Management Relations. He will serve as Chairman of the Emergency Board.

Paul N. Guthrie, an economics professor at the University of North Carolina. He has been a member of numerous Presidential Emergency Boards, involving both railroad and airline labor disputes. He has also served as a labor arbitrator and as a referee for the National Railroad Adjustment Board. He is a past president of the National Academy of Arbitrators.

Ralph W. Yarborough, of Austin, Tex., an attorney, arbitrator, and former U.S. Senator. Yarborough served in the Senate from 1957 to 1971 and was chairman of the Senate Labor and Public Welfare Committee.

Visit of King Hassan II of Morocco

Toasts at the State Dinner.
November 14, 1978

THE PRESIDENT. First of all, let me welcome all of you to the White House. This is a wonderful occasion for us, to have a distinguished visitor, his sister, his two sons, to come and represent a country that has extremely significant historical ties with our own Nation.

When I welcomed King Hassan this morning, I pointed out to the audience on the South Lawn that our Nation declared its independence in 1776. And in 1777 we were sitting here fighting for freedom, a small struggling country with practically no friends in the rest of the world. But one nation came forward and said, "We recognize you as an independent people." And I think all of you here can guess which nation that was. It was Morocco.

This, of course, was in 1777. And now for more than 200 years our country has been honored with the friendship and the alliance and support and partnership with a great people, the Kingdom of Morocco. Ten years later, we signed a treaty of peace and commerce and began a very fruitful trade between our two nations, with the exchange of ambassadors, first of all, and then with merchant seamen, more recently airmen, members of our Navy. This has been a very constant and fruitful interrelationship between two people.

My mother visited Morocco recently. King Hassan tells me that Morocco has recovered from her visit. [*Laughter*] As a matter of fact, my mother is a walking chamber of commerce for Morocco. And I thought she was the greatest supporter of Morocco that I knew, until I sat next to Mrs. Billy Casper. Her husband has played in 8 [golf] tournaments in Morocco. They visited Morocco 20 times. And she says that of all the countries she has ever visited, it's her favorite.

The history, the customs, the tradition, the achievements of Morocco are admirable in every respect. And it is a great honor for us to have King Hassan come and visit here, 11, 12 years since he made his last visit. The first time he came here with his own father as a Crown Prince, and he's brought his oldest son, the Crown Prince, with him this time.

The last time King Hassan came to our country, about 12 years ago, the Middle East was in a time of crisis, indeed war. On this occasion we are struggling to prevent a recurrence of that kind of crisis in the Middle East.

We've made historic progress in recent months. The outcome of the final negotiations for peace between Egypt and Israel is still in doubt. But one of the staunch allies and friends of President Sadat who courageously supported him when he made his historic journey to Jerusalem almost exactly 12 months ago was King Hassan of Morocco. It was not an easy thing for him to do. He was castigated and criticized by some because he expressed his friendship and support for that giant step toward peace. But this is typical of his leadership.

He's been instrumental in giving us advice and counsel. Me, as a new President, I had a lot to learn about the Arab world, about historical interrelationships, about the continent of Africa, the prospects for peace. And in many ways that have never been revealed, he's been very constructive in laying a basis for progress that is now being made.

My wife and the Crown Prince have been speaking tonight in Spanish. The Crown Prince is quite fluent; my wife is still a student. But King Hassan told me that even in years gone by, the Spanish language has been very helpful to our Nation. In 1943, as you well know, in a time of worldwide crisis, President Roosevelt met with the Prime Minister of Great Britain, Churchill, in Casablanca.

It was a highly secret meeting. Intelligence revealed their presence there. The Germans were informed. Fortunately, they had a Spanish translator in Berlin, and the information that reached Hitler was that the President of the United States and the Prime Minister of Great Britain were meeting in the White House. [*Laughter*] So, although this building was in danger of being bombed, President Roosevelt and Prime Minister Churchill escaped unscathed.

That's a true story, as a matter of fact, but a very interesting element from history shows again that in time of crisis, the great nation of Morocco was a place for the resolution of differences and the laying for groundwork for peace.

We are honored, too, because King Hassan has been so diligent and so successful in providing for his own people an expanded opportunity for living a fruitful life. Under his benevolent leadership, the people of Morocco have been granted constitutional government with the holding of elections in a very successful way, the election of a new parliament, including members of the political opposition. And this has been done in such a fine and successful fashion that Morocco has set, indeed, an example for other nations to emulate.

The tremendous natural wealth of

Morocco is still in many instances waiting to be tapped. And its phosphate reserves, its oil reserves, oil shale, uranium reserves, and the great agricultural capability of his country and the human resources are now being developed in a very constructive way in partnership, on occasion, with us. Although the relationships are of mutual benefit, I would have to say in candor that we have benefited much more from our relationship with Morocco than vice versa.

It's a wonderful opportunity to have here a man who understands the continent of Africa, an area where our own interest has just recently begun to be exerted in a constructive fashion. And when the world sat in doubt and the nation of Zaire was threatened with invasion from outside forces, there was one nation, again, that showed leadership and courage. And you don't have to guess long to know that that nation was Morocco, a stabilizing influence there, instant action brought about by strong and competent leadership. And that's, indeed, the example that King Hassan has established for the world to observe.

I would like to say in closing that we are very grateful for this alliance and for the progress that has been achieved in his country, and the benefit that we have derived from it in our Nation.

It's very reassuring to me as a President to know that I can enjoy the friendship and the support, the advice and the counsel and the common purpose which has historically bound our nations together.

And on behalf of the 220 million people of the United States of America, I would like to propose a toast to the people of the Kingdom of Morocco and to their great leader, and a friend of all Americans, King Hassan II. To King Hassan.

KING HASSAN. The efforts after dinner is not good for digestion—[*laughter*]—but I shall try to.

Ladies and gentlemen, I present you the President, Jimmy Carter, not as President of the United States, but as a new, but close and loyal friend of myself and of my country.

I never met the President before. But this morning I felt that there will be many, many strong ties between him and between I, because we are convinced that the democracy and the freedom are the best reasons for people to live, to fight, to win, or to die.

The President told you that Morocco is rich with uranium, phosphate, and perhaps oil. But before, Morocco is rich by his history, is rich by his respect for the dignity and rights of men. And it's why I feel that President Carter and I, we will build a very long and large bridge over the ocean to make our people more close and more allied, allied not against someone, but allied against poorness, against war, against the strengths of the weapons, and allied for the prosperity of our nations and our peoples.

Mr. President, I told you this morning that I visit you with my friendship and my fault of English. And I continue this this evening. [*Laughter*] But I think that the best conclusion is to explain as possible as I can, what is the kind of the friendship between your country and mine.

And through your person, Mr. President, permit me to pray God to save your people and your country and to help you in your mission and in your job.

Ladies and gentlemen, will you please pray God with me to save the United States and the President of America?

Excuse my very bad speech.

THE PRESIDENT. Very wonderful speech. I thank you very much.

NOTE: The President spoke at 9:45 p.m. in the State Dining Room at the White House.

President's Council on Physical Fitness and Sports

Executive Order 12098.   November 14, 1978

PHYSICAL FITNESS AND SPORTS

By the authority vested in me as President by the Constitution of the United States of America, and in order to amend the composition of the President's Council on Physical Fitness and Sports, Executive Order No. 11562, as amended by Executive Order No. 11945, is hereby further amended by revising Section 2(a) to read as follows:

"There is hereby established the President's Council on Physical Fitness and Sports, hereinafter referred to as the Council, which shall be composed of fifteen members appointed by the President. The Chairman shall be designated by the President from among the members. The Council shall meet at the call of the Chairman.".

JIMMY CARTER

The White House,
  November 14, 1978.

[Filed with the Office of the Federal Register, 10:38 a.m., November 15, 1978]

NOTE: The text of the Executive order was released on November 15.

President's Council on Physical Fitness and Sports

*Appointment of 11 Members.
November 15, 1978*

The President today announced the appointment of 11 persons as members of the President's Council on Physical Fitness and Sports. They are:

HENRY AARON, of Atlanta, Ga., the baseball star, now vice president of the Atlanta Braves;

ANITA DE FRANTZ, a staff attorney at the Juvenile Law Center of Philadelphia, and a bronze medalist on the U.S. Olympic rowing team in 1976;

DOROTHY HAMILL, the Olympic gold medalist in ice skating, now with the Ice Capades;

MARY JOANNE JOHNSON, of Phoenix, Ariz., who is active in community affairs and supports a physical fitness program for housewives;

SAMMY LEE, a physician in Orange County, Calif., and an Olympic gold medalist in diving in 1948;

ALFRED J. McGUIRE, a commentator on college basketball for NBC, vice president of a sporting goods firm, and a former professional basketball player;

JAMES A. NICHOLAS, of Scarsdale, N.Y., an orthopedic surgeon and expert on sports medicine;

DINAH SHORE, the television show hostess, sponsor of the Dinah Shore golf tournaments;

CLAUDE E. TERRY, of Atlanta, president of a consulting firm specializing in environmental studies, and an expert on whitewater canoeing and kayaking;

JOSEPH B. SMITH, chairman of the board of Elektra/Asylum Records;

LeRoy T. WALKER, professor of physical education at North Carolina Central and head coach of the U.S. track and field team at the 1976 Olympics.

Margaret Mead

*Statement on the Death of the
Anthropologist.   November 15, 1978*

Margaret Mead's life was impressively full and productive. Beginning with the publication of "Coming of Age in Samoa," half a century ago, she brought the humane insights of cultural anthropology to a public of millions. In her life as in her thought, she went wherever her probing intelligence would take her. Intrepid and independent, she was a model for several generations of young Americans, especially women. She was loved for her compassionate belief that varying cultural patterns express an underlying human unity.

High Carbon Ferrochromium Imports

Proclamation 4608. November 15, 1978

TEMPORARY DUTY INCREASE ON THE IMPORTATION INTO THE UNITED STATES OF CERTAIN HIGH-CARBON FERROCHROMIUM

By the President of the United States of America

A Proclamation

1. Pursuant to section 201(d)(1) of the Trade Act of 1974 (the Trade Act) (19 U.S.C. 2251(d)(1)), the United States International Trade Commission (USITC) on September 5, 1978, reported to the President (USITC Report 201–35) the results of its investigation under section 201(b)(1) of the Trade Act (19 U.S.C. 2251(b)(1)). The USITC determined that ferrochromium, containing over 3 percent by weight of carbon, provided for in item 607.31 of the Tariff Schedules of the United States (TSUS) (19 U.S.C. 1202) is being imported into the United States in such increased quantities as to be a substantial cause of serious injury to the domestic industry producing an article like or directly competitive with the imported article. The USITC recommended the imposition of tariff increases on the column 1 rate of 30 percent ad valorem in the first year declining to 20 percent ad valorem in the fifth year of relief.

2. On November 2, 1978, pursuant to section 202(b)(1) of the Trade Act (19 U.S.C. 2252(b)(1)), and after taking into account the considerations specified in section 202(c) of the Trade Act (19 U.S.C. 2252(c)), I determined to remedy the injury found to exist by the USITC through the proclamation of a temporary duty increase different from that recommended by the USITC. In accordance with section 203(b)(1) of the Trade Act (19 U.S.C. 2253(b)(1)), I transmitted a report to the Congress setting forth my determination and intention to proclaim a temporary duty increase and stating the reasons why my decision differed from the action recommended by the USITC.

3. Section 203(e)(1) of the Trade Act (19 U.S.C. 2253(e)(1)) requires that import relief be proclaimed and take effect within 15 days after the import relief determination date.

4. Pursuant to section 203(a)(1) of the Trade Act (19 U.S.C. 2253(a)(1)), I am providing import relief through the temporary increase of import duty on ferrochromium, containing over 3 percent by weight of carbon, valued less than 38 cents per pound, as hereinafter proclaimed.

NOW, THEREFORE, I, JIMMY CARTER, President of the United States of America, acting under the authority vested in me by the Constitution and the statutes of the United States, including General Headnote 4 of the TSUS (19 U.S.C. 1202), sections 203 and 604 of the Trade Act (19 U.S.C. 2253 and 2483), and in accordance with Articles I and XIX of the General Agreement on Tariffs and Trade (GATT) (61 Stat. (pt. 5) A 12 and 61 Stat. (pt. 5) A 58: 8 UST (pt. 2) 1786), do proclaim that—

(1) Part I of Schedule XX to the GATT is modified to conform to the actions taken in the Annex to this proclamation.

(2) Subpart A, part 2 of the Appendix to the TSUS is modified as set forth in the Annex to this proclamation.

(3) This proclamation shall be effective as to those articles entered, or withdrawn from warehouse, for consumption on or after November 17, 1978, and before the close of November 16, 1981, unless the period of its effectiveness is earlier expressly modified or terminated.

IN WITNESS WHEREOF, I have hereunto set my hand this fifteenth day of November, in the year of our Lord nineteen hundred seventy-eight, and of the Independence of the United States of America the two hundred and third.

JIMMY CARTER

[Filed with the Office of the Federal Register, 10:25 a.m., November 16, 1978]

NOTE: The annex is printed in the FEDERAL REGISTER of November 17, 1978.

Hubert H. Humphrey North-South Scholarship Program

Announcement of a White House Meeting To Discuss the Program's Implementation. November 15, 1978

The President today invited the presidents of 50 U.S. universities to attend a White House meeting on December 5, 1978, to discuss the implementation of the new Hubert H. Humphrey North-South Scholarship program. The invitation was extended on the President's behalf by Charles W. Bray III, Acting Director of the International Communications Agency.

The program will bring young men and women from every developing nation with which we have diplomatic relations to study in U.S. universities for 1 year of postgraduate study as "Humphrey North-South Scholars." In addition, the students will attend a 3-month summer workshop on North-South relations at the Humphrey Institute in Minnesota. Like the Rhodes Scholar, the Humphrey Scholar will be chosen on the basis of merit and potential leadership, but additionally, the Humphrey Scholar will be of modest means and will be dedicated to a career in public service.

The program was announced by the Vice President on October 21, 1978, in a speech to the American Lutheran Church general convention in Moorehead, Minn. The idea for the program was first suggested by the President in Caracas on March 31, 1978. The proposal resulted from an interagency review chaired by the National Security Council staff. Fifty universities throughout the United States have been selected to be eligible to participate in this program.

The program's purpose is to help educate a core group of a new generation of developing world leaders. It is designed to provide education and a common experience for a group of future leaders and by so doing provide a compelling symbol of U.S. interest in the developing world and in the North-South dialog as one of the most significant global challenges of our time. It will seek out talented youth who might otherwise not be able to afford education, thereby demonstrating a special American concern for helping the poor and for promoting equality of people. The purpose of the studies will be to enhance the students' capabilities for public service, in particular to help improve incomes, living standards, and employment and enable them to contribute more effectively to the equitable development of their country.

The program will cost $5 million for about 240 students. It will begin in September 1979 and will be administered by the International Communication Agency.

Interview With the President

Question-and-Answer Session at a Breakfast
With Members of the White House
Correspondents Association.
November 16, 1978

PRESS SECRETARY POWELL. Ladies and gentlemen, let me take a moment to make sure we understand the groundrules, which are few, and just a word about what's involved here.

We thought it might be helpful to you—and of course we always do things that we think will be helpful to us—to provide an opportunity to talk with the President in a somewhat less formal situation than the regular news conference.

We plan to have two of these breakfasts. About half of the people who cover the White House regularly are here today. The other half will be invited to another breakfast within a week or so. The proceedings will be on the record. We will provide a transcript as soon as possible, and there is no embargo on whatever news you are able to glean from this gathering.

Mr. President?

THE PRESIDENT. I don't know who wants to recognize the interrogator. But, Frank [Frank Cormier, Associated Press], I think I'll start with you and Helen [Helen Thomas, United Press International] first.

ANTI-INFLATION PROGRAM

Q. All right. Mr. President, I'm a little curious—I've been away a month and missed a lot—but I wonder if you would place the goals of defending the dollar and fighting inflation above what might be the contradictory goal of political survival.

THE PRESIDENT. Okay. I'll try to answer. I don't think they are contradictory. There's no doubt that the primary domes-

tic concern of the American people, as revealed by every poll that I've seen lately, is inflation. I think part of the reason is that we have made substantial progress on alleviating the previous number one concern, which was unemployment. The latest figures show 5.8 unemployment, which is a substantial reduction from roughly 8 percent, when I came into office.

Also, I think the Congress and I together have had some very constructive legislation passed concerning transportation, education, aid to the cities, including the employment question, and so forth.

But I think that to deal now successfully with a stable dollar and to level off the rate of inflation, hopefully to reduce it in the future, is not only necessary from a nonpolitical basis but also good politics.

Q. How about when the constituencies start hollering at you?

THE PRESIDENT. That's difficult, but it's already a very serious problem. What I'm trying to do, basically, is to build up within the consciousness of the Congress and my own administration a realization of what Americans demand, and that is a very sound, fiscally responsible approach to these special interest demands.

It's much easier for me to have a partner in Congress as legislation and budget decisions are evolving, rather than for me to assume the unfortunate posture of having to veto legislation once it's passed. And I believe that this would make it easier for me next year than it has been the last few days of this year, when I had to veto several bills that had expectations built up because the Congress passed them, which I couldn't accept.

Q. Mr. President, what do you think of all the scare talk—and I mean scare talk—about not only a recession but a depression, and some of which comes from your own people? And a lot of it comes from economists and experts.

THE PRESIDENT. I checked with Charlie Schultze recently, and Schultze's projections are still a growth rate next year, if the inflation package is successful as we anticipate, of about 3 percent. Some have said lower, of course, but if there's one group that has an extreme diversity in analysis, it is economists. And I think that this is something that we do not anticipate, a recession or a depression. If we have a complete and abject failure in our anti-inflation program, then I think a recession or even a depression is a possibility—I won't say a likelihood. But I think we'll be successful.

Q. But how about controls? Is that a last resort? In case of a recession or a depression, would you go for them?

THE PRESIDENT. Well, mandatory wage and price controls, I think, would be counterproductive. And one of the main reasons that I've discounted them is that I don't think they would work. If our Nation was in such a serious state, approaching a national emergency or danger to our own security, there might be aroused in the public consciousness and in the Congress such a commitment to controlling inflation that mandatory wage and price controls would be necessary, as in the case of war, or something of that kind.

One of the differences that exists now with the experiment that Nixon pursued with wage and price controls that were mandatory is that I don't have the legal authority to do it. There would be no way to have a surprise announcement that wage and price controls were being imposed on the economy by the Government now. If that should become necessary in the case of a serious crisis, and the Congress began the long and, I'm sure, disputed debates, then following that a legal right to impose wage and price controls would come. But we don't have that option now.

Q. Well, wouldn't you want it on a standby basis?

THE PRESIDENT. No. I'm not going to request it, even on a standby basis.

Q. Mr. President, just to follow up on that, the argument of it not being practical to talk about wage and price controls now, because, after all, you don't have the authority to impose it, how does that gibe with the fact that you can always have wage and price controls imposed retroactively, so that if companies rushed to raise their prices when talk first started about it, they still wouldn't be affected when you imposed a retroactive date on it?

THE PRESIDENT. I don't mind answering the question, Marty [Martin J. Schram, Newsday], but this is kind of idle talk, because I don't have any intention of asking the Congress for wage and price authority. I don't think the Congress would grant it if I asked. And I have no intention to do it.

Obviously, if you ever should make that decision in case of a crisis, the decision would have to be retroactive. You can't do it prospectively, because that opens up the possibility of massive price increases just in anticipation of controls and also to lay a basis for higher prices in the future. But I don't anticipate that happening under any foreseeable circumstances, as I say, unless our Nation is in a crisis stage and actually our security is in danger. I don't anticipate it.

Q. I just want to follow up on the same subject. A lot of economists think that there will be a recession next year, perhaps not a deep one. And Alfred Kahn said yesterday—he was talking, as Helen said, scare talk—that if your program doesn't work and we just went along as we have been, there would be a deep depression. Is it fair to assume that you'd rather take the chance of a mild recession than what your people seem to think would be the certainty of a deep depression in your program?

THE PRESIDENT. Sam [Sam Donaldson, ABC News], the reason that Alfred Kahn and I get in the posture of having a tiny phrase extracted from an answer is that the questions are extremely hypothetical and all the caveats that are built very carefully around the answer are sometimes ignored. And then on TV and so forth or in the news media a little tiny phrase is used concerning an extreme depression.

I watched on "Issues and Answers" two or three Sundays ago when you asked Alfred Kahn repeatedly, "If you had to choose between the two, which would you go with?" And he said over and over, "I do not anticipate this happening. I'm reluctant to answer your question." You said, "Well, if you answered the question, how would it be?" He finally said it. And it's really kind of an idle thing. And I'm reluctant to say all my caveats and then add two or three "ifs" and then ever answer the question.

I just don't think we're going to have a substantial economic setback next year. I anticipate success with the anti-inflation program. I can't anticipate perfect success, complete success.

I think if we had a complete failure and inflation ran rampant, then the prospect for a recession and maybe a depression would be there. The definition of recession, the way I understand it, is zero growth for two quarters. We anticipate still a growth rate that's fairly substantial next year. Charlie Schultze's projections still, on which we base our budget preparations, is that if our inflation package is moderately successful, then the growth rate next year would average about 3 percent.

Q. Could I just follow up just one more time? The reason I ask is not to trap you into saying, "Aha! Deep depression possibilities."

THE PRESIDENT. Sure.

Q. But I think one of the reasons most people think that your dollar-strengthening program is successful, people around the world said, "Well, he means business." Do you really mean business?

THE PRESIDENT. I meant and do mean business.

Q. All right. And looking ahead—and I'm not predicting, I don't know anything about it, a recession—but if there should come a mild recession, people are going to think, well, will he then, "Oh my goodness, it's mild recession, and I'm going to start pumping the money in." In other words, now, do we reverse policy again, or do you just kind of hold to your course?

THE PRESIDENT. I intend to hold to my course.

Q. Come what may from the standpoint of——

THE PRESIDENT. With any foreseeable circumstance, based on our current projections, I am going to hold my course. Temporary aberrations or pressures from interest groups will have very little effect.

And I think that the Congress has gotten the message on the desire of the American people just as strongly or maybe even more strongly than I have. I'm not going to be taking a fiscally responsible position opposed by a spendthrift Congress. I think we're going to be working in concert to bring about a responsible but very strict fiscal policy.

I might point out to you that we've made good progress already. In 1975, for instance, the Federal deficit was 4½ percent of our GNP—I think 4.6 percent, to be accurate. Our projections for the 1980 fiscal year budget—no, these are calendar years; I'm sorry—1980 calendar year is 1 percent of our GNP, a substantial reduction in the deficit. And I think this is necessary to give people confidence in the future.

And we tend to forget often that controlling inflation is much more beneficial to those who have marginal incomes, those who are retired and live on fixed incomes, than it is to the wealthy or affluent or well-educated, or those who have a flexible opportunity to seek additional means for income and support. The ones who are tightly bound because of illiteracy or because of immobility or because they don't have options on new jobs, or because they have already finished their life's work and are living on a fixed retirement basis, these are the ones that suffer most from inflation.

And when you take a strong stand against inflation, it doesn't mean that you're abandoning your commitment to the well-being of people who need government assistance and government protection most. I think it's a contributing factor to government caring for, caring about and caring for, these who are most vulnerable.

Q. Mr. President, if you're going to reach that goal of 30 billion or less on the deficit——

THE PRESIDENT. I am.

Q.—— we are told that you'll have to find somehow, to cut 15 billion or more off just the cost of current programs scheduled for next year. If you're going to increase defense spending, what on Earth are you going to find in the other parts of the budget to squeeze that much out of?

THE PRESIDENT. We'll find it. We've got overall projections now, of course. Before I made that commitment, which was a very serious commitment and one about which we had a fairly substantial debate, we had excellent projections that showed that it was both feasible and that it would

be accomplished. It's not going to be easy. And there are going to be many disappointed heads of Federal agencies and many disappointed interest groups in our country. But it's going to be fair, equitable, a sharing of some moderate sacrifice. But the benefits to be derived from this policy will be, I think, well recognized and supported. We'll meet that goal.

EGYPTIAN-ISRAELI PEACE NEGOTIATIONS

Q. Mr. President, on the Middle East, sir, do you think a time might come when another summit might be necessary to untangle all the apparently serious problems that are cropping up?

THE PRESIDENT. I really hope not. And this is not something that we are contemplating.

There are two serious problems that we have now that we did not have at Camp David. One is the lack of authority, final authority, granted to the negotiators. Three weeks ago—I think it was 3 weeks ago, 3½ weeks ago—I spent almost all weekend, including late at night, early in the morning, meeting with the Egyptian and Israeli negotiators. We arrived at an ageement on a treaty text. This text was then submitted back to the national leaders and cabinets and others, and was rejected because of what I consider to be minor differences. They were important to the negotiating nations. And at Camp David, on the contrary, I could walk 50 yards or in 2 minutes have a private conversation in my own cabin with either Begin or Sadat; sometimes, if necessary, both together.

That's been one of the most frustrating things. We've had to negotiate a treaty or a settlement several times already; each time someone has rejected the final conclusion.

I would say equally as serious, perhaps even more serious, is that the negotiations have been conducted and are being conducted through the news media. At Camp David, the imposition of a news embargo, where no statements were made unless all three nations—ourselves and the two negotiating nations—agreed, was a very constructive thing. And I think even the press analysis has agreed with that in retrospect—even at the time, even, perhaps. Now that's one of my most serious concerns.

When a text is presented to the Israelis, there is a series of statements made by them that such and such a portion of the text is unacceptable and that we will never change our position on this. And then the same thing happens in a mirror image in Egypt, where public demands are made by different voices there. And it hardens positions, and it makes it almost impossible to present to both nations an accomplished document which they have to either accept or reject in its totality.

You can find in any piece of legislation the Congress passes one paragraph or one phrase or one section to which I, as President, would strenuously object. But still when I look at the totality of the document, I quite often, most often, can sign it. And these two problems are very, very serious.

I will be meeting in a few minutes, right after this meeting, with the Vice President of Egypt. And I met early this week with Defense Minister Weizman. We're trying now to find some resolution of existing differences. But I don't have any intention at this point of going to another summit meeting. And I hope and pray and expect that it will not be necessary.

Q. Mr. President, to follow up on that, through these long weeks and months of the negotiations where you had such a role yourself, how can we expect that if there is agreement between Egypt and Israel—if it was engineered so much by an outside party, yourself, without a continuing commitment and initiative by the principals, how can we expect that to stand?

THE PRESIDENT. Well, I want to make clear that we've not imposed our will on the other leaders as reluctant negotiators. Everything that has been agreed to at Camp David was not only accepted but— I think you could see during the ceremonies here—accepted with enthusiasm, even with celebration. There was, I think, a justified euphoria there of appreciation to one another for having reached an agreement.

It wasn't something that we demanded that the others accept. We don't have any authority to do that and don't want any. We've tried to serve as an avenue of communication and add our good will when we can. This would continue in the future. I think the issues that were established at Camp David and resolved are the basis for a historical breakthrough. And to use King Hassan's language, "You can't make the stream flow backwards." We've made progress that's irreversible, in my opinion.

Now, the differences, compared to what was agreed, are minor, but important, politically and symbolically. Neither side completely trusts the other. This is based on ancient animosities, frequent wars, losses that quite often bubble up to the surface when you are in private talks with either leader. And I think that their mutual trust of me and our country is an important ingredient. If the Egyptians distrust the Israelis' commitment to move forward with self-government and autonomous authority in the West Bank, Gaza, we say, "We trust the Israelis to move, President Sadat. You and we together can use our influence in the future to ensure compliance with the agreement." If the Israelis distrust President Sadat's peaceful intentions, then I can tell Prime Minister Begin, "To the extent that you trust us, you and I will work together to alleviate your concerns about Sadat in the future."

I think these kinds of problems can be partially alleviated by our presence. But there's got to be some building of mutual trust between the two.

It is disappointing to me. I anticipated after Camp David that in just a few days the agreement could be reached. But those ancient distrusts and disputes continually arise. And I think now, next year, maybe years in the future, a moderating, constructive influence by the United States might be necessary, as mutually requested by both parties. I think both the Israelis and Egyptians see that without our presence now, future progress will be much more difficult. Even with our presence, progress is difficult.

Q. May I follow on that?

THE PRESIDENT. You can, yes.

Q. If we do get the agreement and dare look over the horizon, how much do you think that will do to defuse the potential for continued violence by other causes in the Middle East and continued threats against American oil supplies? Would it be—take us a great leap forward away from that?

THE PRESIDENT. Yes, I think it would be a tremendous leap forward, even as it affects nations who presently are adamantly opposed to the peace agreements between Egypt and Israel. Yes, it would alleviate tension. It would help to let the moderate Arab countries, ourselves, and Israel act in concert to engender peace, open ways for economic development that still have not been adequately analyzed. I think that is the key factor in having a stable and a prosperous Middle East.

Q. Mr. President, when you outlined those problems, I've never heard you speak of why you think that those problems have developed. Is it in your view that these things are happening in spite of the good intentions of both sides? Or is there a suggestion there that maybe one side or the other or both have decided that maybe they just can't go along with what was agreed to at Camp David—maybe that Sadat thinks he can't get along with the rest of the Arab world on this, or the Israelis think that somehow they could get a treaty with Egpyt and wind up keeping the land on the West Bank?

THE PRESIDENT. I think both sides are acting in good faith. They obviously want to interpret the agreements as much as proper to their own advantage. We have an inevitable problem in that Camp David, even though it was quite substantive—the texts were quite substantive—had to be embellished or elaborated with specific time schedules, exact drawing of lines between Israel and Egypt, interim withdrawal terms, the make-up of the Egyptian forces on the east bank of the Suez, the time to commence negotiations on the establishment of self-government in the Gaza Strip and West Bank. These kinds of things had to be negotiated in the final peace treaty.

In a few cases it might be necessary to modify the Camp David accords if both sides agree. If both sides don't agree, then our adamant position will be the Camp David accords cannot be abrogated, because this is just as solemn an agreement between those two nations as a future peace treaty will be. And unless both sides agree to modify the Camp David accords, we will insist that those accords be honored meticulously.

In addition to that, though, the progress from Camp David brings up hundreds of detailed decisions. We've put forward our own compromise proposals and our own documents as the original bargaining position. I spread out in my study upstairs, immediately above us, an enormous map of the Sinai—it was probably 10 or 12 feet long and 6 or 8 feet wide—and personally approved the drawing of the interim withdrawal lines and the final borders, even before the Israeli and Egyptian negotiators came here. And that was put forward to the military negotiators, who in effect have adopted what we proposed.

But I think that both sides are acting in good faith. They have political pressures at home. President Sadat legitimately wants to retain his good ties as a political and military leader of the Arab world. The Israelis have to be sure that their security is certain in years ahead. They want to retain an option of the final status of the West Bank and Gaza. This is all included in the Camp David accords.

But I think that it would certainly be obvious that both sides want peace, and I think that's the main hope that we have in spite of these differences.

When you balance the enormous benefits with peace, compared to the horrible consequences of failure, and then look at the tiny differences that exist between them now—on wording and language, linkage, schedules, hilltops, valleys, security outposts—these things are really minuscule in comparison with the advantages of peace. And their common desire for peace is the hope of all three of us, that we'll be successful.

U.S.-SOVIET RELATIONS

Q. Mr. President, let me ask you a general, all-purpose question about our relations with the Soviet Union. We're coming up now, I hope, to a SALT agreement. Brezhnev is getting older and visibly more feeble with each passing year. And the time is coming when he won't be the leader of the Soviet Union.

How do you see our relations with the Soviet Union developing over the rest of this term of office and on into the 1980's?

THE PRESIDENT. I'm determined that our relationships with the Soviet Union will improve as we go into the next 2 years. With every passing week, we have resolved part of the differences concerning SALT. In spite of a couple of ill-advised statements by me that we would be having a SALT agreement within the next few weeks—[*laughter*]—we have made steady progress. And I think that when I do meet with Brezhnev—and I think "when" is a proper word instead of "if;" we don't know exactly when it will be—then the agenda to be discussed would be quite broad.

The centerpiece of it would be to culminate the SALT negotiations with a SALT II agreement. But I think at that time we would be prepared to discuss, I hope without any excessive time pressure and with very good preparation, the broadest range of differences that exist between ourselves and the Soviet Union.

I think that in recent weeks there has been an alleviation of tension between us. And I would like to see that progress continue.

Q. Why is that? Why in the last few weeks?

THE PRESIDENT. I can't say why. I think at the time of the Shcharanskiy trial, there was a combination of differences that probably made us reach a low point, at least in my own administration. And I think since then we've moved forward on better relations, a better understanding, more harmony, and less disputes with the public media.

Q. When you say you'd be prepared to discuss the broadest range of differences that exist between us, could you be more specific about some of the differences you'd like to discuss?

THE PRESIDENT. No, I don't think so, because we've not prepared an agenda yet. But it certainly would not be exclusively limited to SALT. And I think that any differences we have with the Soviets, we ought to put them on the table and discuss them. But the agenda would have to be worked out jointly with them before any announcement of it was made.

HOSPITAL COST CONTAINMENT LEGISLATION

Q. Mr. President, how are you going to get hospital cost containment?

THE PRESIDENT. With a very determined and concerted effort. We were successful last session in finally getting it through the Senate, a fairly good version of it that would accomplish about 60 percent of what we originally wanted. We didn't have an adequate interest among the public in hospital cost containment. I think we'll have more interest next session than we had before. It's obvious that the hospital industry and the medical industry will exert their utmost effort to prevent hospital cost containment being passed.

I've seen recent news stories about the very large financial contributions made to interested Members of Congress. I think just the revelation of these completely legal contributions will induce the entire Congress to say, "Are we responsive to the general public, or are we excessively concerned with the intense lobbying pressure on this legislation?"

I think an open and objective debate with a full focusing of public attention on it will enhance our chances of success.

SPECIAL INTEREST GROUPS

Q. Mr. President, may I follow up somewhat on that? You talked about special interests here this morning. There is concern among some political scientists and observers that one-issue politics and special-interest politics are sort of taking over the two-party system, factionalizing it. Do you share this concern? And do you feel that some of the Senators who lost last week perhaps were victims, at least in part, of one-issue interest groups?

THE PRESIDENT. I'm concerned about it, and I think some of them who lost were victims of single-interest groups, or at least a small combination of interest groups. The only way to avoid that is to have the public more deeply involved in the electoral process, the financing of elections, and the debate precedent to a congressional decision.

The best single thing that could be done in a generic sense is to have public financing of congressional elections. I think it worked very well in the Presidential election. Certainly the result was obviously beneficial to our Nation. [*Laughter*] I think that everybody who participated in that Presidential election of 1976—myself and also the losers—agreed that the public financing system worked very well. It put a limit on a nationwide basis, I think, of $21 million. And, as you know, in one unfortunate election in North Carolina, a third that much was spent in one Senatorial election by one candidate. This is excessive. And so, I think that is a major step forward.

One of the problems with my first 2 years is that the multiplicity of simultaneous issues being addressed often prevented public focusing of attention on a particular issue. I think that we've learned in the process. I think we'll be much more careful in the future of things that are very important, to have more focusing of public attention on those important items.

The Congress, in my opinion, has been very responsible, and one of the pleasant surprises of my own Presidency has been the high level of honesty and competence and detailed knowledge by Members of the Congress and their staffs. When they get any degree of seniority, they have focused on a particular issue in subcommittee work, and I've been very favorably impressed with the quality of the Congress.

I think the results of the 95th Congress corroborate what I've just said. They've made some difficult decisions, and quite often they've done this courageously.

So, although the lobbying effort also exceeds my expectations, unfortunately, I think that those efforts can be met by some factors, certainly the two that I've just described to you.

ARMS EMBARGO AGAINST SOUTH AFRICA

Q. Mr. President, despite the international arms embargo, South Africa is reported to have received, and may still be receiving, weapons shipments through a complex scheme involving the Spanish Government—or allegedly involving the Spanish Government, the British Government, and the Island of Antigua. I'd like to know, sir, if you know whether these allegations are true, and if so, what degree of international cooperation it may have had, and what, if anything, you will do about the Pentagon's apparent failure to police its contractors.

THE PRESIDENT. I've never heard this before. If it should be true, it would be in direct violation of the pledged word of honor of the nations involved, certainly including all those who voted for the arms embargo against South Africa through the United Nations. But I've never heard of that allegation. If it should prove true, and if the Pentagon has any role to play in it, directly or indirectly, I would use my full influence to comply with the U.N. resolution.

Q. Would you support an investigation to determine the accuracy of this allegation?

THE PRESIDENT. Yes, of course I would.

ANTI-INFLATION PROGRAM

Q. Sir, could I return to this question, for a moment, of the domestic economy?

THE PRESIDENT. Yes.

Q. Without questioning for a moment your resolve to get on top of the inflation problem, are you absolutely convinced in your mind that these very high interest rates which are coming along are a good way to do it? I say that, because some businessmen view high interest rates as costs. They do, of course, add to the deficit——

THE PRESIDENT. I know.

Q. ——and they seem to run against the grain of your own political thinking, as far as I can tell.

THE PRESIDENT. Well, I prefer low interest rates. You know, it would be much better for our economy to have lower interest rates. But I think the best way for me to address that hope successfully is to get inflation under control.

The Federal Reserve is properly independent. There's a good combination, I think, of responsibility between myself, the Federal Reserve, and the Congress. I have basic input in the level of budget requests, the size of the budget deficit, the allocation of funds in different ways that the Federal Government allots directly or through local and State governments. And, of course, I have veto power over tax legislation and the right to propose tax legislation. The Congress, on the other hand, can modify my budget. They can propose and do propose, as you know, tax policy. And the Federal Reserve is primarily concerned with the level of money available in the economy at a particular time.

Consumers have a major input, also, in their buying patterns and particularly in the percentage of their income spent versus income retained in savings accounts. I think that the system is balanced as best I can envision it.

The Federal Reserve will obviously modify its interest policy compatible with the amount of money on hand which is related to the inflation rate.

So, I prefer lower interest rates. I'll do everything I can to encourage lower interest rates within the bounds of the law by controlling Federal policy to get inflation under control.

Q. Mr. President, in that connection, would you, fitting in increases in oil and gas prices along the same lines as interest rates—how do increases in oil and gas prices fit into that, into the anti-inflation program?

THE PRESIDENT. As is the case in almost every answer I've given you this morning, there are two sides of the issue in domestic and international affairs—our relations with the Soviets, our relations with Egypt and Israel, our relations with the Congress, controlling inflation versus meeting the needs of our people. Tell me exactly what you asked.

Q. I was wondering how allowing increases in gas and oil prices perhaps would fit in with fighting inflation.

THE PRESIDENT. There again, one of the problems with our economy is excessive imports of oil, in particular, which increase our trade deficit, which lowers the value of the dollar, which increases inflation. It's estimated that every 10-percent drop in the price of the dollar causes a 1 to 1½ percent increase in the inflation rate here at home. Since we imposed the monetary requirements which stabilized the dollar, the dollar's appreciated about 10 percent, which is a major contributing factor to holding down inflation.

Increasing the price of oil and gas, although it costs the consumers more in this country, decreases consumption, causes the consumers to shift to other forms of energy—which doesn't work any particular hardship on them in the long run—cuts down our imports, helps to balance our trade, strengthens the dollar, and controls inflation. So, it's a very complicated process, obviously.

What I proposed to the Congress in April of 1977 was to increase the price of oil to the world market price and refund that increased cost directly back to the consumers as rapidly and as equitably as possible. That would have had minimal inflationary results. It would raise the price of oil, collect the increased price, reduce consumption of oil, give the money right back to the consumers through some mechanism that we proposed. Ours was a reduction in income tax which would be mirrored immediately in income deductions from biweekly paychecks. So, this is the kind of interrelationships that make the economic situation difficult to understand and results uncertain.

I haven't found any easy questions to answer since I've been in this office. They are all difficult. I don't object to the responsibility, and I've enjoyed the job. And I believe that we will be successful because of the basic strength of our country. I think the world looks for us to be responsible, and in addition to solving our own domestic economic problems, we have a responsibility to the world.

The stability of the dollar is important to every nation on Earth. How well we control inflation, how well we stabilize the value of the dollar will determine to a substantial degree the price set for oil by the OPEC nations, for instance. And how much trust other people have in our country on domestic affairs has a direct influence on me, as an able leader, even in political affairs and military affairs that are not directly related to economics. So, the complexity of it is certainly appreciated by me.

But the basic strength of our country, militarily and economically and politically, is the great resource that I have that gives me confidence that, in spite of my own limitations and the complexity of issues, that I might do a good job in the Congress.

Let me say that I'm thankful to you all for coming to meet with me. I've enjoyed it.

Q. Why don't we do it every 2 weeks? [*Laughter*]

THE PRESIDENT. Well, we have a press conference every couple of weeks.

REPORTER. Thank you, Mr. President.

THE PRESIDENT. Thank you very much.

NOTE: The interview began at 8:50 a.m. in the State Dining Room at the White House.

Ambassador at Large

Nomination of W. Beverly Carter, Jr.
November 16, 1978

The President today announced his intention to nominate W. Beverly Carter, Jr., to be Ambassador at Large to head a new State Department Office for Liaison with State and Local Governments. Carter, 57, of Philadelphia, Pa., is Ambassador to the Republic of Liberia.

As head of the Office for Liaison with State and Local Governments, Carter will report directly to the Secretary of State, and will also work closely with Jack Watson, Assistant to the President for Intergovernmental Affairs.

The responsibilities of the new office will include facilitating State and local

governments' priority international interests; arranging briefings and other communications for Governors and key local government leaders on international issues of special interest to them, and conveying their views on such issues to the President and the Secretary of State; assisting senior State and local government officials in planning their official overseas travel and the visits of foreign officials; coordinating assignments with State and local governments for Foreign Service officers; and developing the State Department's capabilities to identify and to report to State and local governments on how other societies at the national or subnational level understand and resolve common problems of major importance.

Prior to his present assignment in Liberia, Carter served as Ambassador to Tanzania (1972–1975) and Deputy Assistant Secretary of State for African Affairs (1969–1972). A career Foreign Service information officer, he has served in public affairs and area positions in both the former USIA and the State Department.

David H. Shinn has been selected as deputy to Ambassador Carter and will be in charge of the new Office until Carter's return in mid-January. Shinn, a career Foreign Service officer, was most recently detailed to the mayor's office in Seattle under the Pearson Amendment domestic assignment program.

National Council on the Humanities

Recess Appointment of Nine Members.
November 16, 1978

The President today announced the recess appointment of nine persons as members of the National Council on the Humanities. Eight of these persons had been nominated on October 4, 1978, but were not confirmed before the Senate adjourned. The ninth person has not been previously announced.

The new appointee is Kay Howe, of Boulder, Colo. Howe, 40, is chairperson of the program in comparative literature at the University of Colorado and teaches in the humanities division of the integrated studies program.

The eight appointees who were announced on October 4 are Charles V. Hamilton, Louis J. Hector, M. Carl Holman, Jacob Neusner, Mary Beth Norton, Sister Joel Read, Leon Stein, and Harriet M. Zimmerman.

Pennsylvania Avenue Development Corporation

Appointment of Two Members of the Board of Directors.   November 16, 1978

The President today announced the reappointment of two members of the Board of Directors of the Pennsylvania Avenue Development Corporation. They are:

Joseph B. Danzansky, who is also being designated Chairman of the Corporation. Danzansky, 64, is president of Giant Food Inc. He is active in community affairs in Washington and has served as chairman of the Mayor's Economic Development Committee of the District of Columbia and as president of the Metropolitan Washington Board of Trade.

Nathaniel Owings, who is also being designated Vice Chairman of the Corporation. Owings, 75, is an architect and city planner. He has been involved with planning for Pennsylvania Avenue since President Kennedy appointed him as Chairman of the President's Advisory Council on Pennsylvania Avenue in 1962.

He has been on the Board of the Pennsylvania Avenue Development Corporation since its establishment in 1973. He has also participated in designing various Washington landmarks.

Anti-Inflation Program

Remarks at a White House Briefing for Civic Leaders.   November 16, 1978

Alfred Kahn and I lately go from one meeting to another, each one better than the one before. And I'm very grateful that you all would come here, literally from all over our country, to meet with me and others in reconfirming our commitment to a common and very important goal.

Other than maintaining the security of our Nation, I don't anticipate having any greater responsibility next year and in the months preceding that than to control inflation in our country. And I think in many ways, our success in this effort will directly affect the security of our country.

We have taken some first steps in some areas, some bold steps in other areas, made some commitments which I intend to keep—some of those under my direct influence, some where I need many partners to guarantee success. This effort is not going to be easy. It has eluded success for many years under all kinds of political leadership, under many different philosophies expressed in economics. And I'm determined not to fail, with your help.

We've had now too high an inflation rate for the last 10 years or more. In the last part of 1977 we had remarkable success, which is possibly a statistical aberration or because of a confluence of beneficial factors that came during that 6-month period. But the general thrust, the general tenor of our economic system has been with too high a rate of inflation.

I'm now preparing the 1980 fiscal year budget. I haven't had a pleasant session yet. [*Laughter*] And I haven't even met with my agency leaders, nor Cabinet members. I've been meeting with my own staff and the directors of the Office of Management and Budget.

The choices that I have to make are very narrow in their scope, very difficult, and every day's session demonstrates vividly that some very benevolent and needy special interest group or some powerful political force is not going to be pleased with the budget decisions that I am already making in a tentative form. I think, however, that each one of those interest groups, no matter how diverse they might be in character, will be benefited by controlling inflation more than they would with a few million dollars' or hundreds of millions of dollars' extra allocation in the 1980 fiscal year budget.

We've already made some progress. In 1975 the Federal deficit was 4½ percent of our gross national product. In 1980, calendar year, the Federal deficit will be 1 percent of our gross national product. And the progress that we are making is steady. It's tenacious. It's a deep commitment. We have decided to hold down Federal Government employment. I think we've had good response from the administrators of our Government.

I met with about 1,200 of the key leaders in the Federal Government this week to let them realize that when we have limited dollars, limited personnel, we have to make each dollar and each person and their influence be more effective. You can't educate a child with waste, with corruption, nor inefficiency. You can't feed a hungry person with waste, corruption, or inefficiency. You can't build a highway or guarantee housing construction with waste, corruption, or inefficiency.

We have a new Inspectors General bill which will continue our struggle against illegalities, improprieties, and corruption in government. This has not been a pleasant nor an easy task. Some of our efforts have been highly publicized—in the General Services Administration, Small Business Administration, and others. But we are eagerly moving now, not only to detect and reveal and to punish those who are violating proprieties of administration but also to stop illegal practices in their tracks and to make sure that every administrator, no matter how subordinate he or she might be, is equally as dedicated as the President or the administrator of a major agency or the Attorney General.

The prevention of corruption and waste is much more effective a way to address it than to let it happen and then punish those who were guilty.

We have now a good basis for an energy policy. We're trying to cut down present and future imports of oil. I think you will see a substantial improvement in 1979 of our balance-of-trade deficit. We are laying the groundwork for even greater success in the future.

We've got an excellent interrelationship with our major trading partners. Our growth rate will be sustained at a moderate level, not as high as it has been in the last few years, but on the same basis, roughly, as our major trading allies, who have had a much slower growth rate in the past.

We have had to address much more closely the proprieties of government and also the priorities of government, what our obligations are, what is proper and decent and fair on the one hand, and in addressing limited resources for the benefit of all to make sure that we put the emphasis on those that are most important.

We've had superb response from the business leaders of our country. I think labor leaders in general have held back with more understandable reticence. They need to be sure that I, as President, and my administration, the Congress, and the business leaders on price standards, will be forthcoming and cooperative before labor can make a long-term 2- , 3-year contractual commitment on the income of their own members. I understand this. We anticipated this. It's not a very serious problem for us. And the first responsibility is on my shoulders.

Each one of you in this room is a leader. Your voice is heard, your influence is felt, your actions are observed by either dozens of other leaders or by hundreds or perhaps even thousands of other leaders.

As you understand from my own key staff members, including Alfred Kahn, what our purposes are, what the bounds are of our activities, what our limitations are, what our problems are, I hope that you will leave here not just having acquiesced in a dormant fashion in complying with our requests and our standards, but leave here as one who is fervently committed to making this program succeed. Use the same degree of enthusiasm, innovation, and leadership in carrying our country toward a more stable and effective and prosperous future as you do in your own particular responsibilities in a business or profession or even your own family life. It would be a serious waste of your time to come here and only be convinced to go home and keep that conviction to yourself. But there is no one here who doesn't have at least a hundred or two hundred or a thousand people perhaps that look to you for guidance and for leadership and who at least share with you the responsibilities of an exalted place in the free enterprise system of our country.

And I hope that you will take the time to compose a personal letter or to make a list of those that you might call on the phone or to take an opportunity to speak to a civic group or professional group on your own initiative and outline the problems that I face as President with limited legal and constitutional authority and how a partnership must be formed to make the anti-inflation fight successful.

I don't intend to fail in this effort. I think in the past I have not been able to address many of the problems adequately. A year and a half ago, as I traveled around the Nation, as pollsters conducted opinion polls, the number one issue was unemployment. Now there's an overwhelming concern about inflation. One of the reasons, obviously, is that we have made great progress in eliminating unemployment or reducing it. We've added almost 7 million net new jobs. We've cut the unemployment rate down now well below 6 percent. I hope we can hold it at that level.

But inflation is the burning issue in the minds of the American people. It is the burning political issue in the country. And I don't have to convince a Congress, all of whose Members have just experienced an election process, that the American people are genuinely concerned about management, efficiency, waste, corruption, inflation, deficits. The Congress is convinced about that.

And I hope that I can avoid any vetoes next year by assuring that as the Congress considers the evolution of legislation, as they consider the evolution of a budget for 1980, they will be partners with me in the fullest sense in holding down inflation.

I might repeat one of the first comments I made, in closing, and that is that I never want to cheat those in our country who are most in need. The responsibility for meeting their needs is an ever-present burden on any President. And I am convinced as well that the ones who suffer most from uncontrolled or excessive inflation are those who are most vulnerable.

Almost everyone in this room has educational and professional and economic advantages, which gives you some flexibility in your choices for a life's work or alternatives for a life's income. But those who are relatively illiterate or uneducated, who are not mobile because of family or other constraints, those who have finished their productive life's earning work and now live on fixed incomes, those are the very ones who are most vulnerable to inflation and who need protection most. And I think the combination of controlling inflation and meeting the legitimate needs of our people, although not an easy task to resolve, that task is certainly feasible.

In closing, I want to thank you for being here. I have a great confidence in our country. What gives me that confidence is its innate strength. And although all of us are legitimately and properly concerned with transient needs and transient questions and transient challenges, there's an underlying strength in the United States of America that gives us all encouragement and all resolve for the future.

Militarily, we're the greatest, strongest nation on Earth. Politically, we're the greatest nation on Earth. Our system of economics, based on the individuality of human beings and an innate freedom and competition, is the greatest, I think, on Earth. And we have productivity, in spite of a slow rate of growth in productivity, that is tremendous. Natural resources, we are blessed in every possible way.

So, that underlying strength of our country and its people gives us courage to know that victory is available to us if we only do our part. I'll do my part, and

I know that I can depend on you to help me. We are partners in this effort. And I don't intend to fail, with your help.

Thank you very much.

NOTE: The President spoke at 2:20 p.m. in the East Room at the White House. Also participating in the briefing was Alfred E. Kahn, Advisor to the President on Inflation.

United States Arms Control and Disarmament Agency

Recess Appointment of George M. Seignious II as Director.　November 16, 1978

The President today announced that he will appoint retired Army Lieutenant General George M. Seignious II as Director of the U.S. Arms Control and Disarmament Agency, effective December 1, 1978. On October 20, 1978, the President anounced his intention to nominate General Seignious for this position when the Senate reconvenes.

Seignious, 57, has served as the "at large" member of the President's SALT negotiating delegation since September 1977.

Student Loan Marketing Association

Appointment of Two Members of the Board of Directors and Designation of Chairman. November 16, 1978

The President has appointed two persons as members of the Board of Directors of the Student Loan Marketing Association. They are:

TERESA P. HUGHES, of Los Angeles, a California Asseemblywoman, formerly a teacher, a professor of education, and legislative consultant to the California State Commission for Teacher Preparation and Licensing;

TOM H. RIDDELL, JR., of Canton, Miss., a farmer and cotton ginner, and member of the board of directors of the Mississippi Bank and of the Mississippi Agriculture and Industrial Board.

The President also announced that he has designated E. T. Dunlap to be Chairman of the Board of Directors of the Student Loan Marketing Association. Dunlap was appointed to the Board last June. He is chancellor of the Oklahoma State Regents for Higher Education.

Anti-Inflation Program

Letter to Heads of the Nation's 500 Largest Corporations.   November 15, 1978

As the leader of one of our country's major businesses, you are fully aware of the grave problems caused by the inflationary pressures we are now experiencing. You are also in a position to do something to reduce those pressures. I am, therefore, writing to ask you for your support.

I intend to do my part. I will do everything in my power to combat inflation. Our fiscal policies will give top priority to containing inflationary pressures. I will rigorously hold down Federal expenditures. I will cut Federal employment. I will achieve significant reductions in the Federal deficit next year and thereafter. I believe that the Congress will cooperate, but if necessary I will veto inflationary spending measures. I will subject special interest legislation to severe scrutiny; and I will undertake an intensive systematic effort to ensure that actions of my Administration, particularly in the area

of regulation, do not raise costs and prices unnecessarily.

Carrying out such a policy of austerity will not be easy; but the task of fighting inflation requires real sacrifices from all of us.

No matter how much I do with Federal fiscal policy and through other actions, we cannot begin to deal successfully with the problems of inflation without your active support.

Our price standard requires your business to hold its average price increase over the next year to one-half of a percentage point below the average annual rate in 1976 and 1977. If uncontrollable cost increases make such deceleration impossible, it requires that you not expand your profit margin.

My anti-inflation program is designed to avoid imposing excessive hardships on any segment of our population. It provides allowances for special situations, where they are really needed. I will not try to mislead you; complying will not be painless. It will take a major and continuing effort on your part. But I believe that effort is worth making for the good of the country—and for the economic health of your own business as well.

This program needs more than a general pledge of support. I am asking your company for an *explicit* statement of your commitment to comply with the price standard. I recognize that you may have questions about how the price standards apply to your firm and may want answers before you can conscientiously declare your intention to comply. The Council on Wage and Price Stability is developing additional guidance you may need to help you determine how you can comply. Staff of the Council will be contacting you very soon to give you this information.

I urge you to send me your personal response to my request as soon as possible.
    Sincerely,

JIMMY CARTER

NOTE: The text of the letter was released on November 17.

Visit of King Hassan II of Morocco

Joint Press Statement. November 17, 1978

At the invitation of President Jimmy Carter, His Majesty Hassan II, King of Morocco, made a state visit to Washington November 14–15, 1978. In the course of this visit, His Majesty had discussions with President Carter as well as with Secretary of State Cyrus Vance and other members of the American Government. The discussions took place in an atmosphere of friendship and of mutual cooperation. They dealt with bilateral relations as well as with major international problems of common interest.

The President and His Majesty noted with satisfaction that the centuries old ties linking the United States and Morocco are developing in an harmonious fashion. The two Chiefs of State reviewed the many areas of cooperation between Morocco and the United States, particularly those relating to cultural, scientific, and technical cooperation. They decided that the development of energy resources is a sector in which new efforts would be mutually advantageous. They agreed to technical exchanges on the exploitation of shale oil reserves and on the utilization of solar energy and other renewable forms of energy. The two countries expect to sign in the near future a bilateral nuclear cooperation agreement. Such an agreement, which will be in the context of the adherence by both parties to the Nonproliferation Treaty, will permit implementation of a contract for construction of a nuclear research reactor.

President Carter and His Majesty King Hassan also agreed that their governments should seek to expand academic exchanges between Morocco and the United States. They agreed that their governments will jointly sponsor a meeting between academic leaders of the two countries to recommend ways in which educational exchanges could be expanded.

The two parties reaffirmed their desire to see private American firms give their support in the various sectors of social and economic development where Morocco is making considerable efforts. They agreed that the required conditions exist in Morocco for a more active American participation and undertook to facilitate such participation. The two Chiefs of State decided that in the near future a mission under the direction of the U.S. Secretary of Commerce would be sent to Morocco in order to explore the possibilities to develop bilateral trade and to increase investments. The mission will include representatives of the private and public sectors.

President Carter and His Majesty King Hassan acknowledged their identity of view concerning the international problems they examined. For Morocco as for the United States, international relations must be founded on respect for national independence and for the territorial integrity of nations, as well as on willingness to contribute by cooperation and dialogue to the establishment of peace in the world. Within this context, the President expressed appreciation for Morocco's non-aligned, independent policy, and His Majesty welcomed American efforts to resolve global problems.

The two Chiefs of State examined the situation in Africa. The President thanked His Majesty for his description of the situation in northwest Africa and expressed his appreciation for the efforts undertaken by Morocco to end the tension existing there and to create conditions for the establishment of fruitful cooperation between the countries of the region. They agreed that the OAU is the most appropriate framework for the resolution of African problems, and they expressed satisfaction at the decision of the OAU to establish a Committee of Wisemen. Reviewing other points of tension which exist in Africa, the two Chiefs of State condemned foreign intervention and the arms races which have been their result.

The two leaders discussed at length recent developments concerning the Middle East. President Carter, after having outlined to His Majesty the status of the discussions currently underway, explained the American objectives in the peace process, and he reiterated the willingness of the United States to continue to play a role leading to the establishment in the region of a just, durable, and global peace. His Majesty the King, in reaffirming that the Palestinian problem constitutes a fundamental element in the search for a solution and for the establishment of peace in the area, explained that the Moroccan position is based on the decisions made at the Arab Summit meeting held at Rabat in 1974.

With respect to the situation in Lebanon, the two parties noted their commitment to respect the sovereignty, unity, and territorial integrity of that country. They renewed their support for the work of national reconciliation undertaken under the aegis of President Sarkis.

His Majesty the King expressed his deep thanks to President Carter for the warm welcome and great friendship shown him during his visit to the United States as well as that extended to the members of the Royal Family and to the Moroccan delegation.

His Majesty invited President Carter to visit Morocco. The President thanked His Majesty and accepted the invitation, with the date and details of the visit to be arranged through diplomatic channels.

Executive Schedule

Executive Order 12099. November 17, 1978

LEVELS IV AND V OF THE EXECUTIVE SCHEDULE

By the authority vested in me as President of the United States of America by Section 5317 of Title 5 of the United States Code, and in order to place the position of Director of Policy Review, Department of Defense, in level IV of the Executive Schedule, Executive Order No. 12076 of August 18, 1978, is amended by deleting "Director of Policy Review, Department of Defense." from Section 1–102(e) and inserting "(r) Director of Policy Review, Department of Defense." in alphabetical order in Section 1–101 thereof.

JIMMY CARTER

The White House,
  November 17, 1978.

[Filed with the Office of the Federal Register, 4:22 p.m., November 17, 1978]

President's Commission on Pension Policy

Executive Order 12100. November 17, 1978

By the authority vested in me as President by the Constitution of the United States of America, it is hereby ordered as follows:

1–101. In order to ratify and reflect the actual effective date of the functioning of the activities of the Commission, Section 1–403 of Executive Order No. 12071 is amended to read "This Order shall be effective on September 21, 1978.".

1–202. In order to ratify and reflect that the Chairman may appoint necessary staff, Section 1–304 of Executive Order No. 12071 is amended to read as follows:

"1–304. The Chairman is authorized to appoint and fix the compensation of a staff, including not more than one position at the GS–18 level, as may be necessary to enable it to carry out its functions. The Chairman may obtain services in accordance with the provisions of Section 3109 of Title 5 of the United States Code, to the extent funds are available therefor.".

JIMMY CARTER

The White House,
November 17, 1978.

[Filed with the Office of the Federal Register, 4:23 p.m., November 17, 1978]

Delegation of Functions to the Secretary of State

Executive Order 12101.   November 17, 1978

PRIVILEGES, IMMUNITIES AND LIABILITY INSURANCE FOR DIPLOMATIC MISSIONS AND PERSONNEL

By the authority vested in me as President of the United States of America by the Diplomatic Relations Act (Public Law 95–393, 92 Stat. 808; 22 U.S.C. 254a *et seq.*) and Section 301 of Title 3 of the United States Code, in order to implement the liability insurance and other requirements relating to diplomatic personnel, I hereby designate and empower the Secretary of State to perform, without the

approval, ratification, or other action of the President, the functions vested or to be vested in the President by Sections 4 and 6 of the Diplomatic Relations Act (92 Stat. 809; 22 U.S.C. 254c and 254e).

JIMMY CARTER

The White House,
November 17, 1978.

[Filed with the Office of the Federal Register, 4:24 p.m., November 17, 1978]

Trade Committees

Executive Order 12102.   November 17, 1978

By the authority vested in me as President of the United States of America by Section 242 of the Trade Expansion Act of 1962, as amended (19 U.S.C. 1872), and Section 411 of the Trade Act of 1974 (19 U.S.C. 2441), in order to adjust the membership of the Trade Policy Committee and the membership of the East-West Foreign Trade Board, it is hereby ordered as follows:

1–101. Executive Order No. 11846, as amended, is further amended as it relates to the membership of the Trade Policy Committee by deleting the following paragraphs in Section 3(a):

"(10) The Assistant to the President for Economic Affairs.

"(11) The Executive Director of the Council on International Economic Policy.";

and substituting therefor:

"(10) The Chairman of the Council of Economic Advisers.

"(11) The Director of the Office of Management and Budget.".

1–102. Executive Order No. 11846, as amended, is further amended as it relates to the membership of the East-West Foreign Trade Board by deleting the following paragraph in Section 7(a):

"(8) The Executive Director of the Council on International Economic Policy.";
and substituting therefor:
"(8) The Chairman of the Council of Economic Advisers.";
and by also deleting:
"(10) The Assistant to the President for Economic Affairs.".

JIMMY CARTER

The White House,
November 17, 1978.

[Filed with the Office of the Federal Register, 4:25 p.m., November 17, 1978]

Federal Deposit Insurance Corporation

Nomination of Irvine H. Sprague To Be a Member of the Board of Directors. November 17, 1978.

The President today announced that he will nominate Irvine H. Sprague, of Stockton, Calif., to be a member of the Board of Directors of the Federal Deposit Insurance Corporation. He would replace George LaMaistre, resigned.

Sprague, 57, is executive director of the Democratic Steering Policy Committee of the U.S. House of Representatives. He was administrative assistant to the House majority whip from 1973 to 1976 and served as a director of FDIC from 1969 to 1972. He was Special Assistant to the President from 1967 to 1968 and deputy director of finance for the State of California from 1963 to 1966.

Digest of Other White House Announcements

The following listing includes the President's daily schedule and other items of general interest as announced by the White House Press Office during the period covered by this issue. Events and announcements printed elsewhere in the issue are not included.

November 11

The President met at the White House with Zbigniew Brzezinski, Assistant to the President for National Security Affairs.

November 12

The President visited former Senator Harold Hughes' farm in Royal Oak, Md. He returned to the White House later the same day.

November 13

The President met at the White House with:

—Dr. Brzezinski;
—Secretary of State Cyrus R. Vance;
—W. Averell Harriman;
—Adm. Stansfield Turner, Director of Central Intelligence, Hamilton Jordan, Assistant to the President, and Dr. Brzezinski.

The White House announced that the President has accepted the very kind invitation of President López Portillo to visit Mexico between February 14–16, 1979. The announcement further stated that President Carter believes that his visit, like the visit of President López Portillo to the United States in February 1977, will further strengthen the unique relationship between two nations that have always shared a common destiny.

November 14

The President met at the White House with:

—Dr. Brzezinski;
—King Hassan II of Morocco, Secretary Vance, Dr. Brzezinski, and other Moroccan and American officials;
—James T. McIntyre, Jr., Director of the Office of Management and Budget;

—Secretary Vance and Israeli Defense Minister Ezer Weizman.

November 15

The President met at the White House with:

—Dr. Brzezinski;

—Senator Robert C. Byrd of West Virginia, who is serving as the President's personal emissary in a November trip which will include visits to countries in North Africa, the Middle East, and the eastern Mediterranean;

—King Hassan II of Morocco;

—the President's Council on Physical Fitness and Sports;

—Secretary of the Treasury W. Michael Blumenthal;

—Ambassador William G. Bowdler, the U.S. Representative to the International Mediation Group for Nicaragua.

November 16

The President met at the White House with:

—Dr. Brzezinski;

—Maj. Gen. Muhammad Husni Mubarak, the Vice President of Egypt, Secretary Vance, Egyptian Ambassador to the United States Ashraf A. Ghorbal, Ambassador at Large Alfred L. Atherton, Jr., Harold H. Saunders, Assistant Secretary of State for Near Eastern and South Asian Affairs, and Dr. Brzezinski;

—Mrs. Carter, for lunch;

—Secretary of Housing and Urban Development Patricia Roberts Harris;

—His Eminence Terence Cardinal Cooke, and Archbishop John R. Quinn, president, Archbishop John R. Roach, vice president, and Bishop Thomas Kelly, general secretary, National Conference of Catholic Bishops.

In a ceremony in the Oval Office, the President received diplomatic credentials from Ambassadors Macky Koreissi Aguibou Tall of the Republic of Mali, Nicolae Ionescu of Romania, Bernard Loustau Lalanne of the Republic of Seychelles, and Khalil Itani of Lebanon.

The President attended the movie "Children of Sanchez" at the MacArthur Theatre in Washington, D.C., in conjunction with the Mexican-American Legal Defense and Educational Fund's 10th anniversary celebration.

November 17

The President met at the White House with:

—Vice President Walter F. Mondale, Secretary Vance, Secretary of Defense Harold Brown, Dr. Brzezinski, and Mr. Jordan;

—Senator Daniel K. Inouye of Hawaii;

—Mrs. Joan Mondale and Livingston L. Biddle, Jr., Chairman of the National Endowment for the Arts, and others who were meeting to discuss the Federal Government's role in the arts;

—a group of editors and news directors (transcript will be printed next week);

—the judicial selection committee of the American Bar Association.

The President attended the 50th birthday party reception for Mickey Mouse, which was hosted by his daughter, Amy, in the East Room at the White House. Included among the guests were handicapped children from the District of Columbia public school system.

The President left the White House for a weekend stay at Camp David, Md.

NOMINATIONS SUBMITTED
TO THE SENATE

NOTE: The Congress having adjourned *sine die* on Sunday, October 15, no nominations were submitted during the period covered by this issue. The first session of the 96th Congress will begin on Monday, January 15, 1979.

CHECKLIST OF WHITE HOUSE
PRESS RELEASES

The following releases of the Office of the White House Press Secretary, distributed during the period covered by this issue, are not included in the issue.

CHECKLIST—Continued

Released November 11, 1978

News conference: on the President's disapproval of S. 2416, H.R. 9937, and H.R. 11545, and the announcement of the 1979 feed grain program—by Jody Powell, Press Secretary to the President, and Stuart E. Eizenstat, Assistant to the President for Domestic Affairs and Policy

ACTS APPROVED BY
THE PRESIDENT

NOTE: The President completed his consideration of acts and joint resolutions passed during the second session of the 95th Congress on November 10.

Interview With the President

Remarks and a Question-and-Answer Session With Editors and News Directors. November 17, 1978

THE PRESIDENT. I'll have to apologize for interrupting your meeting. [*Laughter*]

As we've done on many occasions with groups like this, I generally outline, just in a few minutes, what particular responsibilities I have today, as an example, and then spend all the time we have possible answering your questions.

ADMINISTRATION POLICIES

The major emphasis that we are placing on domestic affairs is to control inflation. And on a daily basis almost—even more—I meet with special groups who come here to the White House for briefings about the parameters of our effort, the degree of possibility for success, what role they can play in making our anti-inflation effort successful, and letting them know what I have done in the past and will do concerning budgets, stabilizing of the dollar, reducing the deficit, establishment of priorities in Government spending, administration, rooting out corruption and waste, as well.

Yesterday I sent out, for instance, a very strong and specific request to the 500 largest business leaders in the Nation. And we are making the same kind of effort with others around the country.

I'm spending a good bit of time each week putting the preliminary decisions down concerning the 1980 fiscal year budget. Following those general discussions with OMB, Office of Management and Budget, then I will meet specifically with the agency heads to go over their appeals, and I'll listen to specific proposals.

We've got a personnel hiring freeze still on. When vacancies occur, they can only fill half the vacancies. That will be maintained until we reach a certain level and then will be modified as I deem it necessary.

In international affairs we are conducting our share of the Mideast negotiations. I met yesterday with Vice President Mubarak from Egypt. After that he met with Defense Minister Weizman of Israel. Weizman has now gone back to Israel, and Mubarak will be going back to Egypt tomorrow. I think this entire process has been much more time-consuming and difficult than I had anticipated, after Camp David had resolved, as Mr. Mubarak said yesterday, 90 percent of all the issues that separate Egypt from Israel.

In a nonpublicized way—not a secret way, but a nonpublicized way—we are continuing our discussions with the Soviet Union on a wide range of subjects, SALT being the most important of all.

And we are also engaged in pursuing our own Nation's influence in Rhodesia, in Namibia, trying to bring about a settlement of the disputes in Nicaragua. We are actively engaged in all of those.

These are some of the kinds of questions that come before me on a daily basis.

I think we've made good success in the last 2 years. The 95th Congress record, I thought, was superb. We have gotten additional good information in the last 24 hours about net farm income going up substantially. The rate of farm exports has been growing regularly. And we've got, I think, in general, a good record there. Unemployment has gone down. We do not anticipate a recession next year. We'll be doing the best we can to have a balanced improvement in the economic situation in our country.

I think it might be best now to answer your questions. And following this, I have a very important meeting with my daughter, Amy, and with Mickey Mouse. [*Laughter*] It's Mickey Mouse's 50th birthday, as you may have heard.

QUESTIONS

RESULTS OF THE ELECTION

Q. Mr. President, does the conservative trend in last week's election concern you about your legislative proposals you are planning for the next year?

THE PRESIDENT. I'm not sure that that's an accurate description. The trend is much less noticeable than was originally thought. There were some Senators defeated who were considered to be liberal. But I think, in balance, the Congress attitude has not substantially changed. And as you know, out of 435 Members in the House, only 12 seats shifted toward the

Republicans, which was, I'm sure, a disappointment to them.

I think, however, that liberals and conservatives, Democrats and Republicans, got a clear message from the electorate—during the campaign, primarily, not just the results of the campaign—that tight budget constraints are in order, control of inflation is the top priority among poor people and also those who are more affluent, and that waste and corruption in government must be rooted out, and an administrative capability and efficiency has to be demonstrated.

So, I think this has been obvious to us. It was obvious to me when I ran for President in the response of audiences and the kinds of questions that I got. And I emphasized this, as you know, in my own campaign platform commitments. But I think that message has come through loud and clear without regard to the political spectrum placement.

VISIT TO MEXICO

Q. Mr. President, your next visit to Mexico—is the oil issue or illegals' entrance on the agenda?

THE PRESIDENT. We have not yet worked out an agenda with President López Portillo. But I don't have any doubt that both those items would be on the agenda, among probably 15 or 20 other things.

Q. Did you hear about the steel wall on the border to stop the illegal entrance into the United States? There is a tremendous protest from Mexican Americans, Spanish leaders.

THE PRESIDENT. You mean the fence that was——

Q. Yes.

THE PRESIDENT. Yes, that was a serious mistake. It was something that I never knew about until I read about it in the newspaper. But any sort of fencing device that would injure people is certainly contrary to my own inclinations.

EMPLOYMENT AND TRAINING PROGRAMS

Q. Continuing on the text of the Mexico border, it seems like down through the years, we've been pouring billions and billions and billions of Federal aid through multitudes of governmental programs into the border. It's seeming to do little more than sustain the status quo of poverty. Isn't it about time for some new approaches to ending double-digit unemployment and three-generation chains of dependency? In other words, doesn't anybody know that what's being done down there is not working?

THE PRESIDENT. The first state visit I had after I became President was from President López Portillo. And Secretary of State Vance, my own wife, and the Vice President have all visited Mexico already. We are deeply aware of a need for closer working relationships between our country and Mexico in a broad range of things.

Q. I'm not talking about Mexico. I am talking about our situation along the border, those of us who live on the border.

THE PRESIDENT. Yes, well, I didn't understand your question. Perhaps you could rephrase it.

Q. Well, it seems like all the money is going just to maintain the status quo, that is not very profitable.

THE PRESIDENT. What kind of money?

Q. CETA money, this kind of program money, welfare money.

THE PRESIDENT. Well, I think that situation probably can be assessed critically throughout the Nation. All of these programs were designed by Congress and ultimately approved by me or my predecessors, with a genuine attempt to focus the aid and to focus the training in jobs where it's most needed.

As you know, in the CETA program, in particular, the basic decisions are made at the local level of government. When I was Governor, I was personally the chairman of the CETA committee in Georgia. Other Governors didn't do that; some do. But the basic decisions on who gets jobs, who gets training, and what responsibilities are placed on those who receive Federal benefits are made by mayors, by private groups, by benevolent organizations, nonprofit groups, by county officials, and Governors. And the Federal Government responsibility is to assure that the laws are not violated.

We have had, since I've been in office, a massive examination or monitoring of the allocation of CETA funds to make sure that illegalities were rooted out. These have been very embarrassing, as you noticed, to several large municipal administrations throughout the country—I think most of them are Democratic; it hadn't been partisan in nature at all.

But the Congress, in this most recent session, has tightened up greatly on the CETA law, and I think that any abuses that have been obvious in the past will be much less likely in the future. That's always a problem with welfare, any kind of aid or education.

OIL PRICE INCREASE AND INFLATION

Q. Mr. President, what would a 10-percent increase in OPEC prices do to your anti-inflation plans?

THE PRESIDENT. It would not help at all. [*Laughter*]

Q. How far would it set it back?

THE PRESIDENT. Well, Secretary Blumenthal is now on a trip to visit with some of the leaders among the OPEC nations. I think the best way that we can prevent an excessive increase in price, whatever it might be, is to prove to those nations that there will be a stable dollar—because they get paid in dollars for oil; that our own leadership, mine in this country and ours throughout the world, will be to stabilize the value of all currencies, that is, to hold down inflation; and also that we are shifting as strongly as possible away from an overdependence on imported oil, which means that a limited supply will meet the needs of those who cannot go to other sources of oil, gas, coal, alternate energy sources.

But I think that in the past 2 years, certainly since I've been in office, the OPEC leaders—Saudi Arabia, Iran, and others—have been very responsible. Most of their foreign holdings are tied to either property or bonds, where inflation hurts them substantially with their net monetary resources.

And we'll do all we can, in addition to what I've already done, to hold down inflation and to stabilize the value of the dollar. And we'll convince them that any unwarranted increase in OPEC prices would have a destabilizing effect on inflation, not only in our country but throughout the world.

FARM SET-ASIDE PROGRAMS

Q. Mr. President, a lot of farmers in Iowa, where I'm from, and I think elsewhere were disappointed that you waited as long as you did to announce the feed grain program and were disappointed in its contents. Could you tell us whether you waited specifically until the election was over to make that announcement, and why you decided against a somewhat more generous program that would have had larger set-asides and higher payments?

THE PRESIDENT. No, I didn't wait until after the election. The normal time for

me to make that announcement was November 15.

Q. I understood that to be the deadline, sir.

THE PRESIDENT. Well, it was. But last year, I think you know, we made the announcement after Christmas.

There was a need for us to get the November figures on crop production and grain supplies on hand, which came in the day before I made the announcement, which was last week. And those results did influence my decision. I waited until then. Mr. Hjort [1] came over to meet with me and my advisers, and we set the standards.

I think that what we established as feed grain regulations and the price level is the best one that I can devise. But there is no way to satisfy the needs of everyone or the desires of everyone or the demands of every interest group, even from us farmers, and I am a farmer familiar with the needs.

We do have a very high level of feed grains on hand, but we are trying as hard as we can to increase our exports and to have stabilized prices. And as I'd like to remind you, farm net income has gone up 25 percent. We will probably export $27 billion in farm supplies this year to other countries. I think we've made very good success in the roughly 1 year that we've had a new agricultural program at hand.

I don't have anything about which to apologize on the feed grain program itself nor the date that it was issued. I think it's been issued in adequate time to plan for next spring's planting, which will come probably no earlier in any part of the country than early March. So, the

---

[1] Howard W. Hjort, Director, Economics, Policy Analysis and Budget, Department of Agriculture.

farmers have adequate time to prepare for next year's planting.

ANTI-INFLATION PROGRAM

Q. Mr. President, today NBC and the Associated Press released the results of their latest poll, which is on the economy and inflation. The poll was taken earlier in the week. Relative to the economy, only 13 percent of those questioned said they felt the economy would get better in the next year; 53 percent said they thought it would get worse. On inflation, 58 percent said that would get worse. What does this tell you about your effort in the anti-inflation program and the work that's ahead?

THE PRESIDENT. It proves how necessary it is. You know, the American people are genuinely concerned about the future of the economy; so am I. And it's not only a burning political issue—which is of secondary importance, but an important thing—but it also is important for me, as President, to make sure I have a prosperous and a strong and secure nation that I lead.

There is no doubt that the number one concern of the American people at this point is inflation. A year and a half ago, the number one concern of the American people was unemployment. And the reason that we have shifted that legitimate concern of the American people is because we've had remarkable and unanticipated success in putting people back to work. We've had a net increase, as you know, of about 7 million jobs since the Congress acted early in 1977.

But I share that concern with them. And many economists have even predicted that we're going to have a recession or depression next year. We don't think we will.

But the best way to prevent a recession is to make sure that our anti-inflation program is effective. I'm dedicated to it. I'll do everything I can, within the legal constraints placed on me as President, to succeed in this effort. And I don't think we'll have a recession. And I am not going to impose any mandatory wage and price controls. Between those two parameters, which are not incompatible, I think we will be successful enough so that the genuine concerns of the American people are not realized.

U.S. TRADE BALANCE

Q. Mr. President, one of the factors, of course, in inflation is our balance of payments vis-a-vis foreign governments. Recently, Dr. Peter Krogh, who is the dean of the Foreign Service School at Georgetown University, said in a speech that he was talking to an American businessman who said that he can't compete with the Japanese; they've got two governments working for them—theirs and ours. And by that he meant that our Government was not doing enough to help in our export programs. Do you have anything to add to that or comment upon that?

THE PRESIDENT. No. I think that we will have a substantial reduction in 1979 in our balance-of-trade deficit; some have estimated a 30- or 35-percent reduction. Our adverse trade balance this year is in the neighborhood of $30 billion. The prime cause of it is $45 billion worth of oil imports.

Under Secretary Kreps, the Commerce Secretary, under my own leadership, we and my whole administration has tried to encourage exports of American products. And they have been increasing.

I just mentioned agricultural exports as an example, since it has already been raised. Last year, in 1977, we had a very low average price for agricultural products. But we still set alltime record in export volume in dollars, $24 billion; this year we'll pass $27 billion.

I just signed a new agricultural export bill, while I was in Kansas recently, that will let us make short-term loans for those who'll buy agricultural products. It authorizes the establishment of trade offices in nations that are potential customers, to let them know about the offer, the excellent products that we have to sell.

I think we're doing everything we can within legal bounds to encourage export sales. The final responsibility, however, is on the producers of those products, in a competitive world market, to sell their own goods. And I don't know the gentleman to whom you refer, but some people say if you put a total barrier against imports, we can have a better chance to sell our exports. That's obviously a fallacious argument. Open trade opportunities are much better for both sides. But in literally dozens of cases every month, I have people, who want to have every possibility to sell their own products, come and ask me to erect trade barriers or tariffs or quotas that would prevent any competition from coming in and challenging them. But Americans benefit greatly from open trade.

And Bob Strauss is now negotiating in Europe for a multilateral trade negotiation agreement, which I think will help. But we're doing all we can to improve exports and to cut down on unnecessary imports, like excessive oil purchases.

WAGE AND PRICE CONTROLS

Q. Mr. President, Senator Nelson of Wisconsin 2 weeks ago suggested that your voluntary wage-price control program would not work and that it be substituted with a mandatory program for the top 400 companies and unions. Why would that not work?

THE PRESIDENT. I don't know of any case where mandatory price and wage controls have ever worked.

I have said that I have no intention of asking the Congress for that authority, which I do not have under the law, nor to impose wage and price controls in a mandatory way—even if I had the authority—except in time of national emergency, when I thought the security of our Nation was endangered. And that's a pretty tight constraint, which I don't ever anticipate occurring while I'm in office.

Even if I asked the Congress for mandatory controls, I don't think we could get 10 percent to support it. It's an idle debate. And as long as I'm in the White House, I have no intention of mandatory price and wage controls.

Q. Even on a limited basis?

THE PRESIDENT. No. We are monitoring the prices of those 400 top producers of goods in our country—500, as a matter of fact. And if they should exceed our voluntary price guidelines, we have some fairly effective measures to use to encourage compliance.

We've asked them to restrict their price increases to one-half percent below the increases they've experienced the last 2 years, and we're getting a very good response from the business community in this early stage. It's not apparent yet, because the details of the standards, which are so very complicated, have not yet been completely devised nor promulgated.

But I think mandatory wage and price controls would be ill-advised. I see no prospect of them being imposed in our country.

EMPLOYMENT AND TRAINING PROGRAMS

Q. With the high unemployment among black teenagers in this country, is the administration going to offer any kind of incentive for the private sector to bear some of the costs of on-the-job training oriented programs?

THE PRESIDENT. Yes. We have more than doubled both the public service job possibilities and also the encouragement of private employment, with Government incentives of all kinds—tax breaks, a sharing of costs of hiring new people and training programs on the job—in the private sector.

We've also had good success from the business leaders—the National Association of Businessmen and others—in putting into effect their own voluntary programs, where the Government is only slightly involved.

We've made some progress. I think the reduction of unemployment has made it possible now to focus more and more on the chronically unemployed—those who are most difficult to employ and the first ones to be fired if things go the wrong way. And as you know, the primary group that has not yet been helped is the young group, minorities in particular.

I think that we have not backed off at all from the level, the very high level of Federal job opportunities and encouragement of private job opportunities that we initiated at the beginning of our employment drive 15 or 18 months ago. Even in spite of inflation, that emphasis is still being maintained.

TEXTILE INDUSTRY

Q. I come from a highly textile part of the country, and they're concerned over the textile tariff bill that you vetoed. What was your particular problem with it, your main objection?

THE PRESIDENT. I think it was completely counterproductive as far as helping the textile industry itself. What it did,

in effect, was say that in the multilateral trade negotiations, which opens up increased opportunities for trade in textile and all other products, that we could not even discuss or negotiate on the subject of textiles. Had that bill been signed into law, the entire effort on multilateral trade negotiations would have broken down.

We've had very good response from the labor unions who represent textile workers, because of the veto. And as you know, in certain areas where textiles are involved, we have negotiated bilateral agreements with individual nations to hold down the level of their textile shipments to us.

But I'm deeply concerned. We have about 60, 65,000 textile jobs in Georgia. And I know in South Carolina and North Carolina—and others have a similar, even more greater dependence.

But I just don't think the bill was advisable at all and, in my opinion, would ultimately hurt the textile industry as badly as it would other industries in our country.

MR. WURFEL. Thank you, sir.

THE PRESIDENT. Thank all of you. I would like, if you don't have any objection, to get a photograph with each one of you. [*Laughter*] That'll take 2 or 3 minutes. But—yes?

CYPRUS NEGOTIATIONS

Q. I'd like to ask you, Mr. President, on the Cyprus issue, do you feel that there has been any progress after lifting the embargo?

THE PRESIDENT. Yes, there has been progress; there has been progress.

Q. Can you be more detailed?

THE PRESIDENT. No. I think this is something that ought to be handled very privately among the leaders involved.

As you know, both in Greece and Turkey, among the Turkish Cypriots and the

Greek Cypriots, they really prefer to negotiate with one another without our country being involved directly. And when a third party is required to organize or to enhance the discussions, almost everyone agrees that it ought to be the United Nations, rather than us.

So, although progress has been made, compared to what it was before the embargo was lifted, I'm not at liberty to discuss the status of the negotiations.

If you all would just come by, and we will get a photograph made.

I want to thank you again for being with us. I didn't thank you at the beginning, but it's very helpful to me to have you come to the White House and meet with my own staff and ask me your good questions.

NOTE: The interview began at 1:17 p.m. in the Cabinet Room at the While House. Walter W. Wurfel is Deputy Press Secretary.

The transcript of the interview was released on November 18.

Leo J. Ryan

Statement on the Death of the Representative From California. *November 19, 1978*

I am saddened by the death of Congressman Leo J. Ryan, an educator who went on to a 22-year career of public service at the local, State, and national levels.

His concern for environmental values led him to the chairmanship of the Government Operations Subcommittee on Environment, Energy, and Natural Resources, where he became an authority on the problems of nuclear waste disposal.

Congressman Ryan had taught in the Watts ghetto to gain an understanding of educational issues in the slums and once

spent a week as a voluntary prisoner to examine penitentiary conditions. It was this drive to get his information at first hand that led to his tragic death.

Rosalynn and I join his family and his constituents in their shock and grief.

NOTE: Congressman Ryan was killed on November 18 by members of the People's Temple, a religious cult, during his investigation of the People's Temple commune in Jonestown, Guyana.

Death of Three Newsmen in Guyana

Statement by the White House Press Secretary. *November 20, 1978*

The President has asked me to convey the shock and grief both he and the First Lady share over the deaths of the three American newsmen in Guyana.

He wishes to express his deepest condolences to the families of Don Harris and Robert Brown, of the National Broadcasting Corporation, and Gregory Robinson, of the San Francisco Examiner. These three men were all hard-driving, talented professionals who lost their lives while pursuing the highest traditions of journalism.

On behalf of the President, Vice President Mondale is personally calling their families to express his sympathies and condolences.

NOTE: The three newsmen were killed on November 18 by members of the People's Temple, while accompanying Congressman Leo J. Ryan on his investigation of the People's Temple commune in Jonestown, Guyana.

Press Secretary Jody Powell read the statement at 2 p.m. to reporters assembled in the Briefing Room at the White House.

First Anniversary of the National Women's Conference

Statement by the President.
November 20, 1978

I take great pleasure in marking the 1-year anniversary of the first National Women's Conference in Houston, Texas. I think the most meaningful manner in which I can take note of that historic occasion is to call, once again, for ratification of the equal rights amendment.

Many women who were delegates to Houston and to the State conventions which preceded the Houston conference were active in the recent successful effort to extend the ratification deadline 3 more years. My administration and members of my family enthusiastically supported that effort.

This week women all over the country who attended the Houston conference are measuring the progress on the plan of action they adopted 1 year ago. I have recently released a report indicating my administration's action in furtherance of that plan for women's equality.

We will continue to work to realize other goals set forth by the women's conference. It is in the national interest for all citizens to participate fully in every part of American life.

Advisory Committee for Trade Negotiations

Appointment of Wayne E. Glenn as a
Member.   November 22, 1978

The President today announced the appointment of Wayne E. Glenn, of Little Rock, Ark., as a member of the Advisory Committee for Trade Negotiations. Glenn, 54, is acting president of the United Paperworkers International Union.

Committee for Purchase from the Blind and Other Severely Handicapped

Appointment of Robert B. Heinemann and
Diane S. Roupe as Members.
November 22, 1978

The President today announced the appointment of two persons as members of the Committee for Purchase from the Blind and Other Severely Handicapped. They are:

ROBERT B. HEINEMANN, Deputy Director for Operations in the Office of Administrative Services and Procurement at the Commerce Department;

DIANE S. ROUPE, vice president for public affairs of Blue Cross and Blue Shield of Greater New York and a director of National Industries for the Severely Handicapped.

Presidential Commission on World Hunger

Appointment of Thomas H. Wyman as a
Member.   November 22, 1978

The President today announced the appointment of Thomas H. Wyman, of Wayzata, Minn., as a member of the Presidential Commission on World Hunger. Wyman is president and chief executive officer of Green Giant Company.

President's Commission on Mental Retardation

Appointment of Six Members.
November 22, 1978

The President today announced the appointment of six persons as members of the President's Commission on Mental Retardation, for terms expiring May 11, 1981. They are:

ANDREW I. T. CHANG, of Aiea, Hawaii, director of the Hawaii Department of Social Services and Housing;

HERBERT J. COHEN, a professor of pediatrics at Albert Einstein College of Medicine in the Bronx and director of Bronx Developmental Services, a community mental retardation services program;

RUTH W. DIGGS, of Norfolk, Va., a professor in the department of special education at Norfolk State College and a former teacher and principal at a school for the mentally retarded;

SHIRLEY C. MILLER, of Atlanta, chairperson of the human rights committee of the Atlanta Association for Retarded Citizens and winner of awards for her work on behalf of the mentally retarded;

EDWARD J. QUILLIGAN, a professor and associate vice president of health affairs at the University of Southern California School of Medicine;

AILEEN A. WEISS, of Columbia, S.C., a speech pathologist and head of the speech and hearing program for the Military Dependent Schools at Fort Jackson, S.C.

National Bible Week

Remarks at a White House Dinner in
Observance of the Week.　November 22, 1978

Last night, in preparation for my introducing the guest performer, I reread the Book of Mark and tried to think ahead about the experience that we had in store for us tonight. It became much more obvious to me than it ever had before that the Bible is not just a spiritual textbook, but it's an excellent and exciting story, a story about Jesus Christ, one of the most exciting stories of all time, which sometimes loses its meaning and its fervor when we take each verse apart and try to analyze or diagram the verse or probe into every single word. There's obviously a time for that, but I think in the process we lose perspective to some degree and forget that Christ was a person who was alive, dynamic, vigorous, strong, with a great sense of humor.

And we have tonight a great performer to tell us this story in a similar fashion to what Mark might have used when he burst forth to bring his Gospel to the world.

As you know, Mark was an intimate friend of Paul, with some ups and downs. He was an intimate friend of Peter. And, as you know, the Gospel means, in itself, "good news."

I've not seen this performance or heard this reading. But I think it is likely that we'll hear the story of Christ told not in a sad, dreary way of an interesting person approaching death, but a vibrant story of a man who was alive during the time he was on Earth and who was alive and is alive after death. So, it's a happy story.

Alec McCowen is a noted performer on his own. A small view of his biography is in the program that you have. He took upon himself the task of memorizing, I believe, 678 verses in Mark. And we're very delighted to have him here with us. I talked to him for a few minutes before we both came in, and he said it was going to be as though he was in his own home and among friends. And, Alec, that's the way we look upon you as well.

Thank you for coming. We look forward to your reading.

NOTE: The President spoke at 6:46 p.m. in the East Room at the White House.

The 38th annual National Bible Week was sponsored by the National Bible Committee, Inc.

Domestic Artificial Baits and Flies Industry

Letter to the Speaker of the House and the President of the Senate Transmitting a Report. November 22, 1978

Dear Mr. Speaker: (Dear Mr. President:)

In accordance with Section 203(b)(2) of the Trade Act of 1974, enclosed is a report to the Congress setting forth my determination that import relief for the U.S. Artificial Bait and Flies Industry is not in the national economic interest and explaining the reasons for my decision.

    Sincerely,

          JIMMY CARTER

IMPORT RELIEF—ARTIFICIAL BAITS AND FLIES

As required under Section 203(b)(2) of the Trade Act of 1974, I am transmitting this report to Congress setting forth my decision with respect to artificial baits and flies covered by the affirmative finding on September 21, 1978, of the U.S. International Trade Commission (USITC) under Section 201(d)(1) of the Trade Act. As I have determined not to provide import relief, I have included the reasons for my decision.

I have determined that the import relief is not in the national economic interest for the following reasons:

1. Because of the existing large difference in prices between imports and like or similar domestically produced artificial baits and flies the import relief recommended by the USITC would not be effective. Domestically made items sell for an average of $6–$7 per dozen. Imports sell for an average of $2–$3 per dozen. Moreover, the level of imports has barely changed over the five years—5.0 million

dozen were imported in 1974 and 5.1 million dozen were imported in 1977 even though, in the interim, import prices dropped 30 percent and domestic prices nearly doubled.

2. Latest (January–April 1978) economic indicators for this industry show an improved market situation. Compared to a similar period last year, domestic shipments are up 1 percent in value, 6 percent in quantity, employment increased 12 percent and the number of hours worked are up 50 percent. Finally, the domestic industry's share of the domestic market has improved.

NOTE: This is the text of identical letters addressed to Thomas P. O'Neill, Jr., Speaker of the House of Representatives, and Walter F. Mondale, President of the Senate.

The text of the letters was released on November 24.

Domestic Artificial Baits and Flies Industry

Memorandum From the President. November 22, 1978

Memorandum for the Special Representative for Trade Negotiations

Subject: Determination Under Section 202(b) of the Trade Act; Artificial Baits and Flies

Pursuant to Section 202(b)(1) of the Trade Act of 1974 (P.L. 93–618, 88 Stat. 1978), I have determined the action I will take with respect to the report of the United States International Trade Commission (USITC) dated September 21, 1978, on the results of its investigation concerning artificial baits and flies provided for in Item 731.60 of the Tariff Schedules of the United States.

After considering all relevant aspects of the case, including those set forth in Section 202(c) of the Trade Act of 1974, I have determined that import relief would not be in the national economic interest. The measure proposed by the USITC (removal of these products from the GSP program thereby raising the tariff on imports from countries eligible for GSP benefits to 12.5%) would not provide relief in view of the large price differences between imports and the domestically produced items and furthermore it would contribute to inflation. In addition, imports have shown little significant increase during the five years examined, while import prices were reduced 30 percent and domestic prices nearly doubled.

This determination is to be published in the FEDERAL REGISTER.

JIMMY CARTER

[Filed with the Office of the Federal Register, 5:03 p.m., November 22, 1978]

NOTE: The text of the memorandum was released on November 24.

Peace Corps

Statement on the Resignation of Carolyn R. Payton as Director. November 24, 1978

I have come to the conclusion that there are unresolvable policy differences between the Director of ACTION, Sam Brown, and the Director of one of its major agencies, the Peace Corps, Dr. Carolyn Payton. In order to carry out the important programs of ACTION and to resolve this serious impasse, I am today accepting the resignation of Dr. Payton as Director of the Peace Corps.

This does not in any way reflect on the competence, integrity, or sincerity of Dr. Payton. I wish to express my appreciation to her for the good service which she has rendered.

Digest of Other White House Announcements

The following listing includes the President's daily schedule and other items of general interest as announced by the White House Press Office during the period covered by this issue. Events and announcements printed elsewhere in the issue are not included.

November 18

The President announced that U.S. Ambassador to the United Nations Andrew Young will lead a delegation to the Republic of Guinea on the occasion of the celebrations of the 20th anniversary of that nation's independence. Ambassador Young will be accompanied by Mayor Kenneth Gibson of Newark, N.J., Deputy Assistant Secretary of State William C. Harrop, Paul C. Porter, a Boston business consultant, and Richard Trabulsi, a Houston businessman. The delegation will depart for Conakry, Guinea, November 20.

November 20

The President met at the White House with:

—Zbigniew Brzezinski, Assistant to the President for National Security Affairs;
—the Cabinet;
—Vice President Walter F. Mondale.

Chancellor Helmut Schmidt of the Federal Republic of Germany telephoned the President in the morning. They discussed the Middle East, the strategic arms limitation talks, the multilateral trade negotiations, and other international economic matters of mutual concern.

November 21

The President met at the White House with:

—Dr. Brzezinski;

—Representative Robert C. Krueger of Texas;

—Ambassador Robert S. Strauss, Special Representative for Trade Negotiations;

—Vice President Mondale, Adm. Stansfield Turner, Director of Central Intelligence, Hamilton Jordan, Assistant to the President, and Dr. Brzezinski;

—Senate Majority Leader Robert C. Byrd;

—Clem Renouf, president of Rotary International;

—Mrs. Carter, for lunch;

—James T. McIntyre, Jr., Director of the Office of Management and Budget.

In a ceremony in the Oval Office, the President received a framed copy of the 1978 Christmas Seals from representatives of the American Lung Association.

The White House announced that Tunisian Prime Minister Hedi Nouira has accepted President Carter's invitation to make an official visit to the United States. The Prime Minister will arrive in Washington November 29 and meet with the President and various other senior United States officials during his visit. Details of the visit are being discussed between the two governments.

November 22

The President met at the White House with:

—Dr. Brzezinski;

—Charles L. Schultze, Chairman of the Council of Economic Advisers.

The President left the White House to spend the Thanksgiving holiday weekend at Camp David, Md.

NOMINATIONS SUBMITTED TO THE SENATE

NOTE: The Congress having adjourned *sine die* on Sunday, October 15, no nominations were submitted during the period covered by this issue. The first session of the 96th Congress will begin on Monday, January 15, 1979.

CHECKLIST OF WHITE HOUSE PRESS RELEASES

NOTE: All releases of the Office of the White House Press Secretary, distributed during the period covered by this issue, have been included in the issue.

ACTS APPROVED BY THE PRESIDENT

NOTE: The President completed his consideration of acts and joint resolutions passed during the second session of the 95th Congress on November 10.

PRESIDENTIAL DOCUMENTS

Week Ending Friday, December 1, 1978

St. Louis, Missouri

*Remarks at the National League of Cities'
1978 Congress of Cities.
November 27, 1978*

*President Tom Moody, thank you for that
introduction. My good friend, soon to be
president, John Rousakis, Vice President
Jessie Rattley, President Bill McNichols, a
great help to me and all of you, I'm sure,
Alan Beals, Governor Teasdale, Senator
Eagleton, Senator Hatch, Senator Jake
Garn—former mayor of Salt Lake City,
and who would have been, perhaps almost
surely, president of this organization had
he not been elected to the U.S. Senate—
members of the board, members of the
National League of Cities:*

I spent this last weekend at Camp
David with 30 relatives, and I'm very
grateful to escape—[laughter]—and to
come and join you in a wonderful city. I
received the congratulations and interest
of my own family. Amy said that when I
got to St. Louis, I would find not only a
beautiful city but one of the finest zoos
in the world. My brother, Billy, pointed
out there's one of the largest breweries in
the world here. [Laughter] I had other
comments from different members of
my family.

So, I want to thank you for inviting
me. It's very good to see so many old

friends and to come in this delightful community to share with you my thoughts
about American cities.

But in a discussion of where we have
been, where we are, and what we must
do to conserve the greatness of our cities,
we must also deal with our number one
economic problem, and that is inflation.

I admired the strength and the viability of our cities when I was a boy growing up in southwest Georgia. I first experienced it as a child when I went from
Archery to Plains and then a little later
to our county seat of Americus and eventually to the metropolis of Atlanta.

After I was elected President I began to
realize more vividly the problems of our
cities. Shortly after the election two men
knocked on my door; I went outside. It
was Mayor Abraham Beame and Governor Carey. I asked them what they
needed. They said, "We need a loan guarantee of $1,650,000,000 and two bus
tickets back to New York." [Laughter]

We have, I think, come a long way since
then.

And I'm in a somewhat better position
both to appreciate and to help the dynamic cities of our Nation since I have
become President. I want you to help me,
and me to help you, build and conserve
cities that are bright, vital, filled with life,
and filled with enterprise. That requires,
as you know, a close cooperation between

2075

cities, counties, States, the Federal Government, private citizens, and our own free enterprise system. Essential to this partnership is a long-term commitment of efficient Federal aid to cities. This is how you and I have worked together already in the last 22 months.

After my election in 1976, I met with the board of the League of Cities. I learned then that your most urgent need was for a comprehensive local public works program. You asked for $3½ billion. At my urging, the Congress added $4 billion to the local public works programs.

We've also nearly tripled the number of CETA jobs, and we have emphasized in every way permanent, private employment. We started the urban development action grant, the UDAG program. The result has been a net gain of more than 6½ million new jobs since I was elected.

More important, our cooperation has resulted in the evolution of our Nation's first comprehensive urban policy—a goal of the National League of Cities for 21 years—a policy of action, not default, to enhance the quality of American cities. I've already initiated much of that program administratively. Following your advice, we made more than 100 changes to existing Federal programs, and I've issued four Executive orders to make these programs more effective.

My first order reversed the disturbing trend of moving Federal jobs and facilities out of cities into the suburbs. I directed the General Services Administration to make every effort to locate new Federal facilities and jobs in central cities. As an example, the Old Post Office Building here in St. Louis is being renovated for Federal offices under this program. Its first level, incidentally, will include restaurants and shops to help draw people downtown.

In talking to the mayor on the way in from the airport, we also discussed a vital UDAG program for this central city— $150 million, matching UDAG grants on roughly a 10-to-1 basis.

We need your help and your initiative to enhance the value of these policies and these programs.

Another Executive order directed a greater share of Federal purchases to bidders from high unemployment areas.

A third Executive order established an urban impact process for any major new Federal initiative. This was a direct result of the National League of Cities' long effort to dramatize the often unforeseen effects of new Federal programs in our cities.

The fourth order established an interagency coordinating committee to target, to package, and to coordinate Federal assistance to cities.

We also reordered the priorities of the Economic Development Administration. When I took office, only 15 percent of EDA funds went to cities. This year half, one-half of EDA funds will go to cities.

I directed the Federal Environmental Protection Agency to change the priorities of its multibillion-dollar waste treatment programs. The new emphasis will be to rehabilitate older systems in disrepair, instead of encouraging urban sprawl with new construction.

We also submitted to Congress 19 bills as the legislative program of our urban policy that you helped to evolve. It was a tough fight, still going on, but we've already won enactment of 13 of those bills. Of course, you deserve much of this credit.

We reauthorized the CETA program. There will be an estimated 660,000 jobs. We toughened requirements in CETA to eliminate fraud and abuse and to ensure that only genuinely disadvantaged workers get those jobs. And we added incentives for businesses which hire and train those same workers.

We passed a targeted employment tax credit for businesses which hire jobless young people. We also included in the tax code a credit for rehabilitation of older industrial and commercial buildings. These were the first major reforms of the tax code explicitly to help businesses and individuals stay in the cities and not move out.

The new surface transportation act, which Brock Adams is discussing with you more thoroughly at this convention, will now let us plan and build balanced transportation systems.

We worked to secure the New York City loan guarantee and initiated other measures that underscore my commitment to cities.

And we added a new emphasis throughout our urban programs to help rebuild the private economic base of our cities. I want to convince everyone that it is good business to invest in the cities.

I'm proud of these accomplishments— [*applause*]—I'm proud of these accomplishments, and you should be proud, too. I certainly couldn't have done it without you. The Congress has responded well. It's just a good beginning for a new and continuing partnership. I want you to know that my commitment to this partnership remains firm. Together, our progress will continue. I will not step back from this job as long as I hold office.

I'm also determined to alleviate another problem that now affects cities and every American more deeply than any other economic problem. That is inflation.

I don't need to tell you how inflation affects our cities. You can see it every week on purchasing invoices, on utility bills, higher salaries, constantly increasing budget costs of the same items. Inflation

eats into maintenance and capital funds, and with restricted budgets your streets, buildings, and parks fall into greater disrepair. The same thing happens throughout our economy. Consumers put off needed purchases; businesses tend to postpone modernization; our factories age a few more years. For every year of this, we become much less productive.

In other words, inflation jeopardizes the economic progress we've made since the recession of 1974–1975, including the fragile recovery of our troubled cities. It means that Federal dollars sent to cities buy less. General revenue sharing, for example, has sent about $6.2 billion each year to States and cities since 1972. But by next year its purchasing power will have dropped one-third. Cities badly need these dollars. And the Federal Government cannot replace all such major losses to inflation.

Plainly, the future of our cities is at stake in our fight against inflation. And just as plainly, the people whom we serve, you and I, want something done. They will not accept Federal and local government indifference about inflation. I have no doubt that the American people want the Federal Government to act. They want greater efficiency, less waste, less corruption. They want restraints on Government spending and Government taxing. Those are demands that I cannot and will not disregard.

Last month I announced a tough program to fight inflation. I chose a course that is politically difficult, but I intend to hold to it.

The 1980 fiscal year budget will be very, very tight. I have pledged to submit a 1980 budget with a deficit of $30 billion or less. That is much less than one-half the deficit of fiscal year 1976, when I was running for office. It will not be an easy task, but I intend to do this without starving useful programs. I will not make wholesale, arbitrary spending cuts. We're simply going line by line, item by item through the budget to limit or to cut those things we cannot afford.

For the cities the impact will be clear. We will do as much as we can within the necessarily severe limits. We can and will propose new programs like the National Development Bank. We will take into account explosive growth in rapidly growing areas that bring about serious problems, as well as we take into account the problems of areas which are in distress.

But there will be little money for new initiatives next year. It will be an austere budget. However, I promise that the cities will bear no more and no less than a fair share of budget restraint.

My responsibility as President to the people of the United States is to demonstrate clearly, when the budget is presented to the Congress, that there is a sound and fair and equitable balance as we meet the needs of urban Americans and rural Americans, to provide for education, jobs, defense, domestic programs, and foreign or international programs. All will be examined very closely; *all* will be examined very closely. And I can assure you that the budget will be fair.

We will continue to streamline Federal aid to cities. When I ran for President, I pledged to make urban programs more efficient, more responsive, simpler, and more targeted, and to be evolved and administered in closer cooperation with you, the local officials of our country. I'm carrying out that pledge to the best of my ability.

I know from personal experience that Federal programs often cost State and local governments too much. And frankly, that is still true today. For example, for the small town of Junior, West Virginia, it took 7 years, $1.7 million, and

five different Federal agencies to build a required sewer and treatment system.

I know that we can do better. And that's why my urban policy emphasizes less processing time, less overhead cost, less paperwork, and better coordination with you and with State officials. OSHA, for instance, has eliminated hundreds, even thousands, of unnecessary regulations. HEW is eliminating, simplifying, or consolidating about 60 percent of its nearly 1,400 planning requirements. EPA is doing the same with over half of its 300 planning requirements. We are doing that throughout the Government.

We need your continued help. You should point out specifically those planning requirements, those reporting requirements that you consider to be unnecessary, too complicated, or required too frequently.

We can also expect to benefit from our review of new Federal regulations for their cost impact. I'm going to use my power as President to stop cold any new regulation that ignores its impact on costs to cities and States. I urge you to contact Jack Watson on my staff directly, or me, if necessary, to point out where this commitment might tend to be violated. We will stop it immediately if you'll let us know.

But I also expect State government and you, the local government officials, to do your part. We've long known the inflationary impact of State or local regulations that restrict competition and raise costs.

Much of the inflation in housing, for example, comes from outmoded building codes. Productivity in building construction in the last 10 years has actually gone down, almost 2 percent each year. We will look to the cities and the counties to encourage local construction companies and unions to attack the problem of productivity directly, to reexamine the cost-inflating work practices and the possibility of adopting new technologies that will combat rising costs. We will look to the localities to attack directly high real estate transaction costs.

Similarly, the States and localities must attack other restraints on competition, both governmental and private. These include the use of licensing to restrict entry into occupations and eliminate competition, restrictions by private groups on advertising of prices by their members, insurance regulations that hold premium costs up, public utility rate structures that fail to encourage conservation and so promote the unnecessary installation of costly additional capacity.

In the next few weeks I will be calling on State and local officials and working closely with you, when necessary, to revise regulations of businesses to increase competition and reduce costs and to follow restrained, prudent tax and spending policies.

In this fight all sectors have a role. I've taken painful action at the Federal level already by reducing Federal spending, putting a cap on Federal employment, putting a cap on Federal salaries, vetoing popular legislation, and performing a tough cost analysis benefit of new regulations.

The most important things that cities can do to fight inflation is to make sure that all goods and services which you procure come only from suppliers who will certify that they are in compliance with Federal wage and price guidelines. The second is for cities themselves to abide by our wage and price standards in negotiating contracts and in setting your own fees. This will not only help hold down costs but set an example for private firms and others in your own localities. I call on you today to follow the guidelines in these two important areas. But these steps alone will not be enough.

Let me repeat what I said earlier: the 1980 budget will be very, very tight. It will disappoint those who do not take inflation seriously. It will disappoint those who expect protection from inflation while someone else bears the burden. It will disappoint those who think only of next year and not the next decade. And it will disappoint those who expect constantly expanding Federal aid and a constantly expanding number of Federal programs and agencies.

We must control inflation. We must bring it down. We must stop it from interfering with our lives, our aspirations, and our hopes for the future. That's why I need your understanding and your cooperation and your help to solve this problem once and for all.

If we fail to control inflation, we face a deeply troubled future. We would erode the commitment of the American public to helping cities, to helping the poor, to helping the elderly, the jobless, the sick, and the weak. That is a prospect we dare not face.

But as we are successful and bring down inflation, with a concerted effort, we can look back on these years with the satisfaction that we built a solid foundation that kept our country prosperous, compassionate, and strong. That will take an unprecedented effort by us all in the next few years. It will take imagination. It will require initiative, a close attention paid to local and unique circumstances. It will require sacrifice. And it will take the patience to realize that we cannot afford everything that we want now.

I believe strongly that we have the will to solve this problem of inflation in America. I believe strongly that the people are ready to make the necessary sacrifices, if only government provides the leadership and the example. I ask only that you help me in this task—that we as partners might end any drift and indecision and lead our cities and our country toward a brighter, more prosperous, and a more secure future. With your help, we will not fail.

Thank you very much.

NOTE: The President spoke at 10:06 a.m. in Monsanto Hall at the Cervantes Convention Center.

In his opening remarks, the President referred to Mayor Tom Moody of Columbus, Ohio, president; Mayor John Rousakis of Savannah, Ga., incoming president; Councilwoman Jessie Rattley of Newport News, Va., incoming first vice president; Mayor William H. McNichols of Denver, Colo., member of the advisory council; and Alan L. Beals, executive director, all of the National League of Cities.

St. Louis, Missouri

Remarks and a Question-and-Answer Session at a Briefing on the Budget for the Board of Directors of the National League of Cities. November 27, 1978

THE PRESIDENT. One of the most gratifying things that has happened since I've been in the White House as President has been the evolution of a good, cooperative partnership arrangement with you. As we've prepared major programs of all kinds, involving health or education, involving transportation, environmental quality, we've tried to work very closely with the officials who represent the cities of our country. This has been especially true as we evolved the urban policy that's now the basis for programs that we are implementing, either through Executive action or through legislative processes. I hope that this can continue, and I certainly expect it to continue.

My feeling is that you are at ease with me and with my own administration, that

when we fail to measure up to your expectations, you let us know without delay—[*laughter*]—and with at least a proper amount of enthusiasm.

And when we are working in harmony, as has almost always been the case, I've appreciated your compliments and the support that you've given our programs. When I've been faced with major questions on international affairs, you've been very supportive. And, of course, our domestic programs, that don't directly affect you as mayors, but affect you in a very comprehensive way through your people—like energy—you've also been extremely helpful. I want to be sure that this is a part of our entire consciousness as a Nation, that not only you and I realize it but also those people who live in your cities, who look to you as elected leaders, and, of course, all of whom I represent as President.

This morning I'll just be here for a few minutes, and then officials of the Office of Management and Budget—Bo Cutter, is Bo Cutter here?—will go into some detail about prospects for the 1980 fiscal year budget. Many of the specific answers can't be given yet. I'm just at this stage getting a briefing from the Office of Management and Budget about some of the issues that will be presented to me later on. I haven't made any decisions at this point. I've not yet met with a single member of my Cabinet nor a single head of another major agency to discuss their own desires for the programs for 1980 fiscal year at all.

But as we go through this process during the next few weeks, it's important to us to know how you feel about the priorities that we will address. And the main purpose of the session this morning is to let Bo Cutter and myself understand your special concerns.

As I pointed out in my speech a few minutes ago, all of us will have to suffer from the restraints on an equitable and fair basis, and that includes domestic and foreign affairs. It includes domestic programs, defense, other issues that have to come before me. I'm going to be incisive, persistent, dedicated, and, I hope, confident in the preparation of the 1980 budget.

All of you have been through budget cycles yourselves. You know what it is to face unlimited demands and limited resources.

As I pointed out earlier, when I ran for President, the budget deficit was more than $66 billion. Since then we've cut taxes about $30 billion on an annual basis. And we've greatly expanded programs and services, many with your guidance and support. On top of that, we've also cut down the budget deficit substantially. And I have no doubt that I will meet the goal of having a budget deficit much less than half what it was when I ran for President—$30 billion or less. We still have some uncertainties remaining. As you well know, with the economic situation as it is, it's almost impossible to predict the rate of revenues to be received next year.

We've been remarkably successful in cutting down the unemployment rate. I think we will have a sustained, moderate growth throughout 1979. I do not anticipate a recession nor a depression, of course. I have no economic advisers who work with me who believe that there will be a recession in 1979. We will have success with the controlling of inflation to the extent that the American people's consciousness is aroused about the need for restraint. And if there is a broad base of support for controlling inflation, the hardship or suffering or sacrifice to be required from any particular group or person will be greatly minimized.

As you know, in the top levels of em-ployment in our Government—those who are appointed by me, the executive level in the Government—there will be zero increases in salaries for them this year. They will have to take, in effect, a salary cut equivalent to the inflation rate for 1978 and also for this coming year. Others have a moderate income increase of about 5½ percent.

I've had to place a hiring freeze in the Federal Government at this point. For every two vacancies which occur, we only permit one of those vacancies to be filled.

And as I've pointed out earlier, I've had to veto several very popular programs with different, very fine, beneficent, and politically influential special interest groups in our country, and that will continue. I think to the extent that the Congress sees my determination and the fairness of my proposals, the number of bills passed or the number of proposals made which I do have to veto in the future will be less.

I know that you're either bipartisan, nonpartisan, or divided between Democrats and Republicans. [*Laughter*] And I think if there's one lesson to have come out of the results of the general election earlier this month, it was that people want government to be competent, I would say frugal to some degree, and to eliminate waste, fraud, and corruption.

As we cut back on unnecessary spending in the Federal Government, using the zero-base budgeting technique which I initiated, it lets us focus the expenditures which are available much more narrowly where the needs are greatest. And I think this, in effect, ensures that our Government will be more efficient and more competent in the future.

The openness of Government is also very crucial. It's good for consumers of all kinds to know what their own Government is doing. There can be no secrecy surrounding how the Federal funds are spent, except when the extreme urgency of national security is involved.

No aspect of the Government will be sacred nor sacrosanct. All of it will be very carefully examined, including the Defense Department, where I will make sure that every dollar spent is very carefully assessed and where we have the greatest return on the money that we spend.

Perhaps you have one or two questions that you could ask me now before I leave. And I'll ask Bo Cutter to take over after I depart, or he might have to help me with some of the questions. But I want to let you know that the budget now is in the formative stage of preparation, and your comments and your advice, either to me directly or through Bo Cutter, will be very helpful to us in establishing our own priorities.

Does anybody have either a comment or a question?

Tom [Mayor Tom Moody of Columbus, Ohio, president, National League of Cities].

Q. Mr. President, you have answered in your remarks today many of the questions which members of the board brought up about the Defense Establishment, about whether the cities would have to bear the whole load. I can pledge to you renewed assurance—we made up our minds before you came—but we will support you in your inflation fight.

THE PRESIDENT. That's great to know. I think whatever you do, as you prepare your own budgets or as you make decisions about purchasing practices, the writing of your own regulations for your cities, or the issuing of licenses or the assessment of fees, when you do this in compliance with the spirit of controlling inflation, I hope that you'll make every effort to get maximum publicity for it, to let the people know that this is a na-

tionwide effort. It would be a mistake for the people of our country to think that I, as President, or the business establishment or labor unions are the only ones who are responsible and the only ones who can act effectively to control inflation.

Yes, Johnny [Mayor John Rousakis of Savannah, Ga., incoming president, National League of Cities].

Where you from? [*Laughter*]

Q. Your favorite city, Savannah. [*Laughter*]

[*At this point, the President attached to his jacket a campaign button for Mayor Rousakis' National League of Cities presidential campaign.*]

THE PRESIDENT. I was going to wait till Wednesday to put it on, but I'll—[*laughter*]——

Q. You will be here to second my nomination? [*Laughter*]

The strength of your commitment towards this partnership in trying to solve the problem of urban America is starting to spill over in some States, but not all. And you don't have that strength of a commitment from the States. Do you propose some new incentives or programs where they can truly become part of this effort? Because they're not.

THE PRESIDENT. Well, in February I'll be meeting again with all the Governors when they come to Washington for their annual meeting with me. And between now and then, Johnny, if you would work with Jack Watson and be specific, not only about the programs where you need better cooperation with the Governors and their administrations but also with us, and even in a confidential way to let us know which States have a great deal to learn or a long way to go, I would be glad to consult individually or collectively with the Governors to assure that the partnership does include all the States.

Jack Watson is in daily contact with the Governors of our Nation. And I'm sure that most of them, all of them—as are you and I and everyone here—really want to do a good job. And there might be at times a lack of communication or a lack of cooperation that's inadvertent. And sometimes a Governor and the mayors in a State can have a very fine and mutually constructive working relationship, because they use a certain technique or a certain attitude, and another Governor may not be aware of this.

So, if you would work through Jack Watson and directly with me before February, I'll put that at the top of my priority—near the top of my priority at least—and work with the Governors to ensure that there is a full partnership including the State governments. I'd be glad to do this.

Tom.

Q. Mr. President, we've always appreciated your willingness to permit us to have input into programs that are being developed. I think this year's going to be very critical, because we have pledged to you that we will support the efforts against inflation, and we'll work with you in taking our fair share of cuts. My question is, do you have some mechanism by which we can offer input, with which we can determine our own priorities as to which programs we think ought to be cut?

THE PRESIDENT. Well, one of the mechanisms, obviously, is this session this morning. Bo Cutter is the primary one in OMB, Office of Management and Budget, that works with me as I make every decision about what will be in the budget. In fact, I would guess that between now and the time the budget goes to the printers, that I will never have a budget session without Bo Cutter being present. And also, of course, Jack Watson is available to work directly with you, and he attends all those sessions as well. Stu Eizen-

stat is the same. You know all these people very, very well.

I think you are right, Tom. In a time of budget restraint, as we face clearly now, cooperation is much more advantageous than even in normal times. And I think that as we evolved the national urban policy this past year, there was a surprising degree of approval of it, after it was concluded, out of all proportion to the new Federal programs or even the new money spent, because everybody felt that it was evolved in cooperation and that we recognized fiscal restraint. And the onerous things about existing Federal programs were identified to be eliminated, and how they could be made efficient was also clearly described.

So, as I make decisions on domestic affairs, not only including direct aid and programs to cities but also the more general ones involving welfare, health, education, transportation, nothing could benefit me more than to have your direct input. So, I would say, through my domestic staff, Stu Eizenstat, Jack Watson, more particularly, and the Office of Management and Budget, and directly with me—through all those mechanisms—we are very eager to have your input.

Maybe one more question or comment, then I'll have to go.

Q. Mr. President, the urban impact analysis potentially, I think, is one of the most powerful friends that the cities could have. At what time will we be able to see those analyses, since they come from the different agencies, and will they extend not only to new programs but to major changes in existing programs, since probably there won't be too many new programs, according to your own words?

THE PRESIDENT. Well, they apply both to new programs and also to changes in existing programs.

Jack, you might answer the question as far as the time.

MR. WATSON. There are two Executive orders that you know about, that the President mentioned this morning. One of them is the urban impact analysis, with which you're familiar and which you're speaking about now. The other one is this new Interagency Coordinating Council, which I chair for the President and which consists of all the major operating program managers of the Government.

As you see urban impacts, prospective or otherwise, flowing out of changes or out of possible new programs, communication with us about those impacts that you see would be the thing to do, either through the Interagency Coordinating Council or through the urban impact analysis process. Both of those work hand in glove, and the two processes, though one of them is handled principally through the Domestic Policy Staff, with Stu, and the other through me, they are, in effect, a single process.

THE PRESIDENT. Also, when you see Federal programs that are excessively financed, I hope you'll let me know about that as well. [*Laughter*]

Thank you very much.

NOTE: The President spoke at 10:40 a.m. in Room 122 at the Cervantes Convention Center.

W. Bowman "Bo" Cutter is Executive Associate Director for Budget of the Office of Management and Budget, and Jack H. Watson, Jr., is Secretary to the Cabinet and Assistant to the President for Intergovernmental Affairs.

Salt Lake City, Utah

Remarks at Mormon Church Ceremonies Honoring Family Unity.   November 27, 1978

President Kimball, President Romney, President Tanner, members of the Council of the Twelve Apostles, distinguished representatives of the governments at all levels, ladies and gentlemen:

This is absolutely beautiful. And I'm very honored, Mr. President, that you would present this to me.

I'm also honored to be here with you in this beautiful place. I came a little earlier than the audience may have known, and I was pleased to watch the absolutely delightful and memorable television spots that remind all of us who are members of families what our duties are, to hear the Primary Children's Chorus singing "I Am a Child of God," to hear the Lamanite Generation, Native Americans, singing "Go, My Son," and then, of course, to come in and meet the Osmond family, which is a very famous and admirable group in our Nation.

It's a pleasure for me to receive this award, representing a typical American family, and I want to thank you for it.

As a matter of fact, I had my typical American family this past weekend at Camp David, 30 of the members of my family. I finally escaped yesterday. [*Laughter*] After 2 or 3 intense days of negotiation, I think we reached a framework for peace among ourselves. [*Laughter*] It was nice to keep my family out of the news for a few days. [*Laughter*] It was one of the most delightful experiences in many years for me.

We have a large family, a close family, an exciting family, and one which has given one another great help and support and encouragement in times of difficulty or excitement or joy or achievement or sorrow.

There's nothing that gives me more pleasure, even as President of the United States, than to have Amy come to me in the evening, when I'm tired and concerned and worried, and put her arms around my neck and give me a kiss. She was born, my first daughter, after Rosalynn and I had been married 21 years. And she now is proud to call herself a double-digit preteenager. [*Laughter*] She's a great young lady and the joy of our lives.

And I was able to have with me in the last few days my two grandsons. And we're expecting, I hope, a new granddaughter in just a few days from now. [*Laughter*]

When I was invited to come here for this special observance of the family—what it means under the guidance of Jesus Christ and the great Nation of the United States of America, supported and strengthened by the Church of Jesus Christ of Latter-day Saints, publicized and promoted by this special week—I wondered what I wanted to say to you. I thought about the early Mormons coming across this country, singing a famous hymn, I think, that originated in England, "Come, Come Ye Saints." I thought about the times of trial in our country, a time when strength was demanded of all of us, a time when we sometimes feel alone.

Only a deep faith could let the words of that song, "All Is Well," ring out. In times when you and your forefathers were persecuted, driven one from another, crossed this land looking for freedom, a chance to worship in your own way, when perhaps you knew that you were about to die, when drought and thirst afflicted you and still the song rang out—"All Is Well." This is indeed a demonstration of an act of faith and a reaffirmation of hope.

I come here as President of a great country. And in that same act of faith and in affirmation of hope, I tell you that our Nation can say all is well. And even the American family can be characterized by the same phrase, all is well. Because as

was your early church in the minds and hearts of your own forefathers, so is our Nation and the family so precious, so dear, so innately good and right and decent and strong, that challenges to us, to our Nation, to the American family can successfully be withstood.

I grew up in an isolated place, 3 miles west of Plains, Georgia, on a farm, where a family was indeed a self-contained community, where every member of the family felt wanted and loved and secure. When I was sad or hurt, my mother was there, my father was there. We worked together. Some plowed a mule; some carried and dropped a seed or fertilizer; some hoed out weeds; some carried water to the field for the others to drink; some took care of the hogs or the cows or the chickens; some kept the home secure. But in every instance each knew that the other one was contributing, and the children understood the function of the parents, and the parents understood and loved the children. There was easy communication among us. And in our relatively primitive, isolated state of living, we were bound together by love.

My first church was my family. I first heard the Bible read in my family. I first heard prayer in my family. I learned about God within the family. My first school was my family. My first government was my family. There, in an embryonic stage of growth, I began to perceive the world around me. And when I had questions, they were answered. When I had doubts, they were resolved. When I had needs, they were met. My family was strong. And there was very little need for services to be derived from government for us.

And since I've served in the State legislature and as Governor of a State and now as President, and participated in international affairs, I've learned more and more that the stronger a family is, the stronger families are, the less role there is to be played by government. Our government spends a great deal of its time and effort, a great deal of your money repairing damages caused by weak or broken families.

We have signs of deteriorating family structures in our country that cause us great concern. And there's not any inherent reason for it. I agree with a rabbi named Heschel, who said, "I've never understood how a father can take care of 12 children, and 12 children can't take care of 1 father."

But when families fail, governments must act. And sometimes they act in error. When massive programs are put together through government, the individuality of human beings is sometimes forgotten and the sensitivity is lost. Our welfare programs, for instance, in some of their aspects, are antifamily. They function only when a father has actually left a home. And sometimes fathers leave homes temporarily, through subterfuge, sometimes permanently, just so a child can be fed.

In our modern, mobile, permissive society, the basic moral strengths that bind families together are sometimes weakened or broken entirely. For every two marriages that took place in the United States last year, there was one divorce. For people born in the early years of this century and later married, only 1 out of 10 marriages resulted in divorce. For Americans born since World War II who married, one out of three marriages results in divorce.

Children are troubled. Teenage suicide has doubled in the last 10 years, and now the second most prevalent cause of death among male teenagers is suicide. Births out of wedlock are increasing rapidly.

I could go on and on. But these brutal and disturbing statistics are caused by a lack of strength among family members. Lily Tomlin says as a joke, "We're all in this alone." And sometimes we feel that in a fast-moving, modern, technological society that we're alone, not as it was in former generations—because of separation of distance—because now we can be alone in a crowded apartment building, because our next-door neighbors remain strangers.

A family is a mutual improvement society. All of us have weaknesses, faults, fears, yearnings, hopes, dreams, ideals that we can't realize alone, and the support and the concern and the understanding and the care and, sometimes, the criticism and punishment in a constructive way help to repair our weaknesses.

I don't know of any man who is more deeply indebted to one's family than am I. I've had great political ambitions. I've traveled widely. And my family has always gone a second mile in giving me their love and their actual support. Never once have I asked my mother, my brother, my sisters, my children, my wife to give me their help or their confidence when they said, "Your ambitions are too great. I've got my own life to live. I'd rather not give you my help."

Your great church epitomizes to me what a family ought to be—a church that believes, through moral imperative, in strong families, in individualism, the right to be different, but the opportunity and even duty to grow as a human being, to prepare oneself for greater service. The relief society organized by your church has brought blessings to tens of thousands of people, not in a highly publicized way, but in a quiet and effective way.

And when your forebears first reached this valley, in less than 3 years there was a new college. At that time there was a common belief in our Nation that women couldn't stand the rigors of college life, but you knew different. And now this State has the highest educational level of any State in the Nation.

The State constitution recognized in 1896 that women and men should have the same civil, political, religious rights and privileges. And we are trying now to spread that same commitment throughout our entire Nation. The recognition of what a human being is, what a human being can be, is important. But a commitment of one person to another to realize that great potential is an element sometimes missing in our modern society.

Many people these days feel alone. There is a Yiddish proverb, a religious proverb, that says, "God gave burdens, also shoulders." A simple proverb—it doesn't say God gave us burdens, but he gave us shoulders strong enough to bear them, it just says, "God gave burdens, also shoulders." We not only have our own shoulders to carry burdens, but we have others to help, not just to carry burdens but, sometimes, shoulders to cry on. Those shoulders let us bear the burdens of life.

And with each generation comes a tremendous challenge, difficulties, and most of those challenges and difficulties are derived from mandatory change. We tend to think the changes that take place in our own life are the greatest that have ever afflicted any generation, but this is not true.

Our early forebears in this Nation offered their lives, all their belongings, even their family security, to achieve freedom, liberty. Later, our Nation was torn by a War Between the States. Pioneers moved West. The changes that took place in individual lives then were much greater than those that take place today.

But we learned in a time of change, no matter which generation it is, that there are some things which do not change. Those things can be described as the elements of a good family—truth, unselfishness, idealism, commitment, courage, understanding, morality, security, love. As a father, I understand those things. As a husband, I understand those things. As President, I understand the same things.

There are legitimate roles for a government to perform: to assure that our Nation lives in peace; to assure that our people have an opportunity for employment, for jobs, to use what talent God might have given them in a sustained and productive way; to eliminate the threats to society, to the family—drugs, crime; to initiate preventive health care; to provide for better education, transportation, security; to cut down on some of the afflictions, such as unwanted pregnancies that lead to abortions, things that deeply religious people and others deplore; to raise the ideals of individuals; and to sustain the ideals and morals of a nation itself.

I know how much less difficult my own duties would be as President if your mammoth crusade for stable and strong families should be successful. That's why I feel a close kinship with you and a partnership with you in achieving this noble purpose.

Each person's sphere of influence need not be great. A father, a mother, a child can change the course of human history, can change the character of a community, a State, or even a nation. If we cling to those things, that should never change.

God gave us burdens, also shoulders, so that we, working together under religious teachings that we study from different perspectives, in a nation committed to individualism and freedom and high purpose, might be successful and that you and I together might enjoy stronger families and a greater and stronger nation.

Thank you very much.

NOTE: The President spoke at 2:24 p.m. at the Mormon Tabernacle after receiving the Family Unity Award, a statuette entitled "Love at Home," from Spencer W. Kimball, president of the Church of Jesus Christ of Latter-day Saints. In his opening remarks, he also referred to President Marion G. Romney, second counselor, and President N. Eldon Tanner, first counselor, of the First Presidency of the Mormon Church.

The ceremonies were held in conjunction with National Family Week, 1978, which was proclaimed by the President on October 20 by Proclamation 4606.

George Moscone and Harvey Milk

Statement on the Death of the Two San Francisco Officials.   November 27, 1978

I know I speak on behalf of the Nation when I express a sense of outrage and sadness at the senseless killings today of San Francisco Mayor George Moscone and Supervisor Harvey Milk.

George Moscone had long and ably served the people of the San Francisco area. At age 33 he became one of the youngest members ever elected to the San Francisco Board of Supervisors. He was elected three times to the California State Senate before becoming San Francisco's mayor in 1976.

In every conversation with Mayor Moscone, I always knew that the people of San Francisco and California were uppermost in his mind and heart. He was a good and kind man, and he will be sorely missed.

Supervisor Milk was a hard-working and dedicated supervisor, a leader of San Francisco's gay community who kept his promise to represent all his constituents.

Rosalynn and I express our deepest sympathies to the families and friends of both men.

Radioactivity Exposure in Utah

Statement Announcing a Review of Earlier Federal Studies.   November 27, 1978

Governor Matheson has expressed his concern over the possible health implications for people in Utah who were exposed to radioactive particles as a result of Defense Department testing of atomic bombs in the 1950's.

The Governor has asked me to review the findings of earlier Federal studies in Utah on the effects of exposure to radioactive particles on health and to determine whether or not a more comprehensive study is indicated.

I am today directing the Secretary of the Department of Health, Education, and Welfare to take the following actions:

—reevaluate the findings of earlier studies conducted in the State to determine whether or not the rate of illness or death from leukemia is disproportionately large in Utah, particularly in the southwestern counties;

—reopen a study conducted in the late 1960's on the incidence of thyroid disease; and

—consult with State officials and consider the possibility of developing a larger, more complete study if indicated.

I have asked Secretary Califano to work closely with the State of Utah as he proceeds, and I have asked the Secretary of Defense to cooperate fully in this endeavor.

American Battle Monuments Commission

Appointment of Nine Members.
November 27, 1978

The President today announced the appointment of nine persons as members of the American Battle Monuments Commission. They are:

ALFRED P. CHAMIE, of Pacific Palisades, Calif., who retired earlier this year as general counsel of the Association of Motion Picture and Television Producers, Inc. Chamie is a former national commander of the American Legion and is a trustee of the American Legion Hollywood Canteen Fund. He has been a member of this Commission since 1971.

GEN. BENJAMIN O. DAVIS, JR., of Alexandria, Va., a retired Air Force general and former Assistant Secretary of Transportation (1971–1975). Davis is a governing trustee of the Air Force Historical Foundation and a member of the President's Commission on Military Compensation.

T. HARRY GATTON, executive vice president of the North Carolina Bankers Association. Gatton is vice chairman of the North Carolina Historical Commission. He was a member of the American Battle Monuments Commission from 1961 to 1969.

GEN. JAMES M. GAVIN, of Chestnut Hill, Mass., a retired Army general and former ambassador to France. Gavin is now a director and consultant to Arthur D. Little, Inc., the industrial research, engineering, and management consulting company.

GEN. ANNA MAE HAYS, Chief of the Army Nurse Corps, the first American woman to be promoted to general or flag officer rank.

ADM. JAMES L. HOLLOWAY III, former Chief of Naval Operations and member of the Joint Chiefs of Staff.

OLIVER E. MEADOWS, national commander of the Disabled American Veterans, formerly staff director of the House Committee on Veterans' Affairs from 1955 to 1976.

JOHN M. POPE, of Americus, Ga., who retired in 1972 after 25 years as owner and operator of Southern Burial Vault Co.

GEN. LOUIS H. WILSON, Commandant of the Marine Corps.

Bill of Rights Day, Human Rights Day and Week, 1978

Proclamation 4609.   November 28, 1978

By the President of the United States of America

A Proclamation

Two great events in the history of human liberty will be commemorated in December: the ratification, on December 15, 1791, of the Bill of Rights of the Constitution of the United States, and the adoption, on December 10, 1948, of the Universal Declaration of Human Rights by the United Nations General Assembly.

The anniversary of the Bill of Rights reminds us that our Nation is a continuing experiment in human freedom. Because of the Bill of Rights, we have been able to weather 187 years of tumultuous social and technological change without losing our fundamental liberties. Indeed, those liberties have actually expanded in scope, and have grown to encompass a steadily larger proportion of our people. We can be proud of what we have achieved. But we cannot be complacent, for too many Americans are still denied a fair opportunity to enjoy the rights and rewards of our society. That is why Bill of Rights Day should be a day of rededication as well as of commemoration.

This year, we mark the 30th anniversary of the Universal Declaration of Human Rights.

The Declaration is the cornerstone of a developing international consensus on human rights. It is also the authoritative statement of the meaning of the United Nations Charter, through which member nations undertake to promote, respect and observe human rights and fundamental freedoms for all, without discrimination. A long and difficult road must be travelled before the reality of human rights in the world matches the words of the Declaration. The Declaration will light that road and give strength to all who follow it.

The Universal Declaration is the heart of a body of important United Nations human rights documents: the Convention on the Prevention and Punishment of the Crime of Genocide, the Convention on the Elimination of All Forms of Racial Discrimination, the Covenant on Civil and Political Rights, and the Covenant on Economic, Social and Cultural Rights. The United States signed the Genocide Convention in 1948 and the Racial Discrimination Convention in 1966. I signed the other two Covenants on October 4, 1977. I hope that the United States Senate will soon approve the Genocide Convention at last, and will undertake early hearings to permit our Nation's adherence to the three remaining instruments. There could be no more appropriate gesture to mark the anniversary of the Universal Declaration.

I also signed the American Convention on Human Rights on June 1, 1977. I am proud that since then, eleven nations of the Americas have ratified it, thus bringing it into force.

The great and noble struggle to realize the rights of all men and women goes on. In the face of injustice and oppression, human beings continue to sacrifice and strive for justice and for human dignity.

Now, THEREFORE, I, JIMMY CARTER, President of the United States of America, do hereby proclaim December 10, 1978, as Human Rights Day and December 15, 1978, as Bill of Rights Day, and call on all Americans to observe Human Rights Week beginning December 10, 1978. Let us reaffirm our dedication to the promise of this Nation for all citizens. And let us renew our efforts as members of the world community on behalf of the human rights of all people everywhere.

IN WITNESS WHEREOF, I have hereunto set my hand this twenty-eighth day of November, in the year of our Lord nineteen hundred seventy-eight, and of the Independence of the United States of America the two hundred and third.

JIMMY CARTER

[Filed with the Office of the Federal Register, 11:18 a.m., November 29, 1978]

Visit of Prime Minister Hedi Nouira of Tunisia

Remarks at the Welcoming Ceremony. November 29, 1978

THE PRESIDENT. It's with a great deal of pleasure that I, on behalf of the people of our country, welcome to the United States a distinguished visitor, Prime Minister Nouira from Tunisia, who comes here representing a great country which has close and longstanding ties of friendship and common purpose with the people of our Nation.

Ever since Tunisia won its independence under the inspired leadership of President Bourguiba, the relations between the two nations have grown ever closer. We share common purposes, common ideals, common hopes, and a common future. This has been especially true during the last 8 years, since Mr. Nouira became Prime Minister of Tunisia.

I think among all those nations who have had a close economic aid relationship with the United States, Tunisia has excelled in the rapid technological and economic development among their people. They have made full and increasing use of the great natural resources and human resources of their country. And along with this economic development has come a very rapid evolution into a leadership role among the developing nations of the world, the Arab community, and within the United Nations especially.

So, the political and economic leadership which has exemplified Tunisia's role accurately expresses the strength and the purpose, the innovation and commitment of the people of that great country.

Tunisia is recognized as having a government and leaders that are at the same time practical and effective and idealistic and never deviating from proper principles of government. This leadership under Prime Minister Nouira and President Bourguiba has also been exemplified by great courage.

As a member of the Arab nation community, as far back as 1965, President Bourguiba called for a recognition of Israel, its right to exist, its right to be recognized as a nation. We have received good advice, good counsel, good support from Tunisia during our own times of effort to bring peace to the Middle East and to the northern portion of the continent of Africa.

I'm looking forward to my opportunity today to discuss with the Prime Minister these same concerns that we share and the same prospects for further progress in the future. We also are exploring ways for increased economic cooperation, military counsel and communication, the sharing, for both peace and security, agricultural development in Tunisia and cultural exchange. At the same time we have Peace Corps volunteers in Tunisia teaching English and performing other roles, there are volunteers from Tunisia now working in Louisiana, teaching French. This is typical of the human, economic, and political interrelationships that exist between our countries.

And again, on behalf of the American people, I welcome Prime Minister Nouira, an experienced statesman, a courageous leader who works with us and for his people for peace, prosperity, and domestic and international justice.

Mr. Prime Minister, welcome to our country.

THE PRIME MINISTER. Mr. President, your words of welcome are a moving testimony of the sympathy and support that the United States has for Tunisia. On behalf of my country, in the name of President Bourguiba, whose work of wisdom you have just saluted, I want to thank you. In my turn I extend to the American people the very friendly greeting of the Tunisian nation.

Coming to Washington, I have the very natural feeling to be among friends of Tunisia. Longstanding relations have drawn our countries ever closer. Humanistic America gave us her support and sympathy during our struggle for national liberation.

Modern Tunisia has found in your country an active solidarity. Since the time when free to shape our destiny, we have worked to secure our economic and social development. And so today we follow this tradition of exchanges, exchange of views and consultation, and thus I have the privilege to reestablish a personal contact with the chief of state for whom

Tunisia has great consideration. It gives me again the opportunity to express to you the deep appreciation we feel for the task you have undertaken for the prosperity of the American people and the advent of peace in the world.

Mr. President, America concerns all of us, all those who want harmonious development in the world, nuclear peace, the suppression of crisis in the Middle East as well as in Africa, the spiritual and material ascent of the Third World, and the making available to men of the phenomenal conquest of technology. All those can only follow with sustained interest everything that the United States is doing at home and overseas.

Since you assumed the leadership of the great American people, new developments have marked the evolution of the world. There is a new will, a new sensitivity inspiring the policies of the United States. We have come to learn the scope of this huge task whose essential objective is to ensure the survival of man and his fulfillment in security and dignity.

In turn, we shall tell you how we feel about the situation in our own geopolitical context, speaking from the perspective of an Arab and African nation, basing ourselves upon our own realities and experience. I look forward to receiving your impressions and those of the American leaders, and I do not doubt that our meetings will have a very fruitful outcome.

As I thank you again, Mr. President, for the great welcome you have extended to me, to my wife, and to my delegation, allow me to renew the best wishes of Tunisia to the 200 million Americans who, for us Tunisians, are 200 million friends.

NOTE: The President spoke at 10:39 a.m. on the South Lawn of the White House. Prime Minister Nouira spoke in French, and his remarks were translated by an interpreter.

Democratic National Committee

Remarks at a White House Briefing for the Organization's Executive Committee and State Chairpersons. November 29, 1978

Well, it's good to come over here and meet with my partners. I think we have had a good first 2 years, a very successful campaign and election earlier this month. And I think we face the future with a realization of difficulties, no greater than the ones we inherited 2 years ago, but with the same degree of common purpose, confidence, and natural strength.

After I finish my very brief remarks, Stu Eizenstat and Alfred Kahn will go into some depth with you and answer questions about what we have in mind concerning the control of inflation, which is our number one economic problem in our country.

I think it's obvious that we are determined to control inflation. It will be a subject of the greatest and most intense analysis, of common concert and effort on the part of all my administrative officials. I think the last results of the November elections showed that the Nation is deeply concerned about it. And we as Democrats know that those who suffer most from uncontrolled inflation are the very ones about whom we care most deeply. Those who are secure, who are influential, who are wealthy, who are highly educated, who are mobile, can accommodate the constant pressures of reduced monetary values much easier than those who are poor, elderly, inarticulate, who have one narrowly defined capability to earn one's living, or who live on a fixed income and can't escape the increasing pressures that grow on them month by month. I don't see any incompatibility between meeting the basic needs of those constituencies and an effort to control inflation.

I think it's obvious to us all that we, in the last 2 years, working with the Democratic Congress, have been surprisingly successful. We have had unprecedented progress made in education, in transportation, sustained construction of housing.

We've reestablished our Nation as a focal point for world peace, for the enhancement of human rights in the most generic sense of the word, both domestically and in foreign affairs. We've tried to bring some order out of chaos in the Government bureaucracy. We've attempted to inspire the Federal workers to more dedicated service even than they had been exemplifying before. We've reduced the Federal deficit. We've strengthened ourselves militarily. And I think we've repaired some of the damage that had been done among the American people in their attitude of distrust and doubt about the veracity or competence of the Federal Government.

We put Americans back to work in an unprecedented way. Never before in the history of our country, even during wartime, have we added so many net new jobs, when 2 years ago Americans were discouraged about an inability to be gainfully employed, to use what talent they had, and to support themselves. And the benefits derived therefrom in reduced unemployment payments, reduced welfare payments, have made available funds to repair our cities and to carry out other programs that I've just described.

This is a much more insidious problem than some of those that I've described already. We've not caused inflation. It's been a chronic problem now for more than 10 years, an average inflation rate of about 6½ percent for the last 10 years. And I said in my speech to the public the other night on television, the 3 years before I became President the average was 8 percent inflation. This is a problem

that's endemic to all the democratic nations, at least, in the world. Some countries face a much higher inflation rate than do we. But I think our ability to deal with it successfully will be one of the most difficult challenges that I have faced.

There's a lot of practical action that can be taken, and we are pursuing those in depth. I won't go into that—because Fred Kahn and Stu Eizenstat can do it best—but there's a symbolic attitude, symbolic acts that can create an attitude in our country that will make it possible for us to be successful. We've got to engender among the American people a realization that it's a common, joint partnership effort, that it's not just something centered in the Federal Government, that it's not something for which we can blame business or industry or labor, but that it's a kind of pressure on our own economy that hurts us all, that's also caused by all of us, and which must be corrected by all of us.

I have a great additional responsibility when I come forward with the 1980 fiscal year budget to make sure that in its most carefully examined way that the analysis shows that it is equitable and fair. And if we err in giving one segment of our economy a special privilege, I want to be (sure)[1] that that segment is the one who needs the special privilege and the services of government most.

I think what we do in our own country will help greatly in other nations as well. The recent effort to strengthen the dollar, for instance, I think will be a major factor when a decision is made by the OPEC nations concerning the price of oil in the future. And the trade relationships that we have with Germany, with Japan, with Great Britain and other nations will be heavily affected in our favor if we show a determination, a resolve, an ability to

---

[1] Printed in the transcript.

correct economic problems that we ourselves have now identified so clearly.

The last thing I want to say to you is that I need your help. There's no way that a President or a Congress or a joint President and Congress or just labor unions or the National Association of Manufacturers or the National Chamber of Commerce can solve the inflation problem alone. A lot of people look to you for leadership in every one of the States represented here. And your clear voice speaking out in consonance with our own, to the extent that my own beliefs and commitments are compatible with yours, can be very, very helpful. I think that public officials, Governors, other elected officials at the State level, mayors, county officials can be very, very effective in dealing with the consequences of inflation.

The more we see each other moving against this threat, the more it strengthens each person's resolve. Politically it's a crucial question. If we fail to deal with our well-recognized economic problems, there will be an inevitable and justifiable adverse reaction among the American people, who look to us for leadership and for proper service. We can't continue to inflict the American people with rapidly increasing inflation and expect them to have confidence in us in the future.

So, it has the advantage, a successful campaign against inflation, of not only benefiting our Nation, not only being a responsibility that is on us individually and collectively, but also a great test of our worth as public servants who have been chosen by our fellow Americans to serve.

I don't intend to fail. It's a challenge that I accept without hesitation. It's part of my responsibility. And with your help I know I'll be successful. As I said to begin with, we're all in it together, and I'm proud to acknowledge that fact.

Thank you very much.

NOTE: The President spoke at 2:31 p.m. in the East Room at the White House.

Stuart E. Eizenstat, Assistant to the President for Domestic Affairs and Policy, and Alfred E. Kahn, Advisor to the President on Inflation, also spoke to the group.

United States Arms Transfer Levels

Statement by the President.
November 29, 1978

Conventional arms transfer restraint is an important objective of this administration and the Congress. To ensure U.S. leadership and to supplement existing legislation, I established for the first time a set of quantitative and qualitative standards by which arms transfer requests considered by this Government would be judged. The principal consideration in the application of these standards is whether the transfer in question promotes our security and the security of our close friends.

I am pleased to announce that this Government has kept its pledge to take the leadership in restraining arms sales. Under the ceiling I established, U.S. Government transfers of weapons and related items to countries other than NATO, Japan, Australia, and New Zealand, which totaled $8.54 billion in FY 1978, were reduced by 8 percent (or approximately $700 million measured in constant dollars) from the comparable FY 1977 level.

When I set this goal last year, I said that I would make further reductions in the next fiscal year. Today, I am announcing an additional cut of approximately $733 million* or 8 percent for FY 1979 measured in constant dollars. This means that for the fiscal year that began on October 1, 1978, and which will end on September 30, 1979, new commitments under the Foreign Military Sales (FMS) and Military Assistance (MAP) programs for weapons and weapons-related items to all countries except NATO, Japan, Australia, and New Zealand will not exceed $8.43 billion. This cut is consistent with our national security interests, including our historic interest in the security of the Middle East.

When I addressed the United Nations General Assembly in October 1977, I emphasized that the United States had taken the first steps at conventional arms restraint, but that we could not go very far alone. Multilateral cooperation remains essential to the achievement of meaningful restraint measures. We continue to believe that all nations have an interest in restraining transfers of conventional weaponry which threaten the stability of

---

*FY 1979 CEILING ON CONVENTIONAL ARMS TRANSFERS

(IN $ MILLIONS)

Fiscal year 1978 ceiling	$8, 551
Inflation (7.2 percent)	+616
Fiscal year 1978 ceiling in fiscal year 1979 dollars	9, 167
Policy reduction	−733
Fiscal year 1979 ceiling	8, 434

various regions of the world and divert recipient resources from other worthy objectives without necessarily enhancing national security. We are making a maximum effort to achieve multilateral cooperation on the arms restraint issue.

My decision on U.S. arms transfer levels for FY 1980 will depend on the degree of cooperation we receive in the coming year from other nations, particularly in the area of specific achievements and evidence of concrete progress on arms transfer restraint.

Budget Rescission and Deferrals

Message to the Congress.   November 30, 1978

To the Congress of the United States:

In accordance with the Impoundment Control Act of 1974, I herewith propose rescission of $75,000 in unneeded funds appropriated to the Foreign Claims Settlement Commission.

In addition, I am reporting four new deferrals of budget authority totalling $889 million and two revisions to previously transmitted deferrals increasing the amount deferred by $21.4 million in budget authority. These items involve the military assistance program and programs in the Departments of Commerce, Defense, Justice, and State.

The details of the rescission proposal and the deferrals are contained in the attached reports.

JIMMY CARTER

The White House,
    November 30, 1978.

NOTE: The attachments detailing the rescission and deferrals are printed in the FEDERAL REGISTER of December 6, 1978.

THE PRESIDENT'S NEWS CONFERENCE OF NOVEMBER 30, 1978

THE PRESIDENT. Good afternoon.

Mr. Cormier [Frank Cormier, Associated Press]?

ANTI-INFLATION PROGRAM

Q. Mr. President, if worse came to worse—and I know that you don't anticipate this eventuality—but if the choice came down to continuing the fight against inflation and reconciling yourself to being a one-term President, which choice would you make? [*Laughter*]

THE PRESIDENT. I would maintain the fight against inflation—and at the same time I would like to add a comment that I believe this is exactly what the American people want. Instead of being an unpopular act, I think it would be a popular act to maintain it. I think we will be successful in leveling off the rate of inflation and then bringing it down, and I don't see any adverse political consequences from doing so.

I'd like to add one other point, and that is that the decisions are not easy ones. As we go into a very tight 1980 fiscal year budget, I'm beginning to see more and more clearly how difficult it will be. But I intend to do it.

DEFENSE SPENDING; WEAPONS SYSTEMS

Q. On that subject, Mr. President, do plan to stay with your pledge to increase your defense budget by 3 percent despite your anti-inflation drive? And also on defense, there are published reports that you're going to change your nuclear strategy to focus more on massive retaliation. Is that true?

THE PRESIDENT. Well, let me answer the last part first. Our nuclear policy basically is one of deterrence; to take actions that are well known by the American people and well known by the Soviets and other nations; that any attack on us would result in devastating destruction by the nation which launched an attack against us. So, the basic policy is one of deterrence.

We, obviously, constantly assess the quality of our own nuclear weapon systems as times change, as technological advances are made, and as the change takes place in the Soviet Union's arsenal. We keep our weapons up to date; we improve our communications and command and information systems. But we will maintain basically a deterrent policy rather than to change the basic policy itself.

The other answer to your question is that our goal and that of other NATO nations is to increase the real level of defense expenditures. This is our goal. Each expenditure on defense, each system for which we spend the taxpayers' money will be much more carefully assessed this year to make sure that we are efficient and effective in the funds that we do expend.

Over the last number of years, including since I've been in office even, the percentage of our total budget and our gross national product that goes into defense has been decreasing. And at the conclusion of the budget cycle, when I make the budget public to the Congress and to the people in about 6 weeks, I know that I'll be responsible to make sure that the social and other domestic needs of our Nation are met, our international obligations are fulfilled, and an adequate defense is assured, and that there be a proper balance among these different, sometimes conflicting, demands.

So, I'll be responsible, and I will assure you and other Americans that when the budget is assessed that I will carry out my responsibilities well.

PEOPLE'S REPUBLIC OF CHINA

Q. Mr. President, I'd like to ask you about China. What is your timetable for reaching full normalization of relations with China, and have the recent events that are now going on in China—have those altered that policy? And do you envision China as a potential military ally at any time against the Soviet Union?

THE PRESIDENT. We don't have any intention of selling any weapons to either China or the Soviet Union. We are improving our relationships with the People's Republic of China as time goes on, even short of complete diplomatic normalization. Our goal, however, is to move toward normalization in accordance with the Shanghai Communique agreements. The attitude of China, the domestic situation in China, has changed, and we watch it with great interest.

TAX REDUCTION BILL

Q. Mr. President, the austerity budget you're now working on is for spending that begins October 1 of next year, as I understand it. In view of that, and in view of the inflationary pressure we have today, would it have been more effective to veto the tax bill, which would have had an immediate impact on the inflationary economy, rather than waiting until next October?

THE PRESIDENT. No, in balance, it would not have been good for our country. It might have had some tendency to control inflation, but at the same time, I think it would have added a tremendous additional tax burden on our people and restrained greatly the normal growth that

we anticipate maintaining throughout next year.

Our growth rate will be reduced somewhat, to maybe below 3 percent. I don't think we'll have a recession. But we took that into very careful account as we put together our overall anti-inflation program.

So, in balance, I decided to sign and to put into effect the tax reduction bill. I think in spite of that, maybe compatibly with that, we'll still be successful in adequately fighting inflation.

STRATEGIC WEAPONS SYSTEMS; CIVIL DEFENSE

Q. Mr. President, is it correct that you have decided to go ahead with the M-X mobile missile and the Trident II in the next budget? And will you comment on the suggestion that that decision, if you take it, the decision on civil defense, is actually a part of a plan to sort of pull the fangs of the anti-SALT people, that it's part of a SALT dance, rather than an independent action?

THE PRESIDENT. I don't think it's part of a SALT dance. I have not decided yet on what types of new weapons systems, if any, we will advocate in the 1980 fiscal year budget for our strategic arms arsenal.

The press reports about a $2 billion civil defense program have been completely erroneous, and I have never been able to find where the origin of that story might have derived. No proposal has even been made to me for a civil defense program of that magnitude.

We are considering the advisability of pursuing some civil defense assessments, including the fairly long-term evacuation of some of our major cities if we should think a nuclear war would be likely, which is obviously not a very likely project in itself, a proposal in itself.

But I have not yet decided when to move on the M-X or if to move on the M-X, what to do about making sure that our present silo missiles are secure. The Soviet missiles, as have ours in recent years, have been improved in their quality, particularly in their accuracy. And this makes the one leg of our so-called triad more vulnerable, that is, the fixed silo missiles.

We are addressing this question with a series of analyses, but I've not yet made a decision on how to do it.

FORMER PRESIDENT NIXON

Q. Mr. President, what do you think about Richard Nixon beginning to speak out on the public issues? Could this become a problem for you?

THE PRESIDENT. I think Mr. Nixon has the same right to speak out as any other American, and it doesn't cause me any concern.

ANTI-INFLATION PROGRAM

Q. Mr. President, there have been a number of reports about the problems that the people who are running your anti-inflation program have been having, and we are now being told that the wage and price guidelines are going to be modified in some cases. How satisfied are you at this point with the way the program has gotten off the ground? And how concerned are you that some of this early confusion is going to make it more difficult to get people to comply with it?

THE PRESIDENT. I am satisfied with the way the anti-inflation program has commenced. Alfred Kahn, who is heading up the entire program, until a week or 10 days ago—I've forgotten the exact time— was completing his service as the Chairman of the Civil Aeronautics Board, and

it's only been that brief period where he's been full-time on the job.

In accordance with the law of our country, whenever new proposals are promulgated from an administrative point of view, as have been the anti-inflation proposals, they have to be published. And after a certain period of time for requisite public comment among those who are most directly affected by a regulation, then the regulations are made final. The time for that public comment has not yet terminated. It won't be until the end of this week. So, as is always the case, as is required by law, we are now in the phase of letting the public and interested groups respond to the proposals that have been made.

I might say that we are moving expeditiously on the anti-inflation effort. My guidelines, expressed to the public in an evening television address, have not been modified at all. Obviously, with more than a thousand different kinds of decisions to be made, there will be some flexibility. And the reason for this public discussion, as I say again, required by law, is to let special groups that might be affected in an unanticipated way have an opportunity to present their case before the regulations are made final.

FORMER PRESIDENT NIXON; HUMAN RIGHTS

Q. Mr. President, I'd like to follow up on Mr. Sperling's [Godfrey Sperling, Jr., Christian Science Monitor] question and ask a more specific Nixon question, if I could.

He was at Oxford University today, and he said of your human rights policy, quite critically, that it is designed to win a lot of publicity and votes, but it won't achieve results. I was wondering if you'd care to respond to that criticism. And secondly, do you see the events in China as an outcome of your human rights policy?

THE PRESIDENT. I could make a career out of responding to all the criticisms—[*laughter*]—that are made and comments made by other political figures, even including ex-Presidents. I don't intend to do so.

I personally think the human rights policy of our Government is well advised and has had broad-ranging, beneficial effect. I don't claim credit for the American human rights policy when political prisoners are released from certain countries or when those countries move toward more democratic means, or even when—as is in the case of China now—there are public and apparently permitted demands or requests for more democratic government policies and enhanced human rights.

But I think our policy is right. It's well founded. It's one that I will maintain tenaciously, and I think it's demonstrated around the world that it's already had good effect.

RELIGIOUS CULTS

Q. Mr. President, I want to ask about Guyana. Do you think that the nature of that cult says anything about America? And secondly, what can the Government do to avoid future Jonestowns?

THE PRESIDENT. Well, I obviously don't think that the Jonestown cult was typical in any way of America. I think these were people who became obsessed with a particular leader's philosophy. They were obviously misled; a tragedy resulted. It did not take place in our own country. In retrospect, all of us can deplore what did occur.

It's unconstitutional for the Government of our country to investigate or to issue laws against any group—no matter how much they might depart from nor-mal custom—which is based on religious belief. The only exception is when there is some substantive allegation that the activities of those religious groups directly violate a Federal law.

I might point out that Congressman Ryan and other Congressmen did go to the Justice Department several weeks or months ago to go into the so-called brainwashing aspects of a few religious cults around the country. My understanding is that the so-called People's Temple was not one of those thought by them at that time to be indulging in brainwashing. It was a recent, late development that no one, so far as I know, was able to anticipate or assess adequately.

So, I don't think that we ought to have an overreaction because of the Jonestown tragedy by injecting government into trying to control people's religious beliefs. And I believe that we also don't need to deplore on a nationwide basis the fact that the Jonestown cult, so-called, was typical of America, because it's not.

EGYPTIAN-ISRAELI PEACE NEGOTIATIONS

Q. Mr. President, where do we stand on a Middle East accord between Egypt and Israel, and what can you or are you doing to try to bring the two parties together?

THE PRESIDENT. Well, we are negotiating and communicating with both the leaders of Israel and Egypt on a constant and sustained basis. I have been dissatisfied and disappointed at the length of time required to bring about a peace treaty that was signed by both Israel and Egypt. I've already outlined in the past my assessment of why this delay has taken place, as contrasted with Camp David. I'm not dealing directly with the principals simultaneously, and a lot of the negotiation has, unfortunately, been conducted through the press because of political reasons, domestically speaking, or other reasons.

Although I'm somewhat discouraged, we are certainly not going to give up on the effort. Tomorrow, I will be meeting with the Prime Minister of Egypt, Mr. Khalil, who's coming, I understand, with a personal message to me from President Sadat.

We have a need, obviously, to get a treaty text pinned down and approved by both governments, and to resolve the very difficult question of the so-called linkage, whether or not certain acts in the West Bank, Gaza Strip have to be taking place at the same time the Sinai agreement is consummated.

But regardless of temporary disappointments and setbacks that we've experienced since Camp David, they are no more serious nor of any greater concern than some that I experienced at Camp David. And we will continue to pursue our efforts to bring about a peace treaty there.

My reason for what optimism I keep is that I know for certain that both President Sadat and Prime Minister Begin want a peace treaty. I know that their people want a peace treaty. And I think as long as this determination on their part is extant, that our own good offices are very likely to be fruitful. So, I will continue the effort, no matter how difficult it might be in the future.

THE NATION'S ECONOMY

Q. Mr. President, it seems that we are all being asked to settle basically for our present standard of living, something that we don't find easy to accept after all these years of expecting more. And does it seem, indeed, from your anti-inflation program, that either one has to get a promotion or

increase his or her productivity greatly; otherwise there could be no more money? And how important is an acceptance of that to the success of your wage-price standards?

THE PRESIDENT. Well, we anticipate that America will continue to be strong, viable, prosperous, progressive, growing in the quality of life of our own citizens measured in a multifaceted way. We don't anticipate a recession or depression next year. The free enterprise system of our country will still reward outstanding effort or outstanding ability, or perhaps good fortune on occasion, and I see no reason for despair at all.

Most people, many people, look upon an effort to control inflation as a negative or adverse factor in our country's life. I don't look on it that way. It takes a strong, viable, dynamic, confident nation to deal successfully with the question of inflation.

This is not something that has recently arisen as a problem. The last 10 years we've had an inflation rate of about $6\frac{1}{2}$ percent, and I just think now it's time for us to make every effort we can to correct it. But I don't think that the American people need to fear that if we are successful in controlling inflation that their lives are going to be constrained or less pleasant or prosperous in the future.

My belief is that to the extent that we are successful in controlling inflation, the quality of life of Americans will be enhanced, not hurt.

SOVIET MIG–23's IN CUBA

Q. Mr. President, I'd like to ask you about the MIG's in Cuba. Have you come to a decision yet on whether the MIG–23's in Cuba represent any increased threat to the United States? Have you asked the Russians to take them out? And do you believe the 1962 understandings with the Soviet Union have been violated?

THE PRESIDENT. There have been MIG–23's in Cuba for a long time. There is a model of the MIG–23 that's been introduced there late last spring which we have been observing since that time.

We would consider it to be a very serious development if the Soviet Union violated the 1962 agreement. When we have interrogated the Soviet Union through diplomatic channels, they have assured us that no shipments of weapons to the Cubans have or will violate the terms of the 1962 agreement. We will monitor their compliance with this agreement very carefully, which we have been doing in the past, both as to the quality of weapons sent there and the quantity of weapons sent there, to be sure that there is no offensive threat to the United States possible from Cuba.

I might add that we have no evidence at all, no allegation that atomic weapons are present in Cuba.

IRAN

Q. Mr. President, is there any reason that you feel that the Shah is justifiably in trouble with his people?

THE PRESIDENT. Well, I think the Shah understands the situation in Iran very clearly and the reasons for some of the problems that he has experienced recently. He has moved forcefully and aggressively in changing some of the ancient religious customs of Iran, for instance, and some of the more conservative or traditional religious leaders deplore this change substantially. Others of the Iranian citizens who are in the middle class, who have a new prosperity brought about by enhanced oil prices and extra income coming into the country, I think, feel that they ought to have a greater share of the

voice in determining the affairs of Iran. Others believe that the democratization of Iran ought to proceed more quickly.

The Shah, as you know, has offered the opposition groups a place in a coalition government. They have rejected that offer and demand more complete removal from the Shah of his authority.

We trust the Shah to maintain stability in Iran, to continue with the democratization process, and also to continue with the progressive change in the Iranian social and economic structure. But I don't think either I or any other national leader could ever claim that we have never made a mistake or have never misunderstood the attitudes of our people. We have confidence in the Shah, we support him and his efforts to change Iran in a constructive way, moving toward democracy and social progress. And we have confidence in the Iranian people to make the ultimate judgments about their own government.

We do not have any intention of interfering in the internal affairs of Iran, and we do not approve any other nation interfering in the internal affairs of Iran.

DEPARTMENT OF ENERGY

Q. The General Accounting Office is currently working on a report to Congress criticizing the Department of Energy intensely for failing to follow through with enforcing some pricing regulations on oil, and, in particular, failing to follow up on some oil fraud situations in Texas that GAO says Department of Energy was aware of 2 or 3 years ago.

What do you think about that, and what do you intend to do to increase the Department of Energy's enforcing actions?

THE PRESIDENT. I'm not familiar with the particular late development that you described, if it is a late development. I know in the past, earlier this year, on several occasions the Department of Energy has taken very strong action to require some of the oil companies to repay consumers or to pay actual fines when they have violated the laws of the American Government.

My own position is probably predictable to you. I will do everything I can to enforce the law and to assure that any members of my Cabinet or any agencies enforce it also. But I'm not familiar with the specific allegation that you described.

Q. If I could follow up, the General Accounting Office report is supposed to come out sometime in December. This is a new report——

THE PRESIDENT. Oh, I see.

Q. ——which is going to say the Department of Energy has consistently failed to respond to these previous reports.

THE PRESIDENT. Well, I would obviously want them to comply completely with the law and do it very rapidly.

CIVIL SERVICE REORGANIZATION

Q. Mr. President, I was looking at the employment figures for the Federal Government. It looks like there are 6,000 more employees now than when you took office, and depending on how you look at it, it looks like there's a net increase in Government agencies—I don't mean advisory commissions, but Government agencies. Now, what's happened to your program to streamline the Government?

THE PRESIDENT. Well, I think we've streamlined it considerably. I would like to go out of office having had no increase in the total Federal employment in spite of the natural and inevitable growth in services delivered to the American people. Some of the mandated programs that I ask Congress to approve by law are expanded by the Congress in a proper way,

but more than I would originally have proposed. And sometimes a program is put forward by the Congress that I did not advocate, that I accept, sometimes reluctantly, sometimes with enthusiasm. But I think that we have made the Government much more efficient.

The new move toward civil service reform is a good example of that potential progress in the future. It's a new law that's just gone into effect. In addition to that, we've put forward five or six reorganization plans, all of which have been approved overwhelmingly by the Congress.

So, my expectation and my goal is to complete my own service as President with substantially enhanced delivery of service to the American people and with no increase in the total employment of the Federal Government.

INTELLIGENCE ACTIVITIES

Q. Mr. President, when you came to office, there was a lot of criticism of the intelligence agencies about the methods they were using, and now since the Iran thing there's a good deal of criticism, it seems, about their evaluation.

How concerned were you about the intelligence evaluations in Iran? And could you give us a general comment about what you think the state of the intelligence arts is today?

THE PRESIDENT. I've said several times that one of the pleasant surprises of my own administration has been the high quality of work done by the intelligence community. When I interrogate them about a specific intelligence item or when I get general assessments of intelligence matters, I've been very pleased with the quality of their work.

Recently, however, I have been concerned that the trend that was established about 15 years ago to get intelligence from electronic means might have been overemphasized, sometimes to the detriment of the assessment of the intelligence derived and also the intelligence derived through normal political channels, not secret intelligence; sometimes just the assessment of public information that's known in different countries around the world. And recently I wrote a note—which is my custom; I write several every day—to the National Security Council, the State Department, and the CIA leaders, and asked them to get together with others and see how we could improve the quality of our assessment program and also, particularly, political assessments.

Since I've been in office, we have substantially modified the order of priorities addressed by the intelligence community in its totality. When I became President, I was concerned, during the first few months, that quite often the intelligence community itself set its own priorities. As a supplier of intelligence information, I felt that the customers, the ones who receive the intelligence information, including the Defense Department, myself, and others, ought to be the ones to say, "This is what we consider to be most important." That effort has been completed, and it's now working very well.

So, to summarize, there is still some progress to be made. I was pleased with the intelligence community's work when I first came into office, and it's been improved since I became President.

MR. CORMIER. Thank you, Mr. President.

THE PRESIDENT. Thank you, Frank, very much. Thank you, everybody.

NOTE: President Carter's fortieth news conference began at 4 p.m. in Room 450 of the Old Executive Office Building. It was broadcast live on radio and television.

The Cyprus Conflict

Message to the Congress Reporting on Progress Toward a Negotiated Settlement. November 30, 1978

To the Congress of the United States:

In accordance with the provisions of Public Law 95–384, I am reporting on progress made toward the conclusion of a negotiated solution to the Cyprus problem.

While direct negotiations between the two Cypriot communities under the auspices of the United Nations Secretary General have not yet resumed, there is a growing awareness, especially among the parties directly concerned, that the time is now ripe for determined action designed to break the Cyprus deadlock. Moreover, it is increasingly accepted that a just and lasting settlement can come only through intensive, sustained face-to-face negotiations. Public statements, general resolutions and intermittent talks are not adequate to solve the Cyprus problem. For this reason our recent efforts have concentrated on encouraging the two Cypriot parties to work with the Secretary General of the United Nations on an early reconvening of intercommunal talks. Repeal of the Turkish arms embargo has created fresh opportunities for progress on the Cyprus issue.

Secretary of State Vance spoke of this policy before the United Nations General Assembly on September 29. "We would welcome and actively support," he said, "a renewed effort by Secretary General Waldheim to help the parties reach agreement on a sovereign, bicommunal, nonaligned federal Republic of Cyprus." To back up this call, Administration officials have been conferring with high-level representatives of both Cypriot communities, with the Turkish, Greek and other friendly governments, and also with principal officers of the United Nations Secretariat. I had a useful discussion of the Cyprus issue with President Kyprianou on October 6, and Secretary Vance met with President Kyprianou, Turkish Cypriot leader Denktash, and the Foreign Ministers of Greece and Turkey on the margin of the United Nations General Assembly.

These contacts and many others have given us a fairly clear picture of the practical possibilities for forward movement and of the aims and objectives of the two sides. Both Greek and Turkish Cypriots have underscored to us their desire to see a resumption of negotiations, although they still differ on how to do it.

In our talks with the Cypriot parties and with United Nations officials, we have gone into some detail on how to bridge the gap between the parties, so as to arrive at a mutually acceptable basis for negotiations. We cannot yet tell whether the efforts of our government, Secretary General Waldheim, and other friendly governments will bear fruit, but we are doing our best to encourage regular intercommunal negotiations early in the new year.

After the arms embargo repeal, the Government of Turkey restated its desire to help negotiate a rapid resolution of the Cyprus problem. Moreover, in his speech to the United Nations General Assembly on October 3, Turkish Foreign Minister Okcun reconfirmed his Government's commitment to withdrawing all of its armed forces from Cyprus, except those mutually agreed upon by the parties concerned, in connection with a final settlement. We believe that Turkey will do its best to help the Secretary General bring about a resumption of the intercommunal negotiations.

The annual General Assembly debate on the Cyprus question took place in the United Nations during the week of November 6. The United States Representa-

tive stated that "enhancing the prospects for sustained and productive negotiations should be our foremost objective," and that, "All parties interested in promoting a settlement on Cyprus should now concentrate their efforts on encouraging these talks and fostering an atmosphere that will contribute to their success." The United States abstained on the resolution adopted by the General Assembly because it contained elements which were clearly not conducive to a resumption of negotiations. As this report was being prepared the Cyprus question was also being considered within the Security Council.

JIMMY CARTER

The White House,
    November 30, 1978.

Sugars, Sirups, and Molasses Imports
Proclamation 4610.   November 30, 1978

MODIFICATION OF QUOTAS ON CERTAIN SUGARS, SIRUPS, AND MOLASSES

By the President of the United States of America

A Proclamation

1. By Proclamation 4334 of November 16, 1974, the President modified Subpart A, Part 10, Schedule 1 of the Tariff Schedules of the United States (19 U.S.C. 1202, hereinafter referred to as the "TSUS") to establish, effective January 1, 1975, following expiration of the Sugar Act of 1948, rates of duty and a quota applicable to sugars, sirups and molasses described in items 155.20 and 155.30 of the TSUS. The President subsequently modified the rates of duty by Proclamation 4463 of September 21, 1976, Procla-

mation 4466 of October 4, 1976, and Proclamation 4539 of November 11, 1977.

2. The President took these actions pursuant to authority vested in him by the Constitution and statutes of the United States, including section 201(a)(2) of the Trade Expansion Act of 1962 (19 U.S.C. 1821(a)(2)), and in conformity with Headnote 2 of Subpart A of Part 10 of Schedule 1 of the TSUS, hereinafter referred to as the "Headnote." The Headnote was part of a trade agreement which embodied the results of the "Kennedy Round" of international trade negotiations. That agreement is known formally as the 1967 Geneva Protocol to the General Agreement on Tariffs and Trade, and the agreement includes, as an Annex, "Schedule XX," a schedule of United States trade concessions made during those negotiations. This agreement was concluded pursuant to section 201(a) of the Trade Expansion Act of 1962 (19 U.S.C. 1821(a)), and was implemented by Proclamation No. 3822, of December 16, 1967 (82 Stat. 1455) which, *inter alia*, added the Headnote to the TSUS.

3. The Headnote provides, in relevant part, as follows:

"(i) . . . if the President finds that a particular rate not lower than such January 1, 1968, rate, limited by a particular quota, may be established for any articles provided for in item 155.20 or 155.30, which will give due consideration to the interests in the United States sugar market of domestic producers and materially affected contracting parties to the General Agreement on Tariffs and Trade, he shall proclaim such particular rate and such quota limitation, . . .

"(ii) . . . any rate and quota limitation so established shall be modified if the President finds and proclaims that such modification is required or appropriate to give effect to the above considerations; . . ."

4. Section 201(a)(2) of the Trade Expansion Act authorizes the President to proclaim the modification or continuance of any existing duty or other import restrictions, or such additional import restrictions as he determines to be required or appropriate to carry out any trade agreement entered into under the authority of that Act, except that pursuant to section 201(b)(2) of the Act, the President may not by proclamation increase a rate of duty to a rate more than 50 percent above the rate existing on July 1, 1934.

5. I find that the modifications hereinafter proclaimed of the quota applicable to items 155.20 and 155.30 of the TSUS are appropriate to carry out the International Sugar Agreement, 1977, and that portion of the Kennedy Round Trade agreement set forth in the Headnote, and as provided for in the Headnote, give due consideration to the interests in the United States sugar market of domestic producers and materially affected contracting parties to the General Agreement on Tariffs and Trade.

Now, THEREFORE, I, JIMMY CARTER, President of the United States of America, acting under the authority vested in me by the Constitution and statutes, including section 201 of the Trade Expansion Act of 1962, and in conformity with Headnote 2, Subpart A of Part 10 of Schedule 1, of the TSUS, do hereby proclaim until otherwise superseded by law:

A. Headnote 3 of Subpart A, Part 10, Schedule 1 of the TSUS is modified to provide as follows:

(3) The total amount of sugars, sirups, and molasses described in items 155.20 and 155.30, the products of all foreign countries, entered, or withdrawn from warehouse, for consumption in any calendar year shall not exceed, in the aggregate, 6,900,000 short tons, raw value. Of this quantity, not more than 210,987 short

tons, raw value, the product of the Republic of China, and not more than 150,544 short tons, raw value, in the aggregate, the products of all foreign countries other than Argentina, Australia, Bangladesh, Barbados, Belize, Bolivia, Brazil, Bulgaria, Canada, Costa Rica, Cuba, Republic of China, Dominican Republic, Ecuador, Egypt, El Salvador, Fiji, Finland, German Democratic Republic, Guatemala, Guyana, Honduras, Hungary, India, Indonesia, Iraq, Jamaica, Japan, Kenya, Republic of Korea, Madagascar, Malawi, Mauritius, Mexico, Mozambique, New Zealand, Nicaragua, Norway, Pakistan, Panama, Paraguay, Peru, Philippines, Portugal, Singapore, South Africa, St. Christopher-Nevis-Anguilla, Swaziland, Sweden, Thailand, Trinidad and Tobago, Uganda, Union of Soviet Socialist Republics, Venezuela, and Yugoslavia, may be entered, or withdrawn from warehouse for consumption in the period between January 1, 1978 and December 31, 1979, inclusive. For the purposes of this headnote, the term "raw value" means the equivalent of such articles in terms of ordinary commercial raw sugar testing 96 degrees by the polariscope as determined in accordance with regulations issued by the Secretary of the Treasury. The principal grades and types of sugar shall be translated into terms of raw value in the following manner:

(i) For articles described in item 155.20, by multiplying the number of pounds thereof by the greater of 0.93, or 1.07 less 0.0175 for each degree of polarization under 100 degrees (and fractions of a degree in proportion).

(ii) For articles described in item 155.-30, by multiplying the number of pounds of the total sugars thereof (the sum of the sucrose and reducing or invert sugars) by 1.07.

(iii) The Secretary of the Treasury shall establish methods for translating sugar into terms of raw value for any special grade or type of sugar for which he determines that the raw value cannot be measured adequately under the above provisions.

B. The provisions of this proclamation shall become effective with respect to articles entered, or withdrawn from warehouse, for consumption on and after the date of publication of this Proclamation in the FEDERAL REGISTER, except that articles which were released under the provisions of section 448(b) of Tariff Act of 1930 (19 U.S.C. 1448(b)) prior to such date shall not be denied entry.

IN WITNESS WHEREOF, I have hereunto set my hand this thirtieth day of November, in the year of our Lord nineteen hundred seventy-eight, and of the Independence of the United States of America the two hundred and third.

JIMMY CARTER

[Filed with the Office of the Federal Register, 2:23 p.m., December 1, 1978]

NOTE: The text of the proclamation was released on December 1.

Federal Initiatives in Rural Areas

Remarks at a White House Briefing for Representatives of Rural Areas. December 1, 1978

This is one group with whom I feel at home.

I was thinking, during lunch, when I was contemplating coming over here to meet with you, that perhaps the two most exciting and gratifying days of my life was when they turned on the electric lights in our house when I was 13 or 14 years old, and when I was inaugurated as President. I think even the days that followed turning on the electric lights, everything was still pleasant. I can't say the same thing about being inaugurated as President. [*Laughter*]

The national Rural Electric Cooperatives have always been close to me, and to my family, as you well know. Those of you who know anything about my background realize this. The formation of the REA during the late thirties opened up a new opportunity for an expanded and productive life. My own family's knowledge and awareness and influence expanded beyond the boundaries of our farm, really for the first time.

My father was an original REA director and frequently in order to fight for the life of the embryonic group, would come to Washington to go to national conventions, marshal the efforts of other farmers, interested groups, and it added a new dimension to his life, and ultimately to mine, as well.

My own sense is that I and my administration have almost complete compatibility with the purposes of the rural electrics today. There may be times when, because of an absence of communication or a difference in technique or perhaps a time schedule, that we don't completely agree on how to address controversial problems, or how to deal with pressures or questions that confront us all. But there's a basic compatibility which I want to maintain and also to enhance and to strengthen.

One of the prerequisites for achieving common purposes is to have constant understanding and communication. I think if you understand what our desires are, what our programs are, what our time schedules are, what our budget constraints are, it's much easier for you to cooperate with us and to help us achieve those common ideals and goals. If there's a doubt or uncertainty or perhaps misinformation on which you base your own assessments, then the concerns are not only unwarranted, but they also prevent our acting in common to improve the quality of life of people who look to you and to me for leadership.

This afternoon you'll get a fairly thorough briefing, to the extent that you desire it, from the leaders in my own administration—Community Services, Labor, Agriculture, of course, Energy, White House staff, and others. And I want you to take full advantage of this to the extent that you are willing and able. We've got some distinguished congressional leaders here, as well, who share with you and me the responsibility for improving the quality of life in small cities and towns, on the farms and ranches of our country.

In many ways, we detect and live with a broad range of interrelated responsibilities: environmental quality, conservation, education, housing, health, transportation, international trade arrangements, the improvement of net income for farm families, enhancing the export of agricultural products, reducing or perhaps even eliminating the disharmonies that sometimes exist between growing suburban regions served by you and the urban regions which also house Americans about whom we are concerned. These kinds of things bind us together, and I think a realization of the complexity of the issues is important for us all.

I know enough about your own background, your own commitments, your own history, your own statesmanship to realize that you have never taken a narrowly focused and selfish position on issues that affect America. It would be easy for you to do it, but you've never done it. And I know in basic considerations of national defense, international relations, what's best for our major cities, you representing the rural areas of our country have always taken an enlightened and constructive and unselfish position.

I have tried since I've been in office to eliminate some of the obstacles that have prevailed in the past which prevent better services by your government and my government for the people who look to you and me for guidance and for leadership and for service. We've tried to eliminate paperwork. We've tried to tear down the barriers that have separated one Federal agency from another and, in the process, have made congressionally mandated programs less effective, and which have at the same time made it much more difficult for Americans who deserve service to acquire it.

This afternoon, we are announcing, to some degree coincidentally with your visit, some improvements in water and sewage grant procedures. We have about a $2½ billion program to give those Americans who don't have adequate water and sewage facilities that opportunity for a better and healthier life.

In the past we've not had common application forms, common accounting forms, common requirements among EPA, EDA, and the Farm Home Administration. That is being corrected.

In the past there have been 16—at least 16—different Federal agencies that prescribed standards that had to be met before progress could be made in meeting these needs of rural people. In the future that will not be the case. There will be one central clearing procedure, and then the standards of all 16 agencies will assume to have been met.

We are trying to take full advantage of employment opportunities in the Department of Labor and perhaps other agencies as well, to prescribe, with a maximum saving for American people, human, additional services in the rural areas to make sure that the people who need a better life can have access effectively to Government programs. We'll be adding about 1,700 or so—I think 1,750—additional employees, without any increase in Federal budget requirements, that will deal

specifically with the alleviation of obstacles that have separated rural communities from a better life.

I won't pursue that any further, because you'll get more specific details about it later. But I would like to close my own remarks by saying that almost every decision made here in the White House over in the Oval Office or by the Congress affects you and the people whom you serve.

Recently in this very room I signed into law five major pieces of legislation establishing for the first time a basis for a national energy policy. Those bills were extremely complicated. They were the final result of tough negotiations by a wide range of interest groups. They had to accommodate even tiny, geographical, unique problems where the Congress had to say, "We don't want to mistreat a particular county in their method of production of natural gas or oil or their special requirements." They deal with electric power production and encourage conservation, shift toward the use of more plentiful supplies of fuels, and also, of course, open the way for research and development to develop new supplies of energy in the years to come.

These legislative acts must be thoroughly studied and understood by you, because along with TVA and other major cooperative groups, you will be directly affected by how these new laws will be administered. And I don't want to make a mistake; I don't want Jim Schlesinger and others to make a mistake in failing to accommodate the special needs that you might have or the special advice and counsel and constructive criticism that you might offer. And if you wait until after a regulation is promulgated or a decision is made, quite often it's very difficult to modify that decision. But if, in the initial stages of the formulation of a policy, your voice is heard and your opinions are assessed, we can much more easily prevent a mistake and make the administration of these laws much more successful.

I might point out that there has been some concern expressed from some of you that this administration has an antinuclear power policy. We do not. I've not done much graduate work, but all my graduate work was done in nuclear engineering. I was one of the very earliest Americans who worked on the development of a way to use nuclear power for peaceful purposes, to produce electricity, power to propel ships. And I still have a strong commitment to the use of nuclear power.

It should be, obviously, produced in a way that's safe, and we've done that in our country. It should be economically feasible, and we are constantly exploring ways to make it more efficient. And, of course, it should be explained very clearly to the American people. We don't want to waste money. And we need to draw a careful delineation between the allocation of major funds for research and development, for systems that might be beneficial in years to come, compared to investments in practical tests or pilot projects that can be assessed at this time.

This principle not only applies to nuclear power but to many others as well; new ways to get photoelectric power generated, new ways to burn coal efficiently and cleanly, even new ways to produce hydroelectric power more efficiently.

Our water projects, which has been a highly controversial issue, is one that we approached with some concern and trepidation. But I think the outcome of a new water policy will be that when we do have Federal funds available to spend—and they're always limited—that they can be spent on projects that are of the highest

possible priority for our country, to make sure that wasteful projects are not built, ones of doubtful advocacy or advisability are not built, but that we do allot those funds in an open and clear way, with an increased involvement by local people like yourselves, that we will make the right decision; and that just because a project was approved 15 or 20 years ago by a then senior Member of Congress, that it doesn't work its way up to the top and find itself built when other projects are much more desirable, much more needed to serve the people that you yourselves represent.

I might also alleviate some concerns. There will be no proposal made to eliminate the REA loan program. There will be no proposals made to move REA out of Agriculture. And whenever you have a concern about a rumor like this that gets started and then has a life of its own, I hope that you will come directly to see me with a delegation or your own very, very fine representatives here in Washington, and put a stop to that kind of rumor once and for all.

I think that you know that Bob Bergland would not mislead you in any way; neither would I. None of us have any inclination to mislead you. And when that kind of concern arises, it seems to fester like a sore, and it needs to be nipped in the bud immediately. And if, on occasion, there is some concern that is legitimate, I have no trepidation about letting you know that we are considering this. We'll work very closely with you in the alleviation of a problem. You'll be partners of ours and not someone who hears about a decision that affects your lives after it's too late for you to change it. I'll never do that. It would be a very serious mistake for me as President to try to evolve any change in the Federal laws, or any major change in the regulations that are issued, or procedures to be followed that affect you, without working it out harmoniously with you and letting you be an integral part of the decisionmaking process.

I'm not here trying to make mistakes. I'm here to avoid making mistakes and to make sure that when I do make a decision, that it is sound and best for our country. And having your counsel and your advice and your participation in making these kinds of decisions is an integral part of my own life as President.

I might say one other thing: I look on you as full partners with me. Almost all of you share a common background with me, having started life in a different world, sometimes with very severe restraints on the quality of our own outlook, with limited spheres of influence. And everyone in this room has now become an acknowledged leader because of ambition, because of good fortune, because of the trust placed in us by our friends, neighbors who have shared a common purpose. I enjoy that same relationship as well.

So, we are partners. We have temporary and transient concerns. We are fighting hard to control inflation. It'll be my top domestic priority for this year. It's a problem that we have suffered for the last 10 years. And it's time for us to do something about it. Budget constraints will be severe. The deficit is going to be cut. And I need your help in this respect as well.

So, in everything that I do, I won't have any hesitancy to call on you to help me achieve the goals that we established for our Nation. And I hope you feel the same ease in asking me to help you when you have a goal to achieve for people whom you serve as well.

We've got a great, strong country. When we do have temporary unemployment, temporary inflationary pressures, temporary budget constraints, we should remember that our Nation is still the strongest on Earth. It's the strongest economically.

We have the best political system, the finest free enterprise system on Earth. We're the strongest militarily, and we're going to stay that way.

Thank you very much.

NOTE: The President spoke at 1:15 p.m. in the East Room at the White House.

Congressional Visit to the People's Republic of China

Announcement of the Visit by a Bipartisan Congressional Delegation. December 1, 1978

The Chinese People's Institute of Foreign Affairs of the People's Republic of China has invited a bipartisan congressional delegation to visit China during December.

The delegation will depart December 1 and return December 18. The group will be led by Senator Harrison A. Williams, Jr., Democrat of New Jersey, who will be accompanied by his wife.

Other members of the group include Senators Henry Bellmon (R-Okla.), Howard Cannon (D-Nev.), Dale Bumpers (D-Ark.), and Donald Riegle, Jr., (D-Mich.), who will be accompanied by their wives.

The Senators will be accompanied by Robert N. Thomson, Special Assistant for Congressional Liaison; Walter Ramsay, Senator Williams' legislative assistant; and Dr. Jerome Korcak, Robert Perito, and Fran Hess, Department of State.

Since the first congressional delegation went to the People's Republic of China in 1972, more than 100 Members of Congress have visited China.

The exchange relationship fulfills that part of the Shanghai Communique in which both sides pledged to foster broader understanding and engage in cultural and scientific exchanges.

This will be the fourth congressional delegation to visit China in 1978.

Designation of National Monuments in Alaska

Statement by the President.
December 1, 1978

Our Nation has been uniquely blessed with a vast land of great natural beauty and abundant resources. Once these gifts seemed limitless. As our people have spread across the continent and the needs for development reach once distant frontiers, we realize how urgent it is to preserve our heritage for future generations.

Today I have taken several actions to protect Alaska's extraordinary Federal lands. Because of the risks of immediate damage to these magnificent areas, I felt it was imperative to protect all of these lands and preserve for the Congress an unhampered opportunity to act next year.

Passing legislation to designate National Parks, Wildlife Refuges, Wilderness Areas, and Wild and Scenic Rivers in Alaska is the highest environmental priority of my administration. There is strong support for such legislation in the Congress. In the 95th Congress, the House of Representatives overwhelmingly passed an Alaska bill. A bill was reported out of the Senate committee, but time ran out and the Senate was unable to finally pass a bill. Because existing "d–2" land withdrawals under the 1971 Alaska Native Claims Settlement Act expire on December 17, much of the land to be protected by legislation would be unprotected and perhaps irrevocably lost if I did not act now.

Accordingly, along with Secretaries Andrus and Bergland, I have taken the following actions:

—I have signed proclamations under the Antiquities Act of 1906, designating as National Monuments 17 of the most critical areas proposed for legislative designation—13 proposed National Parks, two proposed Wildlife Refuges, and two proposed National Forest Wilderness areas.

These areas, totaling approximately 56 million acres, contain resources of unequalled scientific, historic, and cultural value, and include some of the most spectacular scenery and wildlife in the world. The Antiquities Act has been used in the past to preserve such treasures, for example by President Teddy Roosevelt, who designated the Grand Canyon in this way. The Monuments I have created in Alaska are worthy of the special, permanent protections provided by the Antiquities Act. They will remain permanent Monuments until the Congress makes other provisions for the land.

—I have directed Secretary Andrus to proceed with necessary steps to designate National Wildlife Refuges for the remaining 12 proposed refuge areas, an additional 40 million acres.

—Secretaries Andrus and Bergland have already taken steps under Section 204 of the Federal Land Policy and Management Act to withdraw or segregate all of the areas covered by either congressional or administration proposals from mineral entry and selection by the State of Alaska. I have directed that these withdrawals remain in place.

Each of the areas protected by these actions is exceptional and valuable. Among the treasures to be preserved are the Nation's largest pristine river valley, the place where man may first have come into the New World, a glacier as large

2111

as the State of Rhode Island, and the largest group of peaks over 15,000 feet in North America. Breeding areas of the Great Alaska brown bear, caribou, and Dall sheep, and of ducks, geese, and swans that migrate through the other 49 States each year will also be protected.

In addition to preserving these natural wonders, historical sites, and wildlife habitats, our actions will ensure that Alaskan Eskimos, Indians, and Aleuts can continue their traditional way of life, including hunting and fishing.

In Alaska we have a unique opportunity to balance the development of our vital resources required for continued economic growth with protection of our natural environment. We have the imagination and the will as a people to both develop our last great natural frontier and also preserve its priceless beauty for our children and grandchildren.

The actions I have taken today provide for urgently needed permanent protections. However, they are taken in the hope that the 96th Congress will act promptly to pass Alaska lands legislation.

Admiralty Island National Monument

Proclamation 4611.   December 1, 1978

By the President of the United States of America

A Proclamation

Admiralty Island is outstanding for its superlative combination of scientific and historic objects. Admiralty Island contains unique resources of scientific interest which need protection to assure continued opportunities for study.

Admiralty Island has been continuously inhabited by Tlingit Indians for approxi-

mately 10,000 years. Archeological sites and objects are plentiful in the areas of Angoon, Chaik Bay, Whitewater Bay and other bays and inlets on the island. These resources provide historical documentation of continuing value for study. The continued presence of these natives on the island add to the scientific and historical value of the area.

The cultural history of the Tlingit Indians is rich in ceremony and creative arts and complex in its social, legal and political systems. Admiralty provides a unique combination of archeological and historical resources in a relatively unspoiled natural ecosystem that enhances their value for scientific study.

Subsequent to exploration and mapping by Captain George Vancouver at the end of the 18th century, Russian fur traders, Yankee whalers, and miners and prospectors have left objects and sites on Admiralty which provide valuable historical documentation of white settlement and exploitation of the island and its resources. Admiralty Island is rich in historic structures and sites, including whaling stations, canneries, old mining structures and old village sites, for example, Killisnoo Village where a whaling and herring saltery station were established in 1880.

Unusual aspects of the island ecology include its exceptional distribution of animal species, including dense populations of brown bears and eagles, but excluding entirely—because of the island's separation from the mainland—a large number of species indigenous to the general area. This peculiar distribution enhances the island's value for scientific study.

The unique island ecology includes the highest known density of nesting bald eagles (more than are found in all the other States combined); large numbers of Alaska brown bear; and the largest unspoiled coastal island ecosystem in North

America. Admiralty Island was added to the Tongass National Forest in 1909, and specific portions of the island have been designated as bear and eagle management areas and numerous scientific studies of the bear and eagle habitat have been conducted by scientists from around the world. The island is an outdoor living laboratory for the study of the bald eagle and Alaska brown bear.

Protection of the entire island, exclusive of the Mansfield Peninsula, is necessary to preserve intact the unique scientific and historic objects and sites located there. Designation of a smaller area would not serve the scientific purpose of preserving intact this unique coastal island ecosystem.

Hunting and fishing shall continue to be regulated, permitted and controlled in accord with the statutory authorities applicable to the Monument area.

Section 2 of the Act of June 8, 1906 (34 Stat. 225, 16 U.S.C. 431), authorizes the President, in his discretion, to declare by public proclamation historic landmarks, historic and prehistoric structures, and other objects of historic or scientific interest that are situated upon the lands owned or controlled by the government of the United States to be National Monuments, and to reserve as part thereof parcels of land, the limits of which in all cases shall be confined to the smallest area compatible with the proper care and management of the objects to be protected.

Now, THEREFORE, I, JIMMY CARTER, President of the United States of America, by the authority vested in me by section 2 of the Act of June 8, 1906 (34 Stat. 225, 16 U.S.C. 431), do proclaim that there are hereby set apart and reserved as the Admiralty Island National Monument all lands, including submerged lands, and waters owned or controlled by the United States within the boundaries

of the area described on the document entitled "Admiralty Island National Monument (Copper River Meridian)", attached to and forming a part of this Proclamation. The area reserved consists of approximately 1,100,000 acres, and is the smallest area compatible with the proper care and management of the objects to be protected. Lands, including submerged lands, and waters within these boundaries not owned by the United States shall be reserved as a part of the Monument upon acquisition of title thereto by the United States.

All lands, including submerged lands, and all waters within the boundaries of this Monument are hereby appropriated and withdrawn from entry, location, selection, sale or other disposition under the public land laws, other than exchange. There is also reserved all water necessary to the proper care and management of those objects protected by this Monument and for the proper administration of the Monument in accordance with applicable laws.

The establishment of this Monument is subject to valid existing rights, including, but not limited to, valid selections under the Alaska Native Claims Settlement Act, as amended (43 U.S.C. 1601 *et seq.*), and under or confirmed in the Alaska Statehood Act (48 U.S.C. Note preceding Section 21).

Nothing in this Proclamation shall be deemed to revoke any existing withdrawal, reservation or appropriation, including any withdrawal under section 17 (d)(1) of the Alaska Native Claims Settlement Act (43 U.S.C. 1616(d)(1)); however, the National Monument shall be the dominant reservation. Nothing in this Proclamation is intended to modify or revoke the terms of the Memorandum of Understanding dated September 1, 1972, entered into between the State of Alaska and the United States as part of the negotiated settlement of *Alaska* v. *Morton*, Civil No. A–48–72 (D. Alaska, Complaint filed April 10, 1972).

Warning is hereby given to all unauthorized persons not to appropriate, injure, destroy or remove any feature of this Monument and not to locate or settle upon any of the lands thereof.

IN WITNESS WHEREOF, I have hereunto set my hand this first day of December, in the year of our Lord nineteen hundred and seventy-eight, and of the Independence of the United States of America the two hundred and third.

JIMMY CARTER

[Filed with the Office of the Federal Register, 2:53 p.m., December 1, 1978]

NOTE: The attachment and map detailing the boundaries of the Admiralty Island National Monument are printed in the FEDERAL REGISTER of December 5, 1978.

Aniakchak National Monument
Proclamation 4612.   December 1, 1978

By the President of the United States of America

A Proclamation

The Aniakchak Caldera is located in the heart of the Alaska Peninsula. It is so unexpected a feature that it remained unknown to all but the Natives of the region until about 1920. With its average diameter of approximately six miles, Aniakchak is one of the world's largest calderas.

In the interior of the caldera are textbook examples of certain volcanic features such as lava flows, cinder cones, and explosion pits. Also lying within the caldera is Surprise Lake which is fed by warm springs and is uniquely charged with chemicals. Surprise Lake is the source of the Aniakchak River, which cascades through a 1,500 foot gash in the caldera

wall and downward for 27 miles to the Pacific Ocean.

The flanks of the caldera provide a geological and biological continuum by which to make a comparative study of the formation of the caldera and the significant process of biological succession of both plant and animal species occurring in the vicinity of the caldera, an area that was rendered virtually devoid of life forms by a major eruption of the volcano in 1931.

The caldera is also climatologically unique in that, because of its topography and setting, it appears to be able to generate its own weather. A striking phenomenon known as cloud "niagaras" occurs frequently as strong downdrafts form over the caldera walls.

The land withdrawn and reserved by this Proclamation for the protection of the geological, biological, climatological and other phenomena enumerated above supports now, as it has in the past, the unique subsistence culture of the local residents. The continued existence of this culture, which depends on subsistence hunting, and its availability for study, enhance the historic and scientific values of the natural objects protected herein because of the ongoing interaction of the subsistence culture with those objects. Accordingly, the opportunity for local residents to engage in subsistence hunting is a value to be protected and will continue under the administration of the monument.

Section 2 of the Act of June 8, 1906 (34 Stat. 225, 16 U.S.C. 431), authorizes the President, in his discretion, to declare by public proclamation historic landmarks, historic and prehistoric structures, and other objects of historic or scientific interest that are situated upon the lands owned or controlled by the Government of the United States to be national monuments, and to reserve as part thereof parcels of land, the limits of which in all cases shall be confined to the smallest area compatible with the proper care and management of the objects to be protected.

Now, THEREFORE, I, JIMMY CARTER, President of the United States of America, by the authority vested in me by Section 2 of the Act of June 8, 1906 (34 Stat. 225, 16 U.S.C. 431), do proclaim that there are hereby set apart and reserved as the Aniakchak National Monument all lands, including submerged lands, and waters owned or controlled by the United States within the boundaries of the area depicted as the Aniakchak National Monument on the map numbered ANIA–90,006 attached to and forming a part of this Proclamation. The area reserved consists of approximately 350,000 acres, and is the smallest area compatible with the proper care and management of the objects to be protected. Lands, including submerged lands, and waters within these boundaries not owned by the United States shall be reserved as a part of the monument upon acquisition of title thereto by the United States.

All lands, including submerged lands, and all waters within the boundaries of this monument are hereby appropriated and withdrawn from entry, location, selection, sale or other disposition under the public land laws, other than exchange. There is also reserved all water necessary to the proper care and management of those objects protected by this monument and for the proper administration of the monument in accordance with applicable laws.

The establishment of this monument is subject to valid existing rights, including, but not limited to, rights confirmed in Section 15 of the Act of January 2, 1976 (89 Stat. 1145), and valid selections under the Alaska Native Claims Settlement Act, as amended (43 U.S.C. 1601 *et seq.*), and under or confirmed in the Alaska Statehood Act (48 U.S.C. Note preceding Section 21).

Nothing in this Proclamation shall be deemed to revoke any existing withdrawal, reservation or appropriation, including any withdrawal under Section 17(d)(1) of the Alaska Native Claims Settlement Act (43 U.S.C. 1616(d)(1)); however, the national monument shall be the dominant reservation. Nothing in this Proclamation is intended to modify or revoke the terms of the Memorandum of Understanding dated September 1, 1972, entered into between the State of Alaska and the United States as part of the negotiated settlement of *Alaska* v. *Morton,* Civil No. A–48–72 (D. Alaska, Complaint filed April 10, 1972).

The Secretary of the Interior shall promulgate such regulations as are appropriate, including regulation of the opportunity to engage in a subsistence lifestyle by local residents. The Secretary may close the national monument, or any portion thereof, to subsistence uses of a particular fish, wildlife or plant population if necessary for reasons of public safety, administration, or to ensure the natural stability or continued viability of such population.

Warning is hereby given to all unauthorized persons not to appropriate, injure, destroy or remove any feature of this monument and not to locate or settle upon any of the lands thereof.

IN WITNESS WHEREOF, I have hereunto set my hand this first day of December, in the year of our Lord nineteen hundred and seventy-eight, and of the Independence of the United States of America the two hundred and third.

JIMMY CARTER

[Filed with the Office of the Federal Register, 2:54 p.m., December 1, 1978]

NOTE: The maps detailing the boundaries of the Aniakchak National Monument are printed in the FEDERAL REGISTER of December 5, 1978.

Becharof National Monument

Proclamation 4613.   December 1, 1978

By the President of the United States of America

A Proclamation

This monument on the Alaska Peninsula supports one of the densest known populations of the great Alaska brown bear. This area encompasses habitat used by a discrete population of bears for denning and foraging, both north and south of Becharof Lake.

At the southern end of Becharof Lake, several hundred bears concentrate during salmon spawning season. Certain of the bears make their dens in the area on islands a few feet above the water level, a unique phenomenon of great interest in the study of this great carnivore. Deeply worn bear trails also indicate decades of extensive use, making this area important to the study of the bears' long-term habits and population fluctuation. Rich salmon spawning habitats and the presence of such prey species as caribou and moose are key factors in the intensive use of the area by the bears.

The biology of the brown bears, their habitat and associated plant and animal species within the monument, together with other ecological features of the area, combine to offer excellent opportunities for scientific study and research.

The area is interesting and significant geologically, as it contains one of Alaska's most recent volcanically active areas, the Gas Rocks under Mount Peulik. Studies here of recent volcanism may contribute to the growing understanding of this powerful geological force.

The land withdrawn and reserved by this Proclamation for the protection of the geological, biological and other phenomena enumerated above supports now, as it has in the past, the unique subsistence culture of the local residents. The continued existence of this culture, which depends on subsistence hunting, and its availability for study, enhance the historic and scientific values of the natural objects protected herein because of the ongoing interaction of the subsistence culture with those objects. Accordingly, the opportunity for the local residents to engage in subsistence hunting is a value to be protected and will continue under the administration of the monument.

Section 2 of the Act of June 8, 1906 (34 Stat. 225, 16 U.S.C. 431), authorizes the President, in his discretion, to declare by public proclamation historic landmarks, historic and prehistoric structures, and other objects of historic or scientific interest that are situated upon the lands owned or controlled by the Government of the United States to be national monuments, and to reserve as part thereof parcels of land, the limits of which in all cases shall be confined to the smallest area compatible with the proper care and management of the objects to be protected.

Now, THEREFORE, I, JIMMY CARTER, President of the United States of America, by the authority vested in me by Section 2 of the Act of June 8, 1906 (34 Stat. 225, 16 U.S.C. 431), do proclaim that there are hereby set apart and reserved as the Becharof National Monument all lands, including submerged lands, and waters owned or controlled by the United States within the boundaries of the area depicted as Becharof National Monument on the map numbered FWS–81–00–0414 attached to and forming a part of this Proclamation. The area reserved consists of approximately 1,200,000 acres, and is the smallest area compatible with the proper care and management of the objects to be protected. Lands, including submerged lands, and waters within these boundaries not owned by the United

States shall be reserved as a part of the monument upon acquisition of title thereto by the United States.

All lands, including submerged lands, and all waters within the boundaries of this monument are hereby appropriated and withdrawn from entry, location, selection, sale or other disposition under the public land laws, other than exchange. There is also reserved all water necessary to the proper care and management of those objects protected by this monument and for the proper administration of the monument in accordance with applicable laws.

The establishment of this monument is subject to valid existing rights, including, but not limited to, valid selections under the Alaska Native Claims Settlement Act, as amended (43 U.S.C. 1601 *et seq.*), and under or confirmed in the Alaska Statehood Act (48 U.S.C. Note preceding Section 21).

Nothing in this Proclamation shall be deemed to revoke any existing withdrawal, reservation or appropriation, including any public land order effecting a withdrawal under Section 17(d)(1) of the Alaska Native Claims Settlement Act (43 U.S.C. 1616(d)(1)); however, the national monument shall be the dominant reservation. Nothing in this Proclamation is intended to modify or revoke the terms of the Memorandum of Understanding dated September 1, 1972, entered into between the State of Alaska and the United States as part of the negotiated settlement of *Alaska* v. *Morton,* Civil No. A–48–72 (D. Alaska, Complaint filed April 10, 1972).

The Secretary of the Interior shall promulgate such regulations as are appropriate, including regulation of sport hunting, and of the opportunity to engage in a subsistence lifestyle by local residents. The Secretary may close this national monument, or any portion thereof, to subsistence uses of a particular fish, wildlife or plant population or to sport hunting of a particular fish or wildlife population if necessary for reasons of public safety, administration, or to ensure the natural stability or continued viability of such population.

Warning is hereby given to all unauthorized persons not to appropriate, injure, destroy or remove any feature of this monument and not to locate or settle upon any of the lands thereof.

IN WITNESS WHEREOF, I have hereunto set my hand this 1st day of December, in the year of our Lord nineteen hundred and seventy-eight, and of the Independence of the United States of America the two hundred and third.

JIMMY CARTER

[Filed with the Office of the Federal Register, 2:55 p.m., December 1, 1978]

NOTE: The maps detailing the boundaries of the Becharof National Monument are printed in the FEDERAL REGISTER of December 5, 1978.

Bering Land Bridge National Monument

Proclamation 4614.   December 1, 1978

By the President of the United States of America

A Proclamation

The Bering Land Bridge, now overlain by the Chukchi Sea, the Bering Sea and Bering Strait, was the migration route by which many plants, animals, and humans arrived on the North American continent. The monument hereby created has within it an invaluable record of this migration.

There are found here rich archeological sites giving evidence of human migration during the periods the Bridge was water-free. Also found are paleontological sites providing abundant evidence of the migration of plants and animals onto the continent in the ages before the human migrations. The arctic conditions here are favorable to the preservation of this paleontological record from minute pollen grains and insects to the large mammals such as the mammoth.

The monument is also the summering area for a number of Old World bird species, which feed and nest in the area. It is one of the few places in North America where ornithologists are able to study these species.

The diversity of the soils, topography, permafrost action and climate within the monument leads to an excellent representation of varied, yet interrelated tundra plant communities. Their proximity and diversity make the area a prime outdoor laboratory.

The area is also rich in volcanics. Here is the opportunity to study unique Arctic lava flows which erupted through deep permafrost. The tubes and cracks of these flows are now filled with the sheen of permanent ice. In the Devil Mountain area are the uniquely paired maar explosion craters which were formed by violent explosions resulting from the steam pressure released when the hot volcanic ejecta contacted the water and ice that covered this wetland area. These craters are now crystal clear lakes bounded by a shoreline of volcanic ash, cinders and scoria.

The land withdrawn and reserved by this Proclamation for the protection of the geological, archeological, paleontological, biological and other phenomena enumerated above supports now, as it has in the past, the unique subsistence culture of the local residents. The continued existence of this culture, which depends on subsistence hunting, and its availability for study, enhance the historic and scientific values of the natural objects protected herein because of the ongoing interaction of the subsistence culture with those objects. Accordingly, the opportunity for local residents to engage in subsistence hunting is a value to be protected and will continue under the administration of the monument.

Section 2 of the Act of June 8, 1906 (34 Stat. 225, 16 U.S.C. 431), authorizes the President, in his discretion, to declare by public proclamation historic landmarks, historic and prehistoric structures, and other objects of historic or scientific interest that are situated upon the lands owned or controlled by the Government of the United States to be national monuments, and to reserve as part thereof parcels of land, the limits of which in all cases shall be confined to the smallest area compatible with the proper care and management of the objects to be protected.

Now, Therefore, I, Jimmy Carter, President of the United States of America, by the authority vested in me by Section 2 of the Act of June 8, 1906 (34 Stat. 225, 16 U.S.C. 431), do proclaim that there are hereby set apart and reserved as the Bering Land Bridge National Monument all lands, including submerged lands, and waters owned or controlled by the United States within the boundaries of the area depicted as the Bering Land Bridge National Monument on the map numbered BELA–90,006 attached to and forming a part of this Proclamation. The area reserved consists of approximately 2,590,000 acres, and is the smallest area compatible with the proper care and management of the objects to be protected. Lands, including submerged lands, and waters within these boundaries not owned by the United States shall be reserved as a part of the monument upon acquisition of title thereto by the United States.

All lands, including submerged lands, and all waters within the boundaries of this monument are hereby appropriated and withdrawn from entry, location, selection, sale or other disposition under the public land laws, other than exchange. There is also reserved all water necessary to the proper care and management of those objects protected by this monument and for the proper administration of the monument in accordance with applicable laws.

The establishment of this monument is subject to valid existing rights, including, but not limited to, valid selections under the Alaska Native Claims Settlement Act, as amended (43 U.S.C. 1601 *et seq.*), and under or confirmed in the Alaska Statehood Act (48 U.S.C. Note preceding Section 21).

Nothing in this Proclamation shall be deemed to revoke any existing withdrawal, reservation or appropriation, including any withdrawal under Section 17(d)(1) of the Alaska Native Claims Settlement Act (43 U.S.C. 1616(d)(1)); however, the national monument shall be the dominant reservation. Nothing in this Proclamation is intended to modify or revoke the terms of the Memorandum of Understanding dated September 1, 1972, entered into between the State of Alaska and the United States as part of the negotiated settlement of *Alaska* v. *Morton*, Civil No. A–48–72 (D. Alaska, Complaint filed April 10, 1972).

The Secretary of the Interior shall promulgate such regulations as are appropriate, including regulation of the opportunity to engage in a subsistence lifestyle by local residents. The Secretary may close the national monument, or any portion thereof, to subsistence uses of a particular fish, wildlife or plant population if necessary for reasons of public safety, administration, or to ensure the natural stability or continued viability of such population.

Warning is hereby given to all unauthorized persons not to appropriate, injure, destroy or remove any feature of this monument and not to locate or settle upon any of the lands thereof.

IN WITNESS WHEREOF, I have hereunto set my hand this 1st day of December, in the year of our Lord nineteen hundred and seventy-eight, and of the Independence of the United States of America the two hundred and third.

JIMMY CARTER

[Filed with the Office of the Federal Register, 2:56 p.m., December 1, 1978]

NOTE: The maps detailing the boundaries of the Bering Land Bridge National Monument are printed in the FEDERAL REGISTER of December 5, 1978.

Cape Krusenstern National Monument
Proclamation 4615.   December 1, 1978

By the President of the United States of America

A Proclamation

The area of northwest Alaska known as Cape Krusenstern contains an archeological record of great significance. The Cape's bluffs and its series of one hundred fourteen horizontal beach ridges hold an archeological record of every major cultural period associated with habitation of the Alaska coastline in the last 5000 years.

The unglaciated lands lying inland, including the Kakagrak Hills, the Rabbit Creek area and others, have an older archeological record dating back to pre-Eskimo periods of at least 8000 years ago. This continuum of evidence is of great historic and scientific importance in the study of human survival and cultural evolution.

There are in this area examples of other unique natural processes. The climatological conditions are conducive to the formation of Naleds, one spectacular example of which occurs in the area. In the same inland area at Kilikmak Creek is found the only known Alaskan example of a still recognizable Illinoisian glacial esker, a formation which is over 100,000 years old.

The unique geologic process of erosion and sediment transport in this area created and continues to create the beach ridges in which is preserved the archeological record of the beach civilizations. Also found in the area is a wide variety of plant and animal species, from the marine life along the shoreline and its lagoons to the inland populations such as musk-oxen, Dall sheep, caribou and many smaller species.

The land withdrawn and reserved by this Proclamation for the protection of the geological, archeological, biological and other phenomena enumerated above supports now, as it has in the past, the unique subsistence culture of the local residents. The continued existence of this culture, which depends on subsistence hunting, and its availability for study, enhance the historic and scientific values of the natural objects protected herein because of the ongoing interaction of the subsistence culture with those objects. Accordingly, the opportunity for the local residents to engage in subsistence hunting is a value to be protected and will continue under the administration of the monument.

Section 2 of the Act of June 8, 1906 (34 Stat. 225, 16 U.S.C. 431), authorizes the President, in his discretion, to declare by public proclamation historic landmarks, historic and prehistoric structures, and other objects of historic or scientific interest that are situated upon the lands owned or controlled by the Government of the United States to be national monu-

ments, and to reserve as part thereof parcels of land, the limits of which in all cases shall be confined to the smallest area compatible with the proper care and management of the objects to be protected.

Now, Therefore, I, Jimmy Carter, President of the United States of America, by the authority vested in me by Section 2 of the Act of June 8, 1906 (34 Stat. 225, 16 U.S.C. 431), do proclaim that there are hereby set apart and reserved as the Cape Krusenstern National Monument all lands, including submerged lands, and waters owned or controlled by the United States within the boundaries of the area depicted as the Cape Krusenstern National Monument on the map numbered CAKR–90,008 attached to and forming a part of this Proclamation. The area reserved consists of approximately 560,000 acres, and is the smallest area compatible with the proper care and management of the objects to be protected. Lands, including submerged lands, and waters within these boundaries not owned by the United States shall be reserved as a part of the monument upon acquisition of title thereto by the United States.

All lands, including submerged lands, and all waters within the boundaries of this monument are hereby appropriated and withdrawn from entry, location, selection, sale or other disposition under the public land laws, other than exchange. There is also reserved all water necessary to the proper care and management of those objects protected by this monument and for the proper administration of the monument in accordance with applicable laws.

The establishment of this monument is subject to valid existing rights, including, but not limited to, valid selections under the Alaska Native Claims Settlement Act, as amended (43 U.S.C. 1601 *et seq.*), and under or confirmed in the Alaska Statehood Act (48 U.S.C. Note preceding Section 21).

Nothing in this Proclamation shall be deemed to revoke any existing withdrawal under Section 17(d)(1) of the Alaska Native Claims Settlement Act (43 U.S.C. 1616(d)(1)); however, the national monument shall be the dominant reservation. Nothing in this Proclamation is intended to modify or revoke the terms of the Memorandum of Understanding dated September 1, 1972, entered into between the State of Alaska and the United States as part of the negotiated settlement of *Alaska* v. *Morton,* Civil No. A–48–72 (D. Alaska, Complaint filed April 10, 1972).

The Secretary of the Interior shall promulgate such regulations as are appropriate, including regulation of the opportunity to engage in a subsistence lifestyle by local residents. The Secretary may close the national monument, or any portion thereof, to subsistence uses of a particular fish, wildlife or plant population if necessary for reasons of public safety, administration, or to ensure the natural stability or continued viability of such population.

Warning is hereby given to all unauthorized persons not to appropriate, injure, destroy or remove any feature of this monument and not to locate or settle upon any of the lands thereof.

IN WITNESS WHEREOF, I have hereunto set my hand this 1st day of December, in the year of our Lord nineteen hundred and seventy-eight, and of the Independence of the United States of America the two hundred and third.

JIMMY CARTER

[Filed with the Office of the Federal Register, 2:57 p.m., December 1, 1978]

NOTE: The maps detailing the boundaries of the Cape Krusenstern National Monument are printed in the FEDERAL REGISTER of December 5, 1978.

Denali National Monument

Proclamation 4616.   December 1, 1978

By the President of the United States of America

A Proclamation

In the creation of Mount McKinley National Park the southern half of the mountain's massif was inadvertently excluded from the Park. The creation of Denali National Monument will bring within the protection of the National Park System the entirety of this, the highest peak on the North American continent. This face markedly differs from the north side for it has a more gradual rise and a significant system of glaciers. It is also the approach route used historically by those seeking to scale Mount McKinley.

Certain of the glaciers on the south face are among the largest in Alaska, reaching up to 45 miles in length. Yet, only the very uppermost parts are presently within the National Park. Their protection is enhanced by the creation of this monument.

In the southwest area of the monument hereby created are the geologically unique Cathedral Spires. From this granitic pluton mass radiate eight major glacial troughs exhibiting cirques and headwalls rising 5,000 feet from their bases.

The monument also protects significant habitat for the McKinley caribou herd which has provided a basis for scientific study since the early twentieth century. Associated with the herd in this ecosystem are other scientifically important mammals such as grizzly bear, wolf and wolverine.

The Toklat River region includes a unique area of warm springs which attracts an unusual late run of Chum salmon. This run provides an important late fall food source for the grizzly bear population of the area which, because of its accessibility, has been the subject of many scientific studies.

The land withdrawn and reserved by this Proclamation for the protection of the geological, biological and other phenomena enumerated above supports now, as it has in the past, the unique subsistence culture of the local residents. The continued existence of this culture, which depends on subsistence hunting, and its availability for study, enhance the historic and scientific values of the natural objects protected herein because of the ongoing interaction of the subsistence culture with those objects. Accordingly, the opportunity for the local residents to engage in subsistence hunting is a value to be protected and will continue under the administration of the monument.

Section 2 of the Act of June 8, 1906 (34 Stat. 225, 16 U.S.C. 431), authorizes the President, in his discretion, to declare by public proclamation historic landmarks, historic and prehistoric structures, and other objects of historic or scientific interest that are situated upon the lands owned or controlled by the Government of the United States to be national monuments, and to reserve as part thereof parcels of land, the limits of which in all cases shall be confined to the smallest area compatible with the proper care and management of the objects to be protected.

Now, THEREFORE, I, JIMMY CARTER, President of the United States of America, by the authority vested in me by Section 2 of the Act of June 8, 1906 (34 Stat. 225, 16 U.S.C. 431), do proclaim that there are hereby set apart and reserved as the Denali National Monument all lands, including submerged lands, and waters owned or controlled by the United States within the boundaries of the area depicted as the Denali National Monument on the map numbered DENA–90,007 attached to and forming a part of this Proclamation. The area reserved consists of approximately 3,890,000 acres, and is the smallest area compatible with the proper care and management of the objects to be protected. Lands, including submerged lands, and waters within these boundaries not owned by the United States shall be reserved as a part of the monument upon acquisition of title thereto by the United States.

All lands, including submerged lands, and all waters within the boundaries of this monument are hereby appropriated and withdrawn from entry, location, selection, sale or other disposition under the public land laws, other than exchange. There is also reserved all water necessary to the proper care and management of those objects protected by this monument and for the proper administration of the monument in accordance with applicable laws.

The establishment of this monument is subject to valid existing rights, including, but not limited to, valid selections under the Alaska Native Claims Settlement Act, as amended (43 U.S.C. 1601 *et seq.*), and under or confirmed in the Alaska Statehood Act (48 U.S.C. Note preceding Section 21).

Nothing in this Proclamation shall be deemed to revoke any existing withdrawal, reservation or appropriation, including any withdrawal under Section 17 (d)(1) of the Alaska Native Claims Settlement Act (43 U.S.C. 1616(d)(1)); however, the national monument shall be the dominant reservation. Nothing in this Proclamation is intended to modify or revoke the terms of the Memorandum of Understanding dated September 1, 1972, entered into between the State of Alaska and the United States as part of the negotiated settlement of *Alaska* v. *Morton,*

Civil No. A–48–72 (D. Alaska, Complaint filed April 10, 1972).

The Secretary of the Interior shall promulgate such regulations as are appropriate, including regulation of the opportunity to engage in a subsistence lifestyle by local residents. The Secretary may close the national monument, or any portion thereof, to subsistence uses of a particular fish, wildlife or plant population if necessary for reasons of public safety, administration, or to ensure the natural stability or continued viability of such population.

Warning is hereby given to all unauthorized persons not to appropriate, injure, destroy or remove any feature of this monument and not to locate or settle upon any of the lands thereof.

IN WITNESS WHEREOF, I have hereunto set my hand this 1st day of December, in the year of our Lord nineteen hundred and seventy-eight, and of the Independence of the United States of America the two hundred and third.

JIMMY CARTER

[Filed with the Office of the Federal Register, 2:58 p.m., December 1, 1978]

NOTE: The maps detailing the boundaries of the Denali National Monument are printed in the FEDERAL REGISTER of December 5, 1978.

Gates of the Arctic National Monument

Proclamation 4617. December 1, 1978

By the President of the United States of America

A Proclamation

Lying wholly north of the Arctic Circle, the Gates of the Arctic National Monument hereby created preserves an area containing a wide variety of interior arctic geological and biological forms. The essence of the geology of the area is its great diversity. There are excellent examples of glacial action which formed U-shaped valleys and morraine-dammed lakes. In contrast are the fissure-shaped precipices of Ernie Creek and the tilted limestone blocks along the northern edge of the Brooks Range.

Associated with these various land forms is a progression of ecosystems representing a continuum of communities from the boreal spruce forest and riparian shrub thickets in the south to the arctic tussock tundra in the north. These communities of plants and undisturbed animals offer excellent opportunities for study of natural interaction of the species.

The monument also protects a substantial portion of the habitat requirements for the Western Arctic caribou herd which uses ancient routes through the mountains for migration. This herd, which has suffered severe population losses recently, is of great value for the study of the population dynamics relating to both the decline and recovery of the herd.

The archeological and historical significance of the area is demonstrated by the studies which have revealed evidence of human habitation for approximately 7,000 years. Several known traditional Indian-Eskimo trade routes run through the monument area giving the promise of further important archeological discoveries. In the Wiseman and Ernie's Cabin mining regions in the south are offered opportunities for historical study of the life of the Alaskan pioneer miner of the early twentieth century.

The land withdrawn and reserved by this Proclamation for the protection of the biological, geological, archeological, historical, and other phenomena enumerated above supports now, as it has in the past, the unique subsistence culture of the local residents. The continued existence of this culture, which depends upon subsistence hunting, and its availability for study, enhance the historic and scientific values of the natural objects protected herein because of the ongoing interaction of the subsistence culture with those objects. Accordingly, the opportunity for local residents to engage in subsistence hunting is a value to be protected and will continue under the administration of the monument.

Section 2 of the Act of June 8, 1906 (34 Stat. 225, 16 U.S.C. 431), authorizes the President, in his discretion, to declare by public proclamation historic landmarks, historic and prehistoric structures, and other objects of historic or scientific interest that are situated upon the lands owned or controlled by the Government of the United States to be national monuments, and to reserve as part thereof parcels of land, the limits of which in all cases shall be confined to the smallest area compatible with the proper care and management of the objects to be protected.

Now, THEREFORE, I, JIMMY CARTER, President of the United States of America, by the authority vested in me by Section 2 of the Act of June 8, 1906 (34 Stat. 225, 16 U.S.C. 431), do proclaim that there are hereby set apart and reserved as the Gates of the Arctic National Monument all lands, including submerged lands, and waters owned or controlled by the United States within the boundaries of the area depicted as the Gates of the Arctic National Monument on the map numbered GAAR–90,011 attached to and forming a part of this Proclamation. The area reserved consists of approximately 8,220,000 acres, and is the smallest area compatible with the proper care and management of the objects to be protected. Lands, including submerged lands, and waters within these boundaries not owned by the United States shall be reserved as a part of the monument upon acquisition of title thereto by the United States.

All lands, including submerged lands, and all waters within the boundaries of this monument are hereby appropriated and withdrawn from entry, location, selection, sale or other disposition under the public land laws, other than exchange. There is also reserved all water necessary to the proper care and management of those objects protected by this monument and for the proper administration of the monument in accordance with applicable laws.

The establishment of this monument is subject to valid existing rights, including, but not limited to, valid selections under the Alaska Native Claims Settlement Act, as amended (43 U.S.C. 1601 *et seq.*), and under or confirmed in the Alaska Statehood Act (48 U.S.C. Note preceding Section 21).

Nothing in this Proclamation shall be deemed to revoke any existing withdrawal, reservation or appropriation, including any withdrawal under Section 17(d)(1) of the Alaska Native Claims Settlement Act (43 U.S.C. 1616(d)(1)); however, the national monument shall be the dominant reservation. Nothing in this Proclamation is intended to modify or revoke the terms of the Memorandum of Understanding dated September 1, 1972, entered into between the State of Alaska and the United States as part of the negotiated settlement of *Alaska* v. *Morton*, Civil No. A–48–72 (D. Alaska, Complaint filed April 10, 1972).

The Secretary of the Interior shall promulgate such regulations as are appropriate, including regulation of the opportunity to engage in a subsistence lifestyle by local residents. The Secretary may close the national monument, or any portion thereof, to subsistence uses of a particular fish, wildlife or plant population if necessary for reasons of public safety, administration, or to ensure the natural stability or continued viability of such population.

Warning is hereby given to all unauthorized persons not to appropriate, injure, destroy or remove any feature of this monument and not to locate or settle upon any of the lands thereof.

IN WITNESS WHEREOF, I have hereunto set my hand this 1st day of December, in the year of our Lord nineteen hundred and seventy-eight, and of the Independence of the United States of America the two hundred and third.

JIMMY CARTER

[Filed with the Office of the Federal Register, 2:59 p.m., December 1, 1978]

NOTE: The maps detailing the boundaries of the Gates of the Arctic National Monument are printed in the FEDERAL REGISTER of December 5, 1978.

Glacier Bay National Monument

Proclamation 4618.   December 1, 1978

ENLARGING THE GLACIER BAY NATIONAL MONUMENT

By the President of the United States of America

A Proclamation

Glacier Bay National Monument was created by Presidential Proclamation in 1925 and was enlarged in 1939 and again in 1955. It protects the great tidewater glaciers and a dramatic range of plant communities. The enlargement accomplished by this Proclamation furthers the protection of the array of geological and ecological interests in the area.

This addition includes the northwesterly side of Mount Fairweather, the high-est peak in this part of Alaska, and the Grand Plateau Glacier, both significant to students of glaciology.

The Alsek River corridor provides the only pass through the coastal mountain range for 120 miles. This is the route by which large mammals first entered this isolated area and is used by a significant percentage of the Alaska bald eagle population en route to the Klukwan area where they winter.

The addition also protects two botanically significant areas. In the hills flanking Grand Plateau Glacier live the oldest plant communities in southeast Alaska which survive because the area escaped both glaciation and inundation. Also important to the study of ecological succession are the mature aquatic vegetative communities of the pre-neoglacial lakes in the Deception Hills area.

The land withdrawn and reserved by this Proclamation for the protection of the geological, biological, and other phenomena enumerated above supports now, as it has in the past, a unique subsistence culture of the local residents. The continued existence of this culture, which depends on subsistence hunting, and its availability for study, enhances the historic and scientific value of the natural objects protected herein because of the ongoing interaction of the subsistence culture with those objects. Accordingly, the opportunity for local residents to engage in subsistence hunting is a value to be protected and will continue under the administration of the area added to the Glacier Bay National Monument by this Proclamation.

Section 2 of the Act of June 8, 1906 (34 Stat. 225, 16 U.S.C. 431), authorizes the President, in his discretion, to declare by public proclamation historic landmarks, historic and prehistoric structures and other objects of historic or scientific interest that are situated upon the lands owned or controlled by the Government of the United States to be national monuments, and to reserve as part thereof parcels of land, the limits of which in all cases shall be confined to the smallest area compatible with the proper care and management of the objects to be protected.

Now, THEREFORE, I, JIMMY CARTER, President of the United States of America, by the authority vested in me by Section 2 of the Act of June 8, 1906 (34 Stat. 225, 16 U.S.C. 431), do proclaim that there are hereby set apart and reserved for inclusion in the Glacier Bay National Monument all lands, including submerged lands, and waters owned or controlled by the United States within the boundaries of the area depicted as the Enlargement of Glacier Bay National Monument on the map numbered GLBA–90,005 attached to and forming a part of this Proclamation. The area reserved consists of approximately 550,000 acres, and is necessary to ensure the proper care and management of the objects the monument was established to preserve and those added by this Proclamation. Lands, including submerged lands, and waters within these boundaries not owned by the United States shall be reserved as a part of the monument upon acquisition of title thereto by the United States.

All lands, including submerged lands, and all waters within the boundaries of this addition are hereby appropriated and withdrawn from entry, location, selection, sale or other disposition, other than exchange. There is also reserved all water necessary to the proper care and management of those objects protected by this monument and for the proper administration of the monument in accordance with applicable laws.

The establishment of this addition is subject to valid existing rights, including, but not limited to, valid selections under the Alaska Native Claims Settlement Act, as amended (43 U.S.C. 1601 *et seq.*), and under or confirmed in the Alaska Statehood Act (48 U.S.C. Note preceding Section 21).

Nothing in this Proclamation shall be deemed to revoke any existing withdrawal, reservation or appropriation including any withdrawal under Section 17 (d)(1) of the Alaska Native Claims Settlement Act, (43 U.S.C. 1616(d)(1)); however, the national monument shall be the dominant reservation. Furthermore, nothing in this Proclamation is intended to modify or revoke the terms of the Memorandum of Understanding dated September 1, 1972, entered into between the State of Alaska and the United States as part of the negotiated settlement of *Alaska* v. *Morton,* Civil No. A–48–72 (D. Alaska, Complaint filed April 10, 1972).

The Secretary of the Interior shall promulgate such regulations as are appropriate, including regulation of the opportunity to engage in a subsistence lifestyle by local residents. The Secretary may close this addition, or any portion thereof, to subsistence uses of a particular fish, wildlife or plant population if necessary for reasons of public safety, administration, or to ensure the natural stability or continued viability of such population.

Warning is hereby given to all unauthorized persons not to appropriate, injure, destroy or remove any feature of this monument and not to locate or settle upon any of the lands thereof.

IN WITNESS WHEREOF, I have hereunto set my hand this 1st day of December, in the year of our Lord nineteen hundred and seventy-eight, and of the Independence of the United States of America the two hundred and third.

JIMMY CARTER

[Filed with the Office of the Federal Register, 3 p.m., December 1, 1978]

NOTE: The maps detailing the boundaries of the Glacier Bay National Monument are printed in the FEDERAL REGISTER of December 5, 1978.

Katmai National Monument

Proclamation 4619.   December 1, 1978

ENLARGING THE KATMAI NATIONAL MONUMENT

By the President of the United States of America

A Proclamation

In 1912, Mount Katmai gave vent to an extremely violent volcanic eruption. To preserve this excellent example of recent volcanism and ash deposition, Katmai National Monument was established in 1918. In the ensuing years it was recognized that in addition to the volcanoes, the area included a significant population of Alaskan brown bear and important spawning grounds for the Bristol Bay red salmon. The area was enlarged in view of these features in 1931, 1942 and 1969.

Continued research has revealed that the bear population is more mobile than originally believed. By the addition made hereby, a viable gene-pool population of the Alaskan brown bear can be protected free from human harassment. The addition closes a fifteen mile gap between the former monument boundary and the McNeil River State Game Sanctuary thereby completing the protection of the range

of this population of the world's largest carnivore.

The enlargement also protects the headwaters of the drainages which provide the spawning grounds for the red salmon. By protecting the quality of the water in these watersheds, the drama of the salmon run, a phenomenon of great scientific interest over the years, may be perpetuated.

The land withdrawn and reserved by this Proclamation for the protection of the biologic and other phenomena enumerated above supports now, as it has in the past, the unique subsistence culture of the local residents. The continued existence of this culture, which depends on subsistence hunting, and its availability for study, enhance the historic and scientific values of the natural objects protected herein, because of the ongoing interaction of the subsistence culture with those objects. Accordingly, the opportunity for local residents to engage in subsistence hunting is a value to be protected and will continue under the administration of the area added to Katmai National Monument by this Proclamation.

Section 2 of the Act of June 8, 1906 (34 Stat. 225, 16 U.S.C. 431), authorizes the President, in his discretion, to declare by public proclamation historic landmarks, historic and prehistoric structures and other objects of historic or scientific interest that are situated upon the lands owned or controlled by the Government of the United States to be national monuments, and to reserve as part thereof parcels of land, the limits of which in all cases shall be confined to the smallest area compatible with the proper care and management of the objects to be protected.

Now, THEREFORE, I, JIMMY CARTER, President of the United States of America, by the authority vested in me by Section

2 of the Act of June 8, 1906 (34 Stat. 225, 16 U.S.C. 431), do proclaim that there are hereby set apart and reserved for inclusion in the Katmai National Monument all lands, including submerged lands, and waters owned or controlled by the United States within the boundaries of the area depicted as the Enlargement of Katmai National Monument on the map numbered KATM–90,007 attached to and forming a part of this Proclamation. The area reserved consists of approximately 1,370,000 acres, and is necessary to ensure the proper care and management of the objects the monument was established to preserve and those added by this Proclamation. Lands, including submerged lands, and waters within these boundaries not owned by the United States shall be reserved as a part of the monument upon acquisition of title thereto by the United States.

All lands, including submerged lands, and all waters within the boundaries of this addition are hereby appropriated and withdrawn from entry, location, selection, sale or other disposition, other than exchange. There is also reserved all water necessary to the proper care and management of those objects protected by this monument and for the proper administration of the monument in accordance with applicable laws.

The establishment of this addition is subject to valid existing rights, including, but not limited to, valid selections under the Alaska Native Claims Settlement Act, as amended (43 U.S.C. 1601 *et seq.*), and under or confirmed in the Alaska Statehood Act (48 U.S.C. Note preceding Section 21).

Nothing in this Proclamation shall be deemed to revoke any existing withdrawal, reservation or appropriation, including any withdrawal under Section 17(d)(1) of the Alaska Native Claims Settlement Act (43 U.S.C. 1616(d)(1)); however, the national monument shall be the dominant reservation. Furthermore, nothing in this Proclamation is intended to modify, revoke or abrogate the terms of the Memorandum of Understanding dated September 1, 1972, entered into between the State of Alaska and the United States as part of the negotiated settlement of *Alaska* v. *Morton,* Civil No. A–48–72 (D. Alaska, Complaint filed April 10, 1972).

The Secretary of the Interior shall promulgate such regulations as are appropriate, including regulation of the opportunity to engage in a subsistence lifestyle by local residents. The Secretary may close this addition, or any portion thereof, to subsistence uses of a particular fish, wildlife or plant population if necessary for reasons of public safety, administration, or to ensure the natural stability or continued viability of such population.

Warning is hereby given to all unauthorized persons not to appropriate, injure, destroy or remove any feature of this monument and not to locate or settle upon any of the lands thereof.

IN WITNESS WHEREOF, I have hereunto set my hand this 1st day of December, in the year of our Lord nineteen hundred and seventy-eight, and of the Independence of the United States of America the two hundred and third.

JIMMY CARTER

[Filed with the Office of the Federal Register, 3:01 p.m., December 1, 1978]

NOTE: The maps detailing the boundaries of the Katmai National Monument are printed in the FEDERAL REGISTER of December 5, 1978.

Kenai Fjords National Monument

Proclamation 4620.   December 1, 1978

By the President of the United States of America

A Proclamation

Kenai Fjords National Monument borders the Gulf of Alaska and includes the Harding Icefield and extensions of mountain peaks out into the sea. The area holds a significant opportunity for geologic study of mountain building and for scientific study of ecological variations from an icecap environment to a marine shoreline environment.

The Harding Icefield, one of the Nation's major icecaps, continues to carve deep glacial valleys through the Kenai Mountains. The mountains themselves illustrate tectonic movement through uplift and subsidence over geologic time. Former alpine valleys are now fjords, and former mountain peaks are now tips of islands and vertical sea stacks.

Between the fjords, richly varied rain forest habitats offer opportunities to study life forms adaptable to the wet coastal environment. On the land these include mountain goat, black bear, otter, ptarmigan, and bald eagle. The area is extremely rich in sea bird life of interest to ornithologists and in marine mammals which come to feed in the fjords from their hauling and resting places on nearby islands. The recovery of the sea otter population from almost total extermination to relatively natural populations in this area is of continuing scientific interest.

Section 2 of the Act of June 8, 1906 (34 Stat. 225, 16 U.S.C. 431), author-izes the President, in his discretion, to declare by public proclamation historic landmarks, historic and prehistoric structures, and other objects of historic or scientific interest that are situated upon the lands owned or controlled by the Government of the United States to be national monuments, and to reserve as part thereof parcels of land, the limits of which in all cases shall be confined to the smallest area compatible with the proper care and management of the objects to be protected.

Now, THEREFORE, I, JIMMY CARTER, President of the United States of America, by the authority vested in me by Section 2 of the Act of June 8, 1906 (34 Stat. 225, 16 U.S.C. 431), do proclaim that there are hereby set apart and reserved as the Kenai Fjords National Monument all lands, including submerged lands, and waters owned or controlled by the United States within the boundaries of the area depicted as Kenai Fjords National Monument on the map numbered KEFJ–90,008 attached to and forming a part of this Proclamation. The area reserved consists of approximately 570,000 acres, and is the smallest area compatible with the proper care and management of the objects to be protected. Lands, including submerged lands, and waters within these boundaries not owned by the United States shall be reserved as a part of the monument upon acquisition of title thereto by the United States.

All lands, including submerged lands, and all waters within the boundaries of this monument are hereby appropriated and withdrawn from entry, location, selection, sale or other disposition under the public land laws, other than exchange. There is also reserved all water necessary to the proper care and management of those objects protected by this monument and for the proper administration of the monument in accordance with applicable laws.

The establishment of this monument is subject to valid existing rights, including, but not limited to, valid selections under the Alaska Native Claims Settlement Act, as amended (43 U.S.C. 1601 *et seq.*), and under or confirmed in the Alaska Statehood Act (48 U.S.C. Note preceding Section 21).

Nothing in this Proclamation shall be deemed to revoke any existing withdrawal, reservation or appropriation, including any withdrawal under Section 17 (d)(1) of the Alaska Native Claims Settlement Act (43 U.S.C. 1616(d)(1)); however, the national monument shall be the dominant reservation. Nothing in this Proclamation is intended to modify or revoke the terms of the Memorandum of Understanding dated September 1, 1972, entered into between the State of Alaska and the United States as part of the negotiated settlement of *Alaska* v. *Morton,* Civil No. A–48–72 (D. Alaska, Complaint filed April 10, 1972).

The Secretary of the Interior shall promulgate such regulations as are appropriate.

Warning is hereby given to all unauthorized persons not to appropriate, injure, destroy or remove any feature of this monument and not to locate or settle upon any of the lands thereof.

IN WITNESS WHEREOF, I have hereunto set my hand this 1st day of December, in the year of our Lord nineteen hundred and seventy-eight, and of the Independence of the United States of America the two hundred and third.

JIMMY CARTER

[Filed with the Office of the Federal Register, 3:02 p.m., December 1, 1978]

NOTE: The maps detailing the boundaries of the Kenai Fjords National Monument are printed in the FEDERAL REGISTER of December 5, 1978.

Kobuk Valley National Monument

Proclamation 4621.   December 1, 1978

By the President of the United States of America

A Proclamation

The Kobuk Valley and its environs, an area located in the northwest interior of Alaska, contains important archeological data and biological and geological features of great scientific significance.

Archeological features within the area illustrate an unbroken continuum of human adaptation to the natural environment from the early pre-Eskimo people of 10,500 years ago to present-day local residents. Scientists recently discovered more than 100 dwellings occupied in about 1250 A.D., comprising the largest settlement of its kind. The Onion Portage Archeological District is located within the area, and is listed on the National Register of Historic Places. Archeological research at Onion Portage has yielded evidence of more than 10,000 years of human occupation.

The area contains the Great and Little Kobuk Sand Dunes, which lie north of the Arctic Circle and include both active and stabilized dunes. Scientific studies of the dunes show them to be older than 33,000 years, and several plants have been found in association with the dunes environment which are scientifically unusual in the area. The Great Kobuk Sand Dunes attain a height of 100 feet.

The inclusion of the watersheds on the north and south of the Kobuk River protects a uniquely representative series of interrelated plant communities. There is here an essentially unspoiled laboratory for the study of the northern boreal forest.

A rich variety of wildlife also occurs within the area. Major portions of the northwest arctic caribou herd move through the area in spring and fall migrations. The area also includes one of only two significant populations of the Alaskan sheefish. The water environment is habitat for nesting waterfowl, moose, and muskrat. A relatively dense population of grizzly and black bears, wolf, wolverine, fox, otter, and other northern furbearing mammals range over the entire area.

The land withdrawn and reserved by this Proclamation for the protection of the archeological, geological, biological, and other phenomena enumerated above supports now, as it has in the past, the unique subsistence culture of the local residents. The continued existence of this culture, which depends on subsistence hunting, and its availability for study, enhances the historic and scientific values of the natural objects protected herein because of the ongoing interaction of the subsistence culture with these objects. Accordingly, the opportunity for local residents to engage in subsistence hunting is one of the values to be protected and will continue under the administration of the monument.

Section 2 of the Act of June 8, 1906 (34 Stat. 225, 16 U.S.C. 431), authorizes the President, in his discretion, to declare by public proclamation historic landmarks, historic and prehistoric structures, and other objects of historic or scientific interest that are situated upon the lands owned or controlled by the Government of the United States to be national monuments, and to reserve as part thereof parcels of land, the limits of which in all cases shall be confined to the smallest area compatible with the proper care and management of the objects to be protected.

Now, THEREFORE, I, JIMMY CARTER, President of the United States of America, by the authority vested in me by Section 2 of the Act of June 8, 1906 (34 Stat. 225, 16 U.S.C. 431), do proclaim that there are hereby set apart and reserved as the Kobuk Valley National Monument all lands, including submerged lands, and waters owned or controlled by the United States within the boundaries of the area depicted as the Kobuk Valley National Monument on the map numbered KOVA–90,010 attached to and forming a part of this Proclamation. The area reserved consists of approximately 1,710,000 acres, and is the smallest area compatible with the proper care and management of the objects to be protected. Lands, including submerged lands, and waters within these boundaries not owned by the United States shall be reserved as a part of the monument upon acquisition of title thereto by the United States.

All lands, including submerged lands, and all waters within the boundaries of this monument are hereby appropriated and withdrawn from entry, location, selection, sale or other disposition under the public land laws, other than exchange. There is also reserved all water necessary to the proper care and management of those objects protected by this monument and for the proper administration of the monument in accordance with applicable laws.

The establishment of this monument is subject to valid existing rights, including, but not limited to, valid selections under the Alaska Native Claims Settlement Act, as amended (43 U.S.C. 1601 *et seq.*), and under or confirmed in the Alaska Statehood Act (48 U.S.C. Note preceding Section 21).

Nothing in this Proclamation shall be deemed to revoke any existing withdrawal, reservation or appropriation, including any withdrawal under Section 17 (d)(1) of the Alaska Native Claims Settlement Act (43 U.S.C. 1616(d)(1)); however, the national monument shall be the dominant reservation. Nothing in this Proclamation is intended to modify or revoke the terms of the Memorandum of Understanding dated September 1, 1972, entered into between the State of Alaska and the United States as part of the negotiated settlement of *Alaska* v. *Morton,* Civil No. A–48–72 (D. Alaska, Complaint filed April 10, 1972).

The Secretary of the Interior shall promulgate such regulations as are appropriate, including regulation of the opportunity to engage in a subsistence lifestyle by local residents. The Secretary may close the national monument, or any portion thereof, to subsistence uses of a particular fish, wildlife or plant population if necessary for reasons of public safety, administration, or to ensure the natural stability or continued viability of such population.

Warning is hereby given to all unauthorized persons not to appropriate, injure, destroy or remove any feature of this monument and not to locate or settle upon any of the lands thereof.

IN WITNESS WHEREOF, I have hereunto set my hand this 1st day of December, in the year of our Lord nineteen hundred and seventy-eight, and of the Independence of the United States of America the two hundred and third.

JIMMY CARTER

[Filed with the Office of the Federal Register, 3:03 p.m., December 1, 1978]

NOTE: The maps detailing the boundaries of the Kobuk Valley National Monument are printed in the FEDERAL REGISTER of December 5, 1978.

Lake Clark National Monument

Proclamation 4622.   December 1, 1978

By the President of the United States of America

A Proclamation

An area in south-central Alaska contains examples of geological phenomena associated with two major mountains chains, the Alaska Range and the Chigmit Mountains, in an array that includes jagged peaks and two symmetrical, steaming volcanoes. These volcanoes, Redoubt and Iliamna, have been listed on the National Registry of Natural Landmarks.

The area's land forms also contribute to an outstanding example of ecological diversity in zones which remain relatively unspoiled for continued scientific research. Large mammals such as moose, caribou, Dall sheep, grizzly bear, black bear, and wolverine occur in natural populations. Whistling swans nest and rare trumpeter swans assemble in the area. Other birds, including bald eagle, gyrfalcon, osprey, and endangered peregrine falcon, breed within the area. Seabird colonies occur along the coast. One of the most stable natural populations of caribou in Alaska, the Mulchatna herd, calves and migrates within the area, offering significant opportunities for scientific study of this mammal.

Sockeye salmon runs within the area are exceptional. The area includes the upper drainage of the Kvichak River System, which is the single most productive spawning and rearing habitat for red salmon in the world, and the subject of scientific research for many years.

Historical resources of the area are significant. Kijik Village, on the shore of

Lake Clark, is the site marking the first known Russian exploration of the region in the late eighteenth century. The area holds great promise for the discovery of further evidence defining the impact of the Native-European contacts.

The land withdrawn and reserved by this proclamation for the protection of the geological, archeological, historical, biological and other phenomena enumerated above supports now, as it has in the past, the unique subsistence culture of the local residents. The continued existence of this culture, which depends on subsistence hunting, and its availability for study, enhances the historic and scientific values of the natural objects protected herein because of the ongoing interaction of the subsistence culture with these objects. Accordingly, the opportunity for local residents to engage in subsistence hunting is a value to be protected and will continue under the administration of the monument.

Section 2 of the Act of June 8, 1906 (34 Stat. 225, 16 U.S.C. 431), authorizes the President, in his discretion, to declare by public proclamation historic landmarks, historic and prehistoric structures, and other objects of historic or scientific interest that are situated upon the lands owned or controlled by the Government of the United States to be national monuments, and to reserve as part thereof parcels of land, the limits of which in all cases shall be confined to the smallest area compatible with the proper care and management of the objects to be protected.

Now, THEREFORE, I, JIMMY CARTER, President of the United States of America, by the authority vested in me by Section 2 of the Act of June 8, 1906 (34 Stat. 225, 16 U.S.C. 431), do proclaim that there are hereby set apart and reserved as the Lake Clark National Monument all lands, including submerged lands, and waters owned or controlled by the United States within the boundaries of the area depicted as the Lake Clark National Monument on the map numbered LACL–90,-009 attached to and forming a part of this Proclamation. The area reserved consists of approximately 2,500,000 acres, and is the smallest area compatible with the proper care and management of the objects to be protected. Lands, including submerged lands, and waters within these boundaries not owned by the United States shall be reserved as a part of the monument upon acquisition of title thereto by the United States.

All lands, including submerged lands, and all waters within the boundaries of this monument are hereby appropriated and withdrawn from entry, location, selection, sale or other disposition under the public land laws, other than exchange. There is also reserved all water necessary to the proper care and management of those objects protected by this monument and for the proper administration of the monument in accordance with applicable laws.

The establishment of this monument is subject to valid existing rights, including, but not limited to, valid selections under the Alaska Native Claims Settlement Act, as amended (43 U.S.C. 1601 *et seq.*), and under or confirmed in the Alaska Statehood Act (48 U.S.C. Note preceding Section 21).

Nothing in this Proclamation shall be deemed to revoke any existing withdrawal, reservation or appropriation, including any withdrawal under Section 17 (d)(1) of the Alaska Native Claims Settlement Act (43 U.S.C. 1616(d)(1)); however, the national monument shall be the dominant reservation. Nothing in this Proclamation is intended to modify or revoke the terms of the Memorandum of Understanding dated September 1, 1972, entered into between the State of Alaska and the United States as part of the negotiated settlement of *Alaska* v. *Morton,* Civil No. A–48–72 (D. Alaska, Complaint filed April 10, 1972).

The Secretary of the Interior shall promulgate such regulations as are appropriate, including regulation of the opportunity to engage in a subsistence lifestyle by local residents. The Secretary may close the national monument, or any portion thereof, to subsistence uses of a particular fish, wildlife or plant population if necessary for reasons of public safety, administration, or to ensure the natural stability or continued viability of such population.

Warning is hereby given to all unauthorized persons not to appropriate, injure, destroy or remove any feature of this monument and not to locate or settle upon any of the lands thereof.

IN WITNESS WHEREOF, I have hereunto set my hand this 1st day of December, in the year of our Lord nineteen hundred and seventy-eight, and of the Independence of the United States of America the two hundred and third.

JIMMY CARTER

[Filed with the Office of the Federal Register, 3:04 p.m., December 1, 1978]

NOTE: The maps detailing the boundaries of the Lake Clark National Monument are printed in the FEDERAL REGISTER of December 5, 1978.

Misty Fiords National Monument

Proclamation 4623.   December 1, 1978

By the President of the United States of America

A Proclamation

Misty Fiords is an unspoiled coastal ecosystem containing significant scientific and historical features unique in North America. It is an essentially untouched two million-acre area in the Coast Mountains of Southeast Alaska within which are found nearly all of the important geological and ecological characteristics of the region, including the complete range of coastal to interior climates and ecosytems in a remarkably compact area.

Among the objects of geologic importance are extraordinarily deep and long fiords with sea cliffs rising thousands of feet. Active glaciers along the Canadian border are remnants of the massive ice bodies that covered the region as recently as about 10,000 years ago, at the end of the Pleistocene epoch. However, there have been periodic glacial advances and retreats in more recent historic periods. Some of the area has been free from glaciation for only a short period of time, creating the unusual scientific phenomenon of recent plant succession on newly-exposed land with the accompanying animal species. The Behm Canal, the major inlet at the heart of the area, is more than fifty miles long and extraordinary among natural canals for its length and depth.

The watershed of the Unuk River, which comprises the northern portion of the Misty Fiords area, has its headwaters in Canada. It is steeply mountainous and glaciated and contains the full range of ecosystems and climates from interior to coastal. Mineral springs and lava flows add to the uniqueness of the area and its value for scientific investigation. South of the Unuk, the Chickamin River System and the Le Duc River originate in active glaciers and terminate in Behm Canal. Further south, Rudyerd Bay Fiords and Walker Cove are surrounded by high, cold lakes and mountains extending eastward to Canada.

First inhabitants of Misty Fiords may have settled in the area as long ago as 10,000 years. The area contains cultural sites and objects of historical significance, including traditional native hunting and fishing grounds. Later historical evidence includes a mid-1800's military post-port entry on Tongass Island and a salmon cannery in Behm Canal established in the late 1800's.

Misty Fiords is unique in that the area includes wildlife representative of nearly every ecosystem in Southeast Alaska, most notably bald eagles, brown and black bears, moose, wolves, mountain goats and Sitka black-tailed deer. Numerous other bird species nest and feed in the area, notably falcons and waterfowl. Misty Fiords is a major producer of all five species of Pacific salmon and is especially important for king salmon. Numerous other saltwater, freshwater and anadromous fish species and shellfish are plentiful in this area, which is an extraordinarily fertile interface of marine and freshwater environments. Unusual plantlife includes Pacific silver and subalpine fir trees near the northern limit of their range. The area includes an unusual variety of virgin forests, ranging from coastal spruce-hemlock to alpine forests.

As an intact coastal ecosystem, Misty Fiords possesses a collective array of objects of outstanding value for continuing scientific study. The boundaries of the area follow watershed perimeters and include the smallest area compatible with protection of this unique ecosystem and the remarkable geologic and biological objects and features it contains.

Hunting and fishing shall continue to be regulated, permitted and controlled in accord with the statutory authorities applicable to the monument area.

Section 2 of the Act of June 8, 1906 (34 Stat. 225, 16 U.S.C. 431), authorizes

the President, at his discretion, to declare by public proclamation historic landmarks, historic and prehistoric structures, and other objects of historic or scientific interest that are situated upon the lands owned or controlled by the government of the United States to be National Monuments, and to reserve as part thereof parcels of lands, the limits of which in all cases shall be confined to the smallest area compatible with the proper care and management of the objects to be protected.

Now, THEREFORE, I, JIMMY CARTER, President of the United States of America, by the authority vested in me by section 2 of the Act of June 8, 1906, (34 Stat. 225, 16 U.S.C. 431), do proclaim that there are hereby set apart and reserved as the Misty Fiords National Monument all lands, including submerged lands, and waters owned or controlled by the United States within the boundaries of the area described on the document entitled "Misty Fiords National Monument (Copper River Meridian)", attached to and forming a part of this Proclamation. The area reserved consists of approximately 2,285,000 acres, and is the smallest area compatible with the proper care and management of the objects to be protected. Lands, including submerged lands, and waters within these boundaries not owned by the United States shall be reserved as a part of the Monument upon acquisition of title thereto by the United States.

All lands, including submerged lands, and all waters within the boundaries of this Monument are hereby appropriated and withdrawn from entry, location, selection, sale or other disposition under the public land laws, other than exchange. There is also reserved all water necessary to the proper care and management of those objects protected by this Monument and for the proper administration of the

Monument in accordance with applicable laws.

The establishment of this Monument is subject to valid existing rights, including, but not limited to, valid selection under the Alaska Native Claims Settlement Act, as amended (43 U.S.C. 1601 *et seq.*), and under or confirmed in the Alaska Statehood Act (48 U.S.C. Note preceding Section 21).

Nothing in this Proclamation shall be deemed to revoke any existing withdrawal, reservation or appropriation, including any withdrawal under section 17 (d)(1) of the Alaska Native Claims Settlement Act (43 U.S.C. 1616(d)(1)); however, the National Monument shall be the dominant reservation. Nothing in this Proclamation is intended to modify or revoke the terms of the Memorandum of Understanding dated September 1, 1972, entered into between the State of Alaska and the United States as part of the negotiated settlement of *Alaska* v. *Morton,* Civil No. A–48–72 (D. Alaska, Complaint filed April 10, 1972).

Warning is hereby given to all unauthorized persons not to appropriate, injure, destroy or remove any feature of this Monument and not to locate or settle upon any of the lands thereof.

IN WITNESS WHEREOF, I have hereunto set my hand this first day of December, in the year of our Lord nineteen hundred and seventy-eight, and of the Independence of the United States of America the two hundred and third.

JIMMY CARTER

[Filed with the Office of the Federal Register, 3:05 p.m., December 1, 1978]

NOTE: The attachment and map detailing the boundaries of the Misty Fiords National Monument are printed in the FEDERAL REGISTER of December 5, 1978.

Noatak National Monument
Proclamation 4624.   December 1, 1978

By the President of the United States of America

A Proclamation

The Noatak River basin is the largest mountain-ringed river basin in the Nation still virtually unaffected by technological human activity. This basin has been designated as a Biosphere Reserve under the United Nations' auspices, in recognition of its international importance for scientific study and research.

The area includes landforms and ecological variations of scientific interest. The Grand Canyon of the Noatak River is a dissected valley 65 miles long. The area contains the northwesternmost fringe of boreal forest in North America, and is a transition zone and migration route for plants and animals between subarctic and arctic environments. The diversity of the flora is among the greatest anywhere in the earth's northern latitudes.

The Noatak Valley area contains a rich variety of birdlife including several Asian species. The area is crossed twice a year by two-thirds of the Western Arctic caribou herd, and is prime habitat for the barren ground grizzly bear, moose, and several predator species.

Nearly 200 archeological sites, dating as far back in time as 5,000 years, are within the area. They give promise of future discoveries leading to a deeper understanding of the area's prehistory.

The Noatak basin is an area where indigenous plants and animals perpetuate themselves naturally, in a freely functioning ecosystem. Protection of this area will assure the preservation of an essential base against which scientists may judge environmental dynamics of the future.

The land withdrawn and reserved by this Proclamation for the protection of the geological, archeological, biological, and other phenomena enumerated above supports now, as it has in the past, the unique subsistence culture of the local residents. The continued existence of this culture, which depends upon subsistence hunting, and its availability for study, enhances the historic and scientific values of the natural objects protected herein because of the ongoing interaction of the subsistence culture with those objects. Accordingly, the opportunity for local residents to engage in subsistence hunting is a value to be protected and will continue under the administration of the monument.

Section 2 of the Act of June 8, 1906 (34 Stat. 225, 16 U.S.C. 431), authorizes the President, in his discretion, to declare by public proclamation historic landmarks, historic and prehistoric structures, and other objects of historic or scientific interest that are situated upon the lands owned or controlled by the Government of the United States to be national monuments, and to reserve as part thereof parcels of land, the limits of which in all cases shall be confined to the smallest area compatible with the proper care and management of the objects to be protected.

Now, THEREFORE, I, JIMMY CARTER, President of the United States of America, by the authority vested in me by Section 2 of the Act of June 8, 1906 (34 Stat. 225, 16 U.S.C. 431), do proclaim that there are hereby set apart and reserved as the Noatak National Monument all lands, including submerged lands, and waters owned or controlled by the United States within the boundaries of the area depicted as the Noatak National Monument on the map numbered NOAT–90,004 attached to and forming a part of this Proclamation. The area reserved consists of approx-

imately 5,800,000 acres, and is the smallest area compatible with the proper care and management of the objects to be protected. Lands, including submerged lands, and waters within these boundaries not owned by the United States shall be reserved as a part of the monument upon acquisition of title thereto by the United States.

All lands, including submerged lands, and all waters within the boundaries of this monument are hereby appropriated and withdrawn from entry, location, selection, sale or other disposition under the public land laws, other than exchange. There is also reserved all water necessary to the proper care and management of those objects protected by this monument and for the proper administration of the monument in accordance with applicable laws.

The establishment of this monument is subject to valid existing rights, including, but not limited to, valid selections under the Alaska Native Claims Settlement Act, as amended (43 U.S.C. 1601 *et seq.*), and under or confirmed in the Alaska Statehood Act (48 U.S.C. Note preceding Section 21).

Nothing in this Proclamation shall be deemed to revoke any existing withdrawal, reservation or appropriation, including any withdrawal under Section 17 (d) (1) of the Alaska Native Claims Settlement Act (43 U.S.C. 1616(d)(1)); however, the national monument shall be the dominant reservation. Nothing in this Proclamation is intended to modify or revoke the terms of the Memorandum of Understanding dated September 1, 1972, entered into between the State of Alaska and the United States as part of the negotiated settlement of *Alaska* v. *Morton,* Civil No. A–48–72 (D. Alaska, Complaint filed April 10, 1972).

The Secretary of the Interior shall promulgate such regulations as are appropriate, including regulation of the opportunity to engage in a subsistence lifestyle by local residents. The Secretary may close the national monument, or any portion thereof, to subsistence uses of a particular fish, wildlife or plant population if necessary for reasons of public safety, administration, or to ensure the natural stability or continued viability of such population.

Warning is hereby given to all unauthorized persons not to appropriate, injure, destroy or remove any feature of this monument and not to locate or settle upon any of the lands thereof.

IN WITNESS WHEREOF, I have hereunto set my hand this 1st day of December, in the year of our Lord nineteen hundred and seventy-eight, and of the Independence of the United States of America the two hundred and third.

JIMMY CARTER

[Filed with the Office of the Federal Register, 3:06 p.m., December 1, 1978]

NOTE: The maps detailing the boundaries of the Noatak National Monument are printed in the FEDERAL REGISTER of December 5, 1978.

Wrangell-St. Elias National Monument

Proclamation 4625.   December 1, 1978

By the President of the United States of America

A Proclamation

An area of southeastern Alaska adjacent to the International Boundary with Canada contains a variety of landforms, including high mountain peaks and steep canyons, with associated geological, ecological, biological, and historical phenomena of great importance.

The area includes the greatest assemblage of mountain peaks over 14,500 feet in elevation found in the Nation, the Nation's second highest mountain (Mount St. Elias, at 18,008 feet), several inactive and one active volcano (Mount Wrangell), and an active glacial complex, including some of the largest and longest glaciers in the Nation. The high mountain peaks and glaciers offer an excellent opportunity for glaciological studies. The Malaspina Glacier is listed on the National Registry of Natural Landmarks.

Thermal features in the area include the mud cones and hot springs on the western base of Mount Drum. More complete undeveloped river systems exist here than in any other land area in the Nation, with more than 1,000 miles of powerfully running, silt-laden rivers.

Biologically unique subspecies of flora and fauna have developed in the Bremner and Chitina River Valleys. As a result of their isolation by virtue of ice fields and the Copper River, these areas are virtually ecological islands in which development of subspecies is largely unaffected by interchange with outside plant and animal species.

Wildlife populations include the largest population of wild mountain sheep in North America, moose, mountain goat, and a non-migratory population of caribou. The area is the only part of Alaska where four of the five identifiable forms of bear occur, including the interior grizzly, the coastal brown bear, the black bear, and the rare, blue-color phase of the black bear called glacier bear. Along the coast of the Gulf of Alaska bald eagles and a large and varied shorebird population occur.

Cultural development within the area is of interest to archeologists and historians. Three major culture areas converge here, each with distinctive cultural patterns:

the North Athapascans, the Pacific Eskimo, and the Chugach. Mining history is evidenced by the Kennecott Copper works, a National Historic Landmark.

The land withdrawn and reserved by this Proclamation for the protection of the geological, archeological, biological, and other phenomena enumerated above supports now, as it has in the past, a unique subsistence culture of the local residents. The continued existence of this culture, which depends on subsistence hunting, and its availability for study, enhances the historic and scientific values of the natural objects protected herein because of the ongoing interaction of the subsistence culture with those objects. Accordingly, the opportunity for local residents to engage in subsistence hunting is a value to be protected and will continue under the administration of the monument.

Section 2 of the Act of June 8, 1906 (34 Stat. 225, 16 U.S.C. 431), authorizes the President, in his discretion, to declare by public proclamation historic landmarks, historic and prehistoric structures, and other objects of historic or scientific interest that are situated upon the lands owned or controlled by the Government of the United States to be national monuments, and to reserve as part thereof parcels of land, the limits of which in all cases shall be confined to the smallest area compatible with the proper care and management of the objects to be protected.

Now, THEREFORE, I, JIMMY CARTER, President of the United States of America, by the authority vested in me by Section 2 of the Act of June 8, 1906 (34 Stat. 225, 16 U.S.C. 431), do proclaim that there are hereby set apart and reserved as the Wrangell-St. Elias National Monument all lands, including submerged lands, and waters owned or controlled by the United States within the boundaries

of the area depicted as the Wrangell-St. Elias National Monument on the map numbered WRST–90,007 attached to and forming a part of this Proclamation. The area reserved consists of approximately 10,950,000 acres, and is the smallest area compatible with the proper care and management of the objects to be protected. Lands, including submerged lands, and waters within these boundaries not owned by the United States shall be reserved as a part of the monument upon acquisition of title thereto by the United States.

All lands, including submerged lands, and all waters within the boundaries of this monument are hereby appropriated and withdrawn from entry, location, selection, sale or other disposition under the public land laws, other than exchange. There is also reserved all water necessary to the proper care and management of those objects protected by this monument and for the proper administration of the monument in accordance with applicable laws.

The establishment of this monument is subject to valid existing rights, including, but not limited to, valid selections under the Alaska Native Claims Settlement Act, as amended (43 U.S.C. 1601 *et seq.*), and under or confirmed in the Alaska Statehood Act (48 U.S.C. Note preceding Section 21).

Nothing in this Proclamation shall be deemed to revoke any existing withdrawal, reservation or appropriation, including any withdrawal under Section 17 (d)(1) of the Alaska Native Claims Settlement Act (43 U.S.C. 1616(d)(1)); however, the national monument shall be the dominant reservation. Nothing in this Proclamation is intended to modify or revoke the terms of the Memorandum of Understanding dated September 1, 1972, entered into between the State of Alaska and the United States as part of the negotiated settlement of *Alaska* v. *Morton,*

Civil No. A–48–72 (D. Alaska, Complaint filed April 10, 1972).

The Secretary of the Interior shall promulgate such regulations as are appropriate, including regulation of the opportunity to engage in a subsistence lifestyle by local residents. The Secretary may close the national monument, or any portion thereof, to subsistence uses of a particular fish, wildlife or plant population if necessary for reasons of public safety, administration, or to ensure the natural stability or continued viability of such population.

Warning is hereby given to all unauthorized persons not to appropriate, injure, destroy or remove any feature of this monument and not to locate or settle upon any of the lands thereof.

IN WITNESS WHEREOF, I have hereunto set my hand this 1st day of December, in the year of our Lord nineteen hundred and seventy-eight, and of the Independence of the United States of America the two hundred and third.

JIMMY CARTER

[Filed with the Office of the Federal Register, 3:07 p.m., December 1, 1978]

NOTE: The maps detailing the boundaries of the Wrangell-St. Elias National Monument are printed in the FEDERAL REGISTER of December 5, 1978.

Yukon-Charley National Monument

Proclamation 4626.   December 1, 1978

By the President of the United States of America

A Proclamation

The Yukon-Charley National Monument, an area in east-central Alaska, includes a combination of historic and scientific features of great significance. The Upper Yukon River basin contains historic remains of early mining activity, and includes outstanding paleontological resources and ecologically diverse natural resources, offering many opportunities for scientific and historic study and research.

The area provides breeding habitat for the endangered peregrine falcon, and may produce about one-fourth of the known individuals of the *anatum peregrine* subspecies in its northern habitat. Wildlife also include isolated wild populations of Dall sheep, moose, bear, wolf, and other large mammals. Nearly 200 species of birds, including 20 different raptors, are present in the area.

Geological and paleontological features within the area are exceptional, including a nearly unbroken visible series of rock strata representing a range in geologic time from pre-Cambrian to Recent. The oldest exposures contain fossils estimated to be 700 million years old, including the earliest forms of animal life. A large array of Ice Age fossils occurs in the area.

Within the area is the Charley River basin, parts of which were unglaciated, preserving relict Pleistocene plant communities. The Charley River is considered to be one of the cleanest and clearest of the major rivers in Alaska, and thereby offers excellent opportunities for scientific studies. In the upper Charley River basin, artifacts occur dating back possibly 11,000 years, attesting to the presence of ancient hunters who were the ancestors of the modern Athapascan people.

The land withdrawn and reserved by this Proclamation for the protection of the historical, archeological, biological, geological and other phenomena enumerated above supports now, as it has in the past, the unique subsistence culture of the local residents. The continued existence of this culture, which depends on subsistence hunting, and its availability for study, enhance the historic and scientific values of the natural objects protected herein because of the ongoing interaction of the subsistence culture with those objects. Accordingly, the opportunity for the local residents to engage in subsistence hunting is a value to be protected and will continue under the administration of the monument.

Section 2 of the Act of June 8, 1906 (34 Stat. 225, 16 U.S.C. 431), authorizes the President, in his discretion, to declare by public proclamation historic landmarks, historic and prehistoric structures, and other objects of historic or scientific interest that are situated upon the lands owned or controlled by the Government of the United States to be national monuments, and to reserve as part thereof parcels of land, the limits of which in all cases shall be confined to the smallest area compatible with the proper care and management of the objects to be protected.

Now, THEREFORE, I, JIMMY CARTER, President of the United States of America, by the authority vested in me by Section 2 of the Act of June 8, 1906 (34 Stat. 225, 16 U.S.C. 431), do proclaim that there are hereby set apart and reserved as the Yukon-Charley National Monument all lands, including submerged lands, and waters owned or controlled by the United States within the boundaries of the area depicted as the Yukon-Charley National Monument on the map numbered YUCH–90,009 attached to and forming a part of this Proclamation. The area reserved consists of approximately 1,720,000 acres, and is the smallest area compatible with the proper care and management of the objects to be protected. Lands, including submerged lands, and waters within these boundaries not owned by the United States shall be reserved as a part of the monument upon acquisition of title thereto by the United States.

All lands, including submerged lands, and all waters within the boundaries of this monument are hereby appropriated and withdrawn from entry, location, selection, sale or other disposition under the public land laws, other than exchange. There is also reserved all water necessary to the proper care and management of those objects protected by this monument and for the proper administration of the monument in accordance with applicable laws.

The establishment of this monument is subject to valid existing rights, including, but not limited to, valid selections under the Alaska Native Claims Settlement Act, as amended (43 U.S.C. 1601 *et seq.*), and under or confirmed in the Alaska Statehood Act (48 U.S.C. Note preceding Section 21).

Nothing in this Proclamation shall be deemed to revoke any existing withdrawal, reservation or appropriation, including any withdrawal under Section 17 (d)(1) of the Alaska Native Claims Settlement Act (43 U.S.C. 1616(d)(1)); however, the national monument shall be the dominant reservation. Nothing in this Proclamation is intended to modify or revoke the terms of the Memorandum of Understanding dated September 1, 1972, entered into between the State of Alaska and the United States as part of the negotiated settlement of *Alaska* v. *Morton,* Civil No. A–48–72 (D. Alaska, Complaint filed April 10, 1972).

The Secretary of the Interior shall promulgate such regulations as are appropriate, including regulation of the opportunity to engage in a subsistence lifestyle by local residents. The Secretary may close the national monument, or any portion thereof, to subsistence uses of a particular fish, wildlife or plant population if necessary for reasons of public safety, administration, or to ensure the natural stability or continued viability of such population.

Warning is hereby given to all unauthorized persons not to appropriate, injure, destroy or remove any feature of this monument and not to locate or settle upon any of the lands thereof.

IN WITNESS WHEREOF, I have hereunto set my hand this 1st day of December, in the year of our Lord nineteen hundred and seventy-eight, and of the Independence of the United States of America the two hundred and third.

. JIMMY CARTER

[Filed with the Office of the Federal Register, 3:08 p.m., December 1, 1978]

NOTE: The maps detailing the boundaries of the Yukon-Charley National Monument are printed in the FEDERAL REGISTER of December 5, 1978.

Yukon Flats National Monument

Proclamation 4627.   December 1, 1978

By the President of the United States of America

A Proclamation

The Yukon Flats National Monument exemplifies the largest and most complete example of an interior Alaskan solar basin with its associated ecosystem. The mountain-ringed Yukon Flats basin straddles the Arctic Circle and is bisected by the Yukon River.

The physiography of this basin, coupled with the continuous sunlight of the summer months, results in a climatological phenomenon in the basin of warmer summer temperatures and less cloudiness, precipitation and wind than in surrounding areas. These factors produce a lush wetland area which makes the Yukon Flats basin one of North America's most productive wildlife habitats. The pristine ecological nature of the Yukon Flats offers an excellent opportunity for study of the factors contributing to the immense productivity of the solar basin areas.

The Yukon Flats contributes significant populations of several species of waterfowl to all four of the continent's flyways, including 10–25 percent of the North American breeding population of canvasback ducks. This area is also significant for its capacity to provide nesting for ducks displaced from Canadian pothole provinces in drought years. The productivity, migration flows and key habitat for particular species offer abundant scientific research possibilities.

Additionally, the area produces a unique race of salmon which migrate over 2,000 miles from the sea to spawn. This genetic capability is unknown elsewhere.

From prehistoric times, the area's rich populations of furbearers have attracted humans to the area. The establishment of Fort Yukon, the first English speaking settlement in Alaska, was directly related to the Hudson Bay Company's fur trade. The area's preservation offers to the scientist the opportunity to investigate the life and society of the peoples which utilized these resources.

The land withdrawn and reserved by this Proclamation for the protection of the geological, historical, biological and other phenomena enumerated above supports now, as it has in the past, the unique subsistence culture of the local residents. The continued existence of this culture, which depends on subsistence hunting, and its availability for study, enhance the historic and scientific values of the natural objects protected herein because of the ongoing interaction of the subsistence culture with those objects. Accordingly, the opportunity for the local residents to engage in subsistence hunting is a value to be protected and will continue under the administration of the monument.

Section 2 of the Act of June 8, 1906 (34 Stat. 225, 16 U.S.C. 431), authorizes the President, in his discretion, to declare by public proclamation historic landmarks, historic and prehistoric structures, and other objects of historic or scientific interest that are situated upon the lands owned or controlled by the Government of the United States to be national monuments, and to reserve as part thereof parcels of land, the limits of which in all cases shall be confined to the smallest area compatible with the proper care and management of the objects to be protected.

Now, THEREFORE, I, JIMMY CARTER, President of the United States of America, by the authority vested in me by Section 2 of the Act of June 8, 1906 (34 Stat. 225, 16 U.S.C. 431), do proclaim that there are hereby set apart and reserved as the Yukon Flats National Monument all lands, including submerged lands, and waters owned or controlled by the United States within the boundaries of the area depicted as Yukon Flats National Monument on the map numbered FWS–81–00–1514 attached to and forming a part of this Proclamation. The area reserved consists of approximately 10,600,000 acres, and is the smallest area compatible with the proper care and management of the objects to be protected. Lands, including submerged lands, and waters within these boundaries not owned by the United States shall be reserved as a part of the monument upon acquisition of title thereto by the United States.

All lands, including submerged lands, and all waters within the boundaries of this monument are hereby appropriated and withdrawn from entry, location, selection, sale or other disposition under the public land laws, other than exchange. There is also reserved all water necessary to the proper care and management of those objects protected by this monument and for the proper administration of the monument in accordance with applicable laws.

The establishment of this monument is subject to valid existing rights, including, but not limited to, valid selections under the Alaska Native Claims Settlement Act, as amended (43 U.S.C. 1601 *et seq.*), and under or confirmed in the Alaska Statehood Act (48 U.S.C. Note preceding Section 21).

Nothing in this Proclamation shall be deemed to revoke any existing withdrawal, reservation or appropriation, including any public land order effecting a withdrawal under Section 17(d)(1) of the Alaska Native Claims Settlement Act, 43 U.S.C. 1616(d)(1); however, the national monument shall be the dominant reservation. Nothing in this Proclamation is intended to modify or revoke the terms of the Memorandum of Understanding dated September 1, 1972, entered into between the State of Alaska and the United States as part of the negotiated settlement of *Alaska* v. *Morton*, Civil No. A–48–72 (D. Alaska, Complaint filed April 10, 1972).

The Secretary of the Interior shall promulgate such regulations as are appropriate, including regulation of sport hunting, and of the opportunity to engage in a subsistence lifestyle by local residents. The Secretary may close this national monument, or any portion thereof, to subsistence uses of a particular fish, wildlife or plant population or to sport hunting of a particular fish or wildlife population if necessary for reasons of public safety, administration, or to ensure the natural stability or continued viability of such population.

Warning is hereby given to all unauthorized persons not to appropriate, injure, destroy or remove any feature of this monument and not to locate or settle upon any of the lands thereof.

IN WITNESS WHEREOF, I have hereunto set my hand this 1st day of December, in the year of our Lord nineteen hundred and seventy-eight, and of the Independence of the United States of America the two hundred and third.

JIMMY CARTER

[Filed with the Office of the Federal Register, 3:09 p.m., December 1, 1978]

NOTE: The maps detailing the boundaries of the Yukon Flats National Monument are printed in the FEDERAL REGISTER of December 5, 1978.

Outstanding Contributions by Federal Employees

Memorandum From the President.
December 1, 1978

Memorandum for the Heads of Departments and Agencies

On October 19, 1977, I announced a program designed to motivate Federal personnel at all levels to help improve the quality and performance of Government. I asked to be advised of exceptional contributions by both civilian and military personnel so that I might send a personal letter of appreciation to each.

After one full year of operation of this special recognition program, total tangible benefits to the Government have exceeded $210 million. Some 1,380 people, representing 29 departments and agencies, contributed to changes which saved the public an amount equal to the average income taxes of 95,000 Americans. Equally important, there were benefits to the Government and the nation to which no dollar figure can be readily attached—improvements in vital services, scientific achievements, and contributions to the health and well-being of the American people. Particularly outstanding results have been achieved by personnel of the Departments of the Air Force, Navy, and Health, Education, and Welfare, the Environmental Protection Agency, and the National Aeronautics and Space Administration.

These results are gratifying. They prove that given proper motivation and incentive, Federal personnel are eager to contribute to the growth of productivity in Government. It is up to management to use this great resource and to harness the energy, creativity, and ingenuity of those who work in our Government.

I ask all of you, therefore, to provide personal leadership during the year ahead in making full and effective use of the incentive awards authorities to improve Government productivity. And I ask you to continue to emphasize to everyone in your organizations the need for participation in, and support of, this most important effort.

JIMMY CARTER

Visit of Prime Minister Nouira of Tunisia

Joint Communique. December 1, 1978

At the invitation of President Jimmy Carter, Prime Minister Hedi Nouira currently is making an official visit to the United States. He arrived on November 28 and will depart on December 5.

The Prime Minister, who is accompanied by his wife and a delegation which includes Mr. Mohamed Fitouri, Foreign Minister, Mr. Hassan Belkhodja, Minister of Agriculture, and Mr. Mustapha Zaanouni, Minister of Planning, received a warm and friendly welcome.

During his stay the Prime Minister met with President Carter. The discussions were followed by a working luncheon at the White House with the President. The Prime Minister also met with Secretary of State Cyrus Vance and with other government officials and with Members of the Congress.

In the course of his stay in Washington, the Prime Minister also had talks with leaders of economic, financial, and academic institutions. He will also visit agricultural enterprises in Texas, Arizona, and California. He also will meet with the authorities of these states to discuss the utilization of American technology in the development of arid lands, with a view to promoting future Tunisian-American cooperation in this field.

The President and Prime Minister expressed their pleasure at the excellent bilateral relations which have existed for almost two centuries. The President asked the Prime Minister to convey to President Bourguiba his gratitude for the steadfast friendship he has demonstrated for the United States since Tunisia regained its independence.

The President reiterated to the Prime Minister the continuing interest of the United States in the stability, independence and security of Tunisia.

The two leaders agreed to intensify efforts to increase economic cooperation between their two nations, to encourage investment, to promote the transfer of technology, and to develop commercial and cultural exchange.

President Carter congratulated Prime Minister Nouira on the rapid rate of development Tunisia has experienced under the eight years of his administration. Citing Tunisia as a model recipient for sound use of American assistance, the President reiterated his Government's intention to continue and to develop American participation in Tunisia's economic growth.

To this end the United States-Tunisian Joint Commission will meet in Tunis, in late January 1979.

In their discussion of international issues, President Carter and Prime Minister Nouira concentrated especially on the situation in the Middle East. The President expressed his appreciation for the encouragement President Bourguiba and the Prime Minister have given him to continue his personal efforts to facilitate a peace settlement.

The two leaders stressed that participation of the Palestinian people is a fundamental element in the search for peace, and agreed that a comprehensive, just and durable peace must provide for the realization of the legitimate rights for which all Palestinian people have been striving. President Carter stated his belief that Tunisia's constructive approach to international issues gives Tunisia an important role within the international community.

The President assured the Prime Minister that the United States will continue to promote resolution of conflict through peaceful means.

Reviewing the problems of decolonization in Africa both parties expressed their deep worry over the growing deterioration of the situation in southern Africa as a result of the persistence of minority regimes in pursuing the policy and practices of apartheid and racial discrimination. They reaffirmed their commitment to support the rights of self-determination, dignity, and justice for the people of Zimbabwe, Namibia, and South Africa.

The Tunisian delegation expressed its appreciation for the positive action of the United States in its efforts to direct the problems of Rhodesia and Namibia into a channel leading to peaceful settlements and expressed the hope that these efforts soon will prove productive.

The Prime Minister on behalf of President Bourguiba invited President Carter to make a state visit to Tunisia. President Carter accepted this invitation with pleasure. The date will be determined later by mutual agreement.

Communications Satellite Corporation

Nomination of Jesse Hill, Jr., and Joan F. Tobin To Be Members of the Board of Directors. December 1, 1978

The President today announced two persons whom he will nominate as members of the Board of Directors of the Communications Satellite Corporation. They are:

Jesse Hill, Jr., of Atlanta. Hill, 52, is president and chief executive officer of the Atlanta Life Insurance Co., the largest stockholder life insurance company or financial institution controlled and managed by black Americans. He is also president of the Atlanta Chamber of Commerce.

Joan F. Tobin, of Washington, D.C. Tobin, 35, is president of Tobin Enterprises, Inc., which holds major or controlling interests in growth companies, analyzes potential mergers, acquisitions, and partnerships, structures financial arrangements, and actively participates in the management of the component companies. She is also vice president of Tobin International, an export-import business.

Digest of Other White House Announcements

The following listing includes the President's daily schedule and other items of general interest as announced by the White House Press Office during the period covered by this issue. Events and announcements printed elsewhere in the issue are not included.

November 26

The President returned to the White House from a stay at Camp David, Md.

November 27

The President met at the White House with Zbigniew Brzezinski, Assistant to the President for National Security Affairs.

November 28

The President met at the White House with:
—Dr. Brzezinski;
—Secretary of Transportation Brock Adams;
—Vice President Walter F. Mondale, Adm. Stansfield Turner, Director of Central Intelligence, Hamilton Jordan, Assistant to the President, and Dr. Brzezinski;
—Vice President Mondale;
—James T. McIntyre, Jr., Director of the Office of Management and Budget.

The President attended a portion of the meeting of administration officials with Kentucky civic and community leaders which was held in Room 450 of the Old Executive Office Building.

November 29

The President met at the White House with Dr. Brzezinski.

November 30

The President met at the White House with:
—Dr. Brzezinski;
—Secretary of Health, Education, and Welfare Joseph A. Califano, Jr.;
—Mrs. Carter, for lunch;
—South African Foreign Minister Roelof F. Botha.

The President attended a portion of the White House briefing held in the East

Room for newly elected Democratic Members of the House of Representatives.

December 1

The President met at the White House with:

—Vice President Mondale, Secretary of State Cyrus R. Vance, Secretary of Defense Harold Brown, Dr. Brzezinski, and Mr. Jordan;

—a group of editors and news directors (transcript will be printed next week);

—Vice President Mondale and Charles L. Schultze, Chairman of the Council of Economic Advisers;

—Senator James R. Sasser of Tennessee;

—Secretary of the Treasury W. Michael Blumenthal;

—Prime Minister Mustafa Kahlil of Egypt.

NOMINATIONS SUBMITTED TO THE SENATE

NOTE: The Congress having adjourned *sine die* on Sunday, October 15, no nominations were submitted during the period covered by this issue. The first session of the 96th Congress will begin on Monday, January 15, 1979.

CHECKLIST OF WHITE HOUSE PRESS RELEASES

The following releases of the Office of the White House Press Secretary, distributed during the period covered by this issue, are not included in the issue.

Released November 27, 1978

Advanced text: remarks at the National League of Cities' 1978 Congress of Cities

Released December 1, 1978

Fact sheet: rural water and sewer programs initiatives

Fact sheet: designation of National Monuments in Alaska

News conference: on the President's designation of 17 National Monuments in Alaska—by Stuart E. Eizenstat, Assistant to the President for Domestic Affairs and Policy, Secretary of the Interior Cecil D. Andrus, and Assistant Secretary of Agriculture M. Rupert Cutler

ACTS APPROVED BY THE PRESIDENT

NOTE: The President completed his consideration of acts and joint resolutions passed during the second session of the 95th Congress on November 10.

Interview With the President

Remarks and a Question-and-Answer Session With Editors and News Directors.
December 1, 1978

THE PRESIDENT. Hi, everybody. Well, first of all, let me say that it's a pleasure to have you at the White House. This is our 35th meeting, I understand from my briefing this morning, with editors and other news executives from around the country. And it's always a pleasure for us to have a chance to answer your questions, primarily, and let you know what our current problems are, some of which have been chronic problems and, I guess, opportunities for service.

I think for just 2 or 3 minutes, I might outline where we stand on a few major issues, and then spend what time we have available answering your questions.

ADMINISTRATION POLICIES

In domestic affairs, our primary concern at this phase of the year is to prepare the budget for fiscal year 1980, which will commence the 1st of October, next year. It is a very difficult and unpleasant experience to prepare a budget that's going to be as stringent as the one for the upcoming fiscal year.

I meet, ordinarily, with the Office of Management and Budget after they get all their recommendations in. I give them tentative and general guidelines for the allocation of funds, and then each head of an agency or Secretary of the Cabinet has a right to appeal to me if they think that I and OMB have made an improper judgment in the total amount of money available to that agency or the allocation priorities.

The zero-base budgeting technique has helped tremendously to arrange expenditures in a proper order of priority and to incorporate in the same assessment both longstanding commitments for programs and new or innovative programs to be proposed.

So, that's my primary domestic responsibility at this moment.

In foreign affairs, we are continuing our effort to bring about a resolution of the SALT negotiations, pursuing our conventional arms talks with the Soviet Union, trying to reduce the distribution of conventional arms throughout the world, as a matter of fact. We still hope that without much delay, we can meet at the top level between ourselves and the Soviets to sign a SALT II treaty.

I met yesterday with Foreign Minister Pik Botha, from South Africa, to encour-

2149

age him to move expeditiously in the consummation of U.N. Resolution 435, which would grant independence to Namibia, following free and democratic elections to be supervised by the United Nations. He's now going back to get further instructions from Prime Minister—who also happens to be named Botha, as you know.

This afternoon I'll be meeting with the Prime Minister of Egypt, Mr. Kahlil, who is bringing to me a personal message from President Sadat. And following that meeting, we will decide how to persist most effectively in the conclusion of a peace treaty between Egypt and Israel.

As I said in my press conference yesterday, I've been discouraged and disappointed at the slow progress following the Camp David accords in bringing to finality a treaty text, with all the ancillary documents that go with it. But we will be persistent in this effort, tenacious. And the one bright spot in the entire process is that I'm convinced that both the Egyptian and the Israeli people want peace between themselves.

And we are operating under a handicap, because it's very difficult to negotiate with leaders who are far distant from me. I can't consult with them simultaneously on a given paragraph or phrase or issue. And unfortunately, to an increasing degree, the negotiations have taken place through the news media, which in effect makes any backing down on a statement made by a Foreign Minister or a negotiator or a Prime Minister or a President almost a matter of violation of national honor, rather than the quiet negotiation that we did impose at Camp David.

Although discouraged, I've certainly not given up on the prospect for the peace treaty to be concluded.

I think that there are other matters that I could go over with you, concerning China, negotiations on Philippines bases, trying to prevent bloodshed in Nicaragua,

and so forth. But I think that we might best spend our time with my answering your questions. And I am very delighted to have you here.

John [John Pruitt, WXIA–TV, Atlanta, Ga.]—I'll pull my rank and call on a Georgian first. [*Laughter*]

Q. Thank you, Mr. President.

THE PRESIDENT. John, good to see you.

QUESTIONS

EGYPTIAN-ISRAELI PEACE NEGOTIATIONS

Q. Following up on the Middle East statement you made, what is your personal reaction to President Sadat's statement that he will not go to Oslo to accept the Nobel Peace Prize? Are you personally disappointed by that, and what implications does that have to the peace process?

THE PRESIDENT. I'm not surprised that President Sadat will not go to Oslo. I think had the peace treaty been signed prior to December 10, or whatever the date is, that he would have gone. He will send a representative to receive the prize for him. But I don't think it has any particular extra connotation, other than the obvious one, that to receive the peace prize for bringing about a treaty between Israel and Egypt, absent a conclusion of the treaty, he considers to be inappropriate.

I don't think it has any far-reaching connotations that further aggravate the already difficult situation.

Q. Do you think the two can maybe get together again to resolve this?

THE PRESIDENT. That's always an ultimate possibility. I think they both see that there must be some substantive prospect of success before they get together again. We did not have that substantive prospect of success when they met at Camp David. But I think it was an absolutely hopeless case before we decided to go to Camp David. I don't think it's in that degree of extremity now.

MOOD OF THE AMERICAN PUBLIC

Q. How do you assess the mood of the American people today, December 1, 1978?

THE PRESIDENT. I think the mood of the American people was most accurately expressed publicly by the results of the elections this past month. I was pleased with the overall outcome of the elections. Democrats retain a strong majority, at least 60 percent majority in the House, the Senate, and among Governors. So, there is an overall approbation of the policies of our own party.

I think there was an expression of caution about the rampant inflation that people fear. My own sense is that the American people want us to be determined and tenacious in controlling inflation, reducing the rate of inflation over a period of time. I think they recognize the difficulty of it. It can be accomplished without a recession or depression, and at the same time that we meet our international and domestic needs, social programs, defense responsibilities.

There was and is, I think, an approval of our Nation's policy in international affairs, the general sense that we're doing the best we can, not only to provide peace for our own people—we've not had any American shed blood in combat in the last 2 years; maybe we can continue that; I certainly pray that we can—and the fact that we have raised the banner of human rights in a forceful and, I think, effective way; and the fact that we are negotiating under difficult circumstances in places like Namibia, Rhodesia, Nicaragua, the Mideast, Cyprus, in areas where our security is indirectly threatened, but where the peacefulness of other people are more directly enhanced by our efforts.

So, I think in general I feel a sense of fiscal responsibility combined with a brighter hope for the future. I don't think the American people are concerned. I think they recognize, deeply within them, that our country is militarily, politically, and economically the strongest on Earth, and that we are likely to stay that way.

MAYOR RICHARD G. HATCHER OF GARY

Q. Mr. President, Jerry Mastey from WWCA [Radio] in Gary. It's been an open secret for many years now in northwest Indiana that Mayor Richard Hatcher has been under almost constant investigation by the Internal Revenue Service and the FBI. And many times the mayor has claimed——

THE PRESIDENT. So have I, by the way. I've been—[*laughter*].

Q. ——that he's one of the most investigated mayors in history. A two-part question——

THE PRESIDENT. I'm the most investigated President. [*Laughter*] But go ahead. I'll answer.

Q. The first part of the question: Assuming you are aware of those comments, does the fact you offered the mayor a job in your administration in April of this year indicate those reports are without foundation? The second part: Will you at some point in the future offer the mayor another but not necessarily the same position in your administration?

THE PRESIDENT. Well, I wasn't being completely facetious when I pointed out that my income tax returns have been audited in depth every year at an enormous personal expense to me, like $30, $40,000, just—and the upshot of it has been that I've gotten a refund, not nearly so large as my cost, but a refund. Recently

2151

all of my past reports on property tax evaluations have been assessed. And I think I've got to pay a net of about $750 after all that effort. I don't object to it.

But the fact that an investigation is held of a political figure, a controversial and progressive mayor or a President, doesn't mean that there is any substance to the allegations or any illegalities involved. Of course, we were familiar with the fact that investigations were being held concerning Mayor Hatcher at the time I offered him a top position in the White House, and I wish he had accepted. I still have complete confidence in him.

After careful consideration of that offer, he decided to stay in his present position. And I understood his reasons. There are no hard feelings about it. Since he already has assessed a very attractive position in the Government and rejected, I don't have any plans to offer him another position any time soon.

Q. So, the reports that have been circulating since he came into office in 1968 you feel for the most part are without foundation?

THE PRESIDENT. So far as I know. Obviously I have not conducted any investigation. But knowing that the investigations were being conducted, I was willing to offer him a top position, which indicates my attitude.

STATE LEGISLATURE SALARY INCREASES

Q. Mr. President, Joe Fenley from Dayton, Ohio. On Wednesday, the Ohio Senate approved the 28-percent pay increase for the State legislature. The house has yet to vote on that measure. And one State senator who voted against it, who was elected to Congress in November, he's already been threatened with being redistricted out of Congress by 1980. Would

you comment on that in relation to the kind of interjectories with your policy?

THE PRESIDENT. It doesn't help at all. [*Laughter*] My own longstanding belief is that Congress Members and legislative members should not raise their own salaries during current terms of office; that any time a salary increase is voted by public officials after they have been elected, it ought to be delayed in its effective date until after the next election.

Obviously, to increase legislative salaries in Ohio or Illinois or anywhere else by 25 or 30 percent, when we are really trying to hold down wage increases to a 7-percent level, works counter to the best interest of our Nation in controlling inflation. I say that with the full realization that that's an autonomous body and that I don't have any control over it.

But I would hope that legislators around the country would join in with us in exercising restraint during these times when inflation ought to be in the forefront and when elected officials ought to set an example.

ENERGY PROGRAMS

Q. I'd like to ask two questions about energy. What are your plans for Phase II after the present congressional bill takes effect, and how do you plan to deal with the inflationary effects of energy imports increasing and doubling to a hundred billion dollars in costs by 1985?

THE PRESIDENT. Well, we'll continue to try to implement fully the energy proposal I put to the Congress in April of 1977, which would have resulted in about a 4½ million barrel-per-day savings. The bills that were passed, we estimate they'll save about 2.6 million barrels a day, about 60 percent success.

In the so-called Phase II effort, there are many facets involved. One is a successful administration of the very complicated and detailed and far-reaching five bills that I signed into law earlier this year; to take that law and then to implement it is a very major consideration.

Also, in the preparation of the 1980 fiscal year budget and subsequent budgets, that Phase II implementation of energy savings must be consummated, both in the allocation of tax benefits for those who shift to more plentiful supplies of fuel, encouragement of conservation, and the great increase in allocation of basic research and development funds for solar energy and other alternate, more permanent supplies of energy.

As far as the inflationary impact of imported oil, I would say the overriding interest that we had in consummating the energy policy is to reduce dependence on imported oil below what it would have been had there been no energy policy approved by the Congress.

We, at the same time, are trying to hold down the inclination of the OPEC nations to increase the price of oil that we do have to purchase, whatever the level of imports might be. Secretary Blumenthal has just returned from a fairly extensive trip to the Mideast to try to convince them in an open and clear and fair and objective way about the benefits to be derived among the OPEC nations for stable economic circumstances around the world.

We are trying to do our part by controlling inflation in our own country and by stabilizing the value of the dollar. Since the 1st of November, I think was the date, when I approved a new program to strengthen the American dollar, its value has increased about 12 percent, I think, with respect to the deutsche mark, German deutsche mark, and about the same amount with respect to the Swiss franc and the Japanese yen. This is something we've done on our own behalf.

But I think that to the extent that the OPEC nations realize that an increase in the price of oil to an inordinate degree would be counterproductive, it would help to hold down inflationary pressures in the future.

So, to implement and administer the existing laws that have just been passed, major tasks; through budgetary decisions on the allocation of funds for research, development, and shifting toward new energy supplies, a second thing; to reduce imports as much as we can in present and future years; and to hold down the price of oil that is imported—those are the four basic thrusts that we are pursuing.

STEEL IMPORTS

Q. Following up, regarding imports—Jim Blount from Hamilton, Ohio—Armco Steel is located in my area. Of course, speaking of imports, they report this week of foreign import of steel continuing to increase—I think it was 16 percent rate over the last year. I would be interested in your comments if the administration is planning any more action on the trigger price mechanism in order to try to hold that down.

THE PRESIDENT. I think the trigger price mechanism has only been in effect since May of this year. And so far we've been pleased with the results. The basic modification of that program, I think, would be inappropriate so soon. We don't have any plans to do it. We are constantly assessing, however, the trigger price itself, as we look at inflation here and in other countries, look at the price of producing oil in Japan, which is the base nation that we observe, and also as we assess the import levels from different countries.

The last figures that I've actually seen officially were that Japanese exports to us had been reduced substantially since the trigger price mechanism was implemented. I did see some reports in the news media recently that total imports had increased somewhat.

I don't have any present plans to modify the program at all. But we'll be constantly assessing it to see if that's required action in the future.

APPALACHIAN REGIONAL COMMISSION

Q. Mr. President, I'm Eldora Nuzum from Elkins.

THE PRESIDENT. I recognize you.

Q. We're so happy you came to the Forest Festival.

THE PRESIDENT. So am I.

Q. I think you need to get out with the American people more often. The President walked 2 miles in the Forest Festival parade, and everybody loved it. They felt like they were getting to know you.

Now my question. I know you're cutting back on spending the next year, but the Appalachian Regional Commission Act has built new roads in West Virginia, schools and hospitals. We feel that this is an investment, and it's very important to our people in 13 States. Are you planning on cutting back in this direction?

THE PRESIDENT. I can't answer that question yet. I might say that I was chairman of the Appalachian Regional Commission while I was Governor of Georgia, and I'm familiar to that extent with its function and with its superb improvements that it has made in the whole region, 13 States.

Also, [Senator] Jennings Randolph keeps this question constantly before my eyes. I just talked to Jennings a few minutes ago, by the way, to tell him that we were praying for his wife, who's having an operation today.

But I can't answer your question about a specific level of funding for the Appalachian Regional Commission or other items.

I've just about completed all of my preliminary budget sessions on domestic and foreign affairs. I'll have my last one this afternoon and Monday on Defense Department issues. But all I can say is to repeat what I said yesterday at the press conference: that I'll be ultimately responsible to the American people, that when the budget is revealed to the Congress and to the public, that it is fair and well balanced, and that we meet our domestic and defense and foreign needs, and that the restraints are applied equitably among all our people.

But I can't give you an answer yet on exactly how the Appalachian Regional Commission will be treated; just that it'll be treated fairly. And if the Congress, of course, disagrees and can improve the budget or modify it, based on primarily later revelations of inflationary trends and needs, then, of course, I would have to accommodate those changes.

But that's the best answer I can give you, which is not a very good answer.

GOVERNOR AND LIEUTENANT GOVERNOR OF FLORIDA

Q. Mr. President, Bob Jordan from Orlando, Florida. We understand that sometime ago you were interested in bringing Reubin Askew into your administration, our outgoing Governor. We've since learned that he is going into international law. But there's now talk that Lieutenant Governor Williams might find a place in the Agriculture Department. Have you given up on bringing Reubin Askew to Washington, and are you interested in bringing Jim Williams to Washington?

THE PRESIDENT. Well, let me not comment on Jim Williams, because that's one of the things that I would rather avoid, is speculating on who might get jobs when it's all in the formative stage.

When I was first elected President, I offered Reubin Askew almost any Cabinet post that he would like. He's one of the people that has my unbounded admiration. And he chose then to stay and fulfill his term in Florida as Governor. But I have called on him to do several major jobs since I've been President.

One was to bring order out of chaos in the selection of top diplomatic officials. He has personally screened, along with a very fine committee that he and I chose together, every group of prospective ambassadors, for instance. And I think we've got an admirable group now because of Reubin's work.

He will continue on as chairman of that committee. I asked him to do that recently, and he's agreed to do that. Reubin has informed me that he does not want to leave Florida on a full-time basis anytime in the future.

I might add parenthetically that I don't contemplate any vacancies in my Cabinet in the future. I'm well satisfied with the entire group that I have now.

DEFENSE SPENDING

Q. Mr. President, I'm David Feingold of National Public Radio Station WOSU in Columbus, Ohio. I would like to ask a question.

The administration has been directing a lot of talk both to the public and to Congress about the 3-percent increase in defense spending, the M-X cruise missiles, the civil defense plan.

Two questions: Is this a simultaneous campaign to both neutralize anti-SALT feelings in the Senate and also to create more bargaining chips in the SALT talks themselves?

THE PRESIDENT. No. Compared to a year ago, there's a tenfold increase in the interest in the budget itself. When I was preparing the budget for fiscal year 1979, I very seldom got a question from the news media about, "What are you going to propose next January to the Congress?" But now since we are in a program of fiscal restraint, trying to control inflation as one of our top priorities, and so forth, there's a much more intense interest in the Appalachian Regional Commission and defense-level expenditures and others.

This is the same process I went through last year, to decide what level of increase we should have in the Defense Department. As far as specific programs are concerned, the M-X missiles, or civil defense, it's the same process as we had last year.

I have felt for a good while that our civil defense effort should be reassessed. We have primarily observed the Soviets' interest in civil defense, the massive evacuation of their major cities, including Moscow. This causes some concern, that if we should have a seriously deteriorating relationship with the Soviet Union, so that even the prospect of war was extant, that both sides would want to prepare themselves to minimize deaths in case a war should occur. I think this is obviously a very unlikely prospect. But our capability in transportation is certainly equal to or superior to that of the Soviet Union.

And the fact that we are assessing how we would go about partial evacuation of our major cities if war became possibly imminent is, I think, not a radical thing. It's not designed for propaganda purposes. It's not designed to influence the Soviets, or to influence the Congress to approve SALT. It's just a routine matter that is being pursued by me.

I've not made any decisions on it. I've never discussed with anyone funding levels, in spite of some contrary reports in the press and so forth.

So, these are basically routine matters—the level of defense spending; what kind of strategic weapons we should construct in the future; whether they should be primarily cruise missiles, primarily new airplanes, primarily the M-X; whether we should have a multiple aim point type system. It's a routine matter. They're just highly publicized now. But they are not designed for any sort of subterfuge.

STRATEGIC ARMS LIMITATION

Q. Is Dr. Brzezinski becoming more involved in the SALT talks, and how close to signing are you?

THE PRESIDENT. Well, Dr. Brzezinski couldn't possibly be any more closely involved in the SALT talks than he has been from the very first day we commenced them. Any decision made concerning the SALT negotiating position, whether it was a major position 20 months ago or now, or in minor modification in the text of the language, is very carefully considered by Dr. Brzezinski, by Harold Brown, by Secretary Vance, by Paul Warnke, and almost invariably by the Joint Chiefs of Staff themselves, or at least the Chairman of the Joint Chiefs of Staff. And on occasion, I consult with some of the Members of the Congress, particularly those Members of the Senate who will ultimately have to ratify such

an agreement. But his position has been integral from the very beginning, still is, and hasn't changed.

We are much closer to a SALT agreement now than we were before. I think we are down to the last stages of negotiation. Our position and that of the Soviets is clear, and I think if the Soviets want a SALT agreement, the door is open to them to have one.

What their attitude will be to actually concluding an agreement is something that's unpredictable. But I don't see any obstacle now to fairly expeditious passage of agreement on the SALT II treaty.

ELECTION RESULTS IN MINNESOTA

Q. Mr. President, Frank Wright from the Minneapolis Tribune. You mentioned a few minutes ago that you were generally pleased with the election results. On the other side of that coin, have you and the Vice President had any postmortems on what the two of you might have done to prevent the disaster in Minnesota?

THE PRESIDENT. We could have paid less attention to the polls that were published—[laughter]—in some of the newspapers that I won't mention. [Laughter]

I don't know of anything else we could have done. The sharp division within the DFL [Democratic-Farmer-Labor Party] was obvious to the Vice President and to me. We tried, as best we could, to heal those divisions following the primary elections, and were not able to. I, as you know, made one extra trip into Minnesota the last weekend before the elections, hoping it would help to some degree. But I don't know of anything else we could have done to help the candidates, the Democrats in the election.

I was disappointed with the outcome, but we'll work as well as we can with the new Senators and the new Governor on a bipartisan basis, particularly in matters that concern defense, national affairs. And I look forward to getting to know them better. And once the election's over, as far as I'm concerned, I represent all the people, Democrats and Republicans. Just disappointed, don't know anything else we could have done. We'll work with the ones that the Minnesota people elected.

I don't have much time, and I would like very much, if you don't have any objection, to get a photograph with each one of you individually. I might add that I don't have time to answer additional questions as you come by. So, let's just have a handshake, and you can introduce yourself, and we'll send you the photograph.

I've enjoyed it. Thank you very much.

NOTE: The interview began at 10 a.m. in the Cabinet Room at the White House.

The transcript of the interview was released on December 2.

Department of Agriculture

Nomination of Dale E. Hathaway To Be Under Secretary for International Affairs and Commodity Programs. December 4, 1978

The President today announced that he will nominate Dale E. Hathaway to be Under Secretary of Agriculture for International Affairs and Commodity Programs, a new position.

Hathaway is currently an Assistant Secretary of Agriculture, with primary responsibility for international affairs and commodity programs.

Hathaway, 53, was director of the International Food Policy Research Institute before his appointment as Assistant Secretary of Agriculture in March 1977. He has also served as a program adviser in agriculture for the Ford Foundation's Asia and Pacific Program.

United Nations Economic and Social Council

Appointment of William J. Stibravy as U.S. Deputy Representative. December 4, 1978

The President today announced the appointment of William J. Stibravy, of Newark, N.J., as Deputy Representative of the United States on the Economic and Social Council of the United Nations.

Stibravy, 62, is currently Minister-Counselor for Economic and Social Affairs at the U.S. Mission to the United Nations. He is a former director of the Office of International Economic and Social Affairs at the State Department.

William A. Steiger

Statement on the Death of the Representative From Wisconsin. December 4, 1978

The death this morning of Congressman William Steiger deprives the Congress of a youthful but experienced leader.

Congressman Steiger, the youngest Member of Congress when he was elected in 1966, quickly earned the respect of his colleagues. His energy, independence, and good humor will be sorely missed by the people of Wisconsin and by his colleagues.

Rosalynn and I extend our deepest sympathies to Congressman Steiger's wife and family on their loss.

Emergency Board To Investigate an Airline Labor Dispute

Appointment of One Member and Announcement of Extension of the Deadline for the Board's Report. December 4, 1978

The President today announced the appointment of a new member of the Wien Air Alaska emergency board, and an extension of the time within which the board must report on the dispute.

The President appointed Laurence Seibel, a Washington attorney and labor dispute arbitrator, to replace John Gentry, who resigned from the board. Paul Guthrie, already a member of the board, will replace Gentry as Chairman.

The deadline for the board's report is extended from December 2, 1978, to January 15, 1979.

Airplane Crash in Alaska

Statement on the Incident Involving Senator and Mrs. Ted Stevens of Alaska and Others. December 5, 1978

Rosalynn and I were shocked to learn of the tragic plane crash in Alaska yesterday which claimed the lives of five people, including Mrs. Ted Stevens. We join the families of Senator Stevens and Tony Motley in praying for their quick recovery, and we extend to Senator Stevens' family and the families of Richard Sykes, Richard Church, Joe Rudd, and Clarence Kramer our deepest sympathies for their loss.

Hubert H. Humphrey North-South Scholarship Program

Remarks at a White House Meeting on the Program. December 5, 1978

First of all, let me say that I and Senator Muriel Humphrey, John Reinhardt, and others are very delighted to have you here this afternoon for what I believe is the initiation of a very precious and valuable new program for our own country.

It's completely appropriate that the program should have been conceived and named because of and after Senator Hubert Humphrey. He always exemplified what this program is supposed to accomplish, that is, a deep belief in the human spirit, the value of human progress, hope in the face of at least partial discouragement and sometimes even despair, the breaking down of barriers that exist between people because of difference in heritage or race or country of origin or formal opportunity of their families.

Senator Humphrey also believed that the crucial element in the growth of a person was in education, formal education, of course, but the stretching of one's mind and heart in every conceivable way. I think we all realize that to the limit of his great ability, he strove for better international understanding, for peace, for the end of wars and the prevention of war.

I believe that our country has a great deal to offer that has not yet been accepted by people from other nations. I've said on many occasions that in years gone by I always dreaded seeing the United Nations General Assembly convene, because our country was the target of every attack and the butt of every joke from 100 nations on Earth. And it was very embarrassing to me and to all Americans who observed this annual affair.

That has changed. I believe there's a new willingness, in some cases eagerness for the leaders and the ordinary citizens of other nations now to not only learn more about the United States but also to have a closer political, social, cultural relationship with us.

This is a fairly modest program, but it can have a profound impact. And I think it will help a great deal to alleviate the ignorance of other people toward us or about us. Senator Humphrey said that if freedom cannot live with ignorance, then between the two the choice is very clear. And we are trying to alleviate that, whether someone is highly educated but still doesn't understand our country and, therefore, is ignorant about us, or because someone is deprived and very narrow in their opportunities and don't know much about us.

But I think this program will be an avenue toward a greatly magnified opportunity for the enhancement of better relationships. It will mean a lot to a President. We'll have about 250 highly motivated, extremely competent, deserving young people coming from nations all over the Earth, particularly in the Third World, the developing nations, to our country at the graduate level, already being well conversant, through formal education and experience, with their own nations, to come here to learn about ours.

As many of you undoubtedly know, the originator for the concept of the Peace Corps was Hubert Humphrey. And that was a program to send hundreds of young and old Americans to foreign countries to serve and to learn and to take our culture there for examination in the personality of the Peace Corps volunteer.

This is kind of a Peace Corps in reverse; highly motivated, fortunate young people will come to our Nation to serve their countries, to help serve us, and to learn about us. And, of course, we in the process will learn about them.

These scholarships will be eagerly sought. The competition will be high. The value to our country will be great, and if the program works well, the value to the students' countries will be much greater.

We want to make it work and work well. And when the first group comes to our Nation next year, John, I would like—although I haven't talked to you about this—I would like to have them come by in a group and meet with me and to get some acquaintance not only with the President of the United States but with our Government, our Capital City for just a few hours or perhaps a day or two. And then I understand at the end of our program they will go to the Hubert Humphrey Institute in Minnesota to get an encapsulation of what they can do in political motivation when they return back home.

This is not designed to do anything but serve others. And I think the relatively low costs will be greatly magnified. Rabbi Hillel said that one candle can light a thousand others and not diminish itself. And that's what we hope to accomplish in this program; each focal point of high education, knowledge about our Nation, competence, leadership in the persons of the students involved will go back to their own nations and greatly expand their own influence and, directly and indirectly, the beneficial influence of our own country.

And in the process our Nation certainly will not be diminished in the process.

Let me thank you, again, for being willing to come here. The program will be described to you in some detail later on. You'll get a briefing on the East-West relationships and the North-South relationships that presently exist between our country and others. You'll be able not only to learn about the embryonic program but also, hopefully, to give advice, counsel, and constructive criticisms. I think that as we evolve the final arrangements for the program, your voices will be very valuable to us all. Your institutions are great in themselves. I hope this program will add to their greatness.

Thank you, again, for letting me participate. I know Hubert Humphrey, a great man, a great American, would be proud if he knew about what is going on today, and my belief is that he knows.

Thank you very much.

NOTE: The President spoke at 2:16 p.m. in Room 450 of the Old Executive Office Building. John E. Reinhardt is Director of the International Communication Agency.

For an announcement on the meeting and the scholarship program, see page 2038 of this volume.

New York City, New York

Remarks at a Fundraising Dinner for Former New York City Mayor Abraham Beame. December 5, 1978

With me, Abe Beame stands very tall. [*Laughter*]

Several people have asked me why I would leave the White House and come to New York this evening. As a matter of fact, Alfred Kahn was supposed to come. And he got his invitation, and he called me and said, "Mr. President, I've just discovered that a meal and an opera ticket in New York is now up to $2,500. And I think this is one situation you ought to handle personally." [*Laughter*]

I've come because of my admiration and appreciation for Abe Beame. He joined in a unique circumstance that took place in New York City a couple of years ago, where great and profound decisions were made that benefited New York City and our country. The invitation to the Democratic National Convention to come here was one of those decisions, and the decision made by the Democratic National Convention after they got here was the other one. [*Laughter*] But I'm very proud of what you did for me.

I had a chance to visit with Abe Beame many times, both during and after that convention session. When I was a relatively unknown candidate whom no one had the temerity to support publicly, I had a warm reception from Abe Beame. And he was always willing to take a half hour or an hour with his top staff members, either at City Hall or in Gracie Mansion, to sit down with me, just on the chance that I might have some influence in the future, to explain to me the most serious questions on his mind. He is the most unselfish political figure that I have ever known. Never once have I ever heard him even insinuate a request for anything that would benefit Abe Beame. It was always New York City alone.

It was a very impressive performance, because he knew the dismal prospects at that time. He was frustrated when he turned his eyes and his heart and his hand to Washington. And I know that in those early days of the campaign, he not only talked to me but talked to other Democratic candidates as well about how desperately New York City needed a new partnership, not only with Albany but with Washington as well.

And then I was nominated, and then I was elected. And I think the first two visitors I had in Georgia were two desperate-looking men. Mayor Abe Beame was one; Governor Hugh Carey was the other. They came to talk to me about the prospects for the future. I said, "What can I do for you?" And they said, "Mr. President-elect, we need two things. We need $1,685 million, and we need two bus tickets back to New York." [*Laughter*] And I think after those trying and desperate and lonely days, the progress has been great.

I would like to pay tribute this evening, in closing, to a man whom I admire very much as a dedicated, sincere, competent, quiet, modest political leader who learned the intricacies of New York City's affairs under some of the most trying possible conditions. And when many people, even perhaps some of you sitting here, said "Bankruptcy is inevitable; we will never prevail," Abe Beame was staunch and strong and courageous and great. He's got a worthy successor, Ed Koch— and they worked in the transition in a very harmonious way—and a staunch supporter as well, as you know, in Hugh Carey, who's formed a good partnership.

We've still got a long way to go in making clear to the world and to the people here that New York City's financial condition is permanently sound. But because of this unselfish and dedicated and modest man, great strides have already been made that form a basis for inevitable future success.

So, I've come here to pay my respects as President of the United States on behalf of the American people and as a personal friend and admirer to a great man, a good man, a dedicated and un-selfish man, Abe Beame. It's an honor for me to be here.

Thank you.

NOTE: The President spoke at 7:23 p.m. on the Grand Tier level of the Metropolitan Opera House.

Following the dinner, the President attended a Metropolitan Opera production of "Aida." He then returned to Washington, D.C.

Universal Declaration of Human Rights

Remarks at a White House Meeting Commemorating the 30th Anniversary of the Declaration's Signing. December 6, 1978

What I have to say today is fundamentally very simple. It's something I've said many times, including my acceptance speech when I was nominated as President and my inaugural speech when I became President. But it cannot be said too often or too firmly nor too strongly.

As long as I am President, the Government of the United States will continue throughout the world to enhance human rights. No force on Earth can separate us from that commitment.

This week we commemorate the 30th anniversary of the Universal Declaration of Human Rights. We rededicate ourselves—in the words of Eleanor Roosevelt, who was the chairperson of the Human Rights Commission—to the Universal Declaration as, and I quote from her, "a common standard of achievement for all peoples of all nations."

The Universal Declaration and the human rights conventions that derive from it do not describe the world as it is. But these documents are very important, nonetheless. They are a beacon, a guide to a future of personal security, political freedom, and social justice.

For millions of people around the globe that beacon is still quite distant, a glimmer of light on a dark horizon of deprivation and repression. The reports of Amnesty International, the International Commission of Jurists, the International League for Human Rights, and many other nongovernmental human rights organizations amply document the practices and conditions that destroy the lives and the spirit of countless human beings.

Political killings, tortures, arbitrary and prolonged detention without trial or without a charge, these are the cruelest and the ugliest of human rights violations. Of all human rights, the most basic is to be free of arbitrary violence, whether that violence comes from government, from terrorists, from criminals, or from self-appointed messiahs operating under the cover of politics or religion.

But governments—because of their power, which is so much greater than that of an individual—have a special responsibility. The first duty of a government is to protect its own citizens, and when government itself becomes the perpetrator of arbitrary violence against its citizens, it undermines its own legitimacy.

There are other violations of the body and the spirit which are especially destructive of human life. Hunger, disease, poverty are enemies of human potential which are as relentless as any repressive government.

The American people want the actions of their government, our government, both to reduce human suffering and to increase human freedom. That's why— with the help and encouragement of many of you in this room—I have sought

to rekindle the beacon of human rights in American foreign policy. Over the last 2 years we've tried to express these human concerns as our diplomats practice their craft and as our Nation fulfills its own international obligations.

We will speak out when individual rights are violated in other lands. The Universal Declaration means that no nation can draw the cloak of sovereignty over torture, disappearances, officially sanctioned bigotry, or the destruction of freedom within its own borders. The message that is being delivered by all our representatives abroad—whether they are from the Department of State or Commerce or Agriculture or Defense or whatever—is that the policies regarding human rights count very much in the character of our own relations with other individual countries.

In distributing the scarce resources of our foreign assistance programs, we will demonstrate that our deepest affinities are with nations which commit themselves to a democratic path to development. Toward regimes which persist in wholesale violations of human rights, we will not hesitate to convey our outrage, nor will we pretend that our relations are unaffected.

In the coming year, I hope that Congress will take a step that has been long overdue for a generation, the ratification of the Convention on the Prevention and Punishment of the Crime of Genocide. As you know, the genocide convention was also adopted by the United Nations General Assembly 30 years ago this week, 1 day before the adoption of the Universal Declaration. It was the world's affirmation that the lesson of the Holocaust would never be forgotten, but unhappily, genocide is not peculiar to any one historical era.

Eighty-three other nations have ratified the genocide convention. The United

States, despite the support of every President since 1948, has not. In international meetings at the United Nations and elsewhere, when I meet with foreign leaders, we are often asked why. We do not have an acceptable answer.

I urge the United States Senate to observe this anniversary in the only appropriate way, by ratifying the genocide convention at the earliest possible date.

This action must be the first step toward the ratification of other human rights instruments, including those I signed a year ago. Many of the religious and human rights groups represented here have undertaken a campaign of public education on behalf of these covenants. I commend and appreciate your efforts.

Refugees are the living, homeless casualties of one very important failure on the part of the world to live by the principles of peace and human rights. To help these refugees is a simple human duty. As Americans, as a people made up largely of the descendants of refugees, we feel that duty with special keenness.

Our country will do its utmost to ease the plight of stranded refugees from Indochina and from Lebanon and of released political prisoners from Cuba and from elsewhere. I hope that we will always stand ready to welcome more than our fair share of those who flee their homelands because of racial, religious, or political oppression.

The effectiveness of our human rights policy is now an established fact. It has contributed to an atmosphere of change—sometimes disturbing—but which has encouraged progress in many ways and in many places. In some countries, political prisoners have been released by the hundreds, even thousands. In others, the brutality of repression has been lessened. In still others there's a movement toward democratic institu-

tions or the rule of law when these movements were not previously detectable.

To those who doubt the wisdom of our dedication, I say this: Ask the victims. Ask the exiles. Ask the governments which continue to practice repression. Whether in Cambodia or Chile, in Uganda or South Africa, in Nicaragua or Ethiopia or the Soviet Union, governments know that we in the United States care. And not a single one of those who is actually taking risks or suffering for human rights has ever asked me to desist in our support of basic human rights. From the prisons, from the camps, from the enforced exiles, we receive one message: Speak up, persevere, let the voice of freedom be heard.

I'm very proud that our Nation stands for more than military might or political might. It stands for ideals that have their reflection in the aspirations of peasants in Latin America, workers in Eastern Europe, students in Africa, and farmers in Asia.

We do live in a difficult and complicated world, a world in which peace is literally a matter of survival. Our foreign policy must take this into account. Often, a choice that moves us toward one goal tends to move us further away from another goal. Seldom do circumstances permit me or you to take actions that are wholly satisfactory to everyone.

But I want to stress again that human rights are not peripheral to the foreign policy of the United States. Our human rights policy is not a decoration. It is not something we've adopted to polish up our image abroad or to put a fresh coat of moral paint on the discredited policies of the past. Our pursuit of human rights is part of a broad effort to use our great power and our tremendous influence in the service of creating a better world, a world in which human beings can live in peace, in freedom, and with their basic needs adequately met.

Human rights is the soul of our foreign policy. And I say this with assurance, because human rights is the soul of our sense of nationhood.

For the most part, other nations are held together by common racial or ethnic ancestry, or by a common creed or religion, or by ancient attachments to the land that go back for centuries of time. Some nations are held together by the forces, implied forces of a tyrannical government. We are different from all of those, and I believe that we in our country are more fortunate.

As a people we come from every country and every corner of the Earth. We are of many religions and many creeds. We are of every race, every color, every ethnic and cultural background. We are right to be proud of these things and of the richness that lend to the texture of our national life. But they are not the things which unite us as a single people.

What unites us—what makes us Americans—is a common belief in peace, in a free society, and a common devotion to the liberties enshrined in our Constitution. That belief and that devotion are the sources of our sense of national community. Uniquely, ours is a nation founded on an idea of human rights. From our own history we know how powerful that idea can be.

Next week marks another human rights anniversary—Bill of Rights Day. Our Nation was "conceived in liberty," in Lincoln's words, but it has taken nearly two centuries for that liberty to approach maturity.

For most of the first half of our history, black Americans were denied even the most basic human rights. For most of the first two-thirds of our history, women were excluded from the political process. Their rights and those of Native Americans are still not constitutionally guaranteed and enforced. Even freedom of speech has been threatened periodically throughout our history. Only in the last 10 to 12 years have we achieved what Father Hesburgh has called "the legal abandonment of more than three centuries of apartheid." And the struggle for full human rights for all Americans— black, brown, and white; male and female; rich and poor—is far from over.

To me, as to many of you, these are not abstract matters or ideas. In the rural Georgia country where I grew up, the majority of my own fellow citizens were denied many basic rights—the right to vote, the right to speak freely without fear, the right to equal treatment under the law. I saw at first hand the effects of a system of deprivation of rights. I saw the courage of those who resisted that system. And finally, I saw the cleansing energies that were released when my own region of this country walked out of darkness and into what Hubert Humphrey, in the year of the adoption of the Universal Declaration, called "the bright sunshine of human rights."

The American Bill of Rights is 187 years old, and the struggle to make it a reality has occupied every one of those 187 years. The Universal Declaration of Human Rights is only 30 years old. In the perspective of history, the idea of human rights has only just been broached.

I do not draw this comparison because I want to counsel patience. I draw it because I want to emphasize, in spite of difficulties, steadfastness and commitment.

A hundred and eighty-seven years ago, as far as most Americans were concerned, the Bill of Rights was a bill of promises. There was no guarantee that those promises would ever be fulfilled. We did not realize those promises by waiting for history to take its inevitable course. We realized them because we struggled. We realized them because many sacrificed. We realized them because we persevered.

For millions of people around the world today the Universal Declaration of Human Rights is still only a declaration of hope. Like all of you, I want that hope to be fulfilled. The struggle to fulfill it will last longer than the lifetimes of any of us. Indeed, it will last as long as the lifetime of humanity itself. But we must persevere.

And we must persevere by ensuring that this country of ours, leader in the world, which we love so much, is always in the forefront of those who are struggling for that great hope, the great dream of universal human rights.

Thank you very much.

NOTE: The President spoke at 12 noon in the East Room at the White House. Earlier he had hosted a reception and a briefing by administration officials for the human rights activists, Members of Congress, and administration officials involved in human rights policy who were present for the meeting.

Veterans Preference in Employment

White House Statement.   December 6, 1978

On Monday, the Department of Justice lodged an *amicus curiae* brief with the United States Supreme Court in the case of *Massachusetts* v. *Feeney*. In that case the Supreme Court will be reviewing a Federal District Court ruling that the Massachusetts veterans preference law is unconstitutional.

The Attorney General has advised the President that the Justice Department brief in no way conflicts with the President's policy on veterans preference in Federal employment. The President believes that our Nation is deeply indebted to those who have served in our Armed Forces, and that government can and should provide appropriate preferences and benefits to veterans in recognition of this debt. However, as the President has said repeatedly over the past year, he also believes that the existing Federal veterans preference law for nondisabled veterans unduly interferes with employment opportunities for women and minorities and with efficient and businesslike management. That is why the President has proposed significant reforms in the law. His position on reforming the existing Federal veterans preference for nondisabled veterans remains unchanged.

Advisory Commission on Intergovernmental Relations

Appointment of Bill G. King as a Member. December 6, 1978

The President today announced the appointment of Bill G. King, of Huntsville, Ala., as a member of the Advisory Commission on Intergovernmental Relations.

King, 45, is an Alabama State senator, and a former member of the Alabama House of Representatives. He was a member of the Alabama Constitution Commission. He is president and chairman of the board of Public Systems, Inc., a management consulting firm.

George S. Brown

Statement on the Death of the Former Chairman of the Joint Chiefs of Staff. December 6, 1978

I join in mourning the passing of one of this Nation's most respected military leaders, George Brown. From the beginning of his career as a bomber pilot in the Army Air Corps in World War II to his service as an Air Force general and Chairman of the Joint Chiefs of Staff, General Brown served his country with distinction. He preferred a cockpit to sitting behind a desk, but wherever his country needed him, he answered the call with honor.

George Brown was a forthright, courageous man who inspired the men and women he served with and loved his country. He was what he always intended to be, a good soldier.

I extend my deepest sympathy to his wife, Alice, and their three children.

Conference on Security and Cooperation in Europe

**Memorandum From the President.
December 6, 1978**

Memorandum for the Vice President, the Secretary of State, the Secretary of the Treasury, the Secretary of Defense, the Attorney General, the Secretary of the Interior, the Secretary of Agriculture, the Secretary of Commerce, the Secretary of Labor, the Secretary of Health, Education and Welfare, the Secretary of Transportation, the Secretary of Energy, the Director, International Communication Agency, the Administrator, Environmental Protection Agency, the Chairman, Board for International Broadcasting, the Chairman, Commission on Civil Rights, the Chairman, Equal Employment Opportunity Commission, the Chairman, International Trade Commission, the President, National Academy of Sciences, the Chairman, National Endowment for the Arts, the Chairman, National Endowment for the Humanities, the Chairman, National Science Foundation

This Administration attaches the greatest significance to achieving full implementation of the Final Act of the Conference on Security and Cooperation in Europe (CSCE). This document contains solemn political pledges by the leaders of the 35 States of Europe and North America which participated in the 1975 Helsinki Summit—pledges to work toward lowering the barriers between East and West and improving the everyday lives of their people.

I believe that our own record of implementation has been second to none among the 35 participating States, but our work is not complete. The Final Act pledges us to strive constantly for improvement both domestically, in the area of civil and economic rights, and internationally, in the expansion of our cooperation with the other participating States. Other governments, including the Soviet Union, will better understand the depth of our concern for the full implementation of the Helsinki pledges if we demonstrate that we are working hard at home to fulfill even more effectively our side of the Helsinki bargain.

The work of each of your departments and agencies touches upon important aspects of our Final Act commitments, and I ask you to keep these commitments in mind as you develop your programs. You should work with the Department of State, and cooperate with the Commission on Security and Cooperation in Europe, as they carry out their respective responsibilities to assess implementation and identify areas where American performance can be improved. To facilitate this task, I request that you designate an official at the Assistant Secretary or the Deputy Assistant Secretary level to serve as CSCE contact. I will appreciate your full cooperation with the Department of State as it prepares the Administration's semi-annual reports on CSCE implementation as well as offering your full cooperation to the Commission, which is preparing its own special report on United States implementation of the Helsinki Final Act.

JIMMY CARTER

Indochinese Refugees

Memorandum From the President.
December 6, 1978

Presidential Determination No. 79–1

Memorandum for the Secretary of State

Subject: Determination pursuant to Section 2(c)(1) of the Migration and Refugee Assistance Act of 1962, as amended, (The "Act"), authorizing the use of $5,000,000 of funds made available from the United States Emergency Refugee and Migration Assistance Fund.

In order to meet unexpected urgent needs arising in connection with the responsibilty of the United Nations High Commissioner for Refugees to provide care and maintenance for Indochinese refugees in first asylum, I hereby determine, pursuant to Section 2(c)(1) of the Act, that it is important to the national interest that up to $5,000,000 from the United States Emergency Refugee and Migration Assistance fund be made available through the Department of State for this purpose.

The Secretary of State is requested to inform the appropriate committees of the Congress of this Determination and the obligation of funds made under this authority.

The Determination shall be published in the FEDERAL REGISTER.

JIMMY CARTER

[Filed with the Office of the Federal Register, 4:16 p.m., December 13, 1978]

Dinner for Newly Elected Members of Congress

Remarks at the White House Dinner.
December 6, 1978

I'm glad you stood up so I could find Bill Bradley. Everybody at my table said, "We don't want your autograph; we want to meet Bill Bradley." [*Laughter*]

First of all, let me say that we're very delighted, both Rosalynn and me, and Fritz Mondale and his wife, Joan, to have you come to the White House to get acquainted with one another and also to let us get to know some of you.

This is a special night, particularly in the lives of Members of the House of Representatives. It's the last night that you will spend before you begin to run for reelection. [*Laughter*] And we particularly wanted you to spend it with us.

I know everyone here has different ambitions, different thoughts about what Washington will be in your own life. I never came to Washington, except as a tourist, before I came to be inaugurated as President. And what I wanted to discover was how a southerner could come to Washington and run the Federal Government. And I have learned—sometimes the hard way—it's been very intriguing watching [Senator] Russell Long operate. [*Laughter*] I thought eventually I could start taking over, but it hasn't happened yet. [*Laughter*]

All of us have been greatly honored by the finest people on Earth, given a chance to work as Democrats and Republicans, but in harmony when the vital interests of our country are at heart. I know all of us carry in our hearts a great debt of gratitude and commitment to perform well, sometimes under the most difficult circumstances.

Those who have served in the Congress for 5 years or 35 or 38 years almost unanimously have told me that this past year, this year has been the most difficult in the history of the Congress. The issues faced were contentious, sometimes almost irresolvable, required the greatest degree of personal courage and political courage to vote for what the individual Member of the House or Senate knew was best for our Nation.

But that's not a unique circumstance, even though it has been particularly difficult in recent months. I'm sure we'll face similar questions in the future, and I know that all of us are eager to perform in such a way that those who have given us this honor will be pleased.

Our Nation has gone through traumatic experiences in the last decade. Perhaps other than the War Between the States, this has been the most severe trial for our country's government. We had a danger of alienating, perhaps permanently, the people of our country from their own Federal Government. And the interrelationships between the local, State, and Federal levels of government almost threatened to be torn apart and to destroy the system of federalism.

Our country's reputation around the world was damaged severely, and the ideals and principles on which our country was founded were sometimes in doubt.

Again, those are not transient or one-time problems or challenges. We undoubtedly will have similar kinds of threats in the future to world peace, to a better life for Americans, or because of economic problems that might come and might go. One of the things that I and all my predecessors who have lived here— and everyone has lived here except George Washington—have experienced together is that in spite of those things that seem to us to be crises on a daily or weekly or even an annual basis, they tend to disappear in the stretch of history because of the innate greatness and strength of our country.

We're the strongest nation on Earth militarily, and we intend to stay that way. We're the strongest nation on Earth economically; God's blessed us beyond all reasonable expectation, compared to other people on Earth. And, of course, we have the best political system as well. And that blessing that's fallen upon us gives us a great responsibility not only to our own people to maintain a good life, yes, but to maintain the spirit and the ideals and the principles and the compassion and the love, the unselfishness that are the most important components of a person's life. But let our own influence be spread throughout the world in a beneficial way.

We have many difficult problems. Inflation has now become the most important issue in the minds of American people. I think the election results last month indicated that that is true. But we need to meet also the human needs of the American people as we control inflation. Our economic system needs to be strengthened, not permitted to become weaker. And I think the spirit of our government, the reaching out to encompass more and more people in its comprehension and to participate in final decisions that we make finally, is also a very important and difficult challenge for us.

These things are not incompatible. I think they put a greater responsibility on us next year than perhaps in the past in economic affairs. But it requires us to root out fraud, waste, corruption, inefficiency, mismanagement, in order to meet the basic needs of our people without wasting scarce tax funds, which will be more scarce in the future than they have been in the past.

And at the same time we will continue to struggle for peace, not only to maintain the security of our own people, which is the number one priority of our Nation, but also to try to extend a peaceful life to those who have been torn by strife or threatened with even more severe conflict in the future. Not only in the Middle East but in Namibia, Rhodesia, Cyprus, Nicaragua, perhaps even in Iran, the beneficial effect of our government's influence can be a profound resolution of possible catastrophe for others.

And of course, we have tried to raise high the banner of basic human rights, which we all espouse, sometimes forget, take them for granted because we enjoy them, then fail to realize how much they are missed and desired by others throughout the world not so fortunate as we.

So, the greatness of our country is a sustaining factor in our lives, even though we have a difficult problem in making decisions here in Washington.

I think all of you will soon learn, those who haven't had experience in Washington, that in times of the greatest difficulty, partisan labels tend to disappear, and there is a unique partnership among us when those final decisions are made for the benefit of our Nation. Honest differences of opinion can still exist. But I've been extremely pleased, even pleasantly surprised at the extremely high quality and the integrity and the competence and the experience of the Members of the Congress and also the staff members who serve and will serve you.

I think one of the most important things for us all to remember is how the American people feel, what their concerns are, their doubts, their fears, their hopes, their aspirations, their ideals. And we have tried to choose a program tonight that would bring to you a reminder of our origins and of the fact that the Ameri-

cans' voices are the ones we should listen to in the final analysis.

I don't think anyone better expressed the unfulfilled ambitions of deprived Americans better than Woody Guthrie. His songs have inspired us for many years. I first knew about Woody Guthrie through Bob Dylan's recordings. And we have a man tonight, Tom Taylor, who has studied Woody Guthrie's life. He has analyzed the impact of both that life and those songs on the American people. He's been performing for 3 years now, more than 3 years, in countries throughout the world. And he is here tonight—I won't take over his program—to give us a picture, not only of the past life of Woody Guthrie but the present and future impact of his songs, which genuinely come from the hearts and minds of American people.

And before Tom Taylor comes to entertain us, I would like to introduce to you Mrs. Woody Guthrie, who is here tonight. Would she please stand.

And now I'd like to introduce to you Tom Taylor. Is Tom here? [*Laughter*]

[*At this point, the entertainment began. Following its conclusion, the President resumed speaking as follows.*]

I don't know how many of you have ever heard Bob Dylan sing—how many of you have heard Bob Dylan sing "Song to Woody"? Tell the truth. How many of you saw "Bound for Glory"? Well, you are very fortunate tonight in having Tom Taylor let you feel for this few minutes what Woody Guthrie was and what his music is.

He was a man of poverty. I think he was born in Oklahoma, was he not? His family was divided, and he was a working man. He traveled in what some of we consider low circles. His friends were sometimes worse off than he was. But he had a sense that every person, no matter how poor they were, how illiterate they were, how quiet they were, how inarticulate they were, that their lives were meaningful.

And slowly, as people started turning to Guthrie because of his guitar and because of his ability to write words that meant something, he became a natural leader. And he saw the inequality of opportunity in our country for the Native Americans, for the blacks, for the white working class, for those who couldn't speak English well, and began to fight for them. And he would write a song that would tell about the anguish of a downtrodden spirit and sing it on the radio.

And he became persecuted by many of the powerful people in our country. Joe McCarthy tried to still his voice by calling him a Communist. But eventually Woody Guthrie's songs started reaching people's hearts in places of importance, and he became kind of a living legend in our time.

And I think it's good for me as President of our country and you as Members of Congress, future Members, to realize that those cries of anguish, although not quite as prevalent, still exist and that people whom we may not see from the perspective of the White House or the House Office Building or the Senate Office Building still exist. And we might not even meet many of them on a campaign trail, but they look to us together to alleviate their pain and to let their hopes and dreams be realized.

It may be that none of us in this room will ever mean quite as much to America as Woody Guthrie; all he had was not much of an education and an old, beat-up guitar, with a heart full of love for his fellow Americans and also for our great country. I think it's a good story for us to remember, whether you live in the Redwood Forest or the New York Islands or the Gulfstream Waters. And all over the country Woody Guthrie's songs have meant a lot to just common, ordinary, good Americans, who are the strength of our Nation, who are the future of our Nation, and who have trusted us enough to give us a high honor.

Thank you very much.

NOTE: The President spoke at 9:06 p.m. in the East Room at the White House.

Knoxville International Energy Exposition of 1982

Proclamation 4628. December 6, 1978

By the President of the United States of America

A Proclamation

In May 1982, a six-month International Energy Exposition will open in Knoxville, Tennessee, inviting the nations of the world to think anew of man's relationship with the pervasive force of energy which fundamentally shapes the choices people have as to the endurance and enjoyment of life itself. This exposition, whose theme is "Energy Turns the World," will provide a splendid setting in which to explore new technologies to conserve energy, to harness the long-lasting and most renewable sources, and to carry on the search for new sources of energy.

Because of the opportunities which the Exposition offers for a deeper understanding of energy issues and for the stimulation of trade and cultural exchange, this Administration is moving to extend the fullest possible recognition to this event in accordance with Public Law 91–269. On April 26, 1977, I advised the Secretaries of State and Commerce that the Exposition warrants Federal recognition as provided by statute. On April 27, 1977, upon request of the United States, the Bureau of International Expositions officially registered the event as a Special Category exposition by unanimous vote.

Also, in accordance with law, I shall appoint a United States Commissioner General to exercise the responsibility of the United States Government for fulfillment of the Convention of November 22, 1928, Relating to International Expositions, as modified, and to invite the several States of the Union to participate.

Now, THEREFORE, I, JIMMY CARTER, President of the United States of America, in further recognition of this International Energy Exposition, do hereby authorize and direct the Secretary of State to invite, on my behalf, such foreign countries as he may consider appropriate to participate in this event.

IN WITNESS WHEREOF, I have hereunto set my hand this sixth day of December, in the year of our Lord nineteen hundred and seventy-eight, and of the Independence of the United States of America the two hundred and third.

JIMMY CARTER

[Filed with the Office of the Federal Register, 9:58 a.m., December 8, 1978]

NOTE: The text of the proclamation was released on December 7.

Interview With the President

Remarks and a Question-and-Answer Session at a Breakfast With Members of the White House Correspondents Association. December 7, 1978

THE PRESIDENT. First of all, let me say that I'm very glad that you could come and meet with me this morning. I think we've probably delayed this kind of breakfast excessively, and if it works out

well, I'd like to do it on not a schedule, but a basis as determined by you and Jody.

PRESIDENT'S VISIT TO GUADELOUPE

I will be going to Guadeloupe on the 5th and 6th of December [January], taking only one staff person, meeting with the President of France, the Chancellor of Germany, and the Prime Minister of Great Britain. We'll be there for 2 days, we presently plan. And I think all four of us will be taking our wives. It'll be somewhat of a social affair, but we'll be discussing substantive issues.

I don't think there'll be any press conferences during that time. I think we'll just meet privately and discuss the broadest gamut of questions that affect us all.

This is a group that has met periodically, even before I became President, during the economic and other summit conferences, because we are directly related in the administration of Berlin and we have found the private meetings to be very helpful. And at the last meeting, when we were at Bonn, we all decided to explore this possibility, sometime during the late winter, to meet.

So, we will be going there on the 5th and 6th of December.

Q. Of January?

THE PRESIDENT. The 5th and 6th of January, I'm sorry.

Q. Will there be press briefings, Mr. President?

THE PRESIDENT. I don't know yet. I think that they will be minimal, if any, John [John Osborne, The New Republic]. We'll only be there 2 days. I think we'd like just to go and have a chance to meet in an unstructured way. There will not be any agenda prepared ahead of time, and we'll take one staff person. We have got a lot going on in Washington, and I've tried to think about the staff person that could easiest be spared. If you have any suggestions for me— [*laughter*]——

Q. You can take Jody?

THE PRESIDENT.——I'd appreciate it. That sounds like a good suggestion.

QUESTIONS

IRAN

Q. Mr. President, we appreciate this breakfast, and I'd like to ask a question that I might not pose at a broader meeting. As a former Democratic Member of the House who voted for you and who spent 2 years at our embassy in Iran, I find it a little difficult to reconcile your statements about the Shah's concern for human rights, democracy, and liberalization with the pretty well documented record of his regime.

I think that those of us who have been there—and I'm going back tonight— could accept your policy a little better if you were to postulate it on the broader strategic and energy considerations. I'm wondering if you could enlighten us on that, both points, and anything else on the issue.

THE PRESIDENT. I'll try.

There are several basic premises on which our relationship with Iran is postulated. First of all, our bilateral relationships with Iran have been constructive for both countries. We consider the Iranian people's relationship with the West to be very important. Iran has been a stabilizing factor around the Persian Gulf. This stability is valuable in the region. It's valuable in the surrounding territory, reaching certainly as far as Israel and the Mediterranean, and it's important for world peace. Iran has been very helpful to us in economic matters concerning OPEC, and we have a good and longstanding re-

lationship between Presidents—myself and my predecessors—and the Shah himself.

The Shah has attempted, in my opinion, while maintaining order in a very difficult period, to move toward social liberalization, sometimes directly in conflict with the desires of the more traditional religious leaders, and has on several occasions, increasingly, lately, offered to form coalition governments encompassing his political opponents there. These offers have been rejected.

I don't have any apology to offer for the difference in human rights values that our own Nation espouses and those that have been accomplished by the Shah in Iran. There have been abuses. There have been incarcerations of people without formal charge and trial under the Shah's government that would not be acceptable in our own country.

But I think the trend has been, under the Shah, toward democratic principles and social liberalization. Some have thought he moved too fast; some have thought he has moved not long enough— not strongly and rapidly enough, rather. And, of course, there have been instances when human rights violations have occurred as measured by any objective standard. But I might hasten to add that we have those kinds of violations in our own country as well.

Q. Mr. President, I was going to ask you about the Shah. Do you think he could survive now, and how?

THE PRESIDENT. I don't know. I hope so. This is something that is in the hands of the people of Iran. We have never had any intention and don't have any intention of trying to intercede in the internal political affairs of Iran.

We primarily want an absence of violence and bloodshed, and stability. We personally prefer that the Shah maintain a major role in the government, but that's a decision for the Iranian people to make.

Q. Do you think there's still any chance that he'll form a civilian coalition government?

THE PRESIDENT. I think he has offered that publicly. And as you know, yesterday, I believe, he released two of his top political opponents. And I think, I would guess, surmise, that one of the reasons for those political leaders being released was to encourage them and their followers to join in some form of coalition government. That's the Shah's desire that's expressed to me personally by him and through his own Ambassador here, and I take him at his word.

EGYPTIAN-ISRAELI PEACE NEGOTIATIONS

Q. Mr. President, how important is it, do you feel, for Israel to accept a definite target date—by the end of next year, for example—for the transfer to Palestinian autonomy; how important to accept a target date, as opposed to a more general commitment that we will try to bring autonomy as soon as possible; how important in terms of bringing Palestinians into the process, bringing King Hussein of Jordan into the process? How critical do you feel is the issue of persuading the Israelis to accept a definite target date for transfer to autonomy?

THE PRESIDENT. I should make clear that the United States does not have a unilateral position that we try to force or even encourage the Egyptians and Israelis to adopt. Any mutually acceptable agreement which could be concluded between the Egyptians and the Israelis would be satisfactory to us.

My concern, however, is that we would like to see the Camp David accords carried out, first of all, completely. I think any violation of the Camp David accords would set a very serious precedent which would cast doubt upon the present treaty which is being negotiated.

We would also like to see the Camp David accords carried out, not grudgingly, but enthusiastically, in the same spirit that we saw exemplified in the White House when the accords were signed. This has not been the case during the negotiations. There have been unwarranted delays, quibbling over what seems to us to be insignificant language differences, and excessive public statements on both sides that have made the negotiating process excessively difficult.

We have made a proposal to the Israelis and Egyptians of a peace treaty text plus a separate letter which would endorse a definite timetable on the establishment of the self-government in the West Bank and Gaza Strip. The Israelis adopted the peace treaty text after they had previously rejected some of its component parts, and did not adopt the crucial and integral additional letter with few features in it, the most significant being the timetable. The Egyptians consider that the timetable is a mandatory element of a future success.

I'd like to add one other thing: If the Egyptians and Israelis violate the 3-month limit on negotiating this treaty, it will be a very serious matter to us and, I think, to them. That's why I am sending Cy Vance to Egypt, and perhaps then to Israel. If, because of mutual lack of agreement, we go past December 17, it would cast doubt on whether the Egyptians and Israelis would carry out the difficult terms of the upcoming peace treaty, and it would set a precedent that would have far-reaching, adverse effect.

So, we consider the December 17th date to be very, very important, perhaps at this point more important than Prime Minister Begin or President Sadat. I'm going to make that clear to both leaders during Secretary Vance's trip.

But, to summarize by repeating my first statement, we don't have an independent position. Any mutual agreement between the two nations that leads to peace and a peace treaty would be satisfactory to us.

Q. May I just follow that up, sir?

THE PRESIDENT. Yes.

Q. Would you consider the establishment of four new settlements on the West Bank to be a violation of the Camp David agreements?

THE PRESIDENT. Yes, I would.

My interpretation of the Camp David agreements—and, as you know, Prime Minister Begin disagrees with this interpretation—is that there was a moratorium on the establishment of new settlements until the agreements had been reached on how to establish the autonomous government in the West Bank and Gaza Strip. I had never connected in my own mind or in my conversations with either leader the cessation of settlement construction as it related to an Egyptian-Israeli peace treaty concerning the Sinai. It was always connected in my mind and in the original versions and text of the proposals to be connected with the conclusion of discussions on how to establish the modalities and procedures of establishing the elections, self-government in West Bank, Gaza.

I might say I don't want that to be an obstacle to the Egyptian and Israeli progress. But that's my own personal opinion, and that's my recollection of what occurred at Camp David. It's the only extant difference, and it's already been explored in the press.

APPOINTMENTS OF FEDERAL JUDGES

Q. Senator Harry Byrd of Virginia sent you the names of white males for the judgeships there, and when he set up his commissions, he had several white males, one white female, and one black. The blacks did present some names, but the commissions rejected them.

Since that time, the civil rights organizations of Virginia have considered some black names to fill the judgeships. Are you going to consider those black names, or are you going to acquiesce to Virginia's alltime historical policy of never even considering a black for Federal judgeship?

THE PRESIDENT. I have, practically speaking, a great deal of influence on the selection of circuit judges, those above the district judges. And I've established Merit Selection Commissions to recommend to me a balanced list of well-qualified people when every vacancy occurs, and those are, in effect, under my control.

Because of the ability of any Senator to prevent the appointment of a district judge in his or, now, her State, the district judgeships have to be a partnership agreement between the Senators and the President. Either the Senator or I can, in effect, veto the appointment of a judge.

As we have received lists of judges, judge nominees, from the Senators—and they don't come to me, they come to the Attorney General—if they don't encompass women and minority groups, the Attorney General is asking the Senators to reasses their procedures and to broaden the list to encompass women and minority nominees, so that I can have that opportunity for my own selection.

We are proceeding with that aggressively. In some instances, there have been, since this legislation has been pending for so long, there have already been some commitments made by the Senators themselves. I think there have been 18 or 20—I've forgotten; I don't keep up with the list, but it's been growing—of the Senators who have established district or State selection commissions. And I hope that this will continue.

I'm not prepared to comment on an individual State. I have not seen the list, have not been involved in that at all in, you said, Virginia. But my influence will be used to the maximum degree practical in encouraging Senators to cooperate with me in appointing both and recommending both women and blacks, other minority groups, for those district judgeships.

Q. Could I follow that question up, Mr. President?

THE PRESIDENT. Yes.

Q. I wanted to follow up on that a minute.

Senator Byrd has said that he is not going to reconsider anything but what the commission has passed to him—and I do want to congratulate you on setting up these commissions that are formed at the State level—but he has said he's not going to consider any other names.

THE PRESIDENT. I understand.

Well, I might say that if something of that kind cannot be resolved, then there would be no appointment in Virginia, because the way the Senate operates—and this is not my preference—Senator Byrd could tell the Judiciary Committee that any Senate nominee was unacceptable to him, and the Senate Judiciary Committee would not act. That's the present prospect.

But we hope that as the process is demonstrated to be feasible, that—I'm not commenting specifically on Senator Byrd; I'm not familiar with his recommendations yet—but we hope that there will be a growing inclination on the part of the Senators to act in good faith and to accommodate my policy of broadening the appointments.

Q. Mr. President, would it be unfair to have you comment on any number, any specific number of minority or women Federal judges you expect to appoint in that 152 number? You know, that was the figure that was publicized as being the number of slots that you intend to fill, and, of course, you specified that you want minorities and women. But have

you formulated in your own mind any estimate as to how many of that 152—would half be adequate in your estimation, less than half?

THE PRESIDENT. I'm not prepared to answer that question. I don't know. It's not a question of fairness; I just haven't made those decisions yet. The only thing I can say is that I think one of the recent legal journals—I don't know the name of it; I think I sent a copy of it to Jody—assesses what I have done already in that respect. You are welcome to look it over. And, of course, whenever I make a decision on judicial appointments or on the Federal budget or anything else, my action is subject to public scrutiny and public condemnation if I don't perform well. I do the best I can. Sometimes my authority is limited.

If I didn't have to get Senate confirmation of appointees, I could just tell you flatly that 12 percent of all my judicial appointments would be blacks and 3 percent would be Spanish-speaking and 40 percent would be women and so forth. But that's not a matter that's entirely in my hands. I'll do the best I can. And if I fail to satisfy you or others, then I'm certainly a good target for criticism or condemnation. I'll try to avoid that prospect.

WAGE INCREASES FOR PUBLIC OFFICIALS

Q. Mr. President, the first big challenge to your wage and price guideline program seems to be coming not from the Teamsters or one of the other big unions, but from some public officials of Illinois and Ohio at the State and local level. I'm wondering how important you consider that these pay increases be rolled back to the future of your program—in other words, whether smaller people down the line can be expected to adhere to the guidelines if the public officials don't adhere to them?

THE PRESIDENT. Certainly they're important symbolically. I think it's also important that I express myself very clearly through Alfred Kahn [1] or personally when I believe these salary increases violate the standards.

There are extenuating circumstances in some instances. For instance, the city of Chicago has a constitution which prevents any change in a city administrator's salary, elected official's salary, for a 4-year period, and any change in the salary has to be made before the next election so that the public can, in effect, approve the salary increase. Mayor Bilandic called me yesterday afternoon, very concerned about the altercation, and he is sending his city budget officer, I think today, to meet with Alfred Kahn or his people to work out a reasonable resolution of this question.

I think obviously some of the increases proposed have been excessive, but if they can justify the reason for it, if it's an increase that encompasses, say, an 8-year mandatory period of time, and if the change is made prior to an election, where the people that make the change can be condemned or removed from office by the populace, that certainly is an extenuating circumstance.

I'm not trying to comment on percentages or numbers. I'm not familiar with them. But I think it's a very serious challenge.

I might add one thing—not even parenthetically—that we don't have any authority over a city government or a State legislature. There's a limited amount of action that we can take even indirectly. We can't cut off humanitarian funds to a city or to a State, for instance, or cut off highway funds simply because the legislature votes to raise its own salary. But within the bounds of my authority, or

---

[1] Advisor to the President on Inflation.

practicalities of it, we consider this to be a serious challenge, and we are trying to meet it. I think my own statements last Friday and Fred Kahn's statements since then demonstrate that that's a fact.

MIG–23'S IN CUBA

Q. Mr. President, I was looking over the transcript of your answer at the last press conference on the presence of MIG–23's in Cuba, and I'm not quite clear what exactly our intelligence does show with regard to those warplanes. And I wonder if you could answer whether or not we have any indication that there is even one nuclear-capable MIG down there? I'm not talking about whether or not there are any nuclear weapons down there, but whether or not there is a MIG that is capable of carrying nuclear weapons.

And secondly, your answer also seems to imply, the remarks about assessing the quantity and quality of such systems, that if there were perhaps only one or two, that that in itself might not constitute a violation of the '62 understanding we have with the Soviets. And I wonder if you could also comment on that, whether or not just one or two might be okay, but more than that might not be?

THE PRESIDENT. Well, I think it's obvious that there are planes in Cuba that can carry an atomic weapon if they are outfitted to do so, designed specifically to do so, and if the crew is trained to do so. There are many relatively small, commercial-type jets that have a physical capability of carrying a nuclear weapon, which in this modern technological age can be relatively small in weight. But I think that's as far as I want to go with my answer.

You know, the physical capability of picking up that much weight, carrying it to the shores of the United States and dropping it, is certainly there. But whether the planes are outfitted to do it, designed to do it, crews are trained to do it, is an entirely different matter, and we don't have any indication that this is the case. But we are continuing to monitor that circumstance and act accordingly.

Q. Is there some sort of numerical mix or some sort of formula that we have worked out in our minds beyond which we would consider it a violation of the '62 agreement and under which we wouldn't consider it? In other words, if they just had half a squadron or only a couple of planes, well, you know, it's perhaps trouble, but it's not something we're going to call them on?

THE PRESIDENT. Well, there would certainly be a numerical mix that I can't describe and don't have in my mind now that we would consider in violation of the 1962 agreement. And the 1962 agreement was certainly very unclear on this. The technology and the capability of airplanes, almost all the extant airplanes then, have been modified or replaced, and there would be a mix of quality and quantity. Even if I knew, I wouldn't broadcast it publicly. There might be at that time of crisis, which does not presently exist, a difference between ourselves and the Soviet Union, but I don't think I could define it any more clearly.

The Soviets have assured us that they still stand behind the 1962 agreement, have not violated it, and I think my answer at the press conference was carefully worded. And I think it's adequate.

NICARAGUA AND SOUTHERN AFRICA

Q. Mr. President, I was going to ask you about the MIG's also, but I'll switch my question around to South Africa and Nicaragua—[*laughter*]—both places where the United States has had deadlines in concert with other countries to try and bring about some sort of settlement. In both places the deadlines have come and gone, and in both places you are working behind the scenes to try and bring about some kind of peaceful settlement.

Could you start with Nicaragua, and tell us what progress you're making with [President] Somoza?

THE PRESIDENT. We've got a little time. Let me tell you something in generic terms, general terms, that apply to all these efforts.

We don't have to be involved in trying to bring peace to Nicaragua, to Nigeria, to Rhodesia, to Cyprus, to the Mideast, but it's a voluntary responsibility assumed by us. It's in the best interests of the American people. It's certainly in the best interests of those people who are faced with expanded conflict. It's in the best interests of world peace.

The prospects for resolution of all these very difficult questions are sometimes quite undetectable or remote. They're certainly not a sure thing. We have been persistent and, as a nation, sometimes courageous in injecting ourselves into a thankless responsibility to try to induce reluctant adversaries to cooperate and to maintain or to enhance peace, sometimes even to conclude a final agreement that might be permanent in nature.

We're making some progress, I think, in Nicaragua. When we entered the Nicaraguan conflict, blood was being shed, massive violence existed. We tried to induce and were successful up until now in getting other American nations to join in with us, the Dominican Republic, and Guatemala, to get Somoza for the first time even to agree to an outside arbitration group to resolve the differences between himself and his political adversaries in Nicaragua, to stop the violence, to restrain the shipment of arms into Nicaragua to both sides, and to provide peace between Nicaragua and her immediate neighbors.

At that moment several months ago, I think the prospect of Somoza accepting any sort of plebiscite would have been very remote. He has agreed to a plebiscite under certain restraints. My understanding the last few hours is that his opponents have now tentatively agreed at least to those plebiscite terms. A lot of negotiation still needs to be done, but we are making progress.

And in the meantime, we have shifted— I don't say we've done it alone, but we have helped to shift the Nicaraguan circumstance from active and massive bloodshed and violence into a negotiation on the details of a democratic plebiscite, that would be monitored by the United Nations or by the OAS, that would decide on the future government of Nicaragua. We don't know that we'll be successful, but I think that in itself is progress.

The same thing applies in Rhodesia and certainly to a greater and perhaps better extent in Namibia.

Q. Have you been getting positive feedback on the Namibia situation in the last day or so?

THE PRESIDENT. Yes. I think the prospects for Namibian progress were dismal 2 weeks ago. With the Namibian election plan, which is now under way—I think the final results of it, it takes about 4 days to hold an election; first one they've had in a long time—the Secretary General had asked the Prime Minister of South Africa to take full steps—which I don't know have been revealed publicly, and I'm not going to reveal them this morning. The South Africans were very reluctant to accede to the Secretary General's request.

I invited Pik Botha, the Foreign Minister, to come and meet with me privately. I urged him to accept the importunities of the Secretary General. He went back to South Africa, talked to Prime Minister

Botha, Pieter Botha, and they agreed to accept the Secretary General's request.

Q. They did?

THE PRESIDENT. Yes. This has been a kind of a one-sided proposition. Now, of course, the next step is to go to SWAPO and see if they will accept the present terms. There's nothing certain about it.

Our hope is that this elected body in Namibia will be looked upon as an interim step; and that South Africa will retain responsibility for dealing with the United Nations; that United Nations force will be put into Namibia to supervise future elections that would probably take place over, after 5 or 6, maybe 7 months; that the United Nations force will be patently fair and objective; and that the free expression of all the people who live in Namibia be felt in the establishment of a new government, with SWAPO and the Turnhalle group represented in accordance with a majority vote and one-person-one-vote, majority rule. These are the things that we hope for.

We've had less success in Rhodesia. Although the bloodshed has been more than we would want, it's been much less than could have been the case. I think the British retain primary responsibility there from an outside point of view. We've joined in with the British at their request.

Now there's another effort being made more exclusively by the British. We are participating in this. They're exploring the possibility or getting the four powers together under some framework, and we don't know what the outcome will be. In the meantime, we're trying to encourage all of them to minimize bloodshed and violence and move toward, again, majority rule, one person-one vote, free expression for the will of the people in Zimbabwe, as it will be named, and let anyone who wants to run as a candidate do so. These are the kinds of things we want to do with the United Nations, retaining peace there.

But we can't guarantee success in any of these instances, including the Middle East or Cyprus. But we're doing the best we can, and I think to some degree just stabilizing the situation and continuing the negotiations is constructive.

I'll try to keep my other answers briefer.

BILLY CARTER

Q. Could I shift gears, sir?

THE PRESIDENT. Please.

Q. About 6 weeks ago your brother appeared before an Atlanta grand jury that was investigating the Lance affair. And he later told reporters he'd invoked the fifth amendment two or three times and said—I don't know what his—there are various interpretations of his mood at the time—but he called it a Republican, Yankee-inspired investigation. Have you any general reaction to this, sir?

THE PRESIDENT. Not that I would like to express. [*Laughter*] I might say that I promised the American people that I would stay completely aloof from my own business and so forth. I have never discussed this with Billy, although I talk to him frequently about other things, but he understands my commitment. And any dealing with Carter's Warehouse, from my point of view, is done by Mr. Kirbo, and he'll make any statement that's appropriate. But I don't care to comment on it.

Q. Could you comment on his taking the fifth, sir?

THE PRESIDENT. No, I don't care to do that, either.

I've read the news reports, and Billy's explanation was that he was asked by the grand jury to bring the records for a certain date, a period of time, and that when questions were asked of him about financial details outside that period of time, he refused to answer because he did not have

the documents with him. But I've only gotten that from the press. I've never asked either Kirbo or Billy about that.

U.S.-MEXICAN RELATIONS

Q. Mr. President, could I ask you about the Mexican policy that you have under development now? I understand you want to discuss immigration and some other things that have to do with our dealings with the Mexican Government. Can you tell us a little bit about how that's progressing and what you hope to accomplish?

THE PRESIDENT. Yes. In preparation for my visit to Mexico in February, the National Security Council has been assessing all the facets of our Mexican policy—political, economic, and so forth. We began this during the visit of President López Portillo to our country. He was the first foreign visitor that I ever had. And we set up kind of a task force from the Commerce Department, the Treasury Department, the Attorney General's office, and Defense and Agriculture and so forth, and they have met at the sub-Cabinet level, at the Assistant Secretary level on several occasions to explore potential progress between ourselves and Mexico.

I consider our relationship with Mexico to be as important as any other that we have, and my relationship with President López Portillo has been very good.

We've also had negotiations with them earlier this year on the purchase or pricing of natural gas and, perhaps, eventually oil, as those fields are developed. Because of the uncertainty of congressional action on the energy legislation, they were postponed, with agreement on both sides, until after the Congress adjourned. Those will be recommenced, and I would guess we'll do some background work on that before I arrive in

Mexico to conclude, hopefully, these continuing negotiations.

I think that pretty well encompasses what we are doing at this point on Mexico. It's of very great importance to us. There'll be a great deal of staff work and Cabinet-level work between now and February in both nations, and I hope that my own visit with López Portillo can conclude successfully these negotiations on a wide range of subjects.

STRATEGIC ARMS LIMITATION

Q. Could you tell us, Mr. President, about what progress is being made and what the prospects now are towards a SALT agreement? And I wonder if, without attempting to hang you up on any more predictions, you will have one to discuss at Guadeloupe in January?

THE PRESIDENT. I don't know—I doubt if we will have a final agreement to go over with the other European leaders in Guadeloupe, but we will have the SALT proposals that we have in almost final— our proposals, probably, in final form, when we get to Guadeloupe, and an accurate description to the other leaders of the remaining differences, if any, at that time.

I might say that we keep other leaders, certainly including Schmidt, Callaghan, Giscard d'Estaing, briefed very well on the progress of SALT negotiations on a continuing basis, either with direct secret messages from me to them, sometimes on a nonclassified basis in private telephone calls between me and them, and so forth. As you know, many facets of the SALT II agreement apply directly to the European theater, and, as we prepare for SALT III, this has a much more direct effect on the European theater.

I have been pleased recently with the progress being made on SALT. The remaining differences are minor, compared to what they were a year ago, and in my own mind I can see a way to resolve them. If the Soviets are adequately forthcoming, I would guess that any further delay would be minimal.

Q. What steps, say between now and then, can you anticipate in the way of contacts, meetings, and discussion between ourselves and the Soviets?

THE PRESIDENT. I think an almost inevitable progress would be to continue to define the narrowing differences. And there's been steady progress; there never has been a time when we retrogressed on SALT. Then I think there would be a preparation period for a summit meeting, certainly at the Foreign Minister level, between Secretary Vance and Gromyko, and possibly others, and then a summit meeting between myself and Brezhnev, whenever he and I agree there would be a reasonable opportunity for success.

I think because of their attitude, which I have assessed over the last—almost 2 years, President Brezhnev's inclination is not to have a summit meeting unless there is a sure conclusion of SALT in prospect. But I would like to have, if he should come over here, a 4- or 5-day period where we might discuss a broad range of agenda items and not narrowly focus it just on military items. And of course, that would require very careful preparation.

I can't give you any further information. I don't know anything about dates. It's still just a general outline of how it might go about. But that's my present thinking.

PRESS SECRETARY POWELL. About one more question here.

THE PRESIDENT. One more question? All right.

TAX-EXEMPT STATUS FOR PRIVATE
SCHOOLS

Q. Mr. President, the IRS has a plan to penalize schools that desegregate by taking away their tax-exempt status. I wonder if you could comment on whether you favor that plan, or if you do not, what alternative do you think the IRS has, or anyone has, to get these Christian schools and other schools to desegregate?

THE PRESIDENT. I'm not familiar with a new IRS plan. You may know that I come from Georgia—[*laughter*]—and at the time of the civil rights legislation, a lot of schools were set up with the real purpose of circumventing the civil rights laws, which accepted students on a racial basis. At that time, the IRS passed some very restrictive rulings or interpretations of congressional acts or laws that prevented contributions to those schools from being included for tax benefits.

So far as I know, those rulings still apply, and they are very restrictive on the schools in my own area.

Q. They're holding 4 days of hearings right now on a plan that would require schools that are under court order to desegregate, i.e., private schools under court order to desegregate, or schools that have already—how do I phrase it?—that have already—I can't think of the other part of it, I'm sorry. Anyway, the schools that—Oh, I know, schools that set up around 1970, or when court orders in their area, public schools to desegregate, those schools would have to prove that they are having financial arrangements for minority students, and things like that.

THE PRESIDENT. I see. I don't know how to answer that question——

MR. POWELL. Mr. President, I think that that matter is in Treasury. It has not come to the White House at all, even at the staff level, I don't believe. I think I know what you're talking about, but it is at this point completely within the operation of the Treasury Department.

THE PRESIDENT. That probably—since I'm not familiar with it, it'd probably be better for Jody to look it up, talk to me, and then give you an answer. I don't know.

ANTI-INFLATION PROGRAM

MR. POWELL. Let's take one more here from Mr. Deakin [James Deakin, St. Louis Post-Dispatch]. I know you want to talk about inflation a little bit.

Q. You haven't really been asked a question about inflation—I mean, here we are—walk out of here without it. I was struck by something you said at your last press conference.

You were asked whether it wasn't really the case that if we are going to have a real attack on inflation in this country, really do something about it, the American people weren't going to make up their minds to pause in this expansion of expectations, this ever-rising standard of living. And your answer, as I heard it, was pretty much, no, we didn't have to pause like that, we can have our cake and eat it, too. That's what came across to me.

THE PRESIDENT. I might say I don't remember that question, or that answer. But go ahead. [*Laughter*]

Q. It was at your last press conference.

THE PRESIDENT. I remember the press conference. [*Laughter*]

Q. You were there, that's right. So was I.

I'm just wondering whether you really think that. I was struck, for instance, by what seemed to me to be a conflict between that and your whole approach to the energy problem at the beginning, when you were saying, in effect, this country had to cut back on its greed for energy and its sort of wild consumption of energy.

Do you really think, that we can have our cake and eat it, too? I'm talking about the question of sacrifice. Do you think you can sell the American people and have them believe in your inflation program without a major sacrifice?

THE PRESIDENT. I don't think so. I've said many times that the American people are going to have to sacrifice, and my responsibility, within the limited authority that I have, is to balance that sacrifice among the various groups.

No one here can imagine how difficult the last 2 or 3 weeks have been for me in the preparation of the 1980 fiscal year budget. It is a traumatic experience to try to reach the goal that I very carefully set for myself of reducing the deficit, imposing restraints from the Federal Government level as a needed step and also as a guide or example for others to emulate.

I will be judged, when the budget is revealed, as to whether I've done it fairly and objectively and have met my commitments. I intend to do so. But it is a tight budget, and there are going to be inevitable outcries from those who expect to continue things as they have been going in the last few years.

So, I think that the public is fairly well attuned to, as you say, a pause. At the same time, I don't believe we're going to have a recession or a depression. The rate of growth will certainly be much less than it has been in the last few years, when we've had 6 or 7 percent growth rate.

We have some demonstrations of what I say. I think anyone who reads the speech that I made to the National League of Cities would say that it was a very disappointing-type speech from the perspective of mayors expecting increased handouts or generous Federal Government policies in economics. But the response among the mayors, I think, was very supportive of me, both at the time I was there and their subsequent comments to the press.

So, I think that the sacrifice is inevitable. It ought to be reasonably shared. I'm going to persist in setting an example from the point of view of the Federal Government to control the deficit. And when the budget's revealed I think there's going to be a general conviction among the American people that the sacrifice will be imposed as I've described.

Q. Specifically, what you were asked at that press conference, Mr. President, was whether or not the American standard of living was going to have to—the level was going to have to pause.

THE PRESIDENT. I think the answer to the question was whether it was going to——

Q. You said no, that the standard of living would continue to go up. Can we really have a successful campaign against inflation if the American standard of living—we are, after all, victims of our own standard of living—continues to go up?

THE PRESIDENT. Well, you know, I don't want to predict exactly what's going to happen. My belief is that the American standard of living can continue to go up, that the standard of living, however, is not measured simply by the rate of growth of our national product. I think the standard of living is determined by many things: the assurance of peace, stability, the strength of families, the quality of education, the enhancement of basic human rights, harmony among dissident groups.

This will certainly continue to improve. I think that we will not have a recession. We will have a rate of increase of growth in the national product that will even include additional economic benefits, but how fast the GNP grows will be less than it has been in the past.

But I don't think the American people are looking toward a life that's more dismal or with less hope, nor with less quality. But if you measure quality only by how fast someone's income goes up, then I think there is going to be a difference in the future, compared to what it has been in the past.

I haven't given you a very good answer, but it's the best I can do.

Well, let me say I appreciate a chance to meet with you and discuss subjects in more depth. I've taken more time to answer your questions this morning than I would at a press conference. But if you all think that these kind of sessions are beneficial, talk to Jody about it, and I'd be glad to do it additionally in the future.

I thank you all very much.

REPORTER. Thank you, Mr. President.

MR. POWELL. Let me ask, before everyone gets away, if you would, we're making this announcement on the Guadeloupe trip right away. If you didn't mind just holding onto that, particularly the wires, for just a few minutes, let me walk in there and make that announcement. We did it here so you'd have a chance to explore it in a little more depth. I was glad to see that you availed yourselves of that gracious opportunity. [*Laughter*] If you don't mind doing that, I'd appreciate it.

NOTE: The interview began at 8:50 a.m. in the State Dining Room at the White House.

Constitutional Referendum in Spain

Statement by the President.
December 7, 1978

All people who love freedom and believe in democracy won a victory in Spain yesterday.

The Spanish electorate decisively approved in a national referendum the draft democratic constitution placed before them by their elected parliamentary representatives. This occasion marks the culmination of courageous and determined efforts by the Spanish people, their representatives, and King Juan Carlos to establish a framework for Spanish democracy which meets with the approval of all Spaniards.

The success of the transition to democracy in Spain, and the manifest will of Spaniards across the political spectrum to establish a democratic system, have earned the admiration of people the world over who share similar ideals.

Yesterday's referendum symbolizes a remarkable and praiseworthy achievement. We want to congratulate the Spanish people on this occasion, and to reaffirm the hope and support of the American people and their government for continued success in this historic effort.

NOTE: On December 8, the White House announced that the President had spoken that afternoon by telephone with King Juan Carlos of Spain to express personal congratulations on the new Spanish constitution and on the wise and courageous role that the King has played in Spain's transition to democracy.

Budget Deferrals

Message to the Congress.   December 7, 1978

To the Congress of the United States:

In accordance with the Impoundment Control Act of 1974, I herewith report ten new deferrals of budget authority totalling $110.6 million and four revisions to previously transmitted deferrals increasing the amount deferred by $3.3 million. The items involve the military education and training program and programs in the Departments of Agriculture, the Interior, State, and the Treasury, and several independent agencies.

The details of the deferrals are contained in the attached reports.

JIMMY CARTER

The White House,
    December 7, 1978.

NOTE: The attachments detailing the deferrals are printed in the FEDERAL REGISTER of December 13, 1978.

Foreign Claims Settlement Commission of the United States

Recess Appointment of Richard W. Yarborough as a Member.   December 7, 1978

The President today announced the recess appointment of Richard W. Yarborough, of Austin, Tex., as a member of the Foreign Claims Settlement Commission of the United States for a 3-year term. He replaces Robert E. Lee, whose term has expired.

Yarborough, 47, was a Commissioner of the U.S. Indian Claims Commission from 1967 until the termination of the Commission last October.

Assistant Special Counselor on Inflation

Exchange of Letters on the Resignation of S. Lee Kling.   December 7, 1978

To Lee Kling

I have your letter advising me of your need to devote more time to your interests in the private sector.

I want to take this opportunity to personally express my gratitude and appreciation for the contributions you have made to my Administration, especially your tireless dedication to our fight against inflation. I know I can count on your continued support in this effort, as well as your willingness to serve on the Board of Directors of AMTRAK.

I trust that in the days and months ahead I may continue to seek your advice and counsel. You have my warmest wishes for continued success.

Sincerely,

JIMMY CARTER

December 4, 1978

Dear Mr. President:

My experience over the last eight months as your Assistant Special Counselor on Inflation and Deputy to Ambassador Strauss has been extremely rewarding and enjoyable. I want you to know how much I appreciate your making this opportunity possible.

As you have pointed out, inflation is our nation's most crucial economic concern. During the past several months, the groundwork has been laid for a comprehensive and sustained attack on this critical problem. With the guidance of Bob Strauss and your other economic policy advisers, and now with the addition of Alfred Kahn, I know that your program is developing the broad support necessary to insure success.

With this in mind, I am anxious to return now to my work in the private sector. You may rest assured, however, that I will continue to support vigorously and speak on behalf of the anti-inflation program, as well as your other programs which I endorse so enthusiastically.

The experience of working with you and your fine staff has been a privilege I will remember and treasure. Needless to say, I will always be available to assist you in any way possible.

With my deepest devotion and respect,

Sincerely,

S. LEE KLING

[The President, The White House, Washington, D.C. 20500]

NOTE: On the same day, the White House announced that the President will nominate Mr. Kling to be a member of the Board of Directors of the National Railroad Passenger Corporation (AMTRAK).

Golda Meir

Statement on the Death of the Former Israeli Prime Minister.   December 8, 1978

The American people and I join the people of Israel in mourning the loss of former Prime Minister Golda Meir. Throughout one of the most remarkable careers of public leadership in this century, Golda Meir embodied the best in the Israeli spirit—courage and idealism; honest outspokenness and buoyant good humor; strength and compassion and a deep love of her land; proud determination and boundless energy and hard work; and a deep, abiding commitment to peace.

As a young woman, she lived in the city of Milwaukee, and the American people have always felt a special love and affection for Golda Meir. I will always remember her warmth and graciousness when we met in Israel when she was Prime Minister in 1973.

Though she counted Presidents and world leaders among her friends, Golda Meir always understood that great global issues involve the hopes and fears of ordinary men and women, and people all over the world responded to her humanity.

Golda Meir is among that heroic group of men and women, Israel's pioneers, who dreamed of establishing a free and independent Jewish state—and who made that dream come true for millions of people in one of the great stories of human struggle and fulfillment of all time.

On the occasion of her death, it is fitting to note that the nation of Israel, to which she dedicated her life, is strong and free today. We pray that the second great dream of Golda Meir's life, for which she worked and hoped and prayed all her life, will soon be realized: a just and lasting peace in the Middle East.

NOTE: The White House announcement of the members of the U.S. delegation to the funeral of Mrs. Meir is printed on page 2268 of this volume.

Imports of Petroleum and Petroleum Products

Proclamation 4629.   December 8, 1978

By the President of the United States of America

A Proclamation

The Secretary of Energy has advised me that recent legislation has mandated a change in the treatment accorded residual fuel oil imports under the Emergency Petroleum Allocation Act of 1973 (Section 307 of Public Law 95–465). The congressional intent clearly contemplated simultaneous Presidential action to reduce import fees on residual fuel oil. Therefore, the Secretary recommended that I grant additional fee exempt licenses under Proclamation No. 3279, as amended.

The Secretary also recommended changes in the distribution system for the allocation of fee-exempt licenses for imports of residual fuel oil, and changes in the extent to which refunds of license fees may be made for the payment of duties on petroleum and petroleum products.

These changes are consistent with the purposes of Proclamation No. 3279, as amended.

Now, THEREFORE, I, JIMMY CARTER, President of the United States of America, by the authority vested in me by the Constitution and the laws of the United States, including Section 232 of the Trade

Expansion Act of 1962, as amended (19 U.S.C. 1862), do hereby proclaim that:

SECTION 1. Section 3(a)(1)(iii) of Proclamation No. 3279, as amended, is further amended by adding thereto the following:

"*Provided,* that where the applicable duty on a barrel of crude oil, unfinished oil, or finished product entered on or after Sunday, December 17, 1978, exceeds the amount of the fee paid with respect to that barrel, the reduction shall not exceed the amount of the fee nor may any excess duty be used to reduce the fee on any other barrel.".

SEC. 2. Section 4(b)(5) of Proclamation No. 3279, as amended, is further amended by deleting everything after the second sentence.

SEC. 3. Section 4(b) of Proclamation No. 3279, as amended, is further amended by adding thereto a new paragraph (6) as follows:

"(6) With respect to the allocation of imports into District I of residual fuel oil to be used as fuel, the Secretary shall provide until June 30, 1979, for the fair and equitable distribution of such allocation among all persons desiring to import residual fuel oil into District I. For the period beginning July 1, 1979, the Secretary shall provide that the distribution of such allocation shall be based upon a person's actual average calendar day imports in the six calendar months preceding May 1, 1979.".

SEC. 4. Section 8 of Proclamation No. 3279, as amended, is further amended by adding at the end thereof the following unnumbered clause:

"For the period from November 1, 1978 through June 30, 1979, the allocation of residual fuel oil to be used as fuel in District I shall not be subject to the reductions set forth in this Section.".

IN WITNESS WHEREOF, I have hereunto set my hand this eighth day of December, in the year of our Lord nineteen hundred seventy-eight, and of the Independence of the United States of America the two hundred and third.

JIMMY CARTER

[Filed with the Office of the Federal Register, 4:03 p.m., December 8, 1978]

Digest of Other White House Announcements

The following listing includes the President's daily schedule and other items of general interest as announced by the White House Press Office during the period covered by this issue. Events and announcements printed elsewhere in the issue are not included.

December 2

The President met at the White House with Zbigniew Brzezinski, Assistant to the President for National Security Affairs.

December 3

The President hosted a White House reception honoring the recipients of the Kennedy Center Honors. He and Mrs. Carter then went to the Opera House at the John F. Kennedy Center for the Performing Arts to attend the award presentation ceremonies.

December 4

The President met at the White House with:

—Dr. Brzezinski;

—a group of administration officials to discuss the fiscal year 1980 budget;

—Vice President Walter F. Mondale.

The President attended a portion of the meeting of administration officials with the Black Leadership Forum which was held in the Cabinet Room at the White House.

December 5

The President met at the White House with:

—Dr. Brzezinski;
—a group of administration officials to discuss the fiscal year 1980 budget;
—Vice President Mondale, Adm. Stansfield Turner, Director of Central Intelligence, Hamilton Jordan, Assistant to the President, and Dr. Brzezinski;
—a group of administration officials to discuss the fiscal year 1980 budget;
—Senator Paul Hatfield of Montana;
—Senator James B. Pearson of Kansas;
—Governor, and Senator-elect, David H. Pryor of Arkansas.

December 6

The President met at the White House with:

—Dr. Brzezinski;
—a group of administration officials to discuss the fiscal year 1980 budget.

The President declared a major disaster for the State of Louisiana as a result of severe storms and tornadoes, beginning about December 3, which caused extensive public and private property damage.

December 7

The President met at the White House with:

—Dr. Brzezinski;
—Israeli Ambassador to the United States Simcha Dinitz;
—Mrs. Carter, for lunch;
—Frank B. Moore, Assistant to the President for Congressional Liaison.

The President attended a portion of the foreign policy briefing held in the Residence Library for newly elected Senators.

The White House announced that the President of the French Republic, Mr. Valéry Giscard d'Estaing, has invited the President of the United States, Mr. Carter, the Chancellor of the German Federal Republic, Mr. Helmut Schmidt, and the Prime Minister of the United Kingdom, Mr. Callaghan, to personal and informal conversations on political matters and international developments of special interest to their mutual relations. This friendly meeting will take place at Guadeloupe on the 5th and 6th of January 1979. Each chief of state or government will be accompanied by only one assistant.

The White House announced that the President has asked Secretary of the Treasury W. Michael Blumenthal, who is now in Europe, to visit Romania on December 8, at the invitation of the Romanian Government. This visit is part of the continuing consultations between President Carter and President Ceausescu on bilateral relations and international problems that began with President Ceausescu's visit to the United States last April.

December 8

The President met at the White House with:

—Vice President Mondale, Secretary of State Cyrus R. Vance, Secretary of Defense Harold Brown, and Dr. Brzezinski;
—Dr. Brzezinski;
—a group of administration officials to discuss the fiscal year 1980 budget;
—Senator John C. Culver of Iowa;
—Charles L. Schultze, Chairman of the Council of Economic Advisers.

The President left the White House for a visit to Memphis, Tenn.

NOMINATIONS SUBMITTED TO THE SENATE

NOTE: The Congress having adjourned *sine die* on Sunday, October 15, no nominations were submitted during the period covered by this issue. The first session of the 96th Congress will begin on Monday, January 15, 1979.

CHECKLIST OF WHITE HOUSE PRESS RELEASES

The following releases of the Office of the White House Press Secretary, distributed during the period covered by this issue, are not included in the issue.

Released December 5, 1978

Announcement: meeting of the Interdepartmental Task Force on Women

Released December 6, 1978

Briefing: on the administration's human rights policy—by Secretary of State Cyrus R. Vance, Zbigniew Brzezinski, Assistant to the President for National Security Affairs, Anne Wexler, Assistant to the President, and Patricia M. Derian, Assistant Secretary of State

CHECKLIST—Continued

for Human Rights and Humanitarian Affairs

Advance text: remarks at the White House meeting commemorating the 30th anniversary of the signing of the Universal Declaration of Human Rights

News conference: on the National League of Cities' support for the administration's anti-inflation program—by Mayor John Rousakis of Savannah, Ga., president of the National League of Cities, and Alfred E. Kahn, Advisor to the President on Inflation

Released December 7, 1978

News conference: on the President's trip to Guadeloupe—by Press Secretary to the President Jody Powell

Biographical data: S. Lee Kling

ACTS APPROVED BY THE PRESIDENT

NOTE: The President completed his consideration of acts and joint resolutions passed during the second session of the 95th Congress on November 10.

Editor's Note

Note Concerning the Closing Time of This Issue

The President left the White House on Friday afternoon, December 8, for a visit to Memphis, Tenn. Releases issued on the trip will be printed next week.

PRESIDENTIAL DOCUMENTS

Week Ending Friday, December 15, 1978

Memphis, Tennessee

**Remarks at the Opening Session of the 1978
National Democratic Party Conference.
December 8, 1978**

Mr. Chairman, Mr. Vice President, distinguished officials of our various governments in a great country, and fellow Democrats:

What you and I just watched was one of the best network news programs I've seen since I've been President.[1] [*Laughter*]

I have to say that I've not been to very many, and I don't know what I will experience in the future, but so far I like Democratic conventions very much.

It is an honor for me to speak before the most open, honest, progressive, compassionate political organization in the world today, our Democratic Party. And we are also the oldest continuing political party in the world. And after the American people spoke so clearly last month, we are still the majority political party in the United States, and we're going to stay that way.

---

[1] The President was referring to a Democratic National Committee sponsored film called "Partners in Progress," which was shown at the conference prior to his remarks.

Ours is a party of practical dreamers. Thomas Jefferson conceived of the United States of America as no other nation had ever tried to be—dedicated to human fulfillment, where individual liberty was guaranteed. But Thomas Jefferson also founded a university; he collected a national library; he planned beautiful cities; he mapped the wilderness; and as a farmer, he invented a better plow—typical of Democrats. Time and again in our history, the Democratic Party has given new life and new meaning to our Nation's oldest dreams.

When a generation of hard-working Americans was robbed by the Depression of a lifetime of savings, the New Deal restored economic security and vision and brought new hope because of the vision of Franklin D. Roosevelt.

When a devastated Europe was threatened by economic chaos, political fragmentation, and alien ideologies, the Marshall plan and NATO sustained and strengthened our crucial alliance because of the courage of Harry Truman.

And when an uncontrolled arms race threatened the devastation of nuclear war, a test ban treaty took the first crucial steps toward peace under the bold leadership of John F. Kennedy.

When black Americans challenged our Nation's conscience to fulfill the historic pledge of equal rights, a nation finally answered, "We Shall Overcome," and Democrats wrote the promise of equal opportunity in law, led by and inspired by a great Texan, Lyndon B. Johnson.

I'm proud to be a member of the Democratic Party. And I'm also proud to be a member of a party of others who should have been President, like Adlai Stevenson and Hubert Humphrey.

We Democrats share with the founders of this Nation a faith in the good sense and the decency of average Americans. We are a pioneer people who learned early that survival and our dreams depended on hard work and courage and caring for one another. America's founding principle remains the most revolutionary idea in the world today—that all people are born free.

The dreams, the courage, the ideals of the American people have never been lost. But for too many years, some of our leaders did not reflect that faith. The challenge of government in America is to tap the greatness of a free people, but, for a long time, government failed that challenge.

We have passed through a painful decade—a tragic war abroad and bitter division at home; millions in unemployment lines and the highest inflation since the War Between the States; break-ins and buggings, and our Nation's highest public trust betrayed. Democrats will never permit such anguish and embarrassment to happen in the Nation which we love.

For too many years, the most open society in history had a government that operated in secrecy. We pledged an open government in 1976 which the American people could trust.

When government operates in the shadow and is complicated, bloated, and impossible to understand, the best financed, the most powerful, and often the most selfish lobbies have the advantage. Aver-

age citizens, the poor and the weak, who seek no special favors, are denied their rightful voice. We are tearing down the barriers between Americans and our Government. We've already passed new ethics legislation. The Government of the United States today belongs to the people of the United States, and not to the powerbrokers. And we're going to keep it that way. And you can depend on it.

Under this administration, we have restricted the use of wiretaps. No law-abiding American should ever have to live in fear that our Government will open mail, break in a home, or eavesdrop on private conversations. Under this administration, we will honor personal privacy.

Instead of leadership by veto and government by stalemate we now have a new Democratic partnership: President and Congress, Governors and mayors, legislators and local officials. The Congress has rarely had a more able and respected leadership, and certainly no President has ever had two better allies than Speaker Tip O'Neill and Majority Leader Robert Byrd.

For the first time in 200 years, the Nation's second highest office is a position of full responsibility. The Vice President is my eyes and my ears. His wisdom and his rapidly increasing experience have benefited our country time and again, at home and abroad. And I know that each one of you shares my deep respect and gratitude for the leadership of Vice President Fritz Mondale.

Two years ago, the most productive people in the world were governed by a wasteful and an inefficient bureaucracy. Republican Presidential candidates said they wanted to run government in the worst possible way, and that's exactly what they did. We Democrats pledged to have government as good as the American people, and that's exactly what we are doing.

Democrats do not believe that government should solve every problem or substitute for private initiative. But I have seen the power of rural electrification programs transform the life of a young farmboy in the rural South. And I know what it meant to my own people to eliminate typhoid and malaria, polio and cholera. And I've seen, as has my own wife, Rosalynn, retarded youngsters come alive with excitement and pride, learning new skills because a mental health program run by the Government reached out to them with love.

When government fails to deliver promised services, when redtape, paperwork, bureaucratic waste of time and tax dollars, those who suffer most—those who suffer most—are the ones who depend on government the most. We are cutting redtape, throwing out ridiculous regulations, reorganizing government, and eliminating millions of hours of paperwork. We've breathed new energy and initiative into the Federal civil service for the first time in a hundred years. We Democrats are trying to make government competent so that it can be truly compassionate, and we will achieve both those goals together, competence and compassion.

Those who rob from government with waste, theft, fraud, abuse, steal precious resources that could have helped a child get out of poverty with a head start, trained an unemployed youngster for a job, built a decent home for a family, provided legal services for the poor, or nursed an older American back to health. The stolen tax dollars come from every steelworker, every store clerk, every teacher, every farmer. This administration—and the new Inspectors General will help—will continue to root out every instance of fraud and theft and abuse, and we will prosecute the guilty to the full extent of the law.

For too many years, our free enterprise system was hobbled by massive unemployment, inflation, and an energy crisis that grew worse every year. Harry Truman spoke for every Democrat when he said, "We do not propose, like some people, to meet today's problems by saying that they do not exist, and tomorrow's problems by wishing tomorrow would never come."

We have been willing to confront the difficult and the complicated energy problem, and we are now getting it under control. If we join together as a people, I see an America of the future, strong and secure and free of the fear of energy shortages. I see American genius and technology harnessing solar power for millions of homes and buildings and creating thousands of new jobs. And I see America's achievements offering new hope to an energy-starved world.

In the last 2 years, we have created more than 6½ million new jobs, an all-time record. And we're not through yet. We've cut unemployment by more than 25 percent. The Republicans say they favor work, not welfare. But we Democrats have reduced the welfare rolls by 1.3 million Americans, by giving them new jobs. We have already saved more than $20 billion in welfare payments and unemployment compensation. We still have much more to do. Our Democratic partnership will continue to put America back to work.

After a Republican recession and a housing depression, our economy has grown 9½ percent. Last year we built 2 million new homes. Corporate profits have increased, in 2 years, 37 percent. Alben Barkley said, "If you want to live like a Republican, be sure to vote Democratic."

A Republican administration squeezed us farmers—the most productive in the world—by boosting the profits of middlemen, by embargoing shipments of American grain overseas, and by dictating the decisions that farmers should make themselves.

We have ended grain embargoes, once and for all. The Congress has passed a superb new farm bill, and our Democratic Congress and new legislation has untied the farmers' hands. Farm exports, so vital to our balance of trade, broke all records year before last. They're breaking all records this year, and farm income, net farm income, is up 25 percent. We Democrats are committed to what they have long deserved and are now beginning to get—a decent and fair income for American farmers.

And for the first time in 40 years, we have actually deregulated a major industry. Now the airlines are making more money, more Americans are flying, and they are paying less. Now, that's what I call free enterprise under Democrats. And next year—next year—we'll bring similar benefits to Americans by deregulating the surface transportation industry.

Republicans promise tax cuts. We Democrats have cut taxes nearly $25 billion. The Republicans left us the biggest budget deficit in American history. We have added new resources for human needs, strengthened the American dollar overseas, and cut that deficit $30 billion. Large deficits fuel the flames of inflation, so we must cut them even more, and we will, for inflation threatens all our gains and all our hopes for continued growth.

Inflation is robbing those whom we most want and need to help—working families, the pensioner, the widow, and the poor. It breeds a narrow politics of fear. It's an illusion to believe we can preserve a commitment to compassionate and progressive government if we fail to bring inflation under control.

Each of us must do our part, but government must lead. I have set my budget goals. I am determined to meet them. Short-term sacifices must be made. But we will balance those sacrifices fairly. And if we err in this balance, it will be on the side of those who are most in need. That's the way Democrats govern.

By joining together to control inflation now, we can lay the foundation for an extended era of growth and prosperity which all Americans can share—with more stable prices, with new jobs and opportunity, with new security and hope. And as President, I have no alternative except to bring inflation under control. As Democrats and as partners, we will meet this challenge, and we will meet it successfully.

Now, most of us have dreams, the same dreams for our children and our grandchildren—the opportunity to learn in schools that are challenging and which nurture them, to be protected against disease, to grow up in good neighborhoods, to know the taste of clean water and the smell of fresh air and the pleasure of beauty, natural beauty around them. We want a nation, as our Constitution promises, where the only limits on our children are the talents God gave them and their own determination and hard work.

In the past 2 years, we have added more new resources to educate America's children than ever before in our history. Across this country, 500,000 more handicapped children, 200,000 more children of migrant workers, 125,000 children who do not speak English as their native language—all children who have lived on the outskirts of hope too long—will start life now with a better chance because of our Democratic partnership. And for the first time, every young person in our country, everyone who wants to go to college or vocational school is now eligible for a grant or a loan.

No American family should be reduced to poverty, or bankruptcy, or go without needed health care because they cannot afford the cost. We have begun the fight for hospital cost containment. Next year we're going to win that fight. This is one of the essential steps toward reaching the goal that we all share—to protect every American through a comprehensive system of national health care.

People in every American city are struggling to raise their children in safe neighborhoods and safe homes, where teenagers can go to a good job, instead of to a bad street corner, where there is sunlight and open spaces and green parks. These formerly hopeless and lonely children are no longer struggling alone.

Federal resources are not unlimited, but we are targeting new aid, and we have forged a new urban policy. Our Nation's largest city is putting its finances in order and now facing its future with hope because the Democratic Party kept faith with the people of New York. And I'm thankful we did.

We have also begun the fight to bring billions of dollars of private enterprise, private investment to America's cities and also to our rural centers through a National Development Bank. Next year, we're going to win that fight.

Let me say that our national heritage, our natural heritage, is a gift to each generation. We have finally enacted long-awaited strip mining protection. We have strengthened standards for clean water and clean air. And last week, we guaranteed the protection of 114 million acres of our land in Alaska, our most precious wilderness. This doubled our system of national parks. And with your help, this administration will continue to keep faith with the next generation by protecting our environment.

The civil rights revolution liberated both black and white, North and South.

My commitment as President will never be in doubt. I will continue to uphold and vigorously to enforce the spirit and the letter of the laws of this land to ensure equal justice and opportunity for the people of America. I know you share that commitment.

We will not close our eyes to 200 years of systematic discrimination. We will promote effective affirmative action programs. We have already extended the time limits for ratifying the equal rights amendment. Now let us join forces to wipe out discrimination based on sex and make the equal rights amendment the law of the land, and give voting rights to the people of the District of Columbia.

The experience and the wisdom of our older citizens is a priceless resource. Our Democratic partnership has struck down discrimination based on age. Retired Americans deserve a life of dignity and not fear. The social security checks of all Americans are now guaranteed, not only for today but for the rest of the century.

For too many years, the most idealistic people in the world saw our highest ideals betrayed.

Woodrow Wilson spoke for every American when he said: "I would rather belong to a poor nation that was free than to a rich nation that had ceased to be in love with liberty."

Our Nation, conceived in liberty, is standing in defense of human rights. We do not claim easy victories; but brave people around the world who are struggling to taste the freedom that we now enjoy, they now know that they are no longer alone. Thousands of prison doors which once held innocent people have swung open. And as long as I'm President, America will continue to lead the worldwide struggle for basic human rights.

For many years I dreaded the autumn sessions of the United Nations General

Assembly, because I knew that the country which I loved would be vilified and castigated by scores of nations in the developing world. But the peoples of many of those nations now look to America with fresh eyes and new friendship, because we are struggling with them for justice and economic development, for democracy, and for peace.

In our own hemisphere, we have initiated a new era of mutual respect and cooperation with our neighbors. And I am proud that the United States Senate had the courage and vision to demonstrate to the world the greatness and the strength of our Nation by ratifying the Panama Canal treaties.

And I'm also proud that while I have been President, no American has fought or died in combat anywhere on Earth. My deepest prayer is to be able to say when I leave this office, "My country lived in peace."

With its great strength, America is a continuing and it is a persistent force for peace in Cyprus, in Nicaragua, in Namibia, in Rhodesia, and elsewhere. We've seen the President of Egypt and the Prime Minister of Israel, two long-term enemies, stand in the White House and before the Congress and clasp hands in a genuine gesture of peace.

No single individual in our lifetime gave more of her life and her energies and her devotion to the cause of peace than did Golda Meir. The world has lost one of its great, good hearts.

The road to permanent peace in the Middle East, God knows, is difficult and frustrating, with many deadlocks and delays. But after 4 wars, and 3,000 years of hatred, I am confident that our prayers will be answered and Golda Meir's dream will come true, and we will see a treaty of just and durable peace between the nations of Israel and Egypt signed, and signed very soon.

We want peace. And we are reducing our sales of conventional arms and trying to convince other nations to join with us in this commitment. America does not enjoy and does not want the title "Arms Merchant of the World." I would rather the peoples of other nations see the letters "U.S.A." printed on a bag of American wheat than I would on the butt of a rifle.

As President, I know that many depend upon the strength of America for their peace and for their freedom. I am committed to a strong defense. My first career was military, in the submarine force. My greatest responsibility as President is to maintain the security of our Nation. I will continue to keep that commitment. NATO and our other alliances are being strengthened. Under this administration, America's defense forces will remain so strong and well prepared that no nation will ever be tempted to test them and destroy the peace we love.

But we know that even strong defenses cannot give us true security as long as the awesome power of the atom remains a weapon of war. At the end of World War II, the United States was the only nation that possessed an atomic weapon. Today at least five nations share this sobering responsibility. We dare not permit the ability to produce nuclear explosives to become available to dozens of nations, large and small, led either by responsible leaders or perhaps by madmen.

We acted in the Congress last year to halt the spread of weapons-grade uranium and plutonium. Fifty nations led by us are now working together on this program and on this problem. We must and we will continue to prevent the proliferation of nuclear weapons throughout the world.

And finally, let me say that the nuclear arms race matches super power against super power. It is an unending, unwinnable, ever more costly contest. It escalates the risk of ultimate confrontation. It increases the danger that a fatal miscalculation, a tragic accident, or an act of madness could propel the world into nuclear war and wipe out life as we know it on Earth. I am dedicated to bring the nuclear arms race under control.

We have been negotiating daily and we are now negotiating daily with the Soviet Union on a new treaty to limit strategic arms. We hope soon to sign a SALT agreement which will strengthen the security of the United States, will provide for accurate verification, and will substantially reduce the threat of nuclear war.

Once the SALT II treaty is signed—and I believe it will be soon—I will depend on your help to ensure that it is ratified. We have no more urgent responsibility to the next generation of Americans than to act now to reduce the danger of nuclear holocaust. When the history of our time is written, it will be said that you and I, the American people met that responsibility.

Well, we face these and other serious challenges as Democrats and as Americans. But as a party and as a people we have met and we have overcome great challenges before. We will stay true to the promise of the Democratic Party. We will meet our urgent responsibilities. We will strive for competence. We will act with compassion. And we will continue to dream great dreams—and to make those dreams come true.

With the courage and the common sense of the American people as our guide, we will make this Nation what our founders envisioned—a land of liberty and opportunity, proud of its heritage of hope and human dignity, with the potential for greatness that only a free people can fulfill, a symbol of peace and a symbol of liberty to all the world.

Thank you very much.

NOTE: The President spoke at 9:06 p.m. at the Cook Convention Center auditorium. In his opening remarks, he referred to Democratic National Chairman John C. White.

Following his remarks, the President attended a reception for Governors attending the conference in the Cook Convention Center's main lobby.

Memphis, Tennessee

Remarks at the Democratic National Committee's National Finance Council Breakfast. December 9, 1978

I was standing outside in the hall, listening to the introduction of the Cabinet. I had thought our administration had done a good job up until now. But when Cabinet officers still get applause after 2 years, something's wrong. [*Laughter*] The ones that got the most applause are in trouble with me. [*Laughter*]

As a matter of fact, I think that this conference, which I personally did not approve when it was decided in 1976, is turning out to be a very constructive and very productive meeting. It's good for Democratic delegates throughout the Nation to be interested enough to seek a chance to come here and meet with others; some of them at a substantial sacrifice, financially. And I think the enthusiasm that has already been exhibited, the intense interest in issues has certainly been constructive and instructive to me.

The press and others had anticipated sharp divisions, schisms, debates that were not harmonious at all and not constructive. But that has not been the case. I think the more that our own administration has been assessed, the productivity and leadership of the Congress has been assessed, the more the potential opposition and intense criticism has gone away. It's good for us to be observed with a microscope and for every tiny facet of leadership in our Federal Government to be carefully judged and for us to have advice and counsel and criticism when it is deserved.

I know that the approach of this conference has made me much more aware of a need to inventory what we have done and to analyze our own accomplishments and mistakes and to make plans to present, in a factual but in a positive light, what the Democratic administration has brought to our country.

I'm proud of what we've done. I think the best accomplishment that we can observe is the harmony that exists between me and the Congress, between my entire administration and the State and local officials. It's kind of a new era in American politics, the reestablishment of the sense and the system of federalism which was really totally absent the 8 years before I became President.

I was Governor for 4 of those years, and a very active and enthusiastic and eager Governor. And there was no access from me, representing 5 million people in Georgia, to the core of leadership in Washington; even at the sub-Cabinet level, it was almost impossible for me to get an appointment or to discuss issues that were being contemplated for implementation by the Nixon and Ford administrations. But that's been changed. And I think we've seen a building of a foundation, not only for greater accomplishments in the future but also for greater political achievements in the future.

Although we lost some crucial and disappointing campaign efforts last month, the overall outcome of the election showed a massive approbation and con-

fidence among the American people in Democrats. We have more than 60 percent of the Members of the House who are Democrats; more than 60 percent of the Governors and Senators—just about 60 percent, a very heavy majority. And I think that this has been a notable contribution made by John White, a tremendous chairman who has helped to bring us all together.

We've got a long way to go, both politically and in an administrative and leadership capacity. I'm now involved in the most unpleasant portion of my year—it was the same a year ago—the preparation of the Federal budget. But I'm determined to meet the goals that I've set for myself, and I am reassured in those long, tedious sessions by a firm knowledge that you support those goals and that the average American also supports those goals.

I'm perfectly willing, as I see the evolution of the budget toward a final conclusion, to be judged personally on whether it is fair to the American people, whether our obligations overseas are met, our defense commitments are adequate, the social programs are also designed in a proper priority and at a proper level to meet the legitimate needs of our people. And these are not incompatible with the commitment that I have made to control inflation.

We inherited a mess in bureaucratic terms, in budget terms, in the administration of existing social programs, and in the relationships that did exist between the White House and the people of our country, and the White House and the Congress. Any thoughts that go back to 2 or more years ago would prove that what I've just said is true. Two years is not a long time in the historical evolution of a nation. But we've not only achieved things already of which we can be legitimately proud, but we've laid a groundwork or basis for even more progress in the future.

In international affairs, I'm very pleased with what we have done. We have not been afraid to become involved in highly controversial, sometimes hopeless, apparently hopeless efforts to bring peace to others throughout the world. We didn't have to attempt to bring majority rule and democratic government to Namibia and Rhodesia. This has been an intransigent problem for years, even generations. But we've been willing to put my own reputation on the line to risk disappointments and defeats, castigations from all sides, to join in with our Western Allies and try to bring those goals into fruition.

Andy Young in the United Nations has raised a new image of our country to more than a hundred newly formed or small or weak or black or yellow or brown nations. Whereas formerly we were considered to be their prime opponent, we were the target of their attacks, now they look upon us as an ally, as a representative of the finer and decent aspects of life. This is an accomplishment in itself.

And peace generally pervades in southern Africa, even though the threat of violence still exists. We are making some progress in Cyprus. We've got remarkably good progress in Nicaragua. And instead of violence and thousands of people losing their lives in Nicaragua, we joined in, as you know, with the Dominican Republic and Guatemala in what seemed to be an absolutely hopeless case.

And now last night the FAO, representing the Sandinistas, and the Somoza government has decided to sit down and begin negotiating today, not on how to stop massive bloodshed, but on the terms of a plebiscite to determine the government of Nicaragua in the future. We can't say that we've reached complete success, but we were willing to get in and use the tremendous influence of the United States in a beneficial way.

I won't repeat what I said last night about the Middle East. Cy Vance is arriving in Egypt today. He'll be negotiating with President Sadat. He'll go from there to Israel. We hope and pray we'll be successful. We don't have control over that, obviously, because those are two independent and proud nations. But we've used our influence in a beneficial way, and sometimes, as you know, I've been severely criticized by Americans who felt that I was going too far, not going far enough, or taking a biased position. But I think it's accurate to say that both those governments trust us to do our best.

We're trying to reach agreement with the Soviet Union on a SALT II treaty, and we're making good progress. My anticipation is that we will have, soon, a success. This obviously can't be guaranteed, because we don't ever know what the Soviet Government will do. But the differences that still divide us are very tiny compared to the differences that we've already resolved. But we've not been afraid to stand firm. I have never let a time deadline put me in a vulnerable position. We've not been hasty. And I can assure you that when the SALT agreement is presented to the American people, that it will meet the standards that we set forth.

I think we've strengthened alliances that were damaged severely, and we've raised high the banner of human rights.

These are the kinds of things that we have done so far that bring me gratification. But the main thing is the future. And that's where I would like to thank you for what you've done to keep the Democratic Party viable, to keep the Democratic Party together, and to keep the Democratic Party in the forefront of the domestic and foreign commitments that exemplify the greatness of our Nation. In times of extreme need, under John White, under Bob Strauss, both of whom are here, Ken Curtis, you helped financially, and this has been one of the most gratifying aspects of my own relatively brief political life.

When we were in deep distress, you came through with no thought or expectation of benefiting personally. It's the kind of generosity that too often goes unrecognized, but I recognize it, and I thank you for it. You'll never be thanked adequately, but the financial stability of our party is extremely important.

As you know, there again, we inherited a $9 million debt, left over from ancient past campaigns. [*Laughter*] And we've not only tried to keep our party viable financially by tight management and the elimination of waste, but we've also had to pay off those back debts. And I feel deeply indebted to you.

The last thing I want to say is this: We are partners in every sense of the word. If and when we do have success in controlling inflation, or putting our American people back to work, or building homes, or providing better education, or bringing peace to the Mideast, or a good SALT agreement, or better relations with the developing nations of the world, it's not the President who's done it; it's not even the Congress who has done it; it's you, who represent the families and the communities and the towns and cities and counties and States throughout our Nation, that never yield, in spite of disappointing news—sometimes, even embarrassments—coming out of Washington, in your commitment to a finer and greater America.

And I feel a personal sense of gratification to each one of you. And I feel the assurance of future success, because that partnership is sound and because your hopes, your commitments, your unselfishness, your understanding is unvarying.

And as President of the United States, as the titular head of the Democratic Party, I thank you, one and all, from the bottom of my heart.

Thank you.

NOTE: The President spoke at 9:19 a.m. in the Holiday Hall at the Rivermont Holiday Inn.

Memphis, Tennessee

Question-and-Answer Session at the National Democratic Conference Workshop on Defense Policies and Arms Control.   December 9, 1978

GOVERNOR-ELECT RILEY. Mr. President, in behalf of the delegates and guests, press, and those present, we certainly welcome you to this panel. I would want to know, sir, will you have a statement? The other panelists have made a brief statement. If not, we would proceed with questions.

THE PRESIDENT. I think, not knowing what's already been said, it would be better to take advantage of my brief time here and answer questions, Dick.

GOVERNOR-ELECT RILEY. All right, sir. I recognize Delegate Nick Lucy from Iowa, who was in the process of stating a question. Limit it to submarines, if you could. [*Laughter*] Go ahead, Nick.

TRIDENT SUBMARINES

Q. I'd like to commend you for your past submarine record, Mr. President. Having served in submarines myself for 3 years, I can appreciate your efforts in your earlier days, there.

My question was in regard to the Trident submarine program. I've heard when it was discussed initially that it was too expensive, and we could refit present submarines with the same type missile and therefore save a great deal of money. This was, of course, of great concern to all of us.

However, having also served in the submarine service, I'm concerned about the time at sea, that our crews spend there. And it's my understanding, according to the Navy Department—I've received from information to this effect—that even though the ship will spend about 1 percent more time at sea, the crews will spend approximately 35 percent more time at home. This is not only healthy for the crews on these Trident submarines, but it also gives me the impression that it would make us less dependent on overseas bases.

And I'd like to know where we're going with this program and just how the overall cost factor has been adjusted.

THE PRESIDENT. The Trident submarine decision was made, as you know, several years ago. And I've assessed it since I've been President. I think it was a good decision. The ultimate way to measure the cost of a defense system like the submarine missile program is the total lifetime of the offensive or defensive weapon capability, compared to costs, like per missile. I think the Trident is effective. It will permit the use of missiles which have a greater capability, both range and throw weight, which gives us a better deterrent factor. And the cost over the lifetime of the submarine is less than that of the older submarines outfitted with less effective missiles.

Also, as you know, a submarine, even the old fleet-type submarines, the first ones that I was on, have a limited lifetime, as do all other capital-type ships; 25 or 30 years is the maximum. So, we have to plan long ahead of time.

The last thing I'd like to say about the Trident submarine program is that because of the innovations in its design, there were early delays in the delivery of the first few Trident submarines. But my understanding now from the Defense Department is that we will stay on schedule in the future.

Q. Thank you, Mr. President.

THE PRESIDENT. It's a good system.

GOVERNOR-ELECT RILEY. Thank you so much. Any other panelists want to elaborate? All right, sir, the next question. They know who the boss is, I think. [*Laughter*]

NUCLEAR NONPROLIFERATION

Q. Howard Rosen from New Jersey, to any of the panelists. I was particularly pleased to observe the progress of interest in the nuclear nonproliferation efforts. And I wonder, Mr. Carter, if you or any of the other panelists would comment on where they stand now, particularly with respect to India.

THE PRESIDENT. I'd like to let John Culver answer that, because I think this is one area where the Congress really took the initiative. And I'm very proud of the achievements already on our nonproliferation program. And I think John Culver, who's been in the forefront of that effort, probably ought to be the one to answer the question.

GOVERNOR-ELECT RILEY. Senator Culver.

THE PRESIDENT. I thank you, by the way, for having a reception for me, when I was a lonely candidate, in your home. [*Laughter*] Thank you very much.

SENATOR CULVER. Well, let me just say that as someone that has served in the Congress, now, for 14 years and been concerned with the United States taking a leadership in the area of arms control and other initiatives, it's enormously refreshing to have the opportunity to serve with a President who has the degree of commitment to these goals and objectives as President Carter has, not only in the area of increased efforts in bringing about a greater worldwide participation and compliance in nonproliferation treaty, but in other areas such as conventional arms restraint, where the President has been the one to take the leadership, not only by way of unilateral actions on United States conventional arms sales abroad, but certainly by way of appropriately initiating consultation with our allies and on a bilateral basis with the Soviet Union.

And of course, we have, as we've referred to, the very important SALT negotiations now, hopefully nearing fruition. We also have the mutual balanced force reduction efforts that I think we are on the verge of, hopefully, breaking the impasse, say, that's characterized those talks for the last 5 years. And, in addition, we have a situation where the comprehensive test ban treaty, hopefully, will also be coming on line, where we can get a mutually agreeable arrangement with the Soviet Union and the British and ourselves.

Now, the greatest problem, of course, is to get not only participation with regard to participation in the nonproliferation treaty but to get meaningful safeguards, to get meaningful methods of internationally policing those agreements so that they have enough teeth and viability to be credible. How do we monitor the problems of the traffic in terms of the sources for uranium? How do we put limitations on reprocessing of plants?

And I think, here again, the President, with regard to his efforts with the German Government and the French Government in those sales that were involved in Brazil, for example, and also in Pakistan—very courageous leadership by the President, I think—has very substantially reduced the momentum that was threatening to be completely out of control.

We still have some extremely difficult problems with regard to disposal of waste,

with regard to continually working out some sort of international arrangements where there can be assured supplies. And, of course, we had the incredibly difficult problem of working out sufficient progress in these areas to bring enough international public opinion pressure on governments like the French and the Indian and the Chinese, so that we have not only an arms control regime that is effective but that we have maximum participation and involvement. And I don't think one could be working harder in those areas than the President. And we can only do whatever possible in the Congress to support those efforts.

THE PRESIDENT. Let me add one comment. The problem with nonproliferation is that we cannot stand in the way in our own country or in foreign countries of the development of peaceful use of atomic power to produce electricity and for other reasons. We support this program. But there needs to be a commitment on the part of a broad range of countries, not just us by ourselves, to prevent that from resulting in nuclear explosives anywhere.

So, under our own initiative, we now have 50 nations, at the top levels of government, even including heads of state, working on what we call an international fuel cycle study, nuclear fuel cycle study. And this has been going on now for, I think, about 15 months. And out of this will come some definite recommendations and commitments.

These nations, by the way, include the Soviet Union, all our European allies, South Africa, that we deliberately brought into the discussions because we were concerned about their taking the products of regular powerplants and turning them into explosives. This is a new thing that hasn't been well publicized. But it's an ongoing program, and we've been very pleased with that.

GOVERNOR-ELECT RILEY. Thank you, sir. I recognize the delegate to my left.

STRATEGIC WEAPONS SYSTEMS

Q. Governor, my name is Jon Furman, delegate from the 22d CD [Congressional District] in California. I have a question about the new program for mobile-based missiles. My understanding is that in a series of relatively minor and inexpensive changes, the accuracy of our land-based missiles and the accuracy of the Soviet land-based missiles are both increasing dramatically. And we now have or will soon have the ability to destroy most of their land-based missiles, and they similarly now or soon will have the ability to threaten to destroy many of our land-based missiles. And my understanding is that some people in the Defense Department are suggesting a massive new program to this perceived threat or supposed threat of building mobile land-based missiles, either having several hundred missiles in several thousand silos and moving them at night so the Russians don't know where they are, or putting them in planes that can take off and land in short periods of time on short runways. But this program could cost from $30 to $50 billion, could require as much land, I've read, as the entire State of Connecticut.

And I was wondering, since we have our submarine-based forces, 30 submarines, each one having as much nuclear power as any other country in the world except the United States and the Soviet Union; we have our manned bomber forces; and perhaps, hopefully, these mobile land-based missiles might be a subject for SALT II or SALT III controls. How can we justify to our people spending $30 to $50 billion on a massive, new and, I think, unnecessary weapons program

when we are reducing or we may have to reduce CETA jobs and health services and community development funds that—I mean, I'm from Pasadena, and I've seen how important and vital those are to the local cities and the social services?

GOVERNOR-ELECT RILEY. Thank you, sir. Let me ask Dr. Perry if he would, in behalf of Defense—if you would comment, Dr. Perry?

MR. PERRY. I'd make three comments relative to that question. First of all, it is true that both the Soviet Union and the United States have achieved greatly improved accuracies in their ICBM's, and, as a consequence, these ICBM's are capable of targeting silos. Therefore the silos are no longer a safe haven for missiles.

The second comment then, is, to the extent we believe it is desirable to preserve the deterrent effect of an ICBM, we will need to do something to improve that survivability.

The third comment is that the Department of Defense does not have a program which we are ready to recommend to the President yet as to the best way of doing this. And the reason we don't is precisely because of the problems which you cited: the expense, the environmental impact, and the complication of trying to make the missiles sufficiently mobile to give them the degree of survivability that would be realistic. And we're still working on that program.

Q. Do we really need any program at all?

MR. PERRY. The question is whether we can maintain essential equivalence with the forces of the Soviet Union without the ICBM. We have clearly an option of—instead of making the ICBM forces survivable, we have the option of increasing the strength in the submarine forces and the bomber forces. I think that's a trade-off which is the better way to go. Improving the submarine forces and improving the bombing forces are not without expense and not without environmental impact also. So, that's simply a balance which is still in judgment at this time.

THE PRESIDENT. I might say that the answer to the last question—I think it is necessary, and we are trying to accomplish this in two ways, to avoid that imbalance that might evolve if the Soviets ever get a demonstrable advantage over us. The most efficacious way to handle it is by stringent SALT agreements.

In the upcoming SALT agreement, we will have a substantial reduction in the limits. The reduction will not be a constraint on us, because we have not built at the rate the Soviets have. If the SALT II agreement goes through as we contemplate it, the Soviets will have to destroy several hundred of their existing missiles.

And part of the SALT II agreement which has not been publicized is that it outlines or reestablishes officially a commitment to proceed without delay on SALT III. I contemplate a much more drastic cut in overall missile levels of all kinds in SALT III than we will be able to accomplish in SALT II.

As you know, early in 1977 we proposed a drastic cut to the Soviets. They rejected it, in retrospect, I think, primarily because Brezhnev had a great deal of personal investment in the Vladivostok agreement, and he thought we ought to consummate Vladivostok before we moved on more drastic cuts. And if and when Brezhnev and I meet at a summit conference to wrap up the SALT II agreement, high on the agenda will be a SALT III discussion for much more drastic cuts in overall missile levels than SALT II envisions.

Of course, the other facet of it—and much less attractive—is, under any given SALT agreement, no matter what the levels are for bombers, for cruise missiles, for sea-launched ICBM-type missiles, or for silo missiles, or for mobile missiles, to make sure that we do retain this rough equivalency, because if the Soviets have, in the eyes of the world, a demonstrable advantage, if they feel that with relative impunity they can attack us, it puts us at a decided disadvantage in all sorts of political and economic ways. And we would lose our beneficial influence throughout the world for peace and let the Soviets dominate in the minds of those who are looking for strength in their partnership.

So, we're trying to agree completely with you, to cut down on the overall level, to maintain a rough equivalency. And I think in SALT III, we'll be much more successful. My hope is and my tentative belief is that Brezhnev wants the same thing I do, a drastic cut in SALT III.

GOVERNOR-ELECT RILEY. I recognize Senator Culver for comment.

SENATOR CULVER. I think, just so perhaps there's a general agreed understanding of what we are talking about in the particular context of a mobile missile response or a multiple aim point arrangement to a perceived Soviet threat, is the situation where the Soviet heavy missiles, as they continually are MIRVed with more warheads and as the accuracy increases as a rate that we anticipate, it is theoretically possible that sometime in the mid-1980 time frame, 1985, that some Soviet leader could contemplate a first strike on United States land-based missile sites, where we have now some 1,054. This scenario would conceive of a Soviet political leader making the decision in 1985 to initiate a surprise attack, assumedly without warning, against those United States land-based missiles system sites and silos.

And it's expected that the accuracy that could be contemplated and anticipated at that time might reach proportions that would permit them conceivably and theoretically and somehow possibly, technically, to eliminate a very substantial number, perhaps 75, perhaps 80 percent, perhaps 90 percent of that land-based missile force. And under that particular fact situation, there is concern that somehow we do not have sufficient retaliatory capability to maintain credible deterrence against that theoretical threat.

Now, frankly, it's important to keep in mind that at the present time, the United States and our strategic nuclear inventory has 9,200 strategic warheads. The Soviet Union has 4,500. The bomb that we dropped at Hiroshima was 13 kilotons. The smallest bomb we have in our total inventory of 9,200 strategic nuclear warheads today is on the Poseidon submarine, and it is three times, at least, more powerful than Hiroshima.

The Soviet Union has 4,500 strategic nuclear warheads at the present time. As Dr. Perry has indicated, their numbers are likely to increase. But our 9,200 are spread in the submarines, where they're survivable in the ocean deep, and in our bomber force and in our land-based systems. The Soviets have 70 percent of their strategic inventory, those 4,500 on land-based alone.

Now, if you're a Soviet political leader and someone comes in to you and says, "Comrade, I suggest today that we fire all our land-based missiles, that we fire sufficient missiles in our inventory to strike out maybe 80 to 90 percent of that United States land-based system." And you say, "Well, you suggest that?" "Yes." "Well, will they work? Nothing else in the Soviet Union works. We've never tested these and tried. Will they work? Can you confidently tell me that you'll have that de-

gree of accuracy, that they are reliable, that if we fire them, the President of the United States, who sees them coming and has 15 minutes to make the judgment as to where they are going, whether he will launch, on warning—will he launch on warning, the President of the United States? Will he launch under attack? And if he does, those 2,500 missiles of ours, heading for that land-based system, won't have anything to take out when they get there, because ours will all be fired."

Now, if the United States of America sits back and watches the preparation for that surprise attack, does nothing, and in the worst case, accepts that initiated strike, absorbs it, guess what? In our submarine force and in our submarines, it's estimated that even if that system works and they avoid the problems of fratricide, they still have to contend with what's left in our land-based system, what's left in our submarines at sea, what's left in our bomber force that is off the ground and airborne. And you know the total inventory that would be left, even under that inconceivable, mad folly of that theoretical attack that the Soviets may theoretically contemplate but could never confidently execute? We would have remaining, available for an assured retaliatory, destructive strike on the Soviet Union more strategic warheads than the Soviet Union even has today in their total inventory.

So, I think that the threat that we're talking about is theoretical, and we must not let these threats by bloodless war gamers and talk about perception force us into decisions in billions and billions and billions of dollars of overkill or potentially stabilizing actions which create a far less stable international strategic environment.

Now, we have time to study and resolve these issues carefully and prudently and responsibly. Frankly, if we had pushed ahead with the so-called trench plan that was favored only a year ago, we would have had a vulnerable $30 billion system. And yet there were efforts to move forward with that.

Now, what we fear technically, the Soviet leaders cannot rely on. And even endangered Minuteman preserves the advantages of the triad and retaliation, and it justifies the wisdom of our early strategic military doctrine to diversify and give flexibility and survivability to our strategic inventory.

Many problems need to be resolved: cost; environmental impact; technical feasibility, since we're talking about an area that would require the size of Connecticut; security while moving missiles, and of where they are in comparison with alternatives. And when we do the one thing we can be sure of, the Soviet Union will do it tomorrow, and then what kind of security do we have in the world?

And finally, Mr. President, and Mr. Chairman—I don't mean to take too much time, but one last point: that the multiple aim point system, in my judgment, is necessarily tied to the SALT negotiations, because MAP, a multiple aim point system of any kind, without SALT doesn't make sense, since a multiple aim point system would be no good unless the Soviet Union warhead numbers are limited and unless the Soviet Union is prevented from deception on its own systems.

So, both those protections are now currently being negotiated in terms of warhead limitation and restraint on the Soviet inventory and, of course, keeping them within an arms control agreed regime that will afford us opportunities to monitor and to check the nature and pace of the strategic program in the Soviet Union.

GOVERNOR-ELECT RILEY. Thank you, sir.

I recognize the delegate to my right. Yes, ma'am.

STRATEGIC ARMS LIMITATION

Q. Yes, my name is Deborah Hibbard, and I am a delegate from Maine. And I would like to ask Senator Culver two questions that are of great concern to me and, I think, to all of us in this room.

The kind of theoretical maze that you have just articulated terrifies me, because you are talking about us being number one and yet how do we stop this arms race? I think that it's very conceivable that at the same time that you're sitting here describing a first-strike capability over the next 10 years on the part of the Soviet Union, that there is someone there, sitting there being very concerned about the first-strike capability that we have the potential for developing. And what I would like to ask you is, where does this end?

SENATOR CULVER. I think it's really the most valid question that one could pose, because, clearly, I think if we are unable to politically stay on top and cap the insanity of the current arms race and its proliferation, then the mathematical likelihood that mankind will destroy itself becomes increasingly inevitable; that by accident or design and miscalculation, these weapons will be used. And once that is initiated, in any form, in my judgment, it'll be impossible to contain and avoid a total nuclear holocaust.

It seems to me that the President of the United States is embarking most credibly and most courageously in the right directions, and that is to try to seek a cap. Frankly, in my judgment, SALT I and SALT II today we still have not had any meaningful, genuine arms reduction in the history of arms control. What we've done today is seek agreements and achieve agreements in areas where we don't have any competition yet—and those areas that are easy.

Now, even in SALT I, in SALT II, you can make a case, in my judgment, that those agreements, to a great extent, have been vulnerable to the charge that even getting together forces a very careful, obsessive preoccupation with every variation in the respective balance. Any asymmetry in the static indicators on either side are then scrutinized by our negotiators. And if we don't have 10 green peas and we got 4 white ones—and the bean counts, everybody suddenly says we have to be a mirrored image of every conceivable theoretical capability of the other side.

So, the rough equivalence that one can have without total symmetrical relationship is often put aside. And the result of SALT I and even SALT II, to a great extent, one can argue, is to push up development and production in many systems. Now, the problem today is that our political courage and leadership and imagination has not kept pace with the mind-boggling acceleration of technical developments, technological breakthroughs.

In 1970, when the United States had the leadership on MIRV development, many of us in the Congress went to the President and we went to others and we tried to get an agreement with the Soviet Union to not MIRV their weapons. And we couldn't get an agreement on that. We couldn't do it. The Soviets then have gone to MIRVing, MIRVing their heavy systems.

Now, today we meet and say that our land-based systems are vulnerable because the Soviets are MIRVing, and now we got to have a mobile system, the M-X, to deal with that threat. That wasn't created by arms control; it was created because of a lack of an agreement. Now, hopefully, SALT II will set the stage for meaningful, substantial reductions in SALT III, as President Carter has very properly made reference to. And then, and only then, can we hope for substantial reductions.

In SALT II, under the tentative outline of the agreement being contemplated, it would be the first time the Soviet Union would be called upon to dismantle some 300 of their already deployed land-based systems, which is about 10 percent of their current land-based force and not an insignificant thing. But they will be taking out the old and tired systems and not the new ones. And if you can criticize this agreement, that it isn't enough arms control—but you certainly can't criticize the President of the United States, in my judgment, for not doing everything in his power to making it as meaningful as possible.

Q. I guess what really concerns me is that we're caught in this theoretical thinking. And the other thing is that we must remember that 30 years ago we were the ones who exploded that first atomic bomb, and the arms race commenced at that point. And I think that it's up to us to say no. And I'm not very confident in this SALT III and SALT IV and SALT V and SALT VI—you know, always hoping. I think that as long as we feel that we have—somebody feels that they have to maintain an edge, we're caught. And I think that we have to admit that we're caught.

DEFENSE SPENDING

The other question that I would like to ask you is that you made a statement that the military strength of the U.S. must begin with a strong economy. And what I would like to hear you speak to for a minute or two is what is the relationship between defense spending and inflation?

SENATOR CULVER. Well, the question is, our strong defense, as I mentioned in my initial statement, begins with a strong economy at home. And secondly, in that regard, what is the relationship of defense spending to inflation? Well, clearly, defense spending, however much is necessary, is, relatively speaking, the most inflationary dollar you can spend, because there's no market—[*applause*]. And the reason for that is that there is no market for those goods other than a battlefield or a warehouse or a motorpool or wherever it might be.

Now, secondly, as far as the defense budget's effect on the economy, we hear much about job creation. But if we're going to spend Government money to create jobs, there are far more labor-intensive ways to do that, in education and transportation and health policy. And defense spending is not targeted to areas of chronic unemployment, but it's rather mostly white collar and highly technical people in a relative sense.

Now, having said that, I do think that when we speak about security, we have to keep in mind that it's more than just the defense budget. It is the health of our people; it's their morale; it's their political confidence. And it's most importantly the economy, and I think the great challenge that President Carter, of course, has is how to honor, really, essentially, three commitments: one, in a tentative way to increase our defense budget in cooperation with our European allies; secondly, in cooperation with our European allies, to pledge to reduce inflation and the deficit in the United States of America. And it's very hard to reconcile all these inherently conflicting objectives and goals, although they're all equally admirable in many ways in a relative sense.

But clearly—the 3-percent commitment, for example, that's been discussed about—and in fairness to the President, he hasn't made a final decision, it's my understanding; I'm sure he'd want to speak to this—but the 3-percent commitment may conflict with the other two objectives. And even your question of how much you have available in real growth in the budget to spend on defense is ironically related to just how successful you are in dampening down inflation and reducing your deficit, because when we speak of real growth, we're talking about real growth over the rate of inflation.

If you anticipate the rate of inflation to be at 7 percent, you want 3 percent real growth. You've got one figure. If you can get inflation down to 6 percent, you've got 4 percent real growth with the same budget figures and targets.

So, these are moving targets and they're very elusive and they are interrelated. But clearly, I think it's one of the great challenges, of course, to the President to make these allocations of domestic resource recommendations in the document of the Federal budget, so that our true security interest is truly being advanced and the appropriate proportions for defense and the domestic and social needs of America are respected.

Q. Well, with all theory aside, I would just like to say, let it——

Q. Mr. Chairman, there are a lot of people here and the President of the United States. How about getting her off and letting us hear from the President?

THE PRESIDENT. I don't think we can take up all morning for this.

GOVERNOR-ELECT RILEY. Thank you. Thank you, ma'am. Mr. President, would you like to comment?

THE PRESIDENT. I'd like to—I've got to leave in just a minute, and I wanted to say one thing.

We spend about 5 percent of our gross national product on defense. The estimates are that the Soviets spend between 13 and 15 percent of their gross national product on defense. Senator Culver and I are very strong allies, and we're in harmony on almost everything. But to say that we are wasting money or to insinuate that we might be wasting money because we build weapons that are never used and that rust away in the warehouse is exactly what we hope. We build weapons for peace and to let the world know that our Nation is strong. And I hope that when we build a Trident submarine, or when we build ICBM's, or when we build a tank, or when we build a rocket or an airplane, that it will never be used, that it will never be used. And only the accurate knowledge in the Kremlin that we are strong and that we are going to stay strong and not vulnerable is the only guarantee that we will not have to use our weapons and not have to expend the lives of our young people in combat.

And as you well know, there is no way to evolve a budget and to keep it secret. The budget will be revealed to the American people early next year, to the Congress for a decision. And I think we have so far had a very well-balanced assessment of our total resources, and a well-balanced commitment of those resources between international affairs and domestic affairs, between social programs and defense programs.

The last thing I'd like to say is this: It takes two nations to negotiate an agreement. And if I could have unilaterally sat down in the Oval Office and written a SALT agreement, it might be different from what I had to negotiate over the last 20 months with the Soviets.

Again, I think we will have negotiated a very fine SALT II agreement, and we have personnally fought for much more drastic reductions than the Soviets have yet been willing to accept. This is a continuing process. It's been going on for years, even decades. And my commitment is, as I said in my inaugural address, to remove the threat of nuclear weapons completely from the world. I

don't know if I'll accomplish this while I'm in office, but that's my goal. And I'm going to do the best I can to achieve that goal as President of this country.

GOVERNOR-ELECT RILEY. I recognize the delegate to my left.

ARMED FORCES PERSONNEL

Q. Thank you very much. My name is John Morgan, and I'm a delegate from Pennsylvania, from Butler County, North Allegheny County.

Mr. President, in the newspapers and, oh, just generally over the past year, I've just been reading a tremendous amount of things about the Volunteer Army, the condition of the personnel in the Armed Forces in general. I know that when there is no active war, the military doesn't really keep everybody too much in shape. I know there's a difficulty with getting recruits when there's no real concrete threat. But at the same time— I was a draftee myself—I really can't see why or how we can leave the quality of our personnel with these instruments of death that we invent and the great need that we have—I cannot see how we can leave our personnel deteriorate to the point where it's a threat, or even considered to be a threat in the newspapers. I really feel that there's a need for a draft system, that there's a need for a reconsideration of the present volunteer system in the Army that should be made.

Now, part of the problem, it's a question of looking at your own people and saying, well, you know, you're not doing a job. This is terribly difficult, and you don't want to do that. It breaks the morale down right there. But the thing is that it's quite clear to me that the time has now come or is coming in the immediate future where we're going to have to reconsider, partly because of the reductions of the SALT talks and partly because of the change of the physical needs of the amounts and numbers of people in the Armed Forces, we'll have to reconsider whether or not we need a draft system. And I'd like to have your comments concerning that.

THE PRESIDENT. As you know, I think under President Nixon's administration and with the strong support in the Congress, the voluntary military service system was put into effect, and the draft was eliminated. I had some concerns about it then, but it was a decision made, and we are living with it well.

I think the allegations that the present quality of military service personnel is low are erroneous. The military commanders with whom I meet regularly, the assessments of performance that are done on a fairly scientific and objective and accurate basis show that we do have a very high level of quality in our armed services. Sometimes we have coming into the armed services as volunteers young men and women who don't have a high academic background. We have corrective programs in the Armed Forces, as we did to some degree during wartime, to bring their educational level up, to take advantage of the talent that they inherently have.

If our country ever should turn back to a draft system—and this has constantly been under assessment, ever since the voluntary system was initiated—I think Senator Sam Nunn, Senator Stennis, for instance, have been very interested in assessing whether or not it would be advisable—it ought to be substantially different from the draft system we had before.

I never thought it was fair. I thought it was extremely unfair to give exemptions, for instance, for all young Americans who had the financial resources to stay in college. I think in the future if we should have a draft system, it ought to be absolutely universal. And if we have to take a limited number of young people into the Armed Forces, they ought to be on drawing lots; and whether somebody's in college or working on a farm or relatively illiterate, they ought to be handled in the same, exact way.

Q. Mr. President, wouldn't you feel it's now the time to have a universal draft system——

THE PRESIDENT. I don't know about that.

Q. Since it's peacetime?

THE PRESIDENT. I think the answer is the same as you suggested and as I gave. The best thing to do is to constantly assess it. And that is being done. But no conclusions have yet been reached. And I think for the President to express an opinion kind of short circuits the accurate assessment in which I've not yet been involved.

Maybe I can stay for 5 minutes; maybe a short answer.

GOVERNOR-ELECT RILEY. I recognize the delegate to my right.

ENERGY RESEARCH

Q. My name is David Noble from the 17th District in Ohio. And I sincerely agree with what Senator Culver said, that the security of this Nation rests on our economy.

Mr. President, it seems to me that the fundamental tool of our economy is energy. Therefore, I would like to know why we are not making a greater effort to develop the new energy sources that are going to be available to us once we make the tremendous technological effort that's going to be necessary to do things like building satellites in space that can send energy back via microwaves and photoelectric cells.

THE PRESIDENT. Well, I'll be very brief with that. I'm going from here to a meeting on the economy. I'm trying to attend as many of the sessions as I can.

I am personally not in favor at this time of any substantial commitment to a satellite-type power-producing station, because its cost and the technological problems involved are prohibitive. But I would say that our shift toward solar energy is going to be substantial even in the 1980 tight fiscal year budget. And I don't have any final figures and haven't made final decisions, but I would say that that commitment would approach a billion dollars next year, the total involved in solar energy itself.

And with the basic resource of the new energy legislation which opens up vistas now and possibilities for rapid evolution of alternate sources to oil and natural gas, the hopes that you've expressed will be much more feasible. But I think it's a long way in the future before we can start depending upon a space station to provide electricity, say, for Memphis or Plains.

Thank you very much.

Q. Well, we're not going to get there until we start, Mr. President.

THE PRESIDENT. That's right. I agree.

I've got to go. And I want to express my thanks to all of you for letting me come.

NOTE: The President spoke at 9:50 a.m. in Mezzanine Room N at the Cook Convention Center.

Prior to the President's arrival, the members of the panel—David L. Aaron, Deputy Assistant to the President for National Security Affairs, William J. Perry, Under Secretary of Defense for Research and Engineering, and Senator John C. Culver of Iowa—made opening statements. Governor-elect Richard Riley of South Carolina chaired the workshop.

Memphis, Tennessee

Question-and-Answer Session at the National Democratic Conference Workshop on Inflation. December 9, 1978

LIEUTENANT GOVERNOR O'NEILL. The President would like to entertain questions. [*Laughter*]

FOREIGN TRADE

Q. We're still operating under our international trade agreements that were devised in the late 1940's, and, of course, they were originated to rebuild industry in Western Europe and Japan. And they did a magnificent job of it.

However, at the present time, Germany and Japan and Western Europe and all these manufacturing nations are still operating under the systems that we helped them to build in the 1940's, to build their industry. Consequently, our industrial complex is continuously being, not actually reduced, but reduced in comparison with our competitors.

So, what I want to make a strong pitch for is that we place the same restraints on imports into the United States, say, reciprocal restraints as those nations place on our imports into their countries. If we did this, I have a strong feeling that our industry will become much healthier; it would reduce inflation, because our system flourishes on the supply-and-demand theory. It seems to me the only way that we can really stop this business.

I would also like to have this workshop consider the possibility, if they could, of placing some restraint on the increase of interest rates. If 8-percent wage increases are inflationary, then what is a 11¾ percent interest rate? The banking industry can increase their profits by 800 percent. And our purchasing power is being continuously reduced. Thank you.

THE PRESIDENT. That was not in the form of a question, but let me say this: Our administration, primarily under the leadership of Robert Strauss, the Special Trade Representative, has been laboring ever since I've been in office to conclude a multilateral trade negotiation in Europe, to make sure that restraints on shipments from our country to other countries in the world are fair and equitable and balanced. And we have made bilateral agreements—that is, between our country and just one other country—to protect American manufacturers in several areas of production—color television sets, shoes, textiles, and so forth.

We'll continue to do this. But overall, we believe that our Nation is best protected and our workers have a better prospect for progress, higher wages, more jobs, if these international protective devices in the form of tariffs and other obstacles are reduced and not raised.

Our country only exports about 7 percent of our gross national product. There's not a deep commitment on the part of manufacturers in this country to depend upon exports, because we have such an enormous domestic market. A country like Japan has many, many more times of their portion of their production destined for export. Germany exports between 25 and 30 percent of their gross national product.

But what we're trying to do is to lower trade barriers to make more equal those that have discriminated against American production in the future. And there is a difficult negotiating effort being carried on now.

Bob Strauss is reasonably confident, and we'll continue this effort. We want to have more jobs in our country, more sales overseas, less protective barriers, and equality in treatment, and no dumping of foreign goods on American markets. That's what we're working for.

THE NATION'S ECONOMY

LIEUTENANT GOVERNOR O'NEILL. Yes, sir.

Q. Thank you. My name is Jack Scott from the State of Louisiana, the 8th District. I'm a member of the Louisiana legislature in Louisiana. And I'd like to present a viewpoint that hasn't been stressed as much as I would like it here today.

You know, the community I'm from is a small town. We don't have any giant corporations; we don't have a lot of illicit, obscene profits, and things of that sort, where I come from. But one thing we believe in, and where I do come from is we feel like an individual, a business, a government, what have you, cannot really spend more of its resources than it has. It seems to be a very simple principle. And I'd like to go into it in a little greater depth.

You know, so many people that have spoken today have seemed to blame a philosophy of trying to balance the budget for inflation, as though that's the status quo. But, ladies and gentlemen, we haven't had a balanced budget in this country in 10 years. We've only had one in the last 20 years in this country. So, balanced budgeting and applying the principle of your dollars have to somehow pay for themselves has not been the status quo in this country for many, many years. So, you certainly can't blame today's inflation on that philosophy.

Now, I'd like to go through what history can instruct us just a little bit. We had the first $100 billion budget in our country's history in 1946. It took us about 176 years to reach that point. Then just 24 years later we had, in 1970, our first $200 billion budget. And then just 5 years later, our first $300 billion budget; and 2 years later, '77, our first $400 billion. And now we're right at half a trillion dollar budget per year.

Now, if you look at a graph of spending at the Federal level, you'll see that it's running fairly parallel in the early 20th century, starts rising midway, and by the time you get to the seventies, it's going straight up. So, for those of you who feel that spending a great deal through government at the Federal level will cure inflation, you're getting that right now, and you're paying for it.

Now, let me just—I've got two questions, but I'd like to premise it with these remarks. I have a chain of thought I'd like to share with you. It seems to me that when we have a deficit budget, somehow or another government has to cover that deficit. They have to pay their expenses, their costs, their salaries, to do business. So, somehow, that deficit has got to be covered. How is that done?

Number one is by borrowing, selling bonds, securities, what have you, at a high interest rate, so that private investors will buy them. And that bids the interest rates up all over the country. Number two is we print more dollars, and we've been printing dollars, increasing the money supply to something in the neighborhood of 9 percent, as I understand it, per year, the last couple of years, which means that as we print more dollars through the Federal Reserve and put them into circulation, we're watering down the value of all the dollars that are already in circulation, not just in the United States but all over the country, all over the world.

And so, the dollar goes down and declines in all the money markets, the dollar bills that you and I have in our pockets are worth less and less. So, prices go up, because the merchants who are providing goods and services need to get more dollars to cover the same purchasing power they were getting before. And so, when their prices go up, the people start demanding pay raises to keep pace with it, and they get their pay raises, and so, then we do have the spiral that results.

I say wages and prices are a symptom of inflation; they're not inflation themselves, and that's the reason why controls cannot work. That's the reason why I certainly support voluntary plan, because that can't do any great harm. It may even help, but it certainly isn't the solution to inflation. It's right up there in Congress. Now, our politicians cannot blame the farmers, they can't blame the labor unions, you can't blame the oil companies, you can't blame anyone else in the private sector for the very core, root cause of inflation, because the true cause is up in Washington, D.C., with the policy we've had for so many years, of not just deficit spending, but since 1974, we haven't had a single deficit that was less than $30 billion. So, that is——

Q. Question?

Q. All right. With those, my two questions are this: First of all, why was the Nunn amendment to the tax cut bill rejected when you had both the Senate and the House supporting it overwhelmingly, and it called for a balanced budget over a 5-year plan with spending limitations and with tax reductions that would go into effect only if those spending limitations were met?

And secondly, my second question is, how will the wage insurance plan—that's part of the administration's anti-inflation program—how will it be paid for? My understanding is that you'd be paying something like 1 percent over a person who gets no more salary raise than 7 percent, through his salary, which, in my understanding, is that the national payroll and private sector is around a trillion dollars. And if you work it out, it comes out to somewhere in the neighborhood, just on those very basic pieces of mathematics, to about a $10 billion cost of that plan. So, how will that be paid for?

LIEUTENANT GOVERNOR O'NEILL. Thank you very much.

THE PRESIDENT. Let me try to answer the statement first.

We are cutting down the portion of our gross national product that is collected and spent by the Federal Government. I inherited, as you know, a 1976 deficit that was $66 billion. At that time, the Federal Government was taking out of the American economy and putting back 23 percent of our GNP. We are cutting that down to 21 percent, a substantial reduction over what I inherited.

We believe that we are contributing to inflation when we have a high budget deficit. That's one of the reasons that I have pledged myself to continue the downward trend.

The Nunn amendment was not rejected by me—although I did not support it—it was rejected with good unanimity among the House and Senate conferees when the tax legislation was proposed to me.

I think it might be good to let Fred Kahn follow up very briefly and then perhaps either cover the wage insurance question or let Charlie Schultze cover it very quickly. But the essence of it is that the more wage earners and manufacturers who agree to reduce both wage demands and prices, the more that we will be guaranteed that the insurance cost will be minimal or nonexistent. And, of course, the fewer people that agree to hold down wages, the fewer that will be eligible for insurance, if we are not able to control inflation.

Our goal is to control inflation, not to pay off on high insurance payments. But this is a good inducement and a good guarantee for those enlightened workers who say, "We do want to control inflation. We're willing to make some small sacrifice, but we don't want to pay if others don't agree."

So, this is what the wage insurance will do. I hope the Congress will pass it. Perhaps Kahn and Schultze can make brief additional comments.

LIEUTENANT GOVERNOR O'NEILL. Well, Mr. President, we've got a rule that we're going to let the panelists participate and summarize in the last 15 minutes of the segment.

THE PRESIDENT. Very good.

LIEUTENANT GOVERNOR O'NEILL. I'd like to give everybody an opportunity to come up and ask a question. And if you could hold yourselves to a very brief question, I would certainly appreciate it.

MEAT IMPORTS

Q. I'm going to answer the same way—tell you who I am as I did in 1975, fall, to candidate Jimmy Carter then, at Joyce Van Dusen's house in Cedar Rapids. He walked up to the mike and says, "I'm going to be your next President." After he give us the answer period, I told him who I was.

I'm Harry G. Powell, Senior, from Newton Township, the Cannon County, the Third District of the State of Iowa.

LIEUTENANT GOVERNOR O'NEILL. Sir, will you speak right into the microphone, please?

Q. I never had—only twice in my life have I ever talked in one of these. [*Laughter*]

My county is next to the largest pork-producing county in the United States. Delaware is first. Now, agriculture, to me, is one of the greatest part of the economy. You may wonder why I don't go to the Agriculture Department here.

First, my question is going to be directed to Bob Graham, the Governor of Florida, but now I must add our President because he's here. I want to say this before I forget it. This is one of the greatest honors in my life, my 55 years working for the Democratic Party, to be before this great group of people.

In this foreign beef supplies—may fall short of quotas—this is from the Des Moines Register, December 1. I'll be very brief about this, because maybe you and I can help out the President on a veto. The Governor of my State, reported, sent him a wire to not veto it.

This is in the mid-term conference. "No matter"—they're talking about—"No matter what he decides"—that's President Carter—"on the nearest meat import question, Carter could anger either consumers or farmers."

I live on what we call an average size farm, 470 acres. My son farms it, and I help him now, very active in it. Now, we raise corn, beans, cattle, and hogs—and a supplier of meat. How would you—the Governor of my State sent—I believe it is reported—President Carter a message or wire to veto the bill.

How would you, Governor of Florida, you told us here that you raised beef, that you built houses—and I forgot the other one. [*Laughter*] But as a beef grower, how would you—I'll answer you first if you want me to, what I would have done. [*Laughter*] Politically, I don't think it would have been very sound for a President to have signed it. And I don't feel that I would want any of my Presidents to ever have his hands tied on a little thing like this when the meat supplied in now is 1.5 billion. He only raised it to 200 million.

What did you do on this bill—do you send the President? Would you have signed it, vetoed it or not? Now, you raise cattle.

LIEUTENANT GOVERNOR O'NEILL. I've got to stop you, sir.

Q. Okay, sir.

LIEUTENANT GOVERNOR O'NEILL. The Governor-elect will have an opportunity to answer it when we're summarizing. And I'm going to come over to this side of the room and provide the next person an opportunity. Thank you very much.

FEDERAL SPENDING

Q. Good morning, Mr. President, distinguished panelists. I just have four short questions. My name is James Fite from Baltimore, Maryland.

First is that it appears to me that both the Revenue Act of 1978 and the inflation policy, as Mr. Kahn has explained it, are discriminatory, depending on how one earns one's income. For instance, I am an hourly worker and earn my income in that manner. I can't debate the policy. My boss just told me I'd get a 7-percent raise; there's no question in my mind what's going to happen—got to go along with it. Right? I want to know what controls are going to be made on profits, number one.

Number two, I don't understand the economic thinking that says that a continual decline in real wages, which appears to me would mean that the only way we can continue our standard of living is with the extension of consumer debt, which seems to be on the increase—I don't see how that decline or policies that continue to enforce that decline can pull us out of inflation. I just simply don't understand it from your point of view.

Third is, I don't understand how this distinguished panel can sit here and give the presentations they gave to us today without once discussing the military budget and its purposes and reasons for inflation.

My fourth question, sir: I have an internal memorandum from the board of directors of National Association of Manufacturers, which was put out long before your statement was made public on inflation. I also have the statements from the Brookings institute. Now, I understand that in the past the Brookings institute has been very contributory to the policy and thinking and things like that of the government.

I want to know, since the statement of the National Association of Manufacturers is almost word for word the inflation policy as it was described and announced in your speech, I want to know, does this show a shift of thinking away from the policy-type thinking of Arthur Okun, et cetera, toward the National Association of Manufacturers and that type of economic thinking?

LIEUTENANT GOVERNOR O'NEILL. Sir, Thank you very much.

THE PRESIDENT. I won't try to answer all four questions, but I would like to answer the concern about the military budget.

As I said last night in my speech, the number one responsibility above all else of any President is to ensure the safety of our country. Also, a major portion of my time, a substantial portion of my time, is spent in analyzing how the benefits of the influence of a strong United States can be invested economically and politically throughout the world to bring peace to other regions, and to ensure that alien philosophies which absolutely wipe out human rights do not triumph.

I have to match American military strength with that of the Soviet Union. It is a constant problem for me, a constant challenge. It's one I accept readily. Any President in the past or future would have to meet that commitment. The Soviet Union does not have the advantage of

idealism, of freedom, liberty, of honoring independence or nationalist trends in foreign countries. They don't have a commitment to a better life for people built on freedom. They depend substantially on their influence to challenge us on military strength.

We spend about 5 percent of our gross national product on the military. It's been reducing year by year for a long period of time—5 percent. The Soviets spend between 13 percent and 15 percent of their gross national product on the military. We have tried and are trying, not desperately, but with determination, to cut down on the allocation of resources to the military. We can't do it by unilaterally putting ourselves in a vulnerable position versus the Soviet Union.

We have proposed drastic cuts in missiles. We are negotiating in Vienna for what we call mutual and balanced force reductions in the European theater. We are working for a comprehensive test ban. We're trying to eliminate the proliferation of nuclear weapons. We are trying desperately to bring peace and not divisiveness to the Mideast, to Nigeria, to Rhodesia, to Nicaragua, other places around the world.

In the meantime, though, we have got to have a strong defense. We can't bear it alone. We've got to inspire our own military allies to stay strong themselves. We are not trying to take over anybody's territory or run anybody else's affairs, but we cannot afford to be vulnerable.

Now, I hope that every weapon that we purchase will eventually rust. We are not buying weapons to use, and the degree to which we can be demonstrably strong means that we can have peace for our own people and for those around the world.

I do not have any apology to make at all for maintaining a strong defense. As long as I'm in the White House, I will keep a strong defense.

I just want to add one other sentence. My own assessment in history, my own political fortunes will be determined by Americans' judgment. When I make decisions, for instance, on the 1980 budget—has Jimmy Carter been fair; has he been conversant with and sensitive to the social needs of our people; and has he balanced this equitably between defense and other domestic problems, between domestic and international problems—I want to take that responsibility.

And I can guarantee you that I'll do the best I can to have a well-balanced budget and a fair budget. And, as I said last night, if I do make a mistake, it will be on the side of those who are most dependent on the Government, the poor and the deprived and the disadvantaged who are looking for a better life and who can only find a better life, in my opinion, with a Democratic administration.

LIEUTENANT GOVERNOR O'NEILL. Thank you, Mr. President. We're alternating from one side of the room to the other. Sir?

ANTI-INFLATION PROGRAM

Q. Mr. President, Mr. Chairman, ladies and gentlemen of the panel, ladies and gentlemen of the audience, I'm Victor Bussie, president of the Louisiana AFL–CIO. I'm a life-long Democrat, a man who has never voted for a Republican in his life.

I also come to this conference with even better credentials than that. When the national press and all the polls said that Jimmy Carter could not carry Louisiana, I said that he would carry Louisiana. And we worked the State very hard to make sure that Louisiana did go in the right Democratic column, and we helped to elect Jimmy Carter President of the United States.

I also believe strongly in a military service. I served my country during World War II, and would serve again, age permitting, if it became necessary. So, I don't want to be listed as one of those that vacillates between the Democratic and Republican Parties, nor one of those who feels that we spend too much money for defense.

I simply want to say to you that I have a very deep concern, Mr. President, about your program. I'm concerned about the workers, those I represent and those I don't directly represent, but whom I speak for here today. And I feel that I can speak for them, because as I said, when all the polls said that Louisiana would not go for Jimmy Carter, I said it would, because I go among the poor, those who belong to unions and those who don't belong to unions, and I go among the wealthy, those who accept me, from time to time. [*Laughter*]

And I try to find out what goes on in my State so that I can truthfully stand before any audience and say that this is what the people in my State honestly believe. And I want to say to Mr. Scott, who is a very distinguished representative from Louisiana, that if Jimmy Carter balances the national budget under the existing circumstances, Louisiana and every State in the Union and every municipality and every parish or county will go bankrupt the next day, because you cannot live under those conditions. It simply cannot be done. As much as everyone wants the budget balanced, it must be done in a long period of time and under certain considerations, or else the problem will be too great.

I'm concerned about the exemption from the present anti-inflation program, Mr. President, of the cost of food, the cost of energy, the interest rates, the medical care, and things of that type. I'm concerned, too, about your apparent efforts to remove the controls over the cost of gasoline and the cost of natural gas and things of that type, even though I come from a State which produces a substantial amount of that energy.

Nevertheless, I am concerned about what it's going to do. Every man and woman in the country today, with the exception of a few who may have a bus line that runs within several miles of their home, must depend upon gasoline to go to work and to come back home and to do the things that's necessary for the livelihood. They simply cannot, Mr. President, pay a dollar a gallon for gasoline if their wages are going to be limited to a 7-percent increase, and from the 7 percent, we deduct what we call the fringe benefits—the cost of hospitalization, the cost of the money that the Federal Government says the employer must put in the retirement system in order to make it actuarily sound, and the many other things that the program either does or does not cover, based upon who's explaining it to me and what it's supposed to mean in the final analysis.

I can't get a good explanation of what the program is. But from what I've read in the information I've been able to get—and I've diligently sought all of the information that I can get, Mr. President—the program will work to the detriment of the poor working people of our country. And I hope that you will take into consideration our plea that drastic changes be made in the program. We want to share our responsibility. We want to cover that responsibility, but we want everyone else to do the same thing.

We don't want the big corporations——

LIEUTENANT GOVERNOR O'NEILL. Mr. Bussie, I'm going to have to rush you a little bit.

Q. I'm rushing fast as I can, Mr. Chairman. [*Laughter*] We don't want the big corporations of America to go scot free, and that's what they're going to do, if I understand the program. And I say that sincerely, because they can shift profits from one production line to another, and they have many ways of getting by. Don't let them by, Mr. President; make us all do what we have to do in order to make this program a success. That I beg of you, as a man who was your supporter, a longtime Democrat, a good American, I believe—because I've never advocated anything except the free enterprise system, a representative of working men and women and one who tries to speak honestly and sincerely on their behalf.

LIEUTENANT GOVERNOR O'NEILL. Thank you, Mr. Bussie.

I'd like to thank Mr. Bussie for his statement. And then we're going to come back over here. If you have a question, if you could bring it to a conclusion very quickly, again, I'd appreciate it.

THE DEMOCRATIC PARTY

Q. I'm a delegate from northern California and also a staff member of the California Campaign for Economic Democracy, whose chair is Tom Hayden.

The reason I came up here—I think most of my concerns have already been stated—but I joined the Democratic Party when I came back from Vietnam, because I believed it was working for the working people and the poor people of this country. And as I listened and watched this panel criticize, one after another, wages and government, and then I read the white paper put out by the White House on October 24th, which says excessive wage increases were not the cause of the current inflation, but wage moderation is an essential part of the cure—well, I hope the Democratic Party will forget about going after the poor people and the working people and take on the corporate greed in this country, especially in regards to defense and energy. And I would just like a statement from someone at the end about this.

LIEUTENANT GOVERNOR O'NEILL. Okay. Thank you very much.

CONSUMER AFFAIRS

Q. Mr. President, the question that I have is directed mostly to Mrs. Peterson. And I feel somewhat like David in the lion's den, because I've heard from labor, business, et cetera, and I'm espousing the concerns of the consumers out there.

Mr. President, you've shown an interest in the consumers in the recent legislation that was defeated. But I would hope that that interest is going to continue. As an attorney—and I represent the 10th Congressional District of Pennsylvania—I see what inflation is doing to the American family. I do a lot of domestic relations work and see the problems that inflation causes—alcoholism, the inability to pay one's bills. And I suggest that it's the consumers' ignorance as to how to deal in the marketplace that is one of the greatest problems facing the free enterprise system.

Mr. President, you have at your disposal the United States attorneys' offices all over the U.S. And if the Congress of the United States won't give you a consumer advocate, I suggest the Attorney General should put one in every U.S. attorney's office. Problems such as land fraud, problems such as the automobile used-car dealers, clocking odometers, they go beyond the basis of one State to another. We need this help in the marketplace desperately, Mr. President, because I suggest if we can create an atmosphere where our consumers know how to deal in the marketplace, we can stretch that shrinking dollar. And we can save many families, and you can keep your commitment to the American people that you've

been doing such a wonderful job with thus far.

Thank you very much.

LIEUTENANT GOVERNOR O'NEILL. Esther, maybe you'll handle that at the end.

ANTI-INFLATION PROGRAM

Q. Mr. President, I don't have a question. I'm a delegate of Democrats Abroad. And we represent 1.8 million Americans outside the United States. One of the things which has struck me about this discussion has been the fact that nobody has stressed how much the introduction of your anti-inflation program meant to the world outside the United States. Up to that time, and up to Camp David, the rest of the world didn't know where the United States was going. And it was only when Camp David took place, and when the anti-inflation program was introduced, that the rest of the world knew that the United States and the Carter administration was not going to take the same route which has destroyed so many countries around the world, where countries—I travel in Africa, I travel in the Middle East, and I travel all over Europe, and I know countries where there's not double-digit inflation, but there is triple-digit inflation. And those are the countries which now are convinced that the United States is going to be a strong country and it's going to live up to its leadership obligations, and the rest of the free world is now certain that we are going in the right direction.

Thank you, Mr. President.

UNEMPLOYMENT

Q. I am Susan Garner Koenigsberg from Miami, Florida, delegate for the 13th Congressional District. What I came prepared to state, there is no time to state. However, I will say this is a hard act to follow.

Yes, the consumers are unaware, and Esther Peterson has said it very well. And there are problems, social problems, economic problems. But I do want to say one thing, that if we are just looking at inflation alone without concern for the high unemployment rate, we're looking at people, and we are saying, "Oh, you're a consumer, you have to be educated." But do we really realize that if you're working, you're in a recession? If you're not working, you're in a depression? If you don't have the purchasing power, you can't do anything?

The city of Miami has endorsed a proposed bill. I hope that this panel here would take some time, as well as my Governor, who has worked a hundred jobs, and we'd like to provide hundreds of jobs to help to implement the funding of the Humphrey-Hawkins bill. The centerpiece of this bill is actually the priority use of our money supply. And I cannot take the time on this floor to go into it, but we have a great deal of material. And I was wondering if President Carter's attention had been brought to the fact that there is a proposed bill to fund the Humphrey-Hawkins bill, and the name of this proposed bill is the socioeconomic growth act. I don't know if he's aware of it. [*Laughter*]

LIEUTENANT GOVERNOR O'NEILL. I think he's aware of it.

Q. Thank you very much.

THE PRESIDENT. Let me tell the delegates assembled here that I have to leave. I'm trying to go to as many of the sessions as possible.

I have really been impressed with this one. I think that all of you have seen the intense interest in the economic future of our Nation, and the delicate balancing of conflicting issues is one that ultimately arrives on my desk. But you are expressing your views clearly to me in the brief time

I've been here. I'll read very carefully a summary of everything that you say. I've listened to it with an open mind and an open heart, and, of course, participating in the panel are very close advisers for me that I see every day on consumer affairs, economic development, all kinds of economic affairs, and the control of inflation.

But I'm grateful that you've come. I don't believe anyone in this room thinks that the mid-term conference is a waste of time, because we learn from each other. And I think we'll have a greater future as a Democratic Party and a nation, because you have come and contributed your time to teaching us, to learning from us, and to sharing a consistent and a continuing partnership.

Thank you very much for letting me be part of it.

NOTE: The President spoke at 10:45 a.m. in Mezzanine Room M at the Cook Convention Center.

Prior to the President's arrival, members of the panel—including Charles L. Schultze, Chairman of the Council of Economic Advisers, Alfred E. Kahn, Advisor to the President on Inflation, Esther Peterson, Special Assistant to the President for Consumer Affairs, and Governor-elect Bob Graham of Florida—made opening statements. Lieutenant Governor Thomas P. O'Neill III of Massachusetts chaired the workshop.

Memphis, Tennessee

Remarks to Reporters Following a Visit to the Site of the Assassination of Martin Luther King, Jr. December 9, 1978

Q. Can you tell us about your visit here, Mr. President? What prompted you to come? I wonder if you would give us a minute and talk about your visit to the motel here and why you decided to come.

When did you decide to come here, Mr. President?

THE PRESIDENT. Although the memory of Martin Luther King has always been extremely important in inspiring people to pursue the goals that his life was dedicated to accomplish, there's been a growing realization on a worldwide basis of the significance of what he espoused and what he gave his life to accomplish.

As Andy and Coretta were just pointing out, his Nobel Peace Prize speech deplored poverty, racism, and war. And that still is a list of the most significant challenges to any leader in the world.

And I wanted to come here with his widow, Coretta, and with Andy Young, one of his strong supporters, who was here at the time of the tragedy, to let the people of America know and let the people of the world know that I value what Martin Luther King was and what his memory is, not only for myself as a leader of a great country but among the leaders of the world.

REPORTERS. Thank you.

NOTE: The President spoke at approximately 11:45 a.m. at the Lorraine Motel after he had laid a wreath at the site. He was accompanied by Mrs. Martin Luther King, Jr., and U.S. Ambassador to the United Nations Andrew Young.

Commission on Civil Rights
Nomination of Louis Nuñez to Be Staff Director.   December 11, 1978

The President today announced that he will nominate Louis Nuñez, of Silver Spring, Md., to be Staff Director for the Commission on Civil Rights. He would replace John Buggs, resigned.

Nuñez was born October 20, 1931, in New York City. He graduated from City College of New York in 1953. He served in the U.S. Army in Korea and did graduate work at City College and New York University in education and public administration.

Nuñez has been at the Commission on Civil Rights since 1972, serving as Deputy Staff Director until January 1978. Since then he has been Acting Staff Director.

Prior to joining the Commission on Civil Rights, Nuñez was national executive director of ASPIRA of America, a national, nonprofit organization providing education and leadership development programs for Puerto Rican youth.

THE PRESIDENT'S NEWS CONFERENCE OF DECEMBER 12, 1978

THE PRESIDENT. Good morning, everybody.

I do not have an opening statement, so, Ms. Thomas [Helen Thomas, United Press International]?

STRATEGIC ARMS LIMITATION

Q. Mr. President, can you confirm reports that a tentative agreement has been reached on SALT with the Soviets, that you may meet at the summit with Brezhnev in January? And also, if these are true, can you say what caused the breakthrough?

THE PRESIDENT. We've made good progress on SALT. I can't say that we've reached agreement. A statement will be made later on today by the State Department and by the Soviets simultaneously about a possible meeting of the Foreign Ministers.

I think that there has been steady progress made in the last, almost 2 years. I can't recall any time when there was a retrogression or a pause in the commitment to reach a SALT agreement. Our position has been clear. We have harmony, I believe, among the Defense Department, State Department, and the White House on what should be the United States position. If the Soviets are adequately forthcoming, we will have an agreement without further delay. If they are not forthcoming, then we'll continue to negotiate.

Q. And how about the summit?

THE PRESIDENT. I think that as we approach the time when we are sure that the items have been resolved that are still under negotiation, at that time we will have a summit meeting. And at that summit meeting we will discuss not only concluding the SALT agreement officially but also have a broad agenda of other items that are of mutual interest to us and the Soviet Union.

Mr. Cormier [Frank Cormier, Associated Press].

GASOLINE PRICES

Q. Mr. President, do you lean toward or against the decontrolling of gasoline prices at this time of high inflation? It's a two-edged sword, I think.

THE PRESIDENT. It is, and it's one that I haven't yet decided upon. When I presented my comprehensive energy plan to the Congress in April of 1977, inflation, although important, was not the preeminent issue in my mind.

The Secretary of Energy, my own advisers in the White House, and Alfred Kahn, who's responsible for the anti-inflation program, are now assessing all the ramifications of the pricing of gasoline, and, of course, the Congress will be involved in the decision also. But I've not yet reached a decision about what the administration's position will be.

EGYPTIAN-ISRAELI PEACE NEGOTIATIONS

Q. Mr. President, the other day you took a very serious view of Israel and Egypt going past the 17th of this month without concluding a treaty—that's the date they themselves set for it. Now, with 5 days left, what's your belief, or hunch, as to whether they'll meet that deadline? And do you still think it's sort of a "now or never" proposition?

THE PRESIDENT. I don't think it's now or never. And you very accurately described this deadline date as one established by Israel and Egypt in the most solemn commitment at Camp David.

Secretary Vance reports to me, from Cairo, good progress having been made between him and President Sadat. He has not begun further negotiations with the Israelis yet because of Mrs. Meir's funeral. He will return to Egypt, try to conclude his discussions with President Sadat, and then go back to Israel for discussions with the Israelis.

I consider the deadline date to be quite important. If the Egyptians and Israelis cannot keep a commitment on a 3-month conclusion of a peace treaty when they themselves are the only two nations involved, serving as a mediator in the process, then I think it would be very difficult for them to expect the terms of the treaty they are negotiating to be carried out with assurance. It sets a very bad precedent for Israel and Egypt not to reach a conclusion.

I think the differences that presently divide Israel and Egypt are minor, certainly compared to the resolution of major differences in the past. And I believe that President Sadat has reconfirmed his intention, his commitment, to Secretary Vance to conclude the negotiations without further delay. My hope is and my expectation is that the Israelis will have the same attitude.

THE NATIONAL ANTHEM

Q. Mr. President, this may sound like a frivolous question, but I hope you won't think so. But the National Anthem is played at every trashy football game and baseball game and wrestling match and boxing. Don't you think that downgrades it quite a bit to do that incessantly?

THE PRESIDENT. That's not any more frivolous a question than I have gotten in the past. [*Laughter*] And I think it is a very good question.

I personally don't think that frequent playing of the National Anthem downplays its importance. No matter how often I hear the National Anthem, I'm always stirred within myself toward more intense feelings of patriotism and a realization of what our Nation stands for. And I think for audiences at sports events to hear the National Anthem played is good and not contrary to the influence that the National Anthem has on all of us.

ADMINISTRATION ACCOMPLISHMENTS

Q. Mr. President, at year's end, how do you assess the last 11, 11½ months, the pluses and the minuses as you see them, the hits and the errors—and, particularly, would you speak a little bit about the errors?

THE PRESIDENT. Well, as a completely nonbiased analyst, I would say that the pluses far outweigh the minuses. I think any analysis of the accomplishments of the 95th Congress, including those made by the news media representatives here, have been positive, that the accomplishments were substantial, much greater in the final stages of the Congress session

than had been anticipated earlier in the year.

We've still got a lot of unfulfilled expectations and hopes. We have not successfully addressed the question of inflation. It's been greater during the second half of the year than we had anticipated. We have been pleasantly surprised at maintaining the higher and higher level of employment, preventing the unemployment rate from going up. Last year we had 660,000 new jobs created in America in spite of some slowing down in the national economy, which was expected.

In international affairs, our country has injected itself, I think wisely, into regional disputes where we have no control over the outcome. But we've added our good services, in some instances with almost no immediate prospect of success. My own reputation has been at stake and that of our country.

In Nicaragua, I think instead of having violent and massive bloodshed, we now have the parties negotiating directly with one another for the first time on the terms of a plebiscite and whether or not there should be general amnesty. In Namibia, we are making some good progress, I believe. The South Africans have now accepted the terms set up by the Secretary General of the United Nations. We are waiting for SWAPO to respond.* Cyprus, very minimal but steady, increasing prospects. Mideast, you're well acquainted with that. And I think that on SALT and other major international items we have made steady progress.

---

*In fact, SWAPO accepts the relevant United Nations resolutions on Namibia. The President's intention was to call for their continued support. The United States is waiting for South Africa to indicate in definitive terms its acceptance of the proposal and a date for the arrival of the United Nations transition assistance group. [Printed in the transcript.]

So, in balance, I'm pleased with the last 11 months and don't underestimate the difficulties still facing us.

Q. One followup.

THE PRESIDENT. One followup.

Q. Wouldn't you say that your inability to move faster towards your social goals, those social goals that you spelled out during the campaign and since, wouldn't you call that a distinct minus?

THE PRESIDENT. No, I wouldn't. I think we've made excellent progress in social goals. I've just commented on the fact that we've had large numbers of new Americans at work. We've had a net increase of about 7 million in the number of jobs held by Americans. We've reduced the unemployment rate a full 2 percent. We've had a 25-percent increase in the net income of farmers. We've increased exports there. We've had a stabilization of the American dollar, which was surprisingly effective. We also, of course, recognize a continuing problem that's been of greater importance lately for inflation.

So, I think, on balance, the performance has been positive; although we still have very great problems ahead of us.

DEMOCRATIC NATIONAL CONFERENCE

Q. Mr. President, the Democratic Party just spent what seems to some people an enormous amount of money to hold a mini-convention. And I just wonder, some people are already saying perhaps the money would have been better spent in congressional campaigns or Senatorial campaigns. Do you think that was worth the money, and how do you feel about midterm conventions in general?

THE PRESIDENT. For the first time in, I think, more than 10 years, the Democratic National Committee this year did make substantial contributions to the campaigns of congressional candidates. This was a step in the right direction.

This midterm conference was mandated by the 1976 convention. There was no way I could circumvent that mandate. I personally did not favor the midterm conference when it was decided upon in 1976. I was pleasantly surprised. I think, in balance, the conference was worth the money.

My understanding is that additional funds have been raised in Memphis and in other places to adequately pay for the cost of the convention.

I believe it is very important for me, as a President, and also as head of the Democratic Party, to have my success and failures assessed objectively and openly by Democrats representing the grassroots of our party around the Nation. I think that was done in a very forthcoming way. I've observed the deliberations, participated in them with a great deal of interest, and I think in general the policies of my administration were endorsed.

The one single issue concerning budget matters, which was highly disputed, and on which the more liberal members of the party concentrated their efforts, showed that my policies were endorsed by, I think, more than 60 percent. So, I'm very pleased with it. And I don't think there was anyone who went to the conference who couldn't say in its closing hours that they had an adequate opportunity to express their views, either supportive of me or contrary to what I have done.

So, I feel very pleased about it.

NATIONAL HEALTH INSURANCE

Q. Mr. President, to what extent do you feel bound or influenced by the resolution passed by the midterm conference on calling for enactment of national health insurance in the next Congress?

And specifically, will you seek to have comprehensive legislation passed in the next Congress to take effective phases, or will you go at it one piece of legislation at a time?

THE PRESIDENT. The midterm conference decision was compatible with the 1976 convention decisions on the Democratic Party platform concerning comprehensive health care. I favor that campaign commitment and the platform commitment.

There are differences about how to implement a national health care system. Under any circumstances, those policies espoused by Senator Kennedy, those policies espoused by me—the first major implementation or financial assessment for that purpose would be made in 1983. It's necessarily a slow process. I think it's better done step by step, recognizing the ultimate goal and moving as we can afford it and as we can implement it in a very carefully conceived, methodical way, bringing on board the Congress, and also bringing on board, for support, the American people and the different interest groups involved.

So, I think that the policy expressed by the midterm conference was compatible with my own, and that's what I intend to carry out.

OIL INDUSTRY

Q. Mr. President, this goes to your general attitude with the oil industry. Last week, consumer advocate Clarence Ditlow blocked a multimillion dollar price increase in unleaded gasoline by your administration, said you were ignoring the aspect of destroying catalytic converters.

There's been a major increase in home heating fuel at a time when there's a glut of home heating fuel, particularly here in the Northeast—we've had a very mild winter. It looks like some very high-level

deep-sixing of criminal actions against oil companies in Texas is going on at the Energy Administration, gone on for more than a year now.

And lastly, your Justice Department's testimony from the Antitrust Division going along with oil industry acquisition of uranium companies, solar development companies, and coal companies—all of these were decisions that seemed to be opposed to what you promised as a candidate.

Could you give us a general view? Have you changed your view to the oil industry since becoming President?

THE PRESIDENT. No, I've not changed my views at all. We want to have the principles of the national energy plan carried out effectively. The Congress has now given us legislative authority to carry out 60, 65 percent of what I did propose. Any violation by the oil companies of regulations or law will be prosecuted enthusiastically by me, by the Justice Department, and also by the Department of Energy. And, obviously, we are very deeply dedicated to the enforcement of the antitrust laws.

I'm concerned also about the growing investment by the oil companies in competitive areas of energy supply. I expressed this during my own campaign, and I still feel very strongly about this. I think that the Congress itself is now prepared to move more effectively to modify the law when necessary to minimize abuse. But I don't consider my administration at all reticent about carrying out the policies that I espoused during the campaign when I ran for President, and I certainly don't consider them to be reticent at all in enforcing the law.

PRESIDENT'S 1980 CANDIDACY

Q. Mr. President, a yes or no question, and then, if I may, a followup. In your own mind, have you decided yet whether or not you'll seek a second term?

THE PRESIDENT. Yes. [*Laughter*]

Q. You know my followup question. [*Laughter*] When will you share it with us and the American people?

THE PRESIDENT. Later. [*Laughter*]

Q. Later means——

THE PRESIDENT. It means later.

CONSUMER BOYCOTTS; FEDERAL REVENUE SHARING

Q. Mr. President, your anti-inflation fighter, Mr. Kahn, yesterday suggested that one way to fight inflation would be to have organized consumer boycotts against firms which violate your wage-price guidelines. And another suggestion he made was that the Government might consider reducing or withholding Federal revenue sharing money to cities or States where officials in those cities and States violate the wage guidelines.

I was wondering, first of all, would you support a reduction of Federal revenue sharing money to a city or State which didn't observe or which violated your wage-price guidelines? And how do you feel generally about the Government backing consumer boycotts?

THE PRESIDENT. I don't personally favor any organized boycotts. I think that the posture of a prudent purchaser is one that applies to me as President and also ought to apply to the average consumer who is buying retail items and who should be conversant with the relative compliance of suppliers with our wage and price guidelines—the price guidelines in this instance.

As far as withholding revenue sharing funds, I think this would be illegal under the present law. We have had very good response from Governors and mayors in applying the same policies of a prudent purchaser so that the mayor, for instance,

would be restrained against buying items from companies which patently violate the price guidelines. And we are encouraging mayors to take this action, and Governors as well.

I might say that we encourage them with very good results, very good successes. But as far as withholding revenue sharing funds, this would require an act of Congress, and it's not possible under the present law.

Q. Could you reduce Federal revenue sharing funds to a State which didn't comply?

The PRESIDENT. No, we could not do that under the present law.

TRADE WITH COMMUNIST COUNTRIES

Q. Mr. President, we seem to be headed for a record trade deficit this year, at a time when a major new market for U.S. exports is opening in Communist China.

THE PRESIDENT. Yes.

Q. Now, there are a number of restrictions in U.S. trade laws which inhibit our trading with Communist countries, some aspects of the Export-Import Bank Act, the Jackson-Vanik amendment to the 1974 Trade Act.

My question is, do you intend to try to change and remove some of those restrictions next year?

THE PRESIDENT. We are constantly assessing the advisability of maintaining administrative restraints.

Of course, we have to put trade in a proper perspective. We can't assess trade itself completely separated from our overall relationships with Communist countries, particularly those who are potential adversaries of ours, like the Soviet Union.

We want to have increased trade with the Soviet Union and with the People's Republic of China. I think the statistics will show that recently we have had increasing trade with both those countries, compared to last year or several years ago.

If we, in the future, have normal relationships with China, diplomatic relationships, this would open up increased opportunities for trade with those people. In this present time, short of diplomatic relations, we still have major trade missions going to China, Chinese trade missions coming to our country. And I think that this is bearing good results.

We have one more point, and that is security restraints. If there is a sale of high technology items to the Soviet Union, or the People's Republic of China, proposed, then not only do the Commerce Department and the State Department and the National Security Council assess this, but I refer it to the Defense Department as well, to be sure that we are not deliberately or inadvertently giving to those countries a means by which their military capabilities would be greatly escalated. This would be contrary to the existing law.

But within the bounds of those restraints, we are attempting to improve our relationships with the People's Republic of China and with the Soviet Union. And in the process, as part of a stream of increased interrelationships, improved relationships, enhanced trade.

EGYPTIAN-ISRAELI PEACE NEGOTIATIONS

Q. Mr. President, to follow up the earlier question on the Middle East, you said last week that if Prime Minister Begin and President Sadat had been able to negotiate together on some of these questions over the past few weeks, that there would not have been some of the problems that have arisen. My question is, if all else fails, would you consider calling the two leaders back to Camp David or some other place to negotiate directly with you to resolve this matter?

THE PRESIDENT. Well, let me say that

I don't have any present plans to do that. If all else failed and I felt that we could get together again, I would not hesitate to do so. But I don't envision that taking place.

THE DEMOCRATIC PARTY

Q. Mr. President, if I may follow up on the question raised by Mr. Schieffer [Bob Schieffer, CBS News] and Mr. Hurd.[1] Do you sense, Mr. President, that there is a widening schism in the Democratic Party between yourself and Senator Kennedy, who emphasized in Memphis the need for finishing the great agenda of the Democratic Party, as he put it? And do you have any plans to try to conciliate your differences with him or with the labor leaders, who have generally opposed your economic policies?

THE PRESIDENT. First of all, I don't consider there is a schism, a growing schism in the Democratic Party at all. And as a general principle, and almost entirely, Senator Kennedy and I communicate well; we have a good relationship. We espouse the same ultimate goals. We have some differences, which are expected, on exactly how to achieve those goals.

I have a unique perspective in this country as President. I have to look at a much broader range of issues than does Senator Kennedy. He is extremely interested, for instance, in the comprehensive health program, having devoted several years of his legislative life to that position.

Also, I think it's accurate to say that Senator Kennedy represents a family within the Democratic Party which is revered because of his two brothers and the contribution of his family to our party. There's a special aura of appreciation to him that's personified because of the position of his family in our Nation and in our party. This makes him a spokesman, not only in his own right but also over a much

---

[1] The reporter meant to say Ted Knap of the Scripps-Howard News Service.

broader and expected constituency. I recognize it, and I have no objection to that.

I was with Senator Kennedy the night after the Democratic Conference adjourned, I think on Monday (Sunday)[2] night. And the following morning in a nonrelated way, the Office of Management and Budget, Jim McIntyre and my own Domestic Adviser, Stu Eizenstat, met with Senator Kennedy and his staff to try to resolve differences. The differences are minor.

So, I think this is a healthy situation to have within the Democratic Party. And I think that the Congress will be the ultimate judge of whether my budget, as proposed, is fair and balanced and adequate. I have not changed my goals whatsoever. The Democratic Conference endorsed those goals, either unanimously, or with a 60-percent margin on the most controversial of the issues. I am going to have an adequate defense. I'm going to meet our obligations to our allies around the country [world]. And I'm going to cut the budget deficit down below $30 billion, and I'm going to do the best I can to meet the social needs of our Nation. I'm committed to that. That's what I'm going to do. And I have no aversion to an open and public debate, because I think my positions are sound.

But the differences between me and Senator Kennedy are very minor.

IRAN

Q. Mr. President, what will be the domestic and international effect if the Shah fails to maintain power in Iran?

THE PRESIDENT. I fully expect the Shah to maintain power in Iran and for the present problems in Iran to be resolved. Although there have been certainly deplorable instances of bloodshed which we would certainly want to avoid, or see avoided, I think the predictions of doom and disaster that came from some sources have certainly not been realized at all. The Shah has our support and he also has our confidence.

We have no intention of interfering in the internal affairs of Iran, and we have no intention of permitting others to interfere in the internal affairs of Iran. The difficult situation there has been exacerbated by uncontrolled statements made from foreign nations that encourage bloodbaths and violence. This is something that really is deplorable and, I would hope, would cease after this holy season passes.

I think it's good to point out that the Iranian people for 2,500 years, perhaps as long as almost any nation on Earth, have had the ability for stable self-government. There have been changes in the government, yes, sometimes violence, but they have a history of an ability to govern themselves. And because of that and other factors which I've just described, I think the situation in Iran will be resolved successfully.

OIL PRICES

Q. Mr. President, to what extent are you concerned over the prospect of the OPEC nations raising the price of oil this weekend—reports are it'll be in the neighborhood of 5 percent—the impact this would have on inflation? And do you contemplate any future actions to curb oil imports?

THE PRESIDENT. Most of our problems with the adverse trade balances can be attributed to oil imports, although we have other problems as well. I certainly hope that the OPEC nations will decide not to raise the price of oil. If they do, I hope it would be minimal.

[2] Printed in the transcript.

We have tried to convince them that this is in the best interests of the world economy and also in the best interests of the OPEC nations themselves, to have a stable world economy with a minimum of inflation in the future. We're trying to set a good example in our own Nation, both in controlling inflation and also in stabilizing the value of the dollar on which the price of oil is based. The countries in the OPEC nations have suffered somewhat, because for a time the dollar value was going down very rapidly. It has recovered since the first of November.

So, I would hope, first of all—to repeat myself—that there will be no increase in the price of oil. If they must increase the price of oil, I think it ought to be minimal for their own benefit and for the benefit of the world.

EMPLOYMENT AND REVENUE SHARING PROGRAMS

Q. Mr. President, at the Memphis convention some of the mayors expressed concern over the possibility of sharp reductions in employment programs like the CETA program. And also they expressed concern over the possible lack of support, not by you particularly, but by Congress, for programs like the revenue sharing program which is very important to the cities.

Do you foresee, keeping in mind you haven't made your final budget decisions, sharp reductions in either the CETA program or in revenue sharing which is devoted to the cities?

THE PRESIDENT. It depends on what you mean by sharp reductions. I have to say that there will be some tightening of the budget in almost every aspect of American life. There will be some programs that will be expanded; others will be basically kept at the same level. The decisions have not yet been made. I'm conversant with the problems of the cities.

I don't think any administration has ever had a closer consultative relationship with the mayors than our own has had. In the evolution of our urban policy earlier this year, the mayors were full partners in the process, along with Governors and other—and local officials.

So, I can't say. The revenue sharing legislation is a multiyear authorization, and we support the carrying out of the revenue sharing at its present level until this present law expires. I can't foreclose the possibility that it might be modified in the future. My own attitude has always been that with a given amount for revenue sharing, that a greater portion of it should go to the cities and local governments than to the States. That's one modification in the revenue sharing laws that I would espouse.

But the exact level of the CETA programs and other job programs will have to be decided in the next couple of weeks, and I personally favor as much as possible keeping job opportunities open for Americans.

MR. CORMIER. Thank you, Mr. President.

THE PRESIDENT. Thank you, Frank.

NOTE: President Carter's forty-first news conference began at 11 a.m. in Room 450 of the Old Executive Office Building. It was broadcast live on radio and television.

Budget Deferrals
Message to the Congress.   December 12, 1978

To the Congress of the United States:

In accordance with the Impoundment Control Act of 1974, I herewith report two new deferrals totalling $663.8 million and a revision to one previously transmitted deferral increasing the amount deferred by $.2 million in budget authority. These items involve the foreign military credit sales program and programs in the Departments of Commerce and the Interior.

The details of the deferrals are contained in the attached report.

JIMMY CARTER

The White House,
    December 12, 1978.

NOTE: The attachments detailing the deferrals are printed in the FEDERAL REGISTER of December 18, 1978.

Congressional Christmas Ball

Remarks at the White House Function.
December 12, 1978

What I'd like to do this evening is to welcome all of you to a typical President and congressional meeting—[*laughter*]—similar to what we've had all this past 2 years. But this time we thought we'd let the wives see what it's like.

I'm not going to make a speech. But I would like to say that Christmas is a time for love and for friendship, for an assessment of our many blessings and for peace. Our country has been blessed greatly the last 2 years, in great measure because of the superb work and the courage of the Congress of the United States. And I, as President, want to thank you on behalf of the 215 million American people.

We have enjoyed peace for our own Nation and we've worked tirelessly, you and I, to bring peace to others as well. And during this religious season, regardless of your faith, I know that you will join me and all Americans in praying for peace in the Middle East and throughout the world.

This evening is a time for enjoyment and for getting to know each other better. When we had the Democratic Convention, which made a superb choice—[*laughter*]—I was lucky enough to be

blessed with Peter Duchin's music there. He played for the Inauguration, which was a great day for me and for some of you as well. And tonight we have a man who enjoys as much popularity as any bandleader has ever enjoyed in our country, one of the greatest bandleaders of all time, who follows in the footsteps of his father, Eddie Duchin, and who last year, I believe, gave a new Christmas work, "Christmas Music with Peter Duchin." So, he's here to help us help one another enjoy Christmas and enjoy the fellowship of the White House.

On behalf of me and Rosalynn and our whole family, you're welcome, my friends.

NOTE: The President spoke at 9:10 p.m. in the East Room at the White House.

National Conference on Fraud, Abuse and Error

Remarks at the Conference Sponsored by the Department of Health, Education, and Welfare.   December 13, 1978

First of all, let me say that I'm very grateful to all of you for being willing to attend a conference so important as this one. As you may surmise, I get a lot of invitations to make speeches and to attend conferences and conventions. I particularly wanted to be here because of the importance of the subject and because Joe Califano has been in charge of the program and the origin of the idea.

Joe is a superb Secretary, as you well know. When I first asked him to be Secretary of HEW, I said, "There are a couple of things I'd like for you to do. One is to stay away from controversial subjects"—[*laughter*]—"and to carry out specific assignments with complete success."

This past week I asked him to go to the Democratic midterm conference to explain my position on a comprehensive health program. And the last thing I told him was, "Be sure that when the conference is over Senator Kennedy does not get the headlines." [*Laughter*] So, you can see how deeply indebted I am to him.

I am delighted to join with you today in this crucial conference, and I want to commend Joe Califano, as I have done privately, for taking the lead in the efforts of my administration—the lead in the efforts of my administration—to root out fraud and waste and abuse from this Government. This administration has declared war on waste and fraud in Government programs. We've declared war, and with your help we will win that war.

We're concerned with more than saving dollars, as crucial as that is today. We must continue to restore and to rebuild the trust that must exist in any democracy between a free people and their government.

My administration took office after a painful and difficult period in American history. The experience of Vietnam, of Watergate, revelations of wrongdoing in our intelligence communities, the resignation of a Vice President and a President, the indictment and conviction of top Government officials—these events hit the American people like hammer blows, over and over again. Each of those blows shattered just a little bit more the trust and confidence of the American people in their Government and in their elected officials.

Cynicism and distrust eat away at the vitality of a democratic nation. Abraham Lincoln once said, "With public confidence, everything is possible; without it, nothing is possible."

Over the past 2 years, slowly and steadily we have begun to restore the trust and confidence of the American people. But it's not enough for people to have confidence in the good intentions and the personal integrity of those who hold public office. The American people must also know that government is capable of doing its job. Fraud and abuse and waste undermine that precious confidence.

Those who rob from government rob from every steelworker, every farmer, every teacher, every storeclerk, every truckdriver in America. Under this administration, those who rob from the American people, as the Attorney General has so clearly expressed, will be prosecuted to the full extent of the law.

I do not believe that Americans want to go back on the premise of a better life and a fairer society. The heart of America is too big for that. It would contravene my very concept of the principles of government. The American people will not accept callousness toward those among us who are aged or sick or jobless or who are lacking in influence or in education or in opportunity. But neither will the American people accept a massive bureaucracy that is too clumsy or too poorly managed to do the job.

Of course, most of the funds we spend in Federal programs benefit the people for whom they are intended. As a known or suspected part of the total Federal budget, losses through fraud, abuse, and error may be small. But as part of their tax bill to the average American, these losses are huge, and they are demoralizing. The real damage of fraud and abuse cannot be measured just in dollars and cents, for the value of people's trust and faith in their institutions of self-government are priceless.

If we are to be successful in our efforts to make government work better, one myth must be dispelled at the outset—the myth that the values of compassion and the values of efficiency are somehow in opposition to each other. This is just as absurd as imagining that a physician's medical skills are the enemy of their dedication to curing disease. Nothing could be more totally or more dangerously wrong.

When a program is poorly managed, when it is riddled with waste or fraud, the victims are not abstractions, but flesh-and-blood human beings. They are the unemployed teenagers who get shut out of a job. They are the senior citizens who are deprived of adequate medical service. They are the schoolchildren who go without nutritious meals or the taxpayers whose hard-earned money goes down a drain.

When I lived in Plains after retiring from the naval service, I was able to expand my own small family business, processing peanuts because I was able to obtain a Small Business Administration loan when I could not raise private funds. And there are thousands of Americans, many of them members of minority groups or women, who dream of starting a business of their own and seeing it grow and thrive and having that pride of personal independence and accomplishment. It's a cruel hoax to these Americans to see those dreams destroyed by those who abuse and defraud the Small Business Administration.

Those of us who believe that our society has an obligation toward its weakest members, we have the greatest stake in improving the management and efficiency of programs that are designed to meet that obligation. This is especially true when the battle against inflation makes it impossible to bring vast new resources every year to bear on our social problems. There is no room any longer for waste. At such a time as we have now, indeed at any time, efficient management is in itself an act of compassion, for it unlocks new resources to be used for human ends.

There's a second myth, the myth that it is somehow more compassionate, more committed to appropriate another billion

dollars of the taxpayers' money than it is to streamline existing programs so that they deliver an extra billion dollars worth of service. In fact, the latter is preferable in every way. Of course, it saves money, but it does more than that.

Efficient management increases political support for programs which quite often are not popular among those who pay the taxes to support it. It gives the lie to those who prefer to believe that programs that meet human needs cannot work. It inspires and it boosts the morale of government employees who are deeply frustrated when they see their own hard work frittered away through waste and fraud. That's one of the most demoralizing things that can happen to a dedicated worker in private or public life.

I did not select that $1 billion figure at random. This is the amount that Joe Califano has vowed to save in fiscal year 1979, this year, by cutting deeply into waste and fraud in the Department of Health, Education, and Welfare.

Joe's efforts and those of thousands of others working with him at HEW are already showing good results. Project Match is sifting out those on the Federal payroll who are illegally receiving welfare benefits. The project is very new, but it has already repaid its million dollars in costs twice over. Project Integrity is nailing down the thieves and con artists among health care providers.

Thanks to tough management of the student financial aid program, the number of student defaulters is falling instead of rising for the first time in the 10-year history of this program. And the backlog, which hit 400,000 last March, is projected to be at zero at the end of 1980.

The credit for these successes belongs to an active partnership between the Federal Government and the States and the localities.

Similar efforts are under way in other parts of the Federal Government. The Labor Department is attacking the abuses in the CETA program, and Congress is helping. The Agriculture Department is fighting illegal trafficking in food stamps. At the Small Business Administration and the General Services Administration, we are cracking down on fraud and theft. At the Department of Justice, the prosecution of fraud within our Government is now a very high priority.

The headlines generated by these activities do not always make pleasant reading, but these headlines are a sign not that things are getting worse, because corruption and fraud is being exposed, but that they are being improved, because we are determined to continue with that correction and that exposure.

When I campaigned for the Presidency for 2 years all through this Nation, I promised the American people, in response to their importunities, a compassionate and a competent government. I've not swerved from the goal. I did not underestimate then nor do I underestimate now the difficulties. But our expanding attack on waste and fraud is just one facet of a long-term effort to improve the functioning of government, an effort that began the day that I took office. That effort has made progress on many fronts.

I've used the appointment power to place the best people I could find at the top of the departments and the regulatory agencies—reform-minded leaders who are free of the conventional orthodoxies about regulation and administration.

I've embarked on reorganization of the Federal Government, this, as a top priority, to eliminate the waste caused by duplication and bureaucratic overlap.

I submitted, as you know, and the Congress passed the first sweeping reform of the civil service system in its century-long history. This civil service reform gives the departments and agencies a chance to strengthen their total management systems. It gives us the ability to deal firmly with those few who are dishonest or incompetent, and it increases the rewards for the vast majority who are efficient and effective and properly accountable. It's a major step toward building a Federal work force dedicated throughout their normal day's work to competence and integrity at every level.

A year ago, we instituted a program of special recognition for Federal employees at all levels. And we suggested improvements in their lives if they made improvements in doing their government work if their suggestions produced savings of $5,000 or more. We expected good results, but the results have been astounding. In 1 year, 1,380 people in 29 departments and agencies contributed improvements that brought savings already of $210 million—more than the total average income taxes of more than 95,000 American families. These results show that good management and effective use of incentives are as effective in reducing waste and fraud as are enforcement and punishment.

The civil service act provides greatly increased cash awards in itself, both from agencies and from the President, for employees who make significant suggestions, improve government operations, reduce paperwork, or perform special acts or services in the public interest.

We've waded into the thicket of pointless redtape and regulations that waste the time of citizens and of State and local officials. For example, we inherited more than 1,700 separate planning programs and requirements in various grant and aid programs. We are chopping away at these overlapping requirements and have eliminated or consolidated already more than 300 of them just in the last year.

We're still at it, and HEW is setting the pace.

Last year, I asked the heads of the departments and agencies to improve their audit coordination and to increase their reliance on State and local audits whenever possible. A governmentwide effort, led by the Office of Management and Budget and the General Accounting Office, has now come up with a breakthrough in auditing federally assisted programs—a single guide to replace the almost 100 now in use.

We need to bring the same kind of simplicities to our public assistance programs. Today, the welfare system of just one State eats up 3 billion pieces of paper each year and has a thousand different forms. One woman seeking economic aid in another State had to spend 300 hours in 1 year just filling out paperwork to document her needs.

For this reason, I'm asking today Jim McIntyre and Joe Califano to head a major effort to simplify and to streamline the hundreds of complex eligibility requirements which contribute $3 billion each year to the cost of public assistance and other human service programs—an administrative cost over and above what actually goes to the recipients. We will move to simplify these procedures where it really counts, not only at the Federal but at the State and local level.

Where we have the tools to root out fraud and abuse, we have already put them to work. Where those tools did not exist, we are now creating them.

Perhaps the most important new tools in the fight against fraud are the Inspectors General created in six departments and six other agencies of the Federal Government by an act of Congress, which we strongly supported and which I signed into law 8 weeks ago. The Inspectors General will be a powerful new tool

for the discovery, the prevention, and the elimination of fraud. They have broad powers and a significant degree of independence.

I will choose these Inspectors General carefully. I want them to match the high standard set by Tom Morris, the first Inspector General that I appointed at HEW, who has helped save the American taxpayers one-half billion dollars since the beginning of 1977.

I've already directed Jim McIntyre to oversee the systems which the Inspectors General will run. I want to be sure that in each department covered by the law, the auditing and investigative functions are meshed in a smooth and effective way.

And today I'm taking a further step. I have already directed that significant features of the Inspectors General program be extended not just in those 12 departments and agencies but throughout the Federal Government. Each agency and department will prepare a plan for eliminating waste and fraud in its own activities and will designate a single official to be responsible for and to oversee the preparation and the implementation of that plan. I've assigned the Office of Management and Budget responsibility for overseeing this effort.

I'm looking to the Attorney General to ensure that investigations by Inspectors General and their counterparts in other agencies and bureaus are effectively coordinated with other investigative and prosecutorial activities, so that criminal matters receive immediate and efficient attention.

The fight against waste and fraud will require the best efforts of us all—everyone in this room, every Federal, State, and local official, every citizen of our country. New programs and better enforcement will certainly help. But our most important weapon in this struggle is the vigilance and the dedication which we bring to it. I call on all who work in government to join me in this battle.

The stakes are very high. If we succeed—and I believe we will—we will have kept faith with the millions of men, women, and children whose human needs our society has pledged to meet. And we will have kept faith with ourselves. For the ultimate beneficiary of the success of this effort will be democratic self-government in America, this Nation that all of us love.

Thank you very much.

NOTE: The President spoke at 12:53 p.m. in the International Ballroom at the Washington Hilton Hotel to Federal, State, and local officials attending the conference.

Federal Public Assistance Programs

Memorandum From the President.
December 13, 1978

Memorandum for the Secretary of Health, Education, and Welfare, the Secretary of Agriculture, the Secretary of Labor, the Secretary of Housing and Urban Development, the Director, Office of Management and Budget, the Director, Community Services Administration

I am directing today that the Director of the Office of Management and Budget and the Secretary of Health, Education, and Welfare initiate a major interdepartmental review of the Federal policies and procedures for determining applicant eligibility for Federal public assistance programs, including AFDC, SSI, Food Stamps, Medicaid, employment and training, social services, and housing assistance.

A substantial part of the costs of administering these programs is directly tied to eligibility determination. Those procedures, because of complexity and duplication, add to the waste, high error rates, and fraud which hurt every taxpayer, and most importantly, penalize and frustrate those who have legitimate needs.

I hope that this review will produce recommendations which will lead to more consistent and less burdensome government-wide practices to make the eligibility determination process simple, understandable and efficient. Such improvements could also lead to better quality services for those who are eligible to receive them.

All citizens are concerned about making a bold attack on inefficient and wasteful government. Equally important to me, is our ability to assist our needy citizens in a more responsive and compassionate manner. I know that I can count on your support in meeting both these objectives.

JIMMY CARTER

Waste, Fraud, and Error in Government Programs

Memorandum From the President.
December 13, 1978

Memorandum for the Heads of Executive Departments and Agencies

Subject: Steps to Eliminate Waste, Fraud, and Error in Government Programs

The resources of this government must be managed well, free of waste, fraud and inefficiency. The American people believe, and I agree, that managing their tax money is a public trust. That is why I approved a law establishing Offices of

Inspector General in twelve major departments and agencies. Today, I am directing that significant features of the Inspector General program be extended throughout the Federal Government. Eliminating waste, fraud, and error should be as important to you as your program objectives.

First, by January 31, each of you should develop for my review a comprehensive plan setting the course for your agency in this overall effort. You should immediately designate a single official, accountable directly to you, to oversee preparation of the plan and to monitor its implementation for you. The plan should include at a minimum:

- An analysis of all resources now devoted to the audit and investigation functions and the capacity of your department or agency to prevent and deal with problems of waste, fraud and error.
- Your planned approach to using your agency's audit and investigation resources in a concerted effort to deal with issues of waste, fraud and error, especially in those programs and activities you deem most vulnerable.

Second, I expect each of you personally to review and respond to major allegations by the Comptroller General and others of waste, fraud or error.

Third, I would like each of you to submit to me your suggestions on government-wide action I can take to reduce waste, fraud and error.

Fourth, I am assigning the Director of the Office of Management and Budget responsibility for overseeing this program to eliminate fraud and waste for me. He will provide additional guidance as appropriate. He will be responsible for keeping me informed of progress under the program and activities of Inspectors General and their counterparts in the agencies.

Fifth, I have asked the Attorney General to prepare an action plan to assure that investigations by Inspectors General and similar officers are coordinated with other investigative and prosecutorial activities.

Finally, I am directing the Chairman of the Civil Service Commission (or, following its establishment, the Director of the Office of Personnel Management), working with the Attorney General and the Secretary of the Treasury, to improve the training of investigative and audit staffs throughout the Executive Branch.

JIMMY CARTER

Protection of Journalistic Work Products

Statement Announcing Intention To Propose Legislation. December 13, 1978

Of all the basic rights that contribute to human development, one of the most important is the first amendment freedom of the press. A free press independent of government control and expressing a variety of viewpoints is crucial to both democracy and individual liberty.

Since last May, my administration has been trying to explore the proper constitutional way for us and the Congress together to correct the threat of encroachment on freedom of the press that was raised in the *Stanford Daily* case.

As a result of this work, I will soon propose legislation that would restrict police intrusion into news media offices, and would give members of the press notice and an opportunity to challenge requests for the products of their reporting work.

I think this is a major step forward in protecting the integrity of the freedom of the press.

Business Council

Remarks and a Question-and-Answer Session at a Meeting of the Council.
December 13, 1978

THE PRESIDENT. It's a pleasure to be with you tonight. I look around the group, and I think in a close vote the administration could just about equal the business leaders of our country. [*Laughter*] But I would hope that the vote would be unanimous on any controversial issue that affects our country.

I am honored to have this opportunity to come back and talk to you, a group of men and women who helped to shape the economic present and future of our great country. I think I should begin my own remarks as President of our Nation by expressing my deep thanks to you for the help that you've given me and to our Nation's Government since the last time I appeared here. You've given me advice, counsel, sometimes criticism, constructive always, and when I've called on you to help me with matters of great importance, you have never failed to be very forthcoming in your aid to me.

When I faced the difficult political question of the Panama Canal treaties, you responded with superb influence, and I could not have succeeded in having those treaties ratified without the help of those in this room.

You speak with a voice that is carefully monitored and with opinions that are carefully assessed. And I think your own influence at times might be even underestimated by you.

In the civil service reform effort, as you know, the first time in a hundred years, your strong voice as managers, as business leaders, was highly effective in shaping the opinion of the Congress.

Perhaps the most far-reaching and difficult legislation that the Congress has ever considered was the five bills passed to shape the first part of a national energy policy. Again, your advice and counsel was crucial. In fact, in every matter concerning economics you have been in the forefront of my assistance, and I deeply appreciate it. And, of course, in that process you have helped to shape the political posture of our Nation as well.

We have a very good interrelationship between the leaders of the free enterprise system on the one hand, and the leaders of our government on the other. And I think this interrelationship—open, frank, carefully observed, assessed by the public—is proper and advisable and good for our Nation. I've never had any of you or your fellow business leaders approach me on any occasion with a request or a suggestion that I interpreted as President to be selfish or contrary to the best interests of our country. And I thank you for that enlightened attitude as well.

As a matter of fact, on occasion, many of you—John DeButts, Tom Murphy, Irving Shapiro, Ray Jones, and others—have made suggestions to me that in balance might very well have worked counter to the profit margin of their own corporations if they knew that in the process the overall character and strength and well-being of our Nation would be enhanced.

We have made some progress in the last, almost 2 years. The unemployment rate has dropped from 8 percent to about 5.8 percent, and it's leveled off lately. We have been pleased with this. We've added a net of about 7 million new jobs—660,000 new jobs, I believe, in November alone—when predictions were that the jobless rate would go up sharply during the fall. This has resulted in a decrease of about 1,300,000 Americans who were formerly on welfare and are now self-supporting. The fact is that we still have serious unemployment rates among some groups of our country. But among heads of households now 96.6 percent are employed.

We've had economic growth that's been steady. It's increased by 9½ percent since I've been President. Corporate profits, in which some of you have some slight interest, have gone up 37 percent in 2 years. Farm income, which interests me, net farm income has gone up about 25 percent. Exports, both years, hit an alltime high. We expect to set a new record for our Nation next year. We're constantly probing for new markets for America's goods, and I think that we are about to make more progress even than we've achieved in the past.

In the last 2 years we've also reduced taxes $40 billion, but we still have the specter of inflation hanging over our heads, which could very well wipe out all the gains that I've just described. And my number one domestic priority above everything else is to deal successfully with the inflation threat.

In this respect, your assistance will be much more difficult than it has been in the past because of the diversity of action that must be taken and the wide number of people who will be directly involved in an anti-inflation fight. And I think here the business community's influence can help to counterbalance the mandatory sacrifice, that must be well balanced, on many interest groups that have direct and great influence in Washington and in the State and local levels of government. This will not be an easy or quick task even if we succeed beyond our present expectations. It's going to be a long and tenacious effort required, and I need you to join in with me as full partners on a permanent basis. We've seen prices double in the past 11 years. And although we've experienced inflation at a steady rate, 6½ to 7 percent for those 11 years, for a while there were

special factors on which we could blame the high inflation rates—oil price increases, a shortage of consumer goods or raw materials. That has changed, and there's a more broad-ranging reason now for inflation with which we have to deal directly. There are no special factors that we can blame for our problems.

We've also reduced the Federal deficit in the short time that I've been in the White House by about $28 billion. In 1976, the Federal deficit amounted to more than 4 percent of our gross national product. When I complete work on the 1980 fiscal year budget, that Federal deficit will be down about 1 percent of our gross national product.

I think this is a very vivid and clear demonstration of the leadership that the Federal Government must take in setting an example for others to control inflation. And in the process, we have tried to carry out a campaign commitment that I made to reduce the percentage of our gross national product which is collected and spent by the Federal Government. In the past, it was about 23 percent; we're trying to get it down and will succeed, I believe, to about a 21-percent level.

There are some commitments that I have also made to the American public that I intend to honor. One is to maintain a strong defense. We have obligations to our own people for their security, the number one responsibility on the shoulders of any President. We must convince our allies that we stand staunchly with them with a common approach to any outside threat to the Western democratic world.

I think it's accurate to say that when I became President, because of historical events years past, there was a shaky NATO Alliance. Many of our partners there were not convinced of the resolve of America, and we had to commit ourselves to them, not only to set an example but to join with them in a recommitment to vitalize the NATO Alliance. That commitment will be carried out.

We've tried to get Government intrusion into the business community reduced. Many regulations have been eliminated completely. I think the Occupational Safety and Health Administration is much more cognizant of and much more sensitive to the recommendations and criticisms of the business community without reducing its effectiveness in protecting the health and safety of American workers.

We have tried to combine, in many ways, agencies of the Government. Our reorganization efforts so far have been very well received by the Congress. We have had the amazing success in deregulating for the first time in many decades one of America's great industries, that is, airline deregulation. We have more airline passengers now. They pay lower fares. And I think in almost every instance, the profit margins of the airline companies have gone up. I'm very proud that the ICC Chairman, Dan O'Neal, has been staunch in moving to deregulate the trucking industry. I back him in this. I realize the independence of the regulatory agencies, but with my own voice, my own influence, my future appointments to the ICC, my intention is to continue this trend.

We have many challenges ahead of us. Our country still does not have a commitment to exports of our produced goods that prevails the consciousness of the business leaders in other nations like Japan and Germany. And government can help to some degree. But this is primarily a responsibility that falls on your shoulders. And I think if there was a more intense team commitment, it would be to the advantage of our own Nation and our balance of trade. I think it would be to the advantage of your own corporations and businesses, professional alliances in carrying out the purposes for which they were founded.

Productivity is not rising nearly so rapidly as we would like. We are lagging behind other nations in this respect. We are now assessing the varied and very complicated factors that go into the lowered rate of increase of productivity. We hope to make some progress in the future.

I have some engineering and scientific background, and I have been very deeply committed, even in the tightest of budgets, to increase the influence of the Federal Government in enhancing our research and development programs in all the agencies of the Government itself. When Cabinet officers or the heads of agencies were not enthusiastic about this program, I've inspired them to be more committed to it, because I believe that in the long run, a viable research and development commitment by the Federal Government can pay rich dividends in years ahead.

The implementation of authorization we have on energy programs is still to be demonstrated, but we will take full advantage of the authority, new authority that the Congress has now given me, Dr. Schlesinger, and others.

We have recently moved on November 1, under the leadership of Mike Blumenthal, to strengthen the American dollar, its exchange values in international monetary markets. This has been a program that has been successful to date and, I think, has reestablished the confidence in our own Nation's economic commitments, which were shaky at best just a few months before that.

We've got a good team now evolved in giving me economic advice and working closely with me. Bill Miller gives us sound advice, honoring the independence of the Federal Reserve. Mike Blumenthal is the Chairman of the Economic Policy

Group. We have obviously a fine Secretary of Commerce, Juanita Kreps. Alfred Kahn is giving me advice on our anti-inflation effort. And I think we've got a team spirit now, working with Charlie Schultze and others, that can assure that we have a well-balanced and a closely coordinated effort.

You are at liberty to interrelate with this group individually or collectively, and I would certainly appreciate your continuing to do so.

In closing, let me say this: I need your increased help and cooperation. We do not anticipate a recession next year. We don't see any basic imbalances that in the past have preceded a recessionary period. Inventories are in good shape. Recent statistics on housing construction still maintain a very high level in that region of our economy. We have, I think, very good and stable results in retail sales. We've got another $20 billion in tax cuts coming in about 3 weeks, which should revitalize some commitments to the future. But there are predictions of recessions from varied sources which I think can become a self-fulfilling prophecy unless the facts are described accurately to the American people, unless we show the innate confidence that I feel exists in your minds as well as it does in my own.

Our Nation is strong. We had a Cabinet meeting Monday morning, and there was a general consensus there that if we have made one consistent error in economic predictions, it was to underestimate the economic strength and the growth potential of our country.

I might say that just the last few hours, we have promulgated the final regulations on our voluntary wage and price standards. You'll have a chance to assess those thoroughly. I'm not familiar with the details. The general principles are those that I have approved. And I hope that now that that has been done, that

every one of you, without exception, and all those that listen to your voice and whom you can influence, will give me your pledge of compliance with the voluntary wage and price standards.

A number of you have already done so, even though you had not seen the final, conclusive interpretation of the guidelines. But there's no excuse now for you to delay, and it would add a great deal to me and to my influence in controlling inflation if you would do so. If there are some details or portions of the regulations which you find not completely in accordance with your desires, I hope that you will overlook that or accept it in our commitment to improve the stability of our own economy.

I need your help in continuing to design modifications to the anti-inflation program as we go along. With experience I'm sure there will be these kinds of changes to be made, and I need your continued counsel and your beneficial influence.

Very briefly, this describes some of the points that I wanted to make to you. We've made some progress. We've got a long way to go. Our top priority is anti-inflation. You have helped in many ways. Now is the time for you to help much more specifically. And I know the hundreds, the tens of thousands of letters that are being sent out by you personally and by business organizations to which you belong will have a great impact. But your own personal influence and a flat statement that your company will comply with the wage and price guideline standards will be the greatest and best thing you can do.

John DeButts has asked me to yield the floor to him at this point, and I'll be glad to answer just a couple of questions, relying on my advisers to help me with the answers.

John.

Mr. DeButts. Ladies and gentlemen, I asked the President if I could take a moment to say something to you. I cannot say it to you as the chairman of the Business Council, because, by tradition, we in the Business Council do not take positions on anything. However, I would like to say just a word to you, not as the chairman of the council, but as the chairman of AT&T and a businessman and, I hope, a peer of yours.

We all realize that inflation is the biggest problem we have in this country. We all recognize that the solution to inflation is going to require exerted effort on the part of government to reduce their own expenditures, as well as the regulations that impose expenditures on us, labor, and also business. There are some questions about the possible success of the President's program, the wage guideline, voluntary program. I happen to think that the alternatives to the success of that program are far worse—possible mandatory controls. I happen to believe that that program will work, but it only will work if all three of those groups are willing to cooperate and support it.

I happen to believe that the President is sincere and will succeed in his efforts, insofar as government expenditures and reduction of regulatory pressures on us are concerned. I don't know about labor, although one labor leader has spoken out in favor of it. But I believe that it's incumbent upon us in the business community, and I urge each and every one of you to look at this thing as carefully as you can and find a way to comply with the standards established by our President. I think that's the greatest contribution that we can make to solve the problem, and I hope you'll do it.

And now the President has graciously offered to answer questions from the floor for a few moments. So, it's your program.

THE PRESIDENT. Let me say that I be-lieve that labor will cooperate. That's my conviction and also my determination. But it's incumbent on me, first of all, to prove that, as President, I will do what I said I was going to do, and you can depend on that. I'm going to adhere to my published goals on controlling the deficit, on having a tight, tough, competent budget. I'm going to maintain the military strength of our Nation, and I'm going to meet the social needs of our country as well. I think the Congress will cooperate.

And the second thing that labor will be watching very closely is if the business community comes forward with an enthusiastic endorsement proven through action that you are part of the team. Many labor leaders have already come forward to ask how they can help, and we've got some that are doubting. But there's no doubt in my mind that if business and government show that we mean to carry out the anti-inflation program, this will be the greatest incentive possible to bringing labor on board, and my prediction is that they will come on board.

QUESTIONS

DEPARTMENT OF COMMERCE

Q. Mr. President, the press has reported that the administration is giving consideration to eliminating the Department of Commerce. This, of course, is disturbing to many in the business community. And I wonder if you'd care to comment on this, sir.

THE PRESIDENT. Well, I don't have any plans to eliminate the Department of Commerce. We will be exploring every opportunity to consolidate programs to make them more efficient and perhaps to shift major programs from one department to another. There's a limit on what I can do as President under the reorganization authority, and I hate to foreclose any possibility for the future. But there are no plans to eliminate the Department of Commerce.

You're not the first one to bring this to my attention. Juanita Kreps has also inquired about whether or not that was my plan—[*laughter*]—and I am sure she'll feel better about that. But that's one major task that I have no intention to assume for 1979.

There may be some changes made in the Government that Juanita or Mike or Pat Harris, the others won't like, to shift major programs. I'll try to make the Government more effective. But to eliminate that Department is not in my plans.

MINIMUM WAGE LAW

Q. Mr. President, in terms of what an objective is that we both share, that is, control of inflation, I'd like to ask you about the minimum wage law. Since 1956, the minimum wage has gone up 27 percent per year. And in terms of the 1977 amendment to the Fair Labor Standards Act, it's scheduled to go up another 13 percent a year between now and January 1, 1981. What plans, if any, do you have in terms of the administration position to suggest that we rescind those future increases in the minimum wage law?

THE PRESIDENT. We don't have any plans now to do that. Ever since, I guess, the last 30 years, minimum wages have averaged roughly 53 percent of average manufacturing wages. And there has been a trend for the minimum wage to lag behind year by year by year, and then all of a sudden Congress would act and catch up to restore that rough percentage. There may be some considerations going on now in the economic planning group about slight modifications to the basic minimum wage law, but to change it substantially is not in my present plans.

There was quite a debate in the Congress, as you know, about whether to include young people in the minimum wage. I have heard the EPG is considering the advisability of making a change there. It has not got to my desk. So, as far as I'm personally concerned now, I have no plans to do that. I believe the minimum wage ought to be kept at roughly that percentage of the average manufacturing wages, in fairness to the low-paid employees.

Stu, did I get the figure right? Is that roughly correct? Thanks.

Does anyone else have a question?

EGYPTIAN-ISRAELI PEACE NEGOTIATIONS

Q. Sir, are you at liberty to share with us the latest developments in the Middle East, which Secretary Vance is negotiating?

THE PRESIDENT. I can share them with you up until noon today, but I don't know if I can tell you what happened—well, that was 7 or 8 o'clock in Israel. I'll try to be cautious, not to say an inappropriate thing.

Earlier in the fall, we evolved a text for the treaty itself, which, while Prime Minister Begin was over here on a visit, was basically adopted by the Israeli negotiating team. That particular text was not adopted by the Egyptian negotiating team, because they were not present at the time and had no opportunity to do so. There was a mandatory additional agreement, not part of the treaty text, which came under the general aegis of the so-called linkage, that is, whether or not in carrying out the peace treaty concerning the Sinai itself, there would be an equal commitment to carry out the other terms of the Camp David accords in holding elections and establishing a self-government with full autonomy, to use Mr. Begin's words, for the people who live in the West Bank, Gaza Strip. This is something on which the Egyptians had insisted.

The Israeli Cabinet subsequently met and adopted the text of the treaty itself. They did not take any action, therefore rejecting the accompanying document which was an integral part of the mandatory agreement.

President Sadat then objected strongly to certain provisions of the treaty text itself and made public statements that he could not accept them. I sent Secretary Vance over to try to resolve this apparent impasse.

He had very good success in negotiating with President Sadat. With some possible change with which I am not familiar, President Sadat has accepted the text of the treaty. I don't believe there are any exceptions. And he has adopted a time schedule that was originally proposed by Foreign Minister Dayan himself, that a goal would be agreed of holding elections and establishing a self-government in the West Bank, Gaza by the end of 1979. Earlier, they had talked about a much earlier date or even no date. But Sadat was very generous, in my opinion, in adopting basically an original Israeli position.

There is another point that has been at issue and that is the so-called Article VI of the treaty, which we called the priority of obligations. Egypt has longstanding treaty obligations and other agreements with other Arab nations. Israel had insisted upon language in the treaty which clarified the point that the present treaty would be honored and that these other agreements did not interfere in effect with the application or integrity of the treaty now being negotiated.

They had also asked for additional language which, to the Egyptians, meant that all previous treaties would be abrogated and that this treaty would be paramount over any other treaty, which is contrary to what any other nation has ever been asked to do.

That treaty text has remained and has now been accepted by President Sadat, I understand. And there will be an exchange of letters between us and Sadat, based on the opinion of international lawyers and the lawyers at the State Department, about what this particular section means. Israel would not be required to endorse that language.

My understanding from Secretary Vance is that now the Israelis are reluctant to accept the goal, even, for 1979. And Secretary Vance will be meeting with them, since lunch today, after supper their time—I have not had a report from him—and will be meeting with the Israelis tomorrow morning, and then will go to see President Sadat to give him a report on the Israeli position, and will then return back to our country.

So, the essence of it is that at noon, the Egyptians had adopted the treaty text completely and had adopted our proposal on the ancillary documents. And my understanding is that the Israelis have some problem in accepting those ancillary documents, including the interpretation of what Article VI means about the priority of obligations.

I may have told you more than you want to know—[*laughter*]—but that's basically it. We pray that both nations will ultimately accept the same documents.

But it is extremely difficult, one of the most frustrating experiences I have ever had in my life, to try to negotiate at long distance through negotiators here who have limited, sometimes no authority, with the appeal going to the Prime Minister and then to the Cabinet, or going to the Cabinet and then to the President, and with both sides excessively using the public news media to express their positions. Because once they say that this is the Israeli or Egyptian position, it's almost a matter of losing national face for them to modify their positions. Whereas when we were enclosed at Camp David, you didn't have the public esteem involved every time a negotiating point was yielded.

It's just like a business and labor contract dispute being conducted at long distance through the public news media. And this is what we've had to deal with.

But there's a limited amount of time that Secretary Vance can spend on the Mideast peace treaty, as important as it is. We are now facing final negotiations on SALT. We've got the Nicaraguan problems, Nigerian problems. We are trying to work on trade matters. I'm going to have a meeting in Guadaloupe with the leaders of France and Germany and Great Britain. We have numerous other things, as you can well imagine, to do. And Secretary Vance and I have spent hundreds and hundreds of hours trying to bring these two nations together on differences that now are almost completely insignificant, compared to what they've already resolved.

Both nations deserve a lot of credit. I'm not criticizing them, because I know the sensitivity of them. But I'm very frustrated at this point, and I hope that Secretary Vance has better news from Israel for me than I acquired from him at noon.

Maybe one more question, and then I'll leave you to your work.

ECONOMIC ADVISERS

Q. Mr. President, this is really a two-part question. In the case of economic matters, have you or do you intend to appoint a single spokesman to speak for the administration? And in the area of my own particular interest, in commending you for your posture on deregulation, do you also intend to appoint a single spokesman to talk with the business community about deregulation?

THE PRESIDENT. That is a hard question to answer. Mike Blumenthal has always been my financial spokesman, and I think if you had to pick out one person, he would be the spokesman on economic matters. But at this point, Alfred Kahn has a very important and direct relationship with me on everything that concerns anti-inflation. And, of course, in business matters, trade and so forth, it's Juanita Kreps.

There's no incompatibility among these groups. And I think we have, and you've observed, I'm sure, in the last few months, a much more consistent administration policy being promulgated to the public through the press. But I really have a preference in my own method of administration of dealing with several people. I don't like to have just one person who comes to me and reports a consensus from a group. I prefer to have advice from different sources inside and outside the government.

As far as my personal economic advice is concerned, Charlie Schultze is the one I meet with frequently and regularly. He's a part of my staff itself. And I would say that he and Alfred Kahn are in that category. You're sitting next to the man who generally gives me the documents and gives me his final assessment, and that's Stu Eizenstat.

I'm not trying to confuse the issue, but I would say as far as a public statement on financial matters and economic matters, if I had to choose one person, it would be Mike Blumenthal. But Alfred Kahn is now the foremost spokesman on anti-inflation matters itself.

On deregulation, it varies so much, because from one agency to another, most of the regulatory agencies themselves are independent bodies and report legally more to the Congress than they do to me. I can help to shape their basic policy by appointments to those boards—as is the case with Federal judges and so forth—but that's a long-range process—and, through my own public statements, can certainly help modify general attitudes on deregulation.

In the unique case of the airlines, I had a major input because of foreign policy considerations, and we rapidly deregulated the airline industry in international flights. And I think that to the degree that that proved to be successful for the airlines themselves, for passenger loads and so forth, it made it easier for us to pass legislation deregulating the domestic airline industry.

I think on deregulation, I would have to characterize myself as the one who has the broadest perspective and who makes the ultimate judgments, which may disappoint you, but I hope it doesn't. [*Laughter*]

Let me say in closing that I'd like to stay with you. I know you have other business to carry out. But I'm very deeply grateful to you, and I hope that my performance is meeting with your approval. I have many groups and many distinguished Americans who give me aid and assistance, advice and counsel, criticism, and you are in the forefront of those people. I trust your judgment. I will have to make the ultimate decisions that affect our country.

Sometimes a particular request or suggestion of yours runs counter to other interests that I have to accommodate, but in general, I think that we have grown to understand and respect one another in the last 2 years. And I hope that you will feel that through your organizational leaders or directly to me or through my Cabinet officers or agency heads or advisers, that you have a constant access and easy access to the decisionmaking portion of the Federal Government.

I'm indebted to you. I look forward to working with you closely in the future, and I hope that you will not take lightly my direct, personal request that you not only adopt but encourage others to adopt the voluntary guidelines on wages and prices that I have put forward. That is the best thing that you can do for me at this point. And if you fail me in that, then I would be not quite so grateful in the future as I am now. [*Laughter*]

Thank you.

NOTE: The President spoke at 8:42 p.m. in the Grand Ballroom at the Mayflower Hotel.

President's Commission on the Coal Industry

Executive Order 12103.   *December 14, 1978*

By the authority vested in me as President by the Constitution of the United States of America, and in order to modify and continue, in accord with the provisions of the Federal Advisory Committee Act (5 U.S.C. App. I), a balanced forum to review the state of the Nation's coal industry, it is hereby ordered as follows:

1–1. *Establishment.*

1–101. There is established the President's Commission on the Coal Industry.

1–102. The membership of the Commission shall be composed of five persons appointed by the President from citizens in private life. One shall represent the interests of labor, one shall represent management and three shall represent the general public. The labor and management representatives shall be chosen from among candidates recommended by the United Mine Workers of America and the Bituminous Coal Operators Association of America, but shall not be members of these organizations. The President shall designate one of the members representing the general public to chair the Commission.

1–103. The President of the Senate and the Speaker of the House of Representatives may designate three members of their respective Houses to attend and participate in all meetings of the Commission *ex officio*.

1–104. The Secretary of Labor and the Secretary of Energy or their designees may also attend and participate in all meetings of the Commission *ex officio*.

1–2. *Functions.*

1–201. The Commission shall conduct a comprehensive review of the state of the coal industry in the United States with particular emphasis on matters pertaining to productivity, capital investment, and the general economic health of the industry; collective bargaining, grievance procedures, and such other aspects of labor-management relations as the Commission deems appropriate; health, safety and living conditions in the Nation's coal fields; the development and application of new technologies to the industry; the impact on the coal industry of Federal regulations; and such other matters as the Commission deems appropriate.

1–202. The five members appointed by the President shall prepare and transmit a final report of their findings and recommendations to the President, the Secretary of Labor and the Secretary of Energy.

1–203. To assist the Commission in the exercise of its functions, the Commission may sponsor a White House conference on the future of the coal industry.

1–3. *Administration.*

1–301. The Chairman of the Commission is authorized to appoint and fix the compensation of a staff and such other persons as may be necessary to carry out its functions, subject to the applicable provisions of the Federal Advisory Committee Act, including Section 7(d)(2) thereof.

Supergrade staff positions may not include more than one position at the GS–18 level, one position at the GS–17 level, and three positions at the GS–16 level, and shall be subject to the applicable provisions of law, including any applicable provisions of Sections 3324 and 5108 of Title 5 of the United States Code. The Commission may obtain services in accordance with the provisions of Section 3109 of Title 5 of the United States Code, to the extent that funds are available therefor.

1–302. To the extent authorized by law and requested by the Chairman of the Commission or by the Departments of Labor or Energy, the General Services Administration shall provide the Commission with necessary administrative services, facilities and support on reimbursable basis.

1–303. The Department of Labor and the Department of Energy shall, to the extent permitted by law and subject to the availability of funds, provide the Commission with such information, advice, facilities, support, funds and services, including staff, as may be necessary for the effective performance of the Commission's functions.

1–304. The Commission may request any Executive agency to furnish such information or assistance it deems necessary to carry out its functions. Each such agency is authorized, to the extent permitted by law, to furnish such information and assistance to the Commission upon request of the Chairman.

1–305. Each member of the Commission may receive compensation at the rate now or hereafter prescribed by law for GS–15 of the General Schedule for each day such member is engaged in the work of the Commission. Each member may also receive travel expenses, including per diem in lieu of subsistence (5 U.S.C. 5702 and 5703). Individuals designated to attend meetings under Section 1–103 of this

Order may also receive such travel expenses, including per diem in lieu of subsistence, which are permitted by law.

1–306. The functions of the President under the Federal Advisory Committee Act (5 U.S.C. App. I) which are applicable to the Commission, except that of reporting annually to the Congress, shall be performed by the Administrator of General Services.

1–4. *Final Report and Termination.*

1–401. The final report required by Section 1–202 of this Order shall be transmitted not later than one year from the date of this Order.

1–402. The Commission shall terminate one year from the date of this Order.

1–403. Executive Order No. 12062 of May 26, 1978, is revoked.

JIMMY CARTER

The White House,
    December 14, 1978.

[Filed with the Office of the Federal Register,
    11:32 a.m., December 14, 1978]

Meeting With the President of the Commission of the European Communities

White House Statement. **December 14, 1978**

President Carter met today with Roy Jenkins, President of the Commission of the European Communities, at 11 a.m. for about an hour. The talks, which both President Carter and President Jenkins view as an integral part of the close and ongoing consultative process between the United States and the European Communities, were cordial and productive.

Acting Secretary of State Warren Christopher; Zbigniew Brzezinski, Assistant to the President for National Security Affairs; Under Secretary of State

for Economic Affairs Richard Cooper, and Deane Hinton, United States Ambassador to the European Communities, and others participated in the discussion for the United States. On the Communities side, they were joined by Messrs. Fernand Spaak, Head of the Delegation of the European Communities Commission in the United States; Emile Noel, Secretary General of the European Communities Commission; Crispin Tickell, Head of Cabinet to the President of the European Communities Commission, and others. Among major topics which Presidents Carter and Jenkins discussed were the following:

1. *International Trade.* They welcomed the progress being achieved in Geneva on negotiation of a multilateral trade agreement. They expressed the hope that substantial and balanced agreement would be reached before the end of the year. President Carter expressed his determination to seek congressional action to assure continued application of the waiver on countervailing duties. Both President Carter and President Jenkins agreed that the success of the negotiations would promote economic recovery and the extension of international trade between both industrial and developing countries, thus raising living standards and increasing jobs.

2. *European Monetary System.* President Carter indicated that he viewed the European Monetary System (EMS) as an important step toward the European integration that the United States has long supported. The President of the European Commission emphasized that the creation of such a system was designed not only to establish a zone of monetary stability in Europe but also to contribute to greater stability in the world monetary system as a whole, of which a strong dollar is an essential part. He underlined that the European Monetary System was

entirely compatible with the relevant articles of the International Monetary Fund, which enjoyed full European confidence and support.

3. *Science and Technology.* President Carter and the President of the European Commission agreed to explore the possibilities for cooperation between the United States and the European Communities in research in certain areas of science and technology. They both strongly felt the need for the United States and the Community to strengthen their powers of innovation in this field, while cooperating with each other and others to share knowledge and cost to their mutual advantage. The particular areas they had in mind are nuclear fusion, management of radioactive waste, handling and control of fissile materials, and biological and medical research, including definition of standards for use of toxic substances and definition of carcinogens. President Carter indicated that the United States intended to increase its role in strengthening the scientific and technological capacities of developing countries through the intended Foundation for International Technological Cooperation.

Christmas Pageant of Peace

Remarks on Lighting the National Community Christmas Tree. December 14, 1978

THE PRESIDENT. Merry Christmas!

AUDIENCE. Merry Christmas!

THE PRESIDENT. Come on—Merry Christmas, everybody!

AUDIENCE. Merry Christmas!

THE PRESIDENT. That's better.

As you well know, the theme of this year's Pageant of Peace is unity. There is much to divide us in this world. And sometimes we concentrate too much of our attention on those divisions among us. But Christmas is a good time to recall how much unites us as people and also as nations. We are united in our belief in human dignity, in our conviction that the most likely way to find the truth is to free people's minds and consciences, and that the least likely way to find the truth is to silence people's voices and to try to make them deny what they really believe.

Our country is entering a period of healing and of hope. We are joining together as a people again, realizing the strength of a common purpose. We are blessed with warm fires and warm memories and the voices of children singing of joy in the night. I think that God in His great wisdom knew that we needed these things to help us face the cold and sometimes lonely times. We need the joy of children's voices to remind us that the only things that we can truly give to each other are the only things that we truly need—an ear to listen, a heart to care, a word of encouragement, and a hand to help.

At Christmas, we have not only this year's special moments but the rich store of all Christmases past to remember and to use.

When I was growing up, President Franklin Roosevelt was lighting the Nation's Christmas tree. During the difficult years of the Depression, and later during the Second World War, too many of our own Nation's Christmases have been shadowed by war. We are fortunate as we light this Christmas tree tonight that our Nation and most of the nations of the world are not at war.

This is always a matter of concern, the threat of violence in many corners of the globe. But this Christmas is a time of relative calm and also a time of great hope. Two ancient enemies are on the threshold of an agreement that could bring peace to the Middle East. It is my earnest prayer that the day will soon come when all children in the Middle East can play in the sunshine without fear, when their young men and women can turn their energies and talents away from war and death, to making the deserts fruitful and to building, instead of preparing to destroy.

The Prophet Isaiah, who wrote about ancient wars between Israel and her neighbors, tells us that the work of righteousness is peace. The United States has tried this year to help other nations find peace. We have succeeded in several troubled areas in getting people to talk to each other and to work out their differences without resorting to violence and to war.

I hope that the time has passed when people excuse the pain and destruction and death and see war in itself as a demonstration of national heroism. This generation, our generation, has seen too much of war's desolation. We've seen what it can do spiritually, as well as physically, to a people. War is no longer the brave sound of parades and drums and trumpets. We've seen it as it is, the loss of the young in the full flower of their promise, the death of families and entire communities, and the threat of nuclear devastation for the world.

I think the world is more ready than ever before to understand the thrust of Ralph Waldo Emerson's words that peace is victory for both sides. I believe that nations may be ready now to accept the possibility that those whom they have called enemies might live undisturbed on Earth and that we might at last learn to call even enemies brothers and sisters.

Perhaps at last the same fervor and commitment and sense of high purpose with which we once sought victory in war can now be devoted to our search for peace. And then we will truly be able to say in our hearts, for the fulfillment of the ancient promise of peace on Earth, good will toward men.

The evergreen tree that we use at Christmas is a symbol of eternal life, and also of the perpetual renewal of life. As I light our Nation's Christmas tree, and whenever you see a glowing tree this Christmas, I hope that you will see it as a rekindling of our faith and hope and our dedication to the cause of unity and a great nation's influence throughout the world for peace on Earth.

Thank you very much. And now we'll proceed to wish all the world a happy Christmas by lighting the Christmas tree together.

NOTE: The President spoke at 5:44 p.m. on the Ellipse. Following his remarks, he lit the National Community Christmas Tree with the help of his daughter, Amy.

Interview With the President and Mrs. Carter

Question-and-Answer Session With Barbara Walters of the American Broadcasting Company.   December 14, 1978

Ms. WALTERS. This is the Green Room of the White House, decorated for Christmas. We sit here today with President and Mrs. Carter to talk of the Nation, the world, and of themselves.

VIEWS ON THE PRESIDENCY

It was exactly 2 years ago today, on December 14, that I had the pleasure of talking with both of them in Plains, Georgia. And at that time, it was the first interview that they had done together since the election. And it is, today, the only interview that they have done together since that time.

At the conclusion of that conversation, I asked Mr. Carter if there was anything about his new life which gave him apprehension. And here is how his answer went.[1]

---

[1] ABC News later inserted a segment of the interview referred to by Ms. Walters in its broadcast of this interview.

Mr. President, have you in any way, do you think, disappointed the American people, or have you been disappointed in yourself?

THE PRESIDENT. I think our expectations have been realized for the first 2 years, Barbara. There are obviously many things that I do that disappoint certain Americans who would like to move more rapidly toward the goals that we've established for ourselves jointly.

I think our communications and understanding with the American people has continued in an uninterrupted vein, even following the 2 years of intensive campaigning. Our Nation has been at peace. No American has shed blood in a war or combat overseas. We've used our influence, I think, in a beneficial way to try to enhance peace in other parts of the world.

The pressing problem then was unemployment. And we have added a net increase of 7 million jobs to the American economic system. The welfare rolls have been cut down by 1.3 million, and the unemployment rate has dropped 25 percent. We still face the chronic problem of inflation, which hasn't been resolved rapidly enough. We're moving aggressively on it now. And I think I've learned Washington to some degree better than I thought I would, and have a good working relationship with the Congress.

We still have a major agenda ahead for continued peace, economic prosperity, and to enhance the Nation's influence around the world in a beneficial way.

So, I've got my hands full, but I'm pleased with the first 2 years.

Ms. WALTERS. Mrs. Carter, you and I talked a year ago, and at the time we talked about some of the problems the President was having. And you said you didn't think the people perceived him yet as a leader, but you were sure they were going to. Do they now?

MRS. CARTER. I think they do. And I think 2 years ago, when we talked, we were naturally a little bit apprehensive, because it was new to us and we had not been here. But I think you develop a growing confidence about what you're capable of doing. And also, I think at that time we maybe did not realize the breadth of counsel and advice that we would have, experts in all fields and the range of people that are willing to help us.

Ms. WALTERS. Mrs. Carter, your situation is somewhat unique, because the President has always said that you are an equal partner, and you sit in on Cabinet meetings. And tonight, if we ask some political or economic, or questions about foreign policy, I hope that you'll join in. And if you would like to argue with the President, we'd be just delighted. [*Laughter*]

PRESIDENT'S 1980 CANDIDACY

Mr. President, at your press conference on Tuesday—I'm going to start right in with, I think, questions about you that people care most about—you said that you'd made your decision whether or not to run again, but that you wouldn't reveal the decision until later. It is 2 days later. [*Laughter*] Is it late enough?

THE PRESIDENT. No, it's not. I think it's inappropriate now, when I've only been in office 2 years, to begin talking about future political plans, Barbara. It'll be much later than now.

Ms. WALTERS. Much later.

THE PRESIDENT. Yes.

Ms. WALTERS. A lot of people think you're being coy——

THE PRESIDENT. No.

Ms. Walters. ——and that you really are going to run again, and, you know, why aren't you going to say it?

The President. It's too early to make any political announcement about 1980 elections, whether I decide to run or not run. I'm not going to be coy. And I'll make the announcement when I think the political time approaches.

Ms. Walters. Will it be '79?

The President. It may be the end of this year, but not before that——

Ms. Walters. Let me try once, just a little bit——

The President. Not tonight.

Ms. Walters. Not tonight.

——with Mrs. Carter. There are a number of Democrats who might run if they thought your husband wasn't seeking reelection. They may be packing their bags right now. Should they unpack? You're a considerate woman. What do you think they should do?

Mrs. Carter. I don't worry about those. I think people who want to run for President—when Jimmy has run for office on other occasions, we announced it in time for speculation, in time for those to decide that wanted to run against him. But I agree with Jimmy that this is not the time to make the decision, because we don't want people just speculating about everything we're doing, being, preparing for another election. Right now we're doing what needs to be done at this time. And I think that's the way it should be.

Ms. Walters. Mr. President, as an astute politician, you have to be aware that people are talking about Senator Kennedy as a possible candidate. Okay, at this point, he says he's not going to run; we take him at his word. But if he does— oh, you're smiling. Do you take him at his word?

The President. Yes. I take him at his word. But it was a real prospect that

Senator Kennedy would run for President in 1976. When I decided to run several years ahead of time, I was not deterred by that prospect, nor by that of the candidacy of any other person. And I do take him at his word. But my decision will be made on whether I think I can do a good job for the American people, not on the fear or ease of a tough election.

Ms. Walters. If he ran, could you beat him?

The President. I think if I should decide to run, that I would win, yes.

Mrs. Carter. I think Jimmy's going to be President for a long time.

Ms. Walters. I think you've answered our question without answering our question.

Which Republican would give you the toughest fight, do you think—Ronald Reagan, Gerald Ford, George Bush, John Connally, or somebody else, somebody new?

The President. My experience in politics has been that almost every election is a tough election, very close. And if there are wide ranges in popularity at the beginning, the elections tend to narrow. I don't know why exactly. But I think that any nominee that Republicans would put forward would be formidable.

And the best way to win an election is to have a good record in your incumbency, job, and to be determined and tenacious, and, above all, to stay close to the American people. So, I think no matter whom the Republicans choose, the Democrats should be on their toes, willing for a tough campaign, and confident that ultimately we'll win, because we are the best party for the people.

Ms. Walters. But is there any one whom you think would give you the toughest fight?

The President. No, I wouldn't want

to comment on that. If I did, I would want to choose the weakest.

Ms. WALTERS. Would you like to name the weakest?

THE PRESIDENT. [*Laughing*] No, I wouldn't.

ANTI-INFLATION PROGRAM

Ms. WALTERS. Mr. President, we do want to talk about what is going on in foreign policy and what's happening in the Middle East. But, to most Americans watching tonight, what the polls have shown and what I think most of us feel is that the major concern of the American people is inflation, is the shrinking pocketbook.

Now, President Nixon tried to tackle inflation, and he failed. President Ford tried with his WIN program, and he failed. There are many economists today, there are labor leaders and business leaders who feel that your program is inadequate.

As the audience sits out there tonight watching you, why should they have faith that you, Jimmy Carter, are going to make it?

THE PRESIDENT. We've got a sound economic system. We don't have the uncontrollable single factors involved in inflation that we had a few years ago.

The rapidly increasing prices of oil from overseas had quadrupled, as you know, in a short time, back in 1973. There's not a worldwide shortage of raw materials that forced up prices. And now the American growth rate—how rapidly our own economy is increasing—is becoming almost the same as those of our major trading partners. In the last few years, the American growth rate has been perhaps twice as great as most of our trading partners.

Also, we have escalated the anti-inflation fight to a top domestic priority. I inherited a very large Federal budget deficit, which was in 1976 about 4 percent of our gross national product. By the end of the 1980 fiscal year, which I'm working on now, that budget deficit will drop from 4 percent of our GNP down to 1 percent of our GNP, a very substantial improvement. At the same time, we have gotten, I think, good results from our employment program. And I think that recent statistics show that we can have this stringent anti-inflation program without causing a recession.

The last thing I'd like to say is that we have, in addition to proving my determination and effectiveness at the Federal Government level, we've had good response from business. And I think there will be growing response from labor as government and business prove that we mean business and can cooperate. I don't intend to fail.

Ms. WALTERS. A moment ago, you said that if Senator Kennedy did run for President, that you could beat him. What he is beginning to represent is the liberal or the side of certain groups, perhaps blacks and labor leaders and women, who say that in this inflation program, you are cutting many of the very important domestic social programs. Now, you have, particularly this week, been meeting with some members of those different groups. And they seem to feel more assured that you'll be able to keep the social programs.

Okay, which ones are you going to cut, and which ones can you assure them may still stay?

THE PRESIDENT. I can't answer that question tonight. I want to say that Senator Kennedy is a formidable political person, and I don't underestimate his effectiveness and his popularity. But the recent Democratic conference, I think, gave me strong support in my anti-inflation program, not because of unconcern or callousness about the disadvantaged, but because everyone realizes once they study the issue, that the most heavy burden of inflation falls on those who are disadvantaged, the retired person on a fixed income, the poor person who has maybe one job capability and cannot move about, the family that spends almost all of their income on the necessities of life. Those are the ones who suffer most from inflation.

And it's a complete fallacy, which ought to be wiped out, that controlling inflation works against the poor and the disadvantaged. The best thing that I can do for the poor and disadvantaged is to keep the social programs at a constant level or perhaps some modification to make them more efficient, on the one hand, and control the inflationary burden which falls most heavily on them.

DEFENSE SPENDING

Ms. WALTERS. Mr. President, right now you have a very difficult choice to make—there are always difficult choices, but one in particular—whether you stick to your commitment to raise the defense budget about 3 percent, a commitment you made to our NATO Allies; however, to cut this amount so that you can hold the Federal deficit to the $30 billion and also because you are cutting social domestic programs.

We've read that you have very strong advice on both sides. What are you going to do, Mr. President?

THE PRESIDENT. Well, I get strong advice on both sides of almost every issue, Barbara.

The paramount responsibility of any President is the security of the American people, the American Nation. I feel very strongly that I have got to maintain a strong defense. And I'm not going to yield in that commitment.

When I became President, I think it's accurate to say that NATO was weakened and also dispirited. There was a lack of conviction among our European allies and others that we were dedicated to a strong Western Europe, to withstand the potential threat from Eastern Europe and from the Soviet Union. I do not intend to go back on my commitment to NATO.

Ms. WALTERS. It will be approximately a 3-percent defense raise?

THE PRESIDENT. That's correct.

ROLE OF THE FIRST LADY

Ms. WALTERS. Mrs. Carter, as we talk, not just about these matters but about others which we will get to, you have now been in the White House for 2 years. Are there any policies of this administration or any change in the country which you feel reflect your advice to the President?

MRS. CARTER. Barbara, I don't consider myself a force in his decisions, but he does talk to me about the things that he's doing. And I feel compelled to disagree with him at times——

Ms. WALTERS. Could you tell us why?

MRS. CARTER. ——to be supportive when I think he's right. I never have publicly disagreed with him, and I have a very good reason for doing that: because I know Jimmy well and I think that if I made our disagreements public, I would lose all my effectiveness with him. [*Laughter*] I don't think it would help, in any way change his mind about anything.

And while you're talking about the inflation and the social programs for the country, I was thinking about the thing that I'm interested in now, encouraging individuals in their communities to become involved in solving their own problems, because even with large government programs, when we have tried to cure the social ills with massive government programs, we haven't ever been able to do that. And I don't think there's ever going to be enough money. I don't think government can solve all the problems.

So, I'm going to be working, encouraging people in their own communities to assume responsibilities for the problems around them. And I think particularly, now with inflation, that it's going to be important, more important than ever before.

THE PRESIDENT. Barbara, let me say that Rosalynn's somewhat modest and, maybe, properly so because of the proprieties involved. But I don't hesitate to discuss with her every major decision that I have to make, unless it involves a vital and top secret security point, which I do not share with anyone.

But we had a special need to strengthen our ties, for instance, with Latin America. And Rosalynn went on a full diplomatic mission representing me personally and also representing the Nation. She was received hesitantly by some of the seven or eight leaders, but I think at the conclusion of those meetings, they now rely on her substantially to be sure that I understand the sensitivities of the people.

MS. WALTERS. Still—you think they still do?

MRS. CARTER. They do.

THE PRESIDENT. They do. There's no doubt about that. And also when I'm confined to Washington because of pressing duties and she goes out within the United States, she has a much easier relationship with people and can bring back to me an accurate assessment of what the hopes and dreams and fears and concerns of American people are than I could get from any other possible source. So, she is a full partner in that respect.

MS. WALTERS. Did she ever change your mind? Can you think of something where she disagreed and you switched?

THE PRESIDENT. Well, I think a change in emphasis, sometimes in domestic programs involving the elderly or mental health, she's a very effective spokesman, and I think the point she's just made has been a good reminder to me. When I was totally preoccupied with the Federal Government programs to deal with cities and to deal with other problems, Rosalynn continued to emphasize and finally convinced me that the best approach was to involve not only the mayors and the Governors but also just private citizens in dealing with community problems themselves. And she spends a lot of time on that and very effectively.

WAGE AND PRICE CONTROLS

MS. WALTERS. I have one last question on the economy I'd like to ask, and you could almost take a yes and no. You've repeatedly stated your dislike of mandatory wage and price controls. But if Congress sends you legislation granting authority to impose such conditions, as they did with President Nixon in 1970, would you veto such legislation?

THE PRESIDENT. That would be an inconceivable prospect for me that the Congress would submit to me legislation that I opposed for wage and price controls. If it was a stand-by proposal that could only be used in case of a threat to our Nation's security itself, then I would consider signing it. But I have no desire for that kind of stand-by authority.

MS. WALTERS. We'll be back in just a word. Thank you.

EGYPTIAN-ISRAELI PEACE NEGOTIATIONS

Mr. President, Mrs. Carter, may we turn our attention to foreign policy and start with the Middle East, which continues to be a situation that is unsettled.

It does not look now as if the December 17th deadline is going to be met for the peace agreement between Israel and Egypt. What now, Mr. President?

THE PRESIDENT. Well, I'm not giving up on the 17th deadline.

Ms. WALTERS. Really?

THE PRESIDENT. The decision is primarily in the hands now of the Israeli Cabinet. We have worked out with Sadat as approval by him of the treaty text, and the remaining issues involved how rapidly and under what circumstances the provisions of the Camp David accords shall be implemented.

One of the major issues is whether or not a goal should be set, not a fixed, definite requirement that the West Bank, Gaza self-government should be established by the end of 1979. I personally don't see how this could be difficult for the Israelis, since it's not mandatory, but just a goal to be sought. But the decision now is primarily in the hands of the Israelis. Secretary Vance has had thorough discussions with both Sadat and Begin and their other government officials. We don't know what will happen.

I consider the December 17th date to be quite significant. But if we don't succeed in getting an agreement by then— it's certainly a strong possibility—then we will continue tenaciously to pursue the peace prospects and to try to reach an agreement between Israel and Egypt at a later date.

Ms. WALTERS. How? Summit, maybe? What?

THE PRESIDENT. That's always a possibility. But that would not be my preference. I would certainly have no objection, and would encourage at any time President Sadat and Prime Minister Begin getting together themselves. But I think for them to plan on coming over here anytime in the future would probably be a mistake, because I've got other pressing international problems. And

we've really put an extraordinary amount of time and effort in the Mideast, and I just cannot neglect other problems in order to accomplish this goal.

Ms. WALTERS. We've said that Secretary Vance was coming back to put pressure on the Israelis. Other reports said no, it was urgent business. What's the urgent business, if that's it?

THE PRESIDENT. We have got a broad range of things that are now coming to a head. We've got problems between Chile and Argentina concerning territory down there that could erupt into a conflict. We're trying to reach a conclusion on the Nicaraguan question.

I think that the SALT negotiations are coming to a head. Cy will be going to Europe to meet with Gromyko, on the 21st of December, perhaps to plan for a summit meeting between myself and President Brezhnev earlier next year. And there are just such a broad gamut of things that I need Secretary Vance back here. And he and I agreed in a telephone conversation that his work in the Mideast was primarily completed.

The proposition that has been worked out with Egypt is presented clearly to the Israelis. And now it's up to the Israelis to either accept it or reject it.

Ms. WALTERS. You talked of President Sadat being generous in accepting some of the proposals. You didn't mention Prime Minister Begin. This was last night that you said this. Do you consider Mr. Begin to be intransigent?

THE PRESIDENT. Well, we don't know what the Israeli response will be.

Ms. WALTERS. I spoke with Israel this morning, with some key members in Foreign Minister Dayan's office, with his spokesman. And without going through each detail, what they are saying is that they were willing to sign the original agreement, but that President Sadat is now adding new conditions which they consider open up and change the treaty. And, particularly, they object to the fact that the Egyptians are not going to agree to normalization of relations and exchange of ambassadors until 1 year after Palestinian autonomy. And they say that this is not what was originally agreed to, all these new conditions.

THE PRESIDENT. That's not accurate. The way I understand the recent negotiations, at the time the Israelis complete the interim withdrawal, diplomatic relations would be established between Egypt and Israel. The embargo against Israel would be removed, and then when the self-government is established—within a month, not a year—ambassadors themselves would be exchanged.

The original proposal was that Israel would withdraw from El'Arish and from the central part of the Sinai in the interim withdrawal, much earlier than the Camp David accords required, in 2 months and 4 months. Based on that commitment by Israel negotiators, Sadat said he would exchange ambassadors at that time, a month later. Later Israel's Cabinet withdrew their proposal and therefore relieved President Sadat of the obligation to exchange ambassadors early.

But I think that that's a reasonable schedule. Diplomatic relations would be established with Israel immediately, as soon as they made their first interim withdrawal. It's only the exchange of ambassadors themselves that would be delayed.

Ms. WALTERS. Mr. President, if the Middle East talks fail and if you feel that Israel is not forthcoming, might there be a reassessment of the United States policy in Israel?

THE PRESIDENT. No. Our policy with Israel is—and with the Middle East—is that the security of Israel is paramount; the continued existence of Israel, their

ability to protect themselves adequately, and the ability of the Israeli people to live in peace is paramount above anything else that relates to the Mideast.

Ms. WALTERS. In that regard, Israel was reported to be very upset when hearing that Senate Majority Leader Byrd had said that if Israel builds future settlements, the Senate may not increase its foreign aid to Israel. The Israelis said that Senator Byrd came to Israel recently, describing himself as your emissary. And one wonders if the Senator's statement reflects your point of view.

THE PRESIDENT. [*Laughing*] I have never attempted to control Senator Byrd's statements. And I think Senator Byrd speaks from the perspective of the Congress and as the Democratic leader of the Senate.

We have always, so far as I know, adopted as an official American position, with which I agree, that the settlements in the occupied territories are illegal and that they are a genuine obstacle to peace. And whenever the Israelis publicize with varied voices that there will be $35 million spent on new settlements or a billion dollars spent on new settlements or another new settlement's going to be created, it really puts a dampener on cooperation from the Jordanians, from the Palestinians who live in the West Bank, and even from the Egyptians in carrying out the spirit of Camp David.

I know it's a very sensitive issue with Israel. I'm not saying this in a critical way, but I can say with assurance that the Majority Leader was speaking for himself.

Ms. WALTERS. That does not represent your viewpoint?

THE PRESIDENT. Not necessarily. The attitude of the Congress is, I think, not something that I ought to comment upon. I can't say whether I agree or disagree that the majority leader speaks accurately for the Congress.

Ms. WALTERS. What now, Mr. President? Do you plan perhaps to call or have you already telephoned either Prime Minister Begin or President Sadat? Tomorrow there's a Cabinet meeting. What's going to happen maybe to get something either by this Sunday or soon after?

THE PRESIDENT. Well, it's hard for me to answer that question. I've not received any report from Secretary Vance, except very brief dispatch messages. And he will be back in the United States tomorrow afternoon. Of course, as soon as he returns, he'll come and give me a thorough report. But we've done all we could and will continue to do all we can in spite of setbacks and disappointments and frustrations and delays.

We are very deeply committed to carrying out both the letter and the spirit of Camp David. It was a major step forward. We will never give up, no matter how difficult the circumstances, on searching for a peace treaty between Israel and Egypt, to be followed by peace between Israel and all her neighbors.

IRAN

Ms. WALTERS. Mrs. Carter, I hate for us to have to jump from one part of the world to the other, but we have less than an hour in which to talk.

So often when the news comes in about Iran, I remember New Year's Eve, because you and the President spent New Year's Eve in Iran and many reporters like myself were with you. And the President, in his toast at that time, said Mrs. Carter had said this is where she wanted to be New Year's Eve, with the Shah and Empress.

I wonder if you personally have talked with them and what your view is of them, of the Shah in particular, as a ruler?

Mrs. CARTER. I have not talked with them, but I've had correspondence back and forth with Empress Farah. I think they need our support now more than ever. I just feel very concerned about the situation. We had a wonderful visit with them last year. And New Year's Eve was special, because after all the formalities and the dinner, we relaxed with them and with their friends and with a lot of you all, and just enjoyed being there.

THE PRESIDENT. And King Hussein was there.

Mrs. CARTER. King Hussein was there. And it was a fun evening for us, and it's sad that this has happened in the period of 1 year's time.

Ms. WALTERS. Mr. President, there are reports that you've recently sent messages to the Soviet Union, warning them to keep hands off of Iran. Can you confirm these, and can you tell us if you have any information on Russian involvement in Iran?

THE PRESIDENT. Yes, that's accurate.

Ms. WALTERS. You have sent the letters?

THE PRESIDENT. Yes. President Brezhnev and I exchanged messages.

Ms. WALTERS. Recently?

THE PRESIDENT. Within the last few weeks, a couple of weeks. And I made it very clear to them, to the Soviets, that we have no intention of interfering in the internal affairs of Iran and that we have no intention of permitting others to interfere in the internal affairs of Iran.

I think it's good to point out, Barbara, that Iran has a 2,500-year history of statecraft, of managing their own affairs properly. Obviously, they've had ups and downs, as we have in our own country. But there's a certain stability there, a certain inclination and capability of the Iranians to govern themselves that I think is a stabilizing factor. We don't know what changes will take place.

Ms. WALTERS. Have the Russians been involved, sir, that you know of?

THE PRESIDENT. As far as we know, they have not. We monitor the situation closely. Obviously, there is a Communist party there, the Tudeh party, which perhaps is inclined to encourage violence or disruption in order to change the existing government. But the Shah is communicating with opposition leaders. He is committed to a broader base for the government. He is working toward democratic principles and social change. And he has been embattled lately. And we obviously support him fully.

Ms. WALTERS. When we talk about support, what do we mean today, 1978, post-Vietnam, by support? For example, if the Shah does fall, it threatens our oil supply, it threatens Israel's oil supply, it threatens Saudi Arabia, it threatens the whole Persian Gulf. At what point would support turn into action and what kind of action, if any?

THE PRESIDENT. I am not prepared to answer that question.

Ms. WALTERS. Because there is no answer, or because——

THE PRESIDENT. Well, the answer is difficult. But I think just conjecturing on something that's hypothetical like that, assuming all the catastrophes that might possibly occur in the Persian Gulf, is something on which I don't want to comment. I don't think it's going to happen. And if I were to surmise that if it happens, we would do this, it would be interpreted by some as an actual prediction by me that it's going to happen, and I don't think it's going to happen.

Ms. WALTERS. Is support primarily verbal support?

THE PRESIDENT. No. We have treaty agreements with Iran. We have strong defense agreements with Iran. We look on Iran, as do their neighbors, as being a stabilizing factor. Even the Soviet Union shares a long border with Iran. I'm sure they want stability there on their border. Exactly the formation of the government—I can't speak for the Soviets, but I think that for world peace and for the Soviets, and for us, certainly for the entire Middle East-Persian Gulf region, a stability is desirable, and that's what we want, also.

HUMAN RIGHTS

Ms. WALTERS. Mr. President, I want to move—talking about Iran—move to human rights, because some highly placed Iranians close to the Shah have said that your insistence on human rights was a factor in weakening his position. And Henry Kissinger, in a recent interview, said, and I quote, that your human rights campaign is "a weapon aimed primarily at allies and tends to undermine their domestic structure"—a strong statement.

THE PRESIDENT. [*Laughing*] I haven't had any screams of outrage from our allies about our human rights position. It's been clear. It's been public. It's been consistent and well-advised. And I think I speak accurately for the American people in saying that a United States commitment to the enhancement of human rights on a worldwide basis is a sound policy.

There was a very long and thorough debate, for instance, within the NATO Council earlier this week about the advisability of the human rights stand being strongly pursued throughout the world. And there was a consensus among our NATO Allies—approximately 15 nations—that this was a policy that was well-advised for the Western democratic world. And there are many people on the other side of the so-called Iron Curtain who also agree that the strong human rights policy should be pursued, and it will be.

Ms. WALTERS. Sometimes in this area you're damned if you do, and damned if you don't. I hear the other side. People said to me, "You're going to interview the President. Okay, ask him why he doesn't pursue human rights in the Philippines. Ask him why he doesn't do it in Chile. Ask him why he waited so long in Iran." You get both sides.

THE PRESIDENT. Well, I think if you would talk to President Marcos or to President Pinochet that you would find that they have felt the influence of the United States toward enhanced human rights. We also are constantly reminded in our own country that because we have espoused so strongly the human rights commitment, that we reassess what we do in the United States, to be sure we don't violate basic human rights.

And this is an issue now that has become almost a worldwide obsession. I doubt that any world leader goes through a day that he or she doesn't think, "How are we measuring up in world opinion, in the opinion of my own constituents or citizens, as related to my performance on human rights?" I think it ought to be a burning issue.

Ms. WALTERS. Even Mr. Marcos—because that's where you've been criticized, since he's an ally——

THE PRESIDENT. Yes, yes, I think even Mr. Marcos, yes. But I don't want to single him out. There are many, many others. And there have been thousands of people released from prison—I don't want to take credit for it—but I think because there's a growing awareness of the need for human rights.

MRS. CARTER. And I think it's given hope to people all over the world. I see it in traveling, the difference in attitude of people toward our country. I think there's a trust and respect for our country now that was not there before.

Ms. WALTERS. We'll return and talk about some personal matters. I don't know whether that will be easier or harder to answer. We'll be right back.

STRATEGIC ARMS LIMITATION

Mr. President, we seem to be very close to a SALT agreement, and there comes in this the whole question of, can we trust the Russians. The fight in Congress looks as if it's going to be a very tough fight. Some people say it's going to make the Panama Canal debate look like a Sunday school picnic. How do you reassure Congress and the people?

THE PRESIDENT. The SALT agreement, when concluded—and I think it'll be quite soon—will be in the best interests of our country. It will enhance our own security. And whether we trust the Soviets or not, we will have an adequate ability to verify whether or not they comply. So, the American people need not be concerned about that.

Ms. WALTERS. Do you think Congress is going to pass it?

THE PRESIDENT. I believe so, because it's in the best interests of our country. And I think that Congress wants to do what's in the best interests of our country.

Ms. WALTERS. I said that we were going to discuss personal matters. I'd just like to ask a couple of catchall questions before we do.

PATTY HEARST

Mr. President, do you have any plans to pardon Patty Hearst?

THE PRESIDENT. I don't have any plans to treat Patty Hearst as a special case. From time to time, I get recommendations from the Attorney General to change the sentence of dozens of people—sometimes as many as 75 or 80. I always look them over, assess the reasons for the Attorney General's recommendations, and, almost without exception, comply with his recommendation. But I think to treat her as a special case because she is wealthy and her case has been highly publicized would be a mistake. She'll be treated in a routine fashion when the time comes.

Ms. WALTERS. Mrs. Carter, let me ask you, as a mother, how you feel. Have you given the President any advice in this? Is it something you've discussed.

MRS. CARTER. I'm aware of it, and we, I think, have mentioned it a time or two. But we have not discussed it, no.

Ms. WALTERS. Maybe tonight?

MRS. CARTER. Not tonight. [*Laughter*]

ADMINISTRATION OFFICIALS

Ms. WALTERS. Do you plan any new faces in your Cabinet or in the first string of your administration, Mr. President?

THE PRESIDENT. I hope not. I would like to finish my 4-year term and have the same Cabinet that I started with. They are all good.

Ms. WALTERS. And the same people in the White House?

THE PRESIDENT. I don't have any plans to change the people in the White House.

Ms. WALTERS. Now that Hamilton Jordan's wearing a suit and tie? [*Laughter*]

THE PRESIDENT. I might want to improve some of them, but not move them.

VIEWS ON THE PRESIDENCY

Ms. WALTERS. Mr. President, you said that, when you campaigned, that you would never tell a lie. Well, have you ever told a lie since then, even a tiny white lie, even for national security?

THE PRESIDENT. Not that I can recall.

I think one of the biggest responsibilities that I have is to build up confidence in the Government and the Presidency itself. If I should ever tell a lie, even though it would be a small and perhaps inconsequential one to enhance our national security at the particular moment, and later be caught as a liar, it would cast doubt on all the truthful things that I said. And I have never been tempted, in this 2 years, to lie to the American people or to any individual news reporter about a matter that concerned our national security or a matter that concerned any public event.

Ms. WALTERS. Mrs. Carter, I remember we talked 2 years ago about some misconceptions about both you and the President. What, if any, misconceptions do you think that the public or the press has now?

MRS. CARTER. I don't know, Barbara. I think the press has been very fair to me, those who are with me and see me on a daily basis, in presenting what I'm trying to do to the public.

Ms. WALTERS. What about the President? Is he coming off okay?

MRS. CARTER. I think so. I think in the beginning, the press didn't understand him, didn't know what he was trying to do. But I think that we're changing that. I think with the successes that he had in Congress and the things that he has tried to do that have actually come to fruition, people are seeing, the press is projecting what he actually is doing.

Ms. WALTERS. Do you think there are any misconceptions about you, sir?

THE PRESIDENT. I think the misconceptions are decreasing in number. One of the frustrations and challenges and maybe difficulties of being President or a member of the First Family is to have good communication with the American people in both directions, both to learn what the American people think, what they want, and what they expect of us, and also to project accurately what we are trying to do.

And there are obviously many reports that come out in a newspaper, perhaps on a television program, that are completely erroneous, just based on facts that are wrong. And we try to correct those. But I think that the doubt and suspicion about me, because I had not ever lived in Washington, not ever served in the Federal Government, and was a southerner, a Baptist, most of those have been alleviated now with better communication and knowledge of what I have done and a record to be assessed.

And I think there's been a fairly good transition after some, about a year of rough places with the press and with the public. I feel better now than I did 6 months ago.

MRS. CARTER. There are still some frustrations, things that we—they're not misconceptions, but frustrations about things that we want people to know.

Something that happened this week to me, for instance—I went to the opening of a conference on childhood immunization. Joe Califano started a program last year. I called him because I was concerned about it. And Mrs. Dale Bumpers, who's a good friend of mine—her husband was Governor of Arkansas while Jimmy was Governor, now he's in the Senate—had worked on childhood immunization for years. And so we called on Joe Califano. He started a program last April.

The results of that have been dramatic. And we had a meeting this week to talk about what is happening in the country— the immunizations have gone up, the incidence of disease has dropped. We had a great conference, a great meeting. We didn't read one word about it.

It's not so important that I get publicity or that people know what I'm doing. But when people see that and read it, then those who have children who have

not been immunized will think about it; it'll focus some attention on it.

So, those kinds of frustrations we have.

Ms. WALTERS. Well, stories are selective, and it's usually the more sensational ones. And the public complains to the press about that as well.

CHIP AND CARON CARTER

You've talked a great deal about what you've enjoyed in the White House and that, if anything, it's given you two more time to be together, more time with Amy. But one does wonder sometimes about the price that one pays when a husband and a father becomes President.

And I almost feel funny about asking you this, except that it has been written about and talked about so much, and that's the separation of your son Chip and your daughter-in-law Caron, which obviously must grieve you as parents. And it's been suggested that if he had not lived in the White House, that if he had not been exposed to some of the social conditions of living in this city—I'm sure you have read this—that perhaps it wouldn't have happened.

Do you feel a particular responsibility? Do you feel that this may have been the case?

THE PRESIDENT. Do you want me to answer it or Rosalynn? Go ahead, Rosalynn.

MRS. CARTER. I don't think because we live here we are immune from problems that other families have. But I think our family has grown closer together because of the experiences we share. And I love Chip and I love Caron, and I want them both to be happy.

I think that we made some statements about their decision at the time and have not said anything more public about it. But I don't think the—I have been very proud of my children in the way they have reacted. I think they are dependable and responsible, and they've represented our family well. They've represented the country well when they've traveled abroad. And I think things that happen to them, I think they try to lead as normal a life as anybody else.

THE PRESIDENT. We still pray that their marriage will be saved. And they've asked that it not be discussed publicly, and I think it's better for us not to discuss it.

Ms. WALTERS. Fine, sir.

EQUAL RIGHTS AMENDMENT

Let us talk about something that you are involved in as a First Lady and as a woman, Mrs. Carter, and that's the ERA. You've devoted so much time to it. And it seems to be in trouble getting these last three States to ratify.

What do you think can be done? And in your heart of hearts, do you think it's going to pass?

MRS. CARTER. I don't know. If I have had a failure, I think that not being able to ratify the equal rights amendment has been the failure in these past 2 years, because it is so important and we just can't seem to get the message across about it.

We are working very hard now to formulate plans for educating people about what the equal rights amendment is, because I think when people know what it is, they will be for it, that the opposition is so distorted about it and we want to clear up——

Ms. WALTERS. You're still going to continue to work for it.

MRS. CARTER. That's right. And we were fortunate to get the extension. And I hope that in the next 3 years, we can ratify it.

THE PRESIDENT. And I believe we can. Don't you?

MRS. CARTER. I'm hopeful, I'm very hopeful.

Ms. WALTERS. At the mini-convention, there was a resolution that didn't come to the floor at the mini Democratic convention and that is to push for—that the next Supreme Court Justice be a woman. Are you pushing for that? Is that on your top priority, Mrs. Carter?

MRS. CARTER. Well, the opportunity has not arisen yet. [*Laughter*] But I agree with the resolution.

Ms. WALTERS. You do?

PEOPLE'S REPUBLIC OF CHINA

Mr. President, any plans to travel? We know you're going to Guadeloupe. Any plans perhaps to go to China in 1979—so many different things happening there, many different new positions.

THE PRESIDENT. Barbara, the position that I've taken is that both President Nixon and President Ford have gone to China. The Chinese leaders have not seen fit to come here. And I don't intend to go to China until after the Chinese leaders come here.

Ms. WALTERS. Do the changes in China, which seems to be even to a small degree a somewhat more democratic process, allow you to think that we may have any changes in our policy in 1979?

THE PRESIDENT. We have already made great improvements in our relationships with China in recent months because of the changes you describe, with trade missions, increased relationships in research, development, exploration of energy possibilities with them jointly, primarily with the private business community in our own Nation, agricultural assessments, their visits here. This year there are large numbers of Chinese students who will come to our country and to others, which was not the case in the past. So, I think that the opening up of China is beneficial to our country and to the world. I'm very pleased with it.

Ms. Walters. But you don't expect full diplomatic relations in the next year—or do you?

The President. Well, that's something that we are pursuing in accordance with the Shanghai Communique. Our position has been made clear to Premier Hua and Deputy Premier Teng, and whenever the Chinese are ready to move, we are.

BERT LANCE

Ms. Walters. Mr. President, at the opening of this program, we talked about disappointments, possible disappointments that you might contribute to the American people. And you felt that there were not. But in your personal life, one of the disappointments that we're all aware of must have been what happened to your good friend, Mr. Lance.

The President. Yes.

Ms. Walters. In view of the fact that these investigations continue into allegations of possible misdeeds or illegalities, would you still give him your unqualified support, as you did a year ago?

The President. Yes, I would.

Ms. Walters. Would you still say you were proud of him, as you did a year ago?

The President. I am proud of him. Bert is a fine, decent human being. He has probably been investigated with as concentrated an effort as anyone who's ever served in government, with the possible exception of President Nixon during the Watergate trials.

And I don't know anything about the details of the investigations, the technicalities of the law, and so forth. But Bert

did some things which he's acknowledged, like using the bank's airplane, along with customers, to go to the Sugar Bowl game when the University of Georgia played there. It was a technical violation of the law. I'm not trying to make a judgment on what the investigations will reveal. But I know Bert Lance, have confidence in him, and I hope the investigations prove that he is not guilty of any violation of the law, whether technical or otherwise.

Mrs. Carter. He's just a good person.

The President. He really is.

1976 PRESIDENTIAL CAMPAIGN

Ms. Walters. Would you like to clear up a whispered allegation——

The President. Okay, I'll try.

Ms. Walters. ——is this a good time——

The President. Sure.

Ms. Walters. ——just before Christmas, when people are feeling generous? Your peanut business enjoyed a $5 million line of credit from Mr. Lance's bank.

The President. Yes.

Ms. Walters. Now, during the course of the grand jury investigation, there have been some whispered suggestions that some of this money may have found its way illegally into your Presidential campaign. I'm sure you've heard this.

The President. That is absolutely false.

Mrs. Carter. Absolutely.

Ms. Walters. I just wanted to give you the opportunity to assure the American people.

The President. Absolutely false. Every source of money that came into our campaign has been thoroughly revealed, I think, on a monthly basis, all during the campaign. And we never were inclined to put warehouse money into the campaign at all. As a matter of fact, I have a lot more of my personal money in the warehouse than I needed to and it was never taken out for that purpose.

BILLY CARTER

Ms. WALTERS. How did you feel, Mr. President, when your brother Billy told reporters that he took the fifth amendment before a grand jury investigation into the banking securities of Bert Lance? There's brother Billy again.

THE PRESIDENT. If there's one thing I can say, I have enough responsibility trying to be the President of the United States than to be my brother Billy's keeper. He's got a mind of his own and a voice of his own.

I have never discussed this with Billy, because I've pledged to stay away from my business affairs while I'm President. But his explanation was that he was asked by the grand jury to bring records for certain dates of negotiations and business transactions. And when the grand jury asked him about data from other dates of the year, where he didn't have the records, that's when he refused to answer the questions. I presume that's accurate.

VIEWS ON THE PRESIDENCY

Ms. WALTERS. Let's end this section on a happier note. As you look back on these past 2 years, what—if you had to write it in a book, in that first chapter—and I said the happiest day——

THE PRESIDENT. The happiest?

Ms. WALTERS. Yes.

THE PRESIDENT. Well, I think the happiest day was when we came back from Camp David with the agreement.

MRS. CARTER. I think that would have to be.

THE PRESIDENT. And perhaps the unhappiest day was earlier that day—[laugh-

ter]—3 hours before we left Camp David, when I thought the whole thing had failed. So, there were ups and downs then.

But in general, our first 2 years in the White House have been very pleasant, and there's a warmth here brought about by history, by our own family relationship, and by my relationship with the American people, which we deeply appreciate and enjoy. And I hope the whole Nation and the whole world will have the same warmth of spirit, love for one another, commitment to peace and harmony and the realization of the ideals of our country as Christmas approaches, that I feel now in the White House.

Ms. WALTERS. We'll be back with just one more question, Mrs. Carter, Mr. President.

———

Mr. President, Mrs. Carter, we have one final question. The day you left Plains, Georgia, January 19, 1977, still a private citizen but on your way to your inauguration, our White House correspondent, Sam Donaldson—you know Sam Donaldson—asked if you thought you would be a great President. And you answered, "Yes, I will be. I am going to be a great President."

It is now 2 years later, Mr. Carter. Are you a great President?

THE PRESIDENT. [Laughing] Well, one of the things that prepared me for the difficulties and the challenges and the vicissitudes of being President was Sam Donaldson's constant questions during the campaign for 2 years. [Laughter]

Ms. WALTERS. He'll be delighted to hear that.

THE PRESIDENT. They're always difficult to answer.

It's much too early for me to say whether I'll be a good or a great President. That's still my determination and my goal, not for historical glory, but just to make sure that our Nation is greater because I've been President.

I've not given up on it. But it's too early to make that judgment.

MRS. CARTER. I think he's a great President. I think he's going to be a great President. He's strong and courageous and competent. And I think people already see that he fights for what he believes in. He doesn't worry about political consequences. I just think he's a great President already.

THE PRESIDENT. You can see why I love her. [*Laughter*]

MS. WALTERS. I can see why there are many people who are going to be particularly happy that you joined this interview. I wish you happy holidays, and I thank you for being with us today.

THE PRESIDENT. Same to you, Barbara. Thank you.

MRS. CARTER. I enjoyed it.

NOTE: The interview began at 9:32 a.m. in the Green Room at the White House. It was taped for later broadcast on the ABC television network.

Provision of Electronic Communications Services by the United States Postal Service

Announcement of an Administration Policy Study. December 15, 1978

The President has directed Stuart Eizenstat, his assistant for domestic policy, to conduct a formal study to determine the administration's policy regarding the future role of the U.S. Postal Service in providing services by electronic communications. The study is directed toward developing a policy by early spring

so that the administration will be prepared to respond definitively to the congressional committees which are expected to address this matter during the next session.

The following specific policy areas will be addressed:

—the possible future benefits to the Nation of Postal Service involvement in electronic message services and the potential costs to the Nation of establishing Postal Service competition in an industry that has previously been restricted to private competition;

—the impact of electronic communications on postal operations and revenues (both with and without USPS electronic services) and the overall economic impact, including potential reduction in postal costs, of a USPS investment in an electronic system; and

—the options for interconnection between the Postal Service physical delivery network and the electronic message industry.

An interagency coordinating committee, chaired by Eizenstat, met for the first time on December 13 to define the issues to be addressed to establish the administration's position. The Postal Service is represented on the committee and will assist in obtaining the necessary data and related considerations.

The Commerce Department's National Telecommunications and Information Administration, under Henry Geller, will act as lead staff agency for the study. Other departments and agencies represented on the committee are: the Departments of the Treasury, Justice, Agriculture, Commerce, and Labor; the Council of Economic Advisers; the Council on Wage and Price Stability; the National Aeronautics and Space Administration;

and the Office of Management and Budget. In addition, the written views of labor, industry, and the general public will be solicited.

Advisory Committee for Trade Negotiations

Appointment of Glenn E. Watts as a Member. December 15, 1978

The President today announced the appointment of Glenn E. Watts, of Chevy Chase, Md., as a member of the Advisory Committee for Trade Negotiations.

Watts is president of the Communications Workers of America and a member of the executive council of the AFL–CIO.

Board of Foreign Scholarships

Appointment of Four Members. December 15, 1978

The President today announced the appointment of four persons as members of the Board of Foreign Scholarships for 3-year terms. They are:

JEWEL PLUMMER COBB, dean of the college and professor of biological science at Douglass College, Rutgers University, New Brunswick, N.J. (reappointment);

WALTER A. ROSENBLITH, of Brookline, Mass., a provost and institute professor of communications biophysics at Massachusetts Institute of Technology, a fellow of the National Academy of Sciences;

SUSANNE H. RUDOLPH, professor and chair of the department of political science at the University of Chicago, an expert on South Asia;

ALFRED L. STERN, a professor in the division of humanistic studies and the division of natural sciences at Monteith College, Wayne State University, in Detroit, currently on leave serving as Associate Director of the White House Domestic Policy Staff.

Diplomatic Relations Between the United States and the People's Republic of China

Address to the Nation. December 15, 1978

Good evening.

I would like to read a joint communique which is being simultaneously issued in Peking at this very moment by the leaders of the People's Republic of China:

[*At this point, the President read the text of the joint communique, which reads as follows:*]

JOINT COMMUNIQUE ON THE ESTABLISHMENT OF DIPLOMATIC RELATIONS BETWEEN THE UNITED STATES OF AMERICA AND THE PEOPLE'S REPUBLIC OF CHINA

JANUARY 1, 1979

The United States of America and the People's Republic of China have agreed to recognize each other and to establish diplomatic relations as of January 1, 1979.

The United States of America recognizes the Government of the People's Republic of China as the sole legal Government of China. Within this context, the people of the United States will maintain cultural, commercial, and other unofficial relations with the people of Taiwan.

The United States of America and the People's Republic of China reaffirm the principles agreed on by the two sides in the Shanghai Communique and emphasize once again that:

—Both wish to reduce the danger of international military conflict.

—Neither should seek hegemony in the Asia-Pacific region or in any other region of the world and each is opposed to efforts by any other country or group of countries to establish such hegemony.

—Neither is prepared to negotiate on behalf of any third party or to enter into agreements or understandings with the other directed at other states.

—The Government of the United States of America acknowledges the Chinese position that there is but one China and Taiwan is part of China.

—Both believe that normalization of Sino-American relations is not only in the interest of the Chinese and American peoples but also contributes to the cause of peace in Asia and the world.

The United States of America and the People's Republic of China will exchange Ambassadors and establish Embassies on March 1, 1979.

Yesterday, our country and the People's Republic of China reached this final historic agreement. On January 1, 1979, a little more than 2 weeks from now, our two Governments will implement full normalization of diplomatic relations.

As a nation of gifted people who comprise about one-fourth of the total population of the Earth, China plays, already, an important role in world affairs, a role that can only grow more important in the years ahead.

We do not undertake this important step for transient tactical or expedient reasons. In recognizing the People's Republic of China, that it is the single Government of China, we are recognizing simple reality. But far more is involved in this decision than just the recognition of a fact.

Before the estrangement of recent decades, the American and the Chinese people had a long history of friendship. We've already begun to rebuild some of those previous ties. Now our rapidly expanding relationship requires the kind of structure that only full diplomatic relations will make possible.

The change that I'm announcing tonight will be of great long-term benefit to the peoples of both our country and China—and, I believe, to all the peoples of the world. Normalization—and the expanded commercial and cultural relations that it will bring—will contribute to the well-being of our own Nation, to our own national interest, and it will also enhance the stability of Asia. These more

positive relations with China can beneficially affect the world in which we live and the world in which our children will live.

We have already begun to inform our allies and other nations and the Members of the Congress of the details of our intended action. But I wish also tonight to convey a special message to the people of Taiwan—I have already communicated with the leaders in Taiwan—with whom the American people have had and will have extensive, close, and friendly relations. This is important between our two peoples.

As the United States asserted in the Shanghai Communique of 1972, issued on President Nixon's historic visit, we will continue to have an interest in the peaceful resolution of the Taiwan issue. I have paid special attention to ensuring that normalization of relations between our country and the People's Republic will not jeopardize the well-being of the people of Taiwan. The people of our country will maintain our current commercial, cultural, trade, and other relations with Taiwan through nongovernmental means. Many other countries in the world are already successfully doing this.

These decisions and these actions open a new and important chapter in our country's history and also in world affairs.

To strengthen and to expedite the benefits of this new relationship between China and the United States, I am pleased to announce that Vice Premier Teng has accepted my invitation and will visit Washington at the end of January. His visit will give our Governments the opportunity to consult with each other on global issues and to begin working together to enhance the cause of world peace.

These events are the final result of long and serious negotiations begun by President Nixon in 1972, and continued under the leadership of President Ford. The results bear witness to the steady, determined, bipartisan effort of our own country to build a world in which peace will be the goal and the responsibility of all nations.

The normalization of relations between the United States and China has no other purpose than this: the advancement of peace. It is in this spirit, at this season of peace, that I take special pride in sharing this good news with you tonight.

Thank you very much.

NOTE: The President spoke at 9 p.m. from the Oval Office at the White House. The address was broadcast live on radio and television.

Diplomatic Relations Between the United States and the People's Republic of China

United States Statement.   December 15, 1978

As of January 1, 1979, the United States of America recognizes the People's Republic of China as the sole legal government of China. On the same date, the People's Republic of China accords similar recognition to the United States of America. The United States thereby establishes diplomatic relations with the People's Republic of China.

On that same date, January 1, 1979, the United States of America will notify Taiwan that it is terminating diplomatic relations and that the Mutual Defense Treaty between the United States and the Republic of China is being terminated in accordance with the provisions of the Treaty. The United States also states that it will be withdrawing its remaining military personnel from Taiwan within four months.

In the future, the American people and the people of Taiwan will maintain commercial, cultural, and other relations without official government representation and without diplomatic relations.

The Administration will seek adjustments to our laws and regulations to permit the maintenance of commercial, cultural, and other non-governmental relationships in the new circumstances that will exist after normalization.

The United States is confident that the people of Taiwan face a peaceful and prosperous future. The United States continues to have an interest in the peaceful resolution of the Taiwan issue and expects that the Taiwan issue will be settled peacefully by the Chinese themselves.

The United States believes that the establishment of diplomatic relations with the People's Republic will contribute to the welfare of the American people, to the stability of Asia where the United States has major security and economic interest, and to the peace of the entire world.

Diplomatic Relations Between the United States and the People's Republic of China

Remarks at a White House Briefing Following the Address to the Nation.
December 15, 1978

THE PRESIDENT. Well, I wanted to come by and let you know that I believe this to be an extremely important moment in the history of our Nation. It's something that I and my two predecessors have sought avidly. We have maintained our own United States position firmly, and only since the last few weeks has there been an increasing demonstration to us that Premier Hua and Vice Premier Teng have been ready to normalize relations. I think the interests of Taiwan have been adequately protected. One of the briefers will explain the details to you.

Our Ambassador there, Leonard Woodcock, has done a superb job in presenting our own views strongly and clearly to the officials of the People's Republic of China. I will be preparing myself adequately for the visit of Vice Premier Teng. We invited him on one day, he accepted the next, without delay, and I think he's looking forward to this trip with a great deal of anticipation and pleasure.

I have talked personally this evening to Prime Minister Ohira [of Japan]. Early this morning we notified the officials in Taiwan, and we have also notified many of the leaders around the world of this long-awaited development in international diplomacy.

I think that one of the greatest benefits that will be derived from this is the continuation of strong trade, cultural relationships with Taiwan, the people of Taiwan, and a new vista for prosperous trade relationships with almost a billion people in the People's Republic of China. This is also, of course, enhanced by the new opportunities for us to understand the people of China, and to work avidly for peace in that region and for world peace.

This afternoon the Soviet Union officials were notified through their Ambassador here, Mr. Dobrynin. And I think the Soviets were familiar with the fact that we were anticipating normalization whenever the Chinese were willing to meet our reasonable terms, and they were not surprised. As you well know, the Soviet Union and People's Republic of China have diplomatic relations between themselves.

My own assessment is that this will be well received in almost every nation of the world, perhaps all of them, because

it will add to stability. And the Soviets and others know full well, because of our own private explanations to them, not just recently but in months gone by, that we have no desire whatsover to use our new relationships with China to the disadvantage of the Soviets or anyone else. We believe this will enhance stability and not cause instability in Asia and the rest of the world.

I'm very pleased with it. And I obviously have to give a major part of the credit to President Nixon and to President Ford, who laid the groundwork for this successful negotiation. And most of the premises that were spelled out in the Shanghai Communique 6 years ago or more have been implemented now.

You can tell that I'm pleased, and I know that the world is waiting for your accurate explanation of the results.

Q. How did the congressional leaders take it?

THE PRESIDENT. With mixed response. Some of the congressional leaders who were there have long been very strong personal friends of the officials in Taiwan. They are not as thoroughly familiar with the officials in the People's Republic of China.

One of the most long debated issues was whether or not we would peremptorily terminate our defense treaty with Taiwan, or whether we would terminate that treaty in accordance with its own provisions. And the People's Republic officials agreed with our position that we would give Taiwan a 1-year notice and that the defense treaty would prevail throughout 1979. I think that alleviated some of the concerns among the Senators.

And another concern expressed by them was whether or not we could continue cultural relationships, trade relationships with the people of Taiwan. I assured them that we could, that the Chinese knew this. And we will ask the Congress for special legislation quite early in the session to permit this kind of exchange with the people of Taiwan. This would include authorization for the Eximbank and OPEC to guarantee and to help with specific trade negotiations.

I think that many of their concerns have been alleviated, although there certainly will be some Members of the Congress who feel that we should have maintained the status quo.

I'll take just one question.

Q. Mr. President, you said the response to your speech would be "massive applause throughout the Nation." What do you think the response to your speech will be in Taiwan?

THE PRESIDENT. I doubt if there will be massive applause in Taiwan, but we are going to do everything we can to assure the Taiwanese that we put at top— as one of the top priorities in our own relationships with the People's Republic and them—that the well-being of the people of Taiwan will not be damaged.

To answer the other question, I don't think this will have any adverse effect at all on the SALT negotiations as an independent matter. And I think that the Soviets, as I said earlier, have been expecting this development. They were not surprised, and we have kept them informed recently. Their reaction has not been adverse, and we will proceed aggressively as we have in recent months, in fact throughout my own administration, to conclude a successful SALT agreement.

Good night.

NOTE: The President spoke at approximately 9:30 p.m. to reporters assembled in the Briefing Room at the White House. Following his remarks, administration officials held the background briefing on the announcement.

Digest of Other White House Announcements

The following listing includes the President's daily schedule and other items of general interest as announced by the White House Press Office during the period covered by this issue. Events and announcements printed elsewhere in the issue are not included.

December 9

The President announced the members of the delegation to the funeral of former Israeli Prime Minister Golda Meir. They are:

MRS. LILLIAN CARTER, Personal Representative of the President;

CYRUS R. VANCE, U.S. Secretary of State;

MRS. CYRUS VANCE;

SAMUEL W. LEWIS, U.S. Ambassador to Israel;

MRS. SAMUEL W. LEWIS;

JACOB K. JAVITS, U.S. Senator from New York;

ABRAHAM RIBICOFF, U.S. Senator from Connecticut;

DANIEL PATRICK MOYNIHAN, U.S. Senator from New York;

MURIEL HUMPHREY, U.S. Senator from Minnesota;

CLEMENT ZABLOCKI, U.S. Representative from Wisconsin;

SIDNEY R. YATES, U.S. Representative from Illinois;

LEE H. HAMILTON, U.S. Representative from Indiana;

CHARLES RANGEL, U.S. Representative from New York;

BENJAMIN A. GILMAN, U.S. Representative from New York;

STEPHEN J. SOLARZ, U.S. Representative from New York;

ALFRED L. ATHERTON, JR., Ambassador at Large;

HENRY A. KISSINGER, former U.S. Secretary of State;

ARTHUR GOLDBERG, former Associate Justice of the U.S. Supreme Court;

HAROLD H. SAUNDERS, Assistant U.S. Secretary of State;

CARL LEVIN, U.S. Senator-elect from Michigan;

ROBERT GRAHAM, Governor-elect from Florida;

HENRY WALTER MAIER, mayor of Milwaukee;

EDMUND EDELMAN, supervisor, third district, Los Angeles County, Calif.;

SOL C. CHAIKIN, president of the International Ladies' Garment Workers Union, New York City;

BISHOP JOSEPH C. COLES, presiding bishop of the Georgia Area Christian Methodist Episcopal Church, Atlanta, Ga.;

IRWIN S. FIELD, national chairman, United Jewish Appeal, Los Angeles, Calif.;

CHARLOTTE JACOBSON, chairman, World Zionist Organization, American section, New York City;

MAX M. KAMPELMAN, attorney, Washington, D.C.;

ISAIAH L. KENEN, honorary chairman of the American-Israel Public Affairs Committee and editor emeritus, "Near East Report," Washington, D.C.;

STANLEY LOWELL, attorney; immediate past chairman, National Conference on Soviet Jewry; former deputy mayor of New York City;

THEODORE MANN, president of the Conference of Presidents of Major Jewish Organizations, Philadelphia;

GORDON A. MARTIN, JR., attorney, Boston;

RABBI ISRAEL MILLER, vice president of Yeshiva University, New York City;

SAM ROTHBERG, general chairman, Israel Bond Association, Peoria, Ill.;

RABBI HENRY SEIGMAN, executive director, American Jewish Congress, New York City;

MRS. REBECCA SHULMAN, former national president of Hadassah, New York City;

MRS. ISAAC STERN, first vice president of the American Israel Cultural Foundation, New York City;

MARIE SYRKIN, professor emeritus of Brandeis University, now of Los Angeles, Calif.;

MRS. NELLIE WHITE, wife of John White, chairman of the Democratic National Committee, Washington, D.C.;

WILLIAM WINN, president of the Retail Clerks International Association, Washington, D.C.;

MRS. HARRIET ZIMMERMAN, community leader, Atlanta, Ga.;

EDWARD SANDERS, senior adviser to the President and the Secretary of State.

December 10

The President and Mrs. Carter attended the world premiere of the film "Superman," which was shown at the Eisenhower Theater at the John F. Kennedy Center for the Performing Arts in conjunction with a benefit for the Special Olympics.

December 11

The President met at the White House with:

—Zbigniew Brzezinski, Assistant to the President for National Security Affairs;

—the Cabinet;

—Benjamin L. Hooks, executive director, and members of the board of directors of the National Association for the Advancement of Colored People;

—Vice President Walter F. Mondale;

—a group of administration officials to discuss the fiscal year 1980 budget;

—Secretary of Transportation Brock Adams.

December 12

The President met at the White House with:

—Dr. Brzezinski;

—Vice President Mondale, Adm. Stansfield Turner, Director of Central Intelligence, Hamilton Jordan, Assistant to the President, and Dr. Brzezinski;

—Mrs. Carter, for lunch;

—the Intergovernmental Task Force on Water Policy;

—former President Gerald R. Ford.

The President declared a major disaster for the Commonwealth of Kentucky as a result of severe storms and flooding, beginning about December 7, which caused extensive public and private property damage.

December 13

The President met at the White House with Dr. Brzezinski.

December 14

The President met at the White House with:

—Dr. Brzezinski;

—Vice President Mondale, Secretary of the Treasury W. Michael Blumenthal, G. William Miller, Chairman of the Board of Directors, Federal Reserve System, James T. McIntyre, Jr., Director of the Office of Management and Budget, and Charles L. Schultze, Chairman of the Council of Economic Advisers;

—the General Advisory Committee of the United States Arms Control and Disarmament Agency.

The President declared a major disaster for the State of West Virginia as a result of severe storms and flooding, beginning about December 7, which caused extensive public and private property damage.

December 15

The President met at the White House with:

—Vice President Mondale, Secretary of Defense Harold Brown, Dr. Brzezinski, and Mr. Jordan;

—Dr. Brzezinski;

—a group of administration officials to discuss the fiscal year 1980 budget;

—Secretary of State Cyrus R. Vance.

The President received the report of Emergency Board No. 188, which was appointed on September 28 by Executive Order 12085.

The President greeted guests attending the 30th wedding anniversary dinner for Mr. and Mrs. G. C. Davis, Jr., in the State Dining Room at the White House. The Davises are the parents of Annette Carter, the President's daughter-in-law.

The President left the White House for a weekend stay at Camp David, Md.

NOMINATIONS SUBMITTED TO THE SENATE

NOTE: The Congress having adjourned *sine die* on Sunday, October 15, no nominations were submitted during the period covered by this issue. The first session of the 96th Congress will begin on Monday, January 15, 1979.

CHECKLIST OF WHITE HOUSE PRESS RELEASES

The following releases of the Office of the White House Press Secretary, distributed during the period covered by this issue, are not included in the issue.

Released December 8, 1978

Advance text: remarks at the opening session of the 1978 National Democratic Party Conference

Released December 13, 1978

Advance text: remarks at the National Conference on Fraud, Abuse and Error

News conference: on administration initiatives to eliminate fraud and waste in Federal Government programs—by James T. McIntyre, Jr., Director of the Office of Management and Budget

Released December 15, 1978

Announcement: report submittal to the President by Emergency Board No. 188

ACTS APPROVED BY THE PRESIDENT

NOTE: The President completed his consideration of acts and joint resolutions passed during the second session of the 95th Congress on November 10.

PRESIDENTIAL DOCUMENTS

Week Ending Friday, December 22, 1978

Organization of Petroleum Exporting Countries

White House Statement on the Organization's Increase in Oil Prices. December 17, 1978

We regret the OPEC decision and hope that it will be reconsidered before the next steps take effect.

Market conditions do not warrant a price increase of this magnitude, since the current tightness in the world oil market is a temporary situation that does not reflect underlying demand forces.

This large price hike will impede programs to maintain world economic recovery and to reduce inflation. Responsibility for the success of these programs is shared by the oil-producing countries.

NOTE: Earlier, representatives of the member countries meeting in Abu Dhabi, United Arab Emirates, had voted to increase oil prices at 3-month intervals to a total of 14.5 percent by the end of 1979.

Imports of Papermaking Machinery From Finland

Proclamation 4630.   December 15, 1978

REDUCTION OF RATES OF DUTY ON CERTAIN PAPERMAKING MACHINERY

By the President of the United States of America

A Proclamation

Under the Geneva (1967) Protocol to the General Agreement on Tariffs and Trade (GATT), the United States agreed to staged reductions in duty rates on machines for making cellulosic pulp, paper, or paperboard, and parts thereof provided for in items 668.00 and 668.06 of the Tariff Schedules of the United States (TSUS) (19 U.S.C. 1202).

On December 16, 1967, the President modified (in Proclamation No. 3822) the TSUS in order to carry out the Geneva Protocol including staged reductions of column 1 duty rates to 3.5 percent ad valorem on machines for making cellulosic pulp, paper, or paperboard, and parts thereof.

The Republic of Finland has benefitted from those tariff reductions. As a result of a March 13, 1978 ruling by the United States Customs Service the benefits contemplated to accrue to the Republic of Finland from these tariff reductions were substantially reduced.

The restoration of the contemplated benefits of these tariff reductions to the Republic of Finland would promote the foreign trade of the United States and the Republic of Finland. Pursuant to Section 101(a) of the Trade Act of 1974 (the Trade Act) (19 U.S.C. 2111(a)), I have determined that certain existing duties of the United States are unduly burdening and restricting the foreign trade of the United States and that one or more purposes of the Trade Act would be promoted by entering into a trade agreement with the Republic of Finland and restoring those contemplated benefits.

Having complied with the provisions of the Trade Act, including Sections 131 (a), 132, and 133, I have, through my duly empowered representative, on July 21, 1978, entered into a trade agreement with the Republic of Finland entitled "Agreement Supplementary to the General Agreement on Tariffs and Trade" which restores the tariff concessions on certain papermaking machinery and parts thereof affected by the March 13, 1978 United States Customs Service ruling, and which provides that such new concessions shall be applied as if they were included in part I of Schedule XX to the GATT, with the understanding that as soon as practicable these new concessions will be specifically included in Schedule XX.

Now, THEREFORE, I, JIMMY CARTER, President of the United States of America, by the authority vested in me by the Constitution and the statutes of the United States of America, including Sections 101 and 604 of the Trade Act of 1974 (19 U.S.C. 2111 and 2483), and Article II, paragraph 5, of the GATT (61 Stat. (pt. 5) A16) do hereby proclaim:

(1) The TSUS are modified as provided in the Annex to this Proclamation.

(2) Part 1 of Schedule XX to the GATT is modified to conform with the modifications of the TSUS set forth in the Annex to this Proclamation.

(3) The modifications made by this Proclamation shall be effective as to articles entered, or withdrawn, from warehouse, for consumption on or after March 13, 1978, and as to which the liquidations of the entries or withdrawals have not become final and conclusive under Section 514 of the Tariff Act of 1930 (19 U.S.C. 1514).

IN WITNESS WHEREOF, I have hereunto set my hand this fifteenth day of December, in the year of our Lord nineteen hundred seventy-eight, and of the Independence of the United States of America the two hundred and third.

JIMMY CARTER

[Filed with the Office of the Federal Register, 12:03 p.m., December 18, 1978]

NOTE: The annex is printed in the FEDERAL REGISTER of December 19, 1978.

The text of the proclamation was released on December 18.

Imports of Papermaking Machinery From Finland

Executive Order 12104. December 15, 1978

AMENDING THE GENERALIZED SYSTEM OF PREFERENCES

By the authority vested in me as President by the Constitution and statutes of the United States of America, including Title V and Section 604 of the Trade Act of 1974 (88 Stat. 2066, 19 U.S.C. 2461 *et seq.*; 88 Stat. 2073, 19 U.S.C 2483), in order to make conforming changes to the Generalized System of Preferences (GSP) to reflect changes to the Tariff Schedules of the United States proclaimed by me to implement a trade agreement between the United States and Finland entered into on July 21, 1978, it is hereby ordered as follows:

1–101. Annex II of Executive Order No. 11888 of November 24, 1975, as amended, listing articles that are eligible for benefits of GSP when imported from any designated developing country, is further amended by deleting TSUS item numbers 660.94, 661.55, 661.70, and

680.45, and by adding, in numerical sequence, item numbers 660.96, 660.97, 661.54, 661.56, 661.67, 661.68, 680.43, and 680.44.

1–102. The amendments made by this Order shall be effective with respect to articles entered, or withdrawn from warehouse, for consumption on or after March 13, 1978, and as to which the liquidation of the entries or withdrawals have not become final and conclusive under Section 514 of the Tariff Act of 1930 (19 U.S.C. 1514).

JIMMY CARTER

The White House,
    December 15, 1978.

[Filed with the Office of the Federal Register, 12:04 p.m., December 18, 1978]

NOTE: The text of the Executive order was released on December 18.

March of Dimes Birth Defects Prevention Month, January 1979

Statement by the President.
December 18, 1978

Fifteen million persons in America today have birth defects. Low birthweight is the most common root of such problems. It is not only the leading cause of infant mortality in this country, but also a major factor in disability during childhood. Thanks to the medical progress we have made, newborns weighing less than two and one-half pounds now have an almost fifty percent chance of survival. Only a few years ago their chances were less than twenty percent. But even with greatly improved newborn intensive care, many survivors are physically and men-

tally scarred for life. With proper nutrition and adequate care during pregnancy, low birthweight, like so many birth defects, can very often be prevented.

Another 200,000 babies are born each year with structural or metabolic defects. In addition, many disabling and life-shortening disorders have their origin during pregnancy and birth. Many times these are not thought of as birth defects because symptoms may not appear until later in life.

It is my hope that during 1979, the International Year of the Child, we will marshal our best efforts to make reproductive health the focus of our priority national attention. We must assure every child the right to a healthy start in life. We must join with other nations of the world in protecting the well-being of children—the most precious resource of all.

Prevention of birth defects has long been the special mission of the March of Dimes. In every community of this country the March of Dimes has initiated educational and medical service programs to protect the unborn and newborn. It has increased the availability of prenatal care, started and supported programs to improve maternal nutrition, created a nationwide group of genetic centers and established and assisted newborn intensive care units. It has built a productive partnership with the community, the professions and government at all levels—and proved how much can be accomplished by such a cooperative effort.

As we observe January 1979 as March of Dimes Birth Defects Prevention Month, let us thank the March of Dimes for its critical leadership in this vital task, and let us strengthen our national commitment to our children and to their entry into life with a health future.

NOTE: The President signed the statement at an Oval Office ceremony attended by Melanie Brockington, March of Dimes Poster Child, and members of her family. Also present were Charles Marsey, president, and Harry Green, chairman of the board of directors of the National Foundation of the March of Dimes.

Christmas 1978

Message of the President.
December 18, 1978

Rosalynn and I send our warmest wishes to our fellow citizens who celebrate the birth of Christ and who rejoice with us in the coming of the peace He symbolizes.

We welcome this opportunity to offer our thanks to those who have given us their encouragement and prayers.

We also join in this Season's traditional expression of appreciation to God for His blessings in the past year. And we ask for His continuing guidance and protection as we face the challenges of 1979.

We hope that the months ahead will be good to each of you and to our country.

JIMMY CARTER

National Historical Publications and Records Commission

Appointment of John G. Lorenz as a Member. December 19, 1978

The President today announced the appointment of John G. Lorenz, of Bethesda, Md., as a member of the National Historical Publications and Records Commission.

Lorenz, 63, is executive director of the Association of Research Libraries. He is a former Deputy Librarian of Congress.

Garnishment of Moneys Payable to Employees of Executive Agencies and the District of Columbia

Executive Order 12105.   December 19, 1978

By virtue of the authority vested in me by Section 461(a)(1) of the Social Security Act, as added by Section 501(c) of the Tax Reduction and Simplification Act of 1977 (Public Law 95–30, 91 Stat. 158, 42 U.S.C. 661(a)(1)), and Section 301 of Title 3 of the United States Code, and as President of the United States of America, in order to provide for the enforcement of legal obligations to provide child support or make alimony payments incurred by employees of the Executive branch, it is hereby ordered as follows:

1–1.   *Delegation of Authority.*

1–101. The United States Civil Service Commission, in consultation with the Attorney General, the Secretary of Defense with respect to members of the armed forces, and the Mayor of the District of Columbia with respect to employees of the Government thereof, is authorized to promulgate regulations for the uniform implementation of Section 459 of the Social Security Act, as amended (42 U.S.C. 659), hereinafter referred to as the Act.

1–102. The regulations promulgated by the United States Civil Service Commission pursuant to this Order shall:

(a) Be applicable to the Executive branch of the Government as defined in Section 461(a)(1) of the Act (42 U.S.C. 661(a)(1)).

(b) Require the appropriate officials of the Executive branch of the Government to take the actions prescribed by Sections 461(b)(1), 461(b)(3)(A) and 461(c) of the Act (42 U.S.C. 661(b)(1), 661(b)(3)(A) and 661(c)).

(c) Require the appropriate officials of the Executive branch of the Government to issue such rules, regulations and directives as are necessary to implement the regulations of the United States Civil Service Commission.

1–2. *Revocations.*

1–201. Executive Order No. 11881 of October 3, 1975 is revoked.

1–202. All regulations, directives, or actions taken by the United States Civil Service Commission pursuant to Executive Order No. 11881 of October 3, 1975 shall remain in effect until modified, superseded or revoked by the United States Civil Service Commission pursuant to this Order.

JIMMY CARTER

The White House,
    December 19, 1978.

[Filed with the Office of the Federal Register, 10:52 a.m., December 20, 1978]

Diplomatic Relations Between the United States and the People's Republic of China

Interview With Walter Cronkite of the Columbia Broadcasting System. December 19, 1978

TAIWAN

MR. CRONKITE. We have no commitment from Peking that it will not use force to take Taiwan. Secretary of State Vance has said only that we have the expectation that it will not. But if the present Peking Government or some future Peking Government tried to reunify Taiwan by force, would we feel free to use force to help Taiwan resist?

THE PRESIDENT. In the first place, the People's Republic of China does not have the capability of launching a 120-mile attack across the ocean against Taiwan, who are heavily fortified and also heavily armed. And we have made it clear to the People's Republic that after this year, when the treaty does expire, this coming year, that we will sell to Taiwan defensive weapons.

I think it is accurate to say also, Walter, that the major interest that the People's Republic of China has in the Western Pacific is peace and good relationships with us. They know our firm expectations, clearly expressed to them, that the differences between China and Taiwan will be settled peacefully. And I think to violate that understanding with us would be to wipe out all the benefits to them and to Asia of peace and their new relationship with us.

We have, obviously, a desire and a commitment to maintain peace in the Western Pacific. And as would be the case with an altercation between any two peoples, we would certainly be deeply concerned. But I don't want to speculate on under what circumstances we might take military action because I think it's an absolutely unnecessary speculation, because the people of China want peace, they want good relationships with us, and because Taiwan is so strong and will stay strong.

MR. CRONKITE. Well, clearly, if the situation changed drastically in our relations with any of these two other units, the Chinese Government and Taiwan, we can take a new look at the situation, I suppose.

THE PRESIDENT. That's always an option. And I think, as you know, political circumstances change around the world constantly, and we would have to reassess them as they do occur. But I don't have any doubt that we made the right decision. We have made our intentions and our expectations clear to the people of China and to Taiwan.

My reports from Taiwan, in the last day or few hours, has been that they studied the agreements with the People's Republic, that their original concerns have been substantially alleviated, and I don't think that the people of Taiwan are any more concerned about future peace than they were before. In addition, we will maintain trade relationships, cultural relationships with the people of Taiwan, as has been the case in the past.

SOVIET REACTION TO ANNOUNCEMENT

MR. CRONKITE. Have you had any recent conversations with any Soviet officials or have you heard from Moscow as to what their reaction is in the last few hours, bringing us up to date?

THE PRESIDENT. Yes, I've had a personal message delivered to me this afternoon from President Brezhnev expressing his understanding that our commitment is to peace in the entire world, acknowledging the fact that the American position is that our new relationship with the People's Republic of China will contribute to world peace, and acknowledging the fact that the proper relationship between major sovereign nations is to have full diplomatic relations.

So, I would characterize his personal message to me as being very positive in tone. And I can say without any doubt that our new relationship with China will not put any additional obstacles in the way of a successful SALT agreement and also will not endanger our good relationships with the Soviet Union.

VISITS BY CHINESE AND SOVIET LEADERS

MR. CRONKITE. What about the slight protocol problem of timing visits from Teng Hsiao-p'ing, the Vice Chairman, who's due here from Peking on January 29, and a possible visit from Chairman Brezhnev to sign a SALT agreement? Can Chairman Brezhnev come after Teng has been here?

THE PRESIDENT. I can't set the schedule for him. My hope is that President Brezhnev would come before Mr. Teng comes to Washington.

As you know, Secretary Vance will be meeting with Foreign Minister Gromyko day after tomorrow, the 21st, and at that time we'll see if the SALT agreements are coming to a successful conclusion. If so, we will extend immediately again an invitation to President Brezhnev to come here during the middle part of January.

The two visits would, obviously, not overlap or conflict, and I think I'll be well prepared, in studying the prospective agenda, to meet with both of them in the same month.

MR. CRONKITE. What about return visits from you, sir?

THE PRESIDENT. Well, we have not made any plans for that. And I would presume that both leaders might invite me to come to their countries sometime in the future. And I would look with favor on those invitations, but not anytime soon.

STRATEGIC ARMS LIMITATION

MR. CRONKITE. Do you feel that this agreement with China puts any pressure on the Soviet Union to come to any early conclusion with the SALT talks?

THE PRESIDENT. No, I really can't assess any interrelationship between the two. The agreement with China was not designed to put any sort of pressure on the Soviet Union. I think the outcome of the new relationship between ourselves and the billion people of China and their government is constructive and positive and contributes toward the lessening of tension rather than the building up of additional tension. And that applies to our relationship with the Soviet Union as well as to other countries.

CONSULTATION WITH THE CONGRESS

Mr. Cronkite. Mr. President, some Members of Congress, including Democrats and some liberal Republicans, are claiming that you failed to live up to an administration pledge to consult with Congress before taking any such action as you have toward Taiwan and Peking. And now, there's a threat of a court challenge to the constitutionality of your cancelling the treaty without congressional approval. How seriously do you view this? Do you feel that either Congress or the courts could block this arrangement with both Taiwan and Peking?

The President. No. My constitutional responsibility in establishing relationships with foreign countries is clear and cannot be successfully challenged in court.

We have had constant consultations with the Congress over the past 2 years. And our goal in establishing normal relations with China has been made clear on numerous occasions by me personally. When Secretary Vance went to China and came back, he gave the Congress leaders and Members a thorough briefing. Dr. Brzezinski did the same thing after his visit to China. I have met with all the Members of the Congress who would come to sessions here at the White House.

One of the deliberate items on my own agenda in explaining to them and answering their questions was about the terms under which we would normalize relationships with China. I might add that when numerous delegations of congressional leaders have gone to the People's Republic and come back, they have also given me and Secretary of State Vance their views on what ought to be done. Almost invariably their recommendation was to proceed expeditiously with normalization of relations with China.

So, there's been a clear understanding, really ever since 1972, of the policy of our Government toward China, a desire to normalize relations, and also a clear expression of my views both publicly and privately to the Members of Congress about our goals and the plans for accomplishing this goal.

I might say in complete candor that in the last 2 or 3 weeks, when the negotiations were building up to a climax in an unanticipated degree of rapidity of movement, we did not consult with anyone outside of a very tiny group within the executive branch of Government about the prospective success. But what did happen should not be a surprise to anyone. The congressional views were well known to me. My views were well known to the Members of Congress.

U.S.-CHINESE NEGOTIATIONS

Mr. Cronkite. Mr. President, what was the need for such haste? Why could you not have consulted with the congressional leaders first, before making the final commitment?

The President. Well, Walter, my experience in negotiating sensitive and complicated agreements with foreign leaders, including the experience at Camp David and otherwise, is that to negotiate through the news media, through public pronouncements and with wide divergencies of views expressed by different leaders in a country, is not conducive to success. And I'm authorized and directed by the Constitution and my responsibility is to conduct negotiations of this kind.

We did not depart from the established policy of our country that's been extant since President Nixon went to China in 1972. And I think had we caused a public debate in our country about all the ramifications of the negotiations at the very time we were trying to conclude these discussions with the Chinese, it would have resulted in failure. And our country would have lost a wonderful opportunity to a great stride forward and all the benefits that will be derived from this agreement.

So, I don't have any doubt that what I did was right and correct. I don't have any doubts that had we made a public issue of it, it would have complicated the issue unnecessarily.

U.S.-TAIWAN DEFENSE TREATY

MR. CRONKITE. Mr. President, on the matter of the court challenge, the challenge is not your right to recognize or to withdraw recognition of a government, but of your right to cancel a treaty. Does that change your view any of the validity of that challenge?

THE PRESIDENT. No. The treaty is being terminated in exact conformance with the terms of the treaty itself. Had I canceled the treaty or abrogated the treaty peremptorily as of the first day of January—which was the Chinese request to us, or demand from us originally—there may have been some justification for that court challenge. But the treaty provides that either side can terminate the effectiveness of the treaty by giving a 1-year notice. And that's exactly what we are doing with

the people of Taiwan, telling them that after a year the treaty will no longer be in effect. It's completely in accordance with the terms of the treaty itself, Walter.

MR. CRONKITE. Since the Constitution requires the Senate to approve by a two-thirds vote the making of a treaty, you don't feel that there might be an implication in the Constitution that the same two-thirds would apply to canceling a treaty.

THE PRESIDENT. No. I think this gets into a complicated legal discussion, and I'm not qualified for it. But as of the 1st of January, we will have relations with and acknowledge the nationhood of China. And Taiwan will no longer be a nation in the view of our own country. And whether or not a treaty can exist with an entity which is no longer a nation is a legal question in itself. But we have gone a second mile to protect the integrity of our own country by extending the terms of the peace treaty for a full year, even after we recognize the China Mainland Government as the Government.

So, I think that we have more than honored the terms of the treaty, and I see no basis for a successful court challenge. I think what we've done is right. It's better for our country. It's better for the people of China. It does not hurt the people of Taiwan. It's good for world peace. I think we've benefited greatly, and I'm very proud of it.

STRATEGIC ARMS LIMITATION

MR. CRONKITE. Can I ask you just one more real quick one now on the Senate of the United States?

THE PRESIDENT. Okay.

MR. CRONKITE. Do you think that putting the Chinese question on the agenda of the next session of Congress might complicate the confirmation of a SALT treaty?

THE PRESIDENT. No, I think not. What we will ask the Congress to do next session is to pass special legislation to permit us to continue our cultural relations with Taiwan, our trade relations with Taiwan, the application of the Eximbank, and the support of loans to China—to the people of Taiwan, rather, and also to authorize us to sell weapons to Taiwan after the defense treaty expires.

So, I think that even those who oppose the normalization of relations with China will favor the continued relationships with Taiwan, which this legislation will have to authorize. So, I don't think this will complicate the other issues in Congress. They're almost as complicated as they can get anyhow. I don't think this will hurt at all.

MR. CRONKITE. Thank you very much, Mr. President, for taking the time to be with us. Thank you.

THE PRESIDENT. It's a pleasure, Walter. Thank you.

NOTE: The interview began at 4:30 p.m. in the Map Room at the White House. Mr. Cronkite spoke from a studio in New York City. The interview was taped for later broadcast on the CBS television network.

Consumers Opposed to Inflation in the Necessities

Statement Following a Meeting With the Organization.   December 20, 1978

Following our very constructive meeting with COIN, I have asked Alfred E. Kahn, my adviser on inflation, to have the working groups he has assembled cooperate with COIN and other consumer groups to plan additional specific steps to hold down inflation in the sectors of the economy that provide the basic necessities of life. I expect their recommendations soon.

Consumers always seem to be the last to be consulted about the policies that determine what they pay for products and services in the marketplace. COIN has spoken up for consumers throughout this Nation effectively, and I want to hear their views before decisions are made. I want COIN to be a partner in our common effort to control inflation.

NOTE: The President met with leaders of member organizations of the consumer group at the White House on December 19.

River of No Return Wilderness

Letter to the Speaker of the House and the President of the Senate Transmitting Proposed Legislation.   December 20, 1978

Dear Mr. Speaker: (Dear Mr. President:)

In accordance with the Wilderness Act of 1964, I am pleased to transmit a proposal to designate a 1.9 million acre River of No Return Wilderness on portions of the Bitterroot, Boise, Challis, Nezperce, Payette and Salmon National Forests in Idaho.

This proposal fulfills a pledge made in my Environmental Message of May 1977 to review and expand the wilderness recommendation for this area submitted to the Congress by the prior Administration. The additional acreage included in my proposal reflects substantial involvement by concerned government and private organizations and groups at the national, state and local levels.

I strongly urge the Congress to favorably consider this proposal to preserve the outstanding natural qualities of this large undeveloped area for the benefit of present and future generations of Americans.

Sincerely,

JIMMY CARTER

NOTE: This is the text of identical letters addressed to Thomas P. O'Neill, Jr., Speaker of the House of Representatives, and Walter F Mondale, President of the Senate.

Office of Consumer Affairs

Appointment of Rodney E. Leonard as Deputy Director.   December 20, 1978

The President today announced the appointment of Rodney E. Leonard, of Bethesda, Md., as Deputy Director of the Office of Consumer Affairs.

Leonard, 49, is currently serving as Acting Deputy Director. Prior to joining the Office of Consumer Affairs, he was chief executive officer of the Community Nutrition Institute, which he organized in 1970. He was with the Agriculture Department from 1961 to 1968, serving as assistant to the Secretary, Deputy Assistant Secretary for Marketing and Consumer Services, and Administrator of the Consumer and Marketing Service.

President's Council on Physical Fitness and Sports

Appointment of Billy M. Mills as a Member. December 21, 1978

The President today announced the appointment of Billy M. Mills, of Fair Oaks, Calif., as a member of the President's Council on Physical Fitness and Sports. Mills is a former Olympic track star who won a gold medal in the 1964

Olympics. He now works as a life insurance underwriter and is active in community affairs and as a public speaker.

Digest of Other White House Announcements

The following listing includes the President's daily schedule and other items of general interest as announced by the White House Press Office during the period covered by this issue. Events and announcements printed elsewhere in the issue are not included.

December 17

The President returned to the White House from a weekend stay at Camp David, Md.

December 18

The President met at the White House with:

—Zbigniew Brzezinski, Assistant to the President for National Security Affairs;

—Vice President Walter F. Mondale;

—the National Security Council.

The President and Mrs. Carter hosted a Christmas reception in the morning for members of the Secret Service and their families on the State Floor of the White House.

The President and Mrs. Carter hosted a Christmas reception in the evening for members of the White House staff on the State Floor of the White House.

December 19

The President met at the White House with:

—Dr. Brzezinski;

—a group of administration officials to discuss the fiscal year 1980 budget;

—the Energy Coordinating Committee;

—the Joint Chiefs of Staff.

December 20

The President met at the White House with:

—Dr. Brzezinski;

—a group of administration officials to discuss the fiscal year 1980 budget;

—Adm. Stansfield Turner, Director of Central Intelligence, Hamilton Jordan, Assistant to the President, and Dr. Brzezinski;

—a group of Democratic mayors to discuss the fiscal year 1980 budget;

—a group of Governors to discuss the fiscal year 1980 budget.

The President and Mrs. Carter hosted a Christmas reception in the afternoon for members of the Residence staff and their families on the State Floor of the White House.

The President and Mrs. Carter hosted a Christmas reception in the evening for members of the White House press corps on the State Floor of the White House.

December 21

At the President's direction, Deputy Secretary of State Warren Christopher will lead a mission to Taiwan to discuss arrangements regarding the maintenance of commercial, cultural, and other relations between the American and Taiwanese peoples. This mission will coordinate, with the Taiwanese authorities, the general framework within which these unofficial relations are to be conducted after January 1, 1978. The mission to Taiwan will include Adm. Maurice Wiesner, USN, Commander in Chief, Pacific;

Herbert Hansell, Legal Adviser of the Department of State; Deputy Assistant Secretary of State for East Asian and Pacific Affairs Roger Sullivan; Deputy Assistant Secretary of Defense for International Security Affairs Michael Armacost; and Deputy Assistant Secretary of Commerce W. Dean Moran. The delegation will arrive in Taipei on December 27 and leave Taipei on December 29.

The President declared a major disaster for the State of Arizona as a result of severe storms and flooding, beginning about December 17, which caused extensive public and private property damage.

December 22

The President met at the White House with:

—Dr. Brzezinski;

—a group of administration officials to discuss the fiscal year 1980 budget.

The President left the White House for a trip to Atlanta and Plains, Ga.

NOMINATIONS SUBMITTED TO THE SENATE

NOTE: The Congress having adjourned *sine die* on Sunday, October 15, no nominations were submitted during the period covered by this issue. The first session of the 96th Congress will begin on Monday, January 15, 1979.

CHECKLIST OF WHITE HOUSE PRESS RELEASES

The following releases of the Office of the White House Press Secretary, distributed during the period covered by this issue, are not included in the issue.

Released December 20, 1978

Advance text: address before the Foreign Policy Association—by Zbigniew Brzezinski, Assistant to the President for National Security Affairs

CHECKLIST—Continued

Released December 21, 1978

News conference: on the President's trip to Atlanta and Plains, Ga.—by Press Secretary Jody Powell

News conference: on the President's health—by Press Secretary Powell

ACTS APPROVED BY THE PRESIDENT

NOTE: The President completed his consideration of acts and joint resolutions passed during the second session of the 95th Congress on November 10.

Editor's Note

Note Concerning the Closing Time of This Issue

The President left the White House on Friday afternoon, December 22, for a trip to Atlanta and Plains, Ga. Releases issued on the trip will be printed next week.

American Bolt, Nut, and Large Screw Industry

Letter to the Speaker of the House and the President of the Senate Transmitting a Report. December 22, 1978

Dear Mr. Speaker: (Dear Mr. President:)

In accordance with section 203(b)(1) of the Trade Act of 1974, enclosed is a report to the Congress setting forth my decision to modify the import relief recommendation of the U.S. International Trade Commission (USITC) by proclaiming increased tariffs of 15 percent on iron or steel bolts, nuts, and large screws for a three-year period and giving the reasons for my decision. This report also discusses why the import relief I will proclaim differs from that recommended by the USITC.

Sincerely,

JIMMY CARTER

IMPORT RELIEF ACTION

BOLTS, NUTS AND LARGE SCREWS

As required by section 203(b)(1) of the Trade Act of 1974, I am transmitting this report to Congress setting forth the actions I will take with respect to iron or steel bolts, nuts, and large screws covered by the affirmative finding, on November 3, 1978, of the U.S. International Trade Commission (USITC) under section 201(d)(1) of the Trade Act. As my decision provides import relief which differs from that recommended by the USITC, I am setting forth the reasons for such difference.

After considering all relevant aspects of the case, including those considerations set forth in section 202(c) of the Trade Act of 1974, I have determined that import relief in the form of 15 percent tariffs on iron or steel bolts, nuts, and large screws is in the national economic interest and therefore will proclaim this remedy. Under this remedy, tariffs will remain at 15 percent for large screws (including lag screws), and 15 percent plus the current tariffs of 0.2 and 0.1 cent per pound, respectively, for bolts and nuts for a three-year period after which time they will revert to their current levels (which range from less than one percent ad valorem equivalent to 12.5 percent).

As required by statute, this relief must be implemented within 15 days of this determination.

The USITC recommended that tariffs on iron or steel bolts, nuts, and large screws be increased to 20 percent and staged down to 10 percent (except for lag screws where the tariff would revert to its current level of 12.5 percent) over a five-year period.

I have determined that the USITC remedy would not be an appropriate remedy for a number of reasons. The USITC remedy would substantially increase the cost of ferrous fasteners to U.S. consumers, thereby adding to inflationary pressures in the U.S. economy. Due to its shorter duration (three years versus five years as recommended by the USITC) and smaller tariff increases (15 percent versus 20 percent), the remedy I will proclaim will have a smaller inflationary impact on the U.S. economy, while still providing meaningful and necessary relief to the domestic fastener industry.

Given the recent increases in the prices of imported fasteners, the USITC remedy would be overly restrictive on the foreign countries that supply fasteners to the U.S. market. The smaller tariff increases that I will proclaim will mitigate the adverse impact of providing import relief on foreign suppliers of fasteners and on U.S. international economic interests.

The tariff increase remedy I have chosen should enable many domestically produced fasteners to be competitively priced relative to imports. Thus, implementation of this remedy should prevent further erosion of domestic fastener production, shipments, and employment and may allow domestic producers to increase their share of the U.S. fastener market by using currently idle capacity.

NOTE: This is the text of identical letters addressed to Thomas P. O'Neill, Jr., Speaker of the House of Representatives, and Walter F. Mondale, President of the Senate.

American Bolt, Nut, and Large Screw Industry

Memorandum From the President.
December 22, 1978

Memorandum for the Special Representative for Trade Negotiations

Subject: Determination Under Section 202(b) of the Trade Act; Bolts, Nuts, and Large Screws of Iron or Steel

Pursuant to section 202(b)(1) of the Trade Act of 1974 (P.L. 93–618, 88 Stat. 1978), I have determined the action I will take with respect to the report of the United States International Trade Commission (USITC), transmitted to me on November 3, 1978, concerning the results of its investigation of a resolution submitted by the Committee on Ways and Means of the House of Representatives. The USITC investigation pertained to lag screws or bolts, bolts (except mine-roof bolts) and bolts and their nuts imported in the same shipment, nuts, and screws having shanks or threads over 0.24 inch in diameter, all of the foregoing of iron or steel, provided for in items 646.49, 646.54, 646.56, 646.63, and 646.79 of the Tariff Schedules of the United States.

After considering all relevant aspects of the case, including those considerations set forth in section 202(c) of the Trade Act of 1974, I have determined that import relief in the form of 15 percent tariffs on iron or steel bolts, nuts, and large screws is in the national economic interest and therefore will proclaim this remedy. Under this remedy, tariffs will remain at 15 percent for large screws (including lag screws), 15 percent plus the current tariffs of 0.2 and 0.1 cent per pound, respectively, for bolts and nuts for a three-year period after which time they will revert to their current levels (which range from less than one percent ad valorem equivalent to 12.5 percent).

As required by statute, this relief must be implemented within 15 days of this determination.

The USITC recommended that tariffs on iron or steel bolts, nuts, and large screws be increased to 20 percent and staged down to 10 percent (except for lag screws where the tariff would revert to its current level of 12.5 percent) over a five-year period.

I have determined that the USITC remedy would not be an appropriate remedy for a number of reasons. The USITC remedy would substantially increase the cost of ferrous fasteners to U.S. consumers, thereby adding to inflationary pressures in the U.S. economy. Due to its shorter duration (three years versus five years as recommended by the USITC) and smaller tariff increases (15 percent versus 20 percent), the remedy I will proclaim will have a smaller inflationary impact on the U.S. economy, while still providing meaningful and necessary relief to the domestic fastener industry.

Given the recent increases in the prices of imported fasteners, the USITC remedy would be overly restrictive on the foreign countries that supply fasteners to the U.S. market. The smaller tariff increases that I will proclaim will mitigate the adverse impact of providing import relief on foreign suppliers of fasteners and on U.S. international economic interests.

The tariff increase remedy I have chosen should enable many domestically produced fasteners to be competitively priced relative to imports. Thus, implementation of this remedy should prevent further erosion of domestic fastener production, shipments, and employment and allow domestic producers to increase their

share of the U.S. fastener market by using currently idle capacity.

This determination is to be published in the FEDERAL REGISTER.

JIMMY CARTER

[Filed with the Office of the Federal Register, 11:36 a.m., December 26, 1978]

Atlanta, Georgia

Informal Exchange With Reporters Following a Visit With Judy Carter.   December 22, 1978

Q. What do you think of your granddaughter, Mr. President?

THE PRESIDENT. Well, it's a beautiful granddaughter, and we can't possibly have a better Christmas present.

Q. How do you feel, Mr. President?

THE PRESIDENT. I feel better.

Q. Do you?

THE PRESIDENT. Yeah.

Q. How are the SALT talks going, Mr. President?

THE PRESIDENT. I think we're making good progress. There's still a couple of items that have not yet been resolved—I talked to Secretary Vance this afternoon. But we still have good hopes that we'll be successful.

Q. Mr. President, do you have plans to come back to Georgia to speak to the General Assembly during the session?

THE PRESIDENT. I believe so, yes. It hasn't been firmed up yet, but that's a good prospect.

Q. Could there be a SALT announcement tomorrow, Mr. President?

THE PRESIDENT. I can't give you any time schedule, because we don't know how we'll work out the differences. But I talked to Secretary Vance this afternoon, and he was encouraged. But some of the items still have to be referred back to the Politburo by Foreign Minister Gromyko. So, there's no way to anticipate exactly what the rate of agreement might be.

I hope everybody has a good Christmas. It's nice for us to be back in Georgia with a new granddaughter.

REPORTER. Merry Christmas, Mr. President.

NOTE: The exchange began at 7 p.m. outside Crawford W. Long Memorial Hospital. The President and his family had stopped en route to Plains, Ga., to see his daughter-in-law and her recently born daughter, Sarah Rosemary.

Fort Benning, Georgia

Informal Exchange With Reporters on Arrival at Lawson Army Airfield. December 22, 1978

Q. I hope you found your grandchild real well.

THE PRESIDENT. She was very well. We are proud of her.

Q. Good.

THE PRESIDENT. It makes a good Christmas for us.

Q. Fine.

Q. Do we have a SALT treaty?

THE PRESIDENT. We don't know yet. They were still negotiating when the thing broke up last night in Geneva, and I think we will find out today one way or the other.

Q. Does it look hopeful? Are you encouraged?

THE PRESIDENT. It looks hopeful, but there are still some very difficult issues to be resolved. And I am hopeful, yes, but no certainty yet.

Q. Thank you for coming by.

THE PRESIDENT. Thank you, everybody.

Q. Thank you for coming by. Good luck to you. Merry Christmas.

THE PRESIDENT. You have always been so nice to us.

———

THE PRESIDENT. I had a good night last night——

Q. Good. I know you have been in pain.

THE PRESIDENT. ——with the treatment.

Q. Described as miserable.

THE PRESIDENT. It was.

Q. Are you going to have a chitchat with the townspeople in Plains at all?

THE PRESIDENT. I am going very carefully, yes. Yesterday was horrible. I will see how I feel in the morning.

Q. Is there a possibility you are going to have surgery?

THE PRESIDENT. I don't think there is—there is always a possibility, but I think that threat is over. Last night it was a pretty sure thing, but this morning, I was better. I think my prayers were answered. I have gotten advice from everybody in the United States. [*Laughter*]

Q. I'll bet.

NOTE: The exchange began at approximately 8 p.m. Following his remarks, the President went to his home in Plains, Ga.

As printed above, the item follows the White House press release.

Plains, Georgia

Informal Exchange With Reporters Following a Visit With Allie Smith. December 25, 1978

Q. How was your Christmas?

THE PRESIDENT. Our Christmas has been very good. We hope everyone in our country had as good a Christmas as we've had. We've been with our families and with our friends, and we've got peace on Earth right now. We hope we can keep it that way. And we just wish everyone, on behalf of the First Family, a very wonderful holiday season. And I'm sorry all of you can't be with your folks, too.

Q. Mr. President, we haven't really had a chance to talk with you since the SALT negotiations broke up in Geneva. Can you give us any reading on that? What does it look like? Does it seem that the Russians are sort of holding back until they see how the summit by the Chinese leaders here goes?

THE PRESIDENT. We don't know what the Soviets' motivations are. I talked to Secretary Vance yesterday afternoon after he got back home, and he was encouraged with the meetings with the Soviets and also thought that the Israelis and the Egyptians had a good, solid discussion. And it was constructive; he felt very pleased with it. I think we will have a peace treaty for the Middle East, and I think we will have a SALT agreement with the Soviets. It just takes time. The complications of all the issues are not easily resolved. But I still feel hopeful, and I and Secretary Vance both agree that we're not discouraged at all.

Q. Are you still looking at a date in mid-January, or has that been put back?

THE PRESIDENT. My guess is that it's been put back some, but we don't have a definite period. The differences on the SALT agreement have been narrowed considerably in the last week. There are still a couple of issues that will be discussed and resolved, as Secretary Vance announced, through diplomatic channels and through the regular negotiating teams. But I don't foresee any need for another Foreign Ministers meeting, and I think that we have an excellent chance of a fairly early meeting between myself and President Brezhnev. My guess is, though, that it will not be in January. We would be ready in January if the Soviets are.

Q. Have the differences on the encoding and verification been ironed out, Mr. President?

THE PRESIDENT. Parts of those have been ironed out. I think it might be better to let Secretary Vance give you a specific rundown later on on the remaining issues, because they are still under negotiation. And we've had, I think, a fairly well honored agreement with the Soviets that we won't discuss specific issues through the press; we'll let that be done through more private means.

Q. What about your Christmas? What did you get, Mr. President? People would like to know.

THE PRESIDENT. Well, I got some books, and I got a camera, a small camera that I can carry in my pocket, one like I took down the river. And we had all our family together. We got a lot of clothes, got some running outfits when I get recuperated from my physical injury enough to use it. [*Laughter*]

Q. What are you carrying in your hand, what book?

THE PRESIDENT. This is "101 Famous Poems." But we've had a good Christmas.

Q. How are you feeling?

THE PRESIDENT. Much better. I took it easy yesterday, and I think that speeded my recuperation.

Q. Are you going quail hunting?

THE PRESIDENT. I don't think I'm going to go quail hunting. I can't stand the thought of jumping over those terraces in a jeep right this minute. [*Laughter*]

REPORTERS. Merry Christmas to you.

NOTE: The exchange began at 9:25 a.m. outside the home of Allie Smith, Mrs. Carter's mother.

President Houari Boumediene of Algeria

Statement on the Death of the Algerian President. **December 27, 1978**

It is with deep regret that I have learned of the death of His Excellency Houari Boumediene, President of the Algerian Democratic and Popular Republic and President of the Council of the Revolution. President Boumediene played an outstanding role in Algeria's long struggle for independence. His devotion to duty and his contributions as an international statesman are well known. But it is for his efforts to help create and strengthen an independent, self-sufficient Algerian nation that he will be most remembered.

Rosalynn and I extend our condolences to President Boumediene's family and to the Algerian people, who have lost a leader whom the world will long remember.

NOTE: The following announcement was released by the White House Press Office on December 28:

Secretary W. Michael Blumenthal will head the U.S. Delegation to the state funeral of His Excellency Houari Boumediene, President of the Democratic and Popular Republic of Algeria and President of the Council of the Revolution, on December 29, 1978, in Algiers. Mrs. Blumenthal will accompany the Secretary.

Mr. Chip Carter will be the Personal Representative of the President.

Other representatives of the President are:

ULRIC ST. CLAIR HAYNES, JR., U.S. Ambassador to Algeria;

MRS. HAYNES;

MUHAMMAD ALI, WBC World Heavyweight Champion;

HOWARD T. BOYD of Houston, Tex., chairman of the board of El Paso Co.;

CLARK M. CLIFFORD, attorney and former Secretary of Defense;

WILLIAM C. DEMETREE of Orlando, Fla., president, Demetree Builders;

MORRIS DRAPER, Deputy Assistant Secretary of State, Bureau of Near Eastern and South Asian Affairs;

PETER KELLY of Hartford, Conn., attorney;

LOUIS MARTIN, Special Assistant to the President;

JOSEPH NELSON MEREDITH of Fresno, Calif., vice president, Paine, Webber, Jackson and Curtis, Inc.;

JOHN L. MOORE, JR., President and Chairman of the Export-Import Bank;

WILLIAM B. QUANDT, staff member, National Security Council;

SARAH WEDDINGTON, Special Assistant to the President.

Sugars and Sirups Imports

Proclamation 4631. **December 28, 1978**

IMPORT FEES ON SUGAR AND SIRUPS

By the President of the United States of America

A Proclamation

By Proclamation No. 4547 of January 20, 1978, I imposed, on an emergency basis, import fees on certain sugars and sirups. These fees were to be effective pending my further action after receipt of the report of findings and recommendations of the United States International Trade Commission after its conduct of an investigation with respect to this matter pursuant to section 22 of the Agricultural Adjustment Act, as amended (7 U.S.C. 624). The Commission has made its investigation and reported its findings and recommendations to me.

On the basis of the information submitted to me, I find and declare that:

(a) Sugars, described below by use and physical description, are being imported, or are practically certain to be imported, into the United States under such conditions and in such quantities as to render or tend to render ineffective, or materially interfere with, the price support operations being conducted by the Department of Agriculture for sugar cane and sugar beets, or reduce substantially the amount of any product processed in the United States from domestic sugar beets or sugar cane;

(b) The imposition of the import fees hereinafter proclaimed is necessary in order that the entry, or withdrawal from warehouse, for consumption of such sugars will not render or tend to render ineffective, or materially interfere with, the price support operations being conducted by the Department of Agriculture for sugar beets and sugar cane, or reduce substantially the amount of products processed in the United States from such domestic sugar beets or sugar cane.

Now, THEREFORE, I, JIMMY CARTER, President of the United States of America, by the authority vested in me by section 22 of the Agricultural Adjustment Act, as amended, do hereby proclaim that Part 3 of the Appendix to the Tariff Schedules of the United States is amended as follows:

1. Headnote 4 is continued in effect and amended by changing the heading to read "4. Sugars and sirups.—" and by adding paragraph (c) which reads as follows:

(c)(i) The quarterly adjusted fee provided for in items 956.05 and 957.15 shall be the amount of the fee for item 956.15 plus .52 cents per pound.

(ii) The quarterly adjusted fee provided for in item 956.15 shall be the amount by which the average of the daily spot (world) price quotations for raw sugar for the first 20 consecutive market days preceding the 20th day of the month preceding the calendar quarter during which the fee shall be applicable (as reported by the New York Coffee and Sugar Exchange or, if such quotations are not being reported by the International Sugar

Organization), expressed in United States cents per pound, Caribbean ports, in bulk, adjusted to a United States delivered basis by adding applicable duty and attributed costs of 0.90 cents per pound for freight, insurance, stevedoring, financing, weighing and sampling, is less than 15.0 cents per pound: *Provided,* That whenever the average of such daily spot price quotations for 10 consecutive market days within any calendar quarter, adjusted to a United States delivered basis as provided herein, plus the fee then in effect (1) exceeds 16.0 cents, the fee then in effect shall be decreased by one cent, or (2) is less than 14.0 cents, the fee then in effect shall be increased by one cent: *Provided further,* That the fee may not be greater than 50 per centum of the average of such daily spot price quotations for raw sugar.

(iii) The Secretary of Agriculture shall determine the amount of the quarterly fees in accordance with (i) and (ii) hereof and announce such fees not later than the 25th day of the month preceding the calendar quarter during which the fees shall be applicable. The Secretary shall certify the amount of such fees to the Secretary of the Treasury and file notice thereof with the FEDERAL REGISTER prior to the beginning of the calendar quarter during which the fees shall be applicable. The Secretary of Agriculture shall determine and announce any adjustment in the fees made within a calendar quarter in accordance with the first proviso of (ii) hereof, shall certify such adjusted fees to the Secretary of the Treasury, and shall file notice thereof with the FEDERAL REGISTER within 3 market days of the fulfillment of that proviso.

(iv) No adjustment shall be made in any fee in accordance with the first proviso of (ii) during the last ten market days of a calendar quarter.

(v) Any adjustment made in a fee during a quarter in accordance with the first proviso of (ii) hereof shall be applicable only with respect to sugar entered or withdrawn from warehouse for consumption after 12:01 a.m. (local time at point of entry) on the day following the filing of notice thereof with the FEDERAL REGISTER: *Provided,* That such adjusted fee shall not apply to sugar exported (as defined in section 152.1 of the Customs Regulations) on a through bill of lading to the United States from the country of origin before such time.

2. Items 956.05, 956.15 and 957.15 are continued in effect and amended to read as follows:

Item	Articles	Rates of Duty (Section 22 Fees)
	Sugars and sirups derived from sugar cane or sugar beets, except those entered pursuant to a license issued by the Secretary of Agriculture in accordance with headnote 4(a):	
	Principally of crystalline structure or in dry amorphous form, provided for in item 155.20, part 10A, schedule 1:	
956.05....	Not to be further refined or improved in quality.	3.22¢ per lb., adjusted quarterly beginning January 1, 1979, in accordance with headnote 4(c), but not in excess of 50% ad val.
956.15....	To be further refined or improved in quality....	2.70¢ per lb., adjusted quarterly beginning January 1, 1979, in accordance with headnote 4(c), but not in excess of 50% ad val.
957.15....	Not principally of crystalline structure and not in dry amorphous form, containing soluble non-sugar solids (excluding any foreign substance that may have been added or developed in the product) equal to 6% or less by weight of the total soluble solids, provided for in item 155.30, part 10A, schedule 1.....	3.22¢ per lb., of total sugars, adjusted quarterly beginning January 1, 1979, in accordance with headnote 4(c), but not in excess of 50% ad val.

3. The provision of paragraph (c)(iii) of Headnote 4 of Part 3 of the Appendix to the TSUS, as added herein, requiring the determination and announcement by the Secretary of Agriculture not later than the 25th day of the month preceding the calendar quarter during which the fees shall be applicable, shall not apply to the fees to become effective January 1, 1979.

This proclamation shall be effective as of 12:01 a.m. (Eastern Standard Time) on the day following its signing.

IN WITNESS WHEREOF, I have hereunto set my hand this twenty-eighth day of December, in the year of our Lord nineteen hundred and seventy-eight, and of the Independence of the United States of America the two hundred and third.

JIMMY CARTER

[Filed with the Office of the Federal Register, 11:52 a.m., December 29, 1978]

NOTE: The text of the proclamation was released on December 29.

Equal Employment Opportunity Enforcement

Executive Order 12106.   December 28, 1978

TRANSFER OF CERTAIN EQUAL EMPLOYMENT ENFORCEMENT FUNCTIONS

By the authority vested in me as President of the United States of America by Section 9 of Reorganization Plan No. 1 of 1978 (43 FR 19807), in order to effectuate the transfer of certain functions relating to the enforcement of equal employment programs, and in order to make certain technical amendments in other Orders to reflect this transfer of functions, it is hereby ordered as follows:

1-101. The transfer to the Equal Employment Opportunity Commission of certain functions of the Civil Service Commission, relating to enforcement of equal employment opportunity programs as provided by Sections 1, 2, 3 and 4 of Reorganization Plan No. 1 of 1978 (43 FR 19807), shall be effective on January 1, 1979.

1-102. Executive Order No. 11478, as amended, is further amended by deleting the preamble, by substituting "national origin, handicap, or age" for "or national origin" in the first sentence of Section 1, and revising Sections 3, 4, and 5 to read as follows:

"Sec. 3. The Equal Employment Opportunity Commission shall be responsible for directing and furthering the implementation of the policy of the Government of the United States to provide equal opportunity in Federal employment for all employees or applicants for employment (except with regard to aliens employed outside the limits of the United States) and to prohibit discrimination in employment because of race, color, religion, sex, national origin, handicap, or age.

"Sec. 4. The Equal Employment Opportunity Commission, after consultation with all affected departments and agencies, shall issue such rules, regulations, orders, and instructions and request such information from the affected departments and agencies as it deems necessary and appropriate to carry out this Order.

"Sec. 5. All departments and agencies shall cooperate with and assist the Equal Employment Opportunity Commission in the performance of its functions under this Order and shall furnish the Commission such reports and information as it may request. The head of each department or agency shall comply with rules, regulations, orders and instructions issued by the Equal Employment Opportunity Commission pursuant to Section 4 of this Order.".

1-103. Executive Order No. 11022, as amended, is further amended by revising Section 1(b) to read as follows:

"(b) The Council shall be composed of the Secretary of Health, Education, and Welfare, who shall be Chairman, the Secretary of the Treasury, the Secretary of Agriculture, the Secretary of Commerce, the Secretary of Labor, the Secretary of Housing and Urban Development, the Secretary of Transportation, the Administrator of Veterans Affairs, the Director of the Office of Personnel Management, the Director of the Community Services Administration, and the Chairman of the Equal Employment Opportunity Commission.".

1-104. Executive Order No. 11480 of September 9, 1969, is amended by deleting "and the Chairman of the United States Civil Service Commission" in Section 4 and substituting therefor "Director of the Office of Personnel Management, and the Chairman of the Equal Employment Opportunity Commission".

1-105. Executive Order No. 11830 of January 9, 1975, is amended by deleting Section 2 and revising Section 1 to read as follows:

"In accord with Section 501 of the Rehabilitation Act of 1973 (29 U.S.C. 791) and Section 4 of Reorganization Plan No. 1 of 1978 (43 FR 19808), the Interagency Committee on Handicapped Employees is enlarged and composed of the following, or their designees whose positions are Executive level IV or higher:

(1) Secretary of Defense.

(2) Secretary of Labor.

(3) Secretary of Health, Education, and Welfare, Co-Chairman.

(4) Director of the Office of Personnel Management.

(5) Administrator of Veterans Affairs.

(6) Administrator of General Services.

(7) Chairman of the Federal Communications Commission.

(8) Chairman of the Equal Employment Opportunity Commission, Co-Chairman.

(9) Such other members as the President may designate.".

1–106. This Order shall be effective on January 1, 1979.

JIMMY CARTER

The White House,
   December 28, 1978.

[Filed with the Office of the Federal Register,
   · 2:24 p.m., December 29, 1978]

NOTE: The text of the Executive order was released on December 29.

Federal Civil Service Reorganization

Executive Order 12107.   December 28, 1978

RELATING TO THE CIVIL SERVICE COMMISSION AND LABOR-MANAGEMENT IN THE FEDERAL SERVICE

By virtue of the authority vested in me as President by the Constitution and statutes of the United States of America, and by Section 403 of Reorganization Plan No. 2 of 1978 (43 FR 36037), it is hereby ordered as follows:

SECTION 1

IMPLEMENTATION OF REORGANIZATION
PLAN NO. 2 OF 1978

1–1. *Office of Personnel Management.*

1–101. *Establishment of Office of Personnel Management.* The establishment of the Office of Personnel Management and of the positions of Director, Deputy Director, and Associate Directors of that Office, as provided in Sections 101 and 103 of Reorganization Plan No. 2 of 1978, shall be effective on January 1, 1979.

1–102. *Transfer of Functions.* Section 102 of Reorganization Plan No. 2 of 1978, transferring functions to the Director of the Office of Personnel Management, shall be effective on January 1, 1979.

1–2. *Merit Systems Protection Board.*

1–201. *Redesignation of Civil Service Commission.* The redesignation of the Civil Service Commission as the Merit Systems Protection Board and of the Commissioners as Members of the Board as provided in Section 201 of Reorganization Plan No. 2 of 1978 shall be effective on January 1, 1979.

1–202. *Functions of the Merit Systems Protection Board.* The functions of the Merit Systems Protection Board as provided in Section 202 and the savings provisions of Section 203 of Reorganization Plan No. 2 of 1978 shall be effective on January 1, 1979.

1–3. *The Special Counsel.*

1–301. *Establishment of the Office of Special Counsel.* The establishment of the

Office of Special Counsel to the Merit Systems Protection Board as provided in Section 204(a) of Reorganization Plan No. 2 of 1978 shall be effective on January 1, 1979.

1–302. *Functions of the Special Counsel.* The transfer of functions provided for in Section 204(b) and the performance of functions set forth in Section 204(c)–(g) of Reorganization Plan No. 2 of 1978 shall be effective on January 1, 1979.

1–4. *The Federal Labor Relations Authority.*

1–401. *The Establishment of the Federal Labor Relations Authority and the Office of General Counsel.* The establishment of the Federal Labor Relations Authority as provided in Section 301 and of the Office of General Counsel of the Authority as provided in Section 302 of Reorganization Plan No. 2 of 1978 shall be effective on January 1, 1979.

1–402. *The Federal Service Impasses Panel.* The continuation of the Federal Service Impasses Panel established under Executive Order No. 11491, as amended, as a distinct organizational entity within the Federal Labor Relations Authority as provided in Section 303 of Reorganization Plan No. 2 of 1978, shall be effective on January 1, 1979.

1–403. *Functions of the Federal Labor Relations Authority, the General Counsel, and the Federal Service Impasses Panel.* The transfer of functions provided for in Section 304 of Reorganization Plan No. 2 of 1978 shall be effective on January 1, 1979.

1–5. *General.*

1–501. *General Effective Date.* All other provisions of Reorganization Plan No. 2 of 1978 shall be effective on January 1, 1979.

SECTION 2

REDESIGNATIONS, AMENDMENTS TO RULES AND EXECUTIVE ORDERS AND GENERAL PROVISIONS

2–1. *Redesignations.*

2–101. *Office of Personnel Management.* Each of the Executive orders, as amended, listed in this Section under subsections (a) and (b), as applicable, and any other order which relates to functions or areas of responsibility delegated to the Office of Personnel Management, is amended and revised by substituting the words "Office of Personnel Management" for the words "Civil Service Commission" or "United States Civil Service Commission"; by substituting the word "Office" for the word "Commission" wherever the word "Commission" is used as a reference to United States Civil Service Commission; and by substituting the words "Director, Office of Personnel Management" for the words "Chairman, Civil Service Commission", "Chairman, United States Civil Service Commission", "Commissioners" or "Commissioner" wherever they appear.

(a) Executive orders relating to the Civil Service Rules, ethics and other matters of Presidential interest.

Executive Orders Numbered
  8743
  10577, as amended, except for Rules IV and V, as amended in this order,
  10641
  10717
  10927
  11183
  11222
  11315
  11451

11570
11639
11648
11721
11935
12004
12014
12043

(b) Other Executive orders relating to Federal Personnel Management, and membership on Councils, Boards, and Committees.

Executive Orders Numbered

8744
9230
9712
9830
9932
9961
10000
10242
10422
10450
10459
10530
10549
10550
10552
10556
10647
10763
10774, except for Section 3(e)
10804
10826
10880
10903
10973
10982
11103
11171
11203
11219
11228
11264
11348
11355
11422

11434
11438
11490
11512
11521
11552
11561
11579
11589
11603
11609
11636
11639
11744
11817
11890
11895
11899
11938
11955
12008
12015
12027
12049
12067
12070
12089
12105

2-102. *Merit Systems Protection Board.* The provisions of Section 3(e) of Executive Order No. 10774 and Executive Order No. 11787, are hereby amended and revised by substituting the words "Merit Systems Protection Board" for the words "Civil Service Commission" or "Commission" when used as a reference to the Civil Service Commission wherever such words appear.

2-103. *Amending the Civil Service Rules.* Section 101 of Executive Order No. 10577, as amended, is further amended by substituting for Rule II— Appointment Through the Competitive System, a new Sec. 2.4 as follows:

"Sec. 2.4. *Probationary period.* Persons selected from registers of eligibles for career or career-conditional appointment and employees promoted, transferred, or otherwise assigned, for the first time, to supervisory or managerial positions shall be required to serve a probationary period under terms and conditions prescribed by the Office.";

by deleting the last sentence under Rule IV—Prohibited Practices, Sec. 4.3; and

by substituting for Rule V—Regulations, Investigations, and Enforcement, a new Rule V as follows:

"Rule V—REGULATIONS, INVESTIGATIONS, EVALUATION, AND ENFORCEMENT"

"Sec. 5.1. *Civil Service Regulations.* The Director, Office of Personnel Management, shall promulgate and enforce regulations necessary to carry out the provisions of the Civil Service Act and the Veterans' Preference Act, as reenacted in Title 5, United States Code, the Civil Service Rules, and all other statutes and Executive orders imposing responsibilities on the Office. The Director is authorized, whenever there are practical difficulties and unnecessary hardships in complying with the strict letter of the regulation, to grant a variation from the strict letter of the regulation if such a variation is within the spirit of the regulations, and the efficiency of the Government and the integrity of the competitive service are protected and promoted. Whenever a variation is granted the Director shall note the official record to show: (1) the particular practical difficulty or hardship involved, (2) what is permitted in place of what is required by regulation, (3) the circumstances which protect or promote the efficiency of the Government and the integrity of the competitive service, and (4) a statement limiting the application of the variation to the continuation of the conditions which gave rise to it. Like variations shall be granted whenever like conditions exist. All such decisions and information concerning variations noted in the official record shall be published promptly in a Federal Personnel Manual, Letter or Bulletin and in the Director's next annual report.

"Sec. 5.2. *Investigation and Evaluations.* The Director may secure effective implementation of the civil service laws, rules, and regulations, and all Executive orders imposing responsibilities on the Office by:

(a) Investigating the qualifications and suitability of applicants for positions in the competitive service. The Director may require appointments to be made subject to investigation to enable the Director to determine, after appointment, that the requirements of law or the civil service rules and regulations have been met.

(b) Evaluating the effectiveness of: (1) personnel policies, programs, and operations of Executive and other Federal agencies subject to the jurisdiction of the Office, including their effectiveness with regard to merit selection and employee development; (2) agency compliance with and enforcement of applicable laws, rules, regulations and office directives; and (3) agency personnel management evaluation systems.

(c) Investigating, or directing an agency to investigate and report on, apparent violations of applicable laws, rules, regulations, or directives requiring corrective action, found in the course of an evaluation.

(d) Requiring agencies to report, in a manner and at times as the Director may prescribe, personnel information the Director requests relating to civilian employees in the Executive branch of the Government, as defined by Section 311 of the Civil Service Reform Act of 1978, including positions and officers and employees in the competitive, excepted and Senior Executive services, whether permanent, career-conditional, temporary, or emergency.

"Sec. 5.3. *Enforcement.*

(a) The Director is authorized to ensure enforcement of the civil service laws, rules, and regulations, and all applicable Executive orders, by:

(1) Instructing an agency to separate or take other action against an employee serving an appointment subject to investigation when the Director finds that the employee is disqualified for Federal employment. Where the employee or the agency appeals the Director's finding that a separation or other action is necessary, the Director may instruct the agency as to whether or not the employee should remain on duty and continue to receive pay pending adjudication of the appeal: *Provided,* That when an agency separates or takes other action against an employee pursuant to the Director's instructions, and the Director, on the basis of new evidence, subsequently reverses the initial decision as to the employee's qualifications and suitability, the agency shall, upon request of the Director, restore the employee to duty or otherwise reverse any action taken.

(2) Reporting the results of evaluation or investigations to the head of the agency concerned with instructions for any corrective action necessary, including cancellation of personnel actions where appropriate. The Director's findings resulting from evaluations or investigations are binding unless changed as a result of agency evidence and arguments against them. If, during the course of any evaluation or investigation under this Section, the Director finds evidence of matters which come within the investigative and prosecutorial jurisdiction of the Special Counsel of the Merit Systems Protection Board, the Director shall refer this evidence to the Special Counsel for appropriate disposition.

(b) Whenever the Director issues specific instructions as to separation or other corrective action with regard to an employee, including cancellation of a personnel action, the head of the agency concerned shall comply with the Director's instructions.

(c) If the agency head fails to comply with the specific instructions of the Director as to separation or other corrective action with regard to an employee, including cancellation of a personnel action, the Director may certify to the Comptroller General of the United States the agency's failure to act together with such additional information as the Comptroller General may require, and shall furnish a copy of such certification to the head of the agency concerned. The individual with respect to whom such separation or other corrective action was instructed shall be entitled thereafter to no pay or only to such pay as appropriate to effectuate the Director's instructions.

"Sec. 5.4. *Information and Testimony.* When required by the Office, the Merit Systems Protection Board, or the Special Counsel of the Merit Systems Protection Board, or by authorized representatives of these bodies, agencies shall make available to them, or to their authorized representatives, employees to testify in regard to matters inquired of under the civil service laws, rules, and regulations, and records pertinent to these matters. All such employees, and all applicants or eligibles for positions covered by these rules, shall give to the Office, the Merit Systems Protection Board, the Special Counsel, or to their authorized representatives, all information, testimony, documents, and material in regard to the above matters, the disclosure of which is not otherwise prohibited by law or regulation. These employees, applicants, and eligibles shall sign testimony given under oath or affirmation before an officer authorized by law to administer oaths. Employees are performing official duty when testifying or providing evidence pursuant to this section.

2–104. *Effectiveness of Rule Changes.* The amendments to rules shall be effective on January 1, 1979, to the extent provided by law on that date.

2–2. *Revocation of Executive Orders and Delegation of Functions.*

2–201. *Revocation of Executive Orders and Delegation of Functions to the Director.* Executive Orders numbered 10540 and 10561 are revoked and the authority vested in the President by Section 202(c)(1)(C) of the Annual Sick Leave Act of 1951, as amended, and the authority of the President, pursuant to the Civil Service Act of January 16, 1883, to designate official personnel folders in government agencies as records of the Office of Personnel Management and to prescribe regulations relating to the establishment, maintenance and transfers of official personnel folders, are delegated to the Director of the Office of Personnel Management. Any rules, regulations, directives, instructions or other actions taken pursuant to the authority delegated to the Director of the Office of Personnel Management shall remain in effect until amended, modified, or revoked pursuant to the delegations made by this Order.

2–202. *Savings Provision.* All personnel actions and decisions affecting employees or applicants for employment made on or before January 11, 1979, shall continue to be governed by the applicable Executive order, and the rules and regulations implementing that Order, to the same extent as if that Executive order had not been revoked effective January 11, 1979 unless amended, modified or revoked pursuant to this Order.

2–3. *Labor Management Relations in the Federal Service.*

2–301. *Labor Management Relations.* Executive Order No. 11491 of October 29, 1969, as amended by Executive Orders numbered 11616, 11636, 11838, 11901, and 12027, relating to labor-management relations in the Federal service, is further amended as follows:

1. Subsections (g), (h) and (i) of Section 2 are amended and a new subsection (j) is added to read as follows:

"(g) 'Authority' means the Federal Labor Relations Authority;

"(h) 'Panel' means the Federal Service Impasses Panel;

"(i) 'Assistant Secretary' means the Assistant Secretary of Labor for Labor Management Relations; and

"(j) 'General Counsel' means the General Counsel of the Authority.".

2. Section 3(b) is amended—

(a) by substituting for paragraph (6) the following:

"(6) The Tennessee Valley Authority; or"; and

(b) by adding the following:

"(7) personnel of the Federal Labor Relations Authority (including the Office of the General Counsel and the Federal Service Impasses Panel).".

3. Section (d) is amended to read as follows:

"(d) Employees engaged in administering a labor-management relations law or this Order who are otherwise authorized by this Order to be represented by a labor organization shall not be represented by a labor organization which also represents other groups of employees under the law or this Order, or which is affiliated directly or indirectly with an organization which represents such a group of employees.".

4. Section 4 is amended to read as follows:

"Sec. 4. *Powers and Duties of the Federal Labor Relations Authority.*

"(a) [Revoked].

"(b) The Authority shall administer and interpret this Order, decide major policy issues, and prescribe regulations.

"(c) The Authority shall, subject to its regulations:

(1) decide questions as to the appropriate unit for the purpose of exclusive recognition and related issues submitted for its consideration;

(2) supervise elections to determine whether a labor organization is the choice of a majority of the employees in an appropriate unit as their exclusive representative, and certify the results;

(3) decide questions as to the eligibility of labor organizations for national consultation rights;

(4) decide unfair labor practice complaints; and

(5) decide questions as to whether a grievance is subject to a negotiated grievance procedure or subject to arbitration under an agreement as provided in Section 13(d) of this Order.

"(d) The Authority may consider, subject to its regulations:

(1) appeals on negotiability issues as provided in Section 11(c) of this Order;

(2) exceptions to arbitration awards;

(3) appeals from decisions of the Assistant Secretary of Labor for Labor-Management Relations issued pursuant to Section 6(b) of this Order; and

(4) other matters it deems appropriate to assure the effectuation of the purposes of this Order.

"(e) In any matters arising under subsection (c) and (d)(3) of this Section, the Authority may require an agency or a labor organization to cease and desist from violations of this Order and require it to take such affirmative action as the Authority considers appropriate to effectuate the policies of this Order.

"(f) In performing the duties imposed on it by this Section, the Authority may request and use the services and assistance of employees of other agencies in accordance with Section 1 of the Act of March 4, 1915 (38 Stat. 1084, as amended; 31 U.S.C. 686).".

5. The caption of Section 5 is amended to read as follows:

"Sec. 5. *Powers and Duties of the Federal Service Impasses Panel.*"

6. Section 5(a) is amended:

(a) by substituting the words "a distinct organizational entity within the Authority" for the words "an agency within the Council" in the first sentence; and

(b) by substituting the word "Authority" for the word "Council" in the third sentence.

7. Section 6 is amended to read as follows:

"Sec. 6. *Powers and Duties of the Office of the General Counsel and the Assistant Secretary of Labor for Labor-Management Relations.*

"(a) The General Counsel is authorized, upon direction by the Authority, to;

(1) investigate complaints of violations of Section 19 of this Order;

(2) make final decisions as to whether to issue unfair labor practice complaints and prosecute such complaints before the Authority;

(3) direct and supervise all employees in the Office of General Counsel, including employees of the General Counsel in the regional office of the Authority;

(4) perform such other duties as the Authority may prescribe; and

(5) prescribe regulations needed to administer his functions under this Order.

"(b) The Assistant Secretary shall:

(1) decide alleged violations of the standards of conduct for labor organiza-

tions, established in Section 18 of this Order; and

(2) prescribe regulations needed to administer his functions under this Order.

"(c) In any matter arising under paragraph (b) of this Section, the Assistant Secretary may require a labor organization to cease and desist from violations of this Order and require it to take such affirmative action as he considers appropriate to effectuate the policies of this Order.

"(d) In performing the duties imposed on them by this section, the General Counsel and the Assistant Secretary may request and use the services and assistance of employees of other agencies in accordance with Section 1 of the Act of March 4, 1915 (38 Stat. 1084, as amended; 31 U.S.C. 686).".

8. Section 9 is amended:

(a) by substituting the word "Authority" for the word "Council" in the first sentence of subsection (a); and

(b) by substituting the word "Authority" for the words "Assistant Secretary" in subsection (c).

9. Section 10 is amended:

(a) by substituting the word "Authority" for the words "Assistant Secretary" in the last sentence of subsection (b); and

(b) by substituting the word "Authority" for the words "Assistant Secretary" and the word "it" for the word "him", in the first sentence of subsection (d).

10. Section 11 is amended:

(a) by substituting the word "Authority" for the word "Council in paragraph sentence of subsection (a); and

(b) by substituting the word "Authority" for the word "Council" in paragraph (4) of subsection (c).

11. Section 11(d) is revoked.

12. Section 13 is amended:

(a) by substituting the word "Author-

ity" for the word "Council" in the third sentence of subsection (b); and

(b) by substituting the word "Authority" for the words "Assistant Secretary" in the first and second sentence of subsection (d).

13. Section 19(d) is amended by substituting the word "Authority" for the words "Assistant Secretary" in the last sentence.

14. Section 21(a) is amended by substituting the words "Office of Personnel Management" for the words "Civil Service Commission" in the second sentence.

15. Section 22 is amended:

(a) by substituting the words "Office of Personnel Management" for the words "Civil Service Commission" in the first sentence and

(b) by substituting the words "Merit Systems Protection Board" for the words "Civil Service Commission" in the second and third sentences.

16. Section 25(a) is amended:

(a) by substituting the words "Office of Personnel Management" for the words "Civil Service Commission" in the first, second and third sentences; and

(b) by substituting the word "Authority" for the word "Council" in the third sentence.

17. Section 25(b) is amended by substituting the words "Office of Personnel Management" for the words "Department of Labor and Civil Service Commission.".

2-4. *General Provisions.*

2-401. *Study and Report Provisions.* The Director of the Office of Personnel Management is directed to conduct a study of Executive orders listed in Section 2-101(a) and (b) and to coordinate the study with such other agencies as may be named in or affected by these orders. The

Director of Personnel Management and the Director of the Office of Management and Budget are directed to submit a report on or before July 1, 1981 to the President concerning the performance of functions specified in these Executive orders and any other Executive orders affecting the functions or responsibilities of the Office of Personnel Management. The report shall contain specific detailed recommendations for the continuation, modification, revision or revocation of each Executive order.

2–402. *Continuing Effect of this Order.* Except as required by the Civil Service Reform Act of 1978 as its provisions become effective, in accord with Section 7135 of Title 5, United States Code, as amended, and in accord with Section 902 (a) of that Act, the provisions of this Order shall continue in effect, according to its terms, until modified, terminated or suspended.

2–403. *Transfers and Determinations.*

(a) The records, property, personnel and positions, and unexpended balances of appropriations or funds related to Civil Service Commission functions reassigned by this Order that are available, or to be made available, and necessary to finance or discharge the reassigned functions are transferred to the Director of the Office of Personnel Management, the Federal Labor Relations Authority, or the Federal Service Impasses Panel, as appropriate.

(b) The Director of the Office of Management and Budget shall make such determinations, issue such orders and take all actions necessary or appropriate to effectuate the transfers or reassignments provided by this Order, including the transfer of funds, records, property and personnel.

2–404. *Effective Date.* Except as otherwise specifically provided in this Order,

this Order shall be effective on January 1, 1979.

JIMMY CARTER

The White House,
    December 28, 1978.

[Filed with the Office of the Federal Register,
    2:25 p.m., December 29, 1978]

NOTE: The text of the Executive order was released on December 29.

Employee Retirement Income Security Act Transfers

Executive Order 12108.   December 28, 1978

By the authority vested in me as President of the United States of America by Section 109 of Reorganization Plan No. 4 of 1978 (43 FR 47713), it is hereby ordered that the provisions of Reorganization Plan No. 4 of 1978 shall be effective on Sunday, December 31, 1978.

JIMMY CARTER

The White House,
    December 28, 1978.

[Filed with the Office of the Federal Register,
    2:26 p.m., December 29, 1978]

NOTE: The text of the Executive order was released on December 29.

Federal Physicians Comparability Allowance

Executive Order 12109.   December 28, 1978

By the authority vested in me as President of the United States of America by Section 5948 of Title 5 and Section 301 of Title 3 of the United States Code, it is hereby ordered as follows:

1–101. The Director of the Office of Personnel Management is hereby designated and empowered to exercise, in consultation with the Director of the Office of Management and Budget, the authority of the President under Section 5948 of Title 5 of the United States Code, to prescribe regulations, criteria, and conditions with regard to the payment of comparability allowances to recruit and retain certain Federal physicians.

1–102. Until the Office of Personnel Management is established (on or before January 1, 1979), pursuant to Reorganization Plan No. 2 of 1978 (43 FR 36037), the Civil Service Commission shall exercise the authority delegated under this Order to the Director of the Office of Personnel Management.

JIMMY CARTER

The White House,
　December 28, 1978.

[Filed with the Office of the Federal Register,
　2:27 p.m., December 29, 1978]

NOTE: The text of the Executive order was released on December 29.

Federal Advisory Committees

Executive Order 12110.　December 28, 1978

CONTINUANCE OF CERTAIN FEDERAL
ADVISORY COMMITTEES

By the authority vested in me as President by the Constitution and statutes of the United States of America, and in accordance with the provisions of the Federal Advisory Committee Act (5 U.S.C. App. I), it is hereby ordered as follows:

1–101. Each advisory committee listed below is continued until December 31, 1980.

(a) Committee for the Preservation of the White House—Executive Order No. 11145, as amended (Department of the Interior).

(b) President's Commission on White House Fellowships—Executive Order No. 11183, as amended (United States Civil Service Commission).

(c) President's Committee on the National Medal of Science—Executive Order No. 11287, as amended (National Science Foundation).

(d) President's Council on Physical Fitness and Sports—Executive Order No. 11562, as amended (Department of Health, Education, and Welfare).

(e) President's Export Council—Executive Order No. 11753 of December 20, 1973 (Department of Commerce).

(f) President's Committee on Mental Retardation—Executive Order No. 11776 of March 28, 1974 (Department of Health, Education, and Welfare).

(g) Federal Advisory Council on Occupational Safety and Health—Executive Order No. 11807 of September 28, 1974 (Department of Labor).

(h) Presidential Advisory Board on Ambassadorial Appointments, Executive Order No. 11970 of February 5, 1977 (Department of State).

(i) Committee on Selection of Federal Judicial Officers—Executive Order No. 11992 of May 24, 1977 (Department of Justice).

(j) United States Circuit Judge Nominating Commission—Executive Order No. 12059, as amended (Department of Justice).

(k) United States Court of Military Appeals Nominating Commission—Executive Order No. 12063 of June 5, 1978 (Department of Defense).

(l) United States Tax Court Nominating Commission—Executive Order No. 12064 of June 5, 1978 (Department of the Treasury).

(m) Judicial Nominating Commission for the District of Puerto Rico—Executive Order No. 12084, as amended (Department of Justice).

1-102. Notwithstanding the provisions of any other Executive order, the functions of the President under the Federal Advisory Committee Act which are applicable to the committees listed in Section 1-101 of this Order, except that of reporting annually to Congress, shall be performed by the head of the department or agency designated after each committee, in accordance with guidelines and procedures established by the Administrator of General Services.

1-103. The following Executive orders, that established committees which have terminated or whose work is completed, are revoked:

(a) Executive Order No. 11482 of September 22, 1969, establishing a Construction Industry Collective Bargaining Commission.

(b) Executive Order No. 11849 of April 1, 1975, establishing the Collective Bargaining Committee in Construction.

(c) Executive Order No. 11534 of June 4, 1970, establishing the National Council on Organized Crime.

(d) Executive Order No. 11971, as amended, establishing the Committee on Selection of the Director of the Federal Bureau of Investigation.

(e) Executive Order No. 11973 of February 17, 1977, establishing the President's Commission on Mental Health.

(f) Executive Order No. 11998 of June 27, 1977, establishing the President's Commission on Military Compensation.

1-104. Executive Order No. 11984 is superseded.

1-105. This Order shall be effective December 31, 1978.

JIMMY CARTER

The White House,
December 28, 1978.

[Filed with the Office of the Federal Register, 2:28 p.m., December 29, 1978]
NOTE: The text of the Executive order was released on December 29.

United States Relations With the People on Taiwan

Memorandum From the President. December 30, 1978

Memorandum for All Departments and Agencies

Subject: Relations with the People on Taiwan

As President of the United States, I have constitutional responsibility for the conduct of the foreign relations of the nation. The United States has announced that on January 1, 1979, it is recognizing the government of the People's Republic of China as the sole legal government of China and is terminating diplomatic relations with the Republic of China. The United States has also stated that, in the future, the American people will maintain commercial, cultural and other relations with the people of Taiwan without official government representation and without diplomatic relations. I am issuing this memorandum to facilitate maintaining those relations pending the enactment of legislation on the subject.

I therefore declare and direct that:

(A) Departments and agencies currently having authority to conduct or carry out programs, transactions, or other relations with or relating to Taiwan are directed to conduct and carry out those programs, transactions, and relations beginning January 1, 1979, in accordance with such authority and, as appropriate, through the instrumentality referred to in paragraph D below.

(B) Existing international agreements and arrangements in force between the United States and Taiwan shall continue in force and shall be performed and enforced by departments and agencies beginning January 1, 1979, in accordance with their terms and, as appropriate, through that instrumentality.

(C) In order to effectuate all of the provisions of this memorandum, whenever any law, regulation, or order of the United States refers to a foreign country, nation, state, government, or similar entity, departments and agencies shall construe those terms and apply those laws, regulations, or orders to include Taiwan.

(D) In conducting and carrying out programs, transactions, and other relations with the people on Taiwan, interests of the people of the United States will be represented as appropriate by an unofficial instrumentality in corporate form, to be identified shortly.

(E) The above directives shall apply to and be carried out by all departments and agencies, except as I may otherwise determine.

I shall submit to the Congress a request for legislation relative to non-governmental relationships between the American people and the people on Taiwan.

This memorandum shall be published in the FEDERAL REGISTER.

JIMMY CARTER

[Filed with the Office of the Federal Register, 4:26 p.m., January 2, 1979]

Digest of Other White House Announcements

The following listing includes the President's daily schedule and other items of general interest as announced by the White House Press Office during the period covered by this issue. Events and announcements printed elsewhere in the issue are not included.

December 26

The President went to Camp David, Md., following his return to Andrews Air Force Base, Md., from a visit to Plains, Ga.

NOMINATIONS SUBMITTED TO THE SENATE

NOTE: The Congress having adjourned *sine die* on Sunday, October 15, no nominations were submitted during the period covered by this issue. The first session of the 96th Congress will begin on Monday, January 15, 1979.

CHECKLIST OF WHITE HOUSE PRESS RELEASES

NOTE: All releases of the Office of the White House Press Secretary, distributed during the period covered by this issue, have been included in the issue.

ACTS APPROVED BY THE PRESIDENT

NOTE: The President completed his consideration of acts and joint resolutions passed during the second session of the 95th Congress on November 10. The first session of the 96th Congress will begin on Monday, January 15, 1979.

BILL SIGNINGS

See also last page of text in each issue for acts approved